Dictionary

English-Français
French-Anglais

Rosalind Williams

BARNES
&NOBLE
BOOKS
NEW YORK

Copyright © 1982 by Market House Books.
All rights reserved.

This edition published by Marboro Books Corp.,
a division of Barnes & Noble, Inc.,
by arrangement with Pan Books Ltd.

1992 Barnes & Noble Books

ISBN 0-88029-935-5

Printed and bound in the United States of America

M 9 8 7 6 5 4 3 2

Abbreviations/Abréviations

adj adjective, adjectif
admin administration
adv adverb, adverbe
aero aeronautics
aéro aéronautique
anat anatomy, anatomie
arch architecture
art article
astrol astrology, astrologie
astron astronomy, astronomie
auto automobile
aux auxiliary, auxiliaire
bot botany, botanique
chem chemistry
chim chimie
coll colloquial
comm commerce
conj conjunction, conjonction
derog derogatory
econ economics
écon économie
elec electricity
élec électricité
f feminine, féminin
fam familiar, familier
geog geography
géog géographie
geol geology

géol géologie
gramm grammar, grammaire
impol impolite, impoli
interj interjection
invar invariable
m masculine, masculin
math mathematics, mathématiques
med medicine
méd médicine
mil military, militaire
n noun, nom
naut nautical, nautique
péj péjoratif
phone telephone
phot photography, photographie
pl plural, pluriel
pol politics, politique
prep preposition, préposition
pron pronoun, pronom
psych psychology, psychologie
rail railways
rel religion
sing singular, singulier
tech technical, technique
v verb, verbe
V vide (see, voir)
zool zoology, zoologie

French pronunciation

ɑ pate [pɑt]
a rame [ram]
ɛ baie [bɛ]
e pré [pre]
i fiche [fiʃ]
ɔ col [kɔl]
o pot [po]
u route [rut]
y vue [vy]
ə me [mə]
ø deux [dø]
œ jeune [ʒœn]
ɑ̃ vent [vɑ̃]
ɛ̃ fin [fɛ̃]
ɔ̃ ton [tɔ̃]
œ̃ brun [brœ̃]
' hibou ['ibu] (no liaison)
b bière [bjɛr]
d dame [dam]

f faîte [fɛt]
g gant [gɑ̃]
h hola [hɔla]
j pierre [pjɛr]
k conte [kɔ̃t]
l lieu [ljø]
m mon [mɔ̃]
n nid [ni]
p poli [pɔli]
r rage [raʒ]
s sein [sɛ̃]
t tube [tyb]
v vite [vit]
w oui [wi]
z zone [zon]
ɥ lui [lɥi]
ʃ chou [ʃu]
ʒ neige [nɛʒ]
ɲ ligne [liɲ]
ŋ parking [parkiŋ]

In French, the stress always falls on the final syllable of a word or group of words.

Prononciation de l'anglais

a hat [hat]

e bell [bel]

i big [big]

o dot [dot]

ʌ bun [bʌn]

u book [buk]

ə alone [əˈloun]

a: card [ka:d]

ə: word [wə:d]

i: team [ti:m]

o: torn [to:n]

u: spoon [spu:n]

ai die [dai]

ei ray [rei]

oi toy [toi]

au how [hau]

ou road [roud]

eə lair [leə]

iə fear [fiə]

uə poor [puə]

b back [bak]

d dull [dʌl]

f find [faind]

g gaze [geiz]

h hop [hop]

j yell [jel]

k cat [kat]

l life [laif]

m mouse [maus]

n night [nait]

p pick [pik]

r rose [rouz]

s sit [sit]

t toe [tou]

v vest [vest]

w week [wi:k]

z zoo [zu:]

θ think [θiŋk]

ð those [ðouz]

ʃ shoe [ʃu:]

ʒ treasure [ˈtreʒə]

tʃ chalk [tʃo:k]

dʒ jump [dʒʌmp]

ŋ sing [siŋ]

Le signe ' est placé devant la syllabe qui porte l'accent tonique.
Le signe , est placé devant la syllabe qui porte l'accent secondaire.

Guide to the dictionary

Irregular plural forms are shown at the headword and in the text. The following categories of French plural forms are considered regular:

main	mains
prix	prix
cheval	chevaux
feu	feux
seau	seaux

Irregular feminine forms of adjectives are shown at the headword and in the text. The following categories are considered regular:

brun	brune
digne	digne
précieux	précieuse
vif	vive
artificiel	artificielle
ancien	ancienne
premier	première

Irregular verbs marked with an asterisk in the headword list are listed in the verb tables, with the following exceptions:

For verbs ending in -aindre, -eindre, or -oindre see **atteindre**.
For verbs ending in -aître (except **naître**) see **connaître**.
For verbs ending in -cevoir see **apercevoir**.
For verbs ending in -clure see **conclure**.
For verbs ending in -crire see **écrire**.
For verbs ending in -entir (also **dormir**, **partir**, **servir**, **sortir**) see **mentir**.
For verbs ending in -quérir see **acquérir**.
For verbs ending in -uire (except **luire**, **nuire**) see **conduire**.

Adverbs are shown only if their formation is irregular. English adverbs are considered regular if they are formed by adding -*ly* to the adjective. French adverbs are considered regular if they are formed by adding -*ment* to the feminine form of the adjective.

Guide au dictionnaire

Les formes irrégulières au pluriel sont indiquées après le mot cherché et dans le texte. Les catégories suivantes des formes plurielles sont considérées régulières en anglais:

cat	cats
glass	glasses
fly	flies
half	halves
wife	wives

Les formes irrégulières des adjectifs au féminin sont indiquées après le mot cherché et dans le texte. Les catégories suivantes des formes féminines sont considérées régulières:

brun	brune
digne	digne
precieux	précieuse
vif	vive
artificiel	artificielle
ancien	ancienne
premier	première

Les verbes irréguliers se trouvant dans la liste des verbes sont marqués d'un astérisque dans la liste des mots du dictionnaire.

Les adverbes se construisant régulièrement ne sont pas indiqués. Les adverbes anglais sont considérés réguliers s'ils sont construits en ajoutant -ly à l'adjectif. Les adverbes français sont considérés réguliers s'ils sont construits en ajoutant -ment à la forme féminine de l'adjectif.

French irregular verbs

Infinitive	Present	Imperfect	Past Participle	Future
absoudre	absous	absolvais	absous	absoudrai
acquérir	acquiers	acquérais	acquis	acquerrai
aller	vais	allais	allé	irai
apercevoir	aperçois	apercevais	aperçu	apercevrai
assaillir	assaille	assaillais	assailli	assaillirai
asseoir	assieds	asseyais	assis	assiérai
atteindre	atteins	atteignais	atteint	atteindrai
avoir	ai	avais	eu	aurai
battre	bats	battais	battu	battrai
boire	bois	buvais	bu	boirai
bouillir	bous	bouillais	bouilli	bouillirai
braire	brais	brayais	brait	brairai
circoncire	circoncis	circoncisais	circoncis	circoncirai
clore	clos		clos	clorai
conclure	conclus	concluais	conclu	conclurai
conduire	conduis	conduisais	conduit	conduirai
confire	confis	confisais	confit	confirai
connaître	connais	connaissais	connu	connaîtrai
coudre	couds	cousais	cousu	coudrai
courir	cours	courais	couru	courrai
couvrir	couvre	couvrais	couvert	couvrirai
croire	crois	croyais	cru	croirai
croître	croîs	croissais	crû	croîtrai
cueillir	cueille	cueillais	cueilli	cueillerai
devoir	dois	devais	dû	devrai
dire	dis	disais	dit	dirai
dissoudre	dissous	dissolvais	dissous	dissoudrai
échoir	il échoit		échu	il échoira
écrire	écris	écrivais	écrit	écrirai
envoyer	envoie	envoyais	envoyé	enverrai
être	suis	étais	été	serai
faillir			failli	faillirai
faire	fais	faisais	fait	ferai
falloir	il faut	il fallait	fallu	il faudra
foutre	fous	foutais	foutu	foutrai
frire	fris		frit	frirai
fuir	fuis	fuyais	fui	fuirai

Infinitive	Present	Imperfect	Past Participle	Future
gésir	gis	gisais		
haïr	hais	haïssais	haï	haïrai
importer	il importe			
lire	lis	lisais	lu	lirai
luire	luis	luisais	lui	luirai
maudire	maudis	maudissais	maudit	maudirai
mentir	mens	mentais	menti	mentirai
mettre	mets	mettais	mis	mettrai
moudre	mouds	moulais	moulu	moudrai
mourir	meurs	mourais	mort	mourrai
mouvoir	meus	mouvais	mû	mouvrai
naître	nais	naissais	né	naîtrai
nuire	nuis	nuisais	nui	nuirai
offrir	offre	offrais	offert	offrirai
ouïr	ois	oyais	ouï	oirai
ouvrir	ouvre	ouvrais	ouvert	ouvrirai
plaire	plais	plaisais	plu	plairai
pleuvoir	il pleut	il pleuvait	plu	il pleuvra
pouvoir	peux *or* puis	pouvais	pu	pourrai
prendre	prends	prenais	pris	prendrai
résoudre	résous	résolvais	résolu	résoudrai
rire	ris	riais	ri	rirai
savoir	sais	savais	su	saurai
seoir	il sied	il seyait		
souffrir	souffre	souffrais	souffert	souffrirai
suffire	suffis	suffisais	suffi	suffirai
suivre	suis	suivais	suivi	suivrai
surseoir	sursois	sursoyais	sursis	surseoirai
taire	tais	taisais	tu	tairai
tenir	tiens	tenais	tenu	tiendrai
traire	trais	trayais	trait	trairai
tressaillir	tressaille	tressaillais	tressailli	tressaillirai
vaincre	vaincs	vainquais	vaincu	vaincrai
valoir	vaux	valais	valu	vaudrai
venir	viens	venais	venu	viendrai
vêtir	vêts	vêtais	vêtu	vêtirai
vivre	vis	vivais	vécu	vivrai
voir	vois	voyais	vu	verrai
vouloir	veux	voulais	voulu	voudrai

Verbes irréguliers anglais

Infinitif	Prétérit	Participe Passé	Infinitif	Prétérit	Participe Passé
abide	abode	abode	deal	dealt	dealt
arise	arose	arisen	dig	dug	dug
awake	awoke	awoken	do	did	done
be	was	been	draw	drew	drawn
bear	bore	borne	dream	dreamed	dreamed
		or born		*or* dreamt	*or* dreamt
beat	beat	beaten	drink	drank	drunk
become	became	become	drive	drove	driven
begin	began	begun	dwell	dwelt	dwelt
behold	beheld	beheld	eat	ate	eaten
bend	bent	bent	fall	fell	fallen
bet	bet	bet	feed	fed	fed
beware			feel	felt	felt
bid	bid	bidden	fight	fought	fought
		or bid	find	found	found
bind	bound	bound	flee	fled	fled
bite	bit	bitten	fling	flung	flung
bleed	bled	bled	fly	flew	flown
blow	blew	blown	forbid	forbade	forbidden
break	broke	broken	forget	forgot	forgotten
breed	bred	bred	forgive	forgave	forgiven
bring	brought	brought	forsake	forsook	forsaken
build	built	built	freeze	froze	frozen
burn	burnt	burnt	get	got	got
	or burned	*or* burned	give	gave	given
burst	burst	burst	go	went	gone
buy	bought	bought	grind	ground	ground
can	could		grow	grew	grown
cast	cast	cast	hang	hung	hung
catch	caught	caught		*or* hanged	*or* hanged
choose	chose	chosen	have	had	had
cling	clung	clung	hear	heard	heard
come	came	come	hide	hid	hidden
cost	cost	cost	hit	hit	hit
creep	crept	crept	hold	held	held
cut	cut	cut	hurt	hurt	hurt

Infinitif	Prétérit	Participe Passé	Infinitif	Prétérit	Participe Passé
keep	kept	kept	**say**	said	said
kneel	knelt	knelt	**see**	saw	seen
knit	knitted	knitted	**seek**	sought	sought
	or knit	or knit	**sell**	sold	sold
know	knew	known	**send**	sent	sent
lay	laid	laid	**set**	set	set
lead	led	led	**sew**	sewed	sewn
lean	leant	leant			or sewed
	or leaned	or leaned	**shake**	shook	shaken
leap	leapt	leapt	**shear**	sheared	sheared
	or leaped	or leaped			or shorn
learn	learnt	learnt	**shed**	shed	shed
	or learned	or learned	**shine**	shone	shone
leave	left	left	**shoe**	shod	shod
lend	lent	lent	**shoot**	shot	shot
let	let	let	**show**	showed	shown
lie	lay	lain	**shrink**	shrank	shrunk
light	lit	lit	**shut**	shut	shut
	or lighted	or lighted	**sing**	sang	sung
lose	lost	lost	**sink**	sank	sunk
make	made	made	**sit**	sat	sat
may	might		**sleep**	slept	slept
mean	meant	meant	**slide**	slid	slid
meet	met	met	**sling**	slung	slung
mow	mowed	mown	**slink**	slunk	slunk
must			**slit**	slit	slit
ought			**smell**	smelt	smelt
pay	paid	paid		or smelled	or smelled
put	put	put	**sow**	sowed	sown
quit	quitted	quitted			or sowed
	or quit	or quit	**speak**	spoke	spoken
read	read	read	**speed**	sped	sped
rid	rid	rid		or speeded	or speeded
ride	rode	ridden	**spell**	spelt	spelt
ring	rang	rung		or spelled	or spelled
rise	rose	risen	**spend**	spent	spent
run	ran	run	**spill**	spilt	spilt
saw	sawed	sawn		or spilled	or spilled
		or sawed	**spin**	spun	spun

Infinitif	Prétérit	Participe Passé	Infinitif	Prétérit	Participe Passé
spit	spat	spat	**swim**	swam	swum
spilt	split	split	**swing**	swung	swung
spread	spread	spread	**take**	took	taken
spring	sprang	sprung	**teach**	taught	taught
stand	stood	stood	**tear**	tore	torn
steal	stole	stolen	**tell**	told	told
stick	stuck	stuck	**think**	thought	thought
sting	stung	stung	**throw**	threw	thrown
stink	stank	stunk	**thrust**	thrust	thrust
	or stunk		**tread**	trod	trodden
stride	strode	stridden	**wake**	woke	woken
strike	struck	struck	**wear**	wore	worn
string	strung	strung	**weave**	wove	woven
strive	strove	striven	**weep**	wept	wept
swear	swore	sworn	**win**	won	won
sweep	swept	swept	**wind**	wound	wound
swell	swelled	swollen	**wring**	wrung	wrung
		or swelled	**write**	wrote	written

Glossary of menu terms

France is the home of the most elegant cooking in the world. French-speaking people take eating seriously, and visitors can find a great variety of good food in many different kinds of eating establishments. **Cafés, restaurants, bistros, charcuteries** (delicatessens), and that popular import from the United States, **le drugstore,** can provide nourishment almost around the clock. French meals are **petit déjeuner** (breakfast), **déjeuner** (lunch), and **diner** (dinner). Breakfast is usually only coffee and a roll; if you need more sustenance, stock up on fruit and cheese from a food store the night before. Lunch and dinner are both large meals. If you aren't up to both, eat from a delicatessen or market for one of them.

Menus will list **hors d'oeuvre** (appetizers); **potages** or **soupes** (soups); **entrées** (main courses) including **poissons** (fish), **volailles** (poultry), **oeufs** (eggs), and **viandes** (meats); **légumes** (vegetables); and **entremets** (desserts). **Volailles** usually means chicken (**poulet**) but may include duck (**canard**), or quail (**cailles**) or one of many other birds; if you're fussy, ask. Desserts may also include cheeses (**fromages**) and fruits and so on (**fruits et les autres**).

A complete meal (not including drinks and tip) at a set price is **prix fixe.** A tip is called **service** and is either **compris** (included on the check) or **pas compris** (not included). Look at the menu or the sign on the café wall to see which way the establishment works. In a restaurant serving both ways, you must pay extra for **drinks** on the **à la carte** menu, but the **service** is usually **compris.**

Hors d'Oeuvre (Appetizers, but sometimes served as main courses as well)

artichaut entier whole artichoke

assiette de charcuterie cold cuts that most Americans will recognize in the Italian version as antipasto, but meat only in France

assiette de crudités raw sliced vegetables, often served with an oil and vinegar sauce or dip

caviar sturgeon caviar; expensive

céleri remoulade celery with a mayonnaise sauce (anything *remoulade* is in a mayonnaise sauce)

champignons à la greque mushrooms with an oil, vinegar, and herb dressing

coeur de palmier hearts of palm

coquilles au crabe, or **colin,** or **langouste,** or **saumon** medallions of crab, or hake, or spiny lobster, or salmon garnished with mayonnaise

coquilles St. Jacques bay scallops in creamy sauce served in large scallop shells

escargots snails, usually dressed in herb or butter or cognac sauce and served in their shells

feuilles de vigne vine leaves stuffed with rice

filets de hareng de la baltique crème herring in sour cream

moules remoulade mussels in mayonnaise sauce

oeufs de lumps lumpfish caviar; less expensive than **caviar**

pâté finely chopped meat cooked with a variety of other ingredients and spices

pâté imperial egg roll in the Vietnamese style (Vietnamese food is to French as Chinese is to American)

quiche non-sweet custard in a pastry shell with any of many ingredients: spinach, bacon, onion

salade niçoise anchovies, eggs, black and green olives, peppers, tomatoes, green beans, and usually tuna; a very popular dish, ubiquitous in **charcuteries**

salade piemontaine like salade niçoise except with radishes instead of anchovies

salade verte green salad; also served as a side dish with the main course or, more rarely, as a last course

sardines à l'huile sardines in oil (**huile** is oil)

saucissons sausages: **à l'ail,** with garlic; **sec,** dry (actually rather moist and tender)

saucissons chaud lyonnais hot sausages Lyonnais style, which means they are usually white

saumon fumé smoked salmon or lox, very popular and expensive

terrine de canard sauvage wild smoked duck pâté

le thon mayonnaise tuna with mayonnaise, or, tunafish salad

Potages or Soupes (Soups)

bisque shellfish soup

bouillabaisse fish and shellfish stew

bouillon any clear soup stock

consommé de volaille chicken soup (clear)

consommé madrilène chicken stock flavored with tomato juice, lemon rind, and spices

petite marmite hearty soup of chicken, beef, and vegetables

potage crème Saint-Germain cream of pea soup

sorbet tomate gazpacho-type soup

soup à l'oignon onion soup

vichyssoise cream of leek and potato soup, usually served cold; pronounce the last ''s''

Entrées (Main Courses)

Poissons (Fish)

bar bass

crevettes shrimp

daurade gilthead bream, a popular fish with white flesh and a delicate taste

filet de maquerreaux mackerel filet

filet de sole the one and only

grenouilles frogs' legs

homard lobster

limande meunière lemon sole or flounder sautéed in oil and butter

poire d'avocat au crabe avocado stuffed with crab meat

raie skatefish: **au beurre noir** (browned butter and vinegar sauce); **au beurre blanc** (butter sauce with shallots and spices)

truite au bleu de meunière trout in oil and butter

turbot also called turbot in English, but not usually available in the U.S.; light, white-fleshed salt-water fish

Volailles (Poultry)

cailles aux raisins quail with raisins, a popular recipe for these tiny birds, usually served two to an order

caneton aux cerises duckling with cherries

coq au vin chicken with vegetables in red wine sauce

coquelet sauté sautéed baby rooster

fricassé de volailles aux cepes wings and backs of a bird cooked with mushrooms

pardix partridge

poulet à la Kiev chicken Kiev

poulet imperial Vietnamese chicken

poulet rôti au froid chicken roasted on a rotisserie and served cold

Oeufs (Eggs)

oeufs à la coque boiled eggs: **brouillé** (scrambled); **en gelée** (in aspic, often a first course); **sur le plat** (fried)

Viandes (Meats)

bifteck steak: **entrecôte** (usually a good cut); **pavé** (a thick steak often served **au poivre,** with pepper and very spicy);

filet mignon (same as in English); **à l'échalote** (with shallots); **chateau briant frite** (chateaubriand with French-fried potatoes — most steaks are served with French-fried potatoes automatically in France); **steak tartare** or **cru** (raw chopped steak); **steak frites** (fried) is the national dish; **bleu** means meat is still almost raw, just heated up; **saignant** is rare; **au point** is medium; **bien cuit** is well done; French restaurants have difficulty cooking **au point** steaks

boeuf burguignonne stew of beef chunks, vegetables and burgundy wine sauce

boeuf en gelée sliced beef in a jelled sauce

boeuf Stroganoff same as in English

boudin blood sausage

brochette de mouton shish kebab: mutton on a skewer, broiled

carre de porc florentine ribs of pork in the Italian style with spinach and cheese

jambon ham: **Parme** (red and uncooked); **de Prague** (Polish); other varieties are named for the place they were made, such as Virginia, York, and various French provinces

jarret de veau veal knuckles, sometimes **au citron** (with lemon)

l'andouillette intestines of pork, often mixed with other parts of the animal — liver, heart — and chopped and wrapped into a sausage

l'escalope panne spaghetti filet, rib, or leg of an animal with spaghetti

lapin en papilotte rabbit cooked wrapped in paper or foil

osso bucco Italian dish of braised chucks of meat

pieds de porc pigs' feet

tournedos de veau medallions of veal, usually broiled or sautéed

les tripes au vin blanc tripe (usually pork) in white wine

vol au vent de ris de veau veal sweetbreads served in pastry shell

Légumes (Vegetables)

asperges fraiches fresh asparagus

choux blanc; choux rouge white or red cabbage

concombres cucumbers

girolles one of many varieties of mushrooms

haricots rouges; haricots verts kidney beans and string beans

maïs corn

petits pois tiny green peas

poireaux leeks, often served **vinaigrette** as an appetizer

pommes mayonnaise potato salad

radis beurre radishes with butter and salt

vapeur riz steamed or boiled rice

Entremets (Desserts)

crème caramel caramel custard

crème chantilly whipped cream lightly sweetened

crème fraiche slightly soured sweet cream

crème de marrons pureed chestnuts in cream

gâteau cake

glaces ice creams

meringue glaces chantilly meringue filled with chocolate ice cream and topped with whipped cream

omelette norvegienne baked Alaska

pêche ou banane melba poached peach or banana with vanilla ice cream, raspberry puree, and kirsch

poire belle Hélène pear with ice cream, a cookie, and hot chocolate sauce

profiterolles au chocolate cream puffs filled with ice cream and covered with chocolate sauce; supposedly Napoleon's favorite dessert

salade au citron green salad dressed with sliced lemon dressing; refreshing after a big meal

sorbets sherbets

tarte aux fruits fruit tarts: small pastries filled with custard and topped with glazed fruits

Fromages (Cheeses)

Cheeses are almost always offered as dessert in cafés and restaurants. Among the great varieties of cheeses commonly offered are: Camembert, Cantal, Gruyère, St. Paulin, Pont l'Eveque, Gorgonzola, Munster, Brie de Meaux, and a special favorite with the French, goat cheese under the blanket name of Chèvre. **Fromage aux herbes** is mild white cheese with various herbs.

Fruits

ananas pineapple; **l'ananas au sirop** (pineapple in syrup)
fraises strawberries
framboises raspberries
melon nature plain melon in season

pamplemousse grapefruit
plum au rhum plum in rum sauce
poire au vin rouge pear poached in red wine
prunneaux au sirop prunes in syrup

Boissons (Drinks)

Restaurants have a variety of **vin** (wine), usually including house liters and demi-liters of Beaujolais, côte de Rhone, and others. After-dinner **liqueurs** are also called **digestifs** and **plus cafés.** Ask for **de l'eau** for a glass or carafe of water. **De l'eau mineral** is mineral water, a popular alternative to wine with dinner. Common French brands include Perrier, Vittel, Vichy, and Evian.

Note: Sometimes you will see a cooking style noted on a menu that puzzles even the French. Some regions of France are used to connote a style known primarily to the chef. Or there are simply esoteric designations, such as **Limousin** (done with onions, shallots, mushrooms, and seasonings). If you know some of the basic words for French foods, you will be able to understand an explanation by restaurant employees.

English–Français

A

a [ə], **an** *art* un, une.
aback [ə'bak] *adv* **be taken aback** être déconcerté.
abandon [ə'bandən] *v* abandonner; (*hope, etc.*) renoncer à.
abashed [ə'baʃt] *adj* décontenancé, confus.
abate [ə'beit] *v* (*storm*) s'apaiser; (*fever*) baisser; (*courage*) diminuer. **abatement** *n* suppression *f*; réduction *f*.
abattoir ['abətwaɪ] *n* abattoir *m*.
abbey ['abi] *n* abbaye *f*. **abbess** *n* abbesse *f*. **abbot** *n* abbé *m*.
abbreviate [ə'briːvieit] *v* abréger. **abbreviation** *n* abréviation *f*.
abdicate ['abdikeit] *v* (*king, etc.*) abdiquer; (*give up*) renoncer à. **abdication** *n* abdication *f*; renonciation *f*.
abdomen ['abdəmən] *n* abdomen *m*. **abdominal** *adj* abdominal.
abduct [əb'dʌkt] *v* enlever. **abduction** *n* enlèvement *n*.
aberration [abə'reiʃən] *n* aberration *f*. **aberrant** *adj* aberrant.
abet [ə'bet] *v* encourager. **abettor** *n* complice *m, f*.
abeyance [ə'beiəns] *n* **be in abeyance** rester en suspens. **fall into abeyance** tomber en désuétude.
abhor [əb'hoɪ] *v* abhorrer. **abhorrence** *n* horreur *f*. **abhorrent** *adj* odieux.
*abide [ə'baid] *v* (*tolerate*) supporter. **abide by** (*rule*) se conformer à; (*promise*) rester fidèle à.
ability [ə'biləti] *n* capacité *f*; talent *m*. **to the best of one's ability** de son mieux.
abject [,abdʒekt] *adj* abject; misérable; (*apology*) servile. **in abject poverty** dans la misère noire.

ablaze [ə'bleiz] *adv, adj* en feu.
able ['eibl] *adj* capable. **be able** pouvoir; (*know how to*) savoir. **able-bodied** *adj* robuste.
abnormal [ab'noːml] *adj* anormal. **abnormality** *n* anomalie *f*; malformation *f*.
aboard [ə'boɪd] *adv* à bord. *prep* à bord de. **go aboard** s'embarquer.
abode [ə'boud] *V* **abide**. *n* demeure *f*; (*law*) domicile *m*.
abolish [ə'boliʃ] *v* abolir; supprimer. **abolition** *n* abolition *f*; suppression *f*.
abominable [ə'bominəbl] *adj* abominable. **abomination** *n* abomination *f*.
Aborigine [abə'ridʒini] *n* aborigène *m, f*.
abort [ə'boɪt] *v* avorter. **abortion** *n* avortement *m*. **have an abortion** se faire avorter. **abortive** *adj* manqué.
abound [ə'baund] *v* abonder.
about [ə'baut] *adv* (*approximately*) vers, environ; (*here and there*) çà et là; (*around*) autour. *prep* (*concerning*) au sujet de; (*around*) autour de. **about to** sur le point de. **what is it about?** de quoi s'agit-il?
above [ə'bʌv] *adv, prep* au-dessus (de). **above all** surtout. **above-mentioned** *adj* ci-dessus.
abrasion [ə'breiʒən] *n* frottement *m*; (*med*) écorchure *f*. **abrasive** *nm, adj* abrasif.
abreast [ə'brest] *adv* de front. **keep abreast of** se tenir au courant de.
abridge [ə'bridʒ] *v* abréger. **abridgment** *n* résumé *m*.
abroad [ə'broɪd] *adv* à l'étranger.
abrupt [ə'brʌpt] *adj* soudain; brusque; (*slope*) abrupt.
abscess ['abses] *n* abcès *m*.
abscond [əb'skond] *v* s'enfuir.
absent ['absənt] *adj* absent. **absent-minded** *adj* distrait. **absent-mindedness** *n* distraction *f*. **absence** *n* absence *f*. **in the**

absence of faute de. **absentee** *n* absent, -e *m, f*.
absolute [ˈabsəluːt] *adj* absolu; complet, -ète. **absolutely** *adv* absolument, tout à fait.
absolve [abˈzolv] *v* absoudre; (*law*) acquitter. **absolution** *n* absolution *f*.
absorb [abˈzoːb] *v* absorber. **absorbent** *adj* absorbant. **absorbing** *adj* (*book, etc.*) passionnant. **absorption** *n* absorption *f*.
abstain [abˈstein] *v* s'abstenir. **abstention** *n* abstention *f*. **abstinence** *n* abstinence *f*.
abstract [ˈabstrakt; *v* abˈstrakt] *adj* abstrait. *n* abstrait *m*; résumé *m*. *v* isoler. **abstraction** *n* (*removal*) extraction *f*; (*absent-mindedness*) distraction *f*; (*concept*) abstraction *f*.
absurd [abˈsəːd] *adj* absurde.
abundance [əˈbandəns] *n* abondance *f*. **abundant** *adj* abondant. **abundantly** *adv* abondamment; (*grow*) à foison; (*completely*) tout à fait.
abuse [əˈbjuːz; *n* əˈbjuːs] *v* (*misuse*) abuser de; (*insult*) injurier, insulter. *n* abus *m*; insultes *f pl*. **abusive** *adj* abusif; injurieux.
abyss [əˈbis] *n* abîme *m*.
academy [əˈkadəmi] *n* académie *f*. **academic** *adj* académique; théorique; (*studies*) scolaire, universitaire.
accede [akˈsiːd] *v* **accede to** agréer.
accelerate [akˈseləreit] *v* accélérer. **acceleration** *n* accélération *f*. **accelerator** *n* accélérateur *m*.
accent [ˈaksənt] *n* accent *m*. *v also* **accentuate** accentuer.
accept [akˈsept] *v* accepter. **acceptable** *adj* acceptable. **acceptance** *n* acceptation *f*; approbation *f*.
access [ˈakses] *n* accès *m*. **accessible** *adj* accessible. **accession** *n* accession *f*; (*to throne*) avènement *m*.
accessory [akˈsesəri] *nm, adj* accessoire.
accident [ˈaksidənt] *n* accident *m*. **by accident** par hasard. **accidental** *adj* accidentel.
acclaim [əˈkleim] *v* acclamer. *n also* **acclamation** acclamation *f*.
acclimatize [əˈklaimətaiz] *v* acclimater; habituer.
accolade [ˈakəleid] *n* accolade *f*.
accommodate [əˈkomədeit] *v* loger; (*adapt*) accommoder. **accommodating** *adj* obligeant. **accommodation** *n* logement *m*, chambres *f pl*.

accompany [əˈkampəni] *v* accompagner. **accompaniment** *n* accompagnement *m*. **accompanist** *n* accompagnateur, -trice *f*.
accomplice [əˈkamplis] *n* complice *m, f*.
accomplish [əˈkamplif] *v* accomplir; réaliser. **accomplished** *adj* (*skilled*) doué; accompli. **accomplishment** *n* accomplissement *m*; talent *m*.
accord [əˈkoːd] *v* (s')accorder. *n* accord *m*. **of one's own accord** de son plein gré. **accordance** *n* conformité *f*. **in accordance with** conformément à. **according to** selon.
accordion [əˈkoːdiən] *n* accordéon *m*.
accost [əˈkost] *v* accoster.
account [əˈkaunt] *n* compte *m*; (*report*) exposé *m*. **on account of** à cause de. **on no account** en aucun cas. **take into account** tenir compte de. *v* **account for** justifier; expliquer. **accountant** *n* comptable *m, f*.
accrue [əˈkruː] *v* revenir; s'accumuler. **accrued interest** intérêt couru *m*.
accumulate [əˈkjuːmjuleit] *v* (s')accumuler. **accumulation** *n* accumulation *f*.
accurate [ˈakjurət] *adj* exact, précis. **accuracy** *n* exactitude *f*, précision *f*.
accuse [əˈkjuːz] *v* accuser. **accusation** *n* accusation *f*. **accusing** *adj* accusateur, -trice.
accustom [əˈkastəm] *v* habituer.
ace [eis] *n* as *m*.
ache [eik] *v* faire mal. *n* douleur *f*.
achieve [əˈtʃiːv] *v* (*task*) accomplir; (*aim*) atteindre. **achievement** *n* (*feat*) exploit *m*; (*completion*) exécution *f*.
acid [ˈasid] *nm, adj* acide.
acknowledge [əkˈnolidʒ] *v* reconnaître; (*letter, etc.*) accuser réception de, répondre à. **acknowledgment** *n* reconnaissance *f*; (*of error*) aveu *m*; (*receipt*) reçu *m*.
acne [ˈakni] *n* acné *f*.
acorn [ˈeikoːn] *n* gland *m*.
acoustic [əˈkuːstik] *adj* acoustique. **acoustics** *pl n* acoustique *f sing*.
acquaint [əˈkweint] *v* (*inform*) aviser. **acquaint with** mettre au courant de. **be acquainted with** (*a fact*) savoir; (*a place or person*) connaître. **become acquainted with** faire la connaissance de. **acquaintance** *n* connaissance *f*; relation *f*.
acquiesce [akwiˈes] *v* acquiescer. **acquiescence** *n* consentement *m*.

3

acquire [ə'kwaiə] v acquérir; prendre. **acquired taste** goût qui s'acquiert m.

acquisition n acquisition f. **acquisitive** adj âpre au gain.

acquit [ə'kwit] v acquitter. **acquittal** n acquittement m.

acrid ['akrid] adj âcre; (biting) acerbe.

acrimony ['akriməni] n acrimonie f. **acrimonious** adj acrimonieux.

acrobat ['akrəbat] n acrobate m. f. **acrobatic** adj acrobatique. **acrobatics** pl n acrobatie f sing.

across [ə'kros] prep en travers de, à travers; de l'autre côté. adv (width) de large. **go across** traverser.

acrylic [ə'krilik] adj acrylique.

act [akt] n acte m, action f; (law) loi f; (theatre) acte m. **in the act of** en train de. v agir; (theatre) jouer. **act the fool** faire l'idiot. **acting** adj (temporary) suppléant, par intérim; (theatre) acteur m. **actress** n actrice f.

action ['akʃən] n action f; (law) procès m; (mil) combat m. **out of action** hors d'usage.

active ['aktiv] adj actif. **activate** v activer. **activity** n activité f.

actual ['aktʃuəl] adj réel; (factual) positif. **actually** adv effectivement; à vrai dire.

actuary ['aktjuəri] n actuaire m.

acumen [ə'kjuːmen] n perspicacité f.

acupuncture ['akjupʌnktʃə] n acupuncture f.

acute [ə'kjuːt] adj aigu, -guë; (mind) pénétrant; (pain, etc.) vif.

adamant ['adəmənt] adj inflexible.

Adam's apple [adəm'zapl] n pomme d'Adam f.

adapt [ə'dapt] v (s')adapter. **adaptable** adj adaptable. **adaptation** n adaptation f. **adaptor** n (elec) prise multiple f.

add [ad] v ajouter; (numbers) additionner. **addition** n addition f. **in addition** de plus. **in addition to** en plus de. **additional** adj additionnel; supplémentaire.

addendum [ə'dendəm] n addendum m invar.

adder ['adə] n vipère f.

addict ['adikt; v ə'dikt] n (drugs) toxicomane m, f; fanatique m, f. v **become addicted to** s'adonner à. **addiction** n (med) dépendance f.

additive ['aditiv] nm, adj additif.

address [ə'dres] n adresse f; (talk) discours m. v (s')adresser (à).

adenoids ['adənoidz] pl n végétations adénoides f pl.

adept [ə'dept] adj expert, versé.

adequate ['adikwət] adj suffisant.

adhere [əd'hiə] v adhérer. **adherent** n adhérent, -e m, f. **adhesion** n adhérence f. **adhesive** nm, adj adhésif.

adjacent [ə'dʒeisənt] adj adjacent, contigu, -guë.

adjective ['adʒiktiv] n adjectif m.

adjoin [ə'dʒoin] v être contigu à. **adjoining** adj voisin.

adjourn [ə'dʒəin] v ajourner; (meeting) suspendre la séance; (move) se retirer.

adjudicate [ə'dʒuːdikeit] v juger. **adjudication** n jugement m. **adjudicator** n juge m.

adjust [ə'dʒʌst] v ajuster; (s')adapter; (correct) régler. **adjustment** n réglage m.

ad-lib [ad'lib] adv à volonté. v improviser.

administer [əd'ministə] v administrer; (business, etc.) gérer. **administration** n administration f; gestion f. **administrative** adj administratif. **administrator** n administrateur, -trice m, f.

admiral ['admərəl] n amiral m. **Admiralty** n ministère de la Marine m.

admire [əd'maiə] v admirer. **admirable** adj admirable. **admiration** n admiration f. **admiring** adj admiratif.

admit [əd'mit] v (let in) laisser entrer; (acknowledge) admettre. **admission** n admission f.

adolescence [adə'lesns] n adolescence f. **adolescent** n, adj adolescent, -e.

adopt [ə'dopt] v adopter. **adopted** adj (child) adoptif. **adoption** n adoption f.

adore [ə'doː] v adorer. **adorable** adj adorable. **adoration** n adoration f.

adorn [ə'doːn] v orner, parer.

adrenalin [ə'drenəlin] n adrénaline f.

adrift [ə'drift] adv à la dérive. **come adrift** (wire, etc.) se détacher.

adroit [ə'droit] adj adroit.

adulation [adju'leiʃən] n adulation f.

adult ['adʌlt] n(m+f), adj adulte.

adulterate [ə'dʌltəreit] v adultérer, falsifier.

adultery [ə'dʌltəri] n adultère m. **adulterer** n adultère m, f.

advance [əd'vains] v (s')avancer. n avance f. **advance booking office** location f. **book in advance** retenir à l'avance. **luggage in advance** bagages enregistrés m pl.

advantage [əd'vɑːntidʒ] *n* avantage *m*. **take advantage of** profiter de. **advantageous** *adj* avantageux.

advent ['ædvənt] *n* venue *f*. **Advent** *n* (*rel*) Avent *m*.

adventure [əd'ventʃə] *n* aventure *f*. **adventurer** *n* aventurier, -ère *m, f*. **adventurous** *adj* aventureux.

adverb ['ædvəːb] *n* adverbe *m*.

adversary ['ædvəsəri] *n* adversaire *m, f*.

adverse ['ædvəːs] *adj* défavorable, hostile. **adversity** *n* adversité *f*.

advertise ['ædvətaiz] *v* (*comm*) faire de la publicité (pour); (*newspaper, etc*.) insérer une annonce. **advertisement** *n* (*comm*) réclame *f*, publicité *f*; (*newspaper*) annonce *f*. **advertising** *n* publicité *f*.

advise [əd'vaiz] *v* conseiller; recommander; (*inform*) aviser. **advice** *n* conseils *m pl*; avis *m*. **advisable** *adj* recommandable. **adviser** *n* conseiller, -ère *m, f*. **advisory** *adj* consultatif.

advocate ['ædvəkeit] *v* recommander.

aerial ['eəriəl] *adj* aérien. *n* antenne *f*.

aerodynamics [eərədai'næmiks] *n* aérodynamique *f*.

aeronautics [eərə'nɔːtiks] *n* aéronautique *f*.

aeroplane ['eərəplein] *n* avion *m*.

aerosol ['eərəsɔl] *n* bombe *f*; (*perfume*) atomiseur *m*.

aesthetic [iːs'θetik] *adj* esthétique.

affair [ə'feə] *n* affaire *f*. **have an affair with** avoir une liaison avec.

affect[1] [ə'fekt] *v* (*influence*) affecter, toucher.

affect[2] [ə'fekt] *v* (*feign*) affecter, feindre. **affected** *adj* affecté, maniéré.

affection [ə'fekʃən] *n* affection *f*. **affectionate** *adj* affectueux.

affiliate [ə'filieit] *v* affilier. **affiliated company** filiale *f*. **affiliation** *n* affiliation *f*.

affinity [ə'finəti] *n* affinité *f*.

affirm [ə'fəːm] *v* affirmer. **affirmative** *nm, adj* affirmatif.

affix [ə'fiks: *n* 'æfiks] *v* apposer; (*stick*) coller. *n* (*gramm*) affixe *m*.

afflict [ə'flikt] *v* affliger. **affliction** *n* affliction *f*; infirmité *f*.

affluent ['æfluənt] *adj* abondant; riche. **affluence** *n* abondance *f*; richesse *f*.

afford [ə'fɔːd] *v* avoir les moyens d'acheter; (*provide*) fournir.

affront [ə'frʌnt] *v* insulter. *n* affront *m*.

afield [ə'fiːld] *adv* **far afield** très loin. **farther afield** plus loin.

afloat [ə'flout] *adv* à flot.

afoot [ə'fut] *adv* **there's something afoot** il se prépare quelque chose.

aforesaid [ə'fɔːsed] *adj* susdit.

afraid [ə'freid] *adj* effrayé. **be afraid** avoir peur; (*polite regret*) regretter.

afresh [ə'freʃ] *adv* de nouveau. **start afresh** recommencer.

Africa ['æfrikə] *n* Afrique *f*. **African** *adj* africain; *n* Africain, -e *m, f*.

aft [ɑːft] *adv* sur or à l'arrière.

after ['ɑːftə] *prep, conj* après. *adv* après; ensuite. **after all** après tout.

after-effect *n* suite *f*.

aftermath ['ɑːftəmɑːθ] *n* conséquences *f pl*.

afternoon [ɑːftə'nuːn] *n* après-midi *m*.

afterthought ['ɑːftəθɔːt] *n* pensée après coup *f*.

afterwards ['ɑːftəwədz] *adv* ensuite.

again [ə'gen] *adv* de nouveau, encore. **again and again** à plusieurs reprises.

against [ə'genst] *prep* contre. **against the law** contraire à la loi.

age [eidʒ] *n* âge *m*; (*historical*) époque *f*. **for ages** pendant une éternité. **of age** majeur, -e. **under age** mineur, -e. *v* vieillir. **aged** *adj* âgé.

agency ['eidʒənsi] *n* agence *f*, bureau *m*.

agenda [ə'dʒendə] *n* ordre du jour *m*.

agent ['eidʒənt] *n* agent, -e *m, f*; représentant, -e *m, f*.

aggravate [ə'grəveit] *v* aggraver; (*increase*) augmenter; (*annoy*) agacer. **aggravation** *n* aggravation *f*; agacement *m*.

aggregate ['ægrigət] *n* ensemble *m*. *adj* collectif.

aggression [ə'greʃən] *n* agression *f*. **aggressive** *adj* agressif.

aghast [ə'gɑːst] *adj* atterré.

agile ['ædʒail] *adj* agile. **agility** *n* agilité *f*.

agitate ['ædʒiteit] *v* (*shake*) agiter; (*worry*) troubler. **agitated** *adj* inquiet, -ète. **agitation** *n* agitation *f*; émotion *f*. **agitator** *n* agitateur, -trice *m, f*.

agnostic [ag'nɔstik] *n(m+f), adj* agnostique.

ago [ə'gou] *adv* il y a. **two days ago** il y a deux mois.

agog [ə'gɔg] *adj, adv* en émoi. **be all agog** être impatient.

agony ['ægəni] *n* (*mental*) angoisse *f*; (*med*) agonie *f*. **be in agony** souffrir le martyre. **agonizing** *adj* angoissant.

agree [ə'griː] v être d'accord; consentir; (*concur*) convenir, s'accorder. **agreeable** *adj* agréable. **agreement** *n* accord *m*.

agriculture ['agrikʌltʃə] *n* agriculture *f*. **agricultural** *adj* agricole.

aground [ə'graund] *adv* échoué. **run aground** s'échouer.

ahead [ə'hed] *adv* en avant; (*time*) en avance.

aid [eid] *v* aider. **aid and abet** être complice de. *n* aide *f*. **in aid of** au profit de.

aim [eim] *v* viser; aspirer. *n* (*purpose*) but *m*. **take aim (at)** viser. **aimless** *adj* (*person*) sans but; (*action*) futile.

air [eə] *n* air *m*. **by air** par avion. *v* aérer; (*opinion*) faire connaître. **airy** *adj* bien aéré.

airbed ['eəbed] *n* matelas pneumatique *m*.

airborne ['eəbɔːn] *adj* aéroporté. **become airborne** (*aircraft*) décoller.

air-conditioned *adj* climatisé. **air-conditioning** *n* climatisation *f*.

aircraft ['eəkrɑːft] *n* avion *m*. **aircraft-carrier** *n* porte-avions *m invar*.

airfield ['eəfiːld] *n* terrain d'aviation *m*.

air force *n* armée de l'air *f*.

air-hostess *n* hôtesse de l'air *f*.

airing cupboard *n* placard-séchoir *m*.

air lift *n* pont aérien *m*.

airline ['eəlain] *n* ligne aérienne *f*.

airmail ['eəmeil] *n* poste aérienne *f*. **airmail letter** lettre par avion *f*. **by airmail** par avion.

airport ['eəpɔːt] *n* aéroport *m*.

air-raid *n* attaque aérienne *f*. **air-raid shelter** abri antiaérien *m*.

airtight ['eətait] *adj* hermétique.

aisle [ail] *n* (*church*) allée centrale *f*, bas-côté *m*; (*theatre*) passage *m*; (*train, etc.*) couloir central *m*.

ajar [ə'dʒɑː] *adj, adv* entrouvert.

akin [ə'kin] *adj* **be akin to** (*resemble*) tenir de, ressembler à; (*family*) être parent de.

alabaster ['alabɑːstə] *n* albâtre *m*.

alarm [ə'lɑːm] *n* alarme *f*. **alarm clock** *n* réveil *m*. *v* alarmer. **alarmist** *n* alarmiste *m, f*.

alas [ə'las] *interj* hélas!

Albania [al'beinjə] *n* Albanie *f*. **Albanian** *nm, adj* albanais; *n* (*people*) Albanais, -e *m, f*.

albatross ['albatros] *n* albatros *m*.

albino [al'biːnou] *n* albinos *m, f*.

album ['albəm] *n* album *m*.

alchemy ['alkəmi] *n* alchimie *f*. **alchemist** *n* alchimiste *m*.

alcohol ['alkəhol] *n* alcool *m*. **alcoholic** *n(m+f)*, *adj* alcoolique. **alcoholism** *n* alcoolisme *m*.

alcove ['alkouv] *n* (*room*) alcôve *f*; (*wall*) niche *f*.

alderman ['ɔːldəmən] *n* conseiller municipal *m*.

ale [eil] *n* bière *f*.

alert [ə'lɜːt] *adj* alerte; vigilant. *n* alerte *f*. **on the alert** sur le qui-vive. *v* alerter, éveiller l'attention de.

algebra ['aldʒibrə] *n* algèbre *f*. **algebraic** *adj* algébrique.

Algeria [al'dʒiəriə] *n* Algérie *f*. **Algerian** *n* Algérien, -enne *m, f*; *adj* algérien.

Algiers [al'dʒiəz] *n* Alger.

alias ['eiliəs] *adv* alias. *n* faux nom *m*.

alibi ['alibai] *n* alibi *m*.

alien ['eiliən] *n, adj* étranger, -ère. **alien to** contraire à. **alienate** *v* aliéner. **alienation** *n* aliénation *f*; éloignement *m*.

alight¹ [ə'lait] *v* descendre; (*bird*) se poser.

alight² [ə'lait] *adj* allumé; en feu. **set alight** mettre le feu à.

align [ə'lain] *v* (s')aligner. **alignment** *n* alignement *m*.

alike [ə'laik] *adj* semblable. *adv* pareillement, de la même façon. **be alike** se ressembler.

alimentary canal [ali'mentəri] *n* tube digestif *m*.

alimony ['aliməni] *n* pension alimentaire *f*.

alive [ə'laiv] *adj* vivant.

alkali ['alkəlai] *n* alcali *m*. **alkaline** *adj* alcaline.

all [ɔːl] *pron, adj* tout, toute (*pl* tous, toutes). *adv* tout, complètement. **all right** ça va. **All Saints' Day** le Toussaint. **all the same** tout de même. **not at all** pas du tout.

allay [ə'lei] *v* apaiser; (*suspicion*) dissiper.

allege [ə'ledʒ] *v* alléguer. **allegation** *n* allégation *f*. **alleged** *adj* prétendu, allégué; présumé.

allegiance [ə'liːdʒəns] *n* fidélité *f*.

allegory ['aligəri] *n* allégorie *f*. **allegorical** *adj* allégorique.

allergy ['alədʒi] *n* allergie *f*. **allergic** *adj* allergique.

alleviate [ə'liːvieit] *v* soulager.

alley ['ali] *n* ruelle *f*.

alliance [ə'laiəns] *n* alliance *f*.

alligator ['aligeitə] *n* alligator *m*.

alliteration [əlitə'reiʃən] *n* allitération *f*.

allocate ['aləkeit] *v* (*allot*) allouer; (*share*) répartir. **allocation** *n* allocation *f*; (*share*) part *f*.

allot [ə'lot] *v* assigner. **allotment** *n* (*land*) parcelle de terre *f*.

allow [ə'lau] *v* permettre; (*give*) accorder. **allow for** tenir compte de. **allowance** *n* allocation *f*; (*subsistence*) indemnité *f*, pension *f*; (*comm*) rabais *m*.

alloy ['aloi; *v* ə'loi] *n* alliage *m*. *v* allier; faire un alliage de.

allude [ə'luid] *v* faire allusion. **allusion** *n* allusion *f*.

allure [ə'ljuə] *v* attirer. *n* charme *m*. **alluring** *adj* séduisant.

ally ['alai; *v* ə'lai] *n* allié, -ée *m, f*. *v* allier. **allied** *adj* allié; (*connected*) apparenté.

almanac ['oilmənak] *n* almanach *m*.

almighty [oil'maiti] *adj* tout-puissant; (*coll*) fameux.

almond ['aimənd] *n* (*nut*) amande *f*; (*tree*) amandier *m*.

almost ['oilmoust] *adv* presque, à peu près.

alms [aimz] *n* aumône *f*. **almshouse** *n* hospice *m*.

aloft [ə'loft] *adv* en haut.

alone [ə'loun] *adj, adv* seul. **leave alone** laisser tranquille. **let alone** sans parler de.

along [ə'loŋ] *prep* le long de. **alongside** *prep* à côté de.

aloof [ə'luif] *adj* distant. *adv* à l'écart.

aloud [ə'laud] *adv* (*reading*) à voix haute; (*think*) tout haut.

alphabet ['alfəbit] *n* alphabet *m*. **alphabetical** *adj* alphabétique. **in alphabetical order** par ordre alphabétique.

already [oil'redi] *adv* déjà.

Alsatian [al'seiʃən] *n* (*dog*) chien-loup *m*.

also ['oilsou] *adv* aussi.

altar ['oiltə] *n* autel *m*.

alter ['oiltə] *v* changer; (*dress, etc.*) retoucher. **alteration** *n* changement *m*; retouchage *m*.

alternate [oil'təinət; *v* 'oiltəneit] *adj* alternatif, alterné; (*every other*) tous les deux. *v* alterner. **alternating current** courant alternatif *m*. **alternator** *n* alternateur *m*.

alternative [oil'təinətiv] *n* (*of two*) alterna-

tive *f*; (*of several*) choix *m*; autre solution *f*. *adj* autre, alternatif.

although [oil'ðou] *conj* bien que, quoique.

altitude ['altitjuid] *n* altitude *f*.

alto ['altou] *n* (*male*) haute-contre *f*; (*female*) contralto *m*; (*instrument*) alto *m*.

altogether [oiltə'geðə] *adv* (*completely*) entièrement; (*including everything*) en tout.

altruistic [altru'istik] *adj* altruiste.

aluminium [alju'miniəm] *n* aluminium *m*.

always ['oilweiz] *adv* toujours.

am [am] *V* be.

amalgamate [ə'malgəmeit] *v* (*companies*) fusionner; (*metals*) amalgamer. **amalgamation** *n* fusionnement *m*; amalgamation *f*.

amass [ə'mas] *v* amasser.

amateur ['amətə] *n* amateur *m*.

amaze [ə'meiz] *v* stupéfier. **amazed** *adj* stupéfait. **amazement** *n* stupéfaction *f*. **amazing** *adj* stupéfiant, ahurissant.

ambassador [am'basədə] *n* ambassadeur *m*.

amber ['ambə] *n* ambre *f*; (*traffic lights*) feu orange *m*.

ambidextrous [ambi'dekstrəs] *adj* ambidextre.

ambiguous [am'bigjuəs] *adj* ambigu, -guë. **ambiguity** *n* ambiguité *f*.

ambition [am'biʃən] *n* ambition *f*. **ambitious** *adj* ambitieux.

ambivalent [am'bivələnt] *adj* ambivalent. **ambivalence** *n* ambivalence *f*.

amble ['ambl] *v* marcher d'un pas tranquille; (*horse*) ambler. *n* pas tranquille *m*; (*horse*) amble *m*.

ambulance ['ambjuləns] *n* ambulance *f*.

ambush ['ambuʃ] *n* embuscade *f*. **in ambush** en embuscade. *v* attirer dans une embuscade.

ameliorate [ə'miiliəreit] *v* (s')améliorer. **amelioration** *n* amélioration *f*.

amenable [ə'miinəbl] *adj* (*cooperative*) maniable; (*answerable*) responsable.

amend [ə'mend] *v* (s')amender; (*revise*) modifier; (*correct*) corriger. **amendment** *n* amendement *m*; modification *f*.

amenity [ə'miinəti] *n* agrément *m*. **amenities** *pl n* commodités *f pl*.

America [ə'merikə] *n* Amérique *f*; (*United States*) Etats-Unis *m pl*. **American** *n* Américain, -e *m, f*; *adj* américain.

amethyst ['aməθist] n améthyste f.

amiable ['eimiəbl] adj aimable.

amicable ['amikəbl] adj amical; (law) à l'amiable.

amid [ə'mid] prep au milieu de.

amiss [ə'mis] adv de travers. adj mal à propos. **something is amiss** quelque chose ne va pas.

ammonia [ə'mouniə] n (gas) ammoniac m; (liquid) ammoniaque f.

ammunition [amju'niʃən] n munitions f pl.

amnesia [am'niːziə] n amnésie f.

amnesty ['amnəsti] n amnistie f.

amoeba [ə'miːbə] n amibe f.

among [ə'mʌŋ] prep entre, parmi.

amoral [ei'morəl] adj amorale.

amorous ['amərəs] adj amoureux.

amorphous [ə'mɔːfəs] adj amorphe; (ideas, etc.) sans forme.

amount [ə'maunt] n quantité f; (total) montant m. v amount to s'élever à; (be equivalent to) revenir à, équivaloir à.

ampere ['ampeə] n ampère m.

amphetamine [am'fetəmiːn] n amphétamine f.

amphibian [am'fibiən] nm, adj amphibie. **amphibious** adj amphibie.

amphitheatre ['amfiθiətə] n amphithéâtre m.

ample ['ampl] adj (plenty) bien assez de; (large) ample.

amplify ['amplifai] v amplifier; développer. **amplifier** n amplificateur m.

amputate ['ampjuteit] v amputer. **amputation** n amputation f.

Amsterdam [amstə'dam] n Amsterdam.

amuse [ə'mjuːz] v (cause laughter) faire rire; (entertain) distraire. **amuse oneself** s'amuser. **amused** adj amusé. **amusement** n amusement m; distraction f.

an [an] V a.

anachronism [ə'nakrənizəm] n anachronisme m. **anachronistic** adj anachronique.

anaemia [ə'niːmiə] n anémie f. **anaemic** adj anémique.

anaesthetic [anəs'θetik] nm, adj anesthésique. **under anaesthetic** sous anesthésie. **anaesthetist** n anesthésiste m, f. **anaesthetize** v anesthésier.

anagram ['anəgram] n anagramme f.

anal ['einl] adj anal.

analogy [ə'nalədʒi] n analogie f.

analysis [ə'naləsis] n analyse f. **analyse** v

analyser, faire l'analyse de. **analytical** adj analytique.

anarchy ['anəki] n anarchie f. **anarchist** n anarchiste m, f.

anathema [ə'naθəmə] n anathème m. **it is anathema to me** je l'ai en abomination.

anatomy [ə'natəmi] n (med) anatomie f; structure f.

ancestor ['ansestə] n ancêtre m, aïeul, -e m, f. **ancestral** adj ancestral. **ancestry** n ascendance f; ancêtres m pl, aïeux m pl.

anchor ['aŋkə] n ancre f. v (naut) (se) mettre à l'ancre; (fasten) ancrer.

anchovy ['antʃəvi] n anchois m.

ancient ['einʃənt] adj antique; ancien.

ancillary [an'siləri] adj auxiliaire.

and [and] conj et.

Andorra [an'dɔːrə] n Andorre f.

anecdote ['anikdout] n anecdote f.

anemone [ə'neməni] n anémone f.

anew [ə'njuː] adv de nouveau.

angel ['eindʒəl] n ange m. **angelic** adj angélique.

angelica [an'dʒelikə] n angélique f.

anger ['aŋgə] n colère f. v mettre en colère.

angina [an'dʒainə] n angine de poitrine f.

angle ['aŋgl] n angle m; aspect m.

angling ['aŋgliŋ] n pêche à la ligne f. **angler** n pêcheur, -euse m, f.

angry ['aŋgri] adj en colère; furieux. **become angry** se fâcher.

anguish ['aŋgwiʃ] n angoisse f.

angular ['aŋgjulə] adj anguleux.

animal ['animəl] nm, adj animal.

animate ['animət; v 'animeit] adj animé. v animer. **animation** n animation f.

animosity [ani'mositi] n animosité f.

aniseed ['anisiːd] n graine d'anis f; (as modifier) à l'anis.

ankle ['aŋkl] n cheville f.

annals ['anlz] pl n annales f pl.

annex [ə'neks; n 'aneks] v annexer. **annexe** n annexe f.

annihilate [ə'naiəleit] v (mil) anéantir; annihiler. **annihilation** n anéantissement m.

anniversary [ani'vəːsəri] n anniversaire m.

annotate ['anəteit] v annoter. **annotation** n annotation f.

announce [ə'nauns] v annoncer. **announcement** n annonce f; (official) avis m; (of birth, etc.) faire-part m. **announcer** n (radio, TV) speaker, -erine m, f.

annoy [ə'nɔi] v ennuyer, agacer. **annoyance** n mécontentement m; (*nuisance*) tracas m. **annoyed** adj mécontent. **annoying** adj agaçant, ennuyeux.

annual ['ænjuəl] adj annuel. n (*bot*) plante annuelle f; (*children's book*) album m.

annul [ə'nʌl] v (*marriage*) annuler; (*law*) abroger. **annulment** n annulation f; abrogation f.

anode ['ænoud] n anode f.

anomaly [ə'nɔməli] n anomalie f. **anomalous** adj anormal.

anonymous [ə'nɔniməs] adj anonyme. **anonymity** n anonymat m.

anorak ['ænəræk] n anorak m.

another [ə'nʌðə] pron, adj (*different*) un autre; (*extra*) encore un. **one another** l'un l'autre, les uns les autres.

answer ['ænsə] n réponse f; solution f. v répondre (à). **answerable** adj responsable.

ant [ænt] n fourmi f. **anthill** n fourmilière f.

antagonize [an'tægənaiz] v contrarier. **antagonism** n antagonisme m. **antagonist** n antagoniste m, f. **antagonistic** adj opposé.

antecedent [anti'siːdənt] adj antérieur, -e. n antécédent m.

antelope ['antəloup] n antilope f.

antenna [an'tenə] n antenne f.

anthem ['ænθəm] n (*national*) hymne m; motet m.

anthology [an'θɔlədʒi] n anthologie f.

anthropology [anθrə'pɔlədʒi] n anthropologie f. **anthropological** adj anthropologique. **anthropologist** n anthropologiste m, f.

anti-aircraft [anti'eəkraːft] adj antiaérien.

antibiotic [antibai'ɔtik] nm, adj antibiotique.

antibody ['anti,bɔdi] n anticorps m.

anticipate [an'tisipeit] v (*foresee*) prévoir; (*act in advance*) prévenir, anticiper. **anticipation** n attente f; appréhension f. **in anticipation** par anticipation, d'avance.

anticlimax [anti'klaimaks] n chute f.

anticlockwise [anti'klɔkwaiz] adj dans le sens inverse des aiguilles d'une montre.

antics ['antiks] pl n singeries f pl, cirque m sing.

anticyclone [anti'saikloun] n anticyclone m.

antidote ['antidout] n antidote m.

antifreeze ['antifriːz] n antigel m.

antihistamine [anti'histəmin] n antihistaminique m.

antipathy [an'tipəθi] n antipathie f. **antipathetic** adj antipathique.

antique [an'tiːk] adj ancien; antique. n (*ornament*) objet d'art ancien m; (*furniture*) meuble ancien m. **antique dealer** n antiquaire m, f. **antique shop** n magasin d'antiquités m. **antiquated** adj vieilli. **antiquity** n antiquité f.

anti-Semitic [antisə'mitik] adj antisémite. **anti-Semite** n antisémite m, f. **anti-Semitism** n antisémitisme m.

antiseptic [anti'septik] nm, adj antiseptique.

antisocial [anti'souʃəl] adj antisocial.

antithesis [an'tiθəsis] n antithèse f.

antlers ['antləz] pl n bois m pl, ramure f sing.

antonym ['antənim] n antonyme m.

anus ['einəs] n anus m.

anvil ['anvil] n enclume f.

anxious ['aŋkʃəs] adj (*worry*) anxieux; (*desire*) impatient. **anxiety** n anxiété f; grand désir m. **anxiously** adv avec inquiétude; avec impatience.

any ['eni] adj (*interrogative*) du, de la, des; (*negative*) de; (*whichever*) n'importe quel. pron en: *je n'en ai pas*; aucun; n'importe lequel. **anybody** or **anyone** pron n'importe qui; (*somebody*) quelqu'un; (*negative*) personne. **anyhow** or **anyway** adv en tout cas; quand même. **any more** encore (de); (*negative*) plus. **anything** pron n'importe quoi; (*something*) quelque chose; (*negative*) rien. **anywhere** adv n'importe où; (*somewhere*) quelque part; (*negative*) nulle part. **at any rate** en tout cas. **in any case** de toute façon.

apart [ə'paːt] adv à part; à distance; séparément; en pièces. **apart from** en dehors de. **come apart** se défaire. **take apart** démonter. **tell apart** distinguer l'un de l'autre.

apartment [ə'paːtmənt] n (*room*) pièce f; (*flat*) appartement m.

apathy ['apəθi] n apathie f, indifférence f. **apathetic** adj apathique.

ape [eip] n singe m, f. v singer, imiter.

aperture ['apətjuə] n (*phot*) ouverture f; orifice m.

apex ['eipeks] *n* sommet *m*.

aphid ['eifid] *n* aphidé *m*.

aphrodisiac [afrə'diziak] *nm, adj* aphrodisiaque.

apiece [ə'piːs] *adv* chacun; par personne; la pièce.

apology [ə'polədʒi] *n* excuses *f pl*; (*defence*) apologie *f*. **apologize** *v* s'excuser. **be apologetic** se répandre en excuses.

apoplexy ['apəpleksi] *n* apoplexie *f*. **fit of apoplexy** coup de sang *m*.

apostle [ə'posl] *n* apôtre *m*.

apostrophe [ə'postrəfi] *n* apostrophe *f*.

appal [ə'poːl] *v* (*shock*) consterner; (*frighten*) épouvanter. **appalling** *adj* consternant; épouvantable.

apparatus [apə'reitəs] *n* appareil *m*, dispositif *m*.

apparent [ə'parənt] *adj* (*not real*) apparent; (*obvious*) évident, manifeste. **apparently** *adv* apparemment; paraît-il.

apparition [apə'riʃən] *n* apparition *f*.

appeal [ə'piːl] *v* faire (un) appel. **appeal to** (*please*) plaire à; (*request*) s'adresser à. **appealing** *adj* (*moving*) attendrissant; (*attractive*) attirant.

appear [ə'piə] *v* (*be seen*) apparaître, se montrer; (*seem*) paraître. **appearance** *n* apparition *f*; (*aspect*) apparence *f*.

appease [ə'piːz] *v* apaiser. **appeasement** *n* apaisement *m*.

appendix [ə'pendiks] *n* appendice *m*. **appendicitis** *n* appendicite *f*.

appetite ['apitait] *n* appétit *m*. **appetizer** *n* apéritif *m*. **appetizing** *adj* appétissant.

applaud [ə'ploːd] *v* applaudir. **applause** *n* applaudissements *m pl*.

apple ['apl] *n* (*fruit*) pomme *f*; (*tree*) pommier *m*.

apply [ə'plai] *v* appliquer; (*paint, etc.*) mettre; (*ask*) s'adresser; (*refer*) s'appliquer. **appliance** *n* appareil *m*. **applicable** *adj* applicable. **applicant** *n* candidat, -e *m, f*. **application** *n* application *f*; (*job*) demande *f*.

appoint [ə'point] *v* désigner, nommer. **at the appointed time** à l'heure convenue. **appointment** *n* (*meeting*) rendez-vous *m*; (*job*) poste.

apportion [ə'poːʃən] *v* partager, répartir; assigner.

appraise [ə'preiz] *v* estimer, évaluer. **appraisal** *n* évaluation *f*; appréciation *f*.

appreciate [ə'priːʃieit] *v* (*value*) apprécier;

(*be aware of*) se rendre compte de; (*be grateful for*) être reconnaissant de; (*rise in value*) prendre de la valeur. **appreciation** *n* appréciation *f*; reconnaissance *f*.

apprehend [apri'hend] *v* (*arrest*) arrêter, appréhender; (*understand*) comprendre. **apprehension** *n* (*fear*) appréhension *f*; arrestation *f*. **apprehensive** *adj* inquiet, -ète; appréhensif.

apprentice [ə'prentis] *v* placer ou mettre en apprentissage (chez). *n* apprenti, -e *m, f*. **apprenticeship** *n* apprentissage *m*.

approach [ə'proutʃ] *v* (s')approcher (de). *n* approche *f*, accès *m*.

appropriate [ə'prouprieit; *adj* ə'proupriət] *v* s'approprier. *adj* (*name, etc.*) juste, bien choisi; (*correct*) approprié.

approve [ə'pruːv] *v* approuver. **approval** *n* approbation *f*. **on approval** à l'essai.

approximate [ə'proksimeit; *adj* ə'proksimət] *v* se rapprocher (de). *adj* approximatif.

apricot ['eiprikot] *n* (*fruit*) abricot *m*; (*tree*) abricotier *m*.

April ['eiprəl] *n* avril *m*. **April fool** *n* poisson d'avril *m*.

apron ['eiprən] *n* tablier *m*; (*aero*) aire de manœuvre *f*.

apt [apt] *adj* (*fitting*) juste, convenable; (*inclined*) enclin, porté. **aptly** *adv* à propos.

aptitude ['aptitjuːd] *n* aptitude *f*.

aqualung ['akwəlʌŋ] *n* scaphandre autonome *m*.

aquarium [ə'kweəriəm] *n* aquarium *m*.

Aquarius [ə'kweəriəs] *n* Verseau *m*.

aquatic [ə'kwatik] *adj* aquatique.

aqueduct ['akwidʌkt] *n* aqueduc *m*.

Arab ['arəb] *n* Arabe *m, f*. *adj* arabe. **Arabia** *n* Arabie *f*. **Arabian** *or* **Arabic** *adj* arabe.

arable ['arəbl] *adj* arable.

arbitrary ['aːbitrəri] *adj* arbitraire.

arbitrate ['aːbitreit] *v* arbitrer, juger. **arbitration** *n* arbitrage *m*. **arbiter** *n* arbitre *m*.

arc [aːk] *n* arc *m*. **arc lamp** lampe à arc *f*. **arc light** arc voltaïque *m*.

arcade [aː'keid] *n* arcade *m*; (*shopping*) passage.

arch [aːtʃ] *v* (s')arquer. *n* (*church, etc.*) voûte *f*, cintre *m*; (*bridge*) arche *f*.

archaeology [aːki'olədʒi] *n* archéologie *f*. **archaeological** *adj* archéologique. **archaeologist** *n* archéologue *m, f*.

archaic [ɑːˈkeiik] adj archaïque. **archaism** n archaïsme m.

archbishop [ɑːtʃˈbiʃəp] n archevêque m.

archduke [ɑːtʃˈdjuːk] n archiduc m. **archduchess** n archiduchesse f.

archery [ˈɑːtʃəri] n tir à l'arc m. **archer** n archer m.

archetype [ˈɑːkitaip] n archétype m.

archipelago [ɑːkiˈpeləgou] n archipel m.

architect [ˈɑːkitekt] n architecte m. **architecture** n architecture f.

archives [ˈɑːkaivz] pl n archives f pl. **archivist** n archiviste m.

ardent [ˈɑːdənt] adj ardent.

ardour [ˈɑːdə] n ardeur f.

arduous [ˈɑːdjuəs] adj ardu.

are [ɑː] V **be**.

area [ˈeəriə] n aire f; (region) étendue f, région f.

arena [əˈriːnə] n arène f.

argue [ˈɑːgjuː] v se disputer, discuter. **argument** n dispute f; (debate) discussion f; (reasons) argument m.

arid [ˈærid] adj aride. **aridity** n aridité f.

Aries [ˈeəriːz] n Bélier m.

*arise [əˈraiz] v s'élever; (question) se présenter; résulter.

arisen [əˈrizn] V **arise**.

aristocracy [æriˈstokrəsi] n aristocratie f. **aristocrat** n aristocrate m, f. **aristocratic** adj aristocratique.

arithmetic [əˈriθmətik] n arithmétique f, calcul m.

arm[1] [ɑːm] n bras m. **armchair** n fauteuil m. **arm in arm** bras dessus bras dessous. **armpit** n aisselle f.

arm[2] [ɑːm] n arme f. **be up in arms against** s'élever contre. v armer.

armistice [ˈɑːmistis] n armistice m.

armour [ˈɑːmə] n armure f. **suit of armour** armure complète f. **armoured** adj cuirassé, blindé. **armoury** n arsenal m.

army [ˈɑːmi] n armée f.

aroma [əˈroumə] n arome m; (wine) bouquet.

arose [əˈrouz] V **arise**.

around [əˈraund] prep autour de; (approximately) à peu près. adv autour, à l'entour.

arrange [əˈreindʒ] v arranger; (meeting, etc.) fixer; (make plans) s'arranger. **arrangement** n arrangement m. **make arrangements** faire des préparatifs, prendre des mesures.

array [əˈrei] v (adorn) orner; (mil) ranger. n (display) étalage m; (mil) ordre m.

arrears [əˈriəz] pl n arriéré m sing. **in arrears** arriéré; en retard.

arrest [əˈrest] v arrêter. n arrestation f. **under arrest** en état d'arrestation.

arrive [əˈraiv] v arriver. **arrival** n arrivée f; (person) arrivant, -e m, f.

arrogant [ˈærəgənt] adj arrogant. **arrogance** n arrogance f.

arrow [ˈærou] n flèche f.

arse [ɑːs] n (vulgar) cul m.

arsenal [ˈɑːsənl] n arsenal m.

arsenic [ˈɑːsnik] n arsenic m.

arson [ˈɑːsn] n incendie criminel m.

art [ɑːt] n art m; (painting, etc.) beaux-arts m pl; (cunning) artifice m. **art gallery** musée d'art m. **arts and crafts** artisanat m sing. **art school** école des beaux-arts f. **Arts degree** licence ès lettres f. **artful** adj rusé.

artefact [ˈɑːtifakt] n objet fabriqué m.

artery [ˈɑːtəri] n artère f.

arthritis [ɑːˈθraitis] n arthrite f.

artichoke [ˈɑːtitʃouk] n artichaut m.

article [ˈɑːtikl] n article m; objet m.

articulate [ɑːˈtikjuleit; adj ɑːˈtikjulət] v articuler. **articulated lorry** semi-remorque m. adj bien articulé; net, nette. **be articulate** s'exprimer bien. **articulation** n articulation f.

artifice [ˈɑːtifis] n artifice f, stratagème m.

artificial [ɑːtiˈfiʃəl] adj artificiel; synthétique; (affected) factice, forcé. **artificial respiration** respiration artificielle f.

artillery [ɑːˈtiləri] n artillerie f.

artisan [ɑːtiˈzan] n artisan m.

artist [ˈɑːtist] n artiste m, f. **artistic** adj artistique.

as [az] conj (while) comme, tandis que, à mesure que; (because) puisque; (like) comme, en. adv aussi. **as ... as** ... aussi ... que .... **as for** quant à. **as if** comme si. **as it were** pour ainsi dire. **as usual** comme d'habitude. **as well** aussi.

asbestos [azˈbestɒs] n amiante f.

ascend [əˈsend] v monter. **ascension** n ascension f. **Ascension Day** jour de l'Ascension m. **ascent** n ascension f; montée f.

ascertain [asəˈtein] v établir; vérifier.

ascetic [əˈsetik] adj ascétique n ascète m, f.

ash[1] [aʃ] n cendre f. **ashtray** n cendrier m. **Ash Wednesday** mercredi des cendres m.

ash² [aʃ] n (tree) frêne m.

ashamed [ə'ʃeimd] adj honteux. **be ashamed** avoir honte.

ashore [ə'ʃɔ:] adv à terre. **go ashore** débarquer.

Asia ['eiʃə] n Asie f. **Asian** n Asiatique m, f; adj asiatique.

aside [ə'said] adv de côté, à part. n aparté m.

ask [ɑ:sk] v demander; inviter. **ask about** s'informer de. **ask after** demander des nouvelles de. **ask a question** poser une question. **ask for** demander.

askew [ə'skju:] adv de travers.

asleep [ə'sli:p] adj endormi. **be asleep** dormir. **fall asleep** s'endormir.

asparagus [ə'spærəgəs] n asperge f.

aspect ['æspekt] n aspect m; (of house) orientation f.

asphalt ['æsfalt] n asphalte m. v asphalter.

asphyxiate [əs'fiksieit] v (s')asphyxier. **asphyxia** or **asphyxiation** n asphyxie f.

aspire [ə'spaiə] v aspirer, ambitionner. **aspirate** adj aspiré. **aspiration** n aspiration f. **aspiring** adj ambitieux.

aspirin ['æspərin] n aspirine f.

ass [as] n âne. -esse m, f; (coll) imbécile m.

assail [ə'seil] v assaillir. **assailant** n agresseur m.

assassinate [ə'sæsineit] v assassiner. **assassin** n assassin m. **assassination** n assassinat m.

assault [ə'sɔ:lt] n attaque f; (mil) assaut m; (law) voies de fait f pl. v attaquer.

assemble [ə'sembl] v (things) (s')assembler; (people) (se) rassembler; (put together) monter. **assembly** n assemblée f; rassemblement m; montage m. **assembly line** chaîne de montage f.

assent [ə'sent] n assentiment m. v consentir.

assert [ə'sə:t] v (declare) affirmer; (rights, etc.) revendiquer. **assertion** n affirmation f; revendication f.

assess [ə'ses] v évaluer; (payment, etc.) fixer le montant de; (property) calculer la valeur imposable de. **assessment** n évaluation f; calcul m.

asset ['æset] n avantage m. **assets** pl n biens m pl; (comm) actif m sing.

assiduous [ə'sidjuəs] adj assidu. **assiduity** n assiduité f.

assign [ə'sain] v (job, etc.) assigner;

(meaning) attribuer; (person) nommer.

assignation n (meeting) rendez-vous m. **assignment** mission f; (school) devoir m.

assimilate [ə'simileit] v (s')assimiler. **assimilation** n assimilation f.

assist [ə'sist] v aider. **assistance** n aide f; secours m. **assistant** n auxiliaire m; (school) assistant, -e m, f; (shop) vendeur, -euse m, f; (as modifier) adjoint, sous-.

associate [ə'souʃieit] v (s')associer. **be associated with** (things) être associé à; (people) s'associer avec. **association** n association f.

assorted [ə'sɔ:tid] adj assorti. **assortment** n assortiment m; mélange m.

assume [ə'sju:m] v supposer, présumer; (take on) assumer, adopter. **assumption** n supposition f.

assure [ə'ʃuə] v assurer. **assurance** n assurance f.

asterisk ['astərisk] n astérisque m. v marquer d'un astérisque.

asthma ['æsmə] n asthme m. **asthmatic** n(m+f), adj asthmatique.

astonish [ə'stoniʃ] v étonner. **astonishment** n étonnement m.

astound [ə'staund] v stupéfier, abasourdir.

astray [ə'strei] adv, adj. **go astray** s'égarer.

astride [ə'straid] adv à califourchon. prep à califourchon sur.

astringent [ə'strindʒənt] nm, adj astringent.

astrology [ə'strolədʒi] n astrologie f. **astrologer** n astrologue m. **astrological** adj astrologique.

astronaut ['astrənɔ:t] n astronaute m, f.

astronomy [ə'stronəmi] n astronomie f. **astronomer** n astronome m. **astronomical** adj astronomique.

astute [ə'stju:t] adj fin, astucieux. **astuteness** n finesse f, astuce f.

asunder [ə'sʌndə] adv (in two) en deux; (in pieces) en morceaux.

asylum [ə'sailəm] n asile m.

at [at] prep à; chez: chez le docteur; (towards) vers. **at first** d'abord. **at last** enfin. **at least** au moins. **at once** tout de suite.

ate [et] V **eat**.

atheism ['eiθiizəm] n athéisme m. **atheist** n athée m, f. **atheistic** adj athée.

Athens ['æθinz] n Athènes. **Athenian** adj athénien; n Athénien, -enne m, f.

athlete ['æθliːt] n athlète m, f. **athlete's foot** n mycose f. **athletic** adj sportif, athlétique. **athletics** n athlétisme m.

Atlantic [ət'læntik] adj atlantique. **the Atlantic (Ocean)** l'(océan) Atlantique m.

atlas ['ætləs] n atlas m.

atmosphere ['ætməsfɪə] n atmosphère f; ambiance f. **atmospheric** adj atmosphérique.

atom ['ætəm] n atome m; (tiny part) grain m. **atom bomb** bombe atomique f. **atomic** adj atomique. **atomizer** n atomiseur m.

atone [ə'təʊn] v **atone for** expier; réparer. **atonement** n expiation f; réparation f.

atrocious [ə'trəʊʃəs] adj atroce. **atrocity** n atrocité f.

attach [ə'tætʃ] v attacher, joindre. **attached** adj (letter, etc.) ci-joint; (fond) attaché. **attachment** n accessoire m; affection f.

attaché [ə'tæʃeɪ] n attaché, -e m, f. **attaché case** mallette f.

attack [ə'tæk] n attaque f; (med) accès m, crise f. v attaquer, combattre. **attacker** n attaquant m.

attain [ə'teɪn] v atteindre (à). **attainments** pl n résultats m pl.

attempt [ə'tempt] v tenter (de), essayer (de). n tentative f, essai m.

attend [ə'tend] v (meeting) assister à; (school) aller à; servir; faire attention. **attend to** s'occuper de. **attendance** n présence f; (number present) assistance f; service m. **attendant** n gardien, -enne m, f. **attendants** pl n suite f sing.

attention [ə'tenʃən] n attention f; (mil) garde-à-vous m. **pay attention** faire attention. **attentive** adj (caring) prévenant; (listening) attentif.

attic ['ætik] n grenier m. **attic room** mansarde f.

attire [ə'taɪə] v parer (de). n habits m pl; (ceremonial) tenue f.

attitude ['ætɪtjuːd] n attitude f.

attorney [ə'tɜːni] n mandataire m; (US) avoué m. **Attorney General** Procureur Général m.

attract [ə'trækt] v attirer. **attract attention** éveiller l'intérêt. **attraction** n attraction f; (charm) attrait m. **attractive** adj attrayant; (price, etc.) intéressant.

attribute [ə'trɪbjuːt; n 'ætrɪbjuːt] v attribuer; (crime, etc.) imputer. n attribut m. **attribution** n attribution f; imputation f.

attrition [ə'trɪʃən] n usure f.

atypical [eɪ'tɪpɪkl] adj atypique.

aubergine ['əʊbəʒiːn] n aubergine f.

auburn ['ɔːbən] adj auburn invar; roux, rousse.

auction ['ɔːkʃən] n vente aux enchères f. v vendre aux enchères. **auctioneer** n commissaire-priseur m.

audacious [ɔː'deɪʃəs] adj (brave) audacieux; (impudent) effronté. **audacity** n audace f; effronterie f.

audible ['ɔːdəbl] adj audible, distinct.

audience ['ɔːdjəns] n spectateurs m pl, auditeurs m pl; (interview) audience f.

audiovisual [ɔːdɪəʊ'vɪʒʊəl] adj audiovisuel. **audiovisual aids** support audiovisuel m sing.

audit ['ɔːdɪt] v vérifier. n vérification f. **auditor** n expert-comptable m.

audition [ɔː'dɪʃən] n audition f. v auditionner.

auditorium [ɔːdɪ'tɔːrɪəm] n salle f.

augment [ɔːg'ment] v (s')augmenter.

August ['ɔːgəst] n août m.

aunt [ɑːnt] n tante f.

au pair [əʊ 'peə] adv au pair m. **au pair girl** n jeune fille au pair f.

aura ['ɔːrə] n aura f; ambiance f.

auspicious [ɔː'spɪʃəs] adj favorable, de bon augure.

austere [ɔː'stɪə] adj austère. **austerity** n austérité f.

Australia [ɒ'streɪljə] n Australie f. **Australian** n Australien, -enne m, f; adj australien.

Austria ['ɒstrɪə] n Autriche f. **Austrian** n Autrichien, -enne m, f; adj autrichien.

authentic [ɔː'θentɪk] adj authentique. **authenticity** n authenticité f.

author ['ɔːθə] n auteur m.

authority [ɔː'θɒrɪti] n (power) autorité f; (permission) autorisation f. **authoritative** adj (source, etc.) autorisé; (person) autoritaire.

authorize ['ɔːθəraɪz] v autoriser. **authorization** n autorisation f; (legal) mandat m.

autobiography [ɔːtəʊbaɪ'ɒgrəfi] n autobiographie f. **autobiographical** adj autobiographique.

autocratic [ɔːtəʊ'krætɪk] adj autocratique. **autocracy** n autocratie f. **autocrat** n autocrate m.

autograph ['ɔːtəgrɑːf] v dédicacer, signer. n autographe m.

automatic [ɔːtə'mætɪk] adj automatique. n (car) voiture automatique f. **automation** n automatisation f.

automobile ['ɔɪtəməbiɪl] n automobile f.
autonomous [ɔɪ'tɒnəməs] adj autonome.
  autonomy n autonomie f.
autopsy ['ɔɪtɒpsi] n autopsie f.
autumn ['ɔɪtəm] n automne m.
auxiliary [ɔɪg'zɪljəri] n(m+f), adj auxiliaire.
avail [ə'veil] v **avail oneself of** utiliser;
  profiter de. n **to no avail** sans résultat.
available [ə'veiləbl] adj disponible. **availability** n disponibilité f.
avalanche ['avəlɑɪnʃ] n avalanche f.
avarice ['avəris] n avarice f. **avaricious** adj
  avare.
avenge [ə'vendʒ] v venger. **avenge oneself**
  prendre sa revanche.
avenue ['avɪnjuɪ] n avenue f.
average ['avərɪdʒ] n moyenne f. adj moy-
  en.
aversion [ə'vɔɪʃən] n aversion f. **averse**
  adj adversaire (de). **be averse to** avoir
  horreur de.
avert [ə'vɔɪt] v (avoid) prévenir; (turn
  away) écarter; (eyes, etc.) détourner.
aviary ['eivjəri] n volière f.
aviation [eivi'eiʃən] n aviation f.
avid ['avid] adv avide. **avidity** n avidité f.
avocado [avə'kɑɪdəu] n (pear) avocat m;
  (tree) avocatier m.
avoid [ə'void] v éviter. **avoidable** adj évitable.
await [ə'weit] v attendre.
*awake [ə'weik] v (s')éveiller. adj éveillé.
  awake to conscient de.
award [ə'wɔɪd] v décerner; (damages)
  accorder. n récompense f, prix m.
aware [ə'weə] adj conscient; au courant.
  be aware of savoir. **awareness** n conscience f.
away [ə'wei] adv au loin, à une distance
  de; absent. adj (sport) à l'extérieur.
awe [ɔɪ] n crainte révérentielle f. **awe-
  inspiring** adj impressionnant. **awe-struck**
  adj stupéfait. **be in awe of** être intimidé
  par.
awful ['ɔɪful] adj affreux, épouvantable.
  awfully adv (very) vraiment.
awkward ['ɔɪkwəd] adj (difficult) peu
  commode; (situation) délicat; (inconvenient) inopportun; (clumsy) maladroit.
  awkwardness n maladresse f; embarras
  m.
awning ['ɔɪnɪŋ] n (shop) banne f; (tent)
  auvent m; (naut) taud m.
awoke [ə'wəuk] V awake.

awoken [ə'wəukn] V awake.
axe [aks] n hache f.
axiom ['aksiəm] n axiome m.
axis ['aksis] n axe m.
axle ['aksl] n axe m; (mot) essieu m.

B

babble ['babl] v bredouiller; (baby) babiller; (stream) gazouiller. n babil m;
  (noise) rumeur f.
baboon [bə'buɪn] n babouin m.
baby ['beibi] n bébé m. **babyish** adj enfantin.
bachelor ['batʃələ] n célibataire m. **Bachelor of Arts/Science** licencié, -e ès let-
  tres/sciences m, f.
back [bak] n dos, derrière m; (reverse
  side) revers m, verso m; (furthest part)
  fond m. adj arrière. adv en arrière. v
  renforcer; financer; (bet on) parier sur.
  back away se reculer. **back out** (car, etc.)
  sortir en marche arrière; (duty, etc.) se
  dérober (à).
backache ['bakeik] n mal aux reins m.
backdate [,bak'deit] v (cheque) antidater.
  backdated to avec rappel à.
backfire [,bak'faiə] v (mot) pétarader;
  (plan, etc.) échouer.
backgammon ['bak,gamən] n trictrac m.
background ['bakgraund] n fond m,
  arrière-plan m; (social) milieu m. **background music** musique de fond f.
backhand ['bakhand] adj, adv (sport) en
  revers. n revers m.
backlog ['baklog] n arriéré m.
backside [bak'said] n arrière m; (coll)
  derrière m.
backstage ['baksteidʒ] adv derrière la
  scène. **go backstage** aller dans la coulisse.
backstroke ['bakstrouk] n dos crawlé m.
backward ['bakwəd] adj en arrière;
  (retarded) arriéré. **backwardness** n arrié-
  ration mentale f.
backwards ['bakwədz] adv en arrière;
  (hack first) à rebours, à reculons; (in
  reverse order) à l'envers.
backwater ['bak,wɔɪtə] n (place) trou perdu m; (pool) eau stagnante f.

14

bacon ['beikən] *n* bacon *m*. **bacon and eggs** œufs au jambon *m pl*.

bacteria [bak'tiəriə] *pl n* bactéries *f pl*.

bad [bad] *adj* mauvais; (*naughty*) méchant; (*serious*) grave; (*decayed*) gâté, carié. **bad-mannered** *adj* mal élevé. **bad-tempered** *adj* acariâtre. **badly** *adv* mal; (*seriously*) grièvement; (*very much*) absolument.

badge [badʒ] *n* insigne *m*; (*scouting*) badge *m*; (*police, etc.*) plaque *f*.

badger ['badʒə] *n* blaireau *m*. *v* harceler.

badminton ['badmintən] *n* badminton *m*.

baffle ['bafl] *v* déconcerter.

bag [bag] *n* sac *m*. **baggage** *n* bagages *m pl*. **baggy** *adj* bouffant; trop ample.

bagpipes ['bagpaips] *pl n* cornemuse *f sing*.

bail[1] [beil] *n* (*law*) caution *f*. **on bail** sous caution. **stand bail for** se rendre garant de. *v* **bail out** faire mettre en liberté provisoire sous caution.

bail[2] *or* **bale** [beil] *v* **bail out** (*flooded boat*) écoper; (*from aircraft*) sauter en parachute.

bailiff ['beilif] *n* (*law*) huissier *m*; (*of estate*) régisseur *m*.

bait [beit] *n* (*fishing*) amorce *f*; (*lure*) appât *m*. *v* amorcer; (*annoy*) tourmenter.

bake [beik] *v* (*faire*) cuire au four. **baked beans** haricots blancs à la sauce tomate *m pl*. **baker** *n* boulanger, -ère *m, f*. **bakery** *n* boulangerie *f*.

balance ['baləns] *n* equilibre *m*; (*scales*) balance *f*; (*comm*) solde *m*. **balance of payments** balance des paiements *f*. *v* (*se*) tenir en équilibre; (*equal*) équilibrer; (*comm*) balancer; solder. **balance the books** dresser le bilan.

balcony ['balkəni] *n* balcon *m*; (*theatre*) fauteuils de deuxième balcon *m pl*.

bald [boild] *adj* chauve; (*tyre*) lisse; (*style*) plat.

bale[1] [beil] *n* ballot *m*; (*hay*) balle *f*. *v* emballotter.

bale[2] *V* **bail**[2].

ball[1] [boil] *n* balle *f*, boule *f*; (*football*) ballon *m*; (*wool, etc.*) pelote *f*; (*of foot*) plante *f*. **ball bearings** roulement à billes *m sing*. **ball-point pen** stylo bille *m*.

ball[2] [boil] *n* (*dance*) bal *m*. **ballroom** *n* salle de danse *f*.

ballad ['baləd] *n* ballade *f*; (*music*) romance *f*.

ballast ['baləst] *n* (*naut*) lest *m*; (*rail*) ballast *m*. *v* lester; ballaster.

ballet ['balei] *n* ballet *m*. **ballerina** *n* ballerine *f*.

ballistic [bə'listik] *adj* balistique. **ballistic missile** engin balistique *m*.

balloon [bə'luin] *n* ballon *m*. **balloonist** *n* aéronaute *m, f*.

ballot ['balət] *n* scrutin *m*; (*paper*) bulletin de vote *m*. **ballot box** urne électorale *f*. *v* voter au scrutin secret.

bamboo [bam'buɪ] *n* bambou *m*.

ban [ban] *v* interdire. *n* interdit *m*. **put a ban on** interdire.

banal [bə'nail] *adj* banal. **banality** *n* banalité *f*.

banana [bə'nainə] *n* (*fruit*) banane *f*; (*tree*) bananier *m*.

band[1] [band] *n* (*group*) bande *f*; (*music*) orchestre *m*; (*mil*) fanfare *f*. **bandstand** *n* kiosque à musique *m*. **jump on the bandwagon** prendre le train en marche.

band[2] [band] *n* (*strip*) bande *f*.

bandage ['bandidʒ] *n* pansement *m*, bandage *m*. *v* mettre un pansement sur.

bandit ['bandit] *n* bandit *m*.

bandy ['bandi] *adj also* **bandy-legged** bancal, arqué. *v* échanger. **bandy about** faire circuler. **bandy words** discuter.

bang [baŋ] *n* (*noise*) claquement *m*, détonation *f*; (*blow*) coup *m*. *interj* pan! *v* (*hit*) frapper, cogner; (*door*) claquer; (*gun, etc.*) détoner.

bangle ['baŋgl] *n* bracelet *m*, jonc *m*.

banish ['baniʃ] *v* bannir; exiler. **banishment** *n* bannissement *m*, exil *m*.

banister ['banistə] *n* rampe *f*.

banjo ['bandʒou] *n* banjo *m*.

bank[1] [baŋk] *n* (*edge*) bord *m*; (*river*) rive *f*; (*sand*) banc *m*; (*earth, etc.*) talus *m*.

bank[2] [baŋk] *n* banque *f*. **bank account** compte en banque *m*. **bank holiday** jour férié *m*. **bank statement** relevé de compte *m*. *v* mettre en banque. **bank on** compter sur. **bank with** avoir un compte à. **banker** *n* banquier *m*. **banker's order** ordre de virement bancaire *m*.

bankrupt ['baŋkrʌpt] *adj* failli, en faillite. **go bankrupt** faire faillite. *n* failli, -e *m, f*. *v* mettre en faillite. **bankruptcy** *n* faillite *f*.

banner ['banə] *n* bannière *f*.

banquet ['baŋkwit] *n* banquet *m*.

banter ['bantə] *v* plaisanter. *n* badinage *m*.

batter

baptize [bap'taiz] v baptiser. **baptism** n baptême m. **Baptist** n(m+f), adj baptiste.

bar [ba:] n (rod) barreau f, barre f; obstacle m; (law) barreau m; (chocolate) tablette f; (for drinks) bar m, comptoir m; (music) mesure f. v barrer: défendre. prep sauf.

barbarian [ba:'heəriən] n(m+f), adj barbare. **barbaric** or **barbarous** adj barbare. **barbarism** or **barbarity** n barbarie f.

barbecue ['ba:bikju:] n barbecue m. v griller au charbon de bois.

barbed wire [ba:bd] n fil de fer barbelé m.

barber ['ba:bə] n coiffeur pour hommes m.

barbiturate [ba:'bitjurət] n barbiturique m.

bare [beə] v mettre à nu. **bare one's teeth** montrer les dents. adj nu; dénudé. **barefaced** adj éhonté. **barefoot** adv nu-pieds. **the bare necessities** le strict nécessaire m. **barely** adv à peine.

bargain ['ba:gin] n (transaction) marché; (offer) occasion. **into the bargain** par-dessus le marché. v négocier. **bargain for** (expect) s'attendre à. **bargain with** marchander avec.

barge [ba:dʒ] n chaland m, péniche f. v **barge in** faire irruption, entrer sans façons. **barge through** traverser comme un ouragan.

baritone ['baritoun] n baryton m.

bark[1] [ba:k] v (dog) aboyer. n aboiement m.

bark[2] [ba:k] n (tree) écorce f.

barley ['ba:li] n orge f. **barley sugar** sucre d'orge m. **barley water** orgeat m.

barn [ba:n] n grange f.

barometer [bə'romitə] n baromètre m.

baron ['barən] n baron m. **baroness** n baronne f. **baronet** n baronnet m.

barracks ['barəks] n (mil) caserne f. quartier m.

barrage ['bara:ʒ] n barrage m; (of questions) pluie f; (of words) flot m.

barrel ['barəl] n (cask) tonneau m; (gun, etc.) canon m.

barren ['barən] adj stérile; aride. **barrenness** n stérilité f; aridité f.

barricade [bari'keid] n barricade f. v barricader.

barrier ['bariə] n barrière f; (rail) portillon m.

barrister ['baristə] n avocat m.

barrow ['barou] n voiture de quatre saisons f.

barter ['ba:tə] v troquer, faire un troc. n troc m.

base[1] [beis] n base f. v baser. **baseless** adj sans fondement.

base[2] [beis] adj bas, basse; ignoble. **baseness** n bassesse f.

baseball ['beisbo:l] n base-ball m.

basement ['beismənt] n sous-sol m.

bash [baʃ] v cogner. n coup m. **have a bash** (try) essayer un coup.

bashful ['baʃful] adj timide.

basic ['beisik] adj fondamental; (salary, etc.) de base; (chem) basique.

basil ['bazl] n basilic m.

basin ['beisin] n cuvette f; (bowl) bol m; (bathroom) lavabo; (geog) bassin m.

basis ['beisis] n base f.

bask [ba:sk] v (in the sun) se dorer; (in glory, etc.) jouir (de).

basket ['ba:skit] n (shopping) panier m; (linen, etc.) corbeille f. **basketball** n basket m.

bass[1] [beis] n (voice) basse f.

bass[2] [bas] n (freshwater) perche f; (sea) bar m.

bassoon [bə'su:n] n basson m.

bastard ['ba:stəd] n bâtard, -e m. f; (derog) salaud m; (coll) type m.

baste [beist] v (cookery) arroser.

bastion ['bastjən] n bastion m.

bat[1] [bat] n (sport) batte f. **off one's own bat** de sa propre initiative. v frapper; manier la batte. **bat an eyelid** sourciller.

bat[2] [bat] n chauve-souris f.

batch [batʃ] n (loaves) fournée f; (letters) paquet m; (goods) lot m.

bath [ba:θ] n bain m; (tub) baignoire f. **bathchair** n fauteuil roulant m. **bathroom** n salle de bains f. **baths** pl n (swimming) piscine f sing. v baigner; prendre un bain.

bathe [beið] v (se) baigner; (wound) laver. **bather** n baigneur, -euse m. f. **bathing** n baignade f. **bathing costume** maillot m. **bathing trunks** slip de bain m.

baton ['batn] n bâton m; (police) matraque f; (race) témoin m.

battalion [bə'taljən] n bataillon m.

batter[1] ['batə] v battre. **battered** adj délabré.

batter² ['batə] n pâte à frire f; (pancakes) pâte à crêpes f.

battery ['batəri] n (elec) pile f; (mot) batterie f; (mil) batterie f.

battle ['batl] n bataille f. **battlefield** n champ de bataille m. **battlements** pl n remparts m pl. **battleship** n cuirassé m. v se battre, lutter.

bawl [bɔːl] v brailler.

bay¹ [bei] n (geog) baie f.

bay² [bei] v aboyer. n aboi m. **at bay** à distance.

bay³ [bei] n laurier m. **bay leaf** feuille de laurier f.

bayonet ['beiənit] n baïonnette f.

bay window n fenêtre en saillie f.

bazaar [bə'zaː] n (charity sale) vente de charité f; (eastern) bazar m.

*be [biː] v être.

beach [biːtʃ] n plage f. v échouer.

beacon ['biːkən] n phare m; (naut) balise f.

bead [biːd] n perle f; (rosary) grain m.

beak [biːk] n bec m.

beaker ['biːkə] n gobelet m.

beam [biːm] n (arch) poutre f; (light) rayon m, faisceau m; (smile) sourire épanoui m. v rayonner.

bean [biːn] n haricot m; (coffee) grain m. **full of beans** en pleine forme.

*bear¹ [beə] v (carry) porter; (support) soutenir; (tolerate) supporter; (give birth) donner naissance à. **bear right/left** prendre à droit/gauche. **bearable** adj supportable. **bearing** n (behaviour) maintien m; (relation) rapport m; (direction) relèvement m. **lose one's bearings** être désorienté.

bear² [beə] n ours m.

beard [biəd] n barbe f. **bearded** adj barbu.

beast [biːst] n bête f; (person) brute f. **beastly** adj abominable; (unkind) sale.

*beat [biːt] v battre. n battement m; rythme m; (police) ronde f. **beating** n (as punishment) rossée f; (defeat) défaite f.

beaten ['biːtn] V beat.

beauty ['bjuːti] n beauté f. **beautician** n esthéticien, -enne m, f. **beautiful** adj beau, belle; magnifique. **beautify** v embellir.

beaver ['biːvə] n castor m.

became [bi'keim] V become.

because [bi'kɔz] conj parce que. **because of** à cause de.

beckon ['bekən] v faire signe (à).

*become [bi'kʌm] v devenir; (suit) aller à. **becoming** adj convenable; (clothes) seyant.

bed [bed] n lit m; (coal, etc.) couche f; (flowers) parterre m. **bedclothes** pl n literie f. **bedridden** adj alité. **bedroom** n chambre f. **bedside** n chevet m. **bed-sitter** n studio m. **bedspread** n couvre-lit m. **go to bed** se coucher.

bedraggled [bi'dragld] adj débraillé.

bee [biː] n abeille f. **beehive** n ruche f. **have a bee in one's bonnet** avoir une marotte. **make a beeline for** filer droit sur.

beech [biːtʃ] n hêtre m.

beef [biːf] n bœuf m.

been [biːn] V be.

beer [biə] n bière f.

beetle ['biːtl] n coléoptère m.

beetroot ['biːtruːt] n betterave f.

before [bi'fɔː] prep avant; (in front of) devant. adv auparavant, avant. conj avant de, avant que. **beforehand** adv à l'avance.

befriend [bi'frend] v traiter en ami; (help) venir en aide à.

beg [beg] v mendier; (entreat) supplier, demander. **beggar** n mendiant, -e m, f.

began [bi'gan] V begin.

*begin [bi'gin] v commencer. **to begin with** pour commencer. **beginner** n novice m, f. **beginning** n commencement m, début m; origine f.

begrudge [bi'grʌdʒ] v envier. **begrudge doing** faire à contre-cœur.

begun [bi'gʌn] V begin.

behalf [bi'haːf] n part f. **on behalf of** de la part de; en faveur de.

behave [bi'heiv] v se conduire. **behave yourself!** sois sage! **behaviour** n conduite f.

behead [bi'hed] v décapiter.

behind [bi'haind] adv, prep derrière, en arrière (de); (late) en retard. n (coll) postérieur m. **behindhand** adv, adj en retard.

*behold [bi'hould] v voir.

beige [beiʒ] nm, adj beige.

being ['biːiŋ] n existence f; être m. **for the time being** pour le moment.

belated [bi'leitid] adj tardif.

belch [beltʃ] v roter; (smoke, etc.) vomir. n renvoi m.

belfry ['belfri] *n* beffroi *m*; (*church*) clocher *m*.

Belgium ['beldʒəm] *n* Belgique *f*. **Belgian** *n* Belge *m*, *f*; *adj* belge.

Belgrade ['belgreid] *n* Belgrade.

believe [bi'liːv] *v* croire. **believe in** (*God*) croire en; (*ghosts, etc.*) croire à; (*approve of*) être partisan de. **belief** *n* croyance *f*; (*rel*) credo *m*, foi *f*; opinion *f*. **believable** *adj* croyable. **believer** *n* partisan, -e *m*, *f*; (*rel*) croyant, -e *m*, *f*.

bell [bel] *n* cloche *f*, clochette *f*; (*door*) sonnette *f*; (*telephone*) sonnerie *f*; (*bicycle*) timbre *m*.

belligerent [bi'lidʒərənt] *n, adj* belligérant, -e. **belligerence** *n* belligérance *f*.

bellow ['belou] *v* mugir; (*cow*) beugler; (*person*) brailler. *n* mugissement *m*, beuglement *m*; (*person*) hurlement *m*.

bellows ['belouz] *pl n* (*organ*) soufflerie *f* sing; (*fire*) soufflet *m* sing.

belly ['beli] *n* ventre *m*.

belong [bi'loŋ] *v* appartenir; (*club*) être membre (de). **belongings** *pl n* affaires *f pl*.

beloved [bi'lʌvid] *adj* bien aimé. *n* bien-aimé, -e *m*, *f*.

below [bi'lou] *prep* sous, au-dessous de. *adv* en bas, en dessous; (*letters, etc.*) ci-dessous. **hit below the belt** porter un coup bas (à).

belt [belt] *n* ceinture *f*; (*land*) zone *f*, région *f*; (*tech*) courroie *f*. *v* (*slang: hit*) flanquer un gnon à; (*slang: rush*) se carapater.

bench [bentʃ] *n* banc *m*; (*workshop*) établi *m*; (*law*) tribunal *m*.

***bend** [bend] *n* coude *m*; (*road*) virage *m*; (*arm, knee*) pli *m*. *v* (se) courber; plier. **bend over** se pencher. **bend over backwards** se mettre en quatre.

beneath [bi'niːθ] *prep* sous, au-dessous de; (*unworthy*) indigne de. *adv* au-dessous, en bas.

benefactor ['benəfaktə] *n* bienfaiteur *m*. **benefactress** *n* bienfaitrice *f*.

benefit ['benəfit] *n* avantage *m*; (*money*) allocation *f*. **for the benefit of** dans l'intérêt de. **the benefit of the doubt** le bénéfice du doute. *v* faire du bien à; gagner (à). **beneficial** *adj* salutaire.

benevolent [bi'nevələnt] *adj* (*kindly*) bienveillant; (*charitable*) bienfaisant. **benevolence** *n* bienveillance *f*; bienfaisance *f*.

benign [bi'nain] *adj* (*med*) bénin, -igne; (*kindly*) bienveillant.

bent [bent] *V* **bend**. *adj* courbé; (*slang: dishonest*) véreux; (*slang: homosexual*) homosexuel. **be bent on** vouloir absolument. *n* aptitude *f*, disposition *f*.

bequeath [bi'kwiːð] *v* léguer. **bequest** *n* legs *m*.

bereaved [bi'riːvd] *adj* endeuillé. **bereavement** *n* deuil *m*.

beret ['berei] *n* béret *m*.

Berlin [bəː'lin] *n* Berlin.

Bern [bəːn] *n* Berne.

berry ['beri] *n* baie *f*.

berserk [bə'səːk] *adj* fou furieux, folle furieuse. **go berserk** devenir fou furieux; (*with anger*) se mettre en rage.

berth [bəːθ] *n* couchette *f*; (*naut*) mouillage *m*. **give a wide berth to** éviter. *v* (*naut*) mouiller, amarrer.

beside [bi'said] *prep* à côté de. **beside oneself** (*with anger*) hors de soi. **besides** *adv* (*as well*) de plus; (*moreover*) d'ailleurs.

besiege [bi'siːdʒ] *v* (*town*) assiéger; (*pester*) assaillir.

best [best] *adj* le meilleur, la meilleure. **best man** garçon d'honneur *m*. *adv* le mieux. *n* mieux *m*. **at best** au mieux. **do one's best** faire de son mieux. **make the best of** s'accommoder de; profiter de.

bestow [bi'stou] *v* accorder; (*title*) conférer.

bet [bet] *v* parier. *n* pari *m*. **betting shop** bureau de paris *m*.

betray [bi'trei] *v* trahir. **betrayal** *n* trahison *f*.

better ['betə] *adj* meilleur. *nm, adv* mieux. **be better** (*after illness*) aller mieux. **get the better of** triompher de. *v* améliorer, dépasser.

between [bi'twiːn] *prep* entre.

beverage ['bevəridʒ] *n* boisson *f*.

***beware** [bi'weə] *v* prendre garde. *interj* attention (à)!

bewilder [bi'wildə] *v* dérouter, abasourdir. **bewilderment** *n* confusion *f*; abasourdissement *m*.

beyond [bi'jond] *prep* au delà de; (*exceeding*) au-dessus de. *adv* au delà. **be beyond** dépasser.

bias ['baiəs] *n* tendance *f*; préjugé *m*; (*sewing*) biais *m*. *v* influencer; (*prejudice*) prévenir. **biased** *adj* partial. **be biased** avoir un préjugé.

bib [bib] *n* bavoir *m*; (*of apron*) bavette *f*.
Bible ['baibl] *n* Bible *f*. **biblical** *adj* biblique.
bibliography [bibli'ografi] *n* bibliographie *f*. **bibliographer** *n* bibliographe *m*, *f*. **bibliographical** *adj* bibliographique.
biceps ['baiseps] *n* biceps *m*.
bicker ['bikə] *v* se chamailler. **bickering** *n* chamailleries *f*.
bicycle ['baisikl] *n* bicyclette *f*, vélo *m*.
*****bid** [bid] *n* offre *f*; (*auction*) enchère *f*; (*cards*) demande *f*; (*attempt*) tentative *f*. *v* faire une offre *or* enchère (de); (*cards*) demander; (*command*) ordonner; (*greeting*) dire, souhaiter. **bidder** *n* offrant *m*. **bidding** *n* enchères *f pl*; ordre *m*.
bidet ['biːdei] *n* bidet *m*.
biennial [bai'eniəl] *adj* biennal.
bifocals [bai'foukəlz] *pl n* lunettes bifocales *f pl*.
big [big] *adj* grand; gros, grosse.
bigamy ['bigəmi] *n* bigamie. **bigamist** *n* bigame *m*, *f*. **bigamous** *adj* bigame.
bigot ['bigət] *n* fanatique *m*, *f*. **bigoted** *adj* fanatique.
bikini [bi'kiːni] *n* bikini *m*.
bilingual [bai'lingwəl] *adj* bilingue.
bilious ['biljəs] *adj* bilieux. **bilious attack** crise de foie *f*. **biliousness** *n* affection hépatique *f*.
bill[1] [bil] *n* (*hotel, shop*) note *f*; (*restaurant*) addition *f*; (*fuel, etc.*) facture *f*; (*pol*) projet de loi *m*; (*poster*) affiche *f*.
bill[2] [bil] *n* bec *m*.
billiards ['biljədz] *n* billard *m*.
billion ['biljən] *n* (10[12]) billion *m*; (10[9]) milliard *m*.
billow ['bilou] *n* flot *m*; (*sail*) gonflement *m*. *v* (*sail*) se gonfler; (*smoke*) tournoyer.
bin [bin] *n* (*rubbish*) poubelle *f*; (*coal*) coffre *m*; (*wine*) casier *m*.
binary ['bainəri] *adj* binaire.
*****bind** [baind] *v* lier; (*book*) relier; (*neaten edge*) border; (*force*) obliger. *n* (*coll*) barbe *f*.
binding ['baindiŋ] *n* (*book*) reliure *f*; (*tape*) extra-fort *m*; (*skis*) fixation *f*. *adj* obligatoire.
binoculars [bi'nokjuləz] *pl n* jumelles *f pl*.
biography [bai'ografi] *n* biographie *f*. **biographer** *n* biographe *m*, *f*. **biographical** *adj* biographique.
biology [bai'olədʒi] *n* biologie *f*. **biological** *adj* biologique. **biologist** *n* biologiste *m*, *f*.

birch [bəːtʃ] *n* bouleau *m*; (*punishment*) verge *f*.
bird [bəːd] *n* oiseau *m*.
birth [bəːθ] *n* naissance *f*; (*confinement*) accouchement *m*. **birth certificate** acte de naissance *m*. **birth control** contrôle des naissances *m*. **birthday** *n* anniversaire *m*. **birthmark** *n* tache de vin *f*. **birthplace** *n* lieu de naissance *m*. **birth rate** natalité *f*. **give birth to** donner naissance à.
biscuit ['biskit] *n* petit gâteau sec *m*; biscuit *m*.
bishop ['biʃəp] *n* évêque *m*.
bison ['baisən] *n* bison *m*.
bit[1] [bit] *V* **bite**. *n* (*horse*) mors *m*; (*drill*) mèche *f*.
bit[2] [bit] *n* morceau *m*, bout *m*, brin *m*. **a bit** *adv* un peu. **bit by bit** petit à petit. **do one's bit** fournir sa part d'effort.
bitch [bitʃ] *n* (*dog*) chienne *f*; (*slang*) garce *f*.
*****bite** [bait] *v* mordre; (*insect*) piquer. *n* morsure *f*; piqûre *f*; (*mouthful*) bouchée *f*. **biting** *adj* (*remark, etc.*) mordant; (*wind*) cinglant; (*cold*) âpre.
bitten ['bitn] *V* **bite**.
bitter ['bitə] *adj* amer; (*cold*) glacial. **to the bitter end** jusqu'au bout. **bitterness** *n* amertume *f*.
bizarre [bi'zaː] *adj* bizarre.
black ['blak] *adj* noir. *n* noir *m*; (*person*) Noir, -e *m*, *f*. *v* (*comm*) boycotter. **blacken** *v* noircir. **blackness** *n* noirceur *f*; (*darkness*) obscurité *f*.
blackberry ['blakbəri] *n* (*fruit*) mûre *f*; (*bush*) mûrier *m*.
blackbird ['blakbəːd] *n* merle *m*.
blackboard ['blakbɔːd] *n* tableau (noir) *m*.
blackcurrant [,blak'kʌrənt] *n* cassis *m*.
black eye *n* œil poché *m*.
blackhead ['blakhed] *n* point noir *m*.
black ice *n* verglas *m*.
blackleg ['blakleg] *n* jaune *m*.
blackmail ['blakmeil] *n* chantage *m*. *v* faire chanter. **blackmailer** *n* maître-chanteur *m*.
black market *n* marché noir *m*.
blackout ['blakaut] *n* (*med*) étourdissement *m*; (*war*) black-out *m*; (*power cut*) panne d'électricité *f*.
blacksmith ['blaksmiθ] *n* forgeron *m*; (*horses*) maréchal-ferrant *m*.
bladder ['bladə] *n* vessie *f*.

19 blown

blade [bleid] *n* lame *f*; (*oar*) plat *m*; (*grass*) brin *m*; (*propeller*) pale *f*.

blame [bleim] *v* attribuer (à), rejeter la responsabilité (sur); (*censure*) blâmer. *n* responsabilité *f*; blâme *m*.

blank [blæŋk] *adj* blanc, blanche; (*cheque*) en blanc; (*empty*) vide; (*puzzled*) déconcerté. *n* blanc *m*, vide *m*; (*gun*) cartouche à blanc *f*.

blanket ['blæŋkit] *n* couverture *f*. *v* recouvrir; (*muffle*) étouffer.

blare [bleə] *n* vacarme *m*; (*trumpet*) sonnerie *f*. *v* retentir; (*radio, etc.*) beugler.

blaspheme [blas'fiːm] *v* blasphémer. **blasphemous** *adj* blasphématoire. **blasphemy** *n* blasphème *m*.

blast [blɑːst] *n* explosion *f*; (*noise, wind*) coup *m*; (*trumpet*) fanfare *f*; (*steam*) jet *m*. *v* (*rocks*) faire sauter; (*hopes, etc.*) détruire. *interj* la barbe!

blatant ['bleitənt] *adj* (*obvious*) flagrant; (*shameless*) éhonté.

blaze [bleiz] *n* (*flare*) flambée *f*; (*large fire*) incendie *m*; (*sun*) flamboiement *m*; (*anger*) explosion *f*. *v* flamber; flamboyer; (*light*) resplendir. **blazing** *adj* en flammes; (*sun*) éclatant; (*coll*) furibond.

bleach [bliːtʃ] *n* blanchir; (*hair*) décolorer. *n* décolorant *m*; (*household*) eau de Javel *f*.

bleak [bliːk] *adj* (*landscape*) morne, désolé; (*bare*) austère; (*prospect*) triste; (*weather*) froid.

bleat [bliːt] *v* bêler. *n* bêlement *m*.

bled [bled] *V* **bleed**.

*bleed [bliːd] *v* saigner. **bleeding** *n* saignement *m*, hémorragie *f*.

blemish ['blemiʃ] *n* défaut *m*; (*reputation*) souillure *f*; (*fruit*) tache *f*. *v* gâter; (*reputation*) ternir.

blend [blend] *v* (se) mélanger; (*colours*) fusionner; (*colours*) (se) fondre, aller bien ensemble. *n* mélange *m*.

bless [bles] *v* bénir. **bless you!** à vos souhaits! **blessed** (*rel*) béni, bienheureux; (*coll*) sacré. **blessing** *n* bénédiction *f*; (*at meal*) bénédicité; (*benefit*) bien *m*. **what a blessing!** quelle chance!

blew [bluː] *V* **blow²**.

blind [blaind] *adj* aveugle. **blind spot** (*mot*) angle mort *m*. *n* aveugler. *v* (*window*) store *m*; (*mask*) feinte *f*. **the blind** les aveugles *m pl*. **blindness** cécité *f*.

blindfold ['blaindfould] *v* bander les yeux à. *n* bandeau *m*. *adv* les yeux bandés.

blink [bliŋk] *v* cligner des yeux. *n* clignotement *m*. **blinkers** *pl n* œillères *f pl*.

bliss [blis] *n* bonheur suprême *m*. **blissful** *adj* merveilleux, divin.

blister ['blistə] *n* ampoule *f*; (*paint*) boursouflure *f*. *v* se couvrir d'ampoules; se boursoufler.

blizzard ['blizəd] *n* tempête de neige *f*.

blob [blob] *n* goutte *f*.

bloc [blok] *n* (*pol*) bloc *m*.

block [blok] *n* bloc *m*; (*wood*) billot *m*; (*flats*) immeuble *m*; (*houses*) pâté *m*; obstruction *f*. **block letters** majuscules *f pl*. *v* (*obstruct*) bloquer, boucher; (*hinder*) gêner. **blockage** *n* obstruction *f*.

bloke [blouk] *n* (*coll*) type *m*.

blond [blond] *adj* blond. **blonde** *nf, adj* blonde.

blood [blʌd] *n* sang *m*. **bloody** *adj* sanglant, ensanglanté; (*slang*) foutu.

bloodcurdling ['blʌdkəːdliŋ] *adj* à figer le sang.

blood donor *n* donneur, -euse de sang *m, f*.

blood group *n* groupe sanguin *m*.

bloodhound ['blʌdhaund] *n* limier *m*.

blood poisoning *n* empoisonnement du sang *m*.

blood pressure *n* tension *f*. **have high/low blood pressure** faire de l'hypertension/hypotension.

bloodshed ['blʌdʃed] *n* effusion de sang *f*.

bloodshot ['blʌdʃot] *adj* injecté de sang.

bloodstream ['blʌdstriːm] *n* système sanguin *m*.

bloodthirsty ['blʌdθəːsti] *adj* sanguinaire.

bloom [bluːm] *v* fleurir. *n* floraison *f*; (*single flower*) fleur *f*. **in full bloom** en pleine floraison.

blot [blot] *n* tache *f*; (*ink*) pâté *m*. *v* tacher; (*dry*) sécher. **blot out** effacer. **blotting paper** papier buvard *m*.

blouse [blauz] *n* chemisier *m*.

blow¹ [blou] *n* (*hit*) coup. **come to blows** en venir aux mains.

*blow² [blou] *v* souffler; (*trumpet*) sonner; (*whistle*) siffler. **blow away** chasser. **blow off** (faire) s'envoler. **blow one's nose** se moucher. **blow out** (s')éteindre. **blow up** (*explode*) (faire) sauter; (*inflate*) gonfler.

blown [bloun] *V* **blow²**.

blubber ['blʌbə] n blanc de baleine m. v pleurer comme un veau.

blue [bluː] adj bleu; (coarse) grivois. n bleu m. **bluebell** n jacinthe des bois f. **blueprint** n bleu m; plan m.

bluff [blʌf] n bluff m. v bluffer.

blunder ['blʌndə] n bévue f; (coll) gaffe f; (social) impair m. v faire une bévue.

blunt [blʌnt] adj (blade) émoussé; (point) épointé; (frank) carré, brusque. v émousser; épointer.

blur [bləː] n tache floue f. v estomper. **blurred** adj flou.

blush [blʌʃ] v rougir. n rougeur f.

boar [boː] n sanglier m.

board [boːd] v (ship, plane) monter à bord de; (train, bus) monter dans; (lodge) prendre en pension. n (wood) planche f; (meals) pension f; (officials) conseil m; (naut) bord m. **above board** régulier. **across the board** de portée générale. **boardroom** n salle du conseil f. **go on board** (s')embarquer. **on board** à bord. **boarder** n pensionnaire m, f. **boarding card** carte d'embarquement f. **boarding house** pension f. **boarding school** pensionnat m.

boast [boust] v se vanter. n fanfaronnade f. **boastful** adj vantard.

boat [bout] n bateau m. **all in the same boat** tous logés à la même enseigne. **boater** n (hat) canotier m. **boating** n canotage m.

bob¹ [bob] v (up and down) sautiller; (curtsy) faire une révérence. n révérence f.

bob² [bob] v (hair) couper court; (tail) écourter. n (hairstyle) coiffure à la Jeanne d'Arc f.

bobbin ['bobin] n bobine f.

bodice ['bodis] n corsage m.

body ['bodi] n corps m; (corpse) cadavre m. **bodyguard** n garde du corps m. **bodywork** n (mot) carrosserie f.

bog [bog] n marais m. **get bogged down** s'embourber. **boggy** adj marécageux.

bogus ['bougəs] adj faux, fausse.

bohemian [bə'hiːmiən] n(m+f), adj (artist) bohème; (gipsy) bohémien, -enne.

boil¹ [boil] v (faire) bouillir; (vegetables, etc.) cuire à l'eau. **boil down to** revenir à. **boil over** déborder. **boiled egg** œuf à la coque m. **boiler** n chaudière f. **boiler suit** bleus m pl. **boiling point** point d'ébullition m.

boil² [boil] n furoncle m.

boisterous ['boistərəs] adj (person) turbulent; (sea) tumultueux.

bold [bould] adj hardi. **boldness** n hardiesse f.

bolster ['boulstə] n (pillow) traversin m. v **bolster up** soutenir.

bolt [boult] n (door) verrou m; (for nut) boulon m; (dash) bond m. v verrouiller; (food) engouffrer; (run away) se sauver.

bomb [bom] n bombe f. v bomber. **bomber** n (aircraft) bombardier m.

bombard [bəm'baːd] v bombarder. **bombardier** n (mil) caporal d'artillerie m. **bombardment** n bombardement m.

bond [bond] n (agreement) engagement m; (tie) lien m; (comm) bon m; (glue) adhérence f. **bondage** n esclavage m.

bone [boun] n os m; (fish) arête f. **bone china** porcelaine tendre f. **bone-dry** adj absolument sec, absolument sèche. **have a bone to pick with** avoir un compte à régler avec. **boned** or **boneless** adj désossé. **bony** adj osseux; (person) anguleux.

bonfire ['bonfaiə] n feu de joie m.

Bonn [bon] n Bonn.

bonnet ['bonit] n (hat) capote f; (mot) capot m.

bonus ['bounəs] n prime f.

booby trap ['buːbi] n traquenard m; (mil) object piégé m.

book [buk] n livre m; (writing) cahier m; (tickets) carnet m. v retenir, réserver. **booked up** complet, -ète.

bookcase ['bukkeis] n bibliothèque f.

booking ['bukin] n réservation f. **booking office** location f.

book-keeper ['buk,kiːpə] n comptable m, f. **book-keeping** n comptabilité f.

booklet ['buklit] n brochure f.

bookmaker ['bukmeikə] n bookmaker m.

bookmark ['bukmaːk] n marque f.

bookseller ['bukselə] n libraire m, f.

bookshop ['bukʃop] n librairie f.

bookstall ['bukstoːl] n kiosque à livres m.

boom [buːm] v (noise) gronder; (comm) prospérer. n grondement m; (comm) forte hausse f; (econ) boom m.

boost [buːst] v (confidence) renforcer; (comm) faire monter; (publicize) faire de la réclame pour.

boot [buːt] n (shoe) botte f; (mot) coffre m.

booth [buːð] *n* cabine *f*; (*voting*) isoloir *m*.

booze [buːz] (*coll*) *n* boissons alcoolisées *f pl*. *v* biberonner. **booze-up** *n* beuverie *f*.

border ['bɔːdə] *n* (*edge*) bord *m*; (*boundary*) frontière *f*; (*garden*) bordure *f*. **borderline** *n* ligne de démarcation *f*. **borderline case** case limite *m*. *v* border. **border on** (*be adjacent*) avoisiner; (*be almost*) frôler.

bore[1] [bɔː] *v* (*hole*) percer; (*well*) creuser; (*rock*) forer. *n* (*gun*) calibre *m*.

bore[2] [bɔː] *n* (*person*) raseur, -euse *m, f*; (*situation*) corvée *f*. *v* ennuyer. **be bored** s'ennuyer (à). **boredom** *n* ennui *m*. **boring** *adj* ennuyeux.

bore[3] [bɔː] *V* **bear**[1].

born [bɔːn] *adj* né. **be born** naître.

borne [bɔːn] *V* **bear**[1].

borough ['bʌrə] *n* circonscription électorale *f*; (*London*) arrondissement *m*.

borrow ['borou] *v* emprunter (à).

bosom ['buzəm] *n* (*woman*) seins *m pl*; (*of family, etc.*) sein *m*. **bosom friend** ami, -e intime *m, f*.

boss [bos] *n* chef *m*; patron, -onne *m, f. v* régenter. **bossy** *adj* tyrannique.

botany ['botəni] *n* botanique *f*. **botanical** *adj* botanique. **botanist** *n* botaniste *m, f*.

both [bouθ] *adj* les deux. *pron* tous les deux.

bother ['boðə] *v* (*annoy*) ennuyer; (*make effort*) se donner la peine (de). *n* ennui *m*. *interj* zut!

bottle ['botl] *n* bouteille *f*; (*beer*) canette *f*; (*perfume*) flacon *m*; (*baby's*) biberon *m*. **bottle-neck** *n* (*road*) rétrécissement de la chaussée *m*; (*traffic*) embouteillage *m*. **bottle-opener** *n* ouvre-bouteilles *m. v* (*fruit*) mettre en bocal; (*wine*) mettre en bouteilles. **bottle up** contenir.

bottom ['botəm] *n* fond *m*, bas *m*; (*buttocks*) derrière *m*. **bottomless** *adj* sans fond.

bough [bau] *n* rameau *m*.

bought [bɔːt] *V* **buy**.

boulder ['bouldə] *n* rocher *m*.

bounce [bauns] *v* (*faire*) rebondir; (*cheque*) être sans provision. *n* bond *m*.

bound[1] [baund] *v* (*leap*) bondir. *n* bond *m*.

bound[2] [baund] *v* (*limit*) borner. **bounds** *pl n* limites *f pl*, bornes *f pl*.

bound[3] [baund] *V* **bind**. *adj* obligé; sûr; (*tied*) lié.

bound[4] [baund] *adj* **bound for** en route pour; à destination de.

boundary ['baundəri] *n* limite *f*, frontière *f*.

bouquet [buːkei] *n* bouquet *m*.

bourgeois ['buəʒwɑː] *n, adj* bourgeois, -e.

bout [baut] *n* (*illness*) accès *m*; (*fight*) combat *m*; (*period*) période *f*.

bow[1] [bau] *v* (*bend*) (se) courber; (*greeting*) *n* salut *m*.

bow[2] [bou] *n* (*archery*) arc *m*; (*music*) archet *m*; (*ribbon*) nœud *m*. **bow-legged** *adj* aux jambes arquées. **bow tie** nœud papillon *m*. **bow window** fenêtre en saillie *f*.

bow[3] [bau] *n* (*naut*) avant *m*.

bowels ['bauəlz] *pl n* (*anat*) intestins *m pl*; (*of earth, etc.*) entrailles *f pl*.

bowl[1] [boul] *n* bol *m*; (*for water*) cuvette *f*.

bowl[2] [boul] *v* (*cricket, etc.*) lancer; (*bowls*) faire rouler. **bowls** *n* jeu de boules *m*. **bowler** *n* (*cricket*) lanceur *m*; (*hat*) chapeau melon *m*. **bowling alley** bowling *m*. **bowling green** terrain de boules *m*.

box[1] [boks] *n* boîte *f*; (*theatre*) loge *f*. **box number** boîte postale *f*. **box office** guichet *m*.

box[2] [boks] *v* (*sport*) boxer. **boxer** *n* boxeur *m*. **boxing** *n* boxe *f*.

Boxing Day *n* le lendemain de Noël *m*.

boy [boi] *n* garçon *m*; (*son*) fils *m*; (*pupil*) élève *m*. **boyfriend** *n* petit ami *m*. **boyhood** *n* enfance *f*.

boycott ['boikot] *v* boycotter. *n* boycottage *m*.

bra [brɑː] *n* soutien-gorge *m*.

brace [breis] *n* (*dental*) appareil *m*; (*tool*) vilebrequin *m*; (*pair*) paire *f*. **braces** *pl n* bretelles *f pl*. *v* soutenir. **brace oneself** se préparer. **bracing** *adj* fortifiant.

bracelet ['breislit] *n* bracelet *m*.

bracken ['brakən] *n* fougère *f*.

bracket ['brakit] *n* support *m*; (*writing*) parenthèse *f*. *v* mettre entre parenthèses; (*group together*) accoler.

brag [brag] *v* se vanter.

braille [breil] *nm, adj* braille.

brain [brein] *n* cerveau *m*. **brains** *pl n* intelligence *f sing*; (*cookery*) cervelle *f sing*. *adj* cérébral. **brain-child** *n* invention personnelle *f*. **brainwashing** *n* lavage de cerveau *m*; (*coll*) bourrage de crâne *m*.

brainwave n inspiration f. **brainy** adj intelligent.

braise [breiz] v braiser.

brake [breik] n frein m. v freiner.

bramble ['bræmbl] n roncier m; (blackberry bush) ronce des haies f.

branch [braːntʃ] n branche f; (road) embranchement m, bifurcation f; (comm) succursale f. v (road) bifurquer.

brand [brænd] v marquer. n marque f. **brand-new** adj tout neuf, toute neuve.

brandish ['brændiʃ] v brandir.

brandy ['brændi] n cognac m.

brass [braːs] n cuivre jaune m. **brass band** fanfare f.

brassière ['bræsiə] V **bra**.

brave [breiv] adj courageux. v braver. **bravery** n courage m.

brawl [broːl] n rixe f. v se quereller.

brawn [broːn] n (cookery) fromage de tête m; (strength) muscle m.

brazen ['breizn] adj effronté.

breach [briːtʃ] n (gap) brèche f; (violation) infraction f; (promise) violation f; (contract) rupture f. **breach of the peace** attentat à l'ordre public m.

bread [bred] n pain m; (slang: money) fric m. **breadcrumbs** pl n chapelure f sing. **bread-winner** n soutien de famille m.

breadth [bredθ] n largeur m.

*break [breik] v (se) casser; (promise, law, etc.) violer. **break down** (cease functioning) tomber en panne; (cry) fondre en larmes. **breakdown** n panne f; (mental) depression nerveuse f; analyse f. **break into** (house) entrer par effraction; (safe, etc.) forcer. **breakthrough** n découverte sensationnelle f. **break up** (se) briser; (school) entrer en vacances. n pause f; rupture f; interruption f. **breakable** adj cassable, fragile. **breakage** n casse f. **breaker** n (wave) brisant m.

breakfast ['brekfəst] n petit déjeuner m.

breast [brest] n (chest) poitrine f; (woman's) sein m; (chicken) blanc m. **breastfeed** v allaiter. **breast-stroke** n brasse f.

breath [breθ] n haleine f, souffle m. **breathtaking** adj stupéfiant. **out of breath** à bout de souffle.

breathalyser ['breθəlaizə] n alcootest m.

breathe [briːð] v respirer; (sigh) souffler. **breather** n moment de répit m. **breathing** n respiration f.

bred [bred] V **breed**.

*breed [briːd] n espèce f. v (rear) élever; (reproduce) se multiplier; (give rise to) engendrer. **breeding** n élevage m; (manners) savoir-vivre m.

breeze [briːz] n brise f.

brew [bruː] v (beer) brasser; (tea) (faire) infuser; (storm) (se) préparer. n brassage m; infusion f. **brewery** n brasserie f.

bribe [braib] n pot-de-vin m. v suborner, soudoyer. **bribery** n corruption f.

brick [brik] n brique f. **bricklayer** n maçon m. v **brick up** murer.

bride [braid] n mariée f. **bridegroom** n marié m. **bridesmaid** n demoiselle d'honneur f. **bridal** adj nuptial; de mariée.

bridge[1] [bridʒ] n pont m; (naut) passerelle f.

bridge[2] [bridʒ] n (cards) bridge m.

bridle ['braidl] n bride f. **bridle path** sentier m. v (horse) brider; (anger) regimber.

brief [briːf] adj bref, brève. v donner des instructions à. n (law) dossier m. **briefcase** n serviette f. **briefly** adv brièvement.

brigade [bri'geid] n brigade f.

bright [brait] adj (shining) brillant; (well-lit) clair; (colour) vif; (clever) intelligent. **brighten** v faire briller; s'éclaircir; (cheer) (s')égayer. **brightness** n éclat m; (of light) intensité f.

brilliant ['briljənt] adj (clever) brillant; (sun) éclatant. **brilliance** n éclat m.

brim [brim] n bord m. **brimful** adj plein à déborder.

brine [brain] n eau salée f; (cookery) saumure f.

*bring [briŋ] v (person) amener; (object) apporter. **bring about** causer, provoquer. **bring in** faire entrer; introduire; (comm) rapporter. **bring off** (succeed) réussir. **bring out** sortir; (colour, etc.) faire ressortir; (publish) publier. **bring up** (rear) élever; (question) soulever; (vomit) vomir.

brink [briŋk] n bord m. **on the brink of** à deux doigts de.

brisk [brisk] adj vif; (trade) actif.

bristle ['brisl] n poil m. v se hérisser. **bristly** adj aux poils durs.

Britain ['britn] n Grande-Bretagne f. **British** adj britannique. **the British** les Britanniques m pl.

Brittany ['britəni] n Bretagne f.

brittle ['britl] adj fragile.

broad [broɪd] adj (wide) large; vaste; général; (accent) prononcé. **broad bean** fève f. **broad-minded** adj tolérant. **broaden** v (s')élargir. **broadly** adv en gros.

broadcast ['broɪdkɑɪst] v *émettre; (rumour, etc.) répandre. n émission f. adj radiodiffusé; télévisé. **broadcasting** n radiodiffusion f; télévision f.

broccoli ['brɒkəlɪ] n brocoli m.

brochure ['brouʃuə] n brochure f.

broke [brouk] V break. adj (coll) à sec.

broken ['broukn] V break.

broker ['broukə] n courtier m.

bronchitis [brɒŋ'kaitis] n bronchite f.

bronze [brɒnz] n bronze m. v brunir; (se) bronzer.

brooch [broutʃ] n broche f.

brood [bruɪd] v couver; (think) ruminer. n nichée f.

brook [bruk] n ruisseau m.

broom [bruɪm] n (brush) balai m; (bush) genêt m.

broth [brɒθ] n bouillon m.

brothel ['brɒθl] n bordel m.

brother ['brʌðə] n frère m. **brother-in-law** n beau-frère m. **brotherhood** n fraternité f. **brotherly** adj fraternel.

brought [brɒɪt] V bring.

brow [brau] n (forehead) front m; (hill) sommet m.

brown [braun] n brun, marron; (tanned) bronzé. n brun m. v (skin) brunir; (cookery) (faire) dorer. **be browned off** (coll) en avoir marre.

browse [brauz] v (book) feuilleter; (animal) brouter.

bruise [bruɪz] n bleu m, meurtrissure f. v faire un bleu à; (se) meurtrir; (fruit) (s')abîmer.

brunette [bruɪ'net] n brunette f.

brush [brʌʃ] n brosse f; (broom) balai m; (undergrowth) taillis m; (skirmish) accrochage m. v brosser; balayer. **brush against** effleurer. **brush up on** se remettre à.

brusque [brusk] adj brusque.

Brussels ['brʌsəlz] n Bruxelles m. **Brussels sprouts** choux de Bruxelles m pl.

brute [bruɪt] n brute m. **brutal** adj brutal; de brute. **brutality** n brutalité f.

bubble ['bʌbl] n bulle f; (in liquid) bouillon m. v bouillonner; (champagne) pétiller.

Bucharest [buɪkə'rest] n Bucharest.

buck [bʌk] n mâle m. **buck-teeth** pl n

dents de lapin f pl. v lancer une ruade. **buck up** (coll: hurry up) se remuer; (coll: cheer up) ravigoter.

bucket ['bʌkit] n seau m.

buckle ['bʌkl] n (fastening) boucle f; (distortion) gauchissement m, voilure f. v (se) boucler; gauchir, (se) voiler.

bud [bʌd] n bourgeon m; (flower) bouton m. v bourgeonner. **budding** adj (plant) bourgeonnant; (talent) en herbe.

Budapest [buɪdə'pest] n Budapest.

budge [bʌdʒ] v (faire) bouger.

budgerigar ['bʌdʒərigaɪ] n perruche f.

budget ['bʌdʒit] n budget m. v budgétiser. **budget for** prévoir des frais de.

buffalo ['bʌfəlou] n buffle, -esse m, f.

buffer ['bʌfə] n tampon m.

buffet[1] ['bʌfit] n (blow) coup m. v frapper, battre; (waves) ballotter.

buffet[2] ['bufei] n buffet m. **buffet car** voiture-buffet f. **buffet lunch** lunch m.

bug [bʌg] n punaise f; (germ) microbe m; (microphone) micro m. v (room) poser des micros dans; (annoy) embêter.

bugger ['bʌgə] n (vulgar) n con m. interj merde alors! **bugger off**: fous-moi la paix!

bugle ['bjuɪgl] n clairon m.

***build** [bild] v bâtir, construire. **build up** (land) urbaniser; (tension) monter; (develop) se développer. n carrure f. **builder** n entrepreneur m; ouvrier du bâtiment m. **building** n construction f; (thing built) bâtiment m; (offices, etc.) immeuble m. **building site** chantier de construction m. **building society** société immobilière f.

built [bilt] V build.

bulb [bʌlb] n (plant) bulbe m; (elec) ampoule f; (thermometer) cuvette f.

Bulgaria [bʌl'geəriə] n Bulgarie f. **Bulgarian** n (people) Bulgare m, f; nm, adj bulgare.

bulge [bʌldʒ] v bomber; (pocket, etc.) être gonflé (de). n bombement m, gonflement m; (increase) poussée f, augmentation f. **bulging** adj (eyes) protubérant; (pockets) bourru.

bulk [bʌlk] n grosseur f; volume m. **in bulk** en gros. **the bulk of** la plus grande partie de. **bulky** adj encombrant.

bull [bul] n taureau m. **bulldog** n bouledogue m. **bulldozer** n bulldozer m. **bullfight** n corrida f. **bull's eye** (target) noir m, mille m.

bullet ['bulit] n balle f. **bullet-proof** adj pare-balles; (car) blindé.

bulletin ['bulitin] n bulletin m.

bullion ['buliən] n (gold) or en barre m; (silver) argent en lingot m.

bully ['buli] n tyran m; (school) brute m. v tyranniser; intimider; brutaliser.

bum [bʌm] n (coll) arrière-train m. adj moche. v **bum around** fainéanter.

bump [bʌmp] n (blow) heurt m, choc m; (on road) bosse f. v heurter; (head, etc.) cogner. **bump into** (car) tamponner; (meet) rencontrer par hasard. **bumpy** adj (road) bosselé; (ride) cahoteux.

bumper ['bʌmpə] n (mot) pare-chocs m invar. adj sensationnel.

bun [bʌn] n (hair) chignon m.

bunch [bʌntʃ] n (flowers) bouquet m; (grapes) grappe f; (tuft) touffe f; (people) bande f.

bundle ['bʌndl] n paquet m, ballot m. v empaqueter, faire un ballot de.

bungalow ['bʌŋɡələu] n bungalow m.

bungle ['bʌŋɡl] v (coll) bâcler. **bungling** adj maladroit.

bunion ['bʌnjən] n oignon m.

bunk [bʌŋk] n couchette f.

bunker ['bʌŋkə] n (coal) coffre m; (naut) soute f; (golf) bunker m; (mil) blockhaus m.

buoy [bɔi] n bouée f. **buoyancy** n (ship) flottabilité f; (liquid) poussée f. **buoyant** adj flottable; (mood) gai.

burden ['bəːdn] n fardeau m. v charger.

bureau ['bjuərəu] n (desk) secrétaire m; (office) bureau m.

bureaucracy [bjuˈrokrəsi] n bureaucratie f. **bureaucrat** n bureaucrate m, f. **bureaucratic** adj bureaucratique.

burglar ['bəːɡlə] n cambrioleur, -euse m, f. **burglar alarm** sonnerie antivol f. **burglary** n cambriolage m. **burgle** v cambrioler.

Burgundy ['bəːɡəndi] n (wine) bourgogne m.

*****burn** [bəːn] v brûler; (building) incendier. n brûlure f. **burning** adj brûlant; (passion) ardent; (lit) allumé.

burnt [bəːnt] V **burn.**

burrow ['bʌrəu] n terrier m. v creuser.

*****burst** [bəːst] v éclater; (balloon, etc.) crever. **burst in** faire irruption. n explosion f; éclat m.

bury ['beri] v enterrer. **burial** n enterrement m.

bus [bʌs] n autobus m. **bus shelter** abribus m. **bus station** gare routière f. **bus stop** arrêt d'autobus m.

bush [buʃ] n buisson m; (thicket) taillis m. **the bush** (Australia) la brousse f. **bushy** adj touffu.

business ['biznis] n affaires f pl; (enterprise) commerce f; (matter) affaire f. **businessman** n homme d'affaires m. **mind one's own business** se mêler de ses affaires. **businesslike** adj pratique; sérieux.

bust[1] [bʌst] n (anat) buste m; (measurement) tour de poitrine m.

bust[2] [bʌst] adj (coll: broken) fichu. **go bust** faire faillite.

bustle ['bʌsl] v s'affairer. n remue-ménage m.

busy ['bizi] adj occupé. **busybody** n mouche du coche f.

but [bʌt] conj mais. adv (only) seulement. prep (except) sauf. **but for** sans.

butane ['bjuːtein] n butane m.

butcher [butʃə] n boucher m. **butcher's shop** boucherie f. v massacrer; (animal) abattre.

butler ['bʌtlə] n maître d'hôtel m.

butt[1] [bʌt] n (cigarette) mégot m, bout m; (gun) crosse f.

butt[2] [bʌt] n victime f.

butt[3] [bʌt] v (goat) donner un coup de corne à. **butt in** s'immiscer dans la conversation, intervenir. n coup de corne m.

butter ['bʌtə] n beurre m. v beurrer.

buttercup ['bʌtəkʌp] n bouton d'or m.

butterfly ['bʌtəflai] n papillon m; (swimming) brasse papillon f. **have butterflies** (coll) avoir le trac.

buttocks ['bʌtəks] pl n (person) fesses f pl; (animal) croupe f sing.

button ['bʌtn] n bouton m. **buttonhole** n boutonnière f; (flower) fleur f. v (se) boutonner.

buttress ['bʌtris] n (arch) arc-boutant m; (support) soutien m. v soutenir.

*****buy** [bai] v acheter. n **a good/bad buy** une bonne/mauvaise affaire. **buyer** acheteur, -euse m, f.

buzz [bʌz] v bourdonner. n bourdonnement m.

by [bai] prep par; (near) près de; (before) avant; (per) à. adv près. **by and by** bientôt. **by the way** à propos. **go by** passer.

bye-law ['bailɔ:] n arrêté municipal m.
by-election ['baii,lekʃən] n election partielle f.
bypass ['bai,pɑːs] n route de contournement f. v contourner.
bystander ['bai,standə] n spectateur, -trice m, f.

C

cab [kæb] n taxi m; (lorry) cabine f.
cabaret ['kæbərei] n cabaret m; (show) spectacle m.
cabbage ['kæbidʒ] n chou (pl choux) m.
cabin ['kæbin] n cabine f; (hut) cabane f.
cabinet ['kæbinit] n cabinet m; (filing) classeur m; (pol) cabinet m. **cabinet-maker** n ébéniste m. **cabinet minister** membre du cabinet m.
cable ['keibl] n câble m. **cablecar** n téléphérique m. v câbler.
cackle ['kækl] v caqueter; (laugh) glousser. n caquet m; gloussement m.
cactus ['kæktəs] n cactus m.
caddie ['kædi] n caddie m.
cadence ['keidəns] n cadence f; (voice) modulation f.
cadet [kə'det] n élève officier m.
café ['kæfei] n café m.
cafeteria [kæfə'tiəriə] n cafétéria f.
caffeine ['kæfiːn] n caféine f.
cage [keidʒ] n cage f.
cake [keik] n gâteau m; (soap, etc) pain m. **cake shop** pâtisserie f. **it's a piece of cake** c'est du gâteau. **like hot cakes** comme des petits pains. **caked** adj coagulé. **caked with** raidi par.
calamine ['kæləmain] n calamine f. **calamine lotion** lotion calmante à la calamine f.
calamity [kə'læməti] n calamité f.
calcium ['kælsiəm] n calcium m.
calculate ['kælkjuleit] v calculer; (reckon) évaluer. **calculable** adj calculable. **calculated** adj délibéré. **calculating** adj (scheming) calculateur, -trice. **calculation** n calcul m. **calculator** n machine à calculer f, calculatrice f.
calendar ['kæləndə] n calendrier m. **calendar month** mois de calendrier m.

calf¹ [kɑːf] n (animal) veau m.
calf² [kɑːf] n (anat) mollet m.
calibre ['kælibə] n calibre m.
call [kɔːl] n appel m; cri m; visite f. **callbox** n cabine téléphonique f. v appeler; (waken) réveiller; (visit) passer. **be called** s'appeler. **call for** (need) demander; (person) passer prendre. **call off** (cancel) annuler. **call on** (visit) passer voir. **call up** (mil) mobiliser. **caller** n visiteur, -euse m, f; (phone) demandeur, -euse m, f. **calling** n vocation f; (job) métier m.
callous ['kæləs] adj dur, sans pitié.
calm [kɑːm] adj calme. n calme m; période de tranquillité f. v calmer. **calm down** (se) calmer. **calmness** n calme m; sang-froid m.
calorie ['kæləri] n calorie f.
came [keim] V come.
camel ['kæməl] n chameau, -elle m, f. **camel-hair** n poil de chameau m.
camera ['kæmərə] n appareil-photo m; (cine) caméra f.
Cameroon [kæmə'ruːn] n Cameroun m.
camouflage ['kæməflɑːʒ] n camouflage m. v camoufler.
camp¹ [kæmp] v camper. **go camping** faire du camping. n camp m. **camp-bed** n lit de camp m. **campsite** n camping m.
camp² [kæmp] adj affecté; efféminé; (slang: homosexual) pédé.
campaign [kæm'pein] n campagne f. v faire campagne.
campus ['kæmpəs] n campus m.
camshaft ['kæmʃɑːft] n (mot) arbre à cames m.
***can¹** [kæn] v (be able) pouvoir; (know how to) savoir.
can² [kæn] n (oil) bidon m; (beer, fruit) boîte f. **can-opener** n ouvre-boîtes m invar. v mettre en boîte.
Canada ['kænədə] n Canada m. **Canadian** n Canadien, -enne m, f; adj canadien.
canal [kə'næl] n canal m.
canary [kə'neəri] n serin m.
Canberra ['kænbərə] n Canberra.
cancel ['kænsəl] v annuler; (order) décommander; (contract) résilier; (train) supprimer; (cheque) faire opposition à. **cancellation** n annulation f; suppression f.
cancer ['kænsə] n cancer m. **Cancer** n Cancer m.
candid ['kændid] adj franc, franche.
candidate ['kændidət] n candidat m.

candle ['kandl] n (wax) bougie f; (tallow) chandelle f. **candle-light** n lumière de bougie f. **candlestick** n bougeoir m; chandelier m. **candlewick** n chenille de coton f.

candour ['kandə] n franchise f.

candy ['kandı] n (US) bonbons m pl. **candied** adj glacé, confit.

cane [kein] n canne f; (school) verge f. v fouetter.

canine ['keinain] adj canin. n (tooth) canine f.

canister ['kanistə] n boîte f.

cannabis ['kanəbis] n (drug) cannabis m; (plant) chanvre indien m.

cannibal ['kanibəl] n(m+f). adj cannibale. **cannibalism** n cannibalisme m.

cannon ['kanən] n canon m. **cannonball** n boulet de canon m.

canoe [kə'nuː] n canoë m; (sport) kayac m. v faire du canoë; faire du kayac.

canon ['kanən] n canon m. **canonical** adj canonique. **canonize** v canoniser.

canopy ['kanəpi] n baldaquin m, dais m.

canteen [kan'tiːn] n (dining place) cantine f; (flask) bidon m; (cutlery) ménagère f.

canter ['kantə] n petit galop m. v aller au petit galop.

canton ['kantən] n canton m.

canvas ['kanvəs] n toile f.

canvass ['kanvəs] v (pol) faire du démarchage électoral; (for orders, votes) solliciter. **canvasser** n (pol) agent électoral m; (comm) démarcheur m. **canvassing** n démarchage m.

canyon ['kanjən] n cañon m.

cap [kap] n (hat) casquette f; (bottle) capsule f; (pen) capuchon m. v capsuler; surpasser.

capable ['keipəbl] adj capable; (situation) susceptible. **capability** n capacité f; aptitude f.

capacity [kə'pasəti] n capacité f; (status) qualité f.

cape¹ [keip] n (cloak) pèlerine f.

cape² [keip] n (geog) cap m.

caper ['keipə] n (cookery) câpre f.

capital ['kapitl] n (city) capitale f; (letter) majuscule f; (money) capital m. adj capital. **capitalism** n capitalisme m. **capitalist** n capitaliste m, f. **capitalize** v capitaliser; (word) mettre une majuscule à. **capitalize on** tirer parti de.

capitulate [kə'pitjuleit] v capituler. **capitulation** n capitulation f.

capricious [kə'prifəs] adj capricieux.

Capricorn ['kaprikɔːn] n Capricorne m.

capsicum ['kapsikəm] n piment m.

capsize [kap'saiz] v (naut) (faire) chavirer.

capsule ['kapsjuːl] n capsule f.

captain ['kaptin] n capitaine m.

caption ['kapfən] n légende f; (title) sous-titre m.

captive ['kaptiv] n captif, -ive m, f. adj captif. **captivate** v captiver. **captivity** n captivité f.

capture ['kaptfə] v prendre, capturer; (attention) capter. n capture f. **captor** n ravisseur m.

car [kaː] n voiture f; (rail) wagon m. **car park** parking m. **car wash** lave-auto m.

caramel ['karəmel] n caramel m.

carat ['karət] n carat m.

caravan ['karəvan] n caravane f; (gipsy) roulotte f.

caraway ['karəwei] n cumin m, carvi m.

carbohydrates [kaːbə'haidreits] pl n farineux m pl, féculents m pl.

carbon ['kaːbən] n carbone m. **carbon copy** (typing) carbone m; (identical thing) réplique f. **carbon dioxide** gaz carbonique m. **carbon paper** papier carbone m.

carburettor ['kaːbjuretə] n carburateur m.

carcass ['kaːkəs] n carcasse f.

card [kaːd] n carte f; (index) fiche f. **cardboard** n carton m. **card trick** tour de cartes. **it's on the cards** il y a de grandes chances. **play one's cards right** bien mener son jeu.

cardiac ['kaːdiak] adj cardiaque. **cardiac arrest** arrêt du cœur m.

cardigan ['kaːdigən] n cardigan m.

cardinal ['kaːdənl] nm, adj cardinal.

care [keə] v se soucier (de). **care for** (like) aimer; (tend) soigner; (look after) s'occuper de. n soin m, attention f; (worry) souci m. **care of** chez. **take care** faire attention. **take care of** s'occuper de. **carefree** adj sans souci, insouciant. **careful** adj prudent; conscientieux. **be careful!** faites attention! **careless** adj négligent; (work) peu soigné.

career [kə'riə] n carrière f.

caress [kə'res] v caresser. n caresse f.

caretaker ['keəteikə] n gardien, -enne m, f; concierge m, f.

cargo ['kaːgou] n cargaison f.

caricature ['kærikətjuə] *n* caricature *f*. *v* caricaturer. **caricaturist** *n* caricaturiste *m*. *f*.

carnage ['kɑːnidʒ] *n* carnage *m*.

carnal ['kɑːnl] *adj* charnel. **carnal knowledge** (*law*) relations sexuelles *f pl*.

carnation [kɑːˈneiʃən] *n* œillet *m*.

carnival ['kɑːnivəl] *n* carnaval *m*.

carnivorous [kɑːˈnivərəs] *adj* carnivore. **carnivore** *n* carnivore *m*.

carol ['kærəl] *n* chant joyeux *m*. **Christmas carol** chant de Noël *m*.

carpenter ['kɑːpəntə] *n* charpentier *m*. **carpentry** *n* charpenterie *f*.

carpet ['kɑːpit] *n* tapis *m*. **carpet-sweeper** *n* balai mécanique *m*. *v* moquetter.

carriage ['kæridʒ] *n* (*horse-drawn*) voiture *f*; (*rail*) wagon *m*; (*comm*) transport *m*; (*person*) maintien *m*. **carriageway** *n* chaussée *f*. **dual carriageway** route à chaussées séparées *f*.

carrier ['kæriə] *n* (*comm*) entreprise de transports *f*; (*med*) porteur, -euse *m*, *f*. **carrier-bag** *n* sac en plastique *m*.

carrot ['kærət] *n* carotte *f*.

carry ['kæri] *v* porter; transporter. **carry away** emporter. **carrycot** *n* porte-bébé *m*. **carry on** continuer. **carry out** exécuter. **get carried away** (*coll*) s'emballer.

cart [kɑːt] *n* (*horse-drawn*) charrette *f*. **cart-horse** *n* cheval de trait *m*. **turn a cart-wheel** faire la roue. *v* transporter; (*coll*) trimballer.

cartilage ['kɑːtilidʒ] *n* cartilage *m*.

cartography [kɑːˈtogrəfi] *n* cartographie *f*. **cartographer** *n* cartographe *m*, *f*.

carton ['kɑːtən] *n* (*cream, etc.*) pot *m*; (*milk*) carton *m*.

cartoon [kɑːˈtuːn] *n* dessin *m*; (*film*) dessin animé *m*. **cartoonist** *n* dessinateur, -trice *m*, *f*; animateur, -trice *m*, *f*.

cartridge ['kɑːtridʒ] *n* cartouche *f*; (*camera*) chargeur *m*. **cartridge paper** papier à cartouche *f*.

carve [kɑːv] *v* (*meat*) découper; (*wood, etc.*) tailler; sculpter; (*initials*) graver. **carving** *n* sculpture *f*. **carving knife** couteau à découper *m*.

cascade [kæsˈkeid] *n* cascade *f*. *v* tomber en cascade.

case[1] [keis] *n* cas *m*; (*law*) affaire *f*; arguments *m pl*. **in any case** en tout cas. **in case** à tout hasard. **in case of** en cas de. **in that case** dans ce cas-là.

case[2] [keis] *n* (*luggage*) valise *f*; (*crate*) caisse *f*; (*violin, camera, etc.*) étui *m*.

cash [kæʃ] *n* (*money*) argent *m*; (*not cheque*) espèces *f pl*; (*immediate payment*) argent comptant *m*. **cash desk** caisse *f*. **cash register** caisse enregistreuse *f*. *v* encaisser.

cashier[1] [kæˈʃiə] *n* caissier *m*.

cashier[2] [kæˈʃiə] *v* renvoyer; (*mil*) casser.

cashmere [kæʃˈmiə] *n* cachemire *m*.

casino [kəˈsiːnou] *n* casino *m*.

cask [kɑːsk] *n* fût *m*.

casket ['kɑːskit] *n* coffret *m*.

casserole ['kæsəroul] *n* (*dish*) cocotte *f*; (*food*) ragoût en cocotte *m*. *v* cuire en cocotte.

cassette [kəˈset] *n* cassette *f*.

cassock ['kæsək] *n* soutane *f*.

*****cast** [kɑːst] *n* (*mould*) moulage *m*; (*theatre*) distribution *f*; (*throw*) coup *m*. *v* (*throw*) jeter; lancer; (*plaster, etc.*) couler; (*theatre*) distribuer les rôles (de). **cast away** rejeter. **castaway** *n* naufragé, -e *m*, *f*. **casting vote** voix prépondérante *f*. **cast-iron** *adj* en fonte; (*excuse, etc.*) inattaquable.

caste [kɑːst] *n* caste *f*.

castle [kɑːsl] *n* château fort *m*.

castor oil [ˈkɑːstə] *n* huile de ricin *f*.

castrate [kəˈstreit] *v* châtrer; émasculer. **castration** *n* castration *f*.

casual ['kæʒuəl] *adj* (*chance*) fortuit, fait par hasard; (*informal*) sans-gêne, désinvolte. **casually** *adv* par hasard; avec désinvolture.

casualty ['kæʒuəlti] *n* (*injured*) blessé, -e *m*, *f*; (*dead*) mort, -e *m*, *f*; (*of accident*) victime *f*; (*hospital ward*) salle des accidentés *f*.

cat [kæt] *n* chat, chatte *m*, *f*. **cat's eyes** (*road*) cataphotes *m pl*. **catsuit** *n* combinaison-pantalon *f*. **let the cat out of the bag** vendre la mèche.

catalogue ['kætəlog] *n* catalogue *m*. *v* cataloguer.

catalyst ['kætəlist] *n* catalyse *f*.

catamaran [kætəməˈran] *n* catamaran *m*.

catapult ['kætəpʌlt] *n* lance-pierres *m* invar; (*aero, mil*) catapulte *f*. *v* catapulter.

cataract ['kætərakt] *n* cataracte *f*.

catarrh [kəˈtɑː] *n* catarrhe *m*.

catastrophe [kəˈtæstrəfi] *n* catastrophe *f*. **catastrophic** *adj* catastrophique.

catch [kætʃ] v attraper; (by surprise) prendre; (train, etc.) ne pas manquer; (on nail) (s')accrocher; (hear) saisir. **catch fire** prendre feu. **catch on** devenir populaire; (understand) comprendre. **catch up** (se) rattraper. n prise f; (drawback) attrape f; (window) loqueteau m. **catching** adj contagieux.

category ['kætəgəri] n catégorie f. **categorical** adj catégorique. **categorize** v classer par catégories.

cater ['keitə] v **cater for** (needs) pourvoir à. **caterer** n fournisseur m, traiteur m. **catering** n restauration f.

caterpillar ['kætəpilə] n chenille f.

cathedral [kə'θidrəl] n cathédrale f.

cathode ['kæθoud] n cathode f. **cathode ray tube** tube cathodique m.

catholic ['kæθlik] adj (rel) catholique; (tastes, etc.) éclectique. n catholique m, f. **catholicism** n catholicisme m.

catkin ['kætkin] n chaton m.

cattle ['kætl] pl n bétail m sing.

catty ['kæti] adj (slang) vache.

caught [kɔtt] V catch.

cauliflower ['kɔliflauə] n chou-fleur (pl choux-fleurs) m.

cause [kɔːz] v causer. n cause f.

causeway ['kɔzwei] n chaussée f.

caustic ['kɔːstik] adj caustique.

caution ['kɔːʃən] n prudence f; (warning) avertissement m; réprimande f. v avertir. **cautious** adj prudent.

cavalry ['kævəlri] n cavalerie f.

cave [keiv] n caverne f, grotte f. **cave in** s'effondrer; (wall) céder.

caviar ['kæviɑː] n caviar m.

cavity ['kævəti] n cavité f. **cavity wall** mur creux m.

cayenne [kei'en] n cayenne m.

cease [siːs] v cesser. **cease-fire** n cessez-le-feu m invar. **ceaseless** adj incessant. **ceaselessly** adv sans cesse.

cedar ['siːdə] n cèdre m.

cedilla [si'dilə] n cédille f.

ceiling ['siːlin] n plafond m.

celebrate ['seləbreit] v célébrer. **celebrated** adj célèbre. **celebration** n célébration f; (occasion) festivités f pl. **celebrity** n célébrité f.

celery ['seləri] n céleri m. **stick of celery** côte de céleri f.

celestial [sə'lestiəl] adj céleste.

celibate ['selibət] n(m+f), adj célibataire. **celibacy** n célibat m.

cell [sel] n cellule f; (elec) élément m.

cellar ['selə] n cave f.

cello ['tʃelou] n violoncelle m. **cellist** n violoncelliste m, f.

cellular ['seljulə] adj cellulaire; (blanket) en cellular.

cement [sə'ment] n ciment m. **cement-mixer** n bétonnière f. v cimenter.

cemetery ['semətri] n cimetière m.

cenotaph ['senətɑːf] n cénotaphe m.

censor ['sensə] n censeur m. v censurer. **censorship** n censure f.

censure ['senʃə] v blâmer. n critique f.

census ['sensəs] n recensement m.

cent [sent] n cent m. **per cent** pour cent.

centenary [sen'tiːnəri] n, adj centenaire.

centigrade ['sentigreid] adj centigrade.

centimetre ['sentimiːtə] n centimètre m.

centipede ['sentipiːd] n mille-pattes m invar.

central ['sentrəl] adj central. **central heating** chauffage central m. **centralization** n centralisation f. **centralize** v (se) centraliser.

centre ['sentə] n centre m. v centrer. **centre on** (thoughts) se concentrer sur; (problem) tourner autour de.

centrifugal [sen'trifjugəl] adj centrifuge.

century ['sentʃuri] n siècle m.

ceramic [sə'ræmik] adj (en) céramique. **ceramics** n céramique f.

cereal ['siəriəl] n céréale f.

ceremonial [serə'mouniəl] n cérémonial m. adj cérémoniel; de cérémonie. **ceremony** ['serəməni] n (event) cérémonie f; (formality) cérémonies f pl. **stand on ceremony** faire des façons. **ceremonious** adj solennel; (over-polite) cérémonieux.

certain ['sɔːtn] adj certain. **certainly** adv certainement; (willingly) volontiers. **certainty** n certitude f.

certificate [sə'tifikət] n certificat m; diplôme m. **certify** v certifier.

cervix ['sɔːviks] n col de l'utérus m.

cesspool ['sespuːl] n fosse d'aisances f.

chafe [tʃeif] v (rub) frotter; (make sore) gratter.

chaffinch ['tʃæfintʃ] n pinson m.

chain [tʃein] n chaîne f. **chain smoke** fumer cigarette sur cigarette. **chain store** magasin à succursales multiples m.

chair [tʃeə] n chaise f; (university) chaire f; (meeting) présidence. **chairlift** n télésiège m. **chairman** n président. v présider.

29   check

chalet ['ʃalei] n chalet m; (motel) bungalow m.
chalk [tʃɔːk] n craie f. **chalky** adj crayeux.
challenge ['tʃalindʒ] n défi m. v défier;
(sport) inviter; (question) contester.
chamber ['tʃeimbə] n chambre f. **chambermaid** n femme de chambre f. **chamber
music** musique de chambre f. **chamber-
pot** n pot de chambre m.
chameleon [kəmiːliən] n caméléon m.
chamois ['ʃamwɑː] n chamois m. **chamois
leather** peau de chamois f.
champagne [ʃam'pein] n champagne m.
champion ['tʃampiən] n champion, -onne
m, f. v défendre. **championship** n championnat m.
chance [tʃɑːns] n (luck) hasard m; (possibility) chance f; (opportunity) occasion f.
by chance par hasard. adj fortuit. v prendre le risque de.
chancellor ['tʃɑːnsələ] n chancelier m.
chandelier [ʃandə'liə] n lustre m.
change [tʃeindʒ] n changement m; (money) monnaie f. v changer; échanger;
(clothes) se changer. **changeable** adj
changeant; (weather) variable. **changing-
room** n vestiaire m.
channel ['tʃanl] n chenal m; (duct) conduit m; (TV) chaîne f. **the Channel
Islands** les îles anglo-normandes f pl. **the
English Channel** la Manche. v (efforts,
etc.) canaliser.
chant [tʃɑːnt] v (rel) psalmodier; (crowd)
scander. n psalmodie f; chant scandé m.
chaos ['keiɒs] n chaos m. **chaotic** adj
chaotique.
chap¹ [tʃap] v (skin) (se) gercer. n gerçure
f.
chap² [tʃap] n (coll) type m.
chapel ['tʃapəl] n chapelle f.
chaperon ['ʃapəroun] n chaperon m. v
chaperonner.
chaplain ['tʃaplin] n aumônier m.
chapter ['tʃaptə] n chapitre m.
char¹ [tʃɑː] v (burn) carboniser.
char² [tʃɑː] v faire des ménages. **charwoman** n femme de ménage f.
character ['karəktə] n caractère m; (theatre, etc.) personnage m. **characteristic** nf,
adj caractéristique. **characterize** v
caractériser.
charcoal ['tʃɑːkoul] n charbon de bois m.
charge [tʃɑːdʒ] n (law) accusation f; (mil)
charge f; (cost) prix m; responsabilité f;
(battery) charge f. **in charge** responsable.
take charge of se charger de. v (law)

accuser (de); (mil) charger; (person) faire
payer; (amount) demander; (battery) (se)
charger. **charge in/out** entrer/sortir en
coup de vent.
chariot ['tʃariət] n char m.
charity ['tʃarəti] n charité f; (society)
œuvre charitable f. **charitable** adj charitable.
charm [tʃɑːm] n charme m; (on bracelet)
breloque f. v charmer. **charming** adj
charmant.
chart [tʃɑːt] n (map) carte f; (graph, etc.)
graphique m, diagramme m. v (journey)
porter sur la carte; (sales, etc.) faire le
graphique de.
charter ['tʃɑːtə] v (boat, etc.) affréter.
chartered accountant expert-comptable
m. n affrètement; (document) charte f.
charter flight charter m.
chase [tʃeis] v chasser, poursuivre. n
chasse f, poursuite f.
chasm ['kazəm] n gouffre m.
chassis ['ʃasi] n (mot) châssis m.
chaste [tʃeist] adj chaste, pur. **chastity** n
chasteté f.
chastise [tʃas'taiz] v châtier. **chastisement**
n châtiment m.
chat [tʃat] n causette f. v bavarder.
chatter ['tʃatə] v jacasser; (teeth) claquer.
n jacassement m; bavardage m. **chatterbox** n bavard, -e m, f.
chauffeur ['ʃoufə] n chauffeur m.
chauvinism ['ʃouvinizəm] n chauvinisme
m. **chauvinist** n, adj chauvin, -e. **male
chauvinist** (slang) phallocrate m.
cheap [tʃiːp] adj bon marché invar;
(reduced) réduit. **cheapen** v baisser le
prix de; (degrade) déprécier. **cheaply** adv
à bon marché.
cheat [tʃiːt] v (deceive) tromper; (at
games) tricher; frauder. n tricheur, -euse
m, f; fraude f.
check [tʃek] n contrôle m, vérification f;
(restraint) arrêt m; (chess) échec m; (US:
cheque) chèque m; (US: bill) addition f.
checkmate n échec et mat. **checkpoint** n
contrôle m. **checkpoint** n (pattern) carreaux m pl. v vérifier; contrôler;
(restrain) maîtriser. **check-in** n (aero)
enregistrement m. **check-out** n (supermarket) caisse f. **check out** (hotel) régler
sa note. **check-up** n (med) bilan de santé
m. **check up on** (thing) vérifier; (person)
se renseigner sur. **checked** adj (pattern) à
carreaux.

cheek [tʃiːk] n (anat) joue f; (coll: impudence) toupet m. **cheekbone** n pommette f. **cheeky** adj effronté.

cheer [tʃiə] v (shout) acclamer, pousser des hourras. **cheer up** (s')égayer; prendre courage; (comfort) consoler. n gaieté f; (shout) acclamation f. **cheerio!** interj salut! **cheers!** interj à la vôtre! **cheerful** adj gai; (news) réconfortant. **cheerless** adj morne. **cheery** adj joyeux.

cheese [tʃiːz] n fromage m. **cheesecake** n tarte au fromage blanc f. **cheesecloth** n (for clothes) toile à beurre f.

cheetah [tʃiːtə] n guépard m.

chef [ʃef] n chef (de cuisine) m.

chemistry ['kemistri] n chimie f. **chemist** n chimiste m, f; pharmacien, -enne m, f. **chemist's shop** pharmacie f.

cheque or US **check** [tʃek] n chèque m. **chequebook** n chéquier m. **cheque card** carte d'identité bancaire f.

cherish ['tʃeriʃ] v chérir; (hope. etc.) nourrir.

cherry ['tʃeri] n (fruit) cerise f; (tree) cerisier m.

chess [tʃes] n échecs m pl. **chessboard** n échiquier m. **chessman** n pièce f.

chest [tʃest] n (anat) poitrine f; (box) caisse f. **chest of drawers** commode f. **chesty** adj (cough) de poitrine.

chestnut ['tʃesnʌt] n (fruit) châtaigne f, marron m; (tree) châtaignier m, marronnier m. adj (hair) châtain.

chew [tʃuː] v mâcher. **chewing gum** chewing-gum m. **chew over** ruminer. **chew the cud** ruminer. **chew up** mâchonner.

chicken ['tʃikin] n poulet m; (very young) poussin m. **chicken pox** n varicelle f. v **chicken out** (slang) se dégonfler.

chicory ['tʃikəri] n chicorée f.

chief [tʃiːf] n chef m. adj principal; en chef. **chiefly** adv principalement; surtout.

chilblain ['tʃilblein] n engelure f.

child [tʃaild] n pl **children** enfant. **childbirth** n accouchement m. **childhood** n enfance f. **childish** adj puéril. **childless** adj sans enfants.

chill [tʃil] n fraîcheur f, froid m; (fear) frisson m; (med) refroidissement m. v (wine) rafraîchir; (champagne) frapper. **chilled to the bone** transi jusqu'aux os. **chilly** adj froid.

chilli ['tʃili] n piment m.

chime [tʃaim] v carillonner; (hours) sonner. n carillon m.

chimney ['tʃimni] n cheminée f. **chimney pot** tuyau de cheminée m. **chimney sweep** ramoneur m.

chimpanzee [tʃimpən'ziː] n chimpanzé m.

chin [tʃin] n menton m.

china ['tʃainə] n porcelaine f.

China ['tʃainə] n Chine f. **Chinese** nm, adj chinois. **the Chinese** les Chinois m pl.

chink[1] [tʃiŋk] n (slit) fente f; (door) entrebâillement m.

chink[2] [tʃiŋk] n (sound) tintement m, v (faire) tinter.

chip [tʃip] n (fragment) éclat m; (in cup, etc.) ébréchure f; (poker, etc.) jeton m. **chipboard** n bois aggloméré m. **chips** pl n (cookery) frites f pl. v (s')ébrécher. **chip in** (interrupt) mettre son mot; (money) contribuer.

chiropody [ki'rɔpədi] n soins du pied m pl. **chiropodist** n pédicure m, f.

chirp [tʃəːp] v pépier. n pépiement m. **chirpy** adj gai.

chisel ['tʃizl] n ciseau m. v ciseler.

chivalry ['ʃivəlri] n chevalerie f. **chivalrous** adj chevaleresque.

chive [tʃaiv] n ciboulette f.

chlorine ['klɔriːn] n chlore m. **chlorinate** v javelliser.

chloroform ['klɔrəfɔːm] n chloroforme m. v chloroformer.

chlorophyll ['klɔrəfil] n chlorophylle f.

chocolate ['tʃɔkəlit] n chocolat m.

choice [tʃɔis] n choix m. adj (fruit) de choix invar; (word) bien choisi.

choir ['kwaiə] n chœur m; chorale f. **choirboy** n jeune choriste m. **choir-stall** n stalle f.

choke [tʃouk] v (s')étrangler, étouffer; (block) boucher. n (mot) starter m.

cholera ['kɔlərə] n choléra m.

***choose** [tʃuːz] v choisir.

chop[1] [tʃɔp] n (meat) côtelette f; (blow) coup m. v trancher; (wood) couper à la hache; (vegetables, etc.) hacher. **chop down** (tree) abattre. **chopper** n hachoir m.

chop[2] [tʃɔp] v **chop and change** changer constamment. **chop logic** ergoter. **choppy** adj (sea) un peu agité.

chops [tʃɔps] pl n (jaws) mâchoires f pl. **lick one's chops** se lécher les babines.

chopstick ['tʃɔpstik] n baguette f.

chord [kɔːd] n (anat) corde f; (music) accord m.

chore [tʃɔː] n (unpleasant) corvée f.
chores pl n (household) travaux du ménage m pl.
choreography [kɒrɪˈɒɡrəfɪ] n chorégraphie f. **choreographer** n chorégraphe m, f.
chorus [ˈkɔːrəs] n refrain m; (singers) chœur m; (dancers) troupe f. **choral** adj choral.
chose [tʃəʊz] V **choose**.
chosen [ˈtʃəʊzn] V **choose**.
christen [ˈkrɪsn] v baptiser; (nickname) surnommer. **christening** n baptême m.
Christian [ˈkrɪstʃən] n, adj chrétien, -enne. **Christian name** prénom m. **Christianity** n christianisme m.
Christmas [ˈkrɪsməs] n Noël m. **Christmas Day** le jour de Noël m. **Christmas Eve** la veille de Noël f.
chromatic [krəˈmætɪk] adj chromatique.
chrome [krəʊm] n chrome m.
chromium [ˈkrəʊmɪəm] n chrome m. **chromium-plated** adj chromé. **chromium-plating** n chromage m.
chromosome [ˈkrəʊməsəʊm] n chromosome m.
chronic [ˈkrɒnɪk] adj chronique; (coll) atroce.
chronicle [ˈkrɒnɪkl] n chronique f.
chronological [krɒnəˈlɒdʒɪkəl] adj chronologique. **in chronological order** par ordre chronologique.
chrysalis [ˈkrɪsəlɪs] n chrysalide f.
chrysanthemum [krɪˈsænθəməm] n chrysanthème m.
chubby [ˈtʃʌbɪ] adj potelé.
chuck [tʃʌk] (coll) v (throw) lancer; (give up) laisser tomber. **chuck out** (thing) balancer; (person) vider.
chuckle [ˈtʃʌkl] v glousser. n petit rire m.
chunk [tʃʌŋk] n gros morceau m; (bread) quignon m.
church [tʃɜːtʃ] n église f. **churchgoer** n pratiquant, -e m, f. **church hall** salle paroissiale f. **churchyard** n cimetière m.
churn [tʃɜːn] n baratte f. v baratter; (water) (faire) bouillonner. **churn out** (coll: books, etc.) pondre en série.
chute [ʃuːt] n glissière f.
cider [ˈsaɪdə] n cidre m.
cigar [sɪˈɡɑː] n cigare m.
cigarette [sɪɡəˈret] n cigarette f. **cigarette lighter** n briquet m.
cinder [ˈsɪndə] n cendre f. **burnt to a cinder** réduit en cendres.
cine camera [ˈsɪnɪ] n caméra f.

cinema [ˈsɪnəmə] n cinéma m.
cinnamon [ˈsɪnəmən] n cannelle f.
circle [ˈsɜːkl] n cercle m; (theatre) balcon m. v (surround) encercler; (move round) tourner autour de; (aircraft) tourner. **circular** nf, adj circulaire.
circuit [ˈsɜːkɪt] n tour m; (law) tournée f; (elec, sport) circuit m. **circuitous** adj indirect.
circulate [ˈsɜːkjʊleɪt] v (faire) circuler. **circulation** n circulation f; (newspaper) tirage m.
circumcise [ˈsɜːkəmsaɪz] v circoncire. **circumcision** n circoncision f.
circumference [səˈkʌmfərəns] n circonférence f.
circumflex [ˈsɜːkəmfleks] adj circonflexe. n accent circonflexe m.
circumscribe [ˈsɜːkəmskraɪb] v circonscrire.
circumspect [ˈsɜːkəmspekt] adj circonspect.
circumstance [ˈsɜːkəmstəns] n circonstance f. **circumstances** pl n (financial) moyens m pl. **under no circumstances** en aucun cas. **under the circumstances** vu l'état des choses.
circus [ˈsɜːkəs] n cirque m.
cistern [ˈsɪstən] n citerne f; (toilet) chasse d'eau f.
cite [saɪt] v citer. **citation** n citation f.
citizen [ˈsɪtɪzn] n (town) habitant, -e m, f; (state) citoyen, -enne m, f. **citizenship** n citoyenneté f.
citrus [ˈsɪtrəs] n citrus m pl. **citrus fruits** agrumes m pl. **citric acid** acide citrique m.
city [ˈsɪtɪ] n ville f, cité f. **city centre** centre ville m.
civic [ˈsɪvɪk] adj (authorities) municipal; (rights) civique. **civic centre** centre administratif m.
civil [ˈsɪvl] adj civil; poli. **civil engineering** travaux publics m pl. **civil rights** droits civiques m pl. **civil servant** fonctionnaire m, f. **civil service** administration f. **civil war** guerre civile f.
civilian [səˈvɪljən] n, adj civil, -e.
civilization [sɪvɪlaɪˈzeɪʃən] n civilisation f. **civilize** v civiliser.
clad [klæd] adj habillé.
claim [kleɪm] v (right, prize, etc.) revendiquer; (damages) réclamer; (profess) déclarer. n revendication f; réclamation

f; (*insurance*) déclaration de sinistre *f*; (*right*) droit *m*.

clairvoyant [kleə'vɔiənt] *n* voyant, -e *m, f*.

clam [klam] *n* praire *f*.

clamber [klambə] *v* grimper en rampant.

clammy [klami] *adj* moite.

clamour [klamə] *n* clameur *f*. *v* vociférer.

clamp [klamp] *n* pince *f*. crampon *m*. *v* serrer, cramponner. **clamp down on** supprimer; restreindre.

clan [klan] *n* clan *m*.

clandestine [klan'destin] *adj* clandestin.

clang [klaŋ] *n* bruit métallique *m*. *v* résonner. **clanger** *n* (*coll*) gaffe *f*.

clap [klap] *v* applaudir. **clap one's hands** battre des mains. *n* (*noise*) claquement *m*; (*thunder*) coup *m*; (*applause*) applaudissements *m pl*.

claret [klarət] *n* bordeaux *m*.

clarify [klarəfai] *v* (se) clarifier; (*situation*) (s')éclaircir.

clarinet [klarə'net] *n* clarinette *f*.

clarity [klarəti] *n* clarté *f*.

clash [klaʃ] *n* (*bang*) s'entrechoquer; (*conflict*) se heurter; (*colours*) jurer. *n* (*dispute*) accrochage *m*; (*personalities*) incompatibilité *f*; (*noise*) choc *m*.

clasp [klasp] *v* serrer. *n* (*fastening*) fermoir *m*; (*grip*) étreinte *f*.

class [klats] *n* classe *f*; catégorie *f*; (*school*) cours *m*. **class-room** *n* salle de classe *f*. *v* classer.

classic [klasik] *nm*, *adj* classique. **classical** *adj* classique. **classics** *n* humanités *f pl*.

classify [klasifai] *v* classifier. **classification** *n* classification *f*. **classified** *adj* classifié; secret, -ète. **classified advertisement** petite annonce *f*.

clatter [klatə] *n* cliquetis *m*. *v* cliqueter.

clause [klɔz] *n* (*law*) clause *f*; (*gramm*) proposition *f*.

claustrophobia [klɔstrə'foubiə] *n* claustrophobie *f*. **claustrophobe** *n* claustrophobe *m, f*. **claustrophobic** *adj* claustrophobique.

claw [klɔt] *n* griffe *f*; (*lobster*) pince *f*. *v* griffer.

clay [klei] *n* argile *f*.

clean [klin] *adj* propre; net, nette. *adv* entièrement. **clean-shaven** *adj* glabre. *v* nettoyer. **cleaner** *n* (*charwoman*) femme de ménage *f*. **cleaner's** *n* teinturerie *f*. **cleaning** *n* nettoyage *m*; (*housework*)

ménage. **cleanliness** *or* **cleanness** *n* propreté *f*.

cleanse [klenz] *v* nettoyer; purifier. **cleanser** *n* (*cosmetic*) démaquillant *m*.

clear [kliə] *adj* clair; transparent; distinct; (*without obstacles*) libre; (s')éclaircir; clarifier; (*remove obstacles*) débarrasser; (*law*) disculper; (*jump*) franchir. **clearance** *n* (*space*) espace *m*; libre; (*customs*) dédouanement *f*; (*aero*) autorisation *f*. **clearing** *n* clairière *f*. **clearness** *n* clarté *f*.

clef [klef] *n* clef *f*.

clench [klentʃ] *v* empoigner. **clench one's fists/teeth** serrer les poings/dents.

clergy [klɔdʒi] *n* clergé *m*. **clergyman** *n* (*Protestant*) pasteur *m*; (*Catholic*) prêtre *m*.

clerical [klerikəl] *adj* (*office*) d'employé, de bureau; (*rel*) clérical.

clerk [klatk] *n* employé, -e *m, f*.

clever [klevə] *adj* intelligent; (*skilful*) habile; (*smart*) astucieux. **cleverness** *n* intelligence *f*; habileté *f*; astuce *f*.

cliché [kliʃei] *n* cliché *m*.

click [klik] *n* déclic *m*. *v* claquer, faire un déclic.

client [klaiənt] *n* client, -e *m, f*. **clientele** *n* clientèle *f*.

cliff [klif] *n* falaise *f*.

climate [klaimət] *n* climat *m*. **climatic** *adj* climatique.

climax [klaimaks] *n* apogée *m*, point culminant *m*.

climb [klaim] *v* grimper, monter; (*mountain*) gravir. *n* montée *f*. **climbing** *n* (*sport*) alpinisme *m*.

*****cling** [klin] *v* se cramponner; (*stick*) (se) coller.

clinic [klinik] *n* clinique *f*. **clinical** *adj* (*med*) clinique; (*attitude*) objectif.

clink [kliŋk] *v* (faire) tinter. *n* tintement *m*.

clip[1] [klip] *v* (*hedge*) tailler; (*hair*) couper; (*dog*) tondre. *n* (*coll: blow*) taloche *f*; (*cinema*) extrait *m*. **clipping** *n* (*newspaper*) coupure de presse *f*.

clip[2] [klip] *n* attache *f*. *v* attacher.

clitoris [klitəris] *n* clitoris *m*.

cloak [klouk] *n* (*clothing*) cape *f*; (*mask*) manteau *m*. **cloakroom** *n* vestiaire *m*. *v* masquer.

clock [klok] *n* (*large*) horloge *f*; (*small*) pendule *f*. **against the clock** contre la montre. **clock-tower** *n* clocher *m*. **clock-**

wise *adj, adv* dans le sens des aiguilles d'une montre. **clockwork** *adj* mécanique. **like clockwork** comme sur des roulettes.

clog [klog] *n* sabot *m*. *v* boucher.

cloister ['klɔistə] *n* cloître *m*. *v* cloîtrer.

close¹ [klous] *adj* (*near*) proche; (*friend*) intime; (*contest, etc.*) serré; (*atmosphere*) étouffant. *adv* de près. **close by** tout près. **close-fitting** *adj* ajusté. **close-up** *n* gros plan *m*. *n* cul-de-sac *m*. **closely** *adv* de près; attentivement.

close² [klouz] *n* (*end*) fin *f*. *v* (se) fermer; (*block*) boucher; (*finish*) (se) terminer. **close in** approcher; (*enclose*) clôturer. **close up** se rapprocher. **closing** *or* **closure** *n* fermeture *f*.

closet ['klɔzit] *n* placard *m*; (*room*) cabinet *m*. *v* enfermer.

clot [klɔt] *n* caillot *m*. *v* (se) coaguler.

cloth [klɔθ] *n* (*fabric*) tissu *m*; (*linen*) toile *f*; (*cleaning*) chiffon *m*.

clothe [klouð] *v* vêtir, habiller. **clothes** *pl n* vêtements *m pl*. **clothes brush** brosse à habits *f*. **clothes horse** séchoir *m*. **clothes line** corde à linge *f*. **clothes peg** pince à linge *f*. **clothing** *n* vêtements *m*.

cloud [klaud] *n* nuage *m*. **cloudburst** *n* déluge de pluie *m*. *v* (*mind*) (s')obscurcir; (*face*) (s')assombrir. **cloud over** se couvrir de nuages. **cloudless** *adj* sans nuages. **cloudy** *adj* nuageux, couvert; (*liquid*) trouble.

clove¹ [klouv] *n* (*spice*) clou de girofle *m*. **oil of cloves** essence de girofle *f*.

clove² [klouv] *n* (*of garlic*) gousse *f*.

clover ['klouvə] *n* trèfle *m*.

clown [klaun] *n* clown *m*.

club [klʌb] *n* (*weapon*) massue *f*; (*cards*) trèfle; (*society*) club *m*. **club-foot** *n* pied-bot *m*. **clubhouse** *n* pavillon *m*. *v* matraquer. **club together** se cotiser.

clue [klu:] *n* indice *m*; (*crosswords*) définition *f*.

clump [klʌmp] *n* (*trees*) bouquet *m*; (*grass, flowers*) touffe *f*.

clumsy ['klʌmzi] *adj* maladroit, gauche. **clumsiness** *n* maladresse *f*, gaucherie *f*.

clung [klʌŋ] *V* **cling**.

cluster ['klʌstə] *n* (*flowers, stars, fruit*) grappe *f*; groupe *m*. *v* se grouper.

clutch [klʌtʃ] *n* (*grip*) étreinte *f*; (*mot*) embrayage *m*. *v* empoigner, se cramponner à.

clutter ['klʌtə] *n* désordre *m*. *v* encombrer.

coach [koutʃ] *n* (*bus*) car *m*; (*rail*) voiture *f*; (*sport*) entraîneur *m*; (*school*) répétiteur, -trice *m, f*. *v* entraîner; (*for exam*) préparer. **coaching** *n* répétitions *f pl*; entraînement *m*.

coagulate [kou'agjuleit] *v* (se) coaguler. **coagulation** *n* coagulation *f*.

coal [koul] *n* charbon *m*, houille *f*. **coalman** *n* charbonnier *m*. **coalmine** *n* houillère *f*. **coalminer** *n* mineur *m*. **coalmining** *n* charbonnage *m*.

coalition [kouə'liʃən] *n* coalition *f*.

coarse [kɔ:s] *adj* grossier; (*salt, etc.*) gros, grosse. **coarseness** *n* rudesse *f*.

coast [koust] *n* côte *f*. **coastguard** *n* garde maritime *m*. **coastline** *n* littoral *m*. **the coast is clear** la voie est libre. *v* (*mot*) descendre en roue libre. **coastal** *adj* côtier. **coaster** *n* (*mat*) dessous de verre *m*.

coat [kout] *n* manteau *m*; (*animal*) pelage *m*, poil *m*; (*horse*) robe *f*; (*paint, etc.*) couche *f*. **coat hanger** cintre *m*. *v* couvrir; (*cookery*) enrober. **coating** *n* couche *f*.

coax [kouks] *v* cajoler.

cobbler ['kɔblə] *n* cordonnier *m*.

cobra ['koubrə] *n* cobra *m*.

cobweb ['kɔbweb] *n* toile d'araignée *f*.

cocaine [kə'kein] *n* cocaïne *f*.

cock [kɔk] *n* coq *m*; mâle *m*; (*vulgar: penis*) bitte *f*. *v* (*a gun*) armer; (*ears*) dresser.

cockle ['kɔkl] *n* coque *f*.

cockpit ['kɔkpit] *n* poste de pilotage *m*.

cockroach ['kɔkroutʃ] *n* blatte *f*.

cocktail ['kɔkteil] *n* cocktail *m*.

cocky ['kɔki] *adj* suffisant.

cocoa ['koukou] *n* cacao *m*.

coconut ['koukənʌt] *n* noix de coco *f*. **coconut palm** cocotier *m*.

cocoon [kə'ku:n] *n* cocon *m*.

cod [kɔd] *n* morue *f*. **cod-liver oil** huile de foie de morue *f*.

code [koud] *n* code *m*. *v* chiffrer.

codeine ['koudi:n] *n* codéine *f*.

coeducation [kouedju'keiʃən] *n* éducation mixte *f*. **coeducational** *adj* mixte.

coerce [kou'ə:s] *v* contraindre. **coercion** *n* contrainte *f*. **coercive** *adj* coercitif.

coexist [kouig'zist] *v* coexister.

coffee ['kɔfi] *n* café *m*. **black/white coffee** café noir/au lait *m*. **coffee bar** café *m*. **coffee bean** grain de café *m*. **coffee pot** cafetière *f*. **coffee table** table basse *f*.

coffin ['kɔfin] n cercueil m.

cog [kɔg] n dent f.

cognac ['kɔnjak] n cognac m.

cohabit [kou'habit] v cohabiter. **cohabitation** n cohabitation f.

coherent [kou'hiərənt] adj cohérent; (account, etc.) facile à suivre. **coherence** n cohérence f. **coherently** adj avec cohérence.

coil [kɔil] n rouleau m; (elec) bobine f; (med) stérilet m. v (s')enrouler; (snake) se lover.

coin [kɔin] n pièce (de monnaie) f. v (money) frapper; (word, etc.) inventer.

coincide [kouin'said] v coïncider. **coincidence** n coïncidence f. **coincidental** adj de coïncidence.

colander ['kɔləndə] n passoire f.

cold [kould] adj froid. **be cold** (person) avoir froid; (weather) faire froid. **cold-blooded** (animal) à sang froid; (person) insensible. **cold sore** n herpès m. n froid m; (med) rhume m. **have a cold** être enrhumé.

colic ['kɔlik] n colique f.

collaborate [kə'labəreit] v collaborer. **collaboration** n collaboration f. **collaborator** n collaborateur, -trice m, f.

collapse [kə'laps] v s'écrouler, s'effondrer. n effondrement m, écroulement m. **collapsible** adj pliant.

collar ['kɔlə] n (on garment) col m; (dog, etc.) collier m. **collarbone** n clavicule f.

collate [kɔ'leit] v collationner. **collation** n collation f.

colleague ['kɔliːg] n collègue m, f.

collect [kə'lekt] v (s')amasser; (se) rassembler; (as hobby) collectionner; (pick up) ramasser; (gather) recueillir; (call for) passer prendre. adj, adv (US: phone) en P.C.V. **collection** n rassemblement m; (money) quête f; (stamps, etc.) collection f; (mail) levée f. **collective** adj collectif. **collector** n (stamps, etc.) collectionneur, -euse m, f.

college [kɔlidʒ] n collège m; (professional) école f.

collide [kə'laid] v se heurter. **collision** n collision f.

colloquial [kə'loukwiəl] adj familier. **colloquialism** n expression familière f.

colon ['koulon] n (punctuation) deux points m invar.

colonel ['kəːnl] n colonel m.

colony ['kɔləni] n colonie f. **colonial** adj colonial. **colonization** n colonisation f. **colonize** v coloniser.

colossal [kə'lɔsəl] adj colossal.

colour ['kʌlə] n couleur f. **colour bar** discrimination raciale f. **colour-blind** adj daltonien. **colour scheme** combinaison de couleurs f. **colour television** (set) téléviseur couleur m. v colorer; (picture) colorier. **coloured** adj coloré; (picture) en couleur; (person) de couleur. **colourful** adj coloré. **colouring** n (complexion) teint m; coloration f. **colourless** adj incolore.

colt [koult] n poulain m.

column ['kɔləm] n colonne f. **columnist** n journaliste m, f.

coma ['koumə] n coma m. **in a coma** dans le coma.

comb [koum] n peigne m; (bird) crête f. v (hair) peigner; (search) fouiller.

combat ['kɔmbat] n combat m. v combattre. **combatant** n combattant, -e m, f.

combine [kəm'bain; n 'kɔmbain] v combiner; s'unir. n association f. **combination** n combinaison f. **combination lock** serrure à combinaison f.

combustion [kəm'bʌstʃən] n combustion f. **combustible** adj combustible.

*__come__ [kʌm] v venir; arriver. **come across** (find) tomber sur. **come back** revenir. **come-back** n rentrée f. **come down** descendre. **come-down** n déchéance f. **come in** entrer. **come off** se détacher; (succeed) réussir. **come out** sortir. **come to** (from faint) revenir à soi; (total) se monter à.

comedy ['kɔmədi] n comédie f. **comedian** n comique m.

comet ['kɔmit] n comète f.

comfort ['kʌmfət] n confort m; consolation f. v consoler; (soothe) soulager. **comfortable** adj confortable; (person) à l'aise.

comic ['kɔmik] adj comique. n (person) comique m; (magazine) comic m. **comical** adj drôle.

comma ['kɔmə] n virgule f.

command [kə'maind] v commander; ordonner; (respect) exiger. n commandement m; ordre m; (mastery) maîtrise f. **commander** n chef m; (mil) commandant m. **commandment** n commandement m.

commandeer [kɔmən'diə] v réquisitionner.

compile

commando [kəˈmɑːndou] n commando m.

commemorate [kəˈmeməreit] v commémorer. **commemoration** n commémoration f. **commemorative** adj commémoratif.

commence [kəˈmens] v commencer. **commencement** n commencement m.

commend [kəˈmend] v (praise) louer; recommander; (entrust) confier. **commendable** adj louable; recommandable. **commendation** n louange f; recommandation f.

comment [ˈkoment] n observation f, commentaire m. v remarquer. **comment on** commenter, faire des remarques sur. **commentary** n commentaire m; (sport) reportage m. **commentator** n reporter m.

commerce [ˈkoməis] n commerce m. **commercial** adj commercial; de commerce. **commercialize** v commercialiser.

commiserate [kəˈmizəreit] v (illness) témoigner de la sympathie (à); (bad luck) s'apitoyer sur le sort (de). **commiseration** n commisération f.

commission [kəˈmiʃən] n commission f; ordres m pl; (mil) brevet m. v (order) commander; déléguer; (mil) nommer à un commandement. **commissioner** n commissaire m; (police) préfet m.

commit [kəˈmit] v commettre; (entrust) confier. **commit oneself** s'engager. **commit suicide** se suicider. **commitment** n responsabilité f; (comm) engagement m.

committee [kəˈmiti] n commission f, comité m.

commodity [kəˈmodəti] n produit m, marchandise f.

common [ˈkomən] adj commun; ordinaire; vulgaire. **Common Market** Marché Commun m. **commonplace** adj banal. **common-room** n salle commune f. **common sense** bon sens. **commonwealth** n république f; confédération f; (British) Commonwealth m.

commotion [kəˈmouʃən] n commotion f; (noise) agitation f.

communal [ˈkomjunəl] adj (shared) commun; (of community) communautaire.

commune¹ [kəˈmjuːn] v communier; converser intimement.

commune² [ˈkomjuːn] n communauté f; (admin) commune f.

communicate [kəˈmjuːnikeit] v communiquer. **communication** n communication f.

communication cord sonnette d'alarme f.

communicative adj communicatif, bavard.

communion [kəˈmjuːnjən] n communion f.

communism [ˈkomjunizəm] n communisme m. **communist** n(m+f), adj communiste.

community [kəˈmjuːnəti] n communauté f; colonie f. **community centre** foyer socio-éducatif m.

commute [kəˈmjuːt] n (travel) faire la navette; échanger; (law) commuer. **commuter** n banlieusard, -e m, f.

compact¹ [kəmˈpakt; n ˈkompakt] adj compact; concis. v condenser. (powder) poudrier m.

compact² [ˈkompakt] n (agreement) contrat m.

companion [kəmˈpanjən] n compagnon m, compagne f. **companionship** n camaraderie f.

company [ˈkʌmpəni] n compagnie f; (theatre) troupe f.

compare [kəmˈpeə] v (se) comparer. **comparable** adj comparable. **comparative** adj comparatif; relatif. **comparison** n comparaison f.

compartment [kəmˈpaːtmənt] n compartiment m.

compass [ˈkʌmpəs] n boussole f; (naut) compas m; (extent) étendue f. **compasses** pl n (math) compas m sing.

compassion [kəmˈpaʃən] n compassion f. **compassionate** adj compatissant; (leave, etc.) pour raisons de famille.

compatible [kəmˈpatəbl] adj compatible. **compatibility** n compatibilité f.

compel [kəmˈpel] v contraindre, forcer. **compelling** adj irrésistible.

compensate [ˈkompenseit] v compenser; (money) dédommager. **compensation** n compensation f.

compete [kəmˈpiːt] v concourir; (comm) faire concurrence. **competition** n compétition f; (contest) concours m; (rivalry) concurrence f. **competitive** adj (price) compétitif; (selection) par concours. **competitor** n concurrent, -e m, f.

competent [ˈkompətənt] adj compétent; suffisant. **competence** n compétence f.

compile [kəmˈpail] v compiler; (dictionary) composer; (list) dresser. **compilation** n compilation f.

complacent [kəm'pleisnt] *adj* content de soi. **complacency** *n* contentement de soi *m*.

complain [kəm'plein] *v* se plaindre. **complaint** *n* plainte *f*; (*comm*) réclamation *f*; (*med*) maladie *f*.

complement ['kompləmənt] *n* complément *m*. *v* compléter. **complementary** *adj* complémentaire.

complete [kəm'plit] *adj* complet, -ète; (*finished*) achevé. *v* compléter; achever. **completion** *n* achèvement *m*.

complex ['kompleks] *nm, adj* complexe. **complexity** *n* complexité *f*.

complexion [kəm'plekʃən] *n* teint *m*; aspect *m*.

complicate ['komplikeit] *v* compliquer. **complication** *n* complication *f*.

complicity [kəm'plisəti] *n* complicité *f*.

compliment ['komplimənt] *n* compliment *m*. *v* complimenter (de). **complimentary** *adj* flatteur, -euse; (*free*) gracieux. **complimentary copy** exemplaire offert en hommage *m*. **complimentary ticket** billet de faveur *m*.

comply [kəm'plai] *n* se soumettre (à); (*wishes*) se conformer (à); (*request*) accéder (à). **compliant** *adj* accommodant. **in compliance with** conformément à.

component [kəm'pounənt] *n* (*tech*) pièce *f*; (*chem*) composant *m*. *adj* constituant.

compose [kəm'pouz] *v* composer. **composed** *adj* calme. **composer** *n* compositeur, -trice *m, f*. **composition** *n* composition *f*; (*essay*) rédaction *f*.

compost ['kompost] *n* compost *m*. **compost heap** tas de compost *m*.

composure [kəm'pouʒə] *n* sang-froid *m*.

compound[1] ['kompaund] *v* kəm'paund] *n* composé *m*. *adj* composé; (*number*) complexe; (*fracture*) compliqué. *v* composer; (*make worse*) aggraver.

compound[2] ['kompaund] *n* enclos *m*.

comprehend [kompri'hend] *v* comprendre. **comprehensible** *adj* compréhensible. **comprehension** *n* compréhension *f*. **comprehensive** *adj* compréhensif; détaillé; (*insurance*) tous-risques. **comprehensive school** centre d'études secondaires *m*.

compress [kəm'pres, *n* 'kompres] *v* comprimer; (*se*) condenser. *n* compresse *f*. **compression** *n* compression *f*; concentration *f*.

comprise [kəm'praiz] *v* comprendre.

compromise ['komprəmaiz] *v* transiger; (*risk*) compromettre. *n* compromis *m*.

compulsion [kəm'pʌlʃən] *n* contrainte *f*. **compulsive** *adj* (*gambler, etc.*) invétéré; (*psych*) compulsif; (*demand*) coercitif. **compulsory** *adj* obligatoire.

compunction [kəm'pʌŋkʃən] *n* remords *m*.

computer [kəm'pjutə] *n* ordinateur *m*. **computer science** informatique *f*. **computerization** *n* automatisation électronique *f*. **computerize** *v* informatiser.

comrade ['komrid] *n* camarade *m, f*. **comradeship** *n* camaraderie *f*.

concave [kon'keiv] *adj* concave.

conceal [kən'sil] *v* dissimuler, cacher. **concealment** *n* dissimulation *f*.

concede [kən'sid] *v* concéder.

conceit [kən'sit] *n* vanité *f*. **conceited** *adj* vaniteux.

conceive [kən'siv] *v* concevoir; (*understand*) comprendre. **conceivable** *adj* concevable.

concentrate ['konsəntreit] *v* (se) concentrer. *n* (*chem*) concentré *m*. **concentration** *n* concentration *f*. **concentration camp** camp de concentration *m*.

concentric [kon'sentrik] *adj* concentrique.

concept ['konsept] *n* concept *m*.

conception [kən'sepʃən] *n* conception *f*.

concern [kən'sən] *v* concerner; regarder. *n* (*business*) affaire *f*; (*comm*) entreprise *f*; (*anxiety*) inquiétude *f*. **concerned** *adj* inquiet, -ète; affecté; en question. **concerning** *prep* en ce qui concerne.

concert ['konsət; *v* kən'sət] *n* concert *m*. *v* concerter.

concertina [konsə'tinə] *n* concertina *m*.

concerto [kən'tʃətou] *n* concerto *m*.

concession [kən'seʃən] *n* concession *f*; (*comm*) réduction *f*. **concessionary** *adj* concessionnaire; (*cheap*) à prix réduit.

conciliate [kən'silieit] *v* (se) concilier; apaiser. **conciliation** *n* conciliation *f*; apaisement *m*. **conciliatory** *adj* conciliant.

concise [kən'sais] *adj* concis.

conclude [kən'klud] *v* conclure. **concluding** *adj* final. **conclusion** *n* conclusion *f*. **conclusive** *adj* définitif.

concoct [kən'kokt] *v* (*cookery*) confectionner; (*excuse*) fabriquer. **concoction** *n* confection *f*; (*excuse*) combinaison *f*.

concrete ['konkrit] *adj* (*real*) concret,

-ète. *n* béton *m*. **concrete mixer** bétonnière *f*. *v* bétonner.

concur [kən'kɜː] *v* (*agree*) être d'accord; coïncider. **concurrent** *adj* simultané.

concussion [kən'kʌʃən] *n* (*med*) commotion cérébrale *f*. *v* **be concussed** être commotionné.

condemn [kən'dem] *v* condamner. **condemnation** *n* condamnation *f*.

condense [kən'dens] *v* (se) condenser. **condensation** *n* condensation *f*. **condenser** *n* (*elec*) condensateur *m*.

condescend [kondi'send] *v* condescendre, daigner. **condescension** *n* condescendance *f*.

condition [kən'diʃən] *n* condition *f*; (*state*) état *m*. *v* conditionner. **conditional** *nm*, *adj* conditionnel. **be conditional on** dépendre de.

condolences [kən'doulənsiz] *pl n* condoléances *f pl*.

condom ['kondəm] *n* préservatif *m*.

condone [kən'doun] *v* pardonner; fermer les yeux sur.

conducive [kən'djuːsiv] *adj* contribuant. **be conducive to** conduire à.

conduct [kondʌkt; *v* kən'dʌkt] *n* conduite *f*. *v* diriger; (*phys*) conduire. **conduct oneself** se conduire. **conducted tour** excursion accompagnée *f*; visite guidée *f*. **conduction** *n* conduction *f*.

conductor [kən'dʌktə] *n* (*music*) chef d'orchestre *m*; (*bus*) receveur *m*; (*phys*) conducteur *m*. **conductress** *n* (*bus*) receveuse *f*.

cone [koun] *n* cône *m*; (*ice cream*) cornet *m*.

confectioner [kən'fekʃənə] *n* (*cakes*) pâtissier, -ère *m, f*; (*sweets*) confiseur, -euse *m, f*. **confectionery** *n* confiserie *f*; pâtisserie *f*.

confederate [kən'fedərət] *n, adj* confédéré, -e. *v* (se) confédérer. **confederation** *n* confédération *f*.

confer [kən'fəː] *v* conférer. **conference** *n* conférence *f*.

confess [kən'fes] *v* confesser, avouer. **confession** *n* confession *f*; aveu *m*.

confetti [kən'feti] *n* confettis *m pl*.

confide [kən'faid] *v* confier; avouer en confidence. **confide in** (*tell*) se confier à; (*trust*) se fier à. **confidence** *n* (*trust*) confiance *f*; (*self-assurance*) assurance *f*; (*secret*) confidence *f*. **confident** *adj*

assuré. **confidential** *adj* confidentiel. **confidently** *adv* avec confiance.

confine [kən'fain] *v* (*imprison*) enfermer; limiter. **be confined** (*childbirth*) accoucher. **confinement** *n* (*childbirth*) couches *f pl*; emprisonnement *m*.

confirm [kən'fəːm] *v* confirmer. **confirmation** *n* confirmation *f*. **confirmed** *adj* (*liar, etc.*) invétéré; (*bachelor*) endurci.

confiscate ['konfiskeit] *v* confisquer. **confiscation** *n* confiscation *f*.

conflict ['konflikt; *v* kən'flikt] *n* conflit *m*. *v* être en conflit; s'opposer. **conflicting** *adj* incompatible; contradictoire.

conform [kən'fɔːm] *v* (se) conformer. **conformity** *n* conformité *f*.

confound [kən'faund] *v* confondre.

confront [kən'frʌnt] *v* (*present*) confronter; (*face*) affronter. **confrontation** *n* confrontation *f*.

confuse [kən'fjuːz] *v* confondre; (*mix up*) embrouiller. **confused** *adj* confus; embrouillé. **confusing** *adj* déroutant. **confusion** *n* confusion *f*; désordre *m*.

congeal [kən'dʒiːl] *v* (se) figer; (*blood*) (se) coaguler; (*freeze*) (se) congeler.

congenial [kən'dʒiːniəl] *adj* sympathique.

congenital [kən'dʒenitl] *adj* congénital.

congested [kən'dʒestid] *adj* encombré; (*med*) congestionné. **congestion** *n* encombrement *m*; (*med*) congestion *f*.

conglomeration [kənˌgloməˈreiʃən] *n* agglomération *f*.

congratulate [kən'grætjuleit] *v* féliciter. **congratulations** *pl n* félicitations *f pl*.

congregate ['kongrigeit] *v* (se) rassembler. **congregation** *n* assemblée *f*.

congress ['kongres] *n* congrès *m*.

conical ['konikəl] *adj* conique.

conifer ['konifə] *n* conifère *m*. **coniferous** *adj* conifère.

conjecture [kən'dʒektʃə] *v* conjecturer. *n* conjecture *f*. **conjectural** *adj* conjectural.

conjugal ['kondʒugəl] *adj* conjugal.

conjugate ['kondʒugeit] *v* (se) conjuguer. **conjugation** *n* conjugaison *f*.

conjunction [kən'dʒʌŋkʃən] *n* conjonction *f*.

conjunctivitis [kənˌdʒʌŋkti'vaitis] *n* conjonctivite *f*.

conjure ['kʌndʒə; (*appeal to*) kən'dʒuə] *v* (*magic*) faire apparaître; (*appeal to*) conjurer. **conjurer** *n* prestidigitateur, -trice *m, f*. **conjuring** *n* prestidigitation *f*. **conjuring trick** tour de passe-passe *m*.

connect [kə'nekt] v (se) relier. **be connected with** avoir des rapports avec. **connection** n jonction f; (elec) connexion f; relation f; (rail) correspondance f.

connoisseur [kona'sət] n connaisseur, -euse m, f.

connotation [kona'teifən] n connotation f.

conquer ['koŋkə] v conquérir; vaincre. **conqueror** n conquérant m. **conquest** n conquête f.

conscience [konfəns] n conscience f.

conscientious [konfi'enfəs] adj consciencieux. **conscientious objector** objecteur de conscience m.

conscious ['konfəs] adj conscient. **consciousness** n (med) connaissance f; (awareness) conscience f.

conscript ['konskript] nm conscrit. **conscription** n conscription f.

consecrate ['konsikreit] v consacrer. **consecration** n consécration f.

consecutive [kən'sekjutiv] adj consécutif.

consensus [kən'sensəs] n consensus m.

consent [kən'sent] v consentir. n consentement m.

consequence ['konsikwəns] n conséquence f; importance f. **consequent** adj résultant. **consequently** adv par conséquent.

conservative [kən'sərvətiv] adj (pol) conservateur, -trice; modeste; traditionnel. n (pol) conservateur, -trice m, f.

conserve [kən'sərv] v conserver. **conservation** n préservation f; défense de l'environnement f. **conservatoire** n (music) conservatoire m. **conservatory** n (greenhouse) serre f.

consider [kən'sidə] v considérer. **considerable** adj considérable. **considerate** adj prévenant. **consideration** n considération f. **considering** prep étant donné.

consign [kən'sain] v (goods) expédier; (entrust) confier. **consignment** n envoi m.

consist [kən'sist] v consister (en). **consistency** n (of substance) consistance f; (of behaviour, etc.) cohérence f. **consistent** adj logique; compatible.

console [kən'soul] v consoler. **consolation** n consolation f.

consolidate [kən'solideit] v (se) consolider. **consolidation** n consolidation f.

consommé [kən'somei] n consommé m.

consonant ['konsənənt] n consonne f. adj en accord.

conspicuous [kən'spikjuəs] adj remarquable; en vue. **be conspicuous** attirer les regards; se faire remarquer.

conspire [kən'spaiə] v conspirer. **conspiracy** n conspiration f. **conspirator** n conspirateur, -trice m, f.

constable ['kʌnstəbl] n agent de police m. **constabulary** n police f.

constant ['konstənt] adj (unchanging) constant; incessant. n constante f. **constancy** n constance f.

constellation [konstə'leifən] n constellation f.

consternation [konstə'neifən] n consternation f.

constipation [konsti'peifən] n constipation f. **constipated** adj constipé.

constituent [kən'stitjuənt] adj constituant. n élément constitutif m; (pol) électeur, -trice m, f. **constituency** n (pol) circonscription électorale f.

constitute ['konstitjut] v constituer. **constitution** n constitution f. **constitutional** adj constitutionnel.

constraint [kən'streint] n contrainte f.

constrict [kən'strikt] v resserrer. **constriction** n resserrement m.

construct [kən'strʌkt] v construire. **construction** n construction f; interprétation f. **constructive** adj constructif.

consul ['konsəl] n consul m. **consular** adj consulaire. **consulate** n consulat m.

consult [kən'sʌlt] v consulter. **consultant** n consultant m; (med) spécialiste m. **consultation** n consultation f.

consume [kən'sjuːm] v consommer; (fire) consumer. **consumer** n consommateur, -trice m, f. **consumer goods** biens de consommation m pl. **consumption** n consommation f.

contact ['kontakt] n contact m; (acquaintance) connaissance f. **contact lenses** verres de contact m pl. v se mettre en contact avec.

contagious [kən'teidʒəs] adj contagieux.

contain [kən'tein] v contenir. **container** n (box, etc.) récipient m; (transport) conteneur m.

contaminate [kən'tamineit] v contaminer. **contamination** n contamination f.

contemplate ['kontəmpleit] v (consider) envisager; (look at) contempler. **contemplation** n contemplation f. **contemplative** adj contemplatif.

contemporary [kən'tempərəri] n, adj contemporain, -e.

contempt [kən'tempt] n mépris m. **contempt of court** outrage à la Cour m. **contemptible** adj méprisable. **contemptuous** adj dédaigneux.

contend [kən'tend] v (fight) combattre (contre), faire face à; (claim) soutenir. **contention** n dispute f.

content¹ [kɒntent] n contenu m. **contents** pl n contenu m sing; (book) table des matières f.

content² [kən'tent] adj also **contented** content, satisfait. **be content with** se contenter de. **contentment** n contentement m, satisfaction f.

contest [kən'test; n 'kɒntest] v contester; (se) disputer. n (fight) combat m; (sport) lutte f; (competition) concours m. **contestant** n concurrent, -e m f.

context [kɒntekst] n contexte m.

continent [kɒntinənt] n continent m. **continental** adj continental. **continental breakfast** petit déjeuner à la française m. **continental quilt** couette f.

contingency [kən'tindʒənsi] n éventualité f. **contingent** adj contingent.

continue [kən'tinjuː] v continuer; (after pause) reprendre. **continual** adj continuel. **continuation** n continuation f; reprise f; (serial) suite f. **continuity** n continuité f. **continuous** adj continu.

contort [kən'tɔːt] v tordre. **contortion** n (acrobat) contorsion f; (twisting) torsion f.

contour ['kɒntuə] n contour m. **contour line** courbe de niveau f.

contraband ['kɒntrəband] n contrebande f.

contraception [kɒntrə'sepʃən] n contraception f. **contraceptive** nm, adj contraceptif.

contract ['kɒntrakt; v kən'trakt] n contrat m. v (se) contracter. **contraction** n contraction f. **contractor** n entrepreneur m.

contradict [kɒntrə'dikt] v contredire. **contradiction** n contradiction f. **contradictory** adj contradictoire.

contralto [kən'traltou] n contralto m.

contraption [kən'trapʃən] n (coll) machin m.

contrary ['kɒntrəri; (perverse) kən'treəri] adj contraire; (perverse) contrariant. adv contrairement. n contraire m. **on the contrary** au contraire.

contrast [kən'traːst; n 'kɒntraːst] v contraster. n contraste m. **contrasting** adj contrasté.

contravene [kɒntrə'viːn] v enfreindre. **contravention** n violation f.

contribute [kən'tribjut] v contribuer. **contribution** n contribution f. **contributor** n (magazine, etc.) collaborateur, -trice m f; (money) donateur, -trice m, f.

contrive [kən'traiv] v (invent) combiner; (manage) s'arranger (pour). **contrived** adj artificiel.

control [kən'troul] n contrôle m; autorité f. **controls** n commandes f pl. v (restrain) maîtriser; (prices, etc.) contrôler; (business) diriger. **controller** n contrôleur m.

controversy [kən'trɒvəsi] n controverse f. **controversial** adj discuté, discutable.

convalesce [kɒnvə'les] v se remettre. **convalescence** n convalescence f. **convalescent** n, adj convalescent, -e.

convector [kən'vektə] n radiateur à convection m.

convenience [kən'viːnjəns] n commodité f, convenance f. **convenient** adj commode, convenable. **be convenient** convenir (à).

convent [kɒnvənt] n couvent m.

convention [kən'venʃən] n (meeting) convention f; (tradition) usage m. **conventional** adj conventionnel, classique.

converge [kən'vɜːdʒ] v converger. **convergence** n convergence f. **convergent** adj convergent.

converse¹ [kən'vɜːs] v causer. **conversation** n conversation f.

converse² ['kɒnvɜːs] nm, adj contraire, inverse.

convert [kən'vɜːt; n 'kɒnvɜːt] v convertir; (house) aménager. n converti, -e m, f. **conversion** n conversion f; aménagement m.

convertible [kən'vɜːtəbl] n (car) voiture décapotable f.

convex [kɒn'veks] adj convexe.

convey [kən'vei] v transmettre; transporter; communiquer. **conveyance** n transport m. **conveyor belt** tapis roulant m.

convict ['kɒnvikt; v kən'vikt] n forçat m. v déclarer coupable.

conviction [kən'vikʃən] n (law) condamnation f; (belief) conviction f.

convince [kən'vins] v convaincre.

convoy ['kɔnvɔi] *n* convoi *m*.

convulsion [kən'vʌlʃən] *n* (*med*) convulsion *f*. **convulsive** *adj* convulsif.

cook [kuk] *n* cuisinier, -ère *m, f. v* (faire) cuire; faire la cuisine. **cooker** *n* cuisinière *f*. **cookery** *or* **cooking** *n* cuisine *f*. **cookie** *n* (*US*) petit gâteau sec *m*.

cool [kuːl] *adj* (*temperature*) frais, fraîche; calme; (*unfriendly*) froid. *v* (se) rafraîchir, (se) refroidir. **cooler** *n* glacière *f*. **coolness** *n* fraîcheur *f*; froideur *f*; (*calmness*) sang-froid *m*.

coop [kuːp] *n* poulailler *m. v* **coop up** cloîtrer.

cooperate [kou'ɔpəreit] *v* coopérer. **cooperation** *n* coopération *f*. **cooperative** *adj* coopératif.

coordinate [kou'ɔːdineit] *v* coordonner. *adj* coordonné. *n* coordonnée *f*.

cope¹ [koup] *v* se débrouiller. **cope with** s'occuper de; (*solve*) venir à bout de.

cope² [koup] *n* chape *f*.

Copenhagen [koupən'heigən] *n* Copenhague.

copious ['koupiəs] *adj* copieux; abondant.

copper¹ ['kɔpə] *n* (*metal*) cuivre *m*. **coppers** *pl n* (*money*) petite monnaie *f* sing.

copper² ['kɔpə] *n also* **cop** (*slang*) flic *m*.

copulate ['kɔpjuleit] *v* copuler. **copulation** *n* copulation *f*.

copy ['kɔpi] *n* copie *f*; (*phot*) épreuve *f*; (*of book, etc.*) exemplaire *m. v* copier. **copyright** *n* copyright *m*.

coral ['kɔrəl] *n* corail (*pl* -aux) *m*. **coral reef** récif de corail *m*.

cord [kɔːd] *n* cordon *m*; (*windows*) corde *f*.

cordial ['kɔːdiəl] *nm, adj* cordial. **cordiality** *n* cordialité *f*.

cordon ['kɔːdn] *n* cordon *m. v* **cordon off** interdire l'accès à.

corduroy ['kɔːdərɔi] *n* velours côtelé *m*.

core [kɔː] *n* (*fruit*) trognon *m*; (*earth*) noyau *m*; (*problem, etc*) essential *m. v* enlever le trognon de.

cork [kɔːk] *n* liège *m*; (*of bottle*) bouchon *m*. **corkscrew** *n* tire-bouchon *m. v* boucher.

corn¹ [kɔːn] *n* blé *m*; (*US*) maïs *m*. **cornflour** *n* farine de maïs *f*. **cornflower** *n* bleuet *m*. **corn on the cob** épi de maïs *m*.

corn² [kɔːn] *n* (*med*) cor *m*.

corner ['kɔːnə] *n* coin *m*; (*mot*) tournant *m. v* (*coll*) coincer; (*comm*) accaparer.

cornet ['kɔːnit] *n* cornet *m*.

Cornwall ['kɔːnwɔːl] *n* Cornouailles *f*.

coronary ['kɔrənəri] *adj* coronaire. **coronary thrombosis** infarctus (du myocarde) *m*.

coronation [kɔrə'neiʃən] *n* couronnement *m*.

corporal¹ ['kɔːpərəl] *adj* corporel.

corporal² ['kɔːpərəl] *n* caporal-chef *m*.

corporation [kɔːpə'reiʃən] *n* (*town*) conseil municipal *m*; (*comm*) société commerciale *f*.

corps [kɔː] *n* corps *m*.

corpse [kɔːps] *n* cadavre *m*.

correct [kə'rekt] *adj* correct. *v* corriger. **correction** *n* correction *f*.

correlate ['kɔrəleit] *v* correspondre; mettre en corrélation. **correlation** *n* corrélation *f*.

correspond [kɔrə'spɔnd] *v* correspondre. **correspondence** *n* correspondance *f*. **correspondent** *n* correspondant, -e *m, f*.

corridor ['kɔridɔː] *n* couloir *m*.

corroborate [kə'rɔbəreit] *v* corroborer. **corroboration** *n* confirmation *f*.

corrode [kə'roud] *v* (se) corroder. **corrosion** *n* corrosion *f*. **corrosive** *adj* corrosif.

corrugated ['kɔrəgeitid] *adj* ondulé. **corrugated iron** tôle ondulée *f*.

corrupt [kə'rʌpt] *v* corrompre. *adj* corrompu. **corruption** *n* corruption *f*.

corset ['kɔːsit] *n* corset *m*.

Corsica ['kɔːsikə] *n* Corse *f*. **Corsican** *n* Corse *m, f*; *adj* corse.

cosmetic [kɔz'metik] *adj* cosmétique; (*surgery*) plastique. **cosmetics** *pl n* produits de beauté *m pl*.

cosmic ['kɔzmik] *adj* cosmique.

cosmopolitan [kɔzmə'pɔlitən] *n*(*m* + *f*). *adj* cosmopolite.

*cost [kɔst] *v* coûter. *n* coût *m*; frais *m pl*. **cost of living** coût de la vie *m*. **costly** *adj* coûteux.

costume ['kɔstjuːm] *n* costume *m*.

cosy ['kouzi] *adj* douillet, -ette.

cot [kɔt] *n* lit d'enfant *m*.

cottage ['kɔtidʒ] *n* cottage *m*; petite maison *f*; (*thatched*) chaumière *f*. **cottage cheese** fromage maigre *m*.

cotton ['kɔtn] *n* coton *m*; (*thread*) fil *m*. **cotton-wool** *n* ouate *f*.

couch [kautʃ] *n* canapé *m. v* exprimer.

cough [kɔf] *n* toux *f. v* tousser.

could [kud] *V* **can¹**.

council ['kaunsǝl] *n* conseil *m*; *(of town)* conseil municipal *m*. **councillor** *n* conseiller, -ère *m, f*.

counsel ['kaunsǝl] *n* conseil *m*; *(law)* avocat, -e *m, f*. *v* conseiller. **counsellor** *n* conseiller, -ère *m, f*; *(social)* orienteur *m*.

count¹ [kaunt] *v* compter; *(consider)* estimer. *n* compte *m*. **countdown** *n* compte à rebours *m*. **countless** *adj* innombrable.

count² [kaunt] *n* comte *m*. **countess** *n* comtesse *f*.

counter¹ ['kauntǝ] *n (shop, etc.)* comptoir *m*; *(bank)* guichet *m*; *(disc)* jeton *m*.

counter² ['kauntǝ] *adj* contraire. *v (blow)* parer; *(boxing, etc.)* riposter. **counter to** à l'encontre de.

counteract [kauntǝ'rakt] *v* neutraliser.

counterattack ['kauntǝrǝ,tak] *v* contre-attaquer. *n* contre-attaque *f*.

counterfeit ['kauntǝfit] *adj* faux, fausse. *v* contrefaire. *n* faux *m*.

counterfoil ['kauntǝ,foil] *n* talon *m*.

counterpart ['kauntǝ,pɑːt] *n* contrepartie *f*; équivalent *m*; *(person)* homologue *m, f*.

country ['kʌntri] *n* pays *m*; *(not town)* campagne *f*; *(native land)* patrie *f*. **the countryside** la campagne *f*.

county ['kaunti] *n* comté *m*. **county town** chef-lieu *m*.

coup [kuː] *n (pol)* coup d'Etat *m*.

couple ['kʌpl] *n* couple *m*. *v* accoupler; *(animals)* s'accoupler.

coupon ['kuːpon] *n (comm)* bon *m*; *(advertisements, etc.)* coupon *m*.

courage ['kʌridʒ] *n* courage *m*. **courageous** *adj* courageux.

courgette [kuǝ'ʒet] *n* courgette *f*.

courier ['kuriǝ] *n* guide *m*; *(messenger)* courrier *m*.

course [kɔːs] *n* cours *m*; *(naut)* route *f*; *(meal)* plat *m*. **of course** bien entendu.

court [kɔːt] *v (woman)* courtiser; *(favour)* solliciter; *(danger)* s'exposer à. *n* cour *m*; *(tennis)* court *m*; *(other sports)* terrain *m*. **court-martial** *n* conseil de guerre *m*. **court-room** *n* salle de tribunal *f*. **courtyard** *n* cour *f*.

courteous ['kǝːtiǝs] *adj* courtois. **courtesy** *n* courtoisie *f*, politesse *f*.

cousin ['kʌzn] *n* cousin, -e *m, f*.

cove [kouv] *n* anse *f*.

cover ['kʌvǝ] *n* couverture *f*; *(lid)* couver-

cle *m*; *(protective)* housse *f*; *(shelter)* abri *m*. *v* couvrir. **coverage** *n* reportage *m*. **covering** *n (wrapping)* couverture *f*; *(layer)* couche *f*.

cow [kau] *n* vache *f*. **cowboy** *n* cow-boy *m*. **cowslip** *n* primevère *f*.

coward ['kauǝd] *n* lâche *m, f*. **cowardice** *n* lâcheté *f*. **cowardly** *adj* lâche.

cower ['kauǝ] *v* trembler; se blottir.

coy [koi] *adj* timide.

crab [krab] *n* crabe *m*. **crab-apple** pomme sauvage *f*. **crabby** *adj* revêche.

crack [krak] *n (split)* fente *f*; *(glass, china, etc.)* fêlure *f*; *(noise)* craquement *m*. *v (se)* fêler; *(ground)* (se) crevasser; *(ice)* (se) craqueler; *(nut)* casser; *(noise)* (faire) craquer.

cracker ['krakǝ] *n (biscuit)* craquelin *m*; *(firework)* pétard *m*; *(Christmas)* diablotin *m*.

crackle ['krakl] *v* crépiter. *n* crépitement *m*.

cradle ['kreidl] *n* berceau *m*. *v* bercer.

craft [krɑːft] *n (skill)* art *m*; *(job)* métier *m*; *(boat)* barque *f*; *(cunning)* astuce *f*. **craftsman** *n* artisan *m*. **crafty** *adj* astucieux.

cram [kram] *v* fourrer, bourrer; *(people)* (s')entasser; *(for exam)* (faire) bachoter.

cramp [kramp] *n (med)* crampe *f*. **cramped** *adj* à l'étroit.

cranberry ['kranbǝri] *n* canneberge *f*.

crane [krein] *n* grue *f*. **cranefly** *n* tipule *f*. *v* **crane one's neck** tendre le cou.

crank [krank] *n (tech)* manivelle *f*. **crankshaft** *n* vilebrequin *m*.

crap [krap] *n (vulgar)* merde *f*; *(nonsense)* conneries *f pl*. **crappy** *adj* merdique.

crash [kraʃ] *n* fracas *m*; *(car, etc.)* accident *m*, collision *f*. *v (car, etc.)* s'écraser; *(collide)* se percuter; *(smash)* (se) fracasser. **crash course** cours intensif *m*. **crash helmet** casque *m*. **crash landing** atterrissage forcé *m*.

crate [kreit] *n* cageot *m*.

crater ['kreitǝ] *n* cratère *m*; *(bomb)* entonnoir *m*.

cravat [krǝ'vat] *n* foulard *m*.

crave [kreiv] *v* avoir grand besoin de; *(beg)* solliciter. **craving** *n* besoin maladif *m*; désir insatiable *m*.

crawl [krɔːl] *v* ramper; *(cars)* avancer au pas; *(babies)* aller à quatre pattes; *(with lice, etc.)* grouiller. *n (swimming)* crawl *m*.

crayfish ['kreifif] n écrevisse f.

crayon ['kreiən] n crayon de couleur m. v colorier au crayon.

craze [kreiz] n engouement m.

crazy ['kreizi] adj fou, folle. crazy paving dallage irrégulier m.

creak [kri:k] v grincer. n grincement m.

cream [kri:m] nf. adj crème. cream cheese fromage blanc m. v also cream off écrémer. creamy adj crémeux.

crease [kri:s] n pli m. crease-resistant adj infroissable. v (se) froisser.

create [kri:'eit] v créer. creation n création f. creative adj créatif.

creature ['kri:tfə] n créature f; bête f.

credentials [kri'denfəlz] pl n références f pl; pièce d'identité f sing.

credible ['kredəbl] adj croyable; plausible. credibility n crédibilité f.

credit ['kredit] n crédit m; honneur m. credit card carte de crédit f. credits pl n (cinema) générique m sing. v croire, attribuer; (banking) créditer. creditable adj honorable. creditor n créancier, -ère m, f.

credulous ['kredjuləs] adj crédule. credulity n crédulité f.

creed [kri:d] n credo m.

*creep [kri:p] v se glisser. creeper n plante grimpante f. creepy adj qui fait frissonner.

cremate [kri'meit] v incinérer. cremation n crémation f. crematorium n crématorium m.

crêpe [kreip] n crêpe m. crêpe paper papier crêpon m.

crept [krept] V creep.

crescent ['kresnt] n croissant m.

cress [kres] n cresson m.

crest [krest] n crête f; (mark) timbre m. crestfallen adj découragé.

crevice ['krevis] n fissure f.

crew [kru:] n (naut) équipage m; (group) équipe f. v (sailing) être équipier. crew-cut n cheveux en brosse m pl. crew-neck n col ras m.

crib [krib] n (baby's) berceau m; (manger) mangeoire f; (rel) crèche f. v copier.

cricket[1] ['krikit] n (insect) grillon m.

cricket[2] ['krikit] n (sport) cricket m.

crime [kraim] n crime m. criminal n, adj criminel, -elle.

crimson ['krimzn] nm, adj cramoisi.

cringe [krindʒ] v reculer; s'humilier.

crinkle ['krinkl] v (se) froisser. n fronce f.

cripple ['kripl] v estropier; (industry, etc.) paralyser. n estropié, -e m, f.

crisis ['kraisis] n crise f.

crisp [krisp] adj (biscuit) croquant; (snow) craquant; (weather, style) vif. crisps pl n chips f pl.

criterion [krai'tiəriən] n, pl -ria critère m.

criticize ['kritisaiz] v critiquer. critic n critique m. critical adj critique. criticism n critique f.

croak [krouk] v (frog) coasser; (crow) croasser. n coassement m; croassement m.

crochet ['kroufei] n travail au crochet m. v (activity) faire du crochet; (make) faire au crochet. crochet hook crochet m.

crockery ['krokəri] n vaisselle f.

crocodile ['krokədail] n crocodile m.

crocus ['kroukəs] n crocus m.

crook [kruk] n (shepherd's) houlette f; (bend) angle m; (coll) escroc m. crooked ['krukid] adj (bent) courbé; (path) tortueux; (askew) de travers; (dishonest) malhonnête.

crop [krop] n culture f; (harvest) récolte f; (cereals) moisson f; (riding) cravache f. v écourter, tondre; (graze) brouter; (hair) couper ras. crop up survenir.

croquet ['kroukei] n croquet m.

cross [kros] n croix f; hybride m; biais m. adj (angry) fâché; diagonal. v (se) croiser; (go across) traverser; (cheque) barrer.

cross-examine [,krosig'zamin] v interroger. cross-examination n contre-interrogatoire f.

cross-eyed ['kros'aid] adj louche.

crossfire ['kros,faiə] n feux croisés m pl.

crossing ['krosin] n (junction) croisement m; (for pedestrians) passage clouté m; (journey) traversée f.

cross-legged [,kros'legid] adj les jambes croisées.

cross-reference [,kros'refərəns] n renvoi m. cross-refer v renvoyer.

crossroads ['kros,roudz] n carrefour m.

cross section n coupe transversale f; (sample) échantillon m.

crosswind ['kros,wind] n vent de travers m.

crossword ['kros,wə:d] n mots croisés m pl.

crotchet ['krotfit] n noire f. crotchety adj grognon, -onne.

crouch [krautʃ] v s'accroupir. n accroupissement m.

crow[1] [krou] n corneille f. **as the crow flies** à vol d'oiseau. **crowbar** n levier m.

crow[2] [krou] v (cock) chanter; (baby) gazouiller. n chant du coq m.

crowd [kraud] n foule f. v (gather round) s'attrouper; (fill up) (s')entasser. **crowded** adj plein (de monde).

crown [kraun] n couronne f; (road) milieu m; (hat) fond m. v couronner. **crown jewels** joyaux de la couronne m pl. **crown prince** prince héritier m.

crucial [kruːʃəl] adj crucial.

crucify [kruːsifai] v crucifier. **crucifix** n crucifix m. **crucifixion** n crucifixion f, crucifiement m.

crude [kruːd] adj (materials) brut; rudimentaire; (behaviour) grossier. **crudely** adv crûment; imparfaitement.

cruel [kruəl] adv cruel. **cruelty** n cruauté f.

cruise [kruːz] n croisière f. v (ship) croiser; (mot) rouler. **cruising speed** vitesse de croisière f. **cruiser** n (ship) croiseur m.

crumb [krʌm] n miette f.

crumble [krʌmbl] v (to crumbs) (s')émietter; (to dust) (s')effriter; (collapse) s'écrouler.

crumple [krʌmpl] v (se) chiffonner.

crunch [krʌntʃ] v (food) croquer; (snow, etc.) faire craquer. n craquement m. **the crunch** (coll) l'instant critique. **crunchy** adj croquant.

crusade [kruːseid] n croisade f. v faire une croisade.

crush [krʌʃ] v (s')écraser; (clothes) (se) froisser. n cohue f. **crushing** adj (defeat) écrasant; (remark) percutant.

crust [krʌst] n croûte f. **crusty** adj (bread) croustillant; (coll) hargneux.

crutch [krʌtʃ] n béquille f; (support) soutien m.

cry [krai] n cri m. v (shout) crier; (weep) pleurer. **cry out** s'écrier, pousser un cri.

crypt [kript] n crypte f.

crystal [kristl] n cristal m. **crystal-clear** adj clair comme le jour. **crystallize** v (se) cristalliser.

cub [kʌb] n petit, -e m, f; (bear) ourson m; (fox) renardeau m; (lion) lionceau m. **cub scout** louveteau m.

cube [kjuːb] n cube m. v (maths) cuber;

(cookery) couper en cubes. **cubic** adj cubique; (in units) cube.

cubicle [kjuːbikl] n (for changing) cabine f; (for sleeping) alcôve f.

cuckoo [kukuː] n coucou m.

cucumber [kjuːkʌmbə] n concombre m.

cuddle [kʌdl] n étreinte f. v serrer dans les bras; (child) câliner. **cuddle up** se pelotonner.

cue[1] [kjuː] n signal m; (theatre) réplique f.

cue[2] [kjuː] n (billiards) queue de billard f.

cuff[1] [kʌf] n (shirt) manchette f. **cuff-link** n bouton de manchette m. **off the cuff** à l'improviste.

cuff[2] [kʌf] v gifler. n gifle f.

culinary [kʌlinəri] adj culinaire.

culminate [kʌlmineit] v culminer. **culminate in** se terminer par. **culmination** n point culminant m; (success) apogée m.

culprit [kʌlprit] n coupable m, f; (law) accusé, -e m, f.

cult [kʌlt] n culte m.

cultivate [kʌltiveit] v cultiver. **cultivation** n culture f.

culture [kʌltʃə] n culture f. **cultural** adj culturel. **cultured** adj cultivé.

cumbersome [kʌmbəsəm] adj encombrant.

cunning [kʌniŋ] adj astucieux; rusé. n astuce f; ruse f.

cup [kʌp] n tasse f; (prize) coupe f.

cupboard [kʌbəd] n placard m.

curate [kjuərət] n vicaire m.

curator [kjuəreitə] n conservateur m.

curb [kəːb] v refréner; restreindre. n frein m.

curdle [kəːdl] v (milk) (se) cailler; (blood) (se) figer.

cure [kjuə] v guérir; (salt) saler; (smoke) fumer. n remède m; (recovery) guérison f. **curable** adj guérissable.

curfew [kəːfjuː] n couvre-feu m.

curious [kjuəriəs] adj curieux. **curiosity** n curiosité f.

curl [kəːl] v (hair) friser, boucler. **curl up** (s')enrouler; (person, animal) se pelotonner. n boucle f; spirale f. **curler** n (hair) rouleau m. **curly** adj bouclé, frisé.

currant [kʌrənt] n (dried fruit) raisin de Corinthe m; (berry) groseille f; (bush) groseillier m.

currency [kʌrənsi] n monnaie f; (foreign) devise f; circulation f.

current [kʌrənt] adj courant; (fashion, etc.) actuel. **current affairs** questions

d'actualité *f pl. n* courant *m*; tendance *f*.
currently *adv* en ce moment.
curry ['kʌri] *n* curry *m*. **curry powder** poudre de curry *f*. **curried** *adj* au curry.
curse [kəːs] *v* maudire; (*swear*) jurer. *n* malédiction *f*; juron *m*; (*bane*) fléau *m*.
curt [kəːt] *adj* brusque.
curtail [kəːˈteil] *v* écourter; (*expenses*) réduire. **curtailment** *n* raccourcissement *m*; réduction *f*.
curtain ['kəːtn] *n* rideau *m*. **curtain call** rappel *m*. *v* garnir de rideaux.
curtsy ['kəːtsi] *n* révérence *f*. *v* faire une révérence.
curve [kəːv] *n* courbe *f*. *v* (se) courber.
cushion ['kuʃən] *n* coussin *m*. *v* amortir.
custard ['kʌstəd] *n* (*pouring*) crème anglaise *f*; (*with eggs*) flan *m*.
custody ['kʌstədi] *n* garde *f*. **custody** emprisonnement *m*.
custom ['kʌstəm] *n* coutume *f*; (*comm*) clientèle *f*. **customs** *n* douane *f*. **customs officer** douanier *m*. **customary** *adj* habituel. **customer** *n* client, -e *m, f*.
*****cut** [kʌt] *n* (*slit*) coupure *f*; (*stroke*) coup *m*; réduction *f*; (*of clothes*) coupe *f*; (*of meat*) morceau *m*. *v* couper; (*slice*) découper; (*shape*, trim) tailler; réduire. **cutback** *n* réduction *f*. **cut down** (*tree, etc.*) abattre; réduire. **cut glass** cristal taillé *m*. **cut off** couper; isoler. **cut out** (*engine*) caler; (*picture*) découper; (*give up*) supprimer. **cut-price** *adv* à prix réduit.
cute [kjuːt] *adj* (*sweet*) mignon, -onne; (*clever*) rusé.
cutlery ['kʌtləri] *n* couverts *m pl*.
cutlet ['kʌtlit] *n* côtelette *f*.
cutting ['kʌtiŋ] *n* (*rail*) tranchée *f*; (*newspaper*) coupure *f*; (*plant*) bouture *f*. *adj* (*edge*) tranchant; (*wind*) cinglant; (*remark*) mordant.
cycle ['saikl] *n* cycle *m*; bicyclette *f*, vélo *m*. *v* faire de la bicyclette; aller à bicyclette. **cycling** *n* cyclisme *m*. **cyclist** *n* cycliste *m, f*.
cyclone ['saikloun] *n* cyclone *m*.
cylinder ['silində] *n* cylindre *m*. **cylinder head** (*mot*) culasse *f*. **cylindrical** *adj* cylindrique.
cymbal ['simbl] *n* cymbale *f*.
cynic ['sinik] *n* cynique *m, f*. **cynical** *adj* cynique. **cynicism** *n* cynisme *m*.
cypress ['saiprəs] *n* cyprès *m*.

Cyprus ['saiprəs] *n* Chypre *f*. **Cypriot** *n* Cypriote *m, f*; *adj* cypriote.
cyst [sist] *n* (*med*) kyste *m*.
Czechoslovakia [ˌtʃekəsləˈvɑːkiə] *n* Tchécoslovaquie *f*. **Czech** *n* (*people*) Tchèque *m, f*; *nm, adj* tchèque. **Czechoslovak** *n* (*people*) Tchécoslovaque *m, f*; *nm, adj* tchécoslovaque.

D

dab [dab] *n* goutte *f*, petite touche *f*. *v* tamponner; appliquer à petits coups.
dabble ['dabl] *v* (*in water*) barboter; (*politics, etc.*) se mêler un peu (de).
dad [dad] *n* (*coll*) papa *m*.
daffodil ['dafədil] *n* jonquille *f*.
daft [dɑːft] *adj* idiot.
dagger ['dagə] *n* poignard *m*.
daily ['deili] *adj* quotidien. *n* (*newspaper*) quotidien *m*; (*cleaner*) femme de ménage *f*. *adv* tous les jours.
dainty ['deinti] *adj* délicat; (*small*) menu.
dairy ['deəri] *n* laiterie *f*; crèmerie *f*. **dairy farming** industrie laitière *f*. **dairy produce** produits laitiers *m pl*.
daisy ['deizi] *n* marguerite *f*; (*wild*) pâquerette *f*.
dam [dam] *n* barrage *m*. *v* endiguer; construire un barrage (sur).
damage ['damidʒ] *n* dommage *m*. **damages** *pl n* (*law*) dommages-intérêts *m, f v* endommager; (*health, etc.*) abîmer; (*reputation*) nuire à. **damaging** *adj* préjudiciable.
damn [dam] *v* (*rel*) damner; condamner. *interj* (*coll*) zut! *adj also* **damned** (*slang*) fichu. *adv* (*slang*) sacrément. **damn all** (*slang*) zéro. **I don't give a damn** (*slang*) je m'en fiche pas mal. **damnable** *adj* odieux. **damnation** *n* (*rel*) damnation *f*.
damp [damp] *adj* humide; (*skin*) moite. *n also* **dampness** humidité *f*. *v also* **dampen** (*moisten*) humecter; (*noise*) étouffer; (*courage*) refroidir. **damp-course** *n* couche isolante *f*. **put a damper on** jeter un froid sur.
damson ['damzən] *n* (*fruit*) prune de Damas *f*; (*tree*) prunier de Damas *m*.
dance [dɑːns] *v* danser. *n* danse *f*; bal *m*.

decant

dance floor piste de danse *f.* **dancer** *n* danseur, -euse *m, f.* **dancing** *n* danse *f.*

dandelion ['dændi,laiən] *n* pissenlit *m.*

dandruff ['dændrəf] *n* pellicules *f pl.*

danger ['deindʒə] *n* danger *m.* **be in danger of** risquer de. **danger money** prime de risque *f.* **on the danger list** dans un état critique. **dangerous** *adj* dangereux.

dangle ['dængl] *v* (*be hanging*) pendre; (*let hang*) balancer.

Danish ['deiniʃ] *nm, adj* danois. **Dane** *n* Danois, -e *m, f.*

dare [deə] *v* oser; (*challenge*) défier. **I dare say** sans doute. **n** défi *m.*

daring ['deəriŋ] *n* audace *f. adj* audacieux.

dark [dɑːk] *adj* obscur; (*colour*) foncé; (*hair*) brun. **be dark** (*night*) faire nuit. **dark horse** quantité inconnue *f.* **darkroom** *n* (*phot*) chambre noire *f. n* obscurité *f;* nuit *f.* **in the dark** (*ignorant*) dans le noir. **darken** *v* (s')obscurcir; (*sky*) (s')assombrir; foncer. **darkness** *n* obscurité *f,* ténèbres *f pl.*

darling ['dɑːliŋ] *n, adj* chéri, -e.

darn [dɑːn] *v* (*socks*) repriser; (*clothes*) raccommoder. **n** reprise *f.* **darning** *n* raccommodage *m.*

dart [dɑːt] *n* (*game*) fléchette *f;* (*sewing*) pince *f.* **dartboard** *n* cible *f. v* s'élancer; (*rays*) darder.

dash [dæʃ] *n* (*drop*) goutte *f;* (*writing*) tiret *m;* (*rush*) élan *m. v* (*rush*) se précipiter; (*throw*) (se) jeter; (*hopes*) anéantir. **dashboard** *n* (*mot*) tableau de bord *m.* **dashing** *adj* plein de panache.

data ['deitə] *n* données *f pl.* **data processing** *n* informatique *f.*

date¹ [deit] *n* date *f;* (*meeting*) rendez-vous *m.* **out of date** (*invalid*) périmé; (*old-fashioned*) démodé. **up to date** moderne; (*books, etc.*) à jour. *v* dater; fixer la date de; (*boyfriend, etc.*) sortir avec. **dated** *adj* démodé.

date² [deit] *n* (*fruit*) datte *f;* (*tree*) dattier *m.*

daub [dɔːb] *v* barbouiller.

daughter ['dɔːtə] *n* fille *f.* **daughter-in-law** *n* belle-fille *f.*

daunt [dɔːnt] *v* décourager. **dauntless** *adj* intrépide.

dawdle ['dɔːdl] *v* traîner.

dawn [dɔːn] *n* aube *f;* point du jour *m. v* (*day*) poindre; (*hope*) naître. **dawn on** venir à.

day [dei] *n* jour *m,* journée *f.* **day after** lendemain *m.* **day before** veille *f.* **daylight** *n* jour *m.* **day-to-day** *adj* journalier.

daydream ['deidriːm] *v* rêvasser. **n** rêvasserie *f.*

daze [deiz] *v* hébéter; (*from blow*) étourdir; (*shock*) abasourdir. **n** hébétement *m;* étourdissement *m;* stupéfaction *f.*

dazzle ['dæzl] *v* éblouir. **n** lumière aveuglante *f.*

dead [ded] *adj* mort. *adv* absolument. **dead-beat** *adj* (*coll*) claqué. **dead end** impasse *f.* **deadline** *n* date limite *f;* heure limite *f.* **deadlock** *n* impasse *f.* **deadpan** *adj, adv* sans expression. **deaden** *v* amortir; (*pain*) calmer. **deadly** *adj* mortel.

deaf [def] *adj* sourd. **deaf-mute** *n* sourd-muet, sourde-muette *m, f.* **deafen** *v* rendre sourd, (*noise*) assourdir. **deafness** *n* surdité *f.*

*deal [diːl] *n* quantité *f;* (*bargain*) marché *m;* (*cards*) donne *f.* **a good deal** beaucoup. *v* (*cards*) distribuer. **deal in** être dans le commerce de. **deal with** (*comm*) négocier avec; (*handle*) se charger de; (*book, report, etc.*) traiter de. **dealer** *n* négociant *m;* (*cards*) donneur *m.* **dealings** *pl n* (*comm*) opérations *f pl;* (*people*) relations *f pl.*

dealt [delt] *V* **deal.**

dean [diːn] *n* doyen *m.*

dear [diə] *n, adj* cher, chère. **oh dear!** oh là là! **dearly** *adv* cher, chèrement.

death [deθ] *n* mort *f.* **death certificate** acte de décès *m.* **death duties** droits de succession *m pl.* **death penalty** peine de mort *f.* **death toll** chiffre des morts *m.* **deathly** *adj* cadavérique; mortel.

debase [di'beis] *v* avilir; (*lower quality*) rabaisser. **debasement** *n* avilissement *m;* baisse *f.*

debate [di'beit] *v* discuter. *n* débat *m;* discussion *f.* **debatable** *adj* contestable.

debit ['debit] *n* débit *m. v* débiter; porter au débit.

debris ['deibriː] *n* débris *m pl.*

debt [det] *n* dette *f.* **get into debt** s'endetter. **debtor** *n* débiteur, -trice *m, f.*

decade ['dekeid] *n* décade *f.*

decadent ['dekədənt] *adj* décadent. **decadence** *n* décadence *f.*

decant [di'kænt] *v* décanter. **decanter** *n* carafe *f.*

decapitate [di'kapi‚teit] v décapiter. **decapitation** n décapitation f.

decay [di'kei] v (rot) pourrir; décliner; tomber en ruines; (tooth) se carier. n pourrissement m; décadence f, carie f. **decaying** adj en pourriture; en décadence.

decease [di'siːs] n décès m. v décéder. **deceased** n, adj défunt, -e.

deceit [di'siːt] n tromperie f. **deceitful** adj trompeur, -euse. **deceitfully** adv fausse-ment. **deceitfulness** n fausseté f.

deceive [di'siːv] v tromper.

December [di'sembə] n décembre m.

decent ['diːsnt] adj (dress) décent; (respectable) convenable; (coll: nice) chic. **decency** n décence f; convenances f pl; (kindness) gentillesse f.

deceptive [di'septiv] adj trompeur. **deception** n tromperie f; illusion f.

decibel ['desi‚bel] n décibel m.

decide [di'said] v (se) décider. **decided** adj résolu; incontestable; marqué. **deciding** adj décisif.

deciduous [di'sidjuəs] adj à feuilles cad-uques.

decimal ['desiməl] adj décimal. n décimale f. **decimal point** virgule f. **decimalization** n décimalisation f. **decimalize** v décimaliser.

decipher [di'saifə] v déchiffrer.

decision [di'siʒən] n décision f. **decisive** adj décisif; (manner) décidé.

deck [dek] n (naut) pont m; (records) table de lecture f. **deck-chair** m transat m. v orner.

declare [di'kleə] v déclarer. **declaration** n déclaration f.

decline [di'klain] n déclin m; (prices) baisse f. v décliner; baisser. **declension** n déclinaison f.

decompose [‚diːkəm'pouz] v (se) décom-poser. **decomposition** n décomposition f.

decorate ['dekə‚reit] v décorer; orner; (room, house) peindre et tapisser. **deco-rating** n décoration intérieure f. **decora-tion** n décoration f; ornement m; (room) décor m. **decorative** adj décoratif. **deco-rator** n décorateur m.

decoy ['diːkoi; v di'koi] n leurre m; (per-son) compère m. v leurrer.

decrease [di'kriːs] v diminuer, décroître. n diminution f, décroissance f.

decree [di'kriː] n décret m. v décréter.

decrepit [di'krepit] adj décrépit; (building)

délabré. **decrepitude** n décrépitude f; délabrement m.

dedicate ['dedi‚keit] v dédier; consacrer. **dedication** dédicace f; consécration f; dévouement m.

deduce [di'djuːs] v déduire. **deduction** n déduction f.

deduct [di'dʌkt] v déduire; (numbers) soustraire; (from wage) prélever (sur). **deductible** adj déductible. **deduction** n déduction f; prélèvement m.

deed [diːd] n action f; (law) contrat m. **deed poll** acte unilatéral m.

deep [diːp] adj profond; (broad) large; (sound) grave. adv profondément. **deep-freeze** n congélateur m. **deep-seated** adj profondément enraciné. **deepen** v (s')approfondir.

deer [diə] n cerf m, biche f.

deface [di'feis] v mutiler; (poster, etc.) barbouiller.

default [di'fɔːlt] n défaut m. **in default of** faute de. v faire défaut; être en défaut.

defeat [di'fiːt] v vaincre, battre. n défaite f. **defeatist** n(m+f), adj défaitiste.

defect [di'fekt] n défaut m. v faire défection. **defection** n défection f. **defective** adj défectueux. **defector** n transfuge m, f.

defend [di'fend] v défendre. **defence** n défense f. **defenceless** adj sans défense. **defendant** n défendeur, -eresse m, f. **defending** adj (champion) en titre; (law) de la défense.

defensive [di'fensiv] n défensive f. adj défensif.

defer [di'fɜː] v (put off) différer. **deferment** n ajournement m; suspension f.

defiant [di'faiənt] adj rebelle; provocant. **defiance** n défi m. **in defiance of** au mépris de. **defiantly** adv d'un air or ton de défi.

deficient [di'fiʃənt] adj insuffisant. **be deficient in** manquer de. **deficiency** n manque f; (med) carence f.

deficit ['defisit] n déficit m.

define [di'fain] v définir. **definition** n défi-nition f; délimitation f; (clearness) net-teté f. **definitive** adj définitif.

definite ['definit] adj certain; déterminé; manifeste; (gramm) défini. **definitely** adv sans aucun doute; catégoriquement.

deflate [di'fleit] v (tyre, etc.) dégonfler; (person) démonter. **deflation** n (econ) déflation f; dégonflement m.

deform [di'fɔ:m] v déformer. **deformation** n déformation f. **deformed** adj difforme. **deformity** n difformité f.

defraud [di'frɔ:d] v (state) frauder; (person) escroquer.

defrost [di:'frɔst] v (refrigerator, etc.) dégivrer; (frozen food) décongeler.

deft [deft] adj habile. **deftness** n habileté f.

defunct [di'fʌŋkt] adj défunt.

defy [di'fai] v défier.

degenerate [di'dʒenə.reit; n, adj di'dʒenərit] v dégénérer. n, adj dégénéré, -e. **degeneracy** or **degeneration** n dégénérescence f.

degrade [di'greid] v dégrader. **degradation** n (person) avilissement m; dégradation f.

degree [di'gri:] n degré m; (university) licence f. **by degrees** petit à petit.

dehydrate [di:'haidreit] v déshydrater. **dehydration** n déshydratation f.

de-icer [di:'aisə] n dégivreur m. **de-ice** v dégivrer.

deity ['di:iti] n divinité f, déité f.

dejected [di'dʒektid] adj abattu. **dejection** n abattement m.

delay [di'lei] v (make late) retarder; (put off) différer. n délai m; retardement m; (rail) retard m. **delaying** adj dilatoire.

delegate ['deligeit; n, adj 'deligit] v déléguer. n, adj délégué, -e. **delegation** n délégation f; nomination f.

delete [di'li:t] v rayer. **deletion** n (act) suppression f; (word, phrase, etc.) rature f.

deliberate [di'libərət; v di'libəreit] adj (intentional) délibéré; réfléchi; mesuré. v délibérer (sur). **deliberately** adv exprès; avec mesure. **deliberation** n délibération f.

delicate ['delikət] adj délicat; (health) fragile. **delicacy** n délicatesse f; (food) friandise f.

delicious [di'liʃəs] adj délicieux.

delight [di'lait] n grand plaisir m, joie f. v enchanter; se délecter (à). **delighted** adj ravi. **delightful** adj charmant, ravissant.

delinquency [di'liŋkwənsi] n délinquance f. **delinquent** n, adj délinquant, -e.

delirious [di'liriəs] adj délirant. **be delirious** (med) avoir le délire; (crowd, etc.) être en délire. **delirium** n délire m.

deliver [di'livə] v (message) remettre; (goods) livrer; (letters) distribuer; (save) délivrer; (speech) prononcer; (woman) accoucher. **deliverance** n délivrance f. **delivery** n livraison f; distribution f; (speech) débit m; accouchement m.

delta ['deltə] n delta m.

delude [di'lu:d] v tromper. **delude oneself** se faire des illusions. **deluded** adj induit en erreur. **delusion** n illusion f; (psych) fantasme m.

deluge ['delju:dʒ] n déluge n. v inonder.

delve [delv] v creuser, fouiller.

demand [di'ma:nd] v exiger, réclamer. n exigence f; (claim) réclamation f; (comm) demande f. **be in demand** être demandé.

democracy [di'mɔkrəsi] n démocratie f. **democrat** n démocrate m, f. **democratic** adj démocratique.

demolish [di'mɔliʃ] v démolir. **demolition** n démolition f.

demon ['di:mən] n démon m. **demoniacal** adj démoniaque.

demonstrate ['demən.streit] v démontrer; (machine, etc.) faire une démonstration de; (pol) manifester. **demonstration** n démonstration f; manifestation f. **demonstrative** adj démonstratif.

demoralize [di'mɔrə.laiz] v démoraliser. **become demoralized** perdre courage. **demoralization** n démoralisation f.

demure [di'mjuə] adj modeste, sage.

den [den] n tanière f, repaire m.

denim ['denim] n toile de jean f. **denims** pl n (jeans) blue-jean m sing.

Denmark ['denma:k] n Danemark m.

denomination [di.nɔmi'neiʃən] n dénomination f; (money) valeur f; (rel) secte f. **denominator** n dénominateur m.

denote [di'nout] v dénoter.

denounce [di'nauns] v dénoncer.

dense [dens] adj dense; (coll: stupid) bouché. **density** n densité f.

dent [dent] n bosselure f. v bosseler, cabosser.

dental [dentl] adj dentaire. **dental surgeon** chirurgien dentiste m.

dentist ['dentist] n dentiste m, f. **dentistry** n art dentaire m.

denture ['dentʃə] n dentier m.

denude [di'nju:d] v dénuder.

denunciation [di.nʌnsi'eiʃən] n dénonciation f.

deny [di'nai] v nier; refuser. **denial** n dénégation f; (accusation, etc.) démenti m.

deodorant [di:'oudərənt] nm, adj déodorant, désodorisant.

depart [di'pɑːt] v partir. **depart from** (*leave*) quitter; (*deviate*) s'écarter de. **departure** n départ m. **departure lounge** salle de départ f.

department [di'pɑːtmənt] n département m; (*shop*) rayon m; (*school, university*) section f; domaine m; (*comm*) service m. **department store** grand magasin m.

depend [di'pend] v dépendre. **depend on** dépendre de; (*rely*) compter sur. **dependant** n personne à charge f. **dependence** n dépendance f. **dependent** adj dépendant.

depict [di'pikt] v (*words*) peindre; (*picture*) représenter. **depiction** n peinture f; représentation f.

deplete [di'pliːt] v réduire. **depletion** n réduction f.

deplore [di'plɔː] v déplorer. **deplorable** adj déplorable.

deport [di'pɔːt] v déporter; expulser. **deportation** n déportation f; expulsion f. **deportment** n maintien m.

depose [di'pouz] v déposer. **deposition** n déposition f.

deposit [di'pɒzit] v déposer; n dépôt m; (*against damage*) caution f; (*token payment*) acompte m. **deposit account** compte de dépôt m. **depositor** n déposant, -e m, f.

depot [depou] n dépôt m.

deprave [di'preiv] v dépraver. **depravity** n dépravation f.

depreciate [di'priːʃi̩eit] v (se) déprécier. **depreciation** n dépréciation f.

depress [di'pres] v déprimer; (*press down*) appuyer sur. **depression** n dépression f; découragement m; (*econ*) crise f.

deprive [di'praiv] v priver. **deprivation** n privation f.

depth [depθ] n profondeur f; (*breadth*) largeur f; intensité f.

deputy [depjuti] n adjoint, -e m, f. **deputation** n délégation f. **deputize for** assurer l'intérim de.

derail [di'reil] v (faire) dérailler. **derailment** n déraillement m.

derelict ['derilikt] adj abandonné, délaissé.

deride [di'raid] v railler. **derision** n dérision f. **derisive** adj moqueur. **derisory** adj (*offer, etc.*) dérisoire.

derive [di'raiv] v (*gain*) trouver, tirer. **be derived from** dériver de, provenir de. **derivation** n dérivation f.

derogatory [di'rogətəri] adj dénigrant, désobligeant.

descend [di'send] v descendre. **descend to** (*crime, etc.*) s'abaisser à. **descendant** n descendant, -e m, f. **descent** n descente f; origine f.

describe [di'skraib] v décrire. **description** n description f. **descriptive** adj descriptif.

desert[1] ['dezət] n désert m.

desert[2] [di'zəːt] v déserter, abandonner. **deserted** adj désert. **deserter** n déserteur m. **desertion** n désertion f; abandon m.

deserts[3] [di'zəːts] n pl dû. m. get one's just deserts avoir ce que l'on mérite.

deserve [di'zəːv] v mériter.

design [di'zain] n modèle m, plan m; (*pattern*) dessin m; (*comm*) design m; (*machine, etc.*) conception f; (*intention*) dessein m. v dessiner; projeter; concevoir. **designer** n (*comm*) concepteur-projeteur m; (*art*) dessinateur, -trice m, f.

designate ['dezigneit] v désigner. **designation** n désignation f.

desire [di'zaiə] n désir m. v désirer. **desirable** adj désirable.

desk [desk] n bureau m; (*school*) pupitre m.

desolate ['desələt] adj désert; sombre; (*person*) affligé. **desolation** n désolation f.

despair [di'speə] n désespoir m. v désespérer.

desperate ['despərət] adj désespéré. **desperation** n désespoir m.

despise [di'spaiz] v mépriser.

despite [di'spait] prep malgré.

despondent [di'spondənt] adj découragé. **despondency** n découragement m.

despot ['despot] n despote m. **despotic** adj despotique.

dessert [di'zəːt] n dessert m. **dessertspoon** n cuiller à dessert f.

destination [desti'neiʃən] n destination f.

destine ['destin] v destiner. **destiny** n destin m.

destitute ['destitjuːt] adj indigent. **destitution** n dénuement m.

destroy [di'stroi] v détruire. **destroyer** n (*ship*) contre-torpilleur m. **destruction** n destruction f. **destructive** adj destructeur, -trice; destructif.

detach [di'tatʃ] v détacher. **detachable** adj détachable. **detached** adj détaché; (*unbiased*) objectif; indifférent. **detached house** maison individuelle f. **detachment** n détachement m; séparation f.

detail ['diːteil] n détail m. v détailler; (*mil*) affecter.

detain [di'tein] v retenir; (*law*) détenir.

detect [di'tekt] v découvrir; distinguer. **detective** n agent de la sûreté m. **detective story** roman policier m. **detector** n detecteur m.

detention [di'tenʃən] n détention f; (*school*) retenue f.

deter [di'təː] v décourager; dissuader; (*prevent*) détourner. **deterrent** n force de dissuasion f.

detergent [di'təːdʒənt] nm, adj détersif.

deteriorate [di'tiəriəˌreit] v (se) détériorer. **deterioration** n détérioration f.

determine [di'təːmin] v déterminer; fixer; décider. **determination** n détermination f. **determined** adj déterminé; résolu.

detest [di'test] v détester.

detonate ['detəˌneit] v (faire) détoner. **detonation** n détonation f. **detonator** n détonateur m.

detour [diˈtuə] n détour m. v faire un détour.

detract [di'trakt] v **detract from** diminuer. **detriment** ['detrimənt] n détriment m. **detrimental** adj nuisible.

devalue [diːˈvaljuː] v dévaluer. **devaluation** n dévaluation f.

devastate ['devəˌsteit] v (*town, etc.*) dévaster; (*person*) terrasser. **devastating** adj (*power*) dévastateur, -trice; (*effect*) accablant. **devastation** n dévastation f.

develop [di'veləp] v (se) développer; contracter. **development** n développement m; exploitation f.

deviate ['diːviˌeit] v dévier. **deviation** n déviation f.

device [di'vais] n appareil m; (*scheme*) formule f.

devil ['devl] n diable m. **talk of the devil!** quand on parle du loup! **devilish** adj diabolique.

devise [di'vaiz] v inventer; (*plan*) combiner.

devious ['diːviəs] adj détourné, tortueux.

devoid [di'void] adj dénué.

devolution [ˌdiːvəˈluːʃən] n (*pol*) décentralisation f.

devote [di'vout] v consacrer. **devoted** adj dévoué. **devotion** n dévouement m.

devour [di'vauə] v dévorer.

devout [di'vaut] adj (*person*) pieux; (*earnest*) fervent.

dew [djuː] n rosée f.

dexterous ['dekstrəs] adj adroit. **dexterity** n adresse f.

diabetes [ˌdiəˈbiːtiːz] n diabète m. **diabetic** n(m+f), adj diabétique.

diagnose [ˌdiəgˈnouz] v diagnostiquer. **diagnosis** n diagnostic m. **diagnostic** adj diagnostique.

diagonal [dai'agənəl] adj diagonal. n diagonale f.

diagram ['daiəˌgram] n diagramme m; (*math*) figure f. **diagrammatic** adj schématique.

dial ['daiəl] n cadran m. v (*number*) faire. **dial direct** appeler par l'automatique. **dial 999** appeler Police Secours. **dialling code** indicatif m. **dialling tone** tonalité f.

dialect ['daiəlekt] n dialecte m; (*rural*) patois m.

dialogue ['daiəlog] n dialogue m.

diameter [dai'amitə] n diamètre m. **diametrically opposed** diamétralement opposé.

diamond ['daiəmənd] n (*gem*) diamant m; (*cards*) carreau m; (*shape*) losange m.

diaper ['daiəpə] n (*US*) couche f.

diaphragm ['daiəˌfram] n diaphragme m.

diarrhoea [ˌdaiəˈriə] n diarrhée f.

diary ['daiəri] n (*record*) journal m; (*appointments*) agenda m.

dice [dais] n dé m. v couper en dés. **dice with death** jouer avec la mort.

dictate [dik'teit] v dicter. **dictation** n dictée f. **dictator** n dictateur m. **dictatorship** n dictature f.

dictionary ['dikʃənəri] n dictionnaire m.

did [did] V do.

die [dai] v mourir. **be dying** se mourir. **be dying to** mourir d'envie de. **be dying for** avoir une envie folle de. **die down** s'apaiser. **die out** disparaître.

diesel ['diːzəl] n diesel m. **diesel oil** gas-oil m. **diesel train** autorail m.

diet ['daiət] n (*restricted*) régime m; (*normal food*) nourriture f. v suivre un régime.

differ ['difə] v différer; ne pas être d'accord. **difference** n différence f. **different** adj différent; (*another*) autre. **differential** adj différentiel. **differentials** pl n (*salary*) écarts salariaux m pl. **differentiate** v distinguer.

difficult ['difikəlt] adj difficile. **difficulty** n difficulté f.

*dig [dig] v creuser; (dog) fouiller. dig up déterrer. n (archaeol) fouille f; (coll: remark) coup de patte m; (with elbow) coup de coude m.

digest [dai'dʒest] v digérer. digestion n digestion f.

digit ['didʒit] n (math) chiffre m; (finger) doigt m. digital adj (clock, etc.) à affichage numérique.

dignified ['dignifaid] adj digne.

dignity ['digniti] n dignité f.

digress [dai'gres] v s'éloigner. digression n digression f.

digs [digz] pl n chambre f sing, logement m sing.

dilapidated [di'lapi,deitid] adj délabré.

dilate [dai'leit] v (se) dilater. dilation n dilatation f.

dilemma [di'lemə] n dilemme m.

diligent ['dilidʒent] adj assidu; laborieux. diligence n assiduité f, zèle m.

dilute [dai'luːt] v diluer. adj dilué.

dim [dim] adj (light) faible; (sound) vague; (coll: stupid) bouché. take a dim view of voir d'un mauvais œil. v (light) baisser; (sound) affaiblir. dimness n faiblesse f, obscurité f.

dimension [di'menʃən] n dimension f. two-/three-dimensional à deux/trois dimensions.

diminish [di'miniʃ] v diminuer.

diminutive [di'minjutiv] adj (small) tout petit; (gramm) diminutif. n diminutif m.

dimple ['dimpl] n fossette f.

din [din] n vacarme m.

dine [dain] v dîner. diner n (person) dîneur, -euse m, f; dining car wagon-restaurant m. dining room salle à manger f.

dinghy ['dingi] n youyou m; (with sail) dériveur m.

dingy ['dindʒi] adj miteux.

dinner ['dinə] n dîner m; (midday meal) déjeuner m. dinner jacket smoking m.

dinosaur ['dainəsot] n dinosaure m.

diocese ['daiəsis] n diocèse m.

dip [dip] v (into water, etc.) plonger; (go down) baisser. n (coll: bathe) baignade f; (in ground) déclivité f. dip-stick n jauge f. diphthong ['difθoŋ] n diphtongue f.

diploma [di'ploumə] n diplôme m.

diplomacy [di'plouməsi] n diplomatie f. diplomat n diplomate m. diplomatic adj diplomatique; (person) diplomate.

dire [daiə] adj terrible; extrême. in dire straits dans une situation désespérée.

direct [di'rekt] adj direct. direct object complément direct m. v diriger; adresser; (instruct) charger. adv directement. direction n direction f; instruction f. directly adv directement; (immediately) tout de suite. director n directeur, -trice m, f; (theatre) metteur en scène m; (film, TV, etc.) réalisateur, -trice m, f. directory n (phone) annuaire m; (addresses) répertoire m. directory enquiries renseignements m pl.

dirt [dəːt] n saleté f, crasse f.

dirty ['dəːti] adj sale; (vulgar) grossier. v salir.

disability [disə'biləti] n incapacité f; infirmité f. disabled adj infirme, handicapé.

disadvantage [disəd'vaintidʒ] n désavantage m. at a disadvantage dans une position désavantageuse.

disagree [disə'griː] v ne pas être d'accord; (be different) ne pas concorder; (food, etc.) ne pas convenir (à). disagreeable adj désagréable. disagreement n désaccord m.

disappear [disə'piə] v disparaître. disappearance n disparition f.

disappoint [disə'point] v decevoir. disappointment n déception f.

disapprove [disə'pruːv] v désapprouver. disapproval n désapprobation f. disapproving adj désapprobateur, -trice m, f.

disarm [dis'aːm] v désarmer. disarmament n désarmement m. disarming adj (smile) désarmant.

disaster [di'zaːstə] n désastre m, catastrophe f. disastrous adj désastreux.

disband [dis'band] v (se) disperser.

disbelief [disbi'liːf] n incrédulité f.

disc or US disk [disk] n disque m.

discard [dis'kaːd; n 'diskaːd] v se débarrasser de; abandonner; (cards) se défausser de. n défausse f.

discern [di'səːn] v discerner. discernible adj perceptible. discerning adj judicieux. discernment n discernement n.

discharge [dis'tʃaːdʒ; v (patient, employee) renvoyer; (gun) tirer; (cargo) décharger; (duty) remplir; (law, mil) libérer. n renvoi m; (elec) décharge f; (med) pertes f pl.

disciple [di'saipl] n disciple m.

discipline ['disiplin] n discipline f. v discipliner; punir. disciplinary adj disciplinaire.

disclaim [dis'kleim] *v* désavouer.

disclose [dis'klouz] *v* divulguer, révéler. **disclosure** *n* divulgation *f.*, révélation *f.*

discolour [dis'kʌlə] *v* (se) décolorer; *(from white)* jaunir. **discolouration** *n* décoloration *f.*; jaunissement *m.*

discomfort [dis'kʌmfət] *n* malaise *m.* gêne *f.*

disconcert [diskən'sə:t] *v* déconcerter.

disconnect [diskə'nekt] *v* disjoindre; *(gas, phone, etc.)* couper; *(television, etc.)* débrancher. **disconnected** *adj* (*thoughts, etc.*) décousu.

disconsolate [dis'konsələt] *adj adj* inconsolable.

discontented [diskən'tentid] *adj* mécontent. **discontent** *or* **discontentment** *n* mécontentement *m.*

discontinue [diskən'tinju:] *v* cesser; interrompre.

discord ['diskɔːd] *n* discorde *f.*; *(music)* dissonance *f.* **discordant** *adj* discordant; dissonant.

discotheque [diskətek] *n* discothèque *f.*

discount [diskaunt] *n* remise *f.* escompte *m.* **at a discount** au rabais. **discount store** magasin de demi-gros *m.* *v* ne pas tenir compte de.

discourage [dis'kʌridʒ] *v* décourager. **become discouraged** se laisser décourager. **discouragement** *n* désapprobation *f.*

discover [dis'kʌvə] *v* découvrir. **discovery** *n* découverte *f.*

discredit [dis'kredit] *v* discréditer. *n* discrédit *m.*

discreet [dis'kri:t] *adj* discret, -ète. **discretion** *n* discrétion *f.* **use your own discretion** c'est à vous de juger. **discretionary** *adj* discrétionnaire.

discrepancy [dis'krepənsi] *n* divergence *f.* désaccord *m.*

discrete [dis'kri:t] *adj* discret, -ète.

discriminate [dis'krimi,neit] *v* distinguer; *(unfairly)* établir une discrimination. **discrimination** *n* distinction *f.*; discrimination *f.*; discernement *m.*

discus ['diskəs] *n* disque *m.*

discuss [dis'kʌs] *v* discuter. **discussion** *n* discussion *f.*

disdain [dis'dein] *n* dédain *m.* **disdainful** *adj* dédaigneux. **disdainfully** *adv* avec dédain.

disease [di'zi:z] *n* maladie *f.* **diseased** *adj* malade.

disembark [disim'ba:k] *v* débarquer. **disembarkation** *n* débarquement *m.*

disengage [disin'geidʒ] *v* dégager; *(tech)* débrayer. **disengaged** *adj* libre; débrayé.

disentangle [disin'taŋgl] *v* débrouiller.

disfigure [dis'figə] *v* défigurer. **disfigurement** *n* défigurement *m.*

disgrace [dis'greis] *n* honte *f.*; *(disfavour)* disgrâce *f.* **in disgrace** (*child, etc.*) en pénitence. *v* faire honte à; déshonorer. **disgraceful** *adj* honteux, scandaleux. **disguise** [dis'gaiz] *v* déguiser. *n* déguisement *m.*; masque *m.* **in disguise** déguisé.

disgust [dis'gʌst] *n* dégoûter. **disgusting** *adj* dégoûtant, écœurant.

dish [diʃ] *n* plat *m.* **do the dishes** faire la vaisselle. **dishcloth** *n* lavette *f.* **dishwasher** *n* lave-vaisselle *m* invar. *v* **dish up** servir.

dishearten [dis'ha:tn] *v* décourager.

dishevelled [di'ʃevəld] *adj* échevelé.

dishonest [dis'onist] *adj* malhonnête. **dishonesty** malhonnêteté *f.*

dishonour [dis'onə] *n* déshonneur *m.* *v* déshonorer. **dishonourable** *adj* déshonorant.

disillusion [disi'lu:ʒən] *n* désillusionner. *n* désillusion *f.*

disinfect [disin'fekt] *v* désinfecter. **disinfectant** *nm, adj* désinfectant. **disinfection** *n* désinfection *f.*

disinherit [disin'herit] *v* déshériter.

disintegrate [dis'inti,greit] *v* (se) désintégrer. **disintegration** *n* désintégration *f.*

disinterested [dis'intristid] *adj* désintéressé.

disjointed [dis'dʒointid] *adj* décousu.

disk *V* **disc**.

dislike [dis'laik] *v* ne pas aimer. *n* aversion *f.* **take a dislike to** prendre en grippe.

dislocate ['dislə,keit] *v* disloquer. **dislocation** *n* dislocation *f.*

dislodge [dis'lodʒ] *v* faire bouger.

disloyal [dis'loiəl] *adj* déloyal. **disloyalty** *n* déloyauté *f.*

dismal [dizməl] *adj* morne, lugubre.

dismantle [dis'mantl] *v* démonter.

dismay [dis'mei] *n* consternation *f.* *v* consterner.

dismiss [dis'mis] *v* (*send away*) renvoyer, congédier; *(meeting)* dissoudre; *(reject)* écarter. **dismissal** *n* renvoi *m.* congédiement *m.*

dismount [dɪsˈmaʊnt] v descendre.
disobey [dɪsəˈbeɪ] v désobéir à. **disobedience** n désobéissance f. **disobedient** adj désobéissant.
disorder [dɪsˈɔːdə] n désordre m; (med) trouble m. **disorderly** adj désordonné.
disorganized [dɪsˈɔːɡənaɪzd] adj désorganisé.
disown [dɪsˈəʊn] v renier.
disparage [dɪsˈpærɪdʒ] v dénigrer. **disparagement** n dénigrement m. **disparaging** adj désobligeant.
disparity [dɪsˈpærɪti] n disparité f.
dispassionate [dɪsˈpæʃənɪt] adj calme; impartial. **dispassionately** adv sans émotion; impartialement.
dispatch [dɪsˈpætʃ] v expédier. n expédition f; (report) dépêche f.
dispel [dɪsˈpel] v dissiper.
dispense [dɪsˈpens] v distribuer, administrer; (medicine) préparer. **dispense with** se passer de. **dispensary** n pharmacie f. **dispensation** n (decree) décret m; (rel) dispense f.
disperse [dɪsˈpɜːs] v (se) disperser; (se) dissiper. **dispersal** n dispersion f.
displace [dɪsˈpleɪs] v déplacer. **displacement** n déplacement m.
display [dɪsˈpleɪ] v étaler; (courage, etc.) faire preuve de. n exposition f; (comm) étalage m; (courage, etc.) manifestation f.
displease [dɪsˈpliːz] v déplaire à. **displeasure** n mécontentement m.
dispose [dɪsˈpəʊz] v disposer. **dispose of** se débarrasser de. **disposable** adj à jeter. **disposal** n disposition f; (rubbish) enlèvement m; (bomb) désamorçage m. **disposition** n tempérament m; inclination f.
disproportion [dɪsprəˈpɔːʃən] n disproportion f. **disproportionate** adj disproportionné.
disprove [dɪsˈpruːv] v réfuter.
dispute [dɪsˈpjuːt] n dispute f, (argument) discussion f; (industrial) conflit m. **beyond dispute** incontestable. v contester; discuter. **disputable** adj discutable.
disqualify [dɪsˈkwɒlɪfaɪ] v disqualifier. **disqualification** n disqualification f.
disregard [dɪsrəˈɡɑːd] v (ignore) mépriser; négliger. n indifférence f; mépris.
disreputable [dɪsˈrepjʊtəbl] adj louche; (clothes) miteux.
disrespect [dɪsrəˈspekt] n manque de respect m. **disrespectful** adj irrespec-

tueux. **be disrespectful to** manquer de respect envers.
disrupt [dɪsˈrʌpt] v perturber, interrompre. **disruption** n perturbation f; interruption f. **disruptive** adj perturbateur, -trice.
dissatisfied [dɪsˈsætɪsfaɪd] adj mécontent. **dissatisfaction** n mécontentement m.
dissect [dɪsˈekt] v disséquer. **dissection** n dissection f.
dissent [dɪsˈent] v différer. n dissentiment m. **dissension** n dissension f.
dissident [ˈdɪsɪdənt] n, adj dissident, -e. **dissidence** n dissidence f.
dissimilar [dɪsˈsɪmɪlə] adj dissemblable. **dissimilarity** n dissemblance f.
dissociate [dɪsˈəʊsɪeɪt] v dissocier. **dissociation** n dissociation f.
dissolve [dɪˈzɒlv] v (se) dissoudre.
dissuade [dɪsˈweɪd] v dissuader. **dissuasion** n dissuasion f.
distance [ˈdɪstəns] n distance f. **in the distance** au loin. **distant** adj lointain, éloigné; (reserved) distant.
distaste [dɪsˈteɪst] n dégoût m. **distasteful** adj déplaisant.
distemper [dɪsˈtempə] n (paint) détrempe f. v peindre en détrempe.
distended [dɪsˈtendɪd] adj (med) dilaté; distendu. **distension** n dilatation f; distension f.
distil [dɪsˈtɪl] v (se) distiller. **distillery** n distillerie f.
distinct [dɪsˈtɪŋkt] adj distinct; net, nette. **distinction** n distinction f. **distinctive** adj distinctif.
distinguish [dɪsˈtɪŋɡwɪʃ] v distinguer; caractériser.
distort [dɪsˈtɔːt] v déformer. **distortion** n distorsion f; déformation f.
distract [dɪsˈtrækt] v distraire. **distracting** adj gênant. **distraction** n distraction f; interruption f.
distraught [dɪsˈtrɔːt] adj éperdu.
distress [dɪsˈtres] n douleur f; affliction f; (poverty, danger) détresse f. v affliger. **distressing** adj pénible.
distribute [dɪsˈtrɪbjuːt] v distribuer; (share) répartir. **distribution** n distribution f; répartition f. **distributor** n (mot) distributeur m.
district [ˈdɪstrɪkt] n (of town) quartier m; (admin) arrondissement m; (of country) région f. **district nurse** infirmière visiteuse f.

distrust [dis'trʌst] v se méfier de. n méfiance f. **distrustful** adj méfiant.

disturb [dis'tə:b] v déranger; troubler. **disturbance** n dérangement m; (noise) tapage m. **disturbing** adj inquiétant.

disuse [dis'ju:s] n désuétude f. **fall into disuse** tomber en désuétude. **disused** adj désaffecté.

ditch [ditʃ] n fossé m.

ditto ['ditou] adv idem.

divan [di'van] n divan m.

dive [daiv] v plonger. n plongeon m; (submarine) plongée f. **diver** n plongeur m. **diving board** plongeoir m.

diverge [dai'və:dʒ] v diverger. **divergence** n divergence f. **divergent** adj divergent.

diverse [dai'və:s] adj divers. **diversity** n diversité f.

divert [dai'və:t] v détourner; (traffic) dévier; (amuse) divertir. **diversion** n déviation f; divertissement m. **create a diversion** faire une diversion.

divide [di'vaid] v (se) diviser; (se) séparer. **divided** adj (country) désuni. **dividers** pl n compas à pointes sèches m sing. **dividing** adj (wall, etc.) mitoyen. **divisible** adj divisible. **division** n division f; séparation f.

dividend ['dividend] n dividende m.

divine [di'vain] adj divin. **divinity** n divinité f; théologie f.

divorce [di'vo:s] n divorce m. v divorcer (avec). **divorcee** n divorcé, -e m, f.

divulge [dai'vʌldʒ] v divulguer.

dizzy ['dizi] adj pris de vertige; (height) vertigineux. **dizziness** n vertige m.

***do** [du:] v faire; (suffice) suffire (à); (coll: cheat) refaire. **do away with** supprimer. **do up** (clothes) (se) fermer; (parcel) emballer; (house) remettre à neuf. **do without** se passer de. **how do you do?** (on introduction) enchanté. **that will do!** ça suffit!

docile ['dousail] adj docile.

dock[1] [dok] n (ships) dock m, bassin m. **dockyard** n chantier naval m. v mettre à quai; (space) s'arrimer. **docker** n docker m.

dock[2] [dok] n (law) banc des accusés m.

dock[3] [dok] v écourter; (wages) rogner.

doctor ['doktə] n docteur m, médecin m; (university) docteur m. **doctorate** n doctorat m.

doctrine ['doktrin] n doctrine f.

document ['dokjumənt] n document m. v

documenter. **documentary** nm, adj documentaire. **documentation** n documentation f.

dodge [dodʒ] v (s')esquiver; (tax) éviter de payer. n détour m; (sport) esquive f; (coll: trick) truc m. **dodgy** adj délicat; douteux.

dog [dog] n chien m. **dog-eared** adj écorné. **dogfish** n chien de mer m. **dog rose** églantine f. v (follow) suivre de près; (plague) harceler.

dogged ['dogid] adj tenace. **doggedly** adv avec ténacité.

dogma ['dogma] n dogme m. **dogmatic** adj dogmatique.

do-it-yourself [,du:itjo:'self] n bricolage m.

dole [doul] n allocation de chômage f. **on the dole** au chômage. v **dole out** distribuer.

doll [dol] n poupée f. v **doll up** bichonner.

dollar ['dolə] n dollar m.

dolphin ['dolfin] n dauphin m.

domain [də'mein] n domaine m.

dome [doum] n dôme m.

domestic [də'mestik] adj domestique; (not foreign) intérieur. **domestic science** arts ménagers m pl. n domestique.

dominate ['domi,neit] v dominer. **dominance** n dominance f. **dominant** adj dominant. **domination** n domination f.

domineering [domi'niəriŋ] adj dominateur, -trice.

dominion [də'minjən] n dominion m, territoire m.

domino ['dominou] n domino m.

don [don] v revêtir.

donate [də'neit] v faire don de; (blood) donner. **donation** n don m.

done [dʌn] V do.

donkey ['doŋki] n âne, -esse m, f.

donor ['dounə] n (med) donneur, -euse m, f; (charity) donateur, -euse m, f.

doom [du:m] n condamner. n destin m. **doomed** adj voué à l'échec.

door [do:] n porte f; (car, train) portière f. **doorbell** n sonnette f. **doorknob** n poignée de porte f. **door-knocker** n heurtoir m. **doormat** n essuie-pieds m invar. **doorstep** n pas de porte m. **door-to-door** adj, adv à domicile. **doorway** n embrasure de porte f.

dope [doup] v doper. n dopant m; (slang: drugs) drogue f; (slang: person) andouille f.

dormant ['dɔːmənt] *adj* en sommeil.

dormitory ['dɔːmitəri] *n* dortoir *m*. **dormitory town** ville dortoir *f*.

dormouse ['dɔːˌmaus] *n, pl* **-mice** loir *m*.

dose [dəus] *n* dose *f*. *v* administrer un médicament à. **dosage** *n* dosage *m*; (*on bottle*) posologie *f*.

dot [dot] *n* point *m*. *v* pointiller. **dotted line** pointillé *m*.

dote [dəut] *v* **dote on** raffoler de. **dotage** *n* (*senility*) gâtisme *m*.

double ['dʌbl] *adj, adv* double; deux fois. *n* double *m*. *v* doubler; plier en deux. **double-barrelled** [,dʌbl'barəld] *adj* (*coll: name*) à rallonges; (*gun*) à deux coups.

double bass [beis] *n* contrebasse *f*.

double bed *n* grand lit *m*.

double cream *n* crème à fouetter *f*.

double-cross [,dʌbl'kros] *v* (*coll*) doubler.

double-decker [,dʌbl'dekə] *n* autobus à impériale *m*.

double dutch *n* baragouin *m*. **talk double dutch** baragouiner.

double-glazing [,dʌbl'gleiziŋ] *n* doubles fenêtres *f pl*.

double-jointed [,dʌbl'dʒɔintid] *adj* désarticulé.

double room *n* chambre à deux personnes *f*.

doubt [daut] *n* doute *m*. **no doubt** sans doute. *v* douter (de). **doubtful** *adj* douteux; incertain. **doubtless** *adv* sans aucun doute.

dough [dəu] *n* pâte *f*; (*slang: money*) fric *m*. **doughnut** *n* beignet *m*.

dove [dʌv] *n* colombe *f*. **dovecote** *n* colombier *m*.

Dover ['dəuvə] *n* Douvres.

dowdy ['daudi] *adj* sans élégance; démodé.

down¹ [daun] *adv* en bas; (*to ground*) par terre. *prep* en bas de; (*along*) le long de. *v* (*coll: drink*) s'envoyer. **down tools** cesser le travail.

down² [daun] *n* duvet *m*. **downy** *adj* duveté.

downcast ['daun,kɑːst] *adj* abattu.

downfall ['daun,fɔːl] *n* chute *f*.

downhearted [,daun'hɑːtid] *adj* abattu.

downhill [,daun'hil] *adj* en pente. **go downhill** descendre la pente; (*deteriorate*) être sur le déclin; (*business*) péricliter.

down payment *n* acompte *m*.

downpour ['daun,pɔː] *n* averse *f*.

downright ['daun,rait] *adj* catégorique. *adv* carrément; purement et simplement.

downstairs ['daun,steəz; *adv* ,daun'steəz] *adj* (*ground floor*) du rez-de-chaussée; (*below*) en bas. *adv* au rez-de-chaussée; en bas. **go downstairs** descendre.

downstream [,daun'striːm] *adv* en aval. **go downstream** descendre le courant.

down-to-earth [,dauntə'əːθ] *adj* terre à terre.

downtrodden ['daun,trodn] *adj* opprimé.

downward ['daunwəd] *adj* vers le bas; (*glance*) baissé.

downwards ['daunwədz] *adv* vers le bas, en bas.

dowry ['dauəri] *n* dot *f*.

doze [dəuz] *v* sommeiller. *n* somme *m*.

dozen ['dʌzn] *n* douzaine *f*.

drab [drab] *adj* terne.

draft¹ [drɑːft] *n* (*letter*) brouillon *m*; (*sketch*) ébauche *f*; (*money*) retrait *m*; (*mil*) détachement *m*. *v* faire le brouillon de; (*plan*) esquisser; (*comm*) rédiger; (*mil*) détacher.

draft² *V* **draught**.

drag [drag] *v* traîner; (*river*) draguer. *n* résistance; (*coll: bore*) corvée *f*; (*coll: smoke*) bouffée *f*. **in drag** en travesti.

dragon ['dragən] *n* dragon *m*. **dragonfly** *n* libellule *f*.

drain [drein] *n* (*pipe*) égout *m*; (*grid*) bouche d'égout *f*. *v* drainer, vider. **draining board** égouttoir *m*. **drainpipe** *n* tuyau d'écoulement *m*. **drainage** *n* drainage *m*; (*in town*) système d'égouts *m*.

drama ['drɑːmə] *n* drame *m*; art dramatique *m*. **dramatic** *adj* dramatique; (*effect*) théâtral. **dramatist** *n* dramaturge *m*. **dramatize** *v* adapter pour la scène; (*exaggerate*) dramatiser.

drank [draŋk] *V* **drink**.

drape [dreip] *v* draper. **drapes** *pl n* (*US*) rideaux *m pl*.

draper ['dreipə] *n* marchand de nouveautés *m*. **draper's shop** magasin de nouveautés *m*. **drapery** *n* draperie *f*.

drastic ['drastik] *adj* énergique, radical.

draught *or US draft* [drɑːft] *n* courant d'air *m*; (*drink*) coup *m*. **draughts** *pl n* dames *f pl*. **draught beer** bière à la pression *f*. **draughtboard** *n* damier *m*. **draught excluder** bourrelet *m*. **draughtsman** *n* dessinateur *m*.

*draw [drɔː] *v* (*art*) dessiner; (*pull*) tirer; (*attract*) attirer; (*be equal*) être ex aequo.

draw back reculer. **draw near** s'approcher (de). **draw out** prolonger. **draw up** (*plan*) dresser. n (*sport*) match nul m; (*lottery*) tirage au sort m.
drawback ['drɔːbak] n inconvénient m.
drawbridge ['drɔːbrɪdʒ] n pont-levis m.
drawer [drɔːr] n tiroir m.
drawing ['drɔːɪŋ] n dessin m. **drawing board** planche à dessin f. **drawing pin** punaise f. **drawing room** salon m.
drawl [drɔːl] n voix traînante f. v parler d'une voix traînante.
drawn [drɔːn] V **draw**.
dread [dred] v redouter. n terreur f. **dreadful** adj épouvantable, atroce. **dreadfully** adv terriblement.
*dream [driːm] n rêve m. v rêver; (*imagine*) songer. **dreamy** adj rêveur. -euse.
dreamt [dremt] V **dream**.
dreary ['drɪəri] adj morne; monotone.
dredge [dredʒ] v draguer. n drague f.
dregs [dregz] pl n lie f sing.
drench [drentʃ] v tremper.
dress [dres] n robe; (*clothing*) tenue f. **dress circle** premier balcon m. **dressmaker** n couturière f. **dressmaking** n couture f. **dress rehearsal** répétition générale f. v (s')habiller; (*salad*) assaisonner; (*wound*) panser. **dress up as** se déguiser en. **dressy** adj élégant.
dresser[1] ['dresə] n (*furniture*) buffet m.
dresser[2] ['dresə] n (*theatre*) habilleur, -euse f.
dressing ['dresɪŋ] n (*wound*) pansement m; (*cookery*) assaisonnement m. **dressing gown** robe de chambre f. **dressing room** (*theatre*) loge f; (*in house*) dressing-room m. **dressing table** coiffeuse f.
drew [druː] V **draw**.
dribble ['drɪbl] v (*child*) baver; (*liquid*) couler lentement; (*sport*) dribbler. n bave f; petite goutte f; dribble m.
dried [draɪd] adj séché; déshydraté; (*milk*) en poudre. **dried fruit** fruits secs m pl.
drier ['draɪə] n séchoir m.
drift [drɪft] v dériver, aller à la dérive. n (*heap*) amoncellement m; (*deviation*) dérive f; (*gist*) but m. **driftwood** n bois flotté m.
drill [drɪl] v (*hole*) forer; (*tooth*) fraiser. n foret m; fraise f; (*mil*) exercice m.
*drink [drɪŋk] v boire. n boisson f. **drinkable** adj potable. **drinking water** eau potable f.

drip [drɪp] v dégoutter. n (*drop*) goutte f; (*coll: person*) nouille f; (*med*) goutte-à-goutte m invar. **drip-dry** adj (*on label*) ne pas repasser. **dripping** n (*fat*) graisse f.
*drive [draɪv] v conduire; (*push*) chasser; (*nail*) enfoncer. n (*trip*) promenade en voiture f; (*to house*) allée f; (*energy*) dynamisme m. **driver** n conducteur, -trice m, f. **driving** n conduite f. **driving licence** permis de conduire m. **driving school** auto-école f. **driving test** examen du permis de conduire m.
drivel ['drɪvl] v radoter. n radotage m.
driven ['drɪvn] V **drive**.
drizzle ['drɪzl] v bruiner. n bruine f.
drone [droun] v ronronner, vrombir; (*bee*) bourdonner. n ronronnement m, vrombissement m; bourdonnement m.
droop [druːp] v s'affaisser, retomber.
drop [drop] n (*liquid*) goutte f; (*fall*) baisse f. v (*fall*) tomber; (*let fall*) laisser tomber; (*price*) baisser. **drop off** (*sleep*) s'endormir. **dropper** n compte-gouttes m invar. **droppings** pl n crottes f pl; (*bird*) fiente f sing.
drought [draut] n sécheresse f.
drove [drouv] V **drive**.
drown [draun] v (se) noyer.
drowsy ['drauzi] adj somnolent. **grow drowsy** s'assoupir. **drowsiness** n somnolence f.
drudgery ['drʌdʒəri] n corvée f.
drug [drʌg] n drogue f. **be on drugs** se droguer. **drug addict** drogué, -e m, f. v droguer.
drum [drʌm] n tambour m; (*oil*) tonnelet m. **drumstick** n baguette de tambour f; (*chicken*) pilon m. v tambouriner. **drummer** n tambour m.
drunk [drʌŋk] V **drink**. adj ivre. **get drunk** s'enivrer. n aussi **drunkard** ivrogne, -esse m, f. **drunkenness** n ivresse f.
dry [draɪ] adj sec, sèche; (*wit*) caustique; (*dull*) aride. **dry-clean** v nettoyer à sec. **dry cleaner's** teinturerie f. **dry rot** pourriture sèche f. **dry ski slope** piste artificielle f. v sécher. **dry up** se dessécher, se tarir; (*dishes*) essuyer la vaisselle.
dual ['djuəl] adj double.
dubbed [dʌbd] adj (*film*) doublé. **dubbing** n doublage m.
dubious ['djuːbiəs] adj douteux.
Dublin ['dʌblɪn] n Dublin.

duchess [ˈdʌtʃis] n duchesse f.

duck[1] [dʌk] n canard m. **duckling** n caneton, canette m, f. **duckpond** n mare aux canards f.

duck[2] [dʌk] v (dodge) se baisser subitement; (submerge) plonger.

duct [dʌkt] n conduite f; (anat) conduit m.

dud [dʌd] adj raté; faux, fausse.

due [djuː] adj dû, due. (suitable) qui convient. **be due** devoir arriver. adv droit. **dues** pl n droits m pl.

duel [ˈdjuəl] n duel m. v se battre en duel. **duellist** n duelliste m.

duet [djuˈet] n duo m.

dug [dʌg] V dig.

duke [djuːk] n duc m.

dull [dʌl] adj terne; (sound) sourd; (weather) gris. (se) ternir; (s')assourdir; (blunt) (s')émousser.

dumb [dʌm] adj muet, muette; (slang: stupid) bête, -asse. **dumbbell** n haltère m. **dumbfound** v confondre. **dumbness** n mutisme m.

dummy [ˈdʌmi] n (comm) factice m; (dressmaker's) mannequin m; (ventriloquist's) pantin m; (baby's) sucette f. **dummy run** coup d'essai m.

dump [dʌmp] n (tip) décharge f. (coll: place) trou. **be down in the dumps** avoir le cafard. v déposer.

dumpling [ˈdʌmpliŋ] n (savoury) boulette de pâte f. (fruit) chausson m.

dunce [dʌns] n âne m. **dunce's cap** bonnet d'âne m.

dune [djuːn] n dune f.

dung [dʌŋ] n crotte f; (manure) fumier m.

dungarees [ˌdʌŋgəˈriːz] pl n salopette f sing.

dungeon [ˈdʌndʒən] n cachot m.

Dunkirk [ˈdʌnkəːk] n Dunkerque.

duplicate [ˈdjuːplikeit; n, adj ˈdjuːplikət] v faire un double de; (photocopy) polycopier. n double m. adj en double; (comm) en duplicata.

durable [ˈdjuərəbl] adj solide; durable.

duration [djuˈreiʃən] n durée f.

during [ˈdjuəriŋ] prep pendant.

dusk [dʌsk] n crépuscule m. **dusky** adj sombre.

dust [dʌst] n poussière f. **dustbin** n poubelle f. **dustman** n éboueur m. **dustpan** n pelle à poussière f. **dust sheet** housse f. v épousseter. **duster** n chiffon m. **dusty** adj poussiéreux.

Dutch [dʌtʃ] nm, adj hollandais, néerlandais. **the Dutch** les Hollandais m pl, les Néerlandais m pl.

duty [ˈdjuːti] n devoir m; (job) fonction f; (tax) droit m. **duty-free** exempté de douane. **duty-free shop** magasin hors-taxe m. **off duty** libre. **on duty** de service. **dutiful** adj respectueux; consciencieux.

duvet [ˈduːvei] n couette f.

dwarf [dwɔːf] n, adj nain, -e m, f. v écraser.

***dwell** [dwel] v habiter. **dwell on** s'arrêter sur. **dwelling** n habitation f.

dwelt [dwelt] V dwell.

dwindle [ˈdwindl] v diminuer.

dye [dai] n teinture f. v teindre.

dyke [daik] n (ditch) fossé m; (barrier) digue f.

dynamic [daiˈnamik] adj dynamique. **dynamism** n dynamisme m.

dynamite [ˈdainəmait] n dynamite f.

dynamo [ˈdainəmou] n dynamo f.

dynasty [ˈdinəsti] n dynastie f.

dysentery [ˈdisəntri] n dysenterie f.

dyslexia [disˈleksiə] n dyslexie f. **dyslexic** n(m+f), adj dyslexique.

dyspepsia [disˈpepsiə] n dyspepsie f.

E

each [iːtʃ] adj chaque. pron chacun, -e. **each other** l'un l'autre, les uns les autres.

eager [ˈiːgə] adj avide; ardent; impatient. **eagerness** n désir ardent m; impatience f.

eagle [ˈiːgl] n aigle m.

ear[1] [iə] n oreille f. **earache** n mal d'oreille m. **eardrum** n tympan m. **earmark** v réserver; (money) assigner. **earphones** pl n casque m sing. **earring** n boucle d'oreille f. **earshot** n portée de voix f.

ear[2] [iə] n (grain) épi m.

earl [əːl] n comte m.

early [ˈəːli] adv de bonne heure, tôt. adj tôt; prématuré; précoce.

earn [əːn] v gagner; mériter. **earnings** pl n salaire m sing; profits m pl.

earnest [ˈəːnist] adj sérieux; ardent; sincère. **in earnest** sérieusement.

earth [ɜːθ] n terre f; (of fox) terrier m. **earthenware** n faïence f. **earthquake** n tremblement de terre m. v (elec) mettre à la terre.

earwig ['ɪəwɪɡ] n perce-oreille m.

ease [iːz] n aise f; (easiness) aisance f. **at ease** à l'aise; (mil) repos. **with ease** facilement. v (pain) soulager; calmer; diminuer; (relax) se détendre.

easel ['iːzl] n chevalet m.

east [iːst] n est m. adj (also easterly, eastern) oriental; d'est; à l'est. adv à or vers l'est. **eastbound** adj est invar.

Easter ['iːstə] n Pâques f pl. **Easter egg** œuf de Pâques m.

easy ['iːzɪ] adj facile. **easy chair** fauteuil m. **easy-going** adj accommodant. **take it easy** ne pas se fatiguer. **easily** adv sans difficulté; sans aucun doute. **easiness** n facilité f.

*eat [iːt] v manger. **eat out** aller au restaurant. **eat up** finir. **eatable** adj mangeable.

eaten ['iːtn] V eat.

eavesdrop ['iːvzdrɒp] v écouter de façon indiscrète. **eavesdropper** n oreille indiscrète f.

ebb [eb] n reflux m. v refluer; (courage, etc.) décliner.

ebony ['ebənɪ] n ébène f.

eccentric [ik'sentrik] n(m+f), adj excentrique. **eccentricity** n excentricité f.

ecclesiastical [iklɪzɪ'astikl] adj ecclésiastique.

echo ['ekou] n écho m. v répercuter; répéter; résonner.

eclair [ei'kleə] n éclair m.

eclipse [i'klips] n éclipse f. v éclipser.

ecology [i'kɒlədʒɪ] n écologie f. **ecological** adj écologique. **ecologist** n écologiste m, f.

economy [i'kɒnəmɪ] n économie f. **economic** adj économique; (profitable) rentable. **economical** adj économe, économique. **economics** n économique f. **economist** n économiste m, f. **economize** v économiser.

ecstasy ['ekstəsɪ] n extase f. **ecstatic** adj extasié. **be ecstatic about** s'extasier sur.

eczema ['eksimə] n eczéma m.

edge [edʒ] n bord m; (of blade) tranchant m. **on edge** énervé. v border; (move) se glisser. **edging** n bordure f. **edgy** adj énervé.

edible ['edəbl] adj comestible.

Edinburgh ['edinbərə] n Edimbourg.

edit ['edit] v (text) éditer; (film) monter; (magazine) diriger. **editor** n rédacteur, -trice m, f, éditeur, -trice m, f; (newspaper) rédacteur, -trice en chef m, f. **editorial** n éditorial m. adj éditorial. **editorial staff** rédaction f.

edition [i'diʃən] n édition f.

educate ['edjuˌkeit] v instruire. **educated** adj instruit; cultivé. **education** n éducation f; (teaching) enseignement m; (studies) études f pl. **educational** adj (methods) pédagogique; (game, etc.) éducatif.

eel [iːl] n anguille f.

eerie ['iərɪ] adj étrange; sinistre.

effect [i'fekt] n effet m. **take effect** (drug) faire son effet; (rule, etc.) entrer en vigueur. v effectuer. **effective** adj efficace. **effectiveness** n efficacité f.

effeminate [i'feminət] adj efféminé.

effervescent [ˌefə'vesənt] adj effervescent; (drink) gazeux. **effervescence** n effervescence f; (drink) pétillement m.

efficient [i'fiʃənt] adj efficace; compétent. **efficiency** n efficacité f; compétence f.

effigy ['efidʒɪ] n effigie f.

effort ['efət] n effort m. **effortless** adj facile.

egg [eɡ] n œuf m. **egg-cup** n coquetier m. **egg-shaped** adj ovoïde. **eggshell** n coquille d'œuf f.

egotism ['eɡətizm] n égotisme m. **egotist** n égotiste m, f.

Egypt ['iːdʒipt] n Egypte f. **Egyptian** n Egyptien, -enne m, f; adj égyptien.

eiderdown ['aidədaun] n édredon m.

eight [eit] nm, adj huit. **eighth** n(m+f), adj huitième.

eighteen [ei'tiːn] nm, adj dix-huit. **eighteenth** n(m+f), adj dix-huitième.

eighty ['eiti] nm, adj quatre-vingts. **eightieth** n(m+f), adj quatre-vingtième.

either ['aiðə] adj l'un ou l'autre; (each) chaque. pron l'un ou l'autre. adv non plus. conj ou. **either ... or ...** ou ... ou ....

ejaculate [i'dʒakjuleit] v éjaculer; (shout) s'exclamer. **ejaculation** n éjaculation f; exclamation f.

eject [i'dʒekt] v éjecter; expulser. **ejection** n éjection f; expulsion f. **ejector seat** siège éjectable m.

eke [iːk] v **eke out** (add to) augmenter; (make last) faire durer.

elaborate [i'labərət; v i'labəreit] adj compliqué, minutieux. v élaborer; donner des détails. **elaborately** adv en détail.

elapse [i'laps] v s'écouler.

elastic [i'lastik] nm, adj élastique. **elastic band** n élastique m. **elasticity** n élasticité f.

elated [i'leitid] adj transporté. **elation** n exultation f.

elbow ['elbou] n coude m. **elbow grease** (coll) huile de coude f.

elder¹ ['eldə] n. adj aîné, -e.

elder² ['eldə] n sureau m. **elderberry** n baie de sureau f.

elderly ['eldəli] adj âgé.

eldest ['eldist] adj aîné.

elect [i'lekt] v élire; choisir. adj futur. **election** n élection f. **electoral** adj électoral. **electorate** n électorat m.

electric [ə'lektrik] adj électrique. **electric blanket** couverture chauffante f. **electric fire** radiateur électrique m. **electric shock** décharge électrique f. **electrical** adj électrique. **electrician** n électricien m. **electricity** n électricité f. **electrify** v électriser; (rail) électrifier.

electrocute [i'lektrəkjuːt] v électrocuter. **electrocution** n électrocution f.

electrode [i'lektroud] n électrode f.

electronic [elək'tronik] adj électronique. **electronics** n électronique f.

elegant ['eligənt] adj élégant. **elegance** n élégance f.

elegy ['elidʒi] n élégie f.

element ['eləmənt] n élément m; (elec) résistance f. **elementary** adj élémentaire.

elephant ['elifənt] n éléphant m.

elevate ['eliveit] v élever. **elevation** n élévation f; altitude f. **elevator** n (US) ascenseur m.

eleven [i'levn] nm, adj onze. **eleventh** n(m+f), adj onzième.

elf [elf] n elfe m. **elfin** adj d'elfe.

eligible ['elidʒəbl] adj éligible.

eliminate [i'limineit] v éliminer. **elimination** n élimination f.

elite [ei'liːt] n élite f.

ellipse [i'lips] n ellipse f. **elliptical** adj elliptique.

elm [elm] n orme m.

elocution [elə'kjuːʃən] n élocution f.

elope [i'loup] v s'enfuir.

eloquent ['eləkwənt] adj éloquent. **eloquence** n éloquence f.

else [els] adv autre, d'autre. **or else** autrement, ou bien. **elsewhere** adv ailleurs.

elude [i'luːd] v éluder, échapper à. **elusive** adj insaisissable.

emaciated [i'meisieitid] adj émacié. **emaciation** n émaciation f.

emanate ['eməneit] v émaner. **emanation** n émanation f.

emancipate [i'mansipeit] v émanciper. **emancipation** n émancipation f.

embalm [im'baːm] v embaumer.

embankment [im'baŋkmənt] n (rail) talus m; (river) quai m; (canal) digue f.

embargo [im'baːgou] n embargo m.

embark [im'baːk] v (s')embarquer. **embark on** commencer; s'engager dans. **embarkation** n embarquement m.

embarrass [im'barəs] v embarrasser, gêner. **embarrassment** n embarras m, gêne f.

embassy ['embəsi] n ambassade f.

embellish [im'beliʃ] v embellir. **embellishment** n embellissement m.

ember ['embə] n charbon ardent m. **embers** pl n braise f sing.

embezzle [im'bezl] v détourner. **embezzlement** n détournement de fonds m. **embezzler** n escroc m.

embitter [im'bitə] v (person) aigrir; (relationship) envenimer.

emblem ['embləm] n emblème m.

embody [im'bodi] v exprimer; réunir. **embodiment** n incarnation f, personnification f.

emboss [im'bos] v (metal) repousser; (paper, etc.) gaufrer. **embossed** adj (letterhead, etc.) en relief.

embrace [im'breis] v (s')embrasser. n enlacement m.

embroider [im'broidə] v broder; (truth) broder sur. **embroidery** n broderie f. **embroidery silk** soie à broder f.

embryo ['embriou] n embryon m. **in embryo** (project, etc.) en germe.

emerald ['emərəld] n émeraude f.

emerge [i'məːdʒ] v émerger, surgir.

emergency [i'məːdʒənsi] n cas urgent m; (med) urgence f. **emergency exit** sortie de secours f. **emergency landing** atterrissage forcé m. **in case of emergency** en cas d'urgence.

emigrate ['emigreit] v émigrer. **emigration** n émigration f.

eminent ['eminənt] adj éminent. **eminence** n distinction f.

emit [i'mit] *v* émettre.

emotion [i'mouʃən] *n* émotion *f*. **emotional** *adj* (*state*) émotionnel; (*shock*) émotif. **emotionally** *adv* avec émotion.

empathy ['empəθi] *n* communion d'idées *f*.

emperor ['empərə] *n* empereur *m*. **empress** *n* impératrice *f*.

emphasis ['emfəsis] *n* accent *m*; importance *f*. **emphasize** *v* appuyer sur; accentuer. **emphatic** *adj* énergique.

empire ['empaiə] *n* empire *m*.

empirical [im'pirikəl] *adj* empirique.

employ [im'ploi] *v* employer. **employee** *n* employé, -e *m, f*. **employer** *n* patron, -onne *m, f*. **employment** *n* emploi *m*. **employment agency** agence de placement *f*.

empower [im'pauə] *v* autoriser.

empty ['empti] *adj* vide; vacant. **empty-handed** *adj* bredouille. *v* vider. **emptiness** *n* vide *m*.

emu ['imjur] *n* émeu *m*.

emulate ['emjuleit] *v* imiter. **emulation** *n* émulation *f*.

emulsion [i'mʌlʃən] *n* émulsion *f*.

enable [i'neibl] *v* permettre à.

enact [i'nakt] *v* (*play*) jouer; (*decree*) décréter.

enamel [i'naməl] *n* émail (*pl* -aux) *m*. *v* émailler.

enamour [i'namə] *v* enchanter. **be enamoured of** *v* être épris de.

encase [in'keis] *v* recouvrir (de).

enchant [in'tʃant] *v* enchanter. **enchanting** *adj* ravissant. **enchantment** *n* enchantement *m*.

encircle [in'səːkl] *v* entourer.

enclose [in'klouz] *v* enclore; (*surround*) entourer; (*in letter*) joindre. **enclosed** *adj* ci-joint. **enclosure** *n* enceinte *f*; (*document*) pièce jointe *f*.

encore ['oŋkoɪ] *nm, interj* bis. *v* bisser.

encounter [in'kauntə] *v* affronter, rencontrer. *n* rencontre *f*.

encourage [in'kʌridʒ] *v* encourager. **encouragement** *n* encouragement *m*.

encroach [in'kroutʃ] *v* empiéter. **encroachment** *n* empiétement *m*.

encumber [in'kʌmbə] *v* encombrer. **encumbrance** *n* embarras *m*.

encyclopedia [insaiklə'piːdiə] *n* encyclopédie *f*.

end [end] *n* (*tip*) bout *m*; (*finish*) fin *f*.

end product (*comm*) produit fini *m*; (*result*) résultat *m*. **make ends meet** joindre les deux bouts. *v* finir; (*se*) terminer.

ending *n* fin *f*; (*of word*) terminaison *f*.

endless *adj* interminable; incessant.

endanger [in'deindʒə] *v* mettre en danger; compromettre.

endeavour [in'devə] *n* effort *m*. *v* s'efforcer (de).

endemic [en'demik] *adj* endémique. *n* endémie *f*.

endive ['endiv] *n* endive *f*; (*curly*) chicorée *f*.

endorse [in'dois] *v* (*cheque, etc.*) endosser; approuver. **endorsement** *n* endossement *m*; sanction *f*; (*mot*) contravention *f*.

endow [in'dau] *v* doter (de); (*prize, etc*) fonder. **endowment** *n* dotation *f*; fondation *f*.

endure [in'djuə] *v* supporter; (*last*) durer. **endurance** *n* endurance *f*, résistance *f*.

enemy ['enəmi] *n* ennemi, -e *m, f*.

energy ['enədʒi] *n* énergie *f*. **energetic** *adj* énergique.

enfold [in'fould] *v* envelopper.

enforce [in'fois] *v* (*law*) faire obéir; (*discipline*) imposer.

engage [in'geidʒ] *v* (*s'*)engager; (*employee*) embaucher; (*clutch*) s'embrayer. **engaged** *adj* fiancé; occupé. **get engaged** se fiancer. **engagement** *n* rendez-vous *m invar*; fiançailles *f pl*; (*actor*) engagement *m*.

engine ['endʒin] *n* machine *f*; moteur *m*. **engine driver** mécanicien *m*. **engine room** (*on ship*) salle des machines *f*.

engineer [endʒi'niə] *n* ingénieur *m*; (*mechanic*) technicien *m*. *v* machiner. **engineering** *n* ingénierie *f*.

England ['ingland] *n* Angleterre *f*. **English** *nm, adj* anglais. **the English** les Anglais.

engrave [in'greiv] *v* graver. **engraver** *n* graveur *m*. **engraving** *n* gravure *f*.

engrossed [in'groust] *adj* absorbé.

engulf [in'gʌlf] *v* engouffrer.

enhance [in'hans] *v* mettre en valeur, rehausser.

enigma [i'nigmə] *n* énigme *f*. **enigmatic** *adj* énigmatique.

enjoy [in'dʒoi] *v* aimer; (*good health, etc.*) jouir de. **enjoy oneself** s'amuser. **enjoyable** *adj* agréable. **enjoyment** *n* plaisir *m*.

enlarge [in'laidʒ] *v* (*s'*)agrandir. **enlargement** *n* agrandissement *m*.

enlighten [in'laitn] v éclairer. **enlightenment** n éclaircissement m.

enlist [in'list] v (s')engager; recruter. **enlistment** n engagement m.

enmity ['enmɪti] n inimitié f.

enormous [i'nɔːməs] adj énorme. **enormously** adv énormément.

enough [i'nʌf] adj, adv, n assez. **be enough** suffire.

enquire [in'kwaɪə] V inquire.

enrage [in'reidʒ] v mettre en rage.

enrich [in'rɪtʃ] v enrichir; (soil) fertiliser.

enrol [in'rəul] v (s')inscrire; (mil) (s')enrôler. **enrolment** n inscription f; enrôlement m.

ensign ['ensain] n (emblem) insigne m; (flag) drapeau m; (naut) pavillon m.

enslave [in'sleɪv] v asservir. **enslavement** n asservissement m.

ensue [in'sjuː] v s'ensuivre.

ensure [in'ʃuə] v assurer.

entail [in'teil] v occasionner, comporter.

entangle [in'tæŋgl] v empêtrer, emmêler.

enter ['entə] v entrer (dans); (register) inscrire. **enter for** (exam) (se) présenter à.

enterprise ['entəpraiz] n entreprise f; initiative f. **enterprising** adj entreprenant.

entertain [entə'tein] v (amuse) divertir; (guests) recevoir; (idea) considérer. **entertainer** n artiste m, f. **entertainment** n divertissement m.

enthral [in'θrɔːl] v captiver.

enthusiasm [in'θuːziazəm] n enthousiasme m. **enthusiast** n enthousiaste m, f. **enthusiastic** adj enthousiaste, passionné.

entice [in'tais] v attirer, entraîner. **enticing** adj attrayant; (food) alléchant.

entire [in'taiə] adj entier. **in its entirety** en entier.

entitle [in'taitl] v autoriser, donner droit à; (book) intituler.

entity ['entɪti] n entité f.

entrails ['entreilz] pl n entrailles f pl.

entrance¹ ['entrəns] n entrée f.

entrance² [in'trɑːns] v ravir.

entrant ['entrənt] n (competition, exam) candidat, -e m, f; (race) concurrent, -e m, f; (profession) débutant, -e m, f.

entreat [in'triːt] v supplier. **entreaty** n supplication f.

entrench [in'trentʃ] v (mil) retrancher. **entrenched** adj (custom) implanté; indélogeable.

entrepreneur [ˌɔntrəprə'nəː] n entrepreneur m.

entrust [in'trʌst] v confier; (with task) charger.

entry ['entri] n entrée f; (on list) inscription f. **entry form** feuille d'inscription f. **no entry** (road) sens interdit; (gate, etc.) défense d'entrer.

entwine [in'twain] v (s')entrelacer.

enunciate [i'nʌnsieit] v articuler; (theory) énoncer. **enunciation** n articulation f; énonciation f.

envelop [in'veləp] v envelopper.

envelope ['envələup] n enveloppe f.

environment [in'vaiərənmənt] n milieu m, environnement m.

envisage [in'vizidʒ] v (foresee) prévoir; (imagine) envisager.

envoy ['envoi] n envoyé, -e m, f.

envy ['envi] n envie f. v envier. **enviable** adj enviable. **envious** adj envieux. **enviously** adv avec envie.

enzyme ['enzaim] n enzyme f.

ephemeral [i'femərəl] adj éphémère.

epic ['epik] adj épique. n épopée f.

epidemic [epi'demik] n épidémie f. adj épidémique.

epilepsy ['epilepsi] n épilepsie f. **epileptic** n(m+f). adj épileptique. **epileptic fit** crise d'épilepsie f.

epilogue ['epilog] n épilogue m.

Epiphany [i'pifəni] n Epiphanie f. fête des Rois f.

episcopal [i'piskəpəl] adj épiscopal.

episode ['episəud] n épisode m. **episodic** adj épisodique.

epitaph ['epitɑːf] n épitaphe f.

epitome [i'pitəmi] n modèle m; quintessence f. **epitomize** v incarner.

epoch ['iːpok] n époque f.

equable ['ekwəbl] adj égal.

equal ['iːkwəl] adj égal, -e. v égaler. **equality** n égalité f. **equalize** v égaliser.

equanimity [ekwə'nimɪti] n sérénité f.

equate [i'kweit] v assimiler; (make equal) égaler. **equation** n équation f.

equator [i'kweitə] n équateur m. **equatorial** adj équatorial.

equestrian [i'kwestriən] adj équestre. n cavalier, -ère m, f.

equilateral [iːkwi'lætərəl] adj équilatéral.

equilibrium [ˌiːkwi'libriəm] n équilibre m.

equinox ['ekwinoks] n équinoxe m. **equinoctial** adj équinoxial.

equip [i'kwip] v équiper. **equipment** n équipement m; matériel m.

equity ['ekwəti] n équité f.

equivalent [i'kwivələnt] nm, adj équivalent.

era ['iərə] n ère f; époque f.

eradicate [i'radi,keit] v extirper, supprimer.

erase [i'reiz] v effacer; (with rubber) gommer. **eraser** n gomme f.

erect [i'rekt] adj droit. v (statue, etc.) ériger; (build) bâtir; (tent, etc.) dresser. **erection** n érection f; construction f.

ermine ['əːmin] n hermine f.

erode [i'roud] v éroder, ronger. **erosion** n érosion f. **erosive** adj érosif.

erotic [i'rɔtik] adj érotique.

err [əː] v se tromper; (sin) pécher.

errand ['erənd] n course f. **errand boy** garçon de courses m.

erratic [i'ratik] adj irrégulier.

error ['erə] n erreur f.

erudite ['erudait] adj savant. **erudition** n érudition f.

erupt [i'rʌpt] v (volcano) entrer en éruption; (quarrel) éclater. **eruption** n éruption f.

escalate ['eskə,leit] v (s')intensifier. **escalation** n escalade f. **escalator** n escalier roulant m.

escalope ['eskə,lɔp] n escalope f.

escape [is'keip] v (s')échapper (à). n fuite f, évasion f.

escort ['eskɔːt; v is'kɔːt] n escorte f. v escorter.

esoteric [esə'terik] adj ésotérique.

especial [i'speʃəl] adj particulier. **especially** adv particulièrement, surtout.

espionage ['espiə,naːʒ] n espionnage m.

esplanade [,esplə'neid] n esplanade f.

essay ['esei] n essai m; (school) rédaction f, dissertation f. **essayist** n essayiste m, f.

essence ['esns] n essence f.

essential [i'senʃəl] adj essentiel. **essentials** pl n essentiel m sing.

establish [i'stabliʃ] v établir; fonder. **establishment** n établissement m; fondation f.

estate [i'steit] n propriété f; (houses) lotissement m; (law) biens m pl. **estate agent** agent immobilier m. **estate car** break m.

esteem [i'stiːm] v estimer. n estime f.

estimate ['estimət; v 'esti,meit] n évaluation f; (comm) devis m. v estimer. **estimation** n jugement m; (esteem) estime f.

estuary ['estjuəri] n estuaire m.

eternal [i'təːnl] adj éternel. **eternity** n éternité f.

ether ['iːθə] n éther m.

ethereal [i'θiəriəl] adj éthéré.

ethical ['eθikl] adj moral. **ethics** pl n morale f sing.

ethnic ['eθnik] adj ethnique.

etiquette ['eti,ket] n étiquette f.

etymology [,eti'mɔlədʒi] n étymologie f. **etymological** adj étymologique.

Eucharist ['juːkərist] n Eucharistie f.

eunuch ['juːnək] n eunuque m.

euphemism ['juːfə,mizəm] n euphémisme m. **euphemistic** adj euphémique.

euphoria [juː'fɔːriə] n euphorie f. **euphoric** adj euphorique.

Europe ['juərəp] n Europe f. **European** n Européen, -enne m, f; adj européen. **European Economic Community (EEC)** Communauté Economique Européenne (CEE) f.

euthanasia [,juːθə'neiziə] n euthanasie f.

evacuate [i'vakju,eit] v évacuer. **evacuation** n évacuation f. **evacuee** n évacué, -e m, f.

evade [i'veid] v éviter. **evasion** n fuite f. **evasive** adj évasif.

evaluate [i'valju,eit] v évaluer. **evaluation** n évaluation f.

evangelical [,iːvan'dʒelikəl] adj évangélique. **evangelist** n évangéliste m.

evaporate [i'vapə,reit] v s'évaporer; (fade away) se volatiliser. **evaporated milk** lait concentré m. **evaporation** n évaporation f.

eve [iːv] n veille f.

even ['iːvən] adj (surface) uni; régulier; égal; (number) pair. adv même; (more, etc.) encore. **even so** quand même. **even-tempered** adj placide. v égaliser.

evening ['iːvniŋ] n soir m, soirée f. **evening class** cours du soir m. **evening dress** (man) tenue de soirée f; (woman) robe du soir f.

evensong ['iːvən,sɔŋ] n office du soir m.

event [i'vent] n évènement m; cas m; (race) course f. **in the event of** en cas de; au cas où. **eventful** adj mouvementé.

eventual [i'ventʃuəl] adj qui s'ensuit. **eventuality** n éventualité f. **eventually** adv finalement.

ever ['evə] adv jamais; (always) toujours.

evergreen ['evəgriːn] *adj* vert, à feuilles persistantes. *n* arbre vert *m*.

everlasting [,evə'lɑːstɪŋ] *adj* éternel.

every ['evrɪ] *adj* (*all*) tous les, toutes les; (*each*) chaque, tout. **everybody** *or* **everyone** *pron* tout le monde. **everyday** *adj* banal; de tous les jours. **every other day** tous les deux jours, un jour sur deux. **everything** *pron* tout. **everywhere** *adv* partout.

evict [i'vɪkt] *v* expulser. **eviction** *n* expulsion *f*.

evidence ['evɪdəns] *n* évidence *f*; (*testimony*) témoignage *m*; signe *m*. **give evidence** témoigner. **evident** *adj* évident. **evidently** *adv* évidemment; à ce qu'il paraît.

evil ['iːvl] *adj* mauvais. *n* mal *m*.

evoke [i'vouk] *v* évoquer. **evocation** *n* évocation *f*. **evocative** *adj* évocateur, -trice.

evolve [i'vɒlv] *v* (se) développer. **evolution** *n* évolution *f*. **evolutionary** *adj* évolutionniste.

ewe [juː] *n* brebis *f*.

exacerbate [ɪg'zasə,beit] *v* exacerber.

exact [ɪg'zakt] *adj* exact. *v* exiger. **exacting** *adj* exigeant; (*task*) astreignant. **exactly** *adv* précisément, exactement.

exaggerate [ɪg'zadʒə,reit] *v* exagérer; accentuer. **exaggeration** *n* exagération *f*.

exalt [ɪg'zɒlt] *v* élever; (*praise*) exalter.

examine [ɪg'zamin] *v* examiner; (*law*) interroger. **examination** *n* examen *m*. **examiner** *n* examinateur, -trice *m*, *f*.

example [ɪg'zɑːmpl] *n* exemple *m*. **for example** par exemple. **set a good example** donner l'exemple.

exasperate [ɪg'zaspə,reit] *v* exaspérer. **exasperation** *n* exaspération *f*.

excavate ['ekskə,veit] *v* excaver; (*dig*) creuser; (*archaeol*) fouiller, faire des fouilles. **excavation** *n* creusage *m*; fouille *f*.

exceed [ik'siːd] *v* dépasser. **exceedingly** *adv* extrêmement.

excel [ik'sel] *v* briller; surpasser. **excellence** *n* excellence *f*. **excellent** *adj* excellent.

Excellency ['eksələnsɪ] *n* Excellence *f*.

except [ik'sept] *prep* sauf, excepté; (*but*) sinon. *v* excepter. **exception** *n* exception *f*. **take exception to** s'offenser de. **exceptional** *adj* exceptionnel.

excerpt ['eksɜːpt] *n* extrait *m*.

excess [ik'ses] *n* excès *m*. **excess fare** supplément *m*. **excess luggage** excédent de bagages *m*. **excessive** *adj* excessif.

exchange [iks'tʃeindʒ] *v* échanger; faire un échange (de). *n* échange *m*; (*phone*) central *m*; (*finance*) change *m*. **exchange rate** taux de change *m*.

exchequer [iks'tʃekə] *n* ministère des finances *m*.

excise ['eksaiz] *n* taxe *f*; (*department*) régie *f*. **excise duties** contributions indirectes *f pl*.

excite [ik'sait] *v* exciter. **excited** *adj* excité, agité. **get excited** s'exciter, s'agiter. **excitement** *n* excitation *f*. **exciting** *adj* passionnant.

exclaim [ik'skleim] *v* s'exclamer, s'écrier.

exclamation [,eksklə'meiʃən] *n* exclamation *f*. **exclamation mark** point d'exclamation *m*.

exclude [ik'skluːd] *v* exclure. **exclusion** *n* exclusion *f*. **exclusive** *adj* exclusif; select; (*dates, numbers, etc.*) exclusivement; (*price, charge*) non compris.

excommunicate [ekskə'mjuːni,keit] *v* excommunier. **excommunication** *n* excommunication *f*.

excrete [ik'skriːt] *v* excréter. **excrement** *n* excrément *m*. **excretion** *n* excrétion *f*.

excruciating [ik'skruːʃieitiŋ] *adj* (*pain*) atroce; (*noise*) infernal.

excursion [ik'skɜːʃən] *n* excursion *f*.

excuse [ik'skjuːz] *v* excuser. **excuse me!** excusez-moi! *n* excuse *f*. **excusable** *adj* excusable.

execute ['eksi,kjuːt] *v* exécuter; accomplir. **execution** *n* exécution *f*; (*of duties*) exercice *m*. **executioner** *n* bourreau *m*.

executive [ig'zekjutiv] *adj* (*power*) exécutif; (*job*) administratif. *n* (*person*) cadre *m*; (*group*) bureau *m*.

exemplify [ig'zempli,fai] *v* exemplifier.

exempt [ig'zempt] *adj* exempt. *v* exempter. **exemption** *n* exemption *f*.

exercise ['eksə,saiz] *n* exercice *m*. **exercises** *pl n* (*physical*) gymnastique *f sing*. **exercise book** cahier *m*. *v* exercer.

exert [ig'zɜːt] *v* exercer; (*force*) employer. **exert oneself** se dépenser; s'appliquer. **exertion** *n* effort *m*; exercice *m*; emploi *m*.

exhale [eks'heil] *v* (*give off*) exhaler; (*breathe out*) expirer.

exhaust [ig'zɔːst] *v* épuiser. *n* (*system*) échappement *m*; (*pipe*) tuyau d'échappement *m*. **exhaustion** *n* épuise-

ment *m*. **exhaustive** *adj* complet, -ète.
exhaustively *adv* à fond.
exhibit [ig'zibit] *v* exposer; (*skill, etc.*)
faire preuve de. *n* objet exposé *m*. **exhibition** *n* exposition *f*. **make an exhibition
of oneself** se donner en spectacle. **exhibitionist** *n*(*m*+*f*). *adj* exhibitionniste.
exhibitor *n* exposant, -e *m. f*.
exhilarate [ig'zilə,reit] *v* vivifier, stimuler.
exhilaration *n* ivresse *f*.
exile ['eksail] *v* exiler. *n* exil *m*; (*person*)
exilé, -e *m. f*. **go into exile** s'exiler.
exist [ig'zist] *v* exister; (*live*) vivre. **existence** *n* existence *f*. **existentialism** *n* existentialisme *m*. **existing** *adj* (*current*)
actuel.
exit ['egzit] *n* sortie *f*.
exonerate [ig'zonə,reit] *v* (*from blame*)
disculper; (*from obligation*) exempter.
exoneration *n* disculpation *f*; exemption
f.
exorbitant [ig'zorbitənt] *adj* exorbitant.
exorcise ['eksor,saiz] *v* exorciser. **exorcism**
n exorcisme *m*. **exorcist** *n* exorciste *m*.
exotic [ig'zotik] *adj* exotique.
expand [ik'spænd] *v* (se) dilater; (se)
développer; (s')étendre. **expansion** *n*
expansion *f*; développement *m*. **expansive** *adj* expansif.
expanse [ik'spæns] *n* étendue *f*.
expatriate [eks'peitrieit; *n.* *adj*
eks'peitriət] *v* expatrier. *n. adj* expatrié,
-e.
expect [ik'spekt] *v* attendre; supposer;
(*demand*) exiger. **expectancy** *or* **expectation** *n* attente *f*.
expedient [ik'spiidiənt] *adj* (*convenient*)
opportun; politique. *n* expédient *m*.
expedition [,ekspi'difən] *n* expédition *f*.
expel [ik'spel] *v* expulser; (*school*)
renvoyer.
expenditure [ik'spenditfə] *n* dépense *f*.
expense [ik'spens] *n* frais *m pl*. **at the
expense of** aux dépens de. **expense
account** frais de représentation *m pl*.
expensive *adj* cher. **be expensive** coûter
cher.
experience [ik'spiəriəns] *n* expérience *f. v*
(*encounter*) rencontrer; (*feel*) éprouver.
experienced *adj* expérimenté.
experiment [ik'speriment] *n* expérience *f*.
v faire une expérience; expérimenter.
experimental *adj* expérimental.
expert ['ekspə:t] *nm. adj* expert.

expertise [,ekspə'ti:z] *n* adresse *f*.
expire [ik'spaiə] *v* expirer. **expiry** *n* expiration *f*.
explain [ik'splein] *v* expliquer. **explanation** *n* explication *f*. **explanatory** *adj*
explicatif.
expletive [ek'splitiv] *n* (*oath*) juron *m*;
exclamation *f*.
explicit [ik'splisit] *adj* explicite.
explode [ik'sploud] *v* (faire) exploser.
explosion *n* explosion *f*. **explosive** *nm,
adj* explosif.
exploit ['eksploit; *v* ik'sploit] *n* exploit *m. v*
exploiter. **exploitation** *n* exploitation *f*.
explore [ik'splo:] *v* explorer. **exploration**
n exploration *f*. **explorer** *n* explorateur,
-trice *m. f*.
exponent [ik'spounənt] *n* interprète *m*.
export [ik'spo:t; *n* 'ekspo:t] *v* exporter. *n*
exportation *f*. **exporter** *n* (*person*)
exportateur, -trice *m. f*; (*country*) pays
exportateur *m*.
expose [ik'spouz] *v* exposer; révéler;
(*uncover*) découvrir. **exposure** *n* exposition *f*; (*phot*) pose *f*. **die of exposure**
mourir de froid.
express [ik'spres] *v* exprimer. *n* (*train*)
rapide *m. adj, adv* exprès. **expression** *n*
expression *f*. **expressive** *adj* expressif.
expulsion [ik'spʌlʃən] *n* expulsion *f*;
(*school*) renvoi *m*.
exquisite ['ekswizit] *adj* exquis.
extend [ik'stend] *v* (s')étendre; (se) prolonger. **extension** *n* prolongation *f*; (*flex.
etc.*) rallonge *f*; (*to house*) agrandisse-
ments *m pl*; (*phone*) poste *m*. **extensive**
adj étendu; considérable.
extent [ik'stent] *n* étendue *f*, longueur *f*;
(*range*) importance *f*; (*degree*) mesure *f*.
exterior [ik'stiəriə] *nm. adj* extérieur, -e.
exterminate [ik'stə:mi,neit] *v* exterminer.
extermination *n* extermination *f*.
external [ik'stə:nl] *adj* externe, extérieur,
-e. **for external use only** pour l'usage
externe.
extinct [ik'stiŋkt] *adj* (*species*) disparu;
(*volcano*) éteint. **extinction** *n* extinction *f*.
extinguish [ik'stiŋgwiʃ] *v* éteindre; (*hopes*)
anéantir. **extinguisher** *n* extincteur *m*.
extort [ik'sto:t] *v* extorquer. **extortion** *n*
extorsion *f*. **extortionate** *adj* exorbitant.
extra ['ekstrə] *adj* de plus; supplémentaire; de réserve. *n* supplément *m*;
(*theatre, cinema*) figurant, -e *m. f*.

extract [ik'strakt; *n* 'ekstrakt] *v* extraire; (*tooth*) arracher. *n* extrait *m*. **extraction** *n* extraction *f*.

extradite ['ekstrədait] *v* extrader. **extradition** *n* extradition *f*.

extramural [,ekstrə'mjuərəl] *adj* (*course*) hors faculté; (*district*) extra-muros.

extraordinary [ik'strɔːdənəri] *adj* extraordinaire.

extravagant [ik'stravəgənt] *adj* (*person*) dépensier; (*taste*) dispendieux; (*ideas, dress*) extravagant. **extravagance** *n* prodigalité *f*; (*expensive thing*) folie *f*; extravagance *f*.

extreme [ik'striːm] *nm, adj* extrême. **extremist** *n*(*m+f*), *adj* extrémiste. **extremity** *n* extrémité *f*.

extricate ['ekstri,keit] *v* dégager; tirer.

extrovert ['ekstrəvəːt] *n, adj* extraverti, -e.

exuberant [igʼzjuːbərənt] *adj* exubérant. **exuberance** *n* exubérance *f*.

exude [igʼzjuːd] *v* exsuder, suinter.

exult [igʼzʌlt] *v* se réjouir. **exultant** *adj* triomphant. **exultation** *n* exultation *f*.

eye [ai] *n* œil (*pl* yeux) *m*. **as far as the eye can see** à perte de vue. **keep an eye on** surveiller. *v* regarder. **eyeball** ['aibɔːl] *n* globe oculaire *m*. **eyebrow** ['aibrau] *n* sourcil *m*. **eye-catching** ['ai,katʃin] *adj* accrocheur, -euse. **eyelash** ['ailaʃ] *n* cil *m*. **eyelid** ['ailid] *n* paupière *f*. **eye shadow** *n* fard à paupières *m*. **eyesight** ['aisait] *n* vue *f*. **eyesore** ['aisɔː] *n* horreur *f*. **eyewitness** ['ai,witnis] *n* témoin oculaire *m*.

F

fable ['feibl] *n* fable *f*.

fabric ['fabrik] *n* tissu *m*. **fabricate** *v* fabriquer. **fabrication** *n* fabrication *f*.

fabulous ['fabjuləs] *adj* fabuleux; (*coll: wonderful*) formidable.

façade [fə'saːd] *n* façade *f*.

face [feis] *n* visage *m*, figure *f*. **facecloth** *n* gant de toilette *m*. **facelift** *n* lifting *m*. **face pack** masque de beauté *m*. **face-to-face** *nm, adv* face à face. **face value** (*coin*)

valeur nominale *f*. **at face value** au pied de la lettre. **in the face of** face à, devant. *v* **faire face** à; (*building*) donner sur. **face the facts** regarder les choses en face.

facet ['fasit] *n* facette *f*.

facetious [fə'siːʃəs] *adj* facétieux.

facial ['feiʃəl] *adj* facial. *n* soin de visage *m*.

facilitate [fə'sili,teit] *v* faciliter.

facility [fə'silati] *n* facilité *f*. **facilities** *pl n* installations *f pl*, équipements *m pl*.

facing ['feisin] *n* (*sewing*) revers *m*; (*building*) revêtement *m*.

facsimile [fak'simili] *n* fac-similé *m*.

fact [fakt] *n* fait *m*; réalité *f*. **as a matter of fact** à vrai dire. **in fact** en fait. **factual** *adj* basé sur les faits.

faction ['fakʃən] *n* faction *f*.

factor ['faktə] *n* facteur *m*.

factory ['faktəri] *n* usine *f*; (*smaller*) fabrique *f*.

faculty ['fakəlti] *n* faculté *f*; aptitude *f*.

fad [fad] *n* marotte *f*. **faddy** *adj* capricieux.

fade [feid] *v* (*light*) baisser; (*colour*) passer; (*flower*) se faner; (*sound*) s'affaiblir.

fag [fag] *n* (*coll*) *n* (*cigarette*) sèche *f*; (*boring task*) barbe *f*. **fag end** (*of cigarette*) mégot *m*. **fagged out** claqué.

fail [feil] *v* (*not succeed*) échouer; (*grow weak*) faiblir, baisser; (*neglect*) manquer (de). *n* échec *m*. **without fail** à coup sûr; inévitablement. **failing** *n* défaut *m*. **failure** *n* échec *m*; (*person*) raté, -e *m, f*; (*breakdown*) panne *f*.

faint [feint] *adj* faible; (*colour*) pâle; (*idea*) vague. **I haven't the faintest idea** je n'en ai pas la moindre idée. *v* s'évanouir. *n* évanouissement *m*.

fair[1] [feə] *adj* juste, équitable; (*average*) passable; (*hair*) blond; (*skin*) clair; (*fine*) beau, belle. **by fair means or foul** par tous les moyens. **fair copy** copie au propre *f*. **fair-sized** *adj* assez grand. **play fair** jouer franc jeu. **fairly** *adv* avec justice; (*reasonably*) assez. **fairness** *n* justice *f*; blondeur *f*.

fair[2] [feə] *n* foire *f*. **fairground** *n* champ de foire *m*.

fairy ['feəri] *n* fée *f*. *adj* féerique. **fairy lights** guirlande électrique *f*. **fairy tale** conte de fées *m*.

faith [feiθ] *n* foi *f*. **have faith in** avoir confiance en. **faithful** *adj* fidèle. **faithfulness** *n* fidélité *f*.

fake [feik] *n (picture)* faux *m*; article truqué *m*; *(person)* imposteur *m*. *adj* faux, fausse; *(photo, interview, etc.)* truqué; falsifié. *v* faire un faux de; truquer; falsifier; *(illness)* faire semblant (de).

falcon [folkən] *n* faucon *m*.

***fall** [foːl] *v* tomber. **fall apart** tomber en morceaux; *(plans, life, etc.)* se désagréger. **fall back on** avoir recours à. **fall through** échouer. *n* chute *f*; *(US)* automne *m*; *(price, etc.)* baisse *f*.

fallacy [faləsi] *n* erreur *f*.

fallen [foːlən] *V* **fall**.

fallible [faləbl] *adj* faillible. **fallibility** *n* faillibilité *f*.

fallow [faləu] *adj (land)* en jachère; *(idea, etc.)* en friche.

false [foːls] *adj* faux, fausse; artificiel. **false alarm** fausse alerte *f*. **false teeth** fausses dents *f pl*. **under false pretences** par des moyens frauduleux. **falsehood** *n* mensonge *m*. **falseness** *n* fausseté *f*. **falsify** *v* falsifier. **falsification** *n* falsification *f*.

falsetto [foːlsetou] *n* fausset *m*.

falter [foːltə] *v* chanceler; *(voice)* hésiter.

fame [feim] *n* renommée *f*.

familiar [fəmiljə] *adj* familier. **be familiar with** bien connaître. **familiarity** *n* familiarité *f*. **familiarize** *v* familiariser.

family [faməli] *n* famille *f*. **family allowance** allocations familiales *f pl*. **family planning** planning familial *m*. **family tree** arbre généalogique *m*.

famine [famin] *n* famine *f*.

famished [famiʃt] *adj* affamé. **be famished** *(coll)* avoir une faim de loup.

famous [feiməs] *adj* célèbre; *(coll: excellent)* fameux.

fan¹ [fan] *n* fan *m, f*. passionné, -e *m, f*. admirateur, -trice *m, f*. **fan club** club de fans *m*.

fan² [fan] *n* ventilateur *m*; *(hand-held)* éventail *m*. **fan belt** courroie de ventilateur *f*. **fan heater** radiateur soufflant *m*. *v* éventer.

fanatic [fənatik] *n* fanatique *m, f*. **fanatical** *adj* fanatique.

fancy [fansi] *n* caprice *m*; *(desire)* envie *f*; imagination *f*. *v (imagine)* se figurer, croire; avoir envie de. **fancy oneself** se gober. *adj* de fantaisie. **fancy dress** travesti *m*. **fanciful** *adj* imaginaire; fantasque, bizarre.

fanfare [fanfeə] *n* fanfare *f*.

fang [faŋ] *n (dog)* croc *m*; *(snake)* crochet *m*.

fantastic [fantastik] *adj* fantastique.

fantasy [fantəsi] *n* fantaisie *f*.

far [faː] *adv* loin; *(much)* beaucoup. *adj* lointain; *(opposite)* autre. **as far as** jusqu'à, autant que. **far and wide** partout. **far away** *adv* au loin. **faraway** *adj* lointain. **Far East** Extrême Orient *m*. **far-fetched** *adj* tiré par les cheveux. **far-off** *adj* éloigné. **far-reaching** *adj* d'une grande portée. **so far so good** jusqu'ici ça va.

farce [faːs] *n* farce *f*. **farcical** *adj* risible, grotesque.

fare [feə] *n* prix du billet *m*. **fare stage** section *f*.

farewell [feəwel] *nm, interj* adieu.

farm [faːm] *n* ferme *f*. **farmhouse** *n* ferme *f*. **farmland** *n* terres cultivées *f pl*. **farmyard** *n* cour de ferme *f*. *v* cultiver; être fermier. **farmer** *n* fermier *m*. **farmer's wife** fermière *f*. **farming** *n* agriculture *f*.

fart [faːt] *(vulgar)* *n* pet *m*. *v* péter.

farther [faːðə] *adv* plus loin. *adj* plus lointain.

farthest [faːðist] *adv* le plus loin. *adj* le plus lointain.

farthing [faːðiŋ] *n* sou *m*.

fascinate [fasineit] *v* fasciner. **fascination** *n* fascination *f*.

fascism [faʃizəm] *n* fascisme *m*. **fascist** *n(m+f)*. *adj* fasciste.

fashion [faʃən] *n* mode *f*; *(manner)* façon *f*. **after a fashion** tant bien que mal. **fashion show** présentation de collections *f*. **in fashion** à la mode. *v* façonner. **fashionable** *adj* à la mode.

fast¹ [faːst] *adj* rapide; *(colour)* bon teint *invar*. **be fast** *(clock, etc.)* avancer. *adv* vite; *(securely)* ferme. **fast asleep** profondément endormi.

fast² [faːst] *v* jeûner. *n* jeûne *m*.

fasten [faːsn] *v* (s')attacher; *(close)* (se) fermer. **fastener** *or* **fastening** *n* attache *f*; fermeture *f*.

fastidious [fastidiəs] *adj* méticuleux, exigeant.

fat [fat] *n* graisse *f*; *(on meat)* gras *m*. *adj* gros, grosse; gras, grasse. **get fat** grossir. **fatten** *v* engraisser. **fattening** *adj (food)* qui fait grossir.

fatal [feitl] *adj* fatal, mortel. **fatality** *n* mort *m*; accident mortel *m*.

fate [feit] n sort m. fated adj destiné; (condemned) voué au malheur. fateful adj fatal.

father ['fɑːðə] n père m. Father Christmas le père Noël. father-in-law n beau-père m. fatherland n patrie f. v engendrer. fatherhood n paternité f. fatherly adj paternel.

fathom ['faðəm] n brasse f. v fathom out sonder.

fatigue [fə'tiːg] n fatigue f. v fatiguer.

fatuous ['fatjuəs] adj imbécile, stupide.

fault [fɔːlt] n (failing) défaut m; (blame) faute f. at fault fautif. faultless adj impeccable; irréprochable. faulty adj défectueux.

fauna ['fɔːnə] n faune f.

favour ['feivə] n faveur f; service m; avantage m. be in favour of être partisan de. v favoriser; préférer. favourable adj favorable; (wind, etc.) propice. favourite n, adj favori, -ite.

fawn [fɔːn] n faon m. adj fauve.

fear [fiə] n peur f. crainte f. v craindre. fearful adj (terrible) affreux; (frightened) peureux. fearless adj intrépide.

feasible ['fiːzəbl] adj faisable; plausible. feasibility n possibilité f; plausibilité f.

feast [fiːst] n festin m; (rel) fête f.

feat [fiːt] n exploit m.

feather ['feðə] n plume f. feather bed lit de plume m. feathery adj plumeux.

feature ['fiːtʃə] n trait m, caractéristique f; specialité f. feature film grand film m. v (faire) figurer; (make prominent) mettre en vedette.

February ['februəri] n février m.

fed [fed] V feed.

federal ['fedərəl] nm, adj fédéral.

federate ['fedəˌreit] v (se) fédérer. adj fédéré. federation n fédération f.

fee [fiː] n droits m pl, frais m pl; (doctor, etc.) honoraires m pl.

feeble ['fiːbl] adj faible; (excuse) pauvre. feebleness n faiblesse f.

*feed [fiːd] v (se) nourrir; (machine, fire) alimenter. be fed up (coll) en avoir marre. n nourriture f; (baby's) tétée f. biberon m. feedback n feed-back m.

*feel [fiːl] v (se) sentir; (touch) palper; (think) avoir l'impression. n toucher m; sensation f. feeler n antenne f. feeling n sentiment m; sensation f.

feet [fiːt] V foot.

feign [fein] v feindre, simuler.

feline ['fiːlain] n, adj félin, -e.

fell¹ [fel] V fall.

fell² [fel] v abattre.

fellow ['felou] n compagnon m; (coll) type m; (of society) membre m. fellowship n amitié f; association f.

felony ['feləni] n crime m. felon n criminel, -elle m, f.

felt¹ [felt] V feel.

felt² [felt] n feutre m. felt-tip pen feutre m.

female ['fiːmeil] adj femelle, féminin. n femelle f; (person) femme f.

feminine ['feminin] nm, adj féminin. femininity n féminité f. feminism n féminisme m. feminist n féministe m, f.

fence [fens] n clôture f; (horse-racing) obstacle m. v clôturer; (sport) faire de l'escrime. fencing n (sport) escrime f.

fend [fend] v fend for oneself se débrouiller. fend off parer; (attacker) repousser.

fender ['fendə] n garde-feu m invar; (US) garde-boue m invar.

fennel ['fenl] n fenouil m.

ferment [fə'ment; n 'fɜːment] v (faire) fermenter. n ferment m; agitation f. fermentation n fermentation f.

fern [fɜːn] n fougère f.

ferocious [fə'rouʃəs] adj féroce. ferocity n férocité f.

ferret ['ferit] n furet m. v fureter. ferret out dénicher.

ferry ['feri] n ferry m; (smaller) bac m. v transporter.

fertile ['fɜːtail] adj (land) fertile; (person) fécond. fertility n fertilité f; fécondité f. fertilization n fertilisation f. fertilize v fertiliser; féconder. fertilizer n engrais m.

fervent ['fɜːvənt] adj fervent. fervour n ferveur f.

fester ['festə] v suppurer; (anger, etc.) couver.

festival ['festəvəl] n festival m; (rel) fête f. festoon [fə'stuːn] v festonner. n feston m.

fetch [fetʃ] v aller chercher; (person) amener; (thing) apporter; (sell for) rapporter. fetching adj ravissant.

fête [feit] n fête f.

fetid ['fiːtid] adj fétide.

fetish ['fetiʃ] n fétiche m.

fetter ['fetə] v entraver. fetters pl n entraves f pl; (irons) fers m pl.

feud [fjuːd] n querelle f. v se quereller.

feudal ['fjuːdl] *adj* féodal.

fever ['fiːvə] *n* fièvre *f*. **feverish** *adj* fiévreux.

few [fjuː] *nm, adj* peu (de). **a few** quelques; quelques-uns, quelques-unes. **quite a few** pas mal (de). **fewer** *nm, adj* moins (de). **fewest** le moins (de).

fiancé [fi'onsei] *n* fiancé *m*. **fiancée** *n* fiancée *f*.

fiasco [fi'askou] *n* fiasco *m*.

fib [fib] *n* blague *f. v* raconter des blagues.

fibre ['faibə] *n* fibre *f*. **fibreglass** *n* fibre de verre *f*.

fickle ['fikl] *adj* inconstant.

fiction ['fikʃən] *n* (*stories*) romans *m pl*; (*invention*) fiction *f*. **fictional** *or* **fictitious** *adj* fictif.

fiddle ['fidl] *n* violon *m*; (*coll: fraud*) combine *f. v* jouer du violon; (*coll: cheat*) traficoter; (*coll: falsify*) truquer. **fiddle with** tripoter. **fiddly** *adj* minutieux.

fidelity [fi'deləti] *n* fidélité *f*.

fidget ['fidʒit] *v* se trémousser. **fidgety** *adj* remuant.

field [fiːld] *n* champ *m*; (*sport*) terrain *m*; (*of knowledge, etc.*) domaine *f*. **field glasses** jumelles *f pl*. **field marshal** maréchal *m*. **fieldwork** *n* recherches sur le terrain *f pl*.

fiend [fiːnd] *n* démon *m*; (*coll: enthusiast*) enragé, -e *m, f*. **fiendish** *adj* diabolique.

fierce [fiəs] *adj* féroce; violent; (*struggle*) acharné. **fierceness** *n* férocité *f*; violence *f*; acharnement *m*.

fiery ['faiəri] *adj* ardent, brûlant; (*temper*) violent.

fifteen [fif'tiːn] *nm, adj* quinze. **fifteenth** *n(m+f), adj* quinzième.

fifth [fifθ] *n(m+f), adj* cinquième.

fifty ['fifti] *nm, adj* cinquante. **fifty-fifty** *adj, adv* moitié-moitié. cinquante pour cent. **fiftieth** *n(m+f), adj* cinquantième.

fig [fig] *n* (*fruit*) figue *f*; (*tree*) figuier *m*.

***fight** [fait] *v* se battre, combattre; (*argue*) se disputer. *n* combat *m*; (*struggle*) lutte *f*.

figment ['figmənt] *n* création *f*. **figment of the imagination** invention *f*.

figure [figə] *n* figure *f*; (*number*) chiffre *m*; (*slimness*) ligne *f*; (*human*) forme *f*. **figurehead** *n* figure de proue *f*; (*derog*) prête-nom *m*. **figure skating** patinage artistique *m. v* (*appear*) figurer; (*think*)

penser. **figure out** arriver à comprendre. **figurative** *adj* figuré.

filament ['filəmənt] *n* filament *m*.

file[1] [fail] *n* (*folder*) dossier *m*; (*card index*) fichier *m*; (*in office*) classeur *m*. **in single file** à la file. *v* classer; (*claim, etc.*) déposer, intenter. **file past** défiler; passer un à un. **filing** *n* classement *m*. **filing cabinet** classeur *m*. **filing clerk** documentaliste *m, f*.

file[2] [fail] *n* lime *f. v* limer. **filings** *pl n* limaille *f sing*.

filial ['filial] *adj* filial.

fill [fil] *v* (se) remplir; (*tooth*) plomber. **fill in** (*form*) remplir; (*hole*) boucher. **fill up** (*petrol tank*) faire le plein; (*cup, etc.*) remplir.

fillet ['filit] *n* filet *m*. **fillet steak** tournedos *m. v* désosser.

filling ['filiŋ] *n* plombage *m*; (*of pie, etc.*) garniture *f. adj* (*food*) substantiel. **filling station** poste d'essence *m*.

film [film] *n* film *m*; (*phot*) pellicule *f*; (*layer*) couche *f*. **film star** vedette *f*. **filmstrip** *n* film fixe *m. v* filmer.

filter ['filtə] *n* filtre *m*. **filter paper** papier filtre *m*. **filter-tipped** *adj* à bout filtre. *v* filtrer; purifier.

filth [filθ] *n* saleté *f*. **filthy** *adj* crasseux; (*language*) ordurier.

fin [fin] *n* nageoire *f*.

final ['fainl] *adj* (*last*) dernier; définitif. *n* finale *f*. **finalist** *n* finaliste *m, f*. **finalize** *v* mettre la dernière main à. **finally** *adv* enfin, finalement.

finance [fai'nans] *n* finance *f. v* financer. **financial** *adj* financier. **financial year** année budgétaire *f*. **financier** *n* financier *m*.

finch [fintʃ] *n* fringillidé *m*.

***find** [faind] *v* trouver. **find out** se renseigner (sur); découvrir. *n* trouvaille *f*. **findings** *pl n* conclusions *f pl*.

fine[1] [fain] *adj* fin, délicat; (*sunny, excellent*) beau, belle. *adv* bien. **fine arts** beaux arts *m pl*. **finely** *adv* magnifiquement; (*small*) menu. **finery** *n* parure *f*.

fine[2] [fain] *n* amende *f. v* **be fined** avoir une amende.

finesse [fi'nes] *n* finesse *f*; (*cards*) impasse *f*.

finger ['fingə] *n* doigt *m*. **finger bowl** rince-doigts *m invar*. **fingermark** *n* trace de doigt *f*. **fingernail** *n* ongle *m*. **finger-**

print *n* empreinte digitale *f*. fingertip *n* bout du doigt *m*. *v* toucher.

finish [ˈfiniʃ] *v* finir, (se) terminer. finishing line ligne d'arrivée *f*. finishing touch touche finale *f*. in fin *f*; (sport) arrivée *f*; surface *f*.

finite [ˈfainait] *adj* fini.

Finland [ˈfinlənd] *n* Finlande *f*. Finn *n* Finlandais, -e *m, f*; (Finnish speaker) Finnois, -e *m, f*. Finnish *adj* finlandais; *nm, adj* (language) finnois.

fir [fəː] *n* sapin *m*. fir cone pomme de pin *f*.

fire [faiə] *n* feu *m*; (uncontrolled) incendie *m*. set fire to mettre le feu à. *v* (enthusiasm, etc.) enflammer; (pottery) cuire; (gun) tirer; (coll: dismiss) vider.

fire alarm *n* avertisseur d'incendie *m*.

firearm [ˈfaiəɑːm] *n* arme à feu *f*.

fire brigade *n* pompiers *m pl*.

fire door *n* porte anti-incendie *f*.

fire drill *n* exercice anti-incendie *m*.

fire engine *n* pompe à incendie *f*.

fire escape *n* (stairs) escalier de secours *m*; (ladder) échelle d'incendie *f*.

fire exit *n* sortie de secours *f*.

fire extinguisher *n* extincteur *m*.

fire-guard [ˈfaiəgɑːd] *n* garde-feu *m invar*.

firelight [ˈfaiəlait] *n* lueur du feu *f*.

fireman [ˈfaiəmən] *n* pompier *m*.

fireplace [ˈfaiəpleis] *n* cheminée *f*.

fireproof [ˈfaiəpruːf] *v* ignifuger. *adj* ignifuge.

fireside [ˈfaiəsaid] *n* foyer *m*.

fire station *n* caserne de pompiers *f*.

firewood [ˈfaiəwud] *n* bois à brûler *m*.

firework [ˈfaiəwəːk] *n* feu d'artifice *m*.

firing squad *n* peloton d'exécution *m*.

firm¹ [fəːm] *adj* ferme; solide. firmness *n* fermeté *f*; solidité *f*.

firm² [fəːm] *n* (comm) compagnie *f*, firme *f*.

first [fəːst] *n, adj* premier. *adv* d'abord; pour la première fois. at first d'abord. first aid premiers secours *m pl*. first-class *adj* (ticket) de première classe; (mail) tarif normal. first floor premier étage *m*. first-hand *adj* de première main. first name prénom *m*. first-rate *adj* excellent, de premier ordre. in the first place en premier lieu.

fiscal [ˈfiskəl] *adj* fiscal.

fish [fiʃ] *n* poisson *m*. *v* pêcher. fish out extirper. fishy *adj* (coll) louche.

fishbone [ˈfiʃboun] *n* arête *f*.

fish cake *n* croquette de poisson *f*.

fisherman [ˈfiʃəmən] *n* pêcheur *m*.

fish fingers *pl n* bâtonnets de poisson *m pl*.

fishing [ˈfiʃiŋ] *n* pêche *f*. fishing boat barque de pêche *f*. fishing line ligne de pêche *f*. fishing rod canne à pêche *f*. fishing tackle attirail de pêche *m*. go fishing aller à la pêche.

fishmonger [ˈfiʃmʌŋgə] *n* marchand de poisson *m*.

fishpond [ˈfiʃpond] *n* étang à poissons *m*.

fish shop *n* poissonnerie *f*.

fish slice *n* pelle à poisson *f*.

fish tank *n* aquarium *m*.

fission [ˈfiʃən] *n* fission *f*.

fissure [ˈfiʃə] *n* fissure *f*.

fist [fist] *n* poing *m*. fistful *n* poignée *f*.

fit¹ [fit] *adj* (suitable) convenable; (competent) capable; (worthy) digne; (healthy) en bonne santé. *v* (clothes, etc.) aller à; ajuster; (match) correspondre à; équiper; (faire) entrer. fitness *n* santé *f*, forme *f*; aptitudes *f pl*. fitter *n* (tech) monteur *m*; (clothes) essayeur, -euse *m, f*. fitting *adj* approprié. fitting room salon d'essayage *m*. fittings *pl n* installations *f pl*.

fit² [fit] *n* accès *m*, crise *f*. fitful *adj* intermittent; (sleep) troublé.

five [faiv] *nm, adj* cinq.

fix [fiks] *v* fixer; arranger; réparer. *n* (coll) embêtement *m*; (slang: drugs) piqûre *f*. fixation *n* fixation *f*. fixed *adj* fixe. fixture *n* installation *f*; (sport) épreuve *f*.

fizz [fiz] *v* pétiller. *n* pétillement *m*. fizzy *adj* pétillant.

flabbergasted [ˈflabəgɑːstid] *adj* (coll) sidéré.

flabby [ˈflabi] *adj* mou, molle; (person) flasque.

flag¹ [flag] *n* drapeau *m*; (naut) pavillon *m*. flagpole *n* mât *m*. flagship *n* vaisseau amiral *m*. *v* flag down héler.

flag² [flag] *v* languir; (tire) s'alanguir; (interest) faiblir.

flagon [ˈflagən] *n* grande bouteille *f*; (jug) cruche *f*.

flagrant [ˈfleigrənt] *adj* flagrant.

flair [fleə] *n* flair *m*.

flake [fleik] *n* (snow, etc.) flocon *m*; (paint, plaster, etc.) écaille *f*. *v* s'écailler; (skin) peler. flake out (coll) tomber dans les pommes. flaky *adj* floconneux; (pastry) feuilleté.

flamboyant [flam'bɔiənt] *adj* flamboyant.
flame [fleim] *n* flamme *f*. **burst into flames** s'enflammer. *v* flamber. **flaming** *adj* ardent; (*slang*) foutu. **flammable** *adj* inflammable.
flamingo [flə'miŋgou] *n* flamant *m*.
flan [flan] *n* tarte *f*.
flank [flaŋk] *n* flanc *m*. *v* flanquer.
flannel ['flanl] *n* (*fabric*) flanelle *f*; (*facecloth*) gant de toilette *m*. **flannels** *pl n* pantalon de flanelle *m sing*. *v* (*slang*) baratiner.
flap [flap] *v* battre; (*sails*) claquer; (*coll*) paniquer. *n* (*envelope*, *etc.*) rabat *m*; battement *m*; claquement *m*; (*table*) abattant *m*; (*coll*) panique *f*.
flare [fleə] *n* signal lumineux *m*; (*clothes*) évasement *m*. *v* s'enflammer; (*clothes*) (s')évaser. **flare up** (*anger*, *etc.*) éclater; (*person*) s'emporter; (*fire*) s'embraser.
flash [flaʃ] *n* éclat *m*, éclair *m*; (*phot*) flash *m*. **flashback** *n* flashback *m invar*. **flash bulb** ampoule de flash *f*. **flash cube** cube-flash *m*. **flashlight** *n* (*torch*) lampe électrique *f*; *v* (*light*) projeter, (*intermittently*) clignoter, (*sparkle*) étinceler; (*show off*) étaler; (*mot*) faire un appel de phares. **flashy** *adj* tapageur, -euse; adj
flask [flɑsk] *n* flacon *m*; thermos ® *m*.
flat[1] [flat] *adj* plat; (*tyre*, *battery*) à plat; (*music*) faux, fausse; (*beer*) éventé. *n* (*music*) bémol *m*. **flat-fish** *n* poisson plat *m*. **flat-footed** *adj* aux pieds plats. **flat rate** taux fixe *m*. **go flat out** (*car*) être à sa vitesse de pointe. **work flat out** travailler d'arrache-pied. **flatly** *adv* carrément, catégoriquement. **flatten** *v* (s')aplatir; (*smooth*) (s')aplanir.
flat[2] [flat] *n* appartement *m*. **flatlet** *n* studio *m*.
flatter [flatə] *v* flatter. **flatterer** *n* flatteur, -euse *m*, *f*. **flattering** *adj* flatteur, -euse. **flattery** *n* flatterie *f*.
flatulence ['flatjuləns] *n* flatulence *f*.
flaunt [flɔint] *v* étaler, faire étalage de. **flaunt oneself** poser.
flautist ['flɔitist] *n* flûtiste *m*, *f*.
flavour ['fleivə] *n* goût *m*; (*ice-cream*, *etc.*) parfum *m*. *v* parfumer; assaisonner. **flavouring** *n* parfum *m*; assaisonnement *m*.
flaw [flɔi] *n* défaut *m*. **flawed** *adj* imparfait. **flawless** *adj* parfait.

flax [flaks] *n* lin *m*. **flaxen** *adj* de lin.
flea [fliː] *n* puce *f*.
fleck [flek] *n* (*colour*) moucheture *f*; particule *f*. *v* moucheter.
fled [fled] *V* flee.
*****flee** [fliː] *v* fuir; s'enfuir (de).
fleece [fliːs] *n* toison *f*. *v* (*coll*) tondre. **fleecy** *adj* (*cloud*) floconneux; (*woolly*) laineux.
fleet [fliːt] *n* flotte *f*.
fleeting ['fliːtiŋ] *adj* fugace, passager.
Flemish ['flemiʃ] *nm*, *adj* flamand. **the Flemish** les Flamands *m pl*.
flesh [fleʃ] *n* chair *f*. **flesh-coloured** *adj* couleur chair *invar*. **in the flesh** en chair et en os. **fleshy** *adj* charnu.
flew [fluː] *V* fly[1].
flex [fleks] *n* fil souple *m*; (*telephone*) cordon *m*. *v* fléchir; (*muscles*) tendre. **flexibility** *n* flexibilité *f*. **flexible** *adj* flexible, souple.
flick [flik] *v* donner un petit coup à. **flick through** (*book*) feuilleter. *n* petit coup *m*; (*with finger*) chiquenaude *f*. **the flicks** (*coll*) le ciné *m*.
flicker ['flikə] *v* danser, trembloter. *n* vacillement *m*; (*of hope*, *etc.*) lueur *f*.
flight[1] [flait] *n* (*of bird*, *etc.*) vol *m*; (*of stairs*) escalier *m*. **flight path** trajectoire *f*.
flight[2] [flait] *n* (*fleeing*) fuite *f*.
flimsy ['flimzi] *adj* peu solide; (*cloth*, *paper*) léger, mince; (*excuse*) piètre.
flinch [flintʃ] *v* broncher.
*****fling** [fliŋ] *v* lancer, jeter. **have one's fling** se payer du bon temps.
flint [flint] *n* silex *m*.
flip [flip] *v* donner un petit coup à. **flip through** (*book*) feuilleter. *n* petit coup *m*; (*with finger*) chiquenaude *f*. **flipping** *adv* (*coll*) fichu.
flippant ['flipənt] *adj* désinvolte. **flippancy** *n* désinvolture *f*.
flipper ['flipə] *n* (*seal*, *etc.*) nageoire *f*; (*swimmer's*) palme *f*.
flirt [fləit] *v* flirter. *n* flirteur, -euse *m*, *f*. **flirtation** *n* flirt *m*.
flit [flit] *v* voleter. **do a moonlight flit** déménager à la cloche de bois.
float [flout] *v* (*faire*) flotter; (*swimmer*) faire la planche. *n* (*fishing*) flotteur *m*; (*in procession*) char *m*.
flock[1] [flok] *n* (*animals*) troupeau *m*; (*birds*) volée *f*; (*people*) foule *f*. *v* s'attrouper.

flock² [flɒk] n (wool) bourre de laine f; (cotton) bourre de coton f.

flog [flɒg] v flageller. **flogging** n flagellation f; (law) fouet m.

flood [flʌd] n inondation f; (sudden rush) déluge m. **open the floodgates** ouvrir les vannes. v inonder; (river) (faire) déborder. **flooding** n inondation f.

*floodlight [flʌd̩laɪt] v illuminer. n projecteur m. **floodlighting** n illumination f; éclairage m.

floor [flɔː] n plancher m; (ground) sol m; (storey) étage m. **floorboard** n planche f. v terrasser; stupéfier.

flop [flɒp] n (coll) fiasco m. v s'effondrer; (coll) faire fiasco. **floppy** adj flottant; (hat) à bords flottants.

flora [flɔːrə] n flore f.

floral [flɔːrəl] adj floral.

florist [flɒrɪst] n fleuriste m, f.

flounce¹ [flaʊns] v **flounce in/out** entrer/sortir dans un mouvement d'humeur. n geste impatient m.

flounce² [flaʊns] n (of dress) volant m.

flounder¹ [flaʊndə] v patauger.

flounder² [flaʊndə] n flet m.

flour [flaʊə] n farine f. **floury** adj enfariné; (potatoes) farineux.

flourish [flʌrɪʃ] v prospérer; (wave) brandir. n fioriture f; (gesture) moulinet m. **flourishing** adj florissant.

flout [flaʊt] v se moquer de.

flow [floʊ] v couler; circuler. n écoulement m; circulation f. **flow chart** organigramme m. **flowing** adj gracieux; (hair, etc.) flottant.

flower [flaʊə] n fleur f. **flower arrangement** composition florale f. **flower bed** plate-bande f. **flowerpot** n pot à fleurs m. **flower show** floralies f pl. v fleurir. **flowery** adj fleuri.

flown [floʊn] V **fly¹**.

flu [fluː] n grippe f.

fluctuate [flʌktjueɪt] v fluctuer, varier. **fluctuating** n fluctuation f, variation f.

flue [fluː] n tuyau m, conduit m.

fluent [fluːənt] adj coulant. **fluency** n aisance f. **fluently** adv couramment.

fluff [flʌf] n (on animal, bird) duvet m; (from fabric) peluche f. v (coll: fail) louper. **fluffy** adj duveteux; pelucheux.

fluid [fluːɪd] nm, adj fluide.

fluke [fluːk] n coup de chance m, hasard extraordinaire m.

flung [flʌŋ] V **fling**.

fluorescent [fluəˈresnt] adj fluorescent. **fluorescence** n fluorescence f.

fluoride [fluəˈraɪd] n fluor m.

flush¹ [flʌʃ] n (blush) rougeur f; (burst) éclat m. v rougir; (wash out) nettoyer à grande eau; (toilet) tirer la chasse. **flushed** adj rouge.

flush² [flʌʃ] adj à ras (de); (slang: rich) plein de fric.

fluster [flʌstə] v énerver. **get flustered** s'énerver. n agitation f.

flute [fluːt] n flûte f.

flutter [flʌtə] v voleter; (wings) battre; (heart) palpiter. n battement m; palpitation f; agitation f.

flux [flʌks] n flux m. **be in a state of flux** changer sans arrêt.

*fly¹ [flaɪ] v voler; (aeroplane) piloter; (kite) faire voler; (time) passer vite; (flee) fuir. **fly across** or **over** survoler. **fly away** s'envoler. **flyaway** adj (hair) difficile. **flyleaf** n page de garde f. **flyover** n (mot) autopont m. **flysheet** n feuille volante f. **flywheel** n (tech) volant m. n also **flies** (on trousers) braguette f.

fly² [flaɪ] n mouche f.

foal [foʊl] n poulain m.

foam [foʊm] n mousse f; (sea, animal) écume f. **foam rubber** caoutchouc mousse m. v mousser; écumer. **foamy** adj mousseux; écumeux.

focal [foʊkəl] adj focal. **focal point** foyer m; (of attention) point central m.

focus [foʊkəs] n foyer m; (of interest) centre m. **in focus** au point. v (phot, etc.) mettre au point; (rays) (faire) converger; concentrer.

fodder [fɒdə] n fourrage m.

foe [foʊ] n ennemi, -e m, f.

foetus [fiːtəs] n fœtus m. **foetal** adj fœtal.

fog [fɒg] n brouillard m. **fogbound** adj bloqué par le brouillard. **foghorn** n corne de brume f. **foglamp** n (mot) phare antibrouillard m. **foggy** adj brumeux. **it's foggy** il fait du brouillard.

foible [foɪbl] n marotte f.

foil¹ [foɪl] v déjouer.

foil² [foɪl] n feuille de métal f; (cooking) papier d'aluminium m.

foil³ [foɪl] n (fencing) fleuret m.

foist [foɪst] v refiler.

fold¹ [foʊld] n pli m. v (se) plier. **fold one's arms** se croiser les bras. **fold up** plier; (coll: collapse) s'écrouler. **folder** n dossier *m.* chemise *f.* **folding** *adj* pliant. **folding door** porte en accordéon *f.*

fold² [fould] *n* (*sheep*) parc à moutons *m.*

foliage ['fouliidʒ] *n* feuillage *m.*

folk [fouk] *n* pl gens *f pl.* **folk** danse folklorique *f.* **folklore** *n* folklore *m.* **folk music** musique folk *f.* **folks** *pl n* (*coll*) famille *f sing.* **folk singer** chanteur, -euse de folk *m. f.*

follicle ['folikl] *n* follicule *m.*

follow ['folou] *v* suivre; (*result*) s'ensuivre. **follow up** exploiter; (faire) suivre. **follower** *n* disciple *m.*

folly ['foli] *n* folie *f.*

fond [fond] *adj* tendre, affectueux. **be fond of** aimer. **fondness** *n* (*for person*) affection *f*; (*for thing*) prédilection *f.*

fondant ['fondənt] *n* fondant *m.*

fondle ['fondl] *v* caresser.

font [font] *n* fonts baptismaux *m pl.*

food [fuːd] *n* nourriture *f.* aliments *m pl.* **food poisoning** intoxication alimentaire *f.* **foodstuffs** *pl n* aliments *m pl.*

fool [fuːl] *n* imbécile *m. f.* **foolproof** *adj* infaillible. *v* (*deceive*) duper. **fool around** faire l'imbécile. **foolhardy** *adj* téméraire. **foolish** *adj* idiot. **foolishly** *adv* bêtement. **foolishness** *n* bêtise *f.*

foolscap ['fuːlskap] *n* papier pot *m.*

foot [fut] *n, pl* **feet** pied *m;* (*bird, animal*) patte *f;* (*of page*) bas *m.* **get off on the right/wrong foot** être bien/mal parti. **on foot** à pied. **put one's foot in it** mettre les pieds dans le plat.

foot-and-mouth disease *n* fièvre aphteuse *f.*

football ['futbɔːl] *n* (*game*) football *m;* (*ball*) ballon *m.* **footballer** *n* footballeur *m.*

footbridge ['futbridʒ] *n* passerelle *f.*

foothold ['futhould] *n* prise de pied *f.*

footing ['futiŋ] *n* position *f;* relations *f pl.* **equal footing** pied d'égalité *m.*

footlights ['futlaits] *pl n* rampe *f sing.*

footnote ['futnout] *n* note en bas de la page *f.*

footpath ['futpɑːθ] *n* sentier *m.*

footprint ['futprint] *n* empreinte du pied *f.*

footstep ['futstep] *n* pas *m.*

footwear ['futweə] *n* chaussures *f pl.*

for [fɔː] *prep* pour; (*exchange*) contre; (*distance*) pendant. *conj* car.

forage ['foridʒ] *v* fourrager. *n* fourrage *m.*

forbade [fɔːˈbad] *V* **forbid.**

*forbear [fɔːˈbeə] *v* s'abstenir. **forbearance** *n* patience *f.*

*forbid [fɔːˈbid] *v* défendre, interdire. **forbidding** *adj* menaçant. (*look*) rébarbatif.

forbidden [fɔːˈbidn] *V* **forbid.**

force [fɔːs] *n* force *f.* **in force** en vigueur. *v* forcer; imposer; (*thrust*) pousser. **force-feed** *v* nourrir de force. **forceful** *adj* énergique, puissant. **forcibly** *adv* de force.

forceps ['fɔːseps] *pl n* forceps *m sing.*

ford [fɔːd] *n* gué *m.* **v** passer à gué.

fore [fɔː] *adj* antérieur, de devant. *n* (*naut*) avant *m.* **come to the fore** se faire remarquer. *adv* à l'avant.

forearm ['fɔːrɑːm] *n* avant-bras *m invar.*

forebears ['fɔːbeəz] *pl n* ancêtres *m pl.*

foreboding [fɔːˈboudiŋ] *n* pressentiment *m.*

*forecast ['fɔːkɑːst] *n* prévision *f.* **weather forecast** bulletin météorologique *m. v* prévoir.

forecourt ['fɔːkɔːt] *n* avant-cour *m;* (*of garage*) devant *m.*

forefathers ['fɔːfɑːðəz] *pl n* ancêtres *m pl.*

forefinger ['fɔːfiŋgə] *n* index *m.*

forefront ['fɔːfrʌnt] *n* premier rang *m.*

foregone ['fɔːgon] *adj* **be a foregone conclusion** être à prévoir.

foreground ['fɔːgraund] *n* premier plan *m.*

forehand ['fɔːhand] *n* (*tennis*) coup droit *m.*

forehead ['forid] *n* front *m.*

foreign ['forən] *adj* étranger. **foreigner** *n* étranger, -ère *m. f.*

foreleg ['fɔːleg] *n* jambe antérieure *f;* patte de devant *f.*

foreman ['fɔːmən] *n* contremaître *m.*

foremost ['fɔːmoust] *adj* principal. **first and foremost** tout d'abord.

forename ['fɔːneim] *n* prénom *m.*

forensic [fəˈrensik] *adj* (*medicine*) légal; (*evidence*) médico-légal.

forerunner ['fɔːrʌnə] *n* précurseur *m.*

*foresee [fɔːˈsiː] *v* prévoir. **forseeable** *adj* prévisible.

foreshadow [fɔːˈʃadou] *v* présager.

foresight ['fɔːsait] *n* prévoyance *f.*

foreskin ['fɔːskin] *n* prépuce *m.*

forest ['forist] *n* forêt *f.* **forester** *n* forestier *m.* **forestry** *n* sylviculture *f.* **Forestry Commission** Eaux et Forêts *f pl.*

forestall [fɔrstɔːl] v devancer, anticiper.
foretaste [fɔːteist] n avant-goût m.
***foretell** [fɔːtel] v prédire.
forethought [fɔːθɔːt] n prévoyance.
forever [fəreivə] adv toujours.
foreword [fɔːwɜːd] n avant-propos m.
forfeit [fɔːfit] v perdre. n peine f; (game) gage m.
forgave [fəgeiv] V **forgive**.
forge¹ [fɔːdʒ] v (counterfeit) contrefaire; (metal) forger. n forge f. **forger** n faussaire m, f; (law) contrefacteur m. **forgery** n (act) contrefaçon f; (thing forged) faux m.
forge² [fɔːdʒ] v **forge ahead** pousser de l'avant.
***forget** [fəget] v oublier. **forget-me-not** n myosotis m. **forgetful** adj distrait.
***forgive** [fəgiv] v pardonner. **forgiveness** n pardon m; clémence f.
forgiven [fəgivn] V **forgive**.
***forgo** [fɔːgou] v renoncer à.
forgot [fəgot] V **forget**.
forgotten [fəgotn] V **forget**.
fork [fɔːk] n (cutlery) fourchette f; (branch) fourche f; (roads) embranchement m. v (road) bifurquer. **fork out** (slang: pay) allonger. **forked** adj fourchu.
forlorn [fəlɔːn] adj malheureux; abandonné.
form [fɔːm] n forme f; (document) formulaire m; (bench) banc m; (school) classe f. v (se) former. **formation** n formation f. **formative** adj formateur, -trice.
formal [fɔːml] adj (dress) de cérémonie; officiel; (person, manner) compassé; (in form only) formel. **formality** n formalité f.
format [fɔːmat] n format m.
former [fɔːmə] adj (previous) ancien; (first) premier. pron celui-là, celle-là. **formerly** adv autrefois.
formidable [fɔːmidəbl] adj redoutable.
formula [fɔːmjulə] n formule f.
formulate [fɔːmjuleit] v formuler. **formulation** n formulation f.
***forsake** [fəseik] v abandonner.
forsaken [fəseikn] V **forsake**.
forsook [fəsuk] V **forsake**.
fort [fɔːt] n fort m.
forte [fɔːtei] n fort m.
forth [fɔːθ] adv en avant. **and so forth** et ainsi de suite. **forthcoming** adj à venir, prochain; (person) ouvert. **forthright** adj franc, franche. **forthwith** adv sur-le-champ.

fortify [fɔːtifai] v fortifier. **fortification** n fortification f.
fortitude [fɔːtitjuːd] n courage m.
fortnight [fɔːtnait] n quinzaine f. **fortnightly** adv tous les quinze jours.
fortress [fɔːtris] n forteresse f.
fortuitous [fɔːtjuːitəs] adj fortuit.
fortunate [fɔːtjunət] adj heureux. **be fortunate** avoir de la chance. **fortunately** adv heureusement.
fortune [fɔːtʃən] n fortune f; (luck) chance f. **fortune-teller** n diseur, -euse de bonne aventure m, f.
forty [fɔːti] nm, adj quarante. **forty winks** un petit somme. **fortieth** n(m+f), adj quarantième.
forum [fɔːrəm] n forum m; (meeting) tribune f.
forward [fɔːwəd] adj en avant; (impudent) effronté. **come forward** se présenter. v expédier; (send on) faire suivre. **please forward** prière de faire suivre.
forwards [fɔːwədz] adv en avant.
fossil [fɔsl] n fossile m. **fossilized** adj fossilisé.
foster [fɔstə] v (child) élever; encourager; (idea) entretenir.
fought [fɔːt] V **fight**.
foul [faul] adj infect; (language) ordurier; (weather) sale. **foul play** acte criminel m; (sport) jeu déloyal m. n (sport) coup défendu. v infecter; (entangle) (s')emmêler.
found¹ [faund] V **find**.
found² [faund] v fonder. **foundation** n fondation f; base f; fondement m. **founder** n fondateur, -trice m, f.
founder [faundə] v (ship) sombrer; (collapse) s'effondrer.
foundry [faundri] n fonderie f.
fountain [fauntin] n fontaine f. **fountain pen** stylo à encre m.
four [fɔː] nm, adj quatre. **foursome** n (game) partie à quatre f; deux couples m pl. **on all fours** à quatre pattes. **fourth** n(m+f), adj quatrième.
fourteen [fɔːtiːn] nm, adj quatorze. **fourteenth** n(m+f), adj quatorzième.
fowl [faul] n volaille f.
fox [fɔks] n renard m. **foxglove** n digitale f. **foxhunting** n chasse au renard f. **foxtrot** n slow m. v (coll) mystifier.
foyer [fɔiei] n foyer m.

fraction ['frakʃən] n fraction f. **fractionally** adv un tout petit peu.

fracture ['fraktʃə] n fracture f. v (se) fracturer.

fragile ['fradʒail] adj fragile. **fragility** n fragilité f.

fragment ['fragmənt] n fragment m. **fragmented** adj morcelé.

fragrant ['freigrənt] adj parfumé. **fragrance** n parfum m.

frail [freil] adj frêle, fragile. **frailty** n fragilité f; (moral) faiblesse f.

frame [freim] n cadre m; (house) charpente f; (car) châssis m; (spectacles) monture f; (film) image f. **frame of mind** humeur f. **framework** n charpente f; structure f. v encadrer.

franc [fraŋk] n franc m.

France [fraɪns] n France f.

franchise ['frantʃaiz] n droit de suffrage m.

frank [fraŋk] adj franc, franche. **frankness** n franchise f.

frantic [frantik] adj frénétique; (person) hors de soi.

fraternal [frə'təɪnl] adj fraternel. **fraternity** n fraternité f; (community) confrérie f. **fraternize** v fraterniser.

fraud [froɪd] n (law) fraude f; (deception) supercherie f; (financial) escroquerie f; (person) imposteur m. **fraudulent** adj frauduleux.

fraught [froɪt] adj (tense) tendu. **fraught with** chargé de.

fray¹ [frei] v (s')effilocher; (cuff, etc.) (s')effranger.

fray² [frei] n rixe f.

freak [friːk] n phénomène m; anomalie f. **freak of nature** accident de la nature m. adj insolite, inattendu.

freckle ['frekl] n tache de son f. **freckled** adj taché de son.

free [friː] adj libre; gratuit. **free-for-all** n mêlée générale f. **freehand** adj, adv à main levée. **freehold** n propriété foncière libre f. **freelance** n, adj indépendant, -e. **freemason** n francmaçon m. **freestyle** n nage libre f. **of one's own free will** de son propre gré. v libérer. **freedom** n liberté f.

freesia ['friːziə] n freesia m.

***freeze** [friːz] v geler; (food) congeler; (prices, etc.) bloquer. n gel m; blocage m. **freezer** n congélateur m. **freezing** adj glacial. **freezing point** point de congélation m.

freight [freit] n fret m; transport m; (goods) marchandises f pl. **freight train** train de marchandises m. v affréter; transporter. **freighter** n (ship) cargo m; (aircraft) avion-cargo m.

French [frentʃ] nm, adj français. **the French** les Français m pl. **French bean** haricot vert m. **French dressing** vinaigrette f. **French horn** cor d'harmonie m. **French-polish** v vernir à l'alcool. **french fries** n pommes frites f pl.

frenzy ['frenzi] n frénésie f. **frenzied** adj frénétique.

frequent ['friːkwənt; v friˈkwent] adj fréquent. v fréquenter. **frequency** n fréquence f. **frequently** adv fréquemment.

fresco ['freskou] n fresque f.

fresh [freʃ] adj frais, fraîche; (new) nouveau, -elle. **freshwater** adj (fish) d'eau douce. **freshen up** faire un brin de toilette. **freshness** n fraîcheur f.

fret¹ [fret] v se tracasser. **fretful** adj agité; (child) pleurnicheur, -euse.

fret² [fret] v découper, chantourner. **fretsaw** n scie à découper f. **fretwork** n découpage m.

friar ['fraiə] n frère m, moine m.

friction ['frikʃən] n friction f; désaccord m.

Friday ['fraidei] n vendredi m.

fridge [fridʒ] n (coll) frigo m.

friend [frend] n ami, -e m, f. **make friends with** devenir ami avec. **friendliness** n bienveillance f. **friendly** adj amical; (kind) gentil, -ille. **friendship** n amitié f.

frieze [friːz] n frise f.

frigate ['frigit] n frégate f.

fright [frait] n effroi m, peur f. **frighten** v effrayer. **be frightened** avoir peur. **frightening** adj effrayant. **frightful** adj affreux.

frigid ['fridʒid] adj glacial; (manner) froid; (woman) frigide. **frigidity** n froideur f; frigidité f.

frill [fril] n (dress) ruche f; (shirt) jabot m. **frilly** adj à fanfreluches.

fringe [frindʒ] n frange f; (edge) bord m. **fringe benefits** avantages supplémentaires m pl. v franger; border.

frisk [frisk] v gambader; (search) fouiller. **frisky** adj vif.

fritter¹ ['fritə] v **fritter away** gaspiller.

fritter² ['fritə] n (cookery) beignet m.

frivolity [friˈvoliti] n frivolité f. **frivolous** adj frivole.

frizz [friz] v (hair) friser. **frizzy** adj crépu.

fro [frou] adv **to and fro** de long en large. **go to and fro between** aller et venir entre.

frock [frɔk] n robe f.

frog [frɔg] n grenouille f. **frogman** n homme-grenouille m. **frogs' legs** cuisses de grenouille f pl.

frolic ['frɔlik] v folâtrer. n ébats m pl.

from [frɔm] prep de; (starting from) à partir de; (extract) dans, à.

front [frʌnt] n devant m, avant m; (mil, weather) front m; (promenade) front de mer m. **in front of** devant. adj de devant, en avant; (first) premier. **front view** vue de face f. **frontage** n façade f; (shop) devanture f.

frontier ['frʌntiə] n frontière f.

frost [frɔst] n gelée f. **frostbite** n gelure f. v geler. **frosted glass** verre dépoli m. **frosty** adj glacial.

froth [frɔθ] n écume f, mousse f. v écumer, mousser. **frothy** adj écumeux, mousseux.

frown [fraun] n froncement de sourcils m. v froncer les sourcils, se renfrogner. **frown on** désapprouver.

froze [frouz] V freeze.

frozen ['frouzn] V freeze. adj gelé. **frozen food** aliments congelés m pl.

frugal ['fruːgəl] adj (meal, etc.) frugal; (person) économe. **frugality** n frugalité f.

fruit [fruːt] n fruit m. **fruit cake** cake m. **fruit machine** machine à sous f. **fruit salad** salade de fruits f. **fruitful** adj fructueux. **fruition** n réalisation f. **fruitless** adj stérile.

frustrate [frʌ'streit] v frustrer; (plans, etc.) faire échouer. **frustration** n frustration f.

fry [frai] v (faire) frire. **fried** adj frit. **fried egg** œuf sur le plat m. **frying** n friture f. **frying pan** poêle f.

fuchsia ['fjuːʃə] n fuchsia m.

fuck [fʌk] (vulgar) v baiser. **fuck off!** va te faire foutre!

fudge [fʌdʒ] n fondant m.

fuel ['fjuəl] n combustible m; (mot) carburant m. **fuel gauge** indicateur de niveau de carburant m. **fuel pump** pompe à essence f. v (stove, etc.) alimenter; (aircraft) (se) ravitailler en combustible.

fugitive ['fjuːdʒitiv] n, adj fugitif, -ive.

fulcrum ['fulkrəm] n pivot m.

fulfil [ful'fil] v accomplir; exécuter; satisfaire. **fulfilment** n accomplissement m; exécution f; contentement m.

full [ful] adj plein; complet, -ète. **full blast** adv (radio, etc.) à pleines tubes. **full-length** adj (picture) en pied; (film) long métrage. **full moon** pleine lune f. **full name** nom et prénoms. **full-scale** adj de grande envergure. **full stop** point m. **full-time** adj, adv à plein temps. **fully** adv entièrement.

fumble ['fʌmbl] v (feel) tâtonner; (search) fouiller.

fume [fjuːm] v fumer; (coll: rage) être furibond. **fumes** pl n vapeurs f pl.

fun [fʌn] n amusement m. **for fun** pour rire. **funfair** n fête foraine f. **have fun** bien s'amuser. **make fun of** se moquer de.

function ['fʌŋkʃən] n fonction f; réception f. v fonctionner. **functional** adj fonctionnel.

fund [fʌnd] n fond m, caisse f. **funds** pl n fonds m pl.

fundamental [fʌndə'mentl] adj fondamental.

funeral ['fjuːnərəl] n enterrement m; (state) funérailles f pl. **funeral parlour** dépôt mortuaire m. **funeral service** service funèbre m.

fungus ['fʌŋgəs] n, pl **fungi** champignon m.

funnel ['fʌnl] n (pouring) entonnoir m; (ship) cheminée f.

funny ['fʌni] adj drôle; bizarre.

fur [fəː] n fourrure f; (kettle) incrustation f. v s'incruster. **furrier** n fourreur m. **furry** adj à poil.

furious ['fjuəriəs] adj furieux.

furnace ['fəːnis] n fourneau m.

furnish ['fəːniʃ] v (house, etc.) meubler; (supply) fournir. **furnishings** pl n mobilier m sing.

furniture ['fəːnitʃə] n meubles m pl, mobilier m.

furrow ['fʌrou] n sillon m; (brow) ride f. v sillonner; rider.

further ['fəːðə] adv (farther) plus loin; (more) davantage. adj (farther) plus lointain; additionnel. **further education** enseignement post-scolaire m. **furthermore** en outre. **until further notice** jusqu'à nouvel ordre. v avancer.

furthest ['fəːðist] adv le plus loin. adj le plus lointain.

furtive ['fəːtiv] adj furtif.

fury ['fjʊəri] *n* fureur *f*.

fuse¹ [fjuːz] *v* (*blend*) fusionner; (*melt*) fondre; (*elec*) faire sauter. **fused** *adj* (*plug*) avec fusible incorporé. *n* (*elec*) plomb *m*. **fuse box** boîte à fusibles *f*. **fuse wire** fusible *m*.

fuse² [fjuːz] *v* (*bomb*) amorcer. *n* amorce *f*.

fuselage ['fjuːzəlɑːʒ] *n* fuselage *m*.

fusion ['fjuːʒən] *n* fusion *f*.

fuss [fʌs] *n* façons *f pl*; agitation *f*. **make a fuss** faire des histoires. *v* (*worry*) se tracasser. **fussy** *adj* tatillon, -onne; (*overelaborate*) tarabiscoté.

futile ['fjuːtail] *adj* futile, vain. **futility** *n* futilité *f*.

future ['fjuːtʃə] *n* avenir *m*; (*gramm*) futur *m*. **in future** à l'avenir. *adj* futur, à venir. **futuristic** *adj* futuriste.

fuzz [fʌz] *n* (*hair*) cheveux crépus *m pl*; (*on body*) duvet *m*; (*slang: police*) flicaille *f*. **fuzzy** *adj* crépu; (*photo*) flou.

G

gabble ['gabl] *v* brédouiller. *n* baragouin *m*.

gable ['geibl] *n* pignon *m*.

gadget ['gadʒit] *n* gadget *m*.

gag¹ [gag] *v* bâillonner. *n* bâillon *m*.

gag² [gag] (*coll*) *n* (*joke*) plaisanterie *f*. *v* plaisanter.

gaiety ['geiəti] *n* gaieté *f*.

gain [gein] *n* gain *m*, profit *m*. *v* gagner; (*speed, weight*) prendre; (*clock, watch*) avancer.

gait [geit] *n* démarche *f*.

gala ['gɑːlə] *n* gala *m*.

galaxy ['galəksi] *n* galaxie *f*.

gale [geil] *n* coup de vent *m*.

gallant ['galənt] *adj* courageux; noble; (*to women*) galant. **gallantry** *n* courage *m*; galanterie *f*.

gall-bladder ['gɔːl bladə] *n* vésicule biliaire *f*.

galleon ['galiən] *n* galion *m*.

gallery ['galəri] *n* galerie *f*; (*spectators*) tribune *f*; (*theatre*) dernier balcon *m*.

galley ['gali] *n* (*ship*) galère *f*; (*kitchen*) cuisine *f*.

gallon ['galən] *n* gallon *m*.

gallop ['galəp] *n* galop *m*. *v* galoper.

gallows ['galouz] *n* gibet *m*.

gallstone ['gɔːlstoun] *n* calcul biliaire *m*.

galore [gə'lɔː] *adv* (*coll*) à gogo.

galvanize ['galvanaiz] *v* galvaniser. **galvanize into action** donner le coup de fouet à.

gamble ['gambl] *v* jouer. **gamble on** compter sur. *n* jeu (de hasard) *m*; entreprise risquée *f*. **gambler** *n* joueur, -euse *m, f*. **gambling** *n* jeu *m*.

game [geim] *n* jeu *m*; (*of cards, tennis, etc*.) partie *f*; (*hunting*) gibier *m*. **gamekeeper** *n* garde-chasse *m*. **games** (*school*) sport *m*. *adj* courageux. **be game for** être prêt à.

gammon ['gamən] *n* jambon salé *m*; (*smoked*) jambon fumé *m*.

gang [gan] *n* bande *f*. *v* **gang up on se** liguer contre. **gangster** *n* gangster *m*.

gangrene ['gangriːn] *n* gangrène *f*.

gangway ['ganwei] *n* passage *m*; (*naut*) passerelle *f*.

gaol *V* **jail**.

gap [gap] *n* trou *m*, vide *m*.

gape [geip] *v* (*stare*) rester bouche bée; (*open wide*) bâiller. **gaping** *adj* béant.

garage ['garɑːʒ] *n* garage *m*.

garbage ['gɑːbidʒ] (*US*) *n* ordures *f pl*. **garbage can** poubelle *f*.

garble ['gɑːbl] *v* déformer, embrouiller. **garbled** *adj* confus; incompréhensible.

garden ['gɑːdn] *n* jardin *m*. **garden party** garden-party *f*. **gardens** *n* parc *m sing*, jardin public *m sing*. **gardener** *n* jardinier, -ère *m, f*. **gardening** *n* jardinage *m*.

gargle ['gɑːgl] *v* se gargariser. *n* gargarisme *m*.

gargoyle ['gɑːgoil] *n* gargouille *f*.

garland ['gɑːlənd] *n* guirlande *f*. *v* enguirlander.

garlic ['gɑːlik] *n* ail (*pl* aulx) *m*.

garment ['gɑːmənt] *n* vêtement *m*.

garnish ['gɑːniʃ] *v* garnir. *n* garniture *f*.

garrison ['garisn] *n* garnison *f*. *v* mettre en garnison.

garter ['gɑːtə] *n* jarretière *f*; (*for socks*) fixe-chaussette *m*; (*US*) jarretelle *f*. **garter belt** (*US*) porte-jarretelles *m invar*.

gas [gas] *n* gaz *m*; (*US: petrol*) essence *f*. **gasmask** *n* masque à gaz *m*. **gas ring** (*cooker*) brûleur *m*. **gasworks** *n* usine à gaz *f*. *v* asphyxier. **gaseous** *adj* gazeux. **gassy** *adj* gazeux.

gash [gaʃ] n entaille f. v entailler.
gasket ['gaskit] n joint (d'étanchéité) m.
gasoline ['gasə,lin] n (US) essence f.
gasp [gaisp] v haleter; (from surprise) avoir le souffle coupé. n halètement m; souffle m.
gastric ['gastrik] adj gastrique. **gastric ulcer** ulcère de l'estomac m. **gastroenteritis** n gastro-entérite f.
gastronomic [gastrə'nomik] adj gastronomique. **gastronomy** n gastronomie f.
gate [geit] n (garden) porte f; (field) barrière f; (iron) grille f; (airport) sortie f. **gatecrash** v s'introduire sans invitation. **gateway** n porte f.
gateau ['gatou] n gâteau m.
gather ['gaðə] v ramasser; (people) (se) rassembler; (sewing) froncer; (infer) déduire. **gathering** n rassemblement m, réunion f.
gaudy ['goidi] adj criard.
gauge [geidʒ] n (instrument) jauge f; (rail) écartement m; (measurement) calibre m. v jauger, mesurer.
gaunt [goint] adj décharné; (face) creux; (grim) lugubre.
gauze [goiz] n gaze f.
gave [geiv] V **give**.
gay [gei] adj gai; (slang) homo. n (slang) homosexuel, -elle m, f.
gaze [geiz] n regard fixe m. v regarder.
gazelle [gə'zel] n gazelle f.
gazetteer [gazə'tiə] n index géographique m.
gear [giə] n (equipment) matériel m; (belongings) affaires f pl; (mot) vitesse f. **gearbox** n boîte de vitesses f. **gear lever** levier de vitesse m. **in gear** en prise. v adapter; préparer.
geese [giis] V **goose**.
gelatine ['dʒelə,tiin] n gélatine f.
gelignite [dʒelig,nait] n gélignite f.
gem [dʒem] n gemme f; (delightful thing) bijou (pl -oux) m, perle f.
Gemini ['dʒemini] n Gémeaux m pl.
gender ['dʒendə] n genre m.
gene [dʒiin] n gène m.
genealogy [dʒiiniˌalədʒi] n généalogie f. **genealogical** adj généalogique.
general ['dʒenərəl] nm, adj général. **general election** élections législatives f pl. **general hospital** centre hospitalier m. **general knowledge** connaissances générales f pl. **general practitioner** généraliste

m. **in general** en général. **generalization** n généralisation f. **generalize** v généraliser.
generate ['dʒenəreit] v engendrer; produire. **generation** n génération f; production f. **generator** n (elec) génératrice f; (steam) générateur m.
generic [dʒi'nerik] adj générique.
generous ['dʒenərəs] adj généreux. **generosity** n générosité f.
genetic [dʒi'netik] adj génétique. **genetics** n génétique f.
Geneva [dʒi'niivə] n Genève. **Lake Geneva** le lac Léman.
genial ['dʒiiniəl] adj cordial.
genital ['dʒenitl] adj génital. **genitals** pl n organes génitaux m pl.
genius ['dʒiinjəs] n génie m.
genteel [dʒen'tiil] adj distingué.
gentle ['dʒentl] adj doux, douce; (light) léger. **gentleman** n monsieur m (pl messieurs) m; (courteous man) gentleman m. **gentleness** n douceur f.
gentry ['dʒentri] n petite noblesse f.
gents [dʒents] n (sign) messieurs m.
genuine ['dʒenjuin] adj véritable, authentique; sincère.
genus ['dʒiinəs] n genre m.
geography [dʒi'ografi] n géographie f. **geographer** n géographe m, f. **geographical** adj géographique.
geology [dʒi'olədʒi] n géologie f. **geological** adj géologique. **geologist** n géologue m, f.
geometry [dʒi'omətri] n géométrie f. **geometrical** adj géométrique.
geranium [dʒə'reiniəm] n géranium m.
geriatric [dʒeri'atrik] adj gériatrique. **geriatrics** n gériatrie f.
germ [dʒəim] n (med) microbe m; germe m.
Germany ['dʒəiməni] n Allemagne f. **German** nm, adj allemand; n (people) Allemand, -e m, f. **German measles** rubéole f. **Germanic** adj germanique.
germinate ['dʒəimineit] v (faire) germer. **germination** n germination f.
gerund ['dʒerənd] n gérondif m.
gesticulate [dʒe'stikju,leit] v gesticuler. **gesticulation** n gesticulation f.
gesture ['dʒestʃə] n geste m. v faire signe.
*get [get] v avoir; obtenir; recevoir; (fetch) aller chercher; (go) aller; (become) devenir. **get across** (cross) traverser; communiquer. **get at** (reach) atteindre; (tease) s'en prendre à. **getaway** n fuite f.

get back (*return*) revenir; (*recover*) retrouver. get down descendre. get down to se mettre à. get off descendre. get on continuer; (*horse, etc.*) monter (*sur*); (*agree*) s'accorder. get out sortir. get up se lever.

geyser ['giːzə] *n* geyser *m*; (*water-heater*) chauffe-bain *m invar*.

ghastly ['gɑːstli] *adj* horrible; (*pale*) blême.

gherkin ['gɜːkin] *n* cornichon *m*.

ghetto ['getou] *n* ghetto *m*.

ghost [goust] *n* fantôme *m*. ghostly *adj* spectral.

giant ['dʒaiənt] *nm, adj* géant.

gibberish ['dʒibərif] *n* baragouin *m*.

gibe [dʒaib] *n* raillerie *f*. *v* gibe at railler.

giblets ['dʒiblits] *pl n* abattis *m pl*.

giddy ['gidi] *adj* (*dizzy*) pris de vertige; (*height*) vertigineux; (*scatterbrained*) étourdi. giddiness *n* vertiges *m pl*.

gift [gift] *n* cadeau *m*; (*talent*) don *m*. gift token chèque-cadeau *m*. gifted *adj* doué.

gigantic [dʒai'gantik] *adj* gigantesque.

giggle ['gigl] *v* rire nerveusement, glousser. *n* gloussement *m*. get the giggles avoir le fou rire.

gill [gil] *n* (*fish*) branchie *f*; (*mushroom*) lamelle *f*.

gilt [gilt] *n* dorure *f*. *adj* doré.

gimmick ['gimik] *n* (*coll*) truc *m*.

gin [dʒin] *n* gin *m*.

ginger ['dʒindʒə] *n* gingembre *m*. gingerbread *n* pain d'épice *m*. *adj* (*hair*) roux, rousse.

zingerly ['dʒindʒəli] *adv* avec précaution.

gipsy ['dʒipsi] *n* bohémien, -enne *m, f*.

giraffe [dʒi'rɑːf] *n* girafe *f*.

girder ['gɜːdə] *n* poutre *f*.

girdle ['gɜːdl] *n* ceinture *f*; (*corset*) gaine *f*. *v* ceindre.

girl [gɜːl] *n* fille *f*; (*pupil*) élève *f*. girlfriend *n* petite amie *f*. girlhood *n* enfance *f*.

girth [gɜːθ] *n* (*tree*) circonférence *f*; (*waist, etc.*) tour *m*; (*saddle*) sangle *f*.

gist [dʒist] *n* essentiel *m*.

*give [giv] *v* donner; offrir; céder. give-and-take *n* concessions mutuelles *f pl*. give away faire cadeau de; révéler. give back rendre. give in se rendre. give off émettre. give out distribuer. give up abandonner. give way céder; (*collapse*) s'affaisser.

given ['givn] *V* give.

glacier ['glasiə] *n* glacier *m*. glaciation *n* glaciation *f*.

glad [glad] *adj* heureux. gladden *v* réjouir. gladly *adv* avec plaisir.

glamour ['glamə] *n* prestige *m*, éclat *m*; (*person*) fascination *f*. glamorous *adj* (*life*) brillant; (*person*) séduisant; (*job*) prestigieux; (*dress*) splendide.

glance [glɑːns] *n* coup d'œil *m*. *v* jeter un coup d'œil.

gland [gland] *n* glande *f*. glandular *adj* glandulaire. glandular fever mononucléose infectieuse *f*.

glare [gleə] *v* lancer un regard furieux; (*light*) éblouir. *n* regard furieux *m*; éblouissement *m*.

glass [glɑːs] *n* verre *m*. glasses *pl n* lunettes *f pl*. glassworks *n* verrerie *f*. glassy *adj* vitreux.

glaze [gleiz] *v* (*window*) vitrer; (*pottery, etc.*) vernisser; (*cookery*) glacer. *n* vernis *m*; glaçage *m*. glazier *n* vitrier *m*.

gleam [gliːm] *v* luire. *n* lueur *f*. gleaming *adj* brillant.

glean [gliːn] *v* glaner.

glee [gliː] *n* joie *f*. gleeful *adj* joyeux.

glib [glib] *adj* désinvolte. glibly *adv* avec aisance, avec désinvolture.

glide [glaid] *v* (*aero*) planer; (*slide*) glisser. *n* vol plané *m*; glissement *m*. glider *n* planeur *m*.

glimmer ['glimə] *v* luire faiblement; miroiter. *n* faible lueur *f*; miroitement *m*.

glimpse [glimps] *v* entrevoir. *n* vision rapide *f*.

glint [glint] *v* étinceler. *n* reflet *m*.

glisten ['glisn] *v* briller.

glitter ['glitə] *v* scintiller. *n* scintillement *m*.

gloat [glout] *v* jubiler.

globe [gloub] *n* globe *m*. globe artichoke artichaut *m*. globe-trotter *n* globe-trotter *m*. global *adj* global; universel.

gloom [gluːm] *n* obscurité *f*; mélancolie *f*. gloomy *adj* sombre, lugubre.

glory ['glɔːri] *n* gloire *f*; splendeur *f*. glorify *v* glorifier. glorious *adj* magnifique, glorieux.

gloss [glos] *n* lustre *m*; (*paint*) brillant *m*. glossy *adj* brillant, lustré.

glossary ['glosəri] *n* glossaire *m*.

glove [glʌv] *n* gant *m*. glove compartment vide-poches *m invar*.

glow [glou] v rougeoyer. n rougeoiement m. **glowing** adj rougeoyant; (words) chaleureux.

glucose ['glu:kous] n glucose m.

glue [glu:] n colle f. v coller.

glum [glʌm] adj triste.

glut [glʌt] n surplus m.

glutton ['glʌtən] n glouton, -onne m, f. **gluttonous** adj glouton. **gluttony** gloutonnerie f.

gnarled [na:ld] adj noueux.

gnash [naʃ] v gnash one's teeth grincer les dents.

gnat [nat] n moucheron m.

gnaw [nɔ:] v ronger. **gnawing** adj tenaillant.

gnome [noum] n gnome m.

*go [gou] v aller; (leave) partir; (work) marcher; (become) devenir; (make sound) faire. **go away** s'en aller. **go back** retourner. **go-between** n intermédiaire m, f. **go by** passer; (judge by) se fonder sur. **go down** descendre; (temperature, etc.) baisser. **go in** entrer. **go off** (food) se gâter; (cease to like) perdre le goût de. **go on** continuer. **go out** sortir. **go up** monter. **go with** (match) s'assortir avec. **go without** se passer de. n essor m; (try) coup m. it's your go c'est à toi de jouer. **on the go** sur la brèche.

goad [goud] v aiguillonner. n aiguillon m.

goal [goul] n but m. **goalkeeper** n gardien de but m. **goal post** montant de but m.

goat [gout] n chèvre f. **act the goat** (coll) faire l'imbécile.

gobble ['gobl] v engloutir.

goblin ['goblin] n lutin m.

god [god] n dieu m. **goddaughter** n filleule f. **godfather** n parrain m. **godmother** n marraine f. **godsend** n aubaine f. **godson** n filleul m. **goddess** n déesse f.

goggles ['goglz] pl n lunettes protectrices f pl.

gold [gould] n or m. **goldfinch** n chardonneret m. **goldfish** n poisson rouge m. **goldfish bowl** bocal m. **gold mine** mine d'or f. **goldsmith** n orfèvre m. **golden** adj d'or, doré. **golden opportunity** occasion magnifique f. **golden rule** règle d'or f. **golden syrup** mélasse raffinée f.

golf [golf] n golf m. **golf course** terrain de golf m. **golfer** n golfeur, -euse m, f.

gondola ['gondələ] n gondole f. **gondolier** n gondolier m.

gone [gon] V go.

gong [goŋ] n gong m.

gonorrhoea [gonə'riə] n blennorragie f.

good [gud] adj bon, bonne; (person) brave; (well-behaved) sage. **good afternoon** bonjour; (later) bonsoir. **goodbye** interj au revoir. **good evening** bonsoir. **good-for-nothing** nm, adj propre à rien. **Good Friday** vendredi saint m. **goodlooking** adj beau, belle. **good morning** bonjour. **goodnight** interj bonsoir; (bedtime) bonne nuit. **goodwill** n bonne volonté f; (comm) incorporels m pl. n bien m. **be no good** ne servir à rien. **for good** pour de bon. **goodness** n bonté f.

goods [gudz] pl n (comm) marchandises f pl; articles m pl; (law) biens m pl. n **goods train** train de marchandises m.

goose [gu:s] n, pl geese oie f.

gooseberry ['guzbəri] n (fruit) groseille à maquereau f; (bush) groseiller m. **play gooseberry** tenir la chandelle.

gore [gɔ:] v encorner.

gorge [gɔːdʒ] n gorge f. v se gorger.

gorgeous ['gɔːdʒəs] adj magnifique.

gorilla [gə'rilə] n gorille m.

gorse [gɔːs] n ajonc m.

gory ['gɔːri] adj sanglant.

gospel ['gospəl] n évangile m.

gossip ['gosip] n (chat) bavardage m; (unkind) commérage m; (person) commère f. v bavarder; (unkindly) potiner.

got [got] V get.

Gothic ['goθik] adj gothique.

goulash ['gu:laʃ] n goulache f.

gourd [guəd] n gourde f.

gourmet ['guəmei] n gourmet m.

gout [gaut] n goutte f.

govern ['gʌvən] v gouverner; administrer; déterminer. **governess** n gouvernante f. **government** n gouvernement m. **governor** n gouverneur m; (school) administrateur, -trice m, f; (coll: boss) patron m.

gown [gaun] n robe f; (law, university) toge f.

grab [grab] v saisir. n mouvement vif pour saisir m.

grace [greis] n grâce f; (before meal) bénédicité m. **graceful** adj gracieux, élégant. **gracious** adj gracieux; courtois.

grade [greid] n catégorie f; échelon m; qualité f; (mark) note f. v classer.

gradient ['greidiənt] n (measurement) inclinaison f; (slope) pente f.

gradual ['grædjuəl] *adj* graduel.

graduate ['grædju.eit; *n. adj* 'grædjuət] *v* graduer; (*university*) obtenir sa licence. *n. adj* licencié, -e.

graffiti [grə'fiːtiː] *pl n* graffiti *m pl*.

graft [grɑːft] *n* greffe *f. v* greffer.

grain [grein] *n* grain *m*; (*wood*) fibre *f*.

gram [græm] *n* gramme *m*.

grammar ['græmə] *n* grammaire *f*. **grammar school** lycée *m*. **grammatical** *adj* grammatical.

gramophone ['græməfoun] *n* phonographe *f*.

granary ['grænəri] *n* grenier *m*.

grand [grænd] *adj* magnifique; grandiose. **grandeur** *n* splendeur *f*.

grandchild ['græntʃaild] *n* petit-enfant, petite-enfant *m. f*.

grand-dad ['grændad] *n also* **grandpa** (*coll*) pépé.

granddaughter ['grændɔːtə] *n* petite-fille *f*.

grandfather ['græn,faːðə] *n* grand-père *m*.

grandma ['grænmɑː] *n also* **granny** (*coll*) mémé *f*.

grandmother ['græn,mʌðə] *n* grande-mère *f*.

grandparent ['græn,peərənt] *n* grand-parent *m*.

grand piano *n* piano à queue *m*.

grandson ['grænsʌn] *n* petit-fils *m*.

grandstand ['grænstænd] *n* tribune *f*.

grand total *n* somme globale *f*.

granite ['grænit] *n* granit *m*.

grant [grɑːnt] *v* accorder; admettre. *n* subvention *f*; (*student*) bourse *f*.

granule ['grænjuːl] *n* granule *m*. **granulated sugar** sucre semoule *m*.

grape [greip] *n* raisin *m*. **grapevine** *n* vigne *f*; (*coll*) téléphone arabe *f*.

grapefruit ['greipfruːt] *n* pamplemousse *m*.

graph [grɑːf] *n* graphique *f*. **graph paper** papier quadrillé *m*; papier millimétré *m*. **graphic** *adj* graphique; (*description*) vivant.

grapple ['græpl] *v* **grapple with** affronter résolument.

grasp [grɑːsp] *v* saisir. *n* prise *f*; compréhension *f*. **grasping** *adj* avare.

grass [grɑːs] *n* herbe *f*; (*lawn*) gazon *m*. **grasshopper** *n* sauterelle *f*. **grass snake** couleuvre *f*. **grassy** *adj* herbeux.

grate¹ [greit] *n* grille de foyer *f*. **grating** *n* grille *f*.

grate² [greit] *v* (*food*) râper; (*metal*) (faire) grincer. **grater** *n* râpe *f*.

grateful ['greitful] *adj* reconnaissant.

gratify ['grætifai] *v* satisfaire; faire plaisir à. **gratifying** *adj* agréable.

gratitude ['grætitjuːd] *n* reconnaissance *f*.

gratuity [grə'tjuːiti] *n* pourboire *m*.

grave¹ [greiv] *n* tombe *f*. **gravedigger** *n* fossoyeur *m*. **gravestone** *n* pierre tombale *f*. **graveyard** *n* cimetière *m*.

grave² [greiv] *adj* grave.

gravel ['grævəl] *n* gravier *m. v* couvrir de gravier.

gravity ['grævəti] *n* (*physics*) pesanteur *f*; (*seriousness*) gravité *f*.

gravy ['greivi] *n* jus de viande *m*; sauce *f*.

graze¹ [greiz] *v* (*scrape*) écorcher; (*touch*) frôler. *n* écorchure *f*.

graze² [greiz] *v* (*animal*) brouter, paître.

grease [griːs] *n* graisse *f*. **grease-paint** *n* fard gras *m*. **greaseproof paper** papier parcheminé *m. v* graisser. **greasy** *adj* graisseux; (*hair, road*) gras, grasse.

great [greit] *adj* grand; magnifique. **Great Britain** Grande-Bretagne *f*. **greatly** *adv* fort, très. **greatness** *n* grandeur *f*.

Greece [griːs] *n* Grèce *f*. **Greek** *nm, adj* grec, grecque; *n* (*people*) Grec, Grecque *m, f*.

greed [griːd] *n* avidité *f*; (*for food*) gourmandise *f*. **greedy** *adj* avide; (*for food*) vorace.

green [griːn] *adj* vert; naïf, naïve; (*bacon*) non fumé. *n* vert *m*; (*grass*) gazon *m*. **greenfly** *n* puceron *m*. **greengage** *n* reineclaude *f*. **greengrocer's** *n* fruiterie *f*. **greenhouse** *n* serre *f*; **green light** feu vert *m*. **greens** *pl n* légumes verts *m pl*. **have green fingers** avoir le pouce vert. **greenery** *n* verdure *f*.

Greenland ['griːnlənd] *n* Groenland *m*. **Greenlander** *n* Groenlandais, -e *m, f*.

greet [griːt] *v* saluer, accueillir. **greeting** *n* salutation *f*. **greetings card** carte de vœux *f*.

gregarious [gri'geəriəs] *adj* grégaire.

grenade [grə'neid] *n* grenade *f*.

grew [gruː] *V* grow.

grey [grei] *nm, adj* gris. **greyhound** *n* lévrier, levrette *m, f*. **go grey** (*hair*) grisonner.

grid [grid] *n* grille *f*; (*elec*) réseau *m*.

grief [griːf] *n* chagrin *m*.

grieve [griːv] *v* (*upset*) peiner; (*sorrow*) s'affliger. **grieve for** pleurer. **grievance** *n* grief *m*; injustice *f*. **grievous** *adj* affreux; grave. **grievous bodily harm** coups et blessures *m pl*.

grill [gril] *v* (faire) griller. *n* gril *m*; (*meal*) grillade *f*. **grillroom** *n* rôtisserie *f*.

grille [gril] *n* grille *f*.

grim [grim] *adj* sinistre; (*coll*) désagréable. **grimly** *adv* d'un air mécontent.

grimace [gri'meis] *n* grimace *f*. *v* grimacer.

grime [graim] *n* crasse *f*. **grimy** *adj* crasseux.

grin [grin] *n* sourire *m*. *v* sourire.

*****grind** [graind] *v* (*coffee, etc.*) moudre; (*crush*) écraser; (*knife*) aiguiser; (*teeth*) grincer. *n* grincement *m*; (*coll*) boulot *m*. **grinder** *n* broyeur *m*, moulin *m*.

grip [grip] *n* (*of hand*) poigne *f*, prise *f*; (*bag*) trousse *f*. *v* saisir; (*hold*) serrer; (*tyres*) adhérer. **gripping** *adj* passionnant.

gripe [graip] *n* colique *f*. *v* (*coll*) rouspéter.

grisly ['grizli] *adj* macabre; horrible.

gristle [grisl] *n* cartilage *m*. **gristly** *adj* cartilagineux.

grit [grit] *n* sable *m*; gravillon *m*; (*coll: courage*) cran *m*. *v* (*teeth*) serrer; (*road*) répandre du gravillon sur.

groan [groun] *n* (*pain*) gémissement *m*; (*dismay*) grognement *m*. *v* gémir; grogner.

grocer ['grousə] *n* épicier, -ère *m*, *f*. **grocer's** *n* (*shop*) épicerie *f*. **groceries** *pl n* provisions *f pl*.

groin [groin] *n* aine *f*.

groom [gruːm] *n* (*for horse*) palefrenier *m*; (*of bride*) marié *m*. *v* (*horse*) panser; préparer.

groove [gruːv] *n* cannelure *f*, rainure *f*; (*record*) sillon *m*. *v* canneler.

grope [group] *v* tâtonner. **grope for** chercher à tâtons.

gross [grous] *adj* (*not net*) brut; flagrant; obèse; (*coarse*) grossier. *n* grosse *f*.

grotesque [grə'tesk] *nm, adj* grotesque.

grotto ['grotou] *n* grotte *f*.

ground¹ [graund] *V* grind.

ground² [graund] *n* terre *f*; (*area*) terrain *m*. **ground floor** rez-de-chaussée *m*. **ground frost** gelée blanche *f*. **grounds** *pl n* parc *m sing*; motifs *m pl*; (*coffee*) marc *m sing*. **groundsheet** *n* tapis de sol *m*. **groundwork** *n* base *f*. *v* (*aircraft*) retenir

au sol; fonder; (*ship*) s'échouer. **groundless** *adj* sans fond.

group [gruːp] *n* groupe *m*. *v* (se) grouper.

grouse¹ [graus] *n* grouse *f*.

grouse² [graus] (*coll*) *v* rouspéter. *n* grief *m*.

grove [grouv] *n* bocage *m*.

grovel ['grovl] *v* ramper.

*****grow** [grou] *v* pousser; grandir; (*become*) devenir; cultiver. **grown-up** *n*(*m+f*). *adj* adulte. **growth** *n* croissance *f*; (*thing grown*) pousse *f*; (*med*) grosseur *f*.

growl [graul] *v* grogner. *n* grognement *m*.

grown [groun] *V* grow.

grub [grʌb] *n* larve *f*; (*slang: food*) bouffe *f*. **grubby** *adj* sale.

grudge [grʌdʒ] *v* donner à contre-cœur. *n* rancune *f*. **bear a grudge against** en vouloir à. **grudgingly** *adv* de mauvaise grâce.

gruelling ['gruəliŋ] *adj* exténuant.

gruesome ['gruːsəm] *adj* horrible.

gruff [grʌf] *adj* bourru.

grumble ['grʌmbl] *v* grommeler. *n* grognement *m*.

grumpy ['grʌmpi] *adj* maussade.

grunt [grʌnt] *v* grogner. *n* grognement *m*.

guarantee [garən'tiː] *n* garantie *f*. *v* garantir. **guarantor** *n* garant, -e *m*, *f*.

guard [gaːd] *n* garde *f*; (*rail*) chef de train *m*. **guard dog** chien de garde *m*. **guard's van** fourgon *m*. *v* garder; défendre. **guarded** *adj* (*remark, etc.*) prudent. **guardian** *n* gardien, -enne *m*, *f*; (*of child*) tuteur, -trice *m*, *f*. **guardian angel** ange gardien *m*.

Guernsey ['gəːnzi] *n* Guernesey *m*.

guerrilla [gə'rilə] *n* guérillero *m*. **guerrilla warfare** guérilla *f*.

guess [ges] *n* conjecture *f*. **at a guess** au jugé. **guesswork** *n* conjecture *f*. *v* deviner; estimer; supposer; (*believe*) croire.

guest [gest] *n* invité, -e *m*, *f*; (*hotel*) client, -e *m*, *f*. **guesthouse** *n* pension de famille *f*. **guest room** chambre d'ami *f*.

guide [gaid] *n* guide *m*; manuel *m*; (*girl*) éclaireuse *f*. **guidebook** *n* guide *m*. **guide dog** chien d'aveugle *m*. *v* guider. **guidance** *n* conseils *m pl*. **guided** *adj* (*missile*) téléguidé. **guided tour** visite guidée *f*.

guild [gild] *n* confrérie *f*; (*craftsmen, etc.*) guilde *f*.

guillotine ['gilətiːn] *n* (*beheading*) guillotine *f*; (*paper*) massicot *m*. *v* guillotiner; massicoter.

guilt [gilt] *n* culpabilité *f.* **guilty** *adj* coupable.

Guinea ['gini] *n* Guinée *f.*

guinea pig *n* cochon d'Inde *m;* (*for experiment*) cobaye *m.*

guitar [gi'ta:] *n* guitare *f.* **guitarist** *n* guitariste *m, f.*

gulf [gʌlf] *n* golfe *m;* (*abyss*) gouffre *m.*

gull [gʌl] *n* mouette *f.*

gullet ['gʌlit] *n* œsophage *m;* (*throat*) gosier *m.*

gullible ['gʌləbl] *adj* crédule. **gullibility** *n* crédulité *f.*

gully ['gʌli] *n* ravine *f.*

gulp [gʌlp] *v* avaler; (*food*) engloutir; (*drink*) lamper. *n* (*food*) bouchée *f;* (*drink*) gorgée *f;* (*action*) coup (de gosier) *m.*

gum[1] [gʌm] *n* (*glue*) gomme *f.* **gumboots** *pl n* bottes de caoutchouc *f pl.* *v* gommer.

gum[2] [gʌm] *n* (*mouth*) gencive *f.*

gun [gʌn] *n* pistolet *m;* (*rifle*) fusil *m.* **gunfire** *n* fusillade *f.* **gunman** *n* bandit armé *m.* **gunpowder** *n* poudre à canon *f.* **gunrunning** *n* contrebande d'armes *f.* **gunshot wound** blessure de balle *f.*

gurgle ['gə:gl] *v* gargouillis *m.* *v* gargouiller.

gush [gʌʃ] *v* jaillir. *n* jaillissement *m.* **gushing** *adj* (*person*) trop exubérant.

gust [gʌst] *n* (*wind*) rafale *f;* (*smoke*) bouffée *f;* (*laughter*) éclat *m.* *v* souffler en bourrasque.

gut [gʌt] *n* (*anat*) boyau *m.* **guts** *pl n* (*coll*) cran *m sing.* *v* vider.

gutter ['gʌtə] *n* (*roof*) gouttière *f;* (*street*) caniveau *m.*

guy[1] [gai] *n* (*coll*) type *m.*

guy[2] [gai] *n* (*rope*) corde de tente *f.*

gymnasium [dʒim'neiziəm] *n* gymnase *m.* **gymnast** *n* gymnaste *m, f.* **gymnastic** *adj* gymnastique. **gymnastics** *n* gymnastique *f.*

gynaecology [gainə'kolədʒi] *n* gynécologie *f.* **gynaecological** *adj* gynécologique. **gynaecologist** *n* gynécologue *m, f.*

gypsum ['dʒipsəm] *n* gypse *m.*

gyrate [,dʒai'reit] *v* tournoyer. **gyration** *n* giration *f.*

gyroscope ['dʒairə,skoup] *n* gyroscope *m.*

H

haberdasher ['habədaʃə] *n* mercier, -ère *m, f.* **haberdashery** *n* mercerie *f.*

habit ['habit] *n* habitude *f;* (*clothes*) habit *m.* **habitual** *adj* habituel.

habitable ['habitəbl] *adj* habitable.

habitat ['habitat] *n* habitat *m.*

hack[1] [hak] *v* hacher, tailler. *n* entaille *f.* **hacksaw** *n* scie à métaux *f.*

hack[2] [hak] *n* (*horse*) cheval de selle *m;* (*writer*) nègre *m.*

hackneyed ['haknid] *adj* usé, rebattu.

had [had] *V* have.

haddock ['hadək] *n* églefin *m.*

haemorrhage ['heməridʒ] *n* hémorragie *f.*

haemorrhoids ['hemərɔidz] *pl n* hémorroïdes *f pl.*

hag [hag] *n* (*coll*) chameau *m.*

haggard ['hagəd] *adj* hagard.

haggle ['hagl] *v* marchander, chicaner. **haggling** *n* marchandage *m.*

Hague [heig] *n* **The Hague** La Haye.

hail[1] [heil] *n* grêle *f.* **hailstone** *n* grêlon *m.* *v* grêler.

hail[2] [heil] *v* saluer; (*taxi*) héler. **hail from** être originaire de.

hair [heə] *n* cheveux *m pl;* (*single strand*) cheveu *m;* (*of body, animal*) poil *m;* (*animal coat*) pelage *m.* **hairy** *adj* velu; (*person*) hirsute.

hairbrush ['heəbrʌʃ] *n* brosse à cheveux *f.*

haircut ['heəkʌt] *n* coupe *f.* **have a haircut** se faire couper les cheveux.

hairdresser ['heə,dresə] *n* coiffeur, -euse *m, f.* **hairdresser's** *n* salon de coiffure *m.* **hairdressing** *n* coiffure *f.*

hair-dryer ['heə,draiə] *n* sèche-cheveux *m.*

hairnet ['heənet] *n* filet à cheveux *m.*

hair-piece ['heə,pi:s] *n* postiche *m.*

hairpin ['heəpin] *n* épingle à cheveux *f.* **hairpin bend** virage en épingle à cheveux *m.*

hair-raising ['heə,reiziŋ] *adj* horrifique.

hair spray *n* laque *f.*

hairstyle ['heəstail] *n* coiffure *f.*

Haiti ['heiti] *n* Haïti *f.*

hake [heik] *n* colin *m.*

half [ha:f] *n* moitié *f;* demi, -e *m, f.* **go halves** se mettre de moitié. **in half** en deux. *adj* demi. *adv* à moitié, à demi.

half-and-half *adv* moitié-moitié.

half-baked [,haɪf'beɪkt] (coll) adj (idea) à la noix; (person) mal dégrossi.

half-breed ['haɪfbriːd] n (person) métis, -isse m, f; (horse) demi-sang m invar.

half-hearted [,haɪf'haɪtɪd] adj (person) sans enthousiasme; (attempt) sans conviction.

half-hour [haɪf'auə] n demi-heure f.

half-mast [,haɪf'maɪst] n at half-mast en berne.

half-open [,haɪf'oupən] adj entrouvert.

half-price [haɪf'praɪs] adj, adv demi-tarif; à moitié prix.

half-term [,haɪf'tɜːm] n congé de demi-trimestre m.

half-time [,haɪf'taɪm] adv, adj à mi-temps.

halfway [,haɪf'weɪ] adj à mi-chemin. **meet halfway** (compromise) couper la poire en deux.

half-wit ['haɪfwɪt] n idiot, -e m, f.

halibut ['halɪbət] n flétan m.

hall [hɔːl] n vestibule m; (room) salle f; (corridor) couloir m.

hallmark ['hɔːlmaɪk] n poinçon m; (of genius, etc.) sceau m. v poinçonner.

hallowed ['haloud] adj saint, sanctifié.

Halloween [halou'iːn] n veille de la Toussaint f.

hallucination [hə,luːsɪ'neɪʃən] n hallucination f.

halo ['heɪlou] n auréole f; (astron) halo m.

halt [hɔːlt] n halte f. v faire halte; (car, etc.) faire arrêter; interrompre.

halter ['hɔːltə] n licou m.

halve [haɪv] v diviser en deux; réduire de moitié.

ham [ham] n jambon m.

hamburger ['hambɜːgə] n hamburger m.

hammer ['hamə] n marteau m. v marteler. **hammer in** enfoncer. **hammer out** (disputes, etc.) démêler.

hammock ['hamək] n hamac m.

hamper¹ ['hampə] v gêner.

hamper² ['hampə] n panier m.

hamster ['hamstə] n hamster m.

hand [hand] n main f; (worker) travailleur, -euse m, f; (clock) aiguille f; (measure) paume f; (coll: assistance) coup de main m. **by hand** à la main. **keep one's hand in** garder la main. **on the other hand** par contre. **to hand** sous la main. v passer. **hand down** transmettre. **hand in** remettre. **hand over** céder. **handful** n poignée f.

handbag ['handbag] n sac à main m.

handbook ['handbuk] n manuel m; guide m.

handbrake ['handbreɪk] n frein à main m.

handcuff ['handkʌf] v mettre les menottes à. **handcuffs** pl n menottes f pl.

handicap ['handɪkap] n handicap m. v handicaper.

handicraft ['handɪkraɪft] n artisanat m.

handiwork ['handɪwɜːk] n œuvre f, ouvrage m.

handkerchief ['haŋkətʃɪf] n mouchoir m.

handle ['handl] n (broom, etc.) manche m; (door, drawer) poignée f; (basket) anse f. v manier; (control) manœuvrer. **handlebars** pl n guidon m sing.

handmade [,hand'meɪd] adj fait main.

hand-out ['handaut] n (leaflet) prospectus m; charité f. v **hand out** distribuer.

hand-pick [hand'pik] v trier sur le volet.

handrail ['handreɪl] n rampe f.

handshake ['handʃeɪk] n poignée de main f.

handsome ['hansəm] adj beau, belle.

handstand ['hand,stand] n **do a handstand** faire l'arbre droit.

handwriting ['hand,raɪtɪŋ] n écriture f. **handwritten** adj manuscrit.

handy ['handi] adj (useful) commode; accessible; (to hand) sous la main; adroit.

*****hang** [haŋ] v pendre; (picture, etc.) accrocher. **hang around** rôder. **hang fire** traîner en longueur. **hang-gliding** n vol libre m. **hangman** n bourreau m. **hang on** (coll: wait) attendre; (hold out) tenir bon; dépendre de. **hangover** n (slang) gueule de bois f. **hang up** accrocher; (phone) raccrocher. **hang-up** n (coll) complexe m.

hanger n cintre m.

hangar ['haŋə] n hangar m.

hanker ['haŋkə] v **hanker for** or **after** aspirer à. **hankering** n envie f.

haphazard [,hap'hazəd] adj (fait) au petit bonheur.

happen ['hapən] v arriver, se passer. **happening** n événement m.

happy ['hapi] adj heureux. **happy birthday/Christmas!** joyeux anniversaire/Noël! **happy-go-lucky** adj insouciant. **happily** adv tranquillement; joyeusement. **happiness** n bonheur m.

harass ['harəs] v harceler.

harbour ['haɪbə] n port m. v héberger; (hope, suspicions, etc.) entretenir.

hard [haɪd] *adj* dur; difficile. *adv* fort,
ferme. **hard-and-fast** *adj* (*rule*) absolu;
inflexible. **hardback** *n* livre relié m. **hard-
boiled** *adj* (*egg*) dur. **hard-hearted** *adj*
impitoyable. **hard up** (*coll*) fauché. **hardware** *n* (*ironmongery*) quincaillerie f;
(*computers*) hardware m. **try hard** faire
un gros effort. **work hard** travailler dur.
harden *v* durcir. **hardness** *n* dureté f; difficulté f. **hardship** *n* épreuves f pl; privation f.

hardly ['haɪdli] *adv* à peine.

hardy ['haɪdi] *adj* robuste; (*plant*) résistant au gel; (*bold*) hardi.

hare [heə] *n* lièvre m. **hare-brained** *adj*
(*person*) écervelé; (*scheme*) insensé. **hare-
lip** *n* bec-de-lièvre m.

haricot ['harikou] *n* haricot blanc m.

harm [haɪm] *n* mal m. *v* faire du mal à.
harmful *adj* nuisible. **harmless** *adj* innocent; pas méchant.

harmonic [haɪˈmɔnik] *nm*. *adj*
harmonique.

harmonica [haɪˈmɔnikə] *n* harmonica m.

harmonize ['haɪmɔnaiz] *v* (s')harmoniser.

harmony ['haɪmɔni] *n* harmonie f. **harmonious** *adj* harmonieux.

harness ['haɪnis] *n* harnais m. *v*
harnacher; (*power, etc.*) exploiter.

harp [haɪp] *n* harpe f. **harpist** *n* harpiste
m, f.

harpoon [haɪˈpuɪn] *n* harpon m. *v* harpon-
ner.

harpsichord ['haɪpsiˌkɔɪd] *n* clavecin m.

harrowing ['harouiŋ] *adj* poignant; (*cry*)
déchirant.

harsh [haɪʃ] *adj* dur; (*texture*) rêche,
rugueux; (*sound*) discordant, criard.
harshness *n* dureté f; rugosité f; discor-
dance f.

harvest ['haɪvist] *n* moisson f; (*fruit*)
récolte f; (*grapes*) vendange f. *v* moissonner; récolter; vendanger.

has [haz] *V* **have**.

hash [haʃ] *n* (*food*) hachis m; (*coll: mess*)
gâchis m.

hashish ['haʃiːʃ] *n* haschich m.

haste [heist] *n* hâte f. **hasten** *v* (se) hâter.
hastily *adv* en hâte; sans réfléchir. **hasty**
adj hâtif; rapide.

hat [hat] *n* chapeau m.

hatch¹ [hatʃ] *v* (faire) éclore; (*plot*) ourdir.

hatch² [hatʃ] *n* (*canteen*) passe-plats m
invar; (*naut*) écoutille f. **hatchback** *adj*
(*car*) avec hayon arrière m.

hatchet ['hatʃit] *n* hachette f.

hate [heit] *v* haïr, détester. *n also* **hatred**
haine f. **pet hate** (*coll*) bête noire f. **hate-
ful** *adj* haïssable. odieux.

haughty ['hɔɪti] *adj* hautain. **haughtiness** *n*
hauteur f.

haul [hɔɪl] *v* traîner; (*naut*) haler. *n* (*fish*)
prise f; (*stolen goods*) butin m. **haulage** *n*
(*transport*) roulage m; (*naut*) halage m.

haunch [hɔɪntʃ] *n* hanche f. **haunches** *pl n*
derrière m *sing*.

haunt [hɔɪnt] *v* hanter. *n* repaire m.
haunting *adj* obsédant.

***have** [hav] *v* avoir; (*meal*) prendre;
(*cause to be*) faire. **have on** (*wear*) porter;
(*coll: tease*) faire marcher. **have to**
devoir, être obligé de.

haven ['heivn] *n* havre m.

haversack ['havəsak] *n* havresac m, sac à
dos m.

havoc ['havək] *n* ravages m pl. **play havoc
with** désorganiser complètement.

hawk [hɔɪk] *n* faucon m.

hawthorn ['hɔɪθɔɪn] *n* aubépine f.

hay [hei] *n* foin m. **go haywire** (*plans*) mal
tourner; (*machine*) se détraquer. **hay
fever** rhume des foins m. **haystack** *n*
meule de foin f.

hazard ['hazəd] *n* risque m; (*chance*)
hasard m. *v* hasarder, risquer. **hazardous**
adj hasardeux, risqué.

haze [heiz] *n* brume f. **hazy** *adj* brumeux;
vague.

hazel ['heizl] *n* noisetier m. **hazel-nut** *n*
noisette f. *adj* (*colour*) noisette *invar*.

he [hiː] *pron* il; (*emphatic*) lui. **he who**
celui qui. *n* (*coll*) mâle m.

head [hed] *n* tête f; (*leader*) chef m; (*coin*)
face f. *adj* principal. *v* se diriger; venir en
tête de; intituler. **headed** *adj* (*paper*) à
en-tête. **heading** *n* titre m. **heady** *adj*
capiteux.

headache ['hedeik] *n* mal de tête m. **have
a headache** avoir mal à la tête.

headfirst [ˌhedˈfəɪst] *adv* la tête la première.

headlamp ['hedlamp] *n also* **headlight**
(*mot*) phare m.

headland ['hedlənd] *n* promontoire m.

headline ['hedlain] *n* (*newspaper*)
manchette f; (*news*) grand titre m.

headlong ['hedloŋ] *adv* la tête la première; (*rush*) à toute allure.

headmaster [ˌhedˈmɑːstə] n directeur m. **headmistress** n directrice f.

head-on adj, adv de plein fouet.

headphones [ˈhedfəunz] n casque m sing.

headquarters [ˌhedˈkwɔːtəz] n bureau principal m.

headrest [ˈhedrest] n appui-tête m.

headscarf [ˈhedskɑːf] n foulard m.

headstrong [ˈhedstrɒŋ] adj têtu.

headway [ˈhedwei] n progrès m.

heal [hiːl] v guérir; (wound) (se) cicatriser.

health [helθ] n santé f. **health foods** aliments naturels m pl. **healthy** adj sain, en bonne santé; (appetite) robuste.

heap [hiːp] n tas m. v entasser, empiler.

*****hear** [hiə] v entendre. **hear from** avoir des nouvelles de. **hear of** entendre parler de. **hearing** n (sense) ouïe f; audition f. **hearing aid** appareil acoustique m. **hearsay** n oui-dire m invar.

heard [hɜːd] V **hear**.

hearse [hɜːs] n corbillard m.

heart [hɑːt] n cœur m. **by heart** par cœur. **set one's heart on** vouloir à tout prix. **to one's heart's content** tout son content. **hearten** v encourager. **heartless** adj cruel. **hearty** adj (welcome, etc.) chaleureux; (meal) copieux.

heart attack n crise cardiaque f.

heartbeat [ˈhɑːtbiːt] n battement de cœur m.

heart-breaking [ˈhɑːtbreikiŋ] adj navrant. **heart-broken** adj navré.

heartburn [ˈhɑːtbɜːn] n brûlures d'estomac f pl.

heart failure n arrêt du cœur m.

heartfelt [ˈhɑːtfelt] adj sincère.

hearth [hɑːθ] n foyer m. **hearthrug** n devant de foyer m.

heart-throb [ˈhɑːtθrɒb] n (coll) idole f.

heart-to-heart adj, adv à cœur ouvert. n **have a heart-to-heart** parler à cœur ouvert.

heartwarming [ˈhɑːtwɔːmiŋ] adj réconfortant.

heat [hiːt] n chaleur f; (sport) épreuve éliminatoire f. **heatwave** n vague de chaleur f. v chauffer. **heated** adj chauffé; (argument) passionné. **heater** n appareil de chauffage m. **heating** n chauffage m.

heath [hiːθ] n lande f.

heathen [ˈhiːðən] n, adj païen, -enne.

heather [ˈheðə] n bruyère f.

heave [hiːv] v (lift) lever avec effort; (pull) tirer avec effort; (sea) se soulever; (sigh) pousser; (retch) avoir des haut-le-cœur. n (sea) houle f; haut-le-cœur m invar; effort m.

heaven [ˈhevn] n ciel m. **heavenly** adj céleste; (excellent) divin.

heavy [ˈhevi] adj lourd; (rain) fort; (cold) gros, grosse. **heavyweight** nm, adj poids lourd. **heaviness** n lourdeur f.

Hebrew [ˈhiːbruː] n (people) Hébreu m, (language) hébreu m. adj hébreu, hébraïque.

heckle [ˈhekl] v chahuter; interrompre. **heckler** n interrupteur, -trice m, f. **heckling** n interpellations f pl.

hectare [ˈhektɑː] n hectare m.

hectic [ˈhektik] adj mouvementé, très bousculé.

hedge [hedʒ] n haie f. v entourer d'une haie; (be evasive) répondre à côté; (bet) couvrir.

hedgehog [ˈhedʒhɒg] n hérisson m.

heed [hiːd] v faire attention à. n attention f. **heedless** adj étourdi, insouciant.

heel [hiːl] n talon m. v (shoe) remettre un talon à.

hefty [ˈhefti] adj (person) costaud; (heavy) lourd; (large) gros, grosse.

heifer [ˈhefə] n génisse f.

height [hait] n hauteur f; (person) taille f; (aircraft) altitude f; (of success, etc.) sommet m, point culminant m. **heighten** v augmenter; (make higher) relever.

heir [eə] n héritier m. **heiress** n héritière f. **heirloom** n héritage m.

held [held] V **hold**.

helicopter [ˈhelikɒptə] n hélicoptère m.

hell [hel] n enfer m. **go to hell!** (impol) va te faire voir! **hell for leather** au triple galop. **hellish** adj infernal.

hello [həˈləu] interj bonjour! (coll) salut! (phone) allô!

helm [helm] n barre f. **be at the helm** tenir la barre.

helmet [ˈhelmit] n casque m.

help [help] n aide f, secours m. interj au secours! v aider; (at meal, etc.) servir; (prevent oneself from) s'empêcher de. **can I help you?** (in shop) vous désirez? **help yourself!** servez-vous! **it can't be helped!** tant pis! **helper** n aide m, f. **helpful** adj utile, efficace. **helping** n portion f. **helpless** adj impuissant.

Helsinki [ˈhelsiŋki] n Helsinki.

hem [hem] n ourlet m. v ourler.

hemisphere ['hemi,sfiə] n hémisphère m.

hemp [hemp] n (plant) chanvre m; (drug) haschich m.

hen [hen] n poule f; femelle f. **henhouse** n poulailler m. **hen party** réunion de femmes f. **henpecked** adj mené par le bout du nez.

hence [hens] adv (therefore) d'où; (from now) d'ici. **henceforth** adv désormais.

henna ['henə] n henné m.

her [həː] pron elle; (direct object) la; (indirect object) lui. adj son, sa; (pl) ses.

herald ['herəld] n héraut m. v annoncer. **heraldic** adj héraldique. **heraldry** n héraldique f.

herb [həːb] n herbe f. **herbal** adj d'herbes.

herd [həːd] n troupeau m. v mener. **herd together** s'attrouper.

here [hiə] adv ici. **hereafter** adv ci-après. **here and now** en ce moment même. **here and there** ça et là. **here goes!** allons-y! **here is/are** voici. **here, there, and everywhere** un peu partout.

hereditary [hi'redətəri] adj héréditaire. **heredity** [hi'redəti] n hérédité f.

heresy ['herəsi] n hérésie f. **heretic** n hérétique m, f. **heretical** adj hérétique.

heritage ['heritidʒ] n héritage m.

hermit ['həːmit] n ermite m.

hernia ['həːniə] n hernie f.

hero ['hiərou] n héros m. **heroine** n héroïne f. **hero-worship** n culte du héros m. **heroic** adj héroïque. **heroism** n héroïsme m.

heroin ['herouin] n héroïne f.

heron ['herən] n héron m.

herring ['heriŋ] n hareng m.

hers [həːz] pron le sien, la sienne.

herself [həː'self] pron se; (emphatic) elle-même. **by herself** toute seule.

hesitate ['heziteit] v hésiter. **hesitant** adj hésitant. **hesitation** n hésitation f.

heterosexual [hetərə'seksʃuəl] n, adj hétérosexuel, -elle.

hexagon ['heksəgən] n hexagone m. **hexagonal** adj hexagonal.

heyday ['heidei] n (of person) apogée m; (of thing) âge d'or m.

hiatus [hai'eitəs] n lacune f.

hibernate ['haibəneit] v hiberner. **hibernation** n hibernation f.

hiccup ['hikʌp] n hoquet m. **have hiccups** avoir le hoquet. v hoqueter.

hid [hid] V **hide**[1].

*****hide**[1] [haid] v see cacher. **hide-and-seek** n cache-cache m. **hide-out** n cachette f.

hide[2] [haid] n peau f; (leather) cuir m.

hidden ['hidn] V **hide**[1].

hideous ['hidiəs] adj hideux.

hiding[1] ['haidiŋ] n **be in hiding** se tenir caché. **go into hiding** se cacher. **hiding place** cachette f.

hiding[2] ['haidiŋ] n (beating) correction f.

hierarchy ['haiərɑːki] n hiérarchie f. **hierarchical** adj hiérarchique.

hi-fi ['hai,fai] n hi-fi f invar; (system) chaîne hi-fi f.

high [hai] adj haut; (speed) grand; (price, etc.) élevé. adv (en) haut. **highly** adv (very) fort; (recommend) chaudement.

highbrow ['haibrau] n, adj intellectuel, -elle.

high chair n chaise haute f.

high-frequency [,hai'friːkwənsi] adj de haute fréquence.

high-heeled [,hai'hiːld] adj à hauts talons.

high jump n saut en hauteur m.

highland ['hailənd] n région montagneuse f. **the Highlands** (Scotland) les Highlands m pl.

highlight ['hailait] v mettre en lumière. n (art) rehaut m; (hair) reflet m; (of evening, etc.) clou m.

Highness ['hainis] n Altesse f.

high-pitched [,hai'pitʃd] adj aigu, -uë.

high-rise block n tour f.

high-speed [,hai'spiːd] adj ultra-rapide.

high-spirited [,hai'spiritid] adj plein d'entrain. **high spirits** entrain m.

high street n rue principale f.

highway ['haiwei] n grande route f; voie publique f. **highway code** code de la route m. **highwayman** n voleur de grand chemin m.

hijack ['haidʒak] v détourner. n détournement m.

hike [haik] n excursion à pied f. v excursionner à pied. **hiker** n excursionniste à pied m, f. **hiking** n randonnées à pied f pl.

hilarious [hi'leəriəs] adj (merry) hilare; (funny) désopilant. **hilarity** n hilarité f.

hill [hil] n colline f; (slope) côte f. **hillside** n flanc de coteau m. **hilly** adj accidenté.

him [him] pron lui; (direct object) le.

himself [him'self] pron se; (emphatic) lui-même. **by himself** tout seul.

hind [haind] *adj* postérieur, -e; de derrière. **hindsight** *n* sagesse rétrospective *f*.
hinder ['hində] *v* gêner, entraver. **hindrance** *n* gêne *f*, entrave *f*.
Hindu [hin'du:] *n* Hindou, -e *m, f*. *adj* hindou. **Hinduism** *n* hindouisme *m*.
hinge [hindʒ] *n* charnière *f*; (*door*) gond *m*. *v* **hinge on** dépendre de.
hint [hint] *n* allusion *f*; (*tip*) conseil *m*; (*trace*) nuance *f*. *v* laisser entendre, insinuer.
hip [hip] *n* hanche *f*.
hippopotamus [hipə'potəməs] *n* hippopotame *m*.
hire [haiə] *v* louer; (*person*) engager. **hire out** louer. *n* location *f*; (*boat*) louage *m*. **for hire** à louer. **hire purchase** achat à crédit *m*.
his [hiz] *adj* son, sa; (*pl*) ses. *pron* le sien, la sienne.
hiss [his] *v* siffler. *n* sifflement *m*.
history ['histəri] *n* histoire *f*. **historian** *n* historien, -enne *m, f*. **historic** *adj* historique.
*hit [hit] *n* coup *m*; succès *m*. coup réussi *m*; (*slang*: *song*) tube *m*. *v* frapper; (*bump*) (se) heurter; (*reach*) atteindre. **hit-or-miss** *adj* au petit bonheur.
hitch [hitʃ] *n* (*obstacle*) anicroche *f*. *v* (*lift*) remonter; (*fasten*) accrocher. **hitch-hike** *v* faire de l'auto stop. **hitch-hiker** *n* auto-stoppeur, -euse *m, f*. **hitch-hiking** *n* auto-stop *m*.
hitherto [hiðə'tu:] *adv* jusqu'ici.
hive [haiv] *n* ruche *f*.
hoard [hɔːd] *n* réserve *f*; trésor *m*. *v* amasser.
hoarding ['hɔːdiŋ] *n* (*advertising*) panneau d'affichage *m*; (*fence*) palissade *f*.
hoarse [hɔːs] *adj* enroué, rauque. **hoarsely** *adv* d'une voix rauque. **hoarseness** *n* enrouement *m*.
hoax [houks] *n* canular *m*.
hobble ['hobl] *v* clopiner; (*horse*) entraver.
hobby ['hobi] *n* passe-temps *m*.
hock¹ [hok] *n* jarret *m*.
hock² [hok] *n* vin du Rhin *m*.
hockey ['hoki] *n* hockey *m*. **hockey stick** crosse de hockey *f*.
hoe [hou] *n* houe *f*. *v* biner.
hog [hog] *n* porc *m*. *v* (*coll*) accaparer, monopoliser.
hoist [hoist] *v* hisser. *n* treuil *m*; (*for goods*) monte-charge *m invar*.

*hold¹ [hould] *n* prise *f*; influence *f*. **get hold of** saisir. *v* tenir; contenir; (*have*) avoir. **holdall** *n* fourre-tout *m invar*. **hold back** (se) retenir. **hold forth** pérorer. **hold on** (*wait*) attendre; maintenir en place; (*grip*) tenir bon. **hold out** tendre; (*resist*) tenir bon. **hold up** (*raise*) lever; (*support*) soutenir; (*delay*) retarder. **hold-up** *n* retard *m*; (*traffic*) bouchon *m*; (*robbery*) hold-up *m invar*. **holder** *n* (*person*) détenteur, -trice *m, f*; (*for object*) support *m*.
hold² [hould] *n* (*naut*) cale *f*.
hole [houl] *n* trou *m*; (*rabbit*) terrier *m*. *v* (se) trouer.
holiday ['holədi] *n* vacances *f pl*; (*day off*) jour de congé *m*. **holiday-maker** *n* vacancier, -ère *m, f*. **holiday resort** villégiature *f*.
Holland ['holənd] *n* Hollande *f*.
hollow ['holou] *adj, adv* creux. *n* creux *m*; (*in ground*) dépression *f*. *v* creuser.
holly ['holi] *n* houx *m*. **hollyhock** *n* rose trémière *f*.
holster ['houlstə] *n* étui de revolver *m*.
holy ['houli] *adj* saint. **holiness** *n* sainteté *m*.
homage ['homidʒ] *n* hommage *m*. **pay homage to** rendre hommage à.
home [houm] *n* maison *f*, foyer *m*. **at home** chez soi. **make oneself at home** faire comme chez soi. *adv* à la maison; (*right in*) à fond. **go home** rentrer. *adj* familial; domestique; (*not foreign*) intérieur, -e, national. **homeless** *adj* sans abri.
homely *adj* simple, confortable; (*US*: *ugly*) laid.
home address *n* domicile permanent *m*; adresse personnelle *f*.
homecoming ['houm.kʌmiŋ] *n* retour *m*.
home-grown [houm'groun] *adj* du jardin.
home help *n* aide ménagère *f*.
homeland ['houmland] *n* patrie *f*.
home-made [houm'meid] *adj* fait à la maison.
Home Office *n* ministère de l'Intérieur *m*.
home rule *n* autonomie *f*.
homesick ['houmsik] *adj* nostalgique. **homesickness** *n* mal du pays *m*; nostalgie *f*.
homework ['houmwə:k] *n* devoirs *m pl*.
homicide ['homisaid] *n* homicide *m*. **homicidal** *adj* homicide.

homogeneous [homə'dʒiːniəs] *adj* homogène.

homosexual [homə'sekʃuəl] *n, adj* homosexuel, -elle. **homosexuality** *n* homosexualité *f*.

honest ['onist] *adj* honnête; sincère; franc, franche. **honesty** *n* honnêteté *f*; sincérité *f*.

honey ['hʌni] *n* miel *m*. **honeycomb** *n* rayon de miel *m*. **honeymoon** *n* lune de miel *f*. **honeysuckle** *n* chèvrefeuille *m*.

honour ['onə] *n* honneur *m*. *v* honorer. **honorary** *adj* honoraire. **honourable** *adj* honorable.

hood [hud] *n* capuchon *m*; (*car roof*) capote *f*; (*US: car bonnet*) capot *m*.

hoof [huːf] *n* sabot *m*.

hook [huk] *n* crochet *m*; (*on dress*) agrafe *f*; (*fishing*) hameçon *m*. *v* accrocher; agrafer; (*fishing*) prendre. **hooked** *adj* crochu.

hooligan ['huːligən] *n* voyou *m*. **hooliganism** *n* vandalisme *m*.

hoop [huːp] *n* cerceau *m*; (*for barrel*) cercle *m*.

hoot [huːt] *v* (*owl*) hululer; (*car*) klaxonner; (*boo*) huer. *n* hululement *m*; coup de klaxon *m*; huée *f*. **hooter** *n* klaxon *m*; (*factory*) sirène *f*.

hop[1] [hop] *v* sauter à cloche-pied; (*jump*) sauter, sautiller. *n* saut *m*, sautillement *m*; (*coll: dance*) sauterie *f*.

hop[2] [hop] *n* (*bot*) houblon *m*.

hope [houp] *n* espoir *m*. *v* espérer. **hopeful** *adj* plein d'espoir; encourageant. **hopeless** *adj* désespéré; (*coll: bad*) nul.

horde [hoːd] *n* horde *f*.

horizon [hə'raizn] *n* horizon *m*.

horizontal [hori'zontl] *adj* horizontal. *n* horizontale *f*.

hormone ['hoːmoun] *n* hormone *f*.

horn [hoːn] *n* corne *f*; (*music*) cor *m*; (*car, etc.*) klaxon *m*.

hornet ['hoːnit] *n* frelon *m*.

horoscope ['horəskoup] *n* horoscope *m*.

horrible ['horibl] *adj* horrible, affreux.

horrid ['horid] *adj* méchant, vilain.

horrify ['horifai] *v* horrifier. **horrific** *adj* horrifique.

horror ['horə] *n* horreur *f*. *adj* (*story, film, etc.*) d'épouvante.

horse [hoːs] *n* cheval *m*.

horseback ['hoːsbak] *n* **on horseback** à cheval.

horse-box ['hoːsboks] *n* fourgon à chevaux *m*.

horse chestnut *n* (*nut*) marron d'Inde *m*; (*tree*) marronnier d'Inde *m*.

horse-drawn ['hoːsdroːn] *adj* à chevaux.

horsefly ['hoːsflai] *n* taon *m*.

horsehair ['hoːsheə] *n* crin *m*.

horseman ['hoːsmən] *n* cavalier *m*.

horsepower ['hoːs,pauə] *n* cheval-vapeur *m*.

horseradish ['hoːs,radiʃ] *n* raifort *m*.

horseshoe ['hoːʃʃuː] *n* fer à cheval *m*.

horsewoman ['hoːs,wumən] *n* cavalière *f*.

horticulture ['hoːtikʌltʃə] *n* horticulture *f*. **horticultural** *adj* horticole.

hose [houz] *n* tuyau *m*; (*mot*) durite *f*; (*stockings*) bas *m pl*. *v* arroser au jet.

hosiery ['houziəri] *n* bas *m pl*; (*business*) bonneterie *f*.

hospitable [ho'spitəbl] *adj* hospitalier.

hospital ['hospitl] *n* hôpital *m*. **hospitalize** *v* hospitaliser.

hospitality [,hospi'taliti] *n* hospitalité *f*.

host[1] [houst] *n* hôte *m*. **hostess** *n* hôtesse *f*.

host[2] [houst] *n* (*crowd*) foule *f*.

hostage ['hostidʒ] *n* otage *m*.

hostel ['hostəl] *n* foyer *m*. **youth hostel** auberge de jeunesse *f*.

hostile ['hostail] *adj* hostile. **hostility** *n* hostilité *f*.

hot [hot] *adj* chaud; (*curry, etc.*) fort; (*temper*) violent. **be hot** (*person*) avoir chaud; (*weather*) faire chaud. **hot dog** hot-dog *m*. **hot-house** *n* serre *f*. **hotplate** *n* chauffe-plats *m invar*. **hot-tempered** *adj* emporté. **hot-water bottle** bouillotte *f*.

hotel [hou'tel] *n* hôtel *m*.

hound [haund] *n* chien de meute *m*. *v* chasser, s'acharner sur.

hour ['auə] *n* heure *f*. **hourglass** *n* sablier *m*. **hourly** *adj, adv* toutes les heures.

house [*n* haus; *v* hauz] *n* maison *f*; (*theatre*) salle *f*. *v* loger.

houseboat ['hausbout] *n* péniche aménagée *f*.

housebound ['hausbaund] *adj* confiné chez soi.

housecoat ['hauskout] *n* peignoir *m*.

household ['haushould] *n* maison *f*, ménage *m*.

housekeeper ['haus,kiːpə] *n* gouvernante *f*. **housekeeping** *n* (*work*) ménage *m*; (*money*) argent du ménage *m*.

housemaid ['hausmeid] *n* bonne *f.*
house-to-house *adj, adv* porte à porte.
house-trained ['haustreind] *adj* propre.
house-warming ['haus,wɔːmiŋ] *n* **have a house-warming (party)** pendre la crémaillère.
housewife ['hauswaif] *n* ménagère *f.*
housework ['hauswɔːk] *n* ménage *m.*
housing ['hauziŋ] *n* logement *m.* **housing estate** cité *f.*
hovel ['hɔvəl] *n* taudis *m.*
hover ['hɔvə] *v* planer; (*person*) rôder. **hovercraft** *n* aéroglisseur *m.*
how [hau] *adv* comment, comme. **how are you?** comment allez-vous? **how do you do?** bonjour; (*on introduction*) enchanté. **how much?** combien?
however [hau'evə] *conj* cependant. *adv* de quelque manière que.
howl [haul] *v* hurler. *n* hurlement *m.*
hub [hʌb] *n* moyeu *m*; pivot *m.* **hubcap** *n* (*mot*) enjoliveur *m.*
huddle ['hʌdl] *v* se blottir. *n* petit groupe *m.*
hue [hjuː] *n* teinte *f.*
huff [hʌf] *n* **in a huff** froissé.
hug [hʌg] *v* étreindre. *n* étreinte *f.*
huge [hjuːdʒ] *adj* énorme.
hulk [hʌlk] *n* épave *f*, carcasse *f*; (*derog: person*) mastodonte *m.* **hulking** *adj* balourd.
hull [hʌl] *n* (*naut*) coque *f.*
hum [hʌm] *v* bourdonner; (*tune*) fredonner; (*engine*) vrombir. *n* bourdonnement *m*; vrombissement *m.* **humming-bird** *n* oiseau-mouche *m.*
human ['hjuːmən] *nm, adj* humain. **human being** être humain *m.*
humane [hjuː'mein] *adj* humain.
humanity [hjuː'manəti] *n* humanité *f.* **humanitarian** *n(m+f), adj* humanitaire.
humble ['hʌmbl] *adj* humble. *v* humilier.
humdrum ['hʌmdrʌm] *adj* monotone.
humid ['hjuːmid] *adj* humide. **humidity** *n* humidité *f.*
humiliate [hjuː'milieit] *v* humilier. **humiliation** *n* humiliation *f.*
humility [hjuː'miləti] *n* humilité *f.*
humour ['hjuːmə] *n* humour *m*; (*mood*) humeur *f.* *v* ménager. **humorist** *n* humoriste *m, f.* **humorous** *adj* humoristique.
hump [hʌmp] *n* bosse *f.* **humpbacked** *adj* (*bridge*) en dos d'âne. *v* arrondir, voûter.

hunch [hʌntʃ] *v* arrondir, voûter. *n* pressentiment *m.* **hunchback** *n* bossu, -e *m, f.* **hunchbacked** *adj* bossu.
hundred ['hʌndrəd] *nm, adj* cent. **hundreds** *pl n* (*coll*) centaines *f pl.* **hundredth** *n(m+f), adj* centième.
hung [hʌŋ] *V* hang.
Hungary ['hʌŋgəri] *n* Hongrie *f.* **Hungarian** *nm, adj* hongrois; *n* (*people*) Hongrois, -e *m, f.*
hunger ['hʌŋgə] *n* faim *f.* *v* avoir faim. **be hungry** avoir faim. **hungrily** *adv* avidement.
hunt [hʌnt] *n* chasse *f*; (*search*) recherche *f.* *v* chasser; chercher. **hunting** *n* chasse *f.* **huntsman** *n* chasseur *m.*
hurdle ['hɔːdl] *n* obstacle *m*; (*sport*) haie *f.*
hurl [hɔːl] *v* jeter, précipiter. **hurl abuse** lancer des injures.
hurricane ['hʌrikən] *n* ouragan *m.*
hurry ['hʌri] *n* hâte *f.* **be in a hurry** être pressé. *v* (faire) se dépêcher, (se) presser. **hurried** *adj* précipité, pressé. **hurriedly** *adv* précipitamment.
*hurt [hɔːt] *v* faire mal (à), blesser. *n* mal *m.* *adj* blessé.
husband ['hʌzbənd] *n* mari *m.*
hush [hʌʃ] *n* silence *m.* *interj* chut! *v* faire taire. **hush up** (*news*) étouffer. **hushed** *adj* étouffé.
husk [hʌsk] *n* (*wheat*) balle *f*; (*rice, maize*) enveloppe *f*; (*nut*) écale *f.* *v* (*grain*) vanner; (*rice, maize*) décortiquer; écaler.
husky ['hʌski] *adj* enroué. **huskily** *adj* d'une voix rauque. **huskiness** *n* enrouement *m.*
hussar [hə'zaː] *n* hussard *m.*
hustle ['hʌsl] *v* (se) bousculer. *n* bousculade *f.* **hustle and bustle** tourbillon *m.*
hut [hʌt] *n* hutte *f.*
hutch [hʌtʃ] *n* clapier *m.*
hyacinth ['haiəsinθ] *n* jacinthe *f.*
hybrid ['haibrid] *nm, adj* hybride.
hydraulic [hai'drɔːlik] *adj* hydraulique.
hydrocarbon [,haidrou'kaːbən] *n* hydrocarbure *m.*
hydro-electric [,haidroui'lektrik] *adj* hydro-électrique.
hydrofoil ['haidroufoil] *n* hydrofoil *m.*
hydrogen ['haidrədʒən] *n* hydrogène *m.*
hyena [hai'iːnə] *n* hyène *f.*
hygiene ['haidʒiːn] *n* hygiène *f.* **hygienic** *adj* hygiénique.

hymn [him] n hymne f. **hymn-book** n livre de cantiques m.

hyphen ['haifən] n trait d'union m.

hypnosis [hip'nousis] n hypnose f. **under hypnosis** en état d'hypnose. **hypnotic** adj hypnotique. **hypnotism** n hypnotisme m. **hypnotist** n hypnotiseur, -euse m, f. **hypnotize** v hypnotiser.

hypochondria [haipə'kondriə] n hypochondrie f. **hypochondriac** n(m+f), adj hypochondriaque.

hypocrisy [hi'pokrəsi] n hypocrisie f. **hypocrite** n hypocrite m, f. **hypocritical** adj hypocrite.

hypodermic [haipə'dəːmik] adj hypodermique. n seringue hypodermique f.

hypothesis [hai'poθəsis] n, pl -ses hypothèse f. **hypothetical** adj hypothétique.

hysterectomy [histə'rektəmi] n hystérectomie f.

hysteria [his'tiəriə] n hystérie f. **hysterical** adj hystérique; (laughter, crying) convulsif. **hysterics** pl n (crying) crise de nerfs f sing; (laughter) crise de rire f sing.

I

I [ai] pron je; (emphatic) moi.

ice [ais] n glace f; (on road) verglas m. **iceberg** n iceberg m. **ice-cold** adj glacé. **ice cream** glace f. **ice cube** glaçon m. **ice rink** patinoire f. **ice-skate** n patin à glace m. **ice-skating** n patinage sur glace m. v (chill) rafraîchir; (cake) glacer. **ice over** or **up** (lake) geler; (windscreen, etc.) givrer. **iced** adj glacé; (champagne) frappé; (melon) rafraîchi. **icing** n glaçage m. **icing sugar** sucre glace m. **icy** adj glacial; (road) verglacé.

Iceland ['aislənd] n Islande f. **Icelander** n Islandais, -e m, f. **Icelandic** nm, adj. islandais.

icicle ['aisikl] n glaçon m.

icon ['aikon] n icône f.

idea [ai'diə] n idée f.

ideal [ai'diəl] nm, adj idéal. **idealist** n idéaliste m, f. **idealistic** adj idéaliste.

identical [ai'dentikəl] adj identique. identical **twins** vrais jumeaux m pl, vraies jumelles f pl.

identify [ai'dentifai] v identifier. **identify with** s'identifier à or avec. **identification** n identification f; (papers) pièce d'identité f.

identity [ai'dentiti] n identité f. **identity card** carte d'identité f. **identity parade** séance d'identification f.

ideology [aidi'olədʒi] n idéologie f.

idiom ['idiəm] n (expression) idiotisme m; (language) idiome m. **idiomatic** adj idiomatique.

idiosyncrasy [,idiə'siŋkrəsi] n particularité f.

idiot ['idiət] n idiot, -e m, f. **idiotic** adj idiot.

idle ['aidl] adj (doing nothing) désœuvré; (lazy) oisif; (machine) en repos; (talk, etc.) oiseux. v fainéanter; (engine) tourner au ralenti. **idleness** n désœuvrement m; (laziness) paresse f.

idol ['aidl] n idole f. **idolatry** n idolâtrie f. **idolize** v idolâtrer.

idyllic [i'dilik] adj idyllique.

if [if] conj si. **as if** comme si. **if not** sinon. **if so** s'il en est ainsi.

ignite [ig'nait] v (light) mettre le feu à; (catch fire) prendre feu.

ignition [ig'nifən] n ignition f; (mot) allumage m. **ignition key** clef de contact f. **ignition switch** contact m. **turn on the ignition** mettre le contact.

ignorant ['ignərənt] adj ignorant. **ignorance** n ignorance f.

ignore [ig'noː] v (remark, etc.) ne pas relever; (person) faire semblant de ne pas reconnaître; (rule) ne pas respecter.

ill [il] adj (sick) malade; (bad) mauvais, nm, adv mal. **ill-at-ease** adj mal à l'aise. **ill-bred** or **ill-mannered** adj mal élevé. **ill-gotten gains** biens mal acquis m pl. **ill-treat** v maltraiter. **illness** n maladie f.

illegal [i'liːgəl] adj illégal.

illegible [i'ledʒəbl] adj illisible.

illegitimate [ili'dʒitimit] adj illégitime. **illegitimacy** n illégitimité f.

illicit [i'lisit] adj illicite.

illiterate [i'litərit] n, adj illettré, -e. **illiteracy** n analphabétisme m.

illogical [i'lodʒikəl] adj illogique.

illuminate [i'luːmineit] v éclairer; (building) illuminer. **illumination** n éclairage m; illumination f.

illusion [i'lurʒən] *n* illusion *f*.

illustrate ['iləˌstreit] *v* illustrer. **illustration** *n* illustration *f*. **illustrator** *n* illustrateur, -trice *m, f*.

illustrious [i'lʌstriəs] *adj* illustre.

image ['imidʒ] *n* image *f*; *(public personality)* image de marque *f*; *(double)* portrait vivant *m*. **imagery** *n* images *f pl*.

imagine [i'madʒin] *v* (s')imaginer. **imaginary** *adj* imaginaire. **imagination** *n* imagination *f*. **imaginative** *adj* plein d'imagination.

imbalance [im'baləns] *n* déséquilibre *m*.

imbecile ['imbəsiːl] *n* imbécile *m, f*.

imitate ['imiˌteit] *v* imiter. **imitation** *n* imitation *f*.

immaculate [i'makjulit] *adj* impeccable; *(rel)* immaculé.

immaterial [ˌimə'tiəriəl] *adj* insignifiant, indifférent.

immature [ˌimə'tjuə] *adj* pas mûr. **be immature** *(person)* manquer de maturité. **immaturity** *n* manque de maturité *f*.

immediate [i'miːdiət] *adj* immédiat. **immediately** *adv* tout de suite; directement.

immense [i'mens] *adj* immense.

immerse [i'məːs] *v* immerger, plonger. **immersion** *n* immersion *f*. **immersion heater** chauffe-eau électrique *m invar*.

immigrate ['imiˌgreit] *v* immigrer. **immigrant** *n* immigrant, -e *m, f*. **immigration** *n* immigration *f*.

imminent ['iminənt] *adj* imminent.

immobile [i'moubail] *adj* immobile. **immobilize** *v* immobiliser.

immoral [i'morəl] *adj* immoral. **immorality** *n* immoralité *f*.

immortal [i'moːtl] *adj* immortel. **immortality** *n* immortalité *f*. **immortalize** *v* immortaliser.

immovable [i'muːvəbl] *adj* fixe; inflexible.

immune [i'mjuːn] *adj* immunisé. **immunity** *n* immunité *f*. **immunization** *n* immunisation *f*. **immunize** *v* immuniser.

imp [imp] *n* diablotin *m*.

impact ['impakt] *n* impact *m*.

impair [im'peə] *v* détériorer, abîmer.

impale [im'peil] *v* empaler.

impart [im'paːt] *v* communiquer; *(give)* donner.

impartial [im'paːʃəl] *adj* impartial. **impartiality** *n* impartialité *f*.

impasse [am'paːs] *n* impasse *f*.

impassive [im'pasiv] *adj* impassible.

impatient [im'peiʃənt] *adj* impatient. **get impatient** s'impatienter. **impatience** *n* impatience *f*.

impeach [im'piːtʃ] *v* accuser; *(question)* mettre en doute. **impeachment** *n* accusation *f*; *(US)* procédure d'impeachment *f*.

impeccable [im'pekəbl] *adj* impeccable.

impede [im'piːd] *v* empêcher, gêner.

impediment [im'pedimənt] *n* obstacle *m*. **speech impediment** défaut d'élocution *m*.

impel [im'pel] *v* pousser, obliger.

impending [im'pendiŋ] *adj* imminent; menaçant.

imperative [im'perətiv] *adj* urgent, impérieux. *n* impératif *m*.

imperfect [im'pəːfikt] *adj* imparfait; défectueux. *n* imparfait *m*.

imperial [im'piəriəl] *adj* impérial; majestueux. **imperialism** *n* impérialisme *m*.

impersonal [im'pəːsənl] *adj* impersonnel.

impersonate [im'pəːsəˌneit] *v* se faire passer pour; *(theatre)* imiter. **impersonation** *n* imitation *f*.

impertinent [im'pəːtinənt] *adj* impertinent. **impertinence** *n* impertinence *f*.

impervious [im'pəːviəs] *adj* imperméable; *(to criticism, etc.)* fermé.

impetuous [im'petjuəs] *adj* impétueux.

impetus [impətəs] *n* impulsion *f*, élan *m*.

impinge [im'pindʒ] *v* **impinge on** empiéter sur; affecter.

implement ['implimənt; *v* 'impliment] *n* instrument *m*. **implements** *pl n* matériel *m sing*. *v* exécuter.

implication [impli'keiʃən] *n* insinuation *f*, implication *f*.

implicit [im'plisit] *adj* implicite; absolu.

implore [im'ploː] *v* implorer. **imploring** *adj* suppliant.

imply [im'plai] *v* (laisser) supposer; suggérer; insinuer. **implied** *adj* implicite, tacite.

impolite [impə'lait] *adj* impoli.

import [im'poːt] *n* *(comm)* importation *f*; sens *m*; importance *f*. *v* *(comm)* importer; signifier.

importance [im'poːtəns] *n* importance *f*. **important** *adj* important.

impose [im'pouz] *v* imposer; *(fine, etc.)* infliger. **impose on** abuser de. **imposition** *n* imposition *f*.

impossible [im'posəbl] *nm, adj* impossible.

impostor [im'postə] *n* imposteur *m*.

impotent ['impətənt] *adj* impuissant.
impotence *n* impuissance *f*.

impound [im'paund] *v* confisquer.

impoverish [im'povəriʃ] *v* appauvrir.

impregnate ['impreg,neit] *v* imprégner.
impregnation *n* imprégnation *f*.

impress [im'pres] *v* impressionner; (*print*)
imprimer. **impression** *n* impression *f*.
impressive *adj* impressionnant.

imprint [im'print; *n* 'imprint] *v* imprimer.
n empreinte *f*.

imprison [im'prizn] *v* emprisonner.
imprisonment *n* emprisonnement *m*.

improbable [im'probəbl] *adj* improbable;
(*story, etc.*) invraisemblable.

impromptu [im'promptjuː] *adv, adj*
impromptu.

improper [im'propə] *adj* indécent;
malhonnête; incorrect.

improve [im'pruːv] *v* (s')améliorer; perfectionner. **improvement** *n* amélioration *f*;
progrès *m*.

improvise ['imprə,vaiz] *v* improviser.
improvisation *n* improvisation *f*.

impudent ['impjudənt] *adj* impudent.
impudence *n* impudence *f*.

impulse ['impʌls] *n* impulsion *f*. **impulsive**
adj impulsif; irréfléchi.

impure [im'pjuə] *adj* impur. **impurity** *n*
impureté *f*.

in [in] *prep* dans; en; (*town*) à. *adv* (*inside*)
dedans; (*at home*) chez soi.

inability [,inə'biləti] *n* incapacité *f*.

inaccessible [,inak'sesəbl] *adj* inaccessible.

inaccurate [in'akjurit] *adj* inexact. **inaccuracy** *n* inexactitude *f*.

inactive [in'aktiv] *adj* inactif, peu actif.
inaction *n* inaction *f*. **inactivity** *n* inactiv-
ité *f*.

inadequate [in'adikwit] *adj* insuffisant.
inadequacy *n* insuffisance *f*.

inadvertent [,inəd'vəːtənt] *adj* inattentif.
inadvertently *adv* par inadvertance.

inane [in'ein] *adj* inepte. **inanity** *n* ineptie
f.

inanimate [in'animit] *adj* inanimé.

inarticulate [,inaː'tikjulit] *adj* (*sound*) inarticulé; (*person*) incapable de s'exprimer.

inasmuch [,inəz'mʌtʃ] *adv* **inasmuch as**
attendu que.

inaudible [in'oːdəbl] *adj* inaudible.

inaugurate [i'noːgju,reit] *v* inaugurer.

inaugural *adj* inaugural. **inauguration** *n*
inauguration *f*.

inborn [,in'boːn] *adj* inné; congénital.

incapable [in'keipəbl] *adj* incapable.

incendiary [in'sendiəri] *adj* incendiaire.
incendiary device dispositif incendiaire
m.

incense¹ ['insens] *n* encens *m*.

incense² [in'sens] *v* courroucer, exaspérer.
incensed by outré de.

incentive [in'sentiv] *n* objectif *m*, stimulant *m*.

incessant [in'sesənt] *adj* incessant.

incest ['insest] *n* inceste *m*. **incestuous** *adj*
incestueux.

inch [intʃ] *n* pouce *m*. **inch by inch** petit à
petit. *v* **inch forward** avancer petit à petit.

incident ['insidənt] *n* incident *m*; épisode
m. **incidental** *adj* accessoire; accidental.
incidental music musique de fond *f*. **incidentally** *adv* (*by the way*) à propos.

incinerator [in'sinə,reitə] *n* incinérateur
m. **incinerate** *v* incinérer. **incineration** *n*
incinération *f*.

incite [in'sait] *v* pousser, inciter.

incline [in'klain] *v* (s')incliner. **be inclined
to** incliner à. *n* pente *f*. **inclination** *n*
inclination *f*; (*hill*) inclinaison *f*.

include [in'kluːd] *v* inclure, comprendre.
including *prep* y compris. **inclusion** *n*
inclusion *f*. **inclusive** *adj* inclus.

incognito [in'kognitou] *adv* incognito.

incoherent [,inkə'hiərənt] *adj* incohérent.
incoherently *adv* sans cohérence.

income ['inkʌm] *n* revenu *m*. **income tax**
impôt sur le revenu *m*. **private income**
rente *f*.

incompatible [inkəm'patəbl] *adj* incompatible. **incompatibility** *n* incompatibilité
f.

incompetent [in'kompitənt] *adj* incompétent. **incompetence** *n* incompétence *f*.

incomplete [,inkəm'pliːt] *adj* incomplet,
-ète.

incomprehensible [in,kompri'hensəbl] *adj*
incompréhensible.

inconceivable [inkən'siːvəbl] *adj* inconcevable.

incongruous [in'kongruəs] *adj* incongru;
peu approprié.

inconsiderate [,inkən'sidərit] *adj* incon-
sidéré; (*person*) sans égards.

inconsistent [,inkən'sistənt] *adj* inconsis-
tant. **inconsistency** *n* inconsistance *f*.

incontinence [in'kɔntinəns] n incontinence f. **incontinent** adj incontinent.

inconvenience [inkən'viːnjəns] n inconvénient m; (trouble) dérangement m. v déranger. **inconvenient** adj inopportun, incommode.

incorporate [in'kɔːpəreit] v incorporer, contenir; (comm) fusionner.

incorrect [inkə'rekt] adj incorrect.

increase [in'kriːs] v augmenter; (s')intensifier. n augmentation f. **increasing** adj croissant. **increasingly** adv de plus en plus.

incredible [in'kredəbl] adj incroyable.

incredulous [in'kredjuləs] adj incrédule. **incredulity** n incrédulité f.

increment ['inkrəmənt] n augmentation f.

incriminate [in'krimineit] v incriminer. **incriminating** adj compromettant; (evidence, etc.) à conviction.

incubate ['inkjuːbeit] v incuber, couver. **incubation** n incubation f. **incubator** n couveuse f.

incur [in'kəː] v encourir; contracter; (risk) courir.

incurable [in'kjuərəbl] adj incurable.

indecent [in'diːsnt] adj indécent. **indecency** n indécence f.

indeed [in'diːd] adv en effet, vraiment.

indefinite [in'definit] adj indéfini, indéterminé.

indelible [in'deləbl] adj indélébile; (memory, etc.) ineffaçable.

indemnity [in'demnəti] n indemnité f.

indent [in'dent] v denteler; (printing) renfoncer. **indentation** n dentelure f; renfoncement m.

independent [indi'pendənt] adj indépendant. **independence** n indépendance f.

index ['indeks] n index m, catalogue m; (ratio) indice m. **index finger** index m. **index-linked** adj indexé. v classer; (book) mettre un index à.

India ['indjə] n Inde f. **Indian** n Indien, -enne m, f; adj indien. **Indian ink** encre de Chine f.

indicate ['indikeit] v indiquer. **indication** n indication f, signe m. **indicative** nm, adj indicatif. **indicator** n indicateur m; (mot) clignotant m.

indict [in'dait] v accuser. **indictment** n mise en accusation f.

indifferent [in'difrənt] adj indifférent; (derog) médiocre. **indifference** n indifférence f.

indigenous [in'didʒinəs] adj indigène.

indigestion [indi'dʒestʃən] n dyspepsie f, indigestion f.

indignant [in'dignənt] adj indigné. **get indignant** s'indigner. **indignantly** adv avec indignation. **indignation** n indignation f.

indignity [in'dignəti] n indignité f.

indirect [indi'rekt] adj indirect.

indiscreet [indi'skriːt] adj indiscret, -ète. **indiscretion** n indiscrétion f.

indiscriminate [indi'skriminit] adj fait au hasard; (blind) aveugle.

indispensable [indi'spensəbl] adj indispensable.

indisposed [indi'spouzd] adj (ill) indisposé; (unwilling) peu disposé. **indisposition** n indisposition f.

individual [indi'vidjuəl] adj individuel; original. n individu m. **individuality** n individualité f.

indoctrinate [in'doktrineit] v endoctriner. **indoctrination** n endoctrination f.

indolent ['indolənt] adj indolent. **indolence** n indolence f.

indoor ['indoː] adj d'intérieur; (swimming pool, etc.) couvert. **indoors** adv à l'intérieur, à la maison.

induce [in'djuːs] v persuader; provoquer; (med: labour) déclencher. **inducement** n encouragement m; (incentive) motif m.

indulge [in'dʌldʒ] v satisfaire; (give way to) céder à. **indulge in** se livrer à. **indulgence** n indulgence f; satisfaction f. **indulgent** adj indulgent.

industry ['indəstri] n industrie f; zèle m. **industrial** adj industriel. **industrial action** action revendicative f. **industrialize** v industrialiser. **industrious** adj industrieux.

inebriated [i'niːbrieitid] adj ivre.

inedible [in'edibl] adj non comestible.

inefficient [ini'fiʃnt] adj inefficace; incompétent. **inefficiency** n inefficacité f; incompétence f.

inept [i'nept] adj inepte.

inequality [ini'kwɔləti] n inégalité f.

inert [i'nəːt] adj inerte. **inertia** n inertie f.

inevitable [in'evitəbl] adj inévitable.

inexpensive [inik'spensiv] adj pas cher.

inexperienced [inik'spiəriənst] adj inexpérimenté.

infallible [in'faləbl] adj infaillible.

infamous ['infəməs] *adj* infâme. **infamy** *n* infamie *f*.

infancy ['infənsi] *n* petite enfance *f*; (*of idea, etc.*) enfance *f*.

infant ['infənt] *n* bébé *m*; enfant en bas âge *m, f*. **infantile** *adj* enfantin, infantile.

infantry ['infəntri] *n* infanterie *f*.

infatuate [in'fatjueit] *v* **be infatuated with** (*person*) être entiché de; (*idea*) être engoué de. **infatuation** *n* engouement *m*.

infect [in'fekt] *v* infecter. **infection** *n* infection *f*. **infectious** *adj* infectieux, contagieux.

infer [in'fəː] *v* déduire. **inference** *n* déduction *f*.

inferior [in'fiəriə] *n*(*m*+*f*), *adj* inférieur, -e. **inferiority** *n* infériorité *f*.

infernal [in'fəːnl] *adj* infernal.

infest [in'fest] *v* infester. **infestation** *n* infestation *f*.

infidelity [infi'deliti] *n* infidelité *f*.

infiltrate [in'filtreit] *v* (s')infiltrer. **infiltration** *n* infiltration *f*; (*pol*) noyautage *m*.

infinite ['infinit] *nm, adj* infini. **infinity** *n* infinité *f*; (*maths*) infini *m*.

infinitive [in'finitiv] *nm, adj* infinitif.

infirm [in'fəːm] *adj* infirme. **infirmity** *n* infirmité *f*.

inflame [in'fleim] *v* (s')enflammer. **inflammable** *adj* inflammable. **inflammation** *n* inflammation *f*.

inflate [in'fleit] *v* gonfler; (*prices*) faire monter. **inflation** *n* (*econ*) inflation *f*; (*of tyre, etc.*) gonflement *m*.

inflection [in'flekʃən] *n* inflexion *f*; (*word ending*) désinence *f*.

inflict [in'flikt] *v* infliger. **infliction** *n* infliction *f*.

influence ['influəns] *n* influence *f*. *v* influencer. **influential** *adj* influent.

influenza [influ'enzə] *n* grippe *f*.

influx ['inflʌks] *n* flot *m*, afflux *m*.

inform [in'fɔːm] *v* informer. **informative** *adj* instructif. **informer** *n* dénonciateur, -trice *m, f*.

informal [in'fɔːml] *adj* familier; dénué de formalité; (*unofficial*) officieux.

information [infə'meiʃən] *n* renseignements *m pl*.

infra-red [infrə'red] *adj* infrarouge.

infringe [in'frindʒ] *v* enfreindre. **infringe on** empiéter sur. **infringement** *n* infraction *f*.

infuriate [in'fjuərieit] *v* rendre furieux. **infuriating** *adj* exaspérant.

ingenious [in'dʒiːniəs] *adj* ingénieux. **ingenuity** *n* ingéniosité *f*.

ingot ['ingət] *n* lingot *m*.

ingredient [in'griːdjənt] *n* ingrédient *m*.

inhabit [in'habit] *v* habiter. **inhabitant** *n* habitant, -e *m, f*.

inhale [in'heil] *v* inhaler; (*smoke*) avaler; (*perfume*) aspirer.

inherent [in'hiərənt] *adj* inhérent.

inherit [in'herit] *v* hériter (de). **inheritance** *n* héritage *m*; succession *f*.

inhibit [in'hibit] *v* inhiber, gêner. **inhibition** *n* inhibition *f*.

inhuman [in'hjuːmən] *adj* inhumain. **inhumanity** *n* inhumanité *f*.

iniquity [i'nikwəti] *n* iniquité *f*.

initial [i'niʃl] *adj* initial, premier. *n* initiale *f*. *v* parafer.

initiate [i'niʃieit] *v* initier; inaugurer; commencer. **initiation** *n* initiation *f*; commencement *m*; inauguration *f*.

initiative [i'niʃiətiv] *n* initiative *f*.

inject [in'dʒekt] *v* injecter. **injection** *n* injection *f*, piqûre *f*.

injure ['indʒə] *v* blesser. **injury** *n* blessure *f*.

injustice [in'dʒʌstis] *n* injustice *f*.

ink [ink] *n* encre *f*. **ink-well** *n* encrier *m*. *v* encrer.

inkling ['inkliŋ] *n* soupçon *m*.

inland ['inlənd; *adv* in'land] *adj* intérieur, -e. **Inland Revenue** fisc *m*. *adv* à l'intérieur.

in-laws ['in,lɔːz] *pl n* (*coll*) beaux-parents *m pl*, belle-famille *f sing*.

inlay [in'lei] *v* incruster; marqueter. *n* incrustation *f*; marqueterie *f*.

inlet ['inlet] *n* crique *f*.

inmate ['inmeit] *n* occupant, -e *m, f*; (*prison*) détenu, -e *m, f*; hospitalisé, -e *m, f*.

inn [in] *n* auberge *f*. **innkeeper** *n* aubergiste *m, f*.

innate [i'neit] *adj* inné.

inner ['inə] *adj* intérieur, -e; (*thoughts, etc.*) intime. **inner tube** chambre à air *f*.

innocent ['inəsnt] *adj* innocent. **innocence** *n* innocence *f*.

innocuous [i'nokjuəs] *adj* inoffensif.

innovation [inə'veiʃən] *n* innovation *f*.

innuendo [inju'endəu] *n* insinuation *f*.

innumerable [i'njuːmərəbl] *adj* innombrable.

inoculate [i'nɔkju,leit] v inoculer. **inoculation** n inoculation f.

inorganic [,inɔr'ganik] adj inorganique.

input ['input] n (elec) énergie f; (tech) consommation f; (computer) input m.

inquest ['inkwest] n enquête f.

inquire [in'kwaiə] v s'informer (de), demander. **inquiring** adj (mind) curieux; (look) interrogateur, -trice. **inquiry** n (official) enquête f; (individual) demande de renseignements f. **inquiry desk** renseignements m pl.

inquisition [,inkwi'ziʃən] n investigation f. **the Inquisition** l'Inquisition f.

inquisitive [in'kwizətiv] adj curieux.

insane [in'sein] adj (med) aliéné; (crazy) fou, folle. **insanity** n aliénation f; folie f.

insatiable [in'seiʃəbl] adj insatiable.

inscribe [in'skraib] v inscrire, graver. **inscription** n inscription f.

insect ['insekt] n insecte m. **insecticide** n insecticide m.

insecure [,insi'kjuə] adj (future, etc.) incertain; (person) anxieux; (structure) peu solide. **insecurity** n insécurité f.

inseminate [in'semineit] v inséminer. **insemination** n insémination f.

insensitive [in'sensətiv] adj insensible. **insensitivity** n insensibilité f.

inseparable [in'sepərəbl] adj inséparable.

insert [in'sɔːt; n 'insɔːt] v insérer. n insertion f; (page) encart m. **insertion** n insertion f.

inshore [,in'ʃɔː] adj côtier.

inside [,in'said] adv dedans. prep à l'intérieur de. adj intérieur, -e. -e dedans m, intérieur m. **inside out** à l'envers.

insidious [in'sidiəs] adj insidieux.

insight ['insait] n perspicacité f.

insignificant [,insig'nifikənt] adj insignifiant. **insignificance** n insignifiance f.

insincere [,insin'siə] adj hypocrite; faux, fausse.

insinuate [in'sinjueit] v insinuer. **insinuation** n insinuation f.

insipid [in'sipid] adj insipide.

insist [in'sist] v insister; affirmer. **insistence** n insistance f. **insistant** adj insistant. **insistently** adv avec insistance.

insolent ['insələnt] adj insolent. **insolence** n insolence f.

insoluble [in'sɔljubl] adj insoluble.

insomnia [in'sɔmniə] n insomnie f. **insomniac** n(m+f). adj insomniaque.

inspect [in'spekt] v inspecter, examiner. **inspection** n inspection f; examen m. **inspector** n inspecteur, -trice m, f.

inspire [in'spaiə] v inspirer. **inspiration** n inspiration f.

instability [,instə'biləti] n instabilité f.

install [in'stɔːl] v installer. **installation** n installation f.

instalment [in'stɔːlmənt] n (comm) acompte m; (of serial) épisode m.

instance ['instəns] n exemple m, cas m. **for instance** par exemple.

instant ['instənt] adj immédiat; (comm) courant; (coffee) soluble. n instant m. **instantaneous** adj instantané. **instantly** adv sur-le-champ.

instead [in'sted] adv à la place, plutôt. **instead of** au lieu de.

instep ['instep] n (anat) cou-de-pied m; (shoe) cambrure f.

instigate ['instigeit] v inciter; provoquer. **instigation** n instigation f. **instigator** n instigateur, -trice m, f.

instil [in'stil] v insuffler, inculquer.

instinct ['instiŋkt] n instinct m. **instinctive** adj instinctif.

institute ['institjuːt] v instituer, fonder. n institut m. **institution** n institution f; (school, home) établissement m.

instruct [in'strʌkt] v instruire; (order) charger. **instruction** n instruction f; **instructions** pl n directives f pl; (comm) indications f pl; (for use) mode d'emploi m sing. **instructive** adj instructif. **instructor** n professeur m; (skiing) moniteur, -trice m, f.

instrument ['instrəmənt] n instrument m. **instrumental** adj (music) instrumental. **be instrumental in** contribuer à.

insubordinate [,insə'bɔːdənət] adj insubordonné. **insubordination** n insubordination f.

insufficient [,insə'fiʃənt] adj insuffisant.

insular ['insjulə] adj insulaire; (outlook) borné.

insulate ['insjuleit] v isoler. **insulation** n isolation f; (against cold) calorifugeage m; (material) isolant m.

insulin ['insjulin] n insuline f.

insult [in'sʌlt; n 'insʌlt] v insulter. n insulte f.

insure [in'ʃuə] v (faire) assurer. **insurance** n assurance f. **insurance certificate** (mot) carte d'assurance f.

intact [in'takt] *adj* intact.

intake (*intake*) *n* (*tech*) adduction *f*; (*school*) admission *f*; (*food*) consommation *f*.

intangible [in'tandʒəbl] *adj* intangible.

integral ['intigrəl] *adj* intégral; (*part*) intégrant. *n* intégrale *f*.

integrate ['intigreit] *v* intégrer. **integration** *n* intégration *f*.

integrity [in'tegriti] *n* intégrité *f*.

intellect ['intilekt] *n* intellect *m*. **intelligence** *f*. **intellectual** *n. adj* intellectuel, -elle.

intelligent [in'telidʒənt] *adj* intelligent. **intelligence** *n* intelligence *f*; (*information*) renseignements *m pl*. **intelligence test** test d'aptitude intellectuelle *m*.

intelligible [in'telidʒəbl] *adj* intelligible.

intend [in'tend] *v* avoir l'intention (de). **intended** *adj* intentionnel; projeté.

intense [in'tens] *adj* intense; (*person*) véhément. **intensify** *v* (s')intensifier. **intensity** *n* intensité *f*; véhémence *f*. **intensive** *adj* intensif. **intensive care** service de réanimation *m*.

intent¹ [in'tent] *n* intention *f*.

intent² [in'tent] *adj* attentif; résolu; absorbé.

intention [in'tenʃən] *n* intention *f*. **intentional** *adj* intentionnel, voulu.

inter [in'təː] *v* enterrer. **interment** *n* enterrement *m*.

interact [,intər'akt] *v* agir réciproquement. **interaction** *n* interaction *f*.

intercede [,intə'siːd] *v* intercéder.

intercept [,intə'sept] *v* intercepter. **interception** *n* interception *f*.

interchange [,intə'tʃeindʒ] *n* échange *m*; (*motorway*) échangeur *m*. *v* échanger. **interchangeable** *adj* interchangeable.

intercom ['intəkom] *n* interphone *m*.

intercourse ['intəkoːs] *n* relations *f pl*; (*sexual*) rapports *m pl*.

interest ['intrist] *n* intérêt *m*; (*comm*) intérêts *m pl*. *v* intéresser. **be interested in** s'intéresser à.

interfere [,intə'fiə] *v* s'immiscer. **interfere with** (*plans*) contrecarrer; (*work*) empiéter sur; (*meddle*) tripoter. **interference** *n* intrusion *f*; (*radio*) parasites *m pl*. **interfering** *adj* importun.

interim ['intərim] *n* intérim *m*. *adj* provisoire, intérimaire.

interior [in'tiəriə] *adj* intérieur, -e. *n* intérieur *m*.

interjection [,intə'dʒekʃən] *n* interjection *f*.

interlude ['intəluːd] *n* intervalle *m*; (*theatre*) intermède *m*; (*musical*) interlude *m*.

intermediate [,intə'miːdiət] *adj* intermédiaire.

interminable [in'təːminəbl] *adj* interminable.

intermission [,intə'miʃən] *n* interruption *f*; (*cinema*) entracte *m*.

intermittent [,intə'mitənt] *adj* intermittent. **intermittently** *adv* par intermittence.

intern [in'təːn] *v* interner. **internment** *n* internement *m*.

internal [in'təːnl] *adj* interne, intérieur, -e. **internal combustion engine** moteur à explosion *m*.

international [,intə'naʃənl] *adj* international.

interpose [,intə'pouz] *v* intervenir; (*remark, etc.*) intercaler.

interpret [in'təːprit] *v* interpréter. **interpretation** *n* interprétation *f*. **interpreter** *n* interprète *m, f*.

interrogate [in'terəgeit] *v* interroger. **interrogation** *n* interrogation *f*; (*police*) interrogatoire *m*. **interrogator** *n* interrogateur, -trice *m, f*.

interrogative [,intə'rogətiv] *adj* interrogateur, -trice; (*gramm*) interrogatif. *n* interrogatif *m*.

interrupt [,intə'rʌpt] *v* interrompre. **interruption** *n* interruption *f*.

intersect [,intə'sekt] *v* (se) couper; (*math*) (s')intersecter. **intersection** *n* croisement *m*; intersection *f*.

intersperse [,intə'spəːs] *v* parsemer.

interval ['intəvəl] *n* intervalle *m*; (*theatre*) entracte *m*.

intervene [,intə'viːn] *v* intervenir; survenir. **intervention** *n* intervention *f*.

interview ['intəvjuː] *n* entrevue; (*press, radio, etc.*) interview *f*. *v* interviewer.

intestine [in'testin] *n* intestin *m*. **intestinal** *adj* intestinal.

intimate¹ ['intimət] *adj* intime; (*detailed*) approfondi. **intimacy** *n* intimité *f*.

intimate² ['intimeit] *v* faire connaître; suggérer. **intimation** *n* annonce *f*; suggestion *f*.

intimidate [in'timideit] *v* intimider. **intimidation** *n* intimidation *f*.

into ['intu] *prep* dans, en.

intolerable [in'tɔlərəbl] *adj* intolérable.

intolerant [in'tɔlərənt] *adj* intolérant. **intolerance** *n* intolérance *f.*

intonation [ˌintə'neiʃən] *n* intonation *f.*

intoxicate [in'tɔksikeit] *v* enivrer. **intoxicated** *adj* ivre. **intoxication** *n* ivresse *f.*

intransitive [in'transitiv] *nm, adj* intransitif.

intravenous [ˌintrə'viːnəs] *adj* intraveineux.

intrepid [in'trepid] *adj* intrépide.

intricate ['intriket] *adj* complexe, compliqué. **intricacy** *n* complexité *f,* complication *f.*

intrigue ['intriːg; *v* in'triːg] *n* intrigue *f. v* intriguer.

intrinsic [in'trinsik] *adj* intrinsèque.

introduce [ˌintrə'djuːs] *v* présenter, introduire. **introduction** *n* introduction *f,* présentation *f.* **introductory** *adj* préliminaire.

introspective [ˌintrə'spektiv] *adj* introspectif. **introspection** *n* introspection *f.*

introvert ['intrəˌvəːt] *n* introverti, -e *m, f.*

intrude [in'truːd] *v* s'imposer, s'immiscer. **intruder** *n* intrus, -e *m, f.* **intrusion** *n* intrusion *f.*

intuition [ˌintjuː'iʃən] *n* intuition *f.* **intuitive** *adj* intuitif.

inundate ['inʌndeit] *v* inonder. **inundation** *n* inondation *f.*

invade [in'veid] *v* envahir. **invader** *n* envahisseur, -euse *m, f.* **invasion** *n* invasion *f.*

invalid[1] ['invəlid] *n(m+f),* *adj* malade; *(disabled)* infirme, invalide.

invalid[2] [in'valid] *adj* non valide.

invaluable [in'valjuəbl] *adj* inestimable.

invariable [in'veəriəbl] *adj* invariable.

invective [in'vektiv] *n* invective *f.*

invent [in'vent] *v* inventer. **invention** *n* invention *f.* **inventor** *n* inventeur, -trice *m, f.*

inventory ['invəntri] *n* inventaire *m.*

invert [in'vəːt] *v* intervertir, renverser. **inverted commas** guillemets *m pl.* **inversion** *n* inversion *f,* renversement *m.*

invertebrate [in'vəːtibrət] *nm, adj* invertébré.

invest [in'vest] *v* investir, placer. **investment** *n* investissement *m,* placement *m.* **investor** *n* actionnaire *m, f.*

investigate [in'vestigeit] *v* examiner; *(crime)* enquêter sur. **investigation** *n* investigation *f.*

invigorating [in'vigəreitiŋ] *adj* vivifiant, tonifiant.

invincible [in'vinsəbl] *adj* invincible.

invisible [in'vizəbl] *adj* invisible.

invite [in'vait] *v* inviter. **invitation** *n* invitation *f.* **inviting** *adj* engageant, tentant.

invoice ['invɔis] *n* facture *f. v* facturer.

invoke [in'vouk] *v* invoquer. **invocation** *n* invocation *f.*

involuntary [in'vɔləntəri] *adj* involontaire.

involve [in'vɔlv] *v* impliquer, mêler; *(entail)* entraîner. **involved** *adj* compliqué. **involvement** *n* rôle *m;* problème *m.*

inward ['inwəd] *adj* vers l'intérieur; *(thoughts)* intime. **inwardly** *adv* secrètement. **inwards** *adv* vers l'intérieur.

iodine ['aiədiːn] *n* iode *m.*

ion ['aiən] *n* ion *m.*

irate [ai'reit] *adj* furieux.

Ireland ['aiələnd] *n* Irlande *f.* **Irish** *nm, adj* irlandais. **Irish Sea** mer d'Irlande *f.* **the Irish** les Irlandais *m pl.*

iris ['aiəris] *n* iris *m.*

irk [əːk] *v* contrarier. **irksome** *adj* ennuyeux.

iron ['aiən] *n* fer *m.* **Iron Curtain** rideau de fer *m.* **ironmonger's** *n* quincaillerie *f. v* repasser. **iron out** faire disparaître. **ironing** *n* repassage *m.* **ironing board** planche à repasser *f.*

irony ['aiərəni] *n* ironie *f.* **ironic** *adj* ironique.

irrational [i'raʃənl] *adj* pas rationnel, déraisonnable; *(math)* irrationnel.

irregular [i'regjulə] *adj* irrégulier. **irregularity** *n* irrégularité *f.*

irrelevant [i'reləvənt] *adj* sans rapport, hors de propos.

irreparable [i'repərəbl] *adj* irréparable.

irresistible [ˌiri'zistəbl] *adj* irrésistible.

irrespective [ˌiri'spektiv] *adj* **irrespective of** sans tenir compte de.

irresponsible [ˌiri'spɔnsəbl] *adj* irréfléchi.

irrevocable [i'revəkəbl] *adj* irrévocable.

irrigate ['irigeit] *v* irriguer. **irrigation** *n* irrigation *f.*

irritate ['iriteit] *v* irriter. **irritable** *adj* irritable. **irritation** *n* irritation *f.*

is [iz] *V* **be.**

Islam ['izlaːm] *n* Islam *m.* **Islamic** *adj* islamique.

island ['ailənd] n île f; (in road) refuge m.

isolate ['aisəleit] v isoler. **isolation** n isolement m.

issue ['iʃuː] n question f; résultat m; (copy) numéro m; (stamps, etc.) émission f. v distribuer; émettre; (writ, etc.) lancer.

isthmus ['ismas] n isthme m.

it [it] pron (subject) il, elle; (direct object) le, la; (indirect object) lui. **it is** c'est, il est.

italic [i'talik] adj italique. **italics** pl n italique m sing.

Italy ['itəli] n Italie f. **Italian** nm, adj italien; (people) Italien, -enne m, f.

itch [itʃ] n démangeaison f. v démanger.

item ['aitəm] n article m; question f.

itinerary [ai'tinərəri] n itinéraire m.

its [its] adj son, sa; (pl) ses. pron le sien, la sienne.

itself [it'self] pron se; (emphatic) luimême, elle-même. **by itself** en soi; (alone) tout seul.

ivory ['aivəri] n ivoire m. **Ivory Coast** Côte d'Ivoire f.

ivy ['aivi] n lierre m.

janitor ['dʒanitə] n portier m.

January ['dʒanjuəri] n janvier m.

Japan [dʒə'pan] n Japon m. **Japanese** nm, adj japonais. **the Japanese** les Japonais m pl.

jar¹ [dʒaː] n pot m, bocal m.

jar² [dʒaː] v (sound) grincer; (knock) cogner; (shake) ébranler; (irritate) agacer.

jargon ['dʒaːgən] n jargon m.

jasmine ['dʒazmin] n jasmin m.

jaundice ['dʒɔːndis] n jaunisse f.

jaunt [dʒɔːnt] n (coll) balade f.

jaunty ['dʒɔːnti] adj enjoué, vif.

javelin ['dʒavəlin] n javelot m.

jaw [dʒɔː] n mâchoire f. **jawbone** n maxillaire m.

jay [dʒei] n geai m.

jazz [dʒaz] n jazz m.

jealous ['dʒeləs] adj jaloux, -ouse. **jealousy** n jalousie f.

jeans [dʒiːnz] pl n blue-jean m sing.

jeep [dʒiːp] n jeep f.

jeer [dʒiə] v railler, huer. n raillerie f, huée f.

jelly ['dʒeli] n gelée f. **jellyfish** n méduse f.

jeopardize ['dʒepədaiz] v mettre en danger. **jeopardy** n danger m, péril m.

jerk [dʒəːk] n saccade f, secousse f. v tirer brusquement; donner une secousse à. **jerky** adj saccadé. **jerkily** adv par saccades.

jersey ['dʒəːzi] n tricot m. **Jersey** n Jersey f.

jest [dʒest] n plaisanterie f. v plaisanter. **jester** n bouffon m.

jet¹ [dʒet] n jet m. **jet lag** décalage horaire m. **jet-propelled** adj à réaction.

jet² [dʒet] n jais m.

jetty ['dʒeti] n jetée f.

Jew [dʒuː] n Juif, Juive m, f. **Jewish** adj juif.

jewel ['dʒuːəl] n bijou (pl -oux) m. **jeweller** n bijoutier m. **jeweller's** n bijouterie f. **jewellery** n bijoux m pl.

jig [dʒig] n gigue f. v danser la gigue; sautiller.

jigsaw ['dʒigsɔː] n (puzzle) puzzle m; (saw) scie à chantourner f.

jilt [dʒilt] v laisser tomber.

jingle ['dʒiŋgl] n tintement m; (verse) petit couplet m. v (faire) tinter.

jinx [dʒiŋks] n (coll) porte-guigne m. **jinxed** adj ensorcelé.

J

jab [dʒab] v enfoncer. n coup de pointe m; (coll: injection) piqûre f.

jack [dʒak] n (mot) cric m; (cards) valet m. v **jack up** soulever avec un cric.

jackal ['dʒakoːl] n chacal m.

jackdaw ['dʒakdɔː] n choucas m.

jacket ['dʒakit] n (man's) veston m; (woman's) jaquette f; (of book) couverture f. **jacket potato** pomme de terre au four f.

jackpot ['dʒakpot] n gros lot m.

jade [dʒeid] nm jade.

jaded ['dʒeidid] adj épuisé.

jagged ['dʒagid] adj déchiqueté.

jaguar ['dʒaguə] n jaguar m.

jail or **gaol** [dʒeil] n prison f. v emprisonner. **jailer** n geôlier, -ère m, f.

jam¹ [dʒam] v (se) coincer; (cram) entasser; (block) encombrer. n embouteillage m.

jam² [dʒam] n confiture f.

job [dʒɔb] *n* travail (*pl* -aux) *m*; poste *m*.
jobcentre *n* agence pour l'emploi *f*. **job lot** lot d'articles divers *m*.

jockey ['dʒɔki] *n* jockey *m*.

jocular ['dʒɔkjula] *adj* jovial; facétieux.

jodhpurs ['dʒɔdpaz] *pl n* culotte de cheval *f* *sing*.

jog [dʒɔg] *n* (*jerk*) secousse *f*; (*with elbow*) coup de coude *m*. **jogtrot** *n* petit trot *m*. *v* secouer; (*elbow*) pousser; (*memory*) rafraîchir. **jogging** *n* footing *m*. **go jogging** faire du footing.

join [dʒɔin] *v* (se) joindre, (s')unir; devenir membre (de), s'inscrire (à); (*roads, rivers, etc.*) (se) rejoindre. **join in** participer (à). **join up** assembler; (*mil*) s'engager. **joiner** *n* menuisier *m*.

joint [dʒɔint] *n* jointure *f*; (*anat*) articulation *f*; (*of meat*) rôti *m*; (*slang: place*) boîte *f*. *adj* commun. **jointly** *adv* en commun.

joist [dʒɔist] *n* solive *f*.

joke [dʒouk] *n* plaisanterie *f*; (*trick*) farce *f*. *v* plaisanter. **joker** *n* blagueur, -euse *m*, *f*; (*cards*) joker *m*.

jolly ['dʒɔli] *adj* enjoué. *adv* (*coll*) drôlement. **jollity** *n* gaieté *f*.

jolt [dʒɔult] *v* cahoter. *n* secousse *f*, cahot *m*; choc *m*.

jostle ['dʒɔsl] *v* (se) bousculer. *n* bousculade *f*.

jot [dʒɔt] *v* **jot down** noter. *n* iota *m*. **jotter** *n* bloc-notes *m*.

journal ['dʒəːnl] *n* revue *f*; (*comm*) livre de comptes *m*; (*diary*) journal *m*. **journalism** *n* journalisme *m*. **journalist** *n* journaliste *m*, *f*.

journey ['dʒəːni] *n* voyage *m*; (*distance*) trajet *m*. *v* voyager.

jovial ['dʒouviəl] *adj* jovial. **joviality** *n* jovialité *f*.

joy [dʒɔi] *n* joie *f*; plaisir *m*. **joyful** *or* **joyous** *adj* joyeux.

jubilant ['dʒuːbilənt] *adj* débordant de joie. **be jubilant** jubiler. **jubilation** *n* jubilation *f*.

jubilee ['dʒuːbiliː] *n* jubilé *m*.

Judaism ['dʒuːdeiizəm] *n* judaïsme *m*.

judge [dʒʌdʒ] *n* juge *m*. *v* juger. **judging by** à en juger par. **judgment** *n* jugement *m*; discernement *m*.

judicial [dʒuːˈdiʃəl] *adj* judiciaire.

judicious [dʒuːˈdiʃəs] *adj* judicieux.

judo ['dʒuːdou] *n* judo *m*.

jug [dʒʌg] *n* cruche *f*; (*for milk*) pot *m*; (*slang: prison*) taule *f*.

juggernaut ['dʒʌgənɔːt] *n* (*lorry*) mastodonte *m*.

juggle ['dʒʌgl] *v* jongler. **juggler** *n* jongleur, -euse *m*, *f*. **jugglery** *n* jonglerie *f*.

jugular ['dʒʌgjulə] *nf, adj* jugulaire.

juice [dʒuːs] *n* jus *m*. **juicy** *adj* juteux.

jukebox ['dʒuːkbɔks] *n* juke-box *m*.

July [dʒuˈlai] *n* juillet *m*.

jumble ['dʒʌmbl] *v* brouiller. *n* mélange *m*, fouillis *m*. **jumble sale** vente de charité *f*.

jump [dʒʌmp] *n* saut *m*; (*start*) sursaut *m*. *v* sauter; sursauter. **jump at** (*offer, etc.*) sauter sur. **jumped-up** *adj* (*derog*) parvenu. **jumpy** *adj* (*coll*) nerveux.

jumper ['dʒʌmpə] *n* pull *m*.

junction ['dʒʌŋkʃən] *n* jonction *f*; (*roads*) bifurcation *f*; (*rail*) embranchement *m*.

juncture ['dʒʌŋkʃə] *n* conjoncture *f*. **at this juncture** à ce moment-là.

June [dʒuːn] *n* juin *m*.

jungle ['dʒʌŋgl] *n* jungle *f*.

junior ['dʒuːnjə] *adj* (*younger*) cadet, -ette; (*lower rank*) subalterne. *n* cadet, -ette *m*, *f*; (*clerk*) petit commis *m*; (*in names*) fils *m*.

juniper ['dʒuːnipə] *n* genévrier *m*. **juniper berry** baie de genièvre *f*.

junk[1] [dʒʌŋk] *n* bric-à-brac *m invar*; (*coll: rubbish*) camelote *f*. **junk-shop** *n* brocanteur *m*.

junk[2] [dʒʌŋk] *n* (*boat*) jonque *f*.

junta ['dʒʌntə] *n* junte *f*.

jurisdiction [dʒuəris'dikʃən] *n* juridiction *f*.

jury ['dʒuəri] *n* jury *m*. **juror** *n* juré, femme juré *m*, *f*.

just [dʒʌst] *adv* juste; simplement. **have just** venir de: *il vient de partir*. *adj* juste.

justice ['dʒʌstis] *n* justice *f*. **Justice of the Peace** juge de paix *m*.

justify ['dʒʌstifai] *v* justifier. **justifiable** *adj* justifiable. **justification** *n* justification *f*.

jut [dʒʌt] *v* **jut out** saillir, dépasser.

jute [dʒuːt] *n* jute *m*.

juvenile ['dʒuːvənail] *n* adolescent, -e *m*, *f*. *adj* juvénile. **juvenile delinquent** mineur délinquant, mineure délinquante *m*, *f*.

juxtapose [,dʒʌkstəˈpouz] *v* juxtaposer. **juxtaposition** *n* juxtaposition *f*.

K

kaftan ['kaftan] n kaftan m.

kaleidoscope [kə'laidəskoup] n kaléidoscope m.

kangaroo [kaŋgə'ruː] n kangourou m.

karate [kə'rɑːti] n karaté m.

kayak ['kaiak] n kayak m.

kebab [ki'bab] n kébab m.

keel [kiːl] n quille f. v **keel over** (naut) chavirer; (coll: faint) tomber dans les pommes.

keen [kiːn] adj vif; enthousiaste; (sharp) aiguisé; (sight, judgment) pénétrant. **keenly** adv vivement, profondément; avec enthousiasme. **keenness** n finesse f; intensité f; enthousiasme m.

*keep [kiːp] v garder; (observe, maintain) tenir; (support) entretenir; (remain) rester; (food, etc.) se garder. **keep-fit** n culture physique f. **keep on** continuer. **keep out!** (on notice) défense d'entrer! **keepsake** n souvenir m. **keep up with** suivre; aller aussi vite que. **keeper** n gardien, -enne m, f.

keg [keg] n tonnelet m.

kennel ['kenl] n niche f. **kennels** pl n chenil m sing.

kept [kept] V keep.

kerb [kəːb] n bordure du trottoir f.

kernel ['kəːnl] n (nut) amande f; (seed) graine m.

kerosene ['kerəsiːn] n kérosène m.

ketchup ['ketʃəp] n ketchup m.

kettle ['ketl] n bouilloire f. **kettledrum** n timbale f.

key [kiː] n clef f; (piano) touche f; (music) ton m. **keyboard** n clavier m. **keyhole** n trou de serrure m. **key-ring** n porte-clefs m invar. adj clef. v **key up** surexciter.

khaki ['kɑːki] nm, adj kaki.

kick [kik] n coup de pied m; (gun) recul m. v donner un coup de pied (à). **kick off** (football) donner le coup d'envoi; (coll: party, etc.) démarrer. **kick-off** n coup d'envoi m; (coll) démarrage m. **kick out** (coll) flanquer dehors.

kid[1] [kid] n (goat, leather) chevreau m; (coll: child) gosse m, f.

kid[2] [kid] v (coll) faire marcher.

kidnap ['kidnap] v kidnapper. **kidnapper** n kidnappeur, -euse m, f. **kidnapping** n enlèvement m.

kidney ['kidni] n (anat) rein m; (as food) rognon m. **kidney bean** haricot rouge m. **kidney machine** rein artificiel m.

kill [kil] v tuer. **killjoy** n rabat-joie m invar. **killer** n tueur, -euse m, f; assassin m. **killing** n meutre m; massacre m.

kiln [kiln] n four m.

kilo ['kiːlou] n kilo m.

kilogram ['kiləgram] n kilogramme m.

kilometre ['kiləmiːtə] n kilomètre m.

kilt [kilt] n kilt m.

kin [kin] n parents m pl. **kinship** n parenté f.

kind[1] [kaind] adj aimable, gentil, -ille. **kind-hearted** adj bon, bonne. **kindness** n bonté f. **gentillesse** f.

kind[2] [kaind] n genre m; (brand) marque f. **in kind** en nature.

kindergarten ['kindəgaːtn] n jardin d'enfants m.

kindle ['kindl] v (s')allumer, (s')enflammer.

kindred ['kindrid] n parents m pl. adj (related) apparenté; similaire. **kindred spirit** âme sœur f.

kinetic [kin'etik] adj cinétique.

king [kiŋ] n roi m; (draughts) dame f. **kingfisher** n martin-pêcheur m. **kingdom** n royaume m; (plant, animal) règne m.

kink [kiŋk] n (rope) entortillement m; (hair) crêpelure f. v s'entortiller. **kinky** adj crêpelé; bizarre.

kiosk ['kiɔsk] n kiosque m.

kipper ['kipə] n hareng fumé m.

kiss [kis] v (s')embrasser. n baiser m. **kiss of life** bouche à bouche m.

kit [kit] n (equipment) matériel m; (sport) affaires f pl; (tools, first-aid, etc.) trousse f; (do-it-yourself) kit m. v **kit out** équiper.

kitchen ['kitʃin] n cuisine f. **kitchen sink** évier m.

kite [kait] n cerf-volant m; (bird) milan m.

kitten ['kitn] n chaton m.

kitty ['kiti] n cagnotte f.

kleptomania [kleptə'meiniə] n kleptomanie f. **kleptomaniac** n(m+f). adj kleptomane.

knack [nak] n tour de main m, truc m. **get the knack of** attraper le tour de main pour.

knapsack ['napsak] n sac à dos m.

knead [niːd] v pétrir.

knee [niː] n genou (pl -oux) m. **kneecap** n rotule f.

****kneel** [niːl] v s'agenouiller.

knelt [nelt] V kneel.

knew [njuː] V know.

knickers ['nɪkəz] pl n culotte f sing; (briefs) slip m sing.

knife [naɪf] n couteau m. v donner un coup de couteau à.

knight [naɪt] n chevalier m. v faire chevalier. **knighthood** n titre de chevalier m. **get a knighthood** être fait chevalier.

knit [nɪt] v tricoter. **knit together** lier; (bone) se souder. **knitting** n tricot m. **knitting machine** tricoteuse f. **knitting needle** aiguille à tricoter f.

knob [nɒb] n bouton m; (of butter) noix f.

knobbly ['nɒblɪ] adj noueux.

knock [nɒk] n coup m. v frapper; (bump) heurter. **knock down** abattre; (mot) renverser. **knock knees** genoux cagneux m pl. **knock out** (stun) assommer; (from context) éliminer. **knockout** n (boxing) knock-out m. **knock over** renverser. **knocker** n marteau de porte m.

knot [nɒt] n nœud m. v nouer.

****know** [nəʊ] v (facts) savoir; (places, people) connaître; (recognize) reconnaître. **know-all** n (coll) je-sais-tout m. **know-how** n (coll) technique f. **know how to** savoir. **knowing** adj fin; (look) entendu.

knowledge ['nɒlɪdʒ] n connaissance f, savoir m. **knowledgeable** adj bien informé.

known [nəʊn] V know.

knuckle ['nʌkl] n articulation du doigt f.

L

label ['leɪbl] n étiquette f. v étiqueter.

laboratory [lə'bɒrətərɪ] n laboratoire m.

labour ['leɪbə] n travail (pl -aux) m; (workers) main-d'œuvre f. **Labour** m, adj (pol) travailliste. **labour pains** douleurs de l'accouchement f pl. **labour-saving device** appareil ménager m. v peiner. **laborious** adj laborieux. **labourer** n ouvrier m.

laburnum [lə'bəːnəm] n cytise m.

labyrinth ['læbərɪnθ] n labyrinthe m.

lace [leɪs] n dentelle f; (for shoe) lacet m. v lacer; (drink) arroser.

lacerate ['læsəreɪt] v lacérer. **laceration** n (act) lacération f; (tear) déchirure f.

lack [læk] n manque m. v manquer (de). **for lack of** faute de. v manquer (de).

lackadaisical [ˌlækə'deɪzɪkəl] adj apathique; indolent.

lacquer ['lækə] n laque f. v laquer.

lad [læd] n (coll) gars m.

ladder ['lædə] n échelle f. v (stocking) filer. **ladderproof** adj indémaillable.

laden ['leɪdn] adj chargé.

ladle ['leɪdl] n louche f.

lady ['leɪdɪ] n dame f. **ladies** n (sign) dames f. **ladies and gentlemen!** mesdames, messieurs! **ladybird** n coccinelle f. **lady-in-waiting** n dame d'honneur f.

lag¹ [læg] v traîner. n retard m; (time difference) décalage m.

lag² [læg] v calorifuger. **lagging** n calorifuge m.

lager ['lɑːgə] n bière blonde f.

lagoon [lə'guːn] n lagune f.

laid [leɪd] V lay¹.

lain [leɪn] V lie².

lair [leə] n tanière f.

laity ['leɪɪtɪ] n laïcs m pl.

lake [leɪk] n lac m.

lamb [læm] n agneau m.

lame [leɪm] adj boîteux; (excuse, etc.) faible. **be lame** boîter. v estropier. **lamely** adv maladroitement. **lameness** n boîterie f; faiblesse f.

lament [lə'ment] n lamentation f. v se lamenter, pleurer. **lamentable** adj lamentable; regrettable.

laminate ['læmɪneɪt] v laminer. **laminated** adj laminé; (glass) feuilleté; (windscreen) en verre feuilleté.

lamp [læmp] n lampe f. **lamppost** n réverbère m. **lampshade** n abat-jour m invar.

lance [lɑːns] n lance f. v (blister, etc.) ouvrir.

land [lænd] n terre f; (country) pays m. **landlady** n propriétaire f; (boarding house) patronne f. **landlord** n propriétaire m; (pub) patron m. **landmark** n point de repère m. **landscape** n paysage m. v (boat) débarquer; (aircraft) atterrir; (fall) tomber. **landing** n débarquement m; atterrissage m; (between floors) palier m. **landing stage** débarcadère m.

lane [leɪn] n chemin m; (on motorway, etc.) voie f; (line of traffic) file f.

language ['læŋwɪdʒ] n (means of expression) langage m; (of a nation) langue f.

languish ['læŋwɪʃ] v languir.

lanky ['læŋkɪ] adj dégingandé.

lantern ['læntən] n lanterne f.

Laos ['laɒs] n Laos m.

lap¹ [læp] n (sport) tour de piste m. v (wrap) enrouler. **lap over** se chevaucher.

lap² [læp] v (drink) laper; (waves) clapoter.

lap³ [læp] n genoux m pl.

lapel [lə'pel] n revers m.

Lapland ['læplænd] n Laponie f. **Lapp** nm, adj lapon; (people) Lapon, -e m, f.

lapse [læps] n (fault) défaillance f; (time) intervalle m; (of custom) disparition f. v (expire) se périmer; (fall) tomber; (commit fault) faire un écart.

larceny ['lɑːsənɪ] n vol simple m.

larch [lɑːtʃ] n mélèze m.

lard [lɑːd] n saindoux m.

larder ['lɑːdə] n garde-manger m invar.

large [lɑːdʒ] adj grand; gros, grosse. **at large** en liberté; en général. **large-scale** adj à grande échelle; fait sur une grande échelle.

lark¹ [lɑːk] n (bird) alouette f.

lark² [lɑːk] (coll) n blague f. v **lark around** faire le petit fou, faire la petite folle.

larva ['lɑːvə] n, pl **larvae** larve f.

larynx ['lærɪŋks] n larynx m. **laryngitis** n laryngite f.

laser ['leɪzə] n laser m.

lash [læʃ] n coup de fouet m; (thong) mèche f; (of eye) cil m. v (whip) fouetter; (rain, etc.) cingler; (attach) attacher. **lash out** envoyer un coup; (coll: money) lâcher. **lashing** n flagellation f. **lashings of** (coll) des tas de.

lass [læs] n jeune fille f.

lassitude ['læsɪtjuːd] n lassitude f.

lasso [læ'suː] n lasso m. v prendre au lasso.

last¹ [lɑːst] adj dernier. **last-minute** adj de dernière minute. **last night** (evening) hier soir. adv en dernier; finalement; la dernière fois. n dernier, -ière m, f. **at last** enfin. **lastly** adv pour terminer.

last² [lɑːst] v durer. **last out** (person) tenir, (money, food, etc.) faire. **lasting** adj durable.

latch [lætʃ] n loquet m. v fermer au loquet.

late [leɪt] adj en retard; récent; (former) ancien; (dead) feu. adv (not on time) en retard; (not early) tard. **lately** adv récemment. **lateness** n retard m. **later** adj plus tard. **see you later!** à tout à l'heure! **latest** adj (most recent) dernier. **at the latest** au plus tard.

latent ['leɪtənt] adj latent.

lateral ['lætərəl] adj latéral.

lathe [leɪð] n tour m.

lather ['lɑːðə] n mousse f. v (apply soap) savonner; (foam) mousser.

Latin ['lætɪn] nm, adj latin.

latitude ['lætɪtjuːd] n latitude f.

latrine [lə'triːn] n latrine f.

latter ['lætə] adj dernier, deuxième. **the latter** celui-ci, celle-ci m, f.

lattice ['lætɪs] n treillis m; (frame) treillage m.

laugh [lɑːf] v rire. **laugh at** rire de; se moquer de. n rire m; éclat de rire m. **laughable** adj ridicule. **it's no laughing matter** il n'y a pas de quoi rire. **laughing-stock** n risée f. **laughter** n rires m pl.

launch¹ [lɔːntʃ] v lancer. **launching** n lancement m.

launch² [lɔːntʃ] n vedette f; (of warship) chaloupe f.

launder ['lɔːndə] v blanchir. **launderette** n laverie automatique f. **laundry** n (clothes, etc.) linge m; (place) blanchisserie f.

laurel ['lɒrəl] n laurier m.

lava ['lɑːvə] n lave f.

lavatory ['lævətərɪ] n toilettes f pl, cabinets m pl.

lavender ['lævɪndə] n lavande f.

lavish ['lævɪʃ] adj prodigue; somptueux. v prodiguer.

law [lɔː] n loi f; (profession) droit m; justice f. **law-abiding** adj respectueux des lois. **lawsuit** n procès m. **lawful** adj légal, légitime. **lawyer** n avocat m.

lawn [lɔːn] n pelouse f. **lawn-mower** n tondeuse f.

lax [læks] adj relâché. **laxity** n relâchement m.

laxative ['læksətɪv] nm, adj laxatif.

*lay¹ [leɪ] v poser; (eggs) pondre. **layabout** n fainéant, -e m, f. **lay-by** n petite aire de stationnement f. **lay off** (workers) licencier. **lay on** (provide) fournir. **layout** n (of house, etc.) disposition f; (of page) mise en page f. **lay the table** mettre la table.

lay² [lei] *adj* laïque. **layman** *n* profane *m*.

lay³ [lei] *V* **lie³**.

layer ['leiə] *n* couche *f. v (hair)* couper en dégradé.

lazy ['leizi] *adj* paresseux. **laze around** paresser. **laziness** *n* paresse *f.*

***lead¹** [liːd] *v* mener, conduire; être à la tête de; *(sport)* être en tête. **lead on** *(tease)* faire marcher; *(encourage)* amener. **lead up to** conduire à; précéder. *n (sport)* tête *f;* exemple *m; (clue)* piste *f; (for dog)* laisse *f;* rôle principal *m; (elec)* fil *m.* **leader** *n* chef *m;* guide *m; (newspaper)* éditorial *m.* **leadership** *n* direction *f.* **leading** *adj* principal; majeur, -e.

lead² [led] *n* plomb *m; (pencil)* mine *f.*

leaf [liːf] *n* feuille *f;* page *f; (of table)* rallonge *f,* rabat *m. v* **leaf through** feuilleter. **leaflet** *n* prospectus *m.*

league [liːg] *n* ligue *f; (sport)* championnat *m.*

leak [liːk] *n* fuite *f. v* fuir; *(information)* divulguer. **leakage** *n* fuite *f.*

***lean¹** [liːn] *v* (se) pencher; *(support)* (s')appuyer. *n* inclinaison *f.* **leaning** *n* penchant *m.*

lean² [liːn] *nm, adj* maigre. **leanness** *n* maigreur *f.*

leant [lent] *V* **lean¹.**

***leap** [liːp] *n* saut *m,* bond *m.* **by leaps and bounds** à pas de géant. *v* sauter, bondir. **leap-frog** *n* saute-mouton *m.* **leap year** année bissextile *f.*

leapt [lept] *V* **leap.**

***learn** [ləːn] *v* apprendre. **learned** *adj* savant. **learner** *n* débutant, -e *m, f.* **learning** *n* érudition *f.*

learnt [ləːnt] *V* **learn.**

lease [liːs] *n* bail *m. v* louer à bail. **leasehold** *n* bail loué à bail.

leash [liːʃ] *n* laisse *f.*

least [liːst] *adj (amount)* le moins de; *(smallest)* le moindre, la moindre. *pron, adv* le moins. **at least** au moins.

leather ['leðə] *n* cuir *m.* **leathery** *adj* coriace; *(skin)* parcheminé.

***leave¹** [liːv] *v* laisser; *(go away from)* quitter; *(depart)* partir. **be left** rester. **leave out** omettre, exclure. **left-luggage office** consigne *f.* **left-overs** *pl n* restes *m pl.*

leave² [liːv] *n* permission *f; (holiday)* congé *m.*

lecherous ['letʃərəs] *adj* lubrique. **lecher** *n* débauché *m.* **lechery** *n* luxure *f.*

lectern ['lektən] *n* lutrin *m.*

lecture ['lektʃə] *n* conférence *f;* réprimande *f.* **lecture theatre** amphithéâtre *m. v* faire un cours; réprimander. **lecturer** *n* conférencier, -ère *m, f; (university)* maître assistant *m.*

led [led] *V* **lead¹.**

ledge [ledʒ] *n* rebord *m,* saillie *f.*

ledger ['ledʒə] *n* grand livre *m.*

lee [liː] *n* abri *m; (naut)* côté sous le vent *m.* **leeward** *adj, adv* sous le vent.

leech [liːtʃ] *n* sangsue *f.*

leek [liːk] *n* poireau *m.*

leer [liə] *v* lorgner. *n* regard mauvais *m.*

leeway ['liːwei] *n (naut)* dérive *f;* liberté d'action *f.*

left¹ [left] *V* **leave¹.**

left² [left] *nf, adj* gauche. *adv* à gauche. **left-hand** *adj* à gauche. **left-handed** *adj* gaucher, -ère. **left-wing** *adj* de gauche.

leg [leg] *n (person)* jambe *f; (animal)* patte *f; (pork, chicken)* cuisse *f; (lamb)* gigot *m; (furniture)* pied *m.*

legacy ['legəsi] *n* legs *m.*

legal ['liːgəl] *adj* légal; judiciaire. **legality** *n* légalité *f.* **legalize** *v* légaliser.

legend ['ledʒənd] *n* légende *f.* **legendary** *adj* légendaire.

legible ['ledʒəbl] *adj* lisible. **legibility** *n* lisibilité *f.*

legion ['liːdʒən] *n* légion *f.*

legislate ['ledʒisleit] *v* faire des lois, légiférer. **legislation** *n* législation *f.*

legitimate [lə'dʒitimət] *adj* légitime. **legitimacy** *n* légitimité *f.*

leisure ['leʒə] *n* loisir *m.*

lemon ['lemən] *n (fruit)* citron *m; (tree)* citronnier *m. adj (colour)* citron *invar.* **lemonade** *n* limonade *f.* **lemon sole** limande-sole *f.* **lemon tea** thé au citron *m.*

***lend** [lend] *v* prêter.

length [leŋθ] *n* longueur *f; (time)* durée *f; (piece)* morceau *m.* **lengthen** *v* (s')allonger, rallonger. **lengthy** *adj* long, longue.

lenient ['liːniənt] *adj* indulgent. **leniency** *n* indulgence *f.*

lens [lenz] *n* lentille *f; (camera)* objectif *m; (spectacles)* verre *m; (eye)* cristallin *m.* **lens hood** parasoleil *m.*

lent [lent] *V* **lend.**

Lent [lent] *n* Carême *m.*

lentil ['lentil] n lentille f.

Leo ['li:ou] n Lion m.

leopard ['lepəd] n léopard m.

leotard ['li:ətɑ:d] n collant m.

leper ['lepə] n lépreux, -euse m. f. **leprosy** n lèpre f. **leprous** adj lépreux.

lesbian ['lezbiən] n lesbienne f. adj lesbien. **lesbianism** n lesbianisme m.

less [les] nm, adv, prep moins. adj moins de. **less and less** de moins en moins. **lessen** v diminuer. **lesser** adj moindre.

lesson ['lesn] n leçon f. cours m.

lest [lest] conj de peur que.

*let [let] v laisser; (rent out) louer. **let down** (lower) descendre; (disappoint) décevoir; (dress) rallonger. **let-down** n déception f. **let in** faire entrer. **let out** faire sortir; (shout, cry) laisser échapper; (clothes) élargir.

lethal ['li:θəl] adj mortel.

lethargy ['leθədʒi] n léthargie f. **lethargic** adj léthargique.

letter ['letə] n lettre f. **letter-box** n boîte aux lettres f.

lettuce ['letis] n laitue f.

leukaemia [lu:'ki:miə] n leucémie f.

level ['levl] n niveau m; (road, rail) palier m. adj (flat) plat; horizontal; (spoonful) ras; (equal) à égalité. **be level with** être au niveau de; être à la hauteur de. **level crossing** passage à niveau m. **level-headed** adj équilibré. v niveler.

lever ['li:və] n levier m.

levy ['levi] n taxation f, taxe f. v prélever, imposer.

lewd [lu:d] adj obscène.

liable ['laiəbl] adj sujet, -ette; (law) responsable. **be liable to** risquer de. **liability** n responsabilité f; handicap m.

liaison [li:'eizon] n liaison f.

liar ['laiə] n menteur, -euse m. f.

libel ['laibəl] n (act) diffamation f; (writing) libelle m. v diffamer; (insult) calomnier. **libellous** adj diffamatoire.

liberal ['libərəl] adj libéral; généreux. **Liberal** n, adj (pol) libéral, -e.

liberate ['libəreit] v libérer. **liberation** n libération f.

liberty ['libəti] n liberté f. **at liberty** en liberté, libre.

Libra ['li:brə] n Balance f.

library ['laibrəri] n bibliothèque f. **librarian** n bibliothécaire m, f.

libretto [li'bretou] n livret m.

lice [lais] V **louse**.

licence ['laisəns] n permis m; (comm) licence f. **license** v donner une licence à; autoriser. **be licensed** (shop, etc.) détenir une licence. **licensee** n (pub) patron, -onne m. f.

lichen ['laikən] n lichen m.

lick [lik] n coup de langue m. v lécher.

lid [lid] n couvercle m.

lido ['li:dou] n complexe balnéaire m.

*lie¹ [lai] v s'allonger, se coucher; (be lying) être allongé, être couché; (be) être. **lie around** traîner. **lie down** s'allonger, se coucher. **lie in** faire la grasse matinée.

lie² [lai] n mensonge m. v mentir.

Liechtenstein ['liktən,stain] n Liechtenstein m.

lieutenant [lef'tenənt] n lieutenant m.

life [laif] n vie f. **lifeless** adj sans vie, inanimé.

lifebelt ['laifbelt] n bouée de sauvetage f.

lifeboat ['laifbout] n canot de sauvetage m; (on ship) chaloupe de sauvetage f.

lifeguard ['laifgɑ:d] n surveillant de baignade m.

life insurance n assurance-vie f.

life-jacket n gilet de sauvetage m.

lifeline ['laiflain] n main courante f; (diver's) corde de sécurité f.

lifelong ['laiflon] adj de toujours.

life-saving n sauvetage m.

life story n biographie f.

lifetime ['laiftaim] n vie f; éternité f.

lift [lift] n ascenseur m. **give someone a lift** prendre quelqu'un en voiture. v (se) lever, soulever.

ligament ['ligəmənt] n ligament m.

*light¹ [lait] n lumière f; (mot) feu m. adj clair. **light bulb** ampoule f. **lighthouse** n phare m. **light meter** photomètre m. **light-year** n année-lumineuse f. v (set fire to) allumer; (room, etc.) éclairer. **lighten** v (s')éclaircir. **lighter** n (for cigarette) briquet m. **lighting** n éclairage m.

light² [lait] adj léger. **light-headed** adj étourdi. **light-hearted** adj gai, joyeux. **lightweight** adj léger; (boxing) poids léger. **lighten** v alléger. **lightness** n légèreté f.

*light³ [lait] v **light upon** tomber sur.

lightning ['laitnin] n éclair m, foudre f. **lightning conductor** paratonnerre m.

like¹ [laik] adj semblable. prep comme. **be or look like** ressembler à. **liken** v comparer. **likeness** n ressemblance f; forme f; portrait m. **likewise** adv également.

like² [laik] v aimer; (want) vouloir. **likeable** adj sympathique. **liking** n goût m.

likely [laikli] adj probable; plausible. **be likely to** risquer de. adv probablement. **likelihood** n probabilité f.

lilac [lailək] nm, adj lilas.

lily [lili] n lis m. **lily-of-the-valley** n muguet m.

limb [lim] n membre m.

limbo [limbou] n (rel) limbes m pl; oubli m.

lime¹ [laim] n chaux f. **limestone** n pierre à chaux f.

lime² [laim] n (fruit) lime f; (tree) limettier m; (linden) tilleul m. **lime green** nm, adj vert jaune. **lime juice** jus de citron vert m.

limelight [laimˌlait] n **in the limelight** en vedette.

limerick [limərik] n poème humoristique m.

limit [limit] n limite f. v limiter. **limitation** n limitation f. **limitless** adj illimité.

limousine [liməˌziːn] n limousine f.

limp¹ [limp] v boiter.

limp² [limp] adj mou, molle. **limpness** n mollesse f.

limpet [limpit] n patelle f.

line¹ [lain] n ligne f; corde f; (of poem) vers m; (row) rangée f, file f. v régler; (wrinkle) rider. **line up** (s')aligner. **linear** adj linéaire.

line² [lain] v (clothes) doubler; (brakes) garnir.

linen [linin] n lin m; (sheets, etc.) linge m. **linen basket** panier à linge m.

liner [lainə] n linier m.

linger [liŋgə] v (person) s'attarder; (pain, memory, etc.) persister; (dawdle) traîner.

lingerie [læʒəri] n lingerie f.

linguist [liŋgwist] n linguiste m, f. **linguistic** adj linguistique. **linguistics** n linguistique f.

lining [lainiŋ] n (clothes) doublure f; (brakes) garniture f.

link [liŋk] n lien m, liaison f; (of chain) maillon m. v lier.

linoleum [liˈnouliəm] n linoléum m. **lino** n (coll) lino m.

linseed [linˌsiːd] n graines de lin f pl. **linseed oil** huile de lin f.

lint [lint] n tissu ouaté m.

lion [laiən] n lion m. **lioness** n lionne f.

lip [lip] n lèvre f; (edge) bord m. **lip-read**

v lire sur les lèvres. **lipstick** n rouge à lèvres m.

liqueur [liˈkjuə] n liqueur f.

liquid [likwid] nm, adj liquide. **liquidate** v liquider. **liquidation** n liquidation f. **liquidizer** n centrifugeuse f.

liquor [likə] n spiritueux m.

liquorice [likəris] n réglisse f.

lira [liərə] n lire f.

Lisbon [lizbən] n Lisbonne.

lisp [lisp] v zézayer.

list¹ [list] n liste f. v cataloguer, énumérer.

list² [list] v (naut) gîter. n inclinaison f.

listen [lisn] v écouter. **listener** n auditeur, -trice m, f.

listless [listlis] adj sans énergie; indolent, apathique.

lit [lit] V **light¹**, **light²**.

litany [litəni] n litanie f.

literacy [litərəsi] n degré d'alphabétisation m. **be literate** savoir lire et écrire.

literal [litərəl] adj littéral.

literary [litərəri] adj littéraire.

literature [litrətʃə] n littérature f; (brochures) documentation f.

litigation [litiˈgeiʃən] n litige m.

litre [liːtə] n litre m.

litter [litə] n détritus m pl; (zool) portée f; (bedding) litière f. **litter-bin** n boîte à ordures f. v joncher; (make untidy) mettre en désordre.

little [litl] adj (small) petit; (not much) peu de. nm, adv peu. **little by little** peu à peu.

liturgy [litədʒi] n liturgie f. **liturgical** adj liturgique.

live¹ [liv] v vivre; habiter. **live down** faire oublier. **live on** vivre de.

live² [laiv] adj vivant; (broadcast) en direct; (coal) ardent; (wire) sous tension. adv en direct.

livelihood [laivlihud] n gagne-pain m invar.

lively [laivli] adj vif, plein d'entrain. **liveliness** n vivacité f, entrain m.

liven [laivn] v **liven up** égayer, (s')animer.

liver [livə] n foie m.

livestock [laivstok] n bétail m.

livid [livid] adj livide; furieux.

living [liviŋ] adj vivant, en vie. n vie f. **living room** salle de séjour f.

lizard [lizəd] n lézard m.

load [loud] n charge f; (weight) poids m; (coll) tas m. v charger. **loaded** adj chargé;

(*dice*) pipé; (*question*) insidieux; (*slang: rich*) bourré de fric.

loaf¹ [louf] *n* pain *m*.

loaf² [louf] *v* loaf around fainéanter. **loafer** *n* (*coll*) flemmard, -e *m*, *f*.

loan [loun] *n* prêt *m*. *v* prêter.

loathe [louð] *v* détester. **loathing** *n* dégoût *m*. **loathsome** *adj* détestable.

lob [lob] *v* lancer; (*tennis*) lober. *n* lob *m*.

lobby ['lobi] *n* vestibule *m*, foyer *m*; groupe de pression *m*. *v* faire pression (sur).

lobe [loub] *n* lobe *m*.

lobster ['lobstə] *n* homard *m*.

local ['loukəl] *adj* local; du pays. *n* (*coll: pub*) café du coin *m*. **the locals** (*coll: people*) les gens du coin. **locality** *n* (*region*) environs *m pl*; (*place*) lieu *m*. **localize** *v* localiser. **locally** *adv* localement; (*nearby*) dans les environs.

locate [lə'keit] *v* (*find*) repérer, localiser; situer. **location** *n* emplacement *m*; (*cinema*) extérieur *m*. **on location** en extérieur.

lock¹ [lok] *n* serrure *f*; (*canal*) écluse *f*. **locksmith** *n* serrurier *m*. **lock, stock, and barrel** en bloc. **under lock and key** sous clef. *v* fermer à clef; (*tech*) (se) bloquer. **lock away** mettre sous clef. **lock in** enfermer. **lock out** enfermer dehors. **lock up** tout fermer; (*jewels, etc.*) enfermer.

lock² [lok] *n* (*of hair*) mèche *f*; (*curl*) boucle *f*.

locker ['lokə] *n* casier *m*.

locket ['lokit] *n* médaillon *m*.

locomotive [,loukə'moutiv] *n* locomotive *f*. *adj* locomotif. **locomotion** *n* locomotion *f*.

locust ['loukəst] *n* locuste *f*.

lodge [lodʒ] *n* loge *f*; (*small house*) maison de gardien *f*. *v* (se) loger; (*report*) présenter. **lodge a complaint** porter plainte. **lodger** *n* locataire *m*, *f*; (*boarder*) pensionnaire *m*, *f*. **lodgings** *pl n* (*room*) chambre *f sing*; (*flatlet*) logement *m sing*.

loft [loft] *n* grenier *m*. **lofty** *adj* haut, élevé; (*haughty*) hautain.

log [log] *n* bûche *f*. **logbook** *n* registre *m*; (*naut*) livre de bord *m*; (*aero*) carnet de vol *m*; (*mot*) carnet de route *m*. **log cabin** cabane en rondins *f*. *v* noter.

logarithm [logariðəm] *n* logarithme *m*.

loggerheads ['logəhedz] *pl n* **at loggerheads** en désaccord.

logic ['lodʒik] *n* logique *f*. **logical** *adj* logique.

loins [loins] *pl n* reins *m pl*. **loin chop** côte première *f*. **loincloth** *n* pagne *m*.

loiter ['loitə] *v* traîner.

lollipop ['loli,pop] *n* sucette *f*.

London ['lʌndən] *n* Londres *m*.

lonely ['lounli] *adj* seul, solitaire. **loneliness** *n* solitude *f*.

long¹ [loŋ] *adj* long, longue. *adv* longtemps. **as long as** pourvu que. **long-distance** *adj* (*race*) de fond; (*phone*) interurbain. **long-playing record** 33 tours *m invar*. **long-range** *adj* à longue portée; (*weather forecast*) à long terme. **long-sighted** *adj* hypermétrope; (*having foresight*) prévoyant. **long-sleeved** *adj* à manches longues. **long-standing** *adj* de longue date. **long-term** *adj* à long terme. **long-winded** *adj* (*person*) intarissable; (*speech*) interminable.

long² [loŋ] *v* avoir très envie. **long for** désirer ardemment. **longing** *n* désir *m*, envie *f*.

longevity [lon'dʒevəti] *n* longévité *f*.

longitude ['londʒitjuːd] *n* longitude *f*. **longitudinal** *adj* longitudinal.

loo [luː] *n* (*coll*) cabinets *m pl*.

look [luk] *n* regard *m*; (*glance*) coup d'œil *m*; air *m*, allure *f*. *v* regarder; sembler, avoir l'air. **look after** s'occuper de; (*possessions*) prendre soin de. **look at** regarder. **look down on** mépriser. **look for** chercher. **look forward to** attendre avec impatience. **look out** faire attention. **look out of** regarder par. **look up** lever les yeux; (*word, etc.*) chercher; s'améliorer.

loom¹ [luːm] *v* apparaître indistinctement; menacer.

loom² [luːm] *n* métier à tisser *m*.

loop [luːp] *n* boucle *f*. *v* boucler; former une boucle. **loop the loop** (*aero*) faire un looping.

loophole ['luːphoul] *n* (*in law, etc.*) lacune *f*, échappatoire *f*.

loose [luːs] *adj* lâche; (*knot*) desserré; (*tooth*) branlant. **come loose** se desserrer; branler. **get loose** s'échapper. **let loose** lâcher. **loose change** petite monnaie *f*. **loose chippings** gravillons *m pl*. **loose covers** housses *f pl*. **loose-leaf** *adj* à feuilles volantes. **loosely** *adv* lâchement; approximativement. **loosen** *v* relâcher; (se) desserrer; (se) défaire.

loot [luːt] n butin m. v piller. **looter** n pillard m. **looting** n pillage m.

lop [lop] v couper.

lopsided [ˌlopˈsaidid] adj de travers.

lord [loːd] n seigneur m; (as title) lord m.

lorry [ˈlori] n camion m. **lorry-driver** n camionneur m, routier m.

*lose [luːz] v perdre; (watch, clock) retarder. **loser** n perdant, -e m. **lost property** objets trouvés m pl.

loss [los] n perte f. **be at a loss** être embarrassé.

lost [lost] V lose.

lot [lot] n (destiny) sort m; (auction) lot m. **a lot** beaucoup. **lots of** beaucoup de. **quite a lot of** pas mal de. **the lot** tout m.

lotion [ˈlouʃən] n lotion f.

lottery [ˈlotəri] n loterie f.

lotus [ˈloutəs] n lotus m.

loud [laud] adj fort, sonore; (gaudy) voyant. adv fort. **loud hailer** porte-voix m invar. **loud-mouthed** adj braillard. **loud-speaker** n haut-parleur m. **loudly** adv fort. **loudness** n force f.

lounge [laundʒ] n salon m. **lounge suit** complet-veston m. v (on bed) se prélasser; (idle) paresser, flâner. **lounger** n (bed) lit de plage m.

louse [laus] n, pl **lice** [lais] pou (pl poux) m. **lousy** adj pouilleux; (slang: bad) moche, dégueulasse.

lout [laut] n rustre m.

love [lʌv] n amour m; (tennis) zéro m. **fall in love** tomber amoureux. **love affair** liaison f. **make love** faire l'amour. **with love from** (in letter) affectueusement. v aimer. **lovable** adj adorable. **lover** n amant m; (enthusiast) amateur m. **loving** adj affectueux.

lovely [ˈlʌvli] adj charmant, agréable.

low [lou] adj bas, basse; faible. adv bas. **low-cut** adj décolleté. **lowland** n plaine f. **low-lying** adj à basse altitude. **low-paid** adj mal payé. **lowly** adj humble, modeste.

lower [ˈlouə] adj inférieur, -e. v baisser; (on rope) descendre.

loyal [ˈloiəl] adj loyal, fidèle. **loyalty** n loyauté f; fidélité f.

lozenge [ˈlozindʒ] n pastille f.

lubricate [ˈluːbrikeit] v lubrifier; (mot) graisser. **lubricant** nm, adj lubrifiant. **lubrication** n lubrification f; graissage m.

lucid [ˈluːsid] adj lucide. **lucidity** n lucidité f.

luck [lʌk] n chance f, hasard m. **bad luck** malchance f, malheur m. **good luck** bonne chance f, bonheur m. **lucky** adj heureux; (charm) porte-bonheur m invar. **be lucky** avoir de la chance.

lucrative [ˈluːkrətiv] adj lucratif.

ludicrous [ˈluːdikrəs] adj ridicule.

lug [lʌg] v traîner.

luggage [ˈlʌgidʒ] n bagages m pl. **luggage label** étiquette à bagages f. **luggage rack** porte-bagages m invar.

lukewarm [ˈluːkwoːm] adj tiède.

lull [lʌl] n arrêt m; (storm) accalmie f. v apaiser.

lullaby [ˈlʌləbai] n berceuse f.

lumbago [lʌmˈbeigou] n lumbago m.

lumber[1] [ˈlʌmbə] n (wood) bois de charpente m; (junk) bric-à-brac m invar. **lumberjack** n bûcheron m. **lumber yard** chantier de scierie m. v **lumber with** (coll) coller à.

lumber[2] [ˈlʌmbə] v marcher pesamment.

luminous [ˈluːminəs] adj lumineux.

lump [lʌmp] n morceau m, masse f; (med) grosseur f. **lump sum** somme globale f. **lumpy** adj grumeleux.

lunacy [ˈluːnəsi] n folie f, démence f.

lunar [ˈluːnə] adj lunaire.

lunatic [ˈluːnətik] n, adj fou, folle; dément, -e. **lunatic asylum** asile d'aliénés m.

lunch [lʌntʃ] n déjeuner m. v déjeuner.

lung [lʌŋ] n poumon m.

lunge [lʌndʒ] v faire un mouvement brusque en avant. n coup en avant m.

lurch[1] [ləːtʃ] v (person) vaciller, tituber; (car, ship) faire une embardée. n vacillement m; embardée f.

lurch[2] [ləːtʃ] n **leave in the lurch** faire faux bond à.

lure [luə] v attirer par la ruse. n attrait m; (decoy) leurre m.

lurid [ˈluərid] adj affreux, horrible; à sensation.

lurk [ləːk] v (person) se tapir; (danger) menacer; (doubt) persister. **lurking** adj vague.

luscious [ˈlʌʃəs] adj succulent.

lush [lʌʃ] adj luxuriant, riche.

lust [lʌst] n (sexual) luxure f; (for power, etc.) soif f. v **lust after** convoiter; avoir soif de. **lusty** adj vigoureux.

lustre [ˈlʌstə] n lustre m.

lute [luːt] n luth m.

Luxembourg ['lʌksəmbɔːg] *n* Luxembourg *m*.
luxury ['lʌkʃəri] *n* luxe *m*. **luxuriant** *adj* luxuriant. **luxurious** *adj* luxueux.
lynch [lintʃ] *v* lyncher.
lynx [links] *n* lynx *m invar*.
lyre [laiə] *n* lyre *f*.
lyrical ['lirikəl] *adj* lyrique.
lyrics ['liriks] *pl n* paroles *f pl*. **lyricist** *n* parolier, -ère *m. f*.

M

mac [mak] *n (coll)* imper *m*.
macabre [mə'kɑːbr] *adj* macabre.
macaroni [makə'rouni] *n* macaroni *m*.
mace[1] [meis] *n (staff)* masse *f*; *(club)* massue *f*.
mace[2] [meis] *n (spice)* macis *m*.
machine [mə'ʃiːn] *n* machine *f*. **machine-gun** *n* mitrailleuse *f*. **machinery** *n* machinerie *f*; mécanisme *m*.
mackerel ['makrəl] *n* maquereau *m*.
mackintosh ['makin.tɔʃ] *n* imperméable *m*.
mad [mad] *adj* fou, folle; *(angry)* furieux. **madden** *v* rendre fou; exaspérer. **madly** *adv* follement, éperdument. **madness** *n* folie *f*.
madam ['madəm] *n* madame *f*.
Madrid [mə'drid] *n* Madrid *m*.
made [meid] *V* make.
Madeira [mə'diərə] *n (place)* Madère *f*; *(wine)* madère *m*.
magazine [.magə'ziːn] *n* revue *f*, magazine *m*; *(mil)* magasin *m*.
maggot ['magət] *n* ver *m*.
magic ['madʒik] *n* magie *f*. *adj also* **magical** magique. **magician** *n* magicien, -enne *m. f*.
magistrate ['madʒistreit] *n* magistrat *m*.
magnanimous [mag'nanimǝs] *adj* magnanime. **magnanimity** *n* magnanimité *f*.
magnate ['magneit] *n* magnat *m*.
magnet ['magnət] *n* aimant *m*. **magnetic** *adj* magnétique. **magnetism** *n* magnétisme *m*. **magnetize** *v* magnétiser.
magnificent [mag'nifisənt] *adj* magnifique. **magnificence** *n* magnificence *f*.
magnify ['magnifai] *v* grossir. **magnifying**

glass loupe *f*. **magnification** *n* grossissement *m*.
magnitude ['magnitjuːd] *n* ampleur *f*.
magnolia [mag'noulia] *n* magnolia *m*.
magpie ['magpai] *n* pie *f*.
mahogany [mə'hogəni] *n* acajou *m*.
maid [meid] *n* bonne *f*. **old maid** vieille fille *f*.
maiden ['meidən] *n* jeune fille *f*. *adj (first)* premier. **maiden aunt** tante célibataire *f*. **maiden name** nom de jeune fille *m*.
mail [meil] *n (letters)* courrier *m*; *(service)* poste *f*. **mail-bag** *n* sac postal *m*. **mail-box** *n (US)* boîte aux lettres *f*. **mailman** *n (US)* facteur *m*. **mail order** vente par correspondance *f*. **v** envoyer par la poste. **mailing list** liste d'adresses *f*.
maim [meim] *v* estropier.
main [mein] *adj* principal. **main course** plat principal *m*. **mainland** *n* continent *m*. **main-line station** gare de grande ligne *f*. **main road** grande route *f*. **mainstay** *n* soutien *m*. *n (gas, water)* conduite *f*. **in the main** en général. **mains** *n (elec)* secteur *m*.
maintain [mein'tein] *v* maintenir; *(car, family)* entretenir; continuer. **maintenance** *n* maintien *m*; entretien *m*; *(alimony)* pension alimentaire *f*.
maisonette [meizə'net] *n* duplex *m*.
maize [meiz] *n* maïs *m*.
majesty ['madʒəsti] *n* majesté *f*. **majestic** *adj* majestueux.
major ['meidʒə] *adj* majeur, -e. *n (mil)* commandant *m*.
majority [mə'dʒoriti] *n* majorité *f*. **be in the majority** être majoritaire.
***make** [meik] *n* marque *f*. *v* faire; rendre; obliger; arriver à. **make believe** faire semblant. **make out** *(draw up)* dresser; discerner; prétendre. **makeshift** *adj* de fortune. **make up** inventer; *(face)* (se) maquiller; composer; assembler. **make-up** *n* maquillage *m*. **make up for** compenser. **maker** *n* fabricant *m*. **making** *n* fabrication *f*.
maladjusted [malə'dʒʌstid] *adj* inadapté.
malaria [mə'leəriə] *n* malaria *m*.
male [meil] *nm, adj* mâle.
malevolent [mə'levələnt] *adj* malveillant. **malevolence** *n* malveillance *f*. **malevolently** *adv* avec malveillance.
malfunction [mal'fʌŋkʃən] *n* mauvaise fonction *f*. *v* mal fonctionner.

Mali 108

Mali ['mɑːli] *n* Mali *m*.

malice ['malis] *n* malice *f*. **malicious** *adj* méchant, malveillant.

malignant [mə'lignənt] *adj* malfaisant; (*med*) malin, -igne. **malignancy** *n* malfaisance *f*; malignité *f*.

malinger [mə'liŋgə] *v* faire le malade. **malingerer** *n* faux malade, fausse malade *m, f*.

mallet ['malit] *n* maillet *m*.

malnutrition [malnjuˈtriʃən] *n* sous-alimentation *f*.

malt [mɔːlt] *n* malt *m*.

Malta ['mɔːltə] *n* Malte *f*. **Maltese** *nm, adj* maltais. **the Maltese** les Maltais.

maltreat [malˈtriːt] *v* maltraiter. **maltreatment** *n* mauvais traitement *m*.

mammal ['maməl] *n* mammifère *m*.

mammoth ['maməθ] *n* mammouth *m. adj* géant.

man [man] *n, pl* **men** homme *m. v* armer. **manhood** *n* âge d'homme *m*. **manly** *adj* viril.

manage ['manidʒ] *v* (*business, etc.*) gérer, administrer; (*cope*) se débrouiller. **manage to** réussir à. **manageable** *adj* maniable. **management** *n* gestion *f*, administration *f*, direction *f*; (*not workers*) cadres *m pl*. **manager** *n* directeur *m*, gérant *m*. **manageress** *n* directrice *f*, gérante *f*. **managerial** *adj* directorial. **managing director** directeur général *m*.

mandarin ['mandərin] *n* mandarin *m*. **mandarin orange** (*fruit*) mandarine *f*; (*tree*) mandarinier *m*.

mandate ['mandeit] *n* mandat *m*. **mandatory** *adj* obligatoire; (*power, etc.*) mandataire.

mandolin ['mandəlin] *n* mandoline *f*.

mane [mein] *n* crinière *f*.

mange [meindʒ] *n* gale *f*. **mangy** *adj* galeux; (*coll*) minable, miteux.

manger ['meindʒə] *n* mangeoire *f*; (*rel*) crèche *f*.

mangle¹ ['maŋgl] *n* (*wringer*) essoreuse *f. v* essorer.

mangle² ['maŋgl] *v* mutiler, estropier.

mango ['maŋgou] *n* (*fruit*) mangue *f*; (*tree*) manguier *m*.

manhandle [man'handl] *v* maltraiter; (*goods*) manutentionner.

manhole ['manhoul] *n* trou d'homme *m*.

mania ['meiniə] *n* manie *f*. **maniac** *n* (*psych*) maniaque *m, f*; (*coll: madman*) fou, folle *m, f*; (*coll: enthusiast*) mordu *m*.

manicure ['manikjuə] *n* soin des mains *m. v* (*nails*) faire. **manicurist** *n* manucure *m, f*.

manifest ['manifest] *adj* manifeste. *v* manifester. **manifestation** *n* manifestation *f*.

manifesto [mani'festou] *n* manifeste *m*.

manifold ['manifould] *adj* divers; multiple. *n* **exhaust manifold** (*mot*) collecteur d'échappement *m*.

manipulate [mə'nipjuleit] *v* manipuler; manœuvrer. **manipulation** *n* manipulation *f*; manœuvre *f*.

mankind [ˌmanˈkaind] *n* le genre humain *m*.

man-made [ˌmanˈmeid] *adj* synthétique; artificiel.

manner ['manə] *n* manière *f*; attitude *f*; sorte *f*. **manners** *pl n* manières *f pl*.

mannerism ['manəˌrizəm] *n* trait particulier *m*.

manoeuvre *or US* **maneuver** [mə'nuːvə] *n* manœuvre *f. v* manœuvrer.

manor ['manə] *n* manoir *m*.

manpower ['manˌpauə] *n* main-d'œuvre *m*; force physique *f*.

mansion ['manʃən] *n* (*country*) château *m*; (*town*) hôtel particulier *m*.

manslaughter ['manˌslɔːtə] *n* homicide involontaire *m*.

mantelpiece ['mantlpiːs] *n* cheminée *f*.

mantle ['mantl] *n* (*of snow*) manteau *m*; (*cloak*) cape *f*; (*of gas lamp*) manchon *m*.

manual ['manjuəl] *nm, adj* manuel. **manually** *adv* à la main.

manufacture [manjuˈfaktʃə] *n* fabrication *f*; (*clothes*) confection *f. v* fabriquer; confectionner. **manufacturer** *n* fabricant *m*.

manure [mə'njuə] *n* fumier *m*; (*artificial*) engrais *m. v* fumer.

manuscript ['manjuskript] *nm, adj* manuscrit.

many ['meni] *adj* beaucoup de, un grand nombre de. *pron* beaucoup, un grand nombre. **as many** autant (de). **how many** combien (de). **so many** tant (de). **too many** trop (de).

map [map] *n* carte *f*; (*of town*) plan *m. v* faire la carte de. **map out** tracer.

maple ['meipl] *n* érable *m*.

mar [mɑː] *v* gâter.

marathon ['marəθən] *nm, adj* marathon.

marble ['maːbl] *n* marbre *m*; (*toy*) bille *f*. *v* marbrer.

march [maːtʃ] *n* marche *f*. *v* marcher au pas. **march-past** défilé *m*.

March [maːtʃ] *n* mars *m*.

marchioness [ˌmaːʃəˈnes] *n* marquise *f*.

mare [meə] *n* jument *f*.

margarine [ˌmaːdʒəˈriːn] *n* margarine *f*.

margin ['maːdʒin] *n* marge *f*. **marginal** *adj* marginal. **marginally** *adv* de très peu.

marguerite [ˌmaːɡəˈriːt] *n* marguerite *f*.

marigold ['mariɡould] *n* souci *m*.

marijuana [mariˈwaːnə] *n* marihuana *f*.

marina [məˈriːnə] *n* marina *f*.

marinade [ˌmariˈneid] *n* marinade *f*. *v* mariner.

marine [məˈriːn] *adj* (*animal, plant*) marin; (*products*) de mer; maritime. *n* (*naut*) marine marchande *f*; (*mil*) fusilier marin *m*.

marital ['maritl] *adj* conjugal, matrimonial.

maritime ['maritaim] *adj* maritime.

marjoram ['maːdʒərəm] *n* marjolaine *f*.

mark[1] [maːk] *n* marque *f*; (*school*) note *f*, point *m*; (*model*) série *f*. **marksman** *n* bon tireur *m*. *v* marquer; (*school*) corriger, noter. **marked** *adj* marqué, sensible. **marking** *n* correction *f*; (*of animal*) marque *f*.

mark[2] [maːk] *n* (*currency*) mark *m*.

market ['maːkit] *n* marché *m*. **market day** jour de marché *m*. **market gardening** culture maraîchère *f*. **market place** place du marché *f*. **market research** étude de marché *f*. **market value** valeur marchande *f*. *v* vendre. **marketing** *n* commercialisation *f*.

marmalade ['maːməleid] *n* confiture d'orange *f*.

maroon[1] [məˈruːn] *adj* bordeaux *invar*.

maroon[2] [məˈruːn] *v* abandonner.

marquee [maːˈkiː] *n* grande tente *f*; (*circus*) chapiteau *m*.

marquess *or* **marquis** ['maːkwis] *n* marquis *m*.

marquetry ['maːkətri] *n* marqueterie *f*.

marriage ['maridʒ] *n* mariage *m*. **by marriage** par alliance. **marriage certificate** extrait d'acte de mariage *m*. **marriage guidance counsellor** conseiller conjugal, conseillère conjugale *m, f*. **marriage licence** dispense de bans *f*.

marrow ['marou] *n* (*of bone*) moelle *f*; (*vegetable*) courge *f*.

marry ['mari] *v* se marier; (*husband, wife*) épouser; (*priest, vicar*) marier. **married** *adj* marié; conjugal. **get married** se marier. **married name** nom de femme mariée *m*.

Mars [maːz] *n* Mars *m*. **Martian** *n* Martien, -enne; *adj* martien.

marsh [maːʃ] *n* marais *m*. **marshland** *n* marécage *m*. **marshmallow** *n* guimauve *f*. **marshy** *adj* marécageux.

marshal ['maːʃəl] *n* (*mil*) maréchal *m*; (*sports, etc.*) membre du service d'ordre *m*. *v* rassembler.

martial ['maːʃəl] *adj* martial.

martin ['maːtin] *n* martinet *m*.

martyr ['maːtə] *n* martyr, -e *m, f*. *v* martyriser. **martyrdom** *n* martyre *m*.

marvel ['maːvəl] *n* merveille *f*. *v* s'étonner (de).

marvellous ['maːvələs] *adj* merveilleux.

marzipan [maziˈpan] *n* pâte d'amandes *f*.

mascara [maˈskaːrə] *n* mascara *m*.

mascot ['maskət] *n* mascotte *f*.

masculine ['maskjulin] *nm, adj* masculin. **masculinity** *n* masculinité *f*.

mash [maʃ] *v* écraser; (*potatoes*) faire en purée. **mashed potatoes** purée *f* sing. *n* (*animal feed*) pâtée *f*; purée *f*.

mask [maːsk] *n* masque *m*. *v* masquer. **masking tape** papier-cache adhésif *m*.

masochist ['masəkist] *n* masochiste *m, f*. **masochism** *n* masochisme *m*. **masochistic** *adj* masochiste.

mason ['meisn] *n* maçon *m*. **masonry** *n* maçonnerie *f*.

masquerade [maskəˈreid] *n* (*pretence*) mascarade *f*. *v* **masquerade as** se faire passer pour.

mass[1] [mas] *n* masse *f*. **mass hysteria** hystérie collective *f*. **mass media** media *m pl*. **mass-produce** *v* fabriquer en série. **mass production** fabrication en série *f*. *v* (se) masser.

mass[2] [mas] *n* (*rel*) messe *f*.

massacre ['masəkə] *n* massacre *m*. *v* massacrer.

massage ['masaːʒ] *n* massage *m*. *v* masser. **masseur** *n* masseur *m*. **masseuse** *n* masseuse *f*.

massive ['masiv] *adj* massif, énorme.

mast [maːst] *n* (*naut*) mât *m*; (*radio, etc.*) pylône *m*.

master ['maːstə] *n* maître *m*; (*teacher*) professeur *m*. **master copy** original *m*. **master key** passe-partout *m invar*. **mas-**

terpiece n chef-d'œuvre m. **master plan**
stratégie d'ensemble f. v maîtriser;
surmonter; (learn, understand) posséder
à fond. **masterly** adj magistral. **mastery** n
maîtrise f, domination f; (skill) virtuosité
f.

mastermind ['mɑːstəmaɪnd] n cerveau m.
v diriger.

masturbate ['mæstəbeɪt] v se masturber.
masturbation n masturbation f.

mat [mæt] n (floor) tapis m; (door) paillasson m; (table) dessous-de-plat m invar;
(cloth) napperon m. **matted** adj (hair)
emmêlé; (cloth) feutré.

match[^1] [mætʃ] n allumette f. **matchbox** n
boîte à allumettes f.

match[^2] [mætʃ] n (sport) match m, partie f;
(equal) égal, -e m, f. v égaler; (clothes)
s'assortir à, aller bien ensemble; (pair)
s'apparier. **matchless** adj sans égal.

mate [meɪt] n mâle, femelle m, f;
camarade m, f; aide f; (coll: friend)
copain, -ine m, f. v (s')accoupler.

material [mə'tɪərɪəl] n (fabric) tissu m;
(substance) matière f; (for book, etc.)
matériaux m pl. **materials** n pl fournitures f pl. adj matériel. **materialist** n
matérialiste m, f. **materialistic** adj matérialiste. **materialize** v se matérialiser.

maternal [mə'təɪnl] adj maternel.

maternity [mə'təɪnəti] n maternité f.
maternity clothes vêtements de grossesse
m pl. **maternity hospital** maternité f.

mathematics [mæθə'mætiks] n mathématiques f pl. **mathematical** adj mathématique. **mathematician** n mathématicien,
-enne m, f. **maths** n (coll) maths f pl.

matinee ['mætineɪ] n matinée f. **matinée
coat** veste de bébé f.

matins ['mætinz] n matines f pl.

matriarch ['meɪtrɪɑːk] n matrone f. **matriarchal** adj matriarcal.

matrimony ['mætrɪməni] n mariage m.
matrimonial adj matrimonial.

matrix ['meɪtriks] n matrice f.

matron ['meɪtrən] n matrone f; (hospital)
infirmière en chef f; (school) infirmière f;
(home) directrice f.

matt [mæt] adj mat.

matter ['mætə] n (substance) matière f;
affaire f; contenu m. **as a matter of fact** à
vrai dire. **matter-of-fact** adj (tone) neutre;
(person) terre à terre. **what's the matter?**
qu'est-ce qu'il y a? v importer. **it doesn't
matter** ça ne fait rien.

mattress ['mætrɪs] n matelas m.

mature [mə'tjuə] adj mûr. v mûrir. **maturity** n maturité f.

maudlin ['mɔːdlɪn] adj larmoyant.

maul [mɔːl] v mutiler, malmener.

mausoleum [mɔːsə'lɪəm] n mausolée m.

mauve [mouv] nm, adj mauve.

maxim ['mæksɪm] n maxime f.

maximum ['mæksɪməm] nm, adj maximum.

****may** [meɪ] v pouvoir.

May [meɪ] n mai m. **May Day** le Premier
mai.

maybe ['meɪbiː] adv peut-être.

mayday ['meɪdeɪ] n mayday m.

mayonnaise [ˌmeɪə'neɪz] n mayonnaise f.

mayor [meə] n maire m.

maze [meɪz] n labyrinthe m.

me [miː] pron moi; (direct object) me.

mead [miːd] n (drink) hydromel m.

meadow ['medou] n pré m.

meagre ['miːgə] adj maigre.

meal[^1] [miːl] n (food) repas m. **make a
meal of** (labour) faire tout un plat de.

meal[^2] [miːl] n (flour) farine f.

****mean**[^1] [miːn] v (signify) vouloir dire;
avoir l'intention (de); destiner.

mean[^2] [miːn] n (not generous) avare;
(unkind) mesquin; (poor) minable. **meanness** n avarice f; mesquinerie f.

mean[^3] [miːn] n milieu m; (math) moyenne
f. adj moyen.

meander [mi'ændə] v (river) serpenter;
(person) errer. n méandre m.

meaning ['miːnɪŋ] n sens m, signification
f. **meaningful** adj significatif. **meaningless**
adj dénué de sens; (senseless) insensé.

means [miːnz] n (way) moyen m; (wealth)
moyens m pl. **by all means** certainement.
by means of au moyen de. **by no means**
pas du tout. **means test** enquête sur les
ressources f.

meant [ment] V **mean**[^1].

meanwhile ['miːnwaɪl] adv en attendant.

measles ['miːzlz] n rougeole f.

measure ['meʒə] n mesure f. **made to
measure** fait sur mesure. v mesurer. **measurement** n mesure f.

meat [miːt] n viande f. **meatball** n
boulette de viande f. **meat pie** pâté en
croûte m.

mechanic [mi'kænik] n mécanicien m.
mechanical adj mécanique. **mechanics** pl
n mécanisme m sing; (sing: science)

mécanique f. **mechanism** n mécanisme m.
mechanize v mécaniser.

medal ['medl] n médaille f. **medallist** n médaillé, -e m, f.

meddle ['medl] v (*interfere*) se mêler (de); toucher (à). **meddlesome** adj indiscret, -ète.

media ['mɪdɪə] pl n media m pl.

mediate ['mɪdɪeɪt] v s'entremettre; servir de médiateur. **mediation** n médiation f. **mediator** n médiateur, -trice m, f.

medical ['medɪkəl] adj médical. **medical officer** médecin du travail m. **medical school** école de médecine f. n visite médicale f, examen médical m. **medicate** v médicamenter. **medicated** adj (*shampoo, etc.*) médical.

medicine ['medsən] n (*science*) médecine f; (*drug*) médicament m. **medicine chest** pharmacie f. **medicinal** adj médicinal.

medieval [medɪˈiːvəl] adj médiéval.

mediocre [mɪdɪˈoukə] adj médiocre. **mediocrity** n médiocrité f.

meditate ['medɪteɪt] v méditer. **meditation** n méditation f. **meditative** adj méditatif.

Mediterranean [medɪtəˈreɪnɪən] adj méditerranéen. n Méditerranée f.

medium ['mɪdɪəm] n milieu m; (*means*) moyen m; (*spirits*) médium m. **happy medium** juste milieu m. adj moyen. **medium-dry** adj (*wine*) demi-sec. **medium wave** (*radio*) onde moyenne f.

medley ['medli] n mélange m; (*music*) pot-pourri m.

meek [miːk] adj doux, douce. **meekness** n douceur f.

****meet** [miːt] v (se) rencontrer; (*by arrangement*) (se) retrouver; (*gather*) se réunir; (*expenses, etc.*) faire face à. **meeting** n réunion f, assemblée f; (*appointment*) rendez-vous m.

megaphone ['megəfoun] n porte-voix m invar.

melancholy ['melənkəli] n mélancolie f. adj also **melancholic** mélancolique.

mellow ['melou] adj moelleux, velouté; (*matured*) mûr. v mûrir; se velouter; (*person*) s'adoucir.

melodrama ['melədrɑːmə] n mélodrame m. **melodramatic** adj mélodramatique. **melodramatically** adv d'un air mélodramatique.

melody ['melədi] n mélodie f. **melodious** adj mélodieux.

melon ['melən] n melon m.

melt [melt] v (se) fondre. **melting** n fusion f.

member ['membə] n membre m. **membership** n adhésion f. **membership card** carte d'adhérent f. **membership fee** cotisation f.

membrane ['membreɪn] n membrane f. **membranous** adj membraneux.

memento [məˈmentou] n souvenir m.

memo ['memou] n (*coll*) note f.

memoirs ['memwaːz] pl n mémoires m pl.

memorable ['memərəbl] adj mémorable.

memorandum [meməˈrandəm] n mémorandum m, note f.

memorial [mɪˈmoːrɪəl] n monument m, mémorial m. adj commémoratif.

memory ['meməri] n (*faculty*) mémoire f; (*thing remembered*) souvenir m. **memorize** v apprendre par cœur.

men [men] V **man**.

menace ['menis] n menace f. v menacer.

menagerie [mɪˈnadʒəri] n ménagerie f.

mend [mend] v raccommoder, réparer. n raccommodage m. **be on the mend** s'améliorer. **mending** n raccommodage m.

menial ['mɪnɪəl] adj (*task*) de domestique; (*person*) servile.

meningitis [menɪnˈdʒaɪtis] n méningite f.

menopause ['menəpɔːz] n ménopause f.

menstrual ['menstruəl] adj menstruel. **menstruate** v avoir ses règles. **menstruation** n menstruation f.

mental ['mentl] adj mental; (*coll: mad*) timbré. **mental arithmetic** calcul mental m. **mental home** or **hospital** clinique psychiatrique f. **mentality** n mentalité f. **mentally** adv mentalement.

menthol ['menθəl] n menthol m.

mention ['menʃən] v mentionner. **don't mention it!** il n'y a pas de quoi! **not to mention** sans compter. n mention f.

menu ['menjuː] n menu m.

mercantile ['məːkənˌtaɪl] adj marchand; commercial.

mercenary ['məːsɪnəri] nm, adj mercenaire.

merchandise ['məːtʃəndaɪz] n marchandises f pl. **merchandizing** n techniques marchandes f pl.

merchant ['məːtʃənt] n négociant m, commerçant m. **merchant navy** marine marchande f.

mercury ['mɜːkjuri] n mercure m.

mercy ['mɜːsi] n pitié f, merci f; (rel) miséricorde f. **at the mercy of** à la merci de.

merciful adj miséricordieux. **merciless** adj impitoyable.

mere [miə] adj simple. **it's a mere formality** ce n'est qu'une formalité.

merge [mɜːdʒ] v se mêler; (comm) fusionner; unifier. **merger** n fusion f.

meridian [mə'ridiən] nm, adj méridien.

meringue [mə'raŋ] n meringue f.

merit ['merit] n mérite m. v mériter.

mermaid ['mɜːmeid] n sirène f.

merry ['meri] adj gai, joyeux; (coll: drunk) éméché. **merry-go-round** n manège m. **merriment** n gaieté f; hilarité f.

mesh [meʃ] n maille f; (network) réseau m; (gears) engrenage m.

mesmerize ['mezməraiz] v hypnotiser.

mess [mes] n désordre m, gâchis m; (dirt) saleté f; (mil) mess m. **make a mess of** gâcher. v **mess up** salir; gâcher, mettre en désordre. **messy** adj en désordre; sale.

message ['mesidʒ] n message m; (errand) course f. **messenger** n messager, -ère m, f.

met [met] V meet.

metabolism [mi'tæbəlizm] n métabolisme m.

metal ['metl] n métal m. **metallic** adj métallique. **metallurgist** n métallurgiste m. **metallurgy** n métallurgie f.

metamorphosis [metə'mɔːfəsis] n métamorphose f.

metaphor ['metəfə] n métaphore f. **metaphorical** adj métaphorique.

metaphysics [metə'fiziks] n métaphysique f. **metaphysical** adj métaphysique.

meteor ['miːtiə] n météore m. **meteoric** adj météorique; (rapid) fulgurant. **meteorite** n météorite m.

meteorology [miːtiə'rolədʒi] n météorologie f. **meteorological** adj météorologique. **meteorologist** n météorologue m. f.

meter ['miːtə] n compteur m.

methane ['miːθein] n méthane m.

method ['meθəd] n méthode f. **methodical** adj méthodique.

Methodist ['meθədist] n méthodiste m, f. **Methodism** n méthodisme m.

methylated spirits ['meθileitid] n alcool à brûler m.

meticulous [mi'tikjuləs] adj méticuleux.

metre ['miːtə] n mètre m. **metric** adj métrique.

metronome ['metrənoum] n métronome m.

metropolis [mə'tropəlis] n métropole f. **metropolitan** adj métropolitain.

mew [mjuː] v miauler. n miaulement m.

mice [mais] V mouse.

microbe ['maikroub] n microbe m.

microfilm ['maikrəfilm] n microfilm m.

microphone ['maikrəfoun] n microphone m.

microscope ['maikrəskoup] n microscope m. **microscopic** adj microscopique.

microwave ['maikrəweiv] n micro-onde f.

mid [mid] adj du milieu. **mid-June, July,** etc. mi-juin, mi-juillet, juillet, etc.

mid-air [mid'eə] n **in mid-air** en plein ciel.

midday [mid'dei] n midi m.

middle ['midl] n milieu m. **in the middle** au milieu. adj du milieu. **middle-aged** adj d'un certain âge. **the Middle Ages** le moyen âge m sing. **middle-class** adj bourgeois. **Middle East** Moyen-Orient m. **middleman** n intermédiaire m. **middle-of-the-road** adj modéré. **middle-sized** adj de grandeur moyenne. **middling** adj comme ci comme ça.

midge [midʒ] n moucheron m.

midget ['midʒit] n nain, -e m, f.

midnight ['midnait] n minuit m.

midriff ['midrif] n diaphragme m; (waist) taille f.

midst [midst] n milieu m. **in our midst** parmi nous. **in the midst of** au milieu de.

midstream [mid'striːm] n **in midstream** au milieu du courant.

midsummer ['mid.sʌmə] n cœur de l'été m. **Midsummer Day** la Saint-Jean f.

midway [mid'wei] adv, adj à mi-chemin.

midweek [mid'wiːk] n milieu de la semaine m.

midwife ['midwaif] n sage-femme f. **midwifery** n obstétrique f.

midwinter [mid'wintə] n milieu de l'hiver m.

might¹ [mait] V may.

might² [mait] n puissance f.

mighty ['maiti] adj puissant; vaste. adv (coll) rudement.

migraine ['miːgrein] n migraine f.

migrate [mai'greit] v émigrer. **migration** n migration f.

mike [maik] n (coll: microphone) micro m.

mild [maild] adj doux, douce. **mildness** n douceur f.

mildew ['mildjuː] n (vine) mildiou m; (plants) rouille f; (cloth) moisissure f.

mile [mail] n mille m. **mileage** n distance en milles f; (petrol) consommation aux cent f. **mileometer** n compteur de milles m. **milestone** n borne f; (of life, etc.) jalon m.

militant ['militənt] n, adj militant, -e.

military ['militəri] adj militaire.

milk [milk] n lait m. **milk chocolate** chocolat au lait m. **milkman** n laitier m. **milk shake** lait parfumé fouetté m. v traire. **milking** n traite f. **milky** adj laiteux.

mill [mil] n moulin m; (larger) minoterie f; (factory) usine f. **like a millpond** comme un lac. **millstone** n meule f; (burden) boulet m. v moudre. **mill round** grouiller autour de. **miller** n meunier m.

millennium [mi'leniəm] n millénaire m. **the millennium** le millénium m.

millet ['milit] n millet m.

milligram ['miligram] n milligramme m.

millilitre ['mili͵liːtə] n millilitre m.

millimetre ['mili͵miːtə] n millimètre m.

milliner ['milinə] n modiste f. **millinery** n modes f pl.

million ['miljən] n million m. **millionaire** n millionnaire m. **millions of** des milliers de. **millionth** n(m+f). adj millionième.

mime [maim] n mime m. v mimer.

mimic ['mimik] n imitateur, -trice m, f. v imiter. **mimicry** n imitation f; (zool) mimétisme f.

minaret [minə'ret] n minaret m.

mince [mins] n (meat) hachis m. **mincemeat** n hachis de fruit secs, de pommes et de graisse m. **mince pie** tarte anglaise au mincemeat f. v hacher; (walk) marcher à petits pas maniérés. **mince words** mâcher ses mots. **mincer** n hachoir m. **mincing** adj affecté.

mind [maind] n esprit m. **bear in mind** tenir compte de. **go out of one's mind** perdre la tête. **have a good mind to** avoir bien envie de. **in mind** dans l'idée. **make up one's mind** décider. **read someone's mind** lire la pensée de quelqu'un. **to my mind** à mon avis. v (look out) faire attention (à). prendre garde (à); (look after) garder. **do you mind?** cela ne vous fait rien? **I don't mind** ça m'est égal. **never mind** ça ne fait rien.

mine¹ [main] pron le mien, la mienne.

mine² [main] n mine f. **minefield** n champ de mines m. **mineshaft** n puits de mine m. **minesweeper** dragueur de mines. m. v extraire; (mil) miner. **miner** n mineur m. **mining** n exploitation minière f. **mining town** ville minière f.

mineral ['minərəl] nm, adj minéral. **minerals** pl n (drinks) boissons gazeuses f pl.

mingle ['miŋgl] v (se) mêler (à).

miniature ['miniətʃə] n miniature f; (bottle) mini-bouteille f. adj miniature; minuscule.

minim ['minim] n blanche f.

minimum ['miniməm] nm, adj minimum. **minimal** adj minime. **minimize** v minimiser.

minister ['ministə] n ministre m. **ministerial** adj ministériel. **ministry** n ministère m.

mink [miŋk] n vison m.

minor ['mainə] adj mineur, -e; (unimportant) petit, secondaire. n mineur, -e m, f.

minority [mai'noriti] n minorité f. **in the minority** en minorité. adj minoritaire.

minstrel ['minstrəl] n ménestrel m.

mint¹ [mint] n (bot) menthe f.

mint² [mint] n Monnaie f. **in mint condition** à l'état neuf. v battre.

minuet [minju'et] n menuet m.

minus ['mainəs] prep moins. **minus quantity** quantité négative f. **minus sign** moins m.

minute¹ ['minit] n minute f. **minutes** pl n compte rendu m sing. v (meeting) rédiger le compte rendu de.

minute² [mai'njuːt] adj (tiny) minuscule; (detailed) minutieux.

miracle ['mirəkl] n miracle m. **miraculous** adj miraculeux.

mirage ['miraːʒ] n mirage m.

mirror ['mirə] n miroir m, glace f; (mot) rétroviseur m. **mirror image** image inverstie f. v refléter.

mirth [məːθ] n hilarité f.

misadventure [misəd'ventʃə] n mésaventure f. **death by misadventure** mort accidentelle f.

misanthropist [miz'anθrəpist] n misanthrope m, f. **misanthropic** adj misanthrope. **misanthropy** n misanthropie f.

misapprehension [misapri'henʃən] *n* malentendu *m*.

misbehave [misbi'heiv] *v* se conduire mal.

miscalculate [mis'kælkjuleit] *v* mal calculer; se tromper.

miscarriage [mis'karidʒ] *n* (*med*) fausse couche *f*; (*plans, etc.*) insuccès *m*. **miscarriage of justice** erreur judiciaire *f*.

miscellaneous [misə'leiniəs] *adj* divers.

mischief ['mistʃif] *n* malice *f*; (*of child*) sottises *f pl*; (*damage*) mal *m*. **get into mischief** faire des sottises. **make mischief** semer la discorde. **mischievous** *adj* espiègle, malicieux.

misconception [miskən'sepʃən] *n* idée fausse *f*.

misconduct [mis'kɔndʌkt] *n* inconduite *f*.

misconstrue [miskən'struː] *v* mal interpréter.

misdeed [mis'diːd] *n* méfait *m*.

misdemeanour [misdi'miːnə] *n* incartade *f*; (*law*) infraction *f*.

miser ['maizə] *n* avare *m, f*. **miserly** *adj* avare.

miserable ['mizərəbl] *adj* (*sad*) malheureux; pitoyable; (*wretched*) misérable; dérisoire.

misery ['mizəri] *n* (*sadness*) tristesse *f*; (*wretchedness*) misère *f*; (*coll: person*) grincheux, -euse *m, f*.

misfire [mis'faiə] *v* rater; (*mot*) avoir des ratés.

misfit ['misfit] *n* inadapté, -e *m, f*.

misfortune [mis'fɔːtʃən] *n* malheur *m*.

misgiving [mis'givin] *n* doute *m*, appréhension *f*.

misguided [mis'gaidid] *adj* malencontreux.

mishap ['mishap] *n* mésaventure *f*.

misinterpret [misin'tɜːprit] *v* mal interpréter. **misinterpretation** *n* interprétation erronée *f*.

misjudge [mis'dʒʌdʒ] *v* mal évaluer; (*person*) méjuger.

****mislay** [mis'lei] *v* égarer.

****mislead** [mis'liːd] *v* tromper. **misleading** *adj* trompeur, -euse.

misnomer [mis'noumə] *n* nom mal approprié *m*.

misogynist [mi'sodʒənist] *n* misogyne *m, f*. **misogyny** *n* misogynie *f*.

misplace [mis'pleis] *v* mal placer; (*lose*) égarer.

misprint ['misprint] *n* coquille *f*.

miss[1] [mis] *v* manquer; (*long for*) regret-

ter. **miss out** sauter; omettre. *n* coup manqué *m*. **missing** *adj* absent, manquant.

miss[2] [mis] *n* mademoiselle *f*; (*abbrev*) Mlle.

misshapen [miʃ'ʃeipən] *adj* difforme.

missile ['misail] *n* projectile *m*; (*mil*) missile *m*.

mission ['miʃən] *n* mission *f*. **missionary** *n* missionnaire *m, f*.

mist [mist] *n* (*weather*) brume *f*; (*on glass*) buée *f*. *v* **mist over** or **up** (s')embuer. **misty** *adj* brumeux; embué.

****mistake** [mi'steik] *n* erreur *f*, faute *f*. **by mistake** par erreur. **make a mistake** faire une faute, se tromper. *v* mal interpréter: ne pas reconnaître; confondre. **mistaken** *adj* erroné. **be mistaken** se tromper, faire erreur.

mistletoe ['misltou] *n* gui *m*.

mistress ['mistris] *n* maîtresse *f*; (*teacher*) professeur *m*.

mistrust [mis'trʌst] *n* méfiance *f*. *v* se méfier de.

****misunderstand** [misʌndə'stand] *v* mal comprendre. **misunderstanding** *n* méprise *f*.

misuse [mis'juːs; *v* mis'juːz] *n* abus *m*; usage impropre *m*. *v* abuser de; employer improprement.

mitigate ['mitigeit] *v* atténuer.

mitre ['maitə] *n* (*rel*) mitre *f*; (*carpentry*) onglet *m*. *v* tailler à onglet.

mitten ['mitn] *n* moufle *f*.

mix [miks] *v* (se) mélanger; (*cookery*) préparer; (*salad*) remuer. **mix up** mélanger; confondre; (*person*) embrouiller. **mix-up** *n* confusion *f*. **mixed** *adj* mixte; assorti. **mixed feelings** sentiments contraires *m pl*. **mixed grill** assortiment de grillades *m*. **mixer** *n* (*cookery*) mixer *m*; (*cement*) malaxeur *m*. **mixture** *n* mélange *m*.

moan [moun] *v* gémir; (*coll: complain*) rouspéter. *n* gémissement *m*; (*complaint*) plainte *f*.

moat [mout] *n* douves *f pl*.

mob [mob] *n* cohue *f*.

mobile ['moubail] *nm, adj* mobile. **mobility** *n* mobilité *f*. **mobilize** *v* mobiliser.

moccasin ['mokəsin] *n* mocassin *m*.

mock [mok] *v* se moquer (de); ridiculiser. *adj* faux, fausse; simulé. **mockery** *n* moquerie *f*; travestissement *m*. **mocking** *adj* moqueur, -euse.

mode [moud] *n* mode *m*.

model ['modl] *n* modèle *m*; *(fashion)* mannequin *m*. *adj* modèle; en miniature. *v* modeler; être mannequin; poser.

moderate ['modərət; *v* 'modəreit] *n*, *adj* modéré, -e. *v* (se) modérer. **moderately** *adv* modérément; *(fairly)* plus ou moins. **moderation** *n* modération *f*. **in moderation** modérément.

modern ['modən] *adj* moderne. **modern languages** langues vivantes *f pl*. **modernization** *n* modernisation *f*. **modernize** *v* moderniser.

modest ['modist] *adj* modeste. **modesty** *n* modestie *f*.

modify ['modifai] *v* modifier; modérer. **modification** *n* modification *f*.

modulate ['modjuleit] *v* moduler. **modulation** *n* modulation *f*.

module ['modjuːl] *n* module *m*.

mohair ['mouheə] *n* mohair *m*.

moist [moist] *adj* moite, humide. **moisten** *v* humecter. **moisture** *n* humidité *f*. **moisturize** *v* humidifier; *(skin)* hydrater.

molasses [mə'lasiz] *n* mélasse *f*.

mold (*US*) *V* **mould**.

mole¹ [moul] *n* (*on skin*) grain de beauté *m*.

mole² [moul] *n* (*zool*) taupe *f*. **molehill** *n* taupinière *f*.

molecule ['molikjuːl] *n* molécule *f*. **molecular** *adj* moléculaire.

molest [mə'lest] *v* molester; *(law)* attenter à la pudeur de.

mollusc ['moləsk] *n* mollusque *m*.

molt (*US*) *V* **moult**.

molten ['moultən] *adj* en fusion.

moment ['moumənt] *n* moment *m*, instant *m*. **at the moment** en ce moment. **momentary** *adj* momentané. **momentous** *adj* considérable.

Monaco ['monəkou] *n* Monaco *f*.

monarch ['monək] *n* monarque *m*. **monarchist** *n* monarchiste *m*, *f*. **monarchy** *n* monarchie *f*.

monastery ['monəstəri] *n* monastère *m*. **monastic** *adj* monastique.

Monday ['mʌndi] *n* lundi *m*.

money ['mʌni] *n* argent *m*, monnaie *f*. **get one's money back** être remboursé. **get one's money's worth** en avoir pour son argent. **money-box** *n* tirelire *f*. **money-lender** *n* prêteur sur gages *m*. **money-making** *adj* lucratif.

mongol ['mongəl] *n*, *adj* (*med*) mongolien, -enne. **mongolism** *n* mongolisme *m*.

mongrel ['mʌngrəl] *n* (*dog*) chien bâtard *m*.

monitor ['monitə] *n* (*device*) moniteur *m*. *v* contrôler.

monk [mʌnk] *n* moine *m*.

monkey ['mʌnki] *n* singe *m*. *v* **monkey around** perdre son temps; faire le idiot.

monogamy [mə'nogəmi] *n* monogamie *f*. **monogamous** *adj* monogame.

monogram ['monəgram] *n* monogramme *m*.

monologue ['monəlog] *n* monologue *m*.

monopolize [mə'nopəlaiz] *v* monopoliser. **monopoly** *n* monopole *m*.

monosyllable ['monəsilabl] *n* monosyllabe *m*. **monosyllabic** *adj* (*word*) monosyllabe; *(reply)* monosyllabique.

monotone ['monətoun] *n* ton monocorde *m*. **monotonous** *adj* monotone. **monotony** *n* monotonie *f*.

monsoon [mon'suːn] *n* mousson *f*.

monster ['monstə] *n* monstre *m*. **monstrosity** *n* monstruosité *f*. **monstrous** *adj* monstrueux; colossal.

month [mʌnθ] *n* mois *m*.

monthly ['mʌnθli] *adj* mensuel. *adv* mensuellement, tous les mois.

monument ['monjument] *n* monument *m*. **monumental** *adj* monumental.

mood¹ [muːd] *n* humeur *f*. **be in the mood for** avoir envie de, être d'humeur à. **moody** *adj* maussade.

mood² [muːd] *n* (*gramm*) mode *m*.

moon [muːn] *n* lune *f*. **moonbeam** *n* rayon de lune *m*. **moonlight** *n* clair de lune *m*. **moonlighting** *n* (*coll*) travail noir *m*.

moor¹ [muə] *n* lande *f*. **moorhen** *n* poule d'eau *f*.

moor² [muə] *v* amarrer, mouiller.

mop [mop] *n* (*floor*) balai laveur *m*; *(dishes)* lavette *f*. **mop of hair** tignasse *f*. *v* essuyer. **mop up** éponger.

mope [moup] *v* se morfondre.

moped ['mouped] *n* cyclomoteur *m*.

moral ['morəl] *adj* moral. moral support soutien moral *m*. *n* (*fable*) morale *f*. **morals** *pl n* moralité *f sing*. **moralist** *n* moraliste *m*, *f*. **morality** *n* moralité *f*. **moralize** *v* moraliser.

morale [mə'raːl] *n* moral *m*.

morbid ['moːbid] *adj* morbide.

more [moː] *adj* (*larger number*) plus de; *(in addition)* encore de. *pron*, *adv* plus, davantage; encore. **all the more** d'autant plus. **and what's more** et qui plus est. **even more** encore plus. **more and more** de plus en plus. **once more** une fois de plus.

moreover [mɔr'rouvə] *adv* de plus; (*besides*) d'ailleurs.

morgue [mɔig] *n* morgue *f.*

Mormon ['mɔtmən] *n, adj* mormon, -e.

morning ['mɔinin] *n* matin *m.* matinée *f.* **morning dress** habit *m.* **morning sickness** nausées matinales *f pl.*

Morocco [mə'rokou] *n* Maroc *m.* **Moroccan** *n* Marocain, -e *m, f; adj* marocain.

moron ['mɔtron] *n* crétin, -e *m. f.* **moronic** *adj* crétin.

morose [mə'rous] *adj* morose.

morphine ['mɔtfiin] *n* morphine *f.*

Morse code [mɔts] *n* morse *m.*

morsel ['mɔtsəl] *n* petit morceau *m.*

mortal ['mɔttl] *nm, adj* mortel. **mortality** *n* mortalité *f.*

mortar ['mɔttə] *n* mortier *m.*

mortgage ['mɔtgidʒ] *n* (*loan*) emprunt-logement *m;* (*law*) hypothèque *f.* *v* hypothéquer.

mortify ['mɔttifai] *v* mortifier. **mortification** *n* mortification *f.*

mortuary ['mɔtfuəri] *n* morgue *f.*

mosaic [mə'zeiik] *n* mosaïque *f.*

Moscow ['moskou] *n* Moscou.

mosque [mosk] *n* mosquée *f.*

mosquito [mə'skiitou] *n* moustique *m.* **mosquito net** moustiquaire *f.*

moss [mos] *n* mousse *f.* **mossy** *adj* moussu.

most [moust] *adj* le plus de; (*majority*) la plupart de. *pron* le plus; la plupart. *adv* le plus; (*very*) bien, fort. **at most** au maximum. **make the most of** profiter de; utiliser au mieux. **mostly** *adv* surtout, pour la plupart; en général.

motel [mou'tel] *n* motel *m.*

moth [moθ] *n* papillon de nuit *m.* **clothes moth** mite *f.* **mothball** *n* boule de naphtaline *f.* **moth-eaten** *adj* mité.

mother ['mʌðə] *n* mère *f.* **mother-in-law** belle-mère *f.* **mother-of-pearl** *n* nacre *f.* **Mother's Day** la fête des Mères *f.* **mother-to-be** *n* future maman *f.* *v* dorloter. **motherhood** *n* maternité *f.* **motherly** *adj* maternel.

motion ['mouʃən] *n* mouvement *m;* (*proposal*) motion *f.* **set in motion** mettre en

marche. *v* faire signe. **motionless** *adj* immobile.

motivate ['moutiveit] *v* motiver; (*person*) pousser. **motivation** *n* motivation *f.*

motive ['moutiv] *n* motif *m;* (*law*) mobile *m. adj* moteur, -trice.

motor ['moutə] *n* moteur *m.* **motorbike** *n* (*coll*) moto *f.* **motorboat** *n* canot automobile *m.* **motorcyclist** *n* motocycliste *m, f.* **motor racing** course automobile *f.* **motorway** *n* autoroute *f.* **motorist** *n* automobiliste *m, f.* **motorize** *v* motoriser.

mottled ['motld] *adj* tacheté.

motto ['motou] *n* devise *f.*

mould¹ *or US* **mold** [mould] *n* (*shape*) moule *m. v* mouler; modeler.

mould² *or US* **mold** [mould] *n* (*fungus*) moisissure *f.* **mouldy** *adj* moisi; (*coll: nasty*) moche. **go mouldy** moisir.

moult *or US* **molt** [moult] *v* muer. *n* mue *f.*

mound [maund] *n* (*natural*) tertre *m;* (*artificial*) remblai *m;* (*heap*) tas *m;* (*burial*) tumulus *m.*

mount¹ [maunt] *v* monter (sur). **mount up** s'accumuler. *n* monture *f;* (*for painting*) carton de montage *m;* (*for machine*) support *m.*

mount² [maunt] *n* mont *m.*

mountain ['mauntən] *n* montagne *f.* **mountaineer** *n* alpiniste *m, f.* **mountaineering** *n* alpinisme *m.* **mountainous** *adj* montagneux; énorme.

mourn [mɔtn] *v* pleurer. **mournful** *adj* (*person*) mélancolique; (*sound*) lugubre. **mourning** *n* deuil *m.*

mouse [maus] *n, pl* **mice** souris *f.* **mousetrap** *n* souricière *f.* **mousy** *adj* timide; (*hair*) châtain clair *invar.*

mousse [mus] *n* mousse *f.*

moustache [mə'statf] *n* moustache *f.*

mouth [mauθ] *n* bouche *f;* (*dog, cat, etc.*) gueule *f;* (*river*) embouchure *f.* **mouth organ** harmonica *m.* **mouthpiece** *n* bec *m;* (*spokesman*) porte-parole *m invar.* **mouthwash** *n* eau dentifrice *f.* **mouthwatering** *adj* appétissant. *v* dire du bout des lèvres. **mouthful** *n* bouchée *f.*

move [muv] *n* mouvement *m;* (*house*) déménagement *m;* (*game*) coup *m;* (*step*) pas *m. v* bouger, (se) déplacer, (se) mouvoir; (*emotionally*) émouvoir; proposer; déménager; (*act*) agir. **move back** reculer; (faire) retourner. **move forward** (faire) avancer. **move in** emménager.

move out déménager. **move over** (s'écarter; (to make room) se pousser. **move up** (faire) monter. **movable** adj mobile. **movement** n mouvement m. **moving** adj émouvant; mobile; (pavement, etc.) roulant.

movie ['muːvi] (US) n film m. **go to the movies** (coll) aller au ciné.

*****mow** [mou] v (lawn) tondre. **mow down** faucher.

mown [moun] V **mow**.

Mr ['mistə] n Monsieur m; (abbrev) M.

Mrs ['misiz] n Madame f; (abbrev) Mme.

much [mʌtʃ] adj beaucoup de. pron, adv beaucoup. **as much** autant (que). **how much** combien (de). **much as** bien que. **so much** tant (de). **too much** trop (de).

muck [mʌk] n (manure) fumier m; (dirt) saleté f. v **muck about** (coll) perdre son temps. **muck in** (slang) mettre la main à la pâte. **muck out** nettoyer. **mucky** adj sale.

mucus ['mjuːkəs] n mucus m. **mucous** adj muqueux.

mud [mʌd] n boue f. **mudguard** n garde-boue m invar. **muddy** adj boueux.

muddle ['mʌdl] n désordre m; confusion f. v brouiller; confondre.

muff [mʌf] n manchon m.

muffle ['mʌfl] v assourdir. **muffle up** emmitoufler. **muffler** n cache-nez m invar; (US: mot) silencieux m.

mug [mʌg] n chope f; (slang: fool) poire f. v agresser. **mugging** n agression f.

muggy ['mʌgi] adj mou, molle.

mulberry ['mʌlbəri] n (fruit) mûre f; (bush) mûrier m.

mule[1] [mjuːl] n (animal) mulet, mule m, f. **mulish** adj têtu.

mule[2] [mjuːl] n (slipper) mule f.

multicoloured [ˌmʌltiˈkʌləd] adj multicolore.

multilingual [ˌmʌltiˈliŋgwəl] adj polyglotte.

multiple ['mʌltipl] nm, adj multiple. **multiple sclerosis** sclérose en plaques f.

multiply ['mʌltiplai] v (se) multiplier. **multiplication** n multiplication f.

multiracial [ˌmʌltiˈreifəl] adj multiracial.

multi-storey [ˌmʌltiˈstoːri] adj (car) à étages.

multitude ['mʌltitjuːd] n multitude f.

mumble ['mʌmbl] v marmotter. n marmottement m.

mummy[1] ['mʌmi] n (corpse) momie f.

mummification n momification f. **mummify** v momifier.

mummy[2] ['mʌmi] n (coll: mother) maman f.

mumps [mʌmps] n oreillons m pl.

munch [mʌntʃ] v mastiquer.

mundane [mʌnˈdein] adj mondain, banal.

municipal [mjuːˈnisipəl] adj municipal. **municipality** n municipalité f.

mural ['mjuərəl] adj mural. n peinture murale f.

murder ['məːdə] n meurtre m. v assassiner. **murderer** n meurtrier, -ère m, f. **murderous** adj meurtrier.

murky ['məːki] adj sombre; (water) trouble.

murmur ['məːmə] n murmure m. v murmurer.

muscle ['mʌsl] n muscle m. **muscular** adj musculaire; (person) musclé.

muse [mjuːz] v méditer, songer. n muse f.

museum [mjuˈziəm] n musée m.

mushroom ['mʌʃrum] n champignon m.

music ['mjuːzik] n musique f. **music centre** chaîne compacte stéréo f. **music hall** music-hall m. **music stand** pupitre à musique m. **musical** adj musical; (gifted) musicien. **musical box** boîte à musique f. **musical** (comedy) comédie musicale f. **musical instrumental** instrument de musique m. **musician** n musicien, -enne m, f.

musk [mʌsk] n musc m.

musket ['mʌskit] n mousquet m. **musketeer** n mousquetaire m.

Muslim ['mʌzlim] n, adj musulman, -e.

muslin ['mʌzlin] n mousseline f.

mussel ['mʌsl] n moule f.

*****must** [mʌst] v devoir. n (coll) chose indispensable f.

mustard ['mʌstəd] n moutarde f. **mustard pot** moutardier m.

muster ['mʌstə] v (se) rassembler, (se) réunir. n assemblée f. **pass muster** être acceptable.

musty ['mʌsti] adj de moisi. **smell musty** sentir le moisi.

mute [mjuːt] adj muet, -ette. n muet, -ette m, f; (music) sourdine f. v assourdir.

mutilate ['mjuːtileit] v mutiler. **mutilation** n mutilation f.

mutiny ['mjuːtini] n mutinerie f; révolte f. v se mutiner; se révolter. **mutinous** adj mutiné; rebelle.

mutter ['mʌtə] n marmonner. n marmonnement m.

mutton ['mʌtn] n mouton m.

mutual ['mjuːtʃuəl] adj mutuel; commun.

muzzle ['mʌzl] n (nose) museau m; (device) muselière f; (gun) bouche f. v museler.

my [mai] adj mon, ma; (pl) mes.

myself [mai'self] pron me; (emphatic) moi-même. **by myself** tout seul.

mystery ['mistəri] n mystère m. **mysterious** adj mystérieux.

mystic ['mistik] n mystique m, f. adj also **mystical** mystique; occulte; surnaturel. **mysticism** n mysticisme m. **mystify** ['mistifai] v rendre perplexe, mystifier.

mystique [mi'stiːk] n mystique f.

myth [miθ] n mythe m. **mythical** adj mythique. **mythological** adj mythologique. **mythology** n mythologie f.

N

nag [nag] v harceler.

nail [neil] n clou m; (anat) ongle m. **bite one's nails** se ronger les ongles. **nailbrush** n brosse à ongles f. **nail-file** n lime à ongles f. **nail polish** vernis à ongles m. **nail-scissors** pl n ciseaux à ongles m pl. v clouer.

naive [nai'iːv] adj naïf. **naivety** n naïveté f.

naked ['neikid] adj nu; dénudé. **nakedness** n nudité f.

name [neim] n nom m. **my name is ...** je m'appelle .... **namesake** n homonyme m. **what's your name?** comment vous appelez-vous? v nommer, appeler; donner un nom à. **nameless** adj sans nom; anonyme; inexprimable. **namely** adv à savoir.

nanny ['nani] n bonne d'enfants f.

nap[1] [nap] n petit somme m. v sommeiller. **catch napping** prendre à l'improviste.

nap[2] [nap] n (of cloth) poil m.

nape [neip] n nuque f.

napkin ['napkin] n serviette f.

nappy ['napi] n couche f.

narcotic [naɪ'kotik] nm, adj narcotique.

narrate [nə'reit] v raconter. **narration** n

narration f. **narrator** n narrateur, -trice m, f.

narrative ['narətiv] n narration f. adj narratif.

narrow ['narou] adj étroit. **narrow-minded** adj borné. v (se) rétrécir. **narrow down** se ramener. **narrowly** adv (only just) de justesse; strictement.

nasal ['neizəl] adj nasal; (voice) nasillard. **nasalize** v nasaliser.

nasturtium [nə'stəːʃəm] n capucine f.

nasty ['naisti] adj (unpleasant) mauvais, vilain; (unkind) méchant.

nation ['neiʃən] n nation f. adj national. **national** n, adj national. **national anthem** hymne national m. **nationalism** n nationalisme m. **nationalist** n nationaliste m, f. **nationality** n nationalité f. **nationalization** n nationalisation f. **nationalize** v nationaliser.

native ['neitiv] adj (town) natal; (language) maternel; indigène; inné. n autochtone m, f; indigène m, f.

nativity [nə'tivəti] n nativité f. **nativity play** miracle de la Nativité m.

natural ['natʃərəl] adj naturel. **naturalism** n naturalisme m. **naturalist** n naturaliste m, f. **naturally** adv naturellement; de nature.

nature ['neitʃə] n nature f. **nature study** histoire naturelle f. **nature trail** circuit forestier éducatif m.

naughty ['noːti] adj méchant. **naughtiness** n désobéissance f.

nausea ['noːziə] n nausée f. **nauseate** v écœurer.

nautical ['noːtikəl] adj nautique.

naval ['neivəl] adj naval; maritime. **naval officer** officier de marine m.

nave [neiv] n nef f.

navel ['neivəl] n nombril m. **navel orange** navel f.

navigate ['navigeit] v naviguer; (steer) diriger. **navigable** adj navigable. **navigation** n navigation f. **navigator** n navigateur m.

navy ['neivi] n marine f. **navy blue** bleu marine.

near [niə] adv près, proche. prep près de. adj proche. v approcher (de). **draw near** s'approcher (de). **in the near future** dans un proche avenir. **nearly** adv presque. **not nearly** loin de.

nearby [niə'bai] adj proche. adv près.

neat [niːt] adj net, nette; soigné; (drink) sec, sèche. **neaten** v ajuster; (tidy) ranger.

neatly *adv* avec soin; (*with skill*) habilement. **neatness** *n* netteté *f*.

necessary ['nesisəri] *adj* nécessaire. **if necessary** s'il le faut. **it is necessary** il faut. **necessitate** *v* nécessiter. **necessity** *n* nécessité *f*. chose nécessaire *f*.

neck [nek] *n* cou *m*; (*of shirt, etc*.) encolure *f*. (*of bottle, vase*) col *m*. **neck and neck** à égalité. **necklace** *n* collier *m*. **neckline** *n* encolure *f*. *v* (*slang*) se peloter.

nectar ['nektə] *n* nectar *m*.

née [nei] *adj* née.

need [nid] *n* besoin *m*. *v* avoir besoin de; demander. **needless** *adj* inutile. **needy** *nm, adj* nécessiteux.

needle ['niːdl] *n* aiguille *f*. **needlework** *n* travaux d'aiguille *m pl*. *v* (*coll*) asticoter.

negative ['negativ] *adj* négatif. *n* (*gramm*) négation *f*; (*photo*) négatif *m*; (*reply*) réponse négative *f*.

neglect [ni'glekt] *v* négliger. *n* manque de soins. **in a state of neglect** à l'abandon. **neglected** *adj* abandonné. **negligible** *adj* négligeable.

negligée ['negliʒei] *n* négligé *m*.

negligence ['neglidʒəns] *n* négligence *f*. **negligent** *adj* négligent.

negotiate [ni'gouʃieit] *v* négocier; (*obstacle*) franchir. **negotiable** *adj* négociable; franchissable. **negotiation** *n* négociation *f*.

Negro ['niːgrou] *nm, adj* nègre. **Negress** *n* négresse *f*.

neigh [nei] *v* hennir. *n* hennissement *m*.

neighbour ['neibə] *n* voisin, -e *m, f*. **neighbourhood** *n* voisinage *m*. **neighbouring** *adj* avoisinant. **neighbourly** *adj* (de) bon voisin.

neither ['naiðə] *adv* ni. **neither ... nor ...** ni ... ni ... *conj* ni non, non plus. *adj, pron* ni l'un ni l'autre.

neon ['niːon] *n* néon *m*.

nephew ['nefjuː] *n* neveu *m*.

nepotism ['nepətizəm] *n* népotisme *m*.

nerve [nəːv] *n* nerf *m*; courage *m*; (*coll: cheek*) toupet *m*. **get on someone's nerves** taper sur les nerfs à quelqu'un. **lose one's nerve** (*coll*) se dégonfler. **nerve-racking** *adj* éprouvant. **nerves** *pl n* (*coll: before performance*) trac *m sing*. **nervous** *adj* nerveux; (*apprehensive*) inquiet, -ète. **nervous breakdown** dépression nerveuse *f*.

nest [nest] *n* nid *m*. **nest egg** pécule *m*. **nest of tables** table gigogne *f*. *v* nicher.

nestle ['nesl] *v* se nicher, se blottir.

net¹ [net] *n* filet *m*. **netball** *n* netball *m*. **net curtains** voilage *m sing*. **network** *n* réseau *m*. *v* prendre au filet.

net² [net] *adj* net.

Netherlands ['neðələndz] *pl n* **the Netherlands** les Pays-Bas *m pl*.

nettle ['netl] *n* ortie *f*. **nettle-rash** *n* urticaire *f*. *v* agacer.

neuralgia [nju'raldʒə] *n* névralgie *f*.

neurosis [nju'rousis] *n* névrose *f*. **neurotic** *adj* névrosé.

neuter ['njuːtə] *nm, adj* neutre. *v* châtrer.

neutral ['njuːtrəl] *adj* neutre. *n* (*mot*) point mort *m*. **in neutral** au point mort. **neutrality** *n* neutralité *f*. **neutralize** *v* neutraliser.

never ['nevə] *adv* (ne ...) jamais. **neverending** *adj* sans fin.

nevertheless [nevəðə'les] *adv* néanmoins, malgré tout.

new [njuː] *adj* nouveau, -elle; (*brand-new*) neuf; (*fresh*) frais, fraîche.

new-born ['njuːbɔːn] *adj* nouveau-né.

newcomer ['njuːkʌmə] *n* nouveau venu, nouvelle venue *m, f*.

New Delhi *n* New Delhi.

new-fangled ['njuːfaŋgld] *adj* nouveau genre.

new-laid ['njuːleid] *adj* (*egg*) du jour.

newly-weds ['njuːliwedz] *pl n* nouveaux mariés *m pl*.

news [njuːz] *n* nouvelles *f pl*; (*press, TV, etc*.) informations *f pl*, actualités *f pl*. **newsagent** *n* marchand, -e de journaux *m, f*. **newsletter** *n* bulletin *m*. **newspaper** *n* journal *m*. **newsreader** *n* speaker, -erine *m, f*.

newt [njuːt] *n* triton *m*.

New Testament *n* Nouveau Testament *m*.

New Year *n* nouvel an *m*. **Happy New Year!** bonne année! **New Year's Day** le jour de l'an *m*. **New Year's Eve** la Saint-Sylvestre *f*.

New Zealand [njuː'ziːlənd] *n* Nouvelle-Zélande *f*. **New Zealander** *n* Néo-Zélandais, -e *m, f*.

next [nekst] *adj* prochain, suivant; (*adjoining*) voisin. *adv* ensuite. *n* prochain, -e *m, f*. **the next day** le lendemain. **next-door** *adj* voisin, d'à côté. **next-of-kin** n plus proche parent m. **next to** à côté de.

nib [nib] n plume f.

nibble ['nibl] v grignoter, mordiller.

nice [nais] adj beau, belle; agréable; (kind) gentil, -ille; (food) bon, bonne. **nicely** adv bien.

niche [nitʃ] n niche f.

nick [nik] n (notch) encoche f; (cut) entaille f; (slang: prison) taule f. **in the nick of time** juste à temps. v entailler; (slang: steal) piquer; (slang: arrest) pincer.

nickel ['nikl] n nickel m; (US: coin) pièce de cinq cents f.

nickname ['nikneim] n surnom m. v surnommer.

Nicosia [nikə'siə] n Nicosie.

nicotine ['nikətiin] n nicotine f.

niece [niis] n nièce f.

niggle ['nigl] v tatillonner. **niggling** adj (detail) insignifiant; (doubt) insinuant; (pain) persistant.

night [nait] n nuit f; (evening) soir m. **night after night** des nuits durant. **work nights** être de nuit.

night-club ['naitklʌb] n boîte de nuit f.

nightdress ['naitdres] n chemise de nuit f.

nightfall ['naitfoil] n tombée du jour f.

nightie ['naiti] n (coll) nuisette f.

nightingale ['naitiŋ,geil] n rossignol m.

night-life ['naitlaif] n vie nocturne f.

night-light ['naitlait] n veilleuse f.

nightly ['naitli] adj de tous les soirs. adv tous les soirs.

nightmare ['naitmeə] n cauchemar m.

night-school ['nait,skuil] n cours du soir m pl.

night-time ['nait,taim] n nuit f.

night-watchman ['nait'wotʃmən] n veilleur de nuit m.

nil [nil] n rien m; (sport) zéro m.

nimble ['nimbl] adj agile; (mind) vif. **nimbleness** n agilité f.

nine [nain] nm, adj neuf. **dressed up to the nines** sur son trente et un. **ninth** n(m+f), adj neuvième.

nineteen [nain'tiin] nm, adj dix-neuf. **nineteenth** n(m+f), adj dix-neuvième.

ninety ['nainti] nm, adj quatre-vingt-dix. **ninetieth** n(m+f), adj quatre-vingt-dixième.

nip¹ [nip] v pincer; (bite) donner un coup de dent à; (coll: go quickly) faire un saut.

nip in the bud tuer dans l'œuf. n pinçon m; (bite) morsure f. **nippy** adj (cold) piquant; (quick) preste.

nip² [nip] n (drop) goutte f.

nipple ['nipl] n mamelon m; (mot) graisseur m.

nit [nit] n lente f; (coll) crétin, -e m, f.

nitrogen ['naitrədʒən] n azote m.

no [nou] adv non; (with comparative) ne ... pas. au aucun, point de, pas de; (on sign) défense de, interdit. **no-claims bonus** bonification pour non-sinistre f. **no more** or **longer** ne ... plus.

noble ['noubl] nm, adj noble. **nobleness** or **nobility** n noblesse f.

nobody ['noubodi] pron (ne ...) personne. n (insignificant person) rien du tout m.

nocturnal [nok'təinəl] adj nocturne.

nod [nod] v faire un signe de tête; (affirmative) faire signe que oui. **nod off** s'endormir. n signe de tête m.

noise [noiz] n bruit m; (loud) tapage m. **noiseless** adj silencieux. **noisy** adj bruyant.

nomad ['noumad] n nomade m, f. **nomadic** adj nomade.

nominal ['nominl] adj nominal; (in name only) de nom.

nominate ['nomineit] v proposer; (appoint) nommer. **nomination** n proposition de candidat f; nomination f.

nonchalant ['nonʃələnt] adj nonchalant. **nonchalance** n nonchalance f.

nonconformist [nonkən'foimist] n(m+f), adj non-conformiste.

nondescript ['nondiskript] adj quelconque.

none [nʌn] pron aucun.

nonentity [non'entəti] n nullité f.

nonetheless [,nʌnðə'les] adv néanmoins.

non-existent [nonig'zistənt] adj non-existant.

non-fiction [non'fikʃən] n littérature non-romanesque f.

non-resident [non'rezidənt] n (hotel) client, -e de passage m, f.

nonsense ['nonsəns] n absurdités f pl, sottises f pl. **nonsensical** adj absurde.

non-smoker [non'smoukə] n (person) non-fumeur m; (rail) compartiment "non-fumeurs" m.

non-stop [non'stop] adj sans arrêt; (train, flight) direct. adv sans arrêt.

noodles ['nuːdlz] pl n nouilles f pl.

noon [nuːn] n midi m.

no-one ['nəʊwʌn] pron (ne . . .) personne.

noose [nuːs] n nœud coulant m; (hangman's) corde f.

nor [nɔː] conj ni.

norm [nɔːm] n norme f.

normal ['nɔːml] adj normal. n normale f.

north [nɔːθ] n nord m. adj also **northerly**, **northern** nord invar; au or du nord. adv au nord. **northbound** adj nord invar. **north-east** nm, adj nord-est. **north-west** nm, adj nord-ouest.

Norway ['nɔːwei] n Norvège f. **Norwegian** nm, adj norvégien; n (people) Norvégien, -enne m, f.

nose [nəʊz] n nez m. **blow one's nose** se moucher. **have a nosebleed** saigner du nez. **nosebag** n musette mangeoire f. **nose-dive** n piqué m. **nose to tail** (cars) pare-choc contre pare-choc. v **nose out** flairer. **nosy** adj (coll) fouinard.

nostalgia [nɒ'stældʒə] n nostalgie f. **nostalgic** adj nostalgique.

nostril ['nɒstrəl] n narine f; (horse, etc.) naseau m.

not [nɒt] adv (ne . . .) pas; non. **I hope not** j'espère que non. **not at all** pas du tout; (acknowledging thanks) de rien.

notable ['nəʊtəbl] adj notable. **notably** adv notamment.

notary ['nəʊtəri] n notaire m.

notch [nɒtʃ] n entaille f; (belt) cran m; (wheel, saw) dent f. v encocher; cranter; denteler.

note [nəʊt] n note f; (short letter) mot m; (money) billet m. **notebook** n carnet m. **notepaper** n papier à lettres m. **noteworthy** adj notable. v noter; (notice) remarquer. **noted** adj célèbre.

nothing ['nʌθiŋ] pron (ne . . .) rien; (with adjective) rien de. n zéro m; (void) néant m. **nothing but** rien que.

notice ['nəʊtis] n (poster) affiche f; (in newspaper) annonce f; (warning) préavis m, délai m; (dismissal) congé m; (resignation) démission f. **notice-board** n panneau d'affichage m. **take no notice of** ne tenir aucun compte de. v s'apercevoir de, remarquer. **noticeable** adj perceptible; évident.

notify ['nəʊtifai] v (make known) notifier, signaler; (inform) aviser. **notification** n avis m, annonce f.

notion ['nəʊʃən] n idée f.

notorious [nəʊ'tɔːriəs] adj notoire. **notoriety** n notoriété f.

notwithstanding [nɒtwiθ'stændiŋ] prep malgré. adv néanmoins.

nougat ['nuːgaː] n nougat m.

nought [nɔːt] n zéro m.

noun [naʊn] n nom m.

nourish ['nʌriʃ] v nourrir. **nourishment** n nourriture f.

novel[1] ['nɒvl] n roman m. **novelist** n romancier, -ère m, f.

novel[2] ['nɒvl] adj nouveau, -elle; original. **novelty** n nouveauté f; innovation f.

November [nə'vembə] n novembre m.

novice ['nɒvis] n novice m, f.

now [naʊ] adv maintenant; (immediately) tout de suite. **from now on** à partir de maintenant. **nowadays** adv de nos jours. **now and then** de temps en temps. **up to now** jusqu'ici.

nowhere ['nəʊweə] adv nulle part.

noxious ['nɒkʃəs] adj nocif.

nozzle ['nɒzl] n ajutage m.

nuance ['njuːɑ̃s] n nuance f.

nuclear ['njuːkliə] adj nucléaire.

nucleus ['njuːkliəs] n noyau m; (of cell) nucléus m.

nude ['njuːd] n, adj nu, -e. **in the nude** nu. **nudist** n nudiste m, f. **nudity** n nudité f.

nudge [nʌdʒ] v pousser du coude. n coup de coude m.

nugget ['nʌgit] n pépite f.

nuisance ['njuːsns] n (thing) ennui m; (person) peste f. **be a nuisance** embêter. **what a nuisance!** (coll) quelle barbe!

null [nʌl] adj nul, nulle. **null and void** nul et non avenu.

numb [nʌm] adj engourdi; (with fear) transi. v engourdir; transir. **numbness** n engourdissement m.

number ['nʌmbə] n nombre m; (of house, page, etc.) numéro m. **number plate** plaque de police f. v compter; (house, etc.) numéroter.

numeral ['njuːmərəl] n chiffre m.

numerate ['njuːmərət] adj **be numerate** savoir compter. **numeracy** n notions de calcul f pl. **numerator** n numérateur m.

numerical [nju'merikl] adj numérique. **in numerical order** dans l'ordre numérique.

numerous ['njuːmərəs] adj nombreux.

nun [nʌn] n religieuse f.

nurse [nəːs] n infirmier, -ère m, f. v (med) soigner; (cradle) bercer; (hope) nourrir. **nursing home** clinique f.

nursery ['nɜːsəri] n (room) nursery f; crèche f; (trees, etc.) pépinière f. **nursery rhyme** comptine f. **nursery school** école maternelle f. **nursery slopes** (skiing) pentes pour débutants f pl.

nurture ['nɜːtʃə] v (rear) élever; (feed) nourrir.

nut [nʌt] n (bot) noix f; (tech) écrou m. **in a nutshell** en un mot. **nutcase** n (slang) dingue m, f. **nutcracker** n casse-noix m invar. **nutmeg** n muscade f.

nutrient ['njuːtriənt] n substance nutritive f.

nutrition [nju'trɪʃən] n nutrition f. **nutritional** adj alimentaire. **nutritious** adj nutritif.

nuzzle ['nʌzl] v (dog) renifler; (pig) fouiner.

nylon ['naɪlon] n nylon m.

nymph [nɪmf] n nymphe f.

O

oak [ouk] n chêne m.

oar [ɔː] n rame f. **oarsman** n rameur m.

oasis [ou'eɪsɪs] n oasis f.

oath [ouθ] n (law) serment m; (expletive) juron m. **take the oath** prêter serment.

oats [outs] pl n avoine f sing. **oatmeal** n flocons d'avoine m pl.

obedient [ə'biːdiənt] adj obéissant. **obedience** n obéissance f.

obelisk ['obəlɪsk] n obélisque m.

obese [ə'biːs] adj obèse. **obesity** n obésité f.

obey [ə'beɪ] v obéir (à).

obituary [ə'bɪtjuəri] n nécrologie f.

object ['obʒɪkt; v əb'ʒekt] n objet m; (gramm) complément m; (aim) but m. v élever une objection (contre); protester. **objection** n objection f. **objectionable** adj insupportable. **objective** nm, adj objectif.

oblige [ə'blaɪdʒ] v obliger. **be obliged to** (have to) être obligé de; (be grateful) être reconnaissant à. **obligation** n obligation f, devoir m. **obligatory** adj obligatoire.

oblique [ə'bliːk] adj oblique; indirect.

obliterate [ə'blɪtəreɪt] v effacer. **obliteration** n effacement m.

oblivion [ə'blɪviən] n oubli m. **oblivious** adj inconscient.

oblong ['oblon] adj oblong, -ongue. n rectangle m.

obnoxious [əb'nokʃəs] adj odieux, détestable.

oboe ['oubou] n hautbois m. **oboist** n hautboïste m, f.

obscene [əb'siːn] adj obscène. **obscenity** n obscénité f.

obscure [əb'skjuə] adj obscur. v obscurcir; (hide) cacher. **obscurity** n obscurité f.

observe [əb'zɜːv] v observer; remarquer. **observant** adj observateur, -trice. **observation** n observation f. **observatory** n observatoire m. **observer** n observateur, -trice m, f.

obsess [əb'ses] v obséder. **obsession** n obsession f.

obsolescent [obsə'lesnt] adj obsolescent. **obsolescence** n obsolescence f. **built-in obsolescence** désuétud · calculée f.

obsolete ['obsəliːt] adj dépassé, désuet, -ète.

obstacle ['obstəkl] n obstacle m.

obstetrics [ob'stetriks] n obstétrique f. **obstetrician** n obstétricien, -enne m, f.

obstinate ['obstɪnət] adj obstiné, têtu. **obstinacy** n obstination f.

obstruct [əb'strʌkt] v obstruer; (hinder) entraver. **obstruction** n obstruction f; obstacle m.

obtain [əb'teɪn] v obtenir, procurer.

obtrusive [əb'truːsɪv] adj importun. **obtrusion** n intrusion f.

obtuse [əb'tjuːs] adj obtus.

obverse ['obvɜːs] n (coin) face f; (statement, etc.) contrepartie f. adj de face; correspondant.

obvious ['obviəs] adj évident.

occasion [ə'keɪʒən] n occasion f; (event) évènement m. v occasionner. **occasional** adj intermittent. **occasionally** adv de temps en temps.

occult ['okʌlt] adj occulte. n **the occult** le surnaturel.

occupy ['okjupaɪ] v occuper. **occupant** or **occupier** n occupant, -e m, f. **occupation** n occupation f; profession f; (trade) métier m. **occupational hazard** risque du métier m. **occupational therapy** ergothérapie f.

occur [ə'kɜː] v (happen) se produire, avoir lieu; (be found) se trouver; (come to mind) venir à l'esprit (de). **occurrence** n évènement m.

ocean ['ouʃən] *n* océan *m.* **oceanic** *adj* océanique.

ochre ['oukə] *n* (*colour*) ocre *m*; (*substance*) ocre *f.*

o'clock [ə'klok] *adv* **one o'clock** une heure. **two/three/etc. o'clock** deux/trois/etc. heures.

octagon ['oktəgən] *n* octogone *m.* **octagonal** *adj* octogonal.

octane ['oktein] *n* octane *m.* **octane number** indice d'octane *m.*

octave ['oktiv] *n* octave *f.*

October [ok'toubə] *n* octobre *m.*

octopus ['oktəpəs] *n* pieuvre *f.*

oculist ['okjulist] *n* oculiste *m. f.*

odd [od] *adj* bizarre, étrange; (*number*) impair; (*from pair*) déparié. **odd jobs** menus travaux *m pl.* **odd man out** exception *f.* **oddity** *n* (*person*) excentrique *m. f*; (*thing*) curiosité *f*; (*oddness*) singularité *f.* **oddment** *n* fin de série *f.*

odds [odz] *pl n* (*betting*) cote *f sing*; chances *f pl.* **be at odds with** ne pas être d'accord avec. **it makes no odds** ça ne fait rien. **odds and ends** bouts *m pl.* restes *m pl.*

ode [oud] *n* ode *f.*

odious ['oudiəs] *adj* odieux.

odour ['oudə] *n* odeur *f.* **odourless** *adj* inodore.

oesophagus [i:'sofəgəs] *n* œsophage *m.*

of [ov] *prep* de. **of it** *or* **them** en: *j'en ai deux.*

off [of] *adj* absent; (*light*) éteint; (*gas, water, etc.*) coupé; (*cancelled*) annulé; (*food*) mauvais. **a day off** un jour de congé. *prep* de. sur; (*distant*) éloigné de.

offal ['ofəl] *n* abats *m pl.*

off chance ['oftʃains] *n* **on the off chance (that)** (*coll*) au cas où.

off-colour [of'kʌlə] *adj* **be off-colour** ne pas être dans son assiette.

offend [ə'fend] *v* offenser, offusquer. **offence** *n* (*law*) délit *m.* **take offence** se froisser. **offender** *n* délinquant, -e *m. f*; contrevenant, -e *m. f.* **offensive** *adj* offensant; déplaisant.

offer ['ofə] *n* offre *f.* *v* offrir, proposer. **offering** *n* offre *f.*

offhand [of'hand] *adj* (*casual*) désinvolte; brusque. *adv* à l'improviste.

office ['ofis] *n* (*place*) bureau *m*; (*post*) fonction *f.* **take office** entrer en fonctions. **officer** *n* officier *m*; (*police*) agent *m.*

official [ə'fiʃəl] *adj* officiel. *n* officiel *m.* fonctionnaire *m. f*; employé, -e *m. f.*

officious [ə'fiʃəs] *adj* empressé.

offing ['ofiŋ] *n* **in the offing** en vue; (*naut*) au large.

off-licence ['oflaisns] *n* magasin de vins et spiritueux *m.*

off-peak [of'pi:k] *adj, adv* aux heures creuses.

off-putting [of'putiŋ] *adj* (*coll*) peu engageant.

off-season [of'si:zn] *n* morte-saison *f. adv, adj* hors-saison.

offset [of'set, 'ofset] *v* contrebalancer. *n* (*printing*) offset *m.*

offshore [of'ʃoi] *adj* (*breeze*) de terre; (*waters*) côtier.

offside [of'said] *n* (*mot: right*) côté droit *m*; (*mot: left*) côté gauche *m*; (*sport*) hors-jeu *m invar.*

offspring ['ofspriŋ] *n* progéniture *f*; résultat *m.*

offstage [of'steidʒ] *adv, adj* dans les coulisses.

off-the-cuff [ofðə'kʌf] *adv, adj* au pied levé.

off-white [of'wait] *nm, adj* blanc cassé *invar.*

often ['ofn] *adv* souvent. **as often as not** le plus souvent. **every so often** de temps en temps.

ogre ['ougə] *n* ogre *m.* **ogress** *n* ogresse *f.*

oil [oil] *n* huile *f*; pétrole *m.* *v* graisser. **oily** *adj* huileux; (*hands, clothes*) graisseux; (*food*) gras, grasse; (*manners*) onctueux.

oilcan ['oilkan] *n* burette à huile *f*; (*storage*) bidon à huile *m.*

oilfield ['oilfiːld] *n* gisement pétrolifère *m.*

oil-fired [oil'faiəd] *adj* à mazout.

oil-painting ['oilpeintiŋ] *n* peinture à l'huile *f.*

oil pump *n* pompe à huile *f.*

oil refinery *n* raffinerie *f.*

oil rig *n* (*at sea*) plate-forme pétrolière *f*; (*on land*) derrick *m.*

oilskin ['oilskin] *n* toile cirée *f.* **oilskins** *pl n* ciré *m sing.* eau de toile cirée.

oil-slick ['oilslik] *n* nappe de pétrole *f.*

oil-tanker [oil'taŋkə] *n* (*ship*) pétrolier *m*; (*lorry*) camion-citerne *m.*

oil-well ['oilwel] *n* puits de pétrole *m.*

ointment ['ointmənt] *n* onguent *m*, pommade *f.*

O.K. [ou'kei] *interj* d'accord!
old [ould] *adj* vieux, vieille; âgé; (*former*) ancien. **he is nine years old** il a neuf ans. **how old is he?** quel âge a-t-il? **old age** vieillesse *f*. **old-age pensioner** retraité, -e *m, f*. **old-fashioned** *adj* démodé, vieux jeu *invar*. **old maid** vieille fille *f*. **old master** (*painting*) tableau de maître *m*. **Old Testament** Ancien Testament *m*. **old wives' tale** conte de bonne femme *m*.
olive ['oliv] *n* (*fruit*) olive *f*; (*tree*) olivier *m*. **olive green** *nm, adj* vert olive. **olive oil** huile d'olive *f*.
Olympic [ə'limpik] *adj* olympique. **Olympic Games** Jeux olympiques *m pl*.
omelette ['omlit] *n* omelette *f*.
omen ['oumən] *n* présage *m*, augure *m*.
ominous ['ominəs] *adj* menaçant, sinistre.
omit [ou'mit] *v* omettre. **omission** *n* omission *f*.
omnipotent [om'nipətənt] *adj* omnipotent.
on [on] *prep* sur, à. *adj* (*elec*) allumé; (*tap*) ouvert. **oncoming** *adj* (*traffic*) qui approche. **onlooker** *n* spectateur, -trice *m, f*. **onset** *n* début *m*; attaque *f*. **onshore** *adj* du large. **onslaught** *n* attaque *f*. **onward(s)** *adj, adv* en avant. **from now onwards** désormais.
once [wʌns] *adv* une fois; (*formerly*) jadis. *conj* une fois que. **at once** tout de suite. **once again** encore une fois. **once and for all** une fois pour toutes.
one [wʌn] *n, adj* un, -e. *pron* un; (*impersonal*) on. **be one up on** avoir l'avantage sur. **one-armed bandit** machine à sous *f*. **one by one** un à un. **one-man band** homme-orchestre *m*. **one-sided** *adj* inégal, partial. **one-way** *adj* à sens unique. **that one** celui-là, celle-là *m, f*. **this one** celui-ci, celle-ci *m, f*. **which one** lequel, laquelle *m, f*.
oneself [wʌn'self] *pron* se; (*emphatic*) soi-même. **by oneself** tout seul.
onion ['ʌnjən] *n* oignon *m*.
only ['ounli] *adj* seul, unique. **only child** enfant unique *m*. *adv* seulement; (ne...) que. *conj* mais.
onus ['ounəs] *n* responsabilité *f*.
onyx ['oniks] *n* onyx *m*.
ooze [uːz] *v* suinter, exsuder.
opal ['oupəl] *n* opale *f*.
opaque [ə'paik] *adj* opaque; obscur. **opacity** *n* opacité *f*; obscurité *f*.
open ['oupən] *v* (s')ouvrir. *adj* ouvert;

(*meeting*) public, -ique; (*question*) non résolu. **open-air** *adj* de or en plein air. **open-minded** *adj* sans parti pris. **open-mouthed** *adj, adv* bouche bée. **open-plan** *adj* sans cloisons.
opening ['oupəniŋ] *n* ouverture *f*; (*door, window*) embrasure *f*; (*ceremony*) inauguration *f*; (*opportunity*) occasion *f*. *adj* inaugural; préliminaire. **opening time** l'heure d'ouverture *f*.
opera ['opərə] *n* opéra *m*. **opera glasses** jumelles de théâtre *f pl*. **opera house** opéra *m*. **opera singer** chanteur, -euse d'opéra *m, f*. **operatic** *adj* d'opéra. **operetta** *n* opérette *f*.
operate ['opəreit] *v* opérer; (*machine*) (faire) marcher. **operable** *adj* opérable. **operating theatre** salle d'opération *f*. **operation** *n* opération *f*; marche *f*, fonctionnement *m*. **in operation** en service; en application. **operational** *adj* opérationnel. **operative** *adj* en vigueur; (*med*) opératoire. **the operative word** le mot clef. **operator** *n* opérateur, -trice *m, f*; (*phone*) standardiste *m, f*.
ophthalmic [of'θalmik] *adj* (*nerve*) ophtalmique; (*surgeon*) ophtalmologique.
opinion [ə'pinjən] *n* opinion *f*. **in my opinion** à mon avis. **opinion poll** sondage d'opinion *m*.
opium ['oupiəm] *n* opium *m*.
opponent [ə'pounənt] *n* adversaire *m, f*.
opportune [opə'tjuːn] *adj* opportun.
opportunity [opə'tjuːnəti] *n* occasion *f*, chance *f*.
oppose [ə'pouz] *v* s'opposer à. **opposed** *adj* opposé. **as opposed to** par opposition à. **opposition** *n* opposition *f*.
opposite ['opəzit] *adj* opposé; d'en face. **the opposite sex** l'autre sexe *m*. *prep* en face de. *n* opposé *m*, contraire *m*.
oppress [ə'pres] *v* opprimer; (*heat, etc.*) oppresser. **oppression** *n* oppression *f*. **oppressive** *adj* tyrannique; (*tax, etc.*) oppressif; (*heat*) accablant. **oppressor** *n* oppresseur *m*.
opt [opt] *v* opter. **opt out** se retirer; choisir de ne pas participer.
optical ['optikl] *adj* optique. **optical illusion** illusion d'optique *f*. **optician** *n* opticien, -enne *m, f*.
optimism ['optimizəm] *n* optimisme *m*. **optimist** *n* optimiste *m, f*. **optimistic** *adj* optimiste.

optimum ['optimǝm] nm, adj optimum.
option ['opʃǝn] n option f, choix m.
optional adj facultatif.
opulent ['opjulǝnt] adj opulent;
abondant. opulence n opulence f;
abondance f.
or [o:] conj ou; (negative) ni. or else ou
bien; (threat) sinon.
oracle ['orǝkl] n oracle m.
oral ['o:rǝl] nm, adj oral.
orange ['orindʒ] n (fruit) orange f; (tree)
oranger m; (colour) orange m. adj (colour) orange; (flavour) d'orange. orangeade n orangeade f.
orator ['orǝtǝ] n orateur, -trice m, f. orate
v discourir. oration or oratory n discours
m.
orbit ['o:bit] n orbite f, v orbiter.
orchard ['o:tʃǝd] n verger m.
orchestra ['o:kǝstrǝ] n orchestre m.
orchestral adj orchestral. orchestrate v
orchestrer. orchestration n orchestration
f.
orchid ['o:kid] n orchidée f.
ordain [o:'dein] v (rel) ordonner; (fate)
décréter. ordination n ordination f.
ordeal [o:'di:l] n supplice m.
order ['o:dǝ] n ordre m; (comm) commande f. in order to pour. out of order
en panne. v ordonner; commander.
orderly ['o:dǝli] adj rangé; méthodique;
en ordre. n (mil) planton m; (med) garçon de salle m.
ordinal ['o:dinl] adj ordinal.
ordinary ['o:dǝnǝri] adj ordinaire, normal; (average) moyen. n ordinaire m. out
of the ordinary hors du commun,
insolite.
ore [o:] n minerai m.
oregano [ori'ga:nou] n origan m.
organ ['o:gǝn] n organe m; (music) orgue
m. organist n organiste m, f.
organic [o:'ganik] adj organique; fondamental.
organism ['o:gǝnizǝm] n organisme m.
organize ['o:gǝnaiz] v organiser. organization n organisation f. organizer n organisateur, -trice m, f.
orgasm ['o:gazǝm] n orgasme m.
orgy ['o:dʒi] n orgie f.
oriental [o:ri'entl] adj oriental, d'Orient.
orientate ['o:rǝnteit] v orienter. orientation n orientation f.
orifice ['orifis] n orifice m.
origin ['oridʒin] n origine f. originate v

être l'auteur de. originate from (person)
être originaire de; (thing) provenir de;
(idea) émaner de. originator n auteur m.
original [ǝ'ridʒǝnl] adj (first) originel;
(idea, play, etc.) original. n original m.
originally adv originairement, à l'origine.
ornament ['o:nǝmǝnt] n (decoration) ornement m; (vase, etc.) bibelot m. v orner,
décorer. ornamental adj ornemental,
décoratif.
ornate [o:'neit] adj très orné.
ornithology [o:ni'θolǝdʒi] n ornithologie
f. ornithological adj ornithologique. ornithologist n ornithologiste m, f.
orphan ['o:fǝn] n, adj orphelin, -e. v rendre orphelin. be orphaned devenir orphelin. orphanage n orphelinat m.
orthodox ['o:θǝdoks] adj orthodoxe.
orthopaedic [o:θǝ'pi:dik] adj orthopédique.
oscillate ['osileit] v osciller; fluctuer.
oscillation n oscillation f.
Oslo ['ozlou] n Oslo.
ostensible [o'stensǝbl] adj prétendu.
ostensibly adv en apparence.
ostentatious [osten'teiʃǝs] adj prétentieux; exagéré. ostentation n ostentation
f.
osteopath ['ostiǝpaθ] n ostéopathe m, f.
ostracize ['ostrǝsaiz] n frapper
d'ostracisme.
ostrich ['ostritʃ] n autruche f.
other ['ʌðǝ] pron, adj autre. adv autrement.
otherwise ['ʌðǝwaiz] adv, conj autrement.
Ottawa ['otǝwǝ] n Ottawa.
otter ['otǝ] n loutre f.
*ought [o:t] v devoir.
our [auǝ] pron nous. adj notre; (pl) nos.
ours [auǝz] pron le nôtre, la nôtre.
ourselves [auǝ'selvz] pron nous; (emphatic) nous-mêmes. by ourselves tout seuls.
oust [aust] v évincer.
out [aut] adj (flower) en fleur; (light, etc.)
éteint. adv dehors. out loud tout haut.
out of en dehors de, hors de; (through)
par; (from) de, sur; (without) sans.
outboard ['autbo:d] n hors-bord m.
outbreak ['autbreik] n début m,
déclenchement m.
outbuilding ['autbildiŋ] n appentis m,
dépendance f.
outburst ['autbǝ:st] n explosion f, accès
m.

outcast ['autkaɪst] n exilé, -e m, f; proscrit, -e m, f.

outcome ['autkʌm] n issue f; conséquence f.

outcry ['autkraɪ] n tollé m.

***outdo** [aut'duː] v surpasser.

outdoor ['autdɔɪ] adj de or en plein air. **outdoors** adv dehors.

outer ['autə] adj extérieur, -e. **outer space** espace cosmique m.

outfit ['autfɪt] n (clothes) tenue f; équipement m; (coll) équipe f.

outgoing ['autgouiŋ] adj (person) ouvert; (tide) descendant; (train, mail, etc.) en partance. **outgoings** pl n dépenses f pl.

***outgrow** [aut'grou] v devenir trop grand pour; perdre or abandonner en grandissant.

outhouse ['authaus] n appentis m.

outing ['autiŋ] n sortie f, excursion f.

outlandish [aut'landiʃ] adj exotique; bizarre.

outlaw ['autlɔː] n hors-la-loi m invar. v proscrire.

outlay ['autleɪ] n frais m pl, dépenses f pl.

outlet ['autlɪt] n sortie f; (comm) débouché m; (for emotions, etc.) exutoire m.

outline ['autlaɪn] n contour m; (summary) esquisse f. v délinéer; esquisser or exposer à grands traits.

outlive [aut'lɪv] v survivre à.

outlook ['autluk] n perspective f; attitude f.

outlying ['autlaiiŋ] adj périphérique; (distant) écarté.

outnumber [aut'nʌmbə] v surpasser en nombre.

out-of-date [autəv'deɪt] adj (ticket, etc.) périmé; (clothes) démodé.

outpatient ['autpeiʃənt] n malade en consultation externe m, f.

outpost ['autpoust] n avant-poste m.

output ['autput] n production f, rendement m; (elec) puissance fournie f.

outrage ['autreɪdʒ] n scandale m. v outrager.

outrageous [aut'reidʒəs] adj scandaleux, outrageant.

outright [aut'raɪt; adj 'autraɪt] adv complètement; catégoriquement; franchement. adj complet, -ète; franc, franche; (winner) incontesté; (sale) au comptant.

outset ['autset] n début m.

outside [aut'saɪd; adj 'autsaɪd] adv dehors, à l'extérieur. prep à l'extérieur de, hors de; (beyond) en dehors de. n extérieur m, dehors m. adj extérieur, -e. **outsider** n étranger, -ère m, f; (horse) outsider m.

outsize [autsaiz] adj (clothes) grande taille invar; énorme.

outskirts ['autskɔɪts] pl n (town) faubourgs m pl; (forest) lisière f sing.

outspoken [aut'spoukən] adj carré. **be outspoken** avoir son franc-parler. **outspokenness** n franc-parler m.

outstanding [aut'standiŋ] adj exceptionnel; mémorable; (debt) impayé.

outstrip [aut'strip] v devancer.

outward ['autwəd] adj vers l'extérieur; (appearance) extérieur, -e. **outward bound** en partance. **outwardly** adv en apparence. **outwards** adv vers l'extérieur.

outweigh [aut'weɪ] v l'emporter sur.

outwit [aut'wɪt] v se montrer plus malin que; (dodge) dépister.

oval ['ouvəl] nm, adj ovale.

ovary ['ouvəri] n ovaire m.

ovation [ou'veiʃən] n ovation f.

oven [ʌvn] n four m. **oven glove** gant isolant m. **ovenproof** adj allant au four. **oven-ready** adj prêt à cuire.

over ['ouvə] adv (par-)dessus; (remaining) en plus. adj fini. prep sur, par-dessus; (above) au-dessus de; (during) au cours de; (more than) plus de. **over and over again** à maintes reprises. **over here** ici. **over there** là-bas.

overall ['ouvərɔːl] adj global; total. n blouse f. **overalls** pl n salopette f sing.

overbalance [ouvə'baləns] v basculer; perdre l'équilibre.

overbearing [ouvə'beəriŋ] adj autoritaire.

overboard ['ouvəbɔːd] adv (fall) à la mer; (throw) par-dessus bord. **go overboard** (coll) s'emballer.

overcast [ouvə'kaɪst] adj couvert.

overcharge [ouvə'tʃaɪdʒ] v faire payer un prix excessif; (elec) surcharger.

overcoat ['ouvəkout] n pardessus m.

***overcome** [ouvə'kʌm] v surmonter, triompher de. **be overcome** by succomber à.

overcrowded [ouvə'kraudid] adj surpeuplé, surchargé. **overcrowding** n surpeuplement m.

***overdo** [ouvə'duː] v exagérer; (overcook) trop cuire.

overdose ['ouvədous] n surdose f.

overdraft ['ouvədraɪft] n découvert m.

*__overdraw__ [ouvə'drɔɪ] v dépasser son crédit. __overdrawn__ adj à découvert.

overdue [ouvə'djuɪ] adj (payment) arriéré; (train, bus) en retard.

overestimate [ouvə'estimeit] v surestimer; exagérer.

overexpose [ouvəik'spouz] v surexposer. __overexposure__ n surexposition f.

overflow [ouvə'flou; n 'ouvəflou] v déborder. n débordement m; (of sink) trop-plein m; (excess) excédent m.

overgrown [ouvə'groun] adj envahi, recouvert.

*__overhang__ [ouvə'haŋ; n 'ouvəhaŋ] v surplomber; faire saillie. n surplomb f. __overhanging__ adj en saillie, en surplomb.

overhaul [ouvə'hɔɪl] v réviser. n révision f.

overhead [ouvə'hed] adv au-dessus; dans le ciel. adj aérien. __overheads__ pl n frais généraux m pl.

*__overhear__ [ouvə'hiə] v surprendre, entendre par hasard.

overheat [ouvə'hiɪt] v surchauffer; (mot) chauffer.

overjoyed [ouvə'dʒɔid] adj ravi.

overland [ouvə'land] adj, adv par voie de terre.

overlap ['ouvəlap; v ouvə'lap] n chevauchement m. v se chevaucher.

*__overlay__ [ouvə'lei; n 'ouvəlei] v recouvrir. n revêtement m.

overleaf [ouvə'liɪf] adv au verso.

overload [ouvə'loud; n 'ouvəloud] v surcharger. n surcharge f.

overlook [ouvə'luk] v (miss) oublier; (house, etc.) donner sur; (ignore) laisser passer.

overnight [ouvə'nait] adv jusqu'au lendemain, pendant la nuit; (suddenly) du jour au lendemain. adj (journey) de nuit; (stay) d'une nuit; (sudden) soudain.

overpower [ouvə'pauə] v subjuguer; dominer. __overpowering__ adj irrésistible; suffocant.

overrated [ouvə'reitid] adj surfait.

*__override__ [ouvə'raid] v passer outre à, outrepasser; annuler. __overriding__ adj prépondérant.

overrule [ouvə'ruɪl] v annuler; rejeter.

*__overrun__ [ouvə'rʌn] v envahir; (go beyond) dépasser.

overseas [ouvə'siɪz] adv outre-mer. adj d'outre-mer; (trade) extérieur, -e.

overseer [ouvə'siə] n contremaître m.

overshadow [ouvə'fadou] v ombrager; (render insignificant) éclipser.

*__overshoot__ [ouvə'fuɪt] v dépasser.

oversight [ouvə'sait] n omission f. __through an oversight__ par négligence.

*__oversleep__ [ouvə'sliɪp] v dormir trop longtemps, se réveiller tard.

overspill ['ouvəspil] n excédent de population m.

overt [ou'vəɪt] adj déclaré. __overtly__ adv ouvertement.

*__overtake__ [ouvə'teik] v (pass) doubler, dépasser; (catch up) rattraper.

*__overthrow__ [ouvə'θrou; n 'ouvəθrou] v renverser, vaincre. n chute f.

overtime [ouvə'taim] n heures supplémentaires f pl.

overtone ['ouvətoun] n note f. sous-entendu m.

overture ['ouvətjuə] n ouverture f.

overturn [ouvə'təɪn] v (se) renverser; (car) capoter.

overweight [ouvə'weit] adj trop lourd. __be overweight__ peser trop.

overwhelm [ouvə'welm] v accabler; (flood) submerger; (conquer) écraser. __overwhelmed__ adj bouleversé, confus, accablé. __overwhelming__ adj accablant; irrésistible; dominant.

overwork [ouvə'wəɪk] n surmenage m. v (se) surmener.

overwrought [ouvə'rɔɪt] adj excédé.

ovulation [ovju'leifn] n ovulation f.

owe [ou] v devoir. __owing__ adj dû, due. __owing to__ à cause de.

owl [aul] n hibou m.

own [oun] adj propre. __get one's own back__ prendre sa revanche. __on one's own__ tout seul. v posséder. __own up__ avouer. __owner__ n propriétaire m, f. __ownership__ n possession f.

ox [oks] n, pl __oxen__ bœuf m. __oxtail__ n queue de bœuf f.

oxygen ['oksidʒən] n oxygène m.

oyster ['oistə] n huître f.

P

pace [peis] *n* pas *m.* **keep pace with** marcher de pair avec. *v* arpenter. **pace up and down** faire les cent pas.

Pacific [pəˈsifik] *nm, adj* Pacifique.

pacify [ˈpasifai] *v* calmer, pacifier. **pacific** *adj* pacifique. **pacifism** *n* pacifisme *m.* **pacifist** *n*(*m*+*f*). *adj* pacifiste.

pack [pak] *n* (*group*) bande *f*; (*hounds*) meute *f*; (*cards*) jeu *m*; (*packet*) paquet *m.* **packhorse** *n* cheval de charge *m. v* emballer; (*cram*) tasser, bourrer; (*suitcase*) faire; (*for holiday*) faire ses bagages. **packed lunch** panier-repas *m.* **packing** *n* emballage *m.*

package [ˈpakidʒ] *n* paquet *m. adj* (*deal, contract*) global; (*holiday, tour*) organisé. *v* emballer.

packet [ˈpakit] *n* paquet *m*; (*sweets*) sachet *m.*

pact [pakt] *n* pacte *m.*

pad[1] [pad] *n* bourrelet *m*; (*writing*) bloc *m*; (*ink*) tampon encreur *m. v* rembourrer, capitonner. **pad out** (*speech, essay*) délayer. **padding** *n* bourre *f*; délayage *m.*

pad[2] [pad] *v* aller à pas feutrés.

paddle[1] [ˈpadl] *n* (*canoe*) pagaie *f*; (*of waterwheel*) aube *f. v* pagayer. **paddle boat** *or* **steamer** bateau à aubes *m. v* pagayer.

paddle[2] [ˈpadl] *v* barboter. **paddling pool** petite piscine *f.*

paddock [ˈpadək] *n* enclos *m*; (*racing*) paddock *m.*

paddy-field [ˈpadifiːld] *n* rizière *f.*

padlock [ˈpadlok] *n* cadenas *m. v* cadenasser.

paediatric [piːdiˈatrik] *adj* de pédiatrie; infantile. **paediatrician** *n* pédiatre *m, f.* **paediatrics** *n* pédiatrie *f.*

pagan [ˈpeigən] *n, adj* paien, -enne.

page[1] [peidʒ] *n* (*book*) page *f.*

page[2] [peidʒ] *n also* **page-boy** (*hotel*) groom *m*; (*court*) page *m. v* (*person*) faire appeler.

pageant [ˈpadʒənt] *n* spectacle historique *m.* **pageantry** *n* apparat *m.*

paid [peid] *V* pay.

pail [peil] *n* seau *m.*

pain [pein] *n* douleur *f.* **pain-killer** *n* calmant *m.* **pains** *pl n* (*trouble*) peine *f sing.* **painstaking** *adj* assidu, soigné. *v* peiner. **painful** *adj* douloureux; (*distressing*) pénible. **painless** *adj* sans douleur; (*easy*) inoffensif.

paint [peint] *n* peinture *f.* **paintbox** *n* boîte de couleurs *f.* **paintbrush** *n* pinceau

m. **paints** *pl n* couleurs *f pl.* **paint-stripper** *n* décapant *m.* **paintwork** *n* peintures *f pl. v* peindre; (*describe*) dépeindre. **painter** *n* peintre *m.* **painting** *n* peinture *f*; (*picture*) tableau *m.*

pair [peə] *n* paire *f*; couple *m. v* (*socks, etc.*) appareiller; (*mate*) (s')accoupler. **pair off** (*people*) s'arranger deux par deux.

pal [pal] *n* (*coll*) copain, copine *m, f.*

palace [ˈpaləs] *n* palais *m.* **palatial** *adj* grandiose.

palate [ˈpalit] *n* palais *m.* **palatable** *adj* acceptable.

pale [peil] *adj* pâle; (*unnaturally*) blême. *v* pâlir; devenir blême. **paleness** *n* pâleur *f.*

palette [ˈpalit] *n* palette *f.*

pall[1] [poːl] *v* perdre son charme (pour).

pall[2] [poːl] *n* drap mortuaire *m*; (*smoke*) voile *m*; (*snow*) manteau *m.*

pallid [ˈpalid] *adj* blafard.

palm[1] [paːm] *n* (*of hand*) paume *f. v* **palm off** (*coll*) refiler (à). **palmist** *n* chiromancien, -enne *m, f.* **palmistry** *n* chiromancie *f.*

palm[2] [paːm] *n* (*tree*) palmier *m.* **Palm Sunday** dimanche des Rameaux *m.*

palpitate [ˈpalpiteit] *v* palpiter. **palpitation** *n* palpitation *f.*

paltry [ˈpoːltri] *adj* misérable.

pamper [ˈpampə] *v* dorloter, choyer.

pamphlet [ˈpamflit] *n* brochure *f.*

pan [pan] *n* casserole *f.*

pancake [ˈpankeik] *n* crêpe *f.* **Pancake Tuesday** mardi gras *m.*

pancreas [ˈpankriəs] *n* pancréas *m.* **pancreatic** *adj* pancréatique.

panda [ˈpandə] *n* panda *m.*

pandemonium [pandiˈmouniəm] *n* tohu-bohu *m.*

pander [ˈpandə] *v* **pander to** se plier à.

pane [pein] *n* vitre *f*, carreau *m.*

panel [ˈpanl] *n* panneau *m*; (*dress*) pan *m*; jury *m*; (*radio, TV*) invités *m pl. v* lambrisser. **panellist** *n* invité, -e *m, f*; membre d'un jury *m.* **panelling** *n* panneaux *m pl.*

pang [paŋ] *n* serrement de cœur *m*; (*conscience*) remords *m pl*; (*hunger*) tiraillement d'estomac *m.*

panic [ˈpanik] *n* panique *f.* **panic-stricken** *adj* affolé. *v* (s')affoler.

panorama [panəˈraːmə] *n* panorama *m.* **panoramic** *adj* panoramique.

pansy ['pænzi] n pensée f.

pant [pænt] v haleter. n halètement m.

panther ['pænθə] n panthère f.

pantomime ['pæntəmaim] n spectacle de Noël m; (mime) pantomime f.

pantry ['pæntri] n garde-manger m invar.

pants [pænts] pl n slip m sing; (coll: trousers) pantalon m sing.

papal ['peipl] adj papal, du Pape.

paper ['peipə] n papier m; (news) journal m; (exam) épreuve f; article m. **paperback** n livre de poche m. **paper bag** pochette f. **paper-boy** n livreur de journaux m. **paper-clip** n trombone m. **paper-knife** n coupe-papier m invar. **paper-mill** n papeterie f. **paper shop** (coll) marchand de journaux m. **paperweight** n presse-papiers m invar; **paperwork** n écritures f pl; (derog) paperasserie f. v (room) tapisser.

paprika [paprikə] n paprika m.

par [paː] n pair m. **be on a par with** aller de pair avec. **feel under par** ne pas se sentir en forme.

parable ['pærəbl] n parabole f.

parachute ['pærəʃuːt] n parachute m. v descendre en parachute; parachuter. **parachutist** n parachutiste m, f.

parade [pə'reid] n défilé m; (ceremony) parade f. v défiler; (display) faire étalage de.

paradise ['pærədais] n paradis m.

paradox ['pærədoks] n paradoxe m. **paradoxical** adj paradoxal.

paraffin ['pærəfin] n paraffine f; (fuel) pétrole m.

paragraph ['pærəgraːf] n paragraphe m. **start a new paragraph** aller à la ligne.

parallel ['pærəlel] nm, adj parallèle. **parallelogram** n parallélogramme m.

paralyse ['pærəlaiz] v paralyser. **paralysis** n paralysie f; immobilisation f. **paralytic** adj paralytique; (slang: drunk) ivre mort.

paramilitary [,pærə'militəri] adj paramilitaire.

paramount ['pærəmaunt] adj souverain, suprême.

paranoia [,pærə'nɔiə] n paranoïa f. **paranoid** adj paranoïde.

parapet ['pærəpit] n parapet m.

paraphernalia [,pærəfə'neiliə] n attirail m.

paraphrase ['pærəfreiz] n paraphrase f. v paraphraser.

paraplegic [,pærə'pliːdʒik] n(m+f). adj paraplégique.

parasite ['pærəsait] n parasite m. **parasitic** adj parasite.

parasol ['pærəsol] n ombrelle f.

paratrooper ['pærə,truːpə] n parachutiste m.

parcel ['paːsəl] n colis m; (portion) parcelle f. **parcel office** bureau de messageries m. **parcel post** service de colis postaux m. v also **parcel up** emballer.

parch [paːtʃ] v (land) dessécher; (person) altérer. **be parched** (coll) mourir de soif.

parchment ['paːtʃmənt] n parchemin m.

pardon ['paːdn] n pardon m; (law) grâce f. v pardonner; gracier. interj pardon?

pare [peə] v réduire; (fruit) peler.

parent ['peərənt] n père, mère m, f. **parents** parents m pl. **parental** adj des parents. **parenthood** n paternité f, maternité f.

parenthesis [pə'renθəsis] n parenthèse f. **in parenthesis** entre parenthèses.

Paris ['pæris] n Paris.

parish ['pæriʃ] n paroisse f; (civil) commune f. **parish church** église paroissiale f. **parishioner** n paroissien, -enne m, f.

parity ['pæriti] n parité f.

park [paːk] n jardin public m; (of mansion) parc m. v (se) garer. **parking** n stationnement m. **parking lot** (US) parking m. **parking meter** parcomètre m. **parking ticket** procès-verbal m.

parliament ['paːləmənt] n parlement m. **parliamentary** adj parlementaire.

parlour ['paːlə] n petit salon m.

parochial [pə'roukiəl] adj paroissial; (derog) de clocher.

parody ['pærədi] n parodie f. v parodier.

parole [pə'roul] n (law) liberté conditionnelle f.

paroxysm ['pærəksizəm] n paroxysme m; (anger) accès m; (joy) transport m.

parrot ['pærət] n perroquet m. **parrot fashion** comme un perroquet.

parsley ['paːsli] n persil m.

parsnip ['paːsnip] n panais m.

parson ['paːsn] n pasteur m. **parson's nose** croupion m. **parsonage** n presbytère m.

part [paːt] n partie f; (behalf) part f, parti m; rôle m; épisode m. **part exchange** reprise en compte f. **part-time** adj, adv à mi-temps, à temps partiel. v (se) séparer; se quitter. **part one's hair** se faire une raie. **part with** se défaire de. **parting** n séparation f; (hair) raie f. **partly** adv partiellement.

***partake** [pɑː'teik] v **partake of** prendre.

partial ['pɑːʃəl] adj partiel; (biased) partial. **be partial to** avoir un faible pour. **partiality** n partialité f; (liking) prédilection f.

participate [pɑː'tisipeit] v participer. **participant** n participant, -e m, f. **participation** n participation f.

participle ['pɑːtisipl] n participe m.

particle ['pɑːtikl] n particule f; (dust, etc.) grain m.

particular [pə'tikjulə] adj particulier; méticuleux; (choosy) pointilleux. n détail m. **in particular** en particulier. **particularity** n particularité f.

partisan [pɑːti'zan] n partisan m.

partition [pɑː'tiʃən] n (in room) cloison f; division f, partage n v cloisonner; diviser, partager.

partner ['pɑːtnə] n (comm) associé, -e m, f; (sport) partenaire m, f; (dancing) cavalier, -ère m, f; (marriage) époux, -ouse m, f. v être l'associé de; être le partenaire de; danser avec. **partnership** n association f. **go into partnership** s'associer.

partridge ['pɑːtridʒ] n perdrix f; (cookery) perdreau m.

party ['pɑːti] n (pol) parti m; (law) partie f; groupe m; (celebration) réunion f, fête f, soirée f. **party line** (phone) ligne commune à deux abonnés f; (pol) ligne du parti f.

pass [pɑːs] v passer; (go beyond) dépasser; (exam) être reçu à. **pass away or on** (die) s'éteindre. **pass out** s'évanouir. **pass round** faire passer; distribuer. v (permit) laissez-passer m invar; (exam) moyenne f; (mountain) col m; (sport) passe f. **passage** [pɑːsidʒ] n passage m; voyage m; (corridor) couloir m.

passenger [pɑːsindʒə] n passager, -ère m, f; (train) voyageur, -euse m, f.

passer-by [pɑːsə'bai] n passant, -e m, f.

passion [paʃən] n passion f. **passionate** adj passionné.

passive [pasiv] nm, adj passif. **passiveness** n passivité f.

Passover [pɑːsouvə] n Pâque des Juifs f.

passport [pɑːspoːt] n passeport m.

password [pɑːswəːd] n mot de passe m.

past [pɑːst] nm, adj passé. prep (time) plus de; (beyond) au delà de; (in front of)

devant. **ten past four** quatre heures dix. adv devant. **go past** passer.

pasta ['pɑːstə] n pâtes f pl.

paste [peist] n pâte f; (meat) pâté m; (glue) colle f; (jewellery) strass m. v coller.

pastel ['pɑːstəl] n pastel m.

pasteurize ['pɑːstʃəraiz] v pasteuriser. **pasteurization** n pasteurisation f.

pastime ['pɑːstaim] n passe-temps m invar.

pastoral ['pɑːstərəl] adj pastoral.

pastry ['peistri] n pâte f; (cake) pâtisserie f. **puff pastry** pâte feuilletée f. **shortcrust pastry** pâte brisée f.

pasture ['pɑːstʃə] n pâture f, pâturage m. v paître.

pasty[1] ['peisti] adj pâteux; (face) terreux.

pasty[2] ['pɑːsti] n petit pâté m.

pat [pat] v tapoter; caresser. n petite tape f; caresse f; (of butter) noix f.

patch [patʃ] n morceau m; (of colour) tache f; (on clothes) pièce f; (of land) parcelle f. **patchwork** n patchwork m. v rapiécer. **patchy** adj inégal.

patent ['peitənt] adj patent. **patent leather** cuir verni m. n brevet m. v faire breveter. **patently** adv manifestement.

paternal [pə'təːnl] adj paternel. **paternity** n paternité f.

path [pɑːθ] n sentier m; (garden) allée f; (of river) cours m; (of missile, etc.) trajectoire f.

pathetic [pə'θetik] adj pitoyable.

pathology [pə'θolədʒi] n pathologie f. **pathological** adj pathologique. **pathologist** n pathologiste m, f.

patient ['peiʃənt] adj patient. n malade m, f; client, -e m, f. **patience** n patience f; (game) réussite f.

patio ['patiou] n patio m.

patriarchal ['peitriɑːkl] adj patriarcal.

patriot ['peitriət] n patriote m, f. **patriotic** adj patriotique; (person) patriote. **patriotism** n patriotisme m.

patrol [pə'troul] n patrouille f. **patrol car** voiture de police f. v patrouiller (dans).

patron ['peitrən] n (arts) protecteur, -trice m, f; (charity) patron, -onne m, f; (shop) client, -e m, f. **patron saint** saint patron, sainte patronne m, f. **patronage** n patronage m. **patronize** v (comm) se fournir chez. **patronizing** adj condescendant.

patter¹ ['patə] v (footsteps) trottiner; (rain) crépiter. n petit bruit m; crépitement m.

patter² ['patə] n (comedian, etc.) bavardage m; (salesman) boniment m.

pattern ['patən] n dessin m, motif m; (sewing) patron m; modèle f. v modeler. **patterned** adj à motifs.

paunch [pɔːntʃ] n panse f.

pauper ['pɔːpə] n indigent, -e m, f.

pause [pɔːz] n pause f; silence m. v faire une pause, s'arrêter un instant; hésiter.

pave [peiv] v paver. **pave the way** préparer le chemin. **pavement** n trottoir m; (US) chaussée f. **paving** n pavage m, dallage m. **paving stone** pavé m.

pavilion [pə'viljən] n pavillon m.

paw [pɔː] n patte f. v donner un coup de patte à; (coll: person) tripoter.

pawn¹ [pɔːn] v mettre en gage. n gage m. **pawnbroker** n prêteur, -euse sur gages m, f. **pawnshop** n mont-de-piété m.

pawn² [pɔːn] n pion m.

*****pay** [pei] v payer; (attention, compliment) faire. **pay back** rembourser. **pay in** verser. **pay off** (debt) régler; (be worthwhile) rapporter. n paie f. **pay-day** n jour de paie m. **pay rise** augmentation de salaire f. **pay-roll** n registre du personnel m. **pay-slip** n feuille de paie f. **payable** adj payable. **payee** n bénéficiaire m, f. **payment** n paiement m; récompense f.

pea [piː] n petit pois m.

peace [piːs] n paix f. **peacemaker** n pacificateur, -trice m, f. **peace offering** cadeau de réconciliation m. **peaceful** adj paisible.

peach [piːtʃ] n (fruit) pêche f; (tree) pêcher m.

peacock ['piːkɔk] n paon m.

peak [piːk] n pic m; sommet m; (on cap) visière f. **peak hours** heures d'affluence f pl, heures de pointe f pl.

peal [piːl] n (bells) carillon m; (thunder) coup m; (laughter) éclat m. v carillonner; (thunder) gronder; éclater.

peanut ['piːnʌt] n cacahouète f.

pear [peə] n (fruit) poire f; (tree) poirier m.

pearl [pɜːl] n perle f; nacre f. v perler. **pearly** adj nacré.

peasant ['peznt] n paysan, -anne m, f.

peat [piːt] n tourbe f.

pebble ['pebl] n caillou m; (on beach) galet m. **pebbledash** n crépi moucheté m. **pebbly** adj caillouteux.

peck [pek] v becqueter, picorer; donner un coup de bec à. n coup de bec m; (coll: kiss) bise f.

peckish ['pekiʃ] adj **feel peckish** (coll) avoir la dent.

peculiar [pi'kjuːljə] adj bizarre; particulier. **peculiarity** n bizarrerie f; particularité f.

pedal ['pedl] n pédale f. v pédaler.

pedantic [pi'dantik] adj pédant.

peddle ['pedl] v colporter; (drugs) faire le trafic de.

pedestal ['pedistl] n piédestal m.

pedestrian [pi'destriən] n piéton m. **pedestrian crossing** passage clouté m. **pedestrian precinct** zone piétonnière f. adj (style) prosaïque.

pedigree ['pedigriː] n pedigree m; (of person) ascendance f. adj de pure race.

pedlar ['pedlə] n colporteur m.

peel [piːl] v (se) peler, éplucher. **peel off** (covering, etc.) décoller. n pelure f. épluchure f; (orange) écorce f; (candied) écorce confite f. **peeler** n éplucheur m. **peelings** pl n pelures f pl, épluchures f pl.

peep [piːp] n coup d'œil m. v jeter un coup d'œil, regarder furtivement. **peeping Tom** voyeur m. **peep out** se montrer.

peer¹ [piə] v regarder d'un air interrogateur. **peer at** scruter du regard.

peer² [piə] n pair m. **peerage** n pairie f. **peerless** adj sans pareil.

peevish ['piːviʃ] adj grincheux, maussade.

peg [peg] n cheville f; (washing) pince f; (coat, hat) patère f; (tent) piquet m. **off the peg** adj prêt-à-porter. v cheviller; (prices) stabiliser.

pejorative [pə'dʒɔrətiv] adj péjoratif.

Peking [piː'kiŋ] n Pékin m.

pelican ['pelikən] n pélican m.

pellet ['pelit] n boulette f; (for gun) plomb m.

pelmet ['pelmit] n (wood) lambrequin m; (fabric) cantonnière f.

pelt¹ [pelt] v bombarder; (coll: rain) tomber des cordes; (coll: run) galoper. n **at full pelt** à toute vitesse.

pelt² [pelt] n peau f; fourrure f.

pelvis ['pelvis] n bassin m. **pelvic** adj pelvien.

pen¹ [pen] n plume f, stylo m. **penfriend** n correspondant, -e m, f. **penknife** n canif m. **pen-name** n pseudonyme m.

pen² [pen] *n (enclosure)* parc *m*. *v* parquer.

penal [piːnl] *adj* pénal. **penal colony** colonie pénitentiaire *f*. **penalize** *v* pénaliser. **penalty** *n* pénalité *f*, peine *f*; *(sport)* pénalisation *f*.

penance [penəns] *n* pénitence *f*.

pencil [pensl] *n* crayon *m*. **pencil-case** *n* trousse *f*. **pencil-sharpener** *n* taille-crayon *m*. *v* crayonner.

pendant [pendənt] *n* pendentif *m*.

pending [pendiŋ] *adj* pendant, en suspens. *prep* en attendant; durant.

pendulum [pendjuləm] *n* pendule *m*.

penetrate [penitreit] *v* pénétrer. **penetrable** *adj* pénétrable. **penetration** *n* pénétration *f*.

penguin [peŋgwin] *n* pingouin *m*.

penicillin [peniˈsilin] *n* pénicilline *f*.

peninsula [pəˈninsjulə] *n* péninsule *f*. **peninsular** *adj* péninsulaire.

penis [piːnis] *n* pénis *m*.

penitent [penitənt] *n, adj* pénitent, -e. **penitence** *n* pénitence *f*.

pennant [penənt] *n* banderole *f*.

penniless [peniləs] *adj* sans le sou.

pension [penʃən] *n* pension *f*; *(from company)* retraite *f*. **pension book** livret de retraite *m*. **pension scheme** caisse de retraite *f*. *v* pensionner. **pension off** mettre à la retraite. **pensioner** *n* retraité, -e *m, f*.

pensive [pensiv] *adj* pensif.

pentagon [pentəgən] *n* pentagone *m*. **pentagonal** *adj* pentagonal.

penthouse [penthaus] *n* appentis *m*. **penthouse flat** appartement de grand standing *m*.

pent-up [pentˈʌp] *adj* refoulé.

penultimate [piˈnʌltimit] *adj* avant-dernier.

people [piːpl] *n* peuple *m*. *pl n* gens *m pl*, *f pl*; personnes *f pl*; *(inhabitants)* peuple *m sing*; *(coll)* famille *f sing*. *v* peupler.

pepper [pepə] *n (spice)* poivre *m*; *(vegetable)* poivron *m*. **peppercorn** *n* grain de poivre *m*. **peppermint** *n (flavour)* menthe *f*; *(sweet)* pastille de menthe *f*. **pepperpot** *n* poivrier *m*. *v* poivrer. **peppery** *adj* poivré.

per [pəː] *prep* par. **per cent** pour cent. **percentage** *n* pourcentage *m*.

perceive [pəˈsiːv] *v* percevoir; *(notice)* remarquer.

perceptible [pəˈseptibl] *adj* perceptible. **perceptibly** *adv* sensiblement.

perception [pəˈsepʃən] *n* perception *f*; sensibilité *f*; perspicacité *f*. **perceptive** *adj* percepteur, -trice; perspicace.

perch [pəːtʃ] *n* perchoir *m*. *v* (se) percher.

percolate [pəːkəleit] *v* passer. **percolator** *n* cafetière à pression *f*.

percussion [pəˈkʌʃən] *n* percussion *f*.

perennial [pəˈreniəl] *adj* perpétuel; *(plant)* vivace. *n* plante vivace *f*.

perfect [pəːfikt] *adj* parfait *nm, adj* parfait. *v* achever, mettre au point. **perfection** *n* perfection *f*; *(perfecting)* perfectionnement *m*. **perfectionist** *n* perfectionniste *m, f*.

perforate [pəːfəreit] *v* perforer. **perforation** *n* perforation *f*.

perform [pəˈfoːm] *v* accomplir, exécuter; *(theatre)* jouer, donner; *(machine)* marcher. **performance** *n (theatre)* représentation *f*, séance *f*; *(of individual)* interprétation *f*; *(sport)* performance *f*; *(of car)* fonctionnement *m*; exécution *f*; *(coll: fuss)* histoire *f*. **performer** *n* artiste *m, f*.

perfume [pəːfjuːm] *n* parfum *m*. *v* parfumer.

perhaps [pəˈhaps] *adv* peut-être.

peril [peril] *n* péril *m*. **perilous** *adj* périlleux.

perimeter [pəˈrimitə] *n* périmètre *m*.

period [piəriəd] *n* période *f*, époque *f*; *(school)* cours *m*; *(menstrual)* règles *f pl*. **periodic** *adj* périodique. **periodical** *nm, adj* périodique.

peripheral [pəˈrifərəl] *adj* périphérique. **periphery** *n* périphérie *f*.

periscope [periskoup] *n* périscope *m*.

perish [periʃ] *v* périr; *(rubber, food)* se détériorer. **be perished** *(coll)* crever de froid. **perishable** *adj* périssable.

perjure [pəːdʒə] *v* **perjure oneself** se parjurer; *(law)* faire un faux serment. **perjurer** *n* parjure *m, f*. **perjury** *n* parjure *m*, faux serment *m*.

perk [pəːk] *v* **perk up** (se) ragaillardir. **perky** *adj* vif, éveillé.

perm [pəːm] *n* permanente *f*. **have a perm** se faire faire une permanente.

permanent [pəːmənənt] *adj* permanent. **permanence** *n* permanence *f*. **permanently** *adv* en permanence, à titre définitif.

permeate [pəːmieit] *v* pénétrer; *(spread)*

se répandre (dans). **permeable** *adj* perméable.

permit [pə'mit; *n* 'pə:mit] *v* permettre. permis *m*; autorisation écrite *f*. **permissible** *adj* permis; acceptable. **permission** *n* permission *f*; autorisation *f*. **permissive** *adj* tolérant; laxiste.

permutation [pə:mju'teiʃən] *n* permutation *f*.

pernicious [pə'niʃəs] *adj* (*med*) pernicieux; nuisible.

perpendicular [,pə:pən'dikjulə] *nf, adj* perpendiculaire.

perpetrate *n* perpétreur. **perpetrate** *v* perpétrer. **perpetration** *n* perpétration *f*. **perpetrator** *n* auteur *m*, coupable *m, f*.

perpetual [pə'petʃuəl] *adj* perpétuel. **perpetuate** [pə'petʃueit] *v* perpétuer. **perpetuation** *n* perpétuation *f*.

perplex [pə'pleks] *v* rendre perplexe; compliquer. **perplexed** *adj* perplexe. **perplexing** *adj* embarrassant. **perplexity** *n* perplexité *f*; complexité *f*.

persecute ['pə:sikju:t] *v* persécuter; tourmenter. **persecution** *n* persécution *f*.

persevere [,pə:si'viə] *v* persévérer. **perseverance** *n* persévérance *f*. **persevering** *adj* persévérant.

persist [pə'sist] *v* persister. **persistence** *n* persistance *f*. **persistent** *adj* continuel; (*person*) persévérant; obstiné.

person ['pə:sn] *n* personne *f*. **personal** *adj* personnel. **personality** *n* personnalité *f*. **personally** *adv* personnellement; en personne.

personify [pə'sonifai] *v* personnifier. **personification** *n* personnification *f*.

personnel [pə:sə'nel] *n* personnel *m*.

perspective [pə'spektiv] *n* perspective *f*.

perspire [pə'spaiə] *v* transpirer. **perspiration** *n* transpiration *f*, sueur *f*.

persuade [pə'sweid] *v* persuader. **persuasion** *n* persuasion *f*. **persuasive** *adj* persuasif; convaincant.

pert [pə:t] *adj* impertinent; (*hat*) coquin.

pertain [pə'tein] *v* se rapporter. **pertinent** *adj* pertinent, approprié.

perturb [pə'tə:b] *v* perturber.

peruse [pə'ru:z] *v* lire attentivement. **perusal** *n* lecture attentive *f*.

pervade [pə'veid] *v* pénétrer dans, s'étendre dans.

perverse [pə'və:s] *adj* pervers; obstiné; contrariant. **perversity** *n* perversité *f*; obstination *f*.

pervert [pə'və:t; *n* 'pə:və:t] *v* pervertir, dénaturer. *n* perverti sexuel, pervertie sexuelle *m, f*. **perversion** *n* perversion *f*.

pessimism ['pesimizəm] *n* pessimisme *m*. **pessimist** *n* pessimiste *m, f*. **pessimistic** *adj* pessimiste.

pest [pest] *n* animal *or* insecte nuisible *m*; (*coll: person*) casse-pieds *m*. **pesticide** *n* pesticide *m*.

pester ['pestə] *v* harceler.

pet [pet] *n* animal familier *m*; (*coll: favourite*) chouchou, -oute *m, f*. (*as endearment*) chou *m*. *adj* favori, -ite. *v* (*coll*) chouchouter; (*slang: sexually*) (se) peloter.

petal ['petl] *n* pétale *m*.

petition [pə'tiʃən] *n* pétition *f*. *v* pétitionner, adresser une pétition à.

petrify ['petrifai] *v* pétrifier de peur.

petrol ['petrəl] *n* essence *f*. **petrol pump** pompe d'essence *f*. **petrol station** station-service *f*. **petrol tank** réservoir d'essence *m*.

petroleum [pə'trouliəm] *n* pétrole *m*.

petticoat ['petikout] *n* jupon *m*; (*slip*) combinaison *f*.

petty ['peti] *adj* mesquin, petit; insignifiant. **petty cash** petite monnaie *f*. **petty officer** second maître *m*. **pettiness** *n* mesquinerie *f*; insignifiance *f*.

petulant ['petjulənt] *adj* irritable. **petulance** *n* irritabilité *f*.

pew [pju:] *n* banc d'église *m*.

pewter ['pju:tə] *n* étain *m*.

phantom ['fantəm] *n* fantôme *m*.

pharmacy ['fɑ:məsi] *n* pharmacie *f*. **pharmaceutical** *adj* pharmaceutique. **pharmacist** *n* pharmacien, -enne *m, f*.

pharynx ['farinks] *n* pharynx *m*. **pharyngitis** *n* pharyngite *f*.

phase [feiz] *n* phase *f*. *v* **phase in** introduire progressivement. **phase out** retirer progressivement.

pheasant ['feznt] *n* faisan *m*.

phenomenon [fə'nomənən] *n*, *pl* -ena phénomène *m*. **phenomenal** *adj* phénoménal.

phial ['faiəl] *n* fiole *f*.

philanthropy [fi'lanθrəpi] *n* philanthropie *f*. **philanthropic** *adj* philanthropique. **philanthropist** *n* philanthrope *m, f*.

philately [fi'latəli] *n* philatélie *f*. **philatelist** *n* philatéliste *m, f*.

philosophy [fi'losəfi] n philosophie f. **philosopher** n philosophe m, f. **philosophical** adj philosophique; (resigned) philosophe. **philosophize** v philosopher.

phlegm [flem] n flegme m.

phlegmatic [fleg'matik] adj flegmatique.

phobia [foun] n phobie f.

phone [foun] (coll) n téléphone m. v téléphoner (à).

phonetic [fə'netik] adj phonétique. **phonetics** n phonétique f.

phoney ['founi] adj (coll) faux, fausse.

phosphate ['fosfeit] n phosphate m.

phosphorescence [fosfə'resəns] n phosphorescence f. **phosphorescent** adj phosphorescent.

phosphorus ['fosfərəs] n phosphore m. **phosphorous** adj phosphoreux.

photo ['foutou] n (coll) photo f.

photocopy ['foutou,kopi] n photocopie f. v photocopier. **photocopier** n photocopieur m. **photocopying** n reprographie f.

photogenic [,foutou'dʒenik] adj photogénique.

photograph ['foutəgraif] n photographie f. **photograph album** album de photos m. v photographier. **photographer** n photographe m, f. **photographic** adj photographique. **photography** n photographie f.

phrase [freiz] n expression f; (gramm) locution f; (music) phrase f. **phrase-book** n recueil d'expressions m. v exprimer.

physical ['fizikəl] adj physique. n (coll) examen médical m.

physician [fi'ziʃən] n médecin m.

physics ['fiziks] n physique f. **physicist** n physicien, -enne m, f.

physiology [,fizi'olədʒi] n physiologie f. **physiological** adj physiologique. **physiologist** n physiologiste m, f.

physiotherapy [,fiziou'θerəpi] n kinésithérapie f. **physiotherapist** n kinésithérapeute m, f.

physique [fi'ziːk] n constitution f; (appearance) physique m.

piano [pi'anou] n piano m. **pianist** n pianiste m, f.

piccolo ['pikəlou] n piccolo m.

pick¹ [pik] n choix m; (best) meilleur, -e m, f. **take one's pick** faire son choix. v choisir; (fruit, flowers) cueillir; (lock) crocheter. **pick at** (food) chipoter. **pick-**

me-up n (coll) remontant m. **pick out** choisir; distinguer; (highlight) rehausser.

pickpocket n pick-pocket m. **pick up** ramasser; (collect) passer prendre; s'améliorer; (learn) apprendre; (coll: arrest) cueillir.

pick² [pik] n (tool) pioche f.

picket ['pikit] n piquet m. **picket line** cordon de piquet de grève m. v organiser un piquet de grève; mettre un piquet de grève.

pickle ['pikl] v conserver dans du vinaigre. **pickles** pl n pickles m pl.

picnic ['piknik] n pique-nique m. v pique-niquer. **picnicker** n pique-niqueur, -euse m, f.

pictorial [pik'toiriəl] adj en images; illustré.

picture ['piktʃə] n image f; (painting) tableau m. **picture frame** cadre m. **picture rail** cimaise f. **pictures** n (coll) cinéma m. **picture window** fenêtre panoramique f. v (s')imaginer; décrire.

picturesque [piktʃə'resk] adj pittoresque.

pidgin ['pidʒən] n pidgin m. **pidgin French** petit-nègre m.

pie [pai] n tourte f, pâté en croûte m.

piece [piːs] n morceau m; (item) pièce f. **piecemeal** adv par bribes, petit à petit. **piecework** n travail à la pièce m. v **piece together** rassembler.

pier [piə] n jetée f; (landing-stage) appontement m.

pierce [piəs] v percer, transpercer. **piercing** adj perçant; glacial.

piety ['paiəti] n piété f.

pig [pig] n cochon m. **pigheaded** adj entêté. **pig-iron** n saumon de fonte m. **pigskin** n peau de porc f. **pigsty** n porcherie f. **pigtail** n natte f.

pigeon ['pidʒən] n pigeon m. **pigeon-hole** n casier m.

pigment ['pigmənt] n pigment m. **pigmentation** n pigmentation f. **pigmented** adj pigmenté.

pike [paik] n (fish) brochet m.

pilchard ['piltʃəd] n pilchard m.

pile¹ [pail] n (heap) pile f, tas m. **piles of** (coll) des masses de. v empiler, entasser. **pile up** (s')amonceler. **pile-up** n carambolage m.

pile² [pail] n (post) pieu m.

pile³ [pail] n (of carpet, etc.) poils m pl.

piles [pailz] pl n (med) hémorroïdes f pl.

placid

pilfer ['pilfə] (*coll*) *v* chaparder. **pilfering** *n* chapardage *m*.

pilgrim ['pilgrim] *n* pèlerin *m*. **pilgrimage** *n* pèlerinage *m*.

pill [pil] *n* pilule *f*.

pillage ['pilidʒ] *n* pillage *m*. *v* piller.

pillar ['pilə] *n* pilier *m*. colonne *f*. **pillar-box** *n* boîte aux lettres *f*.

pillion ['piljən] *n* siège arrière *m*.

pillow ['pilou] *n* oreiller *m*. **pillowcase** *n* taie d'oreiller *f*.

pilot ['pailət] *n* pilote *m*. **pilot-light** *n* veilleuse *f*. **pilot scheme** projet-pilote *m*. *v* piloter.

pimento [pi'mentou] *n* piment *m*.

pimp [pimp] *n* souteneur *m*.

pimple ['pimpl] *n* bouton *m*. **pimply** *adj* boutonneux.

pin [pin] *n* épingle *f*; (*tech*) goupille *f*; (*elec*: *in plug*) fiche *f*. **have pins and needles** avoir des fourmis. **pin-ball** *n* flipper *m*. **pincushion** *n* pelote à épingles *f*. **pin money** argent de poche *m*. **pinpoint** *v* mettre le doigt sur. **pin-stripe** *n* rayure très fine *f*. *v* épingler. **pin down** coincer. **pin up** (*notice*) afficher. **pin-up** *n* pin-up *f invar*.

pinafore ['pinəfɔː] *n* (*apron*) tablier *m*. **pinafore dress** robe-chasuble *f*.

pincers ['pinsəz] *pl n* (*tool*) tenailles *f pl*; (*of crab*) pinces *f pl*.

pinch [pintʃ] *n* pincement *m*; (*of salt*) pincée *f*. **at a pinch** au besoin. *v* pincer; (*shoes, etc.*) serrer; (*coll*: *steal*) chiper.

pine¹ [pain] *n* pin *m*. **pine-cone** *n* pomme de pin *f*.

pine² [pain] *v* languir. **pine for** désirer ardemment.

pineapple ['painapl] *n* ananas *m*.

ping-pong ['piŋpoŋ] *n* ping-pong *m*. **ping-pong ball** balle de ping-pong *f*.

pinion¹ ['pinjən] *n* aileron *m*. *v* lier.

pinion² ['pinjən] *n* (*tech*) pignon *m*.

pink [piŋk] *n* (*colour*) rose *m*; (*flower*) œillet *m*. *adj* rose.

pinnacle ['pinəkl] *n* pinacle *m*.

pioneer [paiə'niə] *n* pionnier *m*; explorateur, -trice *m, f*.

pious ['paiəs] *adj* pieux.

pip¹ [pip] *n* (*seed*) pépin *m*.

pip² [pip] *n* (*phone, etc.*) top *m*. **the pips** le bip-bip *m sing*.

pipe [paip] *n* (*water, etc.*) tuyau *m*; tube *m*; (*for smoking*) pipe *f*; (*music*) pipeau

m. **pipe-cleaner** *n* cure-pipe *m*. **pipeline** *n* pipeline *m*. **in the pipeline** en route. *v* transporter par tuyau. **pipe down** (*coll*) mettre la sourdine. **piping** *n* tuyauterie *f*; (*sewing*) passepoil *m*.

piquant ['piːkənt] *adj* piquant. **piquancy** *n* (*taste*) goût piquant *m*; (*of story*) piquant *m*.

pique [piːk] *n* dépit *m*. *v* dépiter.

pirate ['paiərət] *n* pirate *m*; (*comm*) contrefacteur *m*. *v* contrefaire, piller. **piracy** *n* piraterie *f*; contrefaçon *f*; pillage *m*.

pirouette [piru'et] *n* pirouette *f*. *v* pirouetter.

Pisces ['paisiːz] *n* Poissons *m pl*.

piss [pis] (*impol*) *v* pisser. *n* pisse *f*. **piss off!** fous-moi le camp! **pissed** *adj* (*drunk*) bituré. **be pissed off** en avoir marre.

pistachio [pi'staːtʃiou] *n* pistache *f*.

pistol ['pistl] *n* pistolet *m*.

piston ['pistən] *n* piston *m*.

pit [pit] *n* fosse *f*; mine *f*; (*hole*) trou *m*; (*theatre*) orchestre *m*. *v* trouer, grêler. **pit one's wits against** se mesurer avec.

pitch¹ [pitʃ] *n* (*throw*) lancement *m*; degré *m*; (*music*) ton *m*; (*sport*) terrain *m*. *v* lancer; (*music*) donner le ton de; (*tent*) dresser; (*fall*) tomber. **pitchfork** *n* fourche à foin *f*.

pitch² [pitʃ] *n* poix *f*. **pitch-black** *adj* noir ébène *invar*.

pitfall ['pitfɔːl] *n* piège *m*.

pith [piθ] *n* (*of orange*) peau blanche *f*; (*of plant*) moelle *f*; essence *f*. **pithy** *adj* concis, piquant.

pittance ['pitəns] *n* maigre revenu *m*.

pituitary [pi'tjuːitəri] *adj* pituitaire.

pity ['piti] *n* pitié *f*; (*shame*) dommage *m*. **take pity on** avoir pitié de. **what a pity!** quel dommage! *v* plaindre. **piteous** *adj* pitoyable. **pitiful** *adj* pitoyable; (*bad*) lamentable. **pitiless** *adj* sans pitié. **pitying** *adj* compatissant.

pivot ['pivət] *n* pivot *m*. *v* (faire) pivoter.

placard ['plakaːd] *n* affiche *f*. *v* placarder.

placate [plə'keit] *v* calmer.

place [pleis] *n* endroit *m*. lieu *m*; (*seat, position*) place *f*. **all over the place** partout. **out of place** déplacé; (*remark*) hors de propos. **take place** avoir lieu. *v* placer, mettre; situer; (*order*) passer.

placenta [plə'sentə] *n* placenta *m*.

placid ['plasid] *adj* placide. **placidity** *n* placidité *f*.

plagiarize ['pleidʒəraiz] v plagier. **plagiarism** n plagiat m. **plagiarist** n plagiaire m, f.

plague [pleig] n peste f; (nuisance) fléau m. v harceler, tourmenter.

plaice [pleis] n carrelet m.

plaid [plad] n tissu écossais m. adj écossais.

plain [plein] adj clair; simple; (not patterned) uni; sans beauté; (utter) pur. **plain-clothes** adj en civil. n plaine f.

plaintiff ['pleintif] n demandeur, -eresse m, f.

plaintive [pleintiv] adj plaintif.

plait [plat] n natte f, tresse f. v natter, tresser.

plan [plan] n plan m, projet m. v projeter; organiser; préparer à l'avance. **planning** n planification f; (comm) planning m. **planning permission** permis de construire m.

plane¹ [plein] n (level) plan m; (coll: aeroplane) avion m. adj plan.

plane² [plein] n (tool) rabot. v raboter.

planet ['planit] n planète f. **planetarium** n planétarium m. **planetary** adj planétaire.

plank [plaŋk] n planche f.

plankton ['plaŋktən] n plancton m.

plant [plaint] n (bot) plante f; (tech) matériel m, installation f; (factory) usine f. v planter; (hide) cacher. **plantation** n plantation f.

plaque [plaik] n plaque f.

plasma ['plazmə] n plasma m.

plaster ['plaistə] n plâtre m; (for wound) sparadrap m. **plaster of Paris** plâtre de moulage m. v plâtrer; couvrir. **plasterer** n plâtrier m.

plastic ['plastik] nm, adj plastique. **plastic surgery** chirurgie esthétique f.

plate [pleit] n (dish) assiette f; (of metal) plaque f; (in book) gravure f. v plaquer; (silver) argenter; (gold) dorer. **plateful** n assiettée f.

plateau ['platou] n plateau m.

platform ['platfom] n plate-forme f; (in hall) estrade f, tribune f; (rail) quai m. **platform-soled** adj (shoes) à semelles compensées. **platform ticket** billet de quai m.

platinum ['platinəm] n platine m.

platonic [plə'tonik] adj platonique.

platoon [plə'tuːn] n (mil) section f.

plausible ['plɔːzəbl] adj plausible; (person) convaincant. **plausibility** n plausibilité f.

play [plei] n jeu m; (theatre) pièce f. v jouer. **player** n joueur, -euse m, f. **playful** adj enjoué. **playfulness** n enjouement m, badinage m.

play-back ['pleibak] n réécoute f. **play back** v réécouter.

playboy ['pleiboi] n playboy m.

playground ['pleigraund] n cour de récréation f.

play-group ['pleigruːp] n garderie f.

playing card n carte à jouer f.

playing field n terrain de sport m.

playmate ['pleimeit] n camarade m, f.

play-pen ['pleipen] n parc m.

plaything ['plei,θiŋ] n jouet m.

playtime ['pleitaim] n récréation f.

playwright ['pleirait] n dramaturge m.

plea [pliː] n appel m; (law) argument m; excuse f.

plead [pliːd] v supplier, implorer; (law) plaider; (as excuse) alléguer.

pleasant ['pleznt] adj agréable.

please [pliːz] v plaire (à). **please oneself** faire comme on veut. adv s'il vous plaît. **pleased** adj content. **pleasing** adj plaisant.

pleasure ['pleʒə] n plaisir m. **pleasure boat** bateau de plaisance m. **pleasurable** adj agréable.

pleat [pliːt] n pli m. v plisser.

plectrum ['plektrəm] n plectre m.

pledge [pledʒ] n gage m; promesse f. v engager; promettre.

plenty ['plenti] n abondance f. **plenty of** bien assez de. **plentiful** adj abondant, copieux.

pleurisy ['pluərisi] n pleurésie f.

pliable ['plaiəbl] adj flexible; (person) souple. **pliability** n flexibilité f; souplesse f.

pliers ['plaiəz] pl n pinces f pl, tenailles f pl.

plight [plait] n état critique m, crise f.

plimsoll ['plimsəl] n tennis m.

plod [plod] v marcher d'un pas lourd; (coll: work) bûcher. **plod on** persévérer. **plodder** n (coll) bûcheur m.

plonk [ploŋk] n (coll) vin ordinaire m.

plop [plop] n ploc m. v faire ploc.

plot¹ [plot] n (story, etc) intrigue f; (conspiracy) complot m. v comploter; (route) déterminer.

plot² [plot] n (land) terrain m, lotissement m.

plough [plau] n charrue f. v labourer; (furrow) creuser. **ploughing** n labour m.

pluck [plʌk] n courage m. v (music) pincer; (fruit) cueillir; (fowl) plumer; (eyebrows) épiler. **pluck out** arracher. **pluck up courage** prendre son courage à deux mains. **plucky** adj courageux.

plug [plʌg] n (stopper) bouchon m, tampon m; (sink, bath) bonde f; (elec) fiche f; (mot) bougie f. v boucher. **plug in** (se) brancher.

plum [plʌm] n (fruit) prune f; (tree) prunier m. adj (colour) lie de vin invar. **plum pudding** pudding m.

plumage ['pluːmidʒ] n plumage m.

plumb [plʌm] n plomb m. **plumbline** n fil à plomb m. adj vertical. adv en plein. v sonder. **plumb in** faire le raccordement de. **plumber** n plombier m. **plumbing** n plomberie f.

plume [pluːm] n plume f; (smoke) panache m. v lisser.

plummet ['plʌmit] n plomb m. v plonger; (price, etc.) dégringoler.

plump[1] [plʌmp] adj grassouillet, -ette, potelé. **plumpness** n rondeur f.

plump[2] [plʌmp] v tomber lourdement. **plump for** se décider pour.

plunder ['plʌndə] v piller. n (loot) butin m. **plunderer** n pillard m. **plundering** n pillage m.

plunge [plʌndʒ] n plongeon m; (fall) chute f. **take the plunge** se jeter à l'eau. v plonger; (rush) se jeter; (fall) tomber.

pluperfect [pluː'pəfikt] n plus-que-parfait m.

plural ['pluərəl] nm, adj pluriel.

plus [plʌs] nm, prep plus. adj positif.

plush [plʌʃ] n peluche f. adj pelucheux, (coll) rupin.

ply[1] [plai] v (tool) manier; (trade) exercer; (with questions, etc.) presser; (ship, etc.) faire la navette.

ply[2] [plai] n (wood) feuille f; (wool) fil m; (rope) brin m. **plywood** n contre-plaqué m.

pneumatic [njuˈmatik] adj pneumatique. **pneumatic drill** marteau-piqueur m.

pneumonia [njuˈmouniə] n pneumonie f.

poach[1] [poutʃ] v braconner. **poacher** n braconnier m. **poaching** n braconnage m.

poach[2] [poutʃ] v (egg) pocher.

pocket [ˈpɔkit] n poche f. **pocket-money** n argent de poche m. v empocher.

pod [pɔd] n cosse f.

podgy ['pɔdʒi] adj (coll) rondelet.

poem ['pouim] n poème m.

poet ['pouit] n poète m. **poetess** n poétesse f. **poetic** adj poétique. **poetry** n poésie f.

poignant ['pɔinjənt] adj poignant.

point [pɔint] n point m; (sharp end) pointe f; (decimal) virgule f; (elec: socket) prise f; (meaning) sens m. **beside the point** hors de propos. **come to the point** en venir au fait. **make a point of** ne pas manquer de. **point-blank** adv (shoot) à bout portant; (refuse) tout net; (demand) de but en blanc. **what's the point?** à quoi bon? v indiquer; (aim) pointer, braquer. **point out** (show) montrer; (say) signaler. **pointed** adj pointu; (remark) lourd de sens. **pointless** adj inutile.

poise [pɔiz] n équilibre m; (of body) port m; calme m, assurance f. v tenir en équilibre. **be poised** être en équilibre; être balancé.

poison ['pɔizən] n poison m. v empoisonner. **poisoning** n empoisonnement m. **poisonous** adj toxique; (animal) venimeux; (plant) vénéneux.

poke [pouk] n poussée f, coup m. v pousser, enfoncer; (fire) tisonner. **poker** n tisonnier m.

poker ['poukə] n (cards) poker m. **poker-faced** adj au visage impassible.

Poland ['poulənd] n Pologne f. **Pole** n Polonais, -e m, f. **Polish** nm, adj polonais.

polar ['poulə] adj polaire. **polar bear** ours blanc m. **polarize** v polariser.

pole[1] [poul] n perche f; (fixed) poteau m, mât m. **pole-vault** n saut à la perche m.

pole[2] [poul] n (geog, elec) pôle m. **pole star** étoile polaire f.

police [pəˈliːs] n police f, gendarmerie f. **the police force** la police f, les gendarmes m pl. **policeman** n agent de police m, gendarme m. **police station** poste de police m, gendarmerie f. **policewoman** n femme-agent f.

policy[1] ['pɔləsi] n politique f; ligne f, règle f.

policy[2] ['pɔləsi] n (insurance) police f.

polio ['pouliou] n polio f.

polish ['pɔliʃ] n (shoes) cirage m; (floor, etc.) cire f; (shine) poli m. v polir; cirer, faire briller. **polish off** finir. **polish up** perfectionner.

polite [pəˈlait] *adj* poli. **politeness** *n* politesse *f*.
politics [ˈpolitiks] *n* politique *f*. **political** *adj* politique. **politician** *n* homme politique, femme politique *m, f*.
polka [ˈpolkə] *n* polka *f*.
poll [poul] *n* vote *m*; élection *f*; (survey) sondage *m*. *v* voter. **polling booth** isoloir *m*. **polling day** jour des élections *m*. **polling station** bureau de vote *m*.
pollen [ˈpolən] *n* pollen *m*. **pollinate** *v* féconder. **pollination** *n* pollinisation *f*.
pollute [pəˈluːt] *v* polluer. **pollution** *n* pollution *f*.
polo [ˈpouləu] *n* polo *m*. **polo-neck** *n* col roulé *m*.
polyester [ˌpoliˈestə] *n* polyester *m*.
polygamy [pəˈligəmi] *n* polygamie *f*. **polygamous** *adj* polygame.
polygon [ˈpoligən] *n* polygone *m*.
polystyrene [ˌpoliˈstaiəriːn] *n* polystyrène *m*.
polytechnic [ˌpoliˈteknik] *n* Institut Universitaire de Technologie *m*.
polythene [ˈpoliθiːn] *n* polyéthylène *m*. **polythene bag** sac en plastique *m*.
pomegranate [ˈpomigranit] *n* (fruit) grenade *f*; (tree) grenadier *m*.
pomp [pomp] *n* pompe *f*. **pompous** *adj* pompeux.
pond [pond] *n* étang *m*; (artificial) bassin *m*.
ponder [ˈpondə] *v* réfléchir (à), méditer.
pony [ˈpouni] *n* poney *m*. **pony-tail** *n* queue de cheval *f*. **pony-trekking** *n* randonnée équestre *f*.
poodle [ˈpuːdl] *n* caniche *m*.
poof [puf] *n* (derog) tante *f*, tapette *f*.
pool¹ [puːl] *n* (liquid) flaque *f*; (swimming) piscine *f*.
pool² [puːl] *n* (money) cagnotte *f*; (things) fonds commun *m*; (ideas) réservoir *m*; (comm) pool *m*. *v* mettre en commun; unir.
poor [puə] *adj* pauvre; médiocre; faible. **poorly** [ˈpuəli] *adj* malade. *adv* pauvrement; (badly) mal.
pop¹ [pop] *n* pan *m*, bruit sec *m*; (drink) boisson gazeuse *f*. **popcorn** *n* pop-corn *m*. *v* (balloon) crever; (cork) (faire) sauter. **pop in** entrer en passant.
pop² [pop] *nm, adj* (music, etc.) pop *invar*.
pope [poup] *n* pape *m*.
poplar [ˈpoplə] *n* peuplier *m*.
poplin [ˈpoplin] *n* popeline *f*.

poppy [ˈpopi] *n* pavot *m*, coquelicot *m*.
popular [ˈpopjulə] *adj* populaire. **popularity** *n* popularité *f*. **popularize** *v* populariser.
population [ˌpopjuˈleiʃən] *n* population *f*. **populate** *v* peupler.
porcelain [ˈpoːslin] *n* porcelaine *f*.
porch [poːtʃ] *n* porche *m*.
porcupine [ˈpoːkjupain] *n* porc-épic *m*.
pore¹ [poː] *n* (anat) pore *m*.
pore² [poː] *v* pore over s'absorber dans.
pork [poːk] *n* porc *m*.
pornography [poːˈnogrəfi] *n* pornographie *f*. **pornographic** *adj* pornographique.
porous [ˈpoːrəs] *adj* poreux.
porpoise [ˈpoːpəs] *n* marsouin *m*.
porridge [ˈporidʒ] *n* porridge *m*.
port¹ [poːt] *n* (harbour) port *m*.
port² [poːt] *n* (naut: left) bâbord *m*.
port³ [poːt] *n* (wine) porto *m*.
portable [ˈpoːtəbl] *adj* portatif.
portent [ˈpoːtent] *n* présage *m*.
porter [ˈpoːtə] *n* (rail, etc.) porteur *m*; (in flats, etc.) concierge *m, f*, portier *m*.
portfolio [poːtˈfouliəu] *n* serviette *f*; (pol) portefeuille *f*.
porthole [ˈpoːthoul] *n* hublot *m*.
portion [ˈpoːʃən] *n* portion *f*; partie *f*.
portrait [ˈpoːtrət] *n* portrait *m*.
portray [poːˈtrei] *v* peindre; représenter. **portrayal** *n* peinture *f*; représentation *f*.
Portugal [ˈpoːtjugl] *n* Portugal *m*. **Portuguese** *nm, adj* portugais. **the Portuguese** les Portugais.
pose [pouz] *n* pose *f*. *v* poser. **pose as** se faire passer pour.
posh [poʃ] *adj* chic *invar*.
position [pəˈziʃən] *n* position *f*, place *f*; situation *f*. *v* placer, mettre en place.
positive [ˈpozitiv] *adj* positif; catégorique; réel; sûr, certain.
possess [pəˈzes] *v* posséder. **possession** *n* possession *f*. **possessive** *nm, adj* possessif.
possible [ˈposəbl] *adj* possible. **possibility** *n* possibilité *f*. **possibly** *adv* (perhaps) peut-être.
post¹ [poust] *n* (pole) poteau *m*. *v* afficher.
post² [poust] *n* (sentry, job) poste *m*. *v* poster; (send) affecter. **posting** *n* affectation *f*.
post³ [poust] *n* (mail) poste *f*; (letters) courrier *m*. **post-box** *n* boîte aux lettres *f*. **postcard** *n* carte postale *f*. **post-code** *n* code postal *m*. **postman** *n* facteur *m*.

postmark n cachet de la poste m. **postmarked** adj timbré. **post office** poste f. v envoyer par la poste, poster. **postage** n tarifs postaux m pl. **postage stamp** timbre-poste m. **postal** adj postal, par la poste. **postal order** mandat m.

poster ['pousta] n affiche f. (as decoration) poster m. **poster paint** gouache f.

posterior [po'stiaria] adj postérieur, -e. n (coll) derrière m.

posterity [po'sterati] n postérité f.

postgraduate [poust'gradjuit] adj de troisième cycle. n étudiant, -e de troisième cycle m, f.

posthumous ['postjumas] adj posthume.

post-mortem [poust'mortam] n autopsie f.

postpone [pous'poun] v remettre, ajourner. **postponement** n ajournement m.

postscript ['poussskript] n post-scriptum m.

postulate ['postjuleit; n 'postjulat] v postuler, poser comme principe. n postulat m.

posture ['postja] n posture f; attitude f.

pot [pot] n pot m; (for cooking) marmite f. **pot-roast** n rôti braisé m. **pots and pans** batterie de cuisine f sing. **take pot luck** manger à la fortune du pot. v mettre en pot.

potassium [pa'tasjam] n potassium m.

potato [pa'teitou] n pomme de terre f.

potent ['poutant] adj puissant; (drink) fort.

potential [pa'tenfal] adj potentiel; possible. n (phys, elec, etc) potentiel m; (promise) potentialités f pl.

pot-hole ['pothoul] n (in road) fondrière f; (underground) caverne f, grotte f. **pot-holer** n spéléologue m, f. **pot-holing** n spéléologie f.

potion ['poufan] n potion f.

potter¹ ['pota] v (coll) bricoler.

potter² ['pota] n potier m. **potter's wheel** tour de potier m.

pottery ['potari] n (place, craft) poterie f; (things made) poteries f pl.

potty ['poti] n (coll) pot de bébé m.

pouch [pautf] n petit sac m; (kangaroo) poche f; (tobacco) blague f.

poultice ['poultis] n cataplasme m.

poultry ['poultri] n volaille f.

pounce [pauns] v bondir, sauter. n bond m.

pound¹ [paund] v battre, piler, pilonner, marteler.

pound² [paund] n livre f.

pour [po:] v verser; (flow copiously) couler à flots, ruisseler; (rain) tomber à verse; (people, etc) affluer.

pout [paut] n moue f. v faire la moue.

poverty ['povati] n pauvreté f.

powder ['pauda] n poudre f. **powder puff** houppette f. **powder room** toilettes pour dames f pl. v poudrer; pulvériser. **powdery** adj poudreux.

power ['paua] n (authority, capacity) pouvoir m; (energy, force) puissance f; faculté f. **power cut** coupure de courant f. **power station** centrale électrique f. v faire marcher. **powerful** adj puissant. **powerless** adj impuissant.

practicable ['praktikabl] adj praticable.

practical ['praktikal] adj pratique. **practical joke** farce f.

practice ['praktis] n pratique f; (training) entraînement m; (medicine, etc) exercice m; clientèle f.

practise ['praktis] v pratiquer; s'entraîner (à); (music) travailler, s'exercer (à); (doctor, lawyer) exercer.

practitioner [prak'tifana] n praticien, -enne m, f.

pragmatic [prag'matik] adj pragmatique, dogmatique.

Prague [pra:g] n Prague.

prairie ['preari] n plaine f, prairie f.

praise [preiz] n éloge m. v louer. **praiseworthy** adj louable.

pram [pram] n voiture d'enfant f.

prance [pra:ns] v caracoler.

prank [prank] n frasque f; (joke) farce f.

prattle ['pratl] v jaser, babiller; (chat) jacasser. n babil m; jacasserie f.

prawn [pro:n] n crevette rose f. **prawn cocktail** salade de crevettes f.

pray [prei] v prier. **prayer** n prière f. **prayer-book** n livre de messe m.

preach [pri:tf] v prêcher. **preacher** n prédicateur m. **preaching** n prédication f.

precarious [pri'kearias] adj précaire.

precaution [pri'ko:fan] n précaution f. **take precautions** prendre ses précautions.

precede [pri'si:d] v précéder. **precedence** n préséance f; priorité f. **precedent** n précédent m.

precinct ['pri:siŋkt] n enceinte f; limite f; (shopping) zone commerciale f.

precious ['preʃəs] *adj* précieux.

precipice ['presipis] *n* précipice *m*.

precipitate [pri'sipiteit; *adj* pri'sipitət] *v* (*hasten*) hâter; (*throw*) précipiter. *adj* irréfléchi. **precipitation** *n* précipitation *f*.

précis ['preisi] *n* précis *m*. résumé *m*.

precise [pri'sais] *adj* précis; méticuleux. **precision** *n* précision *f*.

preclude [pri'kluːd] *v* écarter; prévenir; exclure.

precocious [pri'kouʃəs] *adj* précoce. **precocity** *n* précocité *f*.

preconceive [,priːkən'siːv] *v* préconcevoir. **preconception** *n* idée préconçue *f*.

precursor [,priː'kəːsə] *n* (*person*) précurseur *m*; (*thing*) annonce *f*.

predator ['predətə] *n* prédateur *m*. **predatory** *adj* rapace, de prédateur.

predecessor ['priːdisesə] *n* prédécesseur *m*.

predestine [pri'destin] *v* prédestiner. **predestination** *n* prédestination *f*.

predicament [pri'dikəmənt] *n* situation difficile *f*.

predicate ['predikət] *n* prédicat *m*. *v* affirmer.

predict [pri'dikt] *v* prédire. **predictable** *adj* prévisible. **prediction** *n* prédiction *f*.

predominate [pri'domineit] *v* prédominer. **predominance** *n* prédominance *f*. **predominant** *adj* prédominant.

pre-eminent [pri'eminənt] *adj* prééminent. **pre-eminence** *n* prééminence *f*.

preen [priːn] *v* lisser. **preen oneself** *v* pomponner.

prefabricate [pri'fæbrikeit] *v* préfabriquer. **prefab** *n* (*coll*) maison préfabriquée *f*.

preface ['prefis] *n* (*book*) préface *f*; (*speech*) introduction *f*. *v* faire précéder.

prefect ['priːfekt] *n* (*school*) élève chargé de la discipline *m*.

prefer [pri'fəː] *v* préférer, aimer mieux. **preferable** *adj* préférable. **preference** *n* préférence *f*. **preferential** *adj* préférentiel.

prefix ['priːfiks] *n* préfixe *m*. *v* préfixer.

pregnant ['pregnənt] *adj* (*woman*) enceinte; (*animal*) pleine. **pregnancy** *n* (*woman*) grossesse *f*; (*animal*) gestation *f*.

prehistoric [,priːhi'storik] *adj* préhistorique.

prejudice ['predʒədis] *n* préjugé *m*. *v* prévenir; (*damage*) nuire à. **prejudiced** *adj* de parti pris.

preliminary [pri'liminəri] *adj* pré-liminaire; premier. **preliminaries** *pl n* préliminaires *m pl*.

prelude ['preljuːd] *n* prélude *m*.

premarital [priː'mæritl] *adj* avant le mariage.

premature [premə'tʃuə] *adj* prématuré.

premeditate [priː'mediteit] *v* préméditer. **premeditation** *n* préméditation *f*.

premier ['premiə] *adj* premier. *n* premier ministre *m*.

première ['premieə] *n* première *f*.

premise ['premis] *n* prémisse *f*. **premises** *pl n* lieux *m pl*, locaux *m pl*.

premium ['priːmiəm] *n* prime *f*. **premium bond** bon à lots *m*.

premonition [,premə'niʃən] *n* prémonition *f*.

preoccupied [priː'okjupaid] *adj* préoccupé. **preoccupation** *n* préoccupation *f*.

prepare [pri'peə] *v* (se) préparer. **preparation** *n* préparation *f*. **preparations** *pl n* préparatifs *m pl*. **preparatory** *adj* préparatoire; préliminaire. **preparatory school** école primaire privée *f*.

preposition [,prepə'ziʃən] *n* préposition *f*.

preposterous [pri'postərəs] *adj* absurde, ridicule.

prerogative [pri'rogativ] *n* prérogative *f*.

prescribe [pri'skraib] *v* prescrire. **prescription** *n* (*med*) ordonnance *f*; prescription *f*.

presence ['prezns] *n* présence *f*.

present¹ ['preznt] *adj* présent; actuel. *n* présent *m*. **at present** actuellement. **presently** *adv* tout à l'heure.

present² [pri'zent] *v* présenter; (*film, play*) donner; (*gift*) offrir; (*medal*) remettre. *n* cadeau *m*. **presentable** *adj* présentable. **presentation** *n* présentation *f*; (*of gift, medal*) remise *f*. **presenter** *n* présentateur, -trice *m, f*.

preserve [pri'zəːv] *v* conserver; (*from harm*) préserver. **preserved** *adj* en conserve. **preserves** *pl n* conserves *f pl*; (*jam*) confiture *f sing*. **preservation** *n* conservation *f*; préservation *f*. **preservative** *n* agent de conservation *m*.

preside [pri'zaid] *v* présider.

president ['prezidənt] *n* président *m*. **presidency** *n* présidence *f*. **presidential** *adj* présidentiel.

press [pres] *n* presse *f*; (*wine, cider*) pressoir *m*. **press conference** conférence de presse *f*. **press release** communiqué de presse *m*. *v* appuyer (sur), presser; (*iron*) repasser; insister. **press for** faire pression pour. **press-gang** v faire pression sur. **press on** continuer. **press-stud** n bouton-pression m. **press-up** n traction f. **pressing** adj urgent.

pressure ['preʃə] n pression f. **pressure-cooker** n autocuiseur m. **pressure gauge** manomètre m. **pressurize** v (cabin, etc.) pressuriser; (force) contraindre.

prestige [pre'stiːʒ] n prestige m. **prestigious** adj prestigieux.

presume [pri'zjuːm] v présumer. **presumption** n présomption f. **presumptuous** adj présomptueux.

pretend [pri'tend] v faire semblant; (claim) prétendre. **pretence** n feinte f, prétexte m; (claim) prétention f. **pretension** n prétention f. **pretentious** adj prétentieux.

pretext ['priːtekst] n prétexte m.

pretty ['priti] adj joli. adv assez.

prevail [pri'veil] v prévaloir, prédominer. **prevail upon** persuader. **prevailing** adj (wind) dominant; courant, actuel. **prevalent** adj répandu.

prevent [pri'vent] v empêcher. **prevention** n prévention f. **preventive** adj préventif.

preview ['priːvjuː] n avant-première f.

previous ['priːviəs] adj précédent. **previously** adv auparavant.

prey [prei] n proie f. **be a prey to** être en proie à. v **prey on** (animal) faire sa proie de; (fear) ronger.

price [prais] n prix m. **price-list** n tarif m. v fixer le prix de; marquer le prix de. **priceless** adj inestimable.

prick [prik] n piqûre f. v piquer. **prick up one's ears** dresser l'oreille.

prickle ['prikl] n piquant m. v piquer; (sensation) picoter. **prickly** adj hérissé.

pride [praid] n orgueil m; (satisfaction) fierté f. v **pride oneself on** être fier de.

priest [priːst] n prêtre m. **priesthood** n prêtrise f.

prim [prim] adj guindé.

primary ['praiməri] adj (first) primaire, premier; principal. **primary school** école primaire f.

primate ['praimət] n (zool) primate m; (rel) primat m.

prime [praim] adj principal; excellent, de premier choix; (math) premier. **prime minister** premier ministre m. v préparer; (for painting) apprêter. **primer** n apprêt m; (book) premier livre m.

primitive ['primitiv] adj primitif.

primrose ['primrouz] n primevère f.

prince [prins] n prince m. **princely** adj princier. **princess** n princesse f.

principal ['prinsəpəl] adj principal. n (school) directeur, -trice m, f.

principle ['prinsəpl] n principe m. **on principle** par principe.

print [print] n (mark) empreinte f; (type) caractères m pl; (art) gravure f; (phot) épreuve f. **out of print** épuisé. v imprimer; (phot) tirer. **print-out** n listage m. **printed matter** imprimés m pl. **printer** n imprimeur m. **printing** n impression f; (phot) tirage m. **printing press** presse typographique f.

prior ['praiə] adj antérieur, -e. **prior to** antérieurement à. **priority** n priorité f.

prise [praiz] v **prise off/open** enlever/ouvrir en faisant levier; forcer.

prism ['prizm] n prisme m.

prison ['prizn] n prison f. **prisoner** n prisonnier, -ère m, f.

private ['praivət] adj privé; confidentiel; (lesson, car, etc.) particulier; personnel. n simple soldat m. **privacy** n intimité f, solitude f. **privately** adv en privé; à titre personnel.

privet ['privət] n troène m.

privilege ['privilidʒ] n privilège m. **privileged** adj privilégié.

prize [praiz] n prix m. **prizewinner** n lauréat, -e m, f. adj primé. v priser.

probable ['probabl] adj probable; (believable) vraisemblable. **probability** n probabilité f. **probably** adv probablement.

probation [prə'beiʃən] n (law) mise à l'épreuve f, liberté surveillée f. **on probation** (job) engagé à l'essai. **probationary** adj d'essai.

probe [proub] n sonde f; enquête f. v sonder, explorer.

problem ['probləm] n problème m. **problem child** enfant difficile m, f. **problem page** courrier du cœur m. **problematic** adj problématique.

proceed [prə'siːd] v aller, continuer, avancer. **proceed to** se mettre à. **proceeds** pl n produit m sing. **procedure** n procédure f. **proceedings** pl n cérémonie f sing; (law) mesures f pl.

process ['prouses] n processus m; (method) procédé m. **in the process of** en train de, au cours de. v traiter; (phot) développer; (admin) s'occuper de.

procession [prə'seʃən] n cortège m, défilé m.

proclaim [prə'kleim] v proclamer; démontrer. **proclamation** n proclamation f.

procreate ['proukrieit] v procréer. **procreation** n procréation f.

procure [prə'kjuə] v obtenir; (prostitute) procurer.

prod [prod] n petit coup m. v pousser doucement; (rouse) aiguillonner.

prodigal ['prodigəl] adj prodigue.

prodigy ['prodidʒi] n prodige m. **prodigious** adj prodigieux.

produce [prə'djuːs; n 'prodjuːs] v produire; (theatre) mettre en scène. n produits m pl. **producer** n producteur, -trice m, f; metteur en scène m. **product** n produit m. **production** n production f; mise en scène f. **productive** adj productif; fécond. **productivity** n productivité f.

profane [prə'fein] adj profane. v profaner. **profanity** n (oath) juron m.

profess [prə'fes] v professer, affirmer, déclarer.

profession [prə'feʃən] n profession f. **professional** n, adj professionnel, -elle. **professor** [prə'fesə] n professeur m. **professorship** n chaire f.

proficient [prə'fiʃənt] adj compétent. **proficiency** n compétence f.

profile ['proufail] n profil m; (biographical sketch) portrait m.

profit ['profit] n profit m, bénéfice m. **profit-making** adj à but lucratif. v **profit by** or **from** tirer profit de. **profitable** adj rentable; (useful) fructueux.

profound [prə'faund] adj profond. **profoundly** adv profondément.

profuse [prə'fjuːs] adj abondant, profus. **profusely** adv abondamment, à profusion. **profusion** n abondance f, profusion f.

programme ['prougram] n programme m; (broadcast) émission f. v programmer. **programmer** n programmeur, -euse m, f. **programming** n programmation f.

progress ['prougres] n progrès m. **in progress** en cours. **make progress** faire des progrès. v progresser, avancer. **progression** n progression f. **progressive** adj progressif; (outlook, etc.) progressiste.

prohibit [prə'hibit] v interdire, défendre;

(prevent) empêcher. **prohibition** n prohibition f.

project ['prodʒekt; v prə'dʒekt] n projet m; opération f; (school) dossier m. v projeter; (protrude) faire saillie. **projectile** n projectile m. **projecting** adj saillant. **projection** n projection f; saillie f. **projector** n projecteur m.

proletarian [proulə'teəriən] n prolétaire m. adj prolétarien. **proletariat** n prolétariat m.

proliferate [prə'lifəreit] v proliférer. **proliferation** n prolifération f.

prolific [prə'lifik] adj prolifique.

prologue ['proulog] n prologue m.

prolong [prə'loŋ] v prolonger. **prolongation** n (time) prolongation f; (space) prolongement m.

promenade [promə'naːd] n promenade f.

prominent ['prominənt] adj proéminent; important; (striking) frappant. **prominence** n proéminence f; importance f.

promiscuous [prə'miskjuəs] adj léger, immoral; (person) de mœurs faciles. **promiscuity** n promiscuité f.

promise [promis] n promesse f. v promettre. **promising** adj prometteur, -euse.

promontory ['proməntəri] n promontoire m.

promote [prə'mout] v promouvoir; (comm) lancer. **promotion** n promotion f; lancement m.

prompt [prompt] adj rapide, prompt; ponctuel. v pousser, inciter; (theatre) souffler. **prompter** n souffleur, -euse m, f.

prone [proun] adj enclin; (lying) prostré.

prong [proŋ] n dent f.

pronoun ['prounaun] n pronom m.

pronounce [prə'nauns] v prononcer. **pronouncement** n déclaration f. **pronunciation** n prononciation f.

proof [pruːf] n preuve f; (of book, photo, etc.) épreuve f. **proof-read** v corriger les épreuves de. **proof-reading** n correction des épreuves f. adj (resistant) à l'épreuve de.

prop¹ [prop] n support m. v (lean) appuyer; (support) étayer; (financially) soutenir.

prop² [prop] n (coll: theatre) accessoire m.

propaganda [propə'gandə] n propagande f.

propagate ['propəgeit] v (se) propager. **propagation** n propagation f.

propel [prə'pel] v propulser; (push) pousser. **propeller** n hélice f. **propelling pencil** porte-mine m invar.

proper ['prɔpə] adj convenable, correct; (real) véritable. **proper noun** nom propre m. **properly** adv comme il faut.

property ['prɔpəti] n propriété f; (possessions) biens m pl.

prophecy ['prɔfəsi] n prophétie f. **prophesy** v prédire, prophétiser.

prophet ['prɔfit] n prophète m. **prophetic** adj prophétique.

proportion [prə'pɔːʃən] n proportion f; part f. **out of proportion** mal proportionné; hors de proportion. v proportionner. **proportional** adj proportionnel.

propose [prə'pouz] v proposer; (marriage) faire sa demande; (intend) se proposer (de). **proposal** n proposition f; demande en mariage f; projet m. **proposition** n proposition f; affaire f.

proprietor [prə'praiətə] n propriétaire m, f.

propriety [prə'praiəti] n bienséance f; (correctness) justesse f.

propulsion [prə'pʌlʃən] n propulsion f.

prose [prouz] n prose f; (translation) thème m.

prosecute ['prɔsikjuːt] v poursuivre. **prosecution** n poursuites judiciaires f pl; (side) partie plaignante f.

prospect ['prɔspekt; v prə'spekt] n perspective f. **prospects** pl n (of job, etc.) avenir m sing. v prospecter. **prospective** adj futur; possible.

prospectus [prə'spektəs] n prospectus m.

prosper ['prɔspə] v prospérer. **prosperity** n prospérité f. **prosperous** adj prospère.

prostitute ['prɔstitjuːt] n prostituée f. v prostituer. **prostitution** n prostitution f.

prostrate ['prɔstreit; v pro'streit] adj prostré; prostré; (lying) à plat ventre. v (overcome) accabler. **prostrate oneself** se prosterner. **prostration** n prosternation f; (exhaustion) prostration f.

protagonist [prou'tagənist] n protagoniste m.

protect [prə'tekt] v protéger. **protection** n protection f. **protective** adj protecteur, -trice; de protection.

protein ['proutiin] n protéine f.

protest ['proutest; v prə'test] n protestation f. v protester. **protester** n (on march) manifestant, -e m, f.

Protestant ['prɔtistənt] n, adj protestant, -e m, f.

protocol ['proutəkɔl] n protocole m.

prototype ['proutətaip] n prototype m.

protractor [prə'traktə] n rapporteur m.

protrude [prə'truːd] v dépasser, avancer. **protruding** adj saillant, en saillie.

proud [praud] adj fier; orgueilleux.

prove [pruːv] v prouver; se révéler.

proverb ['prɔvəb] n proverbe m. **proverbial** adj proverbial.

provide [prə'vaid] v fournir, pourvoir. **provided that** pourvu que.

provident ['prɔvidənt] adj prévoyant. **providence** n providence f.

province ['prɔvins] n province f; domaine m. **the provinces** la province f sing. **provincial** adj provincial.

provision [prə'viʒən] n (supply) provision f; (providing) fourniture f; (of contract, law, etc.) disposition f. **make provision for** pourvoir aux besoins de. **provisions** pl n provisions f pl. **provisional** adj provisoire.

proviso [prə'vaizou] n stipulation f, condition f.

provoke [prə'vouk] v provoquer. **provocation** n provocation f. **provocative** adj provocant.

prow [prau] n proue f.

prowess ['prauis] n prouesse f.

prowl [praul] v rôder. **prowler** n rôdeur, -euse m f.

proximity [prɔk'siməti] n proximité f.

proxy ['prɔksi] n procuration f. **by proxy** par procuration.

prude [pruːd] n prude f. **prudish** adj prude.

prudent ['pruːdənt] adj prudent. **prudence** n prudence f.

prune¹ [pruːn] n (fruit) pruneau m.

prune² [pruːn] v tailler, élaguer.

pry [prai] v être indiscret. **pry into** fourrer son nez dans. **prying** adj fureteur, -euse.

psalm [saːm] n psaume m.

pseudonym ['sjuːdənim] n pseudonyme m.

psychedelic [,saikə'delik] adj psychédélique.

psychiatry [sai'kaiətri] n psychiatrie f. **psychiatric** adj psychiatrique. **psychiatrist** n psychiatre m, f.

psychic ['saikik] adj métapsychique; (psych) psychique.

psychoanalysis [ˌsaikouəˈnæləsis] *n* psychanalyse *f*. **psychoanalyse** *v* psychanalyser. **psychoanalyst** *n* psychanalyste *m, f*.

psychology [saiˈkɔlədʒi] *n* psychologie *f*. **psychological** *adj* psychologique. **psychologist** *n* psychologue *m, f*.

psychopath [ˈsaikəpæθ] *n* psychopathe *m, f*. **psychopathic** *adj* psychopathe.

psychosis [saiˈkousis] *n* psychose *f*. **psychotic** *n(m+f)*, *adj* psychotique.

psychosomatic [ˌsaikəsəˈmætik] *adj* psychosomatique.

psychotherapy [ˌsaikəˈθerəpi] *n* psychothérapie *f*.

pub [pʌb] *n* pub *m*. **pub-crawl** *n* tournée des bistrots *f*.

puberty [ˈpjuːbəti] *n* puberté *f*.

pubic [ˈpjuːbik] *adj* pubien.

public [ˈpʌblik] *adj* public, -ique. *n* public *m*.

publican [ˈpʌblikən] *n* patron de bistrot *m*.

publication [ˌpʌbliˈkeiʃən] *n* publication *f*.

public bar *n* bar *m*.

public conveniences *pl n* toilettes *f pl*.

public footpath *n* sentier public *m*.

public holiday *n* jour férié *m*.

publicity [pʌbˈlisəti] *n* publicité *f*.

publicize [ˈpʌblisaiz] *v* rendre public; (*advertise*) faire de la publicité pour.

public library *n* bibliothèque municipale *f*.

public relations *pl n* relations publiques *f pl*. **public relations officer** *n* public-relations *m*.

public school *n* collège secondaire privé *m*.

public speaking *n* art oratoire *m*.

public-spirited *adj* be public-spirited faire preuve de civisme.

public transport *n* transport en commun *m*.

publish [ˈpʌbliʃ] *v* publier. **publisher** *n* éditeur, -trice *m, f*. **publishing** *n* édition *f*; publication *f*. **publishing house** maison d'édition *f*.

pucker [ˈpʌkə] *v* (se) plisser; (*sewing*) (faire) goder. *n* (*sewing*) faux pli *m*.

pudding [ˈpudiŋ] *n* dessert *m*.

puddle [ˈpʌdl] *n* flaque d'eau *f*.

puerile [ˈpjuərail] *adj* puéril.

puff [pʌf] *n* bouffée *f*. souffle *m*; (*cake*) feuilleté *m*; (*for powder*) houppe *f*. **puff**

sleeves manches bouffantes *f pl*. *v* souffler. **puff out** *or* **up** (se) gonfler. **puffy** *adj* gonflé.

pull [pul] *n* traction *f*; attraction *f*; (*action*) coup *m*. *v* tirer; (*trigger*) presser; (*muscle*) se déchirer. **pull away** démarrer, s'éloigner. **pull down** baisser, descendre; démolir. **pull off** enlever; (*deal*) conclure; (*trick*) réussir. **pull oneself together** se reprendre. **pull out** (*car, etc.*) déboîter; (*extract*) arracher; (*mil*) retirer. **pull to pieces** démolir. **pull up** (*car, etc.*) s'arrêter; (*socks, etc.*) remonter.

pulley [ˈpuli] *n* poulie *f*.

pullover [ˈpulouvə] *n* pull *m*.

pulp [pʌlp] *n* pulpe *f*. *v* réduire en pulpe. **pulpy** *adj* pulpeux.

pulpit [ˈpulpit] *n* chaire *f*.

pulsate [pʌlˈseit] *v* battre, palpiter; (*music*) vibrer. **pulsation** *n* pulsation *f*, battement *m*.

pulse [pʌls] *n* (*med*) pouls *m*; (*phys, elec*) vibration. *v* battre, palpiter.

pulverize [ˈpʌlvəraiz] *v* pulvériser. **pulverization** *n* pulvérisation *f*.

pump [pʌmp] *n* pompe *f*. *v* pomper. **pump up** gonfler.

pumpkin [ˈpʌmpkin] *n* citrouille *f*.

pun [pʌn] *n* calembour *m*.

punch[1] [pʌntʃ] *n* coup de poing *m*. **punch line** astuce *f*. *v* donner un coup de poing à.

punch[2] [pʌntʃ] *n* (*drink*) punch *m*.

punch[3] [pʌntʃ] *n* (*tool*) poinçonneuse *f*; perforateur *m*. *v* poinçonner; perforer.

punctual [ˈpʌŋktʃuəl] *adj* ponctuel, à l'heure. **punctuality** *n* ponctualité *f*, exactitude *f*.

punctuate [ˈpʌŋktʃueit] *v* ponctuer. **punctuation** *n* ponctuation *f*.

puncture [ˈpʌŋktʃə] *n* (*tyre*) crevaison *f*; (*leather, skin*) piqûre *f*. **have a puncture** crever. *v* crever; piquer.

pungent [ˈpʌndʒənt] *adj* âcre, piquant; (*remark*) mordant. **pungency** *n* âcreté *f*; mordant *m*.

punish [ˈpʌniʃ] *v* punir. **punishment** *n* punition *f*.

punt[1] [pʌnt] *n* (*boat*) bachot *m*.

punt[2] [pʌnt] *v* (*bet*) parier; (*cards*) ponter. **punter** *n* parieur, -euse *m, f*; ponte *m*.

puny [ˈpjuːni] *adj* chétif.

pupil[1] [ˈpjuːpl] *n* élève *m, f*.

pupil[2] [ˈpjuːpl] *n* (*eye*) pupille *f*.

puppet ['pʌpit] n marionnette f.

puppy ['pʌpi] n chiot m.

purchase ['pəːtʃəs] n achat m. v acheter.

pure ['pjuə] adj pur. **purify** v épurer, purifier. **purity** n pureté f.

purée ['pjuərei] n purée f.

purgatory ['pəːgətəri] n purgatoire m.

purge [pəːdʒ] n purge f. v purger. **purgative** nm, adj purgatif.

puritan ['pjuəritən] n, adj puritain, -e. **puritanical** adj puritain.

purl [pəːl] n maille à l'envers f. v tricoter à l'envers.

purple ['pəːpl] nm, adj pourpre, violet.

purpose ['pəːpəs] n (aim) but m; (use) usage m. **on purpose** exprès. **purposeful** adj résolu. **purposely** adv exprès.

purr [pəː] v ronronner. n ronronnement m.

purse [pəːs] n porte-monnaie m invar, bourse f. v **purse one's lips** se pincer les lèvres.

purser ['pəːsə] n commissaire du bord m.

pursue [pə'sjuː] v poursuivre; (seek) rechercher. **pursuer** n poursuivant, -e m, f. **pursuit** n poursuite f; recherche f; occupation f.

pus [pʌs] n pus m.

push [puʃ] n poussée f. **push-chair** n poussette f. v pousser; (press) appuyer (sur). **be pushed for** être à court de.

put [put] v mettre, poser; (say) dire, exprimer; (case, etc.) présenter. **put across** faire comprendre, communiquer. **put away** ranger. **put back** remettre. **put down** déposer; noter; attribuer; (kill) faire piquer. **put off** retarder, renvoyer à plus tard; (distract) dérouter. **put on** mettre. **put out** (fire) éteindre; (bother) déranger; (annoy) contrarier. **put up** (tent) dresser; construire; augmenter; loger; (picture) mettre. **put-up job** (coll) coup monté m. **put up with** supporter.

putrid ['pjuːtrid] adj putride.

putt [pʌt] n putt m. v putter. **putting** n putting m.

putty ['pʌti] n mastic m.

puzzle ['pʌzl] n énigme f; (game) casse-tête m invar. v rendre perplexe. **puzzle out** comprendre; éclaircir. **puzzled** adj perplexe. **puzzling** adj curieux.

pyjamas [pə'dʒaːməz] pl n pyjama m sing.

pylon ['pailən] n pylône m.

pyramid ['pirəmid] n pyramide f.

python ['paiθən] n python m.

Q

quack[1] [kwak] n (duck) coin-coin m. v faire coin-coin.

quack[2] [kwak] n charlatan m.

quadrangle ['kwodraŋgl] n cour f; (math) quadrilatère m.

quadrant ['kwodrənt] n quadrant m.

quadrilateral [kwodrə'latərəl] nm, adj quadrilatère.

quadruped ['kwodruped] nm, adj quadrupède.

quadruple [kwod'ruːpl] nm, adj quadruple. v quadrupler.

quadruplet [kwod'ruːplit] n quadruplé, -e m, f.

quagmire ['kwagmaiə] n bourbier m.

quail[1] [kweil] n (bird) caille f.

quail[2] [kweil] v perdre courage.

quaint [kweint] adj au charme vieillot; bizarre; pittoresque.

quake [kweik] v trembler.

qualify ['kwolifai] v qualifier; obtenir son diplôme; (modify) mitiger. **qualification** n capacité f; réserve f. **qualifications** pl n titres m pl, diplômes m pl. **qualified** adj qualifié, diplômé; mitigé.

quality ['kwoləti] n qualité f.

qualm [kwaːm] n scrupule m; appréhension f; nausée f.

quandary ['kwondəri] n embarras m, dilemme m.

quantify ['kwontifai] v déterminer la quantité de.

quantity ['kwontəti] n quantité f.

quarantine ['kworəntiːn] n quarantaine f. v mettre en quarantaine.

quarrel ['kworəl] n querelle f. v se disputer. **quarrelsome** adj querelleur, -euse.

quarry[1] ['kwori] n (stone) carrière f. v extraire; exploiter (une carrière).

quarry[2] ['kwori] n proie f; (game) gibier m.

quarter ['kwoːtə] n quart m; (of year) trimestre m; (of town) quartier m. **quarter-final** n quart de finale m. **quartermaster** n (naut) maître de manœuvre m. **quarter past two** deux heures et quart. **quarters** pl n (mil) quartiers m pl. **quarter to two** deux heures moins le quart. v diviser en quatre; (mil) caserner. **quarterly** adj trimestriel.

quartet [kwɔːˈtet] n quatuor m.

quartz [kwɔːts] n quartz m.

quash [kwɔʃ] v annuler; rejeter; (riot) étouffer.

quaver ['kweivə] n (music) croche f; tremblement m. v chevroter.

quay [kiː] n quai m.

queasy ['kwiːzi] adj (stomach) délicat. **feel queasy** avoir mal au cœur. **queasiness** n mal au cœur m.

queen [kwiːn] n reine f; (cards) dame f. **Queen Mother** reine mère f.

queer [kwiə] adj étrange; suspect; (slang) homosexuel. n (slang) pédé m.

quell [kwel] v réprimer.

quench [kwentʃ] v (fire) éteindre; (hope) réprimer. **quench one's thirst** se désaltérer.

query ['kwiəri] n question f. n mettre en doute.

quest [kwest] n quête f.

question ['kwestʃən] n question f; doute m. **it's out of the question** il n'en est pas question. **question mark** point d'interrogation m. v interroger; mettre en doute. **questionable** adj douteux. **questioning** n interrogation f. **questionnaire** n questionnaire m.

queue [kjuː] n queue f; file f. **queue-jumper** n resquilleur, -euse m, f. v faire la queue.

quibble ['kwibl] n chicane f. v chicaner.

quick [kwik] adj rapide, prompt. **quicksand** n sable mouvant m. **quickstep** n fox m. **quick-tempered** adj prompt à s'emporter. **quick-witted** adj à l'esprit vif. n vif m. **quicken** v (s')accélérer; stimuler. **quickly** adv vite, sans tarder.

quid [kwid] n (coll) livre f.

quiet ['kwaiət] adj tranquille; (subdued) doux, douce; (voice) bas, basse. n also **quietness** silence m; tranquillité f. **quieten** v calmer. **quietly** adv silencieusement, doucement.

quill [kwil] n penne f; (pen) plume d'oie f; (of porcupine) piquant m.

quilt [kwilt] n édredon piqué m. v ouater, ouatiner.

quince [kwins] n (fruit) coing m; (tree) cognassier m.

quinine [kwiˈniːn] n quinine f.

quinsy ['kwinzi] n amygdalite purulente f.

quintet [kwinˈtet] n quintette m.

quintuplet [kwinˈtuːplit] n quintuplé, -e m, f.

quirk [kwəːk] n bizarrerie f.

***quit** [kwit] v (leave) quitter; (give up) se rendre, renoncer. **quits** adj quitte.

quite [kwait] adv complètement, tout; (fairly) plutôt, assez.

quiver[1] ['kwivə] v trembler, frémir. n frémissement m, tremblement m.

quiver[2] ['kwivə] n (for arrows) carquois m.

quiz [kwiz] n quiz m, jeu-concours m. v interroger.

quizzical ['kwizikl] adj moqueur, -euse; amusant; bizarre.

quorum ['kwɔːrəm] n quorum m.

quota ['kwoutə] n quota m; (share) quote-part f.

quote [kwout] v citer; (reference number) rappeler; (comm) indiquer. **quotation** n citation f; (comm) devis m. **quotation marks** guillemets m pl.

R

rabbi ['rabai] n rabbin m.

rabbit ['rabit] n lapin m.

rabble ['rabl] n cohue f; (derog) populace f.

rabies ['reibiːz] n rage f. **rabid** adj enragé.

race[1] [reis] n (sport) course f. **racecourse** n champ de courses m. **racehorse** n cheval de course m. v (person) faire une course avec; (horse) faire courir; (rush) courir; (pulse) être très rapide. **racing car** voiture de course f. **racing driver** coureur automobile m.

race[2] [reis] n race f. **racial** adj racial. **racialism** or **racism** n racisme m. **racialist** or **racist** n(m+f), adj raciste.

rack [rak] n (bottles) casier m; (food) râtelier m; (shelves) étagère f; (torture) chevalet m. v torturer. **rack one's brains** se creuser la tête.

racket[1] ['rakit] n (sport) raquette f.

racket[2] ['rakit] n (noise) tapage m, vacarme m; (scheme) combine f, escroquerie f.

radar ['reidə] n radar m. **radar trap** piège radar m.

radial ['reidiəl] adj radial. **radial tyre** pneu à carcasse radiale m.

radiant ['reidiənt] *adj* radieux, rayonnant. **radiance** *n* éclat *m*, rayonnement *m*.

radiate ['reidieit] *v* irradier, rayonner; (*heat*) émettre. **radiation** *n* (*heat*) rayonnement *m*; (*light*) irradiation *f*; (*radioactive*) radiation *f*. **radiator** *n* radiateur *m*.

radical ['rædikəl] *nm, adj* radical.

radio ['reidiou] *n* radio *f*, poste *m*. **radio contact** contact radio *m*. **radio station** poste émetteur *m*. **radio wave** onde hertzienne *f*. *v* appeler par radio; signaler par radio.

radioactive [reidiou'æktiv] *adj* radioactif. **radioactivity** *n* radioactivité *f*.

radiography [reidi'ɔgrəfi] *n* radiographie *f*. **radiographer** *n* radiologue *m, f*.

radiology [reidi'ɔlədʒi] *n* radiologie *f*. **radiologist** *n* radiologue *m, f*.

radiotherapy [reidiou'θerəpi] *n* radiothérapie *f*.

radish ['rædiʃ] *n* radis *m*.

radium ['reidiəm] *n* radium *m*.

radius ['reidiəs] *n* rayon *m*.

raffia ['ræfiə] *n* raphia *m*.

raffle ['ræfl] *n* loterie *f*. *v* mettre en loterie.

raft [rɑːft] *n* radeau *m*.

rafter ['rɑːftə] *n* chevron *m*.

rag¹ [ræg] *n* (*piece*) loque *f*; (*for cleaning*) chiffon *m*; (*derog: newspaper*) torchon *m*. **rag doll** poupée de chiffon *f*. **rag-and-bone man** chiffonnier *m*. **rags** *pl n* haillons *m pl*. **ragged** *adj* (*clothes*) en loques; (*edge*) déchiqueté.

rag² [ræg] (*coll*) *v* taquiner. *n* blague *f*.

rage [reidʒ] *n* rage *f*. **be all the rage** faire fureur. *v* (*person*) être furieux; (*storm*) faire rage. **raging** *adj* (*person*) furieux; (*pain*) atroce; (*storm*) déchaîné.

raid [reid] *n* raid *m*; (*police*) descente *f*; (*bandits*) razzia *f*. *v* faire un raid dans; faire une descente dans; razzier; (*orchard*) marauder dans; (*larder*) dévaliser. **raider** *n* pillard *m*.

rail [reil] *n* (*bar*) garde-fou *m*, balustrade *f*; (*for curtains*) tringle *m*; (*for train*) rail *m*. **by rail** par train. **railway** or *US* **railroad** chemin de fer *m*; (*track*) voie ferrée *f*.

railings ['reiliŋz] *pl n* grille *f sing*.

rain [rein] *n* pluie *f*. **rainbow** *n* arc-en-ciel *m*. **raincoat** *n* imperméable *m*. **raindrop** *n* goutte de pluie *f*. **rainfall** *n* hauteur des précipitations *f*. *v* pleuvoir. **rainy** *adj* pluvieux.

raise [reiz] *v* lever; augmenter; (*build, rear*) élever; (*question*) soulever; (*money*) se procurer.

raisin ['reizən] *n* raisin sec *m*.

rake [reik] *n* râteau *m*. *v* (*ground*) ratisser; (*leaves*) râteler. **rake in** (*coll*) amasser.

rally ['ræli] *n* rassemblement *m*; (*mot*) rallye *m*; (*tennis*) échange *m*. *v* (se) rallier; (*get better*) aller mieux. **rally round** venir en aide.

ram [ræm] *n* belier *m*. *v* enfoncer; (*pack in*) tasser; (*car*) emboutir.

ramble ['ræmbl] *n* randonnée *f*. *v* faire une randonnée. **ramble on** discourir.

ramp [ræmp] *n* rampe *f*.

rampage [ræm'peidʒ] *n* **be on the rampage** se déchaîner.

rampant ['ræmpənt] *adj* (*plant*) exubérant; (*heraldry*) rampant. **be rampant** sévir.

rampart ['ræmpɑːt] *n* rempart *m*.

ramshackle ['ræmʃækl] *adj* délabré.

ran [ræn] *V* **run**.

ranch [rɑːntʃ] *n* ranch *m*.

rancid ['rænsid] *adj* rance. **go rancid** rancir.

rancour ['ræŋkə] *n* rancœur *f*.

random ['rændəm] *n* **at random** au hasard. *adj* fait au hasard. **random sample** échantillon prélevé au hasard *m*.

rang [ræŋ] *V* **ring²**.

range [reindʒ] *n* (*scope*) portée *f*; (*mountains*) chaîne *f*; (*extent*) étendue *f*; gamme *f*; choix *m*; (*stove*) fourneau *m*; (*mil*) champ de tir *m*. *v* ranger; (*extend*) s'étendre; (*roam*) parcourir.

rank¹ [ræŋk] *n* rang *m*. **the rank and file** la masse *f*; (*mil*) les hommes de troupe *m pl*. *v* compter, (se) classer.

rank² [ræŋk] *adj* (*smell*) fétide; (*plants*) exubérant; flagrant.

rankle ['ræŋkl] *v* rester sur le cœur.

ransack ['rænsæk] *v* saccager; (*search*) fouiller.

ransom ['rænsəm] *n* rançon *f*. **hold to ransom** rançonner. *v* racheter.

rap [ræp] *v* frapper. *n* petit coup sec *m*.

rape [reip] *n* viol *m*. *v* violer. **rapist** *n* violeur *m*.

rapid ['ræpid] *adj* rapide. **rapids** *pl n* rapides *m pl*. **rapidity** *n* rapidité *f*.

rapier ['reipiə] *n* rapière *f*.

rapport [ra'poːr] *n* rapport *m*.

rapture ['ræptʃə] *n* ravissement *m*, extase *f*. **go into raptures over** s'extasier sur.

rare¹ [reə] adj rare. rarity n rareté f.

rare² [reə] adj (meat) saignant.

rascal ['rɑːskəl] n polisson, -onne m, f; (rogue) coquin m.

rash¹ [raʃ] adj imprudent. rashness n imprudence f.

rash² [raʃ] n (med) éruption f.

rasher ['raʃə] n mince tranche f.

raspberry ['rɑːzbəri] n (fruit) framboise f; (bush) framboisier m.

rat [rat] n rat m. rat poison mort-aux-rats m. rat race foire d'empoigne f.

rate [reit] n taux m; (speed) train m. at any rate en tout cas. ratepayer n contribuable m, f. rates pl n impôts locaux m pl. v évaluer; considérer; se classer.

rather ['rɑːðə] adv plutôt; (fairly) assez, un peu. I would rather ... j'aimerais mieux ...

ratify ['ratifai] v ratifier. ratification n ratification f.

ratio ['reiʃiou] n proportion f. raison f.

ration ['raʃən] n ration f. v rationner. rationing n rationnement n.

rational ['raʃənl] adj raisonnable, rationnel, logique. rationale n raisonnement m. rationalize v justifier après coup; (organize) rationaliser.

rattle ['ratl] n bruit m, fracas m; (chains, etc.) cliquetis m; (toy) hochet m. v faire du bruit; (objects) (faire) s'entrechoquer; (faire) cliqueter; (coll) déconcerter.

raucous ['rɔːkəs] adj rauque.

ravage ['ravidʒ] n ravage m. v ravager.

rave [reiv] v délirer, divaguer; s'extasier (sur). raving adj délirant; furieux.

raven ['reivən] n corbeau m.

ravenous ['ravənəs] adj vorace. be ravenous avoir un faim de loup.

ravine [rə'viːn] n ravin m.

ravish ['raviʃ] v ravir.

raw [rɔː] adj cru; (unprocessed) brut; novice; (sore) à vif. raw deal (coll) sale coup m. raw edge bord coupé m. raw materials matières premières f pl.

ray [rei] n rayon m.

rayon ['reiɔn] n rayonne f.

razor ['reizə] n rasoir m. razor blade lame de rasoir f.

reach [riːtʃ] v atteindre, arriver à; (extend) s'étendre. reach out étendre le bras. n portée f. out of reach hors de portée. within reach à portée.

react [ri'akt] v réagir. reaction n réaction

f. reactionary n(m+f), adj réactionnaire. reactor n réacteur m.

*read [riːd] v lire; étudier. reader n lecteur, -trice m, f; (anthology) recueil de textes m. reading n lecture f.

readjust [riːə'dʒʌst] v rajuster, (se) réadapter. readjustment n réadaptation f, rajustement m.

ready ['redi] adj prêt; prompt. get ready (se) préparer. ready cash argent liquide m. ready-made adj tout fait, tout prêt. readily adv volontiers. readiness n empressement m.

real [riəl] adj réel, vrai. realism n réalisme m. realist n réaliste m, f. realistic adj réaliste. reality n réalité f. really adv vraiment.

realize ['riəlaiz] v se rendre compte de; (make real) réaliser. realization n prise de conscience f; réalisation f.

realm [relm] n domaine m; (kingdom) royaume m.

reap [riːp] v moissonner; (profit) récolter. reaping n moisson f. reaping machine moissonneuse f.

reappear [riːə'piə] v réapparaître. reappearance n réapparition f.

rear¹ [riə] nm, adj arrière. bring up the rear fermer la marche. rear-admiral n contre-amiral m. rearguard n arrière-garde f. rear-view mirror rétroviseur m.

rear² [riə] n (family) élever; (lift up) dresser; (horse, etc.) se cabrer.

rearrange [riːə'reindʒ] v réarranger. rearrangement n réarrangement m.

reason ['riːzn] n raison f. v raisonner. reasonable adj raisonnable. reasoning n raisonnement m.

reassure [riːə'ʃuə] v rassurer. reassurance n réconfort m. reassuring adj rassurant.

rebate ['riːbeit] n (discount) rabais m; remboursement m.

rebel ['rebl] n(m+f), adj rebelle. v se rebeller. rebellion n rébellion f. rebellious adj rebelle; désobéissant.

rebound [ri'baund; n 'riːbaund] v rebondir. n rebond m; ricochet m.

rebuff [ri'bʌf] n rebuffade f. v repousser.

*rebuild [riː'bild] v rebâtir.

rebuke [ri'bjuːk] n reproche m. v réprimander.

recall [ri'kɔːl] v (se) rappeler. n rappel m.

recant [ri'kant] v (se) rétracter; (rel) abjurer.

recap ['riːkap] (*coll*) v faire un résumé (de). n récapitulation f.

recapture [riːˈkaptʃə] v reprendre; (*atmosphere*) recréer. n arrestation f.

recede [riˈsiːd] v s'éloigner; (*tide*) descendre.

receipt [riˈsiːt] n (*receiving*) réception f; (*slip of paper*) reçu m, accusé de réception m.

receive [riˈsiːv] v recevoir. **receiver** n (*phone*) récepteur m; (*law*) administrateur judiciaire m.

recent ['riːsnt] adj récent. **recently** adv récemment.

receptacle [rəˈsɛptəkl] n récipient m.

reception [rəˈsɛpʃən] n réception f. **receptionist** n réceptionniste m, f.

recess [riˈsɛs] n renfoncement m, alcôve f; (*pol, law*) vacances f pl; (*of mind*) recoin m.

recession [rəˈsɛʃən] n (*econ*) récession f; recul m.

recharge [riːˈtʃɑːdʒ] v recharger.

recipe ['rɛsəpi] n recette f.

recipient [rəˈsɪpiənt] n (*letter*) destinataire m, f; (*cheque*) bénéficiaire m, f.

reciprocate [rəˈsɪprəkeit] v retourner; offrir en retour. **reciprocating engine** moteur alternatif m. **reciprocal** nf, adj réciproque.

recite [rəˈsait] v réciter. **recital** n (*music*) récital m. **recitation** n récitation f.

reckless ['rɛkləs] adj insouciant; imprudent. **recklessness** n insouciance f; imprudence f.

reckon ['rɛkən] v compter, calculer; considérer, estimer; (*coll*) penser. **reckoning** n compte m, calcul m; estimation f.

reclaim [riˈkleim] v réclamer; (*land*) assécher, défricher; (*by-product*) récupérer. **reclamation** n réclamation f; assèchement m, défrichement m; récupération f.

recline [riˈklain] v reposer; être allongé.

recluse [rəˈkluːs] n reclus, -e m, f.

recognize ['rɛkəgnaiz] v reconnaître. **recognition** n reconnaissance f. **recognizable** adj reconnaissable.

recoil [rəˈkɔil; n ˈriːkɔil] v reculer; (*spring*) se détendre. n recul m; détente f; dégoût m.

recollect [rɛkəˈlɛkt] v se souvenir (de). **recollection** n souvenir m.

recommence [riːkəˈmɛns] v recommencer.

recommend [rɛkəˈmɛnd] v recommander,

conseiller. **recommendation** n recommandation f.

recompense ['rɛkəmpɛns] n récompense f; (*law*) dédommagement m. v récompenser; dédommager.

reconcile ['rɛkənsail] v réconcilier; (*ideas*) concilier; (*argument*) arranger. **reconcile oneself** se se résigner à. **reconciliation** n réconciliation f; conciliation f.

reconstruct [riːkənˈstrʌkt] v reconstruire; (*crime*) reconstituer. **reconstruction** n reconstruction f; reconstitution f.

record [rəˈkɔːd; n ˈrɛkɔːd] v enregistrer. n disque m; (*sport, etc.*) record m; registre m, rapport m; dossier m. **record-player** n électrophone m. **record token** chèque-disque m. **recorded** adj enregistré. **by recorded delivery** avec avis de réception. **recorder** n (*music*) flûte à bec f. **recording** n enregistrement m.

recount [riˈkaunt] v raconter.

recoup [riˈkuːp] v récupérer.

recover [rəˈkʌvə] v (*get back*) retrouver, récupérer; (*get well*) se remettre, se rétablir. **recovery** n récupération f; (*from illness*) guérison f.

recreation [rɛkriˈeiʃən] n récréation f.

recruit [rəˈkruːt] n recrue f. v recruter. **recruitment** n recrutement m.

rectangle ['rɛktaŋgl] n rectangle m. **rectangular** adj rectangulaire.

rectify ['rɛktifai] v rectifier.

rectum ['rɛktəm] n rectum m.

recuperate [rəˈkjuːpəreit] v (*person*) se rétablir; (*get back*) récupérer. **recuperation** n rétablissement m; récupération f.

recur [riˈkəː] v se reproduire, se retrouver; (*illness*) réapparaître. **recurrence** n répétition f. **recurrent** or **recurring** adj périodique.

red [rɛd] n rouge m. **in the red** à découvert. adj rouge; (*hair*) roux, rousse. **go red** rougir. **redcurrant** n groseille rouge f. **red-handed** adv en flagrant délit. **redhead** n roux, rousse m, f. **red-hot** adj chauffé au rouge. **Red Indian** n peau-rouge m, f. **red tape** paperasserie f.

redirect [riːdaiˈrɛkt] v (*letter, etc.*) faire suivre.

redress [rəˈdrɛs] v redresser. n redressement m. réparation f.

reduce [rə'dʒuːs] v réduire; diminuer; (*lower*) abaisser. **reduction** n réduction f; (*comm*) remise f, rabais m.

redundant [rə'dʌndənt] adj superflu, redondant, en surnombre. **be made redundant** être licencié. **redundancy** n superfluité f; licenciement m.

reed [riːd] n (*bot*) roseau m; (*of wind instrument*) anche f.

reef [riːf] n récif m.

reek [riːk] v puer. n puanteur f.

reel[1] [riːl] n (*thread*) bobine f; (*film*) bande f. v **reel off** débiter.

reel[2] [riːl] v chanceler, tituber.

refectory [rə'fektəri] n réfectoire m.

refer [rə'fəː] v parler; faire allusion; s'appliquer; (*consult*) se reporter; (*pass*) soumettre. **reference** n référence f; allusion f; (*in book*) renvoi m. **reference book** ouvrage de référence m. **reference number** numéro de référence m.

referee [refə'riː] n arbitre m; (*job application*) répondant, -e m, f. v arbitrer.

referendum [refə'rendəm] n référendum m.

refill [riː'fil; n 'riːfil] v recharger. n recharge f, cartouche f.

refine [rə'fain] v affiner, raffiner. **refinement** n (*person*) raffinement m; (*refining*) raffinage m, affinage m; perfectionnement m. **refinery** n raffinerie f, affinerie f.

reflation [riː'fleiʃn] n (*econ*) relance f.

reflect [rə'flekt] v (*light*) refléter; (*mirror*) réfléchir; (*think*) penser; méditer. **reflection** n réflexion f; image f, reflet m. **reflector** n réflecteur m.

reflex [riːfleks] nm, adj réflexe. **reflexive** adj réfléchi.

reform [rə'fɔːm] n réforme f. v (se) réformer. **reformation** n réforme f. **reformed** adj réformé; (*person*) amendé.

refract [rə'frakt] v réfracter. **refraction** n réfraction f.

refrain[1] [rə'frein] v s'abstenir.

refrain[2] [rə'frein] n refrain m.

refresh [rə'freʃ] v rafraîchir; (*rest*) reposer. **refresher course** cours de recyclage m. **refreshments** pl n rafraîchissements pl.

refrigerator [rə'fridʒəreitə] n réfrigérateur m. **refrigerate** v réfrigérer. **refrigeration** n réfrigération f.

refuel [riː'fjuːəl] v (se) ravitailler.

refuge ['refjuːdʒ] n refuge m. **take refuge** se réfugier. **refugee** n réfugié, -e m, f.

refund [riː'fʌnd; n 'riːfʌnd] v rembourser. n remboursement m.

refuse[1] [rə'fjuːz] v refuser. **refusal** n refus m.

refuse[2] ['refjuːs] n détritus m pl, déchets m pl, ordures f pl.

refute [ri'fjuːt] v réfuter.

regain [ri'gein] v regagner; (*health*) recouvrer; (*consciousness*) reprendre.

regal ['riːgəl] adj royal.

regard [rə'gɑːd] v regarder; considérer. **as regards** en ce qui concerne. n égard m, attention f; respect m, estime f. **regards** pl n (*in letter*) amitiés f pl. **regarding** prep quant à. **regardless** adv quand même. **regardless of** sans regarder à.

regatta [rə'gatə] n régate f.

regent ['riːdʒənt] n régent, -e m, f. **regency** n régence f.

regime [rei'ʒiːm] n régime m.

regiment ['redʒimənt] n régiment m. **regimental** adj régimentaire.

region ['riːdʒən] n région f. **regional** adj régional.

register ['redʒistə] n registre m. v (*record*) enregistrer; (*as member, etc.*) s'inscrire; (*birth, death*) déclarer; (*meter*) indiquer; (*letter*) recommander. **registrar** n officier de l'état civil m; (*med*) interne m, f. **registration** n enregistrement m, inscription f. **registration number** numéro d'immatriculation m. **registry office** bureau de l'état civil m.

regress [ri'gres] v régresser; reculer. **regression** n recul m; régression f.

regret [rə'gret] v regretter. n regret m. **regrettable** adj regrettable.

regular ['regjulə] adj régulier; habituel, normal. n habitué, -e m, f. **regularity** n régularité f.

regulate ['regjuleit] v régler. **regulation** n règlement m. adj réglementaire.

rehabilitate [riːhə'biliteit] v réhabiliter; (*for work*) réadapter. **rehabilitation** n réhabilitation f; réadaptation f.

rehearse [rə'həːs] v répéter. **rehearsal** n répétition f.

rehouse [riː'hauz] v reloger.

reign [rein] n règne m. v régner.

reimburse [riːim'bəːs] v rembourser.

rein [rein] n rêne f; (*control*) bride f.

reincarnation [riːinkɑː'neiʃən] n réincarnation f.

rename

reindeer ['reindiə] *n* renne *m*.

reinforce [riin'fots] *v* renforcer. **reinforcement** *n* renforcement *m*. **reinforcements** *pl n* renforts *m pl*.

reinstate [riin'steit] *v* réintégrer. **reinstatement** *n* réintégration *f*.

reinvest [riin'vest] *v* réinvestir.

reissue [rii'fuː] *v* (*book*) rééditer; (*film*) ressortir. *n* réédition *f*.

reject [rə'dʒekt; *n* 'riidʒekt] *v* refuser, rejeter. *n* pièce de rebut *f*. *adj* de rebut. **rejection** *n* refus *m*, rejet *m*.

rejoice [rə'dʒois] *v* (se) réjouir. **rejoicing** *n* réjouissance *f*.

rejoin [rə'dʒoin] *v* rejoindre.

rejuvenate [rə'dʒuːvəneit] *v* rajeunir.

relapse [rə'laps] *n* rechute *f*. *v* rechuter.

relate [rə'leit] *v* raconter; (*be connected*) se rapporter; (*associate*) établir un rapport entre. **related** *adj* apparenté. **relating to** concernant.

relation [rə'leiʃn] *n* (*family*) parent, -e *m, f*; (*connection*) rapport *m*; (*business, etc.*) relation *f*. **relationship** *n* liens de parenté *m pl*; (*personal*) rapports *m pl*, relations *f pl*.

relative ['relətiv] *adj* relatif; respectif. *n* parent, -e *m, f*. **relatively** *adv* relativement; (*rather*) assez. **relativity** *n* relativité *f*.

relax [rə'laks] *v* (se) relâcher; (*person*) (se) détendre; (*rules*) modérer. **relaxation** *n* relâchement *m*; détente *f*, relaxation *f*. **relaxing** *adj* délassant, relaxant.

relay ['riilei; *v* ri'lei] *n* relais *m*. **relay race** course de relais *f*. *v* relayer.

release [rə'liːs] *v* libérer; (*let go*) lâcher; (*record, film*) sortir. *n* libération *f*; sortie *f*.

relegate ['religeit] *v* reléguer. **relegation** *n* relégation *f*.

relent [rə'lent] *v* s'adoucir; revenir sur sa décision. **relentless** *adj* implacable.

relevant ['reləvənt] *adj* pertinent; approprié; significatif. **relevance** *n* rapport *m*; pertinence *f*.

reliable [ri'laiəbl] *adj* sérieux; (*machine*) solide. **reliability** *n* sérieux *m*; sûreté *f*; solidité *f*.

relic ['relik] *n* relique *f*.

relief [rə'liːf] *n* soulagement *m*; (*help*) secours *m*; (*geog, art*) relief *m*. *adj* supplémentaire.

relieve [rə'liːv] *v* soulager; (*help*) secourir;

(*take over*) relayer; (*take away*) débarrasser, décharger.

religion [rə'lidʒən] *n* religion *f*. **religious** *adj* religieux; scrupuleux.

relinquish [rə'liŋkwiʃ] *v* (*give up*) renoncer à, abandonner; (*let go*) lâcher.

relish ['reliʃ] *n* goût *m*, attrait *m*. *v* (*food, drink*) savourer; (*enjoy*) se délecter à.

relive [rii'liv] *v* revivre.

reluctant [rə'lʌktənt] *adj* peu disposé. **reluctance** *n* répugnance *f*. **reluctantly** *adv* à contrecœur.

rely [rə'lai] *v* **rely on** compter sur.

remain [rə'mein] *v* rester. **remainder** *n* reste *m*. **remains** *pl n* restes *m pl*.

remand [rə'maind] *v* renvoyer. *n* renvoi *m*. **on remand** en prévention.

remark [rə'maik] *n* remarque *f*; observation *f*. *v* remarquer; faire une remarque. **remarkable** *adj* remarquable.

remarry [ri'mari] *v* se remarier. **remarriage** *n* remariage *m*.

remedial [rə'miidiəl] *adj* réparateur, -trice; (*teaching, class*) de rattrapage.

remedy ['remədi] *n* remède *m*. *v* remédier à.

remember [ri'membə] *v* se souvenir (de), se rappeler. **remembrance** *n* souvenir *m*.

remind [rə'maind] *v* rappeler. **reminder** *n* mémento *m*; (*comm*) lettre de rappel *f*.

reminiscence [remə'nisns] *n* réminiscence *f*. **reminiscent of** qui rappelle.

remiss [rə'mis] *adj* négligent.

remission [rə'miʃn] *n* rémission *f*; (*law*) remise *f*.

remit [rə'mit] *v* (*law, rel*) remettre; (*money*) envoyer; (*lessen*) (se) relâcher. **remittance** *n* versement *m*, paiement *m*.

remnant ['remnənt] *n* reste *m*; (*fabric*) coupon *m*.

remorse [rə'mois] *n* remords *m*. **remorseless** *adj* sans remords; implacable.

remote [rə'mout] *adj* lointain; isolé; vague. **remote control** télécommande *f*.

remould ['riimould; *v* rii'mould] *n* pneu rechapé *m*. *v* remouler; rechaper.

remove [rə'muiv] *v* enlever; (*move house*) déménager. **removal** *n* enlèvement *m*; déménagement *m*.

remunerate [rə'mjuinəreit] *v* rémunérer. **remuneration** *n* rémunération *f*. **remunerative** *adj* rémunérateur, -trice.

renaissance [rə'neisəns] *n* renaissance *f*.

rename [rii'neim] *v* rebaptiser.

render [rendə] v rendre; remettre; (fat) faire fondre. **rendering** or **rendition** n interprétation f.

rendezvous ['rondivu:] n rendez-vous m. v se retrouver.

renegade ['renigeid] n renégat, -e m, f.

renew [ri'nju:] v renouveler; remplacer. **renewal** renouvellement m; remplacement m; (of subscription) réabonnement m.

renounce [ri'nauns] v renoncer à, renier. **renunciation** n renonciation f. reniement m.

renovate ['renəveit] v rénover, remettre à neuf. **renovation** n rénovation f; remise à neuf f.

renown [rə'naun] n renommée f; renom m. **renowned** adj renommé.

rent [rent] n loyer m. v louer. **rental** n prix de location m.

reopen [ri:'oupən] v rouvrir; (recommence) reprendre. **reopening** n réouverture f.

reorganize [ri:'ɔ:gənaiz] v (se) réorganiser. **reorganization** n réorganisation f.

rep [rep] n (coll) représentant, -e m, f.

repair [ri'peə] v réparer. n réparation f. **beyond repair** irréparable. **in good/bad repair** en bon/mauvais état. **repairer** n réparateur, -trice m, f.

repartee [repa:'ti:] n repartie f.

repatriate [ri:'patrieit] v rapatrier. n rapatrié, -e m, f. **repatriation** n rapatriement m.

*** repay** [ri'pei] v rembourser; récompenser; (debt) s'acquitter de. **repayment** n remboursement m; récompense f.

repeal [rə'pi:l] v abroger, annuler. n abrogation f, annulation f.

repeat [rə'pi:t] v répéter; réciter; (music) reprendre. n répétition f; (broadcast, music) reprise f.

repel [rə'pel] v repousser. **repellent** adj repoussant.

repent [rə'pent] v se repentir (de). **repentance** n repentir m. **repentant** adj repentant.

repercussion [ri:pə'kʌʃən] n répercussion f.

repertoire ['repətwa:] n répertoire m.

repertory ['repətəri] n théâtre de répertoire m. **repertory company** compagnie de répertoire f.

repetition [repə'tiʃn] n répétition f. repeti-

tive adj (person) rabâcheur, -euse; (work) monotone.

replace [rə'pleis] v (substitute) remplacer; (put back) replacer. **replacement** n remplacement m; (person) remplaçant, -e m, f; replacement m.

replay [ri'plei; n 'ri:plei] v rejouer. n match rejoué m.

replenish [rə'pleniʃ] v remplir. **replenishment** n remplissage m.

replica ['replikə] n (picture) réplique f; (document) fac-similé m.

reply [rə'plai] n réponse f. v répondre.

report [rə'pɔ:t] n rapport m, compte rendu m; (press) reportage m; bulletin scolaire m; détonation f. v rapporter; faire un reportage; (notify) signaler; se présenter. **reporter** n reporter m; journaliste m, f.

repose [rə'pouz] n repos m. v (se) reposer.

represent [reprə'zent] v représenter. **representation** n représentation f.

representative [reprə'zentətiv] adj représentatif. n représentant, -e m, f.

repress [rə'pres] v réprimer. **repression** n répression f. **repressive** adj répressif.

reprieve [rə'pri:v] n sursis m; (law) grâce f. v accorder du répit à.

reprimand ['reprimɑ:nd] n réprimande f. v réprimander.

reprint [ri:'print; n 'ri:print] v réimprimer. n réimpression f.

reprisal [rə'praizəl] n représailles f pl.

reproach [rə'proutʃ] n reproche m. v reprocher à. **reproachful** adj réprobateur, -trice.

reproduce [ri:prə'dju:s] v (se) reproduire. **reproduction** n reproduction f. **reproductive** adj reproducteur, -trice.

reprove [rə'pru:v] v (person) blâmer; (action) reprouver. **reproof** n réprimande f.

reptile ['reptail] n reptile m.

republic [rə'pʌblik] n république f. **republican** n, adj républicain, -e.

repudiate [rə'pju:dieit] v répudier; (person) renier. **repudiation** n répudiation f; reniement m.

repugnant [rə'pʌgnənt] adj répugnant. **repugnance** n répugnance f.

repulsion [rə'pʌlʃn] n répulsion f. **repulsive** adj répulsif, répoussant.

repute [rə'pju:t] n réputation f. **reputable** adj honorable, de bonne réputation. **rep-**

utation *n* réputation *f*. **reputed** *adj* réputé, censé.

request [ri'kwest] *n* demande *f*. *v* demander. **request stop** arrêt facultatif *m*.

requiem ['rekwiəm] *n* requiem *m*.

require [ri'kwaiə] *v* (*need*) demander, avoir besoin de; (*order*) exiger. **requirement** *n* (*need*) exigence *f*; condition *f*.

requisition [rekwi'ziʃən] *n* demande *f*; réquisition *f*. *v* réquisitionner.

*****reread** [ri:'ri:d] *v* relire.

re-route [ri:'ru:t] *v* dérouter.

*****rerun** [ri:'rʌn; *n* 'ri:rʌn] *v* (*film*) passer de nouveau; (*race*) courir de nouveau. *n* reprise *f*.

resale [ri:'seil] *n* revente *f*.

rescue ['reskju:] *n* sauvetage *m*; (*help*) secours *m*; (*freeing*) délivrance *f*. *v* sauver; secourir; délivrer. **rescuer** *n* sauveteur *m*.

research [ri'sə:tʃ] *n* recherche *f*. *v* faire des recherches. **researcher** *n* chercheur, -euse *m*, *f*.

*****resell** [ri:'sel] *v* revendre.

resemble [ri'zembl] *v* ressembler à. **resemblance** *n* ressemblance *f*.

resent [ri'zent] *v* s'offusquer de. **resentful** *adj* rancunier. **resentment** *n* ressentiment *m*.

reserve [ri'zə:v] *v* réserver. *n* réserve *f*; (*sport*) remplaçant, -e *m*, *f*. **reservation** *n* réserve *f*; (*booking*) réservation *f*. **reserved** *adj* réservé; (*person*) renfermé.

reservoir ['rezəvwa:] *n* réservoir *m*.

reside [ri'zaid] *v* résider. **residence** *n* résidence *f*; (*hostel*) foyer *m*; (*stay*) séjour *m*. **resident** *n* habitant, -e *m*, *f*; (*in hotel*) pensionnaire *m*, *f*. **residential** *adj* résidentiel.

residue ['rezidju:] *n* reste *m*; (*chem*) résidu *m*. **residual** *adj* restant; résiduaire.

resign [ri'zain] *v* (*from job*) donner sa démission (de), démissionner. **resign oneself to** se résigner à. **resignation** *n* démission *f*; résignation *f*. **resigned** *adj* résigné.

resilient [ri'ziliənt] *adj* (*rubber, etc.*) élastique. **be resilient** (*person*) avoir du ressort. **resilience** *n* élasticité *f*; ressort *m*.

resin ['rezin] *n* résine *f*.

resist [ri'zist] *v* résister (à). **resistance** *n* résistance *f*. **resistant** *adj* résistant.

*****resit** [ri:'sit; *n* 'ri:sit] *v* (*exam*) repasser. *n* deuxième session *f*.

resolute ['rezəlu:t] *adj* résolu.

resolution [rezə'lu:ʃən] *n* résolution *f*.

resolve [rə'zolv] *v* (*s*) résoudre. *n* résolution *f*.

resonant ['rezənənt] *adj* sonore; (*phys*) résonant. **resonance** *n* résonance *f*. **resonate** *v* résonner.

resort [rə'zo:t] *n* recours *m*, ressource *f*; (*place*) station *f*, lieu de vacances *m*. **as a last resort** en dernier ressort. *v* **resort to** avoir recours à.

resound [rə'zaund] *v* retentir, résonner. **resounding** *adj* sonore; (*victory, etc.*) retentissant.

resource [rə'zo:s] *n* ressource *f*. **resourceful** *adj* ingénieux.

respect [rə'spekt] *n* respect *m*; (*aspect*) égard *m*, rapport *m*. **pay one's respects** présenter ses respects. **with respect to** en ce qui concerne. *v* respecter. **respectable** *adj* respectable; (*dress, behaviour*) convenable. **respectful** *adj* respectueux. **respective** *adj* respectif.

respiration [respə'reiʃn] *n* respiration *f*.

respite ['respait] *n* répit *m*.

respond [rə'spond] *v* répondre. **response** *n* réponse *f*. **be responsive** réagir bien.

responsible [rə'sponsəbl] *adj* responsable; digne de confiance. **responsibility** *n* responsabilité *f*.

rest[1] [rest] *n* repos *m*; (*music*) silence *m*; support *m*. *v* (*se*) reposer; (*lean*) (s')appuyer; (*land, put*) (se) poser. **restful** *adj* reposant. **restive** *adj* agité, impatient. **restless** *adj* agité.

rest[2] [rest] *n* **the rest** (*remaining part*) le reste *m*; (*remaining ones*) les autres *m pl*. *v* rester.

restaurant ['restront] *n* restaurant *m*. **restaurant car** (*on train*) wagon-restaurant *m*.

restore [rə'sto:] *v* rendre; (*order, rights, etc.*) rétablir; (*building, etc.*) restaurer. **restoration** *n* rétablissement *m*; restauration *f*.

restrain [rə'strein] *v* retenir; (*temper, etc.*) contenir. **restraint** *n* contrainte *f*; (*moderation*) retenue *f*.

restrict [rə'strikt] *v* restreindre. **restricted** *adj* restreint; confidentiel; (*narrow*) étroit. **restriction** *n* restriction *f*; limitation *f*. **restrictive** *adj* restrictif.

result [rə'zʌlt] *n* résultat *m*; conséquence *f*. *v* résulter. **result in** aboutir à. **resultant** *adj* résultant.

resume [rə'zjuːm] v reprendre. **resumption** n reprise f.

résumé ['reizumei] n résumé m.

resurgence [ri'sɜːdʒəns] n réapparition f.

resurrect [rezə'rekt] v ressusciter; (coll) remettre en service. **resurrection** n résurrection f.

resuscitate [rə'sʌsəteit] v ranimer.

retail ['riːteil] n détail m. v (se) vendre au détail. **retailer** n détaillant, -e m, f.

retain [rə'tein] v (keep) garder; (hold) retenir.

retaliate [rə'talieit] v se venger. **retaliation** n revanche f. **in retaliation** par représailles.

retard [rə'tɑːd] v retarder. **retarded** adj retardé; (mentally) arriéré.

reticent ['retisənt] adj réticent. **reticence** n réticence f.

retina ['retinə] n rétine f.

retinue ['retinjuː] n suite f.

retire [rə'taiə] v se retirer; (from work) prendre sa retraite; (go to bed) se coucher. **retired** adj retraité. **retirement** n retraite f.

retort[1] [rə'tɔːt] v rétorquer. n réplique f.

retort[2] [rə'tɔːt] n (chem) cornue f.

retrace [riː'treis] v reconstituer, retracer. **retrace one's steps** rebrousser chemin.

retract [rə'trakt] v (se) rétracter.

retreat [rə'triːt] n retraite f; (place) asile m. v se retirer; (mil) battre en retraite.

retrial [riː'traiəl] n nouveau procès m.

retrieve [rə'triːv] v récupérer; sauver. **retrieval** n récupération f. **retriever** n (dog) retriever m.

retrograde ['retrəgreid] adj rétrograde.

retrospect ['retrəspekt] n **in retrospect** rétrospectivement. **retrospective** adj rétrospectif.

return [rə'tɜːn] v retourner; (come back) revenir; (give back) rendre; (pol) élire. n retour m; (ticket) aller et retour m; (from investments, etc.) rapport m; (tax) déclaration f. **in return** en revanche. **in return for** en récompense de.

reunite [riːju'nait] v (se) réunir. **reunion** n réunion f.

rev [rev] (mot) n tour m. v **rev up** emballer.

reveal [rə'viːl] v révéler; laisser voir. **revealing** adj révélateur, -trice. **revelation** n révélation f.

revel ['revl] v se délecter (à). **revelry** n festivités f pl.

revenge [rə'vendʒ] n vengeance f. v venger.

revenue ['revinjuː] n revenu m.

reverberate [rə'vɜːbəreit] v (sound) retentir, (se) répercuter; (heat, light) (se) réverbérer. **reverberation** n répercussion f; réverbération f.

reverence ['revərəns] n vénération f. **revere** v révérer. **reverent** adj respectueux.

reverse [rə'vɜːs] adj contraire, opposé. n contraire m, opposé m; (coin) revers m; (page) verso m; (mot) marche arrière f. v renverser, retourner; (order) inverser; (mot) faire marche arrière. **reverse the charges** (phone) téléphoner en P.C.V. **reversal** n renversement m. **reversible** adj réversible.

revert [rə'vɜːt] v revenir, retourner.

review [rə'vjuː] n revue f; révision f; critique f. v passer en revue; réconsidérer; faire la critique de. **reviewer** n critique m.

revise [rə'vaiz] v réviser; corriger. **revision** n révision f.

revive [rə'vaiv] v ranimer; reprendre connaissance; (custom) rétablir; (trade) reprendre. **revival** n reprise f.

revoke [rə'vouk] v révoquer, revenir sur; (withdraw) retirer.

revolt [rə'voult] n révolte f. v (se) révolter. **revolting** adj dégoûtant.

revolution [revə'luːʃən] n révolution f. **revolutionary** n(m+f), adj révolutionnaire. **revolutionize** v révolutionner.

revolve [rə'volv] v (faire) tourner. **revolver** n revolver m. **revolving door** tambour m.

revue [rə'vjuː] n revue f.

revulsion [rə'vʌlʃən] n dégoût m.

reward [rə'wɔːd] n récompense f. v récompenser.

*****rewind** [riː'waind] v (film, tape) réembobiner. **rewinding** n réembobinage m.

*****rewrite** [riː'rait] v récrire; recopier.

Reykjavik ['reikjə,viːk] n Reykjavik.

rhesus ['riːsəs] n rhésus m. **rhesus negative/positive** rhésus négatif/positif.

rhetoric ['retərik] n rhétorique f. **rhetorical** adj rhétorique. **rhetorical question** question pour la forme f.

rheumatism ['ruːmətizəm] n rhumatisme m. **rheumatic** adj rhumatismal.

rhinoceros [rai'nosərəs] n rhinocéros m.

rhododendron [roudə'dendrən] *n* rhododendron *m*.

rhubarb ['ruːbɑːb] *n* rhubarbe *f*.

rhyme [raim] *n* rime *f*; (*poetry*) vers *m pl*. *v* (faire) rimer.

rhythm ['riðəm] *n* rythme *m*. **rhythmic** *adj* rythmique; (*music*) rythmé.

rib [rib] *n* côte *f*.

ribbon ['ribən] *n* ruban *m*. **in ribbons** en lambeaux.

rice [rais] *n* riz *m*. **rice paper** papier de riz *m*. **rice pudding** riz au lait *m*.

rich [ritʃ] *adj* riche. **riches** *pl n* richesses *f pl*. **richness** *n* richesse *f*.

rickety ['rikəti] *adj* branlant.

*****rid** [rid] *v* débarrasser. **get rid of** se débarrasser de. **riddance** *n* débarras *m*.

ridden ['ridn] *V* **ride**.

riddle[1] ['ridl] *n* énigme *f*.

riddle[2] ['ridl] *v* cribler.

*****ride** [raid] *v* monter; (*horse*) monter à cheval. *n* promenade *f*, tour *m*; (*journey*) trajet *m*. **rider** *n* (*horse*) cavalier, -ère *m*, *f*; (*addition*) annexe *f*. **riding** *n* équitation *f*. **riding school** manège *m*.

ridge [ridʒ] *n* (*hills*) faîte *m*; (*roof*) arête *f*; (*on surface*) strie *f*.

ridicule ['ridikjuːl] *n* ridicule *m*. *v* ridiculiser. **ridiculous** *adj* ridicule.

rife [raif] *adj* répandu.

rifle[1] ['raifl] *n* fusil *m*. **rifle range** champ de tir *m*.

rifle[2] ['raifl] *v* piller; (*house, drawer*) dévaliser.

rift [rift] *n* fissure *f*; division *f*.

rig [rig] *n* (*naut*) gréement *m*. **rig-out** *n* (*coll*) tenue *f*. *v* gréer; (*falsify*) truquer. **rigging** *n* gréement *m*; truquage *m*.

right [rait] *adj* (*not left*) droit; juste; approprié; (*correct*) bon, bonne. **be right** avoir raison. *adv* à droite; (*straight*) droit; (*completely*) tout à fait; (*well*) bien. *n* droite *f*; (*entitlement*) droit *m*; (*good*) bien *m*. *v* redresser. **right angle** angle droit *m*. **right-handed** *adj* droitier *m*. **right-of-way** *n* (*public*) droit de passage *m*; (*mot*) priorité *f*. **right-wing** *adj* (*pol*) de droite.

righteous ['raitʃəs] *adj* vertueux; juste.

rightful ['raitfəl] *adj* légitime.

rigid ['ridʒid] *adj* rigide; strict. **rigidity** *n* rigidité *f*.

rigmarole ['rigmərəul] *n* (*coll*) comédie *f*; (*speech*) galimatias *m*.

rigour ['rigə] *n* rigueur *f*. **rigorous** *adj* rigoureux.

rim [rim] *n* bord *m*; (*wheel*) jante *f*.

rind [raind] *n* (*fruit*) peau *f*; (*cheese*) croûte *f*; (*bacon*) couenne *f*.

ring[1] [riŋ] *n* anneau *m*; (*with gem*) bague *f*; cercle *m*, rond *m*; (*circus*) piste *f*; (*boxing*) ring *m*. *v* entourer d'un cercle. **ringleader** *n* meneur *m*. **ring road** route de ceinture *f*.

*****ring**[2] [riŋ] *v* (*bell*) sonner; téléphoner (à); résonner. **ring off** (*phone*) raccrocher. **ring up** (*coll: phone*) donner un coup de fil à. *n* sonnerie *f*; (*coll: phone*) coup de fil *m*.

rink [riŋk] *n* patinoire *f*.

rinse [rins] *v* rincer. *n* rinçage *m*.

riot ['raiət] *n* émeute *f*. *v* faire une émeute.

rip [rip] *v* (se) déchirer. **rip off** *or* **out** arracher. *n* déchirure *f*.

ripe [raip] *adj* mûr. **ripen** *v* mûrir. **ripeness** *n* maturité *f*.

ripple ['ripl] *n* ondulation *f*, ride *f*; (*laughter*) cascade *f*. *v* (se) rider. (faire) onduler.

*****rise** [raiz] *v* (*sun, etc.*) lever *m*; (*increase*) hausse *f*; (*in salary*) augmentation *f*; (*in importance*) essor *m*. **give rise to** engendrer. *v* se lever, s'élever; augmenter, être en hausse; (*rebel*) se soulever. **rising** *adj* levant; en hausse; (*anger*) croissant.

risen ['rizn] *V* **rise**.

risk [risk] *n* risque *m*. **at risk** en danger. *v* risquer. **risky** *adj* risqué.

rissole ['risəul] *n* croquette *f*.

rite [rait] *n* rite *m*.

ritual ['ritjuəl] *nm, adj* rituel.

rival ['raivəl] *n, adj* rival, -e. *v* rivaliser avec. **rivalry** *n* rivalité *f*.

river ['rivə] *n* rivière *f*; (*larger*) fleuve *m*. **riverside** *n* bord de l'eau *m*.

rivet ['rivit] *n* rivet *m*. *v* (*tech*) riveter; fixer, clouer. **riveting** *adj* fascinant.

Riviera [rivi'eərə] *n* **the Riviera** (*French*) la Côte d'Azur *f*; (*Italian*) la Riviera *f*.

road [roud] *n* route *f*; (*to success, etc.*) voie *f*, chemin *m*. **road-block** *n* barrage routier *m*. **road safety** sécurité routière *f*. **roadside** *n* bord de la route *m*. **road sign** panneau de signalisation *m*. **road-works** *pl n* travaux *m pl*.

roam [roum] *v* parcourir, errer.

roar [roː] *v* (*lion*) rugir; (*crowd*) hurler; (*bull, wind*) mugir; (*engine*) vrombir;

(*thunder*) gronder. **roar with laughter**
éclater de rire. *n* rugissement *m*; hurlement *m*; mugissement *m*; vrombissement
m; grondement *m*.
roast [roust] *v* (*meat*) rôtir; (*coffee,
chestnuts*) griller. *nm, adj* rôti.
rob [rob] *v* voler, dévaliser. **robber** *n*
voleur *m*. **robbery** *n* vol *m*.
robe [roub] *n* robe *f*. *v* revêtir.
robin [robin] *n* rouge-gorge *m*.
robot [roubot] *n* robot *m*.
robust [rə'bʌst] *adj* robuste, vigoureux,
solide.
rock[1] [rok] *n* (*stone*) roche *f*; (*hard*) roc
m; (*boulder*) rocher *m*. **rock bun or cake**
rocher *m*. **rock-climbing** *n* varappe *f*.
rock-plant *n* plante alpestre *f*. **rockery**
n rocaille *f*. **rocky** *adj* rocheux, rocailleux.
rock[2] [rok] *n* (*sway*) bercer, (*se*) balancer;
(*shake*) ébranler. *n* (*music*) rock *m*. **rock-
ing-chair** *n* fauteuil à bascule *m*. **rocking-
horse** *n* cheval à bascule *m*.
rocket [rokit] *n* fusée *f*. *v* (*prices*) monter
en flèche.
rod [rod] *n* (*wood*) baguette *f*; (*metal*)
tringle *f*; (*fishing*) canne *f*.
rode [roud] *V* ride.
rodent [roudənt] *n* rongeur *m*.
roe [rou] *n* (*hard*) œufs de poisson *m pl*;
(*soft*) laitance *f*.
rogue [roug] *n* coquin, -e *m, f*. **roguish** *adj*
espiègle.
role [roul] *n* rôle *m*.
roll [roul] *n* rouleau *m*; (*bread*) petit pain
m; (*drums*) roulement *m*; (*register*) liste
f. **roll-call** *n* appel *m*. *v* rouler. **roll in**
(*coll*) affluer; (*coll: person*) s'amener. **roll
over** (*se*) retourner. **roll up** rouler;
(*sleeves*) retrousser. **roller** *n* rouleau *m*.
roller-coaster *n* montagnes russes *f pl*.
roller-skate *n* patin à roulettes *m*. **rolling-
pin** *n* rouleau *m*.
romance [rou'mans] *n* (*love*) idylle *f*,
amour *m*; (*story*) roman à l'eau de rose
m. **Romance** *adj* (*language*) roman.
romantic *n*(*m*+*f*), *adj* romantique.
Romania [ru'meinjə] *n* Roumanie *f*.
Romanian *nm, adj* roumain; (*people*)
Roumain, -e *m, f*.
Rome [roum] *n* Rome. **Roman** *n* Romain,
-e *m, f*. *adj* romain. **Roman Catholic**
n(*m*+*f*), *adj* catholique. **Roman numeral**
chiffre romain *m*.
romp [romp] *n* ébats *m pl*. *v* s'ébattre.
rompers *pl n* barboteuse *f sing*.

roof [ru:f] *n, pl* **roofs** toit *m*. **roof of the
mouth** voûte du palais *f*. **roof-rack** *n*
galerie *f*.
rook [ruk] *n* (*bird*) corneille *f*. *v* (*slang*)
rouler.
room [rum] *n* pièce *f*; (*larger*) salle *f*;
(*hotel*) chambre *f*; (*space*) place *f*. **at
room temperature** (*wine*) chambré. **room-
mate** *n* camarade de chambre *m, f*. **room
service** service des chambres *m*. **roomy**
adj spacieux.
roost [ru:st] *n* perchoir *m*. *v* (*se*) jucher.
rooster *n* coq *m*.
root[1] [ru:t] *n* racine *f*; origine *f*. *v*
(*s'*)enraciner.
root[2] [ru:t] *v* fouiller. **root for** (*slang*)
encourager. **root out** (*find*) dénicher.
rope [roup] *n* corde *f*. **know the ropes** être
au courant. **rope-ladder** *n* échelle de
corde *f*. *v* corder, lier. **rope in** (*coll*)
embringuer. **ropy** *adj* (*coll*) pas fameux.
rosary [rouzəri] *n* chapelet *m*.
rose[1] [rouz] *V* rise.
rose[2] [rouz] *n* rose *f*. **rose-bush** *n* rosier *m*.
rose garden roseraie *f*. **rosewood** *n* bois
de rose *m*. **rosy** *adj* rose.
rosemary [rouzməri] *n* romarin *m*.
rosette [rou'zet] *n* rosette *f*; (*prize*)
cocarde *f*.
rot [rot] *n* pourriture *f*, carie *f*; (*coll: rubbish*) bêtises *f pl*. *v* pourrir. **rotten** *adj*
pourri; (*coll: bad*) moche, sale; (*coll: ill*)
mal fichu.
rota [routə] *n* liste *f*.
rotate [rou'teit] *v* (*faire*) tourner, (*faire*)
pivoter; (*crops*) alterner. **rotary** *adj* rotatif. **rotation** *n* rotation *f*.
rotor [routə] *n* rotor *m*.
rouge [ru:3] *n* rouge *m*.
rough [rʌf] *adj* (*surface*) rugueux; (*coarse*)
rude; brutal, dur; (*draft*) ébauché;
approximatif. **rough-and-ready** *adj* rudimentaire. **rough copy or draft** brouillon
m. *v* **rough it** (*coll*) vivre à la dure. **roughly** *adv* à peu près. **roughness** *n* rugosité *f*;
rudesse *f*; brutalité *f*.
roulette [ru:'let] *n* roulette *f*.
round [raund] *adj* rond. *prep* autour de. *n*
rond *m*; (*of bread*) tranche *f*; (*drinks,
postman, etc.*) tournée *f*; (*game, competition*) partie *f*. **round-necked** *adj* (*pullover*)
ras du cou. **round-shouldered** *adj* voûté. *v*
arrondir. **round off** terminer. **round up**
rassembler; (*figure*) arrondir.

roundabout ['raundəbaut] n (mot) rond-point m; (fair) manège m. adj détourné, indirect.

rouse [rauz] v éveiller; stimuler.

route [ruːt] n itinéraire m.

routine [ruːˈtiːn] n routine f; (theatre) numéro m. adj d'usage; ordinaire.

rove [rouv] v errer (dans), vagabonder.

row[1] [rou] n (side by side) rang m; (queue) file f; (trees, figures) rangée f.

row[2] [rou] v (boat) ramer. n promenade en canot f. **rowing** n (sport) aviron m; (for fun) canotage m. **rowing boat** canot m.

row[3] [rau] n querelle f; (noise) tapage m. v se quereller.

rowdy ['raudi] adj chahuteur, -euse. **rowdiness** n tapage m.

royal ['roiəl] adj royal. **royal blue** bleu roi invar. **royalist** n(m+f). adj royaliste. **royalties** pl n droits d'auteur m pl. **royalty** n royauté f.

rub [rʌb] n frottement m; (with duster) coup de chiffon m. v frotter. **rub in** faire pénétrer; insister sur. **rub out** (s')effacer. **rub up the wrong way** prendre à rebrousse-poil. **rubbing** n (brass, etc.) frottis m.

rubber ['rʌbə] n caoutchouc m; (eraser) gomme f. **rubber band** élastique m. **rubber stamp** tampon m. **rubber tree** arbre à gomme m. **rubbery** adj caoutchouteux.

rubbish ['rʌbiʃ] n détritus m pl, ordures f pl; (derog) camelote f; (nonsense) bêtises f pl.

rubble ['rʌbl] n décombres m pl.

ruby ['ruːbi] n rubis m.

rucksack ['rʌksak] n sac à dos m.

rudder ['rʌdə] n gouvernail m.

rude [ruːd] adj impoli, grossier; (sudden) brusque; (primitif. **rudeness** n impolitesse f, grossièreté f.

rudiment ['ruːdimənt] n rudiment m. **rudimentary** adj rudimentaire.

rueful ['ruːfəl] adj triste. **ruefully** adv avec regret.

ruff [rʌf] n (dress) fraise f; (bird) collier m.

ruffian ['rʌfiən] n voyou m.

ruffle ['rʌfl] v (hair) ébouriffer; (surface) agiter; (clothes) froisser; (worry) troubler.

rug [rʌg] n carpette f, petit tapis m; (blanket) couverture f.

rugby ['rʌgbi] n rugby m.

rugged ['rʌgid] adj (cliff) déchiqueté; (landscape) accidenté; (person) rude; (determination) acharné.

ruin ['ruːin] n ruine f. v ruiner.

rule [ruːl] n règle f; autorité f. **as a rule** normalement. v gouverner; régner; dominer; (lines) régler. **rule out** exclure. **ruler** n souverain, -e m, f; (measuring) règle f. **ruling** n décision f.

rum [rʌm] n rhum m.

rumble ['rʌmbl] n grondement m; (stomach) gargouillement m. v gronder; gargouiller.

rummage ['rʌmidʒ] n fouiller. n **rummage sale** vente de charité f.

rumour ['ruːmə] n rumeur f, bruit m.

rump [rʌmp] n (animal) croupe f; (beef) culotte f. **rump steak** romsteck m.

***run** [rʌn] n course f; (outing) tour m; (track) piste f; séquence f, série f; (demand) ruée f. **in the long run** à la longue. v courir; (flow) couler; (colour) s'étaler; (function) marcher; (organize) diriger; passer. **run away** v se sauver. **runaway** n, adj fugitif, -ive. **run down** v (car, etc.) renverser; (coll) dénigrer. **run-down** adj (coll) à plat, surmené. **run in** v (mot) roder. **run out** expirer, s'épuiser. **run over** (car, etc.) écraser. **runway** n piste f. **runner** n coureur m. **runner bean** haricot à rames m. **runner-up** n second, -e m, f. **running** adj (water, etc.) courant; (in succession) de suite. **running commentary** commentaire suivi m. **running costs** frais d'exploitation m pl.

rung[1] [rʌŋ] V **ring**[2].

rung[2] [rʌŋ] n barreau m.

rupture ['rʌptʃə] n rupture f. v (se) rompre.

rural ['ruərəl] adj rural; de la campagne.

ruse [ruːz] n ruse f.

rush[1] [rʌʃ] n ruée f; hâte f. v se précipiter; (do quickly) dépêcher. **rush hour** heure de pointe f.

rush[2] [rʌʃ] n (bot) jonc m.

rusk [rʌsk] n biscotte f.

Russia ['rʌʃə] n Russie f. **Russian** nm, adj russe; n (people) Russe m, f.

rust [rʌst] n rouille f. v (se) rouiller. **rusty** adj rouillé.

rustic ['rʌstik] adj rustique.

rustle ['rʌsl] v (leaves) (faire) bruire; (paper) froisser. n bruissement m; froissement m.

rut [rʌt] n ornière f. **be in a rut** suivre l'ornière.

ruthless ['ruːθlis] adj impitoyable, sans pitié.

rye [rai] n seigle m.

S

sabbath ['sabəθ] n sabbat m.

sabbatical [sə'batikəl] adj sabbatique. n année sabbatique f.

sable ['seibl] n zibeline f.

sabotage ['sabətaːʒ] n sabotage m. v saboter. **saboteur** n saboteur, -euse f.

sabre ['seibə] n sabre m.

saccharin ['sakərin] n saccharine f.

sachet ['safei] n sachet m.

sack [sak] n sac m. **get the sack** (coll) être sacqué. v (coll) sacquer.

sacrament ['sakrəmənt] n sacrement m.

sacred ['seikrid] adj sacré.

sacrifice ['sakrifais] n sacrifice m. v sacrifier.

sacrilege ['sakrəlidʒ] n sacrilège m. **sacrilegious** adj sacrilège.

sad [sad] adj triste. **sadden** v attrister. **sadly** adv tristement; (very) bien, fort; (unfortunately) fâcheusement. **sadness** n tristesse f.

saddle ['sadl] n selle f. **saddle-bag** n (horse) sacoche de selle f; (bicycle) sacoche de bicyclette f. v seller. **saddle with** (coll) coller à. **saddler** n sellier m. **saddlery** n sellerie f.

sadism ['seidizəm] n sadisme m. **sadist** n sadique m, f. **sadistic** adj sadique.

safari [sə'faːri] n safari m. **safari park** réserve f.

safe [seif] adj (person) en sécurité; (toy, etc.) sans danger; sûr; solide. **safe and sound** sain et sauf. **safe keeping** bonne garde f. **to be on the safe side** par précaution. n coffre-fort m. **safely** adv sans danger; en sûreté. **safety** n sécurité f; solidité f. **safety-belt** n ceinture de sécurité f. **safety first** la sécurité d'abord. **safety-pin** n épingle de sûreté f.

safeguard ['seifgaːd] n sauvegarde f. v sauvegarder.

saffron ['safrən] n safran m.

sag [sag] v s'affaisser, fléchir. n affaissement m, fléchissement m.

saga ['saːgə] n saga f.

sage[1] [seidʒ] nm, adj (wise) sage.

sage[2] [seidʒ] n (herb) sauge f.

Sagittarius [sadʒi'teəriəs] n Sagittaire m.

sago ['seigou] n sagou m; (pudding) sagou au lait m.

said [sed] V say.

sail [seil] n voile f; (trip) tour en bateau m; (windmill) aile f. **sailcloth** n toile à voile f. **set sail** partir. v (leave) partir; (cross) traverser; (boat) piloter. **sail through** (coll) réussir haut la main. **sailing** n navigation f; (sport, hobby) voile f. **sailing boat** bateau à voiles m. **sailor** n marin m.

saint [seint] n saint, -e m, f.

sake [seik] n **for the sake of** pour l'amour de, par égard pour; pour le plaisir de.

salad ['saləd] n salade f. **salad cream** mayonnaise f. **salad dressing** vinaigrette f.

salami [sə'laːmi] n salami m.

salary ['saləri] n traitement m, salaire m. **salary scale** échelle des traitements f.

sale [seil] n vente f; (reductions) soldes m pl. **for sale** à vendre. **on sale** en vente. **sale-room** n salle des ventes f. **sales department** service des ventes m. **salesman** n (shop) vendeur m; représentant m. **salesmanship** n art de la vente m.

saline ['seilain] adj salin. **salinity** n salinité f.

saliva [sə'laivə] n salive f. **salivary** adj salivaire. **salivate** v saliver.

sallow ['salou] adj jaunâtre.

salmon ['samən] n saumon m.

salon ['salon] n salon m.

saloon [sə'luːn] n salle f, salon m. **saloon bar** bar m. **saloon car** conduite intérieure f.

salt [soːlt] n sel m. **salt-cellar** n salière f. v saler. **salty** adj salé.

salute [sə'luːt] n salut m; (guns) salve f. v saluer.

salvage ['salvidʒ] n sauvetage m; récupération f. v sauver; récupérer.

salvation [sal'veifən] n salut m. **Salvation Army** Armée du Salut f.

same [seim] adj, pron même. **all the same** quand même. **at the same time** en même temps.

sample ['saːmpl] n échantillon m; (blood) prélèvement m. v goûter.

sanatorium [sanə'tɔːriəm] *n* sanatorium *m*.

sanctify ['saŋktifai] *v* sanctifier. **sanctification** *n* sanctification *f*.

sanctimonious [saŋkti'mouniəs] *adj* moralisateur, -trice.

sanction ['saŋkʃən] *n* sanction *f*. *v* sanctionner.

sanctity ['saŋktəti] *n* sainteté *f*; inviolabilité *f*.

sanctuary ['saŋktʃuəri] *n* sanctuaire *m*; (*refuge*) asile *m*; (*birds, etc.*) réserve *f*.

sand [sand] *n* sable *m*. **sandbank** *n* banc de sable *m*. **sand-castle** *n* château de sable *m*. **sandpaper** *n* papier de verre *m*. **sandstone** *n* grès *m*. *v* sabler; (*with sandpaper*) frotter au papier de verre. **sandy** *adj* sablonneux; (*beach*) de sable; (*hair*) couleur sable.

sandal ['sandl] *n* sandale *f*.

sandwich ['sanwidʒ] *n* sandwich *m*. **sandwich board** panneau publicitaire *m*. **sandwich course** cours de formation professionnelle *m*.

sane [sein] *adj* sain d'esprit; raisonnable. **sanity** *n* santé mentale *f*.

sang [saŋ] *V* **sing**.

sanitary ['sanitəri] *adj* sanitaire; hygiénique. **sanitary towel** serviette hygiénique *f*.

sank [saŋk] *V* **sink**.

sap [sap] *n* sève *f*.

sapphire ['safaiə] *n* saphir *m*.

sarcasm ['saːkazəm] *n* sarcasme *m*. **sarcastic** *adj* sarcastique.

sardine [saː'diːn] *n* sardine *f*.

Sardinia [saː'diniə] *n* Sardaigne *f*. **Sardinian** *nm, adj* sarde; *n* (*people*) Sarde *m, f*.

sardonic [saː'dɒnik] *adj* sardonique.

sash¹ [saʃ] *n* (*uniform*) écharpe *f*; (*dress*) large ceinture *f*.

sash² [saʃ] *n* (*frame*) chassis à guillotine *m*. **sash-window** *n* fenêtre à guillotine *f*.

sat [sat] *V* **sit**.

Satan ['seitən] *n* Satan *m*. **satanic** *adj* satanique.

satchel ['satʃəl] *n* cartable *m*.

satellite ['satəlait] *n* satellite *m*.

satin ['satin] *n* satin *m*.

satire ['sataiə] *n* satire *f*. **satirical** *adj* satirique. **satirize** *v* faire la satire de.

satisfy ['satisfai] *v* satisfaire; convaincre. **satisfaction** *n* satisfaction *f*. **satisfactory** *adj* satisfaisant.

saturate ['satʃəreit] *v* saturer; (*soak*) trem-

per. **saturation** *n* saturation *f*. **reach saturation point** arriver à saturation.

Saturday ['satədi] *n* samedi *m*.

sauce [sɔːs] *n* sauce *f*; (*slang*) toupet *m*. **saucy** *adj* impertinent; coquin.

saucepan ['sɔːspən] *n* casserole *f*.

saucer ['sɔːsə] *n* soucoupe *f*.

sauerkraut ['sauəkraut] *n* choucroute *f*.

sauna [sɔːnə] *n* sauna *m*.

saunter [sɔːntə] *v* flâner, se balader. *n* flânerie *f*, balade *f*.

sausage ['sɔsidʒ] *n* saucisse *f*. **sausage-meat** *n* chair à saucisse *f*. **sausage roll** friand *m*.

savage ['savidʒ] *adj* féroce, brutal; primitif, sauvage. *n* sauvage *m, f*. *v* attaquer férocement. **savagery** *n* sauvagerie *f*.

save¹ [seiv] *v* sauver; (*put aside*) mettre de côté, garder; économiser, épargner. **savings** *pl n* économies *f pl*. **savings bank** caisse d'épargne *f*.

save² [seiv] *prep* sauf.

saviour ['seivjə] *n* sauveur *m*.

savour ['seivə] *v* savourer. *n* saveur *f*. **savoury** *adj* savoureux, appétissant; (*not sweet*) salé.

saw¹ [sɔː] *V* **see¹**.

***saw²** [sɔː] *n* scie *f*. **sawdust** *n* sciure *f*. **sawmill** *n* scierie *f*. *v* scier.

sawn [sɔːn] *V* **saw²**.

saxophone ['saksəfoun] *n* saxophone *m*.

***say** [sei] *v* dire. **saying** *n* dicton *m*, proverbe *m*.

scab [skab] *n* croûte *f*; (*derog: non-striker*) jaune *m*. *v* se cicatriser; (*derog*) faire le jaune.

scaffold ['skafəld] *n* échafaud *m*. **scaffolding** *n* échafaudage *m*.

scald [skɔːld] *v* échauder, ébouillanter. *n* brûlure *f*. **scalding** *adj* brûlant.

scale¹ [skeil] *n* (*fish, etc.*) écaille *f*; (*deposit*) tartre *m*. **scaly** *adj* écailleux, entartré.

scale² [skeil] *n* échelle *f*; (*music*) gamme *f*. **scale drawing** dessin à l'échelle *m*. *v* escalader. **scale down** réduire (proportionnellement).

scales [skeilz] *pl n* balance *f sing*.

scallop ['skaləp] *n* coquille Saint-Jacques *f*; (*sewing*) feston *m*. **scallop shell** coquille *f*. *v* festonner.

scalp [skalp] *n* cuir chevelu *m*. *v* scalper.

scalpel ['skalpəl] *n* bistouri *m*.

scamper ['skampə] *v* (*child*) galoper; (*mouse*) trottiner.

scampi ['skæmpi] n langoustines f pl.

scan [skæn] v scruter; (glance over) parcourir des yeux; (poetry) (se) scander.

scandal ['skændl] n scandale m; (gossip) cancans m pl. **scandalize** v scandaliser. **scandalous** adj scandaleux.

Scandinavia [‚skændi'neivjə] n Scandinavie f. **Scandinavian** n Scandinave m, f; adj scandinave.

scant [skænt] or **scanty** adj insuffisant.

scapegoat ['skeipgout] n bouc émissaire m.

scar [skɑː] n cicatrice f; (from knife) balafre f. v marquer d'une cicatrice; balafrer.

scarce [skeəs] adj peu abondant; rare. **scarcely** adv à peine. **scarcity** n manque m; rareté f.

scare [skeə] n peur f; alarme f. v effrayer. **be scared** avoir peur. **scarecrow** n épouvantail m.

scarf [skɑːf] n écharpe f; (square) foulard m.

scarlet ['skɑːlit] nf, adj écarlate. **scarlet fever** scarlatine f.

scathing ['skeiðiŋ] adj acerbe, cinglant.

scatter ['skætə] v éparpiller, répandre; (se) disperser. **scatterbrained** adj écervelé.

scavenge ['skævindʒ] v fouiller. **scavenger** n éboueur m; insecte or animal nécrophage m.

scene [siːn] n scène f; (place) lieu m; spectacle m, vue f.

scenery ['siːnəri] n paysage m; (theatre) décor m.

scent [sent] n parfum m; (track) piste f. v parfumer; (smell) flairer.

sceptic ['skeptik] n sceptique m, f. **sceptical** adj sceptique. **scepticism** n scepticisme m.

sceptre ['septə] n sceptre m.

schedule ['fedjuːl] n programme m; (timetable) horaire m. v prévoir.

scheme [skiːm] n plan m, projet m; (plot) complot m; arrangement m. v combiner, comploter.

schizophrenia [‚skitsə'friːniə] n schizophrénie f. **schizophrenic** n(m+f), adj schizophrène.

scholar ['skɒlə] n érudit, -e m, f; (pupil) écolier, -ère m, f. **scholarly** adj érudit. **scholarship** n (award) bourse f; érudition f.

scholastic [skə'læstik] adj scolaire; scolastique.

school¹ [skuːl] n école f; (secondary) collège m, lycée m. **schoolboy** n élève m, écolier m. **school-days** pl n années d'école f pl. **schoolgirl** n élève f, écolière f. **school-leaving age** âge de fin de scolarité m. **school year** année scolaire f. v dresser.

schooling n scolarité f; instruction f; dressage m.

school² [skuːl] n (of fish) banc m.

schooner ['skuːnə] n schooner m.

sciatica [sai'ætikə] n sciatique f. **sciatic** adj sciatique.

science ['saiəns] n science f. **science fiction** n science-fiction f. **scientific** adj scientifique. **scientist** n scientifique m, f.

scintillating ['sintileitiŋ] adj scintillant; (remark, etc.) brillant.

scissors ['sizəz] pl n ciseaux m pl.

scoff¹ [skɒf] v se moquer.

scoff² [skɒf] v (coll) bouffer.

scold [skould] v attraper, gronder. **scolding** n gronderie f.

scone [skɒn] n petit pain au lait m.

scoop [skuːp] n pelle f, cuiller f; (press) scoop m. v (pick up) ramasser; (water) écoper; (hole) creuser.

scooter ['skuːtə] n scooter m; (child's) trottinette f.

scope [skoup] n (range) étendue f; (opportunity) possibilité f.

scorch [skɔːtʃ] n brûlure légère f. v roussir, brûler.

score [skɔː] n (sport) score m; (game) marque f; (subject) titre m; (music) partition f; (twenty) vingtaine f; (cut) rayure f. v marquer; rayer, strier. **scoreboard** n tableau m. **scorer** n marqueur m.

scorn [skɔːn] n mépris m, dédain m. v mépriser, dédaigner. **scornful** adj méprisant, dédaigneux.

Scorpio ['skɔːpiou] n Scorpion m.

scorpion ['skɔːpiən] n scorpion m.

Scotland ['skɒtlənd] n Ecosse f. **Scot** n Ecossais, -e m, f. **Scotch** n whisky m, scotch m. **Scottish** or **Scots** adj écossais.

scoundrel ['skaundrəl] n vaurien m.

scour¹ [skauə] v (clean) récurer. **scourer** n (powder) poudre à récurer f; (pad) tampon abrasif m.

scour² [skauə] v (search) parcourir.

scourge [skɜːdʒ] n fléau m.

scout [skaut] n scout m, éclaireur m. **scoutmaster** n chef scout m. **scouting** n scoutisme m.

scowl [skaul] v se renfrogner. n mine renfrognée f.

scramble ['skræmbl] v avancer avec difficulté; (rush) se bousculer; (eggs, phone) brouiller. n bousculade f.

scrap [skræp] n bout m, fragment m; (metal) ferraille f. **scrap-book** n album m. **scrap-merchant** n ferrailleur m. **scrap paper** n brouillon m. **scraps** pl n restes m pl. v mettre au rebut; abandonner.

scrape [skreip] n (noise) grattement m; (graze) éraflure f. v gratter, racler; érafler. **scrape through** (exam) réussir de justesse.

scratch [skrætʃ] v (for itch) (se) gratter; (with claw) griffer; (graze) érafler; (glass, record, etc.) rayer. n grattement m; éraflure f; rayure f; zéro m.

scrawl [skrɔːl] v gribouiller. n gribouillage m.

scream [skriːm] n cri aigu m, hurlement m. v crier, hurler.

screech [skriːtʃ] n cri strident m, hurlement m; (brakes) grincement m. v crier, hurler; grincer.

screen [skriːn] n (TV, film) écran m; (hospital, room) paravent m; masque m. **screen-play** n scénario m. **screen test** essai filmé m. v masquer, cacher; (film) projeter; protéger.

screw [skruː] n vis m. **screwdriver** n tournevis m. v visser. **screw up** (paper) chiffonner.

scribble ['skribl] v gribouiller, griffonner. **scribble out** raturer. n gribouillage m, griffonage m.

script [skript] n (play) texte m; (film) scénario m; (writing) script m.

scripture ['skriptʃə] n (school) instruction religieuse f; (holy) écriture sainte f.

scroll [skroul] n rouleau m; manuscrit m; (arch) volute f.

scrounge [skraundʒ] (coll) v chiper, taper. **scrounger** n parasite m.

scrub¹ [skrʌb] n nettoyage m. v nettoyer à la brosse, frotter; (coll: cancel) annuler. **scrubbing brush** brosse dure f.

scrub² [skrʌb] n broussailles f pl.

scruff [skrʌf] n **by the scruff of the neck** par la peau du cou.

scruffy ['skrʌfi] adj négligé, débraillé. **scruffiness** n débraillé m.

scrum [skrʌm] n mêlée f.

scruple ['skruːpl] n scrupule m. **scrupulous** adj scrupuleux.

scrutiny ['skruːtəni] n examen minutieux m. **scrutinize** v scruter.

scuffle ['skʌfl] n bagarre f. v se bagarrer.

scull [skʌl] n aviron m, godille f. v ramer, godiller.

scullery ['skʌləri] n arrière-cuisine f.

sculpt [skʌlpt] v sculpter. **sculptor** n sculpteur m. **sculpture** n sculpture f.

scum [skʌm] n écume f; (derog) rebut m.

scurf [skəːf] n pellicules f pl.

scurvy ['skəːvi] n scorbut m.

scuttle¹ ['skʌtl] n (coal) seau à charbon m.

scuttle² ['skʌtl] v (naut) saborder.

scuttle³ ['skʌtl] v courir précipitamment.

scythe [saið] n faux f. v faucher.

sea [siː] n mer f.

sea bed n fond de la mer m.

seafaring ['siːfeəriŋ] adj marin.

seafood ['siːfuːd] n fruits de mer m pl.

sea front n bord de mer m.

seagull ['siːgʌl] n mouette f.

seahorse ['siːhɔːs] n hippocampe m.

seal¹ [siːl] n sceau m, cachet m. v sceller; (stick down) coller; (fate) décider. **sealing wax** cire à cacheter f.

seal² [siːl] n (zool) phoque m. **sealskin** n peau de phoque f.

sea-level n niveau de la mer m.

sea-lion n otarie f.

seam [siːm] n couture f; joint m; (coal) veine f.

seaman ['siːmən] n marin m.

séance ['seiɑ̃s] n séance de spiritisme f.

sear [siə] v flétrir; (burn) brûler. **searing** adj (pain) aigu, -guë.

search [səːtʃ] n recherche f; (of house, etc.) fouille f. **searchlight** n projecteur m. **search-party** n équipe de secours f. **search-warrant** n mandat de perquisition m. v fouiller, chercher. **searching** adj (look) pénétrant; (examination) rigoureux.

sea shell n coquillage m.

seashore ['siːʃɔː] n rivage m, plage f.

seasick ['siːsik] adj **be seasick** avoir le mal de mer. **seasickness** n mal de mer m.

seaside ['siːsaid] n bord de la mer m. **seaside resort** station balnéaire f.

season ['siːzn] n saison f. **season ticket** carte d'abonnement f. v (food) assaisonner; (wood) faire sécher. **seasonal** adj saisonnier. **seasoning** n assaisonnement m.

seat [siːt] n siège m; place f. **seat-belt** n ceinture de sécurité f. v (faire) asseoir; placer.

seaweed ['siːwiːd] n algue f.

seaworthy ['siːwɜːði] adj en état de naviguer.

secluded [si'kluːdid] adj à l'écart, retiré. **seclusion** n solitude f.

second¹ ['sekənd] n (time) seconde f. **second hand** trotteuse f.

second² ['sekənd] n deuxième m, f. second, -e m, f; (comm) article de second choix m. adj, adv deuxième, second. **on second thoughts** réflexion faite. **second-class** adj de deuxième classe; (mail) tarif réduit. **second-hand** adj, adv d'occasion. **second-rate** adj médiocre. **second to none** sans pareil. v appuyer (la motion de). **secondly** adv deuxièmement, en second lieu.

secondary ['sekəndəri] adj secondaire.

secret ['siːkrit] n secret m. adj secret, -ète. **secrecy** n secret m. **secretive** adj réservé, dissimulé. **secretly** adv en secret.

secretary ['sekrətəri] n secrétaire m, f. **secretarial** adj de secrétariat, de secrétaire.

secrete [si'kriːt] v sécréter; (hide) cacher. **secretion** n sécrétion f.

sect [sekt] n secte f. **sectarian** adj sectaire.

section ['sekʃən] n section f, partie f.

sector ['sektə] n secteur m.

secular ['sekjulə] adj séculier, laïque.

secure [si'kjuə] adj solide; sûr, assuré; tranquille. v fixer; se procurer; garantir; assurer. **security** sécurité f; (for loan) caution f.

sedate [si'deit] adj posé, calme. **sedation** n sédation f. **sedative** nm, adj calmant n.

sediment ['sedimənt] n (geol) sédiment m; (wine, etc.) dépôt m.

seduce [si'djuːs] v séduire. **seduction** n séduction f. **seductive** adj séduisant.

*see¹ [siː] v voir. **see to** s'occuper de. **see you later!** à tout à l'heure!

see² [siː] n évêché m.

seed [siːd] n graine f; (source) germe m. **seedless** adj sans pépins. **seedling** n semis m. **seedy** adj miteux; (coll: ill) mal fichu.

*seek [siːk] v chercher, rechercher; demander.

seem [siːm] v sembler, paraître. **seeming** adj apparent. **seemingly** adv apparemment; à ce qu'il paraît.

seen [siːn] V **see¹**.

seep [siːp] v suinter, filtrer. **seepage** n suintement m; (leak) fuite f.

seesaw ['siːsɔː] n bascule f. v osciller.

seethe [siːð] v bouillir, bouillonner. **seething** adj (coll) furibond.

segment ['segmənt] n segment m; (orange, etc.) quartier m.

segregate ['segrigeit] v séparer, isoler. **segregation** n ségrégation f.

seize [siːz] v saisir; (with force) s'emparer de. **seize up** (tech) se gripper; (med) s'ankyloser. **seizure** n saisie f; capture f; (med) crise f.

seldom ['seldəm] adv rarement.

select [si'lekt] v sélectionner, choisir. adj choisi; (club, etc.) fermé. **selection** n sélection f. **selective** adj sélectif.

self [self] n moi m.

self-adhesive adj auto-adhésif.

self-assured adj plein d'assurance. **self-assurance** n assurance f.

self-centred adj égocentrique.

self-coloured adj uni.

self-confident adj sûr de soi. **self-confidence** n confiance en soi f.

self-conscious adj gêné. **self-consciousness** n gêne f.

self-contained adj indépendant.

self-control n maîtrise de soi f. **self-controlled** adj maître de soi, maîtresse de soi.

self-defence n légitime défense f.

self-discipline n discipline personelle f.

self-employed adj **be self-employed** travailler à son compte.

self-evident adj qui va de soi.

self-explanatory adj évident en soi.

self-expression n expression libre f.

self-important adj suffisant. **self-importance** n suffisance f.

self-interest n intérêt personnel m.

selfish ['selfiʃ] adj égoïste. **selfishness** n égoïsme m.

selfless ['selfis] adj désintéressé.

self-opinionated adj opiniâtre.

self-pity n apitoiement sur soi-même m.

self-portrait n autoportrait m.

self-possessed adj assuré. **self-possession** n sang-froid m.

self-raising flour n farine à levure f.

self-respect n respect de soi m.

self-righteous adj pharisaïque. **self-righteousness** n pharisaïsme m.

self-sacrifice n abnégation f.

selfsame ['selfseim] *adj* même.

self-satisfied *adj* content de soi.

self-service *n* libre-service *m*.

self-sufficient *adj* indépendant. **self-suffi- ciency** *n* indépendance *f*.

self-taught *adj* autodidacte.

self-willed *adj* entêté.

*sell [sel] *v* (se) vendre; (*coll*) faire accepter. **sell off** solder, liquider. **seller** *n* vendeur, -euse *m, f*; marchand, -e *m, f*.

sellotape ® ['seləteip] *n* scotch ® *m. v* scotcher.

semantic [sə'mantik] *adj* sémantique. **semantics** *n* sémantique *f*.

semaphore ['seməfoɪ] *n* signaux à bras *m pl*; (*rail*) sémaphore *m*.

semblance ['sembləns] *n* semblant *m*.

semen ['siɪmən] *n* sperme *m*, semence *f*.

semibreve ['semibriɪv] *n* ronde *f*.

semicircle ['semisəɪkl] *n* demi-cercle *m*. **semicircular** *adj* demi-circulaire.

semicolon [,semi'koulən] *n* point-virgule *m*.

semi-conscious *adj* à demi conscient.

semi-detached house *n* maison jumelée *f*.

semifinal [semi'fainl] *n* demi-finale *f*.

seminar ['seminɑɪ] *n* séminaire *m*.

semi-precious *adj* semi-précieux.

semiquaver ['semikweivə] *n* double croche *f*.

semitone ['semitoun] *n* demi-ton *m*.

semolina [,semə'liɪnə] *n* semoule *f*; (*pud- ding*) semoule au lait *f*.

senate ['senit] *n* sénat *m*. **senator** *n* sénateur *m*.

*send [send] *v* envoyer; rendre. **send back** renvoyer. **send for** faire venir; (*mail- order*) se faire envoyer.

senile ['siɪnail] *adj* sénile. **senility** *n* sénilité *f*.

senior ['siɪnjə] *adj* (*age*) aîné; (*rank*) supérieur, -e. *n* aîné, -e *m, f*; (*school*) grand, -e *m, f*. **seniority** *n* (*rank*) supéri- orité *f*; (*service*) ancienneté *f*; priorité d'âge *f*.

sensation [sen'seiʃən] *n* sensation *f*. **sen- sational** *adj* sensationnel; (*newspaper*) à sensation.

sense [sens] *n* sens *m*; sensation *f*; (*feel- ing*) sentiment *m*; (*wisdom*) bon sens *m*. **senses** *pl n* raison *f sing. v* sentir. **sense- less** *adj* insensé; (*unconscious*) sans con- naissance.

sensible ['sensəbl] *adj* sensé, raisonnable; (*clothes*) pratique.

sensitive ['sensitiv] *adj* sensible; suscepti- ble; délicat. **sensitivity** *n* sensibilité *f*; susceptibilité *f*; délicatesse *f*.

sensual ['sensjuəl] *adj* sensuel. **sensuality** *n* sensualité *f*.

sensuous ['sensjuəs] *adj* sensuel.

sent [sent] *V* send.

sentence ['sentəns] *n* (*gramm*) phrase *f*; (*law*) condamnation *f. v* condamner.

sentiment ['sentimənt] *n* sentiment *m*; opinion *f*; sentimentalité *f*. **sentimental** *adj* sentimental.

sentry ['sentri] *n* sentinelle *f*.

separate ['sepərət; *v* 'sepəreit] *adj* séparé; indépendant; différent. *v* (se) séparer; diviser. **separation** *n* séparation *f*.

September [sep'tembə] *n* septembre *m*.

septic ['septik] *adj* septique; (*wound*) infecté. **go septic** s'infecter.

sequel ['siɪkwəl] *n* suite *f*, conséquence *f*.

sequence ['siɪkwəns] *n* ordre *m*; (*cards, music*) séquence *f*; (*series*) suite *f*.

sequin ['siɪkwin] *n* paillette *f*.

serenade [serə'neid] *n* sérénade *f*.

serene [sə'riɪn] *adj* serein. **serenity** *n* sér- énité *f*.

serf [səɪf] *n* serf, serve *m, f*.

sergeant ['sɑɪdʒənt] *n* (*mil*) sergent *m*; (*police*) brigadier *m*. **sergeant-major** *n* sergent-major *m*.

serial ['siəriəl] *n* feuilleton *m. adj* de série. **serialize** *v* adapter en feuilleton; publier en feuilleton.

series ['siəriɪz] *n* série *f*.

serious ['siəriəs] *adj* sérieux, grave. **seri- ousness** *n* sérieux *m*, gravité *f*.

sermon ['səɪmən] *n* sermon *m*.

serpent ['səɪpənt] *n* serpent *m*.

serrated [sə'reitid] *adj* dentelé.

servant ['səɪvənt] *n* domestique *m, f*.

serve [səɪv] *v* servir. **it serves you right** c'est bien fait pour toi.

service ['səɪvis] *n* service *m*; (*mot*) révi- sion *f*. **service area** (*mot*) aire de services *f*. **service charge** service *m*. **serviceman** *n* militaire *m*. **service station** (*mot*) station- service *f. v* réviser. **serviceable** *adj* pra- tique, commode.

serviette [,səɪvi'et] *n* serviette *f*. **serviette ring** rond de serviette *m*.

servile ['səɪvail] *adj* servile. **servility** *n* servilité *f*.

session ['seʃən] n séance f. session f.
****set** [set] n jeu m. série f. collection f. (*people*) groupe m; (*TV*) poste m; (*cinema*) plateau m; (*hair*) mise en plis f; (*tennis*) set m. adj fixe. v (*put*) mettre; (*clock*) régler; fixer; (*mount*) monter; (*jelly, etc.*) prendre; (*sun*) se coucher; (*type*) composer. **set about** se mettre à. **setback** n contretemps m, revers m. **set off** (*leave*) partir; faire exploser; (*enhance*) mettre en valeur. **set out** partir; exposer. **set up** dresser; établir; s'installer. **setting** n cadre m; (*gem*) monture f; (*sun*) coucher m.
settee [se'ti] n canapé m.
settle ['setl] v (*problem, account, etc.*) régler; calmer; (*bird*) se poser; (*person*) s'installer. **settle down** se calmer; s'installer. **settle up** (*bill*) régler. **settlement** n règlement m; accord m; colonie f.
seven ['sevn] nm, adj sept. **seventh** n(m+f). adj septième.
seventeen [sevn'tiin] nm, adj dix-sept. **seventeenth** n(m+f). adj dix-septième.
seventy ['sevnti] nm, adj soixante-dix. **seventieth** n(m+f). adj soixante-dixième.
sever ['sevə] v (*cease*) rompre, cesser; (*cut*) couper.
several ['sevrəl] adj, pron plusieurs.
severe [sə'viə] adj sévère; (*hard*) dur; (*illness*) grave. **severity** n sévérité f; intensité f.
****sew** [sou] v coudre. **sewing** n couture f. **sewing machine** machine à coudre f.
sewage ['sjuidʒ] n vidanges f pl. **sewage farm** champ d'épandage m.
sewer ['sjuə] n égout m.
sewn [soun] V **sew.**
sex [seks] n sexe m. **sexual** adj sexuel. **sexual intercourse** rapports sexuels m pl. **sexuality** n sexualité f.
sextet [seks'tet] n sextuor m.
shabby ['ʃabi] adj râpé, minable; (*behaviour*) mesquin.
shack [ʃak] n cabane f.
shade [ʃeid] n ombre f. nuance f; (*lamp*) abat-jour m invar. v ombrager; (*painting*) ombrer; (*drawing*) hachurer. **shady** adj ombragé; (*dishonest*) louche.
shadow ['ʃadou] n ombre f. **shadow cabinet** cabinet fantôme m. v (*follow*) filer. **shadowy** adj ombragé; indistinct.
shaft [ʃaift] n (*tool*) manche m; (*light*) trait m; (*lift*) cage f; (*mine, ventilation*) puits m; (*spear*) hampe f.

shaggy ['ʃagi] adj hirsute.
****shake** [ʃeik] n secousse f; tremblement m. v secouer; (*bottle*) agiter; trembler; (*weaken*) ébranler. **shake hands** serrer la main. **shake off** se débarrasser de. **shaky** adj tremblant; (*weak, unsure*) chancelant.
shaken ['ʃeikn] V **shake.**
shall [ʃal] aux translated by future tense.
shallot [ʃə'lot] n échalote f.
shallow ['ʃalou] adj peu profond; superficiel.
sham [ʃam] n imitation f; comédie f. adj faux, fausse; feint, simulé. v feindre, simuler; jouer la comédie.
shame [ʃeim] n honte f; (*pity*) dommage m. v faire honte à. **shamefaced** adj honteux; timide. **shameful** adj honteux. **shameless** adj éhonté; impudique.
shampoo [ʃam'puː] n shampooing m. v faire un shampooing à.
shamrock ['ʃamrok] n trèfle m.
shandy ['ʃandi] n panaché m.
shanty[1] ['ʃanti] n (*hut*) baraque f. **shanty town** bidonville m.
shanty[2] ['ʃanti] n chanson de marins f.
shape [ʃeip] n forme f. v façonner; prendre forme. **shapeless** adj informe. **shapely** adj bien fait, bien proportionné.
share [ʃeə] n part f; (*comm*) action f. **shareholder** n actionnaire m, f. v partager.
shark [ʃaik] n requin m.
sharp [ʃaip] adj aigu, -guë; (*point*) pointu; (*edge*) tranchant; (*sudden*) brusque; (*outline*) net, nette; (*pain, wind*) vif. n (*music*) dièse m. **sharpen** v aiguiser; (*pencil*) tailler; (*outline*) rendre plus net. **sharpness** n tranchant m; netteté f.
shatter ['ʃatə] v (*se*) fracasser; briser; ruiner. **shattered** adj bouleversé; (*tired*) éreinté. **shattering** adj bouleversant.
shave [ʃeiv] v (*se*) raser. **shaving** n (*of wood, metal*) copeau m. **shaving brush** blaireau m. **shaving cream** crème à raser f.
shawl [ʃoil] n châle m.
she [ʃiː] pron elle. **she who** celle qui. n (*coll*) femelle f.
sheaf [ʃiːf] n (*corn*) gerbe f; (*papers*) liasse f; (*arrows*) faisceau m.
****shear** [ʃiə] v tondre. **shears** pl n cisailles f pl.

sheath [ʃiːθ] n gaine f; (sword) fourreau m; (scissors) étui m. **sheathe** v rengainer; recouvrir.

*shed[1] [ʃed] v (drop) perdre; (radiate) répandre.

shed[2] [ʃed] n remise f, hutte f.

sheen [ʃiːn] n lustre m, éclat m.

sheep [ʃiːp] n mouton m. **sheep-dog** n chien de berger m. **sheepskin** n peau de mouton f. **sheepish** adj penaud.

sheer[1] [ʃiə] adj pur, absolu; (cliff) à pic; (stockings) extrêmement fin.

sheer[2] [ʃiə] v (naut) faire une embardée.

sheet [ʃiːt] n (bed) drap m; (paper) feuille f; (ice, metal) plaque f. **sheet lightning** éclair en nappe m. **sheet music** partitions f pl.

sheikh [ʃeik] n cheik m.

shelf [ʃelf] n rayon m, étagère f.

shell [ʃel] n coquille f; (tortoise, crab) carapace f; (from beach) coquillage m; (mil) obus m. **shellfish** n coquillage m; (pl: as food) fruits de mer m pl. v (nut, shrimp) décortiquer; (peas) écosser; (mil) bombarder.

shelter [ʃeltə] n abri m. v (s')abriter; protéger; (lodge) recueillir.

shelve [ʃelv] v (project) mettre en sommeil. **shelving** n rayonnage m.

shepherd [ʃepəd] n berger m. **shepherd's pie** hachis Parmentier m.

sheriff [ʃerif] n shérif m.

sherry [ʃeri] n xérès m.

shield [ʃiːld] n bouclier; (screen) écran m. v protéger.

shift [ʃift] n changement m; (work) poste m. **shift key** touche de majuscule f. **shift work** travail en équipe m. v déplacer, bouger; changer (de place). **shifty** adj louche.

shimmer [ʃimə] v miroiter, chatoyer. n miroitement m, chatoiement m.

shin [ʃin] n tibia m.

*shine [ʃain] n éclat m, brillant m. v briller. **shiny** adj brillant, reluisant.

shingle [ʃingl] n galets m pl.

ship [ʃip] n bateau m; (larger) navire m. **shipbuilding** n construction navale f. **shipshape** adj bien rangé. **shipwreck** n naufrage m. **be shipwrecked** faire naufrage. **shipyard** n chantier naval m. v transporter; (send) expédier; (take on) embarquer. **shipment** n cargaison m. **shipping** n navigation f.

shirk [ʃəːk] v esquiver. **shirker** n (coll) tire-au-flanc m invar.

shirt [ʃəːt] n chemise f. **in one's shirt sleeves** en bras de chemise. **shirtwaister** n robe chemisier f.

shit [ʃit] nf, interj (vulgar) merde.

shiver [ʃivə] v frissonner. n frisson m. **shivery** adj frissonnant, fiévreux.

shoal [ʃoul] n (fish) banc m.

shock [ʃok] n choc m; (elec) décharge f. **shock absorber** amortisseur m. **shockproof** adj anti-choc invar. **shock treatment** électrochoc m. v secouer, bouleverser; dégoûter; (scandalize) choquer. **shocking** adj affreux, atroce; scandaleux.

shod [ʃod] V shoe.

shoddy [ʃodi] adj de mauvaise qualité. **shoddiness** n mauvaise qualité f.

*shoe [ʃuː] n chaussure f, soulier m. **shoehorn** n chausse-pied m. **shoe-lace** n lacet de soulier m. **shoemaker** n cordonnier m. **shoe repairer's** cordonnerie f. v (horse) ferrer.

shone [ʃon] V shine.

shook [ʃuk] V shake.

*shoot [ʃuːt] v (fire) tirer, lancer; (kill) abattre; (hit) atteindre d'un coup de fusil; (goal) shooter; (film) tourner; (go quickly) aller en flèche. n (bot) pousse f. **shooting** n fusillade f; (hunting) chasse f.

shop [ʃop] n magasin m; (smaller) boutique f; (in factory) atelier m. **shop assistant** vendeur, -euse m, f. **shop-floor** n ouvriers m pl. **shopkeeper** n marchand, -e. **shoplifting** n vol à l'étalage m. **shopsoiled** adj défraîchi. **shop-steward** n délégué syndical m. **shop-window** n vitrine f. v faire ses courses. **shopping** n achats m pl. **go shopping** faire des courses. **shopping bag** sac à provisions m. **shopping centre** centre commercial m.

shore [ʃoː] n (beach) plage f; (of sea) rivage m; (coast) littoral m.

shorn [ʃoːn] V shear.

short [ʃoːt] adj court; bref, brève; insuffisant; brusque. **in short** en bref. **shortage** n manque m, pénurie f. **shorten** v raccourcir. **shortly** adv bientôt.

shortbread [ʃoːtbred] n sablé m.

short-circuit n court-circuit m. v court-circuiter.

shortcoming [ʃoːtkʌmiŋ] n défaut m.

short cut n raccourci m.

shorthand ['ʃɔːthænd] *n* sténographie *f.* **shorthand typist** sténodactylo *m, f.*

short list *n* liste de candidats sélectionnés *f.*

short-lived [ʃɔːt'lɪvd] *adj* de courte durée.

shorts [ʃɔːts] *pl n* short *m sing.*

short-sighted *adj* myope.

short story *n* nouvelle *f.*

short-tempered *adj* coléreux.

short-term *adj* à court terme.

short wave *n* ondes courtes *f pl.* **à** ou sur ondes courtes.

shot[1] [ʃɔt] *V* shoot.

shot[2] [ʃɔt] *n* coup *m;* (*lead*) plomb *m;* (*try*) essai *m;* photo *f.* **shotgun** *n* fusil de chasse *m.*

should[1] [ʃud] *aux translated by conditional tense.*

should[2] [ʃud] *aux translated by conditional tense of* devoir.

shoulder ['ʃəuldə] *n* épaule *f;* (*road*) accotement *m.* **shoulder-bag** *n* sac à bandoulière *m.* **shoulder-blade** *n* omoplate *f.* *v* endosser.

shout [ʃaut] *n* cri *m.* *v* crier.

shove [ʃʌv] *n* poussée *f.* *v* pousser.

shovel [ʃʌvl] *n* pelle *f.* *v* pelleter.

*****show** [ʃəu] *n* démonstration *f;* (*flowers, etc.*) exposition *f;* (*theatre*) spectacle *m;* apparence *f;* (*ostentation*) parade *f.* **show business** le monde du spectacle *m.* **show-case** *n* vitrine *f.* **show-down** *n* épreuve de force *f.* **show-jumping** *n* concours hippique *m.* **show-room** *n* salle d'exposition *f.* *v* montrer; (*be visible*) se voir. **show in** faire entrer. **show off** (*coll*) crâner. **show up** être visible; (*coll: arrive*) se pointer; (*embarrass*) faire honte à.

shower ['ʃauə] *n* (*rain*) averse *f;* (*bath*) douche *f.* **shower-proof** *adj* imperméable. *v* combler, accabler. **showery** *adj* pluvieux.

shown [ʃəun] *V* show.

shrank [ʃræŋk] *V* shrink.

shred [ʃred] *n* lambeau *m;* (*small amount*) grain *m.* *v* déchiqueter.

shrew [ʃruː] *n* (*zool*) musaraigne *f;* (*woman*) mégère *f.*

shrewd [ʃruːd] *adj* perspicace, astucieux.

shriek [ʃriːk] *n* hurlement *m,* cri perçant *m.* *v* hurler, crier.

shrill [ʃrɪl] *adj* perçant; (*whistle*) strident.

shrimp [ʃrɪmp] *n* crevette *f.*

shrine [ʃraɪn] *n* châsse *f;* lieu saint *m.*

*****shrink** [ʃriŋk] *v* rétrécir; reculer. **shrinkage** *n* rétrécissement *m.*

shrivel ['ʃrɪvl] *v* se ratatiner, se flétrir.

shroud [ʃraud] *n* linceul *m;* (*mist*) voile *m.* *v* ensevelir.

Shrove Tuesday [ʃrouv] *n* mardi gras *m.*

shrub [ʃrʌb] *n* arbrisseau *m,* arbuste *m.* **shrubbery** *n* massif d'arbustes *m.*

shrug [ʃrʌg] *v* hausser (les épaules). *n* haussement d'épaules *m.*

shrunk [ʃrʌŋk] *V* shrink.

shudder ['ʃʌdə] *n* frisson *m;* (*engine*) vibration *f.* *v* frissonner, frémir; vibrer.

shuffle ['ʃʌfl] *n* traîner les pieds; (*cards*) battre. *n* battage *m;* réorganisation *f.*

shun [ʃʌn] *v* fuir, éviter.

shunt [ʃʌnt] *v* (*rail*) aiguiller, manœuvrer.

*****shut** [ʃʌt] *v* fermer. **shut in** enfermer, entourer. **shut up** (*coll*) se taire, faire taire.

shutter ['ʃʌtə] *n* (*window*) volet *m;* (*phot*) obturateur *m.*

shuttle ['ʃʌtl] *n* navette *f.* **shuttlecock** *n* volant *m.* **shuttle service** service de navette *m.*

shy [ʃaɪ] *adj* timide. *v* (*horse*) se cabrer. **shyness** *n* timidité *f.*

Siamese [ˌsaɪə'miːz] *adj* (*cat, twin*) siamois.

sick [sɪk] *adj* malade; (*mind, humour*) malsain. **be sick** vomir. **be sick of** (*coll*) avoir marre de. **feel sick** avoir mal au cœur. **sick bay** infirmerie *f.* **sicken** *v* écœurer. **sicken for** couver. **sickening** *adj* écœurant; (*coll*) agaçant. **sickly** *adj* (*person*) maladif; pâle; (*cake*) écœurant. **sickness** *n* maladie *f;* vomissements *m pl.*

sickle ['sɪkl] *n* faucille *f.*

side [saɪd] *n* côté *m;* (*hill, animal*) flanc *m;* (*edge*) bord *m;* (*team*) équipe *f;* (*in argument, etc.*) camp *m.* *v* **side with** prendre parti pour.

sideboard ['saɪdbɔːd] *n* buffet *m.*

side-effect *n* effet secondaire *m.*

sidelight ['saɪdlaɪt] *n* (*mot*) lanterne *f.*

sideline ['saɪdlaɪn] *n* activité secondaire *f;* (*sport*) touche *f.*

sidelong ['saɪdlɒŋ] *adj, adv* de côté.

side-show *n* attraction *f.*

side-step *v* éviter.

side-street *n* petite rue *f.*

side-track *v* faire dévier.

sidewalk ['saɪdwɔːk] *n* (*US*) trottoir *m.*

sideways ['saɪdweɪz] *adj* oblique. *adv* de côté; (*walk*) en crabe.

siding ['saidiŋ] n (rail) voie de garage f.
sidle ['saidl] v marcher de côté; avancer furtivement. **sidle up to** se glisser vers.
siege [siːdʒ] n siège m.
sieve [siv] n tamis m; (coal) crible m. v tamiser; cribler.
sift [sift] v (food) tamiser; (coal) cribler; (evidence) passer au crible. **sift out** dégager. **sifter** n (flour) saupoudreuse f.
sigh [sai] n soupir m. v soupirer.
sight [sait] n vue f; spectacle m; (on gun) mire f. **sight-read** v déchiffrer. **sightseeing** n tourisme m. v apercevoir.
sign [sain] n signe m; (notice) panneau m. **signpost** n poteau indicateur m. v signer.
signal ['signəl] n signal m. v faire signe (à); faire des signaux.
signature ['signətʃə] n signature f. **signature tune** indicatif musical m.
signify ['signifai] v signifier. **significance** n signification f. **significant** adj significatif; considérable.
silence ['sailəns] n silence m. v réduire au silence, faire taire. **silencer** n silencieux m. **silent** adj silencieux.
silhouette [silu'et] n silhouette f. v be **silhouetted against** se découper contre.
silk [silk] n soie f. **silkworm** n ver à soie m. **silky** adj soyeux.
sill [sil] n rebord m; (mot) bas de marche m.
silly ['sili] adj bête, idiot. **silliness** n sottise f.
silt [silt] n vase f. v **silt up** envaser.
silver ['silvə] n argent m; (cutlery, etc.) argenterie f; (change) monnaie f. adj d'argent; en argent. **silver birch** bouleau argenté m. **silver paper** papier d'argent m. **silversmith** n orfèvre m, f. v argenter. **silvery** adj argenté.
similar ['similə] adj semblable. **similarity** n ressemblance f.
simile ['simili] n comparaison f.
simmer ['simə] v (faire) cuire à feu doux, mijoter; (anger) couver. **simmer down** (coll) se calmer.
simple ['simpl] adj simple. **simpleton** n nigaud. -e m, f. **simplicity** n simplicité f. **simplify** v simplifier. **simply** adv simplement; absolument.
simulate ['simjuleit] v simuler. **simulation** n simulation f.
simultaneous [siməl'teinjəs] adj simultané.
sin [sin] n péché m. v pécher. **sinful** adj

coupable; scandaleux. **sinner** n pécheur. -eresse m, f.
since [sins] prep, adv depuis. conj depuis que; (because) puisque.
sincere [sin'siə] adj sincère. **sincerity** n sincérité f.
sinew ['sinjut] n tendon m.
*****sing** [siŋ] v chanter. **singer** n chanteur, -euse m, f. **singing** n chant m.
singe [sindʒ] v brûler légèrement, roussir. n légère brûlure f.
single ['siŋgl] adj seul; (not double) simple; célibataire. **single bed** lit d'une personne m. **single file** file indienne f. **single-handed** adv tout seul; (sail) en solitaire. **single-minded** adj résolu. **single ticket** aller simple m. **single room** chambre à une f. n (ticket) aller simple m; (record) 45 tours m. **singles** n (sport) simple m. v **single out** distinguer; choisir.
singular ['siŋgjulə] nm, adj singulier.
sinister ['sinistə] adj sinistre.
*****sink** [siŋk] v (go under) couler; (collapse) s'affaisser; (go down) baisser; (mine) creuser. **sink in** (idea, etc.) rentrer, pénétrer. n évier m. **sink unit** bloc-évier m.
sinuous ['sinjuəs] adj sinueux.
sinus ['sainəs] n sinus m invar. **sinusitis** n sinusite f.
sip [sip] n petite gorgée f. v boire à petites gorgées.
siphon ['saifən] n siphon m. v siphonner.
sir [səː] n monsieur m; (knight) sir m.
siren ['saiərən] n sirène f.
sirloin ['səːloin] n aloyau f.
sister ['sistə] n sœur f; religieuse f; (hospital) infirmière en chef f. **sister-in-law** n belle-sœur f.
*****sit** [sit] v (s')asseoir; (clothes) tomber; (committee) être en séance; (exam) passer. **sit down** s'asseoir. **sit-in** n sit-in m invar. **sit up** se redresser; (stay up) ne pas se coucher. **sitting** n séance f; (meal) service m. **sitting room** salon m. **sitting tenant** locataire en place m, f.
site [sait] n emplacement m; (building) chantier m; camping m. v placer.
situation [sitju'eifən] n situation f; emploi m. **situate** v placer, situer.
six [siks] nm, adj six. **sixth** n(m+f), adj sixième. **sixth form** classes de première et terminale f pl.
sixteen [siks'tiːn] nm, adj seize. **sixteenth** n(m+f), adj seizième.

sixty ['siksti] *nm, adj* soixante. **sixtieth** *n*(*m*+*f*), *adj* soixantième.

size [saiz] *n* taille *f*; grandeur *f*; dimensions *f pl*; (*shoes*) pointure *f*. **v size up** mesurer, juger. **sizeable** *adj* assez grand.

sizzle ['sizl] *v* grésiller. *n* grésillement *m*.

skate¹ [skeit] *n* patin *m*. **skateboard** *n* planche à roulettes *f*. *v* patiner. **skater** *n* patineur, -euse *m, f*. **skating** *n* patinage *m*.

skate² [skeit] *n* (*fish*) raie *f*.

skeleton ['skelitn] *n* squelette *m*. *adj* (*staff, etc.*) squelettique. **skeleton key** passe-partout *m invar*.

sketch [sketʃ] *n* croquis *m*; (*rough*) ébauche *f*; (*theatre*) sketch *m*. *v* esquisser. **sketchy** *adj* incomplet, -ète.

skewer ['skjuə] *n* brochette *f*. *v* embrocher.

ski [skiː] *n* ski *m*. **ski-lift** *n* remonte-pente *m*, remontée mécanique *f*. *v* faire du ski. **skier** *n* skieur, -euse *m, f*. **skiing** *n* ski *m*.

skid [skid] *n* dérapage *m*. *v* déraper.

skill [skil] *n* habileté *f*; technique *f*. **skilful** *adj* habile. **skilled** *adj* habile, adroit; (*worker*) qualifié.

skim [skim] *v* (*milk*) écrémer; (*surface*) raser; (*reading*) parcourir.

skimp [skimp] *v* lésiner (sur), économiser. **skimpy** *adj* insuffisant, maigre.

skin [skin] *n* peau *f*. **skin-diving** plongée sous-marine *f*. **skin-tight** *adj* collant. *v* (*animal*) dépouiller; (*fruit, vegetable*) éplucher. **skinny** *adj* maigrelet.

skip [skip] *n* petit saut *m*. *v* gambader; sauter à la corde; (*miss*) sauter. **skipping** *n* saut à la corde *m*. **skipping rope** corde à sauter *f*.

skipper ['skipə] *n* capitaine *m*.

skirmish ['skəːmiʃ] *n* escarmouche *f*.

skirt [skəːt] *n* jupe *f*. *v* contourner. **skirting board** plinthe *f*.

skittle [skitl] *n* quille *f*. **skittles** *n* jeu de quilles *m*.

skull [skʌl] *n* crâne *m*. **skull and crossbones** tête de mort *f*.

skunk [skʌŋk] *n* mouffette *f*.

sky [skai] *n* ciel *m*. **sky-blue** *nm, adj* bleu ciel. **skylark** *n* alouette *f*. **skylight** *n* lucarne *f*. **skyline** *n* ligne d'horizon *f*. **skyscraper** *n* gratte-ciel *m invar*.

slab [slab] *n* bloc *m*, plaque *f*; (*paving*) dalle *f*; (*butcher's*) étal *m*.

slack [slak] *adj* (*loose*) lâche; (*trade*) faible; (*person*) négligent, peu sérieux. *n*

mou *m*. **slacken** *v* (se) relâcher; diminuer. **slacker** *n* (*coll*) flemmard, -e *m, f*.

slacks [slaks] *pl n* pantalon *m sing*.

slag [slag] *n* scories *f pl*. **slag heap** (*mining*) terril *m*.

slalom ['slɑːləm] *n* slalom *m*.

slam [slam] *n* claquement *m*. *v* claquer. **slam on the brakes** freiner à mort.

slander ['slɑːndə] *n* calomnie *f*; (*law*) diffamation *f*. *v* calomnier; diffamer. **slanderous** *adj* calomnieux; diffamatoire.

slang [slaŋ] *n* argot *m*.

slant [slɑːnt] *n* inclinaison *f*; angle *m*. *v* (faire) pencher. **slanting** *adj* incliné, penché.

slap [slap] *n* claque *f*; (*on face*) gifle *f*. *v* donner une claque à; gifler; (*coll: put*) flanquer. **slapdash** *adj* (*person*) négligent; (*work*) bâclé. **slapstick** *n* grosse farce *f*. **slap-up meal** (*coll*) repas fameux *m*.

slash [slaʃ] *n* entaille *f*. *v* entailler, taillader; (*coll: prices*) casser.

slat [slat] *n* lame *f*; (*of blind*) lamelle *f*.

slate [sleit] *n* ardoise *f*. *v* ardoiser; (*coll: criticize*) éreinter.

slaughter ['slɔːtə] *n* abattage *m*; (*people*) carnage *m*. **slaughterhouse** *n* abattoir *m*. *v* abattre; massacrer.

slave [sleiv] *n* esclave *m, f*. **slave-driver** *n* négrier, -ère *m, f*. *v* trimer. **slavery** *n* esclavage *m*.

sledge [sledʒ] *n* luge *f*; (*drawn by animal*) traîneau *m*.

sledgehammer ['sledʒhamə] *n* marteau de forgeron *m*.

sleek [sliːk] *adj* lisse, brillant.

*sleep [sliːp] *n* sommeil *m*. **go to sleep** s'endormir. **sleepwalker** *n* somnambule *m, f*. *v* dormir; (*spend the night*) coucher. **sleep in** faire la grasse matinée. **sleeper** *n* train-couchettes *m*; (*wooden beam*) traverse *f*. **sleeping-bag** *n* sac de couchage *m*. **sleeping-pill** *n* somnifère *m*. **sleepless night** nuit blanche *f*. **sleepy** *adj* endormi, somnolent.

sleet [sliːt] *n* neige fondue *f*.

sleeve [sliːv] *n* manche *f*; (*record*) pochette *f*. **sleeveless** *adj* sans manches.

sleigh [slei] *n* traîneau *m*.

slender ['slendə] *adj* svelte; fin; faible; maigre.

slept [slept] *V* **sleep**.

slice [slais] *n* tranche *f*; partie *f*. *v* couper en tranches.

slick [slik] *adj* (*derog*) facile, superficiel.

slid [slid] *V* **slide**.

*****slide** [slaid] *n* glissade *f*; (*chute*) toboggan *m*; (*microscope*) porte-objet *m*; (*phot*) diapositive *f*; (*hair*) barrette *f*. **slide-rule** *n* règle à calcul *f*. *v* (se) glisser. **sliding** *adj* glissant; (*door, etc.*) coulissant.

slight [slait] *adj* petit, faible; (*person*) mince. *v* offenser. *n* offense *f*. **slightest** *adj* moindre. **slightly** *adv* un peu.

slim [slim] *adj* mince; faible. *v* (faire) maigrir. **slimming** *adj* (*diet, etc.*) amaigrissant.

slime [slaim] *n* vase *f*, limon *m*. **slimy** *adj* visqueux.

*****sling** [slin] *n* (*med*) écharpe *f*; (*weapon*) fronde *f*. *v* lancer; suspendre.

*****slink away** [sliŋk] *v* **slink away** s'en aller furtivement.

slip [slip] *n* erreur *f*; (*of paper*) bout *m*, fiche *f*; (*underskirt*) combinaison *f*. **slip of the tongue** *or* **pen** lapsus *m*. *v* (se) glisser. **slip-knot** *n* nœud coulant *m*. **slip-road** *n* bretelle d'accès *f*. **slipshod** *adj* négligé, négligent. **slipway** *n* cale *f*.

slipper [slipə] *n* pantoufle *f*.

slippery [slipəri] *adj* glissant.

*****slit** [slit] *n* fente *f*, incision *f*. *v* fendre, inciser.

slither [sliðə] *v* glisser, déraper.

slobber [slobə] *v* baver. *n* bave *f*.

sloe [slou] *n* prunelle *f*.

slog [slog] *n* gros effort *m*. *v* travailler très dur; (*ball*) donner un grand coup à.

slogan [slougən] *n* slogan *m*.

slop [slop] *v* (*spill*) répandre; (*overflow*) déborder.

slope [sloup] *n* inclinaison *f*; (*hill*) côte *f*. *v* être incliné. **sloping** *adj* en pente, incliné.

sloppy [slopi] *adj* (*food*) liquide; (*dress*) négligé; (*garment*) mal ajusté; (*coll: work*) bâclé.

slot [slot] *n* fente *f*. **slot-machine** *n* (*vending*) distributeur automatique *m*; (*gambling*) machine à sous *f*. *v* (s')emboîter; (s')insérer.

slouch [slautʃ] *v* se tenir mal.

slovenly [slʌvnli] *adj* négligé.

slow [slou] *adj* lent. *adv* lentement. **in slow motion** au ralenti. **slowcoach** *n* (*coll*) lambin, -e *m, f*. *v* **slow down** ralentir.

slug [slʌg] *n* (*zool*) limace *f*; (*bullet*) balle *f*.

sluggish [slʌgiʃ] *adj* lent, paresseux.

sluice [sluːs] *n* écluse *f*. *v* laver à grande eau.

slum [slʌm] *n* taudis *m*. **slums** *pl n* quartiers pauvres *m pl*.

slumber [slʌmbə] *n* sommeil paisible *m*. *v* dormir paisiblement.

slump [slʌmp] *n* baisse soudaine *f*; récession *f*, crise *f*. *v* s'effondrer.

slung [slʌŋ] *V* **sling**.

slunk [slʌŋk] *V* **slink**.

slur [slə] *n* tache *f*; insulte *f*; (*music*) liaison *f*. *v* mal articuler; (*music*) lier.

slush [slʌʃ] *n* neige fondante *f*.

slut [slʌt] *n* souillon *f*.

sly [slai] *adj* rusé, sournois.

smack¹ [smak] *n* tape *f*, claque *f*; (*sound*) claquement *m*. *v* donner une tape *or* claque à.

smack² [smak] *v* **smack of** sentir. *n* léger goût *m*.

small [smɔːl] *adj* petit; peu nombreux. **feel small** se sentir honteux. **small change** petite monnaie *f*. **smallholding** *n* petite ferme *f*. **smallpox** *n* variole *f*. **small talk** papotage *m*. **n small of the back** creux des reins *m*.

smart [smɑːt] *adj* chic *invar*, élégant; intelligent, astucieux; rapide, vif. *v* brûler, piquer. **smarten up** devenir plus élégant; rendre plus élégant. **smartness** *n* élégance *f*; intelligence *f*.

smash [smaʃ] *n* (*sound*) fracas *m*; accident *m*, collision *f*; (*blow*) coup violent *m*. *v* (se) briser (en mille morceaux), (se) fracasser. **smashing** *adj* (*slang*) formidable.

smear [smiə] *n* tache *f*. *v* (se) salir, barbouiller.

*****smell** [smel] *n* odeur *f*; (*sense*) odorat *m*. *v* sentir; (*sniff*) flairer. **smelly** *adj* malodorant.

smelt [smelt] *V* **smell**.

smile [smail] *n* sourire *m*. *v* sourire.

smirk [smɜːk] *n* petit sourire satisfait *m*. *v* sourire d'un air satisfait.

smock [smok] *n* blouse *f*. **smocking** *n* smocks *m pl*.

smog [smog] *n* brouillard enfumé *m*.

*****smoke** [smouk] *n* fumée *f*. **smoke-screen** *n* paravent *m*. *v* fumer. **smoker** *n* fumeur, -euse *m, f*. **no smoking** défense de fumer. **smoky** *adj* enfumé.

smooth [smuːð] adj lisse; régulier; (person) doucereux. v lisser. **smooth out** faire disparaître. **smoothly** adv facilement, doucement; (move) sans secousses; sans incident.

smother ['smʌðə] v étouffer.

smoulder v couver.

smudge [smʌdʒ] n tache f. v (s')étaler, (se) maculer.

smug [smʌg] adj suffisant.

smuggle ['smʌgl] v passer en contrebande; passer clandestinement. **smuggler** n contrebandier, -ère m, f. **smuggling** n contrebande f.

snack [snak] n casse-croûte m invar. **snack-bar** n snack-bar m.

snag [snag] n inconvénient m, obstacle caché m; (in cloth) accroc m. v accrocher.

snail [sneil] n escargot m.

snake [sneik] n serpent m. v serpenter.

snap [snap] n bruit sec m, claquement m, craquement m; photo f. adj subit, irréfléchi. **snapdragon** n gueule-de-loup f. **snapshot** n photo f. v (se) casser net; (faire) claquer; (dog) essayer de mordre; (person) parler d'un ton brusque.

snare [snɛə] n piège m. v attraper.

snarl [snaːl] n grondement m. v gronder.

snatch [snatʃ] n fragment m; (theft) vol m. v saisir, arracher (à).

sneak [sniːk] v se faufiler; (slang: school) moucharder. **sneak in/out** entrer/sortir furtivement. n (coll) mouchard, -e m, f.

sneer [snɪə] v ricaner. n ricanement m. **sneering** adj ricaneur, -euse.

sneeze [sniːz] n éternuement m. v éternuer.

sniff [snif] n reniflement m. v renifler; (air, aroma) humer.

snigger ['snigə] n petit rire moqueur m. v pouffer de rire.

snip [snip] v couper à petits coups.

snipe [snaip] n bécassine f. v canarder. **sniper** n canardeur m.

snivel ['snivl] v pleurnicher. **snivelling** adj pleurnicheur, -euse.

snob [snob] n snob m, f. **snobbish** adj snob invar.

snooker ['snuːkə] n jeu de billard m.

snoop [snuːp] v (coll) fureter, fourrer son nez.

snooty ['snuːti] adj (coll) hautain.

snooze [snuːz] n roupillon m. v piquer un roupillon.

snore [snɔː] n ronflement m. v ronfler. **snoring** n ronflements m pl.

snorkel ['snɔːkl] n (swimmer) tuba m; (submarine) schnorchel m.

snort [snɔːt] n (person) grognement m; (animal) ébrouement m. v grogner; s'ébrouer.

snout [snaut] n museau m.

snow [snou] n neige f. v neiger. **snow-drift** n congère f. **snowdrop** n perce-neige m. **snow-flake** n flocon de neige m. **snowman** n bonhomme de neige m. **snow-plough** n chasse-neige m invar. **snow-shoe** n raquette f. **snowstorm** n tempête de neige f. v neiger. **be snowed under with** être submergé de. **snowy** adj neigeux; de neige.

snowball ['snoubɔːl] n boule de neige f. v (increase) faire boule de neige.

snub [snʌb] n rebuffade f. v (person) snober; repousser.

snuff [snʌf] n tabac à priser. **snuffbox** n tabatière f. **take snuff** priser.

snug [snʌg] adj douillet, -ette, confortable.

snuggle ['snʌgl] v se blottir, se pelotonner.

so [sou] adv si, tellement, aussi; (thus) ainsi. conj donc. **and so on** et ainsi de suite. **if so** si oui. **is that so?** vraiment? **... or so** à peu près .... **so as to** afin de. **so-called** adj soi-disant invar. **so much or many** tant (de). **so-so** adj (coll) comme ci comme ça. **so that** pour (que). **so what?** et alors?

soak [souk] v (faire) tremper. **soak in** pénétrer. **soak up** absorber. **soaking** n trempage m. **soaking wet** trempé.

soap [soup] n savon m. **soap-box** n tribune improvisée f. **soap-dish** n porte-savon m. **soap opera** (coll) mélo à épisodes m. **soap powder** lessive f. v savonner. **soapy** adj savonneux.

soar [sɔː] v monter en flèche; (hope) grandir.

sob [sob] n sanglot m. v sangloter.

sober ['soubə] adj sérieux; modéré; (not drunk) pas ivre. v **sober up** désenivrer.

soccer ['sokə] n football m.

sociable ['souʃəbl] adj sociable.

social ['souʃəl] adj social; (life, etc.) mondain. **social club** association amicale f. **social science** sciences humaines f pl. **social security** aide sociale f. **social work** assistance sociale f. **socialism** n social-

171   **sound**

isme *m*. **socialist** *n*(*m*+*f*), *adj* socialiste.
socialize *v* fréquenter des gens.
society [sə'saiəti] *n* société *f*.
sociology [sousi'olədʒi] *n* sociologie *f*.
sociological *adj* sociologique. **sociologist**
n sociologue *m, f*.
sock [sok] *n* chaussette *f*.
socket ['sokit] *n* cavité *f*; (*elec*) prise de
courant *f*.
soda ['soudə] *n* (*chem*) soude *f*; (*water*)
eau de Seltz *f*.
sodden ['sodn] *adj* détrempé.
sofa ['soufə] *n* sofa *m*.
Sofia ['soufjə] *n* Sofia.
soft [soft] *adj* doux, douce; (*butter, clay,
etc.*) mou, molle; (*coll*) stupide. **soft-
boiled** (*egg*) à la coque. **soft drink**
boisson non alcoolisée *f*. **soft toy** jouet
de peluche *m*. **soften** *v* (s')adoucir; (*se*)
ramollir. **softness** *n* douceur *f*; mollesse
f.
soggy ['sogi] *adj* détrempé.
soil[1] [soil] *n* sol *m*, terre *f*.
soil[2] *v* salir.
solar ['soulə] *adj* solaire, du soleil.
sold [sould] *V* **sell**.
solder ['soldə] *n* soudure *f*. *v* souder. **soldering iron** fer à souder *m*.
soldier ['souldʒə] *n* soldat *m*. *v* **soldier on**
persévérer.
sole[1] [soul] *adj* seul, unique; exclusif.
sole[2] [soul] *n* (*of shoe*) semelle *f*; (*of foot*)
plante *f*. *v* ressemeler.
sole[3] [soul] *n* (*fish*) sole *f*.
solemn ['soləm] *adj* solennel. **solemnity** *n*
solennité *f*.
solicitor [sə'lisitə] *n* avocat *m*.
solicitude [sə'lisitjuːd] *n* sollicitude *f*.
solid ['solid] *adj* solide; (*not hollow*) plein;
(*line*) continu. *n* solide *m*. **solids** *pl n*
(*food*) aliments solides *m pl*. **solidarity** *n*
solidarité *f*. **solidify** *v* (se) solidifier; (se)
congeler.
solitary ['solitəri] *adj* solitaire; seul,
unique.
solitude ['solitjuːd] *n* solitude *f*.
solo ['soulou] *n* solo *m*. *adj* solo *invar*;
(*flight*) en solitaire. **soloist** *n* soliste *m, f*.
solstice ['solstis] *n* solstice *m*.
soluble ['soljubl] *adj* soluble.
solution [sə'luːʃən] *n* solution *f*.
solve [solv] *v* résoudre, trouver la solution de.
solvent ['solvənt] *adj* (*finance*) solvable. *n*

(*chem*) solvant *m*. **solvency** *n* solvabilité
f.
sombre ['sombə] *adj* sombre, morne.
some [sʌm] *adj* du, de la; (*pl*) des;
certains; (*unspecified*) quelque. *pron*
quelques-uns; (*before verb*) en. *adv* environ. **somebody** or **someone** *pron*
quelqu'un. **somehow** *adv* d'une façon ou
d'une autre. **something** *pron* quelque
chose. **sometime** *adv* un de ces jours.
sometimes *adv* quelquefois. **somewhat**
adv quelque peu. **somewhere** *adv* quelque
part. **somewhere else** ailleurs.
somersault ['sʌməsoːlt] *n* culbute *f*. *v*
faire la culbute.
son [sʌn] *n* fils *m*. **son-in-law** *n* gendre *m*.
sonata [sə'naːtə] *n* sonate *f*.
song [soŋ] *n* chanson *f*; (*birds*) chant *m*.
sonic ['sonik] *adj* sonique. **sonic boom**
détonation supersonique *f*.
sonnet ['sonit] *n* sonnet *m*.
soon [suːn] *adv* bientôt; (*early*) tôt. **as
soon as** dès que. **sooner or later** tôt ou
tard.
soot [sut] *n* suie *f*.
soothe [suːð] *v* calmer, apaiser. **soothing**
adj apaisant; (*ointment*) lénitif.
sophisticated [sə'fistikeitid] *adj* raffiné;
élégant; (*machinery*) sophistiqué.
sopping ['sopiŋ] *adj* trempé.
soprano [sə'praːnou] *n* soprano *m, f*.
sordid ['sordid] *adj* sordide.
sore [soː] *adj* douloureux. **sore point**
point délicat *m*. *n* plaie *f*. **sorely** *adv* (*bit-
terly*) amèrement; (*greatly*) fortement.
soreness *n* endolorissement *m*.
sorrow ['sorou] *n* peine *f*, chagrin *m*. *v* se
lamenter. **sorrowful** *adj* triste, affligé.
sorry ['sori] *adj* désolé; (*plight*) triste. **feel
sorry for** plaindre. *interj* pardon!
sort [soːt] *n* sorte *f*, genre *m*; (*brand*)
marque *f*. *v* trier, classer. **sort out** ranger;
(*problem*) régler; arranger. **sorting office**
bureau de tri *m*.
soufflé ['sufleɪ] *n* soufflé *m*.
sought [soːt] *V* **seek**.
soul [soul] *n* âme *f*. **soul-destroying** *adj*
démoralisant. **soulful** *adj* expressif.
sound[1] [saund] *n* (*noise*) son *m*, bruit *m*.
sound barrier mur du son *m*. **sound
effects** bruitage *m sing*. **soundproof** *adj*
insonorisé. **sound-track** *n* piste sonore *f*.
v sonner, retentir; (*seem*) sembler.
sound[2] [saund] *adj* sain, solide; (*advice*,

etc.) sensé; (*sleep*) profond. **be sound
asleep** être profondément endormi.

sound² [saund] *v* (*depth*) sonder.

soup [suːp] *n* soupe *f*, potage *m*. **soup-
plate** *n* assiette creuse *f*.

sour [sauə] *adj* aigre, acide; (*person*)
acerbe, revêche. *v* (s')aigrir.

source [sɔːs] *n* source *f*.

south [sauθ] *n* sud *m*. *adj also* **southerly,
southern** sud *invar*; au *or* du sud. *adv* au
sud; vers le sud. **southbound** *adj* sud
invar. **south-east** *nm, adj* sud-est. **south-
west** *nm, adj* sud-ouest.

souvenir [suːvəˈniə] *n* souvenir *m*.

sovereign [ˈsɔvrin] *n, adj* souverain, -e.

*sow¹ [sau] *v* semer, ensemencer.

sow² [sau] *n* truie *f*.

sown [soun] *V* **sow¹**.

soya [ˈsɔiə] *n* soja *m*. **soya bean** graine de
soja *f*. **soy sauce** sauce au soja *f*.

spa [spaː] *n* station thermale *f*.

space [speis] *n* espace *m*, place *f*. **space-
man** *n* astronaute *m*. **spaceship** *n* engin
spatial *m*. *v* espacer. **spacious** *adj*
spacieux.

spade¹ [speid] *n* bêche *f*, pelle *f*.

spade² [speid] *n* (*cards*) pique *m*.

spaghetti [spəˈgeti] *n* spaghetti *m pl*.

Spain [spein] *n* Espagne *f*. **Spaniard** *n*
Espagnol, -e *m, f*. **Spanish** *nm, adj*
espagnol.

span [span] *n* envergure *f*, portée *f*;
(*bridge*) travée *f*; (*time*) espace *m*, durée
f. *v* enjamber.

spaniel [ˈspanjəl] *n* épagneul *m*.

spank [spaŋk] *v* donner une fessée *f*.
spanking *n* fessée *f*.

spanner [ˈspanə] *n* clef (à écrous) *f*.

spare [speə] *adj* de réserve, de trop. **spare
part** (*mot*) pièce détachée *f*. **spare-rib** *n*
(*cookery*) côtelette dans l'échine *f*. **spare
room** chambre d'ami *f*. **spare time** temps
libre *m*. **spare tyre** pneu de rechange *m*;
(*coll*) bourrelet *m*. **spare wheel** roue de
secours *f*. *v* se passer de; (*save*) épargner.
sparing *adj* limité, modéré.

spark [spaːk] *n* étincelle *f*. **spark-plug** *n*
bougie *f*. *v* jeter des étincelles. **spark off**
provoquer.

sparkle [ˈspaːkl] *n* scintillement *m*; (*in
eye*) étincelle *f*. *v* étinceler, scintiller.
sparkling *adj* (*drink*) pétillant.

sparrow [ˈsparou] *n* moineau *m*.

sparse [spaːs] *adj* clairsemé. **sparsely** *adv*
peu.

spasm [ˈspazəm] *n* spasme *m*; (*fit*) accès
m. **spasmodic** *adj* (*med*) spasmodique;
irrégulier.

spastic [ˈspastik] *n, adj* handicapé, -e
moteur.

spat [spat] *V* **spit¹**.

spatial [ˈspeiʃl] *adj* spatial.

spatula [ˈspatjulə] *n* spatule *f*.

spawn [spɔːn] *n* frai *m*. *v* frayer.

*speak [spiːk] *v* parler. **speak up** parler
fort. **speaker** *n* orateur *m*; (*loudspeaker*)
haut-parleur *m*.

spear [spiə] *n* lance *f*; (*asparagus*) pointe
f.

special [ˈspeʃəl] *adj* spécial, particulier;
extraordinaire. **specialist** *n* spécialiste *m,
f*. **speciality** *n* spécialité *f*. **specialize** *v* se
spécialiser.

species [ˈspiːʃiːz] *n* espèce *f*.

specify [ˈspesifai] *v* spécifier. **specific** *adj*
précis; (*science*) spécifique. **specification**
n spécification *f*; stipulation *f*.

specimen [ˈspesimin] *n* spécimen *m*;
(*urine*) échantillon *m*; (*blood*) prélèvement *m*.

speck [spek] *n* grain *m*; petite tache *f*.
speckle *v* tacheter.

spectacle [ˈspektəkl] *n* spectacle *m*. **spectacles** *pl n* lunettes *f pl*. **spectacular** *adj*
spectaculaire.

spectator [spekˈteitə] *n* spectateur, -trice
m, f.

spectrum [ˈspektrəm] *n* spectre *m*; (*range*)
gamme *f*.

speculate [ˈspekjuleit] *v* spéculer;
s'interroger. **speculation** *n* spéculation *f*;
conjecture *f*. **speculative** *adj* spéculatif.

sped [sped] *V* **speed**.

speech [spiːtʃ] *n* (*faculty*) parole *f*; articulation *f*; (*address*) discours *m*. **speech day**
distribution des prix *f*. **speech impediment** défaut d'élocution *m*. **speech therapy** orthophonie *f*. **speechless** *adj* muet.

*speed [spiːd] *n* vitesse *f*; rapidité *f*.
speedboat *n* vedette *f*. **speed limit** limitation de vitesse *f*. **speedometer** *n*
compteur de vitesse *m*. *v* (*mot*) conduire
trop vite. **speed along** aller à toute
vitesse. **speed up** aller plus vite; accélérer. **speeding** *n* excès de vitesse *m*. **speedy**
adj rapide.

*spell¹ [spel] *v* épeler; (*write*) écrire; signifier. **spelling** *n* orthographe *f*.

spell¹ [spel] n (*magic*) charme m, formule magique f. **spellbound** adj subjugué, envoûté.

spell² [spel] n période f; (*turn*) tour m.

spelt [spelt] V **spell¹**.

***spend** [spend] v (*money*) dépenser; (*time*) passer. **spendthrift** n dépensier, -ère m, f. **spending** n dépenses f pl. **spending money** argent de poche m.

spent [spent] V **spend**.

sperm [spɜːm] n sperme m.

spew [spjuː] v vomir.

sphere [sfɪə] n sphère f; domaine m. **spherical** adj sphérique.

spice [spais] n épice f. v épicer. **spicy** adj épicé.

spider ['spaidə] n araignée f.

***spike** [spaik] n pointe f.

***spill** [spil] v renverser, (se) répandre.

spilt [spilt] V **spill**.

***spin** [spin] n tournoiement m; (*drying*) essorage m; (*coll: ride*) balade f. v (*wool, etc.*) filer; (*turn*) (faire) tourner, tournoyer. **spin-dry** v essorer. **spin-dryer** n essoreuse f. **spin out** faire durer. **spinning** n filage m. **spinning top** toupie f. **spinning wheel** rouet m.

spinach ['spinidʒ] n (*bot*) épinard m; (*cookery*) épinards m pl.

spindle ['spindl] n (*spinning*) fuseau m, broche f; (*tech*) axe m, tige f. **spindly** adj grêle.

spine [spain] n (*anat*) colonne vertébrale; épine f; (*book*) dos m. **spinal** adj spinal, vertébral. **spiny** adj épineux.

spinster ['spinstə] n célibataire f.

spiral ['spaiərəl] adj en spirale. **spiral staircase** escalier tournant m, in spirale f.

spire [spaiə] n flèche f.

spirit ['spirit] n esprit m; courage m; alcool m. **spirit-level** n niveau à bulle m. **spirited** adj fougueux. **spiritual** adj spirituel. **spiritualism** n spiritisme m. **spiritualist** n spirite m, f.

***spit¹** [spit] n crachat m; salive f. v cracher.

spit² [spit] n (*cookery*) broche f; (*geog*) pointe f.

spite [spait] n rancune f. **in spite of** malgré. v vexer. **spiteful** adj malveillant.

splash [splaʃ] n éclaboussement m; (*sound*) plouf m; (*mark*) éclaboussure f, tache f. v éclabousser.

spleen [spliːn] n (*anat*) rate f; mauvaise humeur f.

splendid ['splendid] adj splendide; excellent. **splendour** n splendeur f.

splice [splais] v épisser.

splint [splint] n éclisse f.

splinter ['splintə] n éclat m; (*in finger*) écharde f. v (se) fendre en éclats, (se) briser en éclats.

***split** [split] n fente f, fissure f. v (se) fendre; (se) diviser; (*share*) (se) partager. **split second** fraction de seconde f.

splutter ['splʌtə] v (*person*) bredouiller; (*engine*) bafouiller; (*fire, fat, etc.*) crépiter. n bredouillement m; bafouillage m; crépitement m.

***spoil** [spoil] v gâter; (*damage*) (s')abîmer. **spoil-sport** n trouble-fête m, f. **spoils** pl n butin m sing.

spoke¹ [spouk] V **speak**.

spoke² [spouk] n rayon m.

spoken ['spoukn] V **speak**.

spokesman ['spouksmən] n porte-parole m invar.

sponge [spʌndʒ] n éponge f; (*cake*) gâteau de Savoie m. **sponge bag** sac de toilette m. v éponger. **sponge on** vivre au crochets de. **spongy** adj spongieux.

sponsor ['sponsə] n personne (f) ou organisme (m) qui assure le patronage; (*for loan*) répondant, -e m, f; (*fund-raising*) donateur, -trice m, f. v patronner. **sponsorship** n patronage m.

spontaneous [spon'teinjəs] adj spontané. **spontaneity** n spontanéité f.

spool [spuːl] n bobine f.

spoon [spuːn] n cuiller f. **spoonful** n cuillerée f.

sporadic [spə'radik] adj sporadique.

sport [spoːt] n sport m. **sports car** voiture de sport f. **sports jacket** veste sport f. **sportsman** n sportif m. **sportswoman** n sportive f. v exhiber. **sporting** adj sportif. **sportive** adj folâtre.

spot [spot] n (*mark*) tache f; (*pimple*) bouton m; (*polka dot*) pois m; (*place*) endroit m; (*small amount*) goutte f, grain m. **on the spot** sur le champ. **spot check** n contrôle intermittent m. **spotlight** n (rayon de) projecteur m. v tacher; (*see*) apercevoir. **spotless** adj immaculé. **spotted** adj tacheté; à pois. **spotty** adj boutonneux.

spouse [spaus] n (*law*) conjoint, -e m, f.

spout [spaut] n bec m; jet m. v (faire) jaillir; (*coll: recite*) débiter.

sprain [sprein] n entorse f. v fouler.

sprang [spræn] V **spring**.

sprawl [sprɔːl] v s'étaler, être affalé.

spray¹ [sprei] n gouttelettes f pl; (from aerosol) pulvérisation f; bombe f, aérosol m. v (water) asperger; vaporiser, pulvériser.

spray² [sprei] n (flowers) gerbe f; branche f.

*****spread** [spred] n propagation f, diffusion f; (span) envergure f; (paste) pâte f; (coll: meal) festin m. v (s')étaler, (s')étendre; (se) propager, (se) communiquer. **spread-eagled** adj vautré. **spread out** (s')étaler; se disperser.

spree [spriː] n fête f.

sprig [sprig] n brin m.

sprightly ['spraitli] adj alerte.

*****spring** [sprin] n (leap) bond m; (coil) ressort m; (water) source f; (season) printemps m. **spring-board** n tremplin m. **spring-cleaning** n grand nettoyage m. **spring onion** ciboule f. v bondir. **spring up** surgir, jaillir. **springy** adj souple.

sprinkle ['sprinkl] v asperger; (sugar, etc.) saupoudrer. **sprinkler** n (garden) arroseur m; (fire) diffuseur m. **sprinkling** n aspersion f; légère couche f.

sprint [sprint] n sprint m. v (sport) sprinter; foncer un sprint.

sprout [spraut] n pousse f, germe m. **Brussels sprouts** choux de Bruxelles m pl. v pousser, germer.

spruce [spruːs] v **spruce up** faire beau or belle.

sprung [sprʌn] V **spring**.

spun [spʌn] V **spin**.

spur [spɜː] n éperon m. **on the spur of the moment** sous l'impulsion du moment. v éperonner.

spurious ['spjuəriəs] adj faux, fausse.

spurn [spɜːn] v repousser.

spurt [spɜːt] n (water) jet m; (energy) sursaut m; effort soudain m. v jaillir.

spy [spai] n espion, -onne m, f. v espionner; (see) apercevoir. **spying** n espionnage m.

squabble ['skwɒbl] n chamaillerie f. v se chamailler.

squad [skwɒd] n escouade f, groupe m.

squadron ['skwɒdrən] n (mil) escadron m; (naut) escadrille f.

squalid ['skwɒlid] adj misérable, sordide; (dirty) sale.

squall [skwɔːl] n rafale f.

squander ['skwɒndə] v gaspiller.

square [skweə] n carré m; (on chessboard, grid) case f; (in town) place f. adj carré; en ordre. v carrer; (settle) régler.

squash [skwɒʃ] n (sport) squash m; (drink) sirop m; (crush) cohue f. v (s')écraser; (together) serrer.

squat [skwɒt] adj ramassé, courtaud. v s'accroupir; (in house) faire du squattage. **squatter** n squatter m.

squawk [skwɔːk] v pousser des gloussements. n gloussement m, cri rauque m.

squeak [skwiːk] n grincement m; (mouse, etc.) petit cri aigu m. v grincer; (mouse) vagir.

squeal [skwiːl] n cri aigu m; (brakes) grincement m. v pousser un cri aigu; grincer.

squeamish ['skwiːmiʃ] adj délicat, facilement dégoûté.

squeeze [skwiːz] n pression f. v presser, serrer; (extract) exprimer.

squid [skwid] n calmar m.

squiggle ['skwigl] n gribouillis m. v gribouiller.

squint [skwint] n (med) strabisme m; (glance) coup d'œil m. v loucher.

squirm [skwɜːm] v se tortiller; (person) avoir un haut-le-corps.

squirrel ['skwirəl] n écureuil m.

squirt [skwɜːt] n jet m. v (faire) jaillir; asperger.

stab [stæb] n coup de couteau m. v poignarder; donner un coup de couteau à.

stabilize ['steibilaiz] v stabiliser. **stabilizer** n stabilisateur m.

stable¹ ['steibl] n écurie f.

stable² ['steibl] adj stable; solide; constant. **stability** n stabilité f; solidité f.

staccato [stə'kaːtou] adv staccato. adj (voice, sounds, etc.) saccadé.

stack [stæk] n (pile) tas m; (hay, etc.) meule f; (chimneys) souche de cheminée f. **stacks of** (coll) un tas de. v empiler, entasser.

stadium ['steidiəm] n stade m.

staff [staːf] n personnel m; bâton m. **staff-room** n (school) salle des professeurs f.

stag [stæg] n cerf m. **stag party** (coll) réunion entre hommes f.

stage [steidʒ] n (theatre) scène f; (platform) estrade f; (point) étape f. **stage fright** trac m. **stage-manager** n régisseur

m. **stage name** nom de théâtre m. **stage whisper** aparté m. v monter; organiser.

stagger ['stagə] v chanceler; (amaze) stupéfier; (payments, etc.) échelonner. **staggering** adj renversant.

stagnant ['stagnənt] adj stagnant. **stagnate** v croupir, stagner. **stagnation** n stagnation f.

staid [steid] adj (person) posé; (opinion) pondéré.

stain [stein] n tache f; colorant m. **stain remover** détachant m. v tacher; (wood) teinter. **stained glass** verre coloré m; (windows) vitraux m pl. **stainless steel** acier inoxydable m.

stair [steə] n marche f. **staircase** n escalier m. **stairs** pl n escalier m sing.

stake¹ [steik] n (post) pieu m; (for execution) bûcher m. v jalonner.

stake² [steik] n (betting) enjeu m; intérêt m. **at stake** en jeu. v jouer.

stale [steil] adj (bread) rassis; (air) confiné; (joke) rebattu. **staleness** n manque de fraîcheur m.

stalemate ['steilmeit] n (chess) pat m; impasse f.

stalk¹ [stoːk] n (plant) tige f; (fruit) queue f.

stalk² [stoːk] v traquer. **stalk in/out** entrer/sortir avec raideur.

stall¹ [stoːl] n (market) éventaire m; kiosque m; (theatre) fauteuil d'orchestre m; (cowshed) stalle f. **stalls** pl n orchestre m sing. v (car, etc.) caler.

stall² [stoːl] v (delay) atermoyer. **stall off** tenir à distance.

stallion ['staljən] n étalon m.

stamina ['staminə] n vigueur f, résistance f.

stammer ['stamə] n bégaiement m. v bégayer.

stamp [stamp] n timbre m; (mark) cachet m; (with foot) trépignement m. **stamp-collecting** n philatélie f. v timbrer, tamponner; (with foot) taper du pied, trépigner.

stampede [stam'piːd] n débandade f; (rush) ruée f. v fuir à la débandade; se ruer.

***stand** [stand] n position f; support m; (comm) étalage m; (at exhibition) stand m. v être debout; (get up) se lever; (put) mettre; (tolerate) supporter; (be based) reposer. **stand for** représenter; tolérer.

stand out ressortir. **standstill** n arrêt m. **come to a standstill** s'immobiliser, s'arrêter. **stand up for** défendre.

standard ['standəd] n norme f, critère m, niveau (voulu) m; (flag) étendard m. adj normal, ordinaire; (comm) standard invar; (measure) étalon invar; correct. **standard lamp** lampadaire m. **standardize** v standardiser.

standing ['standiŋ] adj debout; fixe; permanent. **standing order** (bank) virement automatique m. n importance f; standing m; durée f.

stank [staŋk] V **stink**.

stanza ['stanzə] n strophe f.

staple¹ [steipl] n (papers) agrafe f; (tech) crampon m. v agrafer; cramponner.

staple² [steipl] adj principal; de base.

star [staː] n étoile f; astérisque m; (cinema, etc.) vedette f. **starfish** n étoile de mer f. v étoiler; (film) avoir pour vedette; (person) être la vedette. **stardom** n célébrité f. **starry** adj étoilé.

starboard ['staːbəd] n tribord m.

starch [staːtʃ] n amidon m. v amidonner. **starchy** adj (food) féculent; (person) guindé.

stare [steə] n regard fixe m. v dévisager, regarder fixement.

stark [staːk] adj désolé, austère; (stiff) raide; (utter) pur. **stark naked** complètement nu.

starling ['staːliŋ] n étourneau m.

start [staːt] n commencement m, départ m; (jump) sursaut m. v commencer; (clock, etc.) mettre en marche; (leave) partir; (car) démarrer; sursauter. **starter** n (sport) starter m; (mot) démarreur m; (meal) hors-d'œuvre m.

startle ['staːtl] v faire sursauter. **startling** adj surprenant.

starve [staːv] v manquer de nourriture; (to death) (faire) mourir de faim; (deliberately) affamer; (deprive) priver. **starvation** n inanition f, famine f. **starving** adj affamé. **be starving** (coll) avoir une faim de loup.

state [steit] n état m; pompe f. adj (official) d'État. **statesman** n homme d'État m. v déclarer; formuler; fixer. **stately** adj majestueux. **statement** n déclaration f; (law) déposition f; (bank) relevé m.

static ['statik] adj statique. n (elec, radio, etc.) parasites m pl.

station ['steɪʃən] *n* (*rail*) gare *f*; (*radio, underground*) station *f*; (*position*) poste *m*; (*in life*) rang *m*. *v* poster, placer.

stationary ['steɪʃənərɪ] *adj* stationnaire.

stationer ['steɪʃənə] *n* papetier, -ère *m*, *f*. **stationer's** *n* papeterie *f*. **stationery** *n* articles de bureau *m pl*; papier à lettres *m*.

statistics [stə'tɪstɪks] *n* (*science*) statistique *f*. *pl n* statistiques *f pl*. **statistical** *adj* statistique.

statue ['statjuː] *n* statue *f*.

stature ['statʃə] *n* stature *f*; importance *f*, envergure *f*.

status ['steɪtəs] *n* situation *f*; prestige *m*.

statute ['statjuːt] *n* loi *f*. **statutory** *adj* statutaire; légal.

staunch [stɔːntʃ] *adj* loyal, dévoué.

stay [steɪ] *n* séjour *m*. *v* rester; loger.

steadfast ['stedfɑːst] *adj* ferme; constant.

steady ['stedɪ] *adj* stable, solide; constant, régulier. *v* maintenir; (*person*) reprendre son aplomb; (se) calmer. **steadily** *adv* fermement; progressivement; sans arrêt. **steadiness** *n* stabilité *f*; constance *f*.

steak [steɪk] *n* bifteck *m*; (*of pork, fish*) tranche *f*.

*** steal** [stiːl] *v* voler. **stealing** *n* vol *m*.

stealthy ['stelθɪ] *adj* furtif.

steam [stiːm] *n* vapeur *f*. **steam-roller** *n* rouleau compresseur *m*. *v* fumer; (*cookery*) cuire à la vapeur. **steam up** se couvrir de buée.

steel [stiːl] *n* acier *m*. **steel wool** paille de fer *f*. **steelworks** *n* aciérie *f*. **steely** *adj* dur, d'acier.

steep¹ [stiːp] *adj* raide.

steep² [stiːp] *v* tremper.

steeple ['stiːpl] *n* clocher *m*. **steeplechase** *n* steeple *m*.

steer [stɪə] *v* (*ship*) gouverner; (*car*) conduire; (*person*) guider. **steering** *n* conduite *f*. **steering-wheel** *n* volant *m*.

stem¹ [stem] *n* tige *f*; (*glass*) pied *m*. *v* **stem from** provenir de.

stem² [stem] *v* (*stop*) contenir, endiguer.

stench [stentʃ] *n* puanteur *f*.

stencil ['stensl] *n* pochoir *m*; (*typing*) stencil *m*.

step [step] *n* pas *m*; mesure *f*; (*stair*) marche *f*. **step-ladder** *n* escabeau *m*. *v* faire un pas; marcher. **step up** augmenter, intensifier.

stepbrother ['stepbrʌðə] *n* demi-frère *m*.

stepdaughter ['stepdɔːtə] *n* belle-fille *f*.

stepfather ['stepfɑːðə] *n* beau-père *m*.

stepmother ['stepmʌðə] *n* belle-mère *f*.

stepsister ['stepsɪstə] *n* demi-sœur *f*.

stepson ['stepsʌn] *n* beau-fils *m*.

stereo ['steriəu] *nf*, *adj* stéréo. **stereophonic** *adj* stéréophonique.

stereotype ['steriətaip] *n* stéréotype *m*; (*printing*) cliché *m*. *v* stéréotyper; clicher.

sterile ['sterail] *adj* stérile. **sterility** *n* stérilité *f*. **sterilization** *n* stérilisation *f*. **sterilize** *v* stériliser.

sterling ['stɜːlɪŋ] *n* livres sterling *f pl*. *adj* (*silver*) fin; (*character*) solide.

stern¹ [stɜːn] *adj* sévère.

stern² [stɜːn] *n* arrière *m*.

stethoscope ['steθəskəup] *n* stéthoscope *m*.

stew [stjuː] *n* ragoût *m*. *v* (*meat*) cuire en ragoût; (*fruit*) faire cuire.

steward ['stjuəd] *n* intendant *m*; (*plane, ship*) steward *m*. **stewardess** *n* hôtesse *f*.

stick¹ [stik] *n* bâton *m*; petite branche *f*; (*walking*) canne *f*.

*** stick²** [stik] *v* (*stab*) planter, enfoncer; (*glue*) coller (*put*) mettre; (*get jammed*) être bloqué; (*slang: put up with*) supporter; (*stay*) rester. **stick out** sortir, (faire) dépasser. **stick up for** défendre. **sticky** *adj* poisseux, gluant.

stickler ['stiklə] *n* **be a stickler for** insister sur; être pointilleux sur.

stiff [stif] *adj* raide, rigide; (*hard to move*) dur; (*exam*) difficile; (*cool*) froid. **stiff neck** torticolis *m*. **stiffen** *v* (se) raidir; renforcer. **stiffness** *n* raideur *f*.

stifle ['staifl] *v* étouffer; (*smile, etc.*) réprimer. **stifling** *adj* suffocant.

stigma ['stigmə] *n* stigmate *m*.

stile [stail] *n* échalier *m*.

still¹ [stil] *adv* encore; (*anyway*) quand même; (*sit, stand*) sans bouger. *adj* calme, tranquille. **stillborn** *adj* mort-né. **still life** nature morte. *n* (*cinema*) photo *f*.

still² [stil] *n* alambic *m*; distillerie *f*.

stilt [stilt] *n* échasse *f*. **stilted** *adj* guindé.

stimulus ['stimjuləs] *n*, *pl* **-li** stimulus (*pl* -li) *m*; impulsion *f*, stimulant *m*. **stimulant** *nm*, *adj* stimulant. **stimulate** *v* stimuler. **stimulation** *n* stimulation *f*.

*** sting** [stiŋ] *n* (*insect*) dard *m*; (*wound*) piqûre *f*; (*iodine*) brûlure. *v* piquer; brûler; (*whip*) cingler.

*stink [stiŋk] *n* puanteur *f*. *v* puer, empester.

stint [stint] *n* ration de travail *f*. *v* lésiner sur.

stipulate ['stipjuleit] *v* stipuler. **stipulation** *n* stipulation *f*.

stir [stəː] *n* agitation *f*, sensation *f*. *v* (*tea, etc.*) tourner; (*move*) agiter, remuer; exciter.

stirrup ['stirəp] *n* étrier *m*.

stitch [stitʃ] *n* (*sewing*) point *m*; (*knitting*) maille *f*; (*med*) point de suture *m*; (*pain*) point de côté *m*. *v* coudre; (*med*) suturer.

stoat [stout] *n* hermine *f*.

stock [stok] *n* réserve *f*; (*farm*) cheptel *m*; (*cookery*) bouillon *m*; (*lineage*) souche *f*. **stockbroker** *n* agent de change *m*. **Stock Exchange** Bourse *f*. **stockpile** *v* stocker. **stocks and shares** valeurs *f pl*. **stocktaking** *n* inventaire *m*. *v* approvisionner.

Stockholm ['stokhoum] *n* Stockholm.

stocking ['stokiŋ] *n* bas *m*. **in one's stocking feet** sans chaussures.

stocky ['stoki] *adj* trapu.

stodge [stodʒ] (*coll*) *n* aliment bourratif *m*. **stodgy** *adj* bourratif.

stoical ['stouikl] *adj* stoïque.

stoke [stouk] *v* (*fire*) garnir, alimenter; (*boiler*) chauffer.

stole¹ [stoul] *V* **steal**.

stole² [stoul] *n* étole *f*.

stolen ['stoulən] *V* **steal**.

stomach ['stʌmək] *n* estomac *m*; (*abdomen*) ventre *m*. **stomach-ache** *n* mal à l'estomac *m*. *v* supporter.

stone [stoun] *n* pierre *f*; (*of fruit*) noyau *m*; (*med*) calcul *m*. **stone-cold** *adj* complètement froid. *v* lapider; dénoyauter. **stony** *adj* pierreux; dur.

stood [stud] *V* **stand**.

stool [stuːl] *n* tabouret *m*.

stoop [stuːp] *v* se pencher, se courber; avoir le dos voûté; (*descend*) s'abaisser (jusqu'à).

stop [stop] *n* arrêt *m*. *v* (s')arrêter; cesser; (*block*) boucher; (*prevent*) empêcher. **stop-press** *n* dernière heure *f*. **stop thief!** au voleur! **stop-watch** *n* chronomètre *m*. **stoppage** *n* arrêt *m*; obstruction *f*; (*strike*) grève *f*. **stopper** *n* bouchon *m*.

store [stoː] *n* provision *f*; (*depot*) entrepôt *m*; (*shop*) magasin *m*. *v* mettre en réserve; emmagasiner. **storage** *n* entreposage *m*. **storage space** espace de rangement *m*.

storey ['stoːri] *n* étage *m*.

stork [stoːk] *n* cigogne *f*.

storm [stoːm] *n* tempête *f*; (*thunder*) orage *m*. *v* (*mil*) prendre d'assaut; (*wind, rain*) faire rage; (*person*) fulminer. **stormy** *adj* orageux.

story ['stoːri] *n* histoire *f*.

stout [staut] *adj* gros, grosse; solide; intrépide. *n* stout *m*.

stove [stouv] *n* (*cooker*) fourneau *m*; (*heater*) poêle *m*.

stow [stou] *v* ranger. **stow away** voyager clandestinement. **stowaway** *n* passager clandestin, passagère clandestine *m, f*.

straddle ['stradl] *v* enfourcher, enjamber, être à califourchon (sur).

straggle ['stragl] *v* (*plant*) pousser au hasard; (*hair*) être en désordre; (*village*) s'étendre en longueur. **straggler** *n* traînard, -e *m, f*.

straight [streit] *adj* droit; en ordre; franc, franche. *adv* droit; (*directly*) tout droit. **straight ahead** tout droit. **straight away** tout de suite. **straightforward** *adj* simple; honnête. **straighten** *v* redresser; mettre en ordre.

strain¹ [strein] *n* tension *f*, effort *m*; (*med*) entorse *f*. *v* forcer, tendre fortement; (*med*) froisser, filtrer; s'efforcer, peiner. **strainer** *n* passoire *f*.

strain² [strein] *n* race *f*; tendance *f*.

strait [streit] *n* détroit *m*.

strand¹ [strand] *n* brin *m*, fibre *f*, fil *m*.

strand² [strand] *v* laisser en rade; (*ship*) échouer.

strange [streindʒ] *adj* étrange; (*unfamiliar*) inconnu. **stranger** *n* inconnu, -e *m, f*.

strangle ['straŋgl] *v* étrangler.

strap [strap] *n* lanière *f*, sangle *f*; (*on garment*) bretelle *f*. *v* attacher avec une sangle. **strapping** *adj* costaud.

strategy ['stratədʒi] *n* stratégie *f*. **strategic** *adj* stratégique.

stratum ['strætəm] *n, pl* **-ta** strate *f*, couche *f*.

straw [stroː] *n* paille *f*. **it's the last straw!** c'est le comble!

strawberry ['stroːbəri] *n* (*fruit*) fraise *f*; (*plant*) fraisier *m*.

stray [strei] *n* animal errant *m*. *adj* errant, perdu; isolé. *v* s'égarer, errer.

streak [striːk] *n* raie *f*; tendance *f*. *v* zébrer, strier.

stream [striim] *n* ruisseau *m*; courant *m*; flot *m*, torrent *m*. **streamlined** *adj* (*aero*) fuselé; (*mot*) aérodynamique; (*efficient*) rationalisé. *v* ruisseler; (*school*) répartir par niveau. **streamer** *n* serpentin *m*.

street [striit] *n* rue *f*.

strength [streŋθ] *n* force *f*. **strengthen** *v* fortifier; consolider; augmenter.

strenuous ['strenjuas] *adj* ardu; vigoureux, acharné.

stress [stres] *n* pression *f*; accent *m*; tension *f*; insistance *f*; (*tech*) travail *m*. *v* insister sur; accentuer.

stretch [stretʃ] *n* (*action*) étirement *m*; (*distance*) étendue *f*; période *f*. *v* (s')étirer, (se) tendre; (*reach*) s'étendre. **stretcher** *n* brancard *m*.

stricken ['strikən] *adj* affligé.

strict [strikt] *adj* strict; exact. **strictly** *adv* strictement. **strictly speaking** à proprement parler. **strictness** *n* sévérité *f*; exactitude *f*.

*stride [straid] *n* grand pas *m*. enjambée *f*. *v* marcher à grands pas.

strident ['straidənt] *adj* strident.

strife [straif] *n* conflit *m*; querelles *f pl*.

*strike [straik] *n* (*industry*) grève *f*; (*hit*) coup *m*; (*oil. etc.*) découverte *f*. *v* (*hit*) frapper, heurter; faire grève; (*clock*) sonner; découvrir; (*match*) allumer, frotter. **striker** *n* gréviste *m*, *f*. **striking** *adj* frappant; en grève.

*string [striŋ] *n* ficelle *f*; (*violin, racket, etc.*) corde *f*. **string bag** filet à provisions *m*. **string quartet** quatuor à cordes *m*. **string vest** gilet de coton à grosses mailles *m*. *v* (*beads*) enfiler; (*hang*) suspendre. **stringy** *adj* filandreux.

stringent ['strindʒənt] *adj* rigoureux.

strip¹ [strip] *v* dépouiller; (*undress*) (se) déshabiller; (*bed*) défaire. **strip off** enlever. **strip-tease** *n* strip-tease *m*. **stripper** *n* strip-teaseuse *f*; (*paint*) décapant *m*.

strip² [strip] *n* bande *f*. **strip cartoon** bande dessinée *f*.

stripe [straip] *n* raie *f*, rayure *f*. **striped** *adj* rayé.

*strive [straiv] *v* s'efforcer (de).

strode [stroud] *V* **stride**.

stroke¹ [strouk] *n* coup *m*; (*swimming*) nage *f*; (*mark*) trait *m*; (*med*) attaque d'apoplexie *f*.

stroke² [strouk] *v* caresser. *n* caresse *f*.

stroll [stroul] *n* petite promenade *f*, tour *m*. *v* se promener nonchalamment, flâner.

strong [stroŋ] *adj, adv* fort; solide. **stronghold** *n* bastion *m*; (*mil*) forteresse *f*. **strong-minded** *adj* résolu. **strong-room** *n* chambre forte.

strove [strouv] *V* **strive**.

struck [strʌk] *V* **strike**.

structure ['strʌktʃə] *n* structure *f*; construction *f*. **structural** *adj* structural; de construction.

struggle ['strʌgl] *n* lutte *f*. *v* lutter; (*to escape*) se débattre. **struggle in/out** entrer/sortir avec peine.

strum [strʌm] *v* (*guitar*) racler; (*piano*) tapoter (de).

strung [strʌŋ] *V* **string**.

strut¹ [strʌt] *v* se pavaner.

strut² [strʌt] *n* étai *m*, support *m*.

stub [stʌb] *n* bout *m*; (*tree*) souche *f*; (*cheque*) talon *m*. *v* (*toe, etc.*) cogner. **stub out** écraser.

stubble ['stʌbl] *n* chaume *m*.

stubborn ['stʌbən] *adj* obstiné, opiniâtre. **stubbornness** *n* obstination *f*, opiniâtreté *f*.

stuck [stʌk] *V* **stick²**.

stud¹ [stʌd] *n* clou *m*; (*cheek*) bouton *m*. *v* clouter. **studded with** parsemé de.

stud² [stʌd] *n* écurie *f*; (*farm*) haras *m*. **be at stud** étalonner.

student ['stjuudənt] *n* étudiant, -e *m*, *f*; (*trainee*) stagiaire *m*, *f*.

studio ['stjuudiou] *n* studio *m*.

study ['stʌdi] *n* étude *f*; (*room*) bureau *m*. *v* étudier, faire des études. **studious** *adj* studieux.

stuff [stʌf] *n* choses *f pl*; substance *f*; (*fabric*) étoffe *f*. *v* rembourrer; (*cram*) bourrer; (*thrust*) fourrer; (*cookery*) farcir; (*animal*) empailler. **stuffing** *n* bourre *f*, farce *f*; paille *f*. **stuffy** *adj* mal ventilé; (*person*) collet monté *invar*.

stumble ['stʌmbl] *v* trébucher.

stump [stʌmp] *n* (*tree*) souche *f*; (*limb*) moignon *m*; (*pencil, etc.*) bout *m*; (*cricket*) piquet *m*. *v* (*sport*) mettre hors jeu; (*coll*) coller, faire sécher.

stun [stʌn] *v* étourdir; (*amaze*) abasourdir. **stunning** *adj* stupéfiant; (*coll*) sensationnel.

stung [stʌŋ] *V* **sting**.

stunk [stʌŋk] *V* **stink**.

179 suck

stunt¹ [stʌnt] *v* retarder (la croissance de). **stunted** *adj* rabougri.

stunt² [stʌnt] *n* tour de force *m*; *(aero)* acrobatie *f*; *(trick, publicity)* truc *m*. **stunt man** cascadeur *m*.

stupid ['stjuːpid] *adj* stupide. **stupidity** *n* stupidité *f*.

stupor ['stjuːpə] *n* stupeur *f*.

sturdy ['stəːdi] *adj* robuste, vigoureux. **sturdiness** *n* robustesse *f*, vigueur *f*.

sturgeon ['stəːdʒən] *n* esturgeon *m*.

stutter ['stʌtə] *n* bégaiement *m*. *v* bégayer.

sty [stai] *n* porcherie *f*.

style [stail] *n* style *m*; *(dress)* mode *f*; *(hair)* coiffure *f*; *(type)* genre *m*. *v* créer; *(call)* appeler. **stylish** *adj* élégant, chic *invar.*

stylus ['stailəs] *n* *(tool)* style *m*; *(record player)* pointe de lecture *f*.

suave [swɑːv] *adj* doucereux.

subconscious [sʌb'kɒnʃəs] *nm, adj* subconscient.

subcontract [sʌbkən'trakt] *v* sous-traiter. **subcontractor** *n* sous-traitant *m*.

subdivide [sʌbdi'vaid] *v* (se) subdiviser. **subdivision** *n* subdivision *f*.

subdue [səb'djuː] *v* *(riot)* subjuguer; *(feelings)* contenir; *(light)* adoucir. **subdued** *adj* contenu; faible; *(voice)* bas, basse; *(lighting)* tamisé.

subject [n səb'dʒikt; v səb'dʒekt] *n* sujet *m*; *(school)* matière *f*; *(people)* sujet, -ette *m, f. adj, adv* **subject to** sujet à; à condition de; exposé à. *v* soumettre; exposer. **subjection** *n* sujétion *f*. **subjective** *adj* subjectif.

subjunctive [səb'dʒʌŋktiv] *nm, adj* subjonctif.

sublet [sʌb'let] *v* sous-louer.

sublime [sə'blaim] *nm, adj* sublime.

submarine ['sʌbməriːn] *n* sous-marin *m*.

submerge [səb'məːdʒ] *v* submerger. **submersion** *n* submersion *f*.

submit [səb'mit] *v* (se) soumettre. **submission** *n* soumission *f*. **submissive** *adj* soumis.

subnormal [sʌb'nɔːməl] *adj* au-dessous de la normale; *(person)* arriéré.

subordinate [sə'bɔːdinət] *adj* subalterne; *(gramm)* subordonné. *n* subalterne *m, f*; subordonné, -e *m, f. v* subordonner. **subordination** *n* subordination *f*.

subscribe [səb'skraib] *v* **subscribe to** souscrire à; *(newspaper)* s'abonner à. **subscriber** *n* souscripteur, -trice *m, f*;

abonné, -e *m, f*. **subscription** *n* souscription *f*; *(club)* cotisation *f*; abonnement *m*.

subsequent ['sʌbsikwənt] *adj* ultérieur, -e, suivant; résultant.

subservient [səb'səːviənt] *adj* subalterne; *(derog)* obséquieux.

subside [səb'said] *v* *(land)* s'affaisser; *(flood)* baisser; *(wind)* se calmer. **subsidence** *n* affaissement *m*.

subsidiary [səb'sidiəri] *adj* subsidiaire, accessoire. *n* *(comm)* filiale *f*.

subsidize ['sʌbsidaiz] *v* subventionner. **subsidy** *n* subvention *f*.

subsist [səb'sist] *v* subsister. **subsistence** *n* subsistance *f*.

substance ['sʌbstəns] *n* substance *f*. **substantial** *adj* important, substantiel.

substandard [sʌb'standəd] *adj* de qualité inférieure.

substitute ['sʌbstitjuːt] *n* *(person)* remplaçant, -e *m, f*; *(thing)* succédané *m. v* substituer, remplacer. **substitution** *n* substitution *f*.

subtitle ['sʌbtaitl] *n* sous-titre *m. v* sous-titrer.

subtle ['sʌtl] *adj* subtil. **subtlety** *n* subtilité *f*.

subtract [səb'trakt] *v* soustraire. **subtraction** *n* soustraction *f*.

suburb ['sʌbəːb] *n* faubourg *m*. **suburbs** *pl n* banlieue *f sing*. **suburban** *adj* suburbain.

subvert [səb'vəːt] *v* bouleverser; corrompre. **subversion** *n* subversion *f*. **subversive** *adj* subversif.

subway ['sʌbwei] *n* passage souterrain *m*; *(US)* métro *m*.

succeed [sək'siːd] *v* réussir; *(follow)* succéder à. **succeeding** *adj* suivant; à venir. **success** *n* succès *m*, réussite *f*. **successful** *adj* couronné de succès, qui a réussi. **successfully** *adv* avec succès. **succession** *n* succession *f*. **successive** *adj* successif, consécutif. **successor** *n* successeur *m*.

succinct [sək'siŋkt] *adj* succinct.

succulent ['sʌkjulənt] *adj* succulent.

succumb [sə'kʌm] *v* succomber.

such [sʌtʃ] *adj* tel, pareil; *(so much)* tant (de). **such as** tel que. *adv* si, tellement; *(as)* aussi. *pron* *(those)* ceux, celles; tel, telle.

suck [sʌk] *v* sucer; *(baby)* téter. **suck up to** *(slang)* faire de la lèche à.

sucker ['sʌkə] n (bot) surgeon m; (device) ventouse f; (slang: person) poire f.

suction ['sʌkʃən] n succion f.

sudden ['sʌdən] adj soudain, subit; imprévu. **all of a sudden** tout à coup.

suds [sʌdz] pl n mousse de savon f sing.

sue [suː] v poursuivre en justice.

suede [sweid] n daim m.

suet ['suːit] n graisse de rognon f.

suffer ['sʌfə] v souffrir; (undergo) subir, éprouver; tolérer. **suffering** n souffrance f.

sufficient [sə'fiʃənt] adj assez de, suffisant. **suffice** v suffire (à). **sufficiently** adv suffisamment.

suffix ['sʌfiks] n suffixe m.

suffocate ['sʌfəkeit] v suffoquer, étouffer. **suffocation** n suffocation f; (med) asphyxie f.

sugar ['ʃugə] n sucre m. **sugar-basin** n sucrier m. **sugar-beet** n betterave sucrière f. **sugar-cane** n canne à sucre f. **sugar-lump** n morceau de sucre m. v sucrer. **sugared almond** dragée f. **sugary** adj sucré.

suggest [sə'dʒest] v suggérer. **suggestion** n suggestion f; soupçon m. **suggestive** adj suggestif.

suicide ['suisaid] n suicide m; (person) suicidé, -e m, f. **commit suicide** se suicider. **suicidal** adj suicidaire.

suit [suːt] n (man's) costume m; (woman's) tailleur m; (law) procès m; (cards) couleur f. **suitcase** n valise f. v convenir à, aller à. **suitable** adj qui convient; approprié.

suite [swiːt] n suite f; (furniture) mobilier m.

sulk [sʌlk] v bouder. n bouderie f. **sulky** adj boudeur, -euse.

sullen ['sʌlən] adj maussade, renfrogné. **sullenness** n maussaderie f.

sulphur ['sʌlfə] n soufre m. **sulphuric** adj sulfurique.

sultan ['sʌltən] n sultan m.

sultana [sʌl'tɑːnə] n raisin sec de Smyrne m.

sultry ['sʌltri] adj étouffant, lourd; sensuel.

sum [sʌm] n somme f; (math) calcul m. v **sum up** résumer, récapituler; (person) jauger.

summarize ['sʌməraiz] v résumer, récapituler. **summary** n résumé m.

summer ['sʌmə] n été m. **summer holidays** grandes vacances f pl. **summer-house** n pavillon m.

summit ['sʌmit] n sommet m.

summon ['sʌmən] v faire venir, convoquer, mander. **summon up** rassembler, faire appel à.

summons ['sʌmənz] n sommation f; (law) assignation f. v assigner.

sump [sʌmp] n (mot) carter m.

sumptuous ['sʌmptʃuəs] adj somptueux.

sun [sʌn] n soleil m. v **sun oneself** se chauffer au soleil. **sunny** adj ensoleillé.

sunbathe ['sʌnbeið] v prendre un bain de soleil. **sunbathing** n bains de soleil m pl.

sunbeam ['sʌnbiːm] n rayon de soleil m.

sunburn ['sʌnbəːn] n (tan) bronzage m; (pain) coup de soleil m. **sunburnt** adj bronzé; brûlé.

Sunday ['sʌndi] n dimanche m.

sundial ['sʌndaiəl] n cadran solaire m.

sundry ['sʌndri] adj divers. **all and sundry** n'importe qui. **sundries** pl n articles divers m pl.

sunflower ['sʌnflauə] n tournesol m.

sung [sʌŋ] V sing.

sun-glasses ['sʌnglɑːsiz] pl n lunettes de soleil f pl.

sunk [sʌŋk] V sink.

sunlight ['sʌnlait] n soleil m.

sunrise ['sʌnraiz] n lever du soleil m.

sunset ['sʌnset] n coucher du soleil m.

sunshine ['sʌnʃain] n soleil m. **sunshine roof** (mot) toit ouvrant m.

sunstroke ['sʌnstrouk] n insolation f.

sun-tan ['sʌntan] n bronzage m. **sun-tan lotion/oil** lotion/huile solaire f.

super ['suːpə] adj (coll) formidable.

superannuation [ˌsuːpərənjuˈeiʃən] n retraite f; (payments) versements pour la pension m pl.

superb [suˈpəːb] adj superbe.

supercilious [ˌsuːpəˈsiliəs] adj hautain.

superficial [ˌsuːpəˈfiʃəl] adj superficiel.

superfluous [suˈpəːfluəs] adj superflu.

superhuman [ˌsuːpəˈhjuːmən] adj surhumain.

superimpose [ˌsuːpərimˈpouz] v superposer. **superimposed** adj (phot, etc.) en surimpression.

superintendent [ˌsuːpərinˈtendənt] n directeur, -trice m, f; (police) commissaire m.

superior [suˈpiəriə] n, adj supérieur, -e. **superiority** n supériorité f.

superlative [suːˈpɜːlətɪv] *adj* suprême, sans pareil; (*gramm*) superlatif. *n* superlatif *m*.

supermarket [ˈsuːpəˌmɑːkɪt] *n* supermarché *m*.

supernatural [ˌsuːpəˈnatʃərəl] *nm, adj* surnaturel.

supersede [ˌsuːpəˈsiːd] *v* remplacer, supplanter.

supersonic [ˌsuːpəˈsɒnɪk] *adj* supersonique.

superstition [suːpəˈstɪʃən] *n* superstition *f*. **superstitious** *adj* superstitieux.

supervise [ˈsuːpəvaɪz] *v* surveiller, diriger. **supervision** *n* surveillance *f*, direction *f*. **supervisor** *n* surveillant, -e *m, f*; (*comm*) chef de rayon *m*.

supper [ˈsʌpə] *n* souper *m*; (*evening meal*) dîner *m*.

supple [ˈsʌpl] *adj* souple. **suppleness** *n* souplesse *f*.

supplement [ˈsʌpləmənt] *n* supplément *m*. *v* augmenter, ajouter à. **supplementary** *adj* supplémentaire.

supply [səˈplaɪ] *n* (*stock*) provision *f*; (*fuel, etc.*) alimentation *f*, direction *f*. **supplies** *pl n* provisions *f pl*; matériel *m sing*. *v* fournir; alimenter.

support [səˈpɔːt] *n* appui *m*, soutien *m*. *v* supporter, soutenir; (*financially*) subvenir aux besoins de. **supporter** *n* partisan, -e *m, f*; (*sport*) supporter *m*.

suppose [səˈpəʊz] *v* supposer. **supposed** *adj* prétendu; présumé. **be supposed to** être censé, devoir. **supposedly** *adv* soi-disant. **supposing** *conj* si, à supposer que. **supposition** *n* supposition *f*.

suppress [səˈpres] *v* supprimer, réprimer; (*yawn, etc.*) étouffer. **suppression** *n* suppression *f*, répression *f*; étouffement *m*.

supreme [suːˈpriːm] *adj* suprême. **supremacy** *n* suprématie *f*.

surcharge [ˈsɜːtʃɑːdʒ] *n* surcharge *f*, surtaxe *f*.

sure [ʃʊə] *adj* sûr, certain. **make sure** s'assurer; (*check*) vérifier. **sure enough** effectivement, en effet. **sure-footed** au pied sûr. **surely** *adv* sûrement.

surety [ˈʃʊərəti] *n* caution *f*.

surf [sɜːf] *n* ressac *m*; (*foam*) écume *f*. **surf-board** *n* planche de surf *f*. **surf-boarder** *n* surfeur, -euse *m, f*. **surf-boarding** *or* **surfing** *n* surf *m*. *v* surfer.

surface [ˈsɜːfɪs] *n* surface *f*. **on the surface**

en apparence. *v* (*road*) revêtir; (*swimmer, etc.*) revenir à la surface, faire surface.

surfeit [ˈsɜːfɪt] *n* excès *m*.

surge [sɜːdʒ] *n* vague *f*, montée *f*. *v* déferler.

surgeon [ˈsɜːdʒən] *n* chirurgien *m*. **surgery** *n* (*skill*) chirurgie *f*; (*place*) cabinet *m*; (*time*) consultation *f*. **surgical** *adj* chirurgical.

surly [ˈsɜːli] *adj* revêche.

surmount [səˈmaʊnt] *v* surmonter.

surname [ˈsɜːneɪm] *n* nom de famille *m*.

surpass [səˈpɑːs] *v* surpasser, dépasser.

surplus [ˈsɜːpləs] *n* surplus *m*, excédent *m*. *adj* en surplus.

surprise [səˈpraɪz] *n* surprise *f*. *adj* inattendu. *v* surprendre, étonner.

surrealism [səˈrɪəlɪzəm] *n* surréalisme *m*. **surrealist** *n(m+f)*, *adj* surréaliste. **surrealistic** *adj* surréaliste.

surrender [səˈrendə] *v* (se) rendre; (*documents*) remettre; renoncer à, abandonner. *n* reddition *f*; remise *f*; renonciation *f*.

surreptitious [ˌsʌrəpˈtɪʃəs] *adj* subreptice, furtif.

surround [səˈraʊnd] *v* entourer, encercler. *n* bordure *f*. **surrounding** *adj* environnant. **surroundings** *pl n* alentours *m pl*; (*setting*) cadre *m sing*.

survey [ˈsɜːveɪ; *v* səˈveɪ] *n* vue générale *f*; enquête *f*; (*land*) levé *m*; (*house*) inspection *f*. *v* passer en revue; inspecter; (*land*) arpenter. **surveying** *n* arpentage *m*. **surveyor** *n* (*land*) géomètre *m*; (*house*) expert *m*.

survive [səˈvaɪv] *v* survivre (à). **survival** *n* survie *f*; (*relic*) survivance *f*. **survivor** *n* survivant *m*.

susceptible [səˈseptəbl] *adj* sensible.

suspect [ˈsʌspekt; *v* səˈspekt] *n, adj* suspect, -e. *v* soupçonner.

suspend [səˈspend] *v* suspendre. **suspender** *n* jarretelle *f*. **suspender belt** porte-jarretelles *m invar*. **suspenders** *pl n* (*US*) bretelles *f pl*. **suspense** *n* incertitude *f*; (*book, film*) suspense *m*. **in suspense** en suspens. **suspension** *n* suspension *f*. **suspension bridge** pont suspendu *m*.

suspicion [səˈspɪʃən] *n* soupçon *m*. **suspicious** *adj* soupçonneux; suspect.

sustain [səˈsteɪn] *v* soutenir; (*suffer*) subir.

swab [swɒb] *n* (*mop*) serpillière *f*; (*med: sample*) prélèvement *m*; (*med: pad*) tampon *m*. *v* nettoyer.

swagger ['swagə] *n* air important *m*. *v* plastronner; (*boast*) se vanter.

swallow¹ ['swolou] *v* avaler. **swallow up** engloutir. *n* avalement *m*; (*amount*) gorgée *f*.

swallow² ['swolou] *n* (*bird*) hirondelle *f*.

swam [swam] *V* **swim**.

swamp [swomp] *n* marais *m*. *v* inonder, submerger. **swampy** *adj* marécageux.

swan [swon] *n* cygne *m*.

swank [swaŋk] (*coll*) *n* esbroufe *f*. *v* faire de l'esbroufe. **swank about** se vanter de.

swap *or* **swop** [swop] *n* troc *m*; double *m*. *v* échanger.

swarm [swoːm] *n* essaim *m*; (*ants*) fourmillement *m*. *v* essaimer; fourmiller. **swarm in/out** entrer/sortir en masse.

swarthy ['swoːði] *adj* basané.

swat [swot] *v* écraser.

sway [swei] *n* balancement *m*, oscillation *f*. *v* (se) balancer, osciller; influencer.

*****swear** [swea] *v* jurer. **swear in** assermenter. **swear-word** *n* juron *m*.

sweat [swet] *n* sueur *f*. *v* suer. **sweater** *n* tricot *m*.

swede [swiːd] *n* rutabaga *m*.

Sweden ['swiːdn] *n* Suède *f*. **Swede** *n* Suédois, -e *m, f*. **Swedish** *nm, adj* suédois.

*****sweep** [swiːp] *n* (*chimney*) ramoneur *m*; coup de balai *m*; grand geste *m*; (*curve*) grande courbe *f*. *v* balayer; ramoner. **sweep in/out** entrer/sortir rapidement *or* majestueusement. **sweeping** *adj* large; radical. **sweeping statement** généralisation hâtive *f*.

sweet [swiːt] *adj* doux, douce; (*taste*) sucré; (*kind*) gentil, -ille; (*attractive*) mignon, -onne. *n* bonbon *m*; dessert *m*. **sweetbread** *n* ris de veau *m*. **sweet corn** maïs sucré *m*. **sweetheart** *n* bien-aimé, -e *m, f*. **sweet pea** pois de senteur *m*. **sweetshop** *n* confiserie *f*. **sweeten** *v* sucrer. **sweetly** *adj* (*sing*) mélodieusement; (*smile*) gentiment. **sweetness** *n* goût sucré *m*; douceur *f*.

*****swell** [swel] *n* (*sea*) houle *f*. *v* (se) gonfler, (s')enfler, grossir. **swelling** *n* enflure *f*.

swelter ['sweltə] *v* étouffer de chaleur. **sweltering** *adj* étouffant.

swept [swept] *V* **sweep**.

swerve [swəːv] *v* dévier; (*car, ship*) faire une embardée. *n* embardée *f*.

swift [swift] *adj* prompt, rapide. *n* (*bird*) martinet *m*. **swiftness** *n* rapidité *f*.

swill [swil] *v* laver à grande eau, rincer. *n* (*for pigs*) pâtée *f*.

*****swim** [swim] *v* nager; (*cross*) traverser à la nage. *n* baignade *f*. **swimmer** *n* nageur, -euse *m, f*. **swimming** *n* nage *f*, natation *f*. **swimming baths** *or* **pool** piscine *f*. **swimming costume** maillot de bain *m*.

swindle ['swindl] *n* escroquerie *f*. *v* escroquer. **swindler** *n* escroc *m*.

swine [swain] *n* pourceau *m*; (*impol*) salaud *m*.

*****swing** [swiŋ] *n* balancement *m*; (*pol*) revirement *m*; rythme *m*; (*in playground*) balançoire *f*. **be in full swing** battre son plein. **swing-door** *n* porte battante *f*. *v* (se) balancer, (faire) osciller; (*turn*) virer; influencer.

swipe [swaip] (*coll*) *n* grand coup *m*. *v* (*hit*) frapper à toute volée; (*take*) calotter.

swirl [swəːl] *n* tourbillon *m*, volute *f*. *v* tourbillonner.

swish [swiʃ] *n* bruissement *m*, sifflement *m*. *v* bruire, siffler.

Swiss [swis] *adj* suisse. **Swiss roll** gâteau roulé *m*. **the Swiss** les Suisses.

switch [switʃ] *n* bouton électrique *m*, interrupteur *m*; changement *m*; (*stick*) baguette *f*. **switchboard** *n* standard *m*. *v* changer, échanger; (*rail*) aiguiller. **switch off** éteindre. **switch on** allumer.

Switzerland ['switsələnd] *n* Suisse *f*.

swivel ['swivl] *v* (faire) pivoter. *n* pivot *m*.

swollen ['swoulən] *V* **swell**.

swoop [swuːp] *n* descente (en piqué) *f*. **at one fell swoop** d'un seul coup. *v* fondre, piquer.

swop *V* **swap**.

sword [soːd] *n* épée *f*. **swordfish** *n* espadon *m*.

swore [swoː] *V* **swear**.

sworn [swoːn] *V* **swear**.

swot [swot] (*coll*) *n* bûcheur, -euse *m, f*. *v* bûcher, potasser. **swotting** *n* bachotage *m*.

swum [swʌm] *V* **swim**.

swung [swʌŋ] *V* **swing**.

sycamore ['sikəmoː] *n* sycomore *m*.

syllable ['siləbl] *n* syllabe *f*. **syllabic** *adj* syllabique.

syllabus ['siləbəs] *n* programme *m*.

symbol ['simbl] *n* symbole *m*. **symbolic**

adj symbolique. **symbolism** n symbolisme m. **symbolize** v symboliser.

symmetry ['simitri] n symétrie f. **symmetrical** adj symétrique.

sympathy ['simpəθi] n compassion f; solidarité f. **sympathetic** adj compatissant, bien disposé. **sympathize with** v compatir à, plaindre.

symphony ['simfəni] n symphonie f. **symphonic** adj symphonique.

symposium [sim'pouziəm] n symposium m.

symptom ['simptəm] n symptôme m. **symptomatic** adj symptomatique.

synagogue ['sinəgog] n synagogue f.

synchromesh ['sinkroumeʃ] n synchronisation f.

synchronize ['sinkrənaiz] v synchroniser. **synchronization** n synchronisation f.

syncopate ['sinkəpeit] v syncoper. **syncopation** n syncope f.

syndicate ['sindikit] n syndicat m.

syndrome ['sindroum] n syndrome m.

synonym ['sinənim] n synonyme m. **synonymous** adj synonyme.

synopsis [si'nopsis] n, pl **-ses** résumé m.

syntax ['sintaks] n syntaxe f.

synthesis ['sinθisis] n, pl **-ses** synthèse f. **synthesize** v synthétiser. **synthetic** adj synthétique.

syphilis ['sifilis] n syphilis f.

syringe [si'rindʒ] n seringue f. v seringuer.

syrup ['sirəp] n sirop m; (golden) mélasse raffinée f. **syrupy** adj sirupeux.

system ['sistəm] n système m; méthode f. **systematic** adj systématique.

T

tab [tab] n étiquette f, patte f. **keep tabs on** (coll) avoir à l'œil.

tabby ['tabi] n chat tigré m.

table ['teibl] n table f. **table-cloth** n nappe f. **table-mat** n dessous-de-plat m invar. **table salt** sel fin m. **tablespoon** n cuiller de service f. **tablespoonful** n cuillerée à soupe f. **table tennis** ping-pong m.

table d'hôte [tablə'dout] adj à prix fixe.

tablet ['tablit] n (pill) comprimé m; (stone) plaque f; (soap) pain m.

taboo [ta'bu:] nm, adj tabou. v proscrire.

tabulate ['tabjuleit] v mettre sous forme de table, classifier.

tacit ['tasit] adj tacite.

taciturn ['tasitən] adj taciturne.

tack [tak] n (nail) broquette f; (sewing) point de bâti m; (naut) bord m. v clouer; bâtir; faire un bord. **tacking** n bâtissage m.

tackle ['takl] n (lifting) appareil de levage m; équipement m; (sport) plaquage m. v s'attaquer à; plaquer.

tact [takt] n tact m. **tactful** adj plein de tact, discret, -ète. **tactless** adj peu délicat, indiscret, -ète.

tactics ['taktiks] pl n tactique f sing. **tactical** adj tactique.

tadpole ['tadpoul] n têtard m.

taffeta ['tafitə] n taffetas m.

tag [tag] n étiquette f, patte f; (shoelace) ferret m. v **tag along** (coll) suivre; traîner derrière.

tail [teil] n queue f; (shirt) pan m. **tail-end** n bout m, fin f. **tails** pl n (coin) pile f sing. v (coll) suivre.

tailor ['teilə] n tailleur m. v façonner; adapter.

taint [teint] v infecter, polluer. n infection f; corruption f; (moral) tache f.

***take** [teik] v prendre; (exam) passer; accepter; contenir; (accompany) emmener. **take after** ressembler à. **take away** emporter; soustraire. **take-away** adj (food) à emporter. **take in** prendre; (dress) reprendre; (understand) saisir; inclure, couvrir; (coll: deceive) rouler. **take off** (aero) décoller; (clothes, etc.) enlever. **take-off** n décollage m; pastiche m. **take out** sortir; (insurance) prendre. **take-over** n rachat m.

taken ['teikn] V take.

talcum powder ['talkəm] n talc m.

tale [teil] n conte m, histoire f. **tell tales** (coll) cafarder.

talent ['talənt] n talent m. **talented** adj talentueux, doué.

talk [tɔ:k] n propos m pl; conversation f; (lecture) exposé m. v parler; (chat) causer. **talk about** parler de. **talk into** persuader de. **talk over** discuter. **talkative** adj bavard.

tall [tɔ:l] adj grand; (high) haut. **tallboy** n commode f. **tallness** n grande taille f; hauteur f.

tally ['tali] n compte m. v s'accorder.

talon ['talən] n serre f.

tambourine [tambə'riːn] n tambourin m.

tame [teim] adj apprivoisé; (not exciting) insipide. v apprivoiser; (lion) dompter.

tamper ['tampə] v tamper with toucher à; falsifier.

tampon ['tampon] n tampon m.

tan [tan] n bronzage m. adj ocre. v (hide) tanner; (sun) bronzer, hâler.

tandem ['tandəm] n tandem m.

tangent ['tandʒənt] n tangente f. go off at a tangent partir dans une digression.

tangerine [tandʒə'riːn] nf, adj mandarine.

tangible ['tandʒəbl] adj tangible.

tangle ['tangl] n enchevêtrement m, confusion f. v (s')enchevêtrer, (s')embrouiller.

tank [tank] n réservoir m; (mil) char m. tanker n (lorry) camion-citerne m; (ship) pétrolier m.

tankard ['tankəd] n chope f.

tantalize ['tantəlaiz] v tourmenter. tantalizing adj terriblement tentant.

tantamount ['tantəmaunt] adj tantamount to équivalent à.

tantrum ['trantrəm] n crise de colère f. throw a tantrum piquer une colère.

tap¹ [tap] n petit coup m. tap-dance n claquettes f pl. tap-dancer n danseur, -euse de claquettes m, f. v frapper légèrement, tapoter.

tap² [tap] n robinet m. v (barrel) percer; (tree) inciser; (phone) mettre sur écoute; exploiter.

tape [teip] n ruban m, bande f; (recording) bande magnétique f. tape-measure n mètre à ruban m. tape-recorder n magnétophone m. tapeworm n ténia m. v (record) enregistrer; attacher.

taper ['teipə] n bougie fine f. v (s')effiler. tapered adj fuselé.

tapestry ['tapəstri] n tapisserie f.

tapioca [tapi'oukə] n tapioca m.

tar [taː] n goudron m. v goudronner.

tarantula [tə'rantjulə] n tarentule f.

target ['taːgit] n cible f; objectif m.

tariff ['tarif] n tarif m.

tarmac ® ['taːmak] n macadam goudronné m.

tarnish ['taːniʃ] v (se) ternir. n ternissure f.

tarpaulin [taː'pɔːlin] n bâche f. prélart m.

tarragon ['tarəgən] n estragon m.

tart¹ [taːt] adj aigrelet, acerbe.

tart² [taːt] n tarte f; (small) tartelette f; (slang) poule f.

tartan ['taːtən] n tartan m. adj écossais.

tartar ['taːtə] n tartre m.

task [taːsk] n tâche f.

tassel ['tasəl] n gland m.

taste [teist] n goût m. v goûter; (wine) déguster. taste of avoir un goût de. tasteful adj de bon goût. tasteless adj (flavourless) sans saveur; insipide; (in bad taste) de mauvais goût. tasty adj savoureux.

tattered ['tatəd] adj en lambeaux.

tattoo¹ [tə'tuː] v tatouer. n tatouage m.

tattoo² [tə'tuː] n parade militaire f; (drumming) battements m pl.

tatty ['tati] adj (coll) fatigué, défraîchi.

taught [tɔːt] V teach.

taunt [tɔːnt] n raillerie f. v railler. taunting adj railleur, -euse.

Taurus ['tɔːrəs] n Taureau m.

taut [tɔːt] adj tendu. tautness n tension f.

tawny ['tɔːni] adj fauve.

tax [taks] n impôt m, taxe f. tax-free adj exempt d'impôts. tax haven refuge fiscal m. taxpayer n contribuable m, f. tax return déclaration de revenus f. v imposer, taxer; (patience) mettre à l'épreuve. taxable adj imposable. taxation n taxation f; (taxes) impôts m pl.

taxi ['taksi] n taxi m. taxi-driver n chauffeur de taxi m. taxi rank station de taxis f. v (aero) rouler lentement.

tea [tiː] n thé m; (snack) goûter m.

tea-bag ['tiːbag] n sachet de thé m.

teacake ['tiːkeik] n petit pain brioché m.

tea-cosy ['tiːkouzi] n couvre-théière m.

tea-leaf ['tiːliːf] n feuille de thé f.

teapot ['tiːpot] n théière f.

tea-room ['tiːruːm] n salon de thé m.

tea-set ['tiːset] n service à thé m.

teaspoon ['tiːspuːn] n petite cuiller f. teaspoonful n cuillerée à café f.

tea-towel ['tiːtauəl] n torchon m.

tea-urn ['tiːəːn] n fontaine à thé f.

*teach [tiːtʃ] v apprendre, enseigner. teacher n professeur m; (primary school) instituteur, -trice m, f. teaching n enseignement m.

teak [tiːk] n teck m.

team [tiːm] n équipe f; (horses) attelage m. team-member n équipier, -ère m, f. team spirit esprit d'équipe m. team-work n collaboration f.

*tear¹ [teə] n déchirure f. v (se) déchirer; (snatch) arracher. **tear along/out** filer/sortir à toute allure.

tear² [tiə] n larme f. **burst into tears** fondre en larmes. **tear-gas** n gaz lacrymogène m. **tearful** adj larmoyant.

tease [tiːz] v taquiner. **teasing** n taquineries f pl.

teat [tiːt] n tétine f.

technique [tek'niːk] n technique f. **technical** adj technique. **technicality** n détail technique m. **technician** n technicien, -enne m, f. **technological** adj technologique. **technology** n technologie f.

teddy bear ['tedi‚beə] n nounours m.

tedious ['tiːdiəs] adj ennuyeux.

tee [tiː] n tee m. v **tee off** partir du tee.

teem [tiːm] v (swarm) grouiller; (rain) pleuvoir à verse.

teenage ['tiːneidʒ] adj adolescent. **teenager** n adolescent, -e m, f. **teens** pl n adolescence f sing.

teeth [tiːθ] V tooth.

teethe [tiːð] v faire ses dents. **teething** n dentition f. **teething troubles** difficultés de croissance f pl.

teetotaller [tiː'təutələ] n personne qui ne boit jamais d'alcool f.

telecommunications [‚telikəmjuːni'keiʃənz] pl n télécommunications f pl.

telegram ['teligram] n télégramme m.

telegraph ['teligraːf] n télégraphe m. **telegraph pole** poteau télégraphique m. v télégraphier. **telegraphic** adj télégraphique.

telepathy [tə'lepəθi] n télépathie f. **telepathic** adj télépathique.

telephone ['telifoun] n téléphone m. **telephone box** cabine téléphonique f. **telephone call** coup de téléphone m. **telephone directory** annuaire m. **telephone number** numéro de téléphone m. v téléphoner. **telephonist** n téléphoniste m, f.

telescope ['teliskoup] n télescope m. **telescopic** adj télescopique.

television ['teliviʒən] n télévision f. **televise** v téléviser.

telex ['teleks] n télex m.

*tell [tel] v dire; (story) raconter; (know) savoir. **tell off** (coll) gronder.

temper ['tempə] n tempérament m, humeur f; (anger) colère f. **lose one's temper** se mettre en colère. v tempérer.

temperament ['tempərəmənt] n tempérament m. **temperamental** adj capricieux.

temperate ['tempərət] adj tempéré.

temperature ['tempratʃə] n température f.

tempestuous [tem'pestjuəs] adj orageux.

template ['templət] n patron m.

temple¹ ['templ] n (rel) temple m.

temple² ['templ] n (anat) tempe f.

tempo ['tempou] n tempo m.

temporary ['tempərəri] adj temporaire; provisoire; (secretary) intérimaire.

tempt [tempt] v tenter. **temptation** n tentation f.

ten [ten] nm, adj dix. **tenth** n(m+f), adj dixième.

tenacious [tə'neiʃəs] adj tenace. **tenacity** n ténacité f.

tenant ['tenənt] n locataire m, f. **tenancy** n location f.

tend¹ [tend] v avoir tendance, incliner. **tendency** n tendance f.

tend² [tend] v (look after) garder, soigner.

tender¹ ['tendə] adj tendre; délicat; (heart, bruise) sensible. **tenderize** v attendrir. **tenderness** n tendresse f; (meat) tendreté f.

tender² ['tendə] v offrir; (comm) faire une soumission. n soumission f. **legal tender** cours légal m.

tendon ['tendən] n tendon m.

tendril ['tendril] n vrille f.

tenement ['tenəmənt] n logement m. **tenement block** bâtiment m.

tennis ['tenis] n tennis m. **tennis-court** n court de tennis m.

tenor ['tenə] n (music) ténor m; sens m; (wording) teneur f.

tense¹ [tens] adj tendu, crispé. v tendre. **tension** n tension f.

tense² [tens] n temps m.

tent [tent] n tente f.

tentacle ['tentəkl] n tentacule m.

tentative ['tentətiv] adj hésitant; expérimental; provisoire.

tenterhooks ['tentəhuks] pl n **be on tenterhooks** être sur des charbons ardents.

tenuous ['tenjuəs] adj ténu.

tepid ['tepid] adj tiède. **tepidness** n tiédeur f.

term [təːm] n terme m; (school) trimestre m. **terms** pl n (comm) conditions f pl. **come to terms with** faire face à. **on good/bad terms** en bons/mauvais termes. v appeler.

terminal ['tɔːminɔl] *adj* terminal. *n* terminus *m invar*; (*elec*) borne *f*.

terminate ['tɔːmineit] *v* (se) terminer. **termination** *n* fin *f*.

terminology [tɔːmi'nolɔdʒi] *n* terminologie *f*.

terminus ['tɔːminɔs] *n* terminus *m invar*.

terrace ['terɔs] *n* terrasse *f*; (*houses*) rangée de maisons *f*.

terrain [tɔ'rein] *n* terrain *m*.

terrestrial [tɔ'restriɔl] *adj* terrestre.

terrible ['terɔbl] *adj* terrible; atroce; abominable. **terribly** *adv* (*coll: very*) drôlement.

terrier ['teriɔ] *n* terrier *m*.

terrify ['terifai] *v* terrifier. **terrific** *adj* (*coll: excellent*) formidable; (*coll: extreme*) énorme, terrible.

territory ['teritɔri] *n* territoire *m*. **territorial** *adj* territorial.

terror ['terɔ] *n* terreur *f*. **terrorism** *n* terrorisme *m*. **terrorist** *n*(*m+f*), *adj* terroriste. **terrorize** *v* terroriser.

terse [tɔːs] *adj* laconique.

test [test] *n* essai *m*; (*physical, mental*) épreuve *f*; analyse *f*; (*school*) interrogation *f*. **test card** (*TV*) mire *f*. **test case** (*law*) conflit-test *m*. **test drive** *n* essai de route *m*. **test flight** vol d'essai *m*. **test-tube** *n* éprouvette *f*. *v* essayer, mettre à l'essai; mettre à l'épreuve; analyser; mesurer.

testament ['testɔmɔnt] *n* testament *m*.

testicle ['testikl] *n* testicule *m*.

testify ['testifai] *v* témoigner, porter témoignage.

testimony ['testimɔni] *n* témoignage *m*; déclaration *f*. **testimonial** *n* recommandation *f*.

tetanus ['tetɔnɔs] *n* tétanos *m*.

tether ['teðɔ] *n* longe *f*. *v* attacher.

text [tekst] *n* texte *m*. **textbook** *n* manuel *m*. **textual** *adj* textuel.

textile ['tekstail] *nm, adj* textile.

texture ['tekstjuɔ] *n* contexture *f*; (*wood, paper, etc.*) grain *m*.

Thames [temz] *n* the **Thames** la Tamise *f*.

than [ðɔn] *conj* que, de.

thank [θæŋk] *v* remercier. **thank you** merci. **thanks** *pl n* remerciements *m pl*. **thanksgiving** *n* action de grâce *f*. **thanks to** grâce à. **thankful** *adj* reconnaissant. **thankless** *adj* ingrat.

that [ðat] *adj* ce, cette; (*emphatic*) ce ...

-là, cette ... -là: *ce livre-là*. *pron* cela, ça; ce; (*that one*) celui-là, celle-là; (*who, which*) qui, que, lequel, laquelle; (*when*) où. **that is** c'est-à-dire. *conj* que.

thatch [θatʃ] *n* chaume *m*. **thatched cottage** chaumière *f*.

thaw [θɔː] *v* (faire) dégeler, (faire) fondre. *n* dégel *m*.

the [ðɔ] *art* le, la; (*pl*) les.

theatre ['θiɔtɔ] *n* théâtre *m*. **theatrical** *adj* théâtral.

theft [θeft] *n* vol *m*.

their [ðeɔ] *adj* leur.

theirs [ðeɔz] *pron* le leur, la leur.

them [ðem] *pron* eux, elles; (*direct object*) les; (*indirect object*) leur.

theme [θiːm] *n* thème *m*. **thematic** *adj* thématique.

themselves [ðɔm'selvz] *pron* se; (*emphatic*) eux-mêmes, elles-mêmes. **by themselves** tout seuls.

then [ðen] *adv* alors; (*next*) ensuite, puis; (*in that case*) en ce cas. *n* (*that time*) ce moment-là, cette époque-là.

theology [θi'olɔdʒi] *n* théologie *f*. **theologian** *n* théologien, -enne *m, f*. **theological** *adj* théologique.

theorem ['θiɔrɔm] *n* théorème *m*.

theory ['θiɔri] *n* théorie *f*. **theoretical** *adj* théorique.

therapy ['θerɔpi] *n* thérapie *f*, thérapeutique *f*. **therapeutic** *adj* thérapeutique. **therapist** *n* thérapeute *m, f*.

there [ðeɔ] *adv* y, là; **thereabouts** *adv* environ; (*place*) par là. **thereby** *adv* de cette façon. **there is** *or* **are** il y a; (*showing*) voilà. **thereupon** *adv* sur ce.

therefore ['ðeɔfɔː] *adv* donc.

thermal ['θɔːmɔl] *adj* thermal; (*phys*) thermique. *n* courant ascendant *m*.

thermodynamics [θɔːmoudai'namiks] *n* thermodynamique *f*.

thermometer [θɔ'momitɔ] *n* thermomètre *m*.

thermonuclear [θɔːmou'njukliɔ] *adj* thermonucléaire.

thermos ® ['θɔːmɔs] *n* thermos ® *m*.

thermostat ['θɔːmɔstat] *n* thermostat *m*. **thermostatic** *adj* thermostatique.

these [ðiːz] *adj* ces; (*emphatic*) ces ... -ci: *ces robes-ci*. *pron* ce; ceux-ci, celles-ci.

thesis ['θiːsis] *n, pl* -ses thèse *f*.

they [ðei] *pron* ils, elles; (*emphatic*) eux, elles; (*impersonal*) on.

thump

thick [θik] *adj* épais, -aisse; (*stupid*) bête. **thick-skinned** *adj* peu sensible. **thicken** *v* (s')épaissir. **thickness** *n* épaisseur *f*.

thief [θiːf] *n* voleur, -euse *m, f*.

thigh [θai] *n* cuisse *f*.

thimble ['θimbl] *n* dé à coudre *m*.

thin [θin] *adj* mince, fin; (*person*) maigre; (*liquid*) peu épais, -aisse; (*hair*) clairsemé. *v* (s')éclaircir; (*dilute*) délayer. **thinness** *n* minceur *f*; maigreur *f*.

thing [θiŋ] *n* chose *f*. **things** *pl n* affaires *f pl*. **thingumajig** *n* (*coll*) machin *m*.

****think** [θiŋk] *v* penser; imaginer. **I think so** je pense que oui. **think about** penser à. **think over** réfléchir à.

third [θəːd] *adj* troisième. *n* troisième *m, f*; (*fraction*) tiers *m*; (*musique*) tierce *f*. **third party** (*law*) tiers *m*. **third-party insurance** assurance au tiers *f*. **third-rate** *adj* de qualité très inférieure. **Third World** Tiers-Monde *m*.

thirst [θəːst] *n* soif. *v* avoir soif. **be thirsty** avoir soif.

thirteen [θəːˈtiːn] *nm, adj* treize. **thirteenth** *n*(*m+f*). *adj* treizième.

thirty [ˈθəːti] *nm, adj* trente. **thirtieth** *n*(*m+f*). *adj* trentième.

this [ðis] *adj* ce, cette; (*emphatic*) ce ... -ci, cette ... -ci: *cette maison-ci*. *pron* ceci, ce; (*this one*) celui-ci, celle-ci.

thistle [ˈθisl] *n* chardon *m*.

thong [θɒŋ] *n* lanière *f*.

thorn [θɔːn] *n* épine *f*.

thorough [ˈθʌrə] *adj* profond; minutieux. **thoroughbred** *n* (*horse*) pur-sang *m invar*; bête de race *f*. **thoroughfare** *n* voie publique *f*. **thoroughly** *adv* à fond; (*completely*) tout à fait. **thoroughness** *n* minutie *f*.

those [ðouz] *adj* ces; (*emphatic*) ces ... -là: *ces chaises-là*. *pron* ce; ceux-là, celleslà.

though [ðou] *conj* bien que. *adv* pourtant. **as though** comme si.

thought [θɔːt] *V* **think**. *n* pensée *f*; idée *f*; opinion *f*; considération *f*. **thoughtful** *adj* pensif; sérieux; (*considerate*) prévenant, gentil, -ille. **thoughtless** *adj* étourdi; irréfléchi.

thousand [ˈθauzənd] *nm, adj* mille. **thousandth** *n*(*m+f*). *adj* millième.

thrash [θraʃ] *v* rosser, battre violemment; (*sport, etc.*) battre à plates coutures. **thrash about** se débattre. **thrash out** (*problem, etc.*) débattre de. **thrashing** *n* correction *f*.

thread [θred] *n* fil *m*; (*screw*) pas *m*. *v* enfiler; faire passer. **threadbare** *adj* usé, râpé.

threat [θret] *n* menace *f*. **threaten** *v* menacer.

three [θriː] *nm, adj* trois. **three-dimensional** *adj* à trois dimensions. **three-point turn** demi-tour en trois manœuvres *m*.

thresh [θreʃ] *v* battre. **threshing machine** batteuse *f*.

threshold [ˈθreʃould] *n* seuil *m*.

threw [θruː] *V* **throw**.

thrift [θrift] *n* économie *f*. **thrifty** *adj* économe.

thrill [θril] *n* frisson *m*. *v* transporter. **thriller** *n* roman *or* film à suspense *m*. **thrilling** *adj* palpitant.

thrive [θraiv] *v* se développer bien, pousser bien; prospérer. **thriving** *adj* robuste; prospère.

throat [θrout] *n* gorge *f*. **clear one's throat** s'éclaircir la voix. **throaty** *adj* guttural.

throb [θrɒb] *n* (*heart*) pulsation *f*; (*engine*) vibration *f*. *v* palpiter; vibrer; (*pain*) lanciner.

thrombosis [θrɒmˈbousis] *n* thrombose *f*.

throne [θroun] *n* trône *m*.

throng [θrɒŋ] *n* foule *f*, multitude *f*. *v* affluer, se presser.

throttle [ˈθrɒtl] *v* étrangler. *n* (*tech*) papillon des gaz *m*; (*mot*) accélérateur *m*.

through [θruː] *prep* par; (*place*) à travers; (*time*) pendant. *adv* à travers. *adj* direct. **no through road** impasse *f*. **throughout** *prep* (*place*) partout dans; (*time*) pendant.

****throw** [θrou] *n* jet *m*. *v* jeter, lancer; (*hurl*) projeter. **throw away** jeter; (*waste*) gâcher, gaspiller. **throw out** rejeter; expulser. **throw up** vomir.

thrown [θroun] *V* **throw**.

thrush [θrʌʃ] *n* grive *f*.

****thrust** [θrʌst] *n* poussée *f*; coup *m*. *v* pousser brusquement, enfoncer; imposer.

thud [θʌd] *n* bruit sourd *m*. *v* faire un bruit sourd.

thumb [θʌm] *n* pouce *m*. *v also* **thumb through** feuilleter. **thumb a lift** (*coll*) faire du stop.

thump [θʌmp] *n* bruit lourd *m*; (*blow*) grand coup *m*. *v* cogner (à *or* sur); (*heart*) battre fort; (*person*) assener un coup à.

thunder [ˈθʌndə] n tonnerre m; (noise) fracas m. **thunderstorm** n orage m. **thunderstruck** adj abasourdi. v tonner. **thundery** adj orageux.

Thursday [ˈθəːzdi] n jeudi m.

thus [ðʌs] adv ainsi.

thwart [θwɔːt] v contrecarrer, contrarier.

thyme [taim] n thym m.

thyroid [ˈθairoid] nf. adj thyroïde.

tiara [tiˈɑːrə] n diadème m.

tick[1] [tik] n (mark) coche f; (sound) tic-tac m; (coll) instant m. v cocher; faire tic-tac. **tick off** (coll: scold) attraper. **tick over** (mot) tourner au ralenti.

tick[2] [tik] n (insect) tique f.

ticket [ˈtikit] n billet m; (bus) ticket m; (library) carte f; (label) étiquette f. **ticket collector** contrôleur m. **ticket office** guichet m.

tickle [ˈtikl] v chatouiller. n chatouillement m. **ticklish** adj chatouilleux.

tide [taid] n marée f. **tide-mark** n ligne de marée haute f; (of dirt) ligne de crasse f. v **tide over** dépanner.

tidy [ˈtaidi] adj en ordre, bien rangé; (writing, appearance) net, nette. v ranger. **tidily** adv soigneusement. **tidiness** n propreté f.

tie [tai] n attache f; (neck) cravate f; (link) lien m; (draw) égalité f, match nul m. v attacher; lier; (ribbon, etc.) nouer; faire match nul.

tier [tiə] n étage m; (seating) gradin m.

tiger [ˈtaigə] n tigre m.

tight [tait] adj raide, serré, étroit; (seal) étanche; (coll: drunk) soûl; (coll: mean) radin. **tight-fisted** adj avare. **tightrope** n corde raide f. **tightrope walker** funambule m, f. adv also **tightly** bien; hermétiquement. **tighten** v (se) resserrer; (rope) (se) tendre; (control) renforcer. **tights** pl n collant m sing.

tile [tail] n (roof) tuile f; (wall, floor) carreau m. v couvrir de tuiles; carreler.

till[1] [til] V until.

till[2] [til] n caisse f.

till[3] [til] v labourer.

tiller [ˈtilə] n (naut) barre du gouvernail f.

tilt [tilt] n inclinaison f. v pencher, incliner.

timber [ˈtimbə] n bois d'œuvre m. **timbered** adj (house) en bois.

time [taim] n temps m; (clock) heure f; (occasion) fois f; époque f; moment m; (music) mesure f. **a long time** longtemps.

a short time peu de temps. **at the same time** à la fois. **from time to time** de temps en temps. **in time** à temps; (music) en mesure. **on time** à l'heure. **time bomb** bombe à retardement f. **time-sheet** n feuille de présence f. **time-switch** n minuteur m. **timetable** n (rail) horaire m; (school) emploi du temps m. **time zone** fuseau horaire m. v fixer; (runner, etc.) chronométrer; (programme, etc.) minuter. **timeless** adj éternel. **timely** adj à propos. **timer** n (cooking) compte-minutes m invar.

timid [ˈtimid] adj timide, craintif. **timidity** n timidité f.

timpani [ˈtimpəni] pl n timbales f pl.

tin [tin] n étain m; (can) boîte f; (baking) moule m; (roasting) plat m. **tin foil** papier d'étain m. **tin-opener** n ouvre-boîtes m. **tin soldier** soldat de plomb m. v mettre en boîte. **tinny** adj métallique.

tinge [tindʒ] n teinte f. v teinter.

tingle [ˈtingl] v picoter. n picotement m.

tinker [ˈtinkə] n romanichel, -elle m. f. v bricoler.

tinkle [ˈtinkl] v (faire) tinter. n tintement m.

tinsel [ˈtinsəl] n clinquant m.

tint [tint] n teinte f; (hair) shampooing colorant m. v teinter.

tiny [ˈtaini] adj tout petit, minuscule.

tip[1] [tip] n (end) bout m, pointe f. **on tiptoe** sur la pointe des pieds. v mettre un embout à.

tip[2] [tip] v (se) pencher, incliner; (overturn) (se) renverser; (pour) verser, déverser. n (rubbish) dépotoir m.

tip[3] [tip] n (hint) suggestion f, conseil m; (money) pourboire m. v donner un pourboire (à). **tip off** (warn) prévenir. **tip-off** n (coll) tuyau m.

tipsy [ˈtipsi] adj (coll) éméché.

Tirana [tiˈrɑːnə] n Tirana.

tire[1] [taiə] v (se) fatiguer. **tire out** épuiser. **tired** adj fatigué; las, lasse. **be tired of** en avoir assez de. **tiredness** n fatigue f. **tiresome** adj ennuyeux.

tire[2] (US) V tyre.

tissue [ˈtiʃuː] n tissu m; (handkerchief) mouchoir en papier m. **tissue paper** papier de soie m.

title [ˈtaitl] n titre m; (law) droit m. **title-deed** n titre de propriété m. **title-page** n page de titre f. v intituler. **titled** adj titré.

titter ['titə] n gloussement m. v glousser.
to [tu] prep à; (home, shop) chez; (in order to) pour. **ten to four** quatre heures moins dix. **to-do** n (coll) histoire f.
toad [toud] n crapaud m. **toadstool** n champignon vénéneux m.
toast [toust] n pain grillé m; (speech) toast m. **toast-rack** n porte-toast m. v griller; porter un toast à. **toaster** n grille-pain m invar.
tobacco [tə'bakou] n tabac m. **tobacconist's** n tabac m.
toboggan [tə'bogən] n toboggan m.
today [tə'dei] nm, adv aujourd'hui.
toddler ['todlə] n petit, -e qui commence à marcher m.
toe [tou] n orteil m. **toe-nail** n ongle du pied m. v **toe the line** obéir, se plier.
toffee ['tofi] n caramel m. **toffee-apple** n pomme caramélisée f.
together [tə'geðə] adv ensemble; (simultaneously) à la fois.
toil [toil] n dur travail m. v travailler dur.
toilet ['toilit] n toilettes f pl, cabinets m pl. **toilet-paper** n papier hygiénique m. **toilet water** eau de toilette f.
token ['toukən] n marque f; (disc) jeton m; (voucher) bon m. **as a token of** en gage de. adj symbolique.
Tokyo ['toukiou] n Tokio.
told [tould] V tell.
tolerate ['toləreit] v tolérer, supporter. **tolerable** adj tolérable; passable. **tolerance** or **toleration** n tolérance f. **tolerant** adj tolérant.
toll¹ [toul] n péage m. **toll-gate** n barrière de péage f.
toll² [toul] v sonner.
tomato [tə'maatou] n tomate f.
tomb [tum] n tombeau m. **tombstone** n pierre tombale f.
tomorrow [tə'morou] nm, adv demain. **the day after tomorrow** après-demain.
ton [tʌn] n tonne f.
tone [toun] n ton m; (phone) tonalité f; classe f; sonorité f. v (colour) s'harmoniser. **tone down** baisser, adoucir.
tongs [toŋz] pl n pinces f pl, pincettes f pl.
tongue [tʌŋ] n langue f. **tongue-tied** adj muet, -ette.
tonic ['tonik] adj tonique. n (med) tonique m; (mus) tonique f.
tonight [tə'nait] n, adv cette nuit; (evening) ce soir.

tonsil ['tonsil] n amygdale f. **tonsillitis** n amygdalite f.
too [tu] adv trop; (also) aussi; (moreover) en plus.
took [tuk] V take.
tool [tul] n outil m. **tool-shed** n cabane à outils f.
tooth [tuθ] n, pl teeth dent f. **toothache** n mal de dents m. **have toothache** avoir mal aux dents. **tooth-brush** n brosse à dents f. **toothpaste** n dentifrice m. **toothpick** n cure-dent m. **toothless** adj édenté.
top¹ [top] n haut m; sommet m; (lid) couvercle m; surface f, dessus m; (list) tête f. **at the top of one's voice** à tue-tête. adj du haut; (first) premier; (last) dernier. **top hat** haut-de-forme m. **top-heavy** adj trop lourd du haut. **top secret** ultra-secret, -ète. **topside** n (meat) gîte m. **topsoil** n couche arable f. v surmonter; (exceed) dépasser. **top up** remplir, rajouter.
top² [top] n (toy) toupie f.
topaz ['toupaz] n topaze f.
topic ['topik] n sujet m. **topical** adj d'actualité.
topography [tə'pogrəfi] n topographie f. **topographical** adj topographique.
topple ['topl] v (faire) basculer, (faire) tomber.
topsy-turvy [topsi'tərvi] adj, adv sens dessus dessous.
torch [toitʃ] n (electric) lampe de poche f; (burning) torche f.
tore [toi] V tear¹.
torment ['toiment; v tor'ment] n supplice m. v tourmenter.
torn [toin] V tear¹.
tornado [tor'neidou] n tornade f.
torpedo [tor'piːdou] n torpille f. v torpiller.
torrent ['torənt] n torrent m. **torrential** adj torrentiel.
torso ['toisou] n torse m; (sculpture) buste m.
tortoise ['toitəs] n tortue f. **tortoise-shell** n écaille f.
tortuous ['toitʃuəs] adj tortueux.
torture ['toitʃə] n torture f. v torturer. **torturer** n tortionnaire m.
toss [tos] n lancement m; (coin) coup de pile ou face m. v lancer; (pancake) faire sauter; (s')agiter; (coin) jouer à pile ou face.

tot¹ [tot] *n* (*child*) petit enfant *m*; (*drink*) goutte *f*.

tot² [tot] *v* **tot up** additionner.

total ['toutəl] *nm, adj* total. *v* (*add up*) totaliser; (*add up to*) s'élever à. **totalitarian** *n*(*m*+*f*). *adj* totalitaire.

totter ['totə] *v* chanceler.

touch [tʌtʃ] *n* toucher *m*; contact *m*; (*artist's*) touche *f*. *v* toucher (à), se toucher. **touchy** *adj* susceptible; délicat.

tough [tʌf] *adj* dur; (*strong*) résistant; (*struggle*) acharné. **toughen** *v* rendre plus solide; (*person*) (s')endurcir. **toughness** *n* dureté *f*; résistance *f*.

toupee ['tuːpei] *n* postiche *m*.

tour [tuə] *n* voyage *m*; (*of town, museum, etc.*) visite *f*; (*by musicians*) tournée *f*. *v* visiter. **touring** *or* **tourism** *n* tourisme *m*. **tourist** *n* touriste *m, f*. **tourist's guide** guide touristique *f*.

tournament ['tuənəmənt] *n* tournoi *m*.

tousled ['tauzld] *adj* échevelé.

tow [tou] *n* remorque *f*. *v* remorquer; (*trailer*) tirer. **tow-path** *n* chemin de halage *m*. **tow-rope** *n* remorque *f*.

towards [tə'woːdz] *prep* vers; (*attitude*) envers.

towel ['tauəl] *n* serviette *f*; (*for hands*) essuie-mains *m*. **towel-rail** *n* porte-serviettes *m invar*. **towelling** *n* tissu éponge *m*.

tower ['tauə] *n* tour *f*. *v* **tower over** dominer. **towering** *adj* imposant.

town [taun] *n* ville *f*. **town centre** centre de la ville *m*. **town hall** hôtel de ville *m*. **town planning** urbanisme *m*.

toxic ['toksik] *adj* toxique.

toy [toi] *n* jouet *m*. *adj* petit, miniature; d'enfant. *v* **toy with** jouer avec; (*idea*) caresser.

trace [treis] *n* trace *f*. *v* tracer; (*find*) retrouver; (*through paper*) décalquer. **tracing** *n* calque *m*. **tracing paper** papier-calque *m invar*.

track [trak] *n* (*marks*) trace *f*; (*path*) chemin *m*; (*sport*) piste *f*; (*rail*) voie *f*. **track suit** survêtement *m*. *v* suivre la trace de. **track down** traquer. **tracker** *n* traqueur *m*.

tract¹ [trakt] *n* (*region*) étendue *f*; (*anat*) système *m*.

tract² [trakt] *n* (*treatise*) tract *m*.

tractor ['traktə] *n* tracteur *m*.

trade [treid] *n* commerce *m*; (*job*) métier *m*. **trademark** *n* marque *f*. **tradesman** *n*

commerçant *m*. **trade union** syndicat *m*. **trade-unionist** *n* syndicaliste *m, f*. *v* faire le commerce (de); commercer (avec); échanger. **trade in** faire reprendre. **trader** *n* commerçant, -e *m, f*; négociant, -e *m, f*.

tradition [trə'diʃən] *n* tradition *f*. **traditional** *adj* traditionnel.

traffic ['trafik] *n* (*mot*) circulation *f*; (*aero, naut, etc.*) trafic *m*; commerce *m*. **traffic jam** embouteillage *m*. **traffic-light** *n* feu *m*. **traffic warden** contractuel, -elle *m, f*.

tragedy ['tradʒədi] *n* tragédie *f*. **tragic** *adj* tragique.

trail [treil] *n* traînée *f*; (*tracks*) trace *f*; (*path*) sentier *m*. *v* (*drag*) traîner; (*follow*) suivre la piste de. **trailer** *n* (*mot*) remorque *f*; film publicitaire *m*.

train [trein] *n* train *m*; (*series*) suite *f*; (*of dress*) traîne *f*. *v* (*teach*) former; (*learn*) recevoir sa formation; (*sport*) (s')entraîner; (*animal*) dresser. **trainee** *n* stagiaire *m, f*. **trainer** *n* (*sport*) entraîneur, -euse *m, f*; (*animal*) dresseur, -euse *m, f*; (*shoe*) chaussure de sport *f*. **training** *n* formation *f*; entraînement *m*; dressage *m*.

trait [treit] *n* trait *m*.

traitor ['treitə] *n* traître, -esse *m, f*.

tram [tram] *n* tram *m*.

tramp [tramp] *n* (*person*) clochard, -e *m, f*; (*hike*) randonnée *f*; (*sound*) martèlement des pas *m*. *v* marcher d'un pas lourd.

trample ['trampl] *v* piétiner, fouler aux pieds.

trampoline ['trampəlin] *n* tremplin *m*.

trance [trains] *n* transe *f*.

tranquil ['traŋkwil] *adj* tranquille. **tranquillity** *n* tranquillité *f*. **tranquillize** *v* tranquilliser. **tranquillizer** *n* tranquillisant *m*.

transact [tran'zakt] *v* traiter, régler. **transaction** *n* (*econ*) transaction *f*; (*comm*) opération *f*.

transcend [tran'send] *v* transcender; surpasser. **transcendental** *adj* transcendantal.

transcribe [tran'skraib] *v* transcrire. **transcription** *n* transcription *f*.

transept ['transept] *n* transept *m*.

transfer [trans'fəː; *n* 'transfə] *v* transférer, être transféré. *n* transfert *m*; (*picture*) décalcomanie *f*. **not transferable** personnel.

transfixed [trans'fikst] *adj* cloué sur place.

transform [trans'fo:m] *v* transformer. **transformation** *n* transformation *f.* **transformer** *n* (*elec*) transformateur *m.*

transfuse [trans'fju:z] *v* transfuser. **transfusion** *n* transfusion *f.*

transient ['tranziənt] *adj* transitoire.

transistor [tran'zistə] *n* transistor *m.* **transistorize** *v* transistoriser.

transit ['transit] *n* transit *m.* **in transit** en transit.

transition [tran'ziʃən] *n* transition *f.* **transitional** *adj* de transition.

transitive ['transitiv] *adj* transitif.

transitory ['transitəri] *adj* transitoire.

translate [trans'leit] *v* traduire. **translation** *n* traduction *f*; (*school*) version *f.* **translator** *n* traducteur, -trice *m, f.*

translucent [trans'lu:snt] *adj* translucide. **translucence** *n* translucidité *f.*

transmit [tranz'mit] *v* transmettre; (*broadcast*) émettre. **transmission** *n* transmission *f.* **transmitter** *n* transmetteur *m*; émetteur *m.*

transparent [trans'peərənt] *adj* transparent. **transparency** (*phot*) diapositive *f*; transparence *f.*

transplant [trans'pla:nt; *n* 'transpla:nt] *v* transplanter. *n* transplantation *f.*

transport [trans'po:t; *n* 'transpo:t] *v* transporter. *n* transport *m.* **transportation** *n* transport *m.*

transpose [trans'pouz] *v* transposer. **transposition** *n* transposition *f.*

transverse ['tranzvə:s] *adj* transversal.

transvestite [tranz'vestait] *n* travesti, -e *m, f.*

trap [trap] *n* piège *m.* **trapdoor** *n* trappe *f.* *v* prendre au piège; bloquer.

trapeze [trə'pi:z] *n* trapèze *m.* **trapeze artist** trapéziste *m, f.*

trash [traʃ] *n* (*worthless*) camelote *f*; (*waste*) ordures *f pl.* **trash can** (*US*) poubelle *f.*

trauma ['tro:mə] *n* traumatisme *m*; (*med*) trauma *m.* **traumatic** *adj* traumatisant; (*med*) traumatique.

travel ['travl] *v* voyager; (*go*) aller; (*cover*) parcourir. *n* voyage *m.* **travel agency** agence de voyages *f.* **travel brochure** dépliant touristique *m.* **travel-sickness** *n* mal de la route. **traveller** *n* voyageur, -euse *m, f*; (*comm*) représentant *m.* **traveller's cheque** chèque de voyage *m.*

travesty ['travəsti] *n* simulacre *m,* parodie *f.*

trawler ['tro:lə] *n* chalutier *m.* **trawling** *n* chalutage *m.*

tray [trei] *n* plateau *m.* **tray-cloth** *n* napperon *m.*

treachery ['tretʃəri] *n* traîtrise *f.* **treacherous** *adj* traître, -esse.

treacle ['tri:kl] *n* mélasse *f.*

*****tread** [tred] *n* (bruit de) pas *m*; (*tyre*) chape *f.* *v* marcher. **tread on** mettre le pied sur; (*crush*) écraser du pied.

treason ['tri:zn] *n* trahison *f.*

treasure ['treʒə] *n* trésor *m.* *v* tenir beaucoup à; garder précieusement. **treasurer** *n* trésorier, -ère *m, f.* **treasury** *n* trésorerie *f.*

treat [tri:t] *v* traiter; (*med*) soigner. *n* plaisir *m.* **treatment** *n* traitement *m.*

treatise ['tri:tiz] *n* traité *m.*

treaty ['tri:ti] *n* traité *m.*

treble ['trebl] *adj* triple; de soprano. *n* soprano *m.* *v* tripler. *adv* trois fois plus.

tree [tri:] *n* arbre *m.*

trek [trek] *v* cheminer. *n* randonnée *f.*

trellis ['trelis] *n* treillis *m,* treillage *m.* *v* treillisser.

tremble ['trembl] *v* trembler, frémir. *n* tremblement *m,* frémissement *m.*

tremendous [trə'mendəs] *adj* énorme; (*terrible*) épouvantable; (*coll*: *excellent*) formidable.

tremor ['tremə] *n* tremblement *m.*

trench [trentʃ] *n* tranchée *f.*

trend [trend] *n* tendance *f*; mode *f*; direction *f.* **trendy** *adj* (*coll*) à la mode, dans le vent.

trespass ['trespəs] *v* s'introduire sans permission. *n* entrée non autorisée *f.* **trespasser** *n* intrus, -e *m, f.* **trespassers will be prosecuted** défense d'entrer sous peine de poursuites.

trestle ['tresl] *n* tréteau *m.* **trestle table** table à tréteaux *f.*

trial ['traiəl] *n* (*law*) procès *m*; (*test*) essai *m*; (*trouble*) épreuve *f.* **by trial and error** par tâtonnements. *adj* d'essai.

triangle ['traiangl] *n* triangle *m.* **triangular** *adj* triangulaire.

tribe [traib] *n* tribu *f.* **tribal** *adj* tribal. **tribesman** *n* membre d'une tribu *m.*

tribunal [trai'bju:nl] *n* tribunal *m.*

tributary ['tribjutəri] *n* affluent *m.* *adj* tributaire.

tribute ['tribjuːt] n tribut m.

trick [trik] n tour m; ruse f; (cards) levée f. **do the trick** (coll) faire l'affaire. **trick photograph** photographie truquée f. **trick question** question-piège f. v attraper. **trickery** n ruse f. **tricky** adj délicat, difficile.

trickle ['trikl] n filet m. v couler, dégouliner.

tricycle ['traisikl] n tricycle m.

trifle ['traifl] n bagatelle f; (sweet) diplomate m. v **trifle with** traiter à la légère. **trifling** adj insignifiant.

trigger ['trigə] n détente f, gâchette f. v déclencher, provoquer.

trigonometry [trigə'nomətri] n trigonométrie f.

trill [tril] n trille m. v triller.

trim [trim] adj net, nette; (tidy) bien tenu. **in trim** en forme. v tailler légèrement; (hair) rafraîchir; (decorate) garnir. **trimmings** pl n garnitures f pl; accessoires m pl.

trinket ['triŋkit] n bibelot m.

trio ['triːou] n trio m.

trip [trip] n voyage m; (stumble) faux pas m; (slang: drugs) trip m. v trébucher. **trip up** (faire) trébucher; (on purpose) faire un croche-pied à.

tripe [traip] n tripes f pl; (coll) bêtises f pl.

triple ['tripl] nm, adj triple. v tripler. adv trois fois plus.

triplet ['triplit] n (music) triolet m; (poetry) tercet m; (person) triplé, -e m, f.

tripod ['traipod] n trépied m.

trite [trait] adj banal. **triteness** n banalité f.

triumph ['traiəmf] n triomphe m. v triompher. **triumphant** adj triomphant. **triumphantly** adv triomphalement.

trivial ['triviəl] adj insignifiant; banal. **trivia** or **trivialities** pl n bagatelles f pl.

trod [trod] V tread.

trodden ['trodn] V tread.

trolley ['troli] n chariot m; (shopping) poussette f; (tea) table roulante f.

trombone [trom'boun] n trombone m.

troop [truːp] n bande f, troupe f. troops pl n (mil) troupes f pl. v **troop in/out** entrer/sortir en bande. **trooping the colour** le salut au drapeau.

trophy ['troufi] n trophée m.

tropic ['tropik] n tropique m. **tropical** adj tropical.

trot [trot] n trot m. **on the trot** (coll) de suite. v trotter. **trotter** n pied de porc m.

trouble ['trʌbl] n ennui m; (bother) peine f; difficulté f. **be in trouble** avoir des ennuis. **that's the trouble!** c'est ça l'ennui! **troublemaker** n fauteur, -trice de troubles m, f. **troublesome** adj fatigant, gênant. v (bother) (se) déranger; (upset) affliger, gêner; (worry) inquiéter.

trough [trof] n (drinking) abreuvoir m; (food) auge f; dépression f, creux m.

trousers ['trauzəz] pl n pantalon m sing; (short) culottes f pl. **trouser-suit** n tailleur-pantalon m.

trout [traut] n truite f.

trowel ['trauəl] n truelle f; (gardening) déplantoir m.

truant ['truːənt] n **play truant** faire l'école buissonnière. **truancy** n absence non autorisée f.

truce [truːs] n trêve f. **call a truce** faire trêve.

truck [trʌk] n camion m; (rail) wagon m. **truck-driver** n camionneur m.

trudge [trʌdʒ] v se traîner, marcher péniblement.

true [truː] adj vrai; exact; (accurate) fidèle; réel; (straight) droit; (note) juste. **truly** adv vraiment. **well and truly** bel et bien.

truffle ['trʌfl] n truffe f.

trump [trʌmp] n atout m. **turn up trumps** (coll) faire des merveilles. v couper.

trumpet ['trʌmpit] n trompette f. v (elephant) barrir. **trumpeter** n trompettiste m, f.

truncate [trʌŋ'keit] v tronquer.

truncheon ['trʌntʃən] n matraque f; (police) bâton m.

trunk [trʌŋk] n tronc m; (elephant) trompe f; (case) malle f; (mot) coffre m. **trunk call** communication interurbaine f. **trunk road** route nationale f. **trunks** pl n slip de bain m sing.

truss [trʌs] n (hay) botte f; (fruit) grappe f; (med) bandage herniaire m. v trousser.

trust [trʌst] n confiance f; charge f; (comm) trust m; (law) fidéicommis m. **trustworthy** adj digne de confiance. v avoir confiance en, se fier à; (hope) espérer. **trustee** n (law) fidéicommissaire m; (of school) administrateur, -trice m, f. **trusting** adj confiant. **trusty** adj fidèle.

truth [truːθ] n verité f. **truthful** adj véridique. **truthfulness** n véracité f.

try [trai] n essai m. v essayer; juger; (strain) mettre à l'épreuve; tester. **try on** v essayer. **trying** adj pénible.

tsar [zaɪ] n tsar m.

T-shirt [tiːʃəːt] n T-shirt m.

tub [tʌb] n cuve f, baquet m; (bath) tub m.

tuba [tjuːbə] n tuba m.

tube [tjuːb] n tube m; (rail) métro m. **tubeless** adj (tyre) sans chambre à air.

tuber [tjuːbə] n tubercule m.

tuberculosis [tjubəːkjuˈlousis] n tuberculose f.

tuck [tʌk] n (sewing) rempli m. **tuck-shop** n (school) boutique à provisions f. v mettre. **tuck in** (flap) rentrer; (bedclothes) border; (coll: eat) boulotter. **tuck up** (in bed) border; (skirt) remonter.

Tuesday [tjuːzdi] n mardi m.

tuft [tʌft] n touffe f; (feathers) huppe f.

tug [tʌg] n saccade f; (boat) remorqueur m. **tug-of-war** n lutte à la corde f. v tirer; remorquer.

tuition [tjuˈiʃən] n cours m pl.

tulip [tjuːlip] n tulipe f.

tumble [tʌmbl] n chute f, culbute f. v culbuter, dégringoler; (knock over) faire tomber, renverser. **tumbledown** adj en ruines. **tumble-dryer** n séchoir à air chaud m. **tumble out** tomber en vrac. **tumbler** n verre droit m.

tummy [tʌmi] n (coll) ventre m.

tumour [tjuːmə] n tumeur f.

tumult [tjuːmʌlt] n tumulte m. **tumultuous** adj tumultueux.

tuna [tjuːnə] n also **tunny** thon m.

tune [tjuːn] n air m. **in tune** accordé; (sing) juste. **out of tune** désaccordé; (sing) faux. v régler; (music) accorder. **tuneful** adj mélodieux. **tuner** n (person) accordeur m; (radio) radio-préamplificateur m. **tuning** n réglage m; accord m. **tuning fork** diapason m.

tunic [tjuːnik] n tunique f.

tunnel [tʌnl] n tunnel m. v percer un tunnel.

turban [təːbən] n turban m.

turbine [təːbain] n turbine f.

turbot [təːbət] n turbot m.

turbulent [təːbjulənt] adj turbulent. **turbulence** n turbulence f.

tureen [təˈriːn] n soupière f.

turf [təːf] n gazon m; (sport) turf m. **turf accountant** bookmaker m. v gazonner. **turf out** (coll: thing) bazarder; (coll: person) flanquer à la porte.

turkey [təːki] n dindon m; (cookery) dinde f.

Turkey [təːki] n Turquie f. **Turk** n Turc, Turque m, f. **Turkish** nm, adj turc, turque. **Turkish bath** bain turc m. **Turkish delight** loukoum m.

turmeric [təːmərik] n curcuma m.

turmoil [təːmoil] n agitation f, trouble m.

turn [təːn] n tour m; (in road) tournant m, virage m; (med) crise f; (theatre) numéro m. **do a good turn** rendre un service (à). v (faire) tourner; (se) retourner; changer. **turn away** (se) détourner; refuser, rejeter. **turn down** rejeter; (lower) baisser. **turn off** fermer, éteindre. **turn on** allumer, brancher; attaquer. **turn out** (end up) s'avérer; (light) éteindre; (empty) vider; (expel) mettre à la porte. **turnover** n (comm) roulement m; (cookery) chausson m. **turnstile** n tourniquet m. **turntable** n (record-player) platine f; (trains, etc.) plaque tournante f. **turn up** arriver; (be found) être trouvé; (raise) mettre plus fort, monter. **turning** n (side road) route latérale f; (bend) coude m. **turning point** tournant m, moment décisif m.

turnip [təːnip] n navet m.

turpentine [təːpəntain] n térébenthine f.

turquoise [təːkwoiz] n (stone) turquoise f; (colour) turquoise m. adj (colour) turquoise invar.

turret [tʌrit] n tourelle f.

turtle [təːtl] n tortue marine f. **turn turtle** chavirer. **turtle-neck** (jumper) col montant m.

tusk [tʌsk] n défense f.

tussle [tʌsl] n lutte f. v se battre.

tutor [tjuːtə] n (private) précepteur, -trice m, f; (university) directeur, -trice d'études m, f. v donner des cours particuliers (à).

tuxedo [tʌkˈsiːdou] n smoking m.

tweed [twiːd] n tweed m.

tweezers [twiːzəz] pl n pinces fines f pl.

twelve [twelv] nm, adj douze. **twelfth** n(m+f), adj douzième. **Twelfth Night** la fête des Rois f.

twenty [twenti] nm, adj vingt. **twentieth** n(m+f), adj vingtième.

twice [twais] *adv* deux fois.

twiddle ['twidl] *v* tripoter. **twiddle one's thumbs** se tourner les pouces.

twig [twig] *n* brindille *f*.

twilight ['twailait] *n* crépuscule *m*.

twin [twin] *n, adj* jumeau, -elle. **twin beds** lits jumeaux *m pl.* **twin town** ville jumelée *f.* v jumeler.

twine [twain] *n* ficelle *f. v (weave)* tresser; (s')enrouler; serpenter.

twinge [twindʒ] *n (pain)* élancement *m; (sadness)* pincement *m;* remords *m.*

twinkle ['twiŋkl] *v* scintiller, briller. *n* scintillement *m; (eyes)* pétillement *m.*

twirl [twɜːl] *v* (faire) tournoyer. *n* tournoiement *m.*

twist [twist] *n* torsion *f; (med)* entorse *f; (in wire, etc.)* tortillon *m; (in road)* tournant *m; (story)* coup de théâtre *m. v* (s')entortiller, tordre; *(turn)* tourner; *(road)* serpenter.

twit [twit] *n (slang)* idiot, -e *m. f.*

twitch [twitʃ] *n* tic *m; (pull)* coup sec *m. v* se convulser; avoir un tic; tirer d'un coup sec.

twitter ['twitə] *v* gazouiller. *n* gazouillement *m.*

two [tuː] *nm, adj* deux. **two-faced** *adj* hypocrite. **two-legged** *adj* bipède. **two-time** *v (coll)* doubler.

tycoon [tai'kuːn] *n* magnat *m.*

type [taip] *n* type *m; (sort)* genre *m.* **typesetting** *n* composition *f.* **typewriter** *n* machine à écrire *f. v* taper (à la machine). **typical** *adj* typique. **typing** *n* dactylo *f.* **typist** *n* dactylo *m. f.*

typhoid ['taifɔid] *n* typhoïde *f.*

typhoon [tai'fuːn] *n* typhon *m.*

tyrant ['tairənt] *n* tyran *m.* **tyrannical** *adj* tyrannique. **tyranny** *n* tyrannie *f.*

tyre *or US* **tire** ['taiə] *n* pneu *m.*

U

ubiquitous [juː'bikwitəs] *adj* omniprésent.

udder ['ʌdə] *n* pis *m.* mamelle *f.*

ugly ['ʌgli] *adj* laid, vilain; répugnant. **ugliness** *n* laideur *f.*

ulcer ['ʌlsə] *n* ulcère *m.*

ulterior [ʌl'tiəriə] *adj* ultérieur, -e. **ulterior motive** arrière-pensée *f.*

ultimate ['ʌltimət] *adj* ultime; final; suprême. **ultimately** *adv* à la fin; *(basically)* en fin de compte. **ultimatum** *n* ultimatum *m.*

ultraviolet [ʌltrə'vaiələt] *adj* ultra-violet.

umbilical [ʌm'bilikəl] *adj* ombilical.

umbrage ['ʌmbridʒ] *n* ombrage *m.* **take umbrage** prendre ombrage.

umbrella [ʌm'brelə] *n* parapluie *m.*

umpire ['ʌmpaiə] *n* arbitre *m. v* arbitrer.

umpteen [ʌmp'tiːn] *(coll) adj* je ne sais combien (de). **umpteenth** *adj* énième.

unable [ʌn'eibl] *adj* incapable. **be unable to** *(lack means)* ne pas pouvoir; *(lack knowledge)* ne pas savoir.

unabridged [ʌnə'bridʒd] *adj* intégral.

unacceptable [ʌnək'septəbl] *adj* inacceptable; inadmissible.

unaccompanied [ʌnə'kʌmpənid] *adj* non accompagné; *(music)* sans accompagnement, seul.

unadulterated [ʌnə'dʌltəreitid] *adj* pur.

unaided [ʌn'eidid] *adj* sans aide.

unanimous [juː'naniməs] *adj* unanime. **unanimity** *n* unanimité *f.*

unarmed [ʌn'aːmd] *adj (combat)* sans armes; *(person)* non armé.

unattached [ʌnə'tatʃt] *adj* libre; indépendant.

unattractive [ʌnə'traktiv] *adj* peu attrayant, déplaisant.

unauthorized [ʌn'ɔːθəraizd] *adj* non autorisé.

unavoidable [ʌnə'vɔidəbl] *adj* inévitable.

unaware [ʌnə'weə] *adj* inconscient. **be unaware of** ignorer. **unawares** *adv* à l'improviste.

unbalanced [ʌn'balənst] *adj* mal équilibré; *(mentally)* déséquilibré.

unbearable [ʌn'beərəbl] *adj* insupportable.

unbelievable [ʌnbi'liːvəbl] *adj* incroyable.

*****unbend** [ʌn'bend] *v* redresser; *(person)* se détendre. **unbending** *adj* inflexible.

unbiased [ʌn'baiəst] *adj* impartial.

unbreakable [ʌn'breikəbl] *adj* incassable.

unbridled [ʌn'braidld] *adj* débridé.

unbutton [ʌn'bʌtn] *v* déboutonner.

uncalled-for [ʌn'kɔːldfɔː] *adj* injustifié, déplacé.

uncanny [ʌn'kani] *adj* étrange, troublant.

uncertain [ʌn'sɜːtn] *adj* incertain. **uncertainty** *n* incertitude *f.*

uncle ['ʌŋkl] n oncle m.

uncomfortable [ʌn'kʌmfətəbl] adj inconfortable; mal à l'aise.

uncommon [ʌn'komən] adj rare.

uncompromising [ʌn'komprəmaiziŋ] adj intransigeant.

unconditional [ʌnkən'diʃənl] adj inconditionnel.

unconscious [ʌn'konʃəs] adj (med) sans connaissance; (unaware) inconscient.

unconventional [ʌnkən'venʃənl] adj peu conventionnel.

uncooked [ʌn'kukt] adj non cuit.

uncouth [ʌn'kuːθ] adj grossier.

uncover [ʌn'kʌvə] v découvrir.

uncut [ʌn'kʌt] adj non coupé, non taillé.

undecided [ʌndi'saidid] adj indécis.

undeniable [ʌndi'naiəbl] adj indéniable, incontestable.

under ['ʌndə] adv au-dessous. prep sous; au dessous de; (less) moins de; (according to) selon.

underarm ['ʌndərɑːm] adj, adv par en-dessous.

undercharge [ʌndə'tʃɑːdʒ] v ne pas faire payer assez à.

underclothes ['ʌndəklouðz] pl n sous-vêtements m pl.

undercoat ['ʌndəkout] n couche de fond f.

undercover [ʌndə'kʌvə] adj secret, -ète.

undercut [ʌndə'kʌt] v vendre moins cher que.

underdeveloped [ʌndədi'veləpt] adj sous-développé.

underdog ['ʌndədog] n (loser) perdant m; (oppressed) opprimé m.

underdone [ʌndə'dʌn] adj (meat) saignant; pas assez cuit.

underestimate [ʌndər'estimeit] v sous-estimer. **underestimation** n sous-estimation f.

underfoot [ʌndə'fut] adv sous les pieds.

undergo [ʌndə'gou] v subir, éprouver.

undergraduate [ʌndə'gradjuət] n étudiant, -e m, f.

underground [ʌndə'graund; adj, adv 'ʌndəgraund] adv sous terre; clandestinement. adj sous terre, souterrain; clandestin. n (rail) métro m.

undergrowth ['ʌndəgrouθ] n broussailles f pl.

underhand [ʌndə'hand] adj en sous-main, sournois.

*underlie [ʌndə'lai] v être à la base de. **underlying** adj sous-jacent.

underline [ʌndə'lain] v souligner. **underlining** n soulignage m.

undermine [ʌndə'main] v saper, miner.

underneath [ʌndə'niːθ] prep sous, au-dessous de. nm, adv dessous. adj d'en dessous.

underpaid [ʌndə'peid] adj sous-payé.

underpants ['ʌndəpants] pl n caleçon m sing.

underpass ['ʌndəpɑːs] n (cars) passage inférieur m; (people) passage souterrain m.

underprivileged [ʌndə'prividʒd] adj défavorisé.

underrate [ʌndə'reit] v sous-estimer.

underskirt ['ʌndəskəːt] n jupon m.

understaffed [ʌndə'stɑːft] adj à court de personnel.

*understand [ʌndə'stand] v comprendre; (imply) sous-entendre. **understandable** adj compréhensible. **understanding** n compréhension f; (agreement) accord m.

understate [ʌndə'steit] v minimiser. **make an understatement** ne pas assez dire. **that's an understatement!** c'est peu dire!

understudy ['ʌndəstʌdi] n doublure f. v doubler.

*undertake [ʌndə'teik] v entreprendre, se charger de. **undertaker** n ordonnateur des pompes funèbres m. **undertaking** n entreprise f; promesse f.

undertone ['ʌndətoun] n **in an undertone** à demi-voix.

underwater [ʌndə'wɔːtə] adj sous-marin. adv sous l'eau.

underwear ['ʌndəweə] n sous-vêtements m pl.

underweight [ʌndə'weit] adj (goods) d'un poids insuffisant; (person) trop maigre.

underworld ['ʌndəwəːld] n (criminal) milieu m; (hell) enfers m pl.

*underwrite [ʌndə'rait] v garantir; (insurance) souscrire.

undesirable [ʌndi'zaiərəbl] adj peu souhaitable. n indésirable m, f.

*undo [ʌn'duː] v défaire; (destroy) détruire. **come undone** se défaire. **undoing** n ruine f.

undoubted [ʌn'dautid] adj indubitable.

undress [ʌn'dres] v (se) déshabiller.

undue [ʌn'djuː] adj indu. **unduly** adv trop.

undulate ['ʌndjuleit] v onduler. **undulating** adj onduleux. **undulation** n ondulation f.

unearth [ʌn'ɜːθ] v déterrer. **unearthly** adj surnaturel; (coll: hour) impossible, indu.

uneasy [ʌn'iːzi] adj mal à l'aise; troublé; anxieux.

uneducated [ʌn'edjukeitid] adj sans éducation.

unemployed [ʌnem'ploid] en chômage. **the unemployed** les chômeurs m pl. **unemployment** n chômage m.

unenthusiastic [ʌnenθjuːzi'astik] adj peu enthousiaste.

unequal [ʌn'iːkwəl] adj inégal.

uneven [ʌn'iːvn] adj inégal; (number) impair.

uneventful [ʌni'ventfəl] adj peu mouvementé.

unexpected [ʌneks'pektid] adj inattendu.

unfailing [ʌn'feiliŋ] adj inépuisable; infaillible.

unfair [ʌn'feə] adj injuste. **unfairness** n injustice f.

unfaithful [ʌn'feiθfəl] adj infidèle. **unfaithfulness** n infidélité f.

unfamiliar [ʌnfə'miljə] adj peu familier, inconnu.

unfasten [ʌn'faːsn] v défaire, ouvrir.

unfavourable [ʌn'feivərəbl] adj défavorable.

unfinished [ʌn'finiʃt] adj inachevé; à finir.

unfit [ʌn'fit] adj inapte, impropre; (ill) souffrant.

unfold [ʌn'fould] v déplier; exposer; (story, countryside) se dérouler.

unforeseen [ʌnfɔː'siːn] adj imprévu.

unforgivable [ʌnfə'givəbl] adj impardonnable.

unfortunate [ʌn'fɔːtʃənət] adj malheureux, fâcheux.

unfounded [ʌn'faundid] adj sans fondement; injustifié.

unfriendly [ʌn'frendli] adj froid; hostile.

unfurnished [ʌn'fɜːniʃd] adj non meublé.

ungainly [ʌn'geinli] adj gauche.

ungrateful [ʌn'greitfəl] adj ingrat.

unhappy [ʌn'hapi] adj triste, malheureux. **unhappiness** n tristesse f.

unhealthy [ʌn'helθi] adj malsain; (person) maladif.

unheard-of [ʌn'hɜːdov] adj inouï, sans précédent.

unhurt [ʌn'hɜːt] adj indemne, sain et sauf.

unhygienic [ʌnhai'dʒiːnik] adj non hygiénique.

unicorn ['juːnikɔːn] n licorne f.

unidentified [ʌnai'dentifaid] adj non identifié. **unidentified flying object** (UFO) objet volant non identifié (OVNI) m.

uniform ['juːnifɔːm] nm, adj uniforme. **uniformity** n uniformité f.

unify ['juːnifai] v unifier. **unification** n unification f.

unilateral [juːni'latərəl] adj unilatéral.

unimaginative [ʌni'madʒinətiv] adj peu imaginatif.

unimportant [ʌnim'pɔːtnt] adj peu important.

uninhabited [ʌnin'habitid] adj inhabité.

uninhibited [ʌnin'hibitid] adj sans inhibitions.

unintentional [ʌnin'tenʃənl] adj involontaire.

uninterested [ʌn'intristid] adj indifférent. **uninteresting** adj inintéressant.

union ['juːnjən] n union f; (trade) syndicat m.

unique [juː'niːk] adj unique.

unisex ['juːni,seks] adj (coll) unisexe.

unison ['juːnisn] n unisson m. **in unison** en chœur.

unit ['juːnit] n unité f; bloc m, groupe m.

unite [juː'nait] v (s')unir, unifier. **united** adj uni. **United Kingdom** Royaume-Uni m. **United Nations** Nations Unies f pl. **United States of America** Etats-Unis m pl.

unity ['juːniti] n unité f.

universe ['juːnivɜːs] n univers m. **universal** adj universel.

university [juːni'vɜːsəti] n université f. adj universitaire.

unjust [ʌn'dʒʌst] adj injuste.

unkempt [ʌn'kempt] adj débraillé; (hair) mal peigné.

unkind [ʌn'kaind] adj peu aimable, méchant, cruel. **unkindness** n méchanceté f.

unknown [ʌn'noun] nm, adj inconnu.

unlawful [ʌn'lɔːfəl] adj illégal, illégitime.

unless [ʌn'les] conj à moins que.

unlike [ʌn'laik] adj dissemblable, différent. prep à la différence de.

unlikely [ʌn'laikli] adj peu probable; (story) invraisemblable.

unlimited [ʌn'limitid] adj illimité.

unload [ʌn'loud] v décharger; (get rid of) se défaire de.

unlock [ʌn'lok] v ouvrir.

unlucky [ʌn'lʌki] *adj* malchanceux, malheureux; *(number, etc.)* qui porte malheur.

unmarried [ʌn'marid] *adj* célibataire.

unnatural [ʌn'natʃərəl] *adj* anormal; contre nature.

unnecessary [ʌn'nesəsəri] *adj* inutile; superflu.

unnerving [ʌn'nərviŋ] *adj* déconcertant.

unnoticed [ʌn'noutist] *adj* inaperçu. **go unnoticed** passer inaperçu.

unobtainable [ʌnəb'teinəbl] *adj* impossible à obtenir.

unobtrusive [ʌnəb'truːsiv] *adj* discret, -ète.

unoccupied [ʌn'ɔkjupaid] *adj* inoccupé. *(seat)* libre.

unofficial [ʌnə'fiʃəl] *adj* officieux, non officiel.

unorthodox [ʌn'ɔːθədɔks] *adj* peu orthodoxe.

unpack [ʌn'pak] *v (case)* défaire (sa valise); *(contents)* déballer (ses affaires).

unpaid [ʌn'peid] *adj* impayé, non acquitté; *(worker)* non rétribué.

unpleasant [ʌn'plezŋt] *adj* désagréable, déplaisant.

unpopular [ʌn'pɔpjulə] *adj* impopulaire.

unprecedented [ʌn'presidentid] *adj* sans précédent.

unpredictable [ʌnprə'diktəbl] *adj* imprévisible; incertain.

unqualified [ʌn'kwolifaid] *adj* non qualifié, non diplômé; *(absolute)* sans réserve.

unravel [ʌn'ravəl] *v* (s')effiler; *(mystery)* débrouiller.

unreal [ʌn'riəl] *adj* irréel.

unreasonable [ʌn'riːzənəbl] *adj* déraisonnable; excessif.

unrelenting [ʌnri'lentiŋ] *adj* implacable.

unreliable [ʌnri'laiəbl] *adj* sur qui on ne peut compter; *(machine)* peu fiable; *(source)* douteux.

unrest [ʌn'rest] *n* agitation *f*.

unruly [ʌn'ruːli] *adj* indiscipliné.

unsafe [ʌn'seif] *adj* dangereux.

unsatisfactory [ʌnsatis'faktəri] *adj* peu satisfaisant.

unscrew [ʌn'skruː] *v* (se) dévisser.

unscrupulous [ʌn'skruːpjuləs] *adj* sans scrupules, malhonnête.

unselfish [ʌn'selfiʃ] *adj* non égoïste, désintéressé.

unsettle [ʌn'setl] *v* perturber. **unsettled** *adj* perturbé; incertain; instable.

unsightly [ʌn'saitli] *adj* disgracieux.

unskilled [ʌn'skild] *adj* inexpérimenté. **unskilled worker** manœuvre *m*.

unsound [ʌn'saund] *adj* peu solide; *(health)* précaire; *(reasoning)* mal fondé.

unspeakable [ʌn'spiːkəbl] *adj* indescriptible.

unspecified [ʌn'spesifaid] *adj* non spécifié.

unstable [ʌn'steibl] *adj* instable.

unsteady [ʌn'stedi] *adj* instable, mal assuré.

unstuck [ʌn'stʌk] *adj* **come unstuck** se décoller.

unsuccessful [ʌnsək'sesfəl] *adj* infructueux; *(candidate)* réfusé; *(marriage)* malheureux. **unsuccessfully** *adv* sans succès.

unsuitable [ʌn'suːtəbl] *adj* qui ne convient pas; inopportun; peu approprié.

unsure [ʌn'ʃuə] *adj* incertain.

untangle [ʌn'taŋgl] *v* démêler.

untidy [ʌn'taidi] *adj* négligé, débraillé; *(writing)* brouillon; *(room)* en désordre. **untidiness** *n* débraillé *m*; désordre *m*.

untie [ʌn'tai] *v* défaire.

until [ən'til] *prep* jusqu'à; *(before)* avant. *conj* jusqu'à ce que.

untoward [ʌntə'wɔːd] *adj* fâcheux.

untrue [ʌn'truː] *adj* faux, fausse; inexact.

unusual [ʌn'juːʒuəl] *adj* insolite; bizarre; exceptionnel.

unwanted [ʌn'wɔntid] *adj* superflu; non désiré.

unwell [ʌn'wel] *adj* indisposé, souffrant.

unwilling [ʌn'wiliŋ] *adj* peu disposé. **unwillingly** *adv* à contrecœur.

*unwind [ʌn'waind] *v* (se) dérouler; *(relax)* se détendre.

unwise [ʌn'waiz] *adj* imprudent.

unworthy [ʌn'wəːði] *adj* indigne.

unwrap [ʌn'rap] *v* défaire.

up [ʌp] *adv* en haut, en l'air; *(standing)* debout; *(out of bed)* levé; terminé. **up there** là-haut. **up to** jusqu'à. *prep* dans, sur. **go up** monter. *n* **ups and downs** hauts et bas *m pl*.

upbringing [ʌp'briŋiŋ] *n* éducation *f*.

update [ʌp'deit] *v* mettre à jour.

upheaval [ʌp'hiːvl] *n* bouleversement *m*; *(domestic)* branle-bas *m*; *(pol)* perturbation *f*.

uphill [ʌp'hil] *adj* qui monte; (*struggle*) pénible. *adv* go **uphill** monter.

*****uphold** [ʌp'hould] *v* soutenir, maintenir.

upholster [ʌp'houlstə] *v* rembourrer. **upholstery** *n* tapisserie *f*; (*material*) rembourrage *m*; (*in car*) garniture *f*.

upkeep ['ʌpkiːp] *n* entretien *m*.

uplift [ʌp'lift] *v* élever.

upon [ə'pɔn] *prep* sur.

upper ['ʌpə] *adj* supérieur, -e, du dessus. **upper-class** *adj* aristocratique. **uppermost** *adj* le plus haut; en dessus.

upright ['ʌprait] *adj, adv* droit. *n* montant *m*.

uprising [ʌp'raiziŋ] *n* soulèvement *m*.

uproar ['ʌprɔː] *n* tumulte *m*, vacarme *m*. **uproarious** *adj* tumultueux; hilarant.

uproot [ʌp'ruːt] *v* déraciner.

*****upset** [ʌp'set; *n* 'ʌpset] *v* (*knock over*) renverser; (*plans, etc.*) déranger; (*person*) faire de la peine à, contrarier. *adj* (*angry*) fâché; (*sad*) peiné; (*stomach*) dérangé. *n* désordre *m*; dérangement *m*; chagrin *m*.

upshot ['ʌpʃɔt] *n* résultat *m*.

upside down [ʌpsaidaun] *adv, adj* sens dessus dessous, à l'envers.

upstairs [ʌp'steəz] *adv* en haut. go **upstairs** monter (l'escalier). *adj* du dessus, d'en haut.

upstream [ʌp'striːm; *adj* 'ʌpstriːm] *adv* vers l'amont, en amont; (*swim*) contre le courant. *adj* d'amont.

uptight ['ʌptait] *adj* (*coll*) crispé.

up-to-date [ʌptə'deit] *adj* moderne.

upward ['ʌpwəd] *adj* ascendant. **upwards** *adv* vers le haut, en montant.

uranium [ju'reiniəm] *n* uranium *m*.

urban ['əːbən] *adj* urbain.

urchin ['əːtʃin] *n* polisson, -onne *m, f*.

urge [əːdʒ] *n* désir ardent *m*, forte envie *f. v* pousser, conseiller vivement.

urgent ['əːdʒənt] *adj* urgent; insistant. **urgency** *n* urgence *f*; insistance *f*. **urgently** *adv* d'urgence.

urine ['juːrin] *n* urine *f*. **urinate** *v* uriner.

urn [əːn] *n* urne *f*.

us [ʌs] *pron* nous.

usage ['juːzidʒ] *n* usage *m*.

use [juːs; *v* juːz] *n* usage *m*, emploi *m*. **it's no use** ça ne sert à rien. *v* se servir de, employer. **use up** user, consommer, épuiser. **used** *adj* (*car*) d'occasion. **be used to** être habitué à. **get used to** s'habituer à. **useful** *adj* utile. **useless** *adj* inutile. **user** *n* usager *m*.

usher ['ʌʃə] *n* (*law*) huissier *m*; (*church*) placeur *m. v* **usher in** introduire; inaugurer. **usherette** *n* ouvreuse *f*.

usual ['juːzuəl] *adj* habituel. **as usual** comme d'habitude. **usually** *adv* d'habitude, généralement.

usurp [ju'zəːp] *v* usurper.

utensil [ju'tensl] *n* ustensile *m*.

uterus ['juːtərəs] *n* utérus *m*.

utility [ju'tiləti] *n* utilité *f. adj* utilitaire.

utilize ['juːtilaiz] *v* utiliser.

utmost ['ʌtmoust] *adj* le plus grand; suprême; extrême. *n* plus haut point. **do one's utmost** faire tout son possible.

utter[1] ['ʌtə] *v* proférer; (*cry*) pousser.

utter[2] ['ʌtə] *adj* complet, -ète; pur; (*fool*) fini.

U-turn ['juːtəːn] *n* demi-tour *m*.

V

vacant ['veikənt] *adj* vacant, libre; (*stare*) vague. **vacancy** *n* (*room*) chambre à louer *f*; (*job*) poste *m*. **no vacancies** complet.

vacate [vei'keit] *v* quitter.

vacation [vei'keiʃn] *n* vacances *f pl*.

vaccine ['vaksiːn] *n* vaccin *m*. **vaccinate** *v* vacciner. **vaccination** *n* vaccination *f*.

vacillate ['vasileit] *v* vaciller. **vacillation** *n* indécision *f*, vacillation *f*.

vacuum ['vakjum] *n* vide *m*; (*phys*) vacuum *m*. **vacuum cleaner** aspirateur *m*. **vacuum flask** bouteille thermos ® *f*. **vacuum-packed** *adj* emballé sous vide. *v* passer à l'aspirateur.

vagina [və'dʒainə] *n* vagin *m*. **vaginal** *adj* vaginal.

vagrant ['veigrənt] *n, adj* vagabond, -e. **vagrancy** *n* vagabondage *m*.

vague [veig] *adj* vague, flou, imprécis.

vain [vein] *adj* vain, inutile, futile; (*conceited*) vaniteux. **in vain** en vain.

valiant ['valiənt] *adj* courageux.

valid ['valid] *adj* valide, valable. **validity** *n* validité *f*; force *f*.

Valletta [və'letə] *n* La Valette.

valley ['vali] *n* vallée *f*; (*smaller*) vallon *m*.

value ['valjuː] *n* valeur *f. v* évaluer; apprécier, tenir à. **valuable** *adj* de valeur, précieux. **valuables** *pl n* objets de valeur *m pl*. **valuation** *n* évaluation *f*, expertise *f*.

valve [valv] n soupape f. valve f.

vampire ['vampaiə] n vampire m.

van [van] n camionnette f; (rail) fourgon m.

vandal ['vandl] n vandale m. **vandalism** n vandalisme m. **vandalize** v saccager.

vanilla [və'nilə] n vanille f.

vanish ['vaniʃ] v disparaître.

vanity ['vanəti] n vanité f. **vanity case** sac de toilette m.

vapour ['veipə] n vapeur f. **vaporize** v vaporiser.

varicose veins ['varikous] pl n varices f pl.

variety [və'raiəti] n variété f; quantité f. **variety show** spectacle de variétés m.

various ['veəriəs] adj divers.

varnish ['vaɪniʃ] n vernis m. v vernir.

vary ['veəri] v varier, changer. **vary from** différer de. **variable** nf, adj variable. **variant** n variante f. **variation** n variation f.

vase [vaɪz] n vase m.

vasectomy [və'sektəmi] n vasectomie f.

vast [vaɪst] adj vaste. **vastness** n immensité f.

vat [vat] n cuve f.

Vatican ['vatikən] n Vatican m. **Vatican City** la Cité du Vatican f.

vault[1] [voɪlt] n (cellar) cave f; (tomb) caveau m; (bank) coffre-fort m; (arch) voûte f.

vault[2] [voɪlt] v sauter. n saut m. **vaulting horse** cheval d'arçons m.

veal [viɪl] n veau m.

veer [viə] v tourner, virer.

vegetable ['vedʒtəbl] n légume m. adj végétal. **vegetable garden** potager m. **vegetarian** n, adj végétarien, -enne. **vegetation** n végétation f.

vehement ['viɪmənt] adj ardent; violent. **vehemence** n ardeur f; violence f. **vehemently** adv avec passion; avec violence.

vehicle ['viɪkl] n véhicule m.

veil [veil] n voile m. v voiler.

vein [vein] n veine f.

velocity [vi'losəti] n vélocité f.

velvet ['velvit] n velours m. **velvety** adj velouteux, velouté.

vending machine ['vendiŋ] n distributeur automatique m.

veneer [və'niə] n placage m; (superficiality) vernis m. v plaquer.

venerate ['venəreit] v vénérer. **venerable** adj vénérable. **veneration** n vénération f.

venereal disease [və'niəriəl] n maladie vénérienne f.

Venetian blind [və'niɪʃən] n store vénitien m.

vengeance ['vendʒəns] n vengeance f. **with a vengeance** (coll) pour de bon.

venison ['venisn] n venaison f.

venom ['venəm] n venin m. **venomous** adj venimeux.

vent [vent] n orifice m, trou m. **give vent to** donner libre cours à. v décharger.

ventilate ['ventileit] v ventiler, aérer. **ventilation** n aération f, ventilation f.

ventriloquist [ven'trilakwist] n ventriloque m, f.

venture ['ventʃə] n aventure f; entreprise (risquée) f. v (se) risquer, (se) hasarder.

venue ['venjuɪ] n lieu de rendez-vous m.

verb [vəɪb] n verbe m. **verbal** adj verbal.

verdict ['vəɪdikt] n verdict m.

verge [vəɪdʒ] n bord m. **on the verge of** sur le point de; à deux doigts de. v **verge on** approcher de, frôler.

verify ['verifai] v vérifier. **verification** n vérification f.

vermin ['vəɪmin] n animaux nuisibles m pl; (insects, people) vermine f.

vermouth ['vəɪməθ] n vermouth m.

vernacular [və'nakjulə] adj vernaculaire. n langue vernaculaire f.

versatile ['vəɪsətail] adj aux talents variés; (mind) souple. **versatility** n variété de talents f; souplesse f.

verse [vəɪs] n (stanza) strophe f; (poetry) vers m pl; (bible) verset m.

version ['vəɪʃən] n version f.

versus ['vəɪsəs] prep contre.

vertebra ['vəɪtibrə] n, pl **-brae** vertèbre f. **vertebral** adj vertébral. **vertebrate** nm, adj vertébré.

vertical ['vəɪtikl] adj vertical. n verticale f.

vertigo ['vəɪtigou] n vertige m.

very ['veri] adv très, fort, bien; (absolutely) tout. **very much** beaucoup. adj (exact) même; (extreme) tout; (mere) seul.

vessel ['vesl] n vaisseau m.

vest [vest] n tricot de corps m; (US) gilet m.

vestibule ['vestibjuɪl] n vestibule m.

vestige ['vestidʒ] n vestige m; grain m.

vestry ['vestri] n sacristie f.

vet [vet] (coll) n vétérinaire m, f. v examiner de près.

veteran ['vetərən] n vétéran m. **veteran car** voiture d'époque f. **war veteran** ancien combattant m.

veterinary ['vetərinəri] *adj* vétérinaire. **veterinary surgeon** vétérinaire *m, f.*

veto ['vittou] *n* veto *m.* *v* mettre son veto à.

vex [veks] *v* contrarier, fâcher. **vexation** *n* ennui *m.*

via [vaiə] *prep* par, via.

viable ['vaiəbl] *adj* viable. **viability** *n* viabilité *f.*

viaduct ['vaiədʌkt] *n* viaduc *m.*

vibrate [vai'breit] *v* vibrer. **vibration** *n* vibration *f.*

vicar ['vikə] *n* pasteur *m.* **vicarage** *n* presbytère *m.*

vicarious [vi'keəriəs] *adj* délégué; indirect.

vice[1] [vais] *n* (*evil*) vice *m*; (*fault*) défaut *m.*

vice[2] [vais] *n* (*tool*) étau *m.*

vice-chancellor [vais'tʃainsələ] *n* vice-chancelier *m*; (*university*) recteur *m.*

vice-consul [vais'konsl] *n* vice-consul *m.*

vice-president [vais'prezidənt] *n* vice-president, -e *m, f.*

vice versa [vaisi'vəisə] *adv* vice versa.

vicinity [vi'siniti] *n* environs *m pl*, alentours *m pl.*

vicious ['viʃəs] *adj* (*remark*) méchant; (*attack*) grave; (*animal*) vicieux. **vicious circle** cercle vicieux *m.* **viciousness** *n* méchanceté *f*; brutalité *f.*

victim ['viktim] *n* victime *f.* **victimize** *v* prendre pour victime.

victory ['viktəri] *n* victoire *f.* **victorious** *adj* victorieux.

video-tape ['vidiouteip] *n* bande de magnétoscope *f.* *v* enregistrer sur magnétoscope.

vie [vai] *v* lutter, rivaliser.

Vienna [vi'enə] *n* Vienne.

view [vjut] *n* vue *f.* **in view of** étant donné, vu. **viewfinder** *n* viseur *m.* **viewpoint** *n* point de vue *m.* **with a view to** dans l'intention de, afin de. *v* visiter; considérer; regarder. **viewer** *n* (*TV*) téléspectateur, -trice *m, f*; (*slides*) visionneuse *f.*

vigil ['vidʒil] *n* veille *f.* **vigilance** *n* vigilance *f.* **vigilant** *adj* vigilant.

vigour ['vigə] *n* vigueur *f.* **vigorous** *adj* vigoureux.

vile [vail] *adj* vil; abominable.

villa ['vilə] *n* villa *f*; (*country*) maison de campagne *f.*

village ['vilidʒ] *n* village *m.* **villager** *n* villageois, -e *m, f.*

villain ['vilən] *n* scélérat *m.* **villainy** *n* infamie *f.*

vindictive [vin'diktiv] *adj* vindicatif.

vine [vain] *n* vigne *f.* **vineyard** *n* vignoble *m.*

vinegar ['vinigə] *n* vinaigre *m.*

vintage ['vintidʒ] *n* (*year*) année *f*; (*harvest*) vendange *f.* **vintage car** voiture d'époque *f.* **vintage wine** grand vin *m.*

vinyl ['vainil] *n* vinyle *m.*

viola [vi'oulə] *n* alto *m.*

violate ['vaiəleit] *v* violer. **violation** *n* violation *f.*

violence ['vaiələns] *n* violence *f.* **violent** *adj* violent.

violet ['vaiəlit] *n* (*flower*) violette *f*; (*colour*) violet *m.* *adj* violet, -ette.

violin [vaiə'lin] *n* violon *m.* **violinist** *n* violoniste *m, f.*

viper ['vaipə] *n* vipère *f.*

virgin ['vəidʒin] *nf, adj* vierge. **virginity** *n* virginité *f.*

Virgo ['vəigou] *n* Vierge *f.*

virile ['virail] *adj* viril. **virility** *n* virilité *f.*

virtually ['vəitʃuəli] *adv* en fait, pratiquement.

virtue ['vəitʃui] *n* vertu *f*; mérite *m.* **by virtue of** en vertu de. **virtuous** *adj* vertueux.

virus ['vaiərəs] *n* virus *m.*

visa ['vizə] *n* visa *m.*

viscount ['vaikaunt] *n* vicomte *m.* **viscountess** *n* vicomtesse *f.*

visible ['vizəbl] *adj* visible. **visibility** *n* visibilité *f.*

vision ['viʒən] *n* vision *f.* **visionary** *n(m+f), adj* visionnaire.

visit ['vizit] *n* visite *f*; (*stay*) séjour *m.* *v* (*call on*) aller voir, rendre visite à; (*stay with*) faire un séjour chez; (*place*) aller à; (*go round*) visiter. **visitor** *n* visiteur, -euse *m, f.*

visor ['vaizə] *n* visière *f.*

visual ['viʒuəl] *adj* visuel. **visualize** *v* se représenter.

vital ['vaitl] *adj* vital. **vitality** *n* vitalité *f.* **vitally** *adv* absolument.

vitamin ['vitəmin] *n* vitamine *f.*

vivacious [vi'veiʃəs] *adj* vif, enjoué. **vivacity** *n* vivacité *f.*

vivid ['vivid] *adj* vif, éclatant; (*description*) vivant. **vividness** *n* vivacité *f*, éclat *m*, clarté *f.*

vivisection [vivi'sekʃən] n vivisection f.

vixen ['viksn] n renarde f.

vocabulary [və'kabjuləri] n vocabulaire m; glossaire m.

vocal ['voukəl] adj vocal. **vocalist** n chanteur, -euse m, f.

vocation [vou'keiʃən] n vocation f. **vocational** adj professionnel.

vociferous [və'sifərəs] adj bruyant.

vodka ['vodkə] n vodka f.

voice [vois] n voix f. v exprimer.

void [void] n vide m. adj vide; (law) nul, nulle. v évacuer.

volatile ['volətail] adj (chem) volatil; (person) versatile; (situation) explosif.

volcano [vol'keinou] n volcan m. **volcanic** adj volcanique.

volley ['voli] n volée f; torrent m. **volleyball** n volley m. v (sport) renvoyer une volée.

volt [voult] n volt m. **voltage** n voltage m, tension f.

volume ['voljum] n volume m.

volunteer [volən'tiə] n volontaire m, f. v s'offrir; offrir or fournir spontanément. **voluntary** adj volontaire; (unpaid) bénévole.

voluptuous [və'lʌptʃuəs] adj voluptueux. **voluptuousness** n volupté f.

vomit ['vomit] n vomissement m. v vomir.

voodoo ['vuːduː] nm, adj vaudou.

voracious [və'reiʃəs] adj vorace; avide. **voracity** n voracité f.

vote [vout] n vote m, voix f. **vote of thanks** discours de remerciement m. v voter; élire. **voter** n électeur, -trice m, f.

vouch [vautʃ] v **vouch for** se porter garant de, garantir.

voucher ['vautʃə] n bon m; (receipt) reçu m.

vow [vau] n vœu m. v jurer, vouer.

vowel ['vauəl] n voyelle f.

voyage ['voiidʒ] n voyage (par mer) m. v traverser, voyager (par mer).

vulgar ['vʌlgə] adj vulgaire, grossier. **vulgarity** n vulgarité f, grossièreté f.

vulnerable ['vʌlnərəbl] adj vulnérable.

vulture ['vʌltʃə] n vautour m.

W

wad [wod] n tampon m; (papers) liasse f. **wadding** n bourre f, rembourrage m, ouate f.

waddle ['wodl] v se dandiner. n dandinement m.

wade [weid] v avancer dans l'eau.

wafer ['weifə] n gaufrette f. **wafer-thin** adj mince comme du papier à cigarette.

waft [woft] n (carry) porter; (float) flotter. n bouffée f.

wag [wag] v agiter, remuer. n remuement m.

wage [weidʒ] n salaire m. v **wage war** faire la guerre.

wager ['weidʒə] n pari m. v parier.

waggle ['wagl] v agiter, frétiller.

wagon ['wagən] n chariot m; (rail) wagon m.

waif [weif] n enfant abandonné m.

wail [weil] n gémissement m, vagissement m. v gémir, vagir.

waist [weist] n taille f, ceinture f. **waistband** n ceinture f. **waistcoat** n gilet m. **waistline** n taille f.

wait [weit] n attente f. **lie in wait for** guetter. v attendre; servir. **waiter** n garçon m. **waiting** n attente f. **waiting-list** n liste d'attente f. **waiting-room** n salle d'attente f. **waitress** n serveuse f.

waive [weiv] v renoncer à, abandonner.

wake¹ [weik] n sillage m.

***wake²** [weik] v also **wake up** (se) réveiller.

Wales [weilz] n pays de Galles m.

walk [wok] n promenade f; (gait) démarche f. v (faire) marcher; (go on foot) aller à pied; (for pleasure) se promener; (distance) faire à pied. **walkout** n grève surprise f. **walkover** n walkover m, victoire facile f. **walker** n promeneur, -euse m, f. **walking** n marche à pied f. **walking-stick** n canne f.

wall [wol] n mur m, muraille f. v entourer d'un mur.

wallet ['wolit] n portefeuille m.

wallflower ['wolflauə] n giroflée f. **be a wallflower** faire tapisserie.

wallop ['wolop] n (coll) coup m, beigne f. v cogner, rosser. **walloping** adj sacré.

wallow ['wolou] v se vautrer.

wallpaper ['wolpeipə] n papier peint m. v tapisser.

walnut ['wolnʌt] n (nut) noix f; (tree, wood) noyer m.

walrus ['wɔːlrəs] *n* morse *m*.

waltz [wɔːlts] *n* valse *f*. *v* valser.

wan [wɒn] *adj* pâle.

wand [wɒnd] *n* baguette *f*.

wander ['wɒndə] *v* errer; (*stray*) s'égarer. *n* tour *m*.

wane [wein] *v* décroître; diminuer.

wangle ['wæŋgl] (*col*) *n* combine *f*. *v* resquiller, se débrouiller pour avoir.

want [wɒnt] *n* (*lack*) manque *m*; (*need*) besoin *m*. **for want of** faute de. *v* vouloir, désirer; (*ask for*) demander; (*need*) avoir besoin de. **wanted** *adj* (*police*) recherché.

wanton ['wɒntən] *adj* (*woman*) dévergondé; (*cruelty, etc.*) gratuit. **wantonness** *n* dévergondage *m*; gratuité *f*.

war [wɔː] *n* guerre *f*. **be on the war-path** chercher la bagarre. **war-dance** *n* danse guerrière *f*. **warfare** *n* guerre *f*. **war memorial** monument aux morts *m*. **warship** *n* navire de guerre *m*. **wartime** *n* temps de guerre *m*.

warble ['wɔːbl] *n* gazouillis *m*. *v* gazouiller. **warbler** *n* oiseau chanteur *m*.

ward [wɔːd] *n* (*hospital*) salle *f*; section électorale *f*; (*law*) pupille *m, f*. *v* **ward off** parer.

warden ['wɔːdn] *n* directeur, -trice *m, f*; gardien, -enne *m, f*.

warder ['wɔːdə] *n* gardien de prison *m*. **wardress** *n* gardienne de prison *f*.

wardrobe ['wɔːdroub] *n* garde-robe *f*; (*theatre*) costumes *m pl*.

warehouse ['weəhaus] *n* entrepôt *m*. *v* entreposer.

warm [wɔːm] *adj* chaud; (*welcome, etc.*) chaleureux. *v* (se) chauffer. **warm up** s'échauffer. **warming-pan** *n* bassinoire *f*. **warmth** *n* chaleur *f*; cordialité *f*.

warn [wɔːn] *v* prévenir, avertir. **warning** *n* avertissement *m*; (*written*) avis *m*. **warning light** voyant avertisseur *m*.

warp [wɔːp] *v* (se) voiler, gauchir; pervertir; débaucher. *n* voilure *f*; (*cloth*) chaîne *f*.

warrant ['wɒrənt] *n* (*police*) mandat *m*; justification *f*; (*voucher*) bon *m*. *v* justifier; garantir. **warranty** *n* garantie *f*.

warren ['wɒrən] *n* garenne *f*.

warrior ['wɒriə] *n* guerrier, -ère *m, f*.

Warsaw ['wɔːsɔː] *n* Varsovie.

wart [wɔːt] *n* verrue *f*.

wary ['weəri] *adj* prudent, précautionneux.

was [wɒz] *V* **be**.

wash [wɒʃ] *n* (*clothes*) lavage *m*; (*face, etc.*) toilette *f*; (*paint*) badigeon *m*, lavis *m*. *v* (se) laver. **wash-basin** *n* lavabo *m*. **wash off** or **out** (faire) partir au lavage. **wash-out** *n* (*slang*) fiasco *m*. **wash-room** *n* toilettes *f pl*. **wash up** faire la vaisselle. **washable** *adj* lavable. **washing** *n* lessive *f*. **washing-machine** *n* machine à laver *f*. **washing-powder** *n* lessive *f*. **washing-up** *n* vaisselle *f*.

washer ['wɒʃə] *n* rondelle *f*.

Washington ['wɒʃiŋtən] *n* Washington.

wasp [wɒsp] *n* guêpe *f*.

waste [weist] *n* gaspillage *m*; (*time*) perte *f*; (*scrap*) déchets *m pl*; désert *m*. *adj* de rebut; (*lost*) perdu; (*extra*) superflu. **waste disposal unit** broyeur d'ordures *m*. **waste land** terrain vague *m*. **waste paper** vieux papiers *m pl*. **waste-paper basket** corbeille *f*. *v* gaspiller; perdre. **waste away** dépérir. **wasteful** *adj* gaspilleur, -euse; peu économique.

watch [wɒtʃ] *n* (*time*) montre *f*; garde *f*; surveillance *f*; (*naut*) quart *m*. **keep watch** faire le guet. **watch-dog** *n* chien de garde *m*. **watch-strap** *n* bracelet de montre *m*. *v* regarder; surveiller; faire attention (à); guetter. **watchful** *adj* vigilant.

water ['wɔːtə] *n* eau *f*. *v* (*plant, etc.*) arroser; (*eyes*) larmoyer. **water down** couper d'eau. **watery** *adj* aqueux; (*tea, etc.*) trop faible; pâle; insipide.

water-biscuit *n* craquelin *m*.

water-closet *n* cabinets *m pl*.

water-colour *n* aquarelle *f*.

watercress ['wɔːtəkres] *n* cresson *m*.

waterfall ['wɔːtəfɔːl] *n* chute d'eau *f*.

water-ice *n* sorbet *m*.

watering-can *n* arrosoir *m*.

water-lily *n* nénuphar *m*.

waterlogged ['wɔːtəlɒgd] *adj* (*land*) détrempé; (*wood*) imprégné d'eau.

water-main *n* conduite principale d'eau *f*.

watermark ['wɔːtəmaːk] *n* (*paper*) filigrane *m*; (*tide*) laisse de haute mer *f*.

water-melon *n* melon d'eau *m*.

water-pistol *n* pistolet à eau *m*.

waterproof ['wɔːtəpruːf] *nm, adj* imperméable. *v* imperméabiliser.

water-rate *n* taxe sur l'eau *f*.

watershed ['wɔːtəʃed] *n* moment critique *m*; (*geog*) ligne de partage des eaux *f*.

water-ski *v* faire du ski nautique. *n* ski nautique *m*. **water-skiing** *n* ski nautique *m*.

watertight ['wɔːtətait] adj étanche; (excuse, etc.) inattaquable.

water-way n voie navigable f.

waterworks ['wɔːtəwɜːks] n système hydraulique m.

watt [wɔt] n watt m.

wave [weiv] n (sea) vague f; (hair) ondulation f; (phys. radio, etc.) onde f; geste de la main m. waveband n bande de fréquences f. wavelength n longueur d'ondes f. v agiter, brandir; faire signe de la main; onduler. wavy adj (hair) ondulé; (line) onduleux.

waver ['weivə] v vaciller; trembler; (weaken) lâcher pied.

wax[1] [waks] n cire f. waxwork n personnage en cire m. waxworks n musée de cire m. v cirer. waxy adj cireux.

wax[2] [waks] v croître.

way [wei] n (path) chemin m, voie f; (manner) façon f, manière f; passage m; distance f; direction f, sens m. be in the way gêner. by the way à propos. give way céder; laisser la priorité. on the way en route. this way par ici. under way en cours, en marche. way in entrée f. way out sortie f.

*waylay ['wei'lei] v arrêter au passage.

wayside ['weisaid] n bord de la route. adj au bord de la route.

wayward ['weiwəd] adj capricieux, rebelle.

we [wiː] pron nous.

weak [wiːk] adj faible. weaken v faiblir, (s')affaiblir. weakling n gringalet m. weakness n faiblesse f; point faible m; (liking) faible m.

wealth [welθ] n richesse f; abondance f. wealthy adj riche.

wean [wiːn] v (baby) sevrer. wean off détourner de.

weapon ['wepən] n arme f.

*wear [weə] n usage m; (deterioration) usure f; (clothes) vêtements m pl. wear and tear usure f. v porter; (s')user. wear off passer, se dissiper. wear out épuiser.

weary ['wiəri] adj las, lasse. v (se) lasser. wearily adv avec lassitude. weariness n lassitude f.

weasel ['wiːzl] n belette f.

weather ['weðə] n temps m. weather-beaten adj hâlé. weathercock n girouette f. weather forecast prévisions météorologiques f pl. v (survive) réchapper à.

*weave [wiːv] v tisser; entrelacer;

(through traffic, etc.) se faufiler. n also weaving tissage m.

web [web] n (spider) toile f; (on feet) palmure f; (cloth) tissu m. web-footed adj palmipède.

wedding ['wediŋ] n mariage m; noces f pl. wedding-dress n robe de mariée f. wedding-ring n alliance f.

wedge [wedʒ] n cale f, coin m. v caler; (push in) enfoncer; (jam) coincer.

Wednesday ['wenzdi] n mercredi m.

weed [wiːd] n mauvaise herbe f. weed-killer n désherbant m. v désherber. weeding n désherbage m.

week [wiːk] n semaine f. a week today/tomorrow aujourd'hui/demain en huit. weekday n jour de semaine m. weekend n week-end m.

weekly ['wiːkli] adv chaque semaine, tous les huit jours. nm, adj hebdomadaire.

*weep [wiːp] v pleurer. weeping willow saule pleureur m.

weigh [wei] v peser. weighbridge n pont-bascule m. weight n poids m. lose weight maigrir. put on weight grossir. weight-lifting n haltérophilie f. weighting n indemnité f. weightlessness n apesanteur f.

weir [wiə] n barrage m.

weird [wiəd] adj surnaturel; bizarre. weirdness n étrangeté f.

welcome ['welkəm] adj opportun. be welcome être le bienvenu. you're welcome! (acknowledging thanks) il n'y a pas de quoi! n accueil m. v accueillir; souhaiter la bienvenue à; (news, etc.) se réjouir de.

weld [weld] v souder. n soudure f. welder n soudeur m. welding n soudage m.

welfare ['welfeə] n bien m. Welfare State Etat-providence m. welfare work travail social m.

well[1] [wel] n puits m. v well up monter.

well[2] [wel] adj, adv bien. as well aussi.

well-behaved adj sage, obéissant.

well-being n bien-être m.

well-bred adj bien élevé.

well-built adj solide.

well-informed adj bien informé; instruit.

wellington ['weliŋtən] n botte de caoutchouc f.

well-known adj célèbre.

well-meaning adj bien intentionné.

well-nigh adv presque.

well-off adj riche, aisé.

well-paid adj bien payé.

well-spent adj (time) bien employé.

well-spoken adj poli. be well-spoken avoir une élocution soignée.

well-timed adj opportun.

well-to-do adj aisé, riche.

well-trodden adj battu.

well-worn adj usagé.

Welsh [welʃ] nm, adj gallois. **the Welsh** les Gallois m pl.

went [went] V go.

wept [wept] V weep.

were [wəɪ] V be.

west [west] n ouest m. **the West** l'Occident m. adj also **westerly** occidental: ouest invar; à or de l'ouest. adv à l'ouest, vers l'ouest. **westbound** adj ouest invar.

western ['westən] adj ouest invar; de l'ouest; occidental. n (film) western m.

wet [wet] adj mouillé; (damp) humide; (soaked) trempé; (weather) pluvieux. **wet blanket** rabat-joie m invar. **wet suit** combinaison de plongée f. n pluie f. v mouiller.

whack [wak] (coll) n grand coup m. v donner un grand coup à.

whale [weil] n baleine f.

wharf [wɔːf] n quai m.

what [wɔt] pron (subject) (qu'est-ce) qui; (object) (qu'est-ce) que; (after prep) quoi; (relative) ce qui, ce que. adj quel, quelle. interj quoi!

whatever [wɔtˈevə] pron tout ce que, quoi que. adj, adv quel que soit. **none whatever** pas le moindre.

wheat [wiːt] n blé m, froment m.

wheel [wiːl] n roue f. **wheelbarrow** n brouette f. **wheelchair** n fauteuil roulant m. v pousser, rouler; (turn) tournoyer.

wheeze [wiːz] n respiration bruyante f. v respirer bruyamment. **wheezy** adj poussif, asthmatique.

whelk [welk] n buccin m.

when [wen] adv quand. conj quand, lorsque; (relative) où, que. **whenever** conj chaque fois que.

where [weə] adv où. conj (là) où. **whereabouts** adv où. **whereas** conj alors que. **whereupon** adv sur quoi. **wherever** conj où que; (anywhere) là où; (everywhere) partout où.

whether ['weðə] conj si.

which [witʃ] pron lequel, laquelle; (the one that) celui qui or que, celle qui or

que; (relative) (ce) qui, (ce) que. adj quel, quelle.

whichever [witʃˈevə] pron (quel que soit) celui qui or que, (quelle que soit) celle qui or que. adj n'importe quel; quel que soit . . . que.

whiff [wif] n bouffée f, odeur f.

while [wail] conj pendant que; (as long as) tant que. n quelque temps m. v **while away** passer.

whim [wim] n caprice m.

whimper ['wimpə] n faible geignement m. v pleurnicher, geindre faiblement.

whimsical ['wimzikl] adj capricieux; étrange.

whine [wain] n gémissement m; (siren, etc.) plainte f. v gémir; (complain) se lamenter.

whip [wip] n fouet m. **whip-round** n (coll) collecte f. v fouetter. **whip away/out** enlever/sortir brusquement. **whipping** n correction f.

whippet ['wipit] n whippet m.

whirl [wəːl] n tourbillon m. v (faire) tourbillonner. **whirlpool** n tourbillon m. **whirlwind** n tornade f, trombe f.

whirr [wəː] n (wings) bruissement m; (machinery) vrombissement m. v bruire; vrombir.

whisk [wisk] n (cookery) fouet m. v fouetter; (snatch) enlever brusquement.

whisker ['wiskə] n poil m. **whiskers** pl n moustaches f pl.

whisky ['wiski] n whisky m.

whisper ['wispə] v chuchoter. n chuchotement m.

whist [wist] n whist m. **whist drive** tournoi de whist m.

whistle ['wisl] n sifflet m; (sound) sifflement m. v siffler.

Whit [wit] n also **Whitsun** la Pentecôte f. adj de Pentecôte.

white [wait] adj blanc, blanche. **white elephant** objet superflu m. n blanc m; (person) Blanc, Blanche m, f. **whiten** v blanchir. **whiteness** n blancheur f.

whitewash ['waitwɔʃ] n blanc de chaux m. v blanchir à la chaux; (cover up) justifier, blanchir.

whiting ['waitiŋ] n merlan m.

whittle ['witl] v tailler au couteau. **whittle down** (expenses, etc.) rogner.

whizz [wiz] n sifflement m. **whizz-kid** (coll) petit prodige m. v aller comme une flèche.

who [huː] *pron* (qui est-ce) qui. **whoever** *pron* quiconque; qui que ce soit qui *or* que.

whole [houl] *n* totalité *f*; tout *m*. **on the whole** dans l'ensemble. *adj* entier; intact. **wholehearted** *adj* sans réserve. **wholeheartedly** *adv* de tout cœur. **wholemeal** *adj* (*flour*) brut; (*bread*) complet, -ète. **wholesome** *adj* sain.

wholesale ['houlseil] *n* vente en gros *f*. *adj* de gros; en masse, en bloc. *adv* en gros; en masse.

whom [huːm] *pron* qui; (*relative*) que, lequel, laquelle. **of whom** dont.

whooping cough ['huːpiŋ] *n* coqueluche *f*.

whore [hoː] *n* (*derog*) putain *f*.

whose [huːz] *pron* à qui. *adj* à qui, de qui; (*relative*) dont.

why [wai] *adv, conj* pourquoi. *interj* tiens!

wick [wik] *n* mèche *f*.

wicked ['wikid] *adj* mauvais, méchant, vilain. **wickedness** *n* méchanceté *f*.

wicker ['wikə] *n* osier *m*.

wicket ['wikit] *n* (*cricket*) guichet *m*.

wide [waid] *adj* large; grand; vaste. *adv* loin du but. **wide awake** bien éveillé. **widespread** *adj* répandu. **widely** *adv* largement; (*much*) beaucoup; généralement; radicalement. **widen** *v* (s')élargir.

widow ['widou] *n* veuve *f*. **be widowed** devenir veuf *or* veuve. **widower** *n* veuf *m*.

width [widθ] *n* largeur *f*.

wield [wiːld] *v* manier; brandir; exercer.

wife [waif] *n* femme *f*, épouse *f*.

wig [wig] *n* perruque *f*.

wiggle [wigl] *v* tortiller; agiter, remuer. **wiggly** *adj* (*line*) ondulé.

wild [waild] *adj* sauvage; violent; (*unrestrained*) fou, folle. **like wildfire** comme une traînée de poudre. **wildlife** *n* faune *f*. **wildly** *adv* violemment; fièvreusement; follement.

wilderness ['wildənəs] *n* désert *m*; région sauvage *f*.

wilful ['wilfəl] *adj* (*stubborn*) entêté; volontaire; prémédité.

will¹ [wil] *aux translated by future tense.*

will² [wil] *v* vouloir; léguer. *n* volonté *f*; testament *m*. **against one's will** à contre-cœur. **willpower** *n* volonté *f*.

willing [wiliŋ] *adj* de bonne volonté. **be willing to** être disposé à, vouloir bien. **willingly** *adv* volontiers. **willingness** *n* bonne volonté *f*, empressement *m*.

willow ['wilou] *n* saule *m*. **willow-pattern** *n* motif chinois *m*. **willowy** *adj* svelte.

wilt [wilt] *v* (se) faner, (se) dessécher; (*person*) s'affaiblir.

wily ['waili] *adj* rusé, malin, -igne.

•**win** [win] *n* victoire *f*. *v* gagner. **winner** *n* gagnant, -e *m, f*. **winning** *adj* gagnant; (*smile, etc.*) charmeur, -euse. **winnings** *pl n* gains *m pl*.

wince [wins] *v* tressaillir; grimacer. *n* tressaillement *m*; grimace *f*.

winch [wintʃ] *n* treuil *m*. *v* **winch up/down** monter/descendre au treuil.

wind¹ [wind] *n* vent *m*; (*breath*) souffle *m*; (*med*) vents *m pl*. *v* couper le souffle à. **windy** (*place*) battu par les vents; (*day*) de vent.

•**wind²** [waind] *v* enrouler; (*clock, etc.*) remonter; serpenter. **wind up** (se) terminer; (*comm*) liquider; (*clock, etc.*) remonter. **winder** *n* remontoir *m*. **winding** *adj* sinueux.

wind-break *n* pare-vent *m invar*.

windfall ['windfoːl] *n* fruit abattu par le vent *m*; (*surprise*) aubaine *f*.

wind instrument *n* instrument à vent *m*.

windlass ['windləs] *n* guindeau *m*.

windmill ['wind,mil] *n* moulin à vent *m*.

window ['windou] *n* fenêtre *f*; (*car*) vitre *f*; (*shop*) vitrine *f*; (*cashier's*) guichet *m*. **window-box** *n* jardinière *f*. **window-cleaner** *n* laveur, -euse de vitres *m, f*. **window-dresser** *n* étalagiste *m, f*. **window-shopping** *n* lèche-vitrine *m*. **window-sill** *n* (*inside*) appui de fenêtre *m*; (*outside*) rebord de fenêtre *m*.

windpipe ['windpaip] *n* (*anat*) trachée *f*.

windshield ['windʃiːld] *n* pare-brise *m invar*. **windshield wiper** essuie-glace *m invar*.

wind-sock *n* manche à air *f*.

windswept ['windswept] *adj* venteux, balayé par le vent.

wind tunnel *n* tunnel aérodynamique *m*.

wine [wain] *n* vin *m*. **wineglass** *n* verre à vin *m*. **wine list** carte des vins *f*. **wine-tasting** *n* dégustation *f*. **wine waiter** sommelier *m*.

wing [wiŋ] *n* aile *f*. **wing commander** lieutenant-colonel *m*. **wing-mirror** *n* rétroviseur de côté *m*. **wings** *pl n* (*theatre*) coulisses *f pl*. **wingspan** *n* envergure *f*.

wink [wiŋk] *n* clin d'œil. *v* faire un clin d'œil; (*light*) clignoter.

winkle ['wiŋkl] *n* bigorneau *m*. *v* **winkle out** extirper.

winter ['wintə] *n* hiver *m*. *v* hiverner. **wintry** *adj* d'hiver.

wipe [waip] *n* coup de torchon *m*. *v* essuyer. **wipe out** effacer; anéantir.

wire [waiə] *n* fil *m*; télégramme *m*. **wire-brush** *n* brosse métallique *f*. **wire-cutters** *pl n* cisaille *f sing*. **wireless** *n* T.S.F. *f*. **wire netting** treillis métallique *m*. *v* télégraphier. **wiring** *n* installation électrique *f*. **wiry** *adj* (*hair*) dru; (*person*) noueux.

wisdom ['wizdəm] *n* sagesse *f*; prudence *f*. **wisdom tooth** dent de sagesse *f*.

wise [waiz] *adj* sage; prudent; (*learned*) savant.

wish [wiʃ] *v* souhaiter, désirer. *n* souhait *m*, vœu *m*; désir *m*. **wishbone** *n* bréchet *m*.

wisp [wisp] *n* brin *m*; (*hair*) fine mèche *f*; (*smoke*) mince volute *f*. **wispy** *adj* fin.

wistful ['wistfəl] *adj* nostalgique, mélancolique. **wistfully** *adv* avec nostalgie *or* mélancolie.

wit [wit] *n* esprit *m*; intelligence *f*; (*person*) homme d'esprit, femme d'esprit *m*, *f*. **be at one's wits' end** ne plus savoir que faire.

witch [witʃ] *n* sorcière *f*. **witchcraft** *n* sorcellerie *f*. **witch-doctor** *n* sorcier *m*. **witch-hunt** *n* chasse aux sorcières *f*.

with [wið] *prep* avec; (*having*) à; (*because of*) de; (*despite*) malgré.

*****withdraw** [wið'droː] *v* (se) retirer. **withdrawal** *n* retrait *m*, retraction *f*; (*med*) manque *m*. **withdrawn** *adj* renfermé.

wither ['wiðə] *v* (se) flétrir, (se) faner. **withered** *adj* flétri; desséché; (*limb*) atrophié. **withering** *adj* (*look*) méprisant; (*remark*) cinglant.

*****withhold** [wið'hould] *v* (*keep back*) retenir; (*put off*) remettre; refuser; (*hide*) cacher.

within [wið'in] *adv* dedans, à l'intérieur. *prep* à l'intérieur de; dans; (*less than*) (à) moins de.

without [wið'aut] *prep* sans. *adv* à l'extérieur.

*****withstand** [wið'stand] *v* résister à.

witness ['witnis] *n* (*person*) témoin *m*; (*evidence*) témoignage *m*. *v* (*accident, etc.*) être le témoin de; (*document*) attester l'authenticité de. **witness to** témoigner de.

witty ['witi] *adj* spirituel. **witticism** *n* mot d'esprit *m*.

wizard ['wizəd] *n* magicien *m*.

wobble ['wobl] *v* (faire) trembler, (faire) osciller, (faire) branler. **wobbly** *adj* bancal.

woke [wouk] *V* **wake²**.

woken ['woukn] *V* **wake²**.

wolf [wulf] *n* loup *m*. **wolfhound** *n* chien-loup *m*. **wolf-whistle** sifflement admiratif *m*. *v* **wolf down** engloutir.

woman ['wumən] *n*, *pl* **women** femme *f*. **Women's Lib** (*coll*) M.L.F. *m*. **womanhood** *n* féminité *f*. **womanly** *adj* féminin.

womb [wuːm] *n* utérus *m*.

won [wʌn] *V* **win**.

wonder ['wʌndə] *n* émerveillement *m*; miracle *m*, merveille *f*. **no wonder** (ce n'est) pas étonnant. *v* se demander; (*muse*) songer; (*marvel*) s'émerveiller. **wonderful** *adj* merveilleux.

wood [wud] *n* bois *m*. **wooden** *adj* de *or* en bois; (*stiff*) raide. **woody** *adj* boisé; (*stem*) ligneux.

woodcock ['wudkok] *n* bécasse *f*.

woodcut ['wudkʌt] *n* gravure sur bois *f*.

woodland ['wudlənd] *n* région boisée *f*.

wood-louse *n*, *pl* -lice cloporte *m*.

woodpecker ['wudpekə] *n* pic *m*.

wood-pigeon *n* ramier *m*.

wood-shed *n* bûcher *m*.

wood-wind *n* (*music*) bois *m pl*.

woodwork ['wudwəːk] *n* menuiserie *f*.

woodworm ['wudwəːm] *n* vers du bois *m*.

wool [wul] *n* laine *f*. **woollen** *adj* de *or* en laine. **woolly** *adj* laineux; (*ideas*) confus.

word [wəːd] *n* mot *m*, parole *f*. **be word-perfect** in savoir sur le bout des doigts. **in other words** autrement dit. *v* formuler, rédiger. **wording** *n* termes *m pl*. **wordy** *adj* verbeux.

wore [woː] *V* **wear**.

work [wəːk] *n* travail *m*, œuvre *f*, ouvrage *m*. **out of work** en chômage. **work-force** *n* main d'œuvre *f*. **workman** *n* ouvrier *m*. **workmanship** *n* maîtrise *f*. **work permit** permis de travail *m*. **works** *n* usine *f*. **workshop** *n* atelier *m*. **work-to-rule** *n* grève du zèle *f*. *v* travailler; (*machine, etc.*) (faire) marcher; exploiter. **work out** résoudre; (*plan*) élaborer; calculer. **worker** *n* travailleur, -euse *m*, *f*. **working-class** *adj* ouvrier. **workings** *pl n* mécanisme *m*.

world [wɜːld] n monde m. **First/Second World War** Première/Deuxième guerre mondiale f. **world-wide** adj mondial. **worldly** adj terrestre; matérialiste.

worm [wɜːm] n ver m.

worn [wɔːn] V wear.

worry ['wʌri] n souci m. v (s')inquiéter; (sheep) harceler. **don't worry!** ne vous en faites pas! **worried** adj inquiet, -ète.

worse [wɜːs] adj pire, plus mauvais. adv plus mal. **get worse** empirer, se détériorer. **to make matters worse** pour comble de malheur. n pire m. **worsen** v empirer, se détériorer.

worship ['wɜːʃip] n adoration f; culte m. v adorer, vénérer; faire ses dévotions.

worst [wɜːst] adj le pire, la pire, le plus mauvais, la plus mauvaise. adv le plus mal. n pire m. **at worst** au pis aller.

worsted ['wustid] n worsted m.

worth [wɜːθ] n valeur f. adj **be worth** valoir. **be worth** it valoir la peine. **worthwhile** adj qui en vaut la peine; utile; notable. **worthless** adj qui ne vaut rien. **worthy** adj digne; (effort, cause) louable.

would [wud] aux translated by conditional or imperfect tense.

wound[1] [waund] V wind[2].

wound[2] [wuːnd] n blessure f. v blesser.

wove [wouv] V weave.

woven ['wouvn] V weave.

wrangle ['raŋgl] n dispute f. v se disputer.

wrap [rap] v envelopper; (parcel) emballer. **wrapper** n papier m. **wrapping** n emballage m. **wrapping paper** papier d'emballage m; (fancy) papier cadeau m.

wreath [riːθ] n guirlande f, couronne f.

wreck [rek] n (ship) naufrage m; (car) voiture accidentée f; (person) épave f. v démolir, détruire; (hopes, etc.) ruiner, briser. **wreckage** n débris m pl.

wren [ren] n roitelet m.

wrench [rentʃ] n (tool) clef à écrous f; mouvement de torsion m; (emotional) déchirement m. v tirer violemment, arracher; (med) tordre.

wrestle ['resl] v lutter. **wrestle with** (problem) se débattre avec. **wrestler** n lutteur, -euse m, f; catcheur, -euse m, f. **wrestling** n lutte f, catch m.

wretch [retʃ] n malheureux, -euse m, f; misérable m, f. **wretched** adj misérable; (coll: annoying) maudit.

wriggle ['rigl] v (se) tortiller, remuer; (fish) frétiller.

*****wring** [riŋ] v tordre; (wet clothes) essorer. **wringer** n essoreuse f. **wringing wet** trempé.

wrinkle ['riŋkl] n ride f; (in cloth) pli m. v rider; (se) plisser.

wrist [rist] n poignet m. **wrist-watch** n montre-bracelet f.

writ [rit] n acte judiciaire m. **issue a writ against** assigner.

*****write** [rait] v écrire. **writer** n auteur m, écrivain m, écrivaine f. **writing** n écriture f. **in writing** par écrit. **writing-case** n correspondancier m. **writing-pad** n bloc-notes m. **writing-paper** n papier à lettres m.

writhe [raið] v se tordre, frémir.

written ['ritn] V write.

wrong [roŋ] adj (bad) mal; erroné; incorrect, faux, fausse; (end, side, etc.) mauvais. **be wrong** avoir tort, se tromper; (amiss) ne pas aller. adv mal, n mal m, tort m; injustice f. **wrongful** adj injustifié.

wrought iron [ˌrɔːt'aiən] n fer forgé m.

wrote [rout] V write.

wrung [rʌŋ] V wring.

wry [rai] adj désabusé.

X

xenophobia [ˌzenə'foubiə] n xénophobie f. **xenophobic** adj xénophobe.

Xerox ® ['ziəroks] n (machine) photocopieuse f; (copy) photocopie f. v photocopier.

Xmas ['krisməs] V Christmas.

X-ray ['eksrei] n (photo) radio f; (ray) rayon X m. **have an X-ray** se faire radiographier. v radiographier.

xylophone ['zailəfoun] n xylophone m.

Y

yacht [jot] n yacht m. **yachting** n yachting m.

yank [jaŋk] *n* coup sec *m*. *v* tirer d'un coup sec.

yap [jap] *v* japper. *n* jappement *m*.

yard [jɑːd] *n* cour *f*; (*site*) chantier *m*.

yarn [jɑːn] *n* fil *m*; (*tale*) histoire *f*.

yawn [jɔːn] *v* bâiller; (*hole*) s'ouvrir. *n* bâillement *m*.

year [jiə] *n* an *m*, année *f*. **yearly** *adj* annuel.

yearn [jɔːn] *v* languir (après), aspirer (à). **yearning** *n* désir ardent *m*, envie *f*.

yeast [jiːst] *n* levure *f*.

yell [jel] *n* hurlement *m*. *v* hurler.

yellow [jelou] *nm*, *adj* jaune. *v* jaunir.

yelp [jelp] *v* glapir, japper. *n* glapissement *m*, jappement *m*.

yes [jes] *adv* oui; (*after negative*) si. *n* oui *m* *invar*.

yesterday ['jestədi] *nm*, *adv* hier. **the day before yesterday** avant-hier *m*.

yet [jet] *adv* encore; (*already*) déjà. *conj* cependant, toutefois.

yew [juː] *n* if *m*.

yield [jiːld] *v* produire, rapporter; céder. *n* production *f*, rapport *m*.

yodel ['joudl] *v* jodler. *n* tyrolienne *f*.

yoga ['jougə] *n* yoga *m*.

yoghurt ['jogət] *n* yaourt *m*.

yoke [jouk] *n* joug *m*; (*dress*) empièce-ment *m*. *v* accoupler.

yolk [jouk] *n* jaune *m*.

yonder ['jondə] *adv* là-bas.

you [juː] *pron* (*subject*: *fam*) tu; (*subject*: *pl or fml*) vous; (*after prep*) toi, vous; (*before verb*) te, vous; (*impersonal*) on.

young [jʌŋ] *adj* jeune. *pl n* (*people*) jeunes *m pl*; (*animals*) petits *m pl*. **youngster** *n* jeune *m*.

your [jɔː] *adj* (*fam*) ton, ta, (*pl*) tes; (*pl or fml*) votre, (*pl*) vos; (*impersonal*) son, sa, (*pl*) ses. **yours** *pron* (*fam*) le tien, la tienne; (*pl or fml*) le vôtre, la vôtre.

yourself [jə'self] *pron* (*fam*) te; (*pl or fml*) vous; (*impersonal*) se; (*emphatic*) toi-même, vous-même, soi-même. **by your-self** tout seul.

youth [juːθ] *n* jeunesse *f*; (*boy*) jeune homme *m*. **youth hostel** auberge de la jeunesse *f*.

yo-yo ['joujou] *n* yo-yo *m*.

Yugoslavia [juːgou'slɑːviə] *n* Yougoslavie *f*. **Yugoslav** *adj* yougoslave; *n* Yougos-lave *m*, *f*. **Yugoslavian** *adj* yougoslave.

Z

Zaire [zɑːˈiːə] *n* Zaïre *m*.

zany ['zeini] *adj* (*coll*) toqué.

zeal [ziːl] *n* zèle *m*. **zealous** *adj* zélé; dévoué.

zebra ['zebrə] *n* zèbre *m*. **zebra crossing** passage pour piétons *m*.

zero ['ziərou] *n* zéro *m*.

zest [zest] *n* entrain *m*; saveur *f*.

zigzag ['zigzag] *n* zigzag *m*. *v* zigzaguer.

zinc [ziŋk] *n* zinc *m*.

zip [zip] *n* fermeture éclair *f*. **zip code** (*US*) code postal *m*. *v* **zip up** (se) fermer avec une fermeture éclair.

zodiac ['zoudiak] *n* zodiaque *m*.

zone [zoun] *n* zone *f*. *v* diviser en zones.

zoo [zuː] *n* zoo *m*.

zoology [zou'olədʒi] *n* zoologie *f*. **zoologi-cal** *adj* zoologique. **zoologist** *n* zoologiste *m*, *f*.

zoom [zuːm] *n* vrombissement *m*. **zoom lens** zoom *m*. *v* vrombir. **zoom past/through** (*coll*) passer/traverser en trombe.

French–Anglais

A

à [a] *prep* (*vers*) to; (*position*) at; (*ville*) in; (*d'après*) according to; (*transport*) by; (*pour*) for.

abaisser [abese] *v* lower. **s'abaisser** *v* fall; (*personne*) humble oneself. **abaissement** *nm* fall; (*personne*) subservience; degradation.

abandon [abɑ̃dɔ̃] *nm* desertion; renunciation, giving up; neglect. **à l'abandon** in a state of neglect. **avec abandon** without constraint.

abandonner [abɑ̃dɔne] *v* abandon, give up. **s'abandonner à** give way to, indulge in.

abasourdir [abazurdir] *v* stun. **abasourdissement** *nm* stupefaction.

abat-jour *nm invar* lampshade.

abats [aba] *nm pl* offal *sing*; (*volaille*) giblets *pl*.

abattoir [abatwar] *nm* abattoir.

*abattre [abatrə] *v* pull *or* knock down; (*arbre*) fell; (*tuer*) kill; (*affaiblir*) weaken. **s'abattre** fall, collapse. **abattement** *nm* depression, low spirits *pl*; (*fatigue*) exhaustion; (*rabais*) reduction. **abattu** *adj* exhausted; feeble; depressed.

abbaye [abei] *nf* abbey.

abbé [abe] *nm* abbot. **abbesse** *nf* abbess.

abcès [apsɛ] *nm* abscess.

abdiquer [abdike] *v* abdicate. **abdication** *nf* abdication.

abdomen [abdɔmɛn] *nm* abdomen. **abdominal** *adj* abdominal.

abeille [abɛj] *nf* bee.

abhorrer [abɔre] *v* abhor.

abîme [abim] *nm* abyss, gulf.

abîmer [abime] *v* spoil, damage.

abject [abʒɛkt] *adj* despicable, abject.

abnégation [abnegɑsjɔ̃] *nf* self-denial.

aboiement [abwamɑ̃] *nm* bark.

abois [abwa] *nm pl* **aux abois** at bay.

abolir [abɔlir] *v* abolish. **abolition** *nf* abolition.

abominable [abɔminablə] *adj* abominable. **abomination** *nf* abomination. **avoir en abomination** loathe.

abonder [abɔ̃de] *v* abound, be plentiful. **abondance** *nf* abundance; (*richesse*) wealth. **abondant** *adj* plentiful, profuse; (*cheveux*) thick; (*repas*) copious.

s'abonner [abɔne] *v* subscribe. **abonné, -e** *nm, nf* subscriber; (*gaz, etc.*) consumer. **abonnement** *nm* subscription; (*rail, sport, etc.*) season ticket.

abord [abɔr] *nm* manner; access. **abords** *nm pl* surroundings *pl*. **au premier abord** at first sight. **d'abord** *adv* (at) first.

aborder [abɔrde] *v* approach; (*arriver à*) reach; (*problème, etc.*) tackle. **abordable** *adj* reasonable; approachable; accessible.

aborigène [abɔriʒɛn] *n(m+f)* aborigine. *adj* aboriginal.

aboutir [abutir] *v* succeed. **aboutir à** end up in *or* at, come to. **aboutissement** *nm* result; success.

aboyer [abwaje] *v* bark.

abrasif [abrazif] *nm, adj* abrasive. **abrasion** *nf* abrasion.

abréger [abreʒe] *v* shorten; (*texte*) abridge. **abrégé** *nm* summary.

abreuver [abrœve] *v* (*animal*) water; (*tremper*) soak; (*inonder*) shower, swamp. **s'abreuver** *v* quench one's thirst.

abréviation [abrevjɑsjɔ̃] *nf* abbreviation.

abri [abri] *nm* shelter; protection. **à l'abri** sheltered, safe.

abricot [abriko] *nm* apricot. **abricotier** *nm* apricot (tree).

abriter [abrite] *v* shelter; (*du soleil*) shade. **s'abriter** *v* take cover.

abroger [abrɔʒe] *v* repeal. **abrogation** *nf* repeal.

abrutir [abrytir] *v* exhaust, daze, stupefy.

absent [apsɑ̃], **-e** *nm, nf* absentee. *adj* absent; (*qui manque*) missing. **absence** *nf* absence.

abside [apsid] *nf* apse.

absinthe [apsɛ̃t] *nf* absinthe.

absolu [apsɔly] *nm, adj* absolute.

absorber [apsɔrbe] *v* absorb; (*temps, etc.*) occupy, take up. **absorbant** *adj* absorbing; (*matière*) absorbent. **absorption** *nf* absorption.

*****absoudre** [apsudrə] *v* absolve. **absolution** *nf* absolution.

*****s'abstenir** [apstənir] *v* abstain, refrain. **abstention** *nf* abstention. **abstinence** *nf* abstinence.

abstrait [apstrɛ] *adj* abstract. *nm* abstract; abstract art; abstract artist. **abstraction** *nf* abstraction; abstract idea. **faire abstraction de** disregard.

absurde [apsyrd] *nm, adj* absurd. **absurdité** *nf* absurdity.

abus [aby] *nm* abuse; over-use, over-indulgence. **abuser de** *v* abuse, misuse; exploit; over-use, over-indulge. **abusif** *adj* excessive; improper.

académie [akademi] *nf* academy; school. **académique** *adj* academic.

acajou [akaʒu] *nm* mahogany.

acariâtre [akarjɑtrə] *adj* sour-tempered.

accabler [akable] *v* overwhelm, over-come; (*questions, injures*) shower. **accablant** *adj* overwhelming; (*chaleur, travail*) exhausting. **accablement** *nm* exhaustion; depression.

accaparer [akapare] *v* monopolize; (*absorber*) take up completely.

accéder [aksede] *v* **accéder à** (*lieu*) reach, get to; attain; (*désirs*) comply with.

accélérer [akselere] *v* accelerate, speed up. **accélérateur** *nm* accelerator. **accélération** *nf* acceleration.

accent [aksɑ̃] *nm* accent; emphasis, stress; tone.

accentuer [aksɑ̃tɥe] *v* accent; emphasize, accentuate; intensify.

accepter [aksɛpte] *v* accept; (*être d'accord*) agree. **acceptable** *adj* acceptable; satisfactory. **acceptation** *nf* acceptance.

accès [aksɛ] *nm* access, approach; (*crise*) fit, bout. **accessible** *adj* accessible; (*personne*) approachable.

accessoire [akseswar] *adj* secondary; additional. *nm* accessory.

accident [aksidɑ̃] *nm* accident, mishap. **accidenté** *adj* (*terrain*) uneven. **accidentel** *adj* accidental.

acclamer [aklame] *v* acclaim, cheer. **acclamations** *nf pl* cheers *pl*.

acclimater [aklimate] *v* acclimatize. **s'acclimater** *v* adapt (oneself), become acclimatized.

accommoder [akɔmɔde] *v* adapt; (*cuisine*) prepare. **s'accommoder de** put up with.

accompagner [akɔ̃paɲe] *v* accompany. **accompagnement** *nm* accompaniment.

accomplir [akɔ̃plir] *v* accomplish, carry out, achieve; complete. **accomplissement** *nm* accomplishment, fulfilment; completion.

accord [akɔr] *nm* agreement; harmony; (*musique*) chord. **d'accord** (*fam*) O.K. **être d'accord** agree.

accordéon [akɔrdeɔ̃] *nm* accordion.

accorder [akɔrde] *v* grant, give; (*musique*) tune. **s'accorder** *v* agree; match, be in harmony.

accotement [akɔtmɑ̃] *nm* (*auto*) shoulder, verge. **accotement stabilisé** hard shoulder.

accoucher [akuʃe] *v* give birth. **accouchement** *nm* childbirth, delivery. **accoucheuse** *nf* midwife.

accouder [akude] *v* **s'accouder à** *or* **sur** lean one's elbows on.

*****accourir** [akurir] *v* rush up, hurry.

accoutumer [akutyme] *v* accustom. **s'accoutumer à** get used to.

accroc [akro] *nm* tear; (*tache*) blot; (*anicroche*) hitch.

accrocher [akrɔʃe] *v* catch; (*tableau, etc.*) hang; (*voiture*) bump into. **s'accrocher à** cling to. **accrocheur, -euse** *adj* persistent; (*affiche, etc.*) eye-catching, catchy.

*****accroître** [akrwatrə] *v* increase. **accroissement** *nm* increase.

s'accroupir [akrupir] *v* squat, crouch.

*****accueillir** [akœjir] *v* (*aller chercher*) welcome; receive; meet; (*loger*) accommodate. **accueil** *nm* reception, welcome.

accumuler [akymyle] *v* accumulate. **accumulateur** *nm* accumulator. **accumulation** *nf* accumulation.

accuser [akyze] *v* accuse, blame; accentuate; (*montrer*) show. **accuser réception de** acknowledge receipt of. **accusation** *nf* accusation. **accusé, -e** *nm, nf* accused, defendant.

acerbe [asɛrb] *adj* caustic.

acharner [aʃarne] *v* **s'acharner à** *or* **sur** try desperately to, work furiously at. **s'acharner contre** hound, set oneself against. **acharné** *adj* relentless; determined, set; (*combat*) fierce. **acharnement** *nm* relentlessness; determination; fierceness.

achat [aʃa] *nm* purchase. **faire des achats** go shopping.

acheminer [aʃmine] *v* forward, dispatch; transport. **s'acheminer vers** head for.

acheter [aʃte] *v* buy. **acheteur, -euse** *nm, nf* buyer.

achever [aʃve] *v* finish. **s'achever** end. **achevé** *adj* downright; accomplished. **achèvement** *nm* completion.

acide [asid] *nm, adj* acid. **acidité** *nf* acidity.

acier [asje] *nm* steel. **acier inoxydable** stainless steel. **aciérie** *nf* steelworks.

acné [akne] *nf* acne.

acompte [akɔ̃t] *nm* (*arrhes*) deposit, down payment; (*versement partiel*) instalment.

acoustique [akustik] *adj* acoustic. *nf* acoustics *pl*.

*****acquérir** [akerir] *v* acquire; (*gagner*) win, gain. **acquéreur** *nm* purchaser.

acquiescer [akjese] *v* acquiesce, assent; approve. **acquiescement** *nm* acquiescence; approval.

acquis [aki] *adj* acquired; established. *nm* experience.

acquisition [akizisjɔ̃] *nf* acquisition.

acquit [aki] *nm* receipt.

acquitter [akite] *v* acquit; pay. **s'acquitter de** (*dette*) discharge; (*promesse, tâche*) fulfil. **acquittement** *nm* acquittal; payment; discharge; fulfilment.

âcre [akra] *adj* acrid. **âcreté** *nf* acridity.

acrimonie [akrimoni] *nf* acrimonie. **acrimonieux** *adj* acrimonious.

acrobate [akrobat] *n(m+f)* acrobat. **acrobatie** *nf* acrobatics. **acrobatique** *adj* acrobatic.

acrylique [akrilik] *adj* acrylic.

acte[1] [akt] *nm* action, act; (*jur*) deed, certificate. **acte de décès/mariage/naissance** death/marriage/birth certificate.

acte[2] [akt] *nm* (*théâtre*) act.

acteur [aktœr] *nm* actor. **actrice** *nf* actress.

actif [aktif] *adj* active. *nm* credit.

action [aksjɔ̃] *nf* action, act, deed; (*comm*) share. **actionnaire** *n(m+f)* shareholder.

activer [aktive] *v* speed up; (*chim*) activate. **activiste** *n(m+f)* activist. **activité** *nf* activity. **être en activité** function, be in operation.

actuaire [aktɥɛr] *n(m+f)* actuary.

actualité [aktɥalite] *nf* topicality; current events *pl*. **les actualités** the news *sing*.

actuel [aktɥɛl] *adj* current, present; (*livre, etc.*) topical. **actuellement** *adv* at the moment.

acupuncture [akypɔ̃ktyr] *nf* acupuncture.

adapter [adapte] *v* adapt, fit. **adaptable** *adj* adaptable. **adaptateur** *nm* adapter. **adaptation** *nf* adaptation.

addenda [adɛ̃da] *nm* addenda.

additif [aditif] *nm* additive; (*clause*) rider. **additionner** [adisjone] *v* add (up). **addition** *nf* addition; (*facture*) bill. **additionnel** *adj* additional.

adénoïde [adenoid] *adj* adenoidal. **végétations adénoïdes** *nf pl* adenoids *pl*.

adhérer [adere] *v* adhere, stick. **adhérer à** (*pneu, etc.*) grip; support; (*parti*) join, be a member of. **adhérence** *nf* adhesion; grip. **adhérent, -e** *nm, nf* adherent, member. **adhésif** *nm, adj* adhesive. **adhésion** *nf* support; membership.

adieu [adjø] *nm* farewell. *interj* goodbye! **faire ses adieux** say goodbye.

adjacent [adʒasɑ̃] *adj* adjacent.

adjectif [adʒɛktif] *nm* adjective. *adj* adjectival.

adjoint [adʒwɛ̃], **-e** *nm, nf* assistant.

adjudication [adʒydikasjɔ̃] *nf* sale by auction. **offrir par adjudication** put up for tender.

adjuger [adʒyʒe] *v* auction; (*contrat, etc.*) award. **une fois, deux fois, trois fois, adjugé!** going, going, gone!

*****admettre** [admɛtra] *v* admit; receive; (*candidat*) pass; accept; suppose.

administrer [administre] *v* administer; (*gérer*) manage, run. **administrateur, -trice** *nm, nf* administrator; director. **administratif** *adj* administrative. **administration** *nf* administration; management, government.

admirer [admire] *v* admire. **admirable** *adj* admirable. **admirateur, -trice** *nm, nf* admirer. **admiration** *nf* admiration.

admission [admisjɔ̃] *nf* admission, admittance; entry; acceptance. **admissible** *adj* admissible; acceptable; (*candidat*) eligible.

adolescence [adɔlesɑ̃s] *nf* adolescence. **adolescent, -e** *n, adj* adolescent.

adonner [adɔne] *v* **s'adonner à** devote oneself to; (*boisson, etc.*) take to.

adopter [adɔpte] *v* adopt. **adoptif** *adj* (*enfant*) adopted; (*parent*) adoptive. **adoption** *nf* adoption.

adorer [adɔre] *v* adore; (*rel*) worship. **adorable** *adj* adorable; delightful. **adorateur, -trice** *nm, nf* worshipper. **adoration** *nf* adoration; worship.

adosser [adose] *v* **adosser à** *or* **contre** lean *or* stand against.

adoucir [adusir] *v* soften; sweeten; ease, soothe.

adrénaline [adrenalin] *nf* adrenalin.

adresse¹ [adrɛs] *nf* skill, dexterity.

adresse² [adrɛs] *nf* address. **adresser** *v* address, direct. **s'adresser à** apply to; (*parler*) speak to.

adroit [adrwa] *adj* skilful, deft, clever.

adulation [adylɑsjɔ̃] *nf* adulation.

adulte [adylt] *nm, nf + f), adj* adult.

adultère [adyltɛr] *adj* adulterous. *nm* adultery.

*advenir [advənir] *v* happen. **advenir de** become of.

adverbe [advɛrb] *nm* adverb. **adverbial** *adj* adverbial.

adverse [advɛrs] *adj* opposing, adverse. **adversité** *nf* adversity.

aérer [aere] *v* air; (*terre*) aerate. **aérateur** *nm* ventilator. **aération** *nf* airing; ventilation; aeration.

aérien [aerjɛ̃] *adj* aerial, air. *nm* aerial.

aérodynamique [aerɔdinamik] *adj* aerodynamic, streamlined. *nf* aerodynamics.

aéroglisseur [aerɔglisœr] *nm* hovercraft.

aéronautique [aerɔnotik] *adj* aeronautical. *nf* aeronautics.

aéroport [aerɔpɔr] *nm* airport. **aéroporté** [aerɔpɔrte] *adj* airborne.

aérosol [aerɔsɔl] *nm* aerosol.

affable [afablə] *adj* affable. **affabilité** *nf* affability.

affaiblir [afeblir] *v* weaken. **s'affaiblir** grow weaker; (*son*) fade; (*tempête*) die down. **affaiblissement** *nm* weakening.

affaire [afɛr] *nf* affair, matter, business; transaction, deal. **affaires** *nf pl* (*com-*

merce) business *sing*; (*effets personnels*) things *pl*, belongings *pl*. **avoir affaire à** have to deal with. **faire l'affaire** do nicely, come in handy. **occupe-toi de tes affaires!** mind your own business! **affairé** *adj* busy.

s'affaisser [afese] *v* sink, subside; (*personne*) collapse. **affaissement** *nm* subsidence.

affamer [afame] *v* starve. **affamé** *adj* starving, ravenous.

affecter¹ [afɛkte] *v* feign; (*adopter*) take on, assume. **affectation** *nf* affectation.

affecter² [afɛkte] *v* allocate, assign; (*nommer*) appoint. **affectation** *nf* allocation; appointment.

affecter³ [afɛkte] *v* affect, touch, move.

affection [afɛksjɔ̃] *nf* affection; (*méd*) ailment. **affectionner** *v* be fond of. **affectueux** *adj* affectionate.

affiche [afiʃ] *nf* poster, bill. **afficher** *v* stick up; (*péj*) flaunt, display.

affilier [afilje] *v* affiliate. **affiliation** *nf* affiliation.

affiner [afine] *v* refine.

affinité [afinite] *nf* affinity.

affirmer [afirme] *v* assert, affirm. **affirmatif** *adj* affirmative; positive. **affirmation** *nf* assertion. **affirmative** *nf* affirmative.

affliction [afliksjɔ̃] *nf* affliction.

affliger [afliʒe] *v* distress. **être affligé de** be afflicted with.

affluence [aflyɑ̃s] *nf* crowd.

affoler [afɔle] *v* throw into a panic, terrify. **s'affoler** panic. **affolant** *adj* alarming. **affolé** *adj* panic-stricken. **affolement** *nm* panic.

affranchir [afrɑ̃ʃir] *v* (*lettre*) stamp; (*timbre*) frank; (*libérer*) free, emancipate. **affranchissement** *nm* (*lettre*) postage.

affréter [afrete] *v* charter, hire.

affreux [afrø] *adj* dreadful, horrible, ghastly.

affronter [afrɔ̃te] *v* confront, face, brave.

afin [afɛ̃] *prep* **afin de** so as to, in order to. **afin que** so that, in order that.

Afrique [afrik] *nf* Africa. **africain** *adj* African. **Africain, -e** *nm, nf* African.

agacer [agase] *v* irritate, annoy. **agacement** *nm* irritation, annoyance.

âge [ɑʒ] *nm* age. **quel âge avez-vous?** how old are you? **âgé** *adj* old, elderly. **âgé de quatre ans** four years old.

agence [aʒɑ̃s] *nf* agency, office, bureau.

agenda [aʒɛ̃da] *nm* diary.

s'agenouiller [aʒnuje] v kneel (down).

agent [aʒɑ̃] nm agent; policeman; officer. **agent de change** stockbroker. **agent immobilier** estate agent.

agglomération [aglɔmerɑsjɔ̃] nf built-up area, town; conglomeration.

aggraver [agrave] v aggravate, worsen; (redoubler) increase. **aggravation** nf aggravation, worsening; increase.

agile [aʒil] adj agile, nimble. **agilité** nf agility.

agir [aʒir] v act. **s'agir de** be a matter or question of, be about.

agiter [aʒite] v shake, wave, flap; trouble; debate, discuss. **s'agiter** fidget, get restless. **agitation** nf agitation; restlessness. **agité** adj troubled; restless; (mer) rough.

agneau [aɲo] nm lamb.

agnostique [agnɔstik] n(m+f), adj agnostic.

agoniser [agɔnize] v be dying. **agonie** nf mortal agony; (déclin) death throes pl. **à l'agonie** at death's door.

agrafe [agraf] nf hook; (papiers) staple. **agrafer** v hook, fasten; staple. **agrafeuse** nf stapler.

agrandir [agrɑ̃dir] v enlarge; (développer) expand, extend. **agrandissement** nm (phot) enlargement; expansion, extension.

agréable [agreabla] adj pleasant.

agréer [agree] v accept. **agréer à** please. **agrément** nm charm, pleasantness.

agression [agresjɔ̃] nf aggression; attack. **agressif** adj aggressive.

agricole [agrikɔl] adj agricultural.

agriculture [agrikyltyr] nf agriculture.

agrumes [agrym] nm pl citrus fruits pl.

aguets [agɛ] nm pl **aux aguets** on the look-out.

ahurir [ayrir] v astound. **ahurissement** nm stupefaction.

aide [ɛd] nf help, aid, assistance. n(m+f) assistant. **à l'aide!** help! **à l'aide de** with the help of. **venir en aide à** come to the assistance of.

aider [ede] v help, aid, assist.

aïeux [ajø] nm pl forefathers pl.

aigle [ɛgla] nm eagle.

aiglefin [ɛglafɛ̃] nm haddock.

aigre [ɛgra] adj sour; (son) shrill; (froid) bitter. **aigre-doux, -douce** adj bittersweet; (cuisine) sweet and sour. **aigreur** nf sourness.

aigrir [egrir] v embitter, sour.

aigu, -uë [egy] adj acute, sharp; (son) high-pitched.

aiguille [egɥij] nf needle; (horloge) hand. **travail à l'aiguille** nm needlework.

aiguillon [egɥijɔ̃] nm (insecte) sting; (plante) thorn; stimulus. **aiguillonner** v spur on.

aiguiser [egize] v sharpen; stimulate.

ail [aj] nm, pl **aulx** garlic.

aile [ɛl] nf wing; (moulin) sail. **ailé** adj winged.

ailleurs [ajœr] adv elsewhere. **d'ailleurs** adv besides. **par ailleurs** otherwise.

aimable [ɛmabla] adj kind, nice.

aimant [ɛmɑ̃] nm magnet. **aimanter** v magnetize.

aimer [eme] v like; (d'amour) love. **aimer mieux** prefer.

aine [ɛn] nf groin.

aîné [ene], **-e** adj elder, eldest. nm, nf eldest child; senior.

ainsi [ɛ̃si] adv in this way, thus, so. **ainsi que** just as, as well as. **et ainsi de suite** and so on. **pour ainsi dire** as it were.

air[1] [ɛr] nm air; atmosphere.

air[2] [ɛr] nm (apparence) air, look. **avoir l'air de** look or seem like.

air[3] [ɛr] nm (musique) tune, air; (opéra) aria.

aire [ɛr] nf area.

aise [ɛz] nf pleasure, joy. **à l'aise** at ease, comfortable. **mal à l'aise** ill at ease, uncomfortable. adj glad. **aisance** nf ease; (richesse) affluence. **aisé** adj easy.

aisselle [ɛsɛl] nf armpit.

ajonc [aʒɔ̃] nm gorse.

ajourner [aʒurne] v adjourn, postpone. **ajournement** nm adjournment, postponement.

ajouter [aʒute] v add. **s'ajouter à** add to.

ajuster [aʒyste] v adjust, fit; adapt.

alarme [alarm] nf alarm. **alarmer** v alarm. **alarmiste** n(m+f), adj alarmist.

Albanie [albani] nf Albania. **albanais** nm, adj Albanian. **Albanais, -e** nm, nf Albanian.

albatros [albatros] nm albatross.

album [albɔm] nm album. **album à colorier** colouring book.

alcali [alkali] nm alkali. **alcalin** adj alkaline.

alchimie [alʃimi] nf alchemy. **alchimiste** nm alchemist.

alcool [alkɔl] *nm* alcohol. **alcool à brûler** methylated spirits. **alcoolique** *n(m+f)*, *adj* alcoholic. **alcoolisme** *nm* alcoholism.

alcôve [alkov] *nf* alcove.

aléatoire [aleatwar] *adj* uncertain, chancy.

alentour [alɑ̃tur] *adv* around. **alentours** *nm pl* surroundings *pl*, neighbourhood *sing*.

alerte [alɛrt] *adj* agile, alert, brisk. *nf* alert, alarm, warning. **alerter** *v* alert, notify, warn.

algèbre [alʒɛbrə] *nf* algebra. **algébrique** *adj* algebraic.

Alger [alʒe] *n* Algiers.

Algérie [alʒeri] *nf* Algeria. **algérien** *adj* Algerian. **Algérien, -enne** *nm, nf* Algerian.

algue [alg] *nf* seaweed.

alias [aljɑs] *adv* alias.

alibi [alibi] *nm* alibi.

aliéner [aljene] *v* alienate; (*droits, etc.*) give up. **aliénation** *nf* alienation; (*méd*) derangement. **aliéné, -e** *nm, nf* insane person.

aligner [aliɲe] *v* align, line up. **alignement** *nm* alignment.

aliment [alimɑ̃] *nm* food. **alimentation** *nf* feeding; (*comm*) foodstuffs *pl*. **alimenter** *v* feed, supply.

alinéa [alinea] *nm* paragraph.

aliter [alite] *v* confine to bed. **alité** *adj* bedridden.

allaiter [alete] *v* (*femme*) (breast-)feed; (*animal*) suckle. **allaitement** *nm* (breast-)feeding; suckling.

allée [ale] *nf* path.

alléger [aleʒe] *v* alleviate; (*poids*) lighten, make lighter. **allégement** *nm* alleviation.

allégorie [alegɔri] *nf* allegory. **allégorique** *adj* allegorical.

allègre [alɛgrə] *adj* cheerful, lively. **allégresse** *nf* elation.

alléguer [alege] *v* allege; (*excuse*) put forward. **allégation** *nf* allegation.

alléluia [aleluja] *nm, interj* hallelujah.

Allemagne [almaɲ] *nf* Germany. **allemand** *nm, adj* German. **Allemand, -e** *nm, nf* German.

*aller [ale] *v* go; (*futur*) be going to. **aller à** (*style*) suit; (*mesure*) fit. **aller chercher** fetch. **aller de soi** be obvious. **allez-y!** go on! **allons!** come on! **allons-y!** let's go! **ça va** all right. **comment allez-vous?** how are

you? **s'en aller** go away. *nm* (*trajet*) outward journey; (*billet*) single. **aller-retour** *nm* return.

allergie [alɛrʒi] *nf* allergy. **allergique** *adj* allergic.

allier [alje] *v* ally; unite, combine. **alliage** *nm* alloy. **alliance** *nf* alliance; union; (*bague*) wedding ring; combination. **allié, -e** *nm, nf* ally.

alligator [aligatɔr] *nm* alligator.

allitération [aliterasjɔ̃] *nf* alliteration.

allô [alo] *interj* hello!

allocation [alɔkɑsjɔ̃] *nf* allocation; (*somme*) allowance. **allocation de chômage** unemployment benefit. **allocations familiales** family allowance *sing*.

allocution [alɔkysjɔ̃] *nf* short speech.

allonger [alɔ̃ʒe] *v* lengthen; (*étendre*) stretch out; (*cuisine*) thin. **allonger le cou** crane one's neck.

allouer [alwe] *v* allocate, allot.

allumer [alyme] *v* light; (*lampe, etc.*) turn on. **allumage** *nm* lighting; (*auto*) ignition. **allumette** *nf* match.

allure [alyr] *nf* (*vitesse*) speed, pace; (*démarche*) walk, bearing; air, appearance. **à toute allure** at full speed.

allusion [alyzjɔ̃] *nf* allusion. **faire allusion à** allude to.

almanach [almana] *nm* almanac.

aloi [alwa] *nm* **de bon aloi** respectable, worthy. **de mauvais aloi** of doubtful reputation or quality.

alors [alɔr] *adv* then; so; in that case. **alors même que** even if or though. **alors que** while.

alouette [alwɛt] *nf* lark.

alourdir [alurdir] *v* make heavy, weigh down.

aloyau [alwajo] *nm* sirloin.

alphabet [alfabe] *nm* alphabet. **alphabétique** *adj* alphabetical.

alpinisme [alpinismə] *nm* mountaineering. **alpiniste** *n(m+f)* mountaineer.

altercation [altɛrkɑsjɔ̃] *nf* altercation.

altérer [altere] *v* (*donner soif*) make thirsty; falsify; (*abîmer*) spoil, debase. **altération** *nf* deterioration; falsification.

alterner [altɛrne] *v* alternate. **alternance** *nf* alternation. **alternatif** *adj* alternate; (*élec*) alternating. **alternative** *nf* alternative.

Altesse [altɛs] *nf* Highness.

altier [altje] *adj* haughty.

altitude [altityd] *nf* altitude, height.

alto [alto] *nm* viola.

aluminium [alyminjɔm] *nm* aluminium.

amabilité [amabilite] *nf* kindness.

amadouer [amadwe] *v* coax, cajole.

amaigrir [amegrir] *v* make thin or thinner. **amaigrissant** *adj* (*régime*) slimming. **amaigrissement** *nm* thinness; slimming.

amalgamer [amalgame] *v* combine; (*métal*) amalgamate.

amande [amɑ̃d] *nf* almond. **amandier** *nm* almond (tree).

amant [amɑ̃] *nm* lover.

amarrer [amare] *v* (*naut*) moor; (*fixer*) make fast. **amarrage** *nm* mooring.

amas [amɑ] *nm* heap, mass. **amasser** *v* amass, accumulate.

amateur [amatœr] *nm* (*non-professionnel*) amateur; enthusiast. **d'amateur** *adj* amateurish.

ambassade [ɑ̃basad] *nf* embassy; mission. **ambassadeur, -drice** *nm, nf* ambassador.

ambiance [ɑ̃bjɑ̃s] *nf* atmosphere.

ambidextre [ɑ̃bidɛkstrə] *adj* ambidextrous.

ambigu, -uë [ɑ̃bigy] *adj* ambiguous. **ambiguïté** *nf* ambiguity.

ambition [ɑ̃bisjɔ̃] *nf* ambition. **ambitieux** *adj* ambitious.

ambivalent [ɑ̃bivalɑ̃] *adj* ambivalent. **ambivalence** *nf* ambivalence.

ambre [ɑ̃brə] *nm* amber.

ambulance [ɑ̃bylɑ̃s] *nf* ambulance. **ambulancier** *nm* ambulance man.

ambulant [ɑ̃bylɑ̃] *adj* itinerant, travelling.

âme [ɑm] *nf* soul.

améliorer [ameljɔre] *v* improve. **amélioration** *nf* improvement.

aménager [amenaʒe] *v* fit out *or* up; (*parc*) lay out; develop. **aménagement** *nm* fitting-out; development.

amender [amɑ̃de] *v* amend. **amende** *nf* fine.

amener [amne] *v* bring; cause.

amer [amɛr] *adj* bitter. **amertume** *nf* bitterness.

Amérique [amerik] *nf* America. **américain** *adj* American. **Américain, -e** *nm, nf* American.

améthyste [ametist] *nf, adj* amethyst.

ameublement [amœbləmɑ̃] *nm* furnishing; (*meubles*) furniture.

ami [ami], **-e** *nm, nf* friend. *adj* friendly. **amiable** [amjablə] *adj* amicable.

amiante [amjɑ̃t] *nm* asbestos.

amibe [amib] *nf* amoeba.

amical [amikal] *adj* friendly. **amicale** *nf* association.

amidon [amidɔ̃] *nm* starch. **amidonner** *v* starch.

amiral [amiral] *nm* admiral.

amitié [amitje] *nf* friendship. **amitiés** *nf pl* best wishes *pl*. **prendre en amitié** befriend.

ammoniaque [amɔnjak] *nf* ammonia.

amnésie [amnezi] *nf* amnesia.

amnistie [amnisti] *nf* amnesty.

amoindrir [amwɛ̃drir] *v* reduce, weaken, diminish.

amollir [amɔlir] *v* soften, weaken.

amonceler [amɔ̃sle] *v* pile up, accumulate. **amoncellement** *nm* heap; accumulation.

amont [amɔ̃] *nm* **d'amont** *adj* (*eau*) upstream; (*pente*) uphill. **en amont** *adv* upstream; uphill.

amoral [amɔral] *adj* amoral.

amorcer [amɔrse] *v* bait; (*commencer*) begin. **amorce** *nf* bait; beginning.

amorphe [amɔrf] *adj* (*roche*) amorphous; (*personne*) passive, lifeless.

amortir [amɔrtir] *v* absorb, cushion, deaden; (*dette*) pay off. **amortisseur** *nm* shock absorber.

amour [amur] *nm* love. **amour-propre** *nm* pride, self-esteem. **amoureux** *adj* (*personne*) in love; (*tendre*) loving.

ampère [ɑ̃pɛr] *nm* amp.

amphétamine [ɑ̃fetamin] *nf* amphetamine.

amphibie [ɑ̃fibi] *adj* amphibious. *nm* amphibian.

amphithéâtre [ɑ̃fiteatrə] *nm* amphitheatre; (*université*) lecture theatre.

ample [ɑ̃plə] *adj* ample, full. **ampleur** *nf* (*importance*) scale, extent; fullness.

amplifier [ɑ̃plifje] *v* develop, expand; (*son*) amplify. **amplificateur** *nm* amplifier.

ampoule [ɑ̃pul] *nf* (*élec*) bulb; (*méd*) blister.

amputer [ɑ̃pyte] *v* amputate; (*texte, etc.*) reduce drastically.

Amsterdam [amstɛrdam] *n* Amsterdam.

amuser [amyze] *v* amuse. **s'amuser** enjoy oneself, have fun. **amusement** *nm* entertainment, amusement; pastime.

amygdale [amidal] *nf* tonsil. **amygdalite** *nf* tonsillitis.

an [ā] nm year. **avoir 15 ans** be 15 years old.

anachronisme [anakrɔnism ə] nm anachronism.

anagramme [anagram] nf aı ıgram.

anal [anal] adj anal.

analogie [analɔʒi] nf analogy.

analphabète [analfabɛt] adj illiterate. **analphabétisme** nm illiteracy.

analyser [analize] v analyse; (méd) test. **analyse** nf analysis; test. **analytique** adj analytical.

ananas [anana] nm pineapple.

anarchie [anarʃi] nf anarchy. **anarchiste** n(m+f) anarchist.

anatomie [anatɔmi] nf anatomy.

ancêtre [ɑ̃sɛtrə] n(m+f) ancestor.

anchois [ɑ̃ʃwa] nm anchovy.

ancien, **-enne** adj (vieux) ancient; (d'autrefois) former. nm, nf elder; (élève) old boy, old girl. **ancienneté** nf seniority; great age.

ancre [ɑ̃krə] nf anchor. **ancrer** v anchor.

Andorre [ɑ̃dɔr] nm Andorra.

âne [ɑn] nm donkey, ass.

anéantir [aneɑ̃tir] v annihilate; destroy; (accabler) overwhelm. **anéanti** adj (fatigué) exhausted; overwhelmed. **anéantissement** nm annihilation; destruction; exhaustion.

anecdote [anɛkdɔt] nf anecdote.

anémie [anemi] nf anaemia. **anémique** adj anaemic.

anémone [anemɔn] nf anemone.

anesthésier [anɛstezje] v anaesthetize. **anesthésique** nm, adj anaesthetic. **anesthésiste** n(m+f) anaesthetist.

ange [ɑ̃ʒ] nm angel.

angélique[1] [ɑ̃ʒelik] adj angelic.

angélique[2] [ɑ̃ʒelik] nf angelica.

angine [ɑ̃ʒin] nf sore throat. **angine de poitrine** angina.

angle [ɑ̃glə] nm angle; (coin) corner. **angle droit** right angle.

Angleterre [ɑ̃glətɛr] nf England. **anglais** nm, adj English. **les Anglais** the English.

anglican [ɑ̃glikɑ̃], **-e** n, adj Anglican.

angoisse [ɑ̃gwas] nf anguish, distress; (peur) dread. **angoissant** adj harrowing. **angoissé** adj anguished, distressed.

anguille [ɑ̃gij] nf eel.

anguleux [ɑ̃gylø] adj angular, bony.

anicroche [anikrɔʃ] nf (fam) hitch, snag.

animal[1] [animal] nm animal.

animal[2] [animal] adj animal.

animer [anime] v animate; (discussion, etc.) lead; (pousser) drive, impel; (soirée, etc.) liven up. **s'animer** come to life, liven up. **animateur, -trice** nm, nf compère; (cinéma) animator. **animation** nf animation; liveliness. **animé** adj busy, lively.

animosité [animozite] nf animosity.

anis [ani] nm aniseed.

annales [anal] nf pl annals pl.

anneau [ano] nm ring; (chaîne) link.

année [ane] nf year. **année bissextile** leap year. **année-lumière** nf light year.

annexer [anɛkse] v annex. **annexe** nf annexe.

annihiler [aniile] v destroy, ruin, annihilate. **annihilation** nf annihilation, destruction, ruin.

anniversaire [anivɛrsɛr] nm (naissance) birthday; (événement) anniversary. **anniversaire de mariage** (wedding) anniversary.

annoncer [anɔ̃se] v announce; (prédire) forecast, foreshadow; indicate. **s'annoncer** approach. **s'annoncer bien** look promising. **annonce** nf announcement; sign, indication; (publicité) advertisement.

annoter [anɔte] v annotate. **annotation** nf annotation.

annuaire [anɥɛr] nm annual, yearbook; telephone directory.

annuel [anɥɛl] adj annual.

annuler [anyle] v (rendre nul) nullify; (mariage) annul; (commande, etc.) cancel. **annulation** nf nullification; annulment; cancellation.

anode [anɔd] nf anode.

anodin [anɔdɛ̃] adj insignificant, trivial; (sans danger) harmless.

anomalie [anɔmali] nf anomaly.

anonyme [anɔnim] adj anonymous; impersonal. **anonymat** nm anonymity.

anormal [anɔrmal] adj abnormal.

anse [ɑ̃s] nf handle; (géog) cove.

antagoniste [ɑ̃tagɔnist] n(m+f) antagonist. adj antagonistic. **antagonisme** nm antagonism.

antarctique [ɑ̃tarktik] adj antarctic. **l'Antarctique** nm the Antarctic.

antenne [ɑ̃tɛn] nf antenna; (TV, radio) aerial. **sur** or **à l'antenne** on the air.

antérieur, **-e** [ɑ̃terjœr] adj previous; (patte, membre) front, fore. **antérieur à** prior to.

anthologie [ãtɔlɔʒi] nf anthology.

anthropologie [ãtrɔpɔlɔʒi] nf anthropology. anthropologique adj anthropological. anthropologiste n(m+f) anthropologist.

antiaérien [ãtiaerjɛ̃] adj anti-aircraft; (abri) air-raid.

antialcoolique [ãtialkɔlik] adj against alcohol or alcoholism. ligue antialcoolique nf temperance league.

antibiotique [ãtibjɔtik] nm, adj antibiotic.

antichoc [ãtiʃɔk] adj shockproof.

anticiper [ãtisipe] v anticipate. anticipation nf anticipation. par anticipation in advance.

anticonceptionnel [ãtikɔ̃sɛpsjɔnɛl] adj contraceptive.

anticorps [ãtikɔr] nm antibody.

anticyclone [ãtisiklon] nm anticyclone.

antidater [ãtidate] v backdate.

antidote [ãtidɔt] nm antidote.

antigel [ãtiʒɛl] nm antifreeze.

antihistaminique [ãtiistaminik] nm, adj antihistamine.

antilope [ãtilɔp] nf antelope.

antipathique [ãtipatik] adj unpleasant.

antique [ãtik] adj antique, ancient. antiquaire n(m+f) antique dealer. antiquité nf antiquity. antiquités pl (meubles, etc.) antiques pl.

antisémite [ãtisemit] adj anti-Semitic. n(m+f) anti-Semite. antisémitisme nm anti-Semitism.

antiseptique [ãtisɛptik] nm, adj antiseptic.

antisocial [ãtisɔsjal] adj antisocial.

antithèse [ãtitɛz] nf antithesis. antithétique adj antithetical.

antonyme [ãtɔnim] nm antonym.

antre [ãtr] nm den.

anus [anys] nm anus.

anxiété [ãksjete] nf anxiety. anxieux adj anxious.

août [u] nm August.

apaiser [apeze] v calm, soothe; (soif) quench. s'apaiser die down; calm down; be satisfied.

aparté [aparte] nm aside.

apathie [apati] nf apathy. apathique adj apathetic.

*apercevoir [apɛrsəvwar] v see; (brièvement) catch sight of. s'apercevoir de notice. aperçu nm outline; (coup d'œil) glimpse.

apéritif [aperitif] nm aperitif.

aphrodisiaque [afrɔdizjak] nm, adj aphrodisiac.

aplanir [aplanir] v level; (problèmes) smooth away, iron out.

aplatir [aplatir] v flatten. s'aplatir devant grovel to. aplati adj flat.

aplomb [aplɔ̃] nm self-assurance; balance, equilibrium. d'aplomb adv (stable) steady; (vertical) straight down.

apogée [apɔʒe] nm peak, apogee.

apologie [apɔlɔʒi] nf apologia, defence.

apostrophe [apɔstrɔf] nf apostrophe; (interpellation) rude remark.

apôtre [apotr] nm apostle.

*apparaître [aparɛtr] v appear; seem.

apparat [apara] nm pomp. d'apparat ceremonial.

appareil [aparɛj] nm device, apparatus, appliance; (TV, radio) set; (fam) phone; (dents) brace; (fracture) splint; (anat) system. à l'appareil (téléphone) speaking. appareil-photo nm camera. appareil à sous slot machine.

apparence [aparãs] nf appearance; semblance. en apparence apparently. apparent adj obvious; visible.

apparenter [aparãte] v s'apparenter à ally oneself with; marry into; (ressembler) be similar to.

apparition [aparisjɔ̃] nf appearance; vision, apparition.

appartement [apartəmã] nm flat; (hôtel) suite.

*appartenir [apartənir] v appartenir à belong to; (impersonnel) be up to.

appât [apa] nm (pêche) bait; lure. appâter v lure; (piège) bait.

appeler [aple] v call; summon, send for; telephone. en appeler à/de appeal to/against. s'appeler be called. comment vous appelez-vous? what is your name? appel nm appeal; (cri) call; (école) register. faire appel appeal.

appendice [apɛ̃dis] nm appendix. appendicite nf appendicitis.

appentis [apãti] nm lean-to; (toit) sloping roof.

appétit [apeti] nm appetite. appétissant adj appetizing.

applaudir [aplodir] v applaud. s'applaudir congratulate oneself. applaudissements nm pl applause sing.

appliquer [aplike] v apply. applicable adj applicable. application nf application. appliqué adj industrious.

appointements [apwɛtmɑ̃] *nm pl* salary *sing*.

apporter [apɔrte] *v* bring.

apposer [apoze] *v* affix.

apprécier [apresje] *v* appreciate; value, assess. **appréciable** *adj* appreciable. **appréciation** *nf* assessment.

appréhender [apreɑ̃de] *v* apprehend; (*craindre*) dread. **appréhensif** *adj* apprehensive. **appréhension** *nf* apprehension.

***apprendre** [aprɑ̃drə] *v* learn; (*enseigner*) teach; (*aviser*) inform (of).

apprenti [aprɑ̃ti], -e *nm, nf* apprentice; (*débutant*) beginner. **apprentissage** *nm* apprenticeship.

apprivoiser [aprivwaze] *v* tame. **apprivoisé** *adj* tame.

approbation [aprɔbasjɔ̃] *nf* approval. **approbateur, -trice** *adj* approving.

approcher [aprɔʃe] *v* approach, draw or go near; (*objet*) move near. **s'approcher de** come or go near to, approach. **approche** *nf* approach.

approfondir [aprɔfɔ̃dir] *v* deepen; (*étudier*) go into. **approfondi** *adj* thorough.

approprier [aprɔprije] *v* suit, adapt. **s'approprier** appropriate. **s'approprier à** be appropriate to, suit. **approprié** *adj* appropriate.

approuver [apruve] *v* approve (of).

approvisionner [aprɔvizjɔne] *v* supply.

approximatif [aprɔksimatif] *adj* approximate. **approximation** *nf* approximation.

appui [apɥi] *nm* support. **appui-bras** *nm* armrest.

appuyer [apɥije] *v* press; support; (*poser*) lean, rest. **appuyer sur** press; rest on; stress, accentuate. **s'appuyer sur** rely on.

âpre [ɑprə] *adj* pungent, acrid; (*cruel*) bitter; (*dur*) grim; (*rude*) harsh.

après [aprɛ] *prep* after. *adv* afterwards. **après-demain** *adv* the day after tomorrow. **après-midi** *nm* afternoon. **après-rasage** *nm* after-shave. **d'après** (*selon*) according to; (*suivant*) next, following.

à-propos [aprɔpo] *nm* aptness.

apte [apta] *adj* apte à capable of, fit for. **aptitude** *nf* aptitude, ability.

aquarelle [akwarɛl] *nf* watercolour.

aquarium [akwarjɔm] *nm* aquarium.

aquatique [akwatik] *adj* aquatic.

aqueduc [akdyk] *nm* aqueduct.

aqueux [akø] *adj* aqueous.

arable [arablə] *adj* arable.

arachide [araʃid] *nf* peanut.

araignée [arene] *nf* spider.

arbitrer [arbitre] *v* arbitrate; (*sport*) referee, umpire. **arbitrage** *nm* arbitration. **arbitraire** *adj* arbitrary. **arbitre** *nm* judge; (*sport*) referee, umpire.

arbre [arbrə] *nm* tree; (*tech*) shaft. **arbre à cames** camshaft. **arbre de Noël** Christmas tree. **arbre généalogique** family tree.

arbrisseau [arbriso] *nm* shrub.

arbuste [arbyst] *nm* bush.

arc [ark] *nm* arc; (*arme*) bow; arch. **arc-en-ciel** *nm* rainbow.

arcade [arkad] *nf* archway. **arcades** *nf pl* arcade *sing*, arches *pl*.

archaïque [arkaik] *adj* archaic.

arche¹ [arʃ] *nf* arch.

arche² [arʃ] *nf* (*rel*) ark.

archéologie [arkeɔlɔʒi] *nf* archaeology. **archéologique** *adj* archaeological. **archéologue** *n(m+f)* archaeologist.

archet [arʃɛ] *nm* bow.

archevêque [arʃəvɛk] *nm* archbishop.

archi- [arʃi] *prefix* tremendously, utterly. **archiplein** *adj* (*fam*) chock-a-block.

archiduc [arʃidyk] *nm* archduke.

archipel [arʃipɛl] *nm* archipelago.

architecte [arʃitɛkt] *nm* architect. **architectural** *adj* architectural. **architecture** *nf* architecture.

archives [arʃiv] *nf pl* archives *pl*.

arctique [arktik] *adj* arctic. **l'arctique** *nm* the Arctic.

ardent [ardɑ̃] *adj* burning; passionate; ardent. **ardeur** [ardœr] *nf* ardour; passion.

ardoise [ardwaz] *nf* slate.

ardu [ardy] *adj* arduous.

arène [arɛn] *nf* arena.

arête [arɛt] *nf* fishbone; (*bord*) ridge; (*cube*) edge.

argent [arʒɑ̃] *nm* money; (*métal*) silver. **argent comptant** cash. **argent de poche** pocket money. **argent liquide** ready money. **argenté** *adj* silvery, silvered. **argenterie** *nf* silverware.

argile [arʒil] *nf* clay.

argot [argo] *nm* slang. **argotique** *adj* slang.

argument [argymɑ̃] *nm* argument. **argumenter** *v* argue, reason.

aride [arid] *adj* arid, dry. **aridité** *nf* aridity.

aristocratie [aristɔkrasi] *nf* aristocracy. **aristocrate** *n(m+f)* aristocrat. **aristocratique** *adj* aristocratic.

arithmétique [aritmetik] *nf* arithmetic. *adj* arithmetical.

arme [arm] *nf* weapon, arm. **armes** *nf pl* coat of arms *sing*.

armée [arme] *nf* army. **armée de l'air** air force. **Armée du Salut** Salvation Army.

armer [arme] *v* arm; equip; reinforce; *(fusil)* cock.

armoire [armwar] *nf* cupboard.

armure [armyr] *nf* armour.

arôme [arom] *nm* aroma; fragrance.

arpenter [arpɑ̃te] *v (terrain)* measure; pace up and down. **arpentage** *nm* surveying.

arquer [arke] *v* curve; arch. **arqué** *adj* curved; arched. **avoir les jambes arquées** be bow-legged.

arracher [araʃe] *v* snatch; *(extraire)* pull up *or* out; *(déchirer)* tear off *or* out. **d'arrache-pied** *adv* relentlessly.

arranger [arɑ̃ʒe] *v* arrange; *(régler)* settle; be convenient; *(réparer)* fix. **s'arranger** manage; *(se mettre d'accord)* come to an agreement; *(situation)* work out. **arrangement** *nm* arrangement; agreement.

arrérages [areraʒ] *nm pl* arrears *pl*.

arrestation [arɛstasjɔ̃] *nf* arrest.

arrêt [arɛ] *nm* stop; stopping; judgment. **arrêt d'autobus** bus stop. **arrêt du cœur** cardiac arrest. **arrêt de mort** death sentence.

arrêté [arete] *adj* firm, fixed. *nm* order, decree.

arrêter [arete] *v* stop; *(abandonner)* give up; *(police)* arrest; fix, decide on. **s'arrêter** *(v)* stop.

arrhes [ar] *nf pl* deposit *sing*.

arrière [arjɛr] *nm* rear, back; *(naut)* stern. **en arrière** backwards; *(derrière)* behind. *adj* rear, back. **arrière-goût** *nm* aftertaste. **arrière-pensée** *nf* ulterior motive. **arrière-plan** *nm* background. **arriéré** *adj (comm)* overdue, in arrears; *(personne, pays)* backward.

arriver [arive] *v* arrive; *(se passer)* happen. **arriver à** reach; *(réussir à)* manage. **j'arrive!** I'm coming! **arrivée** *nf* arrival.

arrogance [arɔgɑ̃s] *nf* arrogance. **arrogant** *adj* arrogant.

arrondir [arɔ̃dir] *v* round (off), make rounded. **arrondi** *adj* round.

arrondissement [arɔ̃dismɑ̃] *nm* district.

arroser [aroze] *v* water, spray; *(fam: repas)* wash down. **arrosoir** *nm* watering-can.

arsenal [arsənal] *nm* arsenal.

arsenic [arsənik] *nm* arsenic.

art [ar] *nm* art; *(adresse)* skill. **arts ménagers** domestic science *sing*.

artère [artɛr] *nf* artery. **artériel** *adj* arterial.

arthrite [artrit] *nf* arthritis. **arthritique** *adj* arthritic.

artichaut [artiʃo] *nm* globe artichoke.

article [artikl] *nm* article, item. **article réclame** special offer. **articles de Paris** fancy goods *pl*. **articles de toilette** toiletries *pl*.

articuler [artikyle] *v* articulate. **articulation** *nf (anat)* joint; articulation. **articulation du doigt** knuckle. **articulé** *adj* articulate; jointed.

artifice [artifis] *nm* device, trick, artifice.

artificiel [artifisjɛl] *adj* artificial.

artillerie [artijri] *nf* artillery.

artisan [artizɑ̃] *nm* craftsman, artisan.

artiste [artist] *n(m+f)* artist; *(théâtre)* performer. **artistique** *adj* artistic.

as [ɑs] *nm* ace.

asbeste [asbɛst] *nm* asbestos.

ascendant [asɑ̃dɑ̃] *adj* upward, rising. *nm* influence, ascendancy. **ascendance** *nf* ancestry.

ascenseur [asɑ̃sœr] *nm* elevator.

ascension [asɑ̃sjɔ̃] *nf* ascent.

Asie [azi] *nf* Asia. **asiatique** *adj* Asian. **Asiatique** *n(m+f)* Asian.

asile [azil] *nm* refuge, asylum, sanctuary; *(vieillards)* home.

aspect [aspɛ] *nm* aspect; appearance, look.

asperge [aspɛrʒ] *nf* asparagus.

asperger [aspɛrʒe] *v* spray, sprinkle.

asphalte [asfalt] *nm* asphalt.

asphyxie [asfiksi] *nf* suffocation, asphyxia.

aspirer [aspire] *v* inhale; *(liquide)* suck up. **aspirer à** aspire to, long for. **aspirant, -e** *nm* candidate. **aspirateur** *nm* vacuum cleaner. **aspiration** *nf* aspiration.

aspirine [aspirin] *nf* aspirin.

***assaillir** [asajir] *v* assail, attack.

assainir [asenir] *v* clean up; purify.

assaisonner [asɛzɔne] *v* season. **assaisonnement** *nm* seasoning.

assassiner [asasine] v murder; (pol) assassinate. **assassin, -e** nm, nf murderer; assassin. **assassinat** nm murder; assassination.

assaut [aso] nm assault, attack. **prendre d'assaut** take by storm.

assembler [asɑ̃ble] v assemble. **assemblage** nm assembling, assembly. **assemblée** nf assembly, meeting.

assentiment [asɑ̃timɑ̃] nm assent.

*asseoir [aswar] v sit; establish. s'asseoir (chaise, etc.) sit down; (lit) sit up.

assez [ase] adv enough; (plutôt) rather, fairly. **en avoir assez de** be fed up with.

assidu [asidy] adj assiduous; regular.

assiéger [asjeʒe] v besiege, beset.

assiette [asjɛt] nf plate; (cavalier) seat. **assiette creuse** soup dish. **assiette plate** dinner plate. **ne pas être dans son assiette** be off-colour.

assigner [asiɲe] v assign, allot, allocate; (jur) summons. **assignation** nf assignation; summons.

assimiler [asimile] v assimilate, absorb. **assimiler à** liken to. **assimilation** nf assimilation.

assis [asi] adj sitting, seated.

assises [asiz] nf pl assizes pl.

assister [asiste] v assist. **assister à** attend, witness. **assistance** nf (aide) assistance; (assemblée) audience, attendance. **assistant, -e** nm, nf assistant.

associer [asɔsje] v associate, combine. **s'associer** join together; (comm) form a partnership. **association** nf association; partnership. **associé, -e** nm, nf associate; partner.

assombrir [asɔ̃briːr] v darken; (personne) make gloomy. **assombri** adj gloomy, sombre.

assommer [asɔme] v knock out; (fam) bore stiff.

assortir [asɔrtir] v (couleurs, etc.) match; accompany; (comm) supply. **assorti** adj assorted; matched. **assortiment** nm assortment; arrangement; (vaisselle, etc.) set.

assoupir [asupir] v numb, dull, deaden. **s'assoupir** (s'endormir) doze off. **assoupissement** nm drowsiness.

assourdir [asurdir] v deafen; (amortir) muffle.

assujettir [asyʒetir] v subject, subjugate; (fixer) secure.

assumer [asyme] v assume, take on.

assuré [asyre], **-e** adj assured; certain, sure. nm, nf insured person, policyholder.

assurer [asyre] v assure; (maison, etc.) insure; maintain, provide; (rendre sûr) secure, ensure. **s'assurer** make sure, check; insure oneself. **assurance** nf assurance; self-confidence; (contrat) insurance.

astérisque [asterisk] nm asterisk.

asthme [asmə] nm asthma. **asthmatique** adj asthmatic.

astre [astrə] nm star.

*astreindre [astrɛ̃drə] v force, compel.

astringent [astrɛ̃ʒɑ̃] nm, adj astringent.

astrologie [astrolɔʒi] nf astrology. **astrologique** adj astrological. **astrologue** nm astrologer.

astronaute [astronot] nm(m+f) astronaut.

astronomie [astronɔmi] nf astronomy. **astronome** nm astronomer. **astronomique** adj astronomical.

astucieux [astysjø] adj shrewd. **astuce** nf shrewdness; (truc) trick.

asymétrique [asimetrik] adj asymmetric.

atelier [atalje] nm workshop; (art) studio.

athée [ate] adj atheistic. n(m+f) atheist. **athéisme** nm atheism.

Athènes [atɛn] n Athens. **athénien, -enne** nm, nf Athenian. **Athénien, -enne** nm, nf Athenian.

athlète [atlɛt] n(m+f) athlete. **athlétique** adj athletic. **athlétisme** nm athletics.

atlantique [atlɑ̃tik] adj Atlantic. **l'Atlantique** nm the Atlantic (Ocean).

atlas [atlas] nm atlas.

atmosphère [atmosfɛr] nf atmosphere. **atmosphérique** adj atmospheric.

atome [atom] nm atom. **atomique** adj atomic.

atout [atu] nm trump; (avantage) asset, trump card.

âtre [atrə] nm hearth.

atroce [atros] adj atrocious, dreadful. **atrocité** nf atrocity.

s'attabler [atable] v sit (down) at table.

attacher [ataʃe] v attach; (lier) tie up, fasten. **s'attacher** (fermeture) fasten, do up. **attachant** adj engaging. **attache** nf fastener, string; (lien) tie. **à l'attache** tied up. **attaché** nm attached.

attaquer [atake] v attack; (problème) tackle; (travail) set about. **s'attaquer à** attack. **attaque** nf attack.

attarder [atarde] *v* make late. **s'attarder** *v* linger.

***atteindre** [atɛ̃dr̩] *v* reach; (*balle, etc.*) hit; (*maladie*) affect. **être atteint de** be suffering from. **atteinte** *nf* attack.

atteler [atle] *v* harness. **s'atteler à** get down to.

attenant [atnɑ̃] *adj* adjoining.

attendre [atɑ̃dr̩] *v* wait (for); (*compter sur*) expect. **faire attendre** keep waiting. **s'attendre à** expect. **en attendant** meanwhile.

attendrir [atɑ̃dri̩] *v* (*personne*) move; (*viande*) tenderize. **s'attendrir sur** feel sorry for. **attendrissant** *adj* touching, moving. **attendrissement** *nm* emotion; pity. **attendrisseur** *nm* tenderizer.

attendu [atɑ̃dy] *adj* long-awaited; expected. *prep* considering. **attendu que** seeing that.

attentat [atɑ̃ta] *nm* murder attempt; attack; (*jur*) violation; offence.

attente [atɑ̃t] *nf* wait, waiting; expectation.

attention [atɑ̃sjɔ̃] *nf* attention, care. **avec attention** carefully. **faire attention** take care. **faire attention à** pay attention to. *interj* watch out! careful! **attentif** *adj* attentive; (*scrupuleux*) careful; (*prévenant*) thoughtful.

atténuer [atenɥe] *v* tone down, lighten; (*douleur*) alleviate; (*faute*) mitigate. **s'atténuer** die down, subside.

atterrer [atere] *v* appal.

atterrir [aterir] *v* land. **atterrissage** *nm* landing.

attester [ateste] *v* testify to, attest.

attirail [atiraj] *nm* (*fam*) gear.

attirer [atire] *v* attract; (*appâter*) lure, entice; cause. **attirance** *nf* attraction; lure. **attirant** *adj* attractive.

attiser [atize] *v* poke, stir up.

attitré [atitre] *adj* accredited; regular.

attitude [atityd] *nf* attitude.

attraction [atraksjɔ̃] *nf* attraction.

attrait [atrɛ] *nm* appeal, attraction.

attraper [atrape] *v* catch, get; (*tromper*) take in; (*gronder*) tell off. **attrape** *nf* trick.

attrayant [atrɛjɑ̃] *adj* appealing, attractive.

attribuer [atribɥe] *v* attribute; allocate; accord, award. **s'attribuer** claim. **attribut** *nm* attribute.

attrister [atriste] *v* sadden.

s'attrouper [atrupe] *v* flock together.

au [o] *contraction of* **à le**.

aubaine [oben] *nf* godsend, windfall.

aube[1] [ob] *nf* (*du jour*) dawn.

aube[2] [ob] *nf* (*bateau*) paddle; (*moulin*) vane.

aubépine [obepin] *nf* hawthorn.

auberge [oberʒ] *nf* inn. **auberge de la jeunesse** youth hostel. **aubergiste** *nm* innkeeper, landlord.

aubergine [oberʒin] *nf* aubergine.

aucun [okœ̃] *adj, pron* any, no. **ne … aucun** not any, no, none. **aucunement** *adv* in no way, not in the least.

audace [odas] *nf* audacity, daring. **audacieux** *adj* daring, bold, audacious.

au-delà [odla] *nm, adv* beyond.

au-dessous [odsu] *adv* below, underneath.

au-dessus [odsy] *adv* above, over.

au-devant [odvɑ̃] *adv* ahead. **aller au-devant de** anticipate; (*personne*) go and meet.

audible [odibl̩] *adj* audible.

audience [odjɑ̃s] *nf* audience, hearing.

auditeur [oditœr] *nm, -trice nm, nf* listener.

audition [odisjɔ̃] *nf* (*essai*) audition; recital; (*ouïe*) hearing.

auditoire [oditwar] *nm* audience.

auge [oʒ] *nf* trough.

augmenter [ogmɑ̃te] *v* increase. **augmentation** *nf* increase, rise.

aujourd'hui [oʒurdɥi] *adv* today. **aujourd'hui en huit** today a week today.

aulx [o] *V* **ail**.

aumône [omon] *nf* alms; charity. **aumônier** *nm* chaplain.

auparavant [oparavɑ̃] *adv* before, previously.

auprès [oprɛ] *prep* **auprès de** next to, close to; compared with; in the opinion of.

auquel [okɛl] *contraction of* **à lequel**.

aura [ɔra] *nf* aura.

auréole [ɔreɔl] *nf* halo.

Aurigny [oriɲi] *nf* Alderney.

aurore [ɔrɔr] *nf* dawn, daybreak.

aussi [osi] *adv* too, also; (*comparaison*) as; (*si*) so. **aussi bien** just as well. *conj* therefore.

aussitôt [osito] *adv* straight away. **aussitôt que** as soon as.

austère [ɔster] *adj* austere. **austérité** *nf* austerity.

Australie [ɔstrali] *nf* Australia. **australien** *adj* Australian. **Australien, -enne** *nm, nf* Australian.

autant [otɑ̃] *adv* as much, so much. **autant de** as much as, as many; *(tant)* so much, so many. **autant que** as much as. **autant que possible** as far as possible. **d'autant plus** all the more.

autel [ɔtɛl] *nm* altar.

auteur [otœr] *nm* author, writer; *(musique)* composer.

authentique [ɔtɑ̃tik] *adj* authentic, genuine. **authenticité** *nf* authenticity.

autistique [ɔtistik] *adj* autistic.

auto [ɔto] *nf* car. **auto-école** *nf* driving school. **auto-stop** *nm* hitch-hiking. **faire de l'auto-stop** hitch-hike. **auto-stoppeur, -euse** *nm, nf* hitch-hiker.

autobiographie [ɔtɔbjɔgrafi] *nf* autobiography. **autobiographique** *adj* autobiographical.

autobus [ɔtɔbys] *nm* bus.

autocar [ɔtɔkar] *nm* coach.

autodidacte [ɔtɔdidakt] *adj* self-taught.

autographe [ɔtɔgraf] *nm* autograph.

automatique [ɔtɔmatik] *adj* automatic. **automation** or **automatisation** *nf* automation. **automatiser** *v* automate.

automne [ɔtɔn] *nm* autumn. **automnal** *adj* autumnal.

automobile [ɔtɔmɔbil] *nf* motor car. **l'automobile** *nf* the motor industry; *(sport)* motoring. **automobiliste** *n(m + f)* motorist.

autonome [ɔtɔnɔm] *adj* autonomous. **autonomie** *nf* autonomy.

autopont [ɔtɔpɔ̃] *nm* flyover.

autopsie [ɔtɔpsi] *nf* post-mortem.

autoriser [ɔtɔrize] *v* authorize, give permission. **autorisation** *nf* authorization, permission. **autorisé** *adj* authorized; official.

autorité [ɔtɔrite] *nf* authority. **autoritaire** *n(m + f)*, *adj* authoritarian.

autoroute [ɔtɔrut] *nf* motorway.

autour [otur] *adv* around. *prep* **autour de** around.

autre [otrə] *adj* other; different. **autre chose** something else. **autre part** somewhere else. **d'autre part** on the other hand. *pron* another. **d'autres** others. **rien/personne d'autre** nothing/nobody else.

autrefois [otrəfwa] *adv* in the past. **d'autrefois** of the past.

autrement [otrəmɑ̃] *adv* differently, in another way; *(sinon)* otherwise. **autrement dit** in other words, that is.

Autriche [otriʃ] *nf* Austria. **autrichien** *adj* Austrian. **Autrichien, -enne** *nm, nf* Austrian.

autruche [otryʃ] *nf* ostrich.

autrui [otrɥi] *pron* others.

auvent [ovɑ̃] *nm* awning, canopy.

aux [o] *contraction of* **à les.**

auxiliaire [ɔksiljɛr] *adj* auxiliary, secondary. *n(m + f)* assistant, auxiliary.

auxquels, auxquelles [okel] *contractions of* **à lesquels, à lesquelles.**

aval [aval] *nm* **d'aval** *adj* *(eau)* downstream; *(pente)* downhill. **en aval** *adv* downstream; downhill.

avalanche [avalɑ̃ʃ] *nf* avalanche; torrent, flood.

avaler [avale] *v* swallow.

avancer [avɑ̃se] *v* advance; move *or* bring forward; *(accélérer)* speed up; make progress; *(montre)* gain. **avance** *nf* advance; lead. **à l'avance** in advance, beforehand. **d'avance** in advance. **en avance** *(heure)* early; ahead. **avancement** *nm* promotion; progress.

avant [avɑ̃] *prep* before. *adv* before; *(mouvement)* forward; *(naut)* bow. **avant tout** above all. **d'avant** *adj* previous, earlier. **en avant** *(mouvement)* forward; *(position)* ahead.

avantage [avɑ̃taʒ] *nm* advantage. **avantageux** *adj* worthwhile.

avant-bras *nm invar* forearm.

avant-coureur *nm* forerunner.

avant-dernier, -ère *n, adj* last but one.

avant-garde *nf* avant-garde. **d'avant-garde** *adj* avant-garde.

avant-goût *nm* foretaste.

avant-hier *adv* the day before yesterday.

avant-poste *nm* outpost.

avant-première *nf* preview.

avant-propos *nm invar* foreword.

avant-veille *nf* two days before.

avare [avar] *adj* miserly. *n(m + f)* miser. **avarice** *nf* avarice.

avarie [avari] *nf* damage. **avarié** *adj* rotting, damaged.

avec [avɛk] *prep* with.

avènement [avɛnmɑ̃] *nm* advent; *(roi)* accession.

avenir [avnir] *nm* future. **à l'avenir** from now on.

baie

Avent [avɑ̃] *nm* Advent.

aventure [avɑ̃tyr] *nf* adventure; (*entreprise*) venture. **à l'aventure** at random, aimlessly. **s'aventurer** *v* venture. **aventureux** *adj* adventurous; risky. **aventurier** *nm* adventurer.

avenue [avny] *nf* avenue.

s'avérer [avere] *v* prove to be, turn out to be.

averse [avers] *nf* shower.

aversion [aversjɔ̃] *nf* aversion, loathing. **avoir en aversion** loathe.

avertir [avertir] *v* warn; (*renseigner*) inform. **avertissement** *nm* warning; notice.

aveu [avø] *nm* confession, admission.

aveugle [avœglə] *adj* blind. *n(m+f)* blind person. **aveugler** *v* blind; (*éblouir*) dazzle. **s'aveugler sur** shut one's eyes to. **à l'aveuglette** blindly.

aviateur [avjatœr] *nm* airman. **aviation** *nf* aviation, flying; (*mil*) air force.

avide [avid] *adj* eager, avid; (*cupide*) greedy. **avidité** *nf* eagerness; greed.

avilir [avilir] *v* degrade, debase.

avion [avjɔ̃] *nm* aeroplane. **par avion** by airmail.

aviron [avirɔ̃] *nm* oar; (*sport*) rowing. **faire de l'aviron** row.

avis [avi] *nm* opinion; (*conseil*) advice; notice. **à mon avis** in my opinion. **avis au lecteur** foreword.

aviser [avize] *v* inform, notify; (*apercevoir*) notice. **aviser à** see to. **s'aviser de** realize suddenly; (*oser*) dare to. **avisé** *adj* sensible.

avocat¹ [avɔka], **-e** *nm, nf* (*jur*) barrister, advocate.

avocat² [avɔka] *nm* avocado (pear). **avocatier** *nm* avocado (tree).

avoine [avwan] *nf* oats *pl*.

***avoir¹** [avwar] *v* have; (*obtenir*) get; (*être*) be. **il y a** there is *or* are; (*temps écoulé*) ago. **il n'y a pas de quoi** don't mention it. **qu'est-ce qu'il y a?** what's the matter?

avoir² [avwar] *nm* assets *pl*; (*comm*) credit.

avoisiner [avwazine] *v* border on, be close to. **avoisinant** *adj* neighbouring, nearby.

avorter [avɔrte] *v* abort; (*projet*) fail. **se faire avorter** have an abortion. **avortement** *nm* abortion. **avorteur, -euse** *nm, nf* abortionist.

avouer [avwe] *v* confess, admit. **avoué** *nm* solicitor.

avril [avril] *nm* April.

axe [aks] *nm* axis; (*tech*) axle.

azalée [azale] *nf* azalea.

azote [azɔt] *nf* nitrogen.

B

babiller [babije] *v* (*personne*) chatter; (*ruisseau*) babble; (*oiseau*) twitter. **babillage** *nm* chatter; babble; twitter. **babillard, -e** *nm, nf* chatterbox.

babines [babin] *nf pl* lips *pl*, chops *pl*.

bâbord [babɔr] *nm* (*naut*) port (side).

babouin [babwɛ̃] *nm* baboon.

bac [bak] *nm* ferry-boat; (*récipient*) tub, tray, sink.

baccalauréat [bakalɔrea] *nm* examination equivalent to A-levels.

bâche [baʃ] *nf* canvas cover. **bâche goudronnée** tarpaulin.

bâcler [bakle] *v* hurry through; (*travail*) botch. **bâclé** *adj* slapdash.

bactérie [bakteri] *nf* bacterium (*pl* -ria).

badigeonner [badiʒone] *v* (*mur*) distemper, whitewash; (*méd*) paint. **badigeon** *nm* distemper, whitewash.

badiner [badine] *v* banter; (*avec négatif*) treat lightly, trifle with. **badinage** *nm* banter.

bafouiller [bafuje] *v* splutter; (*bredouiller*) stammer.

bagage [bagaʒ] *nm* bag, piece of luggage. **bagages** *nm pl* luggage *sing*. **bagages à main** hand baggage *sing*.

bagarre [bagar] *nf* fight, fight. **(se) bagarrer** *v* (*fam*) fight, scrap.

bagatelle [bagatɛl] *nf* trifle; (*objet*) trinket.

bagne [baɲ] *nm* hard labour.

bagnole [baɲɔl] *nf* (*fam*) old banger.

bague [bag] *nf* ring.

baguette [bagɛt] *nf* stick; (*musique*) baton; (*pour manger*) chopstick; (*pain*) thin French loaf; (*magique*) wand.

bahut [bay] *nm* chest; (*argot*) school.

bai [bɛ] *adj* bay.

baie¹ [bɛ] *nf* (*géog*) bay.

baie² [bɛ] *nf* (*bot*) berry.

baigner [beɲe] *v* bathe; (*bébé*) bath; (*tremper*) soak. **se baigner** (*mer, piscine*) go swimming; (*se laver*) have a bath. **baignade** *nf* bathe, bathing. **baigneur, -euse** *nm, nf* bather. **baignoire** *nf* bath.

bail [baj] *nm, pl* **baux** lease.

bâiller [baje] *v* yawn; (*couture, col, etc.*) gape; (*porte*) be ajar. **bâillement** *nm* yawn.

bâillonner [bajɔne] *v* gag. **bâillon** *nm* gag.

bain [bɛ̃] *nm* (*baignoire*) bath; (*piscine, mer*) swim, bathe. **bain de foule** walkabout. **bain de mousse** bubble bath. **prendre un bain de soleil** sunbathe.

baïonnette [bajɔnɛt] *nf* bayonet.

baiser [beze] *nm* kiss. *v* (*embrasser*) kiss; (*vulgaire*) screw.

baisser [bese] *v* (*mettre plus bas*) lower; (*décliner*) fall, drop. **se baisser** bend down. **baisse** *nf* fall, drop.

bal [bal] *nm, pl* **bals** dance, ball; (*lieu*) dance hall. **bal costumé** fancy-dress ball.

balader [balade] (*fam*) *v* trail round. **se balader** go for a walk; (*en voiture*) go for a drive. **balade** *nf* walk; drive.

balafrer [balafre] *v* gash. **balafre** *nf* gash; (*cicatrice*) scar. **balafré** *adj* scarred.

balai [balɛ] *nm* broom, brush. **balai mécanique** carpet sweeper.

balance [balɑ̃s] *nf* scales *pl*; (*comm*) balance. **Balance** *nf* Libra.

balancer [balɑ̃se] *v* swing, rock; (*compte*) balance; (*argot*) chuck (out). **se balancer** sway, swing. **balancier** *nm* pendulum. **balançoire** *nf* swing; (*bascule*) seesaw.

balayer [baleje] *v* sweep.

balbutier [balbysje] *v* stammer, mumble.

balcon [balkɔ̃] *nm* balcony; (*théâtre*) dress circle.

baldaquin [baldakɛ̃] *nm* canopy.

baleine [balɛn] *nf* whale.

balise [baliz] *nf* beacon; (*flottante*) buoy.

balistique [balistik] *adj* ballistic. *nf* ballistics.

balivernes [balivɛrn] *nf pl* nonsense *sing*.

ballade [balad] *nf* ballad.

ballant [balɑ̃] *adj* dangling.

balle [bal] *nf* (*projectile*) bullet; (*sport*) ball.

ballet [balɛ] *nm* ballet. **ballerine** *nf* ballerina.

ballon [balɔ̃] *nm* balloon; (*sport*) ball.

ballotter [balɔte] *v* jolt, toss *or* shake about.

balnéaire [balneɛr] *adj* bathing. **station balnéaire** *nf* seaside resort.

balustrade [balystrad] *nf* handrail.

bambou [bɑ̃bu] *nm* bamboo.

banal [banal] *adj* banal, commonplace. **banalité** *nf* banality; (*propos*) platitude.

banane [banan] *nf* banana. **bananier** *nm* banana (tree).

banc [bɑ̃] *nm* bench, seat; (*géol*) layer, bed. **banc d'église** pew. **banc de sable** sandbank. **banc des accusés** dock.

bancal [bɑ̃kal] *adj* wobbly, shaky; (*personne*) bandy-legged.

bandage [bɑ̃daʒ] *nm* bandage.

bande¹ [bɑ̃d] *nf* strip, band; (*magnétophone*) tape; (*méd*) bandage. **bande dessinée** comic strip. **bande sonore** sound-track.

bande² [bɑ̃d] *nf* band, group, gang.

bandeau [bɑ̃do] *nm* (*ruban*) headband; (*yeux*) blindfold.

bander [bɑ̃de] *v* bandage; (*tendre*) stretch. **bander les yeux à** blindfold.

bandit [bɑ̃di] *nm* bandit, thief; (*escroc*) crook.

banlieue [bɑ̃ljø] *nf* suburbs *pl*.

banne [ban] *nf* (*magasin*) awning; (*manne*) hamper.

bannière [banjɛr] *nf* banner.

bannir [banir] *v* banish. **banni, -e** *nm, nf* exile. **bannissement** *nm* banishment.

banque [bɑ̃k] *nf* bank; (*métier*) banking. **banquier** *nm* banker.

banqueroute [bɑ̃krut] *nf* bankruptcy. **faire banqueroute** go bankrupt. **banqueroutier, -ère** *nm, nf* bankrupt.

banquet [bɑ̃kɛ] *nm* banquet.

banquette [bɑ̃kɛt] *nf* seat.

baptême [batɛm] *nm* baptism, christening.

baptiser [batize] *v* baptize, christen.

bar [bar] *nm* bar.

baragouiner [baragwine] *v* (*fam*) gabble; talk gibberish. **baragouin** *nm* gibberish.

baraque [barak] *nf* stand, stall; (*abri*) shed; (*fam: maison*) place.

baratte [barat] *nf* churn. **baratter** *v* churn.

barbare [barbar] *adj* barbarous, barbaric. *nm* barbarian. **barbarie** *nf* barbarity.

barbe [barb] *nf* beard. **barbe à papa** candy floss. **quelle barbe!** (*fam*) what a drag!

barbecue [barbəkju] *nm* barbecue.

barbelé [barbəle] *adj* **fil de fer barbelé** barbed wire.

barbier [barbje] *nm* barber.

barbiturique [barbityrik] *nm* barbiturate.

barboter [barbote] *v* paddle, splash about; (*fam*) pinch. **barboteuse** *nf* rompers *pl*.

barbouiller [barbuje] *v* smear, daub; (*écrire*) scribble. **barbouillis** *nm* daub; scribble.

barbu [barby] *adj* bearded. *nm* bearded man.

barème [barɛm] *nm* list, scale, table.

bariolé [barjɔle] *adj* gaudy, multicoloured.

baromètre [barɔmɛtrə] *nm* barometer.

baron [barɔ̃] *nm* baron. **baronne** *nf* baroness. **baronnet** *nm* baronet.

baroque [barɔk] *adj* weird, strange; (*arch*) baroque. *nm* baroque.

barque [bark] *nf* small boat.

barrage [baraʒ] *nm* (*rivière*) dam; barrier; barricade.

barre [bar] *nf* bar, rod; (*trait*) stroke; (*naut*) helm, tiller.

barreau [baro] *nm* (*échelle*) rung; (*cage, jur*) bar.

barrer [bare] *v* bar, obstruct; (*rayer*) cross (out); (*naut*) steer.

barrette [barɛt] *nf* hair-slide.

barricade [barikad] *nf* barricade. **barricader** *v* barricade.

barrière [barjɛr] *nf* (*porte*) gate; (*clôture*) fence; (*obstacle*) barrier.

baryton [baritɔ̃] *nm, adj* baritone.

bas¹, basse [ba, bas] *adj* low; (*parler*) in a low voice. *nm* bottom. **en bas** down below; (*maison*) downstairs. **basse** *nf* bass.

bas² [ba] *nm* stocking.

basculer [baskyle] *v* fall over, topple; (*renverser*) tip up or out. **bascule** *nf* (*jeu*) see-saw. **cheval/fauteuil à bascule** *nm* rocking-horse/chair.

base [baz] *nf* base; (*fondement*) basis. **de base** basic.

base-ball [bɛzbol] *nm* baseball.

baser [baze] *v* base.

basilic [bazilik] *nm* basil.

basket-ball [baskɛtbol] *nm* basketball.

bassin [basɛ̃] *nm* pond, pool; (*géog*) basin; (*anat*) pelvis; (*naut*) dock.

basson [basɔ̃] *nm* bassoon.

bastille [bastij] *nf* fortress.

bataclan [bataklɑ̃] *nm* (*fam*) junk.

bataille [bataj] *nf* battle, fight. **bataillon** *nm* battalion.

bâtard [batar], **-e** *n, adj* bastard.

bateau [bato] *nm* boat. **bateau à voiles** sailing boat. **bateau de sauvetage** lifeboat.

bâtiment [batimɑ̃] *nm* building; (*naut*) ship.

bâtir [batir] *v* build; (*couture*) tack. **bâti** *nm* frame; tacking.

bâton [batɔ̃] *nm* stick.

battant [batɑ̃] *nm* flap; (*porte*) door; (*cloche*) clapper.

batte [bat] *nf* (*sport*) bat.

battement [batmɑ̃] *nm* beat, beating; interval, pause. **battement de paupières** blink.

batterie [batri] *nf* battery; (*musique*) percussion, drums.

*****battre** [batrə] *v* beat; (*parcourir*) scour; (*cartes*) shuffle. **battre des mains** clap. **battre son plein** be at its height. **se battre** fight.

baux [bo] *V* **bail**.

bavard [bavar], **-e** *adj* talkative. *nm, nf* (*fam*) chatterbox.

bavarder [bavarde] *v* chatter; (*papoter*) gossip. **bavardage** *nm* chatter; gossip.

baver [bave] *v* dribble, slobber. **bave** *nf* dribble, slobber. **bavette** *nf* bib.

béant [beɑ̃] *adj* gaping, wide open.

béat [bea] *adj* smug; (*sourire*) blissful.

beau [bo], **belle** *adj* beautiful, fine, lovely. **bel et bien** well and truly. **de plus belle** all the more. **beauté** *nf* beauty.

beaucoup [boku] *adv* (very) much, a great deal, a lot; (*personnes*) many. **de beaucoup** by far.

beau-fils *nm* son-in-law; (*remariage*) stepson.

beau-frère *nm* brother-in-law.

beau-père *nm* father-in-law; (*remariage*) stepfather.

beaux-arts [bozar] *nm pl* fine arts *pl*.

bébé [bebe] *nm* baby.

bec [bɛk] *nm* beak; (*plume*) nib; (*carafe*) lip; (*théière*) spout.

bécane [bekan] *nf* (*fam*) bike.

bécasse [bekas] *nf* woodcock. **bécassine** *nf* snipe.

bêcher [beʃe] *v* dig. **bêche** *nf* spade.

becqueter [bɛkte] *v* peck.

bedaine [bədɛn] *nf* (*fam*) paunch.

bée [be] *adj* **bouche bée** open-mouthed.

beffroi [befrwa] *nm* belfry.

bégayer [begeje] *v* stammer, stutter.

bégueule [begœl] *nf* prude. *adj* prudish.

béguin [begɛ̃] *nm* bonnet. **avoir le béguin pour** (*fam*) have a crush on, take a fancy to.

beige [bɛʒ] *nm, adj* beige.

beignet [bɛɲɛ] *nm* fritter; (*soufflé*) doughnut.

bel [bɛl] *form of* **beau** *used before vowel or mute* h.

bêler [bele] *v* bleat.

belette [bəlɛt] *nf* weasel.

Belgique [bɛlʒik] *nf* Belgium. **belge** *adj* Belgian. **belge** *n*(*m*+*f*) Belgian.

Belgrade [bɛlgrad] *n* Belgrade.

bélier [belje] *nm* ram. **Bélier** *nm* Aries.

belle [bɛl] *V* **beau.**

belle-fille *nf* daughter-in-law; (*remariage*) stepdaughter.

belle-mère *nf* mother-in-law; (*remariage*) stepmother.

belle-sœur *nf* sister-in-law.

bémol [bemɔl] *nm* flat.

bénédicité [benedisite] *nm* grace.

bénédiction [benediksjɔ̃] *nf* blessing.

bénéfice [benefis] *nm* (*comm*) profit; advantage, benefit. **bénéficiaire** *n*(*m*+*f*) beneficiary; (*chèque*) payee. **bénéficier de** *v* benefit from; (*jouir de*) enjoy; (*obtenir*) get.

bénévole [benevɔl] *adj* voluntary, unpaid.

bénin, -igne [benɛ̃, -iɲ] *adj* mild, slight; (*tumeur*) benign.

bénir [benir] *v* bless. **bénit** *adj* consecrated, holy.

béquille [bekij] *nf* crutch.

bercer [bɛrse] *v* rock; (*apaiser*) lull. **se bercer** delude oneself. **berceau** *nm* cradle. **berceuse** *nf* lullaby.

berger [bɛrʒe] *nm* shepherd; (*chien*) sheepdog. **berger allemand** alsatian. **bergère** *nf* shepherdess.

Berlin [bɛrlɛ̃] *n* Berlin.

Berne [bɛrn] *n* Bern.

besogne [bəzɔɲ] *nf* work.

besoin [bəzwɛ̃] *nm* need. **au besoin** if necessary. **avoir besoin de** need.

bétail [betaj] *nm* livestock; (*bovins*) cattle.

bête [bɛt] *nf* animal, creature, beast. **bête à bon dieu** ladybird. **bête noire** pet hate. **faire la bête** act stupid. *adj* stupid. **bêtise** *nf* stupidity; (*erreur*) blunder; (*action*) silly thing. **dire des bêtises** talk nonsense.

béton [betɔ̃] *nm* concrete. **bétonner** *v* concrete.

betterave [bɛtrav] *nf* beet. **betterave rouge** beetroot. **betterave sucrière** sugar beet.

beugler [bøgle] *v* bellow; (*radio*) blare; (*vache*) low.

beurre [bœr] *nm* butter. **beurrer** *v* butter.

bévue [bevy] *nf* blunder.

biais [bjɛ] *nm* (*détour*) expedient, device; (*aspect*) angle; (*couture*) bias; (*oblique*) slant. **de biais** at an angle; indirectly. **en biais** diagonally, at an angle.

bibelot [biblo] *nm* trinket, knick-knack.

biberon [bibrɔ̃] *nm* feeding bottle. **élevé au biberon** bottle-fed.

Bible [bibl] *nf* Bible. **biblique** *adj* biblical.

bibliographie [biblijɔgrafi] *nf* bibliography.

bibliothécaire [biblijɔtekɛr] *n*(*m*+*f*) librarian.

bibliothèque [biblijɔtɛk] *nf* library; (*meuble*) bookcase.

biceps [bisɛps] *nm* biceps.

biche [biʃ] *nf* doe.

bicyclette [bisiklɛt] *nf* bicycle; (*sport*) cycling. **aller à bicyclette** cycle.

bidon [bidɔ̃] *nm* can, tin.

bien [bjɛ̃] *adv* well; (*très*) very; (*beaucoup*) very much; (*plutôt*) rather; certainly, indeed; (*tout à fait*) properly, carefully. *adj* good; (*beau*) nice. *nm* good; possession. **bien de** much. **bien que** although. **biens** *nm pl* goods *pl*; property *sing*.

bien-aimé [bjɛ̃neme], **-e** *n, adj* beloved.

bien-être [bjɛ̃nɛtra] *nm* well-being.

bienfaisant [bjɛ̃fəzɑ̃] *adj* beneficial; (*personne*) kind. **bienfaisance** *nf* charity.

bienfaiteur [bjɛ̃fɛtœr] *nm* benefactor. **bienfaitrice** *nf* benefactress.

bienheureux [bjɛ̃nœrø] *adj* (*rel*) blessed; happy.

biennal [bjenal] *adj* biennial.

bienséance [bjɛ̃seɑ̃s] *nf* propriety. **bienséant** *adj* proper, seemly.

bientôt [bjɛ̃to] *adv* soon. **à bientôt!** see you!

bienveillance [bjɛ̃vejɑ̃s] *nf* kindness, benevolence. **bienveillant** *adj* benevolent, kindly.

bienvenu [bjɛ̃vny], **-e** *adj* well-chosen. *nm, nf* welcome person *or* thing. **être le bienvenu** be welcome. **bienvenue** *nf* welcome.

bière¹ [bjɛr] *nf* (*boisson*) beer. **bière (à la) pression** draught beer. **bière blonde** lager.

bière² [bjɛr] *nf* coffin.

biffer [bife] *v* cross out.

bifocal [bifɔkal] *adj* bifocal. **lunettes bifocales** *nf pl* bifocals *pl*.

bifteck [biftɛk] *nm* steak.

bifurcation [bifyrkɑsjɔ̃] *nf* fork, branching off. **bifurquer** *v* fork, branch off.

bigame [bigam] *adj* bigamous. *n(m+f)* bigamist. **bigamie** *nf* bigamy.

bigorneau [bigɔrno] *nm* winkle.

bigot [bigo], **-e** *adj* bigoted. *nm, nf* bigot.

bigoudi [bigudi] *nm* curler, roller.

bijou [biʒu] *nm, pl* **-oux** jewel. **bijouterie** *nf* jewellery; (*boutique*) jeweller's. **bijoutier, -ère** *nm, nf* jeweller.

bikini [bikini] *nm* bikini.

bilan [bilɑ̃] *nm* assessment; consequence; (*comm*) balance sheet. **bilan de santé** check-up.

bile [bil] *nf* bile. **se faire de la bile** get worried.

bilingue [bilɛ̃g] *adj* bilingual.

billard [bijar] *nm* billiards; billiard table.

bille [bij] *nf* marble; billiard ball.

billet [bijɛ] *nm* ticket; note. **billet de banque** banknote.

billot [bijo] *nm* block.

binaire [binɛr] *adj* binary.

biner [bine] *v* hoe. **binette** *nf* hoe.

biographie [bjɔgrafi] *nf* biography. **biographe** *n(m+f)* biographer. **biographique** *adj* biographical.

biologie [bjɔlɔʒi] *nf* biology. **biologique** *adj* biological. **biologiste** *n(m+f)* biologist.

bis [bis] *nm, interj* encore. *adv* (*musique*) repeat.

bisannuel [bizanɥɛl] *adj* biennial.

biscornu [biskɔrny] *adj* irregular; (*bizarre*) peculiar.

biscotte [biskɔt] *nf* rusk.

biscuit [biskɥi] *nm* biscuit; (*gâteau*) sponge cake.

bise¹ [biz] *nf* (*vent*) north wind.

bise² [biz] *nf* kiss.

bistouri [bisturi] *nm* scalpel.

bistro [bistro] *nm* pub, café.

bizarre [bizar] *adj* strange, odd. **bizarrerie** *nf* strangeness, oddness.

blafard [blafar] *adj* pale, wan.

blague [blag] *nf* joke; (*farce*) trick. **sans**

blague? really? **blaguer** (*fam*) *v* (*taquiner*) tease; (*plaisanter*) be joking.

blaireau [blɛro] *nm* badger; (*brosse*) shaving brush.

blâmer [blame] *v* blame; reprimand. **blâme** *nm* blame, reprimand.

blanc, blanche [blɑ̃, blɑ̃ʃ] *nm, adj* (*couleur*) white; (*page, etc.*) blank. **blanc cassé** off-white. **blancheur** *nf* whiteness.

blanchir [blɑ̃ʃir] *v* whiten; (*mur*) whitewash; (*toile*) bleach; (*linge*) launder; (*devenir blanc*) go or turn white. **blanchisserie** *nf* laundry.

blasé [blaze] *adj* blasé. **être blasé de** be bored with.

blason [blazɔ̃] *nm* coat of arms; heraldry.

blasphémer [blasfeme] *v* blaspheme. **blasphématoire** *adj* blasphemous. **blasphème** *nm* blasphemy.

blatte [blat] *nf* cockroach.

blé [ble] *nm* wheat, corn.

blêmir [blemir] *v* turn or go pale. **blême** *adj* pallid, wan.

blessé [blese], **-e** *adj* wounded. *nm, nf* casualty.

blesser [blese] *v* hurt, injure, wound. **blessure** *nf* wound.

blet, blette [blɛ, blɛt] *adj* overripe.

bleu [bly] *adj* blue. *nm* blue; (*meurtrissure*) bruise; (*vêtement*) overalls *pl*; (*débutant*) beginner. **bleu marine** navy blue. **bleu roi** royal blue.

bleuet [bly] *nm* cornflower.

blindé [blɛ̃de] *adj* armoured, reinforced.

bloc [blɔk] *nm* (*pierre, bois*) block; (*papier*) pad; group; (*d'éléments*) unit. **à bloc** fully, properly. **en bloc** outright.

blocage [blɔkaʒ] *nm* (*prix, etc.*) freeze; (*blocaille*) rubble.

blocus [blɔkys] *nm* blockade. **faire le blocus de** blockade.

blond [blɔ̃] *adj* fair, blond; (*sable*) golden. **blonde** *nf* blonde.

bloquer [blɔke] *v* block, jam, wedge; group together; (*salaires, etc.*) freeze.

se blottir [blɔtir] *v* snuggle up.

blouse [bluz] *nf* overall; (*chemisier*) blouse.

blue-jean [bludʒin] *nm* jeans *pl*.

bluff [blœf] *nm* (*fam*) bluff. **bluffer** *v* bluff.

bobine [bɔbin] *nf* spool, reel, bobbin; (*élec*) coil. **bobiner** *v* wind.

bocage [bɔkaʒ] *nm* grove; (*géog*) bocage.

bocal [bɔkal] *nm* jar; (*poissons*) bowl.

bock [bɔk] *nm* glass of beer.

bœuf [bœf] *nm* (*animal*) bullock, ox; (*viande*) beef.

bohème [bɔɛm] *n*(*m*+*f*), *adj* bohemian.

*****boire** [bwar] *v* drink; absorb.

bois [bwa] *nm* wood; (*cerf*) antler; (*musique*) wood-wind instrument. **bois de chauffage** firewood. **de** *or* **en bois** wooden. **boisé** *adj* wooded, woody. **boiserie** *nf* panelling.

boisson [bwasɔ̃] *nf* drink. **boisson alcoolisée** alcoholic drink.

boîte [bwat] *nf* box; (*métal*) tin, can. **boîte à lettres** pillar-box. **boîte à ordures** dustbin. **boîte de nuit** night-club. **boîte de vitesses** gearbox.

boiter [bwate] *v* limp. **boiteux** *adj* lame; (*meuble*) wobbly; (*projet*) shaky.

bol [bɔl] *nm* bowl.

bombarder [bɔ̃barde] *v* bombard; bomb. **bombardier** *nm* (*avion*) bomber.

bombe [bɔ̃b] *nf* bomb; aerosol, spray. **bombe atomique** atom bomb.

bomber [bɔ̃be] *v* bulge, stick out; (*route*) camber. **bombé** *adj* rounded, bulging. **bombement** *nm* bulge; camber.

bon, **bonne** [bɔ̃, bɔn] *adj* good; (*agréable*) nice; (*gentil*) kind; (*valable*) valid; (*correct*) right. **à quoi bon?** what's the use? **bon à** *or* **pour** fit for. **de bonne heure** early. **pour de bon** for good. *nm* good person; good part. *interj* right!

bon² [bɔ̃] *nm* form; coupon, voucher; (*titre*) bond.

bon anniversaire *interj* happy birthday!

bonasse [bɔnas] *adj* meek.

bonbon [bɔ̃bɔ̃] *nm* sweet. **bonbon à la menthe** mint.

bond [bɔ̃] *nm* leap, bound; (*balle*) bounce.

bonde [bɔ̃d] *nf* plug, stopper.

bondé [bɔ̃de] *adj* packed, crammed.

bondir [bɔ̃dir] *v* leap (up), jump (up); (*balle*) bounce; (*sursauter*) start.

bon enfant *adj invar* good-natured.

bonheur [bɔnœr] *nm* happiness; joy; (*chance*) luck. **au petit bonheur** haphazardly. **par bonheur** fortunately.

bonhomie [bɔnɔmi] *nf* good nature.

bonhomme [bɔnɔm] *nm* (*fam*) chap, bloke. **bonhomme de neige** snowman. *adj invar* good-natured.

boni [bɔni] *nm* profit.

bonjour [bɔ̃ʒur] *nm*, *interj* hello; (*matin*)

good morning; (*après-midi*) good afternoon.

bon marché *adj invar* cheap.

Bonn [bɔn] *n* Bonn.

bonne [bɔn] *V* **bon¹**. *nf* maid.

bonne année *interj* happy New Year!

bonne-maman *nf* (*fam*) granny, grandma.

bonnet [bɔnɛ] *nm* hat, bonnet; (*soutien-gorge*) cup. **bonnet d'âne** dunce's cap. **bonnet de bain** bathing cap. **bonneterie** *nf* hosiery.

bon-papa [bɔ̃papa] *nm* (*fam*) grand-dad, grandpa.

bon sens *nm* common sense.

bonsoir [bɔ̃swar] *nm*, *interj* good evening; (*en se couchant*) goodnight.

bonté [bɔ̃te] *nf* kindness, goodness.

bord [bɔr] *nm* edge, side; (*verre*) rim. **à bord** on board, aboard. **à ras bord** to the brim. **au bord de** (*lac, etc.*) by, alongside; (*larmes, ruine*) on the verge *or* brink of. **au bord de la mer** at the seaside. **bord du trottoir** kerb. **bordure** *nf* edge, border.

bordeaux [bɔrdo] *nm* Bordeaux. **bordeaux rouge** claret. *adj invar* maroon.

bordel [bɔrdɛl] *nm* brothel.

border [bɔrde] *v* edge; (*rue*) line; (*lit*) tuck in.

bordereau [bɔrdəro] *nm* note, slip; (*relevé*) statement.

borgne [bɔrɲə] *adj* one-eyed; (*louche*) shady.

borner [bɔrne] *v* limit; (*terrain*) mark out. **se borner à** content oneself with, confine oneself to. **borne** *nf* limit; (*kilométrique*) milestone. **sans bornes** limitless. **borné** *adj* narrow-minded; limited.

bosquet [bɔskɛ] *nm* copse.

bosse [bɔs] *nf* bump, lump; (*bossu*) hump. **avoir la bosse de** (*fam*) be good at, have a flair for.

bosseler [bɔsle] *v* emboss; (*déformer*) dent. **bosselé** *adj* dented, battered; (*sol*) bumpy. **bosselure** *nf* dent.

bossu, **-e** [bɔsy] *adj* hunchbacked. *nm*, *nf* hunchback.

bot [bo] *adj* **pied bot** club foot.

botanique [bɔtanik] *adj* botanical. *nf* botany. **botaniste** *n*(*m*+*f*) botanist.

botte¹ [bɔt] *nf* boot. **botte de caoutchouc** wellington, gumboot. **bottillon** *nm* bootee.

botte² [bɔt] *nf* bunch, bundle.

botte³ [bɔt] *nf* (*escrime*) thrust.

botter [bɔte] *v* put boots on; (*fam, sport*) kick.

bousculer

Bottin ® [bɔtɛ̃] nm directory.

bouc [buk] nm goat. **bouc émissaire** scapegoat.

boucaner [bukane] v (viande) cure; (peau) tan.

bouche [buʃ] nf mouth. **bouche à bouche** nm invar kiss of life. **bouchée** nf mouthful.

boucher¹ [buʃe] v block; (bouteille) cork; (trou) plug, fill up. **boucher le passage** be in the way. **bouché** adj (temps) cloudy; (argot) stupid, thick.

boucher² [buʃe] nm butcher. **boucherie** nf butcher's.

bouchon [buʃɔ̃] nm stopper, top; (liège) cork; (évier) plug; (auto) traffic jam.

boucler [bukle] v (fermer) buckle, fasten up; complete; (cheveux) curl. **boucler la boucle** (aéro) loop the loop; come full circle; complete. **boucle** nf buckle; curl; (ruban, etc.) loop. **boucle d'oreille** ear-ring. **bouclé** adj curly.

bouclier [buklije] nm shield.

bouddhisme [budismə] nm Buddhism. **bouddhiste** adj nm(m+f), adj Buddhist.

bouder [bude] v sulk. **boudeur, -euse** adj sulky.

boudin [budɛ̃] nm black pudding.

boue [bu] nf mud.

bouée [bwe] nf buoy. **bouée de sauvetage** lifebuoy.

boueux [bwø] adj muddy. nm dustman.

bouffer [bufe] v puff out; (fam) eat. **bouffant** adj (manche) full; (pantalon, etc.) baggy. **bouffe** nf (argot) grub. **bouffée** nf puff; (vent) gust; (parfum) whiff.

bouffir [bufir] v puff up. **bouffi** adj bloated, swollen; (yeux) puffy. **bouffissure** nf puffiness.

bouffon, -onne [bufɔ̃, -ɔn] adj comical. nm buffoon, clown. **bouffonnerie** nf clowning.

bouger [buʒe] v move, stir.

bougie [buʒi] nf candle; (auto) spark plug. **bougeoir** nm candlestick.

***bouillir** [bujir] v boil. **bouilloire** nf kettle.

bouillon [bujɔ̃] nm broth, stock; (bulle) bubble. **bouillon cube** stock cube.

bouillonner [bujɔne] v bubble, foam, seethe.

bouillotte [bujɔt] nf hot-water bottle.

boulanger [bulɑ̃ʒe] nm baker. **boulangerie** nf baker's, bakery.

boule [bul] nf ball. **boule de neige** snowball. **boules** nf pl (jeu) bowls sing.

bouleau [bulo] nm birch.

bouledogue [buldɔg] nm bulldog.

boulet [bulɛ] nm cannon-ball.

boulette [bulɛt] nf pellet.

boulevard [bulvar] nm boulevard.

bouleverser [bulvɛrse] v (renverser) turn upside down; disrupt, change completely; (personne) overwhelm, distress deeply. **bouleversement** nm upheaval.

boulon [bulɔ̃] nm bolt. **boulonner** v bolt.

boulot¹, -otte [bulo, -ɔt] adj plump.

boulot² [bulo] nm (fam) work.

boulotter [bulɔte] v (fam) eat.

bouquet¹ [bukɛ] nm bouquet, bunch; (arbres) clump. **c'est le bouquet!** that's the last straw!

bouquet² [bukɛ] nm (crevette) prawn.

bouquin [bukɛ̃] nm (fam) book. **bouquiniste** nm second-hand bookseller.

bourbe [burb] nf mire, mud. **bourbeux** adj miry, muddy.

bourdon [burdɔ̃] nm bumble-bee; (musique) drone.

bourdonner [burdɔne] v hum, buzz. **bourdonnement** nm buzz, hum.

bourg [bur] nm market town.

bourgeois, -e adj middle-class; (péj) bourgeois, conventional. nm, nf middle-class person. **bourgeoisie** nf middle class.

bourgeon [burʒɔ̃] nm bud. **bourgeonner** v bud.

bourgogne [burgɔɲ] nm burgundy.

bourrade [burad] nf thump, prod.

bourrage [buraʒ] nm stuffing, filling.

bourrasque [burask] nf gust of wind.

bourre [bur] nf stuffing, wadding.

bourreau [buro] nm torturer; executioner.

bourrelet [burlɛ] nm (porte, etc.) draught excluder; (chair) roll.

bourrer [bure] v stuff, cram.

bourriche [buriʃ] nf hamper.

bourru [bury] adj surly, gruff.

bourse [burs] nf purse; (d'étudiant) grant. **la Bourse** the Stock Exchange.

boursoufler [bursufle] v puff up. **se boursoufler** (peinture) blister. **boursouflé** adj puffy, swollen; blistered; (style) turgid. **boursouflure** nf puffiness; blister; turgidity.

bousculer [buskyle] v jostle; (heurter) bump into; (renverser) knock over. **bousculade** nf hustle, crush; (hâte) rush.

bousiller [buzije] (fam) v (travail) botch; (abîmer) wreck.

boussole [busɔl] nf compass.

bout [bu] nm end, tip; (morceau) piece, bit. **à bout** at the end of one's tether. **à bout de souffle** out of breath. **à bout portant** point-blank. **au bout de** at the end of; (après) after. **au bout du compte** all things considered. **de bout en bout** from start to finish. **jusqu'au bout** to the (bitter) end.

bouteille [butɛj] nf bottle. **en bouteille** bottled.

boutique [butik] nf shop. **boutiquier, -ère** nm, nf shopkeeper.

bouton [butɔ̃] nm button; (élec) switch; (porte) handle; (fleur) bud; (méd) pimple. **bouton de col** collar stud. **bouton de manchette** cuff-link. **bouton d'or** buttercup. **bouton-pression** nm press stud. **boutonner** v button. **boutonneux** adj pimply. **boutonnière** nf buttonhole.

bouture [butyr] nf cutting. **faire des boutures** take cuttings.

bouvier [buvje] nm herdsman.

bovin [bɔvɛ̃] adj bovine. **bovins** nm pl cattle pl.

boxer [bɔkse] v box. **boxe** nf boxing. **boxeur** nm boxer.

boyau [bwajo] nm gut; passageway. **boyaux** nm pl entrails pl.

boycotter [bɔjkɔte] v boycott. **boycottage** nm boycott.

bracelet [braslɛ] nm bracelet; (montre) strap. **bracelet-montre** nm wristwatch.

braconner [brakɔne] v poach. **braconnage** nm poaching. **braconnier** nm poacher.

braguette [bragɛt] nf (pantalon) fly.

braille [braj] nm braille.

brailler [braje] v bawl, yell.

*****braire** [brɛr] v bray.

braise [brɛz] nf embers pl.

braiser [breze] v braise.

brancard [brɑ̃kar] nm stretcher; (bras) shaft.

branche [brɑ̃ʃ] nf branch.

brancher [brɑ̃ʃe] v plug in, connect up.

brandir [brɑ̃dir] v brandish.

branle-bas [brɑ̃lba] nm invar bustle, commotion.

branler [brɑ̃le] v be shaky or unsteady; (dent) be loose. **branle** nm swing. **mettre en branle** set in motion, get moving.

braquer [brake] v aim, point; (auto) turn (the wheel).

bras [bra] nm arm; (tech) handle; (travailleur) worker. **bras dessus, bras dessous** arm in arm. **en bras de chemise** in shirt sleeves.

brasero [brazero] nm brazier.

brasier [brazje] nm inferno.

brasse [bras] nf breast-stroke. **brasse papillon** butterfly.

brassée [brase] nf armful.

brasser [brase] v stir, mix; (bière) brew. **brasserie** nf brewery; (café) brasserie.

brave [brav] adj good, nice; brave, courageous.

braver [brave] v brave, defy, stand up to.

bravoure [bravur] nf bravery.

break [brɛk] nm estate car.

brebis [brɑbi] nf ewe, sheep. **brebis galeuse** black sheep.

brèche [brɛʃ] nf breach, gap.

bredouiller [brɑduje] v stammer, mumble. **bredouille** adj empty-handed.

bref, brève [brɛf, brɛv] adj brief, short. **(en) bref** in short.

breloque [brɑlɔk] nf charm.

Bretagne [brɑtaɲ] nf Brittany.

bretelle [brɑtɛl] nf strap. **bretelles** nf pl braces pl.

breuvage [brœvaʒ] nm drink, beverage.

brevet [brɑvɛ] nm certificate, diploma; (d'invention) patent. **breveter** v patent.

bribe [brib] nf scrap, snatch, bit.

bricoler [brikɔle] v potter about, do odd jobs; (réparer) mend. **bricolage** nm do-it-yourself; makeshift repair. **bricoleur** nm handyman.

brider [bride] v bridle, restrain. **bride** nf bridle, rein; (bonnet) string, strap. **à bride abattue** (fam) flat out. **tenir en bride** keep a tight rein on.

bridge [bridʒ] nm bridge.

brièvement [brijɛvmɑ̃] adv briefly. **brièveté** nf brevity.

brigade [brigad] nf brigade; (police) squad; (équipe) team.

brigand [brigɑ̃] nm (péj) crook; (enfant) rascal. **brigandage** nm (armed) robbery.

brigue [brig] nf intrigue. **briguer** v covet, crave; solicit.

brillant [brijɑ̃] adj brilliant; (luisant) shiny, bright; outstanding, excellent. nm brilliance; shine, brightness.

briller [brije] v shine, sparkle.

brin [brɛ̃] nm sprig; (herbe) blade; (fil) strand. **un brin de** a bit of.

231 **bureau**

brindille [brɛ̃dij] *nf* twig.
brioche [brijɔʃ] *nf* bun.
brique [brik] *nf* brick.
briquet [brikɛ] *nm* cigarette lighter.
brise [briz] *nf* breeze.
briser [brize] *v* break, smash; (*espérance,
rebelle*) crush. **brise-lames** *nm invar*
breakwater.
britannique [britanik] *adj* British. **les
Britanniques** the British.
broc [bro] *nm* pitcher.
brocanter [brɔkɑ̃te] *v* deal in second-
hand goods. **brocante** *nf* second-hand
goods *pl*; (*commerce*) second-hand trade.
brocanteur, -euse *nm, nf* second-hand
dealer.
broche [brɔʃ] *nf* (*bijou*) brooch; (*cuisine*)
spit; (*tech*) pin.
broché [brɔʃe] *adj* **livre broché** paperback
book.
brochet [brɔʃɛ] *nm* pike.
brochette [brɔʃɛt] *nf* (*broche*) skewer;
(*plat*) kebab.
brochure [brɔʃyr] *nf* brochure, booklet.
brocoli [brɔkɔli] *nm* broccoli.
broder [brɔde] *v* embroider. **broder sur**
elaborate on. **broderie** *nf* embroidery.
broncher [brɔ̃ʃe] *v* (*cheval*) stumble. **sans
broncher** (*sans peur*) without flinching;
(*sans faute*) without faltering.
bronchite [brɔ̃ʃit] *nf* bronchitis.
bronzer [brɔ̃ze] *v* tan; (*métal*) bronze.
bronzage *nm* suntan. **bronze** *nm* bronze.
brosser [brɔse] *v* brush. **brosse** *nf* brush;
(*cheveux*) crew-cut. **brosse à
cheveux/dents/ongles** hair/tooth/
nailbrush.
brouette [bruɛt] *nf* wheelbarrow.
brouhaha [bruaa] *nm* hubbub.
brouillard [brujar] *nm* fog. **il fait du
brouillard** it's foggy.
brouiller [bruje] *v* (*troubler*) blur; (*mêler*)
mix *or* muddle up. **se brouiller** become
confused; (*se fâcher*) fall out. **brouille** *nf*
quarrel.
brouillon, -onne [brujɔ̃, -ɔn] *adj* untidy;
unsystematic. *nm* rough copy.
broussailles [brusɑj] *nf pl* undergrowth
sing, scrub *sing*. **broussailleux** *adj* bushy.
brouter [brute] *v* graze.
broyer [brwaje] *v* grind, crush.
bru [bry] *nf* daughter-in-law.
bruiner [brɥine] *v* drizzle. **bruine** *nf* drizzle.

bruire [brɥir] *v* rustle; (*eau*) murmur.
bruissement *nm* rustle; murmur.
bruit [brɥi] *nm* noise; rumour; (*histoires*)
fuss. **bruitage** *nm* sound effects *pl*.
brûler [bryle] *v* burn. **brûlant** *adj* burning,
scorching; (*objet*) red hot; (*liquid*) boiling hot. **brûlure** *nf* burn.
brume [brym] *nf* mist. **brumeux** *adj*
misty.
brun [brœ̃] *adj* brown, dark. *nm* brown.
brune *nf* brown ale; (*femme*) brunette.
brunir [brynir] *v* darken; (*peau*) tan, get
sunburnt.
brusque [brysk] *adj* brusque, abrupt.
brusquerie *nf* brusqueness, abruptness.
brut [bryt] *adj* crude, raw, rough; (*comm*)
gross. **brute** *nf* brute.
brutal [brytal] *adj* rough, brutal; (*franc*)
blunt, plain. **brutalité** *nf* brutality.
brutaliser [brytalize] *v* bully, ill-treat.
Bruxelles [brysɛl] *n* Brussels.
bruyant [brɥijɑ̃] *adj* noisy.
bruyère [brɥijɛr] *nf* heather.
Bucarest [bykarɛst] *n* Bucharest.
buccin [byksɛ̃] *nm* whelk.
bûche [byʃ] *nf* log; (*fam*) blockhead.
bûcher[1] [byʃe] *nm* (*remise*) woodshed;
(*supplice*) stake.
bûcher[2] [byʃe] *v* (*fam*) swot.
bûcheron [byʃrɔ̃] *nm* woodcutter, lumberjack.
Budapest [bydapɛst] *n* Budapest.
budget [bydʒɛ] *nm* budget.
buée [bɥe] *nf* steam, condensation.
couvert de buée misted up.
buffet [byfɛ] *nm* buffet; (*meuble*) sideboard. **buffet de cuisine** dresser.
buffle [byflə] *nm* buffalo.
buisson [bɥisɔ̃] *nm* bush.
bulbe [bylbə] *nm* bulb. **bulbeux** *adj* bul-
bous.
Bulgarie [bylgari] *nf* Bulgaria. **bulgare**
nm, adj Bulgarian. **Bulgare** *nm, nf* Bulgarian.
bulle [byl] *nf* bubble; (*méd*) blister.
bulletin [byltɛ̃] *nm* bulletin; ticket; certificate; (*école*) report. **bulletin de vote** ballot paper. **bulletin météorologique** weather report.
bungalow [bœ̃galo] *nm* bungalow; (*motel*)
chalet.
bureau [byro] *nm* (*meuble*) desk; (*cabinet*)
study; (*lieu*) office; (*section*) department.
bureau de location booking office. **bureau**

de poste post office. **bureau de vote** polling station.

bureaucratie [byrokrasi] *nf* bureaucracy. **bureaucrate** *n(m+f)* bureaucrat. **bureaucratique** *adj* bureaucratic.

buriner [byrine] *v* engrave.

burlesque [byrlɛsk] *adj* comical, ludicrous.

buste [byst] *nm* bust, chest.

but [by] *nm* goal, aim. **de but en blanc** point-blank, suddenly.

buter [byte] *v* stumble; (*sport*) score a goal; (*mur*) prop up. **se buter à** bump into. **buté** *adj* stubborn.

butin [bytɛ̃] *nm* booty, spoils.

butoir [bytwar] *nm* buffer.

butte [byt] *nf* mound. **être en butte à** be exposed to.

buvard [byvar] *nm* blotting paper.

buvette [byvɛt] *nf* refreshment bar.

buveur [byvœr], **-euse** *nm*, *nf* drinker.

byzantin [bizɑ̃tɛ̃] *adj* Byzantine.

C

c' [s] *V* **ce**[2].

ça [sa] *informal contraction of* **cela**.

çà [sa] *adv* **çà et là** here and there.

cabale [kabal] *nf* cabal.

cabane [kaban] *nf* hut, shed, cabin. **cabane à outils** toolshed. **cabane en rondins** log cabin.

cabaret [kabarɛ] *nm* night-club, cabaret.

cabillaud [kabijo] *nm* fresh cod.

cabine [kabin] *nf* cabin; (*réduit*) cubicle, booth. **cabine de bain** beach hut. **cabine téléphonique** telephone box.

cabinet [kabinɛ] *nm* (*bureau*) office; (*médecin, dentiste*) surgery; (*meuble, pol*) cabinet. **cabinet de débarras** box-room. **cabinet de toilette** toilet. **cabinet de travail** study.

câble [kɑbl] *nm* cable. **câbler** *v* cable.

cabosser [kabose] *v* dent.

se cabrer [kabre] *v* rear up; rebel.

cabriole [kabrijɔl] *nf* caper; (*danse*) cabriole; (*culbute*) somersault. **cabrioler** *v* caper about.

cacahouette [kakawɛt] *nf* peanut.

cacao [kakao] *nm* cocoa.

cachemire [kaʃmir] *nm* cashmere.

cacher [kaʃe] *v* hide, conceal. **cache-cache** *nm invar* hide-and-seek. **cache-col** *or* **cache-nez** *nm invar* scarf. **se cacher de** hide from.

cachet [kaʃɛ] *nm* seal, stamp; (*comprimé*) tablet; style. **cachet de la poste** postmark. **cacheter** *v* seal.

cachette [kaʃɛt] *nf* hiding-place. **en cachette** on the quiet, secretly.

cachot [kaʃo] *nm* dungeon.

cactus [kaktys] *nm invar* cactus (*pl* -ti).

cadavre [kadavrə] *nm* corpse; (*animal*) carcass. **cadavéreux** *or* **cadavérique** *adj* deathly.

cadeau [kado] *nm* present, gift.

cadenas [kadna] *nm* padlock. **cadenasser** *v* padlock.

cadence [kadɑ̃s] *nf* rhythm; (*musique*) cadence; (*vitesse*) rate. **cadencé** *adj* rhythmic.

cadet, -ette [kadɛ, -ɛt] *adj* younger, youngest. *nm, nf* (*famille*) youngest child; junior.

cadran [kadrɑ̃] *nm* dial, face. **cadran solaire** sundial.

cadre [kadrə] *nm* frame; (*milieu*) setting; (*formulaire*) space; scope, limits *pl*; context; (*responsable*) executive. **les cadres** management *sing*.

cadrer [kadre] *v* tally, conform; (*phot*) centre.

caduc, -uque [kadyk] *adj* (*feuilles*) deciduous; (*jur*) null and void; (*périmé*) outmoded.

cafard [kafar] *nm* (*insecte*) cockroach; (*tristesse*) depression; (*mouchard*) sneak. **avoir le cafard** be down in the dumps. **cafarder** *v* sneak, tell tales.

café [kafe] *nm* coffee; (*lieu*) café. **café au lait** white coffee. **café noir** *or* **nature** black coffee. **café soluble** instant coffee. **caféine** [kafein] *nf* caffeine.

cafetière [kaftjɛr] *nf* coffee-pot.

cage [kaʒ] *nf* cage; (*tech*) casing. **cage à poules** hen-coop.

cagneux [kaɲø] *adj* knock-kneed.

cagnotte [kaɲɔt] *nf* kitty.

cagoule [kagul] *nf* hood.

cahier [kaje] *nm* notebook, exercise book.

cahin-caha [kaɛ̃kaa] *adv* (*fam*) so-so.

cahot [kao] *nm* jolt, bump. **cahotant** *or* **cahoteux** *adj* bumpy. **cahoter** *v* jolt.

caille [kɑj] *nf* quail.

cailler [kɑje] v (lait) curdle; (sang) clot. **caillé** nm curds pl. **caillot** nm clot.

caillou [kɑju] nm, pl -oux stone, pebble. **caillouteux** adj stony, pebbly.

caisse [kɛs] nf box, case; (argent) cash-box, till; (guichet) cash-desk; (tambour) drum. **caisse d'épargne** savings bank. **caissier, -ère** nm, nf cashier.

cajoler [kaʒɔle] v coax, cajole; (câliner) make a fuss of.

cake [kɛk] nm fruit cake.

calamité [kalamite] nf calamity, disaster.

calcaire [kalkɛr] adj chalky; (eau) hard. nm limestone.

calcium [kalsjɔm] nm calcium.

calculer [kalkyle] v calculate, work out. **calcul** nm calculation, sum; arithmetic.

cale¹ [kal] nf (naut) hold; (plan incliné) slipway. **cale sèche** dry dock.

cale² [kal] nf wedge.

caleçon [kalsɔ̃] nm underpants pl. **caleçon de bain** bathing trunks pl.

calembour [kalɑ̃bur] nm pun.

calendrier [kalɑ̃drije] nm calendar; (programme) timetable, schedule.

calepin [kalpɛ̃] nm notebook.

caler [kale] v wedge; prop up, support; (moteur) stall; (fam) give up.

calfeutrer [kalføtre] v stop up; (pièce) draughtproof.

calibre [kalibrə] nm calibre; (qualité) grade; (grosseur) size; (instrument) gauge. **calibrer** v gauge; grade.

califourchon [kalifurʃɔ̃] nm **à califourchon** astride.

câlin [kɑlɛ̃] adj cuddly; tender. nm cuddle. **câliner** v fondle, cuddle. **câlinerie** nf tenderness; caress.

calleux [kalø] adj callous.

calmant [kalmɑ̃] adj soothing. nm tranquillizer; (analgésique) pain-killer.

calmar [kalmar] nm squid.

calme [kalmə] adj quiet, calm, peaceful. nm stillness, peace, calmness.

calmer [kalme] v calm, soothe. **se calmer** calm down; (diminuer) ease, subside.

calomnier [kalɔmnje] v slander; (par écrit) libel. **calomnie** nf slander; libel. **calomnieux** adj slanderous; libellous.

calorie [kalɔri] nf calorie.

calorifuger [kalɔrifyʒe] v lag, insulate. **calorifugeage** nm lagging, insulation.

calquer [kalke] v trace; copy exactly. **calque** nm tracing; exact copy. **papier-calque** nm tracing paper.

calvitie [kalvisi] nf baldness.

camarade [kamarad] n(m+f) companion, friend. **camarade de jeu** playmate.

cambrer [kɑ̃bre] v arch, bend. **se cambrer** arch one's back. **cambrure** nf curve, arch.

cambrioler [kɑ̃brijɔle] v break into, burgle. **cambriolage** nm burglary. **cambrioleur** nm burglar.

camée [kame] nm cameo.

caméléon [kamele5] nm chameleon.

camelote [kamlɔt] nf (fam) junk.

caméra [kamera] nf cine-camera.

Cameroun [kamrun] nm Cameroon.

camion [kamjɔ̃] nm truck. **camion-citerne** nm tanker. **camionnette** nf van. **camionneur** nm truck driver.

camoufler [kamufle] v camouflage; (cacher) conceal; disguise. **camouflage** nm camouflage.

camp [kɑ̃] nm camp; (parti) side. **camp de concentration** concentration camp.

campagne [kɑ̃paɲ] nf country, countryside; (pol, mil, etc.) campaign. **campagnard, -e** n, adj rustic.

camper [kɑ̃pe] v camp. **se camper** plant oneself. **campeur, -euse** nm, nf camper. **camping** nm camping; (lieu) campsite.

campus [kɑ̃pys] nm campus.

Canada [kanada] nm Canada. **canadien** adj Canadian. **Canadien, -enne** nm, nf Canadian.

canaille [kanɑj] adj coarse. nf scoundrel, rogue.

canal [kanal] nm channel; (artificiel, anat) canal. **canaliser** v channel.

canapé [kanape] nm sofa, settee; (cuisine) canapé.

canard [kanar] nm duck; false report; (musique) false note. **canardeau** nm duckling. **canardière** nf duck-pond.

canari [kanari] nm canary.

cancan [kɑ̃kɑ̃] nm gossip. **cancaner** v gossip. **cancanier, -ère** nm, nf gossip, scandalmonger.

cancer [kɑ̃ser] nm cancer. **Cancer** nm Cancer. **cancérigène** adj carcinogenic.

cancre [kɑ̃krə] nm (fam) dunce.

candeur [kɑ̃dœr] nf naivety.

candidat [kɑ̃dida] -e nm, nf candidate, applicant.

candide [kɑ̃did] adj naive, ingenuous.

cane [kan] nf (female) duck. **caneton** nm duckling.

canevas [kanva] *nm* (*toile*) canvas; (*ébauche*) framework.
caniche [kaniʃ] *nm* poodle.
canif [kanif] *nm* penknife.
canin [kanɛ̃] *adj* canine.
caniveau [kanivo] *nm* gutter.
canne [kan] *nf* cane; walking stick. **canne à pêche** fishing rod. **canne à sucre** sugar cane.
canneler [kanle] *v* flute. **cannelure** *nf* groove.
cannelle [kanɛl] *nf* cinnamon.
canoë [kanɔe] *nm* canoe. **faire du canoë** go canoeing.
canon¹ [kanɔ̃] *nm* gun, cannon; (*tube*) barrel.
canon² [kanɔ̃] *nm* canon; model.
cañon [kanɔ̃] *nm* canyon.
canoniser [kanɔnize] *v* canonize.
canot [kano] *nm* boat, dinghy. **canot automobile** motor boat. **canot de sauvetage** lifeboat. **canot pneumatique** rubber dinghy. **canotage** *nm* boating, rowing. **faire du canotage** go boating *or* rowing. **canotier** *nm* boater.
cantatrice [kɑ̃tatris] *nf* singer.
cantine [kɑ̃tin] *nf* canteen.
canton [kɑ̃tɔ̃] *nm* canton, district; section.
cantonnier [kɑ̃tɔnje] *nm* road-mender.
canular [kanylar] *nm* hoax. **faire un canular à** hoax, play a hoax on.
caoutchouc [kautʃu] *nm* rubber. **caoutchouc mousse** foam rubber. **caoutchouteux** *adj* rubbery.
cap [kap] *nm* cape; headland.
capable [kapablə] *adj* capable, able.
capacité [kapasite] *nf* capacity; ability.
cape [kap] *nf* cape, cloak.
capitaine [kapitɛn] *nm* captain.
capital [kapital] *adj* major, chief; fundamental. *nm* capital; fund. **capitale** *nf* capital (letter); capital (city). **capitaliser** *v* amass, accumulate. **capitalisme** *nm* capitalism. **capitaliste** *n*(*m*+*f*), *adj* capitalist.
capiteux [kapitø] *adj* heady; (*femme*) alluring.
capitonner [kapitɔne] *v* pad. **capitonnage** *nm* padding. **capitonné de** lined with.
caporal [kapɔral] *nm* corporal.
capot [kapo] *nm* (*auto*) bonnet *or* US hood.
capote [kapɔt] *nf* (*auto*) hood; (*manteau*) greatcoat.

câpre [kɑprə] *nf* caper.
caprice [kapris] *nm* whim, caprice. **capricieux** *adj* capricious, temperamental.
Capricorne [kaprikɔrn] *nm* Capricorn.
capsule [kapsyl] *nf* capsule; (*pistolet*) cap.
capter [kapte] *v* win, gain; (*émission*) pick up.
captieux [kapsjø] *adj* specious.
captif [kaptif], **-ive** *n*, *adj* captive. **captivité** *nf* captivity.
captiver [kaptive] *v* captivate, fascinate.
capuchon [kapyʃɔ̃] *nm* hood; (*stylo*) cap.
capucine [kapysin] *nf* nasturtium.
caquet [kakɛ] *nm* cackle. **caqueter** *v* cackle.
car¹ [kar] *nm* coach.
car² [kar] *conj* because, for.
carabine [karabin] *nf* rifle.
caractère [karaktɛr] *nm* character, nature. **caractériser** *v* characterize. **caractéristique** *nf*, *adj* characteristic.
carafe [karaf] *nf* carafe, decanter.
caramboler [karɑ̃bɔle] *v* collide with. **carambolage** *nm* pile-up.
caramel [karamɛl] *nm* caramel; (*dur*) toffee.
carapace [karapas] *nf* shell.
carat [kara] *nm* carat.
caravane [karavan] *nf* caravan.
carbone [karbɔn] *nm* carbon.
carboniser [karbɔnize] *v* (*forêt*) burn to the ground; (*cuisine*) burn to a cinder. **carbonisé** *adj* charred.
carburant [karbyrɑ̃] *nm* fuel.
carburateur [karbyratœr] *nm* carburettor.
carcasse [karkas] *nf* carcass; (*charpente*) frame.
cardiaque [kardjak] *adj* cardiac. **être cardiaque** have heart trouble, suffer from heart disease.
cardinal [kardinal] *nm*, *adj* cardinal.
carême [karɛm] *nm* fast. **Carême** *nm* Lent.
carence [karɑ̃s] *nf* deficiency.
carène [karɛn] *nf* hull.
caresser [karese] *v* caress, stroke; (*projet*) toy with. **caresse** *nf* caress.
cargaison [kargɛzɔ̃] *nf* cargo.
caricaturer [karikatyre] *v* caricature. **caricature** *nf* caricature.
carier [karje] *v* decay. **carie** *nf* tooth decay.

carillon [karijɔ̃] *nm* chime. **carillonner** *v* chime, ring. **carillonneur** *nm* bell-ringer.

carnage [karnaʒ] *nm* carnage.

carnassier [karnasje] *adj* carnivorous. *nm* carnivore.

carnaval [karnaval] *nm* carnival.

carnet [karnɛ] *nm* notebook. **carnet de chèques** chequebook. **carnet de billets/timbres** book of tickets/stamps.

carnivore [karnivɔr] *adj* carnivorous. *nm* carnivore.

carotte [karɔt] *nf* carrot.

carpette [karpɛt] *nf* rug.

carquois [karkwa] *nm* quiver.

carré [kare] *adj* square; (*franc*) straight, forthright. *nm* square. **carrément** *adv* bluntly, straight.

carreau [karo] *nm* (*mur, sol*) tile; (*vitre*) pane; (*tissu*) check; (*papier*) square; (*cartes*) diamond.

carrefour [karfur] *nm* crossroads.

carreler [karle] *v* tile; (*papier*) square. **carrelage** *nm* tiling.

carrelet [karlɛ] *nm* plaice.

carrer [kare] *v* square. **se carrer** ensconce oneself.

carrière[1] [karjɛr] *nf* (*pierre*) quarry.

carrière[2] [karjɛr] *nf* (*profession*) career.

carrosse [karos] *nm* coach. **carrosserie** *nf* (*auto*) body, bodywork.

carrure [karyr] *nf* build; stature.

cartable [kartablə] *nm* schoolbag, satchel.

carte [kart] *nf* card; (*géog*) map; menu. **carte à jouer** playing card. **carte de crédit** credit card. **carte des vins** wine list. **carte d'identité** identity card. **carte postale** postcard.

cartilage [kartilaʒ] *nm* cartilage; (*viande*) gristle. **cartilagineux** *adj* cartilaginous; gristly.

carton [kartɔ̃] *nm* cardboard; (*boîte*) box. **cartouche** [kartuʃ] *nf* cartridge; (*cigarettes*) carton.

carvi [karvi] *nm* caraway.

cas [kɑ] *nm* case; situation. **au cas où** in case. **cas limite** borderline case. **cas urgent** emergency. **en aucun cas** under no circumstances. **en tout cas** in any case. **faire cas de** attach importance to.

cascade [kaskad] *nf* waterfall; torrent. **cascadeur** *nm* stuntman.

case [kɑz] *nf* (*papier, échiquier*) square; compartment; hut.

caser [kɑze] *v* find a place for; fix up;

(*fam*) put. **se caser** settle down; find a job.

caserne [kazɛrn] *nf* barracks. **caserne de pompiers** fire station.

casier [kazje] *nm* compartment; (*courrier*) pigeon-hole; (*fermant à clef*) locker; (*bouteilles*) rack. **casier judiciaire** police record.

casino [kazino] *nm* casino.

casque [kask] *nm* helmet; (*à écouteurs*) headphones *pl*.

casquette [kaskɛt] *nf* cap.

casse [kɑs] *nf* breakage, damage. **mettre à la casse** scrap.

casser [kase] *v* break; (*jur*) annul, quash. **casse-cou** *nm invar* (*fam*) reckless person. **casse-croûte** *nm invar* snack. **cassenoisettes** *nm invar* nutcracker. **cassepieds** *n*(*m*+*f*) *invar* (*fam*) nuisance. **cassable** *adj* breakable. **cassant** *adj* brittle; brusque, abrupt. **cassure** *nf* break.

casserole [kasrɔl] *nf* saucepan.

cassette [kasɛt] *nf* casket; (*magnétophone*) cassette.

cassis [kasis] *nm* blackcurrant.

cassonade [kasɔnad] *nf* brown sugar.

caste [kast] *nf* caste.

castor [kastɔr] *nm* beaver.

cataloguer [kataloge] *v* catalogue, list. **catalogue** *nm* catalogue, list.

catalyseur [katalizœr] *nm* catalyst.

catamaran [katamarɑ̃] *nm* catamaran.

cataphote [katafɔt] *nm* reflector; (*route*) cat's-eye.

cataplasme [kataplasmə] *nm* poultice.

cataracte [katarakt] *nf* cataract.

catarrhe [katar] *nm* catarrh.

catastrophe [katastrɔf] *nf* disaster, catastrophe.

catch [katʃ] *nm* wrestling. **catcheur, -euse** *nm, nf* wrestler.

catéchisme [kateʃismə] *nm* catechism. **aller au catéchisme** go to Sunday school.

catégoriser [kategɔrize] *v* categorize. **catégorie** *nf* category. **catégorique** *adj* categorical.

cathédrale [katedral] *nf* cathedral.

cathode [katɔd] *nf* cathode.

catholique [katɔlik] *n*(*m*+*f*), *adj* Catholic. **catholicisme** *nm* Catholicism.

cauchemar [koʃmar] *nm* nightmare. **cauchemardesque** *adj* nightmarish.

cause [koz] *nf* cause; (*jur*) case, brief. **à cause de** because of. **en cause** in question. **pour cause de** on account of.

causer¹ [koze] v (occasionner) cause.

causer² [koze] v (bavarder) chat, talk. **causant** adj (fam) talkative. **causerie** nf chat, talk.

caustique [kostik] adj caustic.

cauteleux [kotlø] adj wily.

caution [kosjɔ̃] nf guarantee; (jur) bail; support. **sous caution** on bail.

cautionnement [kosjɔnmɑ̃] nm guarantee.

cavalerie [kavalri] nf cavalry.

cavalier [kavalje], **-ère** adj offhand. nm, nf (cheval) rider; (bal) partner. nm escort; (échecs) knight.

cave¹ [kav] nf cellar.

cave² [kav] adj hollow, sunken.

caveau [kavo] nm vault.

caverne [kavɛrn] nf cave. **caverneux** adj cavernous.

caviar [kavjar] nm caviar.

cavité [kavite] nf cavity.

ce¹ [sə], **cette** adj (ci) this; (là) that.

ce² [sə], **c'** pron it; (homme) he; (femme) she. **ce que** or **qui** what, which.

ceci [səsi] pron this.

cécité [sesite] nf blindness.

céder [sede] v give up or in; (fléchir, succomber) give way.

cédille [sedij] nf cedilla.

cèdre [sɛdrə] nm cedar.

***ceindre** [sɛ̃drə] v encircle; (mettre) put on.

ceinture [sɛ̃tyr] nf belt; (gaine) girdle; (écharpe) sash; (anat) waist. **ceinture de sécurité** seat or safety belt.

cela [səla] pron that; it. **cela** or **ça ne fait rien** it doesn't matter.

célèbre [selɛbrə] adj famous. **célébrité** nf celebrity.

célébrer [selebre] v celebrate. **célébration** nf celebration.

celer [sle] v conceal.

céleri [sɛlri] nm celery.

céleste [selɛst] adj celestial, heavenly.

célibataire [selibatɛr] adj single. nm bachelor, single man. nf single girl or woman. **célibat** nm celibacy.

cellule [selyl] nf cell.

celte [sɛlt] adj also **celtique** Celtic. **Celte** n(m+f) Celt.

celui, celle [səlɥi, sɛl] pron the one. **celui-ci, celle-ci** this one; (dernier) the latter. **celui-là, celle-là** that one; (premier) the former.

cendre [sɑ̃drə] nf ash. **cendrier** nm ashtray.

cène [sɛn] nm (rel) Communion. **la Cène** the Last Supper.

censé [sɑ̃se] adj supposed.

censeur [sɑ̃sœr] nm censor; critic; (lycée) deputy head.

censurer [sɑ̃syre] v (film, etc.) censor; (critiquer) censure. **censure** nf censorship; censure.

cent [sɑ̃] nm, adj a hundred. **faire les cent pas** pace up and down. **pour cent** per cent. **une centaine (de)** about a hundred. **centième** n(m+f), adj hundredth.

centenaire [sɑ̃tnɛr] adj hundred-year-old. n(m+f) centenarian. nm centenary.

centigrade [sɑ̃tigrad] adj centigrade.

centime [sɑ̃tim] nm centime.

centimètre [sɑ̃timɛtrə] nm centimetre; (ruban) tape measure.

central [sɑ̃tral] adj central. nm telephone exchange. **centrale** nf power station. **centraliser** [sɑ̃tralize] v centralize. **centralisation** nf centralization.

centre [sɑ̃trə] nm centre. **centre commercial** shopping centre. **centre-ville** nm town centre.

cep [sɛp] nm stock.

cependant [səpɑ̃dɑ̃] conj however, nevertheless.

céramique [seramik] nf, adj ceramic. **la céramique** ceramics.

cerceau [sɛrso] nm hoop.

cercle [sɛrklə] nm circle; club; (étendue) range. **cercle vicieux** vicious circle. **cercueil** [sɛrkœj] nm coffin.

céréale [sereal] nf cereal.

cérébral [serebral] adj cerebral; mental.

cérémonie [seremɔni] nf ceremony. **faire des cérémonies** stand on ceremony; (fam) make a fuss. **sans cérémonie** informal, informally. **cérémonieux** adj ceremonious, formal.

cerf [sɛr] nm stag. **cerf-volant** nm kite.

cerise [səriz] nf cherry. **cerisier** nm cherry (tree).

cerner [sɛrne] v encircle, surround. **avoir les yeux cernés** have rings under one's eyes.

certain [sɛrtɛ̃] adj certain; definite. **certains** pron, adj some, certain. **certainement** adv certainly; most probably.

certes [sɛrt] adv indeed, most certainly; admittedly.

certifier [sɛrtifje] v certify; (signature) witness; assure. **certificat** nm certificate.

certitude [sɛrtityd] *nf* certainty.

cerveau [sɛrvo] *nm* brain; (*intelligence*) mind; (*personne*) mastermind.

cervelle [sɛrvɛl] *nf* brains *pl*.

Cervin [sɛrvɛ̃] *nm* Matterhorn.

ces [se] *adj* (*ci*) these; (*là*) those.

cesse [sɛs] *nf* **sans cesse** continually; incessantly.

cesser [sese] *v* stop, cease. **faire cesser** put a stop to.

cet [sɛt] *form of* ce¹ *used before vowel or mute h.*

cette [sɛt] *V* ce¹.

ceux, celles [sø, sɛl] *pron* the ones, those. **ceux-ci, celles-ci** these; (*derniers*) the latter. **ceux-là, celles-là** those; (*premiers*) the former.

chacal [ʃakal] *nm, pl* **-als** jackal.

chacun [ʃakœ̃] *pron* each; (*tout le monde*) everyone.

chagrin [ʃagrɛ̃] *adj* despondent; morose. *nm* sorrow, grief.

chagriner [ʃagrine] *v* distress, worry.

chahut [ʃay] *nm* rumpus. **chahuter, -euse** *n, adj* rowdy.

chaîne [ʃɛn] *nf* chain; (*montagnes*) range; (*usine*) production line; (*TV*) channel.

chair [ʃɛr] *nf* flesh. **chair à saucisse** sausage-meat. **chair de poule** goose-flesh.

chaire [ʃɛr] *nf* (*rel*) pulpit; (*université*) chair.

chaise [ʃɛz] *nf* chair.

chaland [ʃalɑ̃] *nm* barge.

châle [ʃal] *nm* shawl.

chalet [ʃalɛ] *nm* chalet.

chaleur [ʃalœr] *nf* heat, warmth; fervour. **chaleureux** *adj* warm.

chaloupe [ʃalup] *nf* launch. **chaloupe de sauvetage** lifeboat.

chalumeau [ʃalymo] *nm* (*tech*) blowlamp; (*musique*) pipe.

chalut [ʃaly] *nm* trawl. **pêcher au chalut** trawl. **chalutier** *nm* trawler.

se chamailler [ʃamaje] *v* (*fam*) squabble. **chamailleur, -euse** *adj* quarrelsome.

chambellan [ʃɑ̃bɛlɑ̃] *nm* chamberlain.

chambranle [ʃɑ̃brɑ̃l] *nm* frame; (*cheminée*) mantelpiece.

chambre [ʃɑ̃brə] *nf* room; (*à coucher*) bedroom; (*tech, admin*) chamber; (*pol*) house. **chambre d'ami** spare room. **chambre d'enfants** nursery. **chambre noire** dark-room. **chambrer** *v* (*vin*) bring to room temperature; (*personne*) corner.

chameau [ʃamo] *nm* camel.

chamois [ʃamwa] *nm* chamois. *adj invar* buff.

champ [ʃɑ̃] *nm* field. **champ d'aviation** airfield. **champ de courses** racecourse. **champ de foire** fairground.

champagne [ʃɑ̃paɲ] *nm* champagne.

champêtre [ʃɑ̃pɛtrə] *adj* rural.

champignon [ʃɑ̃piɲɔ̃] *nm* mushroom; (*vénéneux*) toadstool; (*terme générique*) fungus; (*fam*) accelerator.

champion, -onne [ʃɑ̃pjɔ̃, -ɔn] *nm, nf* champion. *adj* (*fam*) first-rate. **championnat** *nm* championship.

chance [ʃɑ̃s] *nf* luck; (*possibilité*) chance. **avoir de la chance** be lucky. **pas de chance!** hard luck! **chanceux** *adj* lucky.

chanceler [ʃɑ̃sle] *v* totter, falter. **chancelant** *adj* unsteady, shaky.

chancelier [ʃɑ̃səlje] *nm* chancellor.

chandail [ʃɑ̃daj] *nm* sweater.

chandelle [ʃɑ̃dɛl] *nf* candle. **chandelier** *nm* candlestick.

changer [ʃɑ̃ʒe] *v* change; exchange; (*modifier*) alter. **change** *nm* exchange; (*taux*) exchange rate. **changeant** *adj* changeable. **changement** *nm* change; alteration.

chanoine [ʃanwan] *nm* canon.

chanson [ʃɑ̃sɔ̃] *nf* song.

chant [ʃɑ̃] *nm* singing; (*chanson*) song. **chant de Noël** Christmas carol.

chanter [ʃɑ̃te] *v* sing. **faire chanter** blackmail. **chantage** *nm* blackmail. **chanteur, -euse** *nm, nf* singer.

chantier [ʃɑ̃tje] *nm* yard, site; (*route*) roadworks *pl*. **chantier naval** shipyard.

chantonner [ʃɑ̃tɔne] *v* hum, croon.

chanvre [ʃɑ̃vrə] *nm* hemp.

chaos [kao] *nm* chaos.

chape [ʃap] *nf* (*pneu*) tread; (*rel*) cope.

chapeau [ʃapo] *nm* hat. **chapeau melon** bowler hat.

chapelain [ʃaplɛ̃] *nm* chaplain.

chapelet [ʃaplɛ] *nm* rosary.

chapelle [ʃapɛl] *nf* chapel.

chapelure [ʃaplyr] *nf* breadcrumbs *pl*.

chaperon [ʃaprɔ̃] *nm* chaperon. **chaperonner** *v* chaperon.

chapitre [ʃapitrə] *nm* chapter; subject.

chaque [ʃak] *adj* every, each.

char [ʃar] *nm* (*mil*) tank; (*carnaval*) float.

charabia [ʃarabja] *nm* (*fam*) gibberish.

charbon [ʃarbɔ̃] *nm* coal. **charbon de bois** charcoal. **charbonnage** *nm* coal-mining. **charbonnier** *nm* coalman.

charcuterie [ʃarkytri] nf (magasin) pork butcher's, delicatessen; (viande) cooked pork meats. **charcutier, -ère** nm, nf pork butcher.

chardon [ʃardɔ̃] nm thistle.

chardonneret [ʃardɔnrɛ] nm goldfinch.

charger [ʃarʒe] v load; (mil, élec) charge. **charger de** ask to, put in charge of. **se charger de** see to, take care of. **charge** nf load; charge; responsibility; (frais) expense. **à charge de** on condition that. **chargé** adj loaded, laden; (rempli, occupé) full, heavy. **chargement** nm loading.

chariot [ʃarjo] nm trolley; (charrette) wagon; (tech) carriage.

charité [ʃarite] nf charity; (gentillesse) kindness.

charivari [ʃarivari] nm hullabaloo.

charlatan [ʃarlatɑ̃] nm charlatan; (médecin) quack.

charmer [ʃarme] v charm, enchant. **charmant** adj charming, delightful. **charme** nm charm; (magique) spell.

charnel [ʃarnɛl] adj carnal.

charnière [ʃarnjɛr] nf hinge.

charnu [ʃarny] adj fleshy.

charpente [ʃarpɑ̃t] nf framework, structure; (carrure) build. **charpenté** adj built.

charrette [ʃarɛt] nf cart.

charrue [ʃary] nf plough.

charte [ʃart] nf charter.

chasse [ʃas] nf hunting, hunt; (au fusil) shooting; (poursuite) chase; (d'eau) flush. **tirer la chasse** pull the chain.

châsse [ʃɑs] nf shrine.

chasser [ʃase] v hunt; (au fusil) shoot; (faire partir) drive out, chase away; (dissiper) dispel. **chasse-neige** nm invar snowplough. **chasseur** nm hunter; (hôtel) page.

châssis [ʃɑsi] nm frame; (auto) chassis.

chaste [ʃast] adj chaste. **chasteté** nf chastity.

chat, chatte [ʃa, ʃat] nm, nf cat. **chaton** nm (zool) kitten; (bot) catkin.

châtaigne [ʃatɛɲ] nf chestnut. **châtaignier** nm chestnut (tree).

châtain [ʃatɛ̃] adj chestnut, auburn.

château [ʃato] nm castle; (manoir) mansion.

châtier [ʃatje] v punish; refine. **châtiment** nm punishment.

chatouiller [ʃatuje] v tickle. **chatouille-**

-ment nm tickle. **chatouilleux** adj ticklish; (irritable) touchy, sensitive.

chatoyer [ʃatwaje] v glisten, shimmer, sparkle. **chatoiement** nm glistening, shimmer, sparkle.

châtrer [ʃatre] v castrate.

chaud [ʃo] adj warm, hot. nm heat, warmth. **avoir chaud** be warm or hot. **chaudière** nf boiler.

chauffer [ʃofe] v warm (up), heat (up); (moteur) overheat. **chauffe-eau** nm invar water-heater. **chauffe-plats** nm invar hotplate. **chauffage** nm heating. **chauffage central** central heating.

chauffeur [ʃofœr] nm driver; (privé) chauffeur.

chaume [ʃom] nm stubble; (toit) thatch. **chaumière** nf thatched cottage.

chaussée [ʃose] nf road; causeway.

chausser [ʃose] v (mettre) put (shoes) on; (marchand) supply with shoes; (chaussure) fit. **chausse-pied** nm shoehorn. **chaussette** nf sock. **chausson** nm slipper. **chaussure** nf shoe, boot; footwear.

chauve [ʃov] adj bald. **chauve-souris** nf bat.

chauvin [ʃovɛ̃], **-e** nm, nf chauvinist. adj chauvinistic. **chauvinisme** nm chauvinism.

chaux [ʃo] nf lime. **blanchir à la chaux** whitewash.

chavirer [ʃavire] v capsize, overturn.

chef [ʃɛf] nm head; (patron) boss; (tribu) chief; (révolte, etc.) leader; (cuisine) chef. **chef d'équipe** foreman; (sport) captain. **chef de gare** station-master. **chef de train** guard. **chef-d'œuvre** nm masterpiece. **chef d'orchestre** conductor. **chef-lieu** nm county town.

cheik [ʃɛk] nm sheik.

chelem [ʃlɛm] nm (cartes) slam.

chemin [ʃəmɛ̃] nm way, path; (campagne) lane. **chemin de fer** railway. **chemin faisant** on the way. **se mettre en chemin** set off.

chemineau [ʃəmino] nm tramp.

cheminée [ʃəmine] nf chimney; (foyer) fireplace; (encadrement) mantelpiece; (paquebot) funnel.

cheminer [ʃəmine] v walk; (péniblement) trudge along; (eau, sentier) make its way.

chemise [ʃəmiz] nf shirt; (dossier) folder; (tech) lining, jacket. **chemise de nuit** nightdress. **chemisier** nm blouse.

chenal [ʃənal] nm channel; canal.

chêne [ʃɛn] nm oak.

chenille [ʃənij] nf caterpillar.

chèque [ʃɛk] nm check. **chèque-cadeau** nm gift token. **chèque de voyage** traveller's check. **chèque en blanc** blank check. **chéquier** nm check book.

cher [ʃɛr] adj dear; (coûteux) expensive. adv dearly. **coûter/payer cher** cost/pay a lot. **cherté** nf high price or cost.

chercher [ʃɛrʃe] v look for, seek. **chercher à** try to. **chercheur, -euse** nm, nf researcher.

chéri [ʃeri] -e adj beloved. nm, nf darling.

chérir [ʃerir] v cherish.

chérubin [ʃerybɛ̃] nm cherub.

chétif [ʃetif] adj (enfant, etc.) puny; (repas, etc.) meagre.

cheval [ʃəval] nm horse; (auto) horsepower. **à cheval** on horseback; (chaise, etc.) astride, straddling. **cheval à bascule** rocking horse. **cheval de course** racehorse.

chevalerie [ʃəvalri] nf chivalry. **chevaleresque** adj chivalrous.

chevalet [ʃəvalɛ] nm (peinture) easel; (menuiserie) trestle; (violon) bridge.

chevalier [ʃəvalje] nm knight. **chevalière** nf signet ring.

chevaucher [ʃəvoʃe] v be astride, straddle; (tuile, pan) overlap.

chevelu [ʃəvly] adj long-haired, hairy. **chevelure** nf (head of) hair.

chevet [ʃəvɛ] nm bedside.

cheveu [ʃəvø] nm hair. **cheveux** nm pl hair sing. **tiré par les cheveux** far-fetched.

cheville [ʃəvij] nf ankle; (fiche) peg, pin.

chèvre [ʃɛvr] nf goat. **chevreau** nm kid.

chèvrefeuille [ʃɛvrəfœj] nm honeysuckle.

chevron [ʃəvrɔ̃] nm rafter; (motif) chevron.

chevroter [ʃəvrɔte] v quaver.

chez [ʃe] prep at or to the house of; (avec) with, in, among; (docteur, etc.) at, to; (adresse) care of, c/o. **chez soi** at home. **faites comme chez vous!** make yourself at home!

chic [ʃik] nm style. **avoir le chic pour** have the knack of. adj invar smart; (fam) nice, decent. interj great! terrific!

chicaner [ʃikane] v quibble. **chicanerie** nf quibbling.

chiche [ʃiʃ] adj niggardly, paltry, mean.

chicorée [ʃikɔre] nf (salade) endive; (café) chicory.

chien [ʃjɛ̃] nm dog. **chien d'aveugle** guide dog. **chien de berger** sheepdog. **chien de garde** guard dog. **entre chien et loup** in the twilight. **temps de chien** nm filthy weather. **chienne** nf bitch.

chiffon [ʃifɔ̃] nm rag; (de papier) scrap; (à poussière) duster. **chiffonner** [ʃifɔne] v crumple, crease; (fam) bother, worry.

chiffre [ʃifr] nm figure; total; code. **chiffre d'affaires** turnover.

chiffrer [ʃifre] v code; (évaluer) assess; (pages) number. **se chiffrer à** add up to.

chignon [ʃiɲɔ̃] nm bun.

chimère [ʃimɛr] nf dream, fancy. **chimérique** adj fanciful; imaginary.

chimie [ʃimi] nf chemistry. **chimique** adj chemical. **chimiste** nm(m+f) chemist.

chimpanzé [ʃɛ̃pɑ̃ze] nm chimpanzee.

Chine [ʃin] nf China. **chinois** nm, adj Chinese. **les Chinois** the Chinese.

chiot [ʃjo] nm puppy.

chiper [ʃipe] v (fam) pinch.

chipoter [ʃipɔte] (fam) v haggle, quibble; (manger) pick at.

chips [ʃip] nm pl potato chips pl.

chiquenaude [ʃiknod] nf flick, flip.

chiromancie [kirɔmɑ̃si] nf palmistry. **chiromancien, -enne** nm, nf palmist.

chirurgie [ʃiryrʒi] nf surgery. **chirurgical** adj surgical. **chirurgien** nm surgeon.

chlore [klɔr] nm chlorine. **chlorer** v chlorinate.

chloroforme [klɔrɔfɔrm] nm chloroform. **chloroformer** v chloroform.

chlorophylle [klɔrɔfil] nf chlorophyll.

choc [ʃɔk] nm shock; impact, crash; (conflit) clash.

chocolat [ʃɔkɔla] nm chocolate. **chocolat à croquer** plain chocolate. **chocolat au lait** milk chocolate. **chocolat en poudre** drinking chocolate. adj invar chocolate-coloured.

chœur [kœr] nm chorus; (chanteurs) choir. **en chœur** in chorus.

*****choir** [ʃwar] v fall.

choisir [ʃwazir] v choose, select. **choisi** adj chosen; (raffiné) select.

choix [ʃwa] nm choice, selection. **de choix** choice.

choléra [kɔlera] nm cholera.

cholestérol [kɔlesterɔl] nm cholesterol.

chômer [ʃome] v be idle; (travailleur) be unemployed; (usine, etc.) be at a standstill. **chômage** nm unemployment. **au**

chômage unemployed. **mettre au chômage** make redundant. **chômeur, -euse** nm, nf unemployed person.

chope [ʃɔp] nf tankard.

choquer [ʃɔke] v shock, appal; (offusquer) offend; (commotionner) shake up; (heurter) knock, clink. **se choquer** be shocked.

choral [kɔral] adj choral. nm chorale. **chorale** nf choral society, choir.

chorégraphie [kɔregrafi] nf choreography. **chorégraphe** n(m+f) choreographer.

chose [ʃoz] nf thing. nm (fam) thingumajig. **être tout chose** (fam) feel peculiar.

chou [ʃu] nm, pl **choux** cabbage; (ruban) rosette; (cuisine) puff. **chou de Bruxelles** Brussels sprout. **chou-fleur** nm cauliflower.

choucas [ʃuka] nm jackdaw.

chouchou, -oute [ʃuʃu, -ut] nm, nf (fam) pet.

choucroute [ʃukrut] nf sauerkraut.

chouette[1] [ʃwɛt] adj, interj (fam) smashing, great.

chouette[2] [ʃwɛt] nf owl.

choyer [ʃwaje] v pamper; cherish.

chrétien [kretjɛ̃] adj Christian. **Chrétien, -enne** nm, nf Christian.

christianisme [kristjanismə] nm Christianity.

chromatique [krɔmatik] adj chromatic.

chrome [krom] nm chromium, chrome. **chromé** adj chromium-plated.

chromosome [krɔmozom] nm chromosome.

chronique[1] [krɔnik] adj chronic.

chronique[2] [krɔnik] nf chronicle; (journal) column.

chronologique [krɔnɔlɔʒik] adj chronological.

chronométrer [krɔnɔmetre] v time. **chronomètre** nm stopwatch.

chrysalide [krizalid] nf chrysalis.

chrysanthème [krizɑ̃tɛm] nm chrysanthemum.

chuchoter [ʃyʃote] v whisper. **chuchotement** nm whisper.

chuinter [ʃɥɛ̃te] v hiss softly; (chouette) hoot.

chut [ʃyt] interj hush!

chute [ʃyt] nf fall; (ruine) collapse, downfall. **chute d'eau** waterfall.

Chypre [ʃipra] n Cyprus.

ci [si] adv this; here. **ci-après** adv below. **ci-contre** adv opposite. **ci-dessous** below.

ci-dessus adv above. **ci-devant** adv formerly. **ci-inclus** adj enclosed. **ci-joint** adj enclosed, attached.

cible [siblə] nf target.

ciboule [sibul] nf spring onion. **ciboulette** nf chive.

cicatrice [sikatris] nf scar.

cidre [sidrə] nm cider.

ciel [sjɛl] nm, pl **ciels** or **cieux** sky; (rel) heaven.

cierge [sjɛrʒ] nm candle.

cigale [sigal] nf cicada.

cigare [sigar] nm cigar. **cigarette** nf cigarette.

cigogne [sigɔɲ] nf stork.

cil [sil] nm eyelash.

cime [sim] nf peak; (montagne) summit; (arbre) top.

ciment [simɑ̃] nm cement. **cimenter** v cement.

cimetière [simtjɛr] nm cemetery, graveyard.

cinéaste [sineast] n(m+f) film-maker.

cinéma [sinema] nm cinema.

cinétique [sinetik] adj kinetic. nf kinetics.

cingler [sɛ̃gle] v lash, whip. **cinglant** adj biting; (pluie) driving. **cinglé** adj (fam) mad, crazy.

cinq [sɛ̃k] nm, adj five. **cinquième** n(m+f), adj fifth.

cinquante [sɛ̃kɑ̃t] nm, adj fifty. **cinquantième** n(m+f), adj fiftieth.

cintrer [sɛ̃tre] v arch; bend. **cintre** nm arch; (vêtements) coat-hanger.

cirage [siraʒ] nm shoe polish.

*** circoncire** [sirkɔ̃sir] v circumcize. **circoncision** nf circumcision.

circonférence [sirkɔ̃ferɑ̃s] nf circumference.

circonflexe [sirkɔ̃flɛks] adj circumflex.

circonscription [sirkɔ̃skripsjɔ̃] nf district; (électorale) constituency.

*** circonscrire** [sirkɔ̃skrir] v confine; (math) circumscribe.

circonspect [sirkɔ̃spɛkt] adj circumspect, cautious.

circonstance [sirkɔ̃stɑ̃s] nf circumstance; occasion. **de circonstance** appropriate.

circuit [sirkɥi] nm circuit; (excursion) tour.

circuler [sirkyle] v circulate; (voiture, piéton) go, move along. **circulaire** nf, adj circular. **circulation** nf circulation; (auto) traffic.

cirer [sire] v polish. **cire** nf wax; (meubles) polish. **ciré** nm oilskin. **cireux** adj waxy.

cirque [sirk] nm circus.

cisaille [sizaj] nf shears pl.

ciseau [sizo] nm chisel. **ciseaux** nm pl scissors pl.

ciseler [sizle] v chisel, carve.

cité [site] nf city, town. **cité universitaire** halls of residence pl.

citer [site] v quote, cite; (jur) summon. **citation** nf quotation; summons.

citerne [sitɛrn] nf tank.

cithare [sitar] nf zither.

citoyen [sitwajɛ̃] -enne nm, nf citizen.

citron [sitrɔ̃] nm, adj lemon. **citron pressé** lemon juice. **citronnade** nf lemon squash. **citronnier** nm lemon tree.

citrouille [sitruj] nf pumpkin.

civette [sivɛt] nf chive.

civière [sivjɛr] nf stretcher.

civil [sivil] adj civil; civilian. nm civilian. **en civil** in plain clothes.

civiliser [sivilize] v civilize. **civilisation** nf civilization.

civique [sivik] adj civic.

clair [klɛr] adj clear; (lumineux) light, bright; (sauce, tissu) thin; (couleur) pale; (évident) plain. adv clearly. nm light. **clair de lune** moonlight.

clairière [klɛrjɛr] nf clearing.

clairon [klɛrɔ̃] nm bugle.

clairsemé [klɛrsəme] adj scattered, sparse.

clairvoyant [klɛrvwajɑ̃] adj perceptive, clear-sighted.

clameur [klamœr] nf clamour.

clan [klɑ̃] nm clan.

clandestin [klɑ̃dɛstɛ̃] adj secret, clandestine, underground.

clapier [klapje] nm hutch.

clapoter [klapɔte] v lap. **clapotement** or **clapotis** nm lapping.

claquemurer [klakmyre] v coop up, shut away.

claquer [klake] v (son) bang, snap, crack; (gifler) slap; (fam: fatiguer) tire out; (fam: mourir) die. **claque** nf slap. **claquement** nm bang, snap, crack.

clarifier [klarifje] v clarify. **clarification** nf clarification.

clarinette [klarinɛt] nf clarinet.

clarté [klarte] nf brightness, clearness; (lumière) light; (netteté) clarity.

classe [klɑs] nf class; (salle) classroom; (école) school. **aller en classe** go to school. **faire la classe** teach. **sans classe** classless.

classer [klɑse] v class, classify; (ranger) file; (élève, fruits) grade. **classement** nm classification; filing; grading. **classeur** nm file; (meuble) filing cabinet.

classifier [klasifje] v classify. **classification** nf classification.

classique [klɑsik] adj classic; (art, musique, etc.) classical; (habituel) usual. nm (ouvrage) classic; (auteur) classicist.

claustrophobie [klostrɔfɔbi] nf claustrophobia.

clavecin [klavsɛ̃] nm harpsichord.

clavicule [klavikyl] nf collarbone.

clavier [klavje] nm keyboard.

clef or **clé** [kle] nf key; (tech) spanner; (musique) clef. **clef de contact** ignition key. **sous clef** under lock and key.

clémence [klemɑ̃s] nf clemency; (temps) mildness. **clément** adj lenient; mild.

clerc [klɛr] nm clerk.

clergé [klɛrʒe] nm clergy.

clérical [klerikal] adj clerical.

cliché [klife] nm cliché; (phot) negative.

client [klijɑ̃], -e nm, nf customer, client; (hôtel) guest; (médecin) patient. **clientèle** nf clientèle; (magasin) customers pl; (médecin) practice; (comm) custom.

cligner [kliɲe] v **cligner les yeux** blink; (fermer à demi) screw up one's eyes. **clignement** nm blink.

clignoter [kliɲɔte] v (yeux) blink; (étoile) twinkle; (vaciller) flicker; (signal) flash. **clignotant** nm (auto) indicator.

climat [klima] nm climate. **climatique** adj climatic.

climatiser [klimatize] v air-condition. **climatisation** nf air-conditioning. **climatiseur** nm air-conditioner.

clin [klɛ̃] nm **clin d'œil** wink.

clinique [klinik] adj clinical. nf nursing home.

clinquant [klɛ̃kɑ̃] adj flashy. nm tinsel.

cliqueter [klikte] v rattle, clatter; (métal) clink, jingle. **cliquetis** nm clatter; clink, jingle.

clitoris [klitɔris] nm clitoris.

clochard [klɔʃar], -e nm, nf (fam) tramp.

cloche [klɔʃ] nf bell; cover.

clocher¹ [klɔʃe] nm church tower, steeple.

clocher² [klɔʃe] v (fam) be wrong.

cloison [klwazɔ̃] nf partition; barrier.

cloître [klwatrə] *nm* cloister.

clopiner [klɔpine] *v* hobble along. **clopin-clopant** *adv* hobbling. **entrer/sortir clopin-clopant** hobble in/out.

cloporte [klɔpɔrt] *nm* wood-louse (*pl* -lice).

***clore** [klɔr] *v* close, end, conclude.

clos [klo] *adj* closed, enclosed. *nm* enclosed field; vineyard.

clôture [klotyr] *nf* (*fermeture*) closure, closing; (*enceinte*) fence.

clou [klu] *nm* nail; (*chaussée*) stud; (*méd*) boil; (*théâtre*) star turn. **clou de girofle** clove.

clouer [klue] *v* nail down, pin down. **cloué au lit** confined to bed. **cloué sur place** rooted to the spot.

clouter [klute] *v* stud.

clovisse [klɔvis] *nf* clam.

clown [klun] *nm* clown.

club [klœb] *nm* club.

coaguler [kɔagyle] *v* congeal; (*sang*) coagulate; (*lait*) curdle.

coalition [kɔalisjɔ̃] *nf* coalition.

coasser [kɔase] *v* croak. **coassement** *nm* croak.

cobaye [kɔbaj] *nm* guinea-pig.

cobra [kɔbra] *nm* cobra.

cocarde [kɔkard] *nf* rosette.

cocasse [kɔkas] *adj* comical.

coccinelle [kɔksinɛl] *nf* ladybird.

cocher[1] [kɔʃe] *v* (*crayon*) tick; (*entaille*) notch.

cocher[2] [kɔʃe] *nm* coachman.

cochon, -onne [kɔʃɔ̃, -ɔn] *nm* pig. **cochon d'Inde** guinea-pig. *adj* (*argot*) dirty. **cochonnerie** (*fam*) *nf* rubbish; (*saleté*) filth; (*tour*) dirty trick.

cocktail [kɔktɛl] *nm* cocktail; cocktail party.

cocon [kɔkɔ̃] *nm* cocoon.

cocotier [kɔkɔtje] *nm* coconut palm.

cocotte[1] [kɔkɔt] *nf* (*poule*) hen; (*péj*: *femme*) tart.

cocotte[2] [kɔkɔt] *nf* casserole.

code [kɔd] *nm* code. **code de la route** highway code. **se mettre en code** (*auto*) dip one's headlights.

cœur [kœr] *nm* heart; courage; (*fruit*) core. **avoir mal au cœur** feel sick. **de bon cœur** willingly. **parler à cœur ouvert** have a heart-to-heart.

coexister [kɔɛgziste] *v* coexist. **coexistence** *nf* coexistence.

coffre [kɔfrə] *nm* chest; (*auto*) trunk. **coffre-fort** *nm* safe.

cognac [kɔnak] *nm* cognac.

cogner [kɔne] *v* hit, knock; (*plus fort*) hammer, bang.

cohabiter [kɔabite] *v* live together.

cohérent [kɔerɑ̃] *adj* coherent, consistent. **cohérence** *nf* coherence, consistency.

cohue [kɔy] *nf* crowd.

coiffer [kwafe] *v* (*mettre*) put (a hat) on; cover. **coiffer quelqu'un** do someone's hair. **se coiffer** do one's hair. **se coiffer de** put on; (*péj*) become infatuated with. **coiffeur** *nm* hairdresser; (*hommes*) barber. **coiffeuse** *nf* hairdresser; (*meuble*) dressing table. **coiffure** *nf* hair-style; (*métier*) hairdressing.

coin [kwɛ̃] *nm* corner; (*lieu*) spot, area. **au coin du feu** by the fireside. **du coin** local.

coincer [kwɛ̃se] *v* wedge, jam.

coïncider [kɔɛ̃side] *v* coincide. **coïncidence** *nf* coincidence.

coin-coin [kwɛ̃kwɛ̃] *nm, interj* quack.

coing [kwɛ̃] *nm* quince.

col [kɔl] *nm* (*vêtement*) collar; (*géog*) pass; (*vase*) neck. **col roulé** polo-neck.

coléoptère [kɔleɔptɛr] *nm* beetle.

colère [kɔlɛr] *nf* anger, rage. **en colère** angry. **coléreux** *adj* quick-tempered.

colimaçon [kɔlimasɔ̃] *nm* snail. **en colimaçon** spiral.

colin [kɔlɛ̃] *nm* hake.

colique [kɔlik] *nf* stomach-ache; colic; diarrhoea.

colis [kɔli] *nm* parcel. **par colis postal** by parcel post.

collaborer [kɔlabɔre] *v* collaborate. **collaborateur, -trice** *nm, nf* collaborator; (*journal*) contributor. **collaboration** *nf* collaboration; contribution.

collant [kɔlɑ̃] *nm* (*bas*) tights *pl*; (*acrobate*) leotard. *adj* sticky; (*vêtement*) close-fitting, clinging.

colle [kɔl] *nf* glue, paste; (*fam*: *question*) poser.

collectif [kɔlɛktif] *adj* collective; (*hystérie*) mass; (*billet*) group. **collectivité** *nf* group; community.

collection [kɔlɛksjɔ̃] *nf* collection.

collectionner [kɔlɛksjɔne] *v* collect. **collectionneur, -euse** *nm, nf* collector.

collège [kɔlɛʒ] *nm* secondary school; college. **collégien** *nm* schoolboy. **collégienne** *nf* schoolgirl.

collègue [kɔleg] *n(m+f)* colleague.

coller [kɔle] *v* stick, cling.

collet [kɔle] *nm* (*piège*) snare; (*tech*) collar, neck. **collet monté** prim, strait-laced.

collier [kɔlje] *nm* (*femme*) necklace; (*animal*) collar.

colline [kɔlin] *nf* hill.

collision [kɔlizjɔ̃] *nf* collision; (*conflit*) clash.

colombe [kɔlɔ̃b] *nf* dove. **colombier** *nm* dovecote.

colonel [kɔlɔnɛl] *nm* colonel.

colonie [kɔlɔni] *nf* colony. **colonie de vacances** holiday camp for children. **colonial** *nm, adj* colonial. **coloniser** *v* colonize.

colonne [kɔlɔn] *nf* column; (*arch*) pillar. **colonne vertébrale** spine.

colorer [kɔlɔre] *v* colour; (*tissu*) dye; (*bois*) stain. **coloration** *nf* colouring. **coloré** *adj* colourful; (*teint*) ruddy. **colorier** *v* colour in.

coloris [kɔlɔri] *nm* colour, colouring.

colosse [kɔlɔs] *nm* giant, colossus. **colossal** *adj* colossal.

colporter [kɔlpɔrte] *v* peddle. **colporteur, -euse** *nm, nf* pedlar.

coma [kɔma] *nm* coma.

combat [kɔba] *nm* fight, combat; (*sport*) match.

***combattre** [kɔbatrə] *v* fight, combat.

combien [kɔbjɛ̃] *adv* (*quantité*) how much; (*nombre*) how many. **combien de temps** how long. **le combien sommes-nous?** what date is it?

combinaison [kɔbinɛzɔ̃] *nf* combination; (*sous-vêtement*) slip; (*astuce*) device, scheme.

combiner [kɔbine] *v* combine; (*élaborer*) devise, plan. **combine** *nf* (*truc*) trick; (*péj*) scheme. **combiné** *nm* (*chim*) compound; (*téléphone*) receiver.

comble[1] [kɔblə] *nm* height, climax, peak; (*toit*) roof timbers *pl*. **c'est le comble!** that's the last straw! **pour comble** to cap it all.

comble[2] [kɔblə] *adj* packed.

combler [kɔble] *v* fill; (*déficit*) make good; (*désir*) fulfil.

combustible [kɔbystiblə] *adj* combustible. *nm* fuel. **combustion** *nf* combustion.

comédie [kɔmedi] *nf* comedy, play; (*fam*) fuss. **comédie musicale** musical. **jouer la comédie** put on an act. **comédien** *nm*

comedian; actor; comedy actor. **comédienne** *nf* comedienne; actress; comedy actress.

comestible [kɔmestiblə] *adj* edible. **comestibles** *nm pl* food *sing*.

comète [kɔmet] *nf* comet.

comique [kɔmik] *adj* comic; (*drôle*) comical. *nm* comedy; (*artiste*) comic.

comité [kɔmite] *nm* committee, board.

commander [kɔmɑde] *v* order; command; control. **commandant** *nm* commander; (*mil*) major; (*naut*) captain. **commande** *nf* order; control. **de commande** affected, forced. **fait sur commande** made to order. **commandement** *nm* command; (*rel*) commandment.

commanditer [kɔmɑdite] *v* finance.

comme [kɔm] *conj* as; (*tel que*) like, such as. *adv* how. **comme ça** like that. **comme ci comme ça** so-so. **comme si** as if, as though. **comme il faut** properly. ... **comme tout** as ... as can be.

commémorer [kɔmemɔre] *v* commemorate. **commémoratif** *adj* commemorative, memorial. **commémoration** *nf* commemoration.

commencer [kɔmɑse] *v* begin, start. **commencement** *nm* beginning, start.

comment [kɔmɑ] *adv* how. **comment allez-vous?** how are you? **comment s'appelle-t-il?** what's his name? *interj* what.

commenter [kɔmɑte] *v* comment on; (*sport*) give a commentary on. **commentaire** *nm* comment; (*exposé*) commentary. **commentateur, -trice** *nm, nf* (*sport*) commentator; (*journal*) correspondent.

commérage [kɔmeraʒ] *nm* gossip.

commerçant [kɔmersɑ], **-e** *adj* commercial; (*rue*) shopping. *nm, nf* shopkeeper, tradesman.

commerce [kɔmers] *nm* trade, commerce, business. **commercial** *adj* commercial. **commerciale** *nf* van.

***commettre** [kɔmetrə] *v* commit.

commis [kɔmi] *nm* assistant; (*bureau*) clerk.

commissaire [kɔmiser] *nm* commissioner; (*surveillant*) steward. **commissaire de police** police superintendent. **commissaire-priseur** *nm* auctioneer.

commissariat [kɔmisarja] *nm* police station.

commission [kɔmisjɔ̃] *nf* commission; message; (*course*) errand; committee. **commissions** *nf pl* shopping.

commissionnaire [kɔmisjɔnɛr] *nm* messenger; (*livreur*) delivery man; (*hôtel*) commissionnaire; (*comm*) agent.

commode [kɔmɔd] *adj* handy, convenient; (*facile*) easy; (*personne*) easygoing. ♦ *nf* chest of drawers. **commodité** *nf* convenience.

commotion [kɔmosjɔ̃] *nf* shock. **commotion cérébrale** concussion. **commotionner** *v* shock, shake.

commun [kɔmœ̃] *adj* common; (*partagé*) shared, communal. **hors du commun** out of the ordinary. **peu commun** uncommon.

communauté [kɔmynote] *nf* community; (*cohabitation*) commune.

commune [kɔmyn] *nf* district, borough; parish. **communal** *adj* local; council.

communiant [kɔmynjɑ̃], **-e** *nm, nf* communicant.

communication [kɔmynikasjɔ̃] *nf* communication; message; telephone call. **communication interurbaine/en PCV/avec préavis** trunk/reverse-charge/personal call.

communion [kɔmynjɔ̃] *nf* communion.

communiquer [kɔmynike] *v* communicate; pass on; transmit. **se communiquer** spread; (*personne*) be communicative.

communisme [kɔmynismə] *nm* communism. **communiste** *n(m+f)*, *adj* communist.

compact [kɔ̃pakt] *adj* compact; dense.

compagnie [kɔ̃paɲi] *nf* company. **compagnon, compagne** *nm, nf* companion.

comparer [kɔ̃pare] *v* compare. **comparable** *adj* comparable. **comparaison** *nf* comparison. **comparatif** *nm, adj* comparative.

compartiment [kɔ̃partimɑ̃] *nm* compartment.

compas [kɔ̃pa] *nm* compass; (*math*) pair of compasses.

compassion [kɔ̃pasjɔ̃] *nf* compassion, sympathy.

compatible [kɔ̃patiblə] *adj* compatible. **compatibilité** *nf* compatibility.

compatir [kɔ̃patir] *v* sympathize. **compatissant** *adj* compassionate, sympathetic.

compenser [kɔ̃pɑ̃se] *v* compensate (for). **compensation** *nf* compensation.

compère [kɔ̃pɛr] *nm* accomplice.

compétent [kɔ̃petɑ̃] *adj* competent. **compétence** *nf* competence.

compétition [kɔ̃petisjɔ̃] *nf* competition; event, race. **compétiteur, -trice** *nm, nf* competitor. **compétitif** *adj* competitive.

compiler [kɔ̃pile] *v* compile. **compilation** *nf* compilation.

complaisance [kɔ̃plɛzɑ̃s] *nf* kindness; servility; indulgence; self-satisfaction. **complaisant** *adj* kind; servile; indulgent; self-satisfied.

complément [kɔ̃plemɑ̃] *nm* complement. **complémentaire** *adj* complementary; additional.

complet, -ète [kɔ̃plɛ, -ɛt] *adj* complete; (*plein*) full. ♦ *nm* suit.

compléter [kɔ̃plete] *v* complete; (*augmenter*) supplement, add to.

complexe [kɔ̃plɛks] *nm, adj* complex. **complexité** *nf* complexity.

complication [kɔ̃plikasjɔ̃] *nf* complication.

complice [kɔ̃plis] *n(m+f)* accomplice. *adj* knowing. **être complice de** be a party to. **complicité** *nf* complicity.

compliment [kɔ̃plimɑ̃] *nm* compliment. **compliments** *nm pl* congratulations *pl*. **complimenter** *v* compliment; congratulate.

compliquer [kɔ̃plike] *v* complicate. **se compliquer** get complicated.

complot [kɔ̃plo] *nm* plot. **comploter** *v* plot.

comporter [kɔ̃pɔrte] *v* consist of; (*impliquer*) entail; include. **se comporter** behave, perform. **comportement** *nm* behaviour, performance.

composer [kɔ̃poze] *v* compose, make up; (*numéro*) dial. **composer avec** come to terms with. **se composer de** consist of. **composé** *nm, adj* compound. **compositeur, -trice** *nm, nf* composer. **composition** *nf* composition.

compote [kɔ̃pɔt] *nf* stewed fruit.

compréhensif [kɔ̃preɑ̃sif] *adj* understanding. **compréhension** *nf* understanding, comprehension.

***comprendre** [kɔ̃prɑ̃drə] *v* understand; consist of, comprise; include. **se faire comprendre** make oneself understood. **compris** *adj* included. **tout compris** all inclusive. **y compris** including.

compresse [kɔ̃prɛs] *nf* compress.

compression [kɔ̃presjɔ̃] *nf* compression; *(réduction)* cut-back.

comprimer [kɔ̃prime] *v* compress; *(réduire)* cut back; *(contenir)* hold back.

***compromettre** [kɔ̃prɔmɛtrə] *v* compromise; *(santé, etc.)* jeopardize. **compromis** *nm* compromise.

comptable [kɔ̃tablə] *adj* accounts; *(responsable)* accountable.

compte [kɔ̃t] *nm* account; number; *(calcul)* count. **compte à rebours** countdown. **compte rendu** report, review. **tenir compte de** take into account.

compter [kɔ̃te] *v* count; *(escompter)* reckon; pay; *(facturer)* charge for. **comptant** *nm, adv* cash.

compteur [kɔ̃tœr] *nm* meter. **compteur de vitesse** speedometer. **compteur kilométrique** milometer.

comptine [kɔ̃tin] *nf* nursery rhyme.

comptoir [kɔ̃twar] *nm* counter; bar.

comte [kɔ̃t] *nm* count. **comtesse** *nf* countess.

comté [kɔ̃te] *nm* county.

concave [kɔ̃kav] *adj* concave.

concéder [kɔ̃sede] *v* concede, grant.

concentrer [kɔ̃sãtre] *v* concentrate. **concentration** *nf* concentration. **concentré** *nm* concentrate, extract.

concentrique [kɔ̃sãtrik] *adj* concentric.

concept [kɔ̃sɛpt] *nm* concept.

conception [kɔ̃sɛpsjɔ̃] *nf* conception; idea.

concerner [kɔ̃sɛrne] *v* concern.

concert [kɔ̃sɛr] *nm* concert. **de concert** together, in unison.

concerté [kɔ̃sɛrte] *adj* concerted.

concertina [kɔ̃sɛrtina] *nm* concertina.

concerto [kɔ̃sɛrto] *nm* concerto.

concession [kɔ̃sesjɔ̃] *nf* concession.

***concevoir** [kɔ̃səvwar] *v* conceive; *(comprendre)* understand; *(rédiger)* express.

concierge [kɔ̃sjɛrʒ] *n(m+f)* caretaker. **conciergerie** *nf* caretaker's lodge.

concilier [kɔ̃silje] *v* reconcile; *(attirer)* win, gain.

concis [kɔ̃si] *adj* concise.

***conclure** [kɔ̃klyr] *v* conclude. **concluant** *adj* conclusive. **conclusion** *nf* conclusion.

concombre [kɔ̃kɔ̃brə] *nm* cucumber.

concorder [kɔ̃kɔrde] *v* agree, tally. **concordance** *nf* agreement. **concorde** *nf* concord.

***concourir** [kɔ̃kurir] *v* compete; converge.

concours [kɔ̃kur] *nm* competition; *(examen)* competitive examination; aid.

concret, -ète [kɔ̃krɛ, -ɛt] *adj* concrete.

concurrence [kɔ̃kyrɑ̃s] *nf* competition. **faire concurrence à** compete with. **concurrent, -e** *nm, nf* competitor; *(examen)* candidate. **concurrentiel** *adj* competitive.

condamner [kɔ̃dane] *v* condemn; *(jur)* sentence; *(porte, etc.)* block up. **condamnation** *nf* condemnation; sentence.

condenser [kɔ̃dɑ̃se] *v* condense. **condensation** *nf* condensation.

condescendre [kɔ̃desɑ̃drə] *v* condescend. **condescendance** *nf* condescension.

condition [kɔ̃disjɔ̃] *nf* condition; *(comm)* term; *(rang)* station. **à condition** on approval. **à condition de** provided that. **conditionnel** *nm, adj* conditional.

conditionner [kɔ̃disjɔne] *v* condition; *(emballer)* package. **conditionnement** *nm* conditioning; packaging.

condoléances [kɔ̃dɔleɑ̃s] *nf pl* condolences *pl*.

conducteur, -trice *nm, nf* driver; *(chef)* leader. *nm (élec)* conductor. **conduction** *nf* conduction.

***conduire** [kɔ̃dɥir] *v (véhicule)* drive; *(emmener)* take; *(guider)* lead; *(élec)* conduct; *(diriger)* run. **se conduire** behave. **conduit** *nm* duct, pipe. **conduite** *nf* driving; running; behaviour; conduct; pipe. **conduite d'eau/de gaz** water/gas main. **conduite intérieure** saloon car.

cône [kon] *nm* core.

confectionner [kɔ̃fɛksjɔne] *v* make. **confection** *nf* making; clothing industry. **de confection** ready-made, off-the-peg.

confédéré [kɔ̃federe] *adj* confederate. **confédération** *nf* confederation.

conférer [kɔ̃fere] *v* confer; compare. **conférence** *nf* conference; *(exposé)* lecture. **conférencier, -ère** *nm, nf* lecturer.

confesser [kɔ̃fese] *v* confess. **confession** *nf* confession.

confetti [kɔ̃feti] *nm* confetti.

confiance [kɔ̃fjɑ̃s] *nf* confidence, trust. **avec confiance** confidently. **avoir confiance en** trust. **confiance en soi** self-confidence. **de confiance** trustworthy. **confiant** *adj* confident.

confidence [kɔ̃fidɑ̃s] *nf* confidence, personal secret. **confidentiel** *adj* confidential.

confier [kɔ̃fje] v confide. **se confier à** (*se livrer*) confide in; (*se fier*) put one's trust in.

confiner [kɔ̃fine] v confine. **confiner à** border on. **confins** nm pl borders pl.

***confire** [kɔ̃fir] v preserve.

confirmer [kɔ̃firme] v confirm. **confirmation** nf confirmation.

confiserie [kɔ̃fizri] nf confectionery; (*magasin*) confectioner's, sweet-shop. **confiseur, -euse** nm, nf confectioner.

confisquer [kɔ̃fiske] v confiscate. **confiscation** nf confiscation.

confit [kɔ̃fi] adj candied.

confiture [kɔ̃fityr] nf jam. **confiture d'oranges** marmalade.

conflit [kɔ̃fli] nm conflict, clash.

confluer [kɔ̃flye] v join, converge. **confluence** nf mingling, confluence.

confondre [kɔ̃fɔ̃drə] v mix up, confuse; (*ennemi*) confound; (*étonner*) astound; join, meet. **se confondre** merge. **se confondre en excuses/remerciements** apologize/thank profusely. **confondu** adj overwhelmed.

conforme [kɔ̃fɔrm] adj **conforme à** true to; in accordance with; in keeping with. **conformément à** in accordance with.

conformer [kɔ̃fɔrme] v model. **se conformer à** conform to. **conformité** nf conformity; similarity.

confort [kɔ̃fɔr] nm comfort. **confortable** adj comfortable.

confrère [kɔ̃frɛr] nm colleague.

confronter [kɔ̃frɔ̃te] v confront; compare. **confrontation** nf confrontation; comparison.

confus [kɔ̃fy] adj confused; (*honteux*) ashamed. **confusion** nf confusion; (*honte*) embarrassment.

congé [kɔ̃ʒe] nm holiday, leave; (*renvoi*) notice. **prendre congé** take one's leave.

congédier [kɔ̃ʒedje] v dismiss.

congeler [kɔ̃ʒle] v freeze. **congélateur** nm freezer.

congestion [kɔ̃ʒɛstjɔ̃] nf congestion. **congestionné** adj congested; (*visage*) flushed.

congrès [kɔ̃grɛ] nm congress.

conifère [kɔnifɛr] nm conifer.

conique [kɔnik] adj conical.

conjoint [kɔ̃ʒwɛ̃], **-e** nm, nf spouse. adj joint.

conjonction [kɔ̃ʒɔ̃ksjɔ̃] nf conjunction.

conjugal [kɔ̃ʒygal] adj conjugal.

conjuguer [kɔ̃ʒyge] v conjugate; combine. **conjugaison** nf conjugation.

connaissance [kɔnɛsɑ̃s] nf knowledge; (*personne*) acquaintance; (*conscience*) consciousness. **sans connaissance** unconscious.

connaisseur [kɔnɛsœr], **-euse** adj expert. nm, nf connoisseur.

***connaître** [kɔnɛtrə] v know; be acquainted or familiar with; (*éprouver*) experience. **faire connaître** make known.

connu [kɔny] adj known; (*répandu*, *fameux*) well-known.

***conquérir** [kɔ̃kerir] v conquer.

conquête [kɔ̃kɛt] nf conquest.

consacrer [kɔ̃sakre] v consecrate; (*dédier*) devote, dedicate. **consacré** adj consecrated, hallowed; accepted, established. **consécration** nf consecration.

conscience [kɔ̃sjɑ̃s] nf consciousness; (*morale*) conscience. **avoir conscience de** be aware of. **consciencieux** adj conscientious. **conscient** adj conscious.

conscription [kɔ̃skripsjɔ̃] nf conscription.

conscrit [kɔ̃skri] nm conscript.

consécutif [kɔ̃sekytif] adj consecutive.

conseil [kɔ̃sɛj] nm advice; (*organisme*) board, council. **conseil d'administration** board of directors. **conseil de guerre** court-martial. **conseiller, -ère** nm, nf adviser; councillor.

conseiller [kɔ̃seje] v recommend; advise.

***consentir** [kɔ̃sɑ̃tir] v consent, agree. **consentement** nm consent.

conséquence [kɔ̃sekɑ̃s] nf consequence, result. **conséquent** adj logical; consistent. **par conséquent** consequently.

conservateur [kɔ̃sɛrvatœr], **-trice** adj conservative. nm, nf (*musée*) curator; (*pol*) Conservative.

conservatoire [kɔ̃sɛrvatwar] nm academy, school.

conserve [kɔ̃sɛrv] nf **en conserve** tinned, canned. **mettre en conserve** can.

conserver [kɔ̃sɛrve] v keep, retain, conserve; (*aliments*, etc.) preserve. **conservation** nf preservation.

considérer [kɔ̃sidere] v consider; regard; respect. **considérable** adj considerable. **considération** nf consideration; reflection; respect.

consigner [kɔ̃sine] v (*par écrit*) record; (*en dépôt*) deposit; (*soldat*) confine to barracks. **consignation** nf deposit; (*comm*) consignment. **consigne** nf orders *pl*; *(bagages)* left-luggage office; *(comm)* deposit. **consigné** *adj (bouteille, etc.)* returnable.

consister [kɔ̃siste] *v* consist. **consister en** consist of. **consistance** *nf* consistency. **consistant** *adj* solid.

consoler [kɔ̃sɔle] *v* console. **consolation** *nf* consolation.

consolider [kɔ̃sɔlide] *v* strengthen, consolidate. **consolidation** *nf* strengthening, consolidation.

consommer [kɔ̃sɔme] *v* consume; use; *(manger)* eat; *(mariage)* consummate. **consommateur, -trice** *nm, nf* consumer; *(café)* customer. **consommation** *nf* consumption; *(café)* drink; consummation. **consommé** *nm* consommé.

consonne [kɔ̃sɔn] *nf* consonant.

conspirer [kɔ̃spire] *v* conspire. **conspirateur, -trice** *nm, nf* conspirator. **conspiration** *nf* conspiracy.

conspuer [kɔ̃spɥe] *v* shout down.

constant [kɔ̃stɑ̃] *adj* constant. **constamment** *adv* constantly. **constance** *nf* constancy.

constater [kɔ̃state] *v* note, notice; *(consigner)* record, certify. **constatation** *nf* observation.

constellation [kɔ̃stelasjɔ̃] *nf* constellation.

consterner [kɔ̃stɛrne] *v* dismay. **consternation** *nf* consternation, dismay.

constipation [kɔ̃stipasjɔ̃] *nf* constipation. **constipé** *adj* constipated.

constituer [kɔ̃stitɥe] *v* constitute; *(fonder)* put together, set up; *(jur)* appoint. **constituant** *adj* constituent. **constitution** *nf* constitution; composition.

construction [kɔ̃stryksjɔ̃] *nf* construction; *(bâtiment)* building. **constructif** *adj* constructive.

*****construire** [kɔ̃strɥir] *v* construct; build.

consul [kɔ̃syl] *nm* consul. **consulat** *nm* consulate.

consulter [kɔ̃sylte] *v* consult. **consultation** *nf* consultation.

consumer [kɔ̃syme] *v* consume; destroy.

contact [kɔ̃takt] *nm* contact; *(auto)* ignition.

contagieux [kɔ̃taʒjø] *adj* contagious, infectious. **contagion** *nf* contagion.

contaminer [kɔ̃tamine] *v* contaminate. **contamination** *nf* contamination.

conte [kɔ̃t] *nm* tale, story. **conte de fée** fairy tale.

contempler [kɔ̃tɑ̃ple] *v* contemplate. **con-**

templatif *adj* contemplative. **contemplation** *nf* contemplation.

contemporain [kɔ̃tɑ̃pɔrɛ̃], **-e** *n, adj* temporary.

contenance [kɔ̃tnɑ̃s] *nf* capacity; attitude. **faire bonne contenance** put on a brave face.

*****contenir** [kɔ̃tnir] *v* contain; *(récipient)* hold.

content [kɔ̃tɑ̃] *adj* pleased, happy; satisfied, content.

contenter [kɔ̃tɑ̃te] *v* satisfy. **se contenter de** content oneself with. **contentement** *nm* contentment, satisfaction.

contenu [kɔ̃tny] *adj* restrained. *nm* content; *(récipient)* contents *pl*.

conter [kɔ̃te] *v* recount, relate. **conteur, -euse** *nm, nf* storyteller.

contester [kɔ̃teste] *v* contest, dispute; protest. **contestable** *adj* questionable. **contestation** *nf* dispute.

contexte [kɔ̃tɛkst] *nm* context.

contigu, -uë [kɔ̃tigy] *adj* adjacent, adjoining.

continent [kɔ̃tinɑ̃] *nm* continent. **continental** *adj* continental.

contingent [kɔ̃tɛ̃ʒɑ̃] *nm* contingent; quota; *(part)* share.

continuer [kɔ̃tinɥe] *v* continue. **continu** *adj* continuous. **continuel** *adj* continual; continuous. **continuité** *nf* continuity; continuation.

contourner [kɔ̃turne] *v* skirt round, bypass; *(façonner)* shape; *(déformer)* twist.

contraception [kɔ̃trasɛpsjɔ̃] *nf* contraception. **contraceptif** *nm, adj* contraceptive.

contracter[1] [kɔ̃trakte] *v (raidir)* tense, contract. **contraction** *nf* contraction.

contracter[2] [kɔ̃trakte] *v* contract; *(dette)* incur; *(alliance)* enter into.

contractuel [kɔ̃traktɥɛl], **-elle** *adj* contractual. *nm, nf* traffic warden.

contradiction [kɔ̃tradiksjɔ̃] *nf* contradiction; debate, argument. **contradictoire** *adj* contradictory.

*****contraindre** [kɔ̃trɛ̃dr] *v* force, compel. **contrainte** *nf* constraint.

contraire [kɔ̃trɛr] *adj* contrary; opposite; conflicting. *nm* opposite. **au contraire** on the contrary.

contrarier [kɔ̃trarje] *v (irriter)* annoy; *(gêner)* thwart. **contrariant** *adj* tiresome; *(personne)* contrary.

contraster [kɔ̃traste] v contrast. **contraste** nm contrast.

contrat [kɔ̃tra] nm contract, agreement.

contravention [kɔ̃travãsjɔ̃] nf (amende) fine; (procès-verbal) parking ticket; (jur) contravention.

contre [kɔ̃tr] prep against; (protection) from; (échange) for; (rapport) to. **par contre** on the other hand.

contre-amiral nm rear admiral.

contre-attaque nf counter-attack. **contre-attaquer** v counter-attack.

contre-avion adj anti-aircraft.

contrebande [kɔ̃trəbãd] nf contraband; (activité) smuggling. **faire la contrebande de** smuggle. **contrebandier, -ère** nm, nf smuggler.

contrebasse [kɔ̃trəbas] nf double bass.

contre-boutant nm buttress.

contrecarrer [kɔ̃trəkare] v thwart.

contrecœur [kɔ̃trəkœr] adv **à contrecœur** grudgingly.

contrecoup [kɔ̃trəku] nm repercussions pl.

*****contredire** [kɔ̃trədir] v contradict.

contrée [kɔ̃tre] nf region.

contrefaçon [kɔ̃trəfasɔ̃] nf forgery, counterfeit, imitation.

*****contrefaire** [kɔ̃trəfer] v counterfeit, forge; disguise; imitate. **contrefait** adj deformed.

contre-interrogatoire nm cross-examination.

contremaître [kɔ̃trəmɛtrə] nm foreman.

contremander [kɔ̃trəmãde] v cancel.

contre-manifestation nf counter-demonstration.

contre-pied nm opposite.

contre-plaqué nm plywood.

contrepoids [kɔ̃trəpwa] nm counterbalance.

contre-poil adv **à contre-poil** the wrong way.

contrepoison [kɔ̃trəpwazɔ̃] nm antidote.

contresens [kɔ̃trəsãs] nm misinterpretation. **à contresens** the wrong way. **à contresens de** against.

contretemps [kɔ̃trətã] nm hitch. **à contretemps** at an inconvenient time.

contre-torpilleur nm destroyer.

*****contrevenir** [kɔ̃trəvnir] v contravene.

contrevent [kɔ̃trəvã] nm shutter.

contre-voie adv **à contre-voie** (rail) on the wrong side.

contribuer [kɔ̃tribɥe] v contribute. **contribuable** n(m+f) taxpayer. **contribution** nf contribution. **contributions** nf pl (à l'état) taxes pl; (à la commune) rates pl; (bureau) tax office sing.

contrôler [kɔ̃trole] v control; (vérifier) check; (argent, or) hallmark. **contrôle** nm control; check, inspection; list; hallmark. **contrôleur** nm inspector; bus conductor; ticket collector.

controverse [kɔ̃trɔvers] nf controversy.

contusion [kɔ̃tyzjɔ̃] nf bruise. **contusionner** v bruise.

*****convaincre** [kɔ̃vɛ̃krə] v convince, persuade; (jur) convict.

convalescence [kɔ̃valesãs] nf convalescence. **convalescent, -e** nm, nf convalescent.

*****convenir** [kɔ̃vnir] v suit; (être utile) be convenient; (être approprié) be suitable; (avouer) acknowledge; admit; (s'accorder) agree on. **convenable** adj fitting, suitable, appropriate; decent, acceptable, proper. **convenance** nf convenience; preference. **les convenances** propriety sing. **convenu** adj agreed.

convention [kɔ̃vãsjɔ̃] nf convention; (accord) understanding; (pacte) agreement. **conventionnel** adj conventional.

converger [kɔ̃verze] v converge.

convers [kɔ̃ver] adj lay.

conversation [kɔ̃versasjɔ̃] nf conversation.

conversion [kɔ̃versjɔ̃] nf conversion.

convertir [kɔ̃vertir] v convert. **converti, -e** nm, nf convert. **convertible** adj convertible.

convexe [kɔ̃veks] adj convex.

conviction [kɔ̃viksjɔ̃] nf conviction.

convier [kɔ̃vje] v invite, urge.

convive [kɔ̃viv] n(m+f) guest.

convocation [kɔ̃vɔkasjɔ̃] nf summons.

convoi [kɔ̃vwa] nm convoy.

convoiter [kɔ̃vwate] v covet. **convoitise** nf lust.

convoquer [kɔ̃vɔke] v (assemblée) convene; (personne) summon.

convulsion [kɔ̃vylsjɔ̃] nf convulsion. **convulsif** adj convulsive.

coopérer [kɔɔpere] v cooperate. **coopératif** adj cooperative. **coopération** nf cooperation. **coopérative** nf cooperative.

coordination [kɔɔrdinasjɔ̃] nf coordination.

coordonner [kɔɔrdɔne] v coordinate.

copain, copine [kɔpɛ̃, kɔpin] *nm, nf* (*fam*) pal, mate.

Copenhague [kɔpənag] *n* Copenhagen.

copier [kɔpje] *v* copy. **copie** *nf* copy; (*examen*) paper.

copieux [kɔpjø] *adj* copious.

copuler [kɔpyle] *v* copulate. **copulation** *nf* copulation.

coq [kɔk] *rm* cock.

coque [kɔk] *nf* shell; (*mollusque*) cockle; (*bateau*) hull.

coquelicot [kɔkliko] *nm* poppy.

coqueluche [kɔklyʃ] *nf* whooping cough.

coquet, -ette [kɔke, -ɛt] *adj* flirtatious; clothes-conscious; charming; (*fam: somme*) tidy.

coquetier [kɔktje] *nm* egg-cup.

coquille [kɔkij] *nf* shell; (*récipient*) scallop; (*erreur*) misprint. **coquille Saint-Jacques** scallop. **coquillage** *nm* shellfish.

coquin [kɔkɛ̃], **-e** *adj* mischievous, naughty. *nm, nf* rascal.

cor [kɔr] *nm* (*musique*) horn; (*méd*) corn. **cor anglais** cor anglais. **cor d'harmonie** French horn.

corail [kɔraj] *nm, pl* **-aux** coral.

corbeau [kɔrbo] *nm* crow.

corbeille [kɔrbɛj] *nf* basket. **corbeille à papier** wastepaper basket.

corbillard [kɔrbijar] *nm* hearse.

cordages [kɔrdaʒ] *nm pl* ropes *pl*, rigging *sing*.

corde [kɔrd] *nf* rope; (*musique, raquette*) string; (*tissu*) thread. **corde à linge** clothes-line. **corde à sauter** skipping-rope. **corde raide** tightrope. **cordes vocales** vocal cords *pl*.

corder [kɔrde] *v* twist; (*raquette*) string.

cordon [kɔrdɔ̃] *nm* cord, string; (*soldats, police*) cordon. **cordonnier** *nm* cobbler.

coriace [kɔrjas] *adj* tough.

corne [kɔrn] *nf* horn. **corne de brume** foghorn.

corneille [kɔrnɛj] *nf* crow.

cornemuse [kɔrnəmyz] *nf* bagpipes *pl*.

cornet [kɔrne] *nm* (*papier, glace*) cone, cornet. **cornet à pistons** cornet.

cornichon [kɔrniʃɔ̃] *nm* gherkin.

Cornouailles [kɔrnwaj] *nf* Cornwall.

cornu [kɔrny] *adj* horned.

corporation [kɔrpɔrasjɔ̃] *nf* guild, corporate body.

corporel [kɔrpɔrɛl] *adj* corporal.

corps [kɔr] *nm* body; (*mil*) corps; (*cadavre*) corpse. **corps à corps** *adv* hand-to-hand. **le corps enseignant/médical** the teaching/medical profession.

corpulent [kɔrpylɑ̃] *adj* stout, corpulent.

corpuscule [kɔrpyskyl] *nm* corpuscle.

correct [kɔrɛkt] *adj* correct, accurate, right. **correction** *nf* correction; (*châtiment*) thrashing; accuracy.

correspondant [kɔrɛspɔ̃dɑ̃], **-e** *adj* corresponding. *nm, nf* correspondent. **correspondance** *nf* correspondence; (*transport*) connection.

correspondre [kɔrɛspɔ̃drə] *v* correspond; connect. **correspondre à** fit, agree with, suit.

corrida [kɔrida] *nf* bullfight.

corridor [kɔridɔr] *nm* corridor.

corriger [kɔriʒe] *v* correct; (*punir*) thrash.

corroborer [kɔrɔbɔre] *v* corroborate. **corroboration** *nf* corroboration.

corroder [kɔrɔde] *v* corrode. **corrodant** *adj* corrosive.

corrompre [kɔrɔ̃prə] *v* corrupt; (*eau, aliments*) taint; (*soudoyer*) bribe. **corrompu** *adj* corrupt.

corruption [kɔrypsjɔ̃] *nf* corruption; bribery; decomposition.

corsage [kɔrsaʒ] *nm* bodice.

corsaire [kɔrozjɔ̃] *nf* corrosion. **corrosif** *adj* corrosive; (*ironie, etc.*) scathing.

Corse [kɔrs] *nf* Corsica. *n(m + f)* Corsican. **corse** *nm, nf* Corsican.

corset [kɔrse] *nm* corset.

cortège [kɔrtɛʒ] *nm* procession.

corvée [kɔrve] *nf* chore; (*mil*) fatigue.

cosmétique [kɔsmetik] *adj* cosmetic.

cosmique [kɔsmik] *adj* cosmic.

cosmopolite [kɔsmɔpɔlit] *adj* cosmopolitan.

cosmos [kɔsmɔs] *nm* cosmos.

cosse [kɔs] *nf* pod, hull.

cossu [kɔsy] *adj* well-off, opulent.

costaud [kɔsto] *adj* strong, sturdy.

costume [kɔstym] *nm* costume, dress; (*complet*) suit.

cote [kɔt] *nf* rating, popularity; (*comm*) quotation; (*courses*) odds *pl*; mark.

côte [kɔt] *nf* (*anat, tricot*) rib; (*pente*) slope, hill; (*littoral*) coast, coastline.

côté [kote] *nm* side; way, direction. **à côté** (*maison, pièce*) next door; (*près*) nearby. **à côté de** beside; compared to. **de côté** sideways; aside.

coteau [kɔto] *nm* hill, slope.

côtelette [kotlɛt] *nf* chop, cutlet.
coter [kɔte] *v* rate, mark; (*comm*) quote.
côtier [kotje] *adj* coastal, inshore.
se cotiser [kɔtize] *v* subscribe; (*groupe*) club together. **cotisant, -e** *nm, nf* (*club*) subscriber; (*pension*) contributor. **cotisation** *nf* subscription; contribution; collection.
coton [kɔtɔ̃] *nm* cotton. **coton à broder/repriser** embroidery/darning thread.
côtoyer [kotwaje] *v* skirt, run alongside; (*frôler*) be close to, be verging on.
cou [ku] *nm* neck. **cou-de-pied** *nm* instep.
couchant [kuʃɑ̃] *adj* setting. *nm* west; sunset.
couche [kuʃ] *nf* layer; (*peinture*) coat; (*bébé*) nappy. **couches** *nf pl* (*méd*) confinement *sing*.
coucher [kuʃe] *v* lay down; (*loger*) put up; (*séjourner*) sleep; (*mettre au lit*) put to bed. **se coucher** go to bed; (*s'étendre*) lie down; (*soleil*) set. *nm* **coucher du soleil** sunset. **couché** *adj* lying down; in bed; (*penché*) sloping. **couchette** *nf* couchette, berth.
coucou [kuku] *nm* cuckoo.
coude [kud] *nm* elbow; (*rivière, tuyau*) bend.
*****coudre** [kudr] *v* sew, stitch.
coudrier [kudrije] *nm* hazel tree.
couenne [kwan] *nf* rind.
couic [kwik] *interj* squeak!
couler [kule] *v* run, flow; (*fuir*) leak; (*bateau*) sink; (*verser*) pour. **se couler** slip. **coulant** *adj* smooth, flowing. **coulé** *nm* (*musique*) slur. **coulée** *nf* casting.
couleur [kulœr] *nf* colour; (*cartes*) suit; (*peinture*) paint.
couleuvre [kulœvrə] *nf* grass snake.
coulisse [kulis] *nf* runner, slide. **coulisses** *nf pl* wings *pl*. **dans les coulisses** behind the scenes. **porte à coulisse** *nf* sliding door.
couloir [kulwar] *nm* corridor; (*voie*) lane; (*pol*) lobby.
coup [ku] *nm* blow, knock; (*pinceau, plume*) stroke; (*bruit*) sound; (*essai*) try; (*tour*) trick. **à coup sûr** definitely. **après coup** afterwards. **du coup** suddenly. **du premier coup** first time. **tout à coup** suddenly.
coupable [kupablə] *adj* guilty. *n(m+f)* culprit.
coup de bec *nm* peck.

coup de coude *nm* nudge.
coup de feu *nm* shot.
coup de fil *nm* (*fam*) phone call.
coup de froid *nm* chill.
coup de main *nm* (*helping*) hand.
coup d'envoi *nm* kick-off.
coup de pied *nm* kick.
coup de poing *nm* punch.
coup de soleil *nm* sunburn.
coup de sonnette *nm* ring.
coup de téléphone *nm* telephone call.
coup de vent *nm* gust.
coup d'œil *nm* glance.
coupe[1] [kup] *nf* (*dessert*) dish; (*boire*) goblet; (*sport*) cup.
coupe[2] [kup] *nf* cut, cutting. **coupe transversale** cross section.
couper [kupe] *v* cut; (*eau, élec, etc.*) cut off; (*traverser*) cross; (*voyage*) break; (*vin*) dilute, blend. **coupe-papier** *nm* paper knife. **coupant** *adj* sharp. **coupure** *nf* cut; (*journal*) cutting; (*courant*) power cut.
couple [kuplə] *nm* couple, pair. **coupler** *v* couple.
couplet [kuplɛ] *nm* verse.
coupon [kupɔ̃] *nm* coupon; (*reste*) remnant.
cour [kur] *nf* court; (*bâtiment*) yard, courtyard; (*école*) playground; (*gare*) forecourt; (*femme*) courtship. **cour de ferme** farmyard. **faire la cour (à)** court.
courage [kuraʒ] *nm* courage; spirit, will. **perdre courage** lose heart. **courageux** *adj* brave, courageous.
couramment [kuramɑ̃] *adv* fluently; commonly.
courant [kurɑ̃] *adj* (*normal*) ordinary, standard; (*fréquent*) common; (*actuel*) current. *nm* current; movement; course. **au courant** well-informed, up to date. **courant d'air** draught.
courbature [kurbatyr] *nf* ache. **courbaturé** *adj* aching, stiff.
courbe [kurb] *adj* curved. *nf* curve.
courber [kurbe] *v* bend, curve. **se courber** bend down; (*saluer*) bow.
courge [kurʒ] *nf* marrow. **courgette** *nf* courgette.
*****courir** [kurir] *v* run; (*sport*) race; (*aller vite*) rush, speed; (*chasser*) hunt; (*parcourir*) roam. **coureur, -euse** *nm, nf* runner; (*sport*) competitor. **coureur automobile** racing driver.

couronner [kurɔne] v crown; (*ceindre*) encircle; award a prize to. **couronne** nf crown; (*fleurs*) wreath. **couronnement** nm coronation.

courrier [kurje] nm mail, letters pl; (*journal*) column, page.

courroie [kurwa] nf belt, strap. **courroie de ventilateur** fan belt.

courroux [kuru] nm wrath.

cours [kur] nm course; (*monnaie*) currency; (*leçon*) class. **au cours de** during. **avoir cours** be current. **cours du change** exchange rate. **en cours** in progress.

course [kurs] nf run, running; (*épreuve*) race; (*achat*) shopping, errand; (*voyage*) journey. **faire des courses** go shopping.

court¹ [kur] adj, adv short. **à court de** short of. **court-circuit** nm short-circuit.

court² [kur] nm tennis court.

courtier [kurtje], **-ère** nm, nf broker.

courtisan [kurtizã] nm courtier; (*flatteur*) sycophant.

courtois [kurtwa] adj courteous.

cousin¹ [kuzɛ̃], **-e** nm, nf cousin. **cousin germain** first cousin.

cousin² [kuzɛ̃] nm gnat.

coussin [kusɛ̃] nm cushion. **coussinet** nm pad; (*tech*) bearing.

cousu [kuzy] adj sewn, stitched.

coût [ku] nm cost.

couteau [kuto] nm knife. **couteau à découper** carving knife. **couteau de poche** pocket knife. **couteau-éplucheur** nm peeler.

coutellerie [kutɛlri] nf cutlery.

coûter [kute] v cost. **coûte que coûte** at all costs. **coûter cher** be expensive. **coûteux** adj expensive.

coutume [kutym] nf custom. **coutumier** adj customary.

couture [kutyr] nf sewing; (*confection*) dressmaking; (*suite de points*) seam. **couturier** nm fashion designer. **couturière** nf dressmaker.

couvent [kuvã] nm convent.

couver [kuve] v (*feu, haine*) smoulder; (*émeute*) brew; (*poule*) brood, sit on; (*œufs*) hatch. **couvée** nf brood, clutch. **couveuse** nf incubator.

couvercle [kuvɛrklə] nm lid, cover, top.

couvert [kuvɛr] adj covered; (*ciel*) overcast. nm place setting; (*restaurant*) cover charge; (*abri*) cover, shelter. **mettre le couvert** lay the table.

couverture [kuvɛrtyr] nf cover; (*lit*) blan-

ket. **couverture chauffante** electric blanket.

*****couvrir** [kuvrir] v cover; (*cacher*) conceal. **se couvrir** (*vêtements*) wrap up; (*chapeau*) put on one's hat; (*ciel*) cloud over. **couvre-feu** nm curfew. **couvre-lit** nm bedspread.

crabe [krab] nm crab.

crac [krak] *interj* crack!

cracher [kraʃe] v spit (out). **crachat** nm spit, spittle. **crachement** nm spitting.

crachiner [kraʃine] v drizzle. **crachin** nm drizzle.

craie [krɛ] nf chalk.

*****craindre** [krɛ̃drə] v fear, be afraid (of). **crainte** [krɛ̃t] nf fear. **craintif** adj timid.

cramoisi [kramwazi] adj crimson.

crampe [krãp] nf cramp.

cramponner [krãpɔne] v clamp; (*fam*) cling to. **se cramponner à** clutch, cling to. **crampon** nm clamp; (*chaussure*) stud.

cran [krã] nm notch; (*fusil*) catch; (*cheveux*) wave; (*fam*) guts pl.

crâne [krɑn] nm skull, head.

crâner [krɑne] (*fam*) v show off. **craneur, -euse** nm, nf show-off.

crapaud [krapo] nm toad.

crapuleux [krapylø] adj (*vie*) dissolute; (*action*) villainous.

craquer [krake] v crack; (*neige*) crunch; (*parquet*) creak; (*bas, pantalon*) rip. **craquement** nm crack, creak.

crasse [kras] nf grime, filth. **crasseux** adj grimy, filthy.

cratère [krater] nm crater.

cravate [kravat] nf tie.

crawl [krol] nm crawl. **dos crawlé** nm backstroke.

crayon [krɛjõ] nm pencil; (*dessin*) pencil sketch. **crayon de couleur** crayon.

crayonner [krɛjɔne] v jot down, scribble; (*dessin*) sketch.

créance [kreãs] nf debt, claim. **créancier, -ère** nm, nf creditor.

créateur [kreatœr] **-trice** adj creative. nm, nf creator.

création [kreasjõ] nf creation.

créature [kreatyr] nf creature.

crèche [krɛʃ] nf crèche; (*rel*) crib.

crédit [kredi] nm credit; bank; trust. **créditer** v credit. **créditeur, -trice** adj credit.

crédule [kredyl] adj gullible. **crédulité** nf gullibility.

créer [kree] *v* create.
crémaillère [kremajɛr] *nf* (*tech*) rack. **pendre la crémaillère** have a house-warming party.
crématoire [krematwar] *nm* crematorium.
crémation *nf* cremation.
crème [krɛm] *nf*, *adj* cream. **crème anglaise** custard. **crème à raser** shaving cream. **crème pâtissière** confectioner's custard. **crèmerie** *nf* dairy. **crémeux** *adj* creamy.
crénelé [krɛnle] *adj* notched; (*bordure*) scalloped; (*mur*) crenellated.
crêpe¹ [krɛp] *nf* (*cuisine*) pancake. **crêperie** *nf* pancake shop *or* café.
crêpe² [krɛp] *nm* (*tissu*) crepe.
crépiter [krepite] *v* crackle.
crépuscule [krepyskyl] *nm* twilight.
cresson [kresɔ̃] *nm* cress.
crête [krɛt] *nf* ridge, crest; (*coq*) comb; (*mur*) top.
creuser [krøze] *v* dig (out), hollow (out); (*problème*) go into thoroughly.
creux [krø] *adj* hollow; (*vide*) empty; (*visage*) gaunt; (*jours*) slack. **heures creuses** off-peak periods *pl. nm* hollow; slack period. **creux des reins** small of the back.
crevaison [krəvɛzɔ̃] *nf* puncture.
crevasser [krəvase] *v* crack; (*mains*) chap. **crevasse** *nf* crack, crevice.
crever [krəve] *v* burst; (*pneu*) puncture; (*fam: fatiguer*) wear out; (*fam: mourir*) die.
crevette [krəvɛt] *nf* shrimp; (*rose*) prawn.
cri [kri] *nm* cry, shout.
criailler [kriaje] *v* squawk, screech; (*bébé*) bawl; (*rouspéter*) grumble.
criard [krijar] *adj* yelling, squawking; (*couleur*) garish; (*son*) piercing.
cribler [krible] *v* sift; (*percer*) riddle. **crible** *nm* sieve, riddle. **passer au crible** examine closely. **criblé de** riddled with; covered with; (*dettes*) crippled with.
cric [krik] *nm* jack. **soulever au cric** jack up.
cricket [krikɛt] *nm* cricket.
cri-cri [krikri] *nm* (*grillon*) cricket.
criée [krije] *nf* auction.
crier [krije] *v* shout, cry, scream; (*oiseau*) call; (*grincer*) squeak, squeal.
crime [krim] *nm* crime. **criminel, -elle** *n*, *adj* criminal.
crin [krɛ̃] *nm* hair, horsehair. **crinière** *nf* mane; (*personne*) mop of hair.
crique [krik] *nf* creek.

criquet [krikɛ] *nm* locust.
crise [kriz] *nf* crisis; (*accès*) attack, fit; (*pénurie*) shortage. **crise cardiaque** heart attack. **crise de foie** bilious attack. **piquer une crise** (*fam*) fly off the handle.
crisper [krispe] *v* tense, clench; (*plisser*) shrivel up. **se crisper** become tense, clench. **crispation** *nf* contraction; (*nervosité*) tension; (*spasme*) twitch. **crispé** *adj* nervous, tense, on edge.
crisser [krise] *v* (*gravier*) crunch; (*freins*) screech; (*soie*) rustle. **crisser des dents** grind one's teeth.
cristal [kristal] *nm* crystal. **cristal taillé** cut glass. **cristallin** *adj* crystalline; (*son*) crystal-clear.
cristalliser [kristalize] *v* crystallize. **cristallisation** *nf* crystallization.
critère [kritɛr] *nm* criterion.
critique [kritik] *adj* critical; crucial. *nf* criticism; (*analyse*) critique, review. *n*(*m+f*) critic. **critiquer** *v* criticize.
croasser [krɔase] *v* caw. **croassement** *nm* caw.
croc [kro] *nm* fang, tooth; (*grappin*) hook. **faire un croc-en-jambe à** trip up.
croche [krɔʃ] *nf* quaver.
crochet [krɔʃɛ] *nm* hook; (*technique*) crochet; detour; (*véhicule*) swerve. **crochets** *nm pl* square brackets *pl*. **faire du crochet** crochet. **vivre aux crochets de** sponge on, live off.
crochu [krɔʃy] *adj* hooked.
crocodile [krɔkɔdil] *nm* crocodile.
crocus [krɔkys] *nm* crocus.
*****croire** [krwar] *v* believe, think. **croire à** *or* **en** believe in.
croisade [krwazad] *nf* crusade.
croiser [krwaze] *v* cross; pass; (*naut*) cruise. **croisé** *adj* double-breasted. **croisement** *nm* crossing; (*carrefour*) crossroads. **croisière** *nf* cruise.
croissance [krwasɑ̃s] *nf* growth, development.
croissant [krwasɑ̃] *nm* crescent; (*pain*) croissant. *adj* growing, increasing, rising.
*****croître** [krwatr] *v* grow, increase; (*rivière, vent*) rise.
croix [krwa] *nf* cross. **croix gammée** swastika.
croquer [krɔke] *v* crunch, munch; (*salade, fruit*) be crisp; (*dessiner*) sketch. **croquant** *adj* crisp, crunchy. **croque-monsieur** *nm invar* toasted cheese and ham sandwich.

croquet [krɔkɛ] nm croquet.

croquis [krɔki] nm sketch.

crosse [krɔs] nf (sport) club, stick; (fusil) butt; (rel) crook.

crotter [krɔte] v dirty, make muddy, soil. **crotte** nf droppings pl, dung.

crouler [krule] v collapse; (délabré) be tumbledown; (empire, etc.) totter. **croulant** adj crumbling, tumbledown.

croupe [krup] nf rump, hindquarters pl; (colline) hilltop. **monter en croupe** ride pillion.

croupir [krupir] v stagnate; (personne) wallow. **croupi** adj stagnant.

croustiller [krustije] v be crisp or crunchy; (pain) be crusty. **croustillant** adj crisp, crunchy; crusty; (grivois) spicy.

croûte [krut] nf (pain) crust; (fromage) rind; (plaie) scab. **croûton** nm crust; (cuisine) crouton.

croyable [krwajablə] adj credible.

croyance [krwajãs] nf belief. **croyant, -e** nm, nf believer.

cru¹ [kry] adj raw, crude; (lumière) harsh; (franc) blunt.

cru² [kry] nm (vignoble) vineyard; (vin) vintage, wine.

cruauté [kryote] nf cruelty.

cruche [kryʃ] nf jug, pitcher.

crucifier [krysifje] v crucify. **crucifixion** nf crucifixion.

crucifix [krysifi] nm crucifix.

crudité [krydite] nf crudeness; harshness. **crudités** nf pl coarse remarks pl; (cuisine) salads pl.

crue [kry] nf swelling, rising.

cruel [kryɛl] adj cruel.

crûment [krymã] adv bluntly.

crustacé [krystase] nm shellfish. **crustacés** nm pl (cuisine) seafood sing.

crypte [kript] nf crypt.

cube [kyb] nm cube; (d'enfant) block, brick. adj cubic. **cubique** adj cubic.

***cueillir** [kœjir] v pick, gather; (attraper) catch.

cuiller [kɥijɛr] nf spoon. **cuiller à café** teaspoon. **cuiller de service** tablespoon. **cuillerée** nf spoonful. **cuillerée à soupe** tablespoonful.

cuir [kɥir] nm leather; (avant tannage) hide. **cuir chevelu** scalp. **cuir suédé** suede. **cuir verni** patent leather.

cuirasse [kɥiras] nf armour; (chevalier) breastplate.

cuirassé [kɥirase] adj armoured. nm battleship.

***cuire** [kɥir] v cook; (pain) bake; (porcelaine) fire; (brûler) smart. **à cuire** adj cooking. **cuire à feu doux** simmer. **cuire à l'eau** boil. **cuire au four** (viande) roast; (pain) bake.

cuisant [kɥizã] adj burning, stinging; (regret) bitter.

cuisine [kɥizin] nf (pièce) kitchen; (art) cookery, cooking. **faire la cuisine** cook. **cuisinier nm** cook. **cuisinière** nf (personne) cook; (fourneau) cooker.

cuisse [kɥis] nf thigh; (cuisine) leg.

cuit [kɥi] adj cooked, ready. **cuit à point** done to a turn.

cuivre [kɥivrə] nm copper. **cuivre jaune** brass.

cul [ky] nm bottom; (vulgaire) arse.

culasse [kylas] nf cylinder head.

culbuter [kylbyte] v somersault; (tomber) tumble, topple; (renverser) knock over. **culbute** nf somersault; tumble, fall; (fam: banque, etc.) collapse.

culinaire [kylinɛr] adj culinary.

culminer [kylmine] v culminate, reach its highest point.

culot [kylo] nm cap, base; (fam) cheek.

culotte [kylɔt] nf short trousers pl; (slip) pants pl.

culpabilité [kylpabilite] nf guilt.

culte [kylt] nm cult, worship.

cultivateur [kyltive] v cultivate. **cultivateur, -trice** nm, nf farmer. **cultivé** adj cultured.

culture [kyltyr] nf (champ, etc.) cultivation; (esprit) culture. **culturel** adj cultural.

cupide [kypid] adj greedy. **cupidité** nf greed.

cure [kyr] nf cure; course of treatment. **curé** [kyre] nm parish priest.

curer [kyre] v clean out; (nez) pick. **curedent** nm toothpick. **cure-pipe** nm pipe cleaner.

curieux, -euse [kyrjø] adj curious; interested, keen; (indiscret) inquisitive. nm strange thing. nm, nf inquisitive person.

curiosité [kyrjozite] nf curiosity; inquisitiveness; (d'une ville, etc.) strange sight or feature; (bibelot) curio.

curry [kyri] nm curry. **au curry** curried.

cuver [kyve] v ferment. **cuve** nf vat, tank. **cuvée** nf vintage. **cuvette** nf basin.

cycle¹ [siklə] nm (révolution) cycle.

cycle² [sikl] nm (bicyclette) cycle. **cyclisme** nm cycling. **cycliste** n(m+f) cyclist.

cyclomoteur [siklɔmɔtœr] nm moped.

cyclone [siklon] nm cyclone.

cygne [siɲ] nm swan.

cylindre [silɛ̃dr] nm cylinder; roller. **cylindrique** adj cylindrical.

cymbale [sɛ̃bal] nf cymbal.

cynique [sinik] adj cynical. nm cynic.

cyprès [siprɛ] nm cypress.

cypriote [siprijɔt] adj Cypriot. **Cypriote** n(m+f) Cypriot.

D

d' [d] V de.

dactylographier [daktilɔgrafje] v type. **dactylo** nf typist. **dactylographie** nf typing.

dague [dag] nm dagger.

daigner [deɲe] v condescend, deign.

daim [dɛ̃] nm (animal) deer; (cuir) suede.

dais [dɛ] nm canopy.

daller [dale] v pave. **dallage** nm paving. **dalle** nf (pierre) slab; (trottoir) paving stone.

daltonien [daltɔnjɛ̃] adj colour-blind. **daltonisme** nm colour-blindness.

damas [dama] nm damask. **prune de Damas** nf damson.

dame [dam] nf lady; (cartes) queen. **dames** nf pl (jeu) draughts sing.

damier [damje] nm draughtboard.

damner [dɑne] v damn. **damnation** nf damnation. **damné** adj (fam) confounded.

se dandiner [dɑ̃dine] v waddle. **dandinement** nm waddle.

Danemark [danmark] nm Denmark.

danger [dɑ̃ʒe] nm danger. **mettre en danger** endanger. **sans danger** adv safely. **dangereux** adj dangerous.

danois [danwa] nm, adj Danish. **Danois, -e** nm, nf Dane.

dans [dɑ̃] prep in; into.

danser [dɑ̃se] v dance. **danse** nf dance; (art) dancing. **danseur, -euse** nm, nf dancer.

dard [dar] nm sting.

darder [darde] v (lancer) shoot; (dresser) point.

dater [date] v date. **date** nf date. **date limite** deadline.

datte [dat] nf date. **dattier** nm date palm.

daube [dob] nf stew, casserole.

dauphin [dofɛ̃] nm dolphin.

davantage [davɑ̃taʒ] adv (plus) more, any more; (plus longtemps) longer, any longer.

de [də], d' prep of; from. **de/du/de la/des** some, any.

dé [de] nm dice. **couper en dés** dice. **dé à coudre** thimble.

débâcle [debɑkl] nf collapse; (mil) rout; (glace) breaking up.

déballer [debale] v unpack. **déballage** nm unpacking.

se débander [debɑde] v disperse, scatter. **débandade** nf scattering. **à la débandade** in disorder.

débarbouiller [debarbuje] v wash. **se débarbouiller** wash one's face.

débarcadère [debarkadɛr] nm landing stage.

débardeur [debardœr] nm docker.

débarquer [debarke] v land; (navire) disembark; (décharger) unload. **débarquement** nm landing; unloading.

débarras [debara] nm lumber room. **bon débarras!** good riddance!

débarrasser [debarase] v rid; (table) clear. **se débarrasser de** get rid of.

débat [deba] nm debate; discussion.

*débattre [debatr] v debate; discuss. **se débattre** struggle.

débaucher [debofe] v lead astray; (ouvriers) lay off, make redundant. **débauche** nf debauchery. **débauché** adj debauched.

débile [debil] adj weak, feeble.

débit¹ [debi] nm (comm) turnover; (fluide) flow, output; (élocution) delivery. **débit de boissons** bar. **débit de tabac** tobacconist's.

débit² [debi] nm debit.

débiter¹ [debite] v (comm) retail; (fluide) produce; recite; (couper) cut up. **débiteur²** nm debit.

déblai [deblɛ] nm clearing. **déblais** nm pl rubble sing, debris sing.

déblayer [debleje] v clear.

déboîter [debwate] v (méd) dislocate; (séparer) disconnect; (auto) pull out. **déboîtement** nm dislocation.

débonnaire [debɔnɛr] *adj* easy-going.

déborder [debɔrde] *v* (*liquide*) overflow; (*dépasser*) go beyond, jut out; (*drap*) untuck. **débordant** *adj* exuberant, unbounded. **débordé de** (*fam*) snowed under with. **débordement** *nm* overflowing; outburst.

déboucher[1] [debuʃe] *v* (*tuyau*) unblock; (*bouteille*) uncork.

déboucher[2] [debuʃe] *v* emerge. **débouché** *nm* opening; (*comm*) outlet.

débourser [deburse] *v* pay out. **débours** *nm* outlay.

debout [dəbu] *adv, adj* standing. **être debout** stand. **se mettre debout** stand up.

déboutonner [debutɔne] *v* unbutton.

débraillé [debraje] *adj* slovenly, untidy. *nm* slovenliness.

débrancher [debrɑ̃ʃe] *v* disconnect; (*appareil électrique*) unplug.

débrayer [debreje] *v* (*auto*) let out the clutch; (*fam*) knock off work.

débris [debri] *nm pl* fragments *pl*; (*restes*) remains *pl*; debris *sing*.

débrouiller [debruje] *v* sort out; (*fils*) disentangle. **se débrouiller** manage, cope.

début [deby] *nm* beginning. **au début** at first. **débuts** *nm pl* début *sing*. **débutant, -e** *nm, nf* beginner. **débuter** *v* start.

deçà [dəsa] *adv* **en deçà de** on this side of.

décade [dekad] *nf* decade.

décadent [dekadɑ̃] *adj* decadent. **décadence** *nf* decadence.

décaler [dekale] *v* shift; (*avancer*) bring forward; (*reculer*) put back. **décalage** *nm* gap; (*temps*) interval; (*concepts*) discrepancy; (*horaire, etc.*) change.

décamper [dekɑ̃pe] *v* (*fam*) clear off.

décanter [dekɑ̃te] *v* (*liquide*) allow to settle; (*verser*) decant. **se décanter** settle; (*idées*) become clear. **décanteur** *nm* decanter.

décapotable [dekapɔtablə] *adj* (*voiture*) convertible.

décéder [desede] *v* die. **décédé, -e** *n, adj* deceased.

déceler [desle] *v* detect; reveal.

décembre [desɑ̃brə] *nm* December.

décent [desɑ̃] *adj* decent; (*acceptable*) proper. **décence** *nf* decency.

déception [desɛpsjɔ̃] *nf* disappointment.

décerner [desɛrne] *v* award.

décès [desɛ] *nm* decease.

*décevoir [desvwar] *v* disappoint.

déchaîner [deʃene] *v* (*colère, etc.*) unleash; (*enthousiasme*) rouse. **se déchaîner** (*personne*) rage; (*tempête*) break out. **déchaînement** *nm* fury.

décharger [deʃarʒe] *v* discharge; (*bagages*) unload; (*tirer*) fire. **décharger de** relieve of, release from. **décharge** *nf* discharge; (*arme*) volley of shots; (*ordures*) rubbish tip.

décharné [deʃarne] *adj* bony, emaciated.

se déchausser [deʃose] *v* take one's shoes off. **déchaussé** *adj* barefooted.

déchéance [deʃeɑ̃s] *nf* decline; degeneration; (*pol*) deposition.

déchet [deʃɛ] *nm* (*reste*) scrap; (*comm*) waste. **déchets** *nm pl* rubbish, waste.

déchiffrer [deʃifre] *v* decipher, decode; (*musique*) sight-read.

déchiqueter [deʃikte] *v* tear to pieces, shred. **déchiqueté** *ai* jagged.

déchirer [deʃire] *v* tear. **déchirant** *adj* heartrending. **déchirure** *nf* tear.

*déchoir [deʃwar] *v* (*se dégrader*) demean oneself; decline.

décibel [desibɛl] *nm* decibel.

décider [deside] *v* decide; persuade; determine. **se décider** (*personne*) make up one's mind; (*question*) be settled. **décidé** *adj* determined; settled. **décidément** *adv* undoubtedly.

décimal [desimal] *adj* decimal. **décimale** *nf* decimal.

décisif [desizif] *adj* decisive.

décision [desizjɔ̃] *nf* decision.

déclarer [deklare] *v* declare, announce; (*naissance*) register. **déclaration** *nf* declaration; (*discours*) statement; (*aveu*) admission; registration.

déclencher [deklɑ̃ʃe] *v* (*mécanisme*) release, activate; (*attaque*) launch; (*entraîner*) trigger off.

déclin [deklɛ̃] *nm* decline; (*jour*) close; (*lune*) wane.

décliner [dekline] *v* decline. **déclinaison** *nf* declension.

décoiffé [dekwafe] *adj* dishevelled.

décoller [dekɔle] *v* unstick; (*avion*) take off. **se décoller** come unstuck. **décollage** *nm* take-off.

décolorer [dekɔlɔre] *v* fade; (*cheveux*) bleach.

décombres [dekɔ̃brə] *nm pl* rubble *sing*.

décommander [dekɔmɑ̃de] *v* cancel.

décomposer [dekɔ̃poze] v split up; (vis-age) distort. **se décomposer** decompose. **décomposition** nf decomposition.

décompte [dekɔ̃t] nf deduction; (compte) breakdown. **décompter** v deduct.

déconcerter [dekɔ̃sɛrte] v disconcert.

décongeler [dekɔ̃ʒle] v thaw out.

déconseiller [dekɔ̃seje] v advise against. **déconseillé** adj inadvisable.

décontracter [dekɔ̃trakte] v relax. **décontraction** nf relaxation.

déconvenue [dekɔ̃vny] nf disappointment.

décor [dekɔr] nm scenery; (maison) décor; (cadre) setting.

décorer [dekɔre] v decorate. **décorateur, -trice** nm, nf decorator. **décoratif** adj decorative. **décoration** nf decoration.

découper [dekupe] v cut out or up. **se découper** stand out.

décourager [dekuraʒe] v discourage. **découragement** nm discouragement.

décousu [dekuzy] adj disjointed; (couture) undone.

découvert [dekuvɛr] adj uncovered; (ter-rain) exposed, open. nm overdraft, defi-cit. **découverte** nf discovery.

*****découvrir** [dekuvrir] v (trouver) discover, find out; (exposer) uncover.

décrasser [dekrase] v clean.

décret [dekrɛ] nm decree. **décréter** v decree, order.

*****décrire** [dekrir] v describe.

décrocher [dekrɔʃe] v take down; (télé-phone) pick up (the receiver).

*****décroître** [dekrwatra] v decrease, decline, (lune) wane. **décroissance** nf decrease, decline.

dédaigner [dedeɲe] v despise, scorn. **dédaigneux** adj scornful, contemptuous. **dédain** [dedɛ̃] nm contempt, scorn.

dédale [dedal] nm maze.

dedans [dədã] adv inside, indoors. nm inside.

dédicace [dedikas] nf dedication. **dédi-cacer** v sign, autograph.

dédier [dedje] v dedicate.

se *dédire [dedir] v go back on (one's word); retract.

dédit [dedi] nm forfeit; retraction.

dédommager [dedɔmaʒe] v compensate. **dédommagement** nm compensation.

déduction [dedyksjɔ̃] nf deduction; con-clusion.

*****déduire** [dedɥir] v (comm) deduct; (con-clure) deduce.

déesse [dees] nf goddess.

*****défaillir** [defajir] v weaken, fail; (s'évanouir) faint. **défaillance** nf (faiblesse) weakness; (incapacité) failure; faint.

*****défaire** [defɛr] v (couture, nœud) undo; (valise) unpack; (construction) dismantle. **se défaire** come undone or apart. **se défaire de** get rid of.

défaite [defɛt] nf defeat.

défalquer [defalke] v deduct.

défaut [defo] nm fault, flaw, defect; (manque) lack. **faire défaut** be lacking; (jur) default.

défection [defɛksjɔ̃] nf desertion, defec-tion.

défectueux [defɛktɥø] adj defective, faulty.

défendre [defãdrə] v (protéger) defend; (interdire) forbid.

défense [defãs] nf defence. **défense de fumer/stationner** no smoking/parking. **défense d'entrer** keep out.

déférer [defere] v defer; (jur) hand over. **déférence** nf deference. **déférent** adj def-erential.

défi [defi] nm challenge; (bravade) defi-ance.

déficeler [defisle] v untie.

déficit [defisit] nm deficit.

défier [defje] v defy, challenge. **se défier de** distrust. **défiance** nf distrust. **défiant** adj distrustful.

défigurer [defigyre] v disfigure, spoil; (vérité) distort; (monument) deface. **défiguration** nf distortion; disfigurement.

défilé [defile] nm procession; (géog) gorge, pass.

définir [definir] v define. **défini** adj defi-nite. **définitif** adj final, definitive. **défini-tion** nf definition; (mots croisés) clue.

défoncer [defɔ̃se] v smash in, break up.

déformer [defɔrme] v deform, distort; (métal, etc.) bend or put out of shape. **déformation** nf deformation, distortion.

défraîchi [defreʃi] adj faded.

défricher [defriʃe] v clear. **défricher le ter-rain** prepare the ground.

défunt [defɛ̃], **-e** n, adj deceased.

dégager [degaʒe] v clear; (libérer) free; (exhaler) give off. **dégagé** adj clear; (allure) casual.

dégarnir [degarnir] v strip, clear, empty. **dégarni** adj bare.

dégât [dega] nm damage.

dégel [deʒɛl] nm thaw. **dégeler** v thaw (out).

dégénérer [deʒenere] v degenerate. **dégénéré** adj degenerate. **dégénérescence** nf degeneration, degeneracy.

dégivrer [deʒivre] v defrost, de-ice. **dégivreur** nm defroster, de-icer.

dégonfler [degɔ̃fle] v deflate. **se dégonfler** go down; (fam) back out. **dégonflé** adj (pneu) flat; (fam) chicken.

dégorger [degɔrʒe] v discharge, pour out; (déboucher) clear out.

dégouliner [deguline] v trickle, drip. **dégoulinade** nf trickle.

dégourdir [degurdir] v warm up. **se dégourdir** stretch one's legs. **dégourdi** adj (fam) smart, bright.

dégoûter [degute] v disgust. **dégoût** nm disgust.

dégoutter [degute] v drip.

dégrader [degrade] v degrade, debase; (mur, monument) deface, damage. **se dégrader** debase oneself; deteriorate. **dégradation** nf degradation.

dégrafer [degrafe] v unfasten.

dégraisser [degrese] v remove the fat or grease from. **dégraissage** nm cleaning.

degré [dəgre] nm degree; stage.

dégringoler [degrɛ̃gɔle] v tumble (down). **dégringolade** nf tumble.

dégriser [degrize] v sober up.

déguenillé [degnije] adj ragged.

déguerpir [degɛrpir] v (fam) clear off.

dégueulasse [degœlas] adj (argot) lousy, rotten, revolting.

déguiser [degize] v disguise. **se déguiser** (en) dress up (as). **déguisé** adj in disguise; (travesti) in fancy dress. **déguisement** nm disguise; fancy dress.

déguster [degyste] v taste, sample; savour, enjoy. **dégustation** nf wine-tasting.

dehors [dəɔr] adv outside, outdoors. **en dehors de** outside; (sauf) apart from. nm outside; appearance.

déjà [deʒa] adv already; (encore) yet.

déjeuner [deʒœne] v have lunch. nm lunch.

delà [dəla] adv **au delà** beyond. **en delà** beyond, outside. **par delà** beyond. prep **au delà de** beyond, over.

délabré [delabre] adj dilapidated, falling down; (vêtements) ragged.

délai [delɛ] nm delay; time limit, deadline. **à bref délai** at short notice; (bientôt) very soon.

délaisser [delese] v abandon; neglect; (jur) relinquish. **délaissement** nm desertion; neglect.

délasser [delase] v refresh, relax. **délassement** nm relaxation.

délavé [delave] adj faded, washed-out.

délayer [deleje] v mix; dilute, thin down; (péj) spin out.

déléguer [delege] v delegate. **délégation** nf delegation. **délégué, -e** nm, nf delegate.

délibérer [delibere] v deliberate, confer, consider. **délibération** nf deliberation; resolution. **délibéré** adj deliberate; resolute.

délicat [delika] adj delicate; refined; scrupulous; sensitive; (difficile) fussy. **délicatesse** nf delicacy; tact; refinement.

délice [delis] nm delight. **délicieux** adj delightful; (goût) delicious.

délier [delje] v untie, loosen. **délié** adj agile; fine, slender.

délinquant, -e nm, adj delinquent. **délinquance** nf delinquency.

délire [delir] nm delirium; frenzy. **avoir le délire** be delirious. **délirer** v be delirious.

délit [deli] nm offence.

délivrer [delivre] v (libérer) free; (débarrasser) relieve; (livrer) issue. **délivrance** nf release; relief; issue.

déloyal [delwajal] adj disloyal; (procédé) unfair. **déloyauté** nf disloyalty; unfairness.

delta [delta] nm delta.

déluge [delyʒ] nm deluge, flood; (pluie) downpour.

déluré [delyre] adj smart, resourceful.

se démailler [demaje] v (bas) ladder; (tricot) unravel.

demain [dəmɛ̃] adv tomorrow. **à demain!** see you tomorrow! **demain en huit** a week tomorrow.

demander [dəmɑ̃de] v ask for; enquire, ask; (médecin, etc.) send for; (avoir besoin de) require, need. **se demander** wonder. **demande** nf request; (emploi) application; (remboursement) claim; (comm) demand. **demandé** adj in demand.

démanger [demɑ̃ʒe] v itch. **démangeaison** nf itch.

démaquiller [demakije] v remove make-up from. **démaquillant** nm make-up remover.

démarche [demarʃ] nf gait; procedure, step; approach.

démarrer [demare] v (auto) start; (partir) move off. **bien démarrer** get off to a good start. **démarreur** nm (auto) starter.

démêler [demele] v untangle. **démêlé** nm dispute.

démembrer [demɑ̃bre] v dismember, carve up.

déménager [demenaʒe] v move (house). **déménagement** nm removal, move. **déménageur** nm removal man.

démence [demɑ̃s] nf madness.

se démener [dmne] v struggle; make an effort.

*démentir [demɑ̃tir] v refute, deny, contradict. **démenti** nm denial.

démesuré [demezyre] adj immoderate; enormous.

*démettre [demetrə] v dislocate; (renvoyer) dismiss. **se démettre** resign.

demeurer [dəmœre] v (rester) remain; (habiter) live. **au demeurant** for all that. **demeure** nf residence. **à demeure** permanent.

demi [dəmi], -e n, adj half. **à demi** adv half.

demi-bouteille nf half-bottle.

demi-cercle nm semicircle. **en demi-cercle** semicircular.

demi-douzaine nf half-dozen. **une demi-douzaine** half-a-dozen.

demi-finale nf semifinal. **demi-finaliste** n(m + f) semifinalist.

demi-frère nm half-brother.

demi-heure nf half-hour. **une demi-heure** half an hour.

demi-pension nf half-board.

demi-sœur nf half-sister.

démission [demisjɔ̃] nf resignation; abdication. **donner sa démission** hand in one's notice. **démissionner** v resign.

demi-tarif nm half-price; (transport) half-fare.

demi-teinte nf half-tone.

demi-tour nm about-turn; (auto) U-turn.

démocratie [demɔkrasi] nf democracy. **démocrate** n(m + f) democrat. **démocratique** adj democratic.

démodé [demɔde] adj old-fashioned.

demoiselle [dəmwazɛl] nf young lady. **demoiselle d'honneur** bridesmaid.

démolir [demɔlir] v demolish; destroy. **démolition** nf demolition.

démon [demɔ̃] nm demon.

démonter [demɔ̃te] v dismantle, take apart; disconcert.

démontrer [demɔ̃tre] v demonstrate. **démonstratif** adj demonstrative. **démonstration** nf demonstration.

démoraliser [demɔralize] v demoralize. **se démoraliser** lose heart. **démoralisation** nf demoralization.

démordre [demɔrdrə] v give up. **ne pas démordre de** stick to.

démunir [demynir] v deprive, divest. **démuni de** without.

dénaturer [denatyre] v distort. **dénaturé** adj unnatural.

dénégation [denegasjɔ̃] nf denial.

dénicher [deniʃe] (fam) v discover; (personne) track down; (objet) unearth.

dénigrer [denigre] v denigrate, run down.

dénivellation [denivɛlasjɔ̃] nf unevenness; (pente) slope; (auto) ramp.

dénombrer [denɔ̃bre] v count; enumerate.

dénominateur [denɔminatœr] nm denominator.

dénommer [denɔme] v name.

dénoncer [denɔ̃se] v denounce; (coupable) give away; (révéler) expose.

dénoter [denɔte] v denote, indicate.

dénouer [denwe] v (nœud) undo; (intrigue) untangle, resolve. **se dénouer** come undone; be resolved. **dénouement** nm outcome; (théâtre) dénouement.

denrée [dɑ̃re] nf foodstuff.

dense [dɑ̃s] adj dense; compact. **densité** [dɑ̃site] nf density.

dent [dɑ̃] nf tooth (pl teeth); (fourche) prong; (roue) cog. **avoir la dent** (fam) be peckish. **avoir une dent contre** have a grudge against. **du bout des dents** half-heartedly. **en dents de scie** serrated. **faire ses dents** teethe. **dentaire** adj dental.

denteler [dɑ̃tle] v indent. **dentelé** adj jagged.

dentelle [dɑ̃tɛl] nf lace.

dentier [dɑ̃tje] nm denture.

dentifrice [dɑ̃tifris] nm toothpaste.

dentiste [dɑ̃tist] n(m + f) dentist.

dénuder [denyde] v strip, bare. **dénudé** adj bare; (crâne) bald.

dénué [denɥe] adj **dénué de** devoid of, lacking in.

déodorant [deɔdɔrɑ̃] *nm, adj* deodorant.

dépanner [depane] *v* fix, repair. **dépannage** *nm* repairing. **service de dépannage** *nm* breakdown service. **dépanneuse** *nf* breakdown lorry.

dépaqueter [depakte] *v* unpack.

dépareillé [depareje] *adj* (*objet*) odd; (*collection*) incomplete.

départ [depar] *nm* departure; (*début*) start.

département [departəmɑ̃] *nm* department.

départir [departir] *v* assign. **se départir de** abandon, depart from.

dépasser [depase] *v* pass; (*auto*) overtake; exceed, go beyond; (*clou, rocher, etc.*) stick out. **dépassé** *adj* outmoded; (*fam*) out of one's depth. **dépassement** *nm* overtaking.

dépaysé [depeize] *adj* disorientated. **sentir dépaysé** not feel at home.

dépêcher [depeʃe] *v* dispatch. **se dépêcher** hurry. **dépêche** *nf* dispatch; telegram.

***dépeindre** [depɛ̃dra] *v* depict.

dépendance [depɑ̃dɑ̃s] *nf* dependence, dependency; subordination; (*bâtiment*) outbuilding. **dépendant de** (*employé*) answerable to; dependent on.

dépendre¹ [depɑ̃dra] *v* **dépendre de** depend on, be dependent on; (*employé*) be answerable to; (*appartenir*) belong to.

dépendre² [depɑ̃dra] *v* take down.

dépens [depɑ̃] *nm pl* costs *pl*. **aux dépens de** at the expense of.

dépenser [depɑ̃se] *v* (*argent*) spend; (*consumer*) use (up). **se dépenser** exert oneself. **dépense** *nf* expenditure, expense; consumption. **dépensier** *adj* extravagant. **être dépensier** be a spendthrift.

dépérir [deperir] *v* decline; (*personne*) waste away; (*plante*) wither.

dépêtrer [depetre] *v* extricate, free.

dépister [depiste] *v* (*découvrir*) detect, track down; (*détourner*) throw off the scent.

dépit [depi] *nm* vexation, resentment. **en dépit de** in spite of.

déplacer [deplase] *v* move, shift; (*air, eau, etc.*) displace. **se déplacer** move (around); (*voyager*) travel. **déplacé** *adj* uncalled-for; out of place. **déplacement** *nm* displacement; moving, movement; travel.

***déplaire** [deplɛr] *v* **déplaire à** be disliked

by, displease. **se déplaire** be unhappy, dislike it. **déplaisant** *adj* unpleasant.

déplaisir *nm* displeasure.

déplantoir [deplɑ̃twar] *nm* trowel.

déplier [deplije] *v* unfold, open out. **dépliant** *nm* leaflet, folder.

déplorer [deplɔre] *v* regret, deplore. **déplorable** *adj* deplorable.

déployer [deplwaje] *v* spread out; (*troupes*) deploy; (*étaler*) display.

se déplumer [deplyme] *v* moult.

déporter [depɔrte] *v* deport. **déportation** *nf* deportation.

déposer¹ [depoze] *v* set or put down; (*argent, sédiment*) deposit; (*admin*) file, register; (*roi*) depose. **déposant, -e** *nm, nf* depositor. **déposition** *nf* deposition.

dépositaire [depozitɛr] *n(m+f)* guardian; agent.

dépôt [depo] *nm* deposit; (*train, autobus*) depot; (*entrepôt*) warehouse; (*garde*) trust.

dépouiller [depuje] *v* strip; (*examiner*) peruse, study. **se dépouiller de** shed. **dépouille** *nf* skin, hide. **dépouillé** *adj* bare.

dépourvu [depurvy] *adj* **dépourvu de** devoid of, lacking in, without. *nm* **au dépourvu** unprepared.

dépraver [deprave] *v* deprave. **dépravation** *nf* depravity.

déprécier [depresje] *v* depreciate; (*dénigrer*) belittle. **dépréciation** *nf* depreciation.

dépression [depresjɔ̃] *nf* depression.

déprimer [deprime] *v* depress.

depuis [dəpɥi] *prep* since, from. *adv* ever since.

députation [depytasjɔ̃] *nf* deputation.

député [depyte] *nm* member of parliament; (*envoyé*) delegate.

déraciner [derasine] *v* (*détruire*) eradicate; (*arbre*) uproot. **déracinement** *nm* eradication.

dérailler [deraje] *v* be derailed. **déraillement** *nm* derailment.

déraisonnable [derezɔnabla] *adj* unreasonable.

déranger [derɑ̃ʒe] *v* disturb; (*coiffure*) ruffle; (*gêner*) trouble; (*routine*) upset. **se déranger** put oneself out; move aside. **dérangement** *nm* trouble; disorder.

déraper [derape] *v* skid. **dérapage** *nm* skid.

derechef [dərəʃef] *adv* once more.

dérégler [deregle] *v* disturb, unsettle, upset. **se dérégler** go wrong. **déréglé** *adj* out of order; (*mœurs*) dissolute; upset. **déréglement** *nm* disturbance; dissoluteness.

dérision [derizjɔ̃] *nf* derision, mockery. **dérisoire** *adj* derisory.

dériver[1] [derive] *v* derive; (*rivière*) divert. **dérivation** *nf* derivation; diversion. **dérivé** *nm* derivative, by-product.

dériver[2] [derive] *v* drift. **dérive** *nf* drift. **à la dérive** adrift.

dernier [dɛrnje], **-ère** *adj* last; (*plus récent*) latest; (*extrême*) utmost; (*pire*) bottom; (*ultime*) top. *nm*, *nf* last. **ce dernier, cette dernière** the latter. **dernièrement** *adv* recently.

dérober [derobe] *v* (*cacher*) hide; (*voler*) steal. **se dérober** shy away; (*échapper*) slip away; (*s'effondrer*) give way. **dérobé** *adj* secret. **à la dérobée** secretly.

déroger [derɔʒe] *v* **déroger à** (*jur*) go against; (*s'abaisser*) lower oneself.

dérouler [derule] *v* unroll, unwind. **se dérouler** (*fil*) unwind, unroll; develop, progress; (*se passer*) take place.

dérouter [derute] *v* (*avion*) divert; disconcert. **déroute** *nf* rout. **déroutement** *nm* diversion.

derrière [dɛrjɛr] *prep* behind. *adv* behind, at the back. *nm* back, rear; (*fam*) behind.

des [de] *contraction of* **de les**.

dès [de] *prep* from, since. **dès lors** from then on, from that moment. **dès que** as soon as.

désabuser [dezabyze] *v* disillusion. **désabusé** *adj* disenchanted. **désabusement** *nm* disillusionment.

désaccord [dezakɔr] *nm* discord; conflict, disagreement; (*contradiction*) discrepancy.

désaffecter [dezafɛkte] *v* close down. **désaffecté** *adj* disused.

désagréable [dezagreablə] *adj* unpleasant.

désagréger [dezagreʒe] *v* disintegrate, break up. **désagrégation** *nf* disintegration.

désagrément [dezagremã] *nm* annoyance, trouble.

se désaltérer [dezaltere] *v* quench one's thirst. **désaltérant** *adj* thirst-quenching.

désappointer [dezapwɛte] *v* disappoint.

désapprobation [dezaprɔbasjɔ̃] *nf* disapproval. **désapprobateur, -trice** *adj* disapproving.

désapprouver [dezapruve] *v* disapprove of.

désarmer [dezarme] *v* disarm.

désarroi [dezarwa] *nm* confusion.

désassorti [dezasɔrti] *adj* unmatching.

désastre [dezastrə] *nm* disaster. **désastreux** *adj* disastrous.

désavantage [dezavɑ̃taʒ] *nm* disadvantage, handicap.

désaveu [dezavø] *nm* disavowal, repudiation; retraction.

désavouer [dezavwe] *v* disown, repudiate. **se désavouer** retract.

désaxé [dezakse] *adj* unbalanced.

descendant [desɑ̃dɑ̃], **-e** *adj* downward, descending. *nm*, *nf* descendant.

descendre [desɑ̃drə] *v* go down, come down; (*transport*) get out or off; (*tomber*) fall; (*baisser*) lower; (*porter*) take down. **descendre de** be descended from.

descente [desɑ̃t] *nf* descent; raid; (*pente*) downward slope. **descente de lit** bedside rug.

description [dɛskripsjɔ̃] *nf* description. **descriptif** *adj* descriptive.

désemparer [dezɑ̃pare] *v* (*naut*) disable. **sans désemparer** without stopping. **désemparé** *adj* bewildered; (*navire, avion*) crippled.

désencombrer [dezɑ̃kɔ̃bre] *v* clear.

désenfler [dezɑ̃fle] *v* go down, become less swollen.

désengager [dezɑ̃gaʒe] *v* free, release; (*mil*) disengage.

désenivrer [dezɑ̃nivre] *v* sober up.

déséquilibré [dezekilibre] *adj* unbalanced.

désert [dezɛr] *adj* deserted. *nm* desert. **déserter** [dezɛrte] *v* desert. **déserteur** *nm* deserter. **désertion** *nf* desertion.

désespérer [dezɛspere] *v* despair, lose hope; (*désoler*) drive to despair. **désespérant** *adj* maddening. **désespéré** *adj* desperate.

désespoir [dezɛspwar] *nm* despair.

déshabiller [dezabije] *v* undress. **déshabillé** *nm* negligee.

désherber [dezɛrbe] *v* weed. **désherbage** *nm* weeding. **désherbant** *nm* weed-killer.

déshériter [dezerite] *v* disinherit; (*désavantager*) deprive.

déshonneur [dezɔnœr] *nm* disgrace, dishonour.

déshonorer [dezɔnɔre] v disgrace, dishonour.

déshydrater [dezidrate] v dehydrate. **déshydratation** nf dehydration.

désigner [dezine] v designate; (montrer) point out; (nommer) name, appoint. **désignation** nf designation; appointment.

désillusionner [dezilyzjɔne] v disillusion. **désillusion** nf disillusionment.

désinfecter [dezɛ̃fɛkte] v disinfect. **désinfectant** nm, adj disinfectant. **désinfection** nf disinfection.

désintégrer [dezɛ̃tegre] v split or break up. **se désintégrer** disintegrate. **désintégration** nf disintegration.

désintéressé [dezɛ̃terese] adj disinterested, unselfish. **désintéressement** nm unselfishness.

désinvolte [dezɛ̃vɔlt] adj casual. **avec désinvolture** casually.

désirer [dezire] v desire, want. **désir** nm desire, wish. **désirable** adj desirable. **désireux de** anxious to.

désobéir [dezɔbeir] v disobey. **désobéissance** nf disobedience. **désobéissant** adj disobedient.

désodorisant [dezɔdɔrizɑ̃] nm, adj deodorant.

désœuvré [dezœvre] adj idle. **désœuvrement** nm idleness.

désoler [dezɔle] v distress, upset; devastate. **désolation** nf distress, grief; devastation. **désolé** sorry, distressed; (endroit) desolate.

désopilant [dezɔpilɑ̃] adj hilarious.

désordonné [dezɔrdɔne] adj disorderly, untidy, muddled.

désordre [dezɔrdrə] nm disorder, untidiness; confusion. **désordres** nm pl disturbances pl.

désorganiser [dezɔrganize] v disorganize, disrupt. **désorganisation** nf disorganization.

désorienter [dezɔrjɑ̃te] v disorientate, bewilder.

désormais [dezɔrmɛ] adv in future, from now on.

désosser [dezɔse] v bone.

desquels, desquelles [dekɛl] contractions of **de lesquels, de lesquelles.**

dessécher [desefe] v dry out, parch; (feuille) wither; (aliments) dehydrate; (amaigrir) emaciate.

dessein [desɛ̃] nm intention, plan. **à dessein** intentionally. **avoir des desseins sur** have designs on.

desserrer [desere] v loosen, release. **desserrer les dents** open one's mouth, speak. **desserré** adj loose.

dessert [desɛr] nm dessert, sweet.

*desservir[1] [deservir] v clear the table; (nuire) harm, do a disservice to.

*desservir[2] [deservir] v (transport) serve; (porte) lead into.

dessin [desɛ̃] nm drawing; (motif) pattern; (contour) outline. **dessin animé** cartoon (film). **dessin humoristique** cartoon. **dessinateur, -trice** nm, nf draughtsman; designer; cartoonist.

dessiner [desine] v draw; design. **se dessiner** stand out; become apparent.

dessous [dəsu] adv under, below. nm bottom, underside. **avoir le dessous** get the worst of it. **dessous de plat** table mat. **dessous de verre** coaster.

dessus [dəsy] adv above, over, on top. nm top. **avoir le dessus** have the upper hand. **dessus de lit** bedspread.

destin [dɛstɛ̃] nm fate, destiny.

destination [dɛstinasjɔ̃] nf destination. **à destination de** bound for.

destiner [dɛstine] v destine; intend. **destinée** nf fate, destiny.

destituer [dɛstitɥe] v dismiss. **destitution** nf dismissal, discharge.

destruction [dɛstryksjɔ̃] nf destruction. **destructif** adj destructive.

désuet, -ète [desɥɛ, -ɛt] adj outdated. **désuétude** nf disuse. **tomber en désuétude** become obsolete.

désunir [dezynir] v divide, disunite.

détacher[1] [detafe] v (dénouer) untie, undo; (ôter) remove; separate. **se détacher** come undone; come off or away; (ressortir) stand out. **se détacher de** renounce. **détachable** adj detachable. **détachement** nm detachment.

détacher[2] [detafe] v clean, remove stains from. **détachant** nm stain remover.

détail [detaj] nm detail; (facture) breakdown; (comm) retail.

détailler [detaje] v explain in detail; (articles) sell separately; (comm) retail. **détaillant, -e** nm, nf retailer. **détaillé** adj detailed.

détective [detɛktiv] nm **détective privé** private detective.

*déteindre [detɛ̃drə] v (au soleil) fade; (au lavage) run.

détendre [detɑ̃drə] v release, loosen. **se détendre** relax.

*****détenir** [detnir] v have, hold; (prisonnier) detain. **détenteur, -trice** nm, nf holder. **détenu, -e** nm, nf prisoner.

détente [detɑ̃t] nf relaxation; (élan) spring; (gâchette) trigger.

détergent [detɛrʒɑ̃] nm, adj detergent.

détériorer [deterjɔre] v damage. **se détériorer** deteriorate. **détérioration** nf damage; deterioration.

déterminer [detɛrmine] v determine; fix; decide. **se déterminer** make up one's mind. **détermination** nf determination; resolution. **déterminé** adj determined; specific.

déterrer [detere] v dig up, unearth.

détester [detɛste] v hate, detest. **détestable** adj loathsome.

détoner [detɔne] v detonate. **détonant, -e** adj explosive. **détonateur** nm detonator.

détonner [detɔne] v clash, be out of place; (musique) go out of tune.

détour [detur] nm detour; (courbe) bend. **sans détours** straight out.

détourner [deturne] v divert; (regard) turn away; (avion) hijack; (argent) embezzle. **détourné** adj indirect, roundabout. **détournement** nm diversion; hijacking; embezzlement.

détraqué [detrake] adj broken down, out of order; (temps) unsettled; (fam: personne) crazy.

détremper [detrɑ̃pe] v soak; dilute, mix with water.

détresse [detrɛs] nf distress.

détritus [detritys] nm pl rubbish sing, refuse sing.

*****détruire** [detrɥir] v destroy; ruin.

dette [dɛt] nf debt.

deuil [dœj] nm mourning; (perte) bereavement.

deux [dø] adj two; (quelques) a couple of; (épelant) double. nm two. **deux-points** nm invar colon. (tous) **les deux** both. **tous les deux jours** every other day. **deuxième** n(m+f), adj second.

dévaler [devale] v rush or hurtle down.

dévaliser [devalize] v burgle, rob.

dévaluer [devalɥe] v devalue. **dévaluation** nf devaluation.

devancer [dəvɑ̃se] v forestall; (question, etc.) anticipate; (coureur) get ahead of, leave behind. **devancier, -ère** nm, nf precursor.

devant [dəvɑ̃] prep in front of, before. adv in front, ahead. nm front. **aller au-devant de** anticipate.

devanture [dəvɑ̃tyr] nf (étalage) window, display; (façade) shop front. **à la devanture** in the window.

dévaster [devaste] v devastate. **dévastation** nf devastation.

développer [devlɔpe] v develop; (industrie, etc.) expand. **se développer** develop, spread. **développement** nm development; expansion.

*****devenir** [dəvnir] v become.

dévergondé [devɛrgɔ̃de] adj shameless; licentious.

déverser [devɛrse] v pour out. **déversoir** nm overflow.

dévêtir [devetir] v undress.

dévier [devje] v deviate, veer off course; divert. **déviation** nf deviation; diversion.

deviner [dəvine] v guess; (énigme) solve. **devinette** nf riddle.

devis [dəvi] nm estimate.

dévisager [devizaʒe] v stare at.

devise [dəviz] nf motto; (comm) slogan. **devises** nf pl currency sing.

dévisser [devise] v unscrew.

dévoiler [devwale] v unveil; reveal, disclose.

*****devoir** [dəvwar] v have to, must; (argent, etc.) owe. nm duty; (école) homework.

dévorer [devɔre] v devour; consume.

dévot [devo], **-e** adj devout, pious. nm, nf pious person. **dévotion** nf devoutness.

se dévouer [devwe] v devote oneself; sacrifice oneself. **dévouement** nm devotion.

dextérité [dɛksterite] nf skill, dexterity.

diabète [djabɛt] nm diabetes. **diabétique** n(m+f), adj diabetic.

diable [djablə] nm devil. **diablerie** nf mischief. **diabolique** adj diabolical.

diablotin [djablɔtɛ̃] nm (enfant) imp; (pétard) cracker.

diadème [djadɛm] nm diadem; (bijou) tiara.

diagnostiquer [djagnɔstike] v diagnose. **diagnostic** nm diagnosis.

diagonal [djagɔnal] adj diagonal. **diagonale** nf diagonal.

dialecte [djalɛkt] nm dialect.

dialogue [djalɔg] nm dialogue, conversation.

diamant [djamɑ̃] nm diamond.

diamètre [djamɛtrə] nm diameter. **diamétralement opposé** diametrically opposed.

diaphragme [djafragmə] nm diaphragm.

diapositive [djapozitiv] nf slide, transparency.

diapré [djapre] adj mottled.

diarrhée [djare] nf diarrhoea.

dictateur [diktatœr] nm dictator. **dictature** nf dictatorship.

dicter [dikte] v dictate. **dictée** nf dictation.

dictionnaire [diksjɔnɛr] nm dictionary.

dicton [diktɔ̃] nm saying.

dièse [djɛz] nm, adj sharp.

diesel [djezɛl] nm diesel.

diète [djɛt] nf diet.

dieu [djø] nm god.

diffamer [difame] v slander; (par écrit) libel. **diffamation** nf slander; libel. **diffamatoire** adj slanderous; libellous.

différence [diferɑ̃s] nf difference. **à la différence de** unlike. **différent** adj different.

différencier [diferɑ̃sje] v differentiate. **différenciation** nf differentiation.

différend [diferɑ̃] nm disagreement, difference of opinion.

différentiel [diferɑ̃sjɛl], **-elle** n, adj differential.

différer [difere] v differ; (renvoyer) defer, postpone.

difficile [difisil] adj difficult. **difficulté** nf difficulty.

difforme [difɔrm] adj deformed. **difformité** nf deformity.

diffuser [difyze] v diffuse, spread; (émission) broadcast.

digérer [dizere] v digest.

digestion [dizɛstjɔ̃] nf digestion.

digitale [dizital] nf **digitale pourprée** foxglove.

digne [diɲ] adj worthy; (grave) dignified.

dignité [diɲite] nf dignity.

dique [dig] nf dyke.

dilapider [dilapide] v squander; (détourner) embezzle.

dilater [dilate] v dilate, distend. **se dilater** swell, expand. **dilatation** nf dilation.

dilemme [dilɛm] nm dilemma.

diluer [dilɥe] v dilute. **dilution** nf dilution.

dimanche [dimɑ̃ʃ] nm Sunday. **dimanche des Rameaux** Palm Sunday.

dimension [dimɑ̃sjɔ̃] nf dimension, size, measurement.

diminuer [diminɥe] v diminish, reduce,

decrease. **diminutif** nm, adj diminutive. **diminution** nf reduction, decrease.

dinde [dɛ̃d] nf turkey. **dindon** nm turkey.

dîner [dine] v have dinner, dine. nm dinner. **dîneur, -euse** nm, nf diner.

dingue [dɛ̃g] (fam) adj barmy, crazy. n(m+f) nutcase.

dinosaure [dinozɔr] nm dinosaur.

diocèse [djɔsɛz] nm diocese.

diphtongue [diftɔ̃g] nf diphthong.

diplomate [diplɔmat] adj diplomatic. n(m+f) diplomat. nm (cuisine) trifle. **diplomatie** nf diplomacy. **diplomatique** adj diplomatic.

diplôme [diplom] nm diploma; examination.

diplômé [diplome], **-e** adj qualified. nm, nf holder of a diploma.

***dire** [dir] v say, tell. **c'est-à-dire** that is. **vouloir dire** mean.

direct [dirɛkt] adj direct, straight, immediate. nm fast train, express. **directement** adv directly, straight, immediately.

directeur [dirɛktœr] nm director; (responsable) manager; (école) headmaster. **directeur général** managing director. **directrice** nf director; manageress; headmistress.

direction [dirɛksjɔ̃] nf direction; (gestion) management; (auto) steering.

diriger [dirize] v direct; (gérer) run, manage; (arme) point, aim; steer. **se diriger** find one's way. **se diriger vers** head for.

discerner [disɛrne] v discern; distinguish.

disciple [disiplə] nm disciple.

discipline [disiplin] nf discipline. **disciplinaire** adj disciplinary. **discipliner** v discipline, control.

discontinu [diskɔ̃tiny] adj discontinuous; intermittent.

discorde [diskɔrd] nf discord, dissension. **discordant** adj discordant.

discothèque [diskɔtɛk] nf record collection; (club) discotheque.

discours [diskur] nm speech.

discréditer [diskredite] v discredit. **discrédit** nm discredit.

discret, -ète [diskrɛ, -ɛt] adj discreet; quiet, sober; (quantité) discrete. **discrétion** nf discretion. **avec discrétion** discreetly. **discrétionnaire** adj discretionary.

discrimination [diskriminasjɔ̃] nf discrimination.

discussion [diskysjɔ̃] nf discussion; (querelle) argument.

discuter [diskyte] v discuss; question, dispute; (*protester*) argue. **discutable** *adj* debatable; questionable.

disette [dizɛt] *nf* scarcity, shortage.

disgrâce [disgrɑs] *nf* disgrace. **disgracié** *adj* in disgrace.

disgracieux [disgrasjø] *adj* inelegant; (*laid*) unsightly.

disloquer [dislɔke] v (*méd*) dislocate; (*désunir*) dismantle; (*briser*) break up; (*dissoudre*) disperse. **dislocation** *nf* dislocation.

*****disparaître** [disparɛtrə] v disappear, vanish. **faire disparaître** get rid of, remove. **disparition** *nf* disappearance.

disparate [disparat] *adj* disparate, illassorted. **disparité** *nf* disparity.

disparu [dispary], -e *adj* vanished; (*époque*) bygone; (*mort*) dead; (*mil. etc.*) missing. *nm, nf* dead person; missing person.

dispendieux [dispɑ̃djø] *adj* extravagant, expensive.

dispenser [dispɑ̃se] v dispense; exempt. **se dispenser de** avoid, get out of. **dispense** *nf* exemption.

disperser [dispɛrse] v disperse, scatter.

disponible [dispɔniblə] *adj* available, free. **disponibilité** *nf* availability.

dispos [dispo] *adj* alert, in good form.

disposer [dispoze] v arrange, lay out; (*engager*) dispose, incline. **disposer de** have at one's disposal. **se disposer à** be about to, prepare to. **disposition** *nf* arrangement; disposal; (*humeur*) mood; tendancy; aptitude; (*jur*) clause.

dispositif [dispozitif] *nm* device; plan of action.

disputer [dispyte] v fight, contest; (*fam*) tell off. **se disputer** quarrel; fight over. **dispute** *nf* quarrel.

disqualifier [diskalifje] v disqualify; (*discréditer*) dishonour. **disqualification** *nf* disqualification.

disque [disk] *nm* disc; (*musique*) record.

dissemblable [disɑ̃blablə] *adj* dissimilar, different. **dissemblance** *nf* dissimilarity.

disséminer [disemine] v scatter.

dissentiment [disɑ̃timɑ̃] *nm* disagreement.

disséquer [diseke] v dissect.

dissident [disidɑ̃], -e *n, adj* dissident. **dissidence** *nf* dissidence, rebellion.

dissimuler [disimyle] v conceal; disguise. **dissimulation** *nf* dissimulation.

dissiper [disipe] v dispel, disperse; (*gaspiller*) waste, squander. **dissipation** *nf* dissipation; dispersal.

dissocier [disɔsje] v dissociate. **dissociation** *nf* dissociation.

*****dissoudre** [disudrə] v dissolve.

dissuader [disɥade] v dissuade. **dissuasion** *nf* dissuasion.

distance [distɑ̃s] *nf* distance. **distant** *adj* distant.

distiller [distile] v distil. **distillerie** *nf* distillery.

distinct [distɛ̃] *adj* distinct. **distinctif** *adj* distinctive. **distinction** *nf* distinction.

distinguer [distɛ̃ge] v distinguish; honour. **distingué** *adj* distinguished; eminent.

distraction [distraksjɔ̃] *nf* absent-mindedness, lack of attention; (*détente*) recreation, entertainment.

*****distraire** [distrɛr] v distract; (*divertir*) entertain. **se distraire** amuse oneself. **distrait** *adj* absent-minded.

distribuer [distribɥe] v distribute; arrange; (*cartes*) deal; (*courrier*) deliver. **distributeur** *nm* distributor. **distributeur automatique** slot machine. **distribution** *nf* distribution; arrangement; delivery; (*acteurs*) cast.

divaguer [divage] v ramble.

divan [divɑ̃] *nm* divan.

diverger [divɛrʒe] v diverge. **divergence** *nf* divergence.

divers [divɛr] *adj* diverse; different; (*plusieurs*) various, several. **diversité** *nf* diversity, variety.

divertir [divɛrtir] v amuse, entertain. **divertissement** *nm* amusement, entertainment.

dividende [dividɑ̃d] *nm* dividend.

divin [divɛ̃] *adj* divine. **divinité** *nf* divinity.

diviser [divize] v divide. **divisible** *adj* divisible. **division** *nf* division; discord.

divorcer [divɔrse] v get divorced. **divorce** *nm* divorce. **divorcé, -e** *nm, nf* divorcee.

divulguer [divylge] v divulge, disclose.

dix [dis] *nm, adj* ten. **dixième** *n(m+f)*, *adj* tenth.

dix-huit [dizɥit] *nm, adj* eighteen. **dix-huitième** *n(m+f)*, *adj* eighteenth.

dix-neuf [diznœf] *nm, adj* nineteen. **dix-neuvième** *n(m+f)*, *adj* nineteenth.

dix-sept [disɛt] *nm, adj* seventeen. **dix-septième** *n(m+f)*, *adj* seventeenth.

dizaine [dizɛn] *nf* **une dizaine (de)** about ten.

docile [dɔsil] *adj* docile.

docte [dɔktə] *adj* learned.

docteur [dɔktœr] *nm* doctor.

doctrine [dɔktrin] *nf* doctrine.

document [dɔkymɑ̃] *nm* document. **documentaire** *nm, adj* documentary. **documentation** *nf* documentation, information, research. **documenter** *v* document, research.

dodu [dɔdy] *adj* (*fam*) plump, chubby.

dogmatique [dɔgmatik] *adj* dogmatic.

dogme [dɔgmə] *nm* dogma.

doigt [dwa] *nm* finger. **doigt de pied** toe. **doigté** *nm* (*musique*) fingering; tact.

doit [dwa] *nm* debit.

doléances [dɔleɑ̃s] *nf pl* complaints *pl*.

dollar [dɔlar] *nm* dollar.

domaine [dɔmɛn] *nm* domain; property, estate; sphere, field.

dôme [dom] *nm* dome.

domestique [dɔmɛstik] *n(m+f)* servant. *adj* domestic.

domestiquer [dɔmɛstike] *v* domesticate. **domestication** *nf* domestication.

domicile [dɔmisil] *nm* home, place of residence; address.

dominer [dɔmine] *v* dominate; surpass; (*contrôler*) master; prevail; (*donner sur*) overlook. **dominant** *adj* dominant, main. **dominateur, -trice** *adj* domineering. **domination** *nf* domination.

dominion [dɔminjɔn] *nm* dominion.

domino [dɔmino] *nm* domino.

dommage [dɔmaʒ] *nm* harm, damage. **dommages-intérêts** *nm pl* damages *pl*. **quel dommage!** what a pity!

dompter [dɔ̃te] *v* tame; subdue; master. **dompteur, -euse** *nm, nf* tamer.

don [dɔ̃] *nm* gift; talent; (*argent*) donation. **faire don de** donate. **donateur, -trice** *nm, nf* donor.

donc [dɔk] *conj* so, then, thus. **dis donc** I say; tell me. **tais-toi donc!** do be quiet!

donner [dɔne] *v* give; (*cartes*) deal; produce. **donner dans** fall into. **donner pour** present as, make out to be. **donner sur** overlook, open onto. **se donner à** devote oneself to. **donne** *nf* (*cartes*) deal. **donné** *adj* given. **étant donné que** seeing that. **données** *nf pl* data *pl*, facts *pl*. **donneur, -euse** *nm, nf* dealer; (*méd*) donor.

dont [dɔ̃] *pron* whose; (*objet*) of which; (*personne*) of whom.

dorénavant [dɔrenavɑ̃] *adv* from now on.

dorer [dɔre] *v* gild; (*cuisine*) brown; (*peau*) tan. **doré** *adj* gilt; (*blé, etc.*) golden.

dorloter [dɔrlɔte] *v* pamper, cosset.

***dormir** [dɔrmir] *v* sleep, be asleep. **dormir à poings fermés** sleep soundly.

dortoir [dɔrtwar] *nm* dormitory.

dorure [dɔryr] *nf* gilt, gilding.

dos [do] *nm* back; (*livre*) spine.

dose [doz] *nf* dose, dosage.

dossier [dɔsje] *nm* file; (*siège*) back.

dot [dɔt] *nf* dowry.

doter [dɔte] *v* endow; equip.

douane [dwan] *nf* customs *pl*. **exempté de douane** duty-free. **douanier, -ère** *nm, nf* customs officer.

double [dublə] *adj, adv* double. *nm* double; copy; duplicate.

doubler [duble] *v* double; (*école*) repeat; (*film*) dub; (*acteur*) stand in for; (*revêtir*) line; (*auto*) overtake. **doubler le pas** speed up. **doublage** *nm* dubbing; lining. **doublure** *nf* lining; (*acteur*) stand-in, understudy.

douceur [dusœr] *nf* softness; (*clémence*) mildness; (*goût, son, etc.*) sweetness; (*personne*) gentleness.

douche [duʃ] *nf* shower.

douer [dwe] *v* endow. **doué** *adj* gifted, talented.

douille [duj] *nf* socket; cartridge case.

douillet, -ette [dujɛ, -ɛt] *adj* cosy, soft.

douleur [dulœr] *nf* pain; (*chagrin*) sorrow, distress. **douloureux** *adj* painful; distressing.

douter [dute] *v* douter of doubt. **se douter de** suspect. **doute** *nm* doubt. **mettre en doute** question. **sans doute** doubtless. **douteux** *adj* doubtful; uncertain; (*péj*) dubious.

douve [duv] *nf* moat, ditch.

Douvres [duvrə] *n* Dover.

doux, douce [du, dus] *adj* soft; (*clément, pas fort*) mild; (*agréable, sucré*) sweet; (*personne, pente*) gentle.

douze [duz] *nm, adj* twelve. **douzaine** *nf* dozen. **douzième** *n(m+f), adj* twelfth.

doyen, -enne *nm, nf* dean; senior member.

drachme [drakmə] *nf* drachma.

dragée [draʒe] *nf* sugared almond.

dragon [dragɔ̃] *nm* dragon.

draguer [drage] *v* dredge, drag.

dramatiser [dramatize] *v* dramatize. **dramatique** *adj* dramatic.

dramaturge [dramatyrʒ] *nm, nf* dramatist, playwright.

drame [dram] *nm* drama.

drap [dra] *nm* sheet.

drapeau [drapo] *nm* flag.

draper [drape] *v* drape. **draperie** *nf* drapery. **drapier** *nm* draper.

dresser [drese] *v* put up, erect; (*liste, plan*) draw up; (*lever*) raise; (*animal*) train. **dresser l'oreille** prick up one's ears. **se dresser** stand (up); rise (up). **dressage** *nm* training. **dressoir** *nm* dresser.

drogue [drɔg] *nf* drug. **drogué, -e** *nm, nf* drug addict. **se droguer** take drugs.

droit¹ [drwa] *adj* (*côté*) right; (*ligne*) straight; (*vertical*) upright; honest. *adv* straight. **droitier** *adj* right-handed.

droit² [drwa] *nm* right; (*taxe*) duty; (*d'entrée, etc.*) fee, charge; (*jur*) law. **droits d'auteur** royalties *pl*. **droit de passage** right of way.

droite [drwat] *nf* right, right-hand side.

drôle [drol] *adj* funny. **drôlement** *adv* (*fam*) terribly, awfully.

dromadaire [drɔmadɛr] *nm* dromedary.

dru [dry] *adj* thick, dense. *adv* thick and fast; (*pluie*) heavily.

du [dy] *contraction of* **de le**.

dû, due [dy] *adj* owing, due. *nm* due.

duc [dyk] *nm* duke. **duchesse** *nf* duchess.

duel [dɥɛl] *nm* duel.

dûment [dymɑ̃] *adv* duly.

dune [dyn] *nf* dune.

Dunkerque [dœkɛrk] *n* Dunkirk.

duo [dɥo] *nm* duet.

duper [dype] *v* dupe, deceive.

duquel [dykɛl] *contraction of* **de lequel**.

dur [dyr] *adj* hard, stiff, tough; (*pénible*) harsh. *adv* (*fam*) hard. **à la dure** rough. **durcir** *v* harden. **dureté** *nf* hardness.

durer [dyre] *v* last. **durable** *adj* lasting. **durant** *prep* during, for. **durée** *nf* duration, length; (*ampoule, pile, etc.*) life.

duvet [dyvɛ] *nm* down; sleeping-bag.

dynamique [dinamik] *adj* dynamic. *nf* dynamics. **dynamisme** *nm* dynamism.

dynamite [dinamit] *nf* dynamite.

dynamo [dinamo] *nf* dynamo.

dynastie [dinasti] *nf* dynasty.

dysenterie [disɑ̃tri] *nf* dysentery.

dyslexie [disleksi] *nf* dyslexia. **dyslexique** *n(m + f)*, *adj* dyslexic.

dyspepsie [dispɛpsi] *nf* dyspepsia.

E

eau [o] *nf* water. **eau de Javel** bleach. **eau de vie** brandy. **eau douce** fresh water. **eau gazeuse** soda water. **eau minérale** mineral water. **eau potable** drinking water. **eau salée** salt water. **faire eau** leak. **prendre l'eau** leak.

ébahir [ebair] *v* astound. **ébahi** *adj* flabbergasted, dumbfounded. **ébahissement** *nm* astonishment.

ébats [eba] *nm pl* frolics *pl*.

ébaucher [ebofe] *v* sketch out, outline. **s'ébaucher** take shape. **ébauche** *nf* outline, rough draft.

ébène [ebɛn] *nf* ebony.

éberlué [eberlɥe] *adj* astounded, flabbergasted.

éblouir [ebluir] *v* dazzle. **éblouissement** *nm* dazzle; (*méd*) dizzy turn.

éboulement [ebulmɑ̃] *nm* landslide.

ébouriffer [eburife] *v* tousle, ruffle; (*fam*) amaze.

ébranler [ebrɑ̃le] *v* shake; (*affaiblir*) weaken. **s'ébranler** move off. **ébranlement** *nm* (*choc*) shock; weakening.

ébrécher [ebrefe] *v* chip, nick; (*fortune*) break into. **ébréchure** *nf* chip, nick.

ébrouer [ebrue] *v* snort; (*s'agiter*) shake oneself. **ébrouement** *nm* snort.

ébullition [ebylisjɔ̃] *nf* boiling point; (*agitation*) turmoil. **en ébullition** boiling; (*ville, personne*) seething.

écailler [ekaje] *v* scale. **s'écailler** flake, peel. **écaille** *nf* scale; (*peinture*) flake; (*de tortue*) tortoise-shell. **écailleux** *adj* scaly; flaky.

écaler [ekale] *v* shell. **écale** *nf* shell.

écarlate [ekarlat] *nf, adj* scarlet.

écarquiller [ekarkije] *v* open wide.

écart [ekar] *nm* gap; difference; (*contradiction*) discrepancy; (*faute*) lapse. **à l'écart** on one side; (*isolé*) out of the way; (*distant*) aloof. **à l'écart de** well away from. **faire le grand écart** do the splits. **faire un écart** (*cheval*) shy; (*auto*) swerve.

écarter [ekarte] v separate, open; (exclure) dismiss; (éloigner) push aside, lead away from. **s'écarter** (séparer) part; (s'éloigner) move away; deviate, wander. **écarté** adj remote.

ecclésiastique [eklezjastik] adj ecclesiastical. nm ecclesiastic.

écervelé [esɛrvəle], **-e** adj scatterbrained. nm, nf scatterbrain.

échafaud [eʃafo] nm scaffold. **échafaudage** nm scaffolding.

échalier [eʃalje] nm stile.

échalote [eʃalɔt] nf shallot.

échancré [eʃɑ̃kre] adj (robe) V-necked, with a scooped neckline; (côte) indented; (feuille) serrated.

échanger [eʃɑ̃ʒe] v exchange. **échange** nm exchange. **échangeable** adj exchangeable.

échantillon [eʃɑ̃tijɔ̃] nm sample.

échapper [eʃape] v escape. **échapper à** escape (from). **laisser échapper** let out, let slip. **échappatoire** nf loophole, way out. **échappement** nm (auto) exhaust.

écharde [eʃard] nf splinter.

écharpe [eʃarp] nf scarf; (méd) sling; (maire) sash.

échasse [eʃas] nf stilt.

échauder [eʃode] v scald; (laver) wash in hot water; (théière) warm.

échauffer [eʃofe] v make hot; (moteur) overheat; excite. **s'échauffer** (sport) warm up; (s'animer) become heated. **échauffement** nm overheating; warm-up.

échéance [eʃeɑ̃s] nf expiry date; date of payment; term. **échéant** adj due, payable. **le cas échéant** if the case arises.

échec [eʃɛk] nm failure; (revers) setback; (jeu) check. **échec et mat** checkmate. **échecs** nm pl (jeu) chess sing.

échelle [eʃɛl] nf ladder; (carte, etc.) scale.

échelon [eʃlɔ̃] nm rung; step, grade; (niveau) level.

échelonner [eʃlɔne] v space or spread out; (vacances, etc.) stagger.

échevelé [eʃəvle] adj dishevelled; (effréné) wild.

échine [eʃin] nf spine.

échiquier [eʃikje] nm chessboard.

écho [eko] nm echo.

*échoir** [eʃwar] v fall due; expire.

échouer [eʃwe] v fail; (naut) run aground; (aboutir) end up. **faire échouer** foil, thwart.

éclabousser [eklabuse] v splash. **éclaboussure** nf splash; (tache) stain, smear.

éclair [eklɛr] nm flash; (temps) lightning; (cuisine) éclair.

éclaircir [eklɛrsir] v lighten; (soupe, plantes) thin; (question, mystère) explain, clarify. **s'éclaircir** (temps) clear up; thin out, become thin. **éclaircie** nf bright interval, break. **éclaircissement** nm clarification.

éclairer [eklere] v light up; (problème, texte) throw light on; (personne) enlighten. **s'éclairer** light up; (rue, maison, etc.) be lit. **éclairage** nm lighting. **éclaireur** nm scout. **éclaireuse** nf guide.

éclat [ekla] nm brightness; splendour, glamour; fragment, splinter; (rire, colère) burst; (scandale) fuss.

éclater [eklate] v (pneu) burst; (bombe) explode; (briser) break up, shatter; (guerre) break out. **éclater de rire** burst out laughing. **faire éclater** blow up. **éclatant** adj bright; (fort) loud; (victoire) resounding.

éclipse [eklips] nf eclipse. **éclipser** v eclipse.

éclisse [eklis] nf splint.

éclopé [eklɔpe] adj lame.

*éclore** [eklɔr] v hatch; (fleur) open out. **éclosion** nf hatching; (apparition) birth, dawn.

écluse [eklyz] nf lock.

écœurer [ekœre] v nauseate, sicken; disgust. **écœurant** adj disgusting; (gâteau) sickly. **écœurement** nm nausea; disgust; discouragement.

école [ekɔl] nf school. **école de secrétariat** secretarial college. **école maternelle** nursery school. **école normale** college of education. **faire l'école buissonnière** play truant. **écolier** nm schoolboy. **écolière** nf schoolgirl.

écologie [ekɔlɔʒi] nf ecology. **écologique** adj ecological.

*éconduire** [ekɔ̃dɥir] v dismiss; reject.

économe [ekɔnɔm] adj thrifty. **économie** nf economy; (science) economics; (épargne) saving. **faire des économies** save. **économique** adj economic.

économiser [ekɔnɔmize] v economize, save. **économiste** n(m+f) economist.

écoper [ekɔpe] v bale out.

écorce [ekɔrs] nf peel; (arbre) bark. **écorce** nf peel; bark.

écorcher [ekɔrʃe] v (animal) skin; (égratigner) graze, scratch; (frotter) chafe;

(*fam: estamper*) fleece. **écorchure** *nf* graze, scratch.

écorné [ekɔrne] *adj* (*livre*) dog-eared.

Écosse [ekɔs] *nf* Scotland. **écossais** *adj* Scottish, Scots; (*whisky*) Scotch; (*tissu*) tartan. **Écossais, -e** *nm, nf* Scot.

écot [eko] *nm* share.

écouler [ekule] *v* get rid of; (*comm*) move, sell. **s'écouler** (*liquide*) flow, ooze; pass; sell. **écoulement** *nm* flow; (*méd*) discharge; passing.

écourter [ekurte] *v* shorten.

écouter [ekute] *v* listen (to). **écouter aux portes** eavesdrop.

écouteur, -euse [ekutœr, -øz] *nm, nf* listener; eavesdropper. *nm* (*telephone*) receiver. **écouteurs** *nm pl* headphones *pl*.

écran [ekrã] *nm* screen.

écraser [ekraze] *v* crush; (*voiture*) run over; (*accabler*) overcome. **s'écraser** (*voiture, avion*) crash. **se faire écraser** get run over. **écrasant** *adj* overwhelming; (*poids*) crushing; (*travail*) gruelling.

écrémer [ekreme] *v* cream, skim.

écrevisse [ekrəvis] *nf* crayfish.

s'écrier [ekrije] *v* exclaim.

écrin [ekrɛ̃] *nm* jewel case.

***écrire** [ekrir] *v* write. **écrit** *nm* writing. **par écrit** in writing. **écrit** (*examen*) written paper. **par écrit** in writing. **écriteau** *nm* notice. **écritoire** *nf* writing case. **écriture** *nf* writing; (*comm*) entry.

écrivain [ekrivɛ̃] *nm* writer.

s'écrouler [ekrule] *v* collapse, crumble, fall (down). **écroulement** *nm* collapse, fall.

écru [ekry] *adj* raw; (*toile*) unbleached.

écu [eky] *nm* shield.

écueil [ekœj] *nm* reef; (*piège*) pitfall.

écuelle [ekɥɛl] *nf* bowl.

écumer [ekyme] *v* skim; (*mousser*) foam, froth; pillage, scour. **écume** *nf* foam, froth; (*crasse*) scum. **écumeux** *adj* frothy.

écureuil [ekyrœj] *nm* squirrel.

écurie [ekyri] *nf* stable.

écuyer [ekɥije], **-ère** *nm, nf* rider.

eczéma [ɛgzema] *nm* eczema.

édenté [edãte] *adj* toothless.

édifice [edifis] *nm* building; structure. **édifier** [edifje] *v* edify; construct, build.

Edimbourg [edɛ̃bur] *n* Edinburgh.

édit [edi] *nm* edict.

éditer [edite] *v* publish; (*annoter*) edit. **éditeur, -trice** *nm, nf* publisher; editor.

édition *nf* publishing; edition. **éditorial** *nm* leading article.

édredon [edrədɔ̃] *nm* eiderdown.

éducation [edykasjɔ̃] *nf* education; (*familiale*) upbringing. **éducatif** *adj* educational.

éduquer [edyke] *v* educate; (*élever*) bring up.

effacer [efase] *v* erase, obliterate. **s'effacer** fade, wear away; (*s'écarter*) step aside. **effacé** *adj* faded; (*personne*) retiring.

effarer [efare] *v* alarm. **effarement** *nm* alarm.

effaroucher [efaruʃe] *v* scare; shock. **s'effaroucher** take fright; be shocked.

effectif [efektif] *adj* effective, actual, real. *nm* size, strength.

effectuer [efɛktɥe] *v* carry out, make, execute.

efféminé [efemine] *adj* effeminate.

effervescence [efɛrvesãs] *nf* effervescence; agitation, turmoil.

effet [efɛ] *nm* effect; impression; (*comm*) bill. **effets** *nm pl* things *pl*, clothes *pl*. **en effet** indeed.

s'effeuiller [efœje] *v* shed its leaves.

efficace [efikas] *adj* effective; (*personne*) efficient. **efficacité** *nf* effectiveness; efficiency.

effigie [efiʒi] *nf* effigy.

effiler [efile] *v* (*amincir*) taper; (*forme*) streamline; (*étoffe*) fray.

effleurer [eflœre] *v* touch lightly.

s'effondrer [efɔ̃dre] *v* collapse, cave in. **effondrement** *nm* collapse.

s'efforcer [eforse] *v* try hard, do one's best.

effort [efor] *nm* effort; (*tech*) stress.

effrayer [efreje] *v* frighten.

effréné [efrene] *adj* wild, frantic.

effriter [efrite] *v* crumble. .

effroi [efrwa] *nm* terror. **effroyable** *adj* appalling.

effronté [efrɔ̃te] *adj* insolent, cheeky; (*honte*) brazen. **effronterie** *nf* insolence.

égal [egal], **-e** *adj* equal; (*constant*) even. **ça m'est égal** I don't mind. *nm, nf* equal. **également** *adv* equally; (*aussi*) also. **égaler** *v* equal, match. **égalité** *nf* equality; evenness.

égaliser [egalize] *v* equalize; (*sol*) level out.

égard [egar] *nm* respect, consideration. **à l'égard de** (*envers*) towards; concerning. **avoir égard à** take into account.

égarer [egare] *v* lead astray; *(perdre)* mislay. **s'égarer** get lost. **égaré** *adj* lost; *(animal)* stray; *(isolé)* remote; *(éperdu)* distraught.

égayer [egeje] *v* brighten up; *(divertir)* amuse.

église [egliz] *nf* church.

égocentrique [egɔsɑ̃trik] *adj* self-centred.

égoïste [egɔist] *adj* selfish. **égoïsme** *nm* selfishness.

égorger [egɔrʒe] *v* cut the throat of.

égout [egu] *nm* sewer, drain.

égoutter [egute] *v* drain; *(linge)* drip. **égouttoir** *nm* draining board.

égratigner [egratiɲe] *v* scratch, scrape. **égratignure** *nf* scratch.

égrener [egrane] *v (écosser)* shell; *(raisins)* pick off; *(chapelet)* say.

éhonté [eɔ̃te] *adj* shameless, brazen.

éjaculer [eʒakyle] *v* ejaculate. **éjaculation** *nf* ejaculation.

éjecter [eʒɛkte] *v* eject.

élaborer [elabɔre] *v* work out, elaborate.

élaguer [elage] *v* prune. **élagage** *nm* pruning.

élan [elɑ̃] *nm* rush, surge; *(vitesse)* momentum; vigour, spirit. **s'élancer** [elɑ̃se] *v* rush, dash. **élancé** *adj* slender. **élancement** *nm* sharp pain.

élargir [elarʒir] *v* widen, stretch; *(jur)* release.

élastique [elastik] *adj* elastic; flexible. *nm* elastic; rubber band.

élection [elɛksjɔ̃] *nf* election; choice. **élection partielle** by-election.

électoral [elɛktɔral] *adj* electoral. **électorat** *nm* electorate.

électricité [elɛktrisite] *nf* electricity. **électricien** *nm* electrician.

électrique [elɛktrik] *adj* electric.

électriser [elɛktrize] *v* electrify.

électrocuter [elɛktrɔkyte] *v* electrocute. **électrocution** *nf* electrocution.

électrode [elɛktrɔd] *nf* electrode.

électronique [elɛktrɔnik] *adj* electronic. *nf* electronics.

électrophone [elɛktrɔfɔn] *nm* record player.

élégant [elegɑ̃] *adj* elegant. **élégance** *nf* elegance.

élégie [eleʒi] *nf* elegy.

élément [elemɑ̃] *nm* element; fact; *(préfabriqué)* unit. **éléments** *nm pl* rudiments *pl*. **élémentaire** *adj* elementary, basic.

éléphant [elefɑ̃] *nm* elephant.

élevage [elvaʒ] *nm* breeding, rearing; farm. **faire l'élevage de** breed, rear.

élévation [elevasjɔ̃] *nf* elevation; *(action)* raising; erection.

élève [elɛv] *n(m+f)* pupil, student.

élever [elve] *v* raise; *(enfant)* bring up; *(animal)* rear, breed; erect. **s'élever** rise, go up. **s'élever à** add up to. **élevé** *adj* high, lofty. **bien/mal élevé** well-/ill-mannered.

elfe [ɛlf] *nm* elf.

éligible [eliʒiblə] *adj* eligible.

éliminer [elimine] *v* eliminate. **élimination** *nf* elimination.

*****élire** [elir] *v* elect.

élite [elit] *nf* elite.

elle [ɛl] *pron (sujet: personne)* she; *(objet: personne)* her; *(chose, animal)* it. **elle-même** *pron* herself; itself. **elles** *pron (sujet)* they; *(objet)* them. **elles-mêmes** *pron* themselves.

ellipse [elips] *nf* ellipse. **elliptique** *adj* elliptical.

élocution [elɔkysjɔ̃] *nf* elocution, diction. **défaut d'élocution** *nm* speech impediment.

éloge [elɔʒ] *nm* praise. **faire l'éloge de** praise.

éloigner [elwaɲe] *v* remove; move or take away; *(ajourner)* postpone. **s'éloigner** go away. **éloigné** *adj* distant, far. **éloignement** *nm* distance; removal; absence; postponement.

éloquent [elɔkɑ̃] *adj* eloquent. **éloquence** *nf* eloquence.

élu [ely], **-e** *adj* elected, chosen. *nm, nf* elected member or representative.

éluder [elyde] *v* evade, elude.

émaciation [emasjasjɔ̃] *nf* emaciation. **émacié** *adj* emaciated.

émail [emaj] *nm, pl* **-aux** enamel. **émailler** *v* enamel; *(parsemer)* dot.

émanciper [emɑ̃sipe] *v* emancipate, liberate. **émancipation** *nf* emancipation, liberation.

emballer [ɑ̃bale] *v* pack, wrap; *(fam)* thrill. **s'emballer** *(moteur)* race; *(cheval)* bolt; *(fam)* get worked up. **emballage** *nm* packing, wrapping; *(comm)* package.

embarcadère [ɑ̃barkader] *nm* landing stage, pier.

embardée [ɑ̃barde] *nf* swerve. **faire une embardée** swerve.

embargo [ãbargo] nm embargo.

embarquer [ãbarke] v embark, board; (cargaison) load. s'embarquer dans (fam) get involved in. embarquement nm boarding; loading.

embarras [ãbara] nm obstacle; (gêne) embarrassment; (situation difficile) predicament; dilemma. faire des embarras make a fuss.

embarrasser [ãbarase] v hinder, hamper; put in a predicament. s'embarrasser be troubled; (s'emmêler) get tangled up. embarrassant adj awkward. embarrassé adj embarrassed, ill-at-ease; confused.

embaucher [ãboʃe] v take on, hire.

embaumer [ãbome] v embalm; perfume; (sentir bon) be fragrant.

embellir [ãbelir] v make attractive; embellish. embellissement nm embellishment.

embêter [ãbete] (fam) v bother, annoy. s'embêter be fed up. embêtement nm nuisance, annoyance.

emblée [ãble] adv d'emblée straight away.

emblème [ãblɛm] nm emblem.

emboîter [ãbwate] v fit together.

embouchure [ãbuʃyr] nf (fleuve) mouth; (musique) mouthpiece.

embouteiller [ãbuteje] v block. embouteillage nm traffic jam.

emboutir [ãbutir] v crash into.

embrancher [ãbrãʃe] v join up. embranchement nm branch; junction.

embraser [ãbraze] v set ablaze. s'embraser blaze up, flare up. embrasement nm blaze.

embrasser [ãbrase] v embrace; (donner un baiser) kiss.

embrayer [ãbreje] v (auto) let in the clutch. embrayage nm clutch.

embrouiller [ãbruje] v muddle (up); (ficelle) tangle (up).

embryon [ãbrijõ] nm embryo.

embuscade [ãbyskad] nf ambush.

éméché [emeʃe] adj tipsy.

émeraude [emrod] nf, adj emerald.

émerger [emɛrʒe] v emerge.

émerveiller [emɛrveje] v fill with wonder. s'émerveiller de marvel at. émerveillement nm wonder.

*émettre [emɛtrə] v give out, emit; (TV, radio) transmit, broadcast; (monnaie, etc.) issue. émetteur nm transmitter.

émeu [emø] nm emu.

émeute [emøt] nf riot.

émietter [emjete] v crumble; split up, disperse.

émigrer [emigre] v emigrate; (oiseau) migrate. émigrant, -e nm, nf emigrant. émigration nf emigration.

éminent [eminã] adj eminent.

émission [emisjõ] nf (radio, TV) programme, broadcast; emission; issue.

emmagasiner [ãmagazine] v store (up). emmagasinage nm storage.

emmancher [ãmãʃe] v put a handle on; (fam) make a start (on).

emmanchure [ãmãʃyr] nf armhole.

emmêler [ãmele] v tangle; confuse, muddle.

emménager [ãmenaʒe] v move in.

emmener [ãmne] v take (away), (équipe) lead.

emmitoufler [ãmitufle] v muffle up.

émoi [emwa] nm agitation, commotion.

émonder [emõde] v prune.

émotion [emosjõ] nf emotion; (peur) fright. émotif or émotionnel adj emotional.

émousser [emuse] v blunt, dull. émoussé adj blunt.

*émouvoir [emuvwar] v move, affect; (indigner) rouse; (troubler) upset. émouvant adj (compassion) moving, touching; (admiration) stirring.

empailler [ãpaje] v stuff.

empaqueter [ãpakte] v pack, wrap up. empaquetage nm packing.

emparer [ãpare] v s'emparer de seize, take possession of.

empâter [ãpate] v thicken, fatten.

empêcher [ãpeʃe] v prevent, stop. n'empêche (que) all the same.

empereur [ãprœr] nm emperor.

empeser [ãpəze] v starch.

empester [ãpeste] v stink.

s'empêtrer [ãpetre] v get entangled or involved.

empiéter [ãpjete] v encroach.

s'empiffrer [ãpifre] v (fam) stuff oneself.

empiler [ãpile] v pile, stack.

empire [ãpir] nm empire; influence.

empirer [ãpire] v worsen.

empirique [ãpirik] adj empirical.

emplacement [ãplasmã] nm site.

emplâtre [ãplatrə] nm plaster.

emplette [ãplɛt] nf purchase. faire des emplettes do some shopping.

emplir [ɑ̃plir] v fill.

emploi [ɑ̃plwa] nm use; (poste) job, employment. **emploi du temps** timetable, schedule.

employer [ɑ̃plwaje] v use; (ouvrier) employ. **s'employer à** apply oneself to. **employé, -e** nm, nf employee; (bureau) clerk. **employeur, -euse** nm, nf employer.

empoigner [ɑ̃pwaɲe] v grasp, grab; (lecture, etc.) grip.

empoisonner [ɑ̃pwazɔne] v poison; (empester) stink; (fam) annoy, aggravate. **empoisonnement** nm poisoning; (fam) bother.

emporter [ɑ̃pɔrte] v take (away); (entraîner) carry away or along; (gagner) win. **l'emporter sur** get the better of. **s'emporter** lose one's temper. **emporté** adj angry; (personne) quick-tempered. **emportement** nm anger.

s'empourprer [ɑ̃purpre] v flush, turn crimson.

empreindre [ɑ̃prɛ̃dra] v imprint; (marquer) stamp, tinge.

empreinte [ɑ̃prɛ̃t] nf impression; mark, stamp; (animal) track. **empreinte de pas** footprint. **empreinte digitale** fingerprint.

s'empresser [ɑ̃prese] v (se hâter) hurry; (s'affairer) bustle around. **empressé** adj attentive; (péj) over-zealous. **empressement** nm attentiveness; (hâte) eagerness.

emprisonner [ɑ̃prizɔne] v imprison. **emprisonnement** nm imprisonment.

emprunter [ɑ̃prœ̃te] v borrow; derive. **emprunt** nm loan. **d'emprunt** (nom) assumed. **emprunté** adj ill-at-ease, awkward.

ému [emy] adj moved, touched; excited; emotional.

emulsion [emylsjɔ̃] nf emulsion.

en[1] [ɑ̃] prep in; (à) to; (transport) by; (comme) as; (composition) made of; (durée) while, when.

en[2] [ɑ̃] pron of it or them; (lieu) from there; (cause) about it; (des) some, any.

encadrer [ɑ̃kadre] v frame; (entourer) surround; (instruire) train. **encadrement** nm frame; training.

encaisser [ɑ̃kese] v collect; (chèque) cash. **encaisse** nf cash in hand.

enceinte[1] [ɑ̃sɛ̃t] adj pregnant.

enceinte[2] [ɑ̃sɛ̃t] nf enclosure; (mur) surrounding wall; (palissade) fence.

encens [ɑ̃sɑ̃] nm incense.

encercler [ɑ̃serkle] v surround, encircle.

enchaîner [ɑ̃ʃene] v chain up; (lier) link together; continue, carry on. **enchaînement** nm series, chain.

enchanter [ɑ̃ʃɑ̃te] v enchant; (ravir) delight. **enchanté** adj delighted; (salutation) pleased to meet you. **enchantement** nm enchantment; magic; delight.

enchère [ɑ̃ʃer] nf bid. **enchères** nf pl auction sing.

enchérir [ɑ̃ʃerir] v **enchérir sur** (comm) bid higher than; (dépasser) go further than. **enchérisseur, -euse** nm, nf bidder.

enchevêtrer [ɑ̃ʃəvetre] v entangle; confuse, muddle.

enclin [ɑ̃klɛ̃] adj inclined, prone.

enclore [ɑ̃klɔr] v enclose, shut in.

enclos [ɑ̃klo] nm enclosure; (chevaux) paddock.

enclume [ɑ̃klym] nf anvil.

encoche [ɑ̃kɔʃ] nf notch.

encoignure [ɑ̃kɔɲyr] nf corner.

encolure [ɑ̃kɔlyr] nf neck; (comm) collar size.

encombrer [ɑ̃kɔ̃bre] v clutter, obstruct; (ligne téléphonique) block. **s'encombrer de** load oneself with. **encombrant** adj cumbersome. **sans encombre** without mishap. **encombrement** nm congestion; clutter.

à l'encontre [ɑ̃kɔ̃tra] prep **à l'encontre de** against, counter to; contrary to.

encore [ɑ̃kɔr] adv (toujours) still; (de nouveau) again; (en plus) more; (aussi) also; (même) even. **pas encore** not yet.

encorner [ɑ̃kɔrne] v gore.

encourager [ɑ̃kuraʒe] v encourage. **encouragement** nm encouragement.

encourir [ɑ̃kurir] v incur.

encrasser [ɑ̃krase] v clog (up); (salir) dirty.

encre [ɑ̃kra] nf ink.

encroûter [ɑ̃krute] v encrust. **s'encroûter** (fam) get into a rut.

encyclopédie [ɑ̃siklɔpedi] nf encyclopedia.

endémique [ɑ̃demik] adj endemic.

s'endetter [ɑ̃dete] v get into debt. **endetté** adj in debt.

endiablé [ɑ̃djable] adj boisterous, wild.

s'endimancher [ɑ̃dimɑ̃ʃe] v put on one's Sunday best.

endive [ɑ̃div] nf endive; chicory.

endoctriner [ɑ̃dɔktrine] v indoctrinate. **endoctrination** nf indoctrination.

endolori [ɑ̃dɔlɔri] *adj* painful.

endommager [ɑ̃dɔmaʒe] *v* damage. **endommagement** *nm* damage.

*endormir [ɑ̃dɔrmir] *v* send to sleep; *(douleur)* deaden. **s'endormir** *v* fall asleep. **endormi** *adj* asleep.

endosser [ɑ̃dose] *v (vêtement)* put on; *(chèque, etc.)* endorse. **endossement** *nm* endorsement.

endroit [ɑ̃drwa] *nm* place; *(roman, film, etc.)* point, part. **à l'endroit** *(vêtement)* the right side out; *(objet)* the right way round.

*enduire [ɑ̃dɥir] *v* coat. **enduit** *nm* coating.

endurcir [ɑ̃dyrsir] *v* harden.

endurer [ɑ̃dyre] *v* endure. **endurance** *nf* endurance.

énergie [enerʒi] *nf* energy; *(fermeté)* spirit, force. **énergique** *adj* energetic, forceful.

énerver [enɛrve] *v* irritate. **s'énerver** get excited.

enfant [ɑ̃fɑ̃] *n(m+f)* child *(pl* children). **enfant unique** only child. **enfance** *nf* childhood; *(bébé)* infancy. **enfantin** *adj* childlike; *(puéril)* childish.

enfanter [ɑ̃fɑ̃te] *v* give birth (to).

enfer [ɑ̃fɛr] *nm* hell.

enfermer [ɑ̃fɛrme] *v* shut up or in; *(sous clef)* lock up.

enfiler [ɑ̃file] *v* thread; *(fam: vêtement)* slip on; *(rue, etc.)* take.

enfin [ɑ̃fɛ̃] *adv* at last, finally; *(bref)* in short; *(après tout)* after all.

enflammer [ɑ̃flame] *v (allumer)* set fire to; *(irriter)* inflame. **s'enflammer** catch fire; *(colère, désir)* flare up. **enflammé** *adj* blazing; inflamed.

enfler [ɑ̃fle] *v* swell. **enflé** *adj* swollen. **enflure** *nf* swelling.

enfoncer [ɑ̃fɔ̃se] *v (clou, etc.)* drive in; *(porte)* break down. **s'enfoncer** sink, plunge.

enfouir [ɑ̃fwir] *v* bury.

*enfreindre [ɑ̃frɛ̃dr ə] *v* infringe.

*s'enfuir [ɑ̃fɥir] *v* run away.

engager [ɑ̃gaʒe] *v* engage; *(lier)* bind; *(entraîner)* involve; *(clef, etc.)* insert. **s'engager** *(promettre)* commit oneself, undertake; *(mil)* enlist. **engagement** *nm (promesse)* agreement; enlistment; *(acteur)* engagement.

engelure [ɑ̃ʒlyr] *nf* chilblain.

engendrer [ɑ̃ʒɑ̃dre] *v* generate, create.

engin [ɑ̃ʒɛ̃] *nm* machine; *(outil)* tool.

englober [ɑ̃glɔbe] *v* include.

engloutir [ɑ̃glutir] *v (navire)* swallow up; *(manger)* gulp down.

engorger [ɑ̃gɔrʒe] *v* block.

engouffrer [ɑ̃gufre] *v* engulf. *(fam: manger)* wolf down. **s'engouffrer** rush.

engourdir [ɑ̃gurdir] *v* numb; *(esprit)* dull. **engourdi** *adj* numb. **engourdissement** *nm* numbness.

engrais [ɑ̃grɛ] *nm* fertilizer; *(organique)* manure.

engraisser [ɑ̃grese] *v (animal)* fatten up; *(terre)* fertilize.

engrenage [ɑ̃grənaʒ] *nm (tech)* gearing; *(enchaînement)* chain.

engueuler [ɑ̃gœle] *(fam) v* shout at. **s'engueuler** have a row. **engueulade** *nf* shouting at; *(dispute)* row.

enhardir [ɑ̃ardir] *v* embolden. **s'enhardir** become bolder.

énigme [enigmə] *nf (mystère)* enigma; *(devinette)* riddle, puzzle. **énigmatique** *adj* enigmatic.

enivrer [ɑ̃nivre] *v* intoxicate. **s'enivrer** get drunk. **enivrement** *nm* intoxication.

enjamber [ɑ̃ʒɑ̃be] *v* step over; *(pont)* straddle. **enjambée** *nf* stride.

enjeu [ɑ̃ʒø] *nm* stake.

enjôler [ɑ̃ʒole] *v* coax.

enjoliveur [ɑ̃ʒɔlivœr] *nm (auto)* hub cap.

enjoué [ɑ̃ʒwe] *adj* jolly, playful. **enjouement** *nm* jollity, playfulness.

enlacer [ɑ̃lase] *v* entwine. **s'enlacer** *(fils)* intertwine; *(amants)* embrace.

enlaidir [ɑ̃ledir] *v (déparer)* make ugly; *(personne)* become ugly.

enlever [ɑ̃lve] *v* remove, take off or away; kidnap. **s'enlever** come off. **enlèvement** *nm* kidnapping; removal.

enliser [ɑ̃lize] *v* get stuck. **s'enliser** sink.

ennemi [ɛnmi], **-e** *nm, nf* enemy. *adj* hostile. **être ennemi de** be opposed to.

ennui [ɑ̃nɥi] *nm* boredom; *(difficulté)* trouble.

ennuyer [ɑ̃nɥije] *v (lasser)* bore; *(inquiéter)* worry; *(importuner)* bother; *(agacer)* annoy. **s'ennuyer** be bored. **ennuyeux** *adj* boring, annoying.

énoncer [enɔ̃se] *v* state.

enorgueillir [ɑ̃nɔrgœjir] *v* make proud. **s'enorgueillir de** boast about.

énorme [enɔrm] *adj* enormous. **énormément** *adv* tremendously. **énormément de** a tremendous amount of.

s'enquérir [ɑ̃kerir] v inquire. **s'enquérir de** ask after.

enquête [ɑ̃kɛt] nf inquiry; (police) investigation; (sondage) survey; (mort) inquest. **enquêter** v investigate.

enraciné [ɑ̃rasine] adj deep-rooted, entrenched.

enragé [ɑ̃raʒe], **-e** nm, nf (fam) fanatic. adj furious; (fam) mad keen. **enrager** v be furious.

enrayer [ɑ̃reje] v (maladie) check; (machine) jam. **s'enrayer** jam.

enregistrer [ɑ̃rʒistre] v register; (son) record. **enregistrement** nm registration; recording.

s'enrhumer [ɑ̃ryme] v catch a cold. **être enrhumé** have a cold.

enrichir [ɑ̃riʃir] v enrich. **enrichissement** nm enrichment.

enrôler [ɑ̃role] v enrol; (mil) enlist. **enrôlé** nm recruit. **enrôlement** nm enrolment; enlistment.

enroué [ɑ̃rwe] v hoarse.

enseigne [ɑ̃sɛɲ] nf sign; (mil, naut) ensign.

enseigner [ɑ̃seɲe] v teach. **enseignant, -e** nm, nf teacher. **enseignement** nm education; teaching.

ensemble [ɑ̃sɑ̃blə] adv together. nm whole; unity; (groupe) set; (vêtements) outfit. **dans l'ensemble** on the whole. **d'ensemble** overall.

ensemencer [ɑ̃smɑ̃se] v sow.

ensevelir [ɑ̃səvlir] v bury; (cacher) shroud, hide.

ensoleillé [ɑ̃sɔleje] adj sunny.

ensorceler [ɑ̃sɔrsəle] v bewitch, cast a spell on.

ensuite [ɑ̃sɥit] adv then, next; afterwards.

*s'ensuivre [ɑ̃sɥivrə] v follow.

entaille [ɑ̃taj] nf cut, gash, notch. **entailler** v cut, gash, notch.

entamer [ɑ̃tame] v start (on), open; (couper) cut into.

entasser [ɑ̃tase] v pile up; amass; (serrer) cram.

entendre [ɑ̃tɑ̃drə] v hear; (écouter) listen to; (comprendre) understand; intend, mean. **entendre parler de** hear of. **s'entendre** agree; (s'accorder) get on. **entendu** adj agreed; understood. **bien entendu** of course.

entente [ɑ̃tɑ̃t] nf understanding; (accord) agreement; harmony.

enterrer [ɑ̃tere] v bury. **enterrement** nm burial; (cérémonie) funeral.

en-tête [ɑ̃tɛt] nm heading. **papier à lettres à en-tête** nm headed notepaper.

entêté [ɑ̃tete] adj stubborn. **entêtement** nm stubbornness.

enthousiaste [ɑ̃tuzjast] v enthusiast. adj enthusiastic. **enthousiasme** nm enthusiasm. **s'enthousiasmer** v be enthusiastic.

enticher [ɑ̃tiʃe] v **s'enticher de** become infatuated with.

entier [ɑ̃tje] adj entire, whole; intact; absolute. **en entier** totally. **tout entier** entirely, completely.

entité [ɑ̃tite] nf entity.

entonnoir [ɑ̃tɔnwar] nm funnel.

entorse [ɑ̃tɔrs] nf sprain, twist.

entortiller [ɑ̃tɔrtije] v twist, wind; (fam: enjôler) get round. **s'entortiller** twist; get entangled.

entourer [ɑ̃ture] v surround. **entourage** nm circle, entourage; (bordure) surround.

entracte [ɑ̃trakt] nm interval, interlude.

entrailles [ɑ̃traj] nf pl entrails pl.

entrain [ɑ̃trɛ̃] nm spirit, gusto.

entraîner [ɑ̃trene] v carry along; (causer) bring about; (athlète) train; (influencer) lead. **entraînement** nm training; force, impetus. **entraîneur, -euse** nm, nf trainer, coach.

entraver [ɑ̃trave] v hinder; (animal) shackle. **entrave** nf hindrance; shackle.

entre [ɑ̃trə] prep between; (parmi) among; (dans) in.

entrebâillé [ɑ̃trəbaje] adj ajar.

s'entrechoquer [ɑ̃trəʃɔke] v knock together; (verres) clink.

entrecouper [ɑ̃trəkupe] v interrupt, intersperse. **s'entrecouper** intersect.

s'entrecroiser [ɑ̃trəkrwaze] v (fils) intertwine; (lignes) intersect.

entrée [ɑ̃tre] nf entry, entrance; (accès) admission; (début) outset; (cuisine) first course, entrée.

entrefaites [ɑ̃trəfɛt] nf pl **sur ces entrefaites** at that moment.

entrefilet [ɑ̃trəfile] nm paragraph; (journal) item.

entremets [ɑ̃trəmɛ] nm dessert.

*s'entremettre [ɑ̃trəmɛtrə] v intervene. **entremise** nf intervention.

entrepôt [ɑ̃trəpo] nm warehouse.

*entreprendre [ɑ̃trəprɑ̃drə] v undertake;

(*commencer*) begin, embark upon. **entreprenant** *adj* enterprising.

entrepreneur, -euse [ɑ̃trəprənœr, -øz] *nm, nf* contractor. **entrepreneur de pompes funèbres** undertaker.

entreprise [ɑ̃trəpriz] *nf* firm; enterprise, venture.

entrer [ɑ̃tre] *v* enter, go *or* come in. **faire entrer** (*personne*) show in; (*objet*) put in. **laisser entrer** let in.

entre-temps *adv* meanwhile.

*****entretenir** [ɑ̃trətnir] *v* maintain; (*famille*) support; (*sentiment*) keep alive. **s'entretenir** converse; support oneself. **entretien** *nm* maintenance, upkeep; (*subsistance*) keep; discussion, conversation; interview.

*****entrevoir** [ɑ̃trəvwar] *v* make out, glimpse.

entrevue [ɑ̃trəvy] *nf* meeting; interview.

entrouvert [ɑ̃truver] *adj* half-open.

envahir [ɑ̃vair] *v* invade; (*occuper*) overrun. **envahissement** *nm* invasion. **envahisseur, -euse** *nm, nf* invader.

envelopper [ɑ̃vlɔpe] *v* wrap; (*entourer*) envelop, shroud. **enveloppe** *nf* envelope; (*emballage*) wrapping, covering.

envenimer [ɑ̃vnime] *v* poison; aggravate. **s'envenimer** fester.

envergure [ɑ̃vergyr] *nf* scope, range; (*ailes*) wingspan; calibre.

envers[1] [ɑ̃ver] *prep* towards, to.

envers[2] [ɑ̃ver] *nm* wrong side; (*médaille*) reverse. **à l'envers** (*vêtement*) inside out; (*dessus dessous*) upside down; (*devant derrière*) back to front.

envier [ɑ̃vje] *v* envy. **enviable** *adj* enviable. **envie** *nf* desire; envy; (*anat*) birthmark. **avoir envie de** want, fancy. **envieux, -euse** *adj* envious.

environ [ɑ̃virɔ̃] *adv* about. **environs** *nm pl* surroundings *pl*, vicinity *sing*.

environnement [ɑ̃virɔnmɑ̃] *nm* environment.

envisager [ɑ̃vizaʒe] *v* envisage; consider.

envoi [ɑ̃vwa] *nm* sending; (*colis*) parcel, consignment.

s'envoler [ɑ̃vole] *v* fly away; (*avion*) take off; disappear, vanish.

*****envoyer** [ɑ̃vwaje] *v* send. **envoyer chercher** send for. **envoyé, -e** *nm, nf* messenger; (*pol*) envoy; (*journal*) correspondent.

enzyme [ɑ̃zim] *nm* enzyme.

épagneul [epaɲœl] *nm* spaniel.

épais, -aisse [epe, -es] *adj* thick. **épaisseur** *nf* thickness; (*neige, nuit*) depth. **épaissir** *v* thicken.

épancher [epɑ̃ʃe] *v* (*sentiments*) pour out; (*colère*) vent.

épandre [epɑ̃dr] *v* spread.

s'épanouir [epanwir] *v* blossom, open out; (*visage*) light up. **épanoui** *adj* (*fleur*) in full bloom; (*sourire*) radiant.

épargner [eparɲe] *v* save, spare. **épargne** *nf* saving.

éparpiller [eparpije] *v* scatter, disperse.

épars [epar] *adj* scattered.

épater [epate] (*fam*) *v* amaze, stagger. **épatement** *nm* amazement.

épaule [epol] *nf* shoulder.

épave [epav] *nf* wreck, ruin; (*débris*) wreckage.

épée [epe] *nf* sword.

épeler [eple] *v* spell.

éperdu [eperdy] *adj* distraught, frantic; passionate.

éperon [eprɔ̃] *nm* spur. **éperonner** *v* spur on.

éphémère [efemer] *adj* ephemeral, short-lived.

épi [epi] *nm* (*blé*) ear; (*cheveux*) tuft.

épice [epis] *nf* spice.

épicier [episje], **-ère** *nm, nf* grocer. **épicerie** *nf* grocer's; (*aliments*) groceries *pl*.

épidémie [epidemi] *nf* epidemic. **épidémique** *adj* epidemic; contagious.

épier [epje] *v* spy on; (*guetter*) watch for.

épilepsie [epilepsi] *nf* epilepsy. **épileptique** *n*(*m*+*f*), *adj* epileptic.

épiler [epile] *v* remove hair from; (*sourcils*) pluck.

épilogue [epilɔg] *nm* epilogue; conclusion.

épinards [epinar] *nm pl* spinach *sing*.

épine [epin] *nf* (*plante*) thorn; (*animal*) spine, quill. **épine dorsale** backbone. **épineux, -euse** *adj* thorny; (*situation*) tricky.

épingle [epɛ̃glə] *nf* pin. **épingle à cheveux** hairpin. **épingle de nourrice** *or* **sûreté** safety-pin. **épingler** *v* pin.

Épiphanie [epifani] *nf* Twelfth Night, Epiphany.

épique [epik] *adj* epic.

épiscopal [episkɔpal] *adj* episcopal.

épisode [epizɔd] *nm* episode. **épisodique** *adj* episodic, occasional; secondary, minor.

épitaphe [epitaf] *nf* epitaph.

éploré [eplɔre] *adj* tearful, in tears.

éplucher [eplyʃe] *v* (*légumes*) peel; (*salade*) clean; (*texte*) examine closely. **éplucheur** *nm* peeler. **épluchures** *nf pl* peelings *pl*.

épointé [epwɛ̃te] *adj* blunt.

éponger [epɔ̃ʒe] *v* mop (up). **éponge** *nf* sponge.

épopée [epɔpe] *nf* epic.

époque [epɔk] *nf* time; (*passé*) age, era; (*géol*) period.

épouser [epuze] *v* marry. **épouse** *nf* wife.

épousseter [epuste] *v* dust. **époussetage** *nm* dusting.

épouvanter [epuvɑ̃te] *v* terrify, appal. **épouvantable** *adj* dreadful, terrible. **épouvantail** *nm* scarecrow. **épouvante** *nf* terror, dread. **film d'épouvante** *nm* horror film.

époux [epu] *nm* husband.

***éprendre** [eprɑ̃drə] *v* **s'éprendre de** fall in love with.

épreuve [eprœv] *nf* test; (*peine*) ordeal; (*sport*) event; (*texte*) proof; (*phot*) print.

éprouver [epruve] *v* feel, experience; (*subir*) suffer; test. **éprouvette** *nf* test tube.

épuiser [epɥize] *v* exhaust; use up. **épuisé** *adj* worn out; (*comm*) sold out. **épuisement** *nm* exhaustion.

épurer [epyre] *v* purify, refine. **épuration** *nf* purification, refinement.

équateur [ekwatœr] *nm* equator. **équatorial** *adj* equatorial.

équation [ekwasjɔ̃] *nf* equation.

équerre [ekɛr] *nf* set square. **en équerre** at right angles.

équestre [ekɛstrə] *adj* equestrian.

équilatéral [ekɥilateral] *adj* equilateral.

équilibre [ekilibrə] *nm* (*mental*, *tech*) equilibrium; harmony. **en équilibre** balanced. **équilibré** *adj* well-balanced. **équilibrer** *v* balance; counterbalance.

équinoxe [ekinɔks] *nm* equinox.

équiper [ekipe] *v* equip, fit out. **équipage** *nm* crew; equipment. **équipe** *nf* team; (*usine*) shift. **équipement** *nm* equipment.

équitable [ekitablə] *adj* fair.

équitation [ekitasjɔ̃] *nf* riding.

équité [ekite] *nf* equity.

équivalent [ekivalɑ̃] *nm, adj* equivalent.

***équivaloir** [ekivalwar] *v* be equivalent.

équivoque [ekivɔk] *adj* ambiguous; (*louche*) dubious. *nf* ambiguity; doubt.

érable [erablə] *nm* maple.

érafler [erafle] *v* scratch, graze. **éraflure** *nf* scratch, graze.

éraillé [eraje] *adj* scratched; (*voix*) hoarse, rasping.

ère [ɛr] *nf* era.

érection [erɛksjɔ̃] *nf* erection.

éreinter [erɛ̃te] *v* exhaust; (*fam: critiquer*) slate.

ergoter [ɛrgɔte] *v* quibble.

ériger [eriʒe] *v* establish, set up; (*monument*) erect.

ermite [ɛrmit] *nm* hermit.

éroder [erɔde] *v* erode. **érosif** *adj* erosive. **érosion** *nf* erosion.

érotique [erɔtik] *adj* erotic.

errer [ere] *v* wander, stray.

erreur [erœr] *nf* mistake, error.

éruption [erypsjɔ̃] *nf* eruption. **entrer en éruption** erupt.

ès [ɛs] *prep* in the. **licencié ès lettres/sciences** *nm* Bachelor of Arts/Science.

escabeau [ɛskabo] *nm* stool; (*échelle*) step-ladder.

escadron [ɛskadrɔ̃] *nm* squadron.

escalader [ɛskalade] *v* climb, scale. **escalade** *nf* climbing.

escale [ɛskal] *nf* stop; (*naut*) port of call.

escalier [ɛskalje] *nm* staircase, stairs. **escalier de secours** fire escape. **escalier roulant** escalator. **escalier tournant** spiral staircase.

escalope [ɛskalɔp] *nf* escalope.

escamoter [ɛskamɔte] *v* (*esquiver*) dodge, evade; (*carte, etc.*) make disappear; (*fam*) pinch. **escamoteur, -euse** *nm, nf* conjuror.

escarbille [ɛskarbij] *nf* smut.

escargot [ɛskargo] *nm* snail.

escarmouche [ɛskarmuʃ] *nf* skirmish.

escarpé [ɛskarpe] *adj* steep.

escient [ɛsjɑ̃] *nm* **à bon escient** advisedly. **à mauvais escient** ill-advisedly.

esclandre [ɛsklɑ̃drə] *nm* scene.

esclave [ɛsklav] *nm* slave. **esclavage** *nm* slavery.

escompter [ɛskɔ̃te] *v* discount; (*attendre*) expect, count on. **escompte** *nm* discount.

escorte [ɛskɔrt] *nf* escort. **escorter** *v* escort.

escrime [ɛskrim] *nf* fencing. **faire de l'escrime** fence.

escroc [ɛskro] *nm* swindler.

escroquer [ɛskrɔke] *v* swindle. **escroquerie** *nf* swindle, fraud.

espace [ɛspas] *nm* space. **espacer** *v* space out.

espadon [ɛspadɔ̃] *nm* swordfish.

Espagne [ɛspaɲ] *nf* Spain. **espagnol** *nm*, *adj* Spanish. **Espagnol, -e** *nm*, *nf* Spaniard.

espèce [ɛspɛs] *nf* sort, kind; (*bot, zool*) species. **espèces** *nf pl* cash *sing*.

espérer [ɛspere] *v* hope (for). **espérer en** trust in. **espérance** *nf* hope, expectation.

espiègle [ɛspjɛɡlə] *adj* mischievous. **espièglerie** *nf* mischief.

espion, -onne [ɛspjɔ̃, -ɔn] *nm*, *nf* spy. **espionnage** *nm* espionage. **espionner** *v* spy on.

esplanade [ɛsplanad] *nf* esplanade.

espoir [ɛspwar] *nm* hope.

esprit [ɛspri] *nm* spirit; (*pensée*) mind; (*humour*) wit. **avoir l'esprit large/étroit** be broad-/narrow-minded.

esquimau, -aude [ɛskimo, -od] *nm*, *adj* Eskimo. **Esquimau, -aude** *nm*, *nf* Eskimo.

esquisser [ɛskise] *v* sketch, outline. **esquisse** *nf* sketch, outline.

esquiver [ɛskive] *v* dodge, evade. **s'esquiver** slip away.

essai [ɛsɛ] *nm* try, attempt; (*produit, voiture*) trial, test; (*littéraire*) essay. **à l'essai** on trial.

essaim [ɛsɛ̃] *nm* swarm. **essaimer** *v* swarm; (*se disperser*) scatter, spread.

essayer [ɛseje] *v* try; test; (*vêtement*) try on.

essence [ɛsɑ̃s] *nf* (*carburant*)‖ gasoline; (*extrait*) oil, essence.

essentiel [ɛsɑ̃sjɛl] *adj* essential. *nm* main thing, essentials *pl*. **l'essentiel de** the best part of.

essieu [ɛsjø] *nm* axle.

essor [ɛsɔr] *nm* development, expansion; (*oiseau*) flight.

essorer [ɛsɔre] *v* wring (out); (*machine*) spin-dry. **essoreuse** *nf* spin-dryer; (*à rouleaux*) mangle.

essoufflé [ɛsufle] *adj* breathless, out of breath.

essuyer [ɛsɥije] *v* wipe; (*sécher*) dry; (*subir*) suffer. **essuie-glace** *nm* windscreen wiper. **essuie-mains** *nm* hand towel. **essuie-pieds** doormat.

est [ɛst] *nm* east. *adj invar* east; (*région*) eastern; (*direction*) eastward.

estaminet [ɛstaminɛ] *nm* tavern.

estamper [ɛstɑ̃pe] *v* stamp; (*fam*) diddle. **estampe** *nf* engraving, print.

estampille [ɛstɑ̃pij] *nf* stamp.

esthétique [ɛstetik] *adj* aesthetic. **esthéticien, -enne** *nm*, *nf* beautician.

estimer [ɛstime] *v* estimate; value; respect, esteem; consider. **estime** *nf* esteem, respect.

estivant [ɛstivɑ̃], **-e** *nm*, *nf* holiday-maker.

estomac [ɛstɔma] *nm* stomach.

estomper [ɛstɔ̃pe] *v* blur.

estrade [ɛstrad] *nf* platform.

estragon [ɛstraɡɔ̃] *nm* tarragon.

estropier [ɛstrɔpje] *v* cripple. **estropié, -e** *nm*, *nf* cripple.

estuaire [ɛstɥɛr] *nm* estuary.

esturgeon [ɛstyrʒɔ̃] *nm* sturgeon.

et [e] *conj* and.

étable [etablə] *nf* cowshed.

établir [etablir] *v* establish, set up; (*liste, plan*) draw up. **s'établir** become established; (*s'installer*) settle. **établissement** *nm* establishment.

étage [etaʒ] *nm* floor, storey; (*gâteau*) tier. **étagère** *nf* shelf; (*meuble*) set of shelves.

étai [etɛ] *nm* stay, prop.

étain [etɛ̃] *nm* tin; (*alliage*) pewter.

étaler [etale] *v* spread (out); (*comm*) display; parade, flaunt. **s'étaler** stretch out. **étalage** *nm* display; (*vitrine*) shop window. **étalagiste** *n(m+f)* window-dresser.

étalon¹ [etalɔ̃] *nm* (*cheval*) stallion.

étalon² [etalɔ̃] *nm* standard.

étancher [etɑ̃ʃe] *v* stem, staunch; make watertight. **étanche** *adj* watertight. **étanche à l'air** airtight.

étang [etɑ̃] *nm* pond.

étape [etap] *nf* stage; (*arrêt*) stop.

état [eta] *nm* state; condition; (*comm*) statement. **état-major** *nm* (*mil*) staff; (*comm*) senior management.

États-Unis [etazyni] *nm pl* United States *sing*.

étau [eto] *nm* (*tech*) vice.

étayer [eteje] *v* support, prop up.

été [ete] *nm* summer.

*****éteindre** [etɛ̃drə] *v* extinguish; (*lampe, radio, etc.*) switch *or* turn off; (*calmer*) quench. **s'éteindre** (*feu, etc.*) go out; (*mourir*) die out. **éteint** *adj* dull, faded; feeble; (*disparu*) extinct.

étendard [etɑdar] nm standard.

étendre [etɑ̃drə] v extend, expand; (étaler) spread (out), stretch out; dilute. **étendu** adj vast, extensive. **étendue** nf (terre) expanse, area; (pouvoir) scope, extent.

éternel [etɛrnɛl] adj eternal; perpetual.

éternité [etɛrnite] nf eternity.

éternuer [etɛrnɥe] v sneeze. **éternuement** nm sneeze.

éther [etɛr] nm ether.

éthique [etik] adj ethical. nf ethics pl.

ethnique [ɛtnik] adj ethnic.

étinceler [etɛ̃sle] v sparkle, glitter. **étincelle** nf spark. **étincellement** nm sparkle, gleam.

étiquette [etikɛt] nf label; (protocole) etiquette. **étiqueter** v label.

étirer [etire] v stretch.

étoffe [etɔf] nf material. **avoir l'étoffe de** have the makings of.

étoile [etwal] nf star. **étoile de mer** starfish.

étole [etɔl] nf stole.

étonner [etɔne] v surprise, amaze. **étonnement** nm surprise, amazement.

étouffer [etufe] v stifle, suffocate; (bruit) muffle; (sentiments, révolte) suppress. **étouffement** nm suffocation; suppression.

étourdir [eturdir] v stun, daze; (altitude, etc.) make dizzy; (douleur) deaden; (bruit) deafen. **étourderie** nf thoughtlessness. **étourdi** adj scatterbrained, thoughtless. **étourdissement** nm dizzy spell.

étourneau [eturno] nm starling.

étrange [etrɑ̃ʒ] adj strange.

étranger [etrɑ̃ʒe], **-ère** adj foreign; (inconnu) strange, unfamiliar. nm foreign country. **à l'étranger** abroad. nm, nf foreigner; stranger.

étrangler [etrɑ̃gle] v strangle, choke. **étranglement** nm strangulation.

étrave [etrav] nf stem.

*être [ɛtr] v be. **être à** belong to. nm being; (âme) soul. **être humain** nm human being.

*étreindre [etrɛ̃drə] v embrace; (serrer) grasp, grip. **étreinte** nf embrace; grasp, grip.

étrenne [etrɛn] nf New Year's gift.

étrier [etrije] nm stirrup.

étriqué [etrike] adj narrow, cramped, tight.

étroit [etrwa] adj narrow; (vêtement)

tight; (intime) close; strict. **étroitesse** nf narrowness; tightness.

étude [etyd] nf study.

étudier [etydje] v study; examine. **étudiant, -e** nm, nf student.

étui [etɥi] nm case.

étymologie [etimɔlɔʒi] nf etymology. **étymologique** adj etymological.

eucalyptus [økaliptys] nm eucalyptus.

Eucharistie [økaristi] nf Eucharist.

eunuque [ønyk] nm eunuch.

euphémisme [øfemismə] nm euphemism. **euphémique** adj euphemistic.

euphorie [øfɔri] nf euphoria. **euphorique** adj euphoric.

Europe [ørɔp] nf Europe. **européen** adj European. **Européen, -enne** nm, nf European.

euthanasie [øtanazi] nf euthanasia.

eux [ø] pron (sujet) they; (objet) them. **eux-mêmes** pron themselves.

évacuer [evakɥe] v evacuate. **évacuation** nf evacuation. **évacué -e** nm, nf evacuee.

s'évader [evade] v escape.

évaluer [evalɥe] v (bijou) value; (dégâts) assess; estimate.

évangélique [evɑ̃ʒelik] adj evangelical. **évangéliste** nm evangelist.

évangile [evɑ̃ʒil] nm gospel.

s'évanouir [evanwir] v (personne) faint; (disparaître) vanish. **évanouissement** nm loss of consciousness; disappearance.

évaporer [evapore] v evaporate. **évaporation** nf evaporation.

évasé [evaze] adj flared.

évasion [evazjɔ̃] nf escape. **évasif** adj evasive.

éveiller [eveje] v arouse, awaken. **éveil** nm alert, alarm. **en éveil** on the alert. **éveillé** adj alert; awake.

événement [evɛnmɑ̃] nm event.

éventail [evɑ̃taj] nm fan.

éventer [evɑ̃te] v fan, air; discover. **s'éventer** go flat or stale. **éventé** adj stale, flat.

éventrer [evɑ̃tre] v tear open; (taureau) gore.

éventuel [evɑ̃tɥɛl] adj possible. **éventualité** nf possibility, eventuality.

évêque [evɛk] nm bishop.

s'évertuer [evɛrtɥe] v strive, do one's utmost.

évidence [evidɑ̃s] nf evidence; (fait) obvious fact. **en évidence** conspicuous.

évidemment adv obviously, of course.
évident adj obvious, evident.
évider [evide] v hollow out.
évier [evje] nm sink.
évincer [evɛ̃se] v oust.
éviter [evite] v avoid. **évitable** adj avoidable.
évocateur, -trice [evɔkatœr, -tris] adj evocative.
évoluer [evɔlɥe] v evolve, develop; move about, manoeuvre. **évolution** nf evolution, development; movement, manoeuvre.
évoquer [evɔke] v evoke, recall.
exacerber [ɛgzasɛrbe] v exacerbate.
exact [ɛgzakt] adj exact; correct; (vrai) true; precise, accurate; punctual. **exactitude** nf exactness; precision; accuracy; punctuality.
exagérer [ɛgzaʒere] v exaggerate; (abuser) go too far. **exagération** nf exaggeration.
exalter [ɛgzalte] v excite; (glorifier) exalt. **exaltation** nf great excitement. **exalté** adj excited, elated; (imagination) vivid; fanatical.
examen [ɛgzamɛ̃] nm examination; test.
examiner [ɛgzamine] v examine.
exaspérer [ɛgzaspere] v exasperate, aggravate. **exaspération** nf exasperation.
excaver [ɛkskave] v excavate. **excavation** nf excavation.
excéder [ɛksede] v exceed; exasperate. **excédent** nm surplus, excess.
excellent [ɛkselɑ̃] adj excellent. **excellence** nf excellence. **Excellence** nf Excellency.
exceller [ɛksele] v excel.
excentrique [ɛksɑ̃trik] n(m+f), adj eccentric. **excentricité** nf eccentricity.
excepter [ɛksɛpte] v exclude. **excepté** prep except. **exception** nf exception. **exceptionnel** adj exceptional.
excès [ɛksɛ] nm excess; surplus. **excès de vitesse** (auto) speeding. **excessif** adj excessive.
exciter [ɛksite] v excite; (provoquer) arouse; stimulate; (encourager) urge. **s'exciter** (fam) get worked up. **excitation** nf excitement; stimulation.
s'exclamer [ɛksklame] v exclaim. **exclamation** nf exclamation.
*exclure [ɛksklyr] v exclude; (chasser) expel. **exclusif** adj exclusive; sole. **exclusion** nf exclusion; expulsion.

excommunier [ɛkskɔmynje] v excommunicate. **excommunication** nf excommunication.
excréter [ɛkskrete] v excrete. **excrément** nm excrement. **excrétion** nf excretion.
excursion [ɛkskyrsjɔ̃] nf excursion, trip.
excuser [ɛkskyze] v excuse; pardon, forgive. **excusez-moi** I'm sorry. **s'excuser** apologize. **excuse** nf excuse. **excuses** nf pl apology sing.
exécrer [ɛgzekre] v loathe. **exécrable** adj atrocious.
exécuter [ɛgzekyte] v execute, perform, carry out. **exécutif** adj executive. **exécution** nf execution.
exemplaire [ɛgzɑ̃plɛr] adj exemplary. nm copy; specimen.
exemple [ɛgzɑ̃plə] nm example. **par exemple** for example; (surprise) indeed, really.
exempt [ɛgzɑ̃] adj exempt, free. **exempter** v exempt. **exemption** nf exemption.
exercer [ɛgzɛrse] v exercise; practise; (force) exert; (entraîner) train. **s'exercer** practise.
exercice [ɛgzɛrsis] nm exercise; practice; (mil) drill.
exhaler [ɛgzale] v exhale; (odeur) give off; (soupir) utter.
exhiber [ɛgzibe] v exhibit, show, display. **exhibition** nf exhibition; show. **exhibitionniste** n(m+f), adj exhibitionist.
exiger [ɛgziʒe] v demand, insist; (nécessiter) need, require. **exigences** nf pl demands pl, requirements pl.
exigu, -uë [ɛgzigy] adj cramped.
exiler [ɛgzile] v exile, banish. **exil** nm exile.
exister [ɛgziste] v exist; (être) be. **existence** nf existence. **existentialisme** nm existentialism.
exorbitant [ɛgzɔrbitɑ̃] adj exorbitant.
exorciser [ɛgzɔrsize] v exorcize. **exorcisme** nm exorcism. **exorciste** nm exorcist.
exotique [ɛgzɔtik] adj exotic.
expansion [ɛkspɑ̃sjɔ̃] nf expansion. **expansif** adj expansive.
expatrier [ɛkspatrije] v expatriate. **expatrié, -e** n, adj expatriate.
expédier [ɛkspedje] v send, dispatch; (fam) dispose of. **expédient** nm, adj expedient. **expéditeur, -trice** nm, nf sender. **expédition** nf dispatch; (paquet) consignment; (voyage) expedition.

expérience [eksperjɑ̃s] *nf* experience; (*scientifique*) experiment.
expérimenter [eksperimɑ̃te] *v* experiment; test, try out. **expérimental** *adj* experimental. **expérimenté** *adj* experienced.
expert [eksper] *nm*, *adj* expert. **expert-comptable** *nm* chartered accountant.
expier [ekspje] *v* atone for. **expiation** *nf* atonement.
expirer [ekspire] *v* expire; (*air*) breathe out. **expiration** *nf* expiry.
explication [eksplikasjɔ̃] *nf* explanation; (*texte*) analysis, commentary. **explicatif** *adj* explanatory.
explicite [eksplisit] *adj* explicit.
expliquer [eksplike] *v* explain; (*texte*) analyse.
exploit [eksplwa] *nm* exploit.
exploiter [eksplwate] *v* exploit; operate, run.
explorer [eksplɔre] *v* explore; examine. **explorateur, -trice** *nm, nf* explorer. **exploration** *nf* exploration.
exploser [eksploze] *v* explode. **explosif** *nm, adj* explosive. **explosion** *nf* explosion.
exporter [eksporte] *v* export. **exportation** *nf* export.
exposer [ekspoze] *v* expose; exhibit, display; (*expliquer*) explain. **exposant, -e** *nm, nf* exhibitor. **exposé** *nm* talk, account. **exposition** *nf* exhibition; (*à l'air, etc.*) exposure; (*maison*) aspect.
exprès [ekspre] *adj invar* express. *adv* on purpose; specially.
express [ekspres] *nm* fast train.
expression [ekspresjɔ̃] *nf* expression. **expressif** *adj* expressive.
exprimer [eksprime] *v* express.
expulser [ekspylse] *v* expel; (*locataire*) evict. **expulsion** *nf* expulsion; eviction.
exquis [ekski] *adj* exquisite, delightful.
extase [ekstaz] *nf* ecstasy. **extasié** *adj* ecstatic.
extension [ekstɑ̃sjɔ̃] *nf* extension, expansion.
exténuer [ekstenɥe] *v* exhaust.
extérieur, -e [eksterjœr] *adj* outer, external, outside; (*étranger*) foreign. *nm* exterior, outside. **à l'extérieur** outside. **en extérieur** on location.
exterminer [ekstermine] *v* exterminate. **extermination** *nf* extermination.
externe [ekstern] *adj* external. **pour l'usage externe** for external use only. *n(m+f)* day pupil. **externat** *nm* day school.
extinction [ekstɛ̃ksjɔ̃] *nf* extinction. **extincteur** *nm* extinguisher.
extirper [ekstirpe] *v* eradicate; (*arracher*) pull out.
extorquer [ekstɔrke] *v* extort. **extorsion** *nf* extortion.
extra [ekstra] *adj invar* first-rate, top-quality; (*fam*) fantastic. *adv* extra.
extraction [ekstraksjɔ̃] *nf* extraction.
extrader [ekstrade] *v* extradite. **extradition** *nf* extradition.
***extraire** [ekstrer] *v* extract; (*charbon*) mine; (*pierre*) quarry. **extrait** *nm* extract.
extraordinaire [ekstraɔrdiner] *adj* extraordinary; exceptional.
extravagant [ekstravagɑ̃] *adj* extravagant; (*prix*) excessive; (*idée*) crazy. **extravagance** *nf* extravagance.
extraverti [ekstraverti], **-e** *n, adj* extrovert.
extrême [ekstrem] *nm* extreme. *adj* extreme; (*loin*) far; intense; (*suprême*) utmost. **Extrême-Orient** *nm* Far East. **extrémiste** *n(m+f)*, *adj* extremist. **extrémité** *nf* end, tip; limit. **extrémités** *nf pl* (*anat*) extremities (*fig*).
exubérant [egzyberɑ̃] *adj* exuberant. **exubérance** *nf* exuberance.

F

fable [fabl] *nf* fable.
fabricant [fabrikɑ̃] *nm* manufacturer. **fabrication** *nf* manufacture.
fabriquer [fabrike] *v* manufacture, make; (*mensonge*) fabricate. **fabrique** *nf* factory.
fabuleux [fabylø] *adj* fabulous.
fac [fak] *nf* (*argot*) university, college.
façade [fasad] *nf* façade, front.
face [fas] *nf* face; (*côté*) side. **de face** frontal. **en face (de)** opposite. **face à** facing. **faire face à** face.
facétie [fasesi] *nf* joke, trick. **facétieux** *adj* mischievous; humorous.
facette [faset] *nf* facet.
fâcher [faʃe] *v* make angry. **se fâcher** get angry; (*se brouiller*) fall out. **fâché** *adj*

angry; (*désolé*) sorry. **fâcheux** *adj* unfortunate; (*ennuyeux*) annoying.

facile [fasil] *adj* easy; (*spontané*) ready.

faciliter [fasilite] *v* facilitate, make easier. **facilité** *nf* ease, easiness; aptitude; tendency. **facilités** *nf pl* facilities *pl*.

façon [fasɔ̃] *nf* way, manner; (*robe*) cut. **de façon à** so as to. **de toute façon** anyway. **façons** *nf pl* (*conduite*) behaviour *sing*; (*chichis*) fuss *sing*.

façonner [fasɔne] *v* shape, form; (*fabriquer*) manufacture, make.

fac-similé [faksimile] *nm* facsimile.

facteur [faktœr] *nm* factor; postman.

factice [faktis] *adj* artificial, false.

faction [faksjɔ̃] *nf* faction; guard, sentry.

facture [faktyr] *nf* bill; (*comm*) invoice. **facturer** *v* invoice; (*compter*) charge for.

facultatif [fakyltatif] *adj* optional; (*arrêt*) request.

faculté [fakylte] *nf* faculty; (*pouvoir*) power; (*droit*) right; (*argot*) university, college.

fadaises [fadɛz] *nf pl* nonsense *sing*.

fade [fad] *adj* insipid, dull.

fagot [fago] *nm* bundle of sticks. **fagoter** [fagɔte] *v* (*péj*) rig out.

faible [fɛblə] *adj* weak, feeble; (*petit*) low, small, slight. *nm* (*personne*) weakling; (*penchant*) weakness. **faiblesse** *nf* weakness.

faiblir [feblir] *v* weaken, fail.

faïence [fajɑ̃s] *nf* earthenware.

faillible [fajiblə] *adj* fallible. **faillibilité** *nf* fallibility.

***faillir** [fajir] *v* fail. **faillir faire** almost do, narrowly miss doing. **failli, -e** *n, adj* bankrupt. **faillite** *nf* bankruptcy; (*chute*) collapse. **faire faillite** go bankrupt.

faim [fɛ̃] *nf* hunger. **avoir faim** be hungry.

fainéant [fenɛɑ̃], **-e** *adj* lazy, idle. *nm, nf* idler. **fainéantise** *nf* idleness.

***faire** [fɛr] *v* make; do; (*mesurer, temps*) be; (*sport, théâtre*) play; (*paraître*) look; (*dire*) say. **ça ne fait rien** it doesn't matter. **faire faire** have done. **faire-part** *nm invar* announcement. **faire voir** show. **se faire à** get used to.

faisable [fəzablə] *adj* feasible.

faisan [fəzɑ̃] *nm* pheasant.

faisceau [fɛso] *nm* bundle; (*rayon*) beam.

fait¹ [fɛ] *nm* fact; event; act. **au fait** (*à propos*) by the way; (*au courant*) informed. **en fait** in fact. **fait divers** news item.

fait² [fɛ] *adj* made; done; (*mûr*) ripe. **c'est bien fait pour toi!** it serves you right!

faîte [fɛt] *nm* summit, top.

faix [fɛ] *nm* burden.

falaise [falɛz] *nf* cliff.

***falloir** [falwar] *v* be necessary. **il faut le faire** it must be done. **s'en falloir (de)** be lacking.

falsifier [falsifje] *v* falsify, alter. **falsification** *nf* falsification.

famé [fame] *adj* **mal famé** disreputable.

fameux [famø] *adj* famous; first-rate, excellent; (*rude*) real. **pas fameux** not so good.

familial [familjal] *adj* family, domestic.

familiariser [familjarize] *v* familiarize. **familiarité** *nf* familiarity.

familier [familje] *adj* familiar; (*amical*) informal; (*mot*) colloquial. *nm* regular visitor.

famille [famij] *nf* family.

famine [famin] *nf* famine.

fanal [fanal] *nm* lantern.

fanatique [fanatik] *adj* fanatical. *n(m+f)* fanatic.

faner [fane] *v* make hay. **se faner** fade, wither.

fanfare [fɑ̃far] *nf* fanfare, flourish; (*orchestre*) brass band.

fanfaron, -onne [fɑ̃farɔ̃, -ɔn] *adj* boastful.

fange [fɑ̃ʒ] *nf* mire.

fantaisie [fɑ̃tezi] *nf* fantasy, fancy; (*caprice*) whim; extravagance; imagination.

fantastique [fɑ̃tastik] *adj* fantastic; (*bizarre*) weird, uncanny.

fantoche [fɑ̃tɔʃ] *nm* puppet.

fantôme [fɑ̃tom] *nm* ghost, phantom. **cabinet fantôme** *nm* shadow cabinet.

faon [fɑ̃] *nm* fawn.

farce¹ [fars] *nf* joke, prank; (*théâtre*) farce. **farceur, -euse** *nm, nf* practical joker.

farce² [fars] *nf* stuffing.

farcir [farsir] *v* stuff.

fard [far] *nm* make-up.

fardeau [fardo] *nm* burden.

farder [farde] *v* make up; disguise.

farfouiller [farfuje] *v* (*fam*) rummage about.

farine [farin] *nf* flour. **farine d'avoine** oatmeal. **farine de maïs** cornflour. **farineux** *adj* floury.

farouche [faruʃ] *adj* fierce; timid; savage, wild; unsociable.

fart [far] *nm* wax. **farter** *v* wax.

fascicule [fasikyl] *nm* volume; part, instalment.

fasciner [fasine] *v* fascinate. **fascination** *nf* fascination.

fascisme [faʃismə] *nm* fascism. **fasciste** *n*(*m*+*f*), *adj* fascist.

faste [fast] *nm* splendour.

fastidieux [fastidjø] *adj* tedious.

fastueux [fastɥø] *adj* sumptuous, luxurious.

fatal [fatal] *adj* fatal; inevitable. **fatalité** *nf* fate.

fatiguer [fatige] *v* tire, strain; (*agacer*) annoy. **se fatiguer** get tired. **fatigant** *adj* tiring; (*agaçant*) tiresome. **fatigue** *nf* fatigue, tiredness.

fatras [fatra] *nm* jumble.

faubourg [fobur] *nm* suburb.

faucher [foʃe] *v* mow, cut; (*fam*) pinch, nick. **fauché** *adj* (*fam*) broke, hard up.

faucon [fokɔ̃] *nm* falcon; hawk.

faufiler [fofile] *v* tack. **se faufiler** thread *or* edge one's way.

faune [fon] *nm* fauna.

fausser [fose] *v* distort, alter; (*courber*) bend, buckle. **fausser compagnie à** slip away from.

fausset [fosɛ] *nm* falsetto.

faute [fot] *nf* fault; mistake, error; (*jur*) offence. **faute de** for lack of. **fautif** *adj* at fault, guilty; incorrect.

fauteuil [fotœj] *nm* armchair; (*théâtre*) seat. **fauteuil à bascule** rocking chair. **fauteuil roulant** wheelchair.

fauve [fov] *adj* tawny, fawn. *nm* wild animal; (*couleur*) fawn.

faux[1], **fausse** [fo, fos] *adj* false; (*incorrect*) wrong; (*argent, etc.*) fake, forged. **fausse alerte** false alarm. **fausse couche** miscarriage. **faux-filet** *nm* sirloin. **faux pli** crease. **faire faux bond** be out of tune. **faux** falsehood; forgery. **à faux** wrongly. **fausseté** *nf* falseness, falsity.

faux[2] [fo] *nf* scythe.

faveur [favœr] *nf* favour. **billet de faveur** *nm* complimentary ticket. **en faveur de** on behalf of. **favorable** *adj* favourable.

favori, -ite [favɔri, -it] *n*, *adj* favourite. **favoriser** *v* favour.

fébrile [febril] *adj* feverish. **fébrilité** *nf* feverishness.

fécond [fekɔ̃] *adj* fertile; prolific. **fécondité** *nf* fertility.

fécule [fekyl] *nf* starch. **féculent** *adj* starchy.

fédérer [federe] *v* federate. **fédéral** *adj* federal. **fédération** *nf* federation.

fée [fe] *nf* fairy. **féerique** *adj* magical.

*****feindre** [fɛ̃drə] *v* feign. **feindre de** pretend.

fêler [fele] *v* crack. **fêlure** *nf* crack.

féliciter [felisite] *v* congratulate. **félicitations** *nf pl* congratulations *pl*.

félin [felɛ̃] *adj* feline.

femelle [fəmɛl] *adj*, *nf* female.

féminin [feminɛ̃] *adj* feminine, female. *nm* feminine. **féminisme** *nm* feminism. **féministe** *n*(*m*+*f*), *adj* feminist. **féminité** *nf* femininity.

femme [fam] *nf* woman; (*épouse*) wife. **femme de chambre** chambermaid. **femme de ménage** cleaner.

fémur [femyr] *nm* femur.

fendre [fɑ̃drə] *v* split, crack.

fenêtre [fənɛtrə] *nf* window. **fenêtre à guillotine** sash window. **fenêtre en saillie** bay window.

fenouil [fənuj] *nm* fennel.

fente [fɑ̃t] *nf* crack, fissure; (*interstice*) slit; slot.

féodal [feɔdal] *adj* feudal.

fer [fɛr] *nm* iron. **fer à cheval** horseshoe. **fer à repasser** iron. **fer-blanc** *nm* tin. **fer forgé** wrought iron.

férié [ferje] *adj* **jour férié** *nm* public holiday.

ferme[1] [fɛrm] *adj* firm; (*solide*) steady. *adv* hard. **fermeté** *nf* firmness; steadiness.

ferme[2] [fɛrm] *nf* farm; (*maison*) farmhouse. **fermier** *nm* farmer. **fermière** *nf* farmer's wife.

fermenter [fɛrmɑ̃te] *v* ferment. **ferment** *nm* ferment. **fermentation** *nf* fermentation.

fermer [fɛrme] *v* close, shut; (*boucher*) block; (*gaz, eau, etc.*) turn off. **fermer à clef** lock. **fermeture** *nf* fastener, catch; (*action*) closing. **fermeture à glissière** zip.

féroce [ferɔs] *adj* ferocious, fierce. **férocité** *nf* ferocity.

ferraille [feraj] *nf* scrap iron.

ferré [fere] *adj* (*canne*) steel-tipped; (*soulier*) hobnailed. **voie ferrée** *nf* railway track *or* line.

ferroviaire [fɛrɔvjɛr] adj railway.

fertile [fɛrtil] adj fertile. **fertilisation** nf fertilization. **fertiliser** v fertilize. **fertilité** nf fertility.

fervent [fɛrvɑ̃] adj fervent. **ferveur** nm fervour.

fesser [fese] v spank. **fesse** nf buttock. **fesses** nf pl bottom sing. **fessée** nf spanking.

festin [fɛstɛ̃] nm feast.

festival [fɛstival] nm festival.

feston [fɛstɔ̃] nm festoon; (couture) scallop. **festonner** v festoon; scallop.

fête [fɛt] nf festival; (congé) holiday; (rel) feast day; (foire) fair; celebration. **fête des Mères** Mothers' Day. **fête foraine** funfair.

fêter [fete] v celebrate.

fétiche [fetiʃ] nm fetish; mascot.

fétide [fetid] adj fetid.

feu¹ [fø] nm fire; (lumière, lampe) light; (cuisine) ring, burner; (chaleur) heat. **feu d'artifice** firework. **feu de joie** bonfire. **feu de position** sidelight. **feux** nm pl (auto) traffic lights pl.

feu² [fø] adj late, deceased.

feuille [fœj] nf leaf; (papier, etc.) sheet; form; (bulletin) slip. **feuillage** nm foliage. **feuillet** nm (livre) leaf, page.

feuilleter [fœjte] v leaf or skim through. **pâte feuilletée** nf puff pastry.

feuilleton [fœjtɔ̃] nm serial.

feutre [føtrə] nm felt; (stylo) felt-tip pen. **feutré** adj muffled.

fève [fɛv] nf broad bean.

février [fevrije] nm February.

fiacre [fjakrə] nm cab.

fiancé [fjɑ̃se] adj engaged. nm fiancé. **fiancée** nf fiancée.

se fiancer [fjɑ̃se] v get engaged. **fiançailles** nf pl engagement sing.

fiasco [fjasko] nm fiasco.

fibre [fibrə] nf fibre.

ficeler [fisle] v tie up. **ficelle** nf string.

ficher¹ [fiʃe] v (enfoncer) stick, drive in; (mettre en fiche) file. **fiche** nf (cheville) peg; (élec) pin; index card; form, slip. **fichier** nm file.

ficher² [fiʃe] (fam) v do, be up to; (donner) give; (mettre) put. **ficher le camp** clear off. **se ficher de** (se moquer) make fun of; (être indifférent) not care about. **fichu** adj (mauvais) rotten; (perdu) done for; capable, likely.

fiction [fiksjɔ̃] nf fiction. **fictif** adj fictitious; false; imaginary.

fidèle [fidɛl] adj faithful; loyal; (habituel) regular. n(m+f) (rel) believer; regular. **fidélité** nf faithfulness; loyalty; (conjugale) fidelity.

fiel [fjɛl] nm gall.

fiente [fjɑ̃t] nm droppings pl.

fier¹ [fjɛr] adj proud. **fierté** nf pride.

fier² [fje] v se **fier à** trust.

fièvre [fjɛvrə] nf fever. **fiévreux** adj feverish.

figer [fiʒe] v congeal, clot, coagulate; (paralyser) freeze, stiffen.

figue [fig] nf fig. **figuier** nm fig tree.

figure [figyr] nf figure; (visage) face; (image) picture.

figurer [figyre] v represent; appear. **se figurer** imagine. **figurant, -e** nm, nf (cinéma) extra; (théâtre) walk-on; (pantin) puppet. **figuré** adj figurative.

fil [fil] nm thread; (élec) wire; (linge, pêche) line; (bois) grain; (tranchant) edge; current. **fil à plomb** plumbline. **fil de fer** wire.

filament [filamɑ̃] nm filament; (fil) thread.

file [fil] nf line; (auto) lane; (d'attente) queue. **à la file** in single file; one after the other.

filer [file] v spin; prolong, draw out; (liquide, sable) flow, run; (bas) ladder; (fam: courir) fly, dash; (fam: s'en aller) slip away.

filet¹ [filɛ] nm streak; (eau) trickle; (fumée) wisp.

filet² [filɛ] nm (viande, etc.) fillet.

filet³ [filɛ] nm (sport, pêche) net; (bagages) rack. **filet à provisions** string bag.

filial [filjal] adj filial. **filiale** nf subsidiary company.

filigrane [filigran] nm (papier) watermark; (argent, verre, etc.) filigree.

fille [fij] nf girl; (opposé à fils) daughter. **fillette** nf little girl.

filleul [fijœl] nm (garçon) godson; (enfant) godchild. **filleule** nf goddaughter.

film [film] nm film. **film fixe** filmstrip. **filmer** v film.

filou [filu] nm rogue.

filouter [filute] (fam) v diddle; (tricher) cheat; (voler) filch.

fils [fis] nm son; (après nom) junior.

filtrer [filtre] v filter. **filtre** nm filter; (*cigarette*) filter-tip.

fin¹ [fɛ̃] adj fine; (*mince*) thin; (*vue*) sharp; (*personne*) shrewd, astute; (*aliments*) choice; (*habile*) expert. **fines herbes** nf pl mixed herbs pl.

fin² [fɛ̃] nf end; (*but*) purpose. **en fin de compte** in the end. **fin de série** oddment. **final** [final] adj final. **finale** nf (*sport*) final. **finalement** adv in the end, finally. **finaliste** n(m+f) finalist.

finance [finɑ̃s] nf finance. **financer** v finance.

financier [finɑ̃sje] adj financial. nm financier.

finaud [fino] adj wily.

finesse [fines] nf fineness; (*vue*) sharpness; (*broderie*) delicacy; subtlety.

finir [finir] v finish, end; (*arrêter*) stop. **fini** adj finished; (*terminé*) over; (*complet*) utter.

Finlande [fɛ̃lɑ̃d] nf Finland. **finlandais** adj Finnish. **Finlandais, -e** nm, nf Finn.

finnois nm, adj Finnish. **Finnois, -e** nm, nf Finn, Finnish speaker.

fioriture [fjorityr] nf flourish.

firme [firm] nf firm.

fisc [fisk] nm Inland Revenue. **fiscal** adj tax, fiscal.

fission [fisjɔ̃] nf fission.

fissure [fisyr] nf crack, fissure.

fixer [fikse] v fix; decide, settle; arrange, set. **fixation** nf fixation; (*attache*) fastening; (*ski*) binding. **fixe** adj fixed, set.

flacon [flakɔ̃] nm bottle.

flageller [flaʒele] v flog. **flagellation** nf flogging.

flagrant [flagrɑ̃] adj blatant, glaring. **prendre en flagrant délit** catch red-handed.

flairer [flere] v smell, sniff (at); (*discerner*) sense, scent. **flair** nm sense of smell; intuition.

flamand [flamɑ̃] nm, adj Flemish. **les Flamands** the Flemish.

flamant [flamɑ̃] nm flamingo.

flambeau [flɑ̃bo] nm torch; candlestick.

flamber [flɑ̃be] v blaze; (*cheveux*) singe. **flambée** nf blaze; (*colère*, etc.) outburst.

flamboyant [flɑ̃bwajɑ̃] adj blazing, fiery.

flamme [flam] nf flame; (*ardeur*, *éclat*) fire. **flammèche** nf spark.

flan [flɑ̃] nm (*cuisine*) egg custard; (*tech*) mould.

flanc [flɑ̃] nm side, flank.

flanelle [flanɛl] nf flannel.

flâner [flane] v stroll; (*péj*) dawdle.

flanquer [flɑ̃ke] v flank; (*fam*) fling, chuck.

flaque [flak] nf pool. **flaque d'eau** puddle.

flasque [flask] adj flaccid, flabby, limp; (*personne*) spineless.

flatter [flate] v flatter; encourage; (*caresser*) stroke. **se flatter de** delude oneself. **se flatter de** pride oneself on. **flatterie** nf flattery. **flatteur, -euse** adj flattering.

flatulence [flatylɑ̃s] nf flatulence.

fléau [fleo] nm scourge; (*fam*) plague.

flèche [flɛʃ] nf arrow; (*église*) spire. **monter en flèche** soar, rocket. **fléchette** nf dart.

fléchir [fleʃir] v bend, sag; (*personne*) yield.

flegme [flegm] nm composure. **flegmatique** adj phlegmatic.

flet [flɛ] nm flounder.

flétan [fletɑ̃] nm halibut.

flétrir¹ [fletrir] v (*faner*) wither, fade.

flétrir² [fletrir] v condemn; (*marquer*) brand. **flétrissure** nf (*tache*) stain, blemish; brand.

fleur [flœr] nf flower; (*arbre*) blossom; (*meilleur*) prime. **à fleur de** just above, on the surface of. **fleuriste** n(m+f) florist.

fleurir [flœrir] v flower, bloom; blossom; flourish, prosper; decorate with flowers. **fleuri** adj flowery; (*plante*) in flower; (*teint*) florid.

fleuve [flœv] nm river.

flexible [fleksibl] adj flexible.

flibustier [flibystje] nm buccaneer, pirate.

flic [flik] nm (*fam*) copper, policeman.

flirter [flœrte] v flirt. **flirteur, -euse** nm, nf flirt.

flocon [flɔkɔ̃] nm flake.

floral [florali] adj floral.

flore [flor] nf flora.

florissant [florisɑ̃] adj flourishing; (*santé*) blooming.

flot [flo] nm flood, stream. **à flot** afloat. **à flots** in torrents.

flotter [flote] v float; (*brume*) drift; (*parfum*) waft; (*drapeau*) flutter, fly; hesitate. **flottabilité** nf buoyancy. **flottable** adj buoyant. **flottant** adj floating; (*vêtement*) loose; irresolute. **flotte** nf fleet. **flotteur** nm float.

flou [flu] adj blurred; vague.

fluctuer [flyktᵁe] v fluctuate. **fluctuation** nf fluctuation.

fluet, -ette [flyɛ, -ɛt] adj slender.

fluide [flᵁid] nm, adj fluid. **fluidité** nf fluidity, flow.

fluorescent [flyɔresɑ̃] adj fluorescent. **fluorescence** nf fluorescence.

flûte [flyt] nf flute; (pain) long thin loaf. **flûte à bec** recorder. **flûtiste** n(m+f) flautist.

flux [fly] nm flood; (méd) flow; (phys) flux.

fluxion [flyksjɔ̃] nf inflammation, swelling. **fluxion dentaire** gumboil. **fluxion de poitrine** pneumonia.

focal [fɔkal] adj focal.

fœtus [fetys] nm foetus. **fœtal** adj foetal.

foi [fwa] nf faith; (parole) word.

foie [fwa] nm liver.

foin [fwɛ̃] nm hay.

foire [fwar] nf fair.

fois [fwa] nf time. **à la fois** at once. **des fois** (fam) sometimes. **deux fois** twice. **une fois** once.

foisonner [fwazɔne] v abound. **à foison** in abundance.

fol [fɔl] form of **fou** used before vowel or mute h.

folâtre [fɔlɑtrə] adj playful, lively.

folie [fɔli] nf (méd) madness; (bêtise) folly; (dépense) extravagance.

folklore [fɔlklɔr] nm folklore. **folklorique** adj folk; (fam) weird, outlandish.

folle [fɔl] V **fou**.

follet, -ette [fɔlɛ, -ɛt] adj scatter-brained.

follicule [fɔlikyl] nm follicle.

foncer [fɔ̃se] v charge, rush; (fam) tear along; (puits) sink; (couleur) go darker. **foncé** adj dark.

foncier [fɔ̃sje] adj land; fundamental.

fonction [fɔ̃ksjɔ̃] nf function; post, office. **faire fonction de** act as. **fonctionnaire** n(m+f) civil servant. **fonctionnel** adj functional.

fonctionner [fɔ̃ksjɔne] v function, work, operate.

fond [fɔ̃] nm bottom; (pièce) back; (tableau) background; (essentiel) heart, core; (profondeur) depth; (lie) sediment. **à fond** thoroughly. **au fond** deep down, basically. **de fond** basic.

fondamental [fɔ̃damɑ̃tal] adj fundamental, basic.

fondant [fɔ̃dɑ̃] adj melting. nm fondant.

fonder [fɔ̃de] v found; base; (foyer) start,

set up; justify. **se fonder sur** (idée) be based on; (personne) go on. **fondateur, -trice** nm, nf founder. **fondation** nf foundation. **fondement** nm foundation, base, grounds pl.

fonderie [fɔ̃dri] nf foundry.

fondre [fɔ̃drə] v melt; (dans l'eau) dissolve; (statue, etc.) cast; (couleur) merge. **fondre sur** swoop down on.

fondrière [fɔ̃drijɛr] nf pothole, rut.

fonds [fɔ̃] nm fund, collection; (comm) business. nm pl funds pl.

fontaine [fɔ̃tɛn] nf fountain.

fonts [fɔ̃] nm pl **fonts baptismaux** font sing.

football [futbol] nm football. **footballeur** nm footballer.

footing [futiŋ] nm jogging. **faire du footing** go jogging.

for [fɔr] nm **dans son for intérieur** in one's heart of hearts.

forain [fɔrɛ̃] nm (marchand) stallholder; fairground entertainer.

forçat [fɔrsa] nm convict.

force [fɔrs] nf force, strength. **à force de** by dint of.

forcené [fɔrsəne], -e adj (fou) deranged; (acharné) frenzied. nm, nf fanatic, maniac.

forceps [fɔrsɛps] nm forceps pl.

forcer [fɔrse] v force; (claquer) strain, overdo. **forcé** adj forced; inevitable. **forcément** adv inevitably, of course. **pas forcément** not necessarily.

forer [fɔre] v drill, bore. **foreuse** nf drill.

forêt [fɔre] nf forest. **forestier** nm forester.

forfait[1] [fɔrfɛ] nm (sport) withdrawal; serious crime. **déclarer forfait** withdraw.

forfait[2] [fɔrfɛ] nm fixed price; contract. **forfaitaire** adj inclusive.

forger [fɔrʒe] v forge; create, form; (mot) coin; (inventer) contrive, concoct. **forge** nf forge. **forgeron** nm blacksmith.

se formaliser [fɔrmalize] v take offence.

format [fɔrma] nm format, size.

former [fɔrme] v form; make up; (éduquer) train; develop. **formalité** nf formality. **formation** nf formation; training. **forme** nf form; (contour) shape. **être en forme** be fit. **formel** adj formal; definite.

formidable [fɔrmidablə] adj tremendous; (fam) incredible, fantastic.

formuler [fɔrmyle] v formulate; (sentiment) express; (ordonnance) draw up.

285 **fraternel**

formulaire *nm* form. formule *nf* formula; expression; system, method; form.

fort [fɔr] *adj* strong; (*gros*) large; (*bruit*) loud; (*grand*) great; (*violent*) hard; (*doué*) good, able. *adv* loudly; hard; (*très*) very, most; (*beaucoup*) greatly, very much. *nm* strong point, forte; (*forteresse*) fort; (*milieu*) height, depths *pl*.

forteresse [fɔrtərɛs] *nf* fortress, stronghold.

fortifier [fɔrtifje] *v* fortify, strengthen. fortification *nf* fortification.

fortuit [fɔrtɥi] *adj* fortuitous, chance.

fortune [fɔrtyn] *nf* fortune; (*chance*) luck. de fortune makeshift. fortuné *adj* (*riche*) wealthy; (*heureux*) fortunate.

fosse [fos] *nf* pit; (*tombe*) grave. fossé *nm* ditch; (*écart*) gulf. fossette *nf* dimple. fossoyeur *nm* gravedigger.

fossile [fosil] *nm* fossil. *adj* fossilized.

fou [fu], folle *adj* mad; (*fam*) terrific, tremendous. avoir le fou rire have the giggles. *nm*, *nf* lunatic.

foudre [fudr] *nf* lightning. coup de foudre love at first sight.

foudroyer [fudrwaje] *v* strike (down). foudroyant *adj* (*vitesse*, *attaque*) lightning; violent; (*succès*) thundering.

fouet [fwɛ] *nm* whip; (*cuisine*) whisk. fouetter *v* whip.

fougère [fuʒɛr] *nf* fern.

fougue [fug] *nf* ardour, spirit. fougueux *adj* fiery, spirited.

fouiller [fuje] *v* search; (*creuser*) dig, excavate. fouiller dans rummage in, go through. fouille *nf* excavation; search.

fouillis [fuji] *nm* jumble, muddle.

fouir [fwir] *v* dig, burrow.

foulard [fular] *nm* scarf.

foule [ful] *nf* crowd, mob.

fouler [fule] *v* trample, tread; (*méd*) sprain. foulure *nf* sprain.

four [fur] *nm* oven; (*usine*) furnace; (*poterie*) kiln.

fourbe [furb] *adj* deceitful, treacherous. fourberie *nf* deceit, treachery.

fourche [furʃ] *nf* fork; (*foin*) pitchfork; (*anat*) crotch. fourcher *v* split. fourchette *nf* fork. fourchu *adj* forked; (*pied*) cloven.

fourgon [furgɔ̃] *nm* coach, wagon, van.

fourmi [furmi] *nf* ant. avoir des fourmis have pins and needles. fourmilier *nm* anteater. fourmilière *nf* ant-hill.

fourmiller [furmije] *v* swarm.

fourneau [furno] *nm* furnace; (*cuisine*) stove.

fournir [furnir] *v* supply, provide. fourni *adj* bushy, thick. fournisseur *nm* tradesman, stockist; (*comm*) supplier. fournitures *nf pl* supplies *pl*.

fourrer [fure] *v* (*cuisine*) stuff, fill; (*vêtement*) line with fur; (*fam*) shove, stick. fourreau *nm* sheath. fourre-tout *nm invar* (*pièce*) lumber room; (*sac*) holdall. fourreur *nm* furrier. fourrure *nf* fur.

*foutre [futr] (*impol*) *v* do. fous-moi le camp! bugger off! se foutre de not give a damn about. va te faire foutre! fuck off! foutaise *nf* rubbish.

foyer [fwaje] *nm* home; (*âtre*) hearth; (*jeunes*) hostel; (*théâtre*) foyer; (*phys*) focus; (*infection, etc.*) seat, centre.

fracas [fraka] *nm* crash, din.

fracasser [frakase] *v* smash, shatter.

fraction [fraksjɔ̃] *nf* fraction.

fracturer [fraktyre] *v* fracture, break. fracture *nf* fracture.

fragile [fraʒil] *adj* fragile, delicate, frail. fragilité *nf* fragility, frailty.

fragment [fragmɑ̃] *nm* fragment, bit.

frai [frɛ] *nm* spawn.

frais¹, fraîche [frɛ, frɛʃ] *adj* fresh; (*froid*) cool; (*nouveau*) new. fraîcheur *nf* freshness; coolness.

frais² [frɛ] *nm pl* costs *pl*, expenses *pl*.

fraise¹ [frɛz] *nf* (*fruit*) strawberry. fraisier *nm* strawberry plant.

fraise² [frɛz] *nf* (*col*) ruff; (*dentiste*) drill.

framboise [frɑ̃bwaz] *nf* raspberry. framboisier *nm* raspberry bush.

franc¹ [frɑ̃] *nm* franc.

franc², franche [frɑ̃, frɑ̃ʃ] *adj* frank, candid; (*libre*) free; (*pêj*) utter, downright; (*net*) clear. franc-parler *nm invar* outspokenness.

France [frɑ̃s] *nf* France. français *nm*, *adj* French. les Français the French.

franchir [frɑ̃ʃir] *v* (*obstacle*) clear, get over; (*traverser*) cross; pass.

franchise [frɑ̃ʃiz] *nf* frankness; exemption; (*bagages*) allowance.

franco [frɑ̃ko] *adv* post-free, carriage-paid.

frange [frɑ̃ʒ] *nf* fringe.

frapper [frape] *v* hit, strike; (*glacer*) chill, ice; (*porte*) knock.

fraternel [fraternɛl] *adj* brotherly, fraternal. fraternité *nf* brotherhood, fraternity.

fraterniser 286

fraterniser [fratɛrnize] v fraternize.

fraude [frod] nf fraud, cheating. **passer en fraude** smuggle in. **frauder** v defraud, cheat. **frauduleux** adj fraudulent.

frayer [freje] v clear, open up; (poisson) spawn. **frayer avec** mix or associate with.

fredaine [frədɛn] nf mischief.

fredonner [frədɔne] v hum.

frein [frɛ̃] nm brake; (cheval) bit. **frein à main** handbrake. **mettre le frein à** curb, check. **frein** v slow down; (auto) brake; (contrarier) check.

frêle [frɛl] adj frail, flimsy.

frelon [frəlɔ̃] nm hornet.

frémir [fremir] v shudder, tremble; (de froid) shiver. **frémissement** nm shudder, shiver.

frêne [frɛn] nm ash.

frénésie [frenezi] nf frenzy. **frénétique** adj frenzied, frenetic.

fréquence [frekɑ̃s] nf frequency. **fréquent** adj frequent.

fréquenter [frekɑ̃te] v frequent; (amis, etc.) go around with, see often.

frère [frɛr] nm brother; (moine) friar.

fresque [frɛsk] nf fresco.

fret [frɛ] nm freight.

fréter [frete] v charter.

frétiller [fretije] v wriggle; (queue) wag.

friable [frijablə] adj crumbly.

friand [frijɑ̃] adj **friand de** fond of, partial to. **friandise** nf sweet, delicacy.

fricoter [frikɔte] v (fam) cook up.

friction [friksjɔ̃] nf friction. **frictionner** v rub.

frigide [friʒid] adj frigid. **frigidité** nf frigidity.

frigo [frigo] nm (fam) fridge.

frileux [frilø] adj sensitive to cold, chilly.

friper [fripe] v crumple.

fripon, -onne [fripɔ̃, -ɔn] adj cheeky, mischievous. nm, nf (fam) rascal.

*frire [frir] v fry.

frise [friz] nf frieze.

friser [frize] v curl; (frôler) skim; (approcher) verge on. **frisé** adj curly.

frisquet, -ette [friskɛ, -ɛt] adj chilly.

frissonner [frisɔne] v tremble, shudder; (de froid) shiver; (feuillage) rustle. **frisson** nm shiver.

frit [fri] adj fried. **frites** nf pl chips pl. **friteuse** nf chip pan, deep-fryer. **friture** nf frying; fried food.

frivole [frivɔl] adj frivolous. **frivolité** nf frivolity.

froid [frwa] adj cold. nm cold. **avoid froid** be cold. **froideur** nf coldness.

froisser [frwase] v crumple, crease; (personne) offend. **se froisser** take offence.

frôler [frole] v brush against, skim.

fromage [frɔmaʒ] nm cheese. **fromage blanc** cream cheese. **fromage maigre** cottage cheese.

froment [frɔmɑ̃] nm wheat.

froncer [frɔ̃se] v gather. **froncer les sourcils** frown. **fronce** nm gather. **froncement de sourcils** nm frown.

fronde [frɔ̃d] nf sling.

front [frɔ̃] nm front; (anat) forehead. **de front** head-on; (côte à côte) abreast. **faire front à** face up to. **frontal** adj frontal.

frontière [frɔ̃tjɛr] nf frontier, border.

frotter [frɔte] v rub; (nettoyer) scrub; (allumette) strike.

fructueux [fryktɥø] adj fruitful, profitable.

frugal [frygal] adj frugal. **frugalité** nf frugality.

fruit [frɥi] nm fruit. **fruits de mer** seafood sing. **fruits secs** dried fruit sing.

fruste [fryst] adj unpolished, crude.

frustrer [frystre] v frustrate. **frustration** nf frustration.

fugace [fygas] adj fleeting.

fugitif [fyʒitif], **-ive** nm, nf fugitive. adj runaway; (fugace) fleeting.

*fuir [fɥir] v run away, escape; (éviter) shun, avoid; (gaz, liquide) leak. **fuite** nf escape, flight; leak.

fumer [fyme] v smoke; (vapeur) steam. **fumée** nf smoke; steam. **fumeur, -euse** nm, nf smoker.

fumier [fymje] nf dung, manure.

funambule [fynɑ̃byl] n(m+f) tightrope walker.

funèbre [fynɛbrə] adj funeral; (lugubre) mournful, gloomy.

funérailles [fyneraj] nf pl funeral sing.

funeste [fynɛst] adj disastrous; fatal, deadly.

fur [fyr] nm **au fur et à mesure** as, as soon as, as fast as.

furet [fyrɛ] nm ferret.

fureter [fyrte] v ferret about; (fouiller) rummage.

fureur [fyrœr] nf fury, rage; passion, mania. **furibond** adj furious, mad. **furie** nf fury; mania. **furieux** adj furious.

furoncle [fyrɔklə] *nm* boil.

furtif [fyrtif] *adj* furtive.

fusée [fyze] *nf* rocket; *(mine)* fuse; *(tech)* spindle.

fusil [fyzi] *nm* gun, rifle. **fusil de chasse** shotgun. **fusiller** *v* shoot.

fusion [fyzjɔ̃] *nf* fusion; *(métal, glace)* melting.

fusionner [fyzjɔne] *v* merge, amalgamate.

fustiger [fystiʒe] *v* censure.

fût [fy] *nm (arbre)* bole; *(tonneau)* barrel; *(colonne)* shaft.

futaie [fytɛ] *nf* forest, plantation of timber trees.

futaille [fytaj] *nf* barrel.

futile [fytil] *adj* futile; *(frivole)* trivial. **futilité** *nf* futility; triviality.

futur [fytyr] *adj* future, prospective. **future maman** *nf* mother-to-be. **futur mari** *nm* husband-to-be. *nm* future.

fuyant [fᵁijɑ̃] *adj* elusive; *(menton, etc.)* receding.

G

gâcher [gɑʃe] *v (gaspiller)* waste; *(gâter)* spoil; *(travail)* botch. **gâchis** *nm* mess; waste.

gâchette [gɑʃɛt] *nf* trigger.

gaffe [gaf] *nf (impair)* blunder; *(naut)* boat-hook.

gage [gaʒ] *nm* guarantee, security; *(preuve)* proof, evidence; *(jeu)* forfeit. **gages** *nm pl* wages *pl.* **gager** *v* wager; guarantee.

gagner [gaɲe] *v (toucher, mériter)* earn; *(être vainqueur)* win; *(obtenir)* gain; *(arriver à)* reach. **gagnant, -e** *nm, nf* winner.

gai [ge] *adj* cheerful, gay, merry. **gaieté** *nf* gaiety, cheerfulness.

gaillard [gajar] *adj* strong; *(alerte)* lively, sprightly; *(grivois)* ribald. *nm* strapping fellow. **gaillardise** *nf* ribald remark.

gain [gɛ̃] *nm* gain; *(salaire)* earnings *pl.* **gains** *nm pl* profits *pl*; *(jeu)* winnings *pl.*

gaine [gɛn] *nf* sheath; *(vêtement)* girdle. **gainer** *v* sheathe, cover.

galant [galɑ̃] *adj* gallant; courteous; romantic. **galanterie** *nf* gallantry.

galaxie [galaksi] *nf* galaxy.

galbe [galbə] *nm* curve.

gale [gal] *nf* mange, scabies. **galeux** *adj* mangy; *(sordide)* squalid, seedy.

galère [galɛr] *nf* galley.

galerie [galri] *nf* gallery; *(auto)* roof rack.

galet [galɛ] *nm* pebble. **galets** *nm pl* shingle *sing.*

galette [galɛt] *nf (crêpe)* pancake; biscuit; *(gâteau)* cake.

galion [galjɔ̃] *nm* galleon.

Galles [gal] *nf pl* **pays de Galles** *nm* Wales. **gallois** *nm, adj* Welsh. **les Gallois** the Welsh.

gallon [galɔ̃] *nm* gallon.

galon [galɔ̃] *nm* braid; *(mil)* stripe.

galop [galo] *nm* gallop. **petit galop** canter. **galoper** *v* gallop.

galvaniser [galvanize] *v* galvanize.

gambader [gɑ̃bade] *v* gambol, leap about. **gambade** *nf* leap, caper.

gamin [gamɛ̃], **-e** *adj* playful; *(puéril)* childish. *nm, nf (fam)* kid.

gamme [gam] *nf* scale; *(série)* range.

gangrène [gɑ̃grɛn] *nf* gangrene.

gangster [gɑ̃gstɛr] *nm* gangster.

gant [gɑ̃] *nm* glove. **gant de toilette** facecloth, flannel.

garage [garaʒ] *nm* garage. **garagiste** *nm* garage owner; garage mechanic.

garant [garɑ̃], **-e** *nm, nf (personne)* guarantor; *(chose)* guarantee. **se porter garant de** stand bail for.

garantir [garɑ̃tir] *v* guarantee; assure; protect. **garantie** *nf* guarantee.

garce [gars] *nf (impol)* bitch.

garçon [garsɔ̃] *nm* boy; *(magasin)* assistant; *(restaurant)* waiter; *(célibataire)* bachelor. **garçon d'honneur** best man.

garde [gard] *nf* guard; *(jur)* custody; *(surveillance)* care. **garde-à-vous!** *(mil)* attention! **prendre garde** be careful, take care. *nm* guard; *(château)* warden. **garde du corps** bodyguard.

garder [garde] *v (surveiller)* look after, guard; *(conserver, retenir)* keep. **garde-boue** *nm invar* ! fender. **garde-chasse** *nm* gamekeeper. **garde-feu** *nm invar* fireguard. **garde-fou** *nm* railing, parapet. **garde-manger** *nm invar* pantry, larder. **garde-nappe** *nm* tablemat. **garde-robe** *nf* wardrobe. **se garder de** beware of, be careful not to. **garderie** *nf* crèche, day nursery.

gardien [gardjɛ̃], **-enne** nm, nf guard; (prison) warder; (château) warden; (zoo) keeper; (musée) attendant; (défenseur) guardian. **gardien de but** goalkeeper. **gardien de nuit** night watchman.

gare¹ [gar] nf station. **gare routière** bus station.

gare² [gar] interj look out! beware!

garenne [garɛn] nf rabbit warren.

garer [gare] v (voiture) park; (bateau) dock. **se garer** park; (piéton) move aside. **se garer de** avoid.

se gargariser [gargarize] v gargle. **gargarisme** nm gargle.

gargouiller [garguje] v gurgle; (intestin) rumble. **gargouille** nf gargoyle.

garnir [garnir] v (remplir) fill, stock; (équiper) fit; (doubler) line; cover; decorate; (cuisine) garnish. **garnison** nm garrison. **garniture** nf fittings pl; (cuisine) garnish, trimmings pl; (légumes) vegetables pl; lining.

gars [gɑ] nm (fam) lad.

gaspiller [gaspije] v waste. **gaspillage** nm waste. **gaspilleur, -euse** adj wasteful.

gastrique [gastrik] adj gastric.

gastronomie [gastrɔnɔmi] nf gastronomy. **gastronomique** adj gastronomic.

gâteau [gɑto] nm cake; (dessert) gâteau. **petit gâteau** (sec) biscuit.

gâter [gɑte] v spoil, ruin. **se gâter** go bad or off; take a turn for the worse.

gauche [goʃ] adj left; (maladroit) awkward, clumsy. nf left, left-hand side. **gaucher** adj left-handed. **gaucherie** nf awkwardness, clumsiness.

gauchir [goʃir] v warp; (fausser) distort.

gaz [gaz] nm invar gas. **gazeux** adj gaseous; (boisson) fizzy.

gaze [gaz] nf gauze.

gazéifier [gazeifje] v aerate.

gazelle [gazɛl] nf gazelle.

gazon [gazɔ̃] nm lawn; (motte) turf.

gazouiller [gazuje] v (oiseau) chirp; (bébé) gurgle; (ruisseau) babble.

géant [ʒeɑ̃] adj gigantic, giant. nm giant.

*geindre [ʒɛ̃drə] v groan, moan, whine.

gel [ʒɛl] nm frost.

gélatine [ʒelatin] nf gelatine.

geler [ʒəle] v freeze, be frozen. **gelé** adj frozen; (membre) frostbitten. **gelée** nf frost; (cuisine) jelly. **gelure** nf frostbite.

gélignite [ʒelignit] nf gelignite.

Gémeaux [ʒemo] nm pl Gemini sing.

gémir [ʒemir] v groan, moan, whine; (grincer) creak. **gémissement** nm groan, moan.

gemme [ʒɛm] nf gem.

gencive [ʒɑ̃siv] nf gum.

gendarme [ʒɑ̃darm] nm policeman.

gendre [ʒɑ̃drə] nm son-in-law.

gène [ʒɛn] nm gene.

gêne [ʒɛn] nf trouble, bother; embarrassment; (physique) discomfort; financial difficulties pl.

généalogie [ʒenealɔʒi] nf genealogy. **généalogique** adj genealogical.

gêner [ʒene] v bother, embarrass; (obstacle) hamper; inconvenience. **se gêner** put oneself out. **gênant** adj embarrassing, awkward. **gêné** adj embarrassed, uncomfortable; short of money.

général [ʒeneral] nm, adj general. **en général** in general, usually. **général de brigade** brigadier. **généralisation** nf generalization. **généraliser** v generalize. **généraliste** nm general practitioner.

génération [ʒenerasjɔ̃] nf generation. **génératrice** [ʒeneratris] nf generator.

généreux [ʒenerø] adj generous. **générosité** nf generosity.

générique [ʒenerik] adj generic. nm (cinéma) credits pl.

génétique [ʒenetik] adj genetic. nf genetics.

génie [ʒeni] nm genius; spirit. **le génie** (mil) the Engineers. **génial** adj brilliant, inspired.

genièvre [ʒənjɛvrə] nm (arbre) juniper; (fruit) juniper berry; (boisson) gin.

génital [ʒenital] adj genital. **organes génitaux** nm pl genitals pl.

genou [ʒənu] nm, pl **-oux** knee. **à genoux** kneeling.

genre [ʒɑ̃r] nm kind, sort; (gramm) gender; (art, etc.) genre; family, genus. **le genre humain** mankind.

gens [ʒɑ̃] nm pl people pl.

gentiane [ʒɑ̃sjan] nf gentian.

gentil, -ille [ʒɑ̃ti, -ij] adj nice; (personne) kind; (sage) good. **gentillesse** nf kindness; favour. **gentiment** adv nicely; kindly.

génuflexion [ʒenyflɛksjɔ̃] nf genuflexion.

géographie [ʒeɔgrafi] nf geography. **géographe** n(m+f) geographer. **géographique** adj geographical.

geôle [ʒol] nf jail. **geôlier, -ère** nm, nf jailer.

géologie [ʒeɔlɔʒi] nf geology. **géologique** adj geological. **géologue** n(m + f) geologist.

géométrie [ʒeɔmetri] nf geometry. **géomètre** nm surveyor. **géométrique** adj geometrical.

géranium [ʒeranjɔm] nm geranium.

gerbe [ʒɛrb] nf sheaf, bundle; (fleurs) spray; (eau, étincelles) shower.

gercer [ʒɛrse] v chap, crack. **gerçure** nf crack.

gérer [ʒere] v manage. **gérance** nf management. **gérant** nm manager. **gérante** nf manageress.

gériatrie [ʒerjatri] nf geriatrics. **gériatrique** adj geriatric.

germanique [ʒɛrmanik] adj Germanic.

germer [ʒɛrme] v germinate; (plante) sprout, shoot. **germe** nm germ; (source) seed. **germination** nf germination.

gérondif [ʒerɔ̃dif] nm gerund, gerundive.

*gésir [ʒezir] v lie, be lying.

geste [ʒɛst] nm gesture; act, deed.

gesticuler [ʒɛstikyle] v.gesticulate. **gesticulation** nf gesticulation.

gestion [ʒɛstjɔ̃] nf management, administration.

geyser [ʒɛzɛr] nm geyser.

ghetto [gɛto] nm ghetto.

gibet [ʒibɛ] nm gallows.

gibier [ʒibje] nm game.

giboulée [ʒibule] nf shower.

gicler [ʒikle] v spurt, squirt. **giclée** nf spurt, squirt.

gifler [ʒifle] v slap in the face. **gifle** nf slap in the face.

gigantesque [ʒigɑ̃tɛsk] adj gigantic, immense.

gigot [ʒigo] nm leg of lamb.

gigue [ʒig] nf jig.

gilet [ʒile] nm waistcoat; cardigan. **gilet de sauvetage** life-jacket.

gin [dʒin] nm gin.

gingembre [ʒɛ̃ʒɑ̃brə] nm ginger.

girafe [ʒiraf] nf giraffe.

girofle [ʒirɔflə] nm clove.

giron [ʒirɔ̃] nm lap.

girouette [ʒirwɛt] nf weathercock.

gisement [ʒizmɑ̃] nm deposit.

gitan [ʒitɑ̃] adj gipsy. **Gitan, -e** nm, nf gipsy.

gîte [ʒit] nm shelter.

givre [ʒivrə] nm hoar-frost. **givrer** v ice up.

glabre [glɑbrə] adj hairless; (rasé) clean-shaven.

glacer [glase] v freeze; (boissons, etc.) chill; (cuisine) glaze; (gâteau) ice. **glaçage** nm icing. **glace** nf ice; (crème) ice cream; mirror; (vitre) window; (verre) glass. **glacé** adj frozen, icy; (boisson) iced. **glacial** adj icy, frosty. **glacière** nf icebox. **glaçon** nm icicle; (boisson) ice cube.

glacier [glasje] nm glacier. **glaciation** nf glaciation.

glaise [glɛz] nf clay.

gland [glɑ̃] nm acorn; (ornement) tassel.

glande [glɑ̃d] nf gland. **glandulaire** adj glandular.

glaner [glane] v glean.

glapir [glapir] v yelp, squeal.

glisser [glise] v slide, slip; (voilier, patineur) glide; (véhicule) skid. **se glisser** slip, creep. **glissade** nf slide, slip; skid. **glissant** adj slippery. **glissière** nf groove, channel. **à glissière** sliding. **glissoire** nf slide.

globe [glɔb] nm globe. **globe oculaire** eyeball. **global** adj global, overall, total.

gloire [glwar] nf glory; (renommée) fame; distinction, credit. **glorieux** adj glorious. **glorifier** [glɔrifje] v glorify. **se glorifier de** glory in. **glorification** nf glorification.

glossaire [glɔsɛr] nm glossary.

glouglouter [gluglute] v (eau) gurgle; (dindon) gobble. **glouglou** nm gurgling; gobbling.

glousser [gluse] v (poule) cluck; (personne) chuckle. **gloussement** nm cluck; chuckle.

glouton, -onne [glutɔ̃, -ɔn] adj greedy. nm, nf glutton. **gloutonnerie** nf gluttony, greed.

gluant [glyɑ̃] adj sticky.

glucose [glykoz] nm glucose.

glycine [glisin] nf wisteria.

gnome [gnom] nm gnome.

go [go] adv (fam) **tout de go** straight; (dire) straight out.

gobelet [gɔblɛ] nm beaker; (verre) tumbler; (papier) cup.

gober [gɔbe] v swallow whole; (mensonge) swallow, believe. **se gober** fancy oneself.

godasse [gɔdas] nf (fam) shoe.

godet [gɔdɛ] nm pot, jar.

godiche [gɔdiʃ] adj awkward, oafish.

goéland [gɔelɑ̃] nm seagull.

goélette [gɔelɛt] nf schooner.

gogo [gɔgo] *adv* **à gogo** (*fam*) galore.

golf [gɔlf] *nm* golf; (*terrain*) golf course. **golfeur, -euse** *nm, nf* golfer.

golfe [gɔlf] *nm* gulf, bay.

gommer [gɔme] *v* (*effacer*) erase, rub out; (*coller*) gum. **gomme** *nf* eraser, rubber; gum, gommeux *adj* sticky.

gond [gɔ̃] *nm* hinge.

gondole [gɔ̃dɔl] *nf* gondola. **gondolier, -ère** *nm, nf* gondolier.

gonfler [gɔ̃fle] *v* swell; (*d'air*) inflate. **gonflé** *adj* swollen; (*yeux*) puffy; (*ventre*) bloated. **gonflement** *nm* swelling; inflation.

gong [gɔ̃] *nm* gong.

gorge [gɔrʒ] *nf* (*gosier*) throat; (*poitrine*) breast; (*défilé*) gorge; (*rainure*) groove. **gorgée** *nf* mouthful. **petite gorgée** sip. se **gorger** *v* gorge.

gorille [gɔrij] *nm* gorilla.

gosier [gozje] *nm* throat.

gosse [gɔs] *n(m+f)* (*fam*) kid.

gothique [gɔtik] *nm* Gothic.

goudron [gudrɔ̃] *nm* tar. **goudronner** *v* tar.

gouffre [gufrə] *nm* abyss.

goulot [gulo] *nm* neck.

goulu [guly] *adj* greedy.

gourde [gurd] *nf* gourd; (*bidon*) flask; (*fam*) clot.

gourmand [gurmɑ̃] *adj* greedy. **gourmandise** *nf* greed.

gourmet [gurme] *nm* gourmet.

gousse [gus] *nf* pod. **gousse d'ail** clove of garlic.

goût [gu] *nm* taste; (*penchant*) liking; style. **de bon/mauvais goût** in good/bad taste.

goûter [gute] *v* taste; savour, enjoy. **goûter à** taste, sample. *nm* afternoon tea.

goutte [gut] *nf* drop; (*méd*) gout. **goutte-à-goutte** *nm invar* (*méd*) drip. **tomber goutte à goutte** drip. **gouttière** *nf* gutter.

gouvernail [guvεrnaj] *nm* rudder; (*barre*) helm.

gouverner [guvεrne] *v* govern, rule; control; (*naut*) steer. **gouvernante** *nf* housekeeper; (*des enfants*) governess. **gouvernement** *nm* government. **gouverneur** *nm* governor.

grâce [grɑs] *nf* grace; favour; charm; pardon, mercy. **de bonne grâce** willingly. **grâce à** thanks to. **gracieux** *adj* graceful; amiable, kindly.

gracile [grasil] *adj* slender.

grade [grad] *nm* grade; (*échelon*) rank; (*titre*) degree.

gradin [gradɛ̃] *nm* terrace, step; (*théâtre*) tier.

graduer [gradɥe] *v* increase gradually; (*exercices*) grade; (*règle, etc.*) graduate. **graduel** *adj* gradual; progressive.

graffiti [grafiti] *nm pl* graffiti *pl*.

grain [grɛ̃] *nm* grain; (*café*) bean; (*collier*) bead. **grain de beauté** mole. **grain de poivre** peppercorn. **grain de raisin** grape.

graine [grɛn] *nf* seed.

graisser [grese] *v* grease. **graisse** *nf* fat, grease. **graisse de rognon** suet. **graisse de viande** dripping. **graisseux** *adj* greasy, fatty.

grammaire [gramεr] *nf* grammar. **grammatical** *adj* grammatical.

gramme [gram] *nm* gram.

grand [grɑ̃], **-e** *adj* large, big; (*personne*) tall; (*intense, important*) great; (*principal*) main; (*réception, etc.*) grand. *nm, nf* senior *or* older pupil. **grandeur** *nf* greatness; (*dimension*) size.

grand-chose *n(m+f) invar* much.

Grande-Bretagne *nf* Great Britain.

grande ligne *nf* (*rail*) main line.

grandes vacances *nf pl* summer holidays *pl*.

grandiose [grɑ̃djoz] *adj* grand, imposing.

grandir [grɑ̃dir] *v* grow; (*augmenter*) increase; exaggerate; (*grossir*) magnify; (*hausser*) make taller.

grand magasin *nm* department store.

grand-mère *nf* grandmother.

grand ouvert *adj* wide open.

grand-parent *nm* grandparent.

grand-père *nm* grandfather.

grand-route *nf* main road.

grand-voile *nf* mainsail.

grange [grɑ̃ʒ] *nf* barn.

granit [granit] *nm* granite.

graphique [grafik] *adj* graphic. *nm* graph.

grappe [grap] *nf* cluster. **grappe de raisin** bunch of grapes.

gras, grasse [grɑ, grɑs] *adj* fat; (*graisseux*) greasy; (*épais*) thick; rich. **faire la grasse matinée** have a lie-in. *nm* fat. **grassouillet, -ette** *adj* (*fam*) plump, podgy.

gratifier [gratifje] *v* present, give, favour. **gratification** *nf* bonus.

gratin [gratɛ̃] *nm* **au gratin** topped with breadcrumbs or grated cheese.

gratitude [gratityd] *nf* gratitude.

gratter [grate] *v* scratch, scrape. **gratte-ciel** *nm invar* skyscraper.

gratuit [gratᶣi] *adj* free; *(injustifié)* gratuitous.

grave [grav] *adj* serious, grave; *(digne)* solemn; *(son)* deep, low. **gravité** *nf* gravity, seriousness.

graver [grave] *v* engrave; *(disque)* cut. **graver à l'eau-forte** etch. **graveur** *nm* engraver. **gravure** *nf* engraving; *(illustration)* plate; *(réproduction)* print.

gravier [gravje] *nm* gravel.

gravir [gravir] *v* climb.

gré [gre] *nm (volonté)* will; *(goût)* taste, liking.

Grèce [grɛs] *nf* Greece. **grec, grecque** *nm*, *adj* Greek. **Grec, Grecque** *nm*, *nf* Greek.

gréer [gree] *v* rig. **gréement** *nm* rigging.

greffer [grefe] *v* graft; *(organe)* transplant. **greffe** *nf* graft; transplant.

greffier [grefje] *nm* clerk of the court.

grégaire [gregɛr] *adj* gregarious.

grêle[1] [grɛl] *adj* spindly, lanky; *(son)* shrill.

grêle[2] [grɛl] *nf* hail. **grêler** *v* hail. **grêlon** *nm* hailstone.

grelotter [grɔlote] *v* shiver; *(tinter)* jingle.

grenade[1] [grᵊnad] *nf (fruit)* pomegranate. **grenadier** *nm* pomegranate tree.

grenade[2] [grᵊnad] *nf* grenade. **grenade à main** hand grenade. **grenadier** *nm* grenadier.

grenier [grᵊnje] *nm* attic, loft.

grenouille [grᵊnuj] *nf* frog.

grès [grɛ] *nm* sandstone.

grésiller [grezije] *v* sizzle; *(phone, radio)* crackle.

grève[1] [grɛv] *nf (rivière)* bank; *(mer)* shore.

grève[2] [grɛv] *nf* strike. **faire grève** be on strike. **grève de la faim** hunger strike. **grève du zèle** work-to-rule. **grève perlée** go-slow. **se mettre en grève** strike, go on strike. **gréviste** *n(m+f)* striker.

grever [grave] *v* burden, put a strain on.

gribouiller [gribuje] *v* scribble; *(dessiner)* doodle. **gribouillage** *nm* scribble; doodle.

grief [grijɛf] *nm* grievance. **grièvement blessé** seriously injured.

griffer [grife] *v* scratch. **griffe** *nf* claw; signature.

griffonner [grifone] *v* scribble. **griffonnage** *nm* scribble.

grignoter [griɲɔte] *v* nibble (at).

gril [gril] *nm* grill pan.

grille [grij] *nf* grid; *(claire-voie)* grille; *(prison)* bars *pl*; *(clôture)* gate; *(égout)* grating.

griller [grije] *v* grill; *(pain)* toast; *(brûler)* burn, scorch. **grille-pain** *nm invar* toaster. **grillade** *nf* grill.

grillon [grijɔ̃] *nm* cricket.

grimacer [grimase] *v* grimace, pull a face; *(sourire)* grin. **grimace** *nf* grimace.

grimer [grime] *v (théâtre)* make up. **grimage** *nm* make-up.

grimper [grɛ̃pe] *v* climb (up).

grincer [grɛ̃se] *v (métal)* grate; *(bois)* creak. **grincer des dents** gnash one's teeth.

grincheux [grɛ̃ʃø] *adj* grumpy.

grippe [grip] *nf* flu, influenza. **prendre en grippe** take a sudden dislike to.

gris [gri] *adj* grey; *(morne)* dull; *(ivre)* drunk. *nm* grey. **griser** *v* intoxicate. **se griser** get drunk. **grisonner** *v* go grey.

grive [griv] *nf* thrush.

grivois [grivwa] *adj* saucy.

Groënland [grɔenlãd] *nm* Greenland. **Groënlandais, -e** *nm, nf* Greenlander.

grogner [grɔɲe] *v (chien)* growl; *(cochon)* grunt; *(grommeler)* grumble. **grognement** *nm* growl, grunt.

groin [grwɛ̃] *nm* snout.

grommeler [grɔmle] *v* mutter, grumble.

gronder [grɔ̃de] *v (enfant)* scold; *(train, orage)* rumble; *(chien)* growl.

gros, grosse [gro, gros] *adj* big, large; *(personne)* fat; *(épais)* thick, heavy; *(important)* great; *(rude)* coarse. **gros lot** *nm* jackpot. **gros plan** *nm* close-up. **gros titre** *nm* headline. **en gros** fat man; *(principal)* main part, bulk; *(comm)* wholesale. **en gros** wholesale; broadly, roughly. **grosse** *nf* fat woman; *(comm)* gross.

groseille [grozɛj] *nf (rouge)* red currant; *(blanche)* white currant. **groseille à maquereau** gooseberry. **groseillier** *nm* currant bush.

grossier [grosje] *adj* coarse, rough, crude. **grossièreté** *nf* coarseness, crudeness.

grossir [grosir] *v* swell, grow; *(personne)* put on weight; *(augmenter)* increase; exaggerate; *(agrandir)* enlarge, magnify.

grotesque [grɔtɛsk] *adj* grotesque; *(risible)* ludicrous. *nm* grotesque.

grotte [grɔt] *nf* cave; *(artificielle)* grotto.

grouiller [gruje] v mill about. **grouiller de** be swarming or crawling with.

grouper [grupe] v group, put together. **groupe** nm group.

grue [gry] nf crane.

grumeau [grymo] nm lump.

se grumeler [grymle] v go lumpy; (lait) curdle. **grumeleux** adj lumpy.

gué [ge] nm ford. **passer à gué** ford.

guenille [gənij] nf rag.

guépard [gepar] nm cheetah.

guêpe [gɛp] nf wasp. **guêpier** nm wasp's nest; (piège) trap.

guère [gɛr] adv hardly, scarcely; not much.

guérilla [gerija] nf guerrilla warfare. **guérillero** nm guerilla.

guérir [gerir] v (maladie) cure; (blessure) heal; (malade) get better. **guérison** nf recovery.

Guernesey [gɛrnəzɛ] nf Guernsey.

guerre [gɛr] nf war; (stratégie) warfare. **en guerre** at war. **guerre mondiale** world war. **guerrier, -ère** nm nf warrior.

guerroyer [gɛrwaje] v wage war.

guet [gɛ] nm watch. **faire le guet** be on the look-out. **guet-apens** nm ambush, trap.

guetter [gete] v watch (for); (menace) lie in wait for.

gueuler [gœle] v (argot) bawl, yell. **gueule** nf mouth; (fam: figure) face. **gueule de bois** (fam) hangover. **gueule-de-loup** nf snapdragon.

gueux [gø] **gueuse** nm, nf beggar.

gui [gi] nm mistletoe.

guichet [giʃɛ] nm window, counter; (théâtre) box office; (gare) ticket office; (porte) hatch, grille.

guide [gid] nm guide; (livre) guidebook. nf rein; (jeune fille) girl guide. **guider** v guide.

guidon [gidɔ̃] nm handlebars pl.

guigne [giɲ] nf (fam) bad luck.

guillemets [gijmɛ] nm pl inverted commas pl, quotation marks pl. **entre guillemets** in inverted commas.

guilleret, -ette [gijrɛ, -ɛt] adj perky, lively; (propos) saucy.

guillotine [gijɔtin] nf guillotine. **guillotiner** v guillotine.

guimauve [gimov] nf marshmallow.

guindé [gɛ̃de] v (air) stiff; (style) stilted.

Guinée [gine] nf Guinea.

guingois [gɛ̃gwa] adv **de guingois** (fam) askew, lop-sided.

guirlande [girlɑ̃d] nf garland. **guirlande de Noël** tinsel. **guirlande électrique** or **lumineuse** fairy lights pl.

guise [giz] nf **à sa guise** as one pleases. **en guise de** by way of.

guitare [gitar] nf guitar. **guitariste** n(m+f) guitarist.

gymnase [ʒimnaz] nm gymnasium. **gymnaste** n(m+f) gymnast. **gymnastique** nf (sport) gymnastics; exercises pl.

gynécologie [ʒinekɔlɔʒi] nf gynaecology. **gynécologique** adj gynaecological. **gynécologue** n(m+f) gynaecologist.

gypse [ʒips] nm gypsum.

gyroscope [ʒirɔskɔp] nm gyroscope.

H

habile [abil] adj skilful, clever; (malin) cunning. **habileté** nf skill, cleverness.

habiller [abije] v dress, clothe; cover. **s'habiller** get dressed. **s'habiller en** dress up as. **habillement** nm clothing; outfit.

habit [abi] nm (costume) dress, outfit; (soirée) formal dress; (rel) habit. **habits** nm pl clothes pl.

habiter [abite] v live (in). **habitable** adj habitable. **habitant, -e** nm nf inhabitant; (maison) occupant. **habitat** nm habitat. **habitation** nf residence, home; (logement) housing.

habitude [abityd] nf habit; custom. **avoir l'habitude de** be used to. **comme d'habitude** as usual. **d'habitude** usually.

habituer [abitɥe] v accustom. **s'habituer à** get used to. **habitué** nm regular. **habituel** adj usual, habitual.

hâbleur, -euse [ˈɑblœr, -øz] adj boastful. nm, nf braggart. **hâblerie** nf bragging, boasting.

hacher [ˈaʃe] v chop; (menu) mince. **hache** nf axe. **haché** adj minced; (phrases) jerky. **hachette** nf hatchet. **hachis** nm mince. **hachis Parmentier** cottage pie. **hachoir** nm chopper; mincer.

hagard [ˈagar] adj wild, distraught.

haie [ˈɛ] nf hedge; (sport) hurdle, fence; (rangée) line.

haillon [ˈɑjɔ̃] *nm* rag.

haine [ˈɛn] *nf* hatred.

*haïr [ˈair] *v* detest, hate.

Haïti [aiti] *nf* Haiti.

halage [ˈalaʒ] *nm* towing. **chemin de halage** *nm* towpath.

hâle [ˈɑl] *nm* sunburn, tan. **hâlé** *adj* sunburnt, tanned.

haleine [alɛn] *nf* breath. **hors d'haleine** out of breath. **reprendre haleine** get one's breath back.

haler [ˈale] *v* tow; *(ancre)* haul in.

haleter [ˈalte] *v* pant, gasp for breath. **haletant** *adj* panting, breathless.

hall [ˈol] *nm* hall.

halle [ˈal] *nf* covered market.

hallucination [alysinasjɔ̃] *nf* hallucination.

halte [ˈalt] *nf* stop, pause; *(rail)* halt. **faire halte** stop, halt. *interj* stop! halt!

haltérophilie [alterɔfili] *nf* weight-lifting.

hamac [ˈamak] *nm* hammock.

hameau [ˈamo] *nm* hamlet.

hameçon [amsɔ̃] *nm* hook.

hampe [ˈɑ̃p] *nf* pole, shaft.

hamster [ˈamstɛr] *nm* hamster.

hanche [ˈɑ̃ʃ] *nf* hip; *(cheval)* haunch.

handicaper [ˈɑ̃dikape] *v* handicap. **handicap** *nm* handicap. **handicapé, -e** *nm, nf* handicapped person. **handicapé moteur** spastic.

hangar [ˈɑ̃gar] *nm* shed; *(aéro)* hangar.

hanter [ˈɑ̃te] *v* haunt. **hantise** *nf* obsession.

happer [ˈape] *v* snatch, grab.

haras [ˈarɑ] *nm* stud farm.

harassé [ˈarase] *adj* exhausted.

harceler [ˈarsəle] *v* harass, pester.

harde [ˈard] *nf* herd.

hardes [ˈard] *nf pl* old clothes *pl*.

hardi [ˈardi] *adj* bold, daring. **hardiesse** *nf* boldness; effrontery; audacity.

hareng [ˈarɑ̃] *nm* herring. **hareng fumé** kipper.

hargneux [ˈarɲø] *adj* aggressive.

haricot [ˈariko] *nm* bean. **haricot à rames** runner bean. **haricot beurre/blanc/rouge/vert** butter/haricot/kidney/French bean.

harmonica [armɔnika] *nm* harmonica.

harmonie [armɔni] *nf* harmony. **harmonieux** *adj* harmonious. **harmonique** *nm, adj* harmonic. **harmoniser** *v* harmonize.

harnacher [ˈarnaʃe] *v* harness.

harnais [ˈarnɛ] *nm* harness.

harpe [ˈarp] *nf* harp. **harpiste** *n(m+f)* harpist.

harpon [ˈarpɔ̃] *nm* harpoon.

hasard [ˈazar] *nm* chance, luck; risk, hazard; coincidence. **au hasard** at random. **par hasard** by accident. **hasarder** *v* risk.

hasardeux *adj* risky, dangerous.

haschich [ˈaʃiʃ] *nm* hashish.

hâter [ˈɑte] *v* hasten, hurry. **hâte** *nf* haste, hurry; impatience. **à la hâte** hurriedly. **hâtif** *adj* hasty, hurried; precocious, early.

hausser [ˈose] *v* raise. **hausser les épaules** shrug one's shoulders. **hausse** *nf* rise, increase.

haut [ˈo] *adj* high; *(arbre, édifice)* tall; noble. *adv* high; *(fort)* loudly. *nm* top. **à haute voix** aloud. **de haut en bas** downwards; *(regarder)* up and down. **en haut** at the top; *(dessus)* above; *(maison)* upstairs. **haut-de-forme** *nm* top hat. **haut fourneau** blast furnace. **haut-parleur** *nm* loudspeaker.

hautain [ˈotɛ̃] *adj* haughty.

hautbois [ˈobwa] *nm* oboe. **hauboïste** *n(m+f)* oboist.

hauteur [ˈotœr] *nf* height; *(son)* pitch; nobility; *(arrogance)* haughtiness. **à la hauteur de** level with; equal to.

hâve [ˈav] *adj* haggard, gaunt.

havre [ˈavrə] *nm* haven.

havresac [ˈavrəsak] *nm* haversack.

Haye [ˈɛ] *nf* **La Haye** the Hague.

hebdomadaire [ɛbdɔmadɛr] *nm, adj* weekly.

héberger [eberʒe] *v* lodge, take in.

hébéter [ebete] *v* daze, numb. **hébétement** *nm* stupor.

hébraïque [ebraik] *adj* Hebrew.

hébreu [ebrø] *nm, adj* Hebrew. **Hebreu** *nm* Hebrew.

hectare [ɛktar] *nm* hectare.

hein [ˈɛ̃] *interj (fam)* eh?

hélas [ˈelas] *interj* alas!

héler [ˈele] *v* hail.

hélice [elis] *nf* propeller.

hélicoptère [elikɔptɛr] *nm* helicopter.

hémisphère [emisfɛr] *nm* hemisphere.

hémorragie [emɔraʒi] *nf* haemorrhage.

hémorroïdes [emɔroid] *nf pl* haemorrhoids *pl*.

henné [ˈene] *nm* henna.

hennir [ˈenir] v neigh. **hennissement** nm neigh.

héraldique [eraldik] adj heraldic. nf heraldry.

héraut [ˈero] nm herald.

herbe [ɛrb] nf grass; (cuisine) herb. **en herbe** (plante) unripe; (personne) budding. **herbeux** or **herbu** adj grassy. **herbicide** nm weed-killer.

hérédité [eredite] nf heredity. **héréditaire** adj hereditary.

hérésie [erezi] nf heresy.

hérétique [eretik] adj heretical. n(m+f) heretic.

hérisser [ˈerise] v bristle, spike; (personne) ruffle. **se hérisser** stand on end, bristle up. **hérissé** adj bristly, prickly.

hérisson [ˈerisɔ̃] nm hedgehog.

hériter [erite] v inherit. **héritage** nm inheritance; (civilisation) heritage. **héritier** nm heir. **héritière** nf heiress.

hermétique [ɛrmetik] adj sealed; (étanche) watertight; (à l'air) airtight; impenetrable.

hermine [ɛrmin] nf ermine; (animal) stoat.

hernie [ˈɛrni] nf hernia. **hernie discale** slipped disc.

héroïne¹ [erɔin] nf (femme) heroine.

héroïne² [erɔin] nf (drogue) heroin.

héroïsme [erɔismə] nm heroism. **héroïque** adj heroic.

héron [ˈerɔ̃] nm heron.

héros [ˈero] nm hero.

hésiter [ezite] v hesitate. **hésitant** adj hesitant. **hésitation** nf hesitation.

hétéroclite [eterɔklit] adj sundry, assorted; (personne) eccentric.

hétérosexual [eterɔsɛksɥɛl] adj heterosexual.

hêtre [ˈɛtrə] nm beech.

heure [œr] nf time; (mesure) hour. **à l'heure** on time. **deux/trois etc. heures** two/three etc. o'clock. **heure d'affluence** rush hour. **heures creuses** off-peak periods pl. **heures supplémentaires** overtime sing. **tout à l'heure** (passé) just now; (futur) shortly.

heureux [œrø] adj happy; fortunate, lucky.

heurter [ˈœrte] v strike, hit; (sentiments, idées) conflict with, go against. **se heurter** collide; (s'opposer) clash. **heurt** nm collision; clash. **sans heurts** smoothly. **heurtoir** nm door-knocker.

hexagone [ɛgzagɔn] nm hexagon. **hexagonal** adj hexagonal.

hiberner [iberne] v hibernate. **hibernation** nf hibernation.

hibou [ˈibu] nm, pl -oux nm owl.

hideux [ˈidø] adj hideous.

hier [jɛr] adv yesterday. **hier soir** yesterday evening, last night.

hiérarchie [ˈjerarʃi] nf hierarchy. **hiérarchique** adj hierarchical.

hilare [ilar] adj merry, mirthful. **hilarité** nf hilarity.

hindou [ɛ̃du] adj Hindu. **Hindou, -e** nm, nf Hindu. **hindouisme** nm Hinduism.

hippique [ipik] adj horse, equestrian. **concours hippique** nm show-jumping. **hippisme** nm (courses) horse-racing; (équitation) horse-riding.

hippocampe [ipokɑ̃p] nm sea-horse.

hippodrome [ipɔdrom] nm racecourse.

hippopotame [ipɔpɔtam] nm hippopotamus.

hirondelle [irɔ̃dɛl] nf swallow.

hisser [ˈise] v hoist. **se hisser** heave or haul oneself up.

histoire [istwar] nf history; (conte) story; (fam: affaire) business. **histoires** nf pl (fam) fuss sing, trouble sing. **historien, -enne** nm, nf historian. **historique** adj historical; (événement) historic.

hiver [ivɛr] nm winter. **hivernal** adj winter; (temps) wintry.

hocher [ˈɔʃe] v **hocher la tête** (oui) nod; (non) shake one's head. **hochement de tête** nm nod; shake of the head.

hochet [ˈɔʃe] nm rattle.

hockey [ˈɔkɛ] nm hockey.

Hollande [ˈɔlɑ̃d] nf Holland. **hollandais** nm, adj Dutch. **les Hollandais** the Dutch.

homard [ˈɔmar] nm lobster.

homicide [ɔmisid] nm murder. **homicide involontaire** manslaughter.

hommage [ɔmaʒ] nm homage, tribute; (témoignage) token. **hommages** nm pl respects pl.

homme [ɔm] nm man (pl men); (espèce) mankind. **homme à tout faire** odd-job man. **homme d'affaires** businessman. **homme de loi** lawyer. **homme d'État** statesman. **homme-grenouille** nm frogman. **homme politique** politician.

homogène [ɔmɔʒɛn] adj homogeneous.

homonyme [ɔmɔnim] nm homonym; (personne) namesake.

homosexuel [ɔmɔsɛksɥɛl], **-elle** n, adj homosexual. **homosexualité** nf homosexuality.

Hongrie ['ɔ̃gri] nf Hungary. **hongrois** nm, adj Hungarian. **Hongrois, -e** nm, nf Hungarian.

honnête [ɔnɛt] adj honest; decent; (juste) fair, reasonable. **honnêteté** nf honesty; decency; fairness.

honneur [ɔnœr] nm honour; (mérite) credit.

honorer [ɔnɔre] v honour; do credit to; respect. **honorable** adj honourable, worthy. **honoraire** adj honorary.

honte ['ɔ̃t] nf shame; (déshonneur) disgrace. **avoir honte** be ashamed. **faire honte à** put to shame. **honteux** adj (penaud) ashamed; (scandaleux) shameful, disgraceful.

hôpital [ɔpital] nm hospital.

hoquet ['ɔkɛ] nm hiccup. **avoir le hoquet** have hiccups. **hoqueter** v hiccup.

horaire [ɔrɛr] adj hourly. nm timetable.

horde ['ɔrd] nf horde.

horizon [ɔrizɔ̃] nm horizon; (paysage) landscape, view.

horizontal [ɔrizɔ̃tal] adj horizontal. **horizontale** nf horizontal.

horloge [ɔrlɔʒ] nf clock.

hormis ['ɔrmi] prep but, save.

hormone [ɔrmɔn] nf hormone.

horoscope [ɔrɔskɔp] nm horoscope.

horreur [ɔrœr] nf horror. **avoir horreur de** loathe, detest. **faire horreur à** disgust.

horrible [ɔriblə] adj horrible, dreadful.

horrifier [ɔrifje] v horrify.

hors ['ɔr] prep except, apart from. **hors-bord** nm invar speedboat. **hors de** out of; (dehors) outside; (loin de) away from. **être hors de soi** be beside oneself. **hors d'œuvre** nm invar hors d'oeuvre, starter. **hors-jeu** nm, adj invar offside. **hors-la-loi** nm invar outlaw. **hors-taxe** adv, adj invar duty-free.

horticulture [ɔrtikyltyr] nf horticulture. **horticole** adj horticultural. **horticulteur** nm horticulturalist.

hospice [ɔspis] nm home.

hospitalier [ɔspitalje] adj (service) hospital; (accueillant) hospitable. **hospitalité** nf hospitality.

hostile [ɔstil] adj hostile.

hôte [ot] nm host. n(m+f) (invité) guest. **hôtesse** nf hostess. **hôtesse de l'air** nf hostess.

hôtel [otɛl] nm hotel; (particulier) mansion. **hôtel de ville** town hall. **hôtel-Dieu** nm general hospital. **hôtelier, -ère** nm, nf hotelier.

houblon ['ublɔ̃] nm hop.

houe ['u] nf hoe.

houille ['uj] nf coal. **houille blanche** hydro-electric power. **houillère** nf coalmine.

houle ['ul] nf swell. **houleux** adj turbulent, stormy.

houppe ['up] nf tuft, tassel. **houppette** nf powder puff.

houspiller ['uspije] v scold, tell off.

housse ['us] nf cover.

houx ['u] nm holly.

hublot ['yblo] nm porthole.

huer ['ɥe] v boo; (chouette) hoot. **huées** nf pl boos pl.

huile [ɥil] nf oil. **huile de coude** (fam) elbow grease. **huile de ricin** castor oil. **huile solaire** suntan oil. **huiler** v oil. **huileux** adj oily.

huis [ɥi] nm à huis clos in camera.

huissier [ɥisje] nm usher; (jur) bailiff.

huit [ɥit] nm, adj eight. **huit jours a** week. **... en huit** a week on ... **huitaine** nf about eight; about a week. **huitième** n(m+f), adj eighth.

huître [ɥitrə] nf oyster.

humain [ymɛ̃] adj human; (compatissant) humane. nm human. **humanitaire** adj humanitarian. **humanité** nf humanity.

humble [œblə] adj humble.

humecter [ymɛkte] v dampen, moisten.

humer [yme] v smell; (air) inhale.

humeur [ymœr] nf mood, humour; temperament, temper; (colère) bad temper. **d'humeur égale** even-tempered.

humide [ymid] adj damp, moist; (climat) humid. **humidité** nf humidity; dampness, damp.

humilier [ymilje] v humiliate. **humiliation** nf humiliation. **humilité** nf humility, humbleness.

humour [ymur] nm humour; sense of humour. **humoriste** n(m+f) humorist. **humoristique** adj humorous.

huppe ['yp] nf crest.

hurler ['yrle] v yell, roar; (chien) howl. **hurlement** nm yell, roar; howl.

hussard ['ysar] nm hussar.

hutte ['yt] nf hut.

hybride [ibrid] nm, adj hybrid.

hydrate [idrat] *nm* **hydrate de carbone** carbohydrate.

hydraulique [idrolik] *adj* hydraulic.

hydro-électrique [idroelɛktrik] *adj* hydro-electric.

hydrofoil [idrofɔjl] *nm* hydrofoil.

hydrogène [idrɔʒɛn] *nm* hydrogen.

hydromel [idrɔmɛl] *nm* mead.

hydrophile [idrɔfil] *adj* absorbent.

hyène [jɛn] *nf* hyena.

hygiène [iʒɛn] *nf* hygiene. **hygiénique** *adj* hygienic.

hymne [imnə] *nm* hymn. **hymne national** national anthem.

hypermétropie [ipermetrɔpi] *nf* long-sightedness. **hypermétrope** *adj* long-sighted.

hypertension [ipertɑ̃sjɔ̃] *nf* high blood pressure.

hypnose [ipnoz] *nf* hypnosis. **hypnotique** *adj* hypnotic. **hypnotiser** *v* hypnotize. **hypnotiseur** *nm* hypnotist. **hypnotisme** *nm* hypnotism.

hypocondrie [ipokɔ̃dri] *nf* hypochondria. **hypocondriaque** *n(m+f)*, *adj* hypochondriac.

hypocrite [ipokrit] *adj* hypocritical. *n(m+f)* hypocrite. **hypocrisie** *nf* hypocrisy.

hypodermique [ipodɛrmik] *adj* hypodermic.

hypotension [ipotɑ̃sjɔ̃] *nf* low blood pressure.

hypothéquer [ipoteke] *v* mortgage. **hypothèque** *nf* mortgage.

hypothèse [ipotɛz] *nf* hypothesis. **hypothétique** *adj* hypothetical.

hystérectomie [isterɛktɔmi] *nf* hysterectomy.

hystérie [isteri] *nf* hysteria. **hystérique** *adj* hysterical.

I

iceberg [ajsbɛrg] *nm* iceberg.

ici [isi] *adv* (*lieu*) here; (*temps*) now. **d'ici là** before then. **d'ici peu** before long. **par ici** this way.

icône [ikon] *nf* icon.

idéal [ideal] *nm*, *adj* ideal.

idéaliste [idealist] *adj* idealistic. *n(m+f)* idealist.

idée [ide] *nf* idea; (*esprit*) mind. **idée fixe** obsession. **idée lumineuse** brainwave.

identifier [idɑ̃tifje] *v* identify. **identification** *nf* identification.

identique [idɑ̃tik] *adj* identical. **identité** *nf* identity.

idéologie [ideɔlɔʒi] *nf* ideology.

idiome [idjom] *nm* idiom. **idiomatique** *adj* idiomatic.

idiosyncrasie [idjɔsɛ̃krazi] *nf* idiosyncrasy.

idiot [idjo], **-e** *adj* idiotic. *nm*, *nf* idiot. **idiotie** *nf* idiocy, stupidity; (*action, propos*) idiotic or stupid thing.

idiotisme [idjɔtismə] *nm* idiom.

idolâtrer [idɔlɑtre] *v* idolize. **idolâtrie** *nf* idolatry.

idole [idɔl] *nf* idol.

idyllique [idilik] *adj* idyllic.

if [if] *nm* yew.

igloo [iglu] *nm* igloo.

ignifuger [iɲifyʒe] *v* fireproof. **ignifuge** *adj* fireproof.

ignorer [iɲɔre] *v* not know, be unaware of. **ignorance** *nf* ignorance. **ignorant** *adj* ignorant. **ignorant de** unaware of. **ignoré** *adj* unknown.

il [il] *pron* it; (*personne*) he. **il y a** (*sing*) there is; (*pl*) there are.

île [il] *nf* island. **les îles anglo-normandes** the Channel Islands.

illégal [ilegal] *adj* illegal. **illégalité** *nf* illegality.

illégitime [ileʒitim] *adj* illegitimate. **illégitimité** *nf* illegitimacy.

illettré [iletre], **-e** *n*, *adj* illiterate.

illicite [ilisit] *adj* illicit.

illimité [ilimite] *adj* unlimited, boundless.

illisible [ilizibla] *adj* (*écriture*) illegible; (*livre*) unreadable.

illogique [ilɔʒik] *adj* illogical.

illuminer [ilymine] *v* light up, illuminate. **illumination** *nf* illumination, lighting.

illusion [ilyzjɔ̃] *nf* illusion. **illusion d'optique** optical illusion.

illustre [ilystra] *adj* illustrious.

illustrer [ilystre] *v* illustrate. **illustrateur**, **-trice** *nm*, *nf* illustrator. **illustration** *nf* illustration.

ils [il] *pron* they.

image [imaʒ] *nf* image; (*dessin*) picture; reflection.

imaginer [imaʒine] v imagine; (inventer) think up. **s'imaginer** imagine; (croire) think. **imaginaire** adj imaginary. **imaginatif** adj imaginative. **imagination** nf imagination.

imbécile [ɛ̃besil] adj stupid. n(m+f) imbecile.

imbiber [ɛ̃bibe] v saturate, impregnate, soak. **s'imbiber** absorb.

imbu [ɛ̃by] adj imbu de full of, steeped in.

imiter [imite] v imitate; copy; (signature) forge; (ressembler) look like; (célébrité) impersonate. **imitation** nf imitation; forgery; impersonation.

immaculé [imakyle] adj immaculate, spotless.

immanquable [ɛ̃mɑ̃kablə] adj inevitable; infallible.

immatriculer [imatrikyle] v register. **immatriculation** nf registration.

immédiat [imedja] adj immediate.

immense [imɑ̃s] adj vast, immense; (espace) boundless.

immerger [imɛrʒe] v immerse, submerge. **immersion** nf immersion, submersion.

immeuble [imœblə] nm building; (appartements) block of flats; (bureaux) office block.

immigrer [imigre] v immigrate. **immigrant, -e** nm, nf immigrant. **immigration** nf immigration.

imminent [iminɑ̃] adj imminent, impending.

immiscer [imise] v s'immiscer dans interfere with.

immobile [imɔbil] adj immobile, motionless, still. **immobilier** adj property. **immobiliser** v immobilize. **s'immobiliser** come to a standstill.

immonde [imɔ̃d] adj vile, foul; (rel) unclean. **immondices** nf pl refuse sing.

immoral [imɔral] adj immoral. **immoralité** nf immorality.

immortel [imɔrtɛl] adj immortal. **immortaliser** v immortalize. **immortalité** nf immortality.

immuniser [imynize] v immunize. **immunisation** nf immunization. **immunisé** adj immune. **immunité** nf immunity.

impact [ɛ̃pakt] nm impact.

impair [ɛ̃pɛr] adj odd, uneven. nm blunder.

imparfait [ɛ̃parfɛ] nm, adj imperfect.

impartial [ɛ̃parsjal] adj impartial, unbiased. **impartialité** nf impartiality.

impasse [ɛ̃pas] nf dead end, no through road; (situation) impasse, deadlock.

impassible [ɛ̃pasiblə] adj impassive.

impatience [ɛ̃pasjɑ̃s] nf impatience. **impatient** adj impatient; (avide) eager. **impatienter** [ɛ̃pasjɑ̃te] v irritate. **s'impatienter** lose one's patience.

impeccable [ɛ̃pekablə] adj perfect, impeccable.

imper [ɛ̃pɛr] nm (fam) mac.

impératif [ɛ̃peratif] nm, adj imperative.

impératrice [ɛ̃peratris] nf empress.

impérial [ɛ̃perjal] adj imperial. **impériale** nf (autobus) top deck. **autobus à impériale** double-decker.

imperméable [ɛ̃pɛrmeablə] adj waterproof; (roches) impervious. nm raincoat. **imperméabiliser** v waterproof.

impersonnel [ɛ̃pɛrsɔnɛl] adj impersonal.

impertinent [ɛ̃pɛrtinɑ̃] adj impertinent. **impertinence** nf impertinence.

impétueux [ɛ̃petɥø] adj impetuous.

impitoyable [ɛ̃pitwajablə] adj merciless, ruthless.

implicite [ɛ̃plisit] adj implicit.

impliquer [ɛ̃plike] v imply; (mêler) involve.

implorer [ɛ̃plɔre] v implore.

impoli [ɛ̃pɔli] adj impolite.

impopulaire [ɛ̃pɔpylɛr] adj unpopular. **impopularité** nf unpopularity.

importer[1] [ɛ̃pɔrte] v (comm) import. **importation** nf import.

***importer**[2] [ɛ̃pɔrte] v matter. **n'importe** never mind, it doesn't matter. **n'importe comment/où/quand/quel/qui/quoi** anyhow/anywhere/anytime/any/anybody/anything. **importance** nf importance; (grandeur) size, extent. **important** adj important; considerable.

importuner [ɛ̃pɔrtyne] v bother, trouble.

imposer [ɛ̃poze] v impose; (prescrire) set; tax. **imposable** adj taxable. **imposant** adj imposing, impressive.

impossible [ɛ̃posiblə] adj impossible.

imposteur [ɛ̃postœr] nm impostor.

impôt [ɛ̃po] nm tax; taxation.

impotent [ɛ̃potɑ̃], **-e** adj disabled, crippled. nm, nf disabled person. **impotence** nf disability.

imprécis [ɛ̃presi] adj imprecise.

imprégner [ɛ̃preɲe] v impregnate; (air) pervade. **s'imprégner de** absorb, soak up.

impression [ɛpresjɔ̃] *nf* impression; (*imprimerie*) printing. **impressionnable** *adj* impressionable. **impressionnant** *adj* impressive. **impressionner** *v* impress; (*bouleverser*) upset.

imprévu [ɛprevy] *adj* unexpected, unforeseen.

imprimer [ɛprime] *v* print; (*cachet*) stamp; (*marquer*) imprint; publish. **imprimé** *nm* (*poste*) printed matter; (*tissu*) print. **imprimerie** *nf* printing; printing house or works. **imprimeur** *nm* printer.

improbable [ɛprɔbablə] *adj* improbable, unlikely.

impromptu [ɛprɔ̃pty] *adj*, *adv* impromptu.

improviser [ɛprɔvize] *v* improvise. **improvisation** *nf* improvisation.

improviste [ɛprɔvist] *nm* **à l'improviste** without warning, unexpectedly.

imprudent [ɛprydɑ̃] *adj* unwise, foolish, careless. **imprudence** *nf* foolishness, carelessness.

impudent [ɛpydɑ̃] *adj* impudent. **impudence** *nf* impudence.

impuissant [ɛpɥisɑ̃] *adj* powerless; (*effort*) ineffectual; (*sexuellement*) impotent. **impuissance** *nf* impotence.

impulsion [ɛpylsjɔ̃] *nf* impulse; impetus. **impulsif** *adj* impulsive.

impur [ɛpyr] *adj* impure. **impureté** *nf* impurity.

imputer [ɛpyte] *v* impute, attribute; (*frais*) charge.

inaccessible [inaksesiblə] *adj* inaccessible.

inactif [inaktif] *adj* inactive, idle.

inadapté [inadapte], **-e** *nm*, *nf* misfit. *adj* (*psychol*) maladjusted.

inadvertance [inadvertɑ̃s] *nf* oversight. **par inadvertance** inadvertently.

inanimé [inanime] *adj* inanimate; (*personne*) unconscious.

inaperçu [inapersy] *adj* unnoticed. **passer inaperçu** go unnoticed.

inappréciable [inapresjablə] *adj* invaluable; imperceptible.

inapte [inapt] *adj* incapable, unfit.

inarticulé [inartikyle] *adj* inarticulate.

inattendu [inatɑ̃dy] *adj* unexpected.

inaudible [inodiblə] *adj* inaudible.

inaugurer [inogyre] *v* inaugurate; (*plaque*) unveil; (*exposition*) open. **inaugural** *adj* inaugural; (*voyage*) maiden. **inauguration** *nf* inauguration; unveiling; opening.

incapable [ɛkapablə] *adj* incapable, unable.

incapacité [ɛkapasite] *nf* incapacity; incompetence; inability; (*invalidité*) disability.

incendier [ɛsɑ̃dje] *v* set fire to, burn. **incendiaire** *adj* incendiary. **incendie** *nm* fire. **incendie volontaire** arson.

incertain [ɛsɛrtɛ̃] *adj* uncertain. **incertitude** *nf* uncertainty.

incessant [ɛsesɑ̃] *adj* incessant. **incessamment** *adv* very soon.

inceste [ɛsɛst] *nm* incest. **incestueux** *adj* incestuous.

incident [ɛsidɑ̃] *adj* incidental. *nm* incident; (*anicroche*) setback, hitch. **incidemment** *adv* incidentally.

incinérer [ɛsinere] *v* (*ordures*) incinerate; (*cadavre*) cremate. **incinérateur** *nm* incinerator. **incinération** *nf* incineration; cremation.

inciter [ɛsite] *v* incite, encourage.

incliner [ɛkline] *v* slope, tilt; tend, be inclined. **s'incliner** bow. **inclinaison** *nm* slope, incline. **inclination** *nf* inclination.

*****inclure** [ɛklyr] *v* include; (*joindre*) enclose; insert. **inclus** *adj* enclosed; included, inclusive. **inclusion** *nf* inclusion; insertion. **inclusivement** *adv* inclusively.

incognito [ɛkɔnito] *adv* incognito.

incohérent [ɛkɔerɑ̃] *adj* incoherent.

incolore [ɛkɔlɔr] *adj* colourless.

incommoder [ɛkɔmɔde] *v* disturb, bother. **incommode** *adj* inconvenient, awkward; (*siège*) uncomfortable. **incommodité** *nf* inconvenience.

incompatible [ɛkɔ̃patiblə] *adj* incompatible. **incompatibilité** *nf* incompatibility.

incompétent [ɛkɔ̃petɑ̃] *adj* incompetent. **incompétence** *nf* incompetence; (*ignorance*) lack of knowledge.

incomplet, **-ète** [ɛkɔ̃plɛ, -ɛt] *adj* incomplete.

inconcevable [ɛkɔ̃svablə] *adj* inconceivable.

inconfort [ɛkɔ̃fɔr] *nm* discomfort. **inconfortable** *adj* uncomfortable.

inconnu [ɛkɔny], **-e** *adj* unknown; strange. *nm*, *nf* stranger. **l'inconnu** the unknown.

inconscience [ɛkɔ̃sjɑ̃s] *nf* unconsciousness; (*folie*) thoughtlessness, rashness. **inconscient** *adj* unconscious; thoughtless, rash.

inconséquent [ɛ̃kɔ̃sekã] adj inconsistent; (irréfléchi) thoughtless.

inconstant [ɛ̃kɔ̃stã] adj fickle.

incontestable [ɛ̃kɔ̃tɛstablə] adj unquestionable, undeniable.

inconvenant [ɛ̃kɔ̃vnã] adj improper, unseemly.

inconvénient [ɛ̃kɔ̃venjã] nm disadvantage, drawback; risk.

incorporer [ɛ̃kɔrpore] v incorporate; mix.

incorrect [ɛ̃kɔrɛkt] adj incorrect; impolite.

incrédule [ɛ̃kredyl] adj incredulous. n(m+f) (rel) unbeliever. **incrédulité** nf incredulity.

incriminer [ɛ̃krimine] v incriminate.

incroyable [ɛ̃krwajablə] adj incredible.

incuber [ɛ̃kybe] v incubate, hatch. **incubation** nf incubation.

inculper [ɛ̃kylpe] v charge. **inculpation** nf charge.

inculte [ɛ̃kylt] adj uncultivated; (négligé) unkempt.

incurable [ɛ̃kyrablə] adj incurable.

Inde [ɛ̃d] nf India.

indécent [ɛ̃desã] adj indecent. **indécence** nf indecency.

indécis [ɛ̃desi] adj (irrésolu) indecisive; (hésitant) undecided; (douteux) unsettled; vague.

indéfini [ɛ̃defini] adj indefinite.

indemne [ɛ̃dɛmnə] adj unharmed, unhurt.

indemniser [ɛ̃dɛmnize] v compensate, reimburse. **indemnité** nf compensation, indemnity; (frais) allowance.

indépendant [ɛ̃depãdã] adj independent; (appartement) self-contained; (journaliste, etc.) freelance. **indépendance** nf independence.

index [ɛ̃dɛks] nm index; (aiguille) needle, pointer; (doigt) index finger.

indicatif [ɛ̃dikatif] adj indicative. nm (musical) signature tune; (téléphonique) dialling code; (gramm) indicative.

indication [ɛ̃dikasjɔ̃] nf indication; (renseignement) information; instruction, direction. **indicateur** nm indicator; (horaire) timetable; guide; gauge.

indice [ɛ̃dis] nm indication, sign; (clef) clue; index, rating.

indien [ɛ̃djɛ̃] adj Indian. **Indien, -enne** nm, nf Indian.

indifférent [ɛ̃diferã] adj indifferent; (sans importance) immaterial. **indifférence** nf indifference.

indigence [ɛ̃diʒãs] nf poverty. **indigent** adj poor, destitute.

indigène [ɛ̃diʒɛn] n(m+f), adj native.

indigestion [ɛ̃diʒɛstjɔ̃] nf indigestion.

indigne [ɛ̃diɲ] adj unworthy.

indigner [ɛ̃diɲe] v make indignant. **s'indigner** be indignant. **indignation** nf indignation. **indigné** adj indignant.

indiquer [ɛ̃dike] v indicate, show, point out.

indirect [ɛ̃dirɛkt] adj indirect.

indiscipliné [ɛ̃disipline] adj unruly.

indiscret, -ète [ɛ̃diskrɛ, -ɛt] adj indiscreet. **indiscrétion** nf indiscretion.

indispensable [ɛ̃dispãsablə] adj essential.

indisposé [ɛ̃dispoze] adj unwell.

individu [ɛ̃dividy] nm individual. **individualité** nf individuality. **individuel** adj individual; personal, private.

indolent [ɛ̃dɔlã] adj idle, indolent. **indolence** nf idleness, indolence.

indolore [ɛ̃dɔlɔr] adj painless.

*****induire** [ɛ̃dЧir] v infer. **induire en erreur** mislead.

indulgence [ɛ̃dylʒãs] nf indulgence, leniency. **indulgent** adj indulgent, lenient.

industrie [ɛ̃dystri] nf industry. **industrialiser** v industrialize. **industriel** adj industrial.

inébranlable [inebrãlablə] adj steadfast, solid.

inefficace [inefikas] adj (mesure) ineffective; (employé) inefficient.

inégal [inegal] adj (irrégulier) uneven; (différent) unequal. **inégalité** nf inequality; unevenness; difference.

inepte [inɛpt] adj inept.

inerte [inɛrt] adj inert, lifeless; passive, apathetic. **inertie** nf inertia; apathy.

inestimable [inɛstimablə] adj invaluable.

inévitable [inevitablə] adj inevitable; (accident) unavoidable.

inexact [inɛgzakt] adj inaccurate; unpunctual. **inexactitude** nf inaccuracy; unpunctuality.

inexpérimenté [inɛksperimãte] adj (personne) inexperienced; (produit) untested.

infaillible [ɛ̃fajiblə] adj infallible.

infâme [ɛ̃fam] adj infamous; (odieux) vile, despicable. **infamie** nf infamy.

infanterie [ɛ̃fãtri] nf infantry.

infarctus [ɛ̃farktys] nm **infarctus du myocarde** coronary thrombosis.

infatué [ɛ̃fatᵴe] *adj* conceited, vain.

infécond [ɛ̃fekɔ̃] *adj* sterile, infertile. **infécondité** *nf* sterility, infertility.

infect [ɛ̃fɛkt] *adj* vile, revolting.

infecter [ɛ̃fɛkte] *v* infect, contaminate. **s'infecter** turn septic. **infectieux** *adj* infectious. **infection** *nf* infection; (*puanteur*) stench.

inférieur, -e [ɛ̃ferjœr] *adj* (*plus bas*) lower; (*qualité*) inferior; (*quantité*) smaller. *nm, nf* inferior. **infériorité** *nf* inferiority.

infester [ɛ̃fɛste] *v* infest. **infestation** *nf* infestation.

infidèle [ɛ̃fidɛl] *adj* unfaithful; (*inexact*) inaccurate. **infidélité** *nf* unfaithfulness; (*mari, femme*) infidelity; inaccuracy.

s'infiltrer [ɛ̃filtre] *v* infiltrate; (*liquide*) percolate; (*lumière*) filter through. **infiltration** *nf* infiltration.

infime [ɛ̃fim] *adj* tiny, minute.

infini [ɛ̃fini] *adj* infinite; interminable. *nm* infinity. **infinité** *nf* infinity; infinite number. **infinitif** *nm, adj* infinitive.

infirme [ɛ̃firm] *adj* crippled, disabled; (*vieillards*) infirm. *nm, nf* cripple, disabled person. **infirmerie** *nf* (*école*) sick bay. **infirmier, -ère** *nm, nf* nurse. **infirmité** *nf* disability; infirmity.

inflammable [ɛ̃flɑmablə] *adj* inflammable. **inflammation** *nf* inflammation.

inflation [ɛ̃flɑsjɔ̃] *nf* inflation.

inflexion [ɛ̃flɛksjɔ̃] *nf* inflection; (*courbe*) bend.

infliger [ɛ̃fliʒe] *v* inflict; impose.

influencer [ɛ̃flyɑ̃se] *v* influence. **influence** *nf* influence. **influent** *adj* influential.

influer [ɛ̃flye] *v* **influer sur** have an influence on.

informe [ɛ̃fɔrm] *adj* shapeless.

informer [ɛ̃fɔrme] *v* inform. **s'informer** inquire, find out. **information** *nf* information; (*jur*) inquiry. **informations** *nf pl* news *sing*.

infortune [ɛ̃fɔrtyn] *nf* misfortune. **infortuné** *adj* ill-fated, wretched.

infraction [ɛ̃fraksjɔ̃] *nf* offence; (*loi*) infringement, breach.

infroissable [ɛ̃frwasablə] *adj* crease-resistant.

infuser [ɛ̃fyze] *v* (*thé*) brew, infuse.

ingénieur [ɛ̃ʒenjœr] *nm* engineer.

ingénieux [ɛ̃ʒenjø] *adj* ingenious. **ingéniosité** *nf* ingenuity.

ingénu [ɛ̃ʒeny] *adj* naïve, ingenuous.

s'ingérer [ɛ̃ʒere] *v* interfere, meddle. **ingérence** *nf* interference.

ingrat [ɛ̃gra] *adj* ungrateful; (*tâche*) thankless; (*déplaisant*) unattractive. **ingratitude** *nf* ingratitude.

ingrédient [ɛ̃gredjɑ̃] *nm* ingredient.

inhabile [inabil] *adj* clumsy, inept.

inhabité [inabite] *adj* uninhabited, unoccupied.

inhaler [inale] *v* inhale.

inhérent [inerɑ̃] *adj* inherent.

inhiber [inibe] *v* inhibit. **inhibition** *nf* inhibition.

inhumain [inymɛ̃] *adj* inhuman.

inimitié [inimitje] *nf* enmity.

initial [inisjal] *adj* initial. **initiale** *nf* initial.

initiative [inisjativ] *nf* initiative.

initier [inisje] *v* initiate. **initiation** *nf* initiation.

injecter [ɛ̃ʒɛkte] *v* inject. **injection** *nf* injection.

injurier [ɛ̃ʒyrje] *v* abuse, insult. **injure** *nf* abuse, insult. **injurieux** *adj* abusive, insulting.

injuste [ɛ̃ʒyst] *adj* unjust, unfair. **injustice** *nf* injustice, unfairness.

inné [ine] *adj* innate.

innocent [inɔsɑ̃], **-e** *adj* innocent. *nm, nf* innocent (person); idiot, simpleton. **innocence** *nf* innocence.

innovation [inɔvɑsjɔ̃] *nf* innovation.

inoccupé [inɔkype] *adj* unoccupied.

inoculer [inɔkyle] *v* inoculate. **inoculation** *nf* inoculation.

inonder [inɔ̃de] *v* flood; (*tremper*) soak. **inondation** *nf* flood.

inopiné [inɔpine] *adj* unexpected.

inouï [inwi] *adj* incredible, unheard-of.

inoxydable [inɔksidablə] *adj* stainless; (*couteau, etc.*) stainless steel.

inquiéter [ɛ̃kjete] *v* worry, bother. **inquiet, -ète** *adj* worried, anxious. **inquiétude** *nf* worry, anxiety.

inquisition [ɛ̃kizisjɔ̃] *nf* inquisition.

inscription [ɛ̃skripsjɔ̃] *nf* inscription; (*club, cours, etc.*) enrolment, registration.

*inscrire [ɛ̃skrir] *v* write down, enrol, register; (*graver*) inscribe.

insecte [ɛ̃sɛkt] *nm* insect. **insecticide** *nm* insecticide.

insécurité [ɛ̃sekyrite] *nf* insecurity.

inséminer [ɛ̃semine] *v* inseminate. **insémination** *nf* insemination.

insensé [ɛ̃sãse] *adj* insane, crazy.

insensible [ɛ̃sãsiblə] *adj* insensitive; imperceptible. **insensibilité** *nf* insensitivity.

insérer [ɛ̃sere] *v* insert. **s'insérer dans** fit into. **insertion** *nf* insertion.

insidieux [ɛ̃sidjø] *adj* insidious.

insigne [ɛ̃siɲ] *adj* distinguished, notable. *nm* badge, insignia.

insignifiant [ɛ̃siɲifjã] *adj* insignificant. **insignifiance** *nf* insignificance.

insinuer [ɛ̃sinɥe] *v* insinuate, imply. **s'insinuer dans** worm one's way into. **insinuation** *nf* insinuation.

insipide [ɛ̃sipid] *adj* insipid.

insister [ɛ̃siste] *v* insist. **insister sur** stress. **insistance** *nf* insistence. **insistant** *adj* insistent.

insolation [ɛ̃solasjɔ̃] *nf* (*méd*) sunstroke; (*temps*) sunshine.

insolent [ɛ̃solã] *adj* insolent. **insolence** *nf* insolence.

insolite [ɛ̃solit] *adj* strange, unusual.

insomnie [ɛ̃sɔmni] *nf* insomnia. **insomniaque** *n(m+f)*, *adj* insomniac.

insonore [ɛ̃sɔnɔr] *adj* soundproof. **insonoriser** *v* soundproof.

insouciant [ɛ̃susjã] *adj* carefree, happy-go-lucky.

inspecter [ɛ̃spɛkte] *v* inspect. **inspecteur**, **-trice** *nm*, *nf* inspector. **inspection** *nf* inspection.

inspirer [ɛ̃spire] *v* inspire; (*respirer*) breathe in. **inspiration** *nf* inspiration.

instable [ɛ̃stablə] *adj* unstable. **instabilité** *nf* instability.

installer [ɛ̃stale] *v* install; (*pièce*) fit out. **s'installer** settle in (or down); (*emménager*) move in, set up home. **installation** *nf* installation. **installations** *nf pl* fittings *pl*, facilities *pl*; (*usine*) plant *sing*.

instant [ɛ̃stã] *nm* moment, instant. **à l'instant** at this moment; (*passé*) a moment ago. **par instants** at times. **pour l'instant** for the time being. **instantané** *adj* instantaneous; (*café*) instant.

instar [ɛ̃star] *nm* **à l'instar de** after the fashion of.

instigation [ɛ̃stigasjɔ̃] *nf* instigation. **instigateur**, **-trice** *nm*, *nf* instigator.

instinct [ɛ̃stɛ̃] *nm* instinct. **instinctif** *adj* instinctive.

instituer [ɛ̃stitɥe] *v* institute. **institut** *nm* institute. **instituteur**, **-trice** *nm*, *nf* pri-

mary school teacher. **institution** *nf* institution; (*école*) private school.

instruction [ɛ̃stryksjɔ̃] *nf* education. **instructions** *nf pl* instructions *pl*. **instructif** *adj* instructive.

***instruire** [ɛ̃strɥir] *v* teach, instruct; educate; inform.

instrument [ɛ̃strymã] *nm* instrument; (*outil*) tool. **instrumental** *adj* instrumental.

insu [ɛ̃sy] *nm* **à l'insu de** unknown to. **à mon insu** without my knowing it.

insubordonné [ɛ̃sybɔrdɔne] *adj* insubordinate. **insubordination** *nf* insubordination.

insuccès [ɛ̃syksɛ] *nm* failure.

insuffisant [ɛ̃syfizã] *adj* inadequate; (*quantité*) insufficient. **insuffisance** *nf* inadequacy; insufficiency.

insulaire [ɛ̃sylɛr] *adj* insular. *n(m+f)* islander.

insuline [ɛ̃sylin] *nf* insulin.

insulter [ɛ̃sylte] *v* insult. **insulte** *nf* insult.

insupportable [ɛ̃sypɔrtablə] *adj* unbearable, intolerable.

s'insurger [ɛ̃syrʒe] *v* rebel. **insurgé**, **-e** *nm*, *nf* rebel. **insurrection** *nf* revolt.

intact [ɛ̃takt] *adj* intact.

intègre [ɛ̃tɛgrə] *adj* honest. **intégrité** *nf* integrity.

intégrer [ɛ̃tegre] *v* integrate. **intégral** *adj* complete, full; (*texte*) unabridged. **intégration** *nf* integration.

intellect [ɛ̃telɛkt] *nm* intellect. **intellectuel**, **-elle** *n*, *adj* intellectual.

intelligence [ɛ̃teliʒãs] *nf* intelligence; (*compréhension*) understanding. **intelligent** *adj* intelligent, clever.

intelligible [ɛ̃teliʒiblə] *adj* intelligible.

intendant [ɛ̃tãdã] *nm* (*école*) bursar; (*maison*) steward; (*mil*) quartermaster.

intense [ɛ̃tãs] *adj* intense. **intensif** *adj* intensive. **intensifier** *v* intensify. **intensité** *nf* intensity.

intention [ɛ̃tãsjɔ̃] *nf* intention. **à l'intention de** for the benefit of, for. **avoir l'intention de** intend to. **intentionnel** *adj* intentional.

intercéder [ɛ̃tɛrsede] *v* intercede.

intercepter [ɛ̃tɛrsepte] *v* intercept; (*boucher*) block, cut off. **interception** *nf* interception.

***interdire** [ɛ̃tɛrdir] *v* forbid, ban. **interdiction** *nf* ban. **interdit** *adj* prohibited.

intéresser [ɛterese] v interest; concern. **s'intéresser à** be interested in. **intéressant** adj interesting; (offre, prix) attractive.

intérêt [ɛterɛ] nm interest; importance.

intérieur, -e [ɛterjœr] adj inner, internal, inside; (pol) domestic, home. nm interior, inside. **à l'intérieur** inside.

intérim [ɛterim] nm interim. **intérimaire** adj temporary.

interjection [ɛterʒɛksjɔ̃] nf interjection.

interloquer [ɛterlɔke] v dumbfound, take aback.

intermède [ɛtermɛd] nm interlude.

intermédiaire [ɛtermedjɛr] adj intermediate. n(m+f) go-between; (comm) middleman. **sans intermédiaire** directly.

interminable [ɛterminablə] adj endless, interminable.

intermittent [ɛtermitɑ̃] adj intermittent.

internat [ɛterna] nm boarding school.

international [ɛternasjɔnal] adj international.

interne [ɛtern] adj internal. n(m+f) boarder; (méd) houseman, intern. **internement** nm internment. **interner** v intern.

interpeller [ɛterpele] v (appeler) call out to; (apostropher) shout at; question.

interphone [ɛterfɔn] nm intercom.

interposer [ɛterpoze] v interpose. **s'interposer** intervene.

interpréter [ɛterprete] v interpret; (théâtre, musique) perform. **interprétation** nf interpretation. **interprète** n(m+f) interpreter; performer.

interroger [ɛterɔʒe] v question; examine; (police, etc.) interrogate. **interrogatif** nm, adj interrogative. **interrogation** nf questioning, interrogation; question; (école) test. **interrogatoire** nm questioning; (jur) cross-examination.

*interrompre** [ɛterɔ̃prə] v interrupt; (arrêter) break off.

interruption [ɛterypsjɔ̃] nf interruption. **interrupteur** nm switch.

interurbain [ɛteryrbɛ̃] adj (téléphone) long-distance.

intervalle [ɛterval] nm interval; space. **dans l'intervalle** in the meantime.

*intervenir** [ɛtervənir] v intervene; (survenir) take place, occur. **intervention** nf intervention.

intervertir [ɛtervertir] v invert, reverse.

interview [ɛtervju] nf interview.

intestin [ɛtestɛ̃] nm intestine. **intestins** nm

pl bowels pl. adj internal. **intestinal** adj intestinal.

intime [ɛtim] adj intimate; private, personal; (ami) close. n(m+f) close friend. **intimité** nf intimacy; privacy.

intimider [ɛtimide] v intimidate. **intimidation** nf intimidation.

intituler [ɛtityle] v entitle, call. **intitulé** nm title.

intolérable [ɛtolerablə] adj intolerable. **intolérance** nf intolerance. **intolérant** adj intolerant.

intonation [ɛtɔnasjɔ̃] nf intonation.

intoxiquer [ɛtɔksike] v poison. **intoxication** nf poisoning. **intoxiqué, -e** nm, nf addict.

intransitif [ɛtrɑ̃zitif] nm, adj intransitive.

intraveineux [ɛtravenø] adj intravenous.

intrépide [ɛtrepid] adj intrepid, bold.

intriguer [ɛtrige] v intrigue; (comploter) scheme. **intrigue** nf scheme; (film, livre, etc.) plot.

intrinsèque [ɛtrɛ̃sɛk] adj intrinsic.

*introduire** [ɛtrɔdɥir] v introduce; insert; (faire entrer) show in. **s'introduire** get in. **introduction** nf introduction; insertion; admission.

introverti, -e [ɛtrɔverti] adj introverted. nm, nf introvert.

intrus, -e [ɛtry] nm, nf intruder. adj intrusive. **intrusion** nf intrusion.

intuition [ɛtɥisjɔ̃] nf intuition. **intuitif** adj intuitive.

inutile [inytil] adj useless; (effort) pointless; (superflu) needless.

invaincu [ɛvɛ̃ky] adj unbeaten.

invalide [ɛvalid] n(m+f) disabled person. adj disabled. **invalidité** nf disability.

invariable [ɛvarjablə] adj invariable.

invasion [ɛvazjɔ̃] nf invasion.

inventaire [ɛvɑ̃ter] nm inventory; (comm) stocktaking.

inventer [ɛvɑ̃te] v invent; (forger) make up; (imaginer) think up. **inventeur, -trice** nm, nf inventor. **invention** nf invention.

inverse [ɛvers] nm, adj opposite, reverse. **inversement** adv conversely. **inverser** v reverse, invert. **inversion** nf inversion.

invertébré [ɛvertebre] nm, adj invertebrate.

investigation [ɛvestigasjɔ̃] nf investigation.

investir [ɛvestir] v invest. **investissement** nm investment.

invisible [ɛ̃viziblə] *adj* invisible.

inviter [ɛ̃vite] *v* invite, ask. **invitation** *nf* invitation. **invité, -e** *nm, nf* guest.

involontaire [ɛ̃vɔlɔ̃tɛr] *adj* involuntary; unintentional.

invoquer [ɛ̃vɔke] *v* call upon; (*excuse*) put forward.

invraisemblable [ɛ̃vrɛsɑ̃blablə] *adj* unlikely, improbable; incredible.

iode [jɔd] *nm* iodine.

ion [jɔ̃] *nm* ion.

iris [iris] *nm* iris.

Irlande [irlɑ̃d] *nf* Ireland. **irlandais -e**, *adj* Irish. **les Irlandais** the Irish.

ironie [irɔni] *nf* irony. **ironique** *adj* ironic.

irrationnel [irasjɔnɛl] *adj* irrational.

irréel [ireɛl] *adj* unreal.

irréfléchi [irefleʃi] *adj* thoughtless, hasty.

irrégulier [iregylje] *adj* irregular. **irrégularité** *nf* irregularity.

irrésistible [irezistiblə] *adj* irresistible.

irrespect [irɛspɛ] *nm* disrespect. **irrespectueux** *adj* disrespectful.

irrévocable [irevɔkablə] *adj* irrevocable.

irriguer [irige] *v* irrigate. **irrigation** *nf* irrigation.

irriter [irite] *v* irritate; annoy. **irritable** *adj* irritable. **irritation** *nf* irritation.

irruption [irypsjɔ̃] *nf* **faire irruption** burst in.

Islam [islam] *nm* Islam. **islamique** *adj* Islamic.

Islande [islɑ̃d] *nf* Iceland. **islandais** *nm*, *adj* Icelandic. **Islandais, -e** *nm, nf* Icelander.

isoler [izɔle] *v* isolate; (*élec*) insulate. **isolation** *nf* insulation. **isolé** *adj* isolated, lonely, remote. **isolement** *nm* isolation. **isoloir** *nm* polling booth.

issu [isy] *adj* **issu de** descended from.

issue [isy] *nf* (*sortie*) exit; solution; (*fin*) outcome; (*eau*) outlet.

isthme [ismə] *nm* isthmus.

Italie [itali] *nf* Italy. **italien** *nm*, *adj* Italian. **Italien, -enne** *nm, nf* Italian.

italique [italik] *nm* italics *pl. adj* italic.

itinéraire [itinerɛr] *nm* itinerary, route.

ivoire [ivwar] *nm* ivory. **Côte d'Ivoire** *nf* Ivory Coast.

ivre [ivrə] *adj* drunk. **ivresse** *nf* drunkenness; ecstasy, exhilaration. **ivrogne** *n(m+f)* drunkard.

J

j' [ʒ] *V* **je.**

jabot [ʒabo] *nm* (*chemise*) jabot; (*zool*) crop.

jacasser [ʒakase] *v* chatter. **jacasse** *nf* magpie. **jacassement** *nm* chatter.

jachère [ʒaʃɛr] *nf* fallow.

jacinthe [ʒasɛ̃t] *nf* hyacinth. **jacinthe des bois** bluebell.

jade [ʒad] *nm* jade.

jadis [ʒadis] *adv* formerly, long ago.

jaguar [ʒagwar] *nm* jaguar.

jaillir [ʒajir] *v* gush forth, spurt out; (*rires, etc.*) burst out; (*surgir*) spring up. **jaillissement** *nm* spurt, gush.

jais [ʒɛ] *nm* jet.

jalonner [ʒalɔne] *v* mark out; (*border*) line.

jaloux, -ouse [ʒalu, -uz] *adj* jealous. **jalousie** *nf* jealousy; (*store*) blind.

jamais [ʒamɛ] *adv* ever; (*négatif*) never. **à tout jamais** for ever and ever. **ne ... jamais** never.

jambe [ʒɑ̃b] *nf* leg.

jambon [ʒɑ̃bɔ̃] *nm* ham.

jante [ʒɑ̃t] *nf* rim.

janvier [ʒɑ̃vje] *nm* January.

Japon [ʒapɔ̃] *nm* Japan. **japonais** *nm*, *adj* Japanese. **les Japonais** the Japanese.

japper [ʒape] *v* yap. **jappement** *nm* yap.

jaquette [ʒakɛt] *nf* jacket; (*homme*) morning coat.

jardin [ʒardɛ̃] *nm* garden. **jardin d'enfants** nursery school. **jardin maraîcher** market garden. **jardin public** park.

jardiner [ʒardine] *v* garden. **jardinage** *nm* gardening. **jardinier** *nm* gardener. **jardinière** *nf* gardener; (*caisse*) window box.

jargon [ʒargɔ̃] *nm* jargon.

jarret [ʒarɛ] *nm* (*anat*) back of the knee; (*zool*) hock; (*cuisine*) knuckle.

jarretelle [ʒartɛl] *nf* suspender *or US* garter.

jarretière [ʒartjɛr] *nf* garter.

jars [ʒar] *nm* gander.

jaser [ʒaze] *v* chatter; (*médire*) gossip; (*ruisseau*) babble.

jasmin [ʒasmɛ̃] *nm* jasmine.

jatte [ʒat] *nf* bowl.

jauger [ʒoʒe] *v* measure, gauge; (*personne*) size up. **jauge** *nf* gauge; capacity.

jauge d'essence petrol gauge. jauge d'huile dipstick.

jaune [ʒon] adj yellow. nm yellow; (œuf) yolk; (péj) blackleg. jaunir v turn yellow. jaunisse nf jaundice.

javelot [ʒavlo] nm javelin.

jazz [dʒaz] nm jazz.

je [ʒə], j' pron I.

jean [dʒin] nm jeans pl.

jeep [ʒip] nf jeep.

jersey [ʒɛrzɛ] nm jersey, jumper.

Jersey [ʒɛrzɛ] nf Jersey.

jet¹ [ʒɛ] nm (liquide) jet, spurt, stream; (lumière) beam; (pierre) throw; (fam: coup) go.

jet² [dʒɛt] nm (aéro) jet.

jetée [ʒəte] nf jetty; pier.

jeter [ʒəte] v throw.

jeton [ʒətɔ̃] nm token; (jeu) counter.

jeu [ʒø] nm play; game; (série) set; (casino) gambling. jeu de cartes (ensemble) pack of cards; (partie) card game. jeu de mots pun.

jeudi [ʒødi] nm Thursday. jeudi saint Maundy Thursday.

jeun [ʒœ̃] adv à jeun on an empty stomach.

jeune [ʒœn] adj young; (cadet) junior, younger. n(m+f) young person. jeunesse nf youth; (personnes) young people pl.

jeûner [ʒøne] v go without food; (rel) fast. jeûne nm fast.

joaillier [ʒoaje], -ère nm, nf jeweller. joaillerie nf jewellery; (magasin) jeweller's.

jockey [ʒɔkɛ] nm jockey.

jodler [ʒɔdle] v yodel.

joie [ʒwa] nf joy, delight.

*joindre [ʒwɛ̃drə] v join; (unir) combine; (inclure) attach, enclose; (personne) contact.

joint [ʒwɛ̃] nm joint; (auto) gasket; (robinet) washer. adj joint. jointure nf joint.

joli [ʒɔli] adj pretty, nice. joliment adv nicely; (fam) pretty, jolly.

jonc [ʒɔ̃] nm (plante) rush; cane; (bracelet) bangle; (bague) ring.

joncher [ʒɔ̃ʃe] v strew, litter.

jonction [ʒɔ̃ksjɔ̃] nf junction.

jongler [ʒɔ̃gle] v juggle. jonglerie nf juggling, jugglery. jongleur, -euse nm, nf juggler.

jonquille [ʒɔ̃kij] nf daffodil.

joue [ʒu] nf cheek.

jouer [ʒwe] v play; (théâtre) act; (clef, etc.) be loose; (casino) gamble; (argent) stake. jouer de use, make use of. se jouer de (tromper) deceive; (moquer) scoff at. jouet nm toy. joueur, -euse nf player; gambler.

joufflu [ʒufly] adj chubby-cheeked.

joug [ʒu] nm yoke.

jouir [ʒwir] v jouir de enjoy. jouissance nf pleasure, delight; (jur) use.

jour [ʒur] nm day; (lumière) light; (ouverture) gap. de nos jours nowadays. jour de congé day off. jour férié bank holiday. jour ouvrable weekday. le jour de l'An New Year's day. quinze jours a fortnight. vivre au jour le jour live from hand to mouth. journée nf day.

journal [ʒurnal] nm newspaper; magazine, journal; (intime) diary. journalier adj daily; (banal) everyday. journalisme nm journalism. journaliste n(m+f) journalist.

jovial [ʒɔvjal] adj jovial, jolly. jovialité nf joviality, jollity.

joyau [ʒwajo] nm jewel, gem.

joyeux [ʒwajø] adj joyful, merry.

jubilé [ʒybile] nm jubilee.

jubiler [ʒybile] v (fam) be jubilant. jubilation nf jubilation.

jucher [ʒyʃe] v perch.

judaïsme [ʒydaisma] nm Judaism.

judiciaire [ʒydisjɛr] adj judicial.

judicieux [ʒydisjø] adj judicious.

judo [ʒydo] nm judo.

juger [ʒyʒe] v judge; (jur) try; consider; decide. au jugé by guesswork. juge nm judge. juge de paix Justice of the Peace. jugement nm judgment; (jur) sentence.

juif [ʒ⁴if] adj Jewish. Juif, Juive nm, nf Jew.

juillet [ʒ⁴ijɛ] nm July.

juin [ʒ⁴ɛ̃] nm June.

jumeau, -elle [ʒymo, -ɛl] adj twin; (maisons) semi-detached. nm, nf twin. vrais jumeaux, vraies jumelles identical twins. jumelles nf pl binoculars pl. jumeler [ʒymle] v twin; join. jumelé adj double; twin.

jument [ʒymɑ̃] nf mare.

jungle [ʒɔ̃glə] nf jungle.

junte [ʒɔ̃t] nf junta.

jupe [ʒyp] nf skirt. jupon nm waist slip.

jurer [ʒyre] v swear, vow; (couleurs) clash. juré, -e nm, nf juror.

juridique [ʒyridik] *adj* legal. **juridiction** *nf* jurisdiction.

juron [ʒyrɔ̃] *nm* oath, curse.

jury [ʒyri] *nm* jury.

jus [ʒy] *nm* juice. **jus de viande** gravy.

jusant [ʒyzɑ̃] *nm* ebb.

jusque [ʒyskə] *prep* up to. **jusqu'à** up to; (*lieu*) as far as; (*temps*) until; (*même*) even. **jusqu'à ce que** until. **jusqu'au bout** to the bitter end. **jusqu'ici** so far; (*lieu*) up to here; (*temps*) until now. **jusqu'où**? how far?

juste [ʒyst] *adj* just, fair; exact, accurate, right; (*pertinent*) sound; (*musique*) in tune; (*trop petit*) tight, barely enough. *adv* just; exactly; accurately; in tune. **au juste** exactly. **tout juste** only just, barely; exactly. **justesse** *nf* accuracy; soundness.

justice [ʒystis] *nf* justice, fairness; (*pol*) law.

justifier [ʒystifje] *v* justify; prove. **justifiable** *adj* justifiable. **justification** *nf* justification; proof.

jute [ʒyt] *nm* jute.

juteux [ʒytø] *adj* juicy.

juvénile [ʒyvenil] *adj* young, youthful.

juxtaposer [ʒykstapoze] *v* juxtapose. **juxtaposition** *nf* juxtaposition.

K

kaki [kaki] *nm, adj* khaki.

kaléidoscope [kaleidɔskɔp] *nm* kaleidoscope.

kangourou [kɑ̃guru] *nm* kangaroo.

karaté [karate] *nm* karate.

kayak [kajak] *nm* kayak.

kermesse [kɛrmɛs] *nf* fair, bazaar.

kidnapper [kidnape] *v* kidnap. **kidnappeur, -euse** *nm, nf* kidnapper.

kilo [kilo] *nm* kilo.

kilogramme [kilɔgram] *nm* kilogram.

kilomètre [kilɔmɛtrə] *nm* kilometre. **kilométrage** *nm* mileage.

kilowatt [kilɔwat] *nm* kilowatt.

kimono [kimɔno] *nm* kimono.

kinésithérapie [kineziterapi] *nf* physiotherapy. **kinésithérapeute** *n(m+f)* physiotherapist.

kiosque [kjɔsk] *nm* kiosk; (*jardin*) summer-house.

kiwi [kiwi] *nm* kiwi.

klaxon ® [klaksɔn] *nm* horn. **klaxonner** *v* sound one's horn, hoot.

kleptomanie [klɛptɔmani] *nf* kleptomania. **kleptomane** *n(m+f), adj* kleptomaniac.

kyste [kist] *nm* cyst.

L

l' [l] *V* **la, le.**

la [la], **l'** *art* the. *pron* (*personne*) her; (*animal, chose*) it.

là [la] *adv* there; (*ici*) here; (*temps*) then; (*cela*) that. **là-bas** *adv* over there. **là-dedans** *adv* inside, in it. **là-dessous** *adv* underneath. **là-dessus** *adv* on that; (*à ce sujet*) about that; (*alors*) at that point. **là-haut** up there.

laboratoire [labɔratwar] *nm* laboratory.

laborieux [labɔrjø] *adj* (*pénible*) laborious; (*diligent*) hard-working.

labourer [labure] *v* plough. **laboureur** *nm* ploughman.

labyrinthe [labirɛ̃t] *nm* labyrinth, maze.

lac [lak] *nm* lake.

lacer [lase] *v* lace (up). **lacet** *nm* lace; (*route*) sharp bend; (*piège*) snare. **en lacet** winding.

lacérer [lasere] *v* tear up; (*corps*) lacerate. **lacération** *nf* laceration.

lâche [lɑʃ] *adj* loose; (*personne*) cowardly. *n(m+f)* coward. **lâcheté** *nf* cowardice.

lâcher [lɑʃe] *v* release, let go (of); (*ceinture*) loosen; (*fam: abandonner*) give up, drop. **lâcher pied** give way. **lâcher prise** let go.

lacrymogène [lakrimɔʒɛn] *adj* **gaz lacrymogène** *nm* tear-gas.

lacté [lakte] *adj* milky.

lacune [lakyn] *nf* gap.

ladre [lɑdrə] *adj* mean. *n(m+f)* miser.

lagune [lagyn] *nf* lagoon.

laid [lɛ] *adj* ugly. **laideur** *nf* ugliness.

laine [lɛn] *nf* wool. **de laine** woollen. **laineux** *adj* woolly.

laïque [laik] *adj* lay, secular. *nm* layman. **laïques** *nm pl* laity *sing*.

laisse [lɛs] *nf* lead, leash.

laisser [lese] *v* leave; let. **laisser-aller** *nm invar* carelessness. **laissez-passer** *nm invar* pass.

lait [lε] *nm* milk. **lait caillé** curds *pl*. **lait concentré** evaporated milk. **laiterie** *nf* dairy. **laiteux** *adj* milky. **laitier** *nm* milkman.

laiton [lεtɔ̃] *nm* brass.

laitue [lety] *nf* lettuce.

lama [lama] *nm* llama.

lambeau [lãbo] *nm* scrap, shred.

lambrequin [lãbrəkɛ̃] *nm* pelmet.

lame [lam] *nf* (*bande*) strip; (*tranchant*) blade; (*vague*) wave.

se lamenter [lamãte] *v* lament, moan. **lamentable** *adj* lamentable, awful; (*cri*) pitiful. **lamentation** *nf* lament.

lampadaire [lãpader] *nm* standard lamp.

lampe [lãp] *nf* lamp, light. **lampe de poche** torch.

lamper [lãpe] (*fam*) *v* swig. **lampée** *nf* swig.

lance [lãs] *nf* spear.

lancer [lãse] *v* throw, hurl; (*émettre*) send out; (*mettre en mouvement*) launch. **lance-pierres** *nm invar* catapult. **se lancer** (*sauter*) leap; (*se précipiter*) dash. **se lancer dans** embark on.

lanciner [lãsine] *v* throb; obsess, torment.

landau [lãdo] *nm* pram.

lande [lãd] *nf* moor.

langage [lãgaʒ] *nm* language.

langouste [lãgust] *nf* crayfish. **langoustines** *nf pl* scampi *pl*.

langue [lãg] *nf* (*anat*) tongue; language.

languir [lãgir] *v* languish; (*conversation*) flag; (*désirer*) pine, long. **languissant** *adj* (*personne*) listless; (*récit*) dull.

lanière [lanjεr] *nf* strap, thong.

lanterne [lãtεrn] *nf* lantern; lamp, light; (*auto*) sidelight.

Laos [laos] *nm* Laos.

laper [lape] *v* lap (up).

lapin [lapɛ̃] *nm* rabbit.

Laponie [laponi] *nf* Lapland. **lapon** *nm*, *adj* Lapp. **Lapon**, -e *nm*, *nf* Lapp.

lapsus [lapsys] *nm* (*parlé*) slip of the tongue; (*écrit*) slip of the pen.

laque [lak] *nf* lacquer. **laquer** *v* lacquer.

laquelle [lakεl] *V* lequel.

larcin [larsɛ̃] *nm* (*vol*) theft.

lard [lar] *nm* bacon; (*gras*) fat.

large [larʒ] *adj* wide, broad; generous. *nm* width; (*place*) space, room; (*naut*) open

sea. **largement** *adv* widely; generously; (*de loin*) greatly; (*au moins*) at least, easily. **largesse** *nf* generosity. **largeur** *nf* width, breadth.

larme [larm] *nf* tear.

larmoyer [larmwaje] *v* whimper; (*yeux*) water. **larmoyant** *adj* tearful.

larve [larv] *nf* larva, grub.

larynx [larɛ̃ks] *nm* larynx. **laryngite** *nf* laryngitis.

las, lasse [lɑ, lɑs] *adj* weary.

lascif [lasif] *adj* lascivious.

laser [lazεr] *nm* laser.

lasser [lɑse] *v* weary. **se lasser de** grow tired of.

lasso [laso] *nm* lasso. **prendre au lasso** lasso.

latent [latã] *adj* latent.

latéral [lateral] *adj* lateral.

latin [latɛ̃] *nm*, *adj* Latin.

latitude [latityd] *nf* latitude.

laurier [lorje] *nm* laurel; (*cuisine*) bay leaves *pl*.

lavable [lavablə] *adj* washable.

lavabo [lavabo] *nm* washbasin. **lavabos** *nm pl* toilets *pl*.

lavage [lavaʒ] *nm* wash, washing. **lavage de cerveau** brainwashing.

lavande [lavãd] *nf* lavender.

lave [lav] *nf* lava.

laver [lave] *v* wash; (*plaie*) bathe. **lave-vaisselle** *nm invar* dishwasher. **se laver** have a wash. **laverie automatique** *nf* launderette. **lavette** *nf* dishcloth. **laveur de vitres** *nm* window-cleaner.

laxatif [laksatif] *nm*, *adj* laxative.

le [lə], **l'** *art* the. *pron* (*personne*) him; (*animal, chose*) it.

lécher [leʃe] *v* lick. **faire du lèche-vitrines** go window-shopping.

leçon [ləsɔ̃] *nf* lesson.

lecteur, -trice [lεktœr, -tris] *nm*, *nf* reader. **lecture** *nf* reading.

ledit, ladite [lədi, ladit] *adj*, *pl* **lesdits, lesdites** the aforementioned *or* aforesaid.

légal [legal] *adj* legal; official. **légaliser** *v* legalize. **légalité** *nf* legality.

légende [leʒãd] *nf* legend; (*illustration*) caption. **légendaire** *adj* legendary.

léger [leʒe] *adj* light; (*petit*) slight; agile; (*licencieux*) ribald. **à la légère** thoughtlessly; not seriously. **légèreté** *nf* lightness.

légiférer [leʒifere] *v* legislate.

légion [leʒjɔ̃] *nf* legion; vast number. **être légion** be numberless.

législation [leʒislasjɔ̃] *nf* legislation.

légitime [leʒitim] *adj* legitimate, lawful.

legs [lɛg] *nm* legacy.

léguer [lege] *v* bequeath.

légume [legym] *nm* vegetable.

Léman [lemɑ̃] *nm* **lac Léman** *nm* Lake Geneva.

lendemain [lɑ̃dmɛ̃] *nm* day after, next day; future. **le lendemain matin/soir** the next morning/evening.

lent [lɑ̃] *adj* slow. **lenteur** *nf* slowness.

lentille [lɑ̃tij] *nf* lentil; (*optique*) lens.

léopard [leopar] *nm* leopard.

lépreux [leprø], **-euse** *adj* leprous. *nm, nf* leper. **lèpre** *nf* leprosy.

lequel [ləkɛl], **laquelle** *pron, pl* **lesquels, lesquelles** which; (*personne*) who, whom.

les [le] *art the. pron* them.

lesbienne [lɛsbjɛn] *nf* lesbian.

léser [leze] *v* wrong; injure.

lésiner [lezine] *v* skimp.

lessive [lesiv] *nf* washing; (*substance*) washing powder.

lest [lɛst] *nm* ballast.

leste [lɛst] *adj* nimble, sprightly; risqué; (*cavalier*) offhand.

léthargie [letarʒi] *nf* lethargy. **léthargique** *adj* lethargic.

lettre [lɛtrə] *nf* letter. **au pied de la lettre** literally. **lettres** *nf pl* (*université*) arts *pl*; literature *sing*. **lettres de créance** credentials *pl*.

leu [lø] *nm* **à la queue leu leu** in single file.

leucémie [løsemi] *nf* leukaemia.

leur [lœr] *pron* them, to them. *adj* their. **le** *or* **la leur** theirs.

leurrer [lœre] *v* deceive, delude. **leurre** *nm* delusion; (*appât*) lure; (*piège*) trap.

levé [ləve] *nm* survey. *adj* raised.

lever [ləve] *v* raise, lift; (*impôts*) levy; (*séance*) close; (*cuisine*) rise. **se lever** rise, get up. *nm* rising. **lever du soleil** sunrise. **levée** *nf* raising; closing; (*poste*) collection; (*cartes*) trick.

levier [ləvje] *nm* lever. **levier de vitesse** gear lever.

lèvre [lɛvrə] *nf* lip.

lévrier [levrije] *nm* greyhound.

levure [ləvyr] *nf* yeast.

lézard [lezar] *nm* lizard. **lézarde** *nf* crack. **lézarder** *v* crack; (*au soleil*) bask in the sun.

liaison [ljɛzɔ̃] *nf* (*d'affaires*) relationship; contact; (*rapport*) connection, link; (*amoureuse*) affair.

liasse [ljas] *nf* bundle, wad.

libelle [libɛl] *nm* libel; (*satire*) lampoon.

libellule [libelyl] *nf* dragonfly.

libéral [liberal], **-e** *adj* liberal; (*pol*) Liberal. *nm, nf* Liberal.

libérer [libere] *v* release, free, liberate. **libération** *nf* release, liberation.

liberté [liberte] *nf* freedom, liberty. **liberté conditionnelle** parole. **liberté sous caution** bail. **liberté surveillée** probation.

librairie [libreri] *nf* bookshop. **libraire** *n(m+f)* bookseller.

libre [librə] *adj* free. **libre-service** *nm* self-service shop *or* restaurant.

licence [lisɑ̃s] *nf* (*université*) degree; (*comm*) licence; permit. **licencié, -e** *nm, nf* graduate. **licencié ès lettres/sciences** Bachelor of Arts/Science.

licorne [likɔrn] *nf* unicorn.

licou [liku] *nm* halter.

lie [li] *nf* dregs *pl*.

Liechtenstein [liʃtɛnʃtajn] *nm* Liechtenstein.

liège [ljɛʒ] *nm* cork.

lien [ljɛ̃] *nm* (*attache*) bond; (*liaison*) link; (*de famille, etc.*) tie.

lier [lje] *v* tie up, bind; (*relier*) link up; unite; (*cuisine*) thicken.

lierre [ljɛr] *nm* ivy.

lieu [ljø] *nm* place. **au lieu de** instead of. **avoir lieu** take place. **avoir lieu de** have good reason to. **donner lieu à** give rise to. **sur les lieux** at the scene, on the spot. **tenir lieu de** take the place of.

lieutenant [ljøtnɑ̃] *nm* lieutenant. **lieutenant-colonel** *nm* wing commander.

lièvre [ljɛvrə] *nm* hare.

ligament [ligamɑ̃] *nm* ligament.

ligne [liɲ] *nf* line; (*rangée*) row; (*silhouette*) figure. **à la ligne** new paragraph. **hors ligne** outstanding. **ligne d'horizon** skyline.

ligoter [ligɔte] *v* tie, bind.

ligue [lig] *nf* league.

lilas [lila] *nm, adj invar* lilac.

limace [limas] *nf* slug. **limaçon** *nm* snail.

limaille [limaj] *nf* filings *pl*.

limbe [lɛ̃b] *nm* **les limbes** limbo *sing*. **dans les limbes** (*rel*) in limbo; (*projet*) in the air.

limer [lime] v file. **lime** nf file. **lime à ongles** nail-file.

limier [limje] nm bloodhound; (policier) sleuth.

limite [limit] nf limit; (pays) boundary. adj maximum. **cas limite** nm borderline case. **date limite** nf deadline.

limiter [limite] v limit, restrict; (frontière) border. **limitation** nf limitation, restriction.

limon [limɔ̃] nm silt.

limonade [limɔnad] nf lemonade.

lin [lɛ̃] nm flax.

linceul [lɛ̃sœl] nm shroud.

linéaire [lineɛr] adj linear.

linge [lɛ̃ʒ] nm linen; (lessive) washing; (sous-vêtements) underwear; (torchon) cloth. **lingerie** nf lingerie.

lingot [lɛ̃go] nm ingot.

linguistique [lɛ̃ɡ⁴istik] nf linguistics. adj linguistic. **linguiste** n(m+f) linguist.

linoléum [linɔleɔm] nm linoleum. **lino** nm (fam) lino.

lion [ljɔ̃] nm lion. **Lion** nm Leo. **lionceau** nm lion cub. **lionne** nf lioness.

liqueur [likœr] nf liqueur.

liquide [likid] nm, adj liquid. **liquidation** nf liquidation; (règlement) settlement. **liquider** v liquidate; settle.

*****lire¹** [lir] v read.

lire² [lir] nf lira.

lis [lis] nm lily.

Lisbonne [lisbɔn] n Lisbon.

lisible [lizibl] adj (écriture) legible; (livre) readable. **lisibilité** nf legibility.

lisière [lizjɛr] nf edge; (tissu) selvage.

lisse [lis] adj smooth. **lisser** v smooth.

liste [list] nf list.

lit [li] nm bed; (couche) layer. **lit de camp** camp-bed. **lit d'enfant** cot. **lit d'une personne** single bed. **literie** nf bedding.

litanie [litani] nf litany.

litée [lite] nf litter.

litre [litrə] nm litre.

littéraire [literɛr] adj literary.

littéral [literal] adj literal.

littérature [literatyr] nf literature.

littoral [litɔral] adj coastal. nm coast.

livide [livid] adj pallid, livid.

livraison [livrɛzɔ̃] nf delivery; (revue) part, issue.

livre¹ [livr] nm book. **livre à succès** bestseller. **livre de bord** logbook. **livre de poche** paperback. **livre d'images** picture book. **livre d'or** visitors' book.

livre² [livrə] nf pound.

livrer [livre] v deliver; (abandonner) hand over, give up. **se livrer** confide. **se livrer à** (s'adonner) indulge in; (se consacrer) devote oneself to.

livret [livrɛ] nm (musique) libretto; (carnet) booklet, record book.

lobe [lɔb] nm lobe.

local [lɔkal] adj local. nm premises pl. **localiser** v localize; (déterminer) locate; (limiter) confine. **localité** nf locality.

locataire [lɔkatɛr] n(m+f) tenant.

location [lɔkasjɔ̃] nf (maison) renting; (voiture, bateau) hiring. **bureau de location** nm booking office.

locomotive [lɔkɔmɔtiv] nf locomotive, engine.

locuste [lɔkyst] nf locust.

locution [lɔkysjɔ̃] nf phrase.

logarithme [lɔɡaritmə] nm logarithm.

loger [lɔʒe] v lodge; accommodate, put up; (habiter) live. **se loger** find accommodation; (se coincer) get stuck. **loge** nf lodge; (artiste) dressing room; (spectateur) box. **logement** nm housing; accommodation, lodgings pl. **logeur** nm landlord. **logeuse** nf landlady.

logique [lɔʒik] nf logic. adj logical.

logis [lɔʒi] nm dwelling.

loi [lwa] nf law.

loin [lwɛ̃] adv far. **au loin** in the distance. **de loin** from a distance; (de beaucoup) by far. **plus loin** further.

lointain [lwɛ̃tɛ̃] adj distant, remote. nm (tableau) background. **au lointain** in the distance.

loir [lwar] nm dormouse.

loisir [lwazir] nm leisure, spare time.

lombric [lɔ̃brik] nm earthworm.

Londres [lɔ̃drə] n London.

long, longue [lɔ̃, lɔ̃ɡ] adj long. **à long terme** long-term. **à longue portée** long-range. **de longue date** long-standing. **longue-vue** nf telescope. adv **en savoir/dire long** know/say a lot. nm length. **de long en large** back and forth. **le long de** along. nf **à la longue** at last, in the end. **longueur** nf length. **longueur d'onde** wavelength.

longer [lɔ̃ʒe] v border; (sentier, etc.) run alongside; (personne) walk along.

longévité [lɔ̃ʒevite] nf longevity.

longitude [lɔ̃ʒityd] nf longitude.

longtemps [lɔ̃tɑ̃] *adv* (for) a long time, (for) long.

loque [lɔk] *nf* rag.

loquet [lɔkɛ] *nm* latch.

lorgner [lɔrɲe] *v* (*fam*) peer at, eye up.

lors [lɔr] *adv* **dès lors** from then on. **lors de** at the time of. **lors même que** even if.

lorsque [lɔrskə] *conj* when.

losange [lɔzɑ̃ʒ] *nm* diamond.

lot [lo] *nm* (*assortiment*) set, batch; (*portion*) share; (*prix*) prize.

loterie [lɔtri] *nf* lottery, raffle.

lotion [losjɔ̃] *nf* lotion.

lotus [lɔtys] *nm* lotus.

louange [lwɑ̃ʒ] *nf* praise.

louche[1] [luʃ] *adj* dubious, shady. **loucher** *v* have a squint.

louche[2] [luʃ] *nf* ladle.

louer[1] [lwe] *v* (*exalter*) praise. **louable** *adj* praiseworthy.

louer[2] [lwe] *v* rent, hire.

loufoque [lufɔk] *adj* (*fam*) crazy.

loup [lu] *nm* wolf. **loup-cervier** *nm* lynx. **loup-garou** *nm* werewolf.

loupe [lup] *nf* magnifying glass.

louper [lupe] (*fam*) *v* bungle, make a mess of; (*occasion*) miss; (*examen*) fail.

lourd [lur] *adj* heavy; (*temps*) close; (*important*) serious; (*gauche*) clumsy. **lourdeur** *nf* heaviness.

loutre [lutrə] *nf* otter.

louveteau [luvto] *nm* wolf cub; cub scout.

loyal [lwajal] *adj* loyal; (*honnête*) fair. **loyauté** *nf* loyalty; fairness.

loyer [lwaje] *nm* rent.

lubie [lybi] *nf* whim, fad.

lubrifier [lybrifje] *v* lubricate. **lubrifiant** *nm* lubricant. **lubrification** *nf* lubrication.

lucarne [lykarn] *nf* skylight, dormer window.

lucide [lysid] *adj* lucid. **lucidité** *nf* lucidity.

lucratif [lykratif] *adj* lucrative, profitable.

lueur [lɥœr] *nf* glimmer, glow.

luge [lyʒ] *nf* sledge, toboggan.

lugubre [lygybrə] *adj* gloomy, dismal.

lui [lɥi] *pron* (*homme*) him, to him; (*femme*) her, to her; (*chose, animal*) it, to it; (*sujet*) he. **lui-même** *pron* himself; itself.

***luire** [lɥir] *v* gleam, shine. **luisant** *nm* sheen, gloss.

lumbago [lɔ̃bago] *nm* lumbago.

lumière [lymjɛr] *nf* light.

lumineux [lyminø] *adj* luminous.

lundi [lœdi] *nm* Monday.

lune [lyn] *nf* moon. **lune de miel** honeymoon. **lunaire** *adj* lunar.

lunette [lynɛt] *nf* telescope. **lunettes** *nf pl* glasses *pl*. **lunettes de soleil** sunglasses *pl*. **lunettes protectrices** goggles *pl*.

lurette [lyrɛt] *nf* **il y a belle lurette** ages ago.

lustrer [lystre] *v* polish; make shiny. **lustre** *nm* lustre; (*appareil d'éclairage*) chandelier. **lustré** *adj* shiny.

luth [lyt] *nm* lute.

lutin [lytɛ̃] *nm* imp. *adj* impish, mischievous.

lutrin [lytrɛ̃] *nm* lectern.

lutter [lyte] *v* struggle, fight. **lutte** *nf* struggle, fight; (*sport*) wrestling. **lutteur, -euse** *nm, nf* fighter; wrestler.

luxe [lyks] *nm* luxury. **luxueux** *adj* luxurious.

Luxembourg [lyksɑ̃bur] *nm* Luxembourg.

luxure [lyksyr] *nf* lust. **luxurieux** *adj* lascivious.

lycée [lise] *nm* secondary school. **lycéen, -enne** *nm, nf* secondary school pupil.

lyncher [lɛ̃ʃe] *v* lynch.

lynx [lɛ̃ks] *nm* lynx.

lyre [lir] *nf* lyre.

lyrique [lirik] *adj* lyrical.

M

m' [m] *V* **me**.

ma [ma] *V* **mon**.

macabre [makabrə] *adj* macabre.

macaroni [makarɔni] *nm* macaroni.

macédoine [masedwan] *nf* (*fam*) jumble. **macédoine de fruits** fruit salad. **macédoine de légumes** mixed vegetables *pl*.

mâcher [mɑʃe] *v* chew, munch. **mâchoire** *nf* jaw.

machin [maʃɛ̃] (*fam*) *nm* thing, contraption; whatsit. **Machin** *nm* what's-his-name.

machine [maʃin] *nf* machine; (*rail, naut*) engine. **machine à coudre/laver** sewing/washing machine. **machine à écrire** typewriter. **machine à sous** slot machine. **machinal** *adj* mechanical, automatic. **machinerie** *nf* machinery.

macis [masi] nm mace.

maçon [masɔ̃] nm (pierre) mason; (construction) builder; (briques) bricklayer. **maçonner** v build. **maçonnerie** nf masonry; building.

maculer [makyle] v stain. **macule** nf smudge.

madame [madam] nf, pl **mesdames** madam. **Madame** nf (suivi du nom de famille) Mrs.

mademoiselle [madmwazɛl] nf, pl **mesdemoiselles** miss, young lady. **Mademoiselle** nf (suivi du nom de famille) Miss.

madère [madɛr] nm (vin) Madeira. **Madère** nf (île) Madeira.

Madrid [madrid] n Madrid.

madrier [madrije] nm beam.

magasin [magazɛ̃] nm shop; (entrepôt) warehouse; (fusil) magazine. **magasin à succursales multiples** chain store.

magazine [magazin] nm magazine.

magie [maʒi] nf magic. **magicien, -enne** nm, nf magician. **magique** adj magic, magical.

magistral [maʒistral] adj masterly, brilliant; authoritative.

magistrat [maʒistra] nm magistrate.

magnanime [maɲanim] adj magnanimous. **magnanimité** nf magnanimity.

magnat [maɲa] nm tycoon, magnate.

magnétiser [maɲetize] v magnetize. **magnétique** adj magnetic. **magnétisme** nm magnetism.

magnétophone [maɲetɔfɔn] nm tape-recorder.

magnifique [maɲifik] adj magnificent.

mai [mɛ] nm May.

maigre [mɛgrə] adj thin; (viande) lean; (petit) meagre, slight; (médiocre) poor. nm lean meat. **maigreur** nf thinness. **maigrir** v lose weight; (exprès) slim.

maille [maj] nf stitch; (armure) link; (filet) mesh. **maille filée** ladder.

maillet [majɛ] nm mallet.

maillot [majo] nm vest; (sport) jersey; (danse) leotard. **maillot de bain** (homme) swimming trunks pl; (femme) bathing costume.

main [mɛ̃] nf hand. **à la main** by hand. **en venir aux mains** come to blows. **fait main** handmade. **main-d'œuvre** nf labour, manpower. **sous la main** to or at hand.

maint [mɛ̃] adj many (a). **maintes fois** time and again.

maintenant [mɛ̃tnɑ̃] adv now.

***maintenir** [mɛ̃tnir] v maintain; support; (garder) keep. **se maintenir** hold one's own, keep up; continue, persist. **maintien** nm maintenance, upholding; (posture) deportment.

maire [mɛr] nm mayor. **mairie** nf town hall.

mais [mɛ] conj but. nm objection.

maïs [mais] nm maize or US corn.

maison [mɛzɔ̃] nf house; (foyer) home; firm, company; (domestiques) household. adj invar home-made. **maison de repos** convalescent home. **maison de retraite** old people's home. **maison de santé** nursing home.

maître, -esse [mɛtrə, -ɛs] adj main, major. nm master. **être maître de** be in control of. **maître chanteur** blackmailer. **maître de chapelle** choirmaster. **maître d'hôtel** (maison) butler; (hôtel) head waiter. nf mistress. **maîtriser** [mɛtrize] v control, master, overcome. **maîtrise** nf mastery; control. **maîtrise de soi** self-control.

majesté [maʒɛste] nf majesty. **majestueux** adj majestic.

majeur, -e [maʒœr] adj major; (principal) main; (jur) of age.

majorité [maʒɔrite] nf majority. **être majoritaire** be in the majority.

majuscule [maʒyskyl] nf, adj capital.

mal [mal] adv badly; ill; (incorrectement) wrongly; with difficulty. **mal acquis** ill-gotten. **mal à l'aise** ill-at-ease. **mal comprendre** misunderstand. **mal élevé** ill-mannered. **mal interpréter** misinterpret. **pas mal** rather well, not badly. **pas mal de** (fam) quite a lot of. adj invar bad, wrong; (malade) ill; (mal à l'aise) uncomfortable. nm evil; (douleur) pain; (maladie) sickness; (tristesse) sorrow; difficulty, trouble; (dommage) harm. **avoir mal be** in pain, ache. **avoir mal à** have a pain in. **avoir mal aux dents/oreilles** have toothache/earache. **faire du mal à** hurt, harm. **mal de l'air** airsickness. **mal de mer** seasickness. **mal de tête** headache. **mal du pays** homesickness. **se faire mal** hurt oneself.

malade [malad] adj ill, sick. n(m+f) invalid, sick person; (d'un médecin) patient. **maladie** nf illness, disease. **maladif** adj sickly.

maladresse [maladrɛs] nf clumsiness, awkwardness; (*gaffe*) blunder.

maladroit [maladrwa] adj clumsy; (*indélicat*) tactless.

malaise [malɛz] nm discomfort; (*trouble*) uneasiness.

malappris [malapri] adj ill-mannered.

malaria [malarja] nf malaria.

malavisé [malavize] adj unwise, ill-advised.

malchance [malʃɑ̃s] nf misfortune, bad luck. **malchanceux** adj unlucky.

malcommode [malkɔmɔd] adj inconvenient; (*peu pratique*) unsuitable.

mâle [mal] adj male; virile. nm male.

malédiction [malediksjɔ̃] nf curse.

malentendu [malɑ̃tɑ̃dy] nm misunderstanding.

malfaisant [malfəzɑ̃] adj evil, harmful.

malgré [malgre] prep despite, in spite of.

malheur [malœr] nm misfortune; (*épreuve*) hardship; (*accident*) mishap. **malheureux** adj unfortunate; miserable.

malhonnête [malɔnɛt] adj dishonest; (*impoli*) rude. **malhonnêteté** nf dishonesty; rudeness.

Mali [mali] nm Mali.

malice [malis] nf mischief; (*malignité*) malice. **malicieux** adj mischievous.

malin, -igne [malɛ̃, -iɲ] adj cunning, shrewd; (*fam*) difficult; (*mauvais*) malicious; (*méd*) malignant.

malingre [malɛ̃grə] adj sickly, puny.

malle [mal] nf trunk; (*auto*) boot.

malmener [malməne] v manhandle.

malotru [malɔtry], -e nm, nf uncouth person, lout.

malpropre [malprɔprə] adj dirty; (*travail*) slovenly; (*indélicat*) unsavoury. **malpropreté** nf dirtiness; (*propos*) unsavoury remark; (*acte*) low trick.

malsain [malsɛ̃] adj unhealthy.

malséant [malseɑ̃] adj unseemly.

malt [malt] nm malt.

Malte [malt] nf Malta. **maltais** nm, adj Maltese. **les Maltais** the Maltese.

maltraiter [maltrete] v ill-treat, manhandle; misuse.

malveillant [malvejɑ̃, -ɑ̃t] adj malevolent, malicious. **malveillance** nf malevolence.

maman [mamɑ̃] nf (*fam*) mummy, mum.

mamelle [mamɛl] nf (*femme*) breast; (*animal*) teat; (*pis*) udder. **mamelon** nm nipple.

mammifère [mamifɛr] nm mammal.

mammouth [mamut] nm mammoth.

manche¹ [mɑ̃ʃ] nf sleeve. **à manches courtes/longues** short-/long-sleeved. **la Manche** the English Channel. **manchette** nf cuff; (*journal*) headline. **manchon** nm muff.

manche² [mɑ̃ʃ] nm handle. **manche à balai** broomstick; (*aéro*) joystick.

manchot [mɑ̃ʃo] adj one-armed; (*sans bras*) armless. nm penguin.

mandarine [mɑ̃darin] nf mandarin, tangerine.

mandat [mɑ̃da] nm mandate; (*police*) warrant. **mandat-poste** nm postal order. **mandater** v commission; elect.

mandoline [mɑ̃dɔlin] nf mandolin.

manège [manɛʒ] nm (*fête foraine*) roundabout; (*équitation*) riding school; (*jeu*) game.

manette [manɛt] nf lever.

manger [mɑ̃ʒe] v eat; (*fortune*) squander. nm food. **mangeable** adj edible.

mangue [mɑ̃g] nf mango. **manguier** nm mango tree.

maniaque [manjak] adj fussy, fanatical. n(m+f) fanatic.

manie [mani] nf odd habit; (*obsession*) mania.

manier [manje] v handle. **maniable** adj manageable; easily influenced; (*accommodant*) amenable. **maniement** nm handling.

manière [manjɛr] nf way, manner; style. **de manière à** so as to. **d'une manière ou d'une autre** somehow or other. **manières** nf pl manners pl, behaviour sing. **maniéré** adj affected.

manifeste [manifɛst] adj obvious, evident. nm manifesto.

manifester [manifɛste] v show, indicate; (*pol*) demonstrate. **manifestant, -e** nm, nf demonstrator. **manifestation** nf demonstration; expression; appearance.

manipuler [manipyle] v manipulate; (*objet*) handle. **manipulation** nf manipulation; handling.

manivelle [manivɛl] nf crank.

manne [man] nf hamper.

mannequin [mankɛ̃] nm (*personne*) model; (*objet*) dummy.

manœuvre [manœvrə] nf manœuvre, operation; (*intrigue*) scheme. nm labourer. **manœuvrer** v manoeuvre; (*machine*) operate.

manoir [manwar] *nm* manor house.

manquer [mɑ̃ke] *v* miss; (*rater*) make a mess of, botch; (*faire défaut*) be lacking; be absent; (*échouer*) fail. **manquer à** be missed by. **manquer de** lack. **manquer de faire** almost do. **ne pas manquer de** be sure to. **manque** *nm* lack, shortage; (*lacune*) gap; (*méd*) withdrawal.

mansarde [mɑ̃sard] *nf* attic.

manteau [mɑ̃to] *nm* coat.

manuel [manɥɛl] *nm*, *adj* manual.

manuscrit [manyskri] *adj* handwritten. *nm* manuscript.

manutention [manytɑ̃sjɔ̃] *nf* handling.

maquereau[1] [makro] *nm* (*poisson*) mackerel.

maquereau[2] [makro] *nm* (*argot*) pimp.

maquette [makɛt] *nf* model.

maquiller [makije] *v* make up; (*document, etc.*) fake. **maquillage** *nm* make-up.

maquis [maki] *nm* scrub, bush.

maraîcher [mareʃe], **-ère** *nm*, *nf* market gardener.

marais [marɛ] *nm* marsh.

marathon [maratɔ̃] *nm* marathon.

marbre [marbrə] *nm* marble.

marchand [marʃɑ̃], **-e** *nm*, *nf* (*boutiquier*) shopkeeper, tradesman; dealer, merchant. **marchand de journaux** newsagent. **marchand de légumes** greengrocer. **marchand de poissons** fishmonger. *adj* (*valeur*) market; (*navire*) merchant.

marchander [marʃɑ̃de] *v* haggle (over), bargain.

marchandise [marʃɑ̃diz] *nf* merchandise, goods *pl*.

marche [marʃ] *nf* walk, walking; (*mil, etc.*) march; (*machine, véhicule*) running; progress; (*escalier*) step. **marche arrière** reverse. **mettre en marche** start, set going.

marché [marʃe] *nm* market; (*contrat*) bargain, deal. **Marché commun** Common Market. **marché noir** black market.

marcher [marʃe] *v* walk; (*mil*) march; (*mettre le pied*) step, tread; (*fonctionner*) work.

mardi [mardi] *nm* Tuesday. **Mardi gras** Shrove Tuesday.

mare [mar] *nf* (*étang*) pond; (*flaque*) pool.

marécage [marekaʒ] *nm* marsh, bog. **marécageux** *adj* marshy.

maréchal [mareʃal] *nm* marshal, field marshal. **maréchal-ferrant** *nm* blacksmith.

marée [mare] *nf* tide. **marée noire** oil slick.

margarine [margarin] *nf* margarine.

marge [marʒ] *nf* margin. **marginal** *adj* marginal.

marguerite [margərit] *nf* daisy.

mari [mari] *nm* husband.

mariage [marjaʒ] *nm* marriage; (*cérémonie*) wedding.

marié [marje], **-e** *adj* married. *nm* bridegroom. *nf* bride.

marier [marje] *v* marry; (*couleurs, etc.*) blend. **se marier** get married.

marihuana [mariɥana] *nf* marijuana.

marin [marɛ̃] *adj* sea, marine. *nm* sailor.

marina [marina] *nf* marina.

marine [marin] *nf*, *adj invar* navy. **marine marchande** merchant navy.

mariner [marine] *v* marinade. **marinade** *nf* marinade.

marionnette [marjɔnɛt] *nf* puppet.

marital [marital] *adj* marital.

maritime [maritim] *adj* maritime; (*ville*) coastal; (*commerce, etc.*) shipping.

marjolaine [marʒɔlɛn] *nf* marjoram.

mark [mark] *nm* mark.

marmite [marmit] *nf* pot.

marmonner [marmɔne] *v* mumble, mutter.

marmot [marmo] *nm* (*fam*) kid, brat.

marmotter [marmɔte] *v* mumble, mutter.

Maroc [marɔk] *nm* Morocco. **marocain** *adj* Moroccan. **Marocain, -e** *nm*, *nf* Moroccan.

marotte [marɔt] *nf* hobby, craze.

marquer [marke] *v* mark; indicate, show; (*écrire*) write *or* note down; (*événement*) stand out. **marque** *nf* mark; (*comm*) brand, make; (*sport*) score. **de marque** (*produit*) high-class; (*personne*) distinguished, important. **marque de fabrique** trademark.

marqueterie [markətri] *nf* marquetry.

marquis [marki] *nm* marquis *or* marquess. **marquise** *nf* marchioness.

marraine [marɛn] *nf* godmother.

marre [mar] *(fam)* *adv* **en avoir marre** be fed up. **marrant** *adj* funny. **se marrer** *v* laugh.

marron [marɔ̃] *nm* (*couleur*) brown. **marron d'Inde** horse-chestnut. *adj invar* brown. **marronnier** *nm* chestnut tree.

mars [mars] *nm* March.

Mars [mars] *nm* Mars. **martien, -enne** *n, adj* Martian.

marsouin [marswɛ̃] *nm* porpoise.

marsupial [marsypjal] *nm, adj* marsupial.

marteau [marto] *nm* hammer; (*porte*) knocker. **marteau-piqueur** *nm* pneumatic drill.

marteler [martəle] *v* hammer, pound.

martial [marsjal] *adj* martial, warlike.

martinet [martinɛ] *nm* swift.

martin-pêcheur [martɛ̃peʃœr] *nm* king-fisher.

martre [martrə] *nf* marten. **martre zibeline** sable.

martyr [martir], **-e** *nm, nf* martyr. **martyre** *nm* martyrdom; (*souffrance*) agony. **martyriser** *v* (*rel*) martyr; torture; (*bébé*) batter.

mascara [maskara] *nm* mascara.

mascarade [maskarad] *nf* masquerade.

mascotte [maskɔt] *nf* mascot.

masculin [maskylɛ̃] *nm, adj* masculine. **masculinité** *nf* masculinity.

masochiste [mazɔʃist] *n(m+f)* masochist. *adj* masochistic. **masochisme** *nm* masochism.

masquer [maske] *v* hide, mask. **masque** *nm* mask; air, façade. **masque de beauté** face-pack.

massacrer [masakre] *v* massacre; (*animaux*) slaughter; (*fam*) make a mess of. **massacre** *nm* massacre; slaughter.

masse¹ [mas] *nf* mass; (*élec*) earth.

masse² [mas] *nf* (*maillet*) sledge-hammer; (*bâton*) mace.

massepain [maspɛ̃] *nm* marzipan.

masser¹ [mase] *v* assemble, gather together.

masser² [mase] *v* massage. **massage** *nm* massage. **masseur** *nm* masseur. **masseuse** *nf* masseuse.

massif [masif] *adj* massive; solid, heavy. *nm* clump; (*géog*) massif.

massue [masy] *nf* club.

mastic [mastik] *nm* putty.

mastiquer¹ [mastike] *v* (*mâcher*) chew.

mastiquer² [mastike] *v* apply putty to.

mastodonte [mastɔdɔ̃t] *nm* (*camion*) juggernaut; (*personne*) colossus.

se masturber [mastyrbe] *v* masturbate. **masturbation** *nf* masturbation.

mat¹ [mat] *nm* checkmate. *adj invar* checkmated. **faire mât** checkmate.

mat² [mat] *adj* matt, dull.

mât [mɑ] *nm* (*naut*) mast; (*poteau*) pole.

match [matʃ] *nm* match. **match nul** draw.

matelas [matla] *nm* mattress. **matelas pneumatique** air-bed. **matelasser** *v* pad.

matelot [matlo] *nm* sailor.

se matérialiser [materjalize] *v* materialize.

matérialiste [materjalist] *adj* materialistic. *n(m+f)* materialist.

matériaux [materjo] *nm pl* material(s).

matériel [materjɛl] *adj* material. *nm* equipment, materials *pl*; (*tech*) plant.

maternel [maternɛl] *adj* maternal; (*soin, geste*) motherly. **école maternelle** *nf* nursery school. **maternité** *nf* maternity, motherhood; maternity hospital.

mathématique [matematik] *adj* mathematical. **mathématiques** *nf pl* mathematics *sing*. **mathématicien, -enne** *nm, nf* mathematician. **maths** *nf pl* (*fam*) maths *sing*.

matière [matjɛr] *nf* matter; subject; material. **matière grasse** fat. **matières premières** raw materials *pl*.

matin [matɛ̃] *nm* morning. **de bon matin** early in the morning. **matinal** *adj* morning, early. **matinée** *nf* morning; (*théâtre*) afternoon performance, matinée.

matois [matwa] *adj* wily, sly.

matraque [matrak] *nf* truncheon, cosh.

matriarcal [matrijarkal] *adj* matriarchal.

matrice [matris] *nf* matrix; (*utérus*) womb.

matrimonial [matrimɔnjal] *adj* matrimonial.

maturité [matyrite] *nf* maturity.

***maudire** [modir] *v* curse.

mausolée [mozɔle] *nm* mausoleum.

maussade [mosad] *adj* sullen, morose; (*triste*) gloomy.

mauvais [mɔvɛ] *adj* bad; (*erroné*) wrong; (*vilain*) wicked, evil; (*désagréable*) nasty, unpleasant. **mauvaise herbe** *nf* weed.

mauve [mov] *nm, adj* mauve.

maxime [maksim] *nf* maxim.

maximum [maksimɔm] *nm, adj* maximum.

mayonnaise [majɔnɛz] *nf* mayonnaise.

mazout [mazut] *nm* oil.

me [mə], **m'** *pron me*, to me; (*réfléchi*) myself.

méandre [meɑ̃drə] *nm* meander.

mec [mɛk] *nm* (*argot*) bloke.

mécanique [mekanik] *adj* mechanical. *nf* mechanics. **mécanicien, -enne** *nm, nf* mechanic; (*naut, aéro*) engineer.

mécaniser *v* mechanize. **mécanisme** *nm* mechanism; mechanics *pl.*

méchant [meʃɑ̃] *adj* nasty; (*malveillant*) spiteful; (*enfant*) naughty; (*vilain*) wicked. **méchanceté** *nf* nastiness; (*propos*) spiteful remark.

mèche [mɛʃ] *nf* (*bougie*) wick; (*bombe*) fuse; (*cheveux*) lock; (*tech*) bit. **être de mèche avec** be in league with.

mécompte [mekɔ̃t] *nm* (*déception*) disappointment; (*erreur*) miscalculation.

mécontent [mekɔ̃tɑ̃] *adj* discontented, dissatisfied; (*contrarié*) annoyed. **mécontentement** *nm* dissatisfaction. **mécontenter** *v* displease, annoy.

médaille [medaj] *nf* medal.

médecin [mɛdsɛ̃] *nm* doctor. **médecine** *nf* medicine.

media [medja] *nm pl* mass media *pl.*

médiation [medjasjɔ̃] *nf* mediation. **médiateur, -trice** *nm, nf* mediator.

médical [medikal] *adj* medical.

médicament [medikamɑ̃] *nm* medicine.

médication [medikasjɔ̃] *nf* treatment, medication.

médicinal [medisinal] *adj* medicinal.

médiéval [medjeval] *adj* medieval.

médiocre [medjɔkrə] *adj* mediocre, poor. **médiocrité** *nf* mediocrity.

*médire** [medir] *v* speak ill, malign. **médisance** *nf* scandal, gossip.

méditer [medite] *v* meditate, contemplate. **Méditerrané** [meditɛrane] *nf* Mediterranean (Sea). **méditerranéen** *adj* Mediterranean.

méduse [medyz] *nf* jellyfish.

méfait [mefɛ] *nm* misdemeanour. **méfaits** *nm pl* ravages *pl*, damage *sing.*

se méfier [mefje] *v* be careful, look out. **se méfier de** mistrust, be suspicious of; beware of. **méfiance** *nf* distrust. **méfiant** *adj* suspicious.

mégarde [megard] *nf* **par mégarde** accidentally, inadvertently.

mégère [meʒɛr] *nf* shrew.

mégot [mego] *nm* (*fam*) fag end.

meilleur, -e [mɛjœr] *adj, adv* better. **le meilleur, la meilleure** (the) best.

mélancolie [melɑ̃kɔli] *nf* melancholy. **mélancolique** *adj* melancholy, melancholic.

mélanger [melɑ̃ʒe] *v* mix (up); (*couleurs, etc.*) blend. **mélange** *nm* mixture; blend.

mélasse [melas] *nf* treacle.

mêler [mele] *v* mix, mingle; (*cartes*) shuffle; (*impliquer*) involve. **se mêler à** join, mingle with; get involved in. **se mêler de** meddle with, interfere in. **mêle-toi de tes affaires!** mind your own business! **mêlée** *nf* fray, mêlée; (*rugby*) scrum. **mêlée générale** free-for-all.

mélèze [melɛz] *nm* larch.

mélodie [melɔdi] *nf* melody. **mélodieux** *adj* melodious. **mélodique** *adj* melodic.

mélodrame [melɔdram] *nm* melodrama. **mélodramatique** *adj* melodramatic.

melon [məlɔ̃] *nm* melon; (*chapeau*) bowler.

membrane [mɑ̃bran] *nf* membrane.

membre [mɑ̃brə] *nm* (*anat*) limb; (*société*) member.

même [mɛm] *adj* (*semblable*) same; very. *pron* same. *adv* even. **de même** likewise. **quand même** all the same.

mémé [meme] *nf* (*fam*) granny, grandma.

mémento [memɛ̃to] *nm* (*agenda*) engagement diary; note.

mémoire[1] [memwar] *nf* memory.

mémoire[2] [memwar] *nm* memorandum; report; (*comm*) bill; (*exposé*) paper. **mémoires** *nm pl* memoirs *pl.*

mémorable [memɔrablə] *adj* memorable.

mémorandum [memɔrɑ̃dɔm] *nm* memorandum.

menacer [mənase] *v* threaten. **menaçant** *adj* menacing, threatening. **menace** *nf* threat.

ménage [menaʒ] *nm* (*entretien*) housekeeping, housework; married couple; (*communauté*) household. **ménager** *adj* household, domestic. **ménagère** *nf* (*femme*) housewife; (*couverts*) canteen of cutlery.

ménager [menaʒe] *v* spare; (*personne*) show consideration for; (*argent, etc.*) use sparingly or carefully; (*amener*) bring about; arrange. **ménagement** *nm* care, consideration.

mendier [mɑ̃dje] *v* beg (for). **mendiant, -e** *nm, nf* beggar. **mendicité** *nf* begging.

mener [məne] *v* lead; (*emmener*) take; (*enquête, conversation*) conduct; (*affaires, entreprise*) manage, run. **menées** *nf pl* intrigues *pl*. **meneur, -euse** *nm, nf* leader.

ménestrel [menɛstrɛl] *nm* minstrel.

méningite [menɛ̃ʒit] *nf* meningitis.

ménopause [menɔpoz] *nf* menopause.

menottes [mənɔt] *nf pl* handcuffs *pl*.

mensonge [mɑ̃sɔ̃ʒ] *nm* lie. **mensonger** *adj* false.

menstruel [mɑ̃stryɛl] *adj* menstrual. **menstruation** *nf* menstruation.

mensuel [mɑ̃sɥɛl] *adj* monthly. **mensuellement** *adv* monthly.

mensuration [mɑ̃syrasjɔ̃] *nf* measurement.

mental [mɑ̃tal] *adj* mental. **mentalité** *nf* mentality.

menteur, -euse [mɑ̃tœr, -øz] *adj* false; illusory; (*personne*) untruthful. *nm, nf* liar.

menthe [mɑ̃t] *nf* mint.

menthol [mɑ̃tɔl] *nm* menthol.

mention [mɑ̃sjɔ̃] *nf* mention; note; (*examen*) grade, class. **avec mention très bien** with distinction. **mentionner** *v* mention.

***mentir** [mɑ̃tir] *v* lie.

menton [mɑ̃tɔ̃] *nm* chin.

menu [məny] *adj* (*fin*) small, slight; (*peu important*) petty, minor. *adv* finely, small. *nm* menu.

menuisier [mənɥizje] *nm* joiner, carpenter. **menuiserie** *nf* joinery, carpentry, woodwork.

se *méprendre [meprɑ̃drə] *v* make a mistake.

mépris [mepri] *nm* contempt, scorn.

méprise [mepriz] *nf* mistake.

mépriser [meprize] *v* scorn, despise. **méprisable** *adj* contemptible. **méprisant** *adj* contemptuous.

mer [mɛr] *nf* sea; (*marée*) tide. **en mer** at sea.

mercenaire [mɛrsənɛr] *nm, adj* mercenary.

mercerie [mɛrsəri] *nf* haberdashery.

merci [mɛrsi] *interj* thank you; (*refus*) no thank you. **merci beaucoup** *or* **bien** thank you very much. *nm* thank-you, thanks *pl*. *nf* mercy.

mercier [mɛrsje] *, -ère nm, nf* haberdasher.

mercredi [mɛrkrədi] *nm* Wednesday. **mercredi des Cendres** Ash Wednesday.

mercure [mɛrkyr] *nm* mercury.

merde [mɛrd] (*vulgaire*) *nf* shit. *interj* hell! shit!

mère [mɛr] *nf* mother.

méridien [meridjɛ̃] *nm, adj* meridian.

méridional [meridjɔnal] *adj* southern; from the south of France. **Méridional, -e** *nm, nf* Southerner.

meringue [mərɛ̃g] *nf* meringue.

mériter [merite] *v* deserve, merit; (*exiger*) require; (*valoir*) be worth. **mérite** *nm* merit; (*respect*) credit; quality.

merlan [mɛrlɑ̃] *nm* whiting.

merle [mɛrl] *nm* blackbird.

merveille [mɛrvɛj] *nf* wonder, marvel. **à merveille** perfectly, marvellously. **merveilleux** *adj* wonderful, marvellous.

mes [me] *V* **mon.**

mésaventure [mezavɑ̃tyr] *nf* misadventure, misfortune.

mesquin [mɛskɛ̃] *adj* mean, stingy; (*étroit*) petty. **mesquinerie** *nf* meanness; pettiness.

message [mesaʒ] *nm* message. **messager, -ère** *nm, nf* messenger. **messageries** *nf pl* parcels service *sing*. **bureau de messageries** *nm* parcel office.

messe [mes] *nf* mass.

mesurer [məzyre] *v* measure; (*évaluer*) assess; limit, ration. **mesure** *nf* measure; measurement; (*musique*) bar; (*cadence*) time; moderation. **à mesure que** as. **fait sur mesure** made-to-measure. **mesuré** *adj* measured; moderate; (*ton*) steady.

métabolisme [metabolismə] *nm* metabolism.

métal [metal] *nm* metal. **métallique** *adj* metallic. **métallurgie** *nf* metallurgy. **métallurgiste** *nm* metallurgist; (*ouvrier*) metal-worker.

métamorphose [metamɔrfoz] *nf* metamorphosis.

métaphore [metafɔr] *nf* metaphor. **métaphorique** *adj* metaphorical.

métaphysique [metafizik] *adj* metaphysical. *nf* metaphysics.

météore [meteɔr] *nm* meteor. **météorique** *adj* meteoric. **météorite** *nm* meteorite.

météorologie [meteɔrɔlɔʒi] *nf* meteorology. **météorologique** *adj* meteorological, weather. **météorologue** *n(m+f)* meteorologist.

méthane [metan] *nm* methane.

méthode [metɔd] *nf* method. **méthodique** *adj* methodical.

méthodiste [metɔdist] *n(m+f)*, *adj* Methodist. **méthodisme** *nm* Methodism.

méticuleux [metikylø] *adj* meticulous.

métier [metje] *nm* job, trade, profession; technique, experience; (*machine*) loom.

métis, -isse [metis] n, adj half-caste, half-breed. **métisser** v cross.

métrage [metraʒ] nm length; measurement.

mètre [metrə] nm metre; (règle) rule. **mètre à ruban** tape measure. **métrique** adj metric.

metro [metro] nm subway, tube.

métronome [metronɔm] nm metronome.

métropole [metropɔl] nf metropolis. **métropolitain** adj metropolitan.

mets [mɛ] nm dish.

*****mettre** [metrə] v put; (vêtements) put on, wear; (temps) take, spend; suppose. **se mettre à** start. **metteur en scène** nm (théâtre) producer; (cinéma) director.

meubler [mœblə] v furnish; (remplir) fill (out). **meuble** nm piece of furniture. **meubles** nm pl furniture sing.

meugler [møglə] v moo, low. **meuglement** nm lowing.

meule[1] [møl] nf (moudre) millstone; (aiguiser) grindstone.

meule[2] [møl] nf stack, rick. **meule de foin** haystack.

meunier [mønje] nm miller.

meurtre [mœrtrə] nm murder.

meurtrier [mœrtrije], **-ère** nm, nf murderer. adj murderous, lethal.

meurtrir [mœrtrir] v bruise. **meurtrissure** nf bruise.

meute [møt] nf pack.

mi- [mi] prefix half-, mid-. **à mi-chemin** halfway. **à mi-corps** to the waist. **à mi-côte** halfway up or down. **à mi-temps** part-time. **à mi-voix** in an undertone. **mi-janvier, mi-février,** etc. mid-January, mid-February, etc.

miche [miʃ] nf round loaf.

micro [mikro] nm (fam) mike.

microbe [mikrɔb] nm germ, microbe.

microfilm [mikrɔfilm] nm microfilm.

microphone [mikrɔfɔn] nm microphone.

microscope [mikrɔskɔp] nm microscope. **microscopique** adj microscopic.

microsillon [mikrɔsijɔ̃] nm long-playing record.

midi [midi] nm midday, noon; lunchtime; (géog) south. **le Midi** the South of France.

mie [mi] nf soft part of bread.

miel [mjɛl] nm honey. **mielleux** adj (péj) sugary, smooth.

mien [mjɛ̃], **mienne** pron **le mien, la mienne** mine.

miette [mjɛt] nf crumb.

mieux [mjø] adj, adv better. **le** or **la mieux** (the) best.

mièvre [mjɛvrə] adj mawkish, affected.

mignon, -onne [miɲɔ̃, -ɔn] adj sweet, dainty. nm, nf darling.

migraine [migrɛn] nf headache; (méd) migraine.

migration [migrɑsjɔ̃] nf migration.

mijoter [miʒɔte] v simmer; (fam) plot, cook up.

mildiou [mildju] nm mildew.

milieu [miljø] nm middle; environment; (social) circle, background. **au milieu de** in the middle of. **juste milieu** happy medium.

militaire [militɛr] adj military. nm soldier.

militant [militɑ̃], **-e** n, adj militant.

mille[1] [mil] nm, adj invar (a) thousand. **mille-pattes** nm invar centipede. **milliard** nm thousand million. **millième** n(m + f), adj thousandth. **millier** nm thousand or so. **des milliers de** thousands or millions of.

mille[2] [mil] nm mile.

millénaire [milenɛr] nm millennium, thousand years. adj thousand-year-old, ancient.

milligramme [miligram] nm milligram.

millilitre [mililitrə] nm millilitre.

millimètre [milimɛtrə] nm millimetre.

million [miljɔ̃] nm million. **millionnaire** n(m + f) millionaire. **millionième** n(m + f), adj millionth.

mimer [mime] v mime; (imiter) mimic. **mime** nm mime; mimic.

minable [minablə] adj (lieu) seedy, shabby; miserable, wretched; (fam: piètre) pathetic, hopeless.

minauder [minode] v mince, simper.

mince [mɛ̃s] adj thin; (svelte) slim, slender; (insignifiant) slight, small. adv thinly. interj blast! drat! **minceur** nf thinness.

mine[1] [min] nf expression; look, appearance. **avoir bonne/mauvaise mine** look well/unwell. **faire mine de** pretend to, make as if to.

mine[2] [min] nf mine; (crayon) lead. **miner** v (mil) mine; (saper) undermine. **mineur** nm miner. **minage** nm mining.

minerai [minrɛ] nm ore.

minéral [mineral] nm, adj mineral.

mineur, -e [minœr] n, adj minor.

miniature [minjatyr] *nf. adj.* miniature.

minime [minim] *adj* minimal; (*insignifiant*) trivial; (*piètre*) paltry. **minimiser** *v* minimize. **minimum** *nm, adj* minimum.

ministère [minister] *nm* ministry; government. **ministériel** *adj* ministerial. **ministre** *nm* minister.

minorité [minɔrite] *nf* minority. **minoritaire** *adj* minority.

minuit [minɥi] *nm* midnight.

minuscule [minyskyl] *adj* minute, tiny; (*lettre*) small. *nf* small letter.

minute [minyt] *nf* minute; moment, instant.

minutieux [minysjø] *adj* meticulous, minute. **minutie** *nf* meticulousness; (*ouvrage*) minute detail.

mioche [mjɔʃ] *n(m+f)* (*fam*) kid, brat.

miracle [miraklə] *nm* miracle. **miraculeux** *adj* miraculous.

mirage [miraʒ] *nm* mirage.

mirer [mire] *v* mirror. **se mirer** be reflected.

miroir [mirwar] *nm* mirror.

miroiter [mirwate] *v* sparkle, gleam.

misanthrope [mizɑ̃trɔp] *n(m+f)* misanthropist. *adj* misanthropic. **misanthropie** *nf* misanthropy.

mise [miz] *nf* putting; (*enjeu*) stake; (*vêtements*) clothing. **être de mise** be acceptable. **mise en plis** set. **mise en scène** production. **miser** *v* stake, bet.

misérable [mizerablə] *adj* miserable; (*pitoyable*) wretched; (*pauvre*) destitute; (*minable*) paltry. *n(m+f)* wretch.

misère [mizɛr] *nf* (*malheur*) misery, misfortune; poverty. **faire des misères à** (*fam*) be nasty to.

miséricorde [mizerikɔrd] *nf* mercy. **miséricordieux** *adj* merciful.

misogyne [mizɔʒin] *n(m+f)* misogynist. **misogynie** *nf* misogyny.

missile [misil] *nm* missile.

mission [misjɔ̃] *nf* mission. **missionnaire** *n(m+f)* missionary.

mite [mit] *nf* clothes moth. **mité** *adj* moth-eaten. **miteux** *adj* seedy, shabby.

mitoyen [mitwajɛ̃] *adj* dividing, common. **mur mitoyen** party wall.

mitrailleuse [mitrajøz] *nf* machine gun.

mitre [mitrə] *nf* mitre.

mixte [mikst] *adj* mixed; (*école*) coeducational.

mobile [mɔbil] *adj* mobile, moving, movable. *nm* motive; (*art*) mobile. **mobiliser** *v* mobilize. **mobilité** *nf* mobility.

mobilier [mɔbilje] *adj* (*jur*) personal, movable. *nm* furniture.

mocassin [mɔkasɛ̃] *nm* moccasin.

moche [mɔʃ] (*fam*) *adj* (*mauvais*) rotten; (*laid*) ugly.

mode[1] [mɔd] *nf* fashion; style. **à la mode** fashionable.

mode[2] [mɔd] *nm* mode; method; (*gramm*) mood. **mode d'emploi** directions for use.

modeler [mɔdle] *v* model, shape, mould. **modèle** *nm, adj* model.

modérer [mɔdere] *v* moderate, restrain. **se modérer** control oneself. **modération** *nf* moderation; reduction. **modéré** *adj* moderate.

moderne [mɔdɛrn] *adj* modern. **modernisation** *nf* modernization. **moderniser** *v* modernize.

modeste [mɔdɛst] *adj* modest. **modestie** *nf* modesty.

modifier [mɔdifje] *v* modify. **modification** *nf* modification.

modique [mɔdik] *adj* modest, small.

module [mɔdyl] *nm* module.

moduler [mɔdyle] *v* modulate. **modulation** *nf* modulation.

moelle [mwal] *nf* (*anat*) marrow; pith. **moelle épinière** spinal cord. **moelleux** *adj* soft, smooth, mellow.

mœurs [mœr] *nf pl* morals *pl*; customs *pl*; habits *pl*; manners *pl*.

mohair [mɔɛr] *nm* mohair.

moi [mwa] *pron* me; (*sujet*) I. *nm* self, ego. **moi-même** *pron* myself.

moignon [mwaɲɔ̃] *nm* stump.

moindre [mwɛ̃drə] *adj* less; (*plus bas*) lower; (*inférieur*) poorer. **le** or **la moindre** the least, the slightest.

moine [mwan] *nm* monk.

moineau [mwano] *nm* sparrow.

moins [mwɛ̃] *nm, adv* less. **à moins de** barring, unless. **à moins que** unless. **au moins** at least. **du moins** at least. **le** or **la moins** (the) least. **moins de** less (than); (*heure*) before. *prep* minus. **six heures moins dix** ten to six.

mois [mwa] *nm* month. **au mois** by the month, monthly.

moisir [mwazir] *v* go mouldy. **moisi** *adj* mouldy. **sentir le moisi** smell musty. **moisissure** *nf* mould.

moisson [mwasɔ̃] *nf* harvest, crop. **mois-**

sonner v harvest, reap. **moissonneuse-batteuse** nf combine harvester.

moite [mwat] adj moist, clammy.

moitié [mwatje] nf half. **à moitié** half. **moitié moitié** half-and-half.

mol [mɔl] form of **mou** used before a vowel or mute h.

molécule [mɔlekyl] nf molecule. **moléculaire** adj molecular.

molester [mɔleste] v manhandle, maul.

mollasse [mɔlas] (fam) adj lethargic; (flasque) flabby.

molle [mɔl] V **mou**.

mollesse [mɔles] nf softness; (manque de fermeté) limpness; lethargy, lifelessness.

mollet, -ette [mɔlɛ, -ɛt] adj soft; (œuf) soft-boiled. nm (anat) calf.

mollir [mɔlir] v soften; (vent) abate; (fléchir) yield; give way.

mollusque [mɔlysk] nm mollusc.

môme [mom] n(m+f) (fam) kid, brat.

moment [mɔmɑ̃] nm moment; time. **en ce moment** at the moment. **momentané** adj momentary, brief.

momie [mɔmi] nf mummy. **momification** nf mummification. **momifier** v mummify.

mon [mɔ̃], **ma** adj, pl **mes** my.

Monaco [mɔnako] nm Monaco.

monarque [mɔnark] nm monarch. **monarchie** nf monarchy. **monarchiste** n(m+f) monarchist.

monastère [mɔnaster] nm monastery. **monastique** adj monastic.

monceau [mɔ̃so] nm heap, pile.

monde [mɔ̃d] nm world; (gens) people; society, circle. **tout le monde** everybody. **mondain** adj fashionable; society; refined; (rel) worldly. **mondial** adj world-wide.

monétaire [mɔnetɛr] adj monetary.

mongolien [mɔ̃gɔljɛ̃], **-enne** n, adj mongol. **mongolisme** nm mongolism.

moniteur, -trice [mɔnitœr, -tris] nm, nf (sport) instructor; (surveillant) supervisor.

monnaie [mɔnɛ] nf (devises) currency; (pièce) coin; (appoint) change. **monnayer** v mint; (tirer profit de) capitalize on.

monogamie [mɔnɔgami] nf monogamy. **monogame** adj monogamous.

monogramme [mɔnɔgram] nm monogram.

monologue [mɔnɔlɔg] nm monologue.

monopole [mɔnɔpɔl] nm monopoly. **monopoliser** v monopolize.

monosyllabe [mɔnɔsilab] nm monosyllable. **monosyllabique** adj monosyllabic.

monotone [mɔnɔtɔn] adj monotonous. **monotonie** nf monotony.

monseigneur [mɔ̃sɛɲœr] nm Your or His Grace, Your or His Lordship.

monsieur [məsjø] nm, pl **messieurs** gentleman; (titre) sir. **Monsieur** nm (suivi du nom de famille) Mr.

monstre [mɔ̃stra] nm monster. adj (fam) colossal. **monstrueux** adj monstrous. **monstruosité** nf monstrosity.

mont [mɔ̃] nm mount. **mont-de-piété** nm pawnshop.

montagne [mɔ̃taɲ] nf mountain. **montagnes russes** big dipper sing. **montagneux** adj mountainous.

montant [mɔ̃tɑ̃] adj upward, rising; (col, corsage) high. nm (portant) upright; (somme) total.

monter [mɔ̃te] v mount; go up, rise; ascend, climb; (porter) take up; (cheval) ride; (théâtre) put on, produce; assemble; equip. **monter à cheval/bicyclette** ride a horse/bicycle. **monter dans** or **en** get on or into. **se monter à** amount to. **montage** nm assembly; (cinéma) editing. **montée** nf ascent, climb; rise; (côte) hill. **monture** nf frame, setting, mount.

montre [mɔ̃tra] nf watch.. **faire montre de** show, display. **montre-bracelet** nf wristwatch.

montrer [mɔ̃tre] v show. **se montrer** appear; prove to be.

monument [mɔnymɑ̃] nm monument. **monumental** adj monumental.

moquer [mɔke] v **se moquer de** make fun of; (mépriser) not care about. **moquerie** nf mockery.

moral [mɔral] adj moral. nm morale. **morale** or **moralité** nf morality; (mœurs) morals pl; (fable) moral. **moraliser** v moralize. **moraliste** n(m+f) moralist.

morbide [mɔrbid] adj morbid.

morceau [mɔrso] nm piece; (bout) bit; extract, passage.

mordre [mɔrdra] v bite. **mordant** adj biting; (acerbe) scathing, cutting. **mordu** adj (fam) mad keen.

se morfondre [mɔrfɔ̃dra] v mope.

morgue[1] [mɔrg] nf morgue, mortuary.

morgue[2] [mɔrg] nf (arrogance) pride, haughtiness.

319   **moyeu**

moribond [mɔribɔ̃] *adj* dying.

mormon [mɔrmɔ̃], **-e** *n, adj* Mormon.

morne [mɔrn] *adj* gloomy, dismal.

morose [mɔroz] *adj* sullen, morose.

morphine [mɔrfin] *nf* morphine.

mors [mɔr] *nm* bit.

morse¹ [mɔrs] *nm* (*zool*) walrus.

morse² [mɔrs] *nm* Morse code.

morsure [mɔrsyr] *nf* bite.

mort¹ [mɔr], **-e** *adj* dead. *nm, nf* dead person. **morte-saison** *nf* off season. **mort-né** *adj* stillborn.

mort² [mɔr] *nf* death. **mort-aux-rats** *nf* rat poison.

mortalité [mɔrtalite] *nf* mortality; (*taux*) death rate.

mortel [mɔrtɛl] *adj* mortal; fatal; (*poison, etc*.) lethal, deadly.

mortier [mɔrtje] *nm* mortar.

mortifier [mɔrtifje] *v* mortify. **mortification** *nf* mortification.

mortuaire [mɔrtᵆɛr] *adj* mortuary. **dépôt mortuaire** *nm* funeral parlour.

morue [mɔry] *nf* cod.

morveux [mɔrvø], **-euse** *nm, nf* (*argot*) kid, brat.

mosaïque [mɔzaik] *nf* mosaic.

Moscou [mɔsku] *n* Moscow.

mosquée [mɔske] *nf* mosque.

mot [mo] *nm* word; note; (*expression*) saying. **mot de passe** password. **mots croisés** crossword *sing*.

motel [mɔtɛl] *nm* motel.

moteur, **-trice** [mɔtœr, -tris] *nm* motor, engine. **moteur à explosion** internal combustion engine. **moteur à réaction** jet engine. *adj* (*anat*) motor; (*tech*) driving.

motif [mɔtif] *nm* motive, grounds *pl*; (*ornement, musique*) motif.

motion [mosjɔ̃] *nf* motion.

motiver [mɔtive] *v* motivate; justify; (*expliquer*) account for. **motivation** *nf* motivation.

moto [mɔto] *nf* (*fam*) motorbike. **motocycliste** *n*(*m+f*) motorcyclist.

motte [mɔt] *nf* lump; (*terre*) clod; (*gazon*) turf.

mou [mu], **molle** *adj* soft; (*sans fermeté*) limp; (*flasque*) flabby, feeble, weak; lethargic; (*temps*) muggy. *nm* softness. **avoir du mou** be slack.

mouche [muʃ] *nf* fly. **prendre la mouche** (*fam*) get in a huff. **moucheron** *nm* midge.

moucher [muʃe] *v* (*fam*) snub; (*chandelle*) snuff. **se moucher** blow one's nose.

moucheter [muʃte] *v* speckle. **moucheture** *nf* speck, spot.

mouchoir [muʃwar] *nm* handkerchief. **mouchoir en papier** tissue.

*****moudre** [mudr] *v* grind.

moue [mu] *nf* pout. **faire la moue** pout, pull a face.

mouette [mwɛt] *nf* sea-gull.

mouffette [mufɛt] *nf* skunk.

moufle [mufl] *nf* mitten.

mouiller [muje] *v* wet; (*naut*) moor, anchor. **mouillage** *nm* mooring, anchorage. **mouillé** *adj* wet.

moule¹ [mul] *nm* mould.

moule² [mul] *nf* (*zool, cuisine*) mussel.

mouler [mule] *v* mould, cast; (*vêtements*) hug, fit closely.

moulin [mulɛ̃] *nm* mill. **moulin à café** coffee-mill. **moulin à paroles** (*fam*) chatterbox. **moulin à vent** windmill. **moulinet** *nm* (*pêche*) reel.

moulu [muly] *adj* ground.

*****mourir** [murir] *v* die.

mousquet [muskɛ] *nm* musket. **mousquetaire** *nm* musketeer.

mousse¹ [mus] *nf* (*bot*) moss; (*écume*) froth, foam; (*savon*) lather; (*cuisine*) mousse. **mousser** *v* froth, foam; lather; (*vin*) sparkle. **mousseux** *adj* frothy; sparkling. **moussu** *adj* mossy.

mousse² [mus] *nm* cabin boy.

mousseline [muslin] *nf* muslin.

mousson [musɔ̃] *nf* monsoon.

moustache [mustaʃ] *nf* moustache. **moustaches** *nf pl* (*animal*) whiskers *pl*.

moustique [mustik] *nm* mosquito.

moutarde [mutard] *nf* mustard.

mouton [mutɔ̃] *nm* sheep; (*cuisine*) mutton.

*****mouvoir** [muvwar] *v* drive, move. **se mouvoir** move. **mouvant** *adj* changing, shifting. **mouvement** *nm* movement; activity; impulse. **mouvementé** *adj* lively, eventful.

moyen [mwajɛ̃], **-enne** *adj* medium, average; middle. **moyen âge** *nm* Middle Ages *pl*. **Moyen-Orient** *nm* Middle East. *nm* means, way. **au moyen de** by means of. **moyens** *nm pl* means *pl*. **moyenne** *nf* average.

moyennant [mwajɛnɑ̃] *prep* (in return) for.

moyeu [mwajø] *nm* hub.

muer [mɥe] v moult; (*voix*) break.

muet, -ette [mɥɛ, -ɛt] adj silent; (*infirme*) dumb. nm, nf mute, dumb person.

mufle [myfl] nm muzzle; (*argot*) lout.

mugir [myʒir] v bellow, roar; (*vache*) moo.

muguet [mygɛ] nm lily of the valley.

mule [myl] nf mule.

mulet [mylɛ] nm mule.

multicolore [myltikɔlɔr] adj multicoloured.

multiple [myltipl] adj multiple, numerous, many. nm multiple.

multiplier [myltiplije] v multiply; (*augmenter*) increase. **multiplication** nf multiplication.

multitude [myltityd] nf multitude, vast number.

municipal [mynisipal] adj municipal; (*conseil*) local; (*piscine, etc.*) public. **municipalité** nf municipality; town council.

munir [mynir] v **munir de** provide with, equip with. **munitions** nf pl ammunition *sing*.

mur [myr] nm wall; barrier. **muraille** nf high wall.

mûr [myr] adj (*fruit*) ripe; (*personne*) mature.

mural [myral] adj mural. **peinture murale** nf mural.

mûre [myr] nf (*ronce*) blackberry; (*mûrier*) mulberry. **mûrier** nm mulberry bush; blackberry bush.

mûrir [myrir] v ripen; mature.

murmurer [myrmyre] v murmur. **murmure** nm murmur.

musc [mysk] nm musk.

muscade [myskad] nf nutmeg.

muscle [myskl] nm muscle. **musclé** adj muscular.

museau [myzo] nm muzzle; (*porc*) snout.

musée [myze] nm museum; (*d'art*) art gallery.

museler [myzle] v muzzle. **muselière** nf muzzle.

muséum [myzeɔm] nm natural history museum.

musicien, -enne [myzisjɛ̃, -ɛn] nm, nf musician. adj musical.

musique [myzik] nf music; (*mil*) band. **musical** adj musical.

musulman [myzylmɑ̃], -e n, adj Muslim.

mutiler [mytile] v mutilate; (*personne*)

maim. **mutilation** nf mutilation. **mutilé, -e** nm, nf disabled person.

mutin [mytɛ̃] adj mischievous. nm rebel. **se mutiner** [mytine] v mutiny; rebel. **mutiné** adj mutinous. **mutinerie** nf mutiny; rebellion.

mutisme [mytismə] nm silence; (*méd*) dumbness.

mutuel [mytɥɛl] adj mutual.

myope [mjɔp] adj short-sighted. **myopie** nf short-sightedness.

myrtille [mirtij] nf bilberry.

mystère [mistɛr] nm mystery. **mystérieux** adj mysterious.

mystifier [mistifje] v fool, take in.

mystique [mistik] n(m+f) mystic. adj mystical, mystic. **mysticisme** nm mysticism.

mythe [mit] nm myth. **mythique** adj mythical. **mythologie** nf mythology. **mythologique** adj mythological.

N

n' [n] V ne.

nabot, -e [nabo, -ɔt] adj tiny. nm, nf dwarf.

nacre [nakrə] nf mother-of-pearl. **nacré** adj pearly.

nager [naʒe] v swim; float; (*naut*) row. **nage** nf (*action*) swimming; (*manière*) stroke. **nage libre** freestyle. **nageoire** nf (*poisson*) fin; (*phoque*) flipper. **nageur, -euse** nm, nf swimmer.

naguère [nagɛr] adv not long ago; (*autrefois*) formerly.

naïf [naif], -ïve adj naive. nm, nf gullible fool. **naïveté** nf naivety.

nain [nɛ̃], -e n, adj dwarf.

naissance [nɛsɑ̃s] nf birth; source.

*naître [nɛtrə] v be born; (*surgir*) arise, spring up. **faire naître** arouse; create.

nappe [nap] nf tablecloth; (*eau*) sheet; (*brouillard*) blanket. **nappe de pétrole** oil slick. **napperon** nm mat.

narcotique [narkɔtik] nm, adj narcotic.

narine [narin] nf nostril.

narquois [narkwa] adj mocking, derisive.

narrer [nare] v narrate. **narrateur, -trice** nm, nf narrator. **narratif** adj narrative. **narration** nf narration; (*récit*) narrative.

nasal [nazal] *adj* nasal. **nasaliser** *v* nasalize. **naseau** *nm* nostril. **nasillard** *adj* nasal.

natal [natal] *adj* native. **natalité** *nf* birth rate.

natation [natasjɔ̃] *nf* swimming.

natif [natif] *-ive n, adj* native.

nation [nasjɔ̃] *nf* nation. **national, -e n,** *adj* national. **nationalisation** *nf* nationalization. **nationaliser** *v* nationalize. **nationalisme** *nm* nationalism. **nationaliste** *n(m+f)* nationalist. **nationalité** *nf* nationality.

nativité [nativite] *nf* nativity.

natter [nate] *v* plait. **natte** *nf* (*cheveux*) plait; (*paille, etc.*) mat.

naturalisme [natyralismə] *nm* naturalism. **naturaliste** *n(m+f)* naturalist.

nature [natyr] *nf* nature. **en nature** in kind. **nature morte** still life. *adj invar* plain, neat.

naturel [natyrɛl] *adj* natural. *nm* disposition.

naufrage [nofraʒ] *nm* shipwreck; ruin. **naufragé** *adj* shipwrecked.

nausée [noze] *nf* nausea. **avoir la nausée** feel sick. **nauséabond** *adj* nauseating.

nautique [notik] *adj* nautical.

naval [naval] *adj* naval.

navet [navɛ] *nm* turnip; (*fam*) rubbish.

navette [navɛt] *nf* shuttle (service). **faire la navette** commute; go backwards and forwards.

naviguer [navige] *v* (*bateau*) sail; (*avion*) fly; (*piloter*) navigate. **navigateur** *nm* navigator. **navigation** *nf* navigation; traffic.

navire [navir] *nm* ship.

navrer [navre] *v* distress; (*irriter*) annoy. **navré** *adj* sorry; distressed.

ne [nə], **n'** *adv* not. **ne ... guère** scarcely. **ne ... jamais** never. **ne ... pas** not. **ne ... personne** nobody. **ne ... plus** no longer. **ne ... que** only. **ne ... rien** nothing.

né [ne] *adj* born.

néanmoins [neɑ̃mwɛ] *adv* nevertheless, yet.

néant [neɑ̃] *nm* nothing, void.

nébuleux [nebylø] *adj* nebulous, vague; (*ciel*) cloudy.

nécessaire [neseser] *adj* necessary; indispensable. *nm* essentials *pl*. **le nécessaire** what is needed. **nécessité** *nf* necessity. **nécessiter** *v* necessitate.

nécrologie [nekrɔlɔʒi] *nf* (*notice*) obituary; (*liste*) obituary column.

nectar [nɛktar] *nm* nectar.

néerlandais [neɛrlɑ̃dɛ] *nm, adj* Dutch. **les Néerlandais** the Dutch.

nef [nɛf] *nf* nave.

néfaste [nefast] *adj* (*nuisible*) harmful; (*funeste*) unlucky.

négatif [negatif] *nm, adj* negative.

négligé [negliʒe] *adj* neglected; (*tenue*) slovenly; (*travail*) careless. *nm* slovenliness; (*vêtement*) negligee.

négliger [negliʒe] *v* neglect; (*occasion*) miss. **négligeable** *adj* negligible. **négligence** *nf* negligence, carelessness. **négligent** *adj* negligent, careless.

négocier [negɔsje] *v* negotiate. **négoce** *nm* trade. **négociable** *adj* negotiable. **négociant, -e** *nm, nf* merchant. **négociation** *nf* negotiation.

nègre [nɛgr] *nm, adj* Negro. **petit nègre** pidgin French. **négresse** *nf* Negress.

négrier *nm* (*péj*) slave-driver.

neige [nɛʒ] *nf* snow. **neige fondue** sleet. **neiger** *v* snow. **neigeux** *adj* snowy.

nénuphar [nenyfar] *nm* water-lily.

néon [neɔ̃] *nm* neon.

néo-zélandais [neozelɑ̃dɛ] *adj* New Zealand. **Néo-Zélandais, -e** *nm, nf* New Zealander.

nerf [nɛr] *nm* nerve; spirit, energy. **nerveux** *adj* nervous; energetic, vigorous; (*musclé*) sinewy. **nervosité** *nf* nervousness; tension; irritability.

net, nette [nɛt] *adj* neat; (*propre*) clean; (*comm*) net; (*clair*) clear; distinct. *adv* net; frankly; (*sur le coup*) outright; (*s'arrêter*) dead. **netteté** *nf* neatness; clearness.

nettoyer [nɛtwaje] *v* clean. **nettoyer à sec** dry-clean. **nettoyage** *nm* cleaning.

neuf¹ [nœf] *nm, adj* nine. **neuvième** *n(m+f), adj* ninth.

neuf² [nœf] *adj* new. **à neuf** as good as new.

neutre [nøtrə] *nm, adj* neutral; (*genre*) neuter. **neutraliser** *v* neutralize. **neutralité** *nf* neutrality.

neveu [nəvø] *nm* nephew.

névralgie [nevralʒi] *nf* neuralgia.

névrose [nevro... *nf* neurosis. **névrosé** *adj* neurotic.

nez [ne] *nm* nose; flair; (*figure*) face.

ni [ni] *conj* nor, or. **ni ... ni ...** neither ... nor ....

niais [njɛ]. **-e** adj simple, silly. nm, nf simpleton. **niaiserie** nf silliness; (propos) foolish talk.

nicher [niʃe] v nest. **niche** nf niche; (chien) kennel. **nichée** nf brood.

nickel [nikɛl] nm nickel.

Nicosie [nikɔsi] n Nicosia.

nicotine [nikɔtin] nf nicotine.

nid [ni] nm nest. **nid de poule** pot-hole.

nièce [njɛs] nf niece.

nier [nje] v deny.

nigaud [nigo]. **-e** adj silly, simple. nm, nf simpleton.

nimbe [nɛ̃b] nm halo.

nitouche [nituʃ] nf **sainte nitouche** hypocrite. **faire la sainte nitouche** look as if butter wouldn't melt in one's mouth.

niveau [nivo] nm level; (degré) standard. **niveau à bulle** spirit level. **niveau de vie** standard of living.

niveler [nivle] v level, even out.

noble [nɔblə] nm, adj noble. **noblesse** nf nobleness, nobility.

noce [nɔs] nf wedding. **faire la noce** (fam) live it up.

nocif [nɔsif] adj noxious, harmful.

nocturne [nɔktyrn] adj nocturnal.

Noël [nɔɛl] nm Christmas.

nœud [nø] nm knot; (de ruban) bow; (lien) bond; (rail, route) junction. **nœud coulant** slip-knot. **nœud papillon** bow tie.

noir [nwar] adj black; (obscur) dark; (profond) deep. nm black; darkness. **Noir** nm black man. **noire** nf crotchet. **Noire** nf black woman. **noircir** v blacken; darken.

noisette [nwazɛt] nf hazelnut. adj invar hazel. **noisetier** nm hazel tree.

noix [nwa] nf walnut. **noix de beurre** knob of butter. **noix de coco** coconut.

nom [nɔ̃] nm name; (gramm) noun. **nom de baptême** Christian name. **nom de famille** surname. **nom de jeune fille** maiden name. **nom d'emprunt** assumed name. **nom de théâtre** stage name. **nom propre** proper noun.

nomade [nɔmad] adj nomadic. n(m+f) nomad.

nombre [nɔ̃brə] nm number. **nombreux** adj numerous.

nombril [nɔ̃bri] nm navel.

nominal [nɔminal] adj nominal.

nomination [nɔminasjɔ̃] nf appointment, nomination.

nommer [nɔme] v name; (désigner) appoint.

non [nɔ̃] adv no; (pas) not. **non plus** neither. nm invar no.

nonchalant [nɔ̃ʃalɑ̃] adj nonchalant. **nonchalance** nf nonchalance.

non-conformiste [nɔ̃kɔ̃fɔrmist] n(m+f), adj nonconformist.

non-existant [nɔnɛgzistɑ̃] adj non-existent.

nonobstant [nɔnɔpstɑ̃] prep, adv notwithstanding.

nord [nɔr] nm north. adj invar north; (région) northern; (direction) northward. **nord-est** nm, adj invar north-east. **nord-ouest** nm, adj invar north-west.

normal [nɔrmal] adj normal. **normale** nf norm, normal.

norme [nɔrm] nf norm; standard.

Norvège [nɔrvɛʒ] nf Norway. **norvégien** nm, adj Norwegian. **Norvégien, -enne** nm, nf Norwegian.

nos [no] V **notre**.

nostalgie [nɔstalʒi] nf nostalgia. **nostalgique** adj nostalgic.

notable [nɔtablə] adj notable.

notaire [nɔtɛr] nm notary.

notamment [nɔtamɑ̃] adv notably, in particular.

notation [nɔtasjɔ̃] nf notation; (devoir) marking.

noter [nɔte] v (écrire) note down; (remarquer) notice, note; (devoir) mark. **note** nf note; mark; (compte) bill.

notice [nɔtis] nf note; instructions pl.

notifier [nɔtifje] v notify. **notification** nf notification.

notion [nɔsjɔ̃] nf notion.

notoire [nɔtwar] adj well-known; (criminal) notorious. **notoriété** nf fame; notoriety. **notoriété publique** common knowledge.

notre [nɔtrə] adj. pl **nos** our.

nôtre [notrə] pron **le** or **la nôtre** ours.

nouer [nwe] v tie, knot; (amitié, etc.) strike up; (intrigue) build up. **noueux** adj knotty, gnarled.

nouilles [nuj] nf pl noodles pl.

nounou [nunu] nf (fam) nanny.

nounours [nunurs] nm (fam) teddy.

nourrice [nuris] nf nurse. **nourricier** adj nutritive.

nourrir [nurir] v feed, nourish; (espoir, etc.) nurse, harbour. **nourrisson** nm infant. **nourriture** nf food, nourishment.

nous [nu] *pron (sujet)* we; *(objet)* us, to us; *(réfléchi)* ourselves, each other. **nous-mêmes** *pron* ourselves.

nouveau, -elle [nuvo, -ɛl] *adj* new; fresh. **à nouveau** *de* **de nouveau** again. **nouveau-né** *adj* newborn. **Nouveau Testament** *nm* New Testament. **nouveau venu, nouvelle venue** *nm, nf* newcomer. **nouveaux-mariés** *nm pl* newly-weds *pl*. **nouvel an** *nm* New Year. **Nouvelle-Zélande** *nf* New Zealand. *nf* piece of news; *(récit)* short story. **nouvelles** *nf pl* news *sing*. **nouveauté** *nf* novelty; change; *(mode)* fashion.

nouvel [nuvɛl] *form of* **nouveau** *used before a vowel or mute h*.

novateur, -trice [nɔvatœr, -tris] *adj* innovative. *nm, nf* innovator.

novembre [nɔvɑ̃brə] *nm* November.

novice [nɔvis] *adj* inexperienced. *n(m + f)* novice.

noyau [nwajo] *nm (fruit)* stone; nucleus; *(tech)* core; small group.

noyer¹ [nwaje] *nm (arbre, bois)* walnut.

noyer² [nwaje] *v* drown; *(auto)* flood; *(submerger)* swamp. **noyade** *nf* drowning.

nu [ny] *adj* bare; *(sans vêtements)* naked; *(style)* plain. *nm* nude. **mettre à nu** expose, lay bare. **nu-pieds** *adv* barefoot.

nuage [nɥaʒ] *nm* cloud. **nuageux** *adj* cloudy.

nuance [nɥɑ̃s] *nf* nuance; *(couleur)* shade; slight difference. **nuancer** *v* shade.

nucléaire [nykleɛr] *adj* nuclear.

nudité [nydite] *nf* nudity; *(dénuement)* bareness. **nudiste** *n(m + f)* nudist.

nue [ny] *nf* **porter aux nues** praise to the skies. **tomber des nues** be flabbergasted.

nuée [nɥe] *nf* cloud; *(multitude)* horde.

***nuire** [nɥir] *v* **nuire à** harm. **nuisible** *adj* harmful. **animal** *or* **insecte nuisible** *nm* pest.

nuit [nɥi] *nf* night; *(obscurité)* darkness. **cette nuit** *(passé)* last night; *(futur)* tonight. **nuit blanche** sleepless night.

nul, nulle [nyl] *adj (aucun)* no; *(résultat)* nil; *(personne)* useless. **nul et non avenu** null and void. **nulle part** nowhere. *pron* no-one. **nullement** *adv* not at all.

numéral [nymeral] *nm* numeral.

numérique [nymerik] *adj* numerical.

numéro [nymero] *nm* number; *(journal)* issue. **numéro minéralogique** *(auto)* registration number.

numéroter [nymerɔte] *v* number.

nuptial [nypsjal] *adj* bridal, nuptial.

nuque [nyk] *nf* nape of the neck.

nutrition [nytrisjɔ̃] *nf* nutrition. **nutritif** *adj* nutritious, nourishing.

nylon [nilɔ̃] *nm* nylon.

nymphe [nɛ̃f] *nf* nymph.

O

oasis [ɔazis] *nf* oasis.

obéir [ɔbeir] *v* **obéir à** obey. **obéissance** *nf* obedience. **obéissant** *adj* obedient.

obélisque [ɔbelisk] *nm* obelisk.

obèse [ɔbɛz] *adj* obese. **obésité** *nf* obesity.

objecter [ɔbʒɛkte] *v* object; *(raison)* put forward; *(prétexter)* plead. **objection** *nf* objection.

objectif [ɔbʒɛktif] *adj* objective. *nm* objective; *(appareil-photo)* lens.

objet [ɔbʒɛ] *nm* object; *(but)* purpose; subject. **objets trouvés** lost property *sing*.

obliger [ɔbliʒe] *v* oblige; force, compel. **obligation** *nf* obligation; *(devoir)* duty. **obligatoire** *adj* compulsory; *(fam)* inevitable.

oblique [ɔblik] *adj* oblique. **regard oblique** *nm* sidelong glance.

oblitérer [ɔblitere] *v* cancel.

oblong, -ongue [ɔblɔ̃, -ɔ̃g] *adj* oblong.

obscène [ɔpsɛn] *adj* obscene. **obscénité** *nf* obscenity.

obscur [ɔpskyr] *adj* obscure; *(sombre)* dark; humble. **obscurité** *nf* obscurity; darkness.

obscurcir [ɔpskyrsir] *v* obscure; darken.

obséder [ɔpsede] *v* obsess, haunt. **obsédant** *adj* obsessive, haunting. **obsédé, -e** *nm, nf (fam)* fanatic.

obsèques [ɔpsɛk] *nf pl* funeral *sing*.

observateur, -trice [ɔpsɛrvatœr, -tris] *nm, nf* observer. *adj* observant.

observer [ɔpsɛrve] *v* observe; *(regarder)* watch; *(remarquer)* notice. **observation** *nf* observation; remark. **observatoire** *nm* observatory.

obsession [ɔpsesjɔ̃] *nf* obsession.

obstacle [ɔpstaklə] *nm* obstacle; *(hippisme)* fence.

obstétrique [ɔpstetrik] *nf* obstetrics.

s'obstiner [ɔpstine] v insist. **s'obstiner à** persist obstinately in. **obstination** nf obstinacy. **obstiné** adj obstinate.

obstruer [ɔpstrye] v obstruct, block. **obstruction** nf obstruction.

*obtenir [ɔptənir] v obtain, get; (atteindre) achieve.

obturateur [ɔptyratœr] nm (phot) shutter.

obtus [ɔpty] adj obtuse.

obus [ɔby] nm shell.

occasion [ɔkazjɔ̃] nf opportunity, chance; (circonstance) occasion; cause; (comm) bargain; (marché) second-hand market. **d'occasion** second-hand. **occasionnel** adj casual; (fortuit) chance. **occasionner** v cause.

occident [ɔksidɑ̃] nm west. **occidental** adj western.

occulte [ɔkylt] adj occult; secret, hidden.

occuper [ɔkype] v occupy. **s'occuper de** attend to, take care of. **occupant, -e** nm, nf occupant, occupier. **occupation** nf occupation. **occupé** adj busy; (téléphone, toilettes) engaged; (mil) occupied.

océan [ɔseɑ̃] nm ocean. **océanique** adj oceanic.

ocre [ɔkra] nf ochre. nm (couleur) ochre.

octane [ɔktan] nm octane.

octave [ɔktav] nf octave.

octobre [ɔktɔbra] nm October.

octogone [ɔktɔgɔn] nm octagon. **octogonal** adj octagonal.

octroyer [ɔktrwaje] v grant.

oculiste [ɔkylist] n(m+f) oculist.

ode [ɔd] nf ode.

odeur [ɔdœr] nf odour, smell; (agréable) fragrance, scent. **odorant** adj sweet-smelling. **odorat** nm sense of smell.

odieux [ɔdjø] adj obnoxious, odious.

œil [œj] nm, pl **yeux** eye; (expression) look. **œil poché** black eye. **œillade** nf wink. **œillères** nf pl blinkers pl. **œillet** nm carnation; (trou) eyelet.

œsophage [ezɔfaʒ] nm oesophagus.

œuf [œf] nm egg. **œuf à la coque** boiled egg. **œuf du jour** new-laid egg. **œuf dur** hard-boiled egg. **œuf mollet** soft-boiled egg. **œuf poché** poached egg. **œufs brouillés** scrambled eggs pl. **œuf sur le plat** fried egg.

œuvre [œvra] nf work; (tâche) task; charity. **œuvre d'art** work of art.

offenser [ɔfɑ̃se] v offend. **s'offenser** take offence. **offensant** adj offensive. **offense**

nf insult; (rel) trespass. **offensive** nm (mil) offensive.

office [ɔfis] nm office; bureau, agency; (rel) service. **faire office de** act as. **officiel, -elle** n, adj official. **officier** nm officer. **officieux** adj unofficial.

officine [ɔfisin] nf dispensary.

*offrir [ɔfrir] v offer; present; (cadeau) give. **s'offrir** treat oneself to. **offrande** nf offering. **offre** nf offer; (enchères) bid; (comm) tender.

offusquer [ɔfyske] v offend.

ogre [ɔgra] nm ogre. **ogresse** nf ogress.

oie [wa] nf goose.

oignon [ɔɲɔ̃] nm (légume) onion; (bot) bulb.

*oindre [wɛ̃dra] v anoint.

oiseau [wazo] nm bird.

oisif [wazif] adj idle. **oisiveté** nf idleness.

oison [wazɔ̃] nm gosling.

olive [ɔliv] nf olive. **olivier** nm olive tree.

olympique [ɔlɛ̃pik] adj Olympic.

ombrage [ɔ̃braʒ] nm shade. **prendre ombrage** take umbrage. **ombrager** v shade. **ombrageux** adj touchy.

ombre [ɔ̃bra] nf shadow; (ombrage) shade; obscurity, dark. **ombrer** v shade.

omelette [ɔmlɛt] nf omelette.

*omettre [ɔmɛtra] v omit. **omission** nf omission.

omnibus [ɔmnibys] nm slow train.

omnipotent [ɔmnipɔtɑ̃] adj omnipotent.

omoplate [ɔmɔplat] nf shoulder blade.

on [ɔ̃] pron one, (les gens) they, people; (tu, vous) you; (nous) we; (quelqu'un) someone. **on demande ...** wanted. **on-dit** nm invar rumour, hearsay.

oncle [ɔ̃kla] nm uncle.

onde [ɔ̃d] nf wave. **grandes ondes** long wave(s). **ondes courtes/moyennes** short/medium wave(s). **sur les ondes** on the air.

ondoyer [ɔ̃dwaje] v ripple, wave. **ondoyant** adj undulating; (flamme) wavering; (forme) supple.

onduler [ɔ̃dyle] v undulate; (cheveux) be wavy. **ondulant** adj undulating; (pouls) uneven. **ondulation** nf undulation. **ondulé** adj (cheveux) wavy. **onduleux** adj wavy; (movement) sinuous.

ongle [ɔ̃gla] nm nail; (animal) claw.

onguent [ɔ̃gɑ̃] nm ointment.

onyx [ɔniks] nm onyx.

onze [ɔ̃z] nm, adj eleven. **onzième** n(m+f), adj eleventh.

opale [ɔpal] nf opal.

opaque [ɔpak] adj opaque. **opacité** nf opacity.

opéra [ɔpera] nm opera; (édifice) opera house. **opérette** nf operetta.

opérer [ɔpere] v operate; (accomplir) carry out; (effectuer) bring about; (faire) make; (agir) act, work. **se faire opérer** have an operation. **opérateur, -trice** nm, nf operator. **opération** nf operation; (comm) deal; (tech) process. **salle d'opération** nf operating theatre.

ophtalmique [ɔftalmik] adj ophthalmic.

s'opiniâtrer [ɔpinjɑtre] v persist stubbornly. **opiniâtre** adj stubborn, obstinate; persistent. **opiniâtreté** nf stubbornness, obstinacy.

opinion [ɔpinjɔ̃] nf opinion.

opium [ɔpjɔm] nm opium.

opportun [ɔpɔrtœ̃] adj opportune; appropriate. **opportunité** nf timeliness.

opposé [ɔpoze] adj opposite; conflicting, opposing; contrasting. **opposé à** opposed to. nm opposite.

opposer [ɔpoze] v place opposite; contrast. **s'opposer à** oppose. **opposition** nf opposition; conflict; contrast. **par opposition à** as opposed to.

opprimer [ɔprime] v oppress.

opprobre [ɔprɔbr] nm disgrace.

opter [ɔpte] v opt, choose. **option** nf option.

opticien [ɔptisjɛ̃], **-enne** nm, nf optician.

optimiste [ɔptimist] n(m+f) optimist. adj optimistic. **optimisme** nm optimism.

optimum [ɔptimɔm] nm, adj optimum.

optique [ɔptik] adj optical, optic. nf optics.

opulent [ɔpylɑ̃] adj wealthy, rich, opulent. **opulence** nf richness, opulence.

or¹ [ɔr] nm gold. **d'or** golden.

or² [ɔr] conj now.

oracle [ɔrakl] nm oracle.

orage [ɔraʒ] nm storm. **orageux** adj stormy.

oraison [ɔrezɔ̃] nf prayer.

oral [ɔral] nm, adj oral.

orange [ɔrɑ̃ʒ] nf orange. nm, adj invar (couleur) orange. **oranger** nm orange tree.

orateur, -trice [ɔratœr, -tris] nm, nf orator, speaker.

orbite [ɔrbit] nf orbit. **orbiter** v orbit.

orchestre [ɔrkɛstr] nm orchestra; (danse, jazz) band; (théâtre) stalls pl. **orchestral** adj orchestral. **orchestration** nf orchestration. **orchestrer** v orchestrate.

orchidée [ɔrkide] nf orchid.

ordinaire [ɔrdiner] adj ordinary; common; (habituel) usual. nm ordinary.

ordinal [ɔrdinal] adj ordinal.

ordinateur [ɔrdinatœr] nm computer.

ordonner [ɔrdɔne] v order; arrange, organize; (méd) prescribe; (rel) ordain. **ordonnance** nf order; prescription; organization. **ordonné** adj orderly, tidy.

ordre [ɔrdr] nm order. **de premier/deuxième ordre** first-/second-rate. **en ordre** tidy. **ordre du jour** agenda.

ordure [ɔrdyr] nf dirt, filth. **ordures** nf pl rubbish sing. refuse sing; obscenities pl.

oreille [ɔrɛj] nf ear; (ouïe) hearing. **oreiller** nm pillow. **oreillons** nm pl mumps sing.

ores [ɔr] adv **d'ores et déjà** already, here and now.

orfèvre [ɔrfɛvr] nm (argent) silversmith; (or) goldsmith.

organe [ɔrgan] nm organ; instrument; (porte-parole) spokesman, mouthpiece.

organique [ɔrganik] adj organic.

organiser [ɔrganize] v organize. **organisateur, -trice** nm, nf organizer. **organisation** nf organization. **organisme** nm organism; (institution) body.

organiste [ɔrganist] n(m+f) organist.

orgasme [ɔrgasm] nm orgasm.

orge [ɔrʒ] nf barley.

orgie [ɔrʒi] nf orgy; (excès) profusion.

orgue [ɔrg] nm organ.

orgueil [ɔrgœj] nm pride, arrogance. **orgueilleux** adj proud, arrogant.

orient [ɔrjɑ̃] nm east. **oriental** adj eastern, oriental.

orienter [ɔrjɑ̃te] v orientate; direct; (disposer) position, adjust. **orienter vers** turn towards. **s'orienter** find one's bearings. **orientation** nf orientation; direction; positioning; (maison, jardin) aspect. **orientation professionnelle** careers guidance.

origan [ɔrigɑ̃] nm oregano.

origine [ɔriʒin] nf origin. **à l'origine** originally. **originaire** adj original; native. **original** nm, adj original; (péj) eccentric. **originalité** nf originality; eccentricity. **originel** adj original.

orme [ɔrm] nm elm.

ornement [ɔrnəmɑ̃] nm ornament. **orne-**

mental *adj* ornamental. **ornementation** *nf* ornamentation.

orner [ɔrne] *v* decorate; embellish. **orné** *adj* ornate.

ornière [ɔrnjer] *nf* rut.

ornithologie [ɔrnitɔlɔʒi] *nf* ornithology. **ornithologique** *adj* ornithological. **ornithologiste** *n(m+f)* ornithologist.

orphelin [ɔrfalɛ̃], **-e** *n, adj* orphan. **orphelinat** *nm* orphanage.

orteil [ɔrtɛj] *nm* toe.

orthodoxe [ɔrtɔdɔks] *adj* orthodox.

orthographe [ɔrtɔgraf] *nf* spelling. **orthographier** *v* spell.

orthopédique [ɔrtɔpedik] *adj* orthopaedic.

orthophonie [ɔrtɔfɔni] *nf* (*méd*) speech therapy. **orthophoniste** *n(m+f)* speech therapist.

ortie [ɔrti] *nf* nettle.

os [ɔs] *nm* bone. **os à moelle** marrowbone. **trempé jusqu'aux os** soaked to the skin.

osciller [ɔsile] *v* oscillate; (*se balancer*) rock, swing; (*hésiter*) waver; (*prix, etc.*) fluctuate. **oscillation** *nf* oscillation; fluctuation.

oser [oze] *v* dare. **osé** *adj* bold, daring.

osier [ozje] *nm* wicker. **en osier** wickerwork.

ossature [ɔsatyr] *nf* (*corps*) frame; framework; (*visage*) bone structure.

osseux [ɔsø] *adj* bony.

ostentation [ɔstɑ̃tasjɔ̃] *nf* ostentation.

ostraciser [ɔstrasize] *v* ostracize. **ostracisme** *nm* ostracism.

otage [ɔtaʒ] *nm* hostage.

otarie [ɔtari] *nf* sea-lion.

ôter [ote] *v* take away *or* off, remove.

ou [u] *conj* or. **ou bien** or else. **ou ... ou ...** either ... or ....

où [u] *adv* where; (*temps*) when.

ouate [wat] *nf* cotton wool; (*rembourrage*) wadding. **ouater** *v* quilt.

oublier [ublije] *v* forget. **oubli** *nm* oblivion; lapse of memory; omission, oversight.

ouest [west] *nm* west. *adj invar* west; (*région*) western; (*direction*) westward.

oui [wi] *adv, nm invar* yes.

***ouïr** [wir] *v* hear. **ouï-dire** *nm invar* hearsay. **ouïe** *nf* hearing.

ouragan [uragɑ̃] *nm* hurricane.

ourdir [urdir] *v* (*complot*) hatch.

ourler [urle] *v* hem. **ourlet** *nm* hem.

ours [urs] *nm* bear. **ours blanc** polar bear.

outil [uti] *nm* tool, implement. **outillage** *nm* set of tools; equipment. **outiller** *v* provide with tools; equip.

outrager [utraʒe] *v* outrage; insult. **outrage** *nm* insult. **outrage à la pudeur** indecent behaviour. **outrage à magistrat** contempt of court.

outrance [utrɑ̃s] *nf* excess.

outre [utrə] *prep* as well as. **en outre** moreover, besides. **outre-mer** *adv* overseas.

outrer [utre] *v* outrage; exaggerate. **outré** *adj* excessive, overdone; outraged.

ouvert [uver] *adj* open. **ouvertement** *adv* openly, overtly. **ouverture** *nf* opening; (*musique, avance*) overture.

ouvrable [uvrablə] *adj* **jour ouvrable** weekday.

ouvrage [uvraʒ] *nm* work, piece of work.

ouvreuse [uvrøz] *nf* usherette.

ouvrier [uvrije], **-ère** *adj* labour, industrial; working-class. *nm, nf* worker.

***ouvrir** [uvrir] *v* open; (*gaz, robinet, etc.*) turn on. **ouvre-boîte** *nm invar* tin-opener. **ouvre-bouteille** *nm invar* bottle-opener.

ovaire [ɔver] *nm* ovary.

ovale [ɔval] *nm, adj* oval.

ovation [ɔvasjɔ̃] *nf* ovation.

ovulation [ɔvylasjɔ̃] *nf* ovulation.

oxygène [ɔksiʒɛn] *nm* oxygen.

P

pacage [pakaʒ] *nm* pasture.

pacifier [pasifje] *v* pacify. **pacifique** *adj* peaceful, peaceable. **pacifisme** *nm* pacifism. **pacifiste** *n(m+f)*, *adj* pacifist.

Pacifique [pasifik] *nm, adj* Pacific.

pacte [pakta] *nm* pact, treaty.

pagaie [page] *nf* paddle. **pagayer** *v* paddle.

pagaïe [pagaj] *nf* mess; (*cohue*) chaos.

page¹ [paʒ] *nf* (*livre*) page. **à la page** up-to-date.

page² [paʒ] *nm* (*garçon*) page.

pagode [pagɔd] *nf* pagoda.

paie [pɛ] *nf* pay. **paiement** *nm* payment.

païen [pajɛ̃], **-enne** *n, adj* pagan, heathen.

paillasson [pajasɔ̃] *nm* doormat.

paille [pɑj] *nf* straw; (*défaut*) flaw. **paille de fer** steel wool. **paillette** *nf* speck; (*savon*) flake; (*ornement*) sequin; flaw.

pain [pɛ̃] *nm* bread; (*miche*) loaf; (*savon*) bar. **pain bis/complet** brown/wholemeal bread. **pain de mie** sandwich loaf. **pain d'épice** gingerbread. **pain grillé** toast. **petit pain** roll.

pair¹ [pɛr] *nm* peer. **au pair** *adj* au pair. **pairie** *nf* peerage.

pair² [pɛr] *adj* even.

paire [pɛr] *nf* pair.

paisible [pezibl] *adj* peaceful, quiet.

*paître [pɛtrə] *v* graze.

paix [pɛ] *nf* peace.

palace [palas] *nm* luxury hotel.

palais¹ [palɛ] *nm* palace. **palais de justice** law courts *pl*.

palais² [palɛ] *nm* (*anat*) palate.

pâle [pɑl] *adj* pale; (*faible*) faint, weak. **paleur** *nf* paleness.

palefrenier [palfrənje] *nm* groom.

palette [palɛt] *nf* palette; (*aube*) paddle.

palier [palje] *nm* landing; (*étape*) stage.

pâlir [pɑlir] *v* turn pale; (*couleur, etc.*) fade; (*lumière*) grow dim.

palissade [palisad] *nf* fence.

palmarès [palmares] *nm* prize list.

palme [palm] *nf* palm leaf; (*nageur*) flipper. **palmé** *adj* (*patte*) webbed. **palmier** *nm* palm tree. **palmipède** *adj* web-footed.

palombe [palɔ̃b] *nf* wood-pigeon.

palourde [palurd] *nf* clam.

palper [palpe] *v* feel, finger.

palpiter [palpite] *v* (*cœur*) beat; (*violemment*) pound, throb; (*frémir*) quiver. **palpitant** *adj* thrilling. **palpitation** *nf* palpitation.

paludisme [palydism] *nm* malaria.

pâmer [pɑme] *v* **se pâmer de** be overcome with.

pamphlet [pɑ̃flɛ] *nm* lampoon.

pamplemousse [pɑ̃pləmus] *nm* grapefruit.

pan [pɑ̃] *nm* piece; (*côté*) side. **pan de chemise** shirt-tail.

panache [panaʃ] *nm* plume; gallantry. **panaché** [panaʃe] *adj* multicoloured; mixed, motley. *nm* shandy. **panacher** *v* vary; (*mélanger*) blend.

panais [panɛ] *nm* parsnip.

pancarte [pɑ̃kart] *nf* sign; (*manifestation*) placard.

pancréas [pɑ̃kreas] *nm* pancreas. **pancréatique** *adj* pancreatic.

panda [pɑ̃da] *nm* panda.

paner [pane] *v* coat with breadcrumbs.

panier [panje] *nm* basket. **panier à salade** salad shaker; (*fam*) police van, Black Maria. **panier-repas** *nm* packed lunch.

panique [panik] *nf* panic.

panne [pan] *nf* breakdown, failure. **être en panne** break down. **être en panne de** run out of.

panneau [pano] *nm* panel; (*écriteau*) sign. **panneau d'affichage** notice-board. **panneau de signalisation** road sign. **panneau-réclame** *nm* hoarding.

panoplie [panɔpli] *nf* outfit.

panorama [panɔrama] *nm* panorama. **panoramique** *adj* panoramic.

panse [pɑ̃s] *nf* paunch.

panser [pɑ̃se] *v* (*plaie*) dress; bandage; (*cheval*) groom. **pansement** *nm* dressing; bandage; (*sparadrap*) plaster.

pantalon [pɑ̃talɔ̃] *nm* trousers *pl*; pair of trousers.

pantelant [pɑ̃tlɑ̃] *adj* panting; (*cœur*) throbbing.

panthère [pɑ̃tɛr] *nf* panther.

pantomime [pɑ̃tɔmim] *nf* mime.

pantoufle [pɑ̃tuflə] *nf* slipper.

paon [pɑ̃] *nm* peacock.

papa [papa] *nm* (*fam*) dad, daddy.

pape [pap] *nm* pope. **papal** *adj* papal. **papauté** *nf* papacy.

papeterie [papetri] *nf* stationery; (*magasin*) stationer's; (*fabrique*) paper mill. **papetier, -ère** *nm, nf* stationer.

papier [papje] *nm* paper. **papier à lettres** *nm* notepaper. **papier à musique** *nm* manuscript paper. **papier buvard** *nm* blotting paper. **papier calque** *nm* tracing paper. **papier d'aluminium** *nm* kitchen foil. **papier de soie** *nm* tissue paper. **papier de verre** *nm* sandpaper. **papier hygiénique** *nm* toilet paper. **papier millimétré** *nm* graph paper. **papier peint** *nm* wallpaper.

papillon [papijɔ̃] *nm* butterfly; (*police*) parking ticket. **papillon de nuit** moth.

paprika [paprika] *nm* paprika.

paquebot [pakbo] *nm* liner.

pâquerette [pɑkrɛt] *nf* daisy.

Pâques [pɑk] *nm* Easter.

paquet [pakɛ] *nm* packet, pack; (*colis*) parcel; (*tas*) pile, mass. **mettre en paquet** parcel up.

par

par [par] *prep* by; through; (*distribution*) per. **par-ci par-là** here and there; (*temps*) now and then. **par-dessous** *prep*, *adv* under. **par-dessus** *prep*, *adv* over. **par ici/là** this/that way.

parabole [parabɔl] *nf* (*rel*) parable; (*math*) parabola.

parachute [paraʃyt] *nm* parachute. **parachuter** *v* parachute. **parachutiste** *n(m+f)* parachutist; (*mil*) paratrooper.

parade [parad] *nf* parade; (*ostentation*) show. **faire parade de** show off, brag about.

paradis [paradi] *nm* paradise, heaven.

paradoxe [paradɔks] *nm* paradox. **paradoxal** *adj* paradoxical.

paraffine [parafin] *nf* paraffin (wax).

parages [paraʒ] *nm pl* vicinity *sing*. **dans les parages** round about, in the area.

paragraphe [paragraf] *nm* paragraph.

*paraître [parɛtrə] *v* appear; (*sembler*) seem; be visible, show; be published.

parallèle [paralɛl] *nm*, *adj* parallel. *nf* parallel line. **parallélogramme** *nm* parallelogram.

paralyser [paralize] *v* paralyse. **paralysie** *nf* paralysis. **paralytique** *adj* paralytic.

paramilitaire [paramilitɛr] *adj* paramilitary.

paranoïa [paranɔja] *nf* paranoia. **paranoïde** *adj* paranoid.

parapet [parapɛ] *nm* parapet.

paraphraser [parafraze] *v* paraphrase. **paraphrase** *nf* paraphrase.

paraplégique [papleʒik] *n(m+f)*, *adj* paraplegic.

parapluie [paraplɥi] *nm* umbrella.

parasite [parazit] *nm* parasite. **parasites** *nm pl* (*radio*) interference *sing*. *adj* parasitic.

paratonnerre [paratɔnɛr] *nm* lightning conductor.

parc [park] *nm* park; (*château*) grounds *pl*; (*animal*) pen; (*bébé*) play-pen.

parcelle [parsɛl] *nf* fragment, bit. **parcelle de terre** plot of land.

parce que [parskə] *conj* because.

parchemin [parʃəmɛ̃] *nm* parchment. **parcheminé** *adj* wrinkled.

parcomètre [parkɔmɛtrə] *nm* parking meter.

*parcourir [parkurir] *v* travel through, cover; (*livre*) glance through.

parcours [parkur] *nm* distance; (*trajet*) journey; course; (*itinéraire*) route.

pardessus [pardəsy] *nm* overcoat.

pardon [pardɔ̃] *nm* forgiveness, pardon. **demander pardon** apologize. *interj* (*comment*) pardon; (*désolé*) sorry, excuse me. **pardonner** *v* forgive, pardon; excuse.

pareil, -eille [parɛj] *adj* the same, alike; (*tel*) such. *nm*, *nf* equal, peer.

parement [parmɑ̃] *nm* facing.

parent, -e *nm*, *nf* relation. **parents** *nm pl* (*père*, *mère*) parents *pl*. **parenté** *nf* relationship.

parenthèse [parɑ̃tɛz] *nf* parenthesis; digression; (*signe*) bracket. **entre parenthèses** in brackets; incidentally.

parer¹ [pare] *v* (*orner*) adorn; (*robe*) trim; (*préparer*) dress.

parer² [pare] *v* ward off. **pare-balles** *adj invar* bulletproof. **pare-brise** *nm invar* windshield. **pare-chocs** *nm invar* bumper. **pare-étincelles** *nm invar* fireguard. **parer à** deal with; prepare for.

paresseux [parɛsø] *adj* lazy. **paresse** *nf* laziness.

parfait [parfɛ] *adj* perfect; complete; absolute.

parfois [parfwa] *adv* sometimes; occasionally.

parfum [parfœ̃] *nm* perfume, scent; (*glace*) flavour. **parfumer** *v* perfume; flavour.

pari [pari] *nm* bet. **parier** *v* bet.

Paris [pari] *n* Paris.

parité [parite] *nf* parity.

parjure [parʒyr] *adj* false. *nm* perjury, false witness. *n(m+f)* perjurer. **se parjurer** *v* perjure oneself, bear false witness.

parking [parkiŋ] *nm* car park.

parlement [parləmɑ̃] *nm* parliament. **parlementaire** *adj* parliamentary.

parler [parle] *v* talk, speak. **sans parler de** not to mention. **tu parles!** (*fam*) you're telling me! *nm* speech.

parmi [parmi] *prep* among.

parodie [parɔdi] *nf* parody. **parodier** *v* parodier.

paroi [parwa] *nf* wall; (*cloison*) partition; rock face; (*récipient*) inside surface.

paroisse [parwas] *nf* parish. **paroissial** *adj* parish. **salle paroissiale** *nf* church hall. **paroissien, -enne** *nm*, *nf* parishioner.

parole [parɔl] *nf* word; (*faculté*) speech; remark. **parolier, -ère** *nm*, *nf* lyricist.

paroxysme [parɔksismə] *nm* height, climax.

parquer [parke] v (auto) park; (enfermer) pen in; (entasser) pack in.

parquet [parke] nm floor.

parrain [parɛ̃] nm godfather.

parsemer [parsəme] v scatter, sprinkle.

part [par] nf part, portion, share. **à part** (de côté) aside; separately; except for, apart from. **d'autre part** moreover. **de la part de** on behalf of. **faire part de** announce.

partager [partaʒe] v share; divide. **partage** nm share, portion; (distribution) sharing out; division.

partance [partɑ̃s] nf **en partance** outbound. **en partance pour** (bound) for.

partenaire [partənɛr] n(m + f) partner.

parterre [partɛr] nm border, flower-bed; (théâtre) stalls pl.

parti [parti] nm party, side; decision; (mariage) match. **parti pris** prejudice, bias. **prendre le parti de** stand up for. **prendre parti pour** side with. **tirer parti de** take advantage of, put to good use.

partial [parsjal] adj partial, biased. **partialité** nf partiality, bias.

participe [partisip] nm participle.

participer [partisipe] v **participer à** participate in, take part in; (frais) contribute to; (profits, etc.) share in. **participant, -e** nm, nf participant; (concours) entrant. **participation** nf participation; (comm) interest.

particularité [partikylarite] nf particularity, characteristic.

particule [partikyl] nf particle.

particulier [partikylje] adj particular; special, exceptional; (étrange) peculiar; private. nm person, individual.

partie [parti] nf part; (sport, etc.) game; (droit, divertissement) party. **faire partie de** belong to.

partiel [parsjɛl] adj partial.

*__partir__ [partir] v leave, go; (fusil) go off; (commencer) start. **à partir de** from.

partisan [partizɑ̃] -e nm, nf supporter, advocate. **être partisan de** be in favour of.

partition [partisjɔ̃] nf (musique) score.

partout [partu] adv everywhere. **partout où** wherever.

parure [paryr] nf finery; (bijoux) jewels pl; (ensemble) set; (ornement) trimming.

*__parvenir__ [parvənir] v **parvenir à** reach, get to; (réussir) manage to, succeed in.

parvenu, -e nm, nf (péj) upstart.

pas¹ [pa] nm step; (vitesse) pace; (trace) footprint; (géog) pass. **à pas de loup** stealthily. **pas de la porte** doorstep.

pas² [pa] adv not. ne ... **pas** not. **pas du tout** not at all. **pas mal de** (fam) quite a lot of.

passage [pasaʒ] nm passage; change, transition; (traversée) crossing. **passage à niveau** level crossing. **passage clouté** pedestrian crossing. **passage interdit** no thoroughfare. **passage souterrain** subway.

passager [pasaʒe], **-ère** adj passing, brief; (oiseau) migratory; (rue) busy. nm, nf passenger. **passager clandestin** stowaway.

passant [pasɑ̃], **-e** nm, nf passer-by.

passe [pas] nf pass. **en passe de** on the way to.

passé [pase] adj past; (dernier) last. nm past. prep after.

passe-partout nm invar skeleton key.

passeport [paspɔr] nm passport.

passer [pase] v pass; go past; (aller) go; (franchir) get through or over; (examen) sit, take; (temps) spend; (film) show; (cuisine) strain; (traverser) cross. **passer par** go through. **passer prendre** pick up, call for. **passer voir** call on. se **passer** happen, take place; (finir) be over. se **passer de** do without.

passerelle [pasrɛl] nf (pont) foot-bridge; (naut) gangway.

passe-temps nm invar pastime.

passif [pasif] nm, adj passive. **passivité** nf passiveness.

passion [pasjɔ̃] nf passion.

passionné [pasjɔne], **-e** adj passionate. nm, nf fanatic.

passionner [pasjɔne] v fascinate. se **passionner pour** be mad keen on.

passoire [paswar] nf sieve; (plus grande) colander.

pastel [pastɛl] nm, adj invar pastel.

pastèque [pastɛk] nf water-melon.

pasteuriser [pastœrize] v pasteurize. **pasteurisation** nf pasteurization.

pastille [pastij] nf pastille.

pastis [pastis] nm (boisson) pastis; (argot) jam, fix.

pastoral [pastɔral] adj pastoral.

pat [pat] nm stalemate.

pataud [pato] adj clumsy.

patauger [patoʒe] v wade, splash; (se perdre) flounder.

pâte [pɑt] *nf* paste; cream; (*tarte*) pastry; (*à frire*) batter; (*gâteau*) mixture; (*pain*) dough. **pâte à modeler** plasticine ®. **pâte brisée** shortcrust pastry. **pâte dentifrice** toothpaste. **pâte feuilletée** puff pastry. **pâtes** *nf pl* pasta *sing*.

pâté [pɑte] *nm* (*cuisine*) pâté; (*encre*) blot; (*maisons*) block; (*sable*) sand-castle. **pâté en croûte** pie.

patelin [patlɛ̃] *nm* (*fam*) village.

patelle [patɛl] *nf* limpet.

patent [patɑ̃] *adj* patent, obvious.

patenté [patɑ̃te] *adj* licensed.

patère [patɛr] *nf* peg.

paternel [patɛrnɛl] *adj* paternal; (*bienveillant*) fatherly. **paternité** *nf* paternity.

pâteux [pɑtø] *adj* pasty; (*langue*) furred; (*voix*) husky.

pathétique [patetik] *adj* pathetic. *nm* pathos.

pathologie [patɔlɔʒi] *nf* pathology. **pathologique** *adj* pathological. **pathologiste** *n(m+f)* pathologist.

patient [pasjɑ̃], -e *n, adj* patient. **patience** *nf* patience. **patienter** *v* wait.

patin [patɛ̃] *nm* skate; (*luge*) runner. **patin à glace** ice-skate. **patin à roulettes** roller-skate. **patinage** *nm* skating. **patiner** *v* skate; (*auto*) spin. **patineur, -euse** *nm, nf* skater. **patinoire** *nf* ice rink.

patio [patjo] *nm* patio.

pâtir [pɑtir] *v* suffer.

pâtisserie [pɑtisri] *nf* (*magasin*) cake shop; (*gâteau*) pastry, cake; (*métier*) confectionery. **pâtissier, -ère** *nm, nf* confectioner.

patois [patwa] *nm* patois, dialect.

patrie [patri] *nf* homeland.

patrimoine [patrimwan] *nm* inheritance, heritage.

patriote [patrijɔt] *n(m+f)* patriot. *adj* patriotic. **patriotique** *adj* patriotic. **patriotisme** *nm* patriotism.

patron, -onne [patrɔ̃, -ɔn] *nm, nf* proprietor; employer; (*fam*) boss; (*protecteur*) patron; (*naut*) skipper. *nm* pattern. **patronage** *nm* patronage. **patronat** *nm* management. **patronner** *v* support, sponsor.

patrouille [patruj] *nf* patrol. **patrouiller** *v* patrol.

patte [pat] *nf* (*jambe*) leg; (*pied*) paw, foot; (*languette*) flap, tongue. **patte de derrière** hind leg. **patte de devant** foreleg. **patte de mouche** scrawl.

pâture [pɑtyr] *nf* pasture; (*nourriture*) food. **pâturage** *nm* pasture.

paume [pom] *nf* palm.

paupière [popjɛr] *nf* eyelid.

pause [poz] *nf* break, pause. **pause-café** *nf* coffee break.

pauvre [povr] *adj* poor; (*piètre*) weak. *n(m+f)* poor person. **pauvreté** *nf* poverty; poorness; weakness.

se pavaner [pavane] *v* strut about.

paver [pave] *v* pave; (*chaussée*) cobble. **pavé** *nm* paving stone; (*rond*) cobble-stone.

pavillon [pavijɔ̃] *nm* pavilion; lodge; (*villa*) house; (*drapeau*) flag.

pavot [pavo] *nm* poppy.

payer [peje] *v* pay (for). **se payer** (*fam*) treat oneself to. **payable** *adj* payable.

pays [pei] *nm* country, land; region. **du pays** local. **les Pays-Bas** the Netherlands *pl*. **pays de Galles** Wales. **paysage** *nm* landscape; scenery. **paysan, -anne** *nm, nf* peasant.

péage [peaʒ] *nm* toll.

peau [po] *nf* skin; (*cuir*) hide; (*fruit*) peel. **peau de chamois** chamois leather. **peau de mouton** sheepskin. **Peau-Rouge** *n(m+f)* Red Indian.

pêche¹ [pɛʃ] *nf* (*fruit*) peach. **pêcher** *nm* peach tree.

pêche² [pɛʃ] *nf* fishing. **aller à la pêche** go fishing.

pécher [peʃe] *v* sin. **péché** *nm* sin. **pécheur, -eresse** *nm, nf* sinner.

pêcher [peʃe] *v* fish (for); (*attraper*) catch. **pêcheur** *nm* fisherman.

pédagogique [pedagɔʒik] *adj* educational.

pédaler [pedale] *v* pedal. **pédale** *nf* pedal.

pédant [pedɑ̃] *adj* pedantic.

pédéraste [pederast] *nm* homosexual. **pédé** *nm* (*argot*) queer. **pédérastie** *nf* homosexuality.

pédiatre [pedjatrə] *n(m+f)* paediatrician. **pédiatrie** *nf* paediatrics.

pédicure [pedikyr] *n(m+f)* chiropodist.

pedigree [pedigri] *nm* pedigree.

peigner [peɲe] *v* comb. **se peigner** comb one's hair. **mal peigné** dishevelled. **peigne** *nm* comb. **peignoir** *nm* dressing-gown.

*peindre [pɛ̃drə] *v* paint; (*décrire*) depict, portray.

peine [pɛn] *nf* effort, trouble; (*tristesse*) sorrow; difficulty; punishment. **à peine** scarcely, hardly.

peiner [pene] v (s'efforcer) labour, struggle; (affliger) grieve, distress.

peintre [pɛ̃tr] n(m+f) painter. **peinture** nf painting; (surface) paintwork; (matière) paint.

péjoratif [peʒɔratif] adj derogatory.

Pékin [pekɛ̃] n Peking.

pelage [pɔlaʒ] nm coat, fur.

pêle-mêle [pɛlmɛl] adv pell-mell, any old how. nm invar jumble.

peler [pɔle] v peel.

pèlerin [pɛlrɛ̃] nm pilgrim. **pèlerinage** nm pilgrimage. **pèlerine** nf cape.

pélican [pelikã] nm pelican.

pelle [pɛl] nf shovel; (d'enfant) spade. **pelle à ordures** dustpan. **pelleter** v shovel (up).

pelletier [pɛltje], **-ère** nm, nf furrier.

pellicule [pelikyl] nf film. **pellicules** nf pl dandruff sing.

pelote [pɔlɔt] nf ball; (à épingles) pincushion.

se peloter [pɔlɔte] v (fam) pet, neck.

peloton [pɔlɔtɔ̃] nm small ball; group, squad.

pelotonner [pɔlɔtɔne] v (laine) wind into a ball. **se pelotonner** curl up, snuggle up.

pelouse [pɔluz] nf lawn.

peluche [pɔlyʃ] nf plush, fur fabric; (poil, flocon) bit of fluff. **en peluche** fluffy. **pelucheux** adj fluffy.

pelure [pɔlyr] nf peel, peeling.

pénal [penal] adj penal. **pénaliser** v penalize. **pénalité** nf penalty.

penaud [pano] adj sheepish, contrite.

pencher [pãʃe] v tilt, lean (over), slant. **se pencher** lean (over); (se baisser) bend (down). **penchant** nm tendency; (goût) liking. **penché** adj sloping.

pendant¹ [pãdã] adj hanging, drooping; (affaire) pending. nm counterpart, match.

pendant² [pãdã] prep during, for. **pendant que** conj while.

pendentif [pãdãtif] nm pendant.

pendiller [pãdije] v flap about.

pendre [pãdr] v hang; (s'affaisser) sag; (bras, jambes) dangle. **pendaison** nf hanging.

pendule [pãdyl] nf clock. nm pendulum.

pêne [pɛn] nm bolt.

pénétrer [penetre] v penetrate. **pénétrer dans** enter. **pénétrable** adj penetrable. **pénétrant** adj piercing, penetrating;

(pluie) drenching; (esprit, personne) shrewd. **pénétration** nf penetration.

pénible [penibl] adj hard, difficult; (fatigant) tiresome; (douloureux) painful.

péniche [peniʃ] nf barge.

pénicilline [penisilin] nf penicillin.

péninsule [penɛ̃syl] nf peninsula. **péninsulaire** adj peninsular.

pénis [penis] nm penis.

pénitent [penitã], **-e** n, adj penitent. **pénitence** nf penitence; (peine) penance; punishment.

penser [pãse] v think. **penser à** think of or about; (réfléchir) think over. **penser de** think of. **penser faire** be thinking of doing, expect to do. **pensée** nf thought; (bot) pansy. **pensif** adj pensive.

pension [pãsjɔ̃] nf (allocation) pension; (hôtel) guest house; (école) boarding school; (hébergement) board and lodging. **pension complète** full board. **pension de famille** boarding house. **pensionnaire** n(m+f) (école) boarder; (maison) lodger; (hôtel) resident. **pensionnat** nm boarding school.

pentagone [pɛ̃tagon] nm pentagon. **pentagonal** adj pentagonal.

pente [pãt] nf slope. **en pente** sloping, on a slope.

Pentecôte [pãtkot] nf Whitsun. **lundi de Pentecôte** nm Whit Monday.

pénurie [penyri] nf shortage.

pépé [pepe] nm (fam) grandad, grandpa.

pépier [pepje] v chirp, tweet. **pépiement** nm chirping.

pépin [pepɛ̃] nm pip; (fam) snag, hitch. **pépinière** nf nursery.

pépite [pepit] nf nugget.

percepteur, **-trice** [pɛrsɛptœr, -tris] adj perceptive. nm tax collector.

perception [pɛrsɛpsjɔ̃] nf perception; (impôt, etc.) collection; (bureau) tax office. **perceptible** adj perceptible; payable. **perceptif** adj perceptive.

percer [pɛrse] v pierce; (avec perceuse) drill, bore; penetrate; (abcès) burst; (mil, soleil) break through. **perce-neige** nm invar snowdrop. **perce-oreille** nm earwig. **percer des dents** cut one's teeth, be teething. **percée** nf opening, gap. **perceuse** nf drill.

*percevoir [pɛrsəvwar] v perceive; (impôt) collect.

perche¹ [pɛrʃ] nf (poisson) perch.

perche² [pɛrʃ] *nf* pole.

percher [pɛrʃe] *v* perch. **perchoir** *nm* perch.

perclus [pɛrkly] *adj* paralysed.

percussion [pɛrkysjɔ̃] *nf* percussion.

perdre [pɛrdrə] *v* lose; *(gaspiller)* waste; *(manquer)* miss; *(réservoir, etc.)* leak; ruin. **se perdre** get lost; disappear; go to waste. **perdant, -e** *nm, nf* loser. **perdu** *adj* lost, wasted; missed; ruined; isolated.

perdrix [pɛrdri] *nf* partridge.

père [pɛr] *nm* father. **le père Noël** Father Christmas.

perfection [pɛrfɛksjɔ̃] *nf* perfection. **perfectionner** *v* improve, perfect. **perfectionniste** *n(m+f)* perfectionist.

perfide [pɛrfid] *adj* treacherous, false. **perfidie** *nf* perfidy.

perforer [pɛrfɔre] *v* perforate; *(poinçonner)* punch. **perforation** *nf* perforation.

péril [peril] *nm* peril. **périlleux** *adj* perilous.

périmé [perime] *adj* out-of-date.

périmètre [perimetrə] *nm* perimeter; *(zone)* area.

période [perjɔd] *nf* period.

périodique [perjɔdik] *adj* periodic, periodical; *(math, méd)* recurring. *nm* periodical.

péripétie [peripesi] *nf* event, episode.

périphérique [periferik] *adj* peripheral. *nm* ring road. **périphérie** *nf* periphery; *(ville)* outskirts *pl*.

périr [perir] *v* perish, die. **périssable** *adj* perishable.

périscope [periskɔp] *nm* periscope.

périssoire [periswar] *nf* canoe.

perle [pɛrl] *nf* pearl; *(grain)* bead; *(goutte)* drop; *(erreur)* howler.

permanence [pɛrmanɑ̃s] *nf* permanence; *(bureau)* office. **en permanence** permanently; continuously; **être de permanence** be on duty. **permanent** *adj* permanent; continuous. **permanente** *nf* perm.

perméable [pɛrmeablə] *adj* permeable, pervious.

*permettre [pɛrmetrə] *v* allow, permit; *(rendre possible)* enable.

permis [pɛrmi] *adj* permitted. *nm* permit, licence. **permis de conduire** driving licence. **permis de construire** planning permission. **permis de séjour/travail** residence/work permit.

permission [pɛrmisjɔ̃] *nf* permission; *(mil)* leave.

permutation [pɛrmytasjɔ̃] *nf* permutation.

pernicieux [pɛrnisjø] *adj* pernicious; *(nuisible)* harmful.

pérorer [perɔre] *v* hold forth.

peroxyde [pɛrɔksid] *nm* peroxide.

perpendiculaire [pɛrpɑ̃dikylɛr] *nf, adj* perpendicular.

perpétrer [pɛrpetre] *v* perpetrate. **perpétration** *nf* perpetration.

perpétuer [pɛrpetɥe] *v* perpetuate, carry on. **se perpétuer** survive. **perpétuel** *adj* perpetual; constant; permanent. **perpétuité** *nf* perpetuity. **à perpétuité** for ever; *(jur)* for life.

perplexe [pɛrplɛks] *adj* perplexed, puzzled. **perplexité** *nf* perplexity, confusion.

perquisition [pɛrkizisjɔ̃] *nf* search. **perquisitionner** *v* search.

perron [pɛrɔ̃] *nm* steps *pl*.

perroquet [pɛrɔkɛ] *nm* parrot.

perruche [peryʃ] *nf* budgerigar.

perruque [peryk] *nf* wig.

persécuter [pɛrsekyte] *v* persecute; harass. **persécution** *nf* persecution.

persévérer [pɛrsevere] *v* persevere. **persévérance** *nf* perseverance. **persévérant** *adj* persevering.

persienne [pɛrsjɛn] *nf* shutter.

persifler [pɛrsifle] *v* mock. **persiflage** *nm* mockery.

persil [pɛrsi] *nm* parsley.

persister [pɛrsiste] *v* persist. **persister à** persist in. **persistance** *nf* persistence. **persistant** *adj* persistent. **à feuilles persistantes** *(arbre, plante)* evergreen.

personne [pɛrsɔn] *nf* person. *pron* anyone. **ne ... personne** nobody. **personnage** *nm* character; individual; celebrity; important person. **personnalité** *nf* personality.

personnel [pɛrsɔnɛl] *adj* personal. *nm* staff, personnel.

personnifier [pɛrsɔnifje] *v* personify. **personnification** *nf* personification, embodiment.

perspective [pɛrspɛktiv] *nf* perspective; view, angle; *(éventualité)* prospect.

perspicace [pɛrspikas] *adj* shrewd. **perspicacité** *nf* shrewdness, insight.

persuader [pɛrsɥade] *v* persuade; convince. **persuasif** *adj* persuasive. **persuasion** *nf* persuasion; *(croyance)* belief.

perte [pɛrt] nf loss; ruin; (gaspillage) waste. **à perte de vue** as far as the eye can see.

pertinent [pɛrtinɑ̃] adj pertinent, relevant; (juste) apt. **pertinence** nf pertinence, relevance; aptness.

perturbateur, -trice [pɛrtyrbatœr, -tris] adj disruptive. nm, nf troublemaker.

perturber [pɛrtyrbe] v disturb, disrupt; (personne) perturb. **perturbation** nf disturbance, disruption.

pervers [pɛrvɛr] adj perverse; depraved, perverted. **perversion** nf perversion. **perversité** nf perversity; depravity.

pervertir [pɛrvɛrtir] v pervert, corrupt. **perverti, -e** nm, nf pervert.

peser [pəze] v weigh; (appuyer) press. **pesant** adj heavy. **pesanteur** nf heaviness; (phys) gravity; (poids) weight.

pessimiste [pesimist] adj pessimistic. n(m+f) pessimist. **pessimisme** nm pessimism.

peste [pɛst] nf plague; (personne) nuisance, pest.

pet [pɛ] nm (vulgaire) fart.

pétale [petal] nm petal.

pétarader [petarade] v backfire.

pétard [petar] nm banger, firecracker; (mil) explosive charge; (fam: tapage) row, din.

péter [pete] v (vulgaire) fart; (fam: casser) bust; (fam: exploser) burst, go off.

pétiller [petije] v sparkle; (champagne) bubble; (feu) crackle. **pétillant** adj sparkling; bubbly.

petit [pəti], -e adj small, little; (mince) slim, thin; (jeune) young; (court) short; (faible) faint, slight; (mesquin) petty. **petit ami** nm boyfriend. **petit déjeuner** nm breakfast. **petite amie** nf girlfriend. **petite-fille** nf granddaughter. **petit-enfant** nm grandchild. **petit-fils** nm grandson. **petit gâteau** nm biscuit. **petit-pois** nm pea. **à peu petit à petit** little by little. nm, nf young child; small person; (animal) young. **petitesse** nf smallness; pettiness.

pétrin [petrɛ̃] nm mess, fix.

pétrir [petrir] v knead; mould.

pétrole [petrɔl] nm oil, petroleum. **pétrole lampant** paraffin. **pétrolifère** adj oil-bearing. **gisement pétrolifère** nm oilfield.

pétrolier [petrɔlje] adj oil. nm tanker.

pétulant [petylɑ̃] adj vivacious. **pétulance** nf vivacity.

peu [pø] nm little. adv little; (quantité) not much; (nombre) few; (pas très) not very. **à peu près** about; (presque) almost. **peu à peu** little by little.

peupler [pœple] v populate, fill. **peuple** nm people; nation; (foule) crowd.

peuplier [pøplije] nm poplar.

peur [pœr] nf fear; fright. **avoir peur** be frightened or afraid. **faire peur à** frighten, scare. **peureux** adj fearful, timorous.

peut-être [pøtɛtrə] adv perhaps, maybe.

phallus [falys] nm phallus. **phallique** adj phallic. **phallocrate** nm (fam) male chauvinist pig.

phare [far] nm lighthouse; (balise) beacon; (auto) headlight. **phare antibrouillard** fog lamp.

pharmacie [farmasi] nf pharmacy; (magasin) chemist's; (armoire) medicine chest. **pharmaceutique** adj pharmaceutical. **pharmacien, -enne** nm, nf chemist, pharmacist.

pharynx [farɛ̃ks] nm pharynx. **pharyngite** nf pharyngitis.

phase [faz] nf phase; stage.

phénix [feniks] nm phoenix.

phénomène [fenɔmɛn] nm phenomenon (pl -ena); (personne) freak. **phénoménal** adj phenomenal.

philanthropie [filɑ̃trɔpi] nf philanthropy. **philanthrope** n(m+f) philanthropist. **philanthropique** adj philanthropic.

philatélie [filateli] nf philately. **philatéliste** n(m+f) philatelist.

philosophe [filɔzɔf] adj philosophical. n(m+f) philosopher. **philosophie** nf philosophy. **philosophique** adj philosophical.

phobie [fɔbi] nf phobia.

phonétique [fɔnetik] adj phonetic. nf phonetics.

phonographe [fɔnɔgraf] nm gramophone.

phoque [fɔk] nm seal.

phosphate [fɔsfat] nm phosphate.

phosphore [fɔsfɔr] nm phosphorus. **phosphoreux** adj phosphorous.

phosphorescence [fɔsfɔresɑ̃s] nf phosphorescence. **phosphorescent** adj phosphorescent, luminous.

photo [fɔto] nf photo.

photocopier [fɔtɔkɔpje] v photocopy. **photocopie** nf photocopy. **photocopieur** nm photocopier.

photogénique [fɔtɔʒenik] adj photogenic.

photographie [fɔtɔgrafi] nf (image) photograph; (art) photography. **photographe** n(m+f) photographer. **photographier** v

photograph, take a picture of.
photographique adj photographic.
phrase [fraz] nf phrase; (gramm) sentence.
physiologie [fizjɔlɔʒi] nf physiology. **physiologique** adj physiological. **physiologiste** n(m+f) physiologist.
physique[1] [fizik] adj physical. nm physique.
physique[2] [fizik] nf physics. **physicien, -enne** nm, nf physicist.
piaffer [pjafe] v stamp, paw the ground.
piailler [pjaje] v (fam) squawk, screech.
piano [pjano] nm piano. **piano à queue** grand piano. **pianiste** n(m+f) pianist.
piauler [pjole] v whine; (enfant) whimper; (oiseau) cheep.
pic[1] [pik] nm (oiseau) woodpecker; (instrument) pick.
pic[2] [pik] nm (cime) peak. **à pic** sheer; (arriver, tomber) just at the right time.
piccolo [pikɔlo] nm piccolo.
picorer [pikɔre] v peck (at).
picoter [pikɔte] v (yeux) smart, sting; (gorge) tickle; (peau) prickle; (picorer) peck.
pie [pi] nf magpie.
pièce [pjɛs] nf piece; (machine) part; (document) (maison) room; (théâtre) play; (monnaie) coin; (couture) patch. **à la pièce** separately. **pièce détachée** spare part.
pied [pje] nm foot; (table) leg; base; (verre) stem. **à pied** on foot. **au pied de la lettre** literally. **en pied** full-length. **être sur pied** be under way. **mettre les pieds dans le plat** put one's foot in it. **mettre sur pied** set up. **perdre pied** get out of one's depth. **pied bot** club-footed.
piédestal [pjedestal] nm pedestal.
piège [pjɛʒ] nm trap. **piéger** v trap; (engin, etc.) booby-trap. **lettre/voiture piégée** nf letter/car bomb.
pierre [pjɛr] nf stone. **pierre à briquet** flint. **pierre à chaux** limestone. **pierre d'achoppement** stumbling block. **pierre de gué** stepping stone. **pierre ponce** pumice stone. **pierre tombale** tombstone. **pierreux** adj stony.
piété [pjete] nf piety; devotion.
piétiner [pjetine] v (fouler) trample (on); (trépigner) stamp; make no progress.
piéton [pjetɔ̃] nm pedestrian.
piètre [pjɛtrə] adj paltry, very poor.
pieu [pjø] nm post; (pointu) stake.

pieuvre [pjœvrə] nf octopus.
pieux [pjø] adj pious, devout.
pigeon [piʒɔ̃] nm pigeon.
piger [piʒe] (argot) v cotton on, twig. **tu piges?** do you get it?
pigment [pigmɑ̃] nm pigment. **pigmentation** nf pigmentation.
pignon [piɲɔ̃] nm (arch) gable; (tech) pinion.
pile[1] [pil] nf (tas) pile; support; (élec) battery.
pile[2] [pil] nf (pièce) tails pl. **côté pile** nm reverse side. **pile ou face?** heads or tails? **tirer à pile ou face** toss up. adv (fam) dead, exactly.
piler [pile] v crush, pound.
pilier [pilje] nm pillar.
piller [pije] v pillage, plunder. **pillage** nm pillage, looting.
pilote [pilɔt] nm pilot; (auto) driver; guide. adj experimental. **piloter** v pilot; (avion) fly; drive; (personne) show round.
pilule [pilyl] nf pill.
piment [pimɑ̃] nm pimento; piquancy, spice. **piment doux** capsicum. **piment rouge** chilli. **pimenté** adj (plat) hot; (récit) spicy.
pimpant [pɛ̃pɑ̃] adj trim, smart.
pin [pɛ̃] nm pine.
pinacle [pinaklə] nm pinnacle.
pince [pɛ̃s] nf pliers pl; (charbon, sucre) tongs pl; (levier) crowbar; (couture) dart; (crabe) pincer, claw. **pince à épiler** eyebrow tweezers pl. **pince à linge** clothes peg. **pincé** adj stiff; (sourire) tight-lipped. **pincée** nf pinch. **pincer** v pinch, nip; (serrer) grip; (musique) pluck; (fam) catch.
pinceau [pɛ̃so] nm paintbrush.
pingouin [pɛ̃gwɛ̃] nm penguin.
ping-pong [piŋpɔ̃g] nm table tennis.
pinson [pɛ̃sɔ̃] nm chaffinch.
piocher [pjɔʃe] v dig with a pick; (fam) swot; (cartes, etc.) pick up. **pioche** nf pick, pickaxe.
pion [pjɔ̃] nm (jeu) piece; (échecs) pawn; student supervising schoolchildren.
pionnier [pjɔnje] nm pioneer.
pipe [pip] nf pipe.
piquant [pikɑ̃] adj (tige) prickly; (goût) hot, pungent; (vin) tart; (mordant) biting; (sauce, détail) piquant. nm prickle; (hérisson) spine; piquancy.
pique[1] [pik] nf (arme) pike. nm (cartes) spade.

pique² [pik] *nf* cutting remark.

pique-nique [piknik] *nm* picnic. **pique-niquer** *v* picnic. **pique-niqueur, -euse** *nm, nf* picnicker.

piquer [pike] *v* prick; sting; *(insecte, serpent)* bite; *(aiguille, etc.)* jab, stick; excite, arouse; *(fam: voler)* pinch; *(moutarde, etc.)* be hot *or* pungent; *(avion, oiseau)* swoop down. **piquer une colère** fly into a rage. **piquer une crise** throw a fit. **se faire piquer** have an injection. **se piquer** get stung; give oneself an injection; take offence. **piqué** *adj (couture)* quilted; *(marqué)* dotted, pitted; *(fam)* barmy. **piqûre** *nf* prick; sting; bite; injection; *(couture)* stitch; *(trou)* hole.

piquet [pike] *nm* post, stake; *(tente)* peg; *(de grève)* picket.

pirate [pirat] *nm, adj* pirate. **pirate de l'air** hijacker. **piraterie** *nf* piracy.

pire [pir] *adj* worse. **le** *or* **la pire** (the) worst.

pirouette [pirwɛt] *nf* pirouette. **pirouetter** *v* pirouette.

pis¹ [pi] *nm* udder.

pis² [pi] *adj, adv* worse. **de pis en pis** worse and worse. *nm* worst. **au pis aller** if the worst comes to the worst. **pis-aller** *nm invar* makeshift.

piscine [pisin] *nf* swimming pool; *(publique)* baths *pl*.

pissenlit [pisɑ̃li] *nm* dandelion.

pisser [pise] *(vulgaire) v* piss. **pisse** *nf* piss.

pistache [pistaʃ] *nf* pistachio.

piste [pist] *nf* track; *(traces)* trail; *(aéro)* runway; *(ski)* run; *(police)* lead. **piste cavalière** bridle-path. **piste sonore** soundtrack.

pistolet [pistɔlɛ] *nm* pistol, gun.

piston [pistɔ̃] *nm* piston; *(musique)* valve. **avoir du piston** *(fam)* have friends in the right places.

pitié [pitje] *nf* pity. **avoir pitié de** take pity on; *(compâtir)* feel sorry for. **piteux** *adj* pitiful; *(honteux)* shamefaced. **pitoyable** *adj* pitiful.

pitre [pitrə] *nm* clown.

pittoresque [pitɔrɛsk] *adj* picturesque.

pivot [pivo] *nm* pivot. **pivoter** *v* pivot, revolve, swivel round.

placage [plakaʒ] *nm (bois)* veneer; *(pierre)* facing.

placard [plakar] *nm (armoire)* cupboard;

(affiche) notice, placard. **placarder** *v (affiche)* stick up; *(mur)* placard.

place [plas] *nf* place; space; *(siège)* seat; *(prix)* fare; *(ville)* square; *(emploi)* job. **à la place de** instead of; *(personne)* on behalf of. **à ta** *or* **votre place** if I were you. **faire place à** give way to. **sur place** on the spot.

placenta [plasɛ̃ta] *nm* placenta.

placer [plase] *v* place, put; *(argent)* invest; *(vendre)* sell. **se placer** *(debout)* stand; *(assis)* sit; *(avoir lieu)* take place; find a job. **placement** *nm* investment. **placeur** *nm* usher.

placide [plasid] *adj* placid. **placidité** *nf* placidity.

plafond [plafɔ̃] *nm* ceiling.

plage [plaʒ] *nf* beach; *(ville)* seaside resort; *(disque)* track.

plagier [plaʒje] *v* plagiarize. **plagiaire** *n(m + f)* plagiarist. **plagiat** *nm* plagiarism.

plaider [plede] *v* plead.

plaie [plɛ] *nf* wound; *(fam)* nuisance.

***plaindre** [plɛ̃drə] *v* pity, feel sorry for. **se plaindre** moan, complain, grumble.

plaine [plɛn] *nf* plain.

plain-pied [plɛ̃pje] *adv* **de plain-pied avec** on the same level as.

plainte [plɛ̃t] *nf* complaint; *(gémissement)* moan. **plaintif** *adj* plaintive.

***plaire** [plɛr] *v* **plaire à** please; *(convenir à)* suit. **se plaire** be happy, enjoy oneself. **se plaire à** like, delight in. **s'il te** *or* **vous plaît** please.

plaisance [plɛzɑ̃s] *nf* **maison de plaisance** *nf* country house. **navigation de plaisance** *nf* boating; yachting.

plaisant [plɛzɑ̃] *adj* pleasant; amusing. **plaisanter** [plɛzɑ̃te] *v* joke; *(taquiner)* tease. **plaisanterie** *nf* joke.

plaisir [plezir] *nm* pleasure. **faire plaisir à** please, make happy.

plan¹ [plɑ̃] *adj* flat, level, plane. *nm* plane, level; *(cinéma)* shot. **premier plan** foreground.

plan² [plɑ̃] *nm* plan; *(carte)* map.

planche [plɑ̃ʃ] *nf* board, plank; *(rayon)* shelf. **faire la planche** float on one's back. **planche à dessin/repasser** drawing/ironing board. **planche à pain** breadboard.

plancher [plɑ̃ʃe] *nm* floor.

plancton [plɑ̃ktɔ̃] *nm* plankton.

planer [plane] *v* glide, hover; *(monter)* soar. **planer sur** *(danger)* hang over;

(*regard*) look down over. **planeur** nm glider.

planète [planɛt] nf planet. **planétaire** adj planetary. **planétarium** nm planetarium.

plant [plɑ̃] nm seedling, young plant; (*arbres*) plantation; (*légumes, fleurs*) bed.

plantation [plɑ̃tasjɔ̃] nf plantation; (*action*) planting.

plante[1] [plɑ̃t] nf (*bot*) plant. **plante grimpante** creeper.

plante[2] [plɑ̃t] nf (*anat*) sole of the foot.

planter [plɑ̃te] v plant; (*enfoncer*) drive or stick in; (*mettre*) put, stick; (*installer*) put or set up. **planter là** (*fam*) dump, ditch.

planton [plɑ̃tɔ̃] nm orderly.

plantureux [plɑ̃tyrø] adj copious, lavish.

plaque [plak] nf plate, sheet; (*pierre, chocolat*) slab; (*tache*) patch, blotch; (*commémorative*) plaque; (*insigne*) badge. **plaque chauffante** hotplate. **plaque minéralogique** or **d'immatriculation** number plate.

plaquer [plake] v (*bois*) veneer; (*métal*) plate; (*fam*) ditch, chuck; (*aplatir*) plaster down, flatten; (*sport*) tackle.

plasma [plasma] nm plasma.

plastique [plastik] nm, adj plastic.

plat [pla] adj flat; (*fade*) dull; (*cheveux*) straight. **à plat** flat. **plate-bande** nf flowerbed. **plate-forme** nf platform. nm flat part; (*cuisine*) dish; (*partie d'un repas*) course.

plateau [plato] nm tray; (*géog*) plateau; (*théâtre*) stage. **plateau à** or **de fromages** cheeseboard.

platine [platin] nm platinum.

platonique [platonik] adj (*amour*) platonic; vain, futile.

plâtrer [plɑtre] v plaster; (*méd*) set in plaster. **plâtre** nm plaster; (*méd, art*) plaster cast. **plâtrier** nm plasterer.

plausible [plozibl] adj plausible. **plausibilité** nf plausibility.

plectre [plɛktrə] nm plectrum.

plein [plɛ̃] adj full; complete; solid; (*animal*) pregnant. **en plein ...** at the height of ..., in the middle of ... **en plein jour** in broad daylight. **plein air** nm open air. **pleine mer** nf open sea; (*marée*) high tide. adv full. nm **faire le plein** fill up.

pleurer [plœre] v cry; (*yeux*) water; lament, bemoan; (*mort*) mourn. **pleureur, -euse** adj tearful; (*enfant*) whining.

pleurnicher [plœrniʃe] v snivel, whine.

*pleuvoir [pløvwar] v rain.

pli [pli] nm fold; (*faux*) crease; (*couture*) pleat; (*genou*) bend; envelope; (*forme*) shape; habit.

plier [plije] v fold; (*courber*) bend; (*céder*) yield, give way. **se plier à** submit to. **pliant** adj collapsible, folding.

plinthe [plɛ̃t] nf skirting board.

plisser [plise] v (*jupe, etc.*) pleat; (*rider*) pucker, crease.

plomb [plɔ̃] nm lead; (*chasse*) shot; (*élec*) fuse. **à plomb** straight down. **de plomb** leaden; (*sommeil*) heavy. **plombage** nm filling. **plomber** v weight; (*dent*) fill. **plomberie** nf plumbing. **plombier** nm plumber.

plonger [plɔ̃ʒe] v plunge, dive. **plonge** nf washing-up. **plongé dans** adj immersed in, buried in. **plongée** nf diving. **plongée sous-marine** skin-diving. **plongeoir** nm diving board. **plongeon** nm dive. **plongeur, -euse** nm, nf diver; (*restaurant*) washer-up.

plouf [pluf] nm, interj splash.

ployer [plwaje] v bend; (*plancher*) sag; (*céder*) give way.

pluie [plɥi] nf rain; (*averse*) shower.

plume [plym] nf (*oiseau*) feather; (*écrire*) pen; (*bec*) nib. **plumage** nm plumage. **plumer** v pluck; (*argot*) fleece.

plupart [plypar] nf **la plupart** most, the majority. **pour la plupart** mostly.

pluriel [plyrjɛl] nm, adj plural.

plus [ply] adv more. **de** or **en plus** on top, extra, in addition, besides. **de plus en plus** more and more. **le** or **la plus** the most. **ne ... plus** no more; (*temps*) no longer. **plus de** more than, over. **plus-que-parfait** nm pluperfect. conj plus.

plusieurs [plyzjœr] adj several.

plutôt [plyto] adv rather.

pluvieux [plyvjø] adj rainy, wet.

pneu [pnø] nm tyre. **pneu rechapé** remould.

pneumatique [pnømatik] adj pneumatic; (*canot, matelas*) inflatable.

pneumonie [pnømɔni] nf pneumonia.

pochard [pɔʃar], **-e** nm, nf (*argot*) drunk.

poche [pɔʃ] nf pocket; (*sac*) bag; (*zool*) pouch. **de poche** pocket; (*livre*) paperback. **pochette** nf pocket handkerchief; envelope, case.

pocher [pɔʃe] v poach. **pocher un œil à** give a black eye to. **pochade** nf quick sketch. **pochoir** nm stencil.

poêle¹ [pwal] nf frying pan.

poêle² [pwal] nm stove.

poème [pɔɛm] nm poem. **poésie** nf poetry. **poète** nm poet. **poétesse** nf poetess. **poétique** adj poetic.

poids [pwa] nm weight. **poids lourd** heavyweight; (camion) lorry. **prendre du poids** put on weight.

poignant [pwaɲɑ̃] adj poignant, harrowing.

poignard [pwaɲar] nm dagger. **poignarder** v stab, knife.

poigne [pwaɲ] nf grip; (main) hand. **poignée** nf (valise, porte, etc.) handle; (quantité) handful. **poignée de main** handshake. **poignet** nm wrist; (vêtement) cuff.

poil [pwal] nm hair; (brosse) bristle; (tapis, tissu) pile. **à poil** (fam) naked. **poilu** adj hairy.

poinçon [pwɛ̃sɔ̃] nm awl; (or, etc.) die, stamp; (marque) hallmark. **poinçonner** v stamp; hallmark; (billet) punch.

****poindre** [pwɛdrə] v (jour) dawn; (aube) break; (plante) come up.

poing [pwɛ̃] nm fist.

point¹ [pwɛ̃] nm point; (marque) dot; (tache) spot; (ponctuation) full stop; (couture, tricot) stitch. **à point** just right; (bifteck) medium. **au point** (phot) in focus; perfect. **être sur le point de** be just about to. **mettre au point** perfect; (phot) focus; finalize. **point de côté** stitch. **point de mire** focal point. **point de suture** (méd) stitch. **point d'exclamation** exclamation mark. **point d'interrogation** question mark. **point du jour** daybreak. **point mort** (auto) neutral. **point noir** (visage) blackhead; (auto) black spot. **point virgule** semicolon.

point² [pwɛ̃] adv not. **ne ... point** not at all.

pointe [pwɛt] nf point; (bout) tip; (maximum) peak; (soupçon) touch, dash. **sur la pointe des pieds** on tiptoe.

pointer¹ [pwɛte] v (cocher) tick off; (braquer) aim, point; (employé) clock in or out. **pointeur** nm timekeeper.

pointer² [pwɛte] v (piquer) stick; appear; (dresser) soar up.

pointillé [pwɛtije] adj dotted. nm dotted line. **pointiller** v (art) stipple.

pointilleux [pwɛtijø] adj particular.

pointu [pwɛty] adj pointed; (aigu) sharp; (péj) touchy, peevish.

pointure [pwɛtyr] nf size.

poire [pwar] nf pear; (fam) mug. **poirier** nm pear tree.

poireau [pwaro] nm leek.

pois [pwa] nm pea; (point) dot, spot. **pois cassés** split peas pl. **pois chiche** chickpea. **pois de senteur** sweet pea.

poison [pwazɔ̃] nm poison.

poisseux [pwasø] adj sticky.

poisson [pwasɔ̃] nm fish. **poisson d'avril** April fool. **poisson rouge** goldfish. **Poissons** nm pl Pisces sing. **poissonnerie** nm fish shop. **poissonnier, -ère** nm, nf fishmonger.

poitrine [pwatrin] nf chest; (seins) bust; (cuisine) breast.

poivre [pwavrə] nm pepper. **poivre de Cayenne** Cayenne pepper. **poivré** adj peppery; (récit) spicy. **poivrer** v pepper. **poivrier** nm pepper-pot. **poivron** nm pepper.

poix [pwa] nf pitch.

polaire [pɔlɛr] adj polar.

polariser [pɔlarize] v polarize; attract; (concentrer) focus. **se polariser sur** be centred on.

pôle [pol] nm pole.

polémique [pɔlemik] adj controversial. nf controversy, argument.

poli¹ [pɔli] adj polite.

poli² [pɔli] adj polished. nm shine.

police¹ [pɔlis] nf police. **faire la police** keep order.

police² [pɔlis] nf (assurance) policy.

policier [pɔlisje] nm policeman. (roman) detective novel. adj police; detective.

polio [pɔljo] nf polio.

polir [pɔlir] v polish.

polisson, -onne [pɔlisɔ̃, -ɔn] nm, nf rascal. adj (enfant) naughty; (grivois) saucy. **polissonnerie** nf naughty trick; saucy remark or action.

politesse [pɔlites] nf politeness, courtesy; polite remark or gesture.

politique [pɔlitik] adj political. nf (science) politics; (ligne de conduite) policy. **politicien, -enne** nm, nf politician.

polka [pɔlka] nf polka.

pollen [pɔlɛn] nm pollen. **pollinisation** nf pollination.

polluer [pɔlЦe] v pollute. **pollution** nf pollution.

Pologne [pɔlɔɲ] nf Poland. **polonais** nm, adj Polish. **Polonais, -e** nm, nf Pole.

poltron, -onne [pɔltrɔ̃, -ɔn] nm, nf coward. adj cowardly. **poltronnerie** nf cowardice.

polycopier [pɔlikɔpje] v duplicate, stencil.

polyester [pɔliɛstɛr] nm polyester.

polyéthylène [pɔlietilɛn] nm polythene.

polygame [pɔligam] adj polygamous. nm polygamist. **polygamie** nf polygamy.

polyglotte [pɔliglɔt] adj multilingual. n(m+f) polyglot.

polygone [pɔligɔn] nm polygon.

pommade [pɔmad] nf ointment.

pomme [pɔm] nf apple; (laitue, chou) heart; (arrosoir) rose. **pomme à couteau/cuire** eating/cooking apple. **pomme d'Adam** Adam's apple. **pomme de pin** pine cone. **pomme de terre** potato. **pommes frites** chips pl. **pommier** nm apple tree.

pommelé [pɔmle] adj (cheval) dappled.

pommette [pɔmɛt] nf cheekbone.

pompe[1] [pɔ̃p] nf pump. **pompe à incendie** fire engine. **pomper** v pump. **pompier** nm fireman. **pompiste** n(m+f) petrol pump attendant.

pompe[2] [pɔ̃p] nf pomp. **pompeux** adj pompous.

poncer [pɔ̃se] v rub down, sandpaper.

ponctuel [pɔ̃ktЦɛl] adj punctual; (assidu) meticulous. **ponctualité** nf punctuality; meticulousness.

ponctuer [pɔ̃ktЦe] v punctuate. **ponctuation** nf punctuation.

pondérer [pɔ̃dere] v balance. **pondéré** adj level-headed.

pondre [pɔ̃dra] v lay; (œuvre) produce.

poney [pɔnɛ] nm pony.

pont [pɔ̃] nm bridge; (naut) deck. **pont aérien** airlift. **pont-levis** nm drawbridge. **pont suspendu** suspension bridge. **pont tournant** swing bridge.

popeline [pɔplin] nf poplin.

populace [pɔpylas] nf rabble.

populaire [pɔpylɛr] adj popular; (république, etc.) people's, of the people. **populariser** v popularize. **popularité** nf popularity.

population [pɔpylasjɔ̃] nf population.

porc [pɔr] nm pig; (viande) pork. **porc-épic** nm porcupine.

porcelaine [pɔrsəlɛn] nf porcelain, china.

porche [pɔrʃ] nm porch.

porcherie [pɔrʃəri] nf pigsty.

pore [pɔr] nm pore. **poreux** adj porous.

pornographie [pɔrnɔgrafi] nf pornography. **pornographique** adj pornographic.

port[1] [pɔr] nm port; (bassin) harbour.

port[2] [pɔr] nm carriage; postage; (comportement) bearing; (casque, barbe, etc.) wearing.

porte [pɔrt] nf door; (aéro, jardin, écluse) gate; (embrasure) doorway. **mettre à la porte** throw out; (licencier) sack.

porte-avions nm invar aircraft carrier.

porte-bagages nm invar luggage rack.

porte-bébé nm carrycot.

porte-bonheur nm invar lucky charm.

porte-clefs nm invar key ring.

porte d'entrée nf front door.

porte-fenêtre nf French window.

portefeuille [pɔrtəfœj] nm wallet; (pol) portfolio.

portemanteau [pɔrtmɑ̃to] nm coat rack.

porte-mine nm propelling pencil.

porte-monnaie nm invar purse.

porte-parole nm invar spokesman.

porter [pɔrte] v carry; bear; (vêtement) wear; (amener) take; direct, turn; (comm) put down, enter; (ressentir) feel; (inciter) prompt, induce; (coup) strike home. **se porter bien/mal** be well/ill. **portable** adj wearable. **portatif** adj portable. **porté** adj inclined, prone. **portée** nf range, reach; (effet) significance, consequences pl; (animal) litter; (musique) stave. **porteur, -euse** nm, nf bearer; (valises) porter; messenger.

porte-serviettes nm invar towel rail.

porte-voix nm invar megaphone.

portière [pɔrtjɛr] nf door.

portion [pɔrsjɔ̃] nf portion; part.

porto [pɔrto] nm port.

portrait [pɔrtrɛ] nm portrait.

Portugal [pɔrtygal] nm Portugal. **portugais, nm, adj** Portuguese. **les Portugais** the Portuguese.

poser [poze] v put, lay; set down; (question) ask; (tableau, étagères) put up; (art) pose. **se poser** alight, come down; (regard) rest; (question) crop up, arise. **se poser en** pose as. **pose** nf pose; (phot) exposure; affectation; (chauffage, etc.) installation. **posé** adj sedate, staid; (allure) steady.

positif [pozitif] *adj* positive; real; definite.

position [pozisjɔ̃] *nf* position.

posséder [posede] *v* possess, have. **possessif** *nm, adj* possessive. **possession** *nf* possession.

possible [posiblə] *adj* possible; feasible; potential. **possibilité** *nf* possibility.

poste¹ [post] *nf* post; (*bureau*) post office. **mettre à la poste** post. **poste aérienne** air mail. **postal** *adj* postal.

poste² [post] *nm* post; (*emploi*) job; (*TV, radio*) set; (*téléphone*) extension. **poste de police** police station. **poste d'essence** petrol station.

poster [poste] *v* post.

postérieur, -e [posterjœr] *adj* (*temps*) later; (*espace*) back; (*pattes, etc.*) hind. *nm* (*fam*) behind.

postérité [posterite] *nf* posterity.

posthume [postym] *adj* posthumous.

postiche [postiʃ] *adj* false. *nm* hairpiece.

postscolaire [postskolɛr] *adj* **enseignement postscolaire** *nm* further education.

post-scriptum [postskriptɔm] *nm invar* postscript.

postuler [postyle] *v* (*emploi*) apply for; (*poser*) postulate. **postulant, -e** *nm, nf* applicant. **postulat** *nm* postulate.

posture [postyr] *nf* posture, position.

pot [po] *nm* pot; (*verre*) jar; (*lait*) jug; carton; (*fam: chance*) luck. **pot à bière** tankard. **pot-au-feu** *nm invar* stew. **pot-de-vin** *nm* bribe.

potable [potablə] *adj* drinkable; (*fam*) reasonable, decent.

potage [potaʒ] *nm* soup.

potager [potaʒe] *adj* vegetable; (*plante*) edible. *nm* vegetable garden.

potassium [potasjɔm] *nm* potassium.

poteau [poto] *nm* post. **poteau indicateur** signpost. **poteau télégraphique** telegraph pole.

potelé [potle] *adj* plump, chubby.

potence [potɑ̃s] *nf* (*gibet*) gallows; (*support*) bracket.

potentiel [potɑ̃sjɛl] *nm, adj* potential.

poterie [potri] *nf* pottery. **potier** *nm* potter.

potin [potɛ̃] *nm* din, racket. **potins** *nm pl* gossip *sing.* **potiner** *v* gossip.

potion [posjɔ̃] *nf* potion.

potiron [potirɔ̃] *nm* pumpkin.

pou [pu] *nm, pl* **poux** louse (*pl* lice).

poubelle [pubɛl] *nf* bin.

pouce [pus] *nm* thumb; (*orteil*) big toe; (*mesure*) inch.

poudre [pudrə] *nf* powder. **poudre à canon** gunpowder. **poudre de riz** face powder. **poudrer** *v* powder. **poudreux** *adj* dusty. **poudrier** *nm* powder compact.

pouffer [pufe] *v* snigger.

poulain [pulɛ̃] *nm* foal.

poule [pul] *nf* hen; (*cuisine*) fowl. **poulailler** *nm* henhouse. **poulet** *nm* chicken.

pouliche [puliʃ] *nf* filly.

poulie [puli] *nf* pulley.

poulpe [pulp] *nm* octopus.

pouls [pu] *nm* pulse.

poumon [pumɔ̃] *nm* lung.

poupe [pup] *nf* stern.

poupée [pupe] *nf* doll.

pour [pur] *prep* for; (*comme*) as; (*but*) to. **pour cent** per cent. **pour que** so that.

pourboire [purbwar] *nm* tip.

pourceau [purso] *nm* (*péj*) swine.

pourcentage [pursɑ̃taʒ] *nm* percentage.

pourchasser [purʃase] *v* pursue.

pourpre [purprə] *nm, adj* crimson, purple.

pourquoi [purkwa] *conj, adv* why.

pourrir [purir] *v* rot, decay; (*fruit*) go rotten or bad; (*gâter*) spoil. **pourri** *adj* rotten, bad. **pourriture** *nf* rot.

*****poursuivre** [pursɥivrə] *v* pursue; (*harceler*) hound; (*jur*) prosecute; continue, carry on. **poursuite** *nf* pursuit, chase. **poursuites** *nf pl* legal proceedings *pl*. **poursuivant, -e** *nm, nf* pursuer.

pourtant [purtɑ̃] *adv* yet, nevertheless.

pourtour [purtur] *nm* circumference; perimeter.

*****pourvoir** [purvwar] *v* provide, equip, supply. **pourvoir à** provide for, cater for. **pourvoyeur, -euse** *nm, nf* supplier.

pourvu [purvy] *adj* **être pourvu de** (*personne*) be endowed with; (*chose*) be fitted or equipped with. **pourvu que** *conj* provided that, as long as.

pousser [puse] *v* push; (*stimuler, inciter*) drive, urge; continue, pursue; (*cri*) utter, let out; (*grandir*) grow. **pousser du coude** nudge. **pousse** *nf* growth; (*bot*) shoot. **poussé** *adj* advanced; elaborate; (*enquête*) exhaustive. **poussée** *nf* push, thrust; (*prix, pol*) upsurge. **poussette** *nf* push-chair.

poussière [pusjɛr] *nf* dust. **poussiéreux** *adj* dusty.

poussin [pusɛ̃] nm chick.

poutre [putrə] nf beam; (métal) girder.

*pouvoir [puvwar] v can; (permission) may, be allowed to; (capacité) be able to; (possibilité) might, could. n'en plus pouvoir be tired out. n'y rien pouvoir be unable to do anything about it. se pouvoir be possible. nm power; (capacité) ability; influence.

pragmatique [pragmatik] adj pragmatic.

Prague [prag] n Prague.

prairie [preri] nf meadow, grassland; (Amérique) prairie.

praticable [pratikablə] adj practicable, feasible; (chemin) passable.

praticien [pratisjɛ̃], -enne nm, nf practitioner.

pratique¹ [pratik] adj practical; (commode) handy, convenient.

pratique² [pratik] nf practice.

pratiquer [pratike] v practise; (faire) make; (employer) use; (rel) go to church.

pré [pre] nm meadow.

préalable [prealablə] adj preliminary, prior. nm au préalable first.

préavis [preavi] nm (advance) notice.

précaire [prekɛr] adj precarious.

précaution [prekosjɔ̃] nf precaution; (prudence) care, caution.

précédent [presedɑ̃] adj previous. nm precedent.

précéder [presede] v precede.

précepteur [preseptœr] nm tutor. préceptrice nf governess.

prêcher [preʃe] v preach. prêche nm sermon.

précieux [presjø] adj precious; affected.

précipice [presipis] nm precipice, chasm.

précipiter [presipite] v precipitate; (lancer) throw, hurl; (hâter) hasten, speed up. se précipiter rush. précipitamment adv hurriedly, hastily. précipitation nf precipitation; haste. précipité adj hurried, rapid; (décision) hasty; (fuite) headlong.

précis [presi] adj precise. nm précis, summary; (manuel) handbook. précisément adv precisely; exactly; just. préciser v specify, make clear; be more precise (about). se préciser become clear, take shape. précision nf precision; detail, point.

précoce [prekɔs] adj precocious; (fruit, etc.) early; (sénilité) premature. précocité nf precocity; earliness.

préconçu [prekɔ̃sy] adj preconceived.

préconiser [prekɔnize] v recommend; advocate.

précurseur [prekyrsœr] nm precursor.

prédateur, -trice [predatœr, -tris] nm predator. adj predatory.

prédécesseur [predesesœr] nm predecessor.

prédestiner [predestine] v predestine. prédestination nf predestination.

prédicat [predika] nm predicate.

prédicateur [predikatœr] nm preacher.

*prédire [predir] v predict, foretell. prédiction nf prediction.

prédominer [predɔmine] v predominate, prevail. prédominance nf predominance. prédominant adj predominant, prevailing.

prééminent [preeminɑ̃] adj pre-eminent. prééminence nf pre-eminence.

préfabriqué [prefabrike] adj prefabricated.

préface [prefas] nf preface.

préfecture [prefɛktyr] nf prefecture. préfecture de police Paris police headquarters.

préférer [prefere] v prefer. préférable adj preferable. préféré, -e n, adj favourite. préférence nf preference. préférentiel adj preferential.

préfet [prefɛ] nm prefect, chief administrative officer of a French department. préfet de police chief of Paris police.

préfixe [prefiks] nm prefix. préfixer v prefix.

préhistorique [preistɔrik] adj prehistoric.

préjudice [preʒydis] nm harm, wrong; (matériel) loss. au préjudice de at the expense of. préjudiciable adj detrimental.

préjugé [preʒyʒe] nm prejudice.

prélever [prɛlve] v take; (argent) deduct. prélèvement nm taking; deduction. faire un prélèvement de sang take a blood sample.

préliminaire [preliminɛr] adj preliminary. préliminaires nm pl preliminaries pl.

prélude [prelyd] nm prelude.

prématuré [prematyre] adj premature.

préméditer [premedite] v premeditate. préméditation nf premeditation.

premier [prəmje], -ère adj first; (le plus bas) bottom; (le plus haut) top; (le plus important) greatest, foremost; (fondamental) basic; original. premier ministre nm prime minister. premiers secours nm pl first aid sing. nm first; (étage) first

floor. *nf* first; (*cinéma*) première; (*transport*) first class; (*lycée*) lower sixth form.
prémisse [premis] *nf* premise.
prémonition [premɔnisjɔ̃] *nf* premonition.
prenant [prǝnɑ̃] *adj* absorbing, fascinating.
***prendre** [prɑ̃drǝ] *v* take; (*aller chercher*) fetch, pick up; (*attraper*) catch; (*repas*) have; (*acheter*) buy; (*air*) assume, put on; (*manier*) handle; (*durcir*) set. **s'en prendre à** take it out on; blame; attack. **s'y prendre** set about it.
prénom [prenɔ̃] *nm* Christian name.
prénuptial [prenypsjal] *adj* premarital.
préoccuper [preɔkype] *v* (*absorber*) preoccupy; (*inquiéter*) worry. **se préoccuper de** be concerned with *or* about. **préoccupation** *nf* preoccupation; worry.
préparer [prepare] *v* prepare; (*faire*) make; (*apprêter*) get ready; (*réserver*) have in store. **préparatifs** *nm pl* preparations. **préparation** *nf* preparation. **préparatoire** *adj* preparatory.
préposé [prepoze], **-e** *nm, nf* employer, official; (*vestiaire*) attendant.
préposition [prepozisjɔ̃] *nf* preposition.
prérogative [prerɔgativ] *nf* prerogative.
près [prɛ] *adv* near, close. **à cela près** apart from that. **de près** closely. **près de** close to; (*presque*) almost.
présager [prezaʒe] *v* be an omen of; (*prédire*) predict. **présage** *nm* omen.
presbyte [presbit] *adj* long-sighted. **presbytie** *nf* long-sightedness.
***prescrire** [preskrir] *v* prescribe; order; stipulate. **prescription** *nf* prescription; order.
préséance [preseɑ̃s] *nf* precedence.
présence [prezɑ̃s] *nf* presence; (*bureau, école*) attendance.
présent¹ [prezɑ̃] *nm, adj* present. **à présent** now. **d'à présent** of today, present-day.
présent² [prezɑ̃] *nm* present, gift.
présenter [prezɑ̃te] *v* present; introduce; (*exposer*) set out; turn. **se présenter** appear; (*occasion*) arise; (*élection*) stand; (*concours*) go in for; (*examen*) take. **présentable** *adj* presentable. **présentateur, -trice** *nm, nf* presenter. **présentation** *nf* presentation; introduction.
préserver [prezɛrve] *v* protect; save. **préservatif** *nm* condom. **préservation** *nf* preservation, protection.
président [prezidɑ̃] *nm* president;

(*comité*) chairman. **présidence** *nf* presidency. **présidentiel** *adj* presidential.
présider [prezide] *v* preside (over); (*débat*) chair.
présomption [prezɔ̃psjɔ̃] *nf* presumption. **présomptueux** *adj* presumptuous.
presque [prɛskǝ] *adv* almost, nearly; (*guère*) scarcely, hardly.
presqu'île [prɛskil] *nf* peninsula.
presser [prese] *v* press; (*serrer*) squeeze; (*hâter*) speed up, hurry; be urgent. **presse-papiers** *nm invar* paperweight. **se presser** hurry; squeeze up, crowd together. **pressant** *adj* urgent. **presse** *nf* press. **pressé** *adj* hurried, in a hurry; urgent. **pression** *nf* pressure. **à la pression** on draught. **pressoir** *nm* press. **pressuriser** *v* pressurize.
preste [prɛst] *adj* nimble.
prestidigitateur, -trice [prestidiʒitatœr, -tris] *nm, nf* conjuror. **prestidigitation** *nf* conjuring.
prestige [prɛstiʒ] *nm* prestige. **prestigieux** *adj* prestigious.
présumer [prezyme] *v* presume.
prêt¹ [prɛ] *adj* ready. **prêt-à-porter** *nm* ready-to-wear clothes *pl*.
prêt² [prɛ] *nm* loan; advance; (*action*) lending.
prétendre [pretɑ̃drǝ] *v* claim; intend; mean. **prétendant, -e** *nm, nf* candidate. **prétendu** *adj* so-called, alleged. **prétention** *nf* claim, pretension; (*vanité*) pretentiousness. **prétentieux** *adj* pretentious.
prêter [prete] *v* lend; attribute; (*offrir*) give; (*tissu*) stretch. **prête-nom** *nm* figurehead. **prêter attention à** pay attention to. **prêter serment** take an oath. **prêteur, -euse** *nm, nf* lender. **prêteur sur gages** pawnbroker.
prétexte [pretɛkst] *nm* pretext, excuse.
prêtre [prɛtrǝ] *nm* priest. **prêtrise** *nf* priesthood.
preuve [prœv] *nf* proof, evidence.
***prévaloir** [prevalwar] *v* prevail. **se prévaloir de** (*profiter*) take advantage of; (*se flatter*) pride oneself on.
***prévenir** [prevnir] *v* (*avertir*) warn; inform; anticipate; (*éviter*) avert; (*influencer*) prejudice. **prévenance** *nf* kindness, consideration. **prévenant** *adj* kind, considerate. **prévenu, -e** *n, adj* accused.
préventif [prevɑ̃tif] *adj* preventive. **prévention** *nf* prevention; (*jur*) custody; (*préjugé*) prejudice.

prévision [previzjɔ̃] nf prediction, forecast. **prévisions météorologiques** weather forecast sing. **prévisible** adj foreseeable.

*prévoir [prevwar] v anticipate; (temps) forecast; (projeter) plan; (envisager) allow; (jur) provide for. **prévoyance** nf foresight.

prier [prije] v pray; invite, ask; (implorer) beg. **je vous en prie** (de rien) don't mention it; (faites donc) please do. **prière** nf prayer; (demande) request, plea.

prieuré [prijœre] nm priory.

primaire [primɛr] adj primary.

prime¹ [prim] nf premium; bonus; (cadeau) free gift.

prime² [prim] adj first, earliest.

primer¹ [prime] v prevail over, outdo.

primer² [prime] v award a prize to.

primesautier [primsotje] adj impulsive.

primeurs [primœr] nf pl early fruit and vegetables pl.

primevère [primvɛr] nf primrose.

primitif [primitif] adj primitive; original.

primordial [primɔrdjal] adj primordial, essential.

prince [prɛ̃s] nm prince. **princesse** nf princess. **princier** adj princely.

principal [prɛ̃sipal] adj main, principal; (employé) chief, head. nm principal; main point.

principe [prɛ̃sip] nm principle. **par principe** on principle.

printanier [prɛ̃tanje] adj spring, springlike.

printemps [prɛ̃tɑ̃] nm spring, springtime.

priorité [prijɔrite] nf priority; (auto) right of way.

pris [pri] adj (place) taken, occupied; (mains) full; (personne) busy, engaged.

prise [priz] nf hold, grip; capture; (élec: à fiches) plug; (élec: à douilles) socket. **en prise** (auto) in gear. **prise multiple** adapter.

priser [prize] v prize.

prisme [prism] nm prism.

prison [prizɔ̃] nf prison, jail; imprisonment. **prisonnier, -ère** nm, nf prisoner.

privé [prive] adj private.

priver [prive] v deprive. **se priver** deny oneself. **se priver de** do without. **privation** nf deprivation.

privilège [privilɛʒ] nm privilege. **privilégié** adj privileged.

prix [pri] nm price, cost; (récompense) prize. **à tout prix** at all costs. **prix fixe** set price.

probable [prɔbablə] adj probable, likely. **probabilité** nf probability, likelihood.

probe [prɔb] adj honest. **probité** nf integrity.

problème [prɔblɛm] nm problem. **problématique** adj problematic.

procéder [prɔsede] v proceed. **procédé** nm process; conduct, behaviour. **procédure** nf procedure.

procès [prɔsɛ] nm (jur) trial; (poursuite) proceedings pl, lawsuit; (affaire) case. **procès-verbal** nm minutes pl, report.

procession [prɔsesjɔ̃] nf procession.

processus [prɔsesys] nm process.

prochain [prɔʃɛ̃] adj next; (départ, etc.) imminent; (proche) near, nearby. **prochainement** adv soon.

proche [prɔʃ] adj near, close; (village, rue, etc.) nearby. **proches** nm pl close relations pl.

proclamer [prɔklame] v proclaim, declare; announce. **proclamation** nf proclamation.

procréer [prɔkree] v procreate. **procréation** nf procreation.

procurer [prɔkyre] v (fournir) provide; (donner) give; (apporter) bring. **se procurer** get, obtain. **procuration** nf proxy; power of attorney. **procureur** nm public prosecutor, attorney.

prodige [prɔdiʒ] nm wonder, marvel; (personne) prodigy. **prodigieux** adj fantastic, prodigious, phenomenal.

prodigue [prɔdig] adj prodigal, extravagant; generous, lavish. **prodigalité** nf extravagance.

*produire [prɔdɥir] v produce. **se produire** happen. **producteur, -trice** nm, nf producer. **productif** adj productive. **production** nf production; (produit) product. **productivité** nf productivity. **produit** nm product. **produits** nm pl (légumes, etc.) produce sing; (comm) goods pl. **produits chimiques** chemicals pl. **produits de beauté** cosmetics pl.

proéminence [prɔeminɑ̃s] nf prominence. **proéminent** adj prominent.

profane [prɔfan] adj secular, profane. n(m+f) layman. **profaner** v desecrate, profane, debase.

professer [prɔfese] v profess, declare; (enseigner) teach.

professeur [profesœr] *nm* teacher; (*université*) professor.

profession [profesjɔ̃] *nf* profession; occupation.

professionnel [profesjɔnɛl], **-elle** *adj* professional; (*formation*) vocational. *nm, nf* professional; (*ouvrier*) skilled worker.

profil [profil] *nm* profile; contour, outline.

profit [profi] *nm* profit; advantage, benefit. **tirer profit de** profit from. **profitable** *adj* beneficial.

profiter [profite] *v* **profiter à** benefit, be beneficial to. **profiter de** take advantage of.

profond [profɔ̃] *adj* deep; (*sentiment, remarque*) profound. **peu profond** shallow. **profondément** *adv* deeply; profoundly. **profondeur** *nf* depth.

profus [profy] *adj* profuse. **profusion** *nf* profusion.

progéniture [proʒenityr] *nf* offspring.

programme [program] *nm* programme; (*scolaire*) curriculum, syllabus; (*ordinateur*) program. **programmation** *nf* programming. **programmer** *v* programme. **programmeur, -euse** *nm* computer programmer.

progrès [progrɛ] *nm* progress; advance, improvement.

progresser [progrese] *v* progress; advance; make progress. **progressif** *adj* progressive. **progression** *nf* progression; progress. **progressiste** *n(m+f)*, *adj* progressive.

prohiber [proibe] *v* prohibit. **prohibition** *nf* prohibition.

proie [prwa] *nf* prey. **être en proie à** be a prey to; be a victim of.

projecteur [proʒɛktœr] *nm* projector; (*théâtre*) spotlight; (*monument, sport*) floodlight; (*pour chercher*) searchlight.

projectile [proʒɛktil] *nm* missile, projectile.

projection [proʒɛksjɔ̃] *nf* projection.

projet [proʒɛ] *nm* plan; (*ébauche*) draft. **projeter** *v* project; plan.

prolétariat [proletarja] *nm* proletariat. **prolétaire** *nmm* proletarian. **prolétarien** *adj* proletarian.

proliférer [prolifere] *v* proliferate. **prolifération** *nf* proliferation.

prolifique [prolifik] *adj* prolific.

prologue [prolog] *nm* prologue.

prolonger [prolɔ̃ʒe] *v* prolong, extend. **se**

prolonger go on, persist. **prolongation** *nf* prolongation. **prolongement** *nm* extension.

promener [promne] *v* take for a walk. **se promener** go for a walk; (*errer*) wander. **promenade** *nf* walk, stroll; (*en voiture*) drive; (*à cheval*) ride.

promesse [promɛs] *nf* promise.

***promettre** [prometra] *v* promise. **prometteur, -euse** *adj* promising.

promotion [promosjɔ̃] *nf* promotion.

***promouvoir** [promuvwar] *v* promote.

prompt [prɔ̃] *adj* swift, prompt, quick. **promptitude** *nf* swiftness, promptness.

prône [pron] *nm* sermon.

pronom [pronɔ̃] *nm* pronoun.

prononcer [prɔnɔ̃se] *v* pronounce; (*dire*) utter;- (*discours*) deliver. **se prononcer** come to a decision; give an opinion. **prononciation** *nf* pronunciation.

propagande [propagãd] *nf* propaganda.

propager [propaʒe] *v* propagate, spread. **propagation** *nf* propagation.

prophète [profɛt] *nm* prophet. **prophétie** *nf* prophecy. **prophétique** *adj* prophetic. **prophétiser** *v* prophesy.

propice [propis] *adj* favourable.

proportion [proporsjɔ̃] *nf* proportion. **proportionnel** *adj* proportional. **proportionner** *v* proportion, make proportional.

propos [propo] *nm* purpose, intention; subject. *nm pl* talk *sing*; remarks *pl*. **à propos** by the way; (*arriver*) at the right time; (*remarque*) apt. **à propos de** concerning, about.

proposer [propoze] *v* propose; suggest; offer. **se proposer de** intend to. **proposition** *nf* proposal, proposition; suggestion; (*gramm*) clause.

propre [propr] *adj* (*pas sale*) clean; (*net*) neat; (*chien, chat*) house-trained; honest; (*possessif*) own; appropriate, suitable. **propre à** suitable for; (*coutume, etc.*) peculiar to. **proprement** *adv* cleanly; neatly; (*comme il faut*) properly; strictly. **à proprement parler** strictly speaking. **propreté** *nf* cleanness; neatness.

propriétaire [proprijeter] *nm* owner; (*hôtel*) proprietor; (*location*) landlord. *nf* owner; proprietress; landlady. **propriété** *nf* property; (*droit*) ownership; correctness, suitability.

propulser [propylse] *v* propel. **propulseur** *nm* propeller. **propulsion** *nf* propulsion.

*proscrire [prɔskrir] v ban, prohibit; (*personne*) banish, exile. **proscrit, -e** nm, nf outlaw; exile.

prose [proz] nf prose.

prospectus [prɔspɛktys] nm leaflet, brochure.

prospérer [prɔspere] v thrive, flourish; (*personne*) prosper. **prospère** adj thriving, flourishing; prosperous. **prospérité** nf prosperity.

se prosterner [prɔstɛrne] v bow down, prostrate oneself; (*s'humilier*) grovel. **prosternation** nf prostration. **prosterné** adj prostrate.

prostituer [prɔstitЧe] v prostitute. **prostituée** nf prostitute. **prostitution** nf prostitution.

protagoniste [prɔtagɔnist] nm protagonist.

protecteur, -trice [prɔtɛktœr, -tris] adj protective. nm, nf protector; (*art*) patron. **protection** nf protection; patronage.

protéger [prɔteʒe] v protect; patronize, be a patron of.

protéine [prɔtein] nf protein.

protester [prɔteste] v protest; declare. **protestant, -e** n, adj Protestant. **protestation** nf protest.

protocole [prɔtɔkɔl] nm protocol; etiquette.

prototype [prɔtɔtip] nm prototype.

proue [pru] nf bow, prow.

prouesse [prues] nf prowess; (*acte*) feat.

prouver [pruve] v prove.

*provenir [prɔvnir] v **provenir de** come from; be the result of. **provenance** nf origin, source. **en provenance de** (coming) from.

proverbe [prɔvɛrb] nm proverb. **proverbial** adj proverbial.

providence [prɔvidɑ̃s] nf providence.

province [prɔvɛ̃s] nf province. **provincial** adj provincial.

proviseur [prɔvizœr] nm headmaster.

provision [prɔvizjɔ̃] nf stock, supply. **provisions** nf pl provisions pl, food sing.

provisoire [prɔvizwar] adj provisional, temporary.

provoquer [prɔvɔke] v provoke; cause; incite; (*duel*) challenge; (*colère, curiosité*) arouse. **provocant** adj provocative. **provocation** nf provocation.

proximité [prɔksimite] nf proximity.

prude [pryd] nf prude. adj prudish.

prudent [prydɑ̃] adj prudent; (*circonspect*) careful, cautious; (*sage*) sensible. **prudence** nf prudence; care, caution.

prune [pryn] nf plum. **pruneau** nm prune. **prunelle** nf (*bot*) sloe; (*anat*) pupil. **prunier** nm plum tree.

psaume [psom] nm psalm.

pseudonyme [psødɔnim] nm pseudonym.

psychanalyse [psikanaliz] nf psychoanalysis. **psychanalyser** v psychoanalyse. **psychanalyste** n(m+f) psychoanalyst.

psychédélique [psikedelik] adj psychedelic.

psychiatrie [psikjatri] nf psychiatry. **psychiatre** n(m+f) psychiatrist. **psychiatrique** adj psychiatric.

psychique [psiʃik] adj psychic.

psychologie [psikɔlɔʒi] nf psychology. **psychologique** adj psychological. **psychologue** n(m+f) psychologist.

psychopathe [psikɔpat] n(m+f) psychopath.

psychose [psikoz] nf psychosis. **psychotique** n(m+f), adj psychotic.

psychosomatique [psikɔsɔmatik] adj psychosomatic.

psychothérapie [psikɔterapi] nf psychotherapy.

puanteur [pЧɑ̃tœr] nf stink.

puberté [pybɛrte] nf puberty.

pubien [pybjɛ̃] nf puberty.

public, -ique [pyblik] adj public. nm public; audience. **le grand public** the general public.

publicité [pyblisite] nf publicity; (*comm*) advertising; (*annonce*) advertisement. **publicitaire** adj advertising.

publier [pyblije] v publish. **publication** nf publication; publishing.

puce [pys] nf flea. **jeu de puce** nm tiddlywinks. **puceron** nm greenfly.

pucelle [pysɛl] nf virgin.

pudeur [pydœr] nf modesty, decency. **pudique** [pydik] adj modest; discreet.

puer [pЧe] v stink.

puéril [pЧeril] adj childish.

puis [pЧi] adv then.

puiser [pЧize] v draw. **puiser dans** dip into.

puisque [pЧiskə] conj since, seeing that, as.

puissance [pЧisɑ̃s] nf power; (*jur*) authority. **en puissance** potentially. **puissant** adj powerful.

puits [pˁi] *nm* well; (*mine*) shaft.

pull [pyl] *nm* (*fam*) jumper.

pulluler [pylyle] *v* swarm, teem. **pullulation** *nf* swarm, multitude.

pulpe [pylp] *nf* pulp. **pulpeux** *adj* pulpy.

pulsation [pylsɑsjɔ̃] *nf* beat, pulsation. **pulsation du cœur** heartbeat.

pulvériser [pylverize] *v* pulverize; (*liquide*) spray; demolish. **pulvérisateur** *nm* spray. **pulvérisation** *nf* pulverization; spraying; demolition.

punaise [pynɛz] *nf* (*zool*) bug; (*clou*) drawing-pin.

punch [pɔ̃ʃ] *nm* punch.

punir [pynir] *v* punish. **punition** *nf* punishment.

pupille[1] [pypij] *nf* (*anat*) pupil.

pupille[2] [pypij] *n* (*m+f*) ward.

pupitre [pypitrə] *nm* desk; (*rel*) lectern; music stand.

pur [pyr] *adj* pure; (*boisson*) neat; honest; (*absolu*) sheer. **pur-sang** *nm* thoroughbred. **pureté** *nf* purity.

purée [pyre] *nf* (*tomates, etc.*) purée; (*pommes de terre*) mashed potato.

purgatoire [pyrgatwar] *nm* purgatory.

purger [pyrʒe] *v* purge; (*tech*) flush out, drain. **purgatif** *nm, adj* purgative. **purge** *nf* purge.

purifier [pyrifje] *v* purify, cleanse. **purification** *nf* purification.

puritain [pyritɛ̃], **-e** *adj* puritanical. *nm, nf* puritan.

pus [py] *nm* pus.

pusillanime [pyzilanim] *adj* faint-hearted.

putain [pytɛ̃] *nf* (*argot*) whore.

putride [pytrid] *adj* putrid.

puzzle [pœzlə] *nm* jigsaw.

pygmée [pigme] *nm* pygmy.

pyjama [piʒama] *nm* pyjamas *pl*.

pylône [pilon] *nm* pylon.

pyramide [piramid] *nf* pyramid.

python [pitɔ̃] *nm* python.

Q

qu' [k] *V* que.

quadrant [kadrɑ̃] *nm* quadrant.

quadrilatère [kadrilatɛr] *nm* quadrilateral.

quadrillé [kadrije] *adj* squared.

quadrupède [kadryped] *nm, adj* quadruped.

quadrupler [kadryple] *v* quadruple. **quadruple** *nm, adj* quadruple. **quadruplé, -e** *nm, nf* quadruplet.

quai [ke] *nm* quay; (*gare*) platform; (*rivière*) embankment.

qualifier [kalifje] *v* qualify; describe, call. **qualification** *nf* qualification; description, label.

qualité [kalite] *nf* quality; (*don*) skill; (*fonction*) position, capacity.

quand [kɑ̃] *conj, adv* when. **quand même** all the same, nevertheless.

quant [kɑ̃] *adv* **quant à** as for; regarding.

quantité [kɑ̃tite] *nf* quantity, amount; great number, great deal.

quarantaine [karɑ̃tɛn] *nf* quarantine. **mettre en quarantaine** quarantine.

quarante [karɑ̃t] *nm, adj* forty. **quarantième** *n* (*m+f*), *adj* fortieth.

quart [kar] *nm* quarter; (*naut*) watch. **... et quart** quarter past **...... moins le quart** quarter to **.... quart de finale** quarter-final. **quart d'heure** quarter of an hour.

quartier [kartje] *nm* quarter; (*ville*) district, area; (*portion*) piece. **du quartier** local. **quartier général** headquarters.

quartz [kwarts] *nm* quartz.

quasi [kazi] *adv* almost.

quatorze [katɔrz] *nm, adj* fourteen. **quatorzième** *n* (*m+f*), *adj* fourteenth.

quatre [katrə] *nm, adj* four. **à quatre pattes** on all fours. **quatrième** *n* (*m+f*), *adj* fourth.

quatre-vingt-dix *nm, adj* ninety. **quatre-vingt-dixième** *n* (*m+f*), *adj* ninetieth.

quatre-vingts *nm, adj* eighty. **quatre-vingtième** *n* (*m+f*), *adj* eightieth.

quatuor [kwatˁɔr] *nm* quartet.

que[1] *conj* that; (*but*) so that; (*comparaison*) than; (*aussi*) as. **ne ... que** only. **que ... que ...** whether ... or ...

que[2] [kə] *adv* how.

que[3] [kə] *pron* that, which; (*temps*) when; (*personne*) that, whom; (*interrogatif*) what. **qu'est-ce que** or **qui** what.

quel [kɛl], **quelle** *pron, adj* what, which. **quel que** whatever; (*personne*) whoever.

quelconque [kɛlkɔ̃k] *adj* any, some; (*médiocre*) poor; ordinary.

quelque [kɛlkə] *adj, adv* some. **quelque chose** something. **quelquefois** *adv* sometimes. **quelque part** somewhere. **quelque peu** somewhat. **quelques** *adj* some, a few; *(peu de)* few. **quelques-uns, -unes** *pron* some, a few. **quelqu'un** *pron* somebody.

quémander [kemɑ̃de] *v* beg for.

querelle [kərɛl] *nf* quarrel. **se quereller** *v* quarrel. **querelleur, -euse** *adj* quarrelsome.

question [kɛstjɔ̃] *nf* question. **il n'en est pas question** it's out of the question. **questionnaire** *nm* questionnaire. **questionner** *v* question, interrogate.

quêter [kete] *v* collect money; *(chercher)* seek. **quête** *nf* collection; *(recherche)* quest, search. **en quête de** in search of. **faire la quête** collect for charity; *(rel)* take the collection.

queue [kø] *nf* tail; *(file)* queue; *(bout, fin)* end; *(liste)* bottom; *(fleur, fruit)* stalk; *(train)* rear; *(billard)* cue. **faire la queue** queue.

qui [ki] *pron* who; *(objet)* whom; *(chose)* which, that; *(quiconque)* whoever, anyone who. **à** *or* **de qui** *(possessif)* whose.

quiche [kiʃ] *nf* quiche.

quiconque [kikɔ̃k] *pron* whoever; *(personne)* anyone.

quignon [kiɲɔ̃] *nm* hunk of bread; *(croûton)* crust.

quille¹ [kij] *nf (jeu)* skittle; *(fam: jambe)* pin, leg. **jeu de quilles** skittles.

quille² [kij] *nf (naut)* keel.

quincaillerie [kɛ̃kɑjri] *nf* hardware; *(magasin)* hardware shop. **quincaillier, -ère** *nm, nf* ironmonger.

quinine [kinin] *nf* quinine.

quinte [kɛ̃t] *nf* coughing fit; *(musique)* fifth.

quintessence [kɛ̃tesɑ̃s] *nf* quintessence.

quintette [kɛ̃tɛt] *nm* quintet.

quintuplé, -e [kɛ̃typle], *-e nm, nf* quintuplet.

quinze [kɛ̃z] *nm, adj* fifteen. **demain en quinze** a fortnight tomorrow. **quinze jours** a fortnight. **quinzaine** *nf* fortnight. **quinzième** *n(m + f), adj* fifteenth.

quiproquo [kiprɔko] *nm* mistake; *(malentendu)* misunderstanding.

quittance [kitɑ̃s] *nf* receipt.

quitter [kite] *v* leave; *(espoir)* give up. **ne quittez pas** *(téléphone)* hold the line. **se quitter** part. **quitte** *adj* quits, even; *(débarrassé)* clear, rid.

quoi [kwa] *pron* what. **à quoi bon?** what's the use? **avoir de quoi** have (the) means. **il n'y a pas de quoi** don't mention it. **quoi que** whatever.

quoique [kwakə] *conj* although.

quorum [kɔrɔm] *nm* quorum.

quote-part [kɔtpar] *nf* share, quota.

quotidien [kɔtidjɛ̃] *adj* daily; *(banal)* everyday. *nm* daily newspaper.

R

rabâcher [rabɑʃe] *v* harp on, keep repeating.

rabais [rabɛ] *nm* reduction, discount.

rabaisser [rabese] *v* belittle, disparage; reduce.

rabat [raba] *nm* flap.

***rabattre** [rabatrə] *v (fermer)* close; *(faire retomber)* pull *or* turn down; *(drap)* fold back; reduce; deduct. **rabat-joie** *nm invar* spoilsport. **se rabattre** close; *(voiture)* cut in.

rabbin [rabɛ̃] *nm* rabbi.

rabot [rabo] *nm* plane. **raboter** *v* plane; *(fam)* scrape. **raboteux** *adj* uneven, rough.

rabougri [rabugri] *adj* stunted; *(ratatiné)* shrivelled.

racaille [rakaj] *nf* rabble.

raccommoder [rakɔmɔde] *v* mend; *(fam)* reconcile. **se raccommoder** *(fam)* make it up. **raccommodage** *nm (action)* mending; *(endroit)* mend. **raccommodement** *nm (fam)* reconciliation.

raccorder [rakɔrde] *v* join, link up, connect. **raccord** *nm* join, link.

raccourcir [rakursir] *v* shorten; get shorter. **raccourci** *nm (résumé)* summary; *(chemin)* short cut. **en raccourci** in miniature.

raccrocher [rakrɔʃe] *v (téléphone)* hang up, ring off; *(attraper)* grab, get hold of; *(tableau, etc.)* hang up again. **se raccrocher à** cling to; *(relier)* link with.

race [ras] *nf* race; *(animal)* breed; *(famille)* stock, blood. **de race** pedigree, thoroughbred. **racial** *adj* racial. **racisme** *nm* racialism, racism. **raciste** *n(m + f), adj* racialist, racist.

racheter [raʃte] v buy back; (dette) redeem; (otage) ransom; (péché) atone for; (faute) make up for. **rachat** nm redemption; ransom; atonement.

racine [rasin] nf root.

racler [rɑkle] v scrape. **se racler la gorge** clear one's throat. **raclée** nf (fam) thrashing.

racoler [rakɔle] v (prostituée) solicit; (vendeur) tout for.

raconter [rakɔ̃te] v tell, relate. **racontar** nm story, piece of gossip. **raconteur, -euse** nm, nf story-teller, narrator.

se racornir [rakɔrnir] v shrivel up; (durcir) become hard or tough.

radar [radar] nm radar.

rade [rad] nf harbour. **laisser en rade** leave stranded, abandon.

radeau [rado] nm raft.

radial [radjal] adj radial.

radiateur [radjatœr] nm radiator; (à gaz) heater. **radiateur électrique** electric fire. **radiateur soufflant** fan heater.

radiation [radjɑsjɔ̃] nf radiation.

radical [radikal] nm, adj radical.

radier [radje] v cross or strike off.

radieux [radjø] adj radiant.

radin [radɛ̃], -e (fam) adj stingy. nm, nf skinflint.

radio [radjo] nf radio; (méd) X-ray. **radioactif** [radjoaktif] adj radioactive. **radioactivité** nf radioactivity. **radiodiffuser** [radjodifyze] v broadcast. **radiodiffusion** nf broadcasting. **radiographie** [radjografi] nf radiography. **radiographier** v X-ray. **radiologie** [radjɔlɔʒi] nf radiology. **radiothérapie** [radjoterapi] nf radiotherapy.

radis [radi] nm radish.

radium [radjɔm] nm radium.

radoter [radɔte] v (péj) ramble on. **radotage** nm drivel.

radoucir [radusir] v soften. **se radoucir** (personne) calm down; (temps, voix) become milder.

rafale [rafal] nf gust, blast.

raffermir [rafɛrmir] v strengthen; (durcir) harden; (voix) steady. **se raffermir** grow stronger; harden; become steady.

raffiner [rafine] v refine. **raffinage** nm refining. **raffinement** nm refinement. **raffinerie** nf refinery.

raffoler [rafɔle] v **raffoler de** be very fond of.

raffut [rafy] nm (fam) row, racket.

rafistoler [rafistɔle] v patch up.

rafle [raflə] nf police raid. **rafler** v (fam) swipe.

rafraîchir [rafreʃir] v refresh; (visage) freshen up; (refroidir) cool; (vêtement, appartement, etc.) brighten up; (cheveux) trim. **rafraîchissements** nm pl refreshments pl.

rage [raʒ] nf rage; mania; (méd) rabies. **rage de dents** raging toothache. **rager** v fume, be furious. **rageur, -euse** adj hot-tempered.

ragots [rago] nm pl (fam) gossip sing.

ragoût [ragu] nm stew.

raide [rɛd] adj stiff; (cheveux) straight; (corde) tight; (pente) steep; (fam: histoire) far-fetched; (osé) daring. adv steeply. **raideur** nf stiffness; straightness; tightness; steepness. **raidir** v stiffen.

raie[1] [rɛ] nf line; (bande) stripe; (cheveux) parting; (éraflure) scratch.

raie[2] [rɛ] nf (poisson) skate, ray.

raifort [rɛfɔr] nm horse-radish.

rail [raj] nm rail.

railler [raje] v scoff at. **raillerie** nf mockery. **railleur, -euse** adj mocking.

rainure [renyr] nf groove; (plus courte) slot.

raisin [rɛzɛ̃] nm grape. **raisin de Corinthe** currant. **raisin de Smyrne** sultana. **raisin sec** raisin.

raison [rɛzɔ̃] nf reason; (math) ratio. **avoir raison** be right. **raisonnable** adj reasonable; (sensé) sensible. **raisonnement** nm reasoning; argument. **raisonner** v reason; (convaincre) reason with; argue.

rajeunir [raʒœnir] v rejuvenate; modernize; (rafraîchir) brighten up; (personne) look or feel younger.

rajuster [raʒyste] v readjust; rearrange, tidy.

ralenti [ralɑ̃ti] adj slow. nm (cinéma) slow motion; (auto) tick-over. **au ralenti** in slow motion. **tourner au ralenti** tick over, idle.

ralentir [ralɑ̃tir] v slow down.

rallier [ralje] v rally; unite; (gagner) win over. **se rallier à** join, side with.

rallonger [ralɔ̃ʒe] v lengthen, extend. **rallonge** nf extension; (table) leaf. **à rallonges** (fam: nom) double-barrelled.

ramasser [ramase] v pick up; collect; (récolter) gather. **ramassé** adj crouched, huddled up; (trapu) squat; compact.

rame¹ [ram] nf (aviron) oar. **ramer** v row. **rameur** nm oarsman.

rame² [ram] nf train; (papier) ream.

rame³ [ram] nf (branche) stick, stake.

rameau [ramo] nm branch.

ramener [ramne] v bring back; (tirer) draw, pull.

ramier [ramje] nm wood-pigeon.

se ramifier [ramifje] v branch out.

ramollir [ramɔlir] v soften; (courage, etc.) weaken. **ramolli** adj soft.

ramoner [ramɔne] v sweep. **ramoneur** nm chimney-sweep.

ramper [rɑ̃pe] v crawl, creep. **rampe** nf ramp; (côte) slope; (balustrade) handrail; (escalier) banister; (théâtre) footlights pl.

rancart [rɑ̃kar] nm **mettre au rancart** (argot) scrap, chuck out.

rance [rɑ̃s] adj rancid.

rançon [rɑ̃sɔ̃] nf ransom. **rançonner** v hold to ransom.

rancune [rɑ̃kyn] nf spite; grudge.

randonnée [rɑ̃dɔne] nf (voiture) drive; (bicyclette) ride; (pied) walk, hike.

rang [rɑ̃] nm (rangée) row; (place) rank.

ranger [rɑ̃ʒe] v arrange; (à sa place) put away; (en ordre) tidy up; (compter) rank. **se ranger** (s'écarter) pull over; (soldats, etc.) line up; (fam) settle down. **se ranger à** go along with, fall in with. **rangé** adj orderly; settled. **rangée** nf row.

ranimer [ranime] v revive; (feu, amour) rekindle.

rapace [rapas] adj (avide) rapacious; (oiseau) predatory.

rapatrier [rapatrije] v repatriate. **rapatrié, -e** nm, nf repatriate. **rapatriement** nm repatriation.

râper [rɑpe] v (cuisine) grate; (bois) rasp. **râpe** nf grater; rasp. **râpé** adj grated; (usé) threadbare. **râpeux** adj rough.

rapetisser [raptise] v shorten; (vêtement) take up or in; look smaller; (vieillard) shrink; (dénigrer) belittle.

raphia [rafja] nm raffia.

rapide [rapid] adj fast, rapid, quick. nm express train. **rapides** nm pl rapids pl. **rapidité** nf speed, rapidity.

rapiécer [rapjese] v patch, mend.

rappeler [raple] v call back; (faire souvenir) remind, recall. **se rappeler** remember. **rappel** nm recall; reminder.

rapport [rapɔr] nm connection; relation-

ship; (exposé) report; revenue, yield; (math) ratio. **être en rapport avec** (s'accorder) be in keeping with; (comm, etc.) have dealings with. **par rapport à** in relation to; (envers) with regard to.

rapporter [rapɔrte] v bring back; (revenu) yield, bring in; report; (argot) tell tales, sneak. **se rapporter à** relate to, refer to. **s'en rapporter à** rely on. **rapporteur** nm (fam) sneak; (géom) protractor. **rapporteuse** nf (fam) sneak.

rapprocher [raprɔʃe] v bring together; (approcher) bring nearer; compare. **se rapprocher** come together; get closer, approach. **à ras bords** to the brim. **rapprochement** nm comparison; reconciliation; (lien) link, parallel.

raquette [rakɛt] nf racket.

rare [rar] adj rare; (peu) few; (peu abondant) scarce, sparse; exceptional. **rareté** nf rarity.

ras [rɑ] adj short; (cheveux) close-cropped. **à ras bords** to the brim. **au ras de** level with. **en avoir ras le bol** (fam) be fed up with.

raser [rɑze] v shave; (effleurer) skim, scrape; (fam) bore. **se raser** have a shave; (fam) be bored. **rasage** nm shaving. **raseur, -euse** nm, nf (fam) bore.

rasoir nm razor; (fam) bore.

rassasier [rasazje] v satisfy. **se rassasier** eat one's fill. **se rassasier de** tire of.

rassembler [rasɑ̃ble] v collect, assemble, gather (together); (remonter) reassemble.

rassis [rasi] adj stale; (personne) composed, calm.

rassurer [rasyre] v reassure. **se rassurer** put one's mind at ease.

rat [ra] nm rat.

ratatiner [ratatine] v wrinkle, shrivel up.

râteau [rɑto] nm rake.

râtelier [rɑtəlje] nm rack; (fam) set of false teeth.

rater [rate] v (fusil) misfire; (affaire) go wrong; (fam: manquer) miss; (fam: gâcher) mess up; (fam: échouer) fail.

ratifier [ratifje] v ratify. **ratification** nf ratification.

ration [rɑsjɔ̃] nf ration.

rationaliser [rasjɔnalize] v rationalize. **rationnel** adj rational.

rationner [rasjɔne] v ration. **rationnement** nm rationing.

ratisser [ratise] v rake (up).

rattacher [ratafe] *v* fasten again; join; (*relier*) link, relate.

rattraper [ratrape] *v* catch again; (*regagner*, *réparer*) make up for; (*rejoindre*) catch up with.

rature [ratyr] *nf* deletion, erasure.

rauque [rok] *adj* hoarse; (*cri*) raucous.

ravager [ravaʒe] *v* ravage, devastate. **ravages** *nm pl* ravages *pl*, devastation *sing*.

ravaler [ravale] *v* swallow; (*colère*, *larmes*) hold back; (*mur*) restore.

ravauder [ravode] *v* mend.

ravin [ravɛ̃] *nm* ravine, gully.

ravir [ravir] *v* delight; (*enlever*) carry off. **ravissant** *adj* delightful, beautiful. **ravissement** *nm* rapture.

se raviser [ravize] *v* change one's mind.

ravitailler [ravitaje] *v* (*carburant*) refuel; (*vivres*, *etc.*) provide with fresh supplies.

rayer [reje] *v* (*marquer*) line; (*érafler*) scratch; (*biffer*) cross out. **rayé** *adj* (*papier*) ruled, lined; (*tissu*) striped; scratched.

rayon[1] [rɛjɔ̃] *nm* ray, beam; (*roue*) spoke; (*cercle*) radius. **rayon X** X-ray.

rayon[2] [rɛjɔ̃] *nm* (*planche*) shelf; (*comm*) department; (*comptoir*) counter; (*miel*) honeycomb.

rayon[3] [rɛjɔ̃] *nm* row, drill.

rayonne [rɛjɔn] *nf* rayon.

rayonner [rɛjɔne] *v* radiate; (*briller*) shine (forth), be radiant. **rayonnant** *adj* radiant. **rayonnement** *nm* radiance; radiation; influence.

rayure [rejyr] *nf* (*bande*) stripe; (*éraflure*) scratch.

razzia [razja] *nf* raid.

réaction [reaksjɔ̃] *nf* reaction. **moteur à réaction** jet engine. **réacteur** *nm* reactor. **réactionnaire** *n(m+f)*, *adj* reactionary.

réadapter [readapte] *v* readjust; (*méd*) rehabilitate. **réadaptation** *nf* readjustment; rehabilitation.

réagir [reaʒir] *v* react.

réaliser [realize] *v* realize; (*ambition*) fulfil; (*projet*) carry out; (*cinéma*) produce. **réalisateur**, **-trice** *nm*, *nf* director. **réalisation** *nf* realization; fulfilment; production.

réaliste [realist] *adj* realistic. *n(m+f)* realist. **réalisme** *nm* realism.

réalité [realite] *nf* reality.

*****réapparaître** [reaparɛtrə] *v* reappear. **réapparition** *nf* reappearance.

réarranger [rearɑ̃ʒe] *v* rearrange. **réarrangement** *nm* rearrangement.

rébarbatif [rebarbatif] *adj* forbidding, daunting.

rebattu [rəbaty] *adj* hackneyed.

rebelle [rəbɛl] *adj* rebellious; (*cheveux*) unruly; (*virus*) resistant. *n(m+f)* rebel. **se rebeller** *v* rebel. **rébellion** *nf* rebellion.

rebondir [rəbɔ̃dir] *v* bounce, rebound. **rebond** *nm* bounce, rebound. **rebondi** *adj* (*personne*) plump, portly; (*forme*) rounded.

rebord [rəbor] *nm* edge; (*plat*, *assiette*) rim; (*vêtement*) hem. **rebord de fenêtre** window ledge *or* sill.

rebours [rəbur] *nm* **à rebours** the wrong way; (*compter*) backwards. **à rebours de** against.

rebrousser [rəbruse] *v* brush up *or* back. **à rebrousse-poil** the wrong way. **prendre à rebrousse-poil** rub up the wrong way. **rebrousser chemin** turn back, retrace one's steps.

rebuffade [rəbyfad] *nf* rebuff.

rebut [rəby] *nm* scrap. **mettre au rebut** throw out, discard.

rebuter [rəbyte] *v* discourage, put off; (*répugner*) repel.

receler [rəsəle] *v* (*secret*) conceal; (*malfaiteur*) harbour; (*objet volé*) receive.

recensement [rəsɑ̃smɑ̃] *nm* census.

récent [resɑ̃] *adj* recent; (*nouveau*) new. **récemment** *adv* recently.

récépissé [resepise] *nm* receipt.

récepteur, **-trice** [reseptœr, -tris] *adj* receiving. *nm* receiver.

réception [resepsjɔ̃] *nf* reception; (*d'une lettre*, *etc.*) receipt. **réceptionniste** *n(m+f)* receptionist.

récession [resesjɔ̃] *nf* recession.

recette [rəsɛt] *nf* (*cuisine*) recipe; (*comm*) takings *pl*. **recettes** *nf pl* receipts *pl*, revenue *sing*.

*****recevoir** [rəsvwar] *v* receive; (*invité*) entertain; (*contenir*) take, hold. **être reçu** (**à**) (*examen*) pass. **receveur**, **-euse** *nm*, *nf* tax collector; bus conductor.

rechange [rəfɑ̃ʒ] *nm* **de rechange** spare; alternative. **rechange de vêtements** change of clothes.

réchapper [refape] *v* **réchapper de** come through.

recharger [rəfarʒe] *v* (*stylo*, *etc.*) refill; (*fusil*, *etc.*) reload; (*batterie*) recharge. **recharge** *nf* refill.

réchaud [reʃo] nm stove.

réchauffer [reʃofe] v warm up; (cuisine) reheat.

rêche [rɛʃ] adj rough, harsh.

rechercher [rəʃɛrʃe] v seek; (chercher) search for; (viser) strive for, pursue; (s'informer) inquire into. **recherche** nf search; pursuit; investigation; (université) research. **à la recherche de** in search of. **recherché** adj in demand; (soigné) meticulous; (péj) affected.

rechute [rəʃyt] nf relapse.

récif [resif] nm reef.

récipient [resipjɑ̃] nm container, receptacle.

réciproque [resiprɔk] adj reciprocal, mutual.

réciter [resite] v recite. **récit** nm story, account. **récital** nm recital. **récitation** nf recitation.

réclamer [reklame] v (demander) ask for, call for; (protester) complain; (droit, etc.) claim. **réclamation** nf complaint. **réclame** nf (annonce) advertisement; (publicité) advertising. **en réclame** on offer. **faire de la réclame** advertise.

reclus [rəkly], -e nm, nf recluse. adj cloistered.

recoin [rəkwɛ̃] nm nook, recess.

récolter [rekɔlte] v harvest; collect. **récolte** nf harvest, crop; collection.

recommander [rəkɔmɑ̃de] v recommend; (conseiller) advise; (poste) register. **recommandation** nf recommendation. **recommandé** adj recommended; advisable; registered. **en recommandé** by registered post; (avec avis de réception) recorded delivery.

recommencer [rəkɔmɑ̃se] v start again.

récompenser [rekɔ̃pɑ̃se] v reward. **récompense** nf reward.

réconcilier [rekɔ̃silje] v reconcile. **réconciliation** nf reconciliation.

*reconduire [rəkɔ̃dɥir] v (raccompagner) take back; (renouveler) renew.

réconforter [rekɔ̃fɔrte] v comfort; (remonter) fortify. **réconfort** nm comfort.

*reconnaître [rəkɔnɛtrə] v recognize; (avouer) admit, acknowledge; (mil) reconnoitre. **reconnaissable** adj recognizable. **reconnaissance** nf recognition; acknowledgement; (mil) reconnaissance; gratitude. **reconnaissant** adj grateful.

reconstituer [rəkɔ̃stitɥe] v (crime) reconstruct; (édifice) restore. **reconstitution** nf reconstruction; restoration.

*reconstruire [rəkɔ̃strɥir] v rebuild, reconstruct. **reconstruction** nf reconstruction.

record [rəkɔr] nm record.

recours [rəkur] nm recourse, resort. **avoir recours à** resort to.

*recouvrir [rəkuvrir] v cover.

récréation [rekreasjɔ̃] nf recreation; (école) break.

recrue [rəkry] nf recruit.

recruter [rəkryte] v recruit. **recrutement** nm recruitment.

rectangle [rɛktɑ̃glə] nm rectangle, oblong. adj right-angled. **rectangulaire** adj rectangular, oblong.

rectifier [rɛktifje] v rectify, correct; adjust; (rendre droit) straighten.

rectitude [rɛktityd] nf rectitude.

rectum [rɛktɔm] nm rectum.

reçu [rəsy] adj accepted; (candidat) successful. nm receipt.

recueil [rəkœj] nm collection; (poèmes) anthology. **recueil d'expressions** phrasebook.

*recueillir [rəkœjir] v collect, gather; (réfugié) take in; (enregistrer) record, take down. **se recueillir** collect one's thoughts. **recueillement** nm meditation. **recueilli** adj meditative.

reculer [rəkyle] v move back; (fusil) recoil; (mil) retreat; (diminuer) decline, subside; (date, décision) postpone. **reculer devant** (hésiter) shrink from. **recul** nm retreat; recoil; decline; postponement; distance. **reculé** adj remote. **à reculons** backwards.

récupérer [rekypere] v recover; (ferraille, etc.) salvage, retrieve; (heures) make up. **récupération** nf recovery; salvage.

récurer [rekyre] v scour.

rédacteur, -trice [redaktœr, -tris] nm, nf editor; (article) writer. **rédaction** nf (contrat) drafting; writing; editing; (personnel) editorial staff; (école) essay.

rédiger [redize] v write; (contrat) draft, draw up.

*redire [rədir] v repeat. **trouver à redire à** find fault with.

redondant [rədɔ̃dɑ̃] adj redundant, superfluous.

redoubler [rəduble] v increase, intensify; (école) repeat a year.

redouter [rədute] v dread, fear.
redoutable adj formidable.
redresser [rədrɛse] v straighten (up); (relever) right, set upright; rectify. **se redresser** stand up straight.
*réduire [redɥir] v reduce. **se réduire à** amount to; limit oneself to. **se réduire en** be reduced to. **réduction** nf reduction.
réduit [redɥi] adj small-scale, miniature; (prix) reduced. nm tiny room; (recoin) recess.
réel [reel] adj real. nm reality.
*refaire [rəfɛr] v do or make again; (pièce, meuble) do up, renovate. **se refaire** recover.
réfectoire [refɛktwar] nm canteen, refectory.
référence [referɑ̃s] nf reference. **faire référence à** refer to.
référendum [referɛ̃dɔm] nm referendum.
référer [refere] v **se référer à** refer to; consult.
réfléchir [refleʃir] v reflect; (penser) think. **réfléchir à** think over or about. **réfléchi** adj (personne) thoughtful; (action) well thought out; (gramm) reflexive.
réflecteur [reflɛktœr] nm reflector.
reflet [rəflɛ] nm reflection; (lumière) light, glint.
refléter [rəflete] v reflect, mirror.
réflexe [reflɛks] nm, adj reflex.
réflexion [reflɛksjɔ̃] nf reflection; (pensée) thought; remark. **réflexion faite** on second thoughts.
reflux [rəfly] nm ebb.
réformer [reforme] v reform; (mil) discharge. **réforme** nf reform; (rel) reformation; discharge.
refouler [rəfule] v force back, repress.
réfracter [refrakte] v refract. **réfraction** nf refraction.
refrain [rəfrɛ̃] nm refrain.
réfrigérer [refriʒere] v refrigerate. **réfrigérateur** nm refrigerator. **réfrigération** nf refrigeration.
refroidir [rəfrwadir] v cool (down). **refroidissement** nm cooling; (méd) chill.
refuge [rəfyʒ] nm refuge; (pour piétons) traffic island.
se réfugier [refyʒje] v take refuge. **réfugié, -e** nm, nf refugee.
refuser [rəfyze] v refuse; (client) turn away. **être refusé (à)** (examen) fail. **refus** nm refusal.
réfuter [refyte] v refute.

regagner [rəgaɲe] v regain; (argent, etc.) win back; (temps) make up; (lieu) get back to.
regain [rəgɛ̃] nm renewal, revival.
régal [regal] nm, pl **-als** delight, treat. **régaler** v treat.
regarder [rəgarde] v look at; (action) watch; concern, regard. **regarder fixement** stare at, gaze at. **regard** nm look, glance; expression; (égout) manhole. **regard fixe** gaze, stare. **regard furieux** glare.
régate [regat] nf regatta.
régent [reʒɑ̃], **-e** nm, nf regent. **régence** nf regency.
régie [reʒi] nf state control.
régime [reʒim] nm regime; system; government; (méd) diet.
régiment [reʒimɑ̃] nm regiment. **régimentaire** adj regimental.
région [reʒjɔ̃] nf region, area. **régional** adj regional.
régir [reʒir] v govern. **régisseur** nm (théâtre) stage manager; (gérant) steward.
registre [rəʒistrə] nm register.
régler [regle] v settle; adjust, regulate; (papier) rule. **réglage** nm adjustment; (moteur, TV, etc.) tuning. **règle** nf rule; (instrument) ruler. **en règle** (papiers) in order. **règle à calcul** slide rule. **règles** nfpl (méd) period sing. **réglé** adj regular; (papier) lined. **règlement** nm settlement; (règle) rule. **réglementaire** adj regulation; statutory.
réglisse [reglis] nf liquorice.
régner [reɲe] v reign. **règne** nm reign; (bot, zool) kingdom.
regret [rəgrɛ] nm regret. **regrettable** adj regrettable. **regretter** v regret; (personne, pays, etc.) miss; (être désolé) be sorry; deplore.
régulier [regylje] adj regular; (constant) steady; (égal) even. **régularité** nf regularity; steadiness; evenness.
réhabiliter [reabilite] v rehabilitate; restore to favour. **réhabilitation** nf rehabilitation.
rehausser [rəose] v (relever) raise, make higher; (beauté, goût, etc.) enhance, bring out.
rein [rɛ̃] nm kidney. **reins** nm pl back sing.
réincarnation [reɛ̃karnasjɔ̃] nf reincarnation.

reine [rɛn] *nf* queen. **reine-claude** *nf* greengage.

réintégrer [reɛ̃tegre] *v* reinstate; return to. **réintégration** *nf* reinstatement; return.

rejeter [rəʒte] *v* reject; *(relancer)* throw back; *(lave, déchets, etc.)* throw out; *(expulser)* cast out, expel. **se rejeter sur** fall back on. **rejet** *nm* rejection; expulsion; *(bot)* shoot.

***rejoindre** [rəʒwɛ̃drə] *v* rejoin; join; *(rattraper)* catch up with. **se rejoindre** meet.

réjouir [reʒwir] *v* delight, thrill. **se réjouir** be delighted; rejoice. **réjouissance** *nf* rejoicing. **réjouissant** *adj* amusing; *(nouvelle)* cheerful.

relâcher [rəlɑʃe] *v* relax; *(desserrer)* loosen; *(libérer)* release. **relâche** *nf* rest, respite; *(théâtre)* closure; *(naut)* port of call. **relâché** *adj* loose; *(discipline)* lax.

relais [rəlɛ] *nm* relay; *(usine)* shift.

relatif [rəlatif] *adj* relative. **relativité** *nf* relativity.

relation [rəlasjɔ̃] *nf* relationship; *(connaissance)* acquaintance, connection; *(récit)* account. **relations** *nf pl* relations *pl*.

relayer [rəleje] *v* *(remplacer)* relieve, take over from; *(TV, radio)* relay. **se relayer** take turns.

reléguer [rəlege] *v* relegate. **relégation** *nf* relegation.

relevé [rəlve] *adj* raised, elevated; *(manches)* rolled-up; *(col)* turned-up; *(cuisine)* highly-seasoned. *nm* summary, statement; list; *(facture)* bill. **relevé de compte** bank statement.

relever [rəlve] *v* *(redresser)* pick up, stand up; *(remonter)* raise; *(manche)* roll up; *(chaussette)* pull up; *(col)* turn up; *(cuisine)* season; *(relayer)* relieve; *(faute)* find; *(notes)* take down. **relever de** be a matter for, be the concern of. **relève** *nf* relief. **relève de la garde** changing of the guard.

relief [rəljɛf] *nm* relief. **en relief** in relief; *(en-tête)* embossed; *(phot)* three-dimensional. **mettre en relief** bring out, accentuate.

relier [rəlje] *v* link, connect, *(livre)* bind.

religieux [rəliʒjø] *adj* religious. *nm* monk. **religieuse** *nf* nun.

religion [rəliʒjɔ̃] *nf* religion; *(foi)* faith.

relique [rəlik] *nf* relic.

***relire** [rəlir] *v* re-read.

***reluire** [rəlɥir] *v* shine, gleam. **reluisant** *adj* shiny.

remanier [rəmanje] *v* revise, modify.

se remarier [rəmarje] *v* remarry.

remariage *nm* remarriage.

remarquer [rəmarke] *v* notice; *(faire une remarque)* remark. **faire remarquer** point out. **remarquable** *adj* remarkable. **remarque** *nf* remark, comment.

remblai [rɑ̃blɛ] *nm* embankment.

rembourrer [rɑ̃bure] *v* stuff, pad. **rembourrage** *nm* stuffing, padding.

rembourser [rɑ̃burse] *v* repay; *(dépenses)* refund, reimburse. **remboursement** *nm* repayment; refund, reimbursement.

remède [rəmɛd] *nm* remedy, cure. **remédier à** *v* remedy.

remercier [rəmɛrsje] *v* thank. **remerciement** *nm* thanks *pl*.

***remettre** [rəmɛtrə] *v* put back; *(donner)* hand over; *(ajourner)* postpone; *(dette, péché)* remit. **se remettre** recover, get better.

réminiscence [reminisɑ̃s] *nf* reminiscence.

remise [rəmiz] *nf* *(rabais)* discount; *(livraison)* delivery; *(grâce)* remission; *(resserre)* shed; *(ajournement)* postponement.

rémission [remisjɔ̃] *nf* remission.

remonter [rəmɔ̃te] *v* go up (again); return, go back; *(cheval)* remount; *(relever)* raise; *(montre)* wind up; *(moral)* cheer up; *(machine, etc.)* reassemble. **remontant** *nm* tonic. **remontée** *nf* ascent, rise.

remords [rəmɔr] *nm* remorse.

remorquer [rəmɔrke] *v* tow. **remorque** *nf* towing; *(câble)* tow-rope; *(véhicule)* trailer. **en remorque** on tow. **remorqueur** *nm* tugboat.

remous [rəmu] *nm* *(eau)* wash, swirl; *(air)* eddy; *(foule)* bustle; *(agitation)* stir.

rempart [rɑ̃par] *nm* rampart.

remplacer [rɑ̃plase] *v* replace; *(acteur, etc.)* stand in for; be a substitute for. **remplaçant, -e** *nm, nf* replacement; substitute; *(sport)* reserve; *(théâtre)* understudy. **remplacement** *nm* replacement; substitution.

rempli [rɑ̃pli] *adj* full. *nm* *(vêtement)* tuck.

remplir [rɑ̃plir] *v* fill; *(à nouveau)* refill; *(devoir)* fulfil; *(travail)* carry out.

remporter [rãpɔrte] v take away; (*victoire*) win; (*prix*) carry off.

remuer [rəmɥe] v move; (*tourner*) stir. **remue-ménage** nm invar commotion.

rémunérer [remynere] v remunerate, pay. **rémunérateur, -trice** adj remunerative, lucrative. **rémunération** nf remuneration.

renâcler [rənɑkle] v (*animal*) snort; (*personne*) grumble.

renaissance [rənɛsɑ̃s] nf rebirth.

renard [rənar] nm fox.

renchérir [rãʃerir] v (*prix*) get more expensive; (*ajouter*) add, go further; (*péj*) go one better.

rencontrer [rãkɔ̃tre] v meet; (*trouver*) come across; (*obstacle*) come up against, encounter. **rencontre** nf meeting, encounter.

rendez-vous [rãdevu] nm invar appointment; (*lieu*) meeting place. **donner rendez-vous à** make an appointment with.

se *rendormir [rãdɔrmir] v go back to sleep.

rendre [rãdrə] v return, give back; (*achat*) take or send back; render; (*faire*) make; (*mil*) surrender; (*terre*) yield. **se rendre** surrender. **se rendre à** go to. **se rendre compte de** realize. **rendement** nm yield, output.

rêne [rɛn] nf rein.

renégat [rənega], **-e** nm, nf renegade.

renfermer [rãfɛrme] v contain. **renfermé** adj withdrawn. **sentir le renfermé** smell stuffy.

renforcer [rãfɔrse] v reinforce, strengthen; intensify. **renforcement** nm reinforcement, strengthening; intensification.

renfort [rãfɔr] nm reinforcement. **de** or **en renfort** extra, additional. **renforts** nm pl supplies pl.

se renfrogner [rãfrɔɲe] v scowl. **renfrogné** adj sullen, sulky.

rengaine [rãgɛn] nf hackneyed expression.

renier [rənje] v renounce, deny; repudiate, disown; (*promesse*) go back on. **reniement** nm renunciation, denial; repudiation.

renifler [rənifle] v sniff. **reniflement** nm sniff.

renne [rɛn] nm reindeer.

renom [rənɔ̃] nm renown, fame. **renommé** adj renowned, famous. **renommée** nf renown, fame.

renoncer [rənɔ̃se] v **renoncer à** give up, renounce, abandon. **renonciation** nf renunciation.

renoncule [rənɔ̃kyl] nf buttercup.

renouer [rənwe] v tie again; (*conversation, etc.*) renew, resume.

renouveler [rənuvle] v renew. **se renouveler** recur. **renouvellement** nm renewal; recurrence.

rénover [renɔve] v renovate; (*méthodes, etc.*) reform. **rénovation** nf renovation; restoration.

renseigner [rãsɛɲe] v inform, give information to. **se renseigner** find out, make inquiries. **renseignements** nm pl information sing; inquiries pl; (*mil*) intelligence sing.

rente [rãt] nf pension, allowance. **rentes** nf pl private income sing. **rentable** adj profitable.

rentrer [rãtre] v return, go or come back; (*chez soi*) go home; (*entrer*) go in; (*à nouveau*) go back in; (*amener*) bring or take in. **rentrer dans** go into; (*voiture*) crash into; be included in. **rentrée** nf return; reopening; beginning of school term; (*acteur*) comeback.

renverser [rãvɛrse] v (*faire tomber*) knock over; (*mettre à l'envers*) turn upside down; (*gouvernement*) overthrow; (*inverser*) invert, reverse; (*fam*) stagger, astound. **se renverser** overturn. **renversé** adj upside down; inverted. **renversement** nm inversion, reversal; overthrow.

*renvoyer [rãvwaje] v send back; (*employé*) dismiss; (*élève*) expel; (*soldat*) discharge; refer; (*ajourner*) postpone; echo. **renvoi** nm dismissal; expulsion; discharge; cross-reference; postponement; (*rot*) belch.

réorganiser [reɔrganize] v reorganize. **réorganisation** nf reorganization.

repaire [rəpɛr] nm den.

répandre [repãdrə] v (*renverser*) spill; (*disperser*) scatter; (*étendre*) spread; (*odeur, chaleur, etc.*) give off. **répandu** adj widespread.

*reparaître [rəparɛtrə] v reappear.

réparer [repare] v mend, repair; correct; (*compenser*) make up for. **réparation** nf repair; correction; compensation.

repartie [rəparti] nf repartee; (*riposte*) retort.

répartir [repartir] *v* share out, divide up; distribute; (*étaler*) spread. **répartition** *nf* distribution; allocation.

repas [rəpɑ] *nm* meal. **repas léger** snack.

repasser [rəpase] *v* (*frontière*) go back across; (*souvenir, trait*) go (back) over; (*examen*) resit; (*film, émission*) show again; (*au fer*) iron; (*couteau*) sharpen. **repassage** *nm* ironing; sharpening.

se *repentir [rəpãtir] *v* repent. **se repentir** of regret, be sorry for. *nm* repentance. **repentant** *adj* repentant.

répercussion [reperkysjɔ̃] *nf* repercussion.

répercuter [reperkyte] *v* echo; reflect. **se répercuter** reverberate.

repérer [rəpere] *v* locate; (*fam*) spot, discover. **repère** *nm* mark, marker; (*monument, etc.*) landmark.

répertoire [repertwar] *nm* index, list; (*carnet*) notebook; (*théâtre*) repertory; (*chanteur*) repertoire.

répéter [repete] *v* repeat; (*théâtre*) rehearse. **répétiteur, -trice** *nm, nf* tutor. **répétition** *nf* repetition; rehearsal. **répétition générale** dress rehearsal.

répit [repi] *nm* respite.

replacer [rəplase] *v* replace, put back; (*employé*) find a new job for.

replier [rəplije] *v* fold up; (*mil*) withdraw. **se replier** curl up; (*se renfermer*) withdraw. **repli** *nm* fold; withdrawal.

réplique [replik] *nf* reply, retort; counterattack; (*théâtre*) line, cue; (*art*) replica. **répliquer** *v* reply, retort; (*se venger*) retaliate.

répondre [repɔ̃drə] *v* answer, reply; (*réagir*) respond. **répondre de** answer for. **réponse** [repɔ̃s] *nf* answer, reply; (*réaction*) response.

reporter¹ [rəporte] *v* (*ramener*) take back; (*différer*) put off, postpone; transfer; copy out. **se reporter à** refer to; (*penser*) think back to.

reporter² [rəportɛr] *nm* reporter. **reportage** *nm* report; (*sport*) commentary.

repos [rəpo] *nm* rest; pause; (*tranquillité*) peace.

reposer¹ [rəpoze] *v* rest; (*être étendu*) lie. **se reposer** rest; (*compter*) rely. **reposant** *adj* restful.

reposer² [rəpoze] *v* put back; (*question*) repeat, raise again.

repousser [rəpuse] *v* repulse, repel; (*écarter*) push away; reject; (*différer*) put off, postpone; (*cheveux, etc.*) grow again. **repoussant** *adj* repulsive.

*reprendre [rəprɑ̃drə] *v* take back; (*récupérer*) recover, get back; (*recommencer*) resume; (*attraper*) recapture; reprimand. **se reprendre** correct oneself; (*se ressaisir*) pull oneself together.

représailles [rəprezɑj] *nf pl* reprisals *pl*, retaliation *sing*.

représenter [rəprezɑ̃te] *v* represent; (*art*) depict, portray; (*théâtre*) perform. **se représenter** imagine; (*survenir*) occur or arise again; (*à un examen*) resit. **représentant, -e** *nm, nf* representative. **représentatif** *adj* representative. **représentation** *nf* representation; performance.

répressif [represif] *adj* repressive. **répression** *nf* repression.

réprimande [reprimɑ̃d] *nf* reprimand. **réprimander** *v* reprimand.

réprimer [reprime] *v* repress, suppress.

reprise [rəpriz] *nf* (*recommencement*) resumption, renewal; (*film, émission*) repeat; (*affaires, etc.*) recovery; (*chaussette*) darn; (*fois*) occasion, time. **à maintes reprises** many times. **repriser** *v* darn.

reprocher [rəprɔʃe] *v* reproach; criticize. **reproche** *nm* reproach.

reproduction [rəprɔdyksjɔ̃] *nf* reproduction.

*reproduire [rəprɔdɥir] *v* reproduce. **se reproduire** recur.

réprouver [repruve] *v* reprove, condemn.

reptile [rɛptil] *nm* reptile.

républicain [repyblikɛ̃], **-e** *n, adj* republican.

république [repyblik] *nf* republic.

répudier [repydje] *v* repudiate, renounce. **répudiation** *nf* repudiation.

répugnant [repynɑ̃] *adj* repugnant, revolting. **répugnance** *nf* repugnance, loathing.

répulsif [repylsif] *adj* repulsive. **répulsion** *nf* repulsion.

réputation [repytasjɔ̃] *nf* reputation, repute. **réputé** *adj* reputable, renowned; (*prétendu*) reputed.

*requérir [rəkerir] *v* require, call for; (*solliciter*) request.

requête [rəkɛt] *nf* request, petition.

requiem [rekɥijɛm] *nm invar* requiem.

requin [rəkɛ̃] *nm* shark.

requis [rəki] *adj* required, requisite.

réquisition [rekizisjɔ̃] *nf* requisition.
réquisitionner *v* requisition.

rescapé [rɛskape], **-e** *nm, nf* survivor.

réseau [rezo] *nm* network.

réserver [rezɛrve] *v* reserve; (*mettre de côté*) keep, save; (*destiner*) have in store. **réservation** *nf* reservation. **réserve** *nf* reserve; (*restriction*) reservation; (*provision*) stock; (*entrepôt*) storeroom.

réservoir [rezɛrvwar] *nm* tank; (*étang*) reservoir; (*poissons*) fishpond.

résider [rezide] *v* reside. **résidence** *nf* residence. **résidentiel** *adj* residential.

résidu [rezidy] *nm* residue.

se résigner [rezine] *v* resign oneself. **résignation** *nf* resignation.

résilier [rezilje] *v* terminate, cancel.

résille [rezij] *nf* net; (*coiffure*) hairnet.

résine [rezin] *nf* resin.

résister [reziste] *v* **résister à** resist, withstand. **résistance** *nf* resistance. **résistant** *adj* strong, robust.

résolu [rezɔly] *adj* resolute, determined. **résolution** *nf* resolution; solution.

résonner [rezone] *v* resonate, resound. **resonance** *nf* resonance.

***résoudre** [rezudrə] *v* resolve; (*problème*) solve.

respect [rɛspɛ] *nm* respect. **respect de soi** self-respect. **respectable** *adj* respectable. **respecter** *v* respect. **respectif** *adj* respective. **respectueux** *adj* respectful.

respirer [rɛspire] *v* breathe. **respiration** *nf* breathing. **respiration artificielle** artificial respiration.

resplendir [rɛsplɑ̃dir] *v* beam, shine, gleam. **resplendissant** *adj* radiant.

responsable [rɛspɔ̃sablə] *adj* responsible. *n(m+f)* (*coupable*) culprit; (*dirigeant*) official. **responsabilité** *nf* responsibility.

resquiller [rɛskije] *v* get in without paying; jump the queue; (*carotter*) wangle.

se ressaisir [rəsezir] *v* pull oneself together.

ressembler [rəsɑ̃ble] *v* **ressembler à** resemble, be like. **se ressembler** be alike. **ressemblance** *nf* resemblance; similarity.

***ressentir** [rəsɑ̃tir] *v* feel. **se ressentir de** (*personne*) feel the effects of; (*travail*) show the effects of. **ressentiment** *nm* resentment.

resserrer [rəsere] *v* tighten.

ressort[1] [rəsɔr] *nm* spring.

ressort[2] [rəsɔr] *nm* scope, province.

***ressortir** [rəsɔrtir] *v* go *or* come out again; (*retirer*) bring *or* take out again; (*se détacher*) stand out. **ressortir de** be the result of.

ressource [rəsurs] *nf* resource; possibility; (*recours*) resort.

ressusciter [resysite] *v* revive; (*rel, péj*) resurrect.

restant [rɛstɑ̃] *adj* remaining. *nm* rest, remainder.

restaurant [rɛstorɑ̃] *nm* restaurant.

restaurer [rɛstore] *v* restore. **restauration** *nf* restoration.

rester [rɛste] *v* stay, remain; (*subsister*) be left; (*durer*) last. **en rester à** go no further than. **reste** *nm* rest, remainder; (*morceau*) piece left over. **du reste** moreover. **restes** *nm pl* remains *pl*; (*nourriture*) left-overs *pl*.

restituer [rɛstitᴄᴄe] *v* restore; (*rendre*) return.

***restreindre** [rɛstrɛ̃drə] *v* restrict, limit.

restriction [rɛstriksjɔ̃] *nf* restriction. **restrictif** *adj* restrictive.

résulter [rezylte] *v* result. **résultat** *nm* result.

résumer [rezyme] *v* summarize, sum up. **résumé** *nm* summary, résumé.

résurrection [rezyrɛksjɔ̃] *nf* resurrection.

rétablir [retablir] *v* restore; (*réintégrer*) reinstate. **se rétablir** (*malade*) recover. **rétablissement** *nm* recovery; restoration.

retard [rətar] *nm* delay; (*personne*) lateness; (*peuple, enfant*) backwardness. **en retard** late. **retardé** *adj* backward. **retarder** *v* delay; (*remettre*) put back; (*montre*) be slow.

***retenir** [rətnir] *v* hold back; (*garder*) keep, retain; (*retarder*) detain; (*réserver*) book; (*contenir*) restrain.

retentir [rətɑ̃tir] *v* ring, resound, echo. **retentissement** *nm* repercussion; effect.

retenue [rətny] *nf* restraint, reserve; (*prélèvement*) deduction; (*école*) detention.

réticent [retisɑ̃] *adj* reticent; hesitant. **réticence** *nf* reservation.

rétif [retif] *adj* restive.

rétine [retin] *nf* retina.

retirer [rətire] *v* remove, withdraw. **se retirer** retire, withdraw.

retomber [rətɔ̃be] *v* fall (again); (*fusée, etc.*) land, come down; (*pendre*) hang down.

rétorquer [retɔrke] v retort.

retors [rətɔr] adj sly, wily.

retoucher [rətuʃe] v touch up; (*vêtement*) alter. **retouche** nf alteration.

retour [rətur] nm return. **être de retour** be back.

retourner [rəturne] v return; (*renverser*) turn over; (*sens opposé*) turn round.

rétracter [retrakte] v retract.

retrait [rətrɛ] nm withdrawal. **en retrait** set back.

retraite [rətrɛt] nf retreat; (*vieux travailleur*) retirement; pension. **prendre sa retraite** retire.

retraité [rətrete], **-e** adj retired. nm, nf pensioner.

retrancher [rətrɑ̃ʃe] v deduct, take away; (*couper*) cut out or off. **se retrancher** (*mil*) entrench oneself; take refuge.

rétrécir [retresir] (*tissu*) shrink; (*rue*) narrow; (*pupille*) contract. **rétrécissement** nm shrinkage; contraction.

rétribuer [retribɥe] v pay. **rétribution** nf payment.

rétrograder [retrograde] v regress, go backward; (*officier*) demote. **rétrogradation** nf regression; demotion. **rétrograde** adj retrograde, backward.

rétrospectif [retrospektif] adj retrospective. **rétrospectivement** adv in retrospect.

retrousser [rətruse] v (*manche*) roll up; (*lèvre*) curl up; (*jupe, etc.*) hitch up; (*nez*) turn up.

retrouver [rətruve] v find (again); (*personne*) meet, join; (*santé*) regain. **se retrouver** meet up, get together.

rétroviseur [retrovizœr] nm driving mirror.

réunir [reynir] v collect, gather (together); join; (*ennemis, anciens amis*) reunite. **se réunir** unite; (*amis*) get together. **réunion** nf (*séance*) meeting; reunion; collection.

réussir [reysir] v succeed. **réussir à** succeed in; (*examen*) pass; (*air, nourriture*) agree with. **réussi** adj successful. **réussite** nf success; (*cartes*) patience.

revanche [rəvɑ̃ʃ] nf revenge. **en revanche** (*au contraire*) on the other hand; (*en retour*) in return.

revasser [rɛvase] v daydream.

rêve [rɛv] nm dream.

revêche [rəvɛʃ] adj surly.

réveiller [reveje] v wake (up); (*raviver*) rouse, reawaken, revive. **se réveiller** wake up, awake. **réveil** nm waking; (*à la réalité*) awakening; (*pendule*) alarm clock. **réveillé** adj awake.

révéler [revele] v reveal. **révélateur, -trice** adj revealing. **révélation** nf revelation.

revendiquer [rəvɑ̃dike] v claim, demand. **revendication** nf claim, demand.

*revenir [rəvnir] v come back, return. **revenir à** come to, amount to. **revenir à soi** come round. **revenir de** get over. **revenir sur** (*promesse*) go back on; (*passé*) go back over. **revenant, -e** nm, nf ghost. **revenu** nm income, revenue.

rêver [reve] v dream. **rêverie** nf daydream. **rêveur, -euse** adj dreamy.

réverbérer [reverbere] v reverberate, reflect. **réverbération** nf reverberation. **réverbère** nm street lamp.

révérence [reverɑ̃s] nf (*homme*) bow; (*femme*) curtsy; (*respect*) reverence. **faire une révérence** bow; curtsy.

revers [rəvɛr] nm back; (*monnaie*) reverse; (*tissu*) wrong side; (*veste*) lapel; (*manche*) cuff. **réversible** adj reversible.

*revêtir [rəvetir] v assume, take on; (*habiller*) clothe; cover, coat. **revêtement** nm covering, coating; surface.

revirement [rəvirmɑ̃] nm sudden change, reversal.

réviser [revize] v revise; (*examiner*) review; (*voiture, machine*) service, overhaul. **révision** nf revision; review; service.

*revivre [rəvivrə] v relive. **faire revivre** revive.

*revoir [rəvwar] v see again; revise. **au revoir!** goodbye!

révolter [revolte] v revolt, outrage. **se révolter** revolt, rebel. **révolte** nf revolt, rebellion.

révolution [revɔlysjɔ̃] nf revolution. **révolutionnaire** n(m+f), adj revolutionary. **révolutionner** v revolutionize.

revolver [revɔlvɛr] nm gun, revolver.

révoquer [revɔke] v revoke; (*destituer*) dismiss.

revue [rəvy] nf review; (*spectacle*) revue; magazine; (*mil*) inspection.

rez-de-chaussée [redʃose] nm invar ground floor.

rhésus [rezys] nm rhesus. **rhésus négatif/positif** rhesus negative/positive.

rhétorique [retɔrik] nf rhetoric. adj rhetorical.

rhinocéros [rinɔserɔs] *nm* rhinoceros.

rhododendron [rɔdɔdɛ̃drɔ̃] *nm* rhododendron.

rhubarbe [rybarb] *nf* rhubarb.

rhum [rɔm] *nm* rum.

rhumatisme [rymatismə] *nm* rheumatism. **rhumatismal** *adj* rheumatic.

rhume [rym] *nm* cold. **rhume des foins** hay fever.

riant [rjɑ̃] *adj* cheerful, smiling.

ricaner [rikane] *v* snigger, sneer. **ricanement** *nm* snigger, sneer.

riche [riʃ] *adj* rich. *n*(*m*+*f*) rich person. **richesse** *nf* richness; (*argent*) wealth; abundance. **richesses** *nf pl* riches *pl*.

ride [rid] *nf* (*peau*) wrinkle; (*eau*) ripple. **rider** *v* wrinkle; ripple.

rideau [rido] *nm* curtain; (*écran*) screen. **rideau de fer** Iron Curtain.

ridicule [ridikyl] *adj* ridiculous. *nm* ridicule; absurdity. **ridiculiser** *v* ridicule.

rien [rjɛ̃] *pron* nothing; (*quelque chose*) anything. **ça ne fait rien** (*fam*) it doesn't matter. **de rien** (*fam*) not at all, you're welcome. **ne ... rien** nothing. *nm* nothing; (*bagatelle*) trivial thing; (*goutte*) touch, hint.

rigide [riʒid] *adj* rigid, stiff; strict. **rigidité** *nf* rigidity, stiffness; strictness.

rigole [rigɔl] *nf* channel; (*d'écoulement*) drain; (*sillon*) furrow.

rigoler [rigɔle] (*fam*) *v* (*plaisanter*) joke; (*rire*) laugh; (*s'amuser*) have fun. **rigolo, -ote** *adj* funny, comical.

rigoureux [rigurø] *adj* rigorous, (*sévère*) harsh; strict.

rigueur [rigœr] *nf* rigour; (*sévérité*) harshness; strictness; precision. **à la rigueur** if need be; possibly. **de rigueur** compulsory; (*étiquette*) the done thing.

rime [rim] *nf* rhyme. **rimer** *v* rhyme.

rincer [rɛ̃se] *v* rinse. **rinçage** *nm* rinse.

riposter [ripɔste] *v* retort; (*contre-attaquer*) retaliate. **riposte** *nf* retort.

***rire** [rir] *v* laugh; (*plaisanter*) joke; (*s'amuser*) have fun. **se rire de** laugh at. *nm* laugh; (*éclat*) laughter. **petit rire** chuckle. **petit rire nerveux** giggle.

ris [ri] *nm* **ris de veau** sweetbread.

risée [rize] *nf* ridicule; (*personne*) laughing stock.

risquer [riske] *v* risk. **risquer de** may well. **risque-tout** *n*(*m*+*f*) *invar* daredevil. **se risquer** venture. **risque** *nm* risk. **risqué** *adj* risky; (*licencieux*) risqué.

ristourne [risturn] *nf* rebate, refund.

rite [rit] *nm* rite.

rituel [ritɥɛl] *nm, adj* ritual.

rival [rival], **-e** *n, adj* rival. **rivaliser** (*rivalize*) *v* **rivaliser avec** rival, vie with. **rivalité** *nf* rivalry.

rive [riv] *nf* (*mer*) shore; (*rivière*) bank. **rivage** *nm* shore.

river [rive] *v* rivet; (*lier*) bind. **rivet** *nm* rivet.

rivière [rivjɛr] *nf* river.

rixe [riks] *nf* brawl.

riz [ri] *nm* rice. **riz au lait** rice pudding.

robe [rɔb] *nf* dress; (*magistrat*) robe; (*professeur*) gown; (*peau*) skin. **robe-chasuble** *nf* pinafore dress. **robe de chambre** dressing-gown. **robe de grossesse** maternity dress, smock. **robe de mariée** wedding dress. **robe du soir** evening dress.

robinet [rɔbine] *nm* tap.

robot [rɔbo] *nm* robot.

robuste [rɔbyst] *adj* robust.

roc [rɔk] *nm* rock. **rocaille** *nf* (*jardin*) rockery.

roche [rɔʃ] *nf* rock. **rocher** *nm* rock; (*gros bloc*) boulder.

roder [rɔde] *v* (*auto*) run in. **en rodage** running in.

rôder [rode] *v* (*en maraude*) prowl; (*au hasard*) roam. **rôdeur, -euse** *nm, nf* prowler.

rogner [rɔɲe] *v* trim, clip; (*dépense*) whittle down.

rognon [rɔɲɔ̃] *nm* kidney.

rogue [rɔg] *adj* haughty, arrogant.

roi [rwa] *nm* king. **la fête des Rois** Twelfth Night.

roitelet [rwatlɛ] *nm* wren.

rôle [rol] *nm* role, part; (*liste*) roll.

romain [rɔmɛ̃] *adj* Roman. **Romain, -e** *nm, nf* Roman.

roman[1] [rɔmɑ̃] *nm* novel; (*récit*) story. **roman-feuilleton** *nm* serial. **roman policier** detective story. **romans** *nm pl* fiction *sing*. **romancier, -ère** *nm, nf* novelist.

roman[2] [rɔmɑ̃] *adj* (*langue*) Romance; (*arch*) Romanesque.

romanesque [rɔmanɛsk] *adj* (*personne*) romantic; (*récit*) fantastic; (*amour*) storybook.

romantique [rɔmɑ̃tik] *n*(*m*+*f*), *adj* romantic.

romarin [rɔmarɛ̃] nm rosemary.

Rome [rɔm] n Rome.

rompre [rɔ̃prə] v break. **rompu** adj broken; (fatigué) exhausted. **rompu à** experienced in.

romsteck [rɔmstɛk] nm rump steak.

ronce [rɔ̃s] nf bramble; (mûrier) blackberry bush.

rond [rɔ̃] adj round; (gras) chubby, plump; (fam) drunk. **rond-de-cuir** nm clerk. **rond-point** nm roundabout. nm ring; (tranche) slice. **en rond** in a circle. **ronde** nf patrol, rounds pl; (musique) semibreve. **rondelle** nf washer; disc. **rondement** adv (promptement) briskly; frankly. **rondeur** nf roundness; plumpness. **rondin** nm log.

ronfler [rɔ̃fle] v snore; (rugir) roar; (vrombir) hum. **ronflement** nm snore; roar; hum.

ronger [rɔ̃ʒe] v gnaw at, eat into; (malade) sap. **se ronger les ongles** bite one's nails. **rongeur** nm rodent.

ronronner [rɔ̃rɔne] v purr. **ronron** or **ronronnement** nm purr.

roquet [rɔkɛ] nm ill-tempered little dog.

roquette [rɔkɛt] nf rocket.

rosaire [rozɛr] nm rosary.

rosbif [rɔsbif] nm roast beef.

rose [roz] nf rose. nm pink. adj pink; (joues) rosy. **roseraie** nf rose garden. **rosier** nm rose-bush.

roseau [rozo] nm reed.

rosée [roze] nf dew.

rosette [rozɛt] nf rosette; (nœud) bow.

rosser [rɔse] v thrash. **rossée** nf (fam) thrashing, hiding.

rossignol [rɔsiɲɔl] nm nightingale; (fam) piece of junk.

rot [rɔ] nm burp. **roter** v burp.

rotatif [rɔtatif] adj rotary.

rôtir [rotir] v roast. **rôti** nm joint, roast. **rôtisserie** nf steak-house.

rotor [rɔtɔr] nm rotor.

rotule [rɔtyl] nf kneecap.

rouage [rwaʒ] nm cog; part. **rouages** nm pl works pl.

roublard [rublar] adj (fam) crafty, wily.

roucouler [rukule] v coo. **roucoulement** nm coo.

roue [ru] nf wheel. **faire la roue** (se pavaner) strut about; (gymnaste) do a cart-wheel. **roue de secours** spare wheel.

roué [rwe] adj cunning.

rouge [ruʒ] adj red. **rouge-gorge** nm rob-

in. nm red; (fard) rouge. **rouge à lèvres** lipstick. **rougeur** nf redness; (visage) flush, flushing; (de gêne, honte) blush, blushing.

rougeole [ruʒɔl] nf measles.

rougir [ruʒir] v go or turn red, redden; (visage) flush; (de gêne, honte) blush.

rouiller [ruje] v rust, go rusty. **rouille** nf rust. **rouillé** adj rusty.

rouleau [rulo] nm roller; (papier, pellicule, tabac, etc.) roll; (parchemin) scroll. **rouleau à pâtisserie** rolling pin. **rouleau compresseur** steam-roller. **rouleau de papier hygiénique** toilet roll.

rouler [rule] v roll; (enrouler) roll up; (pousser) wheel; (aller) go, run; (conduire) drive; (fam: duper) con, diddle. **roulant** adj moving; (meuble) on wheels; (argot) hilarious. **roulement** nm roll; movement; (bruit) rumble. **roulement à billes** ball bearings pl. **roulette** nf castor; (jeu) roulette.

roulotte [rulɔt] nf caravan.

Roumanie [rumani] nf Romania. **roumain** nm, adj Romanian. **Roumain, -e** nm, nf Romanian.

roupiller [rupije] (fam) v snooze. **roupillon** nm snooze.

rouquin [rukɛ̃], **-e** (fam) nm, nf redhead. adj red-haired.

rouspéter [ruspete] v (fam) moan, grumble.

roussir [rusir] v (brûler) scorch, singe; (feuilles) go brown. **rousseur** nf redness.

route [rut] nf road; (chemin) way; (ligne) route. **en route** on the way. **en route pour** bound for. **se mettre en route** set off. **routier** adj road.

routine [rutin] nf routine. **routinier** adj humdrum, routine.

***rouvrir** [ruvrir] v reopen.

roux, rousse [ru, rus] adj reddish-brown; (cheveux) red, auburn, ginger. nm, nf redhead.

royal [rwajal] adj royal; majestic, regal. **royaliste** n(m+f), adj royalist. **royauté** nf royalty; monarchy.

royaume [rwajom] nm kingdom, realm. **Royaume-Uni** nm United Kingdom.

ruban [rybɑ̃] nm ribbon; band, tape.

rubéole [rybeɔl] nf German measles.

rubis [rybi] nm ruby.

rubrique [rybrik] nf (article) column; (titre) heading.

ruche [ryʃ] *nf* hive.

rude [ryd] *adj* (*pénible*, *dur*) hard, harsh; (*surface*) rough; (*grossier*) crude. **rudement** *adv* harshly; roughly; (*fam*) terribly, awfully. **rudesse** *nf* harshness; roughness; crudeness.

rudiment [rydimɑ̃] *nm* rudiment. **rudimentaire** *adj* rudimentary.

rudoyer [rydwaje] *v* treat roughly.

rue [ry] *nf* street. **rue à sens unique** one-way street. **ruelle** *nf* alley.

ruer [rɥe] *v* kick out. **se ruer** dash, rush, hurl oneself. **se ruer sur** pounce on. **ruée** *nf* rush, stampede.

rugby [rygbi] *nm* rugby.

rugir [ryʒir] *v* roar. **rugissement** *nm* roar.

rugueux [rygø] *adj* rough. **rugosité** *nf* roughness.

ruine [rɥin] *nf* ruin. **ruiner** *v* ruin.

ruisseau [rɥiso] *nm* stream; (*caniveau*) gutter.

ruisseler [rɥisle] *v* stream.

rumeur [rymœr] *nf* (*nouvelle*) rumour; (*son*) murmur, hum, hubbub.

rupture [ryptyr] *nf* rupture, break. **rupture de contrat** breach of contract.

rural [ryral] *adj* rural, country.

ruse [ryz] *nf* (*procédé*) trick, ruse; (*art*) cunning, guile. **ruses de guerre** tactics *pl*. **rusé** *adj* sly, cunning.

Russie [rysi] *nf* Russia. **russe** *nm*, *adj* Russian. **Russe** *n*(*m+f*) Russian.

rustique [rystik] *adj* rustic.

rustre [rystrə] *nm* lout.

rutabaga [rytabaga] *nm* swede.

rythme [ritmə] *nm* rhythm; (*vitesse*) rate. **rythmé** *or* **rythmique** *adj* rhythmic.

S

s' [s] *V* **se**, **si¹**.

sa [sa] *V* **son¹**.

sabbat [saba] *nm* sabbath.

sable¹ [sablə] *nm* sand. **sables mouvants** quicksands *pl*. **sabler** *v* sand. **sableux** *or* **sablonneux** *adj* sandy. **sablier** *nm* hourglass.

sable² [sablə] *nm* sable.

sablé [sablə] *nm* shortbread.

saborder [saborde] *v* scuttle.

sabot [sabo] *nm* (*chaussure*) clog; (*animal*) hoof.

saboter [sabote] *v* sabotage. **sabotage** *nm* sabotage. **saboteur, -euse** *nm*, *nf* saboteur.

sabre [sabrə] *nm* sabre.

sac [sak] *nm* bag; (*à charbon*, *etc.*) sack. **sac à dos** rucksack. **sac à main** handbag. **sac à provisions** shopping bag. **sac de couchage** sleeping bag.

saccade [sakad] *nf* jerk. **par saccades** jerkily, in fits and starts. **saccadé** *adj* jerky.

saccager [sakaʒe] *v* wreck, devastate; (*piller*) ransack. **saccage** *nm* havoc.

saccharine [sakarin] *nf* saccharin.

sacerdoce [sasɛrdɔs] *nm* priesthood.

sachet [saʃɛ] *nm* sachet; (*bonbons*) bag. **sachet de thé** tea-bag.

sacoche [sakɔʃ] *nf* bag; (*cycliste*) saddlebag; (*écolier*) satchel.

sacquer [sake] (*fam*) *v* sack; (*recaler*) fail.

sacrement [sakrəmɑ̃] *nm* sacrament.

sacrer [sakre] *v* consecrate; (*roi*) crown; (*fam*) swear. **sacre** *nm* consecration; (*roi*) coronation. **sacré** *adj* sacred; (*fam*) blasted, damned.

sacrifier [sakrifje] *v* sacrifice. **sacrifice** *nm* sacrifice.

sacrilège [sakrilɛʒ] *nm* sacrilege. *adj* sacrilegious.

sacristie [sakristi] *nf* vestry.

sadique [sadik] *adj* sadistic. *n*(*m+f*) sadist. **sadisme** *nm* sadism.

safari [safari] *nm* safari.

safran [safrɑ̃] *nm* saffron.

saga [saga] *nf* saga.

sagace [sagas] *adj* shrewd. **sagacité** *nf* shrewdness.

sage [saʒ] *adj* wise, sensible; (*enfant*) good; moderate. **sage-femme** *nf* midwife. **sois sage!** be good! behave yourself! *nm* wise man, sage. **sagesse** *nf* wisdom; good behaviour; moderation.

Sagittaire [saʒitɛr] *nm* Sagittarius.

sagou [sagu] *nm* sago.

saigner [seɲe] *v* bleed. **saignant** *adj* bleeding; (*viande*) rare, underdone.

saillir [sajir] *v* jut out, protrude. **saillant** *adj* prominent, protruding; (*frappant*) outstanding. **saillie** *nf* projection; (*boutade*) witticism. **en saillie** overhanging.

sain [sɛ̃] *adj* healthy; (*d'esprit*) sane;

360

(*robuste*) sound. **sain et sauf** safe and
sound.

saindoux [sɛ̃du] *nm* lard.

saint [sɛ̃], **-e** *adj* holy; pious, saintly. *nm*,
nf saint. **Saint-Esprit** *nm* Holy Spirit.
Saint-Jean *nm* Midsummer Day. **saint
patron** patron saint. **Saint-Sylvestre** *nf*
New Year's Eve. **sainteté** *nf* holiness,
sanctity; saintliness.

saisir [sezir] *v* seize, take hold of; (*comprendre*) grasp; (*serrer*) grip. **saisie** *nf*
seizure; capture. **saisissant** *adj* (*spectacle*)
gripping; (*frappant*) striking; (*froid*) biting. **saisissement** *nm* (*frisson*) shiver;
rush of emotion.

saison [sɛzɔ̃] *nf* season. **hors de saison** out
of season; (*prix*) low-season. **saisonnier**
adj seasonal.

salade [salad] *nf* salad; (*laitue*) lettuce;
(*fam*) muddle.

salaire [salɛr] *nm* pay; (*à la semaine*)
wages *pl*; (*au mois*) salary; (*récompense*)
reward.

salami [salami] *nm* salami.

sale [sal] *adj* dirty; (*fam*) nasty, lousy.
saleté *nf* dirt; obscenity; (*sale tour*) dirty
trick; (*fam: camelote*) rubbish.

saler [sale] *v* salt; (*fam*) do, overcharge.
salé *adj* salty; salted; (*fam: grivois*)
spicy; (*fam: sévère*) stiff, steep. **salière** *nf*
salt-cellar.

salin [salɛ̃] *adj* saline. **salinité** *nf* salinity.

salir [salir] *v* dirty, soil; corrupt, sully. **se
salir** get dirty; tarnish one's reputation.

salive [saliv] *nf* saliva. **salivaire** *adj* salivary. **saliver** *v* salivate.

salle [sal] *nf* room; hall; auditorium;
(*hôpital*) ward. **salle à manger** dining
room. **salle d'attente** waiting room. **salle
de bain** bathroom. **salle de bal** ballroom.
salle de classe classroom. **salle de séjour**
living room. **salle des professeurs** staff-
room. **salle d'opération** operating theatre.

salope [salɔp] *nf* (*ouvrier*) overalls *pl*;
(*enfant, femme*) dungarees *pl*; (*ski*)
salopette.

saloperie [salɔpri] *nf* (*argot*) (*camelote*)
rubbish; (*ordure*) muck; (*sale tour*) dirty
trick.

salopette [salɔpɛt] *nf* (*ouvrier*) overalls *pl*;
(*enfant, femme*) dungarees *pl*; (*ski*)
salopette.

saltimbanque [saltɛ̃bɑ̃k] *n(m+f)* acrobat,
member of travelling circus.

salubre [salybrə] *adj* healthy.

saluer [salɥe] *v* greet; (*mil*) salute;
(*acteur*) bow; (*acclamer*) hail.

salut [saly] *nm* (*mil*) salute; (*salutation*)
greeting; (*révérence*) bow; (*sécurité*) safety; (*rel*) salvation. *interj* (*fam: bonjour*)
hi! (*fam: au revoir*) bye! **salutation** *nf*
greeting.

salutaire [salyter] *adj* salutary, beneficial;
profitable; (*sain*) healthy.

samedi [samdi] *nm* Saturday.

sanatorium [sanatɔrjɔm] *nm* sanatorium.

sanctifier [sɑ̃ktifje] *v* hallow, sanctify.
sanctification *nf* sanctification.

sanction [sɑ̃ksjɔ̃] *nf* sanction; (*peine*)
punishment, penalty. **sanctionner** *v* sanction; punish.

sanctuaire [sɑ̃ktɥɛr] *nm* sanctuary.

sandale [sɑ̃dal] *nf* sandal.

sandwich [sɑ̃dwitʃ] *nm* sandwich.

sang [sɑ̃] *nm* blood. **à sang chaud/froid**
warm-/cold-blooded. **sang-froid** *nm invar*
calmness, coolness. **sang-mêlé** *n(m+f)*
invar half-caste.

sanglant [sɑ̃glɑ̃] *adj* bloody; (*visage, habit, etc.*) covered in blood; cruel.

sangle [sɑ̃glə] *nf* strap; (*selle*) girth. **san-
gler** *v* strap up.

sanglier [sɑ̃glije] *nm* boar.

sanglot [sɑ̃glo] *nm* sob. **sangloter** *v* sob.

sangsue [sɑ̃sy] *nf* leech.

sanguin [sɑ̃gɛ̃] *adj* blood; (*visage*) ruddy;
(*tempérament*) fiery. **sanguinaire** *adj*
bloodthirsty.

sanitaire [saniter] *adj* sanitary.

sans [sɑ̃] *prep* without; but for. **sans-abri**
n(m+f) invar homeless person. **sans ça**
or else. **sans faute** without fail. **sans-gêne**
adj invar offhand. **sans quoi** otherwise.
sans-souci *adj invar* carefree.

sansonnet [sɑ̃sɔnɛ] *nm* starling.

santé [sɑ̃te] *nf* health. **à votre santé!**
cheers!

saper [sape] *v* undermine, sap.

sapeur [sapœr] *nm* (*mil*) sapper. **sapeur-
pompier** *nm* fireman.

saphir [safir] *nm* sapphire.

sapin [sapɛ̃] *nm* fir.

sarcasme [sarkasmə] *nm* sarcasm. **sarcastique** *adj* sarcastic.

sarcler [sarkle] *v* weed. **sarclage** *nm* weeding.

Sardaigne [sardɛɲ] *nf* Sardinia. **sarde** *nm*,
adj Sardinian. **Sarde** *n(m+f)* Sardinian.

sardine [sardin] *nf* sardine.

sardonique [sardɔnik] *adj* sardonic.

Satan [satã] *nm* Satan. **satanique** *adj* satanic.

satellite [satelit] *nm* satellite.

satin [satẽ] *nm* satin.

satire [satir] *nf* satire. **faire la satire de** satirize. **satirique** *adj* satirical.

satisfaction [satisfaksjɔ̃] *nf* satisfaction.

*satisfaire [satisfɛr] *v* satisfy. **satisfaire à** satisfy; (*condition*) fulfil. **satisfaisant** *adj* satisfactory. **satisfait** *adj* satisfied.

saturer [satyre] *v* saturate. **saturation** *nf* saturation.

sauce [sos] *nf* sauce; (*jus de viande*) gravy.

saucée [sose] *nf* (*fam*) downpour.

saucisse [sosis] *nf* sausage. **saucisson** *nm* large sausage.

sauf [sof] *adj* unharmed; intact. *prep* except, but; (*à moins de*) unless.

sauge [soʒ] *nf* sage.

saugrenu [sogrəny] *adj* ludicrous.

saule [sol] *nm* willow.

saumon [somɔ̃] *nm* salmon.

saumure [somyr] *nf* brine.

sauna [sona] *nm* sauna.

saupoudrer [sopudre] *v* sprinkle. **saupoudreuse** *nf* dredger.

saut [so] *nm* jump, leap. **saut à la corde** skipping. **saut-de-lit** *nm invar* housecoat. **saut-de-mouton** *nm* flyover. **saut en hauteur/longueur** high/long jump. **saut périlleux** somersault.

sauter [sote] *v* jump, leap; explode; (*fusible*) blow; (*omettre*) skip. **faire sauter** (*mine, etc.*) blow up; (*crêpe*) toss. **saute-mouton** *nm* leapfrog. **saute** *nf* sudden change. **sauté** *adj* sauté. **sauterelle** *nf* grasshopper. **sauterie** *nf* party.

sautiller [sotije] *v* hop; (*enfant*) skip.

sauvage [sovaʒ] *adj* wild; (*brutal, primitif*) savage; unsociable. *n(m+f)* savage; recluse. **sauvagerie** *nf* savagery.

sauvegarder [sovgarde] *v* safeguard. **sauvegarde** *nf* safeguard.

sauver [sove] *v* save, rescue; (*récupérer*) salvage. **sauve-qui-peut** *nm invar* stampede. **se sauver** run away. **sauvetage** *nm* rescue; (*technique*) life-saving; salvage. **sauveur** *nm* saviour.

savant [savã] *adj* learned, scholarly; (*habile*) skilful; (*chien*) performing. *nm* scholar; scientist.

savate [savat] *nf* (*fam*) old shoe *or* slipper; (*maladroit*) clumsy oaf.

saveur [savœr] *nf* (*goût*) flavour; (*piment*) savour.

*savoir [savwar] *v* know; (*être capable de*) know how to. **à savoir** namely, that is. **faire savoir à** inform. **sans le savoir** unknowingly. *nm* learning, knowledge.

savon [savɔ̃] *nm* soap. **savonner** *v* soap, lather. **savonneux** *adj* soapy.

savourer [savure] *v* savour. **savoureux** *adj* tasty; (*histoire*) spicy.

saxophone [saksɔfɔn] *nm* saxophone.

scabreux [skabrø] *adj* indecent, shocking; risky.

scandale [skãdal] *nm* scandal; scene, fuss. **scandaleux** *adj* scandalous. **scandaliser** *v* scandalize, shock.

Scandinavie [skãdinavi] *nf* Scandinavia. **scandinave** *adj* Scandinavian. **Scandinave** *n(m+f)* Scandinavian.

scaphandrier [skafãdrije] *nm* diver.

scarlatine [skarlatin] *nf* scarlet fever.

sceau [so] *nm* seal; (*marque*) stamp.

scélérat [selera], **-e** *nm, nf* villain. *adj* wicked.

sceller [sele] *v* seal.

scénario [senarjo] *nm* scenario; (*dialogue, etc.*) screenplay.

scène [sɛn] *nf* scene; (*estrade, profession*) stage. **mettre en scène** present; (*pièce*) stage; (*film*) direct. **scénique** *adj* theatrical.

sceptique [sɛptik] *adj* sceptical. *n(m+f)* sceptic. **scepticisme** *nm* scepticism.

sceptre [sɛptrə] *nm* sceptre.

schéma [ʃema] *nm* diagram; (*résumé*) outline.

schizophrénie [skizɔfreni] *nf* schizophrenia. **schizophrène** *n(m+f)*, *adj* schizophrenic.

sciatique [sjatik] *nf* sciatica. *adj* sciatic.

scie [si] *nf* saw; (*péj: personne*) bore. **scie à découper** fretsaw. **scie à métaux** hacksaw.

sciemment [sjamã] *adv* knowingly.

science [sjãs] *nf* science; (*savoir*) knowledge. **science-fiction** *nf* science fiction. **scientifique** [sjãtifik] *adj* scientific. *n(m+f)* scientist.

scintiller [sẽtije] *v* sparkle, glitter; (*esprit*) scintillate.

scolaire [skɔlɛr] *adj* school, scholastic. **scolarité** *nf* schooling.

scooter [skutœr] *nm* scooter.

scorpion [skɔrpjɔ̃] *nm* scorpion. **Scorpion** *nm* Scorpio.

scotch¹ [skɔtʃ] *nm* (*boisson*) Scotch.

scotch² ® [skɔtʃ] *nm* sellotape ®.

scrupule [skrypyl] *nm* scruple. **sans scrupules** *adj* unscrupulous. **scrupuleux** *adj* scrupulous.

scruter [skryte] *v* scrutinize, examine.

scrutin [skrytɛ̃] *nm* (*vote*) ballot; (*élection*) poll.

sculpter [skylte] *v* sculpt. **sculpteur** *nm* sculptor. **sculpture** *nf* sculpture.

se [sə], **s'** *pron* (*réfléchi*) oneself; (*homme*) himself; (*femme*) herself; (*chose, animal*) itself; (*au pluriel*) themselves; (*réciproque*) each other.

séance [seɑ̃s] *nf* session; (*réunion*) meeting; (*théâtre*) performance.

séant [seɑ̃] *nm* (*fam*) behind, posterior. *adj* seemly.

seau [so] *nm* bucket.

sec, sèche [sɛk, sɛʃ] *adj* dry; (*raisin, etc.*) dried; (*maigre*) lean; (*dur*) hard, cold; (*bref*) curt; (*alcool*) neat. **nm à sec** dried-up; (*fam*) broke. **au sec** in a dry place. **au secours!** *(argot)* fag. *adv* hard. **sécheresse** *nf* dryness; hardness; coldness; curtness.

sécher [seʃe] *v* dry. **sèche-cheveux** *nm invar* hair-drier. **séchoir** *nm* drier. **séchoir à linge** clothes-horse.

second [səgɔ̃] *adj* second. *nm* second; (*étage*) second floor. *nm* second; (*transport*) second class. **secondaire** *adj* secondary.

secouer [səkwe] *v* shake.

*secourir [səkurir] *v* help.

secours [səkur] *nm* help, aid; (*mil*) relief. **au secours!** help! **de secours** (*de rechange*) spare; (*d'urgence*) emergency.

secousse [səkus] *nf* jolt, bump; shock; (*saccade*) jerk. **par secousses** jerkily.

secret, -ète [səkrɛ, -ɛt] *adj* secret; (*caché*) hidden. *nm* secret; (*silence, discrétion*) secrecy. **en secret** secretly, in secret.

secrétaire [səkretɛr] *n(m+f)* secretary. *nm* (*meuble*) writing desk.

sécréter [sekrete] *v* secrete. **sécrétion** *nf* secretion.

secte [sɛkt] *nf* sect. **sectaire** *adj* sectarian.

secteur [sɛktœr] *nm* sector; (*zone*) area; (*élec*) mains (supply).

section [sɛksjɔ̃] *nf* section; (*autobus*) fare stage.

séculaire [sekylɛr] *adj* a hundred years old; (*très vieux*) age-old; (*jeux, fête, etc.*) occurring once a century.

séculier [sekylje] *adj* secular.

sécurité [sekyrite] *nf* security; (*sûreté*) safety.

sédatif [sedatif] *nm, adj* sedative. **sédation** *nf* sedation.

sédiment [sedimɑ̃] *nm* sediment.

*séduire [sedɥir] *v* seduce; (*attirer*) charm; (*plaire*) appeal to. **séduction** *nf* seduction; charm; appeal. **séduisant** *adj* seductive; appealing, attractive.

segment [sɛgmɑ̃] *nm* segment.

ségrégation [segregasjɔ̃] *nf* segregation.

seigle [sɛglə] *nm* rye.

seigneur [sɛɲœr] *nm* lord.

sein [sɛ̃] *nm* breast; (*milieu*) bosom.

séisme [seismə] *nm* earthquake; (*bouleversement*) upheaval.

seize [sɛz] *nm, adj* sixteen. **seizième** *n(m+f), adj* sixteenth.

séjour [seʒur] *nm* stay; (*demeure*) abode. **séjourner** *v* stay.

sel [sɛl] *nm* salt; (*esprit*) wit; (*piquant*) spice. **sel de cuisine/table** cooking/table salt.

sélection [selɛksjɔ̃] *nf* selection. **sélectif** *adj* selective.

sélectionner [selɛksjone] *v* select.

selle [sɛl] *nf* saddle. **seller** *v* saddle. **sellerie** *nf* saddlery; (*lieu*) harness room. **sellier** *nm* saddler.

selon [səlɔ̃] *prep* according to.

Seltz [sɛls] *nf* **eau de Seltz** soda water.

semaine [səmɛn] *nf* week.

sémantique [semɑ̃tik] *adj* semantic. *nf* semantics.

sémaphore [semafɔr] *nm* semaphore.

sembler [sɑ̃ble] *v* seem. **semblable** *adj* similar; (*tel*) such. **semblable à** like. **semblant** *nm* semblance. **faire semblant de** pretend.

semelle [səmɛl] *nf* sole. **semelle intérieure** insole. **semelles compensées** platform soles *pl*.

semence [səmɑ̃s] *nf* seed.

semer [səme] *v* sow; (*en dispersant*) scatter; (*parsemer*) sprinkle, dot.

semestre [səmɛstrə] *nm* half-year. **semestriel** *adj* half-yearly.

séminaire [seminɛr] *nm* (*université*) seminar; (*rel*) seminary.

semi-précieux *adj* semi-precious.

semoule [səmul] *nf* semolina.

sempiternel [sɛpitɛrnɛl] *adj* never-ending.

sénat [sena] *nm* senate. **sénateur** *nm* senator.

sénile [senil] *adj* senile. **sénilité** *nf* senility.

sens [sɑ̃s] *nm* sense; direction; (*signification*) meaning. **à sens unique** (*rue*) one-way. **bon sens** common sense. **dans le sens des aiguilles d'une montre** clockwise. **sens dessus dessous** upside down. **sens devant derrière** back to front. **sens interdit** no entry.

sensation [sɑ̃sasjɔ̃] *nf* sensation; (*impression*) feeling. **sensationnel** *adj* sensational; (*fam*) fantastic, terrific.

sensé [sɑ̃se] *adj* sensible.

sensible [sɑ̃sibl] *adj* sensitive; perceptible, noticeable; (*cœur*) tender; (*impressionnable*) susceptible. **sensibilité** *nf* sensitivity.

sensuel [sɑ̃sɥɛl] *adj* (*charnel*) sensual; (*esthétique*) sensuous. **sensualité** *nf* sensuality; sensuousness.

sentence [sɑ̃tɑ̃s] *nf* (*jur*) sentence; maxim.

sentier [sɑ̃tje] *nm* path.

sentiment [sɑ̃timɑ̃] *nm* feeling; (*péj*) sentiment. **sentimental** *adj* sentimental.

sentinelle [sɑ̃tinɛl] *nf* sentry.

*****sentir** [sɑ̃tir] *v* feel; (*odeur*) smell; (*goût*) taste; (*pressentir*) sense; (*être conscient de*) be aware of.

*****seoir** [swar] *v* be fitting. **seoir à** become.

séparer [separe] *v* separate; (*diviser*) part, split. **séparation** *nf* separation; parting; division. **séparé** *adj* separated; (*éloigné*) apart.

sept [sɛt] *nm, adj* seven. **septième** *n(m+f), adj* seventh.

septembre [sɛptɑ̃brə] *nm* September.

septentrional [sɛptɑ̃trijɔnal] *adj* northern.

septique [sɛptik] *adj* septic.

séquence [sekɑ̃s] *nf* sequence.

serein [sərɛ̃] *adj* serene, calm.

sérénade [serenad] *nf* serenade.

serf [sɛrf] serve *nm, nf* serf.

sergent [sɛrʒɑ̃] *nm* sergeant.

série [seri] *nf* series; (*ensemble*) set. **de série** standard. **fait en série** mass-produced. **hors série** (*machine*) custom-built; (*qualité*) outstanding.

sérieux [serjø] *adj* serious; (*sage*) responsible; (*sûr*) reliable; (*grand*) considerable. *nm* seriousness. **prendre au sérieux** take seriously.

serin [sərɛ̃] *nm* canary.

seringue [sərɛ̃g] *nf* syringe.

serment [sɛrmɑ̃] *nm* oath.

sermon [sɛrmɔ̃] *nm* sermon.

serpent [sɛrpɑ̃] *nm* snake, serpent. **serpent à sonnettes** rattlesnake.

serpenter [sɛrpɑ̃te] *v* snake, wind.

serre [sɛr] *nf* greenhouse; (*contiguë à une maison*) conservatory; (*griffe*) talon. **serre chaude** hothouse.

serrer [sere] *v* grip; (*dents, poings*) clench; (*vêtement*) be tight; (*nœud, écrou*) tighten; (*rester près de*) keep close to; (*rapprocher*) close up. **serrer la main à** shake hands with. **se serrer** squeeze up, crowd together. **serré** *adj* tight; (*personnes*) packed, crowded; dense.

serrure [seryr] *nf* lock. **serrurier** *nm* locksmith.

servante [sɛrvɑ̃t] *nf* servant, maid.

serveur [sɛrvœr] *nm* (*restaurant*) waiter; (*bar*) barman. **serveuse** *nf* waitress; barmaid.

service [sɛrvis] *nm* service; (*travail*) duty; department; (*ensemble*) set. **être de service** be on duty. **service à thé** tea-set.

serviette [sɛrvjɛt] *nf* (*de toilette*) towel; (*de table*) serviette; (*cartable*) briefcase. **serviette hygiénique** sanitary towel.

servile [sɛrvil] *adj* servile. **servilité** *nf* servility.

*****servir** [sɛrvir] *v* serve; (*dîneur, patron*) wait on; (*client*) attend to; aid. **servir à** be used for; (*être utile*) be useful for. **servir de** act as. **se servir** help oneself. **se servir de** use.

serviteur [sɛrvitœr] *nm* servant.

ses [se] *V* **son**[1].

session [sesjɔ̃] *nf* session.

seuil [sœj] *nm* threshold; (*porte*) doorway; (*dalle*) doorstep.

seul [sœl] *adj* only; (*sans compagnie*) alone; (*isolé*) lonely; (*unique*) single, sole. *adv* by oneself. **seulement** *adv* only.

sève [sɛv] *nf* sap.

sévère [sever] *adj* severe. **sévérité** *nf* severity.

sévir [sevir] *v* act ruthlessly; punish severely; (*régime, fléau*) rage.

sexe [sɛks] *nm* sex. **sexualité** *nf* sexuality.

sexuel *adj* sexual, sex.

sextuor [sɛkstɥɔr] *nm* sextet.

shampooing [ʃɑ̃pwɛ̃] *nm* shampoo.

shérif [ʃerif] *nm* sheriff.

short [ʃɔrt] *nm* shorts *pl*.

si[1] [si], **s'** *conj* if.

si² [si] *adv* so; *(aussi)* as; *(oui)* yes. **si bien que** so that. **si ... que** however.

siamois [sjamwa] *adj* Siamese.

sidérer [sidere] *v (fam)* stagger, shatter.

siècle [sjɛkl] *nm* century; *(époque)* age.

siège [sjɛʒ] *nm* seat; *(organisation)* head-quarters; *(épiscopal)* see; *(mil)* siege. **siège éjectable** ejector seat.

siéger [sjeʒe] *v* be located; *(tenir séance)* sit.

sien, sienne [sjɛ̃, sjɛn] *pron* **le sien, la sienne** *(homme)* his; *(femme)* hers; *(chose, animal)* its own; *(réfléchi)* one's own.

sieste [sjɛst] *nf* siesta; *(petit somme)* nap.

siffler [sifle] *v* whistle; *(serpent, gaz)* hiss. **sifflement** *nm* whistle, hiss. **sifflet** *nm* whistle.

signal [siɲal] *nm* signal.

signaler [siɲale] *v* indicate; *(faire un signe)* signal; *(faire un exposé)* report. **se signaler** stand out, distinguish oneself. **signalement** *nm* description.

signature [siɲatyr] *nf* signature; *(action)* signing.

signe [siɲ] *nm* sign; mark. **faire signe à** beckon. **signet** *nm* bookmark.

signer [siɲe] *v* sign.

signifier [siɲifje] *v* mean, signify. **significatif** *adj* significant. **signification** *nf* significance, meaning.

silence [silɑ̃s] *nm* silence; pause; *(musique)* rest.

silencieux [silɑ̃sjø] *adj* silent. *nm* silencer.

silex [silɛks] *nm* flint.

silhouette [silwɛt] *nf* silhouette, outline; figure.

sillage [sijaʒ] *nm* wake.

sillon [sijɔ̃] *nm* furrow; *(disque)* groove. **sillonner** *v* furrow; *(traverser)* cross.

simagrée [simagre] *nf* pretence. **simagrées** *nf pl* fuss *sing*, play-acting *sing*.

simple [sɛ̃pl] *adj* simple; *(billet)* single. **simplement** *adv* simply; *(seulement)* merely, just. **simplicité** *nf* simplicity. **simplifier** *v* simplify.

simulacre [simylakr] *nm* pretence, show.

simuler [simyle] *v* simulate; feign. **simulation** *nf* simulation. **simulé** *adj* simulated; feigned, sham.

simultané [simyltane] *adj* simultaneous.

sincère [sɛ̃sɛr] *adj* sincere; *(authentique)* genuine, true. **sincérité** *nf* sincerity.

singe [sɛ̃ʒ] *nm* monkey, ape.

singer [sɛ̃ʒe] *v* mimic, ape. **singeries** *nf pl* antics *pl*, clowning *sing*.

singulier [sɛ̃gylje] *adj (gramm)* singular; remarkable; uncommon. *nm* singular. **singularité** *nf* peculiarity. **singulièrement** *adv* remarkably; strangely; particularly.

sinistre [sinistr] *adj* sinister. *nm* disaster; *(assurances)* damage, loss.

sinon [sinɔ̃] *conj* if not; *(autrement)* otherwise; *(sauf)* except, other than.

sinueux [sinɥø] *adj* winding; *(ligne)* sinuous.

sinus [sinys] *nm invar (anat)* sinus. **sinusite** *nf* sinusitis.

siphon [sifɔ̃] *nm* siphon. **siphonner** *v* siphon.

sirène [sirɛn] *nf* siren; *(mythologie)* mermaid.

sirop [siro] *nm* syrup; *(boisson)* squash, cordial. **sirupeux** *adj* syrupy.

siroter [sirɔte] *v* sip.

site [sit] *nm* site; *(environnement)* setting; *(tourisme)* beauty spot, place of interest.

sitôt [sito] *adv* immediately, no sooner. **sitôt que** as soon as.

situer [sitɥe] *v* situate, locate; *(par la pensée)* place. **situation** *nf* situation; position; *(emploi)* job.

six [sis] *nm, adj* six. **sixième** *n(m+f), adj* sixth.

ski [ski] *nm* ski; *(sport)* skiing. **faire du ski** ski, go skiing. **ski nautique** water-skiing. **skieur, -euse** *nm, nf* skier.

slalom [slalom] *nm* slalom.

slip [slip] *nm* briefs *pl*, pants *pl*. **slip de bain** *(homme)* trunks *pl*.

slogan [slɔgɑ̃] *nm* slogan.

smoking [smɔkiŋ] *nm* dinner jacket.

snob [snɔb] *n(m+f)* snob. *adj* snobbish.

sobre [sɔbr] *adj* temperate, abstemious; *(repas)* frugal; *(style)* sober. **sobriété** *nf* temperance; frugality; *(modération)* restraint; sobriety.

sobriquet [sɔbrikɛ] *nm* nickname.

sociable [sɔsjabl] *adj* sociable.

social [sɔsjal] *adj* social. **socialisme** *nm* socialism. **socialiste** *n(m+f), adj* socialist.

société [sɔsjete] *nf* society; club; company. **société anonyme** limited company. **sociétaire** *n(m+f)* member.

sociologie [sɔsjɔlɔʒi] *nf* sociology. **sociologique** *adj* sociological. **sociologue** *n(m+f)* sociologist.

socle [sɔkl] *nm* base; pedestal.

sonore

socquette [sɔkɛt] *nf* ankle sock.

sœur [sœr] *nf* sister; *(rel)* nun.

sofa [sɔfa] *nm* sofa.

soi [swa] *pron* one, oneself. **aller de soi** be obvious, stand to reason. **soi-même** *pron* oneself.

soi-disant *adj invar* so-called. *adv* supposedly.

soie [swa] *nf* silk; *(poil)* bristle.

soif [swaf] *nf* thirst. **avoir soif** be thirsty.

soigner [swaɲe] *v* look after, take care of; *(malade)* treat. **soigné** *adj* neat, tidy; *(consciencieux)* carefully done. **soigneux** *adj* careful; *(soigné)* neat, tidy.

soin [swɛ̃] *nm* care.

soir [swar] *nm* evening. **ce soir** this evening, tonight. **soirée** *nf* evening; party; *(théâtre)* evening performance.

soit [swa] *adv* very well, so be it. *conj* whether; *(à savoir)* that is to say. **soit que** whether. **soit ... soit ...** either ... or

soixante [swasãt] *nm, adj* sixty. **soixantième** *n(m+f)*, *adj* sixtieth.

soixante-dix *nm, adj* seventy. **soixante-dixième** *n(m+f)*, *adj* seventieth.

soja [sɔʒa] *nm* soya.

sol [sɔl] *nm* ground; *(plancher)* floor; *(territoire)* soil.

solaire [sɔlɛr] *adj* solar; *(crème, etc.)* suntan.

soldat [sɔlda] *nm* soldier.

solde [sɔld] *nf* pay.

solde [sɔld] *nm (compte)* balance; *(vente)* sale; *(marchandises)* sale goods *pl*.

sole [sɔl] *nf* sole.

soleil [sɔlɛj] *nm* sun; *(lumière)* sunshine. **il fait du soleil** it's sunny.

solennel [sɔlanɛl] *adj* solemn; ceremonial. **solennité** *nf* solemnity; grand occasion.

solide [sɔlid] *adj* solid; *(sérieux, durable)* sound; robust, sturdy. *nm* solid. **solidarité** *nf* solidarity. **solidement** *adv* solidly; firmly. **solidifier** *v* solidify.

soliste [sɔlist] *n(m+f)* soloist.

solitaire [sɔlitɛr] *adj* solitary; deserted; *(seul, sans compagnie)* lonely. *n(m+f)* recluse. **solitairement** *adv* alone.

solitude [sɔlityd] *nf* solitude; loneliness.

solive [sɔliv] *nf* joist.

solliciter [sɔlisite] *v* appeal to; *(demander)* seek, request.

solo [sɔlo] *nm, adj invar* solo.

soluble [sɔlybla] *adj* soluble.

solution [sɔlysjɔ̃] *nf* solution.

solvable [sɔlvabla] *adj* solvent. **solvabilité** *nf* solvency.

sombre [sɔ̃bra] *adj* dark; *(morne)* sombre, gloomy.

sombrer [sɔ̃bre] *v* sink, founder.

sommaire [sɔmɛr] *adj* brief, basic. *nm* summary.

sommation [sɔmasjɔ̃] *nf (jur)* summons; demand.

somme [sɔm] *nf* **bête de somme** *nf* beast of burden.

somme [sɔm] *nm* nap, snooze. **faire un petit somme** have a nap.

somme [sɔm] *nf* sum, amount. **en somme** all in all; *(en résumé)* in short. **faire la somme de** add up. **somme toute** when all is said and done.

sommeil [sɔmɛj] *nm* sleep; *(envie de dormir)* sleepiness. **avoir sommeil** feel sleepy.

sommeiller [sɔmeje] *v* doze.

sommelier [sɔmalje] *nm* wine waiter.

sommer [sɔme] *v (jur)* summon.

sommet [sɔmɛ] *nm* summit, top.

somnambule [sɔmnãbyl] *n(m+f)* sleepwalker. **somnambulisme** *nm* sleep-walking.

somnifère [sɔmnifɛr] *nm* sleeping-pill.

somnoler [sɔmnɔle] *v* doze. **somnolent** *adj* sleepy, drowsy.

son [sɔ̃], **sa** *adj*, *pl* **ses** *(homme)* his, *(femme)* her; *(chose, animal)* its; *(indéfini)* one's.

son [sɔ̃] *nm (bruit)* sound.

son [sɔ̃] *nm* bran.

sonate [sɔnat] *nf* sonata.

sonder [sɔ̃de] *v (fouiller)* probe; *(naut)* sound; *(personne)* sound out; *(tech)* bore, drill. **sondage** *nm* probe; sounding; drilling; *(d'opinion)* poll. **sonde** *nf* probe; drill.

songer [sɔ̃ʒe] *v (rêver)* dream; reflect. **songer à** consider, think of. **songe** *nm* dream.

songeur, -euse [sɔ̃ʒœr, -øz] *adj* pensive. *nm, nf* dreamer.

sonique [sɔnik] *adj* sonic.

sonner [sɔne] *v (cloche, etc.)* ring; *(trompette, etc.)* sound; *(heure)* strike. **sonnerie** *nf* ringing; *(sonnette)* bell; *(pendule)* chimes *pl*. **sonnette** *nf* bell.

sonnet [sɔnɛ] *nm* sonnet.

sonore [sɔnɔr] *adj* resonant; *(rire, gifle, etc.)* resounding; *(film, onde, effet)* sound.

soprano [sɔprano] *n(m+f)* soprano.

sorcier [sɔrsje] *nm* sorcerer, wizard. **sorcière** *nf* witch. **sorcellerie** *nf* witchcraft, sorcery.

sordide [sɔrdid] *adj* sordid.

sort [sɔr] *nm* fate; (*condition*) lot; (*charme*) spell. **tirer au sort** draw lots.

sorte [sɔrt] *nf* sort, kind. **de la sorte** in that way. **de sorte que** so that. **en quelque sorte** in a way.

*****sortir** [sɔrtir] *v* go out; come out; (*quitter, partir*) leave; (*retirer*) take *or* bring out; (*film, disque*) release. **sortie** *nf* (*endroit, porte*) way out, exit; (*promenade*) outing; (*emportement*) outburst; publication; release. **sortie de secours** emergency exit.

sot, sotte [so, sɔt] *adj* silly, foolish. *nm, nf* fool. **sottise** *nf* silliness; silly thing.

sou [su] *nm* penny. **sans le sou** penniless.

soubresaut [subrəso] *nm* jolt, start.

souche [suʃ] *nf* (*arbre*) stump; (*talon*) stub; (*famille*) founder.

souci¹ [susi] *nm* (*bot*) marigold.

souci² [susi] *nm* (*tracas*) worry; (*préoccupation*) concern.

se soucier [susje] *v* **se soucier de** care about. **soucieux** *adj* concerned.

soucoupe [sukup] *nf* saucer.

soudain [sudɛ̃] *adj* sudden. *adv* suddenly.

soude [sud] *nf* soda.

souder [sude] *v* (*autogène*) weld; (*avec fil à souder*) solder; unite. **se souder** (*os*) knit together. **soudeur** *nm* welder; solderer. **soudure** *nf* welding; soldering; (*substance*) solder; (*endroit*) weld.

soudoyer [sudwaje] *v* bribe.

souffler [sufle] *v* blow; (*bougie*) blow out; (*se reposer*) get one's breath back; (*haleter*) puff, pant; (*dire*) whisper; (*théâtre*) prompt; (*fam: voler*) pinch; (*fam: étonner*) stagger. **souffle** *nm* blow, puff; (*respiration*) breathing; (*haleine*) breath; inspiration. **être à bout de souffle** be out of breath.

soufflet¹ [suflɛ] *nm* bellows *pl*; (*couture*) gusset.

soufflet² [suflɛ] *nm* (*gifle*) slap (in the face). **souffleter** *v* slap (in the face).

*****souffrir** [sufrir] *v* suffer; (*avoir mal*) be in pain; (*supporter*) endure, bear; (*permettre*) allow. **souffrance** *nf* suffering. **en souffrance** pending. **souffrant** *adj* suffering; (*malade*) unwell.

soufre [sufrə] *nm* sulphur.

souhait [swɛ] *nm* wish. **à souhait** to perfection, as well as one could wish. **souhaiter** *v* wish; (*espérer*) hope.

souiller [suje] *v* soil, dirty; (*réputation*) tarnish; (*profaner*) defile. **souillon** *nm* slut. **souillure** *nf* stain.

soûl [su] *adj* drunk. **tout son soûl** to one's heart's content. **soûlard, -e** *nm, nf* (*argot*) drunkard. **soûler** *v* intoxicate. **se soûler** get drunk.

soulager [sulaʒe] *v* relieve; (*conscience*) ease. **soulagement** *nm* relief.

soulever [sulve] *v* raise; (*lever*) lift; (*provoquer*) arouse, stir up. **soulèvement** *nm* uprising.

soulier [sulje] *nm* shoe.

souligner [suliɲe] *v* underline; accentuate, emphasize.

*****soumettre** [sumɛtrə] *v* (*dompter*) subject; (*présenter*) submit. **se soumettre** submit. **soumis** *adj* submissive. **soumission** *nf* submission; (*comm*) tender.

soupape [supap] *nf* valve.

soupçon [supsɔ̃] *nm* suspicion; (*ombre*) touch, hint; (*goutte*) drop. **soupçonner** *v* suspect. **soupçonneux** *adj* suspicious.

soupe [sup] *nf* soup.

soupente [supɑ̃t] *nf* cupboard (under the stairs).

souper [supe] *nm* supper. *v* have supper.

soupir [supir] *nm* sigh. **soupirer** *v* sigh.

soupirail [supiraj] *nm, pl* **-aux** basement window.

souple [suplə] *adj* supple; flexible; (*gracieux*) lithe. **souplesse** *nf* suppleness; flexibility; litheness.

source [surs] *nf* source; (*point d'eau*) spring.

sourcil [sursi] *nm* eyebrow.

sourd, -e *adj* deaf; (*son, couleur*) muted; (*douleur*) dull; (*caché*) hidden. *nm, nf* deaf person.

sourd-muet, sourde-muette *adj* deaf and dumb. *nm, nf* deaf mute.

sourdine [surdin] *nf* mute.

souricière [surisjɛr] *nf* mousetrap.

*****sourire** [surir] *nm* smile. *v* smile.

souris [suri] *nf* mouse.

sournois [surnwa] *adj* underhand, deceitful; (*air*) shifty.

sous [su] *prep* under; (*temps*) within; (*pluie, soleil, etc.*) in.

sous-alimentation *nf* malnutrition.

*souscrire [suskrir] v subscribe; sign.
souscripteur, -trice nm, nf subscriber.
souscription nf subscription.

sous-développé adj underdeveloped.

sous-entendre v imply, infer.
sous-entendu adj understood. nm innuendo.

sous-estimer v underestimate, underrate.
sous-estimation nf underestimation.

sous-jacent adj underlying.

sous-louer v sublet.

sous-marin adj underwater. nm submarine.

sous-payé adj underpaid.

sous-sol nm (maison) basement; (terre) subsoil.

sous-titre nm subtitle. sous-titrer v subtitle.

*soustraire [sustrɛr] v take away; (math) subtract; (cacher) shield. se soustraire à shirk, escape. soustraction nf subtraction.

sous-traiter v subcontract. sous-traitant nm subcontractor.

sous-vêtements nm pl underwear sing.

soutane [sutan] nf cassock.

*soutenir [sutnir] v support; (faire durer) sustain, keep up; (résister à) withstand; (affirmer) uphold. soutenu adj sustained; elevated.

souterrain [sutɛrɛ̃] adj underground. nm underground passage.

soutien [sutjɛ̃] nm support. soutien de famille breadwinner. soutien-gorge nm bra.

*souvenir [suvnir] nm memory; (souvenance) recollection; (objet) memento; (pour touristes) souvenir. v se souvenir (de) remember.

souvent [suvɑ̃] adv often. peu souvent seldom.

souverain [suvrɛ̃], -e adj supreme, sovereign. nm, nf sovereign.

soyeux [swajø] adj silky.

spacieux [spasjø] adj spacious.

spaghetti [spageti] nm pl spaghetti.

sparadrap [sparadra] nm sticking plaster.

spasme [spasmə] nm spasm. spasmodique adj spasmodic.

spatial [spasjal] adj spatial; (voyage, engin, etc.) space.

spatule [spatyl] nf spatula.

speaker, speakerine [spikœr, spikrin] nm, nf announcer.

spécial [spesjal] adj special; (bizarre)

peculiar. spécialement adv particularly, especially; (exprès) specially. se spécialiser v specialize. spécialiste nm(+f) specialist. spécialité nf speciality.

spécieux [spesjø] adj specious.

spécifier [spesifje] v specify, state. spécification nf specification. spécifique adj specific.

spécimen [spesimɛn] nm specimen; (exemplaire) sample copy.

spectacle [spɛktaklə] nm sight, spectacle; (représentation) show. spectaculaire adj spectacular.

spectateur, -trice [spɛktatœr, -tris] nm, nf onlooker; (sport) spectator. spectateurs nm pl (théâtre) audience sing.

spectre [spɛktrə] nm (fantôme) spectre; (phys) spectrum.

spéculer [spekyle] v speculate. spéculatif adj speculative. spéculation nf speculation.

spéléologie [speleɔlɔʒi] nf pot-holing. spéléologue n(m+f) pot-holer.

sperme [spɛrm] nm sperm.

sphère [sfɛr] nf sphere. sphérique adj spherical.

spinal [spinal] adj spinal.

spiral [spiral] adj spiral. spirale nf spiral.

spirite [spirit] n(m+f) spiritualist. spiritisme nm spiritualism.

spirituel [spirituɛl] adj spiritual; (fin) witty.

spiritueux [spirituø] nm (liqueur) spirit.

splendeur [splɑ̃dœr] nf splendour; glory. splendide adj splendid, magnificent.

spongieux [spɔ̃ʒjø] adj spongy.

spontané [spɔ̃tane] adj spontaneous. spontanéité nf spontaneity.

sporadique [spɔradik] adj sporadic.

sport [spɔr] nm sport. de sport sports.

sportif [spɔrtif] adj sports; competitive; (personne) athletic; (attitude) sporting. nm sportsman. sportive nf sportswoman.

square [skwar] nm square with public garden.

squelette [skəlɛt] nm skeleton. squelettique adj skeletal; (très maigre) scrawny; (exposé) sketchy.

stabiliser [stabilize] v stabilize. stabilisateur nm stabilizer.

stable [stablə] adj stable. stabilité nf stability.

stade [stad] nm (étape) stage; (sport) stadium.

stage [staʒ] *nm* training period; training course. **stagiaire** *n(m+f)*, *adj* trainee, student.

stagnant [stagnɑ̃] *adj* stagnant. **stagnation** *nf* stagnation. **stagner** *v* stagnate.

stalle [stal] *nf* stall.

standard [stɑ̃dar] *nm* switchboard. *adj* standard. **standardiser** *v* standardize. **standardiste** *n(m+f)* switchboard operator.

starter [startɛr] *nm* (*auto*) choke; (*sport*) starter.

station [stasjɔ̃] *nf* station; (*halte*) stop; site; (*de vacances*) resort; posture. **station balnéaire** seaside resort. **station de taxis** taxi rank. **station-service** *nf* petrol station.

stationner [stasjɔne] *v* park. **stationnaire** *adj* stationary. **stationnement** *nm* parking.

statique [statik] *adj* static.

statistique [statistik] *nf* statistic; (*science*) statistics. *adj* statistical.

statue [staty] *nf* statue.

stature [statyr] *nf* stature.

statut [staty] *nm* status. **statuts** *nm pl* statutes *pl*, rules *pl*. **statutaire** *adj* statutory.

steeple [stiplə] *nm* steeplechase.

stencil [stɛnsil] *nm* stencil.

sténodactylo [stenɔdaktilo] *nf* (*personne*) shorthand typist; (*emploi*) shorthand typing.

sténographie [stenɔgrafi] *nf* shorthand.

stéréo [stereo] *nf*, *adj* stereo. **stéréophonique** *adj* stereophonic.

stéréotype [stereɔtip] *nm* stereotype.

stérile [steril] *adj* sterile; (*terre*) barren; (*effort*) fruitless. **stérilet** *nm* (*méd*) coil. **stérilisation** *nf* sterilization. **stériliser** *v* sterilize. **stérilité** *nf* sterility; barrenness; fruitlessness.

stéthoscope [stetɔskɔp] *nm* stethoscope.

stigmate [stigmat] *nm* stigma; mark.

stimulant [stimylɑ̃] *adj* stimulating. *nm* stimulant; stimulus (*pl* -li).

stimuler [stimyle] *v* stimulate. **stimulation** *nf* stimulation.

stimulus [stimylys] *nm*, *pl* -li stimulus (*pl* -li).

stipuler [stipyle] *v* stipulate, specify. **stipulation** *nf* stipulation.

stock [stɔk] *nm* stock. **stocker** *v* stock; (*amasser*) stockpile.

Stockholm [stɔkɔlm] *n* Stockholm.

stoïque [stɔik] *adj* stoical. **stoïcisme** *nm* stoicism.

stop [stɔp] *interj* stop! *nm* (*panneau*) stop sign; (*feu*) brake light; (*fam*) hitch-hiking. **faire du stop** hitch-hike.

store [stɔr] *nm* blind; (*magasin*) awning.

strabisme [strabismə] *nm* squint.

strapontin [strapɔ̃tɛ̃] *nm* folding seat.

strate [strat] *nf* stratum (*pl* -ta).

stratégie [strateʒi] *nf* strategy. **stratégique** *adj* strategic.

strict [strikt] *adj* strict; (*tenue*) plain.

strident [stridɑ̃] *adj* strident, shrill.

strié [strije] *adj* streaked; (*en relief*) ridged.

strophe [strɔf] *nf* verse, stanza.

structure [stryktyr] *nf* structure. **structural** *adj* structural.

studieux [stydjø] *adj* studious.

studio [stydjo] *nm* studio; (*logement*) flatlet.

stupéfiant [stypefjɑ̃] *adj* astounding. *nm* drug, narcotic.

stupéfier [stypefje] *v* stun, astound. **stupéfaction** *nf* amazement. **stupéfait** *adj* astounded, dumbfounded.

stupeur [stypœr] *nf* amazement; (*méd*) stupor.

stupide [stypid] *adj* stupid, silly. **stupidité** *nf* stupidity.

style [stil] *nm* style.

stylo [stilo] *nm* pen. **stylo à bille** ball-point pen.

suaire [sɥɛr] *nm* shroud.

suant [sɥɑ̃] *adj* sweaty.

suave [sɥav] *adj* smooth; (*musique*, *etc.*) sweet. **suavité** *nf* smoothness; sweetness.

subalterne [sybaltɛrn] *n(m+f)*, *adj* subordinate.

subconscient [sypkɔ̃sjɑ̃] *nm*, *adj* subconscious.

subdiviser [sybdivize] *v* subdivide. **subdivision** *nf* subdivision.

subir [sybir] *v* undergo; endure; suffer.

subit [sybi] *adj* sudden. **subitement** *adv* suddenly. **subito** *adv* (*fam*) suddenly, at once.

subjectif [sybʒɛktif] *adj* subjective.

subjonctif [sybʒɔ̃ktif] *nm*, *adj* subjunctive.

subjuguer [sybʒyge] *v* captivate.

sublime [syblim] *nm*, *adj* sublime.

submerger [sybmɛrʒe] *v* submerge; (*ennemi*, *émotion*) overwhelm; (*travail*, *etc.*) swamp. **submersion** *nf* submersion.

subordonner [sybɔrdɔne] v subordinate. **subordination** nf subordination. **subordonné, -e** n, adj subordinate.

subreptice [sybrɛptis] adj surreptitious.

subsidiaire [sypsidjɛr] adj subsidiary.

subsister [sybziste] v survive, live; (rester) remain, subsist. **subsistance** nf subsistence, maintenance.

substance [sypstɑ̃s] nf substance. **substantiel** adj substantial.

substituer [sypstitɥe] v substitute. **substitution** nf substitution.

subtil [syptil] adj subtle. **subtilité** nf subtlety.

suburbain [sybyrbɛ̃] adj suburban.

***subvenir** [sybvənir] v **subvenir à** meet, provide for.

subvention [sybvɑ̃sjɔ̃] nf grant, subsidy. **subventionner** v subsidize.

subversion [sybvɛrsjɔ̃] nf subversion. **subversif** adj subversive.

suc [syk] nm juice; essence, pith.

succédané [syksedane] nm substitute.

succéder [syksede] v **succéder à** succeed; (suivre) follow. **succès** nm success. **à succès** successful. **avec succès** successfully. **successeur** nm successor. **successif** adj successive. **succession** nf succession.

succinct [syksɛ̃] adj succinct.

succion [syksjɔ̃] nf suction.

succomber [sykɔ̃be] v succumb, yield; (mourir) die.

succulent [sykylɑ̃] adj succulent, delicious.

succursale [sykyrsal] nf branch.

sucer [syse] v suck. **sucette** nf lollipop; (tétine) dummy.

sucre [sykrə] nm sugar. **sucre d'orge** barley sugar. **sucre en poudre** caster sugar. **sucre glace** icing sugar. **sucre semoule** granulated sugar. **sucré** adj sweet. **sucrer** v sweeten; (thé, café, etc.) put sugar in. **sucrier** nm sugar-basin.

sud [syd] nm south. adj invar south; (région) southern; (direction) southward. **sud-est** nm, adj invar south-east. **sud-ouest** nm, adj invar south-west.

suède [sɥɛd] nm suede.

Suède [sɥɛd] nf Sweden. **suédois** nm, adj Swedish. **Suédois, -e** nm, nf Swede.

suer [sɥe] v sweat. **sueur** nf sweat.

***suffire** [syfir] v suffice, be enough or sufficient. **ça suffit** that will do, that's enough. **suffisant** adj sufficient; (résultat) satisfactory; (personne) self-important.

suffixe [syfiks] nm suffix.

suffoquer [syfɔke] v suffocate, choke. **suffocation** nf suffocation.

suffrage [syfraʒ] nm suffrage; (voix) vote; approbation, approval.

suggérer [sygʒere] v suggest. **suggestif** adj suggestive. **suggestion** nf suggestion.

se suicider [sɥiside] v commit suicide. **suicidaire** adj suicidal. **suicide** nm suicide. **suicidé, -e** nm, nf suicide.

suie [sɥi] nf soot.

suif [sɥif] nm tallow.

suinter [sɥɛ̃te] v ooze.

Suisse [sɥis] nf Switzerland. **les Suisses** the Swiss. **suisse** adj Swiss.

suite [sɥit] nf result, effect; succession, series; (musique, appartement) suite; (feuilleton) next episode, continuation; (roman, film) sequel; coherence, consistency. **de suite** in succession. **faire suite à** follow. **par la suite** afterwards, subsequently. **par suite** consequently. **suite à** (comm) further to. **tout de suite** at once, immediately.

suivant [sɥivɑ̃], -e adj next, following. nm, nf next (one). prep according to.

***suivre** [sɥivrə] v follow; (cours) attend; (en classe) keep up (with). **faire suivre** forward. **suivi** adj consistent; regular; coherent.

sujet, -ette [syʒɛ, -ɛt] adj subject, liable, prone. nm subject; (d'examen) question. **au sujet de** about, concerning. **sujet de** cause for. nm, nf (personne) subject. **sujétion** nf subjection.

sultan [syltɑ̃] nm sultan.

superbe [sypɛrb] adj superb, magnificent.

supercherie [sypɛrʃəri] nf trick.

superficie [sypɛrfisi] nf surface area. **superficiel** [sypɛrfisjɛl] adj superficial.

superflu [sypɛrfly] adj superfluous.

supérieur, -e [sypɛrjœr] adj upper; (hautain, meilleur) superior; (plus grand) greater; (plus haut) higher. nm, nf superior. **supériorité** nf superiority.

superlatif [sypɛrlatif] nm, adj superlative.

supermarché [sypɛrmarʃe] nm supermarket.

supersonique [sypɛrsɔnik] adj supersonic.

superstition [sypɛrstisjɔ̃] nf superstition. **superstitieux** adj superstitious.

suppléant [sypleɑ̃], -e adj temporary. nm, nf deputy; (professeur) supply teacher; (médecin) locum.

suppléer [syplee] *v* supply, provide; (*lacune*) fill in; (*manque*) make up (for); replace. **suppléer à** (*remédier*) make up for; (*remplacer*) substitute for.

supplément [syplemã] *nm* supplement; (*tarif*) extra charge; (*transport*) excess fare. **en supplément** extra. **supplémentaire** *adj* additional, extra, supplementary.

supplice [syplis] *nm* torture; torment. **dernier supplice** execution.

supplier [syplije] *v* implore, entreat.

support [sypɔr] *nm* support; (*moyen*) medium.

supporter [sypɔrte] *v* support; endure, bear; tolerate, put up with; (*résister à*) withstand. **supportable** *adj* bearable; tolerable.

supposer [sypoze] *v* suppose; imply. **supposition** *nf* supposition.

supprimer [syprime] *v* suppress; (*enlever*) remove; (*mot*) delete; abolish, do away with; (*train, etc.*) cancel. **suppression** *nf* suppression; removal; deletion; abolition; cancellation.

suprême [syprɛm] *adj* supreme. **suprématie** *nf* supremacy.

sur [syr] *prep* on; (*par-dessus*) over; (*au-dessus*) above; (*sujet*) about; (*proportion*) out of; (*mesure*) by; (*après*) after. **sur-le-champ** *adv* immediately.

sûr [syr] *adj* sure, certain; (*sans danger*) safe; (*sérieux*) reliable. **à coup sûr** definitely.

surabondance [syrabɔ̃dɑ̃s] *nf* overabundance. **surabondant** *adj* overabundant.

suranné [syrane] *adj* outdated, outmoded.

surcharger [syrʃarʒe] *v* overload. **surcharge** *nf* extra *or* excess load; (*surabondance*) surfeit; (*impôt*) surcharge.

surchauffer [syrʃofe] *v* overheat.

surcroît [syrkrwa] *nm* excess; (*augmentation*) increase. **par surcroît** in addition.

surdité [syrdite] *nf* deafness.

surdose [syrdoz] *nf* overdose.

sureau [syro] *nm* elder. **baie du sureau** elderberry

surélever [syrelve] *v* raise, heighten.

surenchère [syrɑ̃ʃɛr] *nf* higher bid.

surestimer [syrɛstime] *v* overestimate.

sûreté [syrte] *nf* (*sécurité*) safety; (*précision*) reliability; guarantee.

surexposer [syrɛkspoze] *v* overexpose. **surexposition** *nf* overexposure.

surface [syrfas] *nf* surface; (*aire*) surface area. **faire surface** surface.

surfait [syrfɛ] *adj* overrated.

surgeler [syrʒəle] *v* deep-freeze.

surgir [syrʒir] *v* appear suddenly; (*jaillir*) spring up; (*problème, etc.*) arise.

surhumain [syrymɛ̃] *adj* superhuman.

surimpression [syrɛ̃presjɔ̃] *nf* superimposition. **en surimpression** superimposed.

surlendemain [syrlɑ̃dmɛ̃] *nm* next day but one. **le surlendemain** two days later.

surmener [syrməne] *v* overwork. **surmenage** *nm* overwork.

surmonter [syrmɔ̃te] *v* surmount; (*vaincre*) overcome; (*dôme, etc.*) top.

surnaturel [syrnatyrɛl] *nm, adj* supernatural.

surnom [syrnɔ̃] *nm* nickname. **surnommer** *v* nickname.

surnombre [syrnɔ̃brə] *nm* **en surnombre** too many.

surpasser [syrpase] *v* surpass.

surpeuplé [syrpœple] *adj* overpopulated, overcrowded. **surpeuplement** *nm* overpopulation, overcrowding.

surplomb [syrplɔ̃] *nm* overhang. **surplomber** *v* overhang.

surplus [syrply] *nm* surplus. **au surplus** moreover.

*surprendre [syrprɑ̃drə] v surprise; discover, detect; (*prendre*) catch (out). **surpris** *adj* surprised. **surprise** *nf* surprise.

surréaliste [syrrealist] *adj* surrealistic. *n(m + f)* surrealist. **surréalisme** *nm* surrealism.

sursaut [syrso] *nm* start, jump. **sursauter** *v* start, jump.

*sursseoir [syrswar] v **surseoir à** defer, postpone. **sursis** *nm* reprieve.

surtaxer [syrtakse] *v* surcharge. **surtaxe** *nf* surcharge.

surtout [syrtu] *adv* above all; especially, particularly.

surveiller [syrveje] *v* (*garder, épier*) watch; (*contrôler*) supervise. **surveillance** *nf* watch; supervision. **surveillant, -e** *nm, nf* supervisor; (*prison*) warder; (*école*) person in charge of discipline.

*survenir [syrvənir] v occur, take place; (*problème*) arise; (*personne*) arrive unexpectedly.

survêtement [syrvɛtmɑ̃] *nm* tracksuit.

*survivre [syrvivrə] v survive. **survivre à** outlive. **survivance** *nf* survival. **survivant, -e** *nm, nf* survivor.

sus [sy] *adv* en sus in addition.
susceptible [syseptibla] *adj* sensitive, touchy. susceptible à (*possible*) likely to; capable of.
susciter [sysite] *v* arouse; (*obstacles, etc.*) create.
susdit [sysdi] *adj* aforesaid.
suspect [syspɛkt], -e *adj* suspicious; (*douteux*) suspect. suspect de suspected of. *nm, nf* suspect.
suspendre [syspɑ̃drə] *v* suspend; (*fixer, accrocher*) hang (up). suspendu *adj* suspended; hanging.
suspens [syspɑ̃] *nm* en suspens (*projet, etc.*) in abeyance; in suspense; in suspension. suspense *nm* suspense.
suspension [syspɑ̃sjɔ̃] *nf* suspension.
susurrer [sysyre] *v* murmur.
suture [sytyr] *nf* suture. suturer *v* (*méd*) stitch (up).
svelte [svɛlt] *adj* slender.
sycomore [sikɔmɔr] *nm* sycamore.
syllabe [silab] *nf* syllable. syllabique *adj* syllabic.
sylvestre [silvɛstrə] *adj* forest, woodland. sylviculture *nf* forestry.
symbole [sɛ̃bɔl] *nm* symbol. symbolique *adj* symbolic; (*donation, contribution*) nominal. symboliser *v* symbolize. symbolisme *nm* symbolism.
symétrie [simetri] *nf* symmetry. symétrique *adj* symmetrical.
sympathie [sɛ̃pati] *nf* liking; affinity. sympathique *adj* nice, pleasant; (*personne*) likeable, friendly.
symphonie [sɛ̃fɔni] *nf* symphony. symphonique *adj* symphonic.
symposium [sɛ̃pozjɔm] *nm* symposium.
symptôme [sɛ̃ptom] *nm* symptom; sign. symptomatique *adj* symptomatic.
synagogue [sinagɔg] *nf* synagogue.
synchroniser [sɛ̃krɔnize] *v* synchronize. synchronisation *nf* synchronization.
syncoper [sɛ̃kɔpe] *v* (*musique*) syncopate.
syncope *nf* syncopation; (*méd*) black-out, fainting fit.
syndicat [sɛ̃dika] *nm* syndicate; (*ouvrier*) union; association. syndicat d'initiative tourist information bureau. syndical *adj* union. syndicaliste *n(m + f)* trade unionist. syndiqué, -e *nm, nf* union member.
syndrome [sɛ̃drom] *nm* syndrome.
synonyme [sinɔnim] *nm* synonym. *adj* synonymous.
syntaxe [sɛ̃taks] *nf* syntax.

synthèse [sɛ̃tɛz] *nf* synthesis (*pl* -ses).
synthétique *adj* synthetic. synthétiser *v* synthesize.
syphilis [sifilis] *nf* syphilis.
système [sistɛm] *nm* system. systématique *adj* systematic.

T

t' [t] *V* te.
ta [ta] *V* ton[1].
tabac [taba] *nm* tobacco; (*magasin*) tobacconist's. tabac à priser snuff. tabatière *nf* snuffbox.
table [tablə] *nf* table; tablet. faire table rase make a clean sweep. table basse coffee table. table des matières table of contents. table gigogne nest of tables. table roulante trolley.
tableau [tablo] *nm* picture; (*peinture*) painting; scene; (*support, panneau*) board; list; (*graphique*) table, chart. tableau de bord dashboard. tableau noir blackboard.
tablette [tablɛt] *nf* tablet; (*rayon*) shelf; (*chocolat*) bar.
tablier [tablije] *nm* apron.
tabou [tabu] *nm, adj* taboo.
tabouret [taburɛ] *nm* stool.
tache [taʃ] *nf* mark, spot; (*sang, vin, etc.*) stain; (*pâté*) blot. tache de rousseur or son freckle. tacher *v* mark; stain.
tâche [tɑʃ] *nf* task, work. tâcher *v* try, endeavour.
tacheté [taʃte] *adj* speckled, spotted.
tacite [tasit] *adj* tacit.
taciturne [tasityrn] *adj* taciturn.
tact [takt] *nm* tact. avoir du tact be tactful.
tactique [taktik] *nf* tactics *pl*. *adj* tactical.
taffetas [tafta] *nm* taffeta.
taie [tɛ] *nf* taie d'oreiller pillowcase.
taillade [tɑjad] *nf* slash, gash. taillader *v* slash, gash.
taille [tɑj] *nf* size; (*hauteur*) height; (*corps, vêtement*) waist; (*coupe*) cutting, cut; (*tranchant*) edge. à la taille de in keeping with. être de taille à be up to.
tailler [tɑje] *v* cut; (*bois*) carve; (*barbe, haie, etc.*) trim; (*crayon*) sharpen. taille-

crayon nm invar pencil sharpener. **tailleur** nm (personne) tailor; (costume) suit.
taillis [taji] nm copse.

***taire** [tɛr] v conceal, hush up. **faire taire silence. se taire** be quiet.

talc [talk] nm talcum powder.

talent [talɑ̃] nm talent. **talentueux** adj talented.

talon [talɔ̃] nm heel; (chèque) stub; (pain) crust.

talonner [talɔne] v (suivre) follow closely; (harceler) hound; (cheval) spur on.

talus [taly] nm embankment.

tambour [tɑ̃bur] nm drum; (joueur) drummer. **tambourin** nm tambourine. **tambouriner** v drum.

tamis [tami] nm sieve. **tamiser** v sieve, sift; filter.

Tamise [tamiz] nf **la Tamise** the Thames.

tampon [tɑ̃pɔ̃] nm pad, wad; (pour boucher) plug; (pour · règles) tampon; (timbre) stamp; (rail) buffer. **tamponner** v dab, mop; stamp; plug; (heurter) crash into.

tancer [tɑ̃se] v scold, reprimand.

tandem [tɑ̃dɛm] nm tandem; (couple) pair.

tandis [tɑ̃di] conj **tandis que** while; (contraste) whereas.

tangente [tɑ̃ʒɑ̃t] nf tangent.

tangible [tɑ̃ʒiblə] adj tangible.

tanguer [tɑ̃ge] v pitch, reel.

tanière [tanjɛr] nf den, lair.

tanner [tane] v tan; (fam) pester, annoy.

tan-sad [tɑ̃sad] nm pillion.

tant [tɑ̃] adv so much, so. **en tant que** as. **tant de** (quantité) so much; (nombre) so many; (qualité) such. **tant mieux** so much the better. **tant pis** too bad. **tant que** as long as, while. **tant s'en faut** far from it.

tante [tɑ̃t] nf aunt.

tantôt [tɑ̃to] adv this afternoon. **tantôt ... tantôt ...** sometimes ... sometimes ...

taon [tɑ̃] nm horse-fly.

tapage [tapaʒ] nm (vacarme) uproar, din; (scandale) fuss. **tapageur, -euse** adj rowdy; (criard) showy, flashy.

taper [tape] v knock, hit; (battre) beat; (à la machine) type. **taper sur les nerfs de quelqu'un** get on someone's nerves. **tape** nf slap.

tapioca [tapjɔka] nm tapioca.

se tapir [tapir] v crouch; (se cacher) hide away.

tapis [tapi] nm carpet; (carpette) rug; (natte) mat; (table) cloth, covering. **tapis de sol** groundsheet. **tapis roulant** conveyor belt.

tapisser [tapise] v cover; (sol) carpet; (mur) paper. **tapisserie** nf tapestry; (papier peint) wallpaper. **tapissier** nm upholsterer; (maison) interior decorator.

tapoter [tapɔte] v pat, tap.

taquin [takɛ̃] adj teasing. **taquiner** v tease; (inquiéter) bother, worry. **taquinerie** nf teasing.

tard [tar] adv late.

tarder [tarde] v (différer) delay, put off; (être lent) take a long time, be long. **tardif** adj late; (remords, etc.) belated.

tarif [tarif] nm tariff, rate; (tableau) price list; (transport) fare.

tarir [tarir] v run dry, dry up.

tarte [tart] nf tart. **tartelette** nf tart. **tartine** nf slice of bread (and butter). **tartiner** v spread.

tartre [tartrə] nm tartar; (bouilloire) fur.

tas [tɑ] nm pile, heap; (fam: foule) crowd. **un tas de** (fam) loads of, lots of.

tasse [tɑs] nf cup. **tasse à thé/café** tea/coffee cup.

tasser [tɑse] v pack (down), cram. **se tasser** (se serrer) squeeze up; (s'affaisser) settle; (corps) shrink.

tâter [tate] v (palper) feel; (opinion, etc.) sound out; (essayer) try out.

tâtonner [tatɔne] v grop along or around, feel one's way. **par tâtonnements** by trial and error.

tâtons [tatɔ̃] adv **avancer à tâtons** feel one's way along. **chercher à tâtons** feel around for.

tatouer [tatwe] v tattoo. **tatouage** nm tattoo.

taudis [todi] nm slum.

taule [tol] nf (argot: prison) nick.

taupe [top] nf mole.

taureau [tɔro] nm bull. **Taureau** nm Taurus.

taux [to] nm rate; degree, level. **taux de change** exchange rate.

taxer [takse] v tax; (comm) fix the price of; accuse. **taxation** nf taxation. **taxe** nf tax; (douane) duty; fixed price.

taxi [taksi] nm taxi.

Tchécoslovaquie [tʃekɔslɔvaki] nf Czechoslovakia. **tchécoslovaque** nm, adj Czechoslovak. **Tchécoslovaque** n(m+f) Czechoslovak. **tchèque** nm, adj Czech. **Tchèque** n(m+f) Czech.

te [tə], **t'** pron you, to you; (réfléchi) yourself.

technique [tɛknik] adj technical. nf technique. **technicien, -enne** nm, nf technician. **technologie** nf technology. **technologique** adj technological.

teck [tɛk] nm teak.

*****teindre** [tɛ̃drə] v dye; colour, tinge.

teint [tɛ̃] adj dyed. nm complexion, colouring. **teinte** nf shade, tint; colour; (trace) tinge, hint. **teinter** [tɛ̃te] v (verre) tint; (bois) stain. **teinture** [tɛ̃tyr] nf (substance) dye; (action) dyeing. **teinturerie** nf cleaner's.

tel [tɛl], **telle** adj such (a), like, as. **tel que** such as, like. **tel quel** as it stands, as it is. pron one, someone.

télécommande [telekɔmɑ̃d] nf remote control.

télécommunications [telekɔmynikɑsjɔ̃] pl telecommunications pl.

télégramme [telegram] nm telegram.

télégraphier [telegrafje] v telegraph, cable. **télégraphe** nm telegraph. **télégraphique** adj telegraphic; (poteau) telegraph.

télépathie [telepati] nf telepathy. **télépathique** adj telepathic.

téléphérique [teleferik] nm cable-car.

téléphone [telefɔn] nm telephone, phone. **téléphoner** v telephone, phone. **téléphonique** adj telephone. **téléphoniste** n(m+f) telephonist.

télescope [telɛskɔp] nm telescope. **télescopique** adj telescopic.

télésiège [telesjɛʒ] nm chair-lift.

téléski [teleski] nm ski-lift.

téléviser [televize] v televise. **télévision** nf television. **téléviseur** nm television set.

télex [telɛks] nm telex.

tellement [tɛlmɑ̃] adv so (much). **pas tellement** not (very) much.

téméraire [temerɛr] adj rash, reckless. **témérité** nf rashness, recklessness.

témoigner [temwaɲe] v testify; (montrer) show; reveal. **témoigner de** bear witness to. **témoignage** nm evidence, testimony; (récit) account; expression; (cadeau) token. **témoin** nm witness; evidence, testimony; (sport) baton.

tempe [tɑ̃p] nf temple.

tempérament [tɑ̃peramɑ̃] nm tempera-

ment, disposition; constitution. **achat à tempérament** nm hire purchase.

température [tɑ̃peratyr] nf temperature.

tempérer [tɑ̃pere] v temper; (douleur) soothe. **tempéré** adj temperate.

tempête [tɑ̃pɛt] nf storm. **tempétueux** adj stormy, tempestuous.

temple [tɑ̃plə] nm temple; Protestant church.

tempo [tɛmpo] nm tempo.

temporaire [tɑ̃pɔrɛr] adj temporary.

temporel [tɑ̃pɔrɛl] adj temporal, worldly.

temps [tɑ̃] nm time; (météorologie) weather; (musique) beat; (gramm) tense. **à temps** in time. **de temps en temps** now and again. **quel temps fait-il?** what's the weather like?

tenace [tanas] adj stubborn, persistent, tenacious. **ténacité** nf stubbornness, persistence, tenacity.

tenailles [tanaj] nf pl pincers pl. **tenailler** v torture, torment.

tendance [tɑ̃dɑ̃s] nf tendency; (évolution) trend; (opinions) leanings pl. **avoir tendance à** tend to.

tendon [tɑ̃dɔ̃] nm tendon.

tendre[1] [tɑ̃drə] v (raidir) tighten; (tirer sur) stretch; (muscle) tense; (poser) set; (tapisserie, etc.) hang; (présenter) hold out. **tendre à** tend to; (viser à) aim at or to. **tendre le cou** crane one's neck. **tendre l'oreille** prick up one's ears. **tendu** adj taut, tight; tense; (bras) outstretched. **tendu de** hung with.

tendre[2] [tɑ̃drə] adj tender; soft, delicate. **tendresse** nf tenderness, affection. **tendreté** nf tenderness.

ténèbres [tenɛbrə] nf pl darkness sing, gloom sing. **ténébreux** adj dark, gloomy; obscure; mysterious.

*****tenir** [tanir] v hold; (garder) keep; (avoir) have; (magasin, etc.) run; (occuper) take up; (durer) last. **se tenir** (se conduire) behave; (debout) stand. **se tenir à** hold on to. **tenir à** (vouloir) be anxious to, insist on; (aimer) be fond of; (résulter) stem from. **tenir compte de** take into account. **tenir de** take after. **tenir pour** regard as.

tennis [tenis] nm tennis; tennis court. nf pl plimsolls pl.

ténor [tenɔr] nm tenor.

tension [tɑ̃sjɔ̃] nf tension; (méd) blood pressure; (élec) voltage.

tentacule [tɑ̃takyl] *nm* tentacle.
tente [tɑ̃t] *nf* tent.
tenter [tɑ̃te] *v* (*tentation*) tempt; (*tentative*) attempt. **tentation** *nf* temptation. **tentative** *nf* attempt.
tenture [tɑ̃tyr] *nf* hanging; (*rideau*) curtain.
tenu [təny] *adj* **bien tenu** neat, well-kept. **être tenu de** be obliged to. **mal tenu** untidy, neglected. **tenue** *nf* (*habillement*) dress; (*maintien*) posture; (*conduite*) manners *pl*; (*magasin, etc.*) running; control.
ténu [teny] *adj* fine; (*subtil*) tenuous.
térébenthine [terebɑ̃tin] *nf* turpentine.
tergiverser [tɛrʒivɛrse] *v* prevaricate.
terme [tɛrm] *nm* term; (*date limite*) deadline; (*loyer*) rent. **avant terme** prematurely.
terminaison [tɛrminɛzɔ̃] *nf* ending.
terminal [tɛrminal] *adj* terminal. **terminale** *nf* (*classe*) upper sixth.
terminer [tɛrmine] *v* end, finish, terminate.
terminologie [tɛrminɔlɔʒi] *nf* terminology.
terminus [tɛrminys] *nm* terminus.
ternir [tɛrnir] *v* tarnish, dull. **terne** *adj* dull, drab.
terrain [tɛrɛ̃] *nm* ground, land; (*sport*) pitch, field; (*parcelle*) plot, site. **terrain de jeu** playing field. **terrain vague** wasteland.
terrasse [tɛras] *nf* terrace.
terrasser [tɛrase] *v* overcome, overwhelm.
terre [tɛr] *nf* earth; (*sol*) ground; (*étendue, pays*) land. **à terre** ashore. **par terre** on the ground. **terre-à-terre** *adj invar* down-to-earth.
terrestre [tɛrɛstrə] *adj* earthly, terrestrial.
terreur [tɛrœr] *nf* terror.
terrible [tɛribla] *adj* terrible, dreadful; (*fam*) terrific.
terrier [tɛrje] *nm* hole; (*lapin*) burrow; (*renard*) earth; (*race de chien*) terrier.
terrifier [tɛrifje] *v* terrify.
terrine [tɛrin] *nf* earthenware dish; pâté.
territoire [tɛritwar] *nm* territory. **territorial** *adj* territorial.
terroir [tɛrwar] *nm* soil.
terroriser [tɛrɔrize] *v* terrorize. **terrorisme** *nm* terrorism. **terroriste** *n*(*m*+*f*), *adj* terrorist.
tes [te] *V* **ton**[1].
tesson [tesɔ̃] *nm* piece of broken glass.

testament [tɛstamɑ̃] *nm* testament; (*jur*) will.
testicule [tɛstikyl] *nm* testicle.
tétanos [tetanos] *nm* tetanus.
têtard [tɛtar] *nm* tadpole.
tête [tɛt] *nf* head; (*visage*) face; (*devant*) front; (*haut*) top; (*esprit*) mind. **en tête** in front; at the top. **tenir tête à** stand up to. **tête-à-tête** *nm invar* private conversation.
tétine [tetin] *nf* teat; (*vache*) udder; (*sucette*) dummy.
têtu [tety] *adj* stubborn.
texte [tɛkst] *nm* text; passage; subject. **textuel** *adj* textual.
textile [tɛkstil] *nm, adj* textile.
texture [tɛkstyr] *nf* texture.
thé [te] *nm* tea. **théière** *nf* teapot.
théâtre [teɑtrə] *nm* theatre; drama. **théâtral** *adj* theatrical; dramatic.
thème [tɛm] *nm* theme; (*traduction*) prose. **thématique** *adj* thematic.
théologie [teɔlɔʒi] *nf* theology. **théologien, -enne** *nm, nf* theologian. **théologique** *adj* theological.
théorème [teɔrɛm] *nm* theorem.
théorie [teɔri] *nf* theory. **théorique** *adj* theoretical.
thérapeutique [terapøtik] *adj* therapeutic. *nf also* **thérapie** therapy. **thérapeute** *n*(*m*+*f*) therapist.
thermal [tɛrmal] *adj* thermal. **station thermale** *nf* spa.
thermique [tɛrmik] *adj* thermal, heat.
thermodynamique [tɛrmɔdinamik] *nf* thermodynamics.
thermomètre [tɛrmɔmɛtrə] *nm* thermometer.
thermonucléaire [tɛrmɔnykleer] *adj* thermonuclear.
thermos ® [tɛrmos] *nm* thermos flask ®.
thermostat [tɛrmɔsta] *nm* thermostat.
thésauriser [tezɔrize] *v* hoard (money).
thèse [tɛz] *nf* thesis.
thon [tɔ̃] *nm* tuna.
thym [tɛ̃] *nm* thyme.
thyroïde [tirɔid] *nf, adj* thyroid.
tiare [tjar] *nf* tiara.
tic [tik] *nm* tic, twitch; (*manie*) mannerism.
ticket [tikɛ] *nm* ticket.
tic-tac [tiktak] *nm* tick, ticking. **faire tic-tac** tick.

tiède [tjɛd] *adj* lukewarm, tepid; *(doux)* mild.

tien [tjɛ̃], **tienne** *pron* **le tien, la tienne** yours.

tiens [tjɛ̃] *interj* well! *(en donnant)* here! *(en expliquant)* look!

tiers, tierce [tjɛr, tjɛrs] *adj* third. **Tiers-Monde** *nm* Third World. *nm* third; *(jur)* third party. *nf (musique)* third.

tige [tiʒ] *nf* stem, stalk; *(métal)* rod.

tigre [tigr] *nm* tiger. **tigré** *adj (tacheté)* spotted; *(rayé)* striped. **chat tigré** *nm* tabby cat.

tilleul [tijœl] *nm* lime tree.

timbale [tɛ̃bal] *nf* kettledrum; *(gobelet)* metal tumbler. **timbales** *nf pl* timpani *pl*.

timbre [tɛ̃brə] *nm* stamp; *(son)* tone; *(sonnette)* bell. **timbrer** *v* stamp; *(d'un cachet)* postmark.

timide [timid] *adj* timid; *(mal à l'aise)* shy. **timidité** *nf* timidity; shyness.

tintamarre [tɛ̃tamar] *nm* din.

tinter [tɛ̃te] *v* ring; *(clochette)* tinkle; *(clefs, monnaie, etc.)* jingle; *(verres)* chink.

tir [tir] *nm* firing; *(feu)* fire; *(sport)* shooting. **tir à l'arc** archery.

tirailler [tiraje] *v* tug *or* pull at; *(harceler)* plague; *(douleur)* gnaw *or* stab at. **tiraillement** *nm* pulling, tugging; conflict; stabbing *or* gnawing pain.

tirelire [tirlir] *nf* money-box.

tirer [tire] *v* pull, draw; extract, get out, take from; *(fusil)* fire, shoot; *(imprimer)* print. **se tirer de** *(s'échapper)* get out of; *(se débrouiller)* handle, cope with. **tire-bouchon** *nm* corkscrew. **tirage** *nm* printing; *(journal)* circulation; edition; *(loterie)* draw.

tiroir [tirwar] *nm* drawer. **tiroir-caisse** *nm* till.

tisane [tizan] *nf* herb tea.

tisonner [tizɔne] *v* poke. **tisonnier** *nm* poker.

tisser [tise] *v* weave. **tissage** *nm* weaving.

tissu [tisy] *nm* cloth, fabric, material; *(bot, anat)* tissue.

titre [titrə] *nm* title; *(diplôme)* qualification; *(bourse)* bond, security; *(droit)* right, claim. **à ce titre** as such. **à titre de** as, in the capacity of.

tituber [titybe] *v* stagger.

toast [tost] *nm* toast.

toboggan [tɔbɔgɑ̃] *nm* toboggan; *(glissière)* slide, chute.

toi [twa] *pron* you. **toi-même** *pron* yourself.

toile [twal] *nf* cloth; *(grosse)* canvas; linen; cotton; *(araignée)* web. **toile cirée** oilskin. **toile de fond** backcloth, backdrop.

toilette [twalɛt] *nf (soins de propreté)* wash; *(habillement)* outfit, clothes *pl*. **toilettes** *nf pl* toilet *sing*.

toison [twazɔ̃] *nf* fleece.

toit [twa] *nm* roof.

Tokio [tɔkjo] *n* Tokyo.

tôle [tol] *nf* metal sheet. **tôle ondulée** corrugated iron.

tolérer [tɔlere] *v* tolerate; endure, stand. **tolérable** *adj* tolerable. **tolérance** *nf* tolerance, toleration. **tolérant** *adj* tolerant.

tomate [tɔmat] *nf* tomato.

tombe [tɔ̃b] *nf* grave, tomb. **tombeau** *nm* tomb.

tomber [tɔ̃be] *v* fall; *(baisser)* drop; *(pendre)* hang. **laisser tomber** drop. **tomber juste** be exactly right. **tomber sur** come across. **tombée** *nf* fall.

tome [tɔm] *nm* volume.

ton¹ [tɔ̃], **ta** *adj*, *pl* **tes** your.

ton² [tɔ̃] *nm* tone; *(hauteur)* pitch; *(échelle musicale)* key.

tondre [tɔ̃drə] *v* clip; *(mouton)* shear; *(pelouse)* mow. **tondeuse** *nf* shears *pl*; clippers *pl*; lawn-mower. **tondu** *adj* closely-cropped.

tonifier [tɔnifje] *v* tone up, invigorate. **tonifiant** *adj* invigorating, bracing.

tonique [tɔnik] *nm* tonic. *nf (musique)* tonic.

tonne [tɔn] *nf* ton.

tonneau [tɔno] *nm* barrel.

tonner [tɔne] *v* thunder. **tonnerre** *nm* thunder.

topaze [tɔpaz] *nf* topaz.

toper [tɔpe] *v* agree. **tope-là!** *(fam)* it's a deal!

topographie [tɔpɔgrafi] *nf* topography. **topographique** *adj* topographical.

torche [tɔrʃ] *nf* torch.

torcher [tɔrʃe] *v (fam)* wipe.

torchon [tɔrʃɔ̃] *nm* cloth; *(à vaisselle)* tea towel; *(chiffon)* duster.

tordre [tɔrdrə] *v* twist; *(linge, cou)* wring; *(déformer)* distort. **se tordre de douleur/rire** be doubled up with pain/laughter. **tordu** *adj* twisted, crooked.

tornade [tɔrnad] *nf* tornado.

torpille [tɔrpij] *nf* torpedo. **torpiller** *v* torpedo.

torréfier [tɔrefje] *v* roast.

torrent [tɔrā] *nm* torrent. **torrentiel** *adj* torrential.

tors [tɔr] *adj* twisted, crooked.

torse [tɔrs] *nm* torso; (*poitrine*) chest.

tort [tɔr] *nm* wrong; fault; (*dommage*) harm. **à tort** wrongly. **avoir tort** be wrong.

torticolis [tɔrtikɔli] *nm* stiff neck.

tortiller [tɔrtije] *v* twist; (*cheveux, doigts*) twiddle; (*hanches*) wiggle. **se tortiller** wriggle; (*fumée*) curl.

tortue [tɔrty] *nf* tortoise. **tortue de mer** turtle.

tortueux [tɔrtɥø] *adj* (*chemin, etc.*) twisting, winding; (*oblique*) tortuous.

torturer [tɔrtyre] *v* torture. **torture** *nf* torture.

tôt [to] *adv* early, soon. **tôt ou tard** sooner or later.

total [tɔtal] *adj* total; complete, absolute. *nm* total. **totaliser** *v* total. **totalitaire** *adj* totalitarian. **totalité** *nf* whole. **la totalité de** all (of).

toucher [tuʃe] *v* touch; concern, affect; (*être contigu*) adjoin; (*frapper*) hit; contact, reach; (*pension, etc.*) draw; (*chèque*) cash; (*salaire*) get. **toucher à** touch; (*modifier*) meddle with; approach. *nm* touch. **touche** *nf* touch; (*piano*) key.

touffe [tuf] *nf* tuft; (*arbres, fleurs*) clump. **touffu** *adj* bushy, thick; (*roman*) complex.

toujours [tuʒur] *adv* always; (*encore*) still; (*en tout cas*) anyway.

toupet [tupɛ] *nm* (*cheveux*) quiff; (*fam*) nerve, cheek.

toupie [tupi] *nf* spinning-top.

tour[1] [tur] *nf* tower.

tour[2] [tur] *nm* turn; (*excursion*) trip; (*tourisme*) tour; (*poitrine, taille, etc.*) measurement; (*farce, ruse*) trick; (*tech*) lathe. **à tour de rôle** in turn. **faire le tour de** go round. **tour de main** knack. **tour de piste** lap.

tourbe [turb] *nf* peat.

tourbillon [turbijɔ̃] *nm* (*vent*) whirlwind; (*eau*) whirlpool; (*vie, plaisir, etc.*) whirl. **tourbillonner** *v* whirl, swirl.

tourelle [turɛl] *nf* turret.

tourisme [turismə] *nm* (*industrie*) tour-

ism; (*activité*) sightseeing. **touriste** *n(m+f)* tourist. **touristique** *adj* tourist.

tourment [turmã] *nm* agony, torment. **tourmenter** *v* torment. **se tourmenter** fret, worry.

tourmente [turmãt] *nf* storm; (*pol*) upheaval.

tournant [turnã] *adj* (*pivotant*) revolving, swivel; (*escalier*) spiral; (*sinueux*) winding, twisting. *nm* bend; (*moment décisif*) turning point.

tourner [turne] *v* turn; (*film*) make, shoot; (*lait*) turn sour; (*disque, etc.*) revolve, go round; (*moteur*) run. **bien/mal tourner** turn out well/badly. **tourne-disque** *nm* record player. **tournevis** *nm* screwdriver. **tournée** *nf* round; tour.

tournesol [turnəsɔl] *nm* sunflower.

tourniquet [turnikɛ] *nm* (*barrière*) turnstile; (*méd*) tourniquet.

tournoi [turnwa] *nm* tournament.

tournoyer [turnwaje] *v* whirl, swirl.

tournure [turnyr] *nf* turn; turn of phrase; (*apparence*) shape, face.

tourte [turt] *nf* pie.

tourterelle [turtərɛl] *nf* turtle-dove.

Toussaint [tusɛ̃] *nf* All Saints' Day.

tousser [tuse] *v* cough.

tout [tu] *adj*, **toute** *adj*, *pl* **tous**, **toutes** all; (*chaque*) every; (*n'importe quel*) any; (*total*) utmost, full. **de toute façon** in any case. **tous les deux** both. **tous risques** (*assurance*) fully comprehensive. *pron* everything, all. *nm* whole. **du tout** at all. **pas du tout** not at all. *adv* quite, completely; (*très*) very; (*quoique*) though, however. **tout à coup** suddenly. **tout à fait** quite, entirely. **tout à l'heure** (*futur*) presently; (*passé*) just now. **tout au plus/moins** at the very most/least. **tout de même** all the same. **tout de suite** at once. **tout en ...** while .... **tout fait** ready-made. **tout neuf** brand new. **tout-puissant** *adj* omnipotent.

toutefois [tutfwa] *adv* however.

toux [tu] *nf* cough.

toxique [tɔksik] *adj* toxic.

trac [trak] *nm* fit of nerves; (*théâtre*) stage fright.

tracas [traka] *nm* worry, bother. **tracasser** *v* worry, bother.

trace [tras] *nf* trace; mark, sign; (*chemin*) track, path; (*empreinte*) tracks *pl*, trail. **suivre à la trace** track.

tracer [trase] v trace, draw; (*chemin*) mark out.

tract [trakt] nm pamphlet.

tracteur [traktœr] nm tractor.

tradition [tradisjɔ̃] nf tradition. **traditionnel** adj traditional.

*****traduire** [traduir] v translate; express, convey. **traducteur, -trice** nm, nf translator. **traduction** nf translation.

trafic [trafik] nm traffic; (*péj*) dealings pl. **trafiquer** v traffic, trade illicitly.

tragédie [traʒedi] nf tragedy. **tragique** adj tragic.

trahir [trair] v betray; (*forces, etc.*) fail; (*mal exprimer*) misrepresent. **trahison** nf betrayal; (*crime*) treason.

train [trɛ̃] nm train; (*allure*) pace; (*file*) line. **en train** under way. **être en train de** be in the middle of.

train-train nm daily routine.

traîner [trene] v drag; (*mots*) drawl; (*s'attarder*) dawdle, lag behind; (*pendre*) trail; (*s'éterniser*) drag on; (*être éparpillé*) lie around. **se traîner** drag oneself, crawl. **traîneau** nm sledge, sleigh. **traînée** nf streak; (*trace*) trail.

*****traire** [trɛr] v milk.

trait [trɛ] nm line; (*caractéristique*) trait; (*visage*) feature; (*de lumière, satire, etc.*) shaft; (*gorgée*) gulp. **d'un trait** at one go. **trait d'union** hyphen.

traiter [trete] v treat; (*qualifier*) call; (*s'occuper de*) deal with; (*négocier*) have dealings. **traité** nm (*convention*) treaty; (*livre*) treatise. **traitement** nm treatment; salary.

traître, -esse [trɛtrə, -ɛs] adj treacherous. nm, nf traitor. **traîtrise** nf treachery.

trajet [traʒɛ] nm (*voyage*) journey; distance.

trame [tram] nf (*tissu*) thread; (*vie*) texture, web. **tramer** v (*combiner*) plot; (*tisser*) weave.

tramway [tramwɛ] nm tram.

tranchant [trɑ̃ʃɑ̃] adj sharp; (*personne*) assertive. nm cutting edge.

trancher [trɑ̃ʃe] v cut, sever; resolve, settle; contrast sharply. **tranche** nf slice; section; (*bord*) edge. **tranché** adj clearcut, distinct. **tranchée** nf trench.

tranquille [trɑ̃kil] adj quiet; calm, peaceful; (*esprit*) easy, at rest. **laisser tranquille** leave alone. **tranquillisant** nm tranquillizer. **tranquilliser** v reassure. **tranquillité** nf peace, tranquillity.

transaction [trɑ̃zaksjɔ̃] nf transaction; compromise.

transatlantique [trɑ̃zatlɑ̃tik] adj transatlantic. nm (*chaise*) deckchair.

transcender [trɑ̃sɑ̃de] v transcend. **transcendantal** adj transcendental.

*****transcrire** [trɑ̃skrir] v transcribe; copy out. **transcription** nf transcription; copy.

transe [trɑ̃s] nf trance. **transes** nf pl agony sing.

transept [trɑ̃sɛpt] nm transept.

transférer [trɑ̃sfere] v transfer. **transfert** nm transfer.

transformer [trɑ̃sfɔrme] v change, alter; (*radicalement*) transform; convert. **transformateur** nm transformer. **transformation** nf change; transformation; conversion.

transfuge [trɑ̃sfyʒ] n(m+f) renegade.

transfuser [trɑ̃sfyze] v transfuse. **transfusion** nf transfusion.

transiger [trɑ̃ziʒe] v come to an agreement, compromise.

transir [trɑ̃zir] v numb; (*froid*) chill to the bone; (*peur*) transfix. **transi** adj numb with cold; transfixed with fear.

transistor [trɑ̃zistɔr] nm transistor. **transistoriser** v transistorize.

transit [trɑ̃zit] nm transit. **en transit** in transit.

transitif [trɑ̃zitif] adj transitive.

transition [trɑ̃zisjɔ̃] nf transition. **de transition** transitional.

transitoire [trɑ̃zitwar] adj transient, transitory; provisional.

translucide [trɑ̃slysid] adj translucent. **translucidité** nf translucence.

*****transmettre** [trɑ̃smɛtrə] v pass on; (*tech*) transmit. **transmetteur** nm transmitter. **transmission** nf transmission.

transparent [trɑ̃sparɑ̃] adj transparent. **transparaître** v show through. **transparence** nf transparency.

transpirer [trɑ̃spire] v sweat, perspire; (*secret*) come to light. **transpiration** nf perspiration.

transplanter [trɑ̃splɑ̃te] v transplant. **transplantation** nf transplant.

transport [trɑ̃spɔr] nm transport; (*marchandises*) carriage, transportation. **transporter** v carry, convey; (*avec un véhicule*) transport; (*exalter*) carry away.

transposer [trɑ̃spoze] v transpose. **transposition** nf transposition.

transvaser [trɑ̃svaze] v decant.

transversal [trɑ̃svɛrsal] *adj* transverse.
trapèze [trapɛz] *nm* (*sport*) trapeze; (*géom*) trapezium. **trapéziste** *n(m+f)* trapeze artist.
trappe [trap] *nf* trapdoor.
trapu [trapy] *adj* squat, stocky.
traquer [trake] *v* track (down), hunt (out); (*harceler*) hound. **traquenard** *nm* trap; (*embûche*) pitfall.
trauma [troma] *nm* trauma. **traumatique** *adj* traumatic. **traumatisant** *adj* traumatic. **traumatisme** *nm* trauma.
travail [travaj] *nm, pl* **-aux** work; (*métier, tâche*) job; (*méd, ouvriers*) labour. **travaux d'aiguille** needlework *sing*.
travailler [travaje] *v* work; (*vin*) ferment; (*exercer*) practise, work at; (*agir sur*) work on; torment, distract. **travaillé** *adj* (*style*) polished; (*ornement*) intricate; (*façonné*) wrought.
travailleur, -euse [travajœr, -øz] *adj* hard-working. *nm, nf* worker.
travailliste [travajist] *adj* Labour. *n(m+f)* member of the Labour party. **les travaillistes** *nm pl* Labour *sing*.
travers [travɛr] *nm* failing, fault. **à travers** (*milieu*) through; (*surface*) across. **au travers** through. **de travers** (*pas droit*) crooked; (*mal*) wrong. **en travers** across.
traverser [travɛrse] *v* (*surface*) cross; (*milieu*) go through. **traverse** *nf* (*rail*) sleeper; (*tech*) strut, cross-piece. **traversée** *nf* crossing.
traversin [travɛrsɛ̃] *nm* bolster.
travestir [travɛstir] *v* dress up; (*vérité*) misrepresent. **se travestir** (*bal*) put on fancy dress; (*cabaret, psych*) dress up as a woman.
travesti [travɛsti] *-e adj* disguised; (*bal*) fancy-dress. *nm* fancy dress; (*cabaret*) drag artist. *nm, nf* (*psych*) transvestite.
trébucher [trebyʃe] *v* stumble. **faire trébucher** trip up. **trébuchant** *adj* staggering; (*voix*) halting.
trèfle [trɛflə] *nm* clover; (*cartes*) club.
treillis [treji] *nm* trellis, lattice. **treillis métallique** wire netting.
treize [trɛz] *nm, adj* thirteen. **treizième** *n(m+f)*, *adj* thirteenth.
trembler [trɑ̃ble] *v* tremble, shake; (*de froid*) shiver; (*lumière*) flicker. **tremblement** *nm* tremble, tremor; shiver. **tremblement de terre** earthquake.
se trémousser [tremuse] *v* fidget, wriggle; (*se dandiner*) wiggle.

tremper [trɑ̃pe] *v* soak; (*plonger*) dip. **faire trempette** dunk one's bread or sugar.
tremplin [trɑ̃plɛ̃] *nm* spring-board; (*piscine*) diving-board.
trente [trɑ̃t] *nm, adj* thirty. **trentième** *n(m+f)*, *adj* thirtieth.
trépas [trepa] *nm* death. **trépasser** *v* die, pass away.
trépider [trepide] *v* vibrate. **trépidation** *nf* vibration; (*agitation*) flurry.
trépied [trepje] *nm* tripod.
trépigner [trepiɲe] *v* stamp.
très [trɛ] *adv* very; (*devant un participe*) highly, very much.
trésor [trezor] *nm* treasure; (*source*) mine, wealth; (*endroit*) treasury; (*de l'état*) exchequer. **trésorerie** *nf* treasury; finances *pl*, funds *pl*. **trésorier, -ère** *nm, nf* treasurer.
*tressaillir [tresajir] *v* quiver; (*de peur*) shudder; (*de douleur*) wince; (*sursauter*) start; vibrate, shake. **tressaillement** *nm* quiver; shudder; start; vibration.
tresser [trese] *v* (*cheveux*) plait; (*guirlande*) weave; (*corde*) twist. **tresse** *nf* plait; (*cordon*) braid.
tréteau [treto] *nm* trestle.
treuil [trœj] *nm* winch.
trève [trɛv] *nf* (*mil, pol*) truce; respite. **sans trève** unceasingly, relentlessly.
tri [tri] *nm* sorting; selection. **faire le tri de** sort; select. **triage** *nm* sorting, selection.
triangle [trijɑ̃glə] *nm* triangle. **triangulaire** *adj* triangular.
tribord [tribor] *nm* starboard.
tribu [triby] *nf* tribe.
tribunal [tribynal] *nm* court, tribunal.
tribune *nf* (*église*) gallery; (*stade*) stand; platform; (*journal, radio, etc.*) forum.
tribut [triby] *nm* tribute.
tributaire [tribytɛr] *adj* tributary.
tricher [triʃe] *v* cheat. **tricherie** *nf* cheating. **tricheur, -euse** *nm, nf* cheat.
tricot [triko] *nm* (*technique*) knitting; (*vêtement*) jumper. **tricot de corps** vest. **tricoter** *v* knit.
trictrac [triktrak] *nm* backgammon.
tricycle [trisiklə] *nm* tricycle.
trier [trije] *v* sort (out); select. **trier sur le volet** hand-pick.
trille [trij] *nm* trill. **triller** *v* trill.

trimballer [trɛ̃bale] v (fam) cart around.

trimestre [trimɛstrə] nm quarter; (école) term. **trimestriel** adj quarterly; end-of-term.

tringle [trɛ̃glə] nf rod.

trinquer [trɛ̃ke] v clink glasses.

trio [trijo] nm trio.

triompher [trijɔ̃fe] v triumph, win. **triompher de** overcome, conquer. **triomphant** adj triumphant. **triomphe** nm triumph.

tripes [trip] nf pl (cuisine) tripe sing; (fam) guts pl.

triple [triplə] adj triple, treble. nm **le triple** three times as much. **triplé, -e** nm, nf triplet. **tripler** v triple, treble.

tripoter [tripote] v fiddle with; (fouiller) rummage about; (affaire) be involved in.

triste [trist] adj sad, miserable; (sombre) dreary, dismal. **tristesse** nf sadness, sorrow; dreariness.

triton [tritɔ̃] nm newt.

trivial [trivjal] adj (grossier) coarse; (ordinaire) mundane. **trivialité** nf coarseness; coarse remark or detail; mundane nature.

troc [trɔk] nm exchange; (système économique) barter.

trognon [trɔɲɔ̃] nm core.

trois [trwa] nm, adj three. **à trois dimensions** three-dimensional. **trois-quarts** nm pl three quarters. **troisième** n(m+f), adj third.

trombe [trɔ̃b] nf (pluie) downpour; (tornade) whirlwind.

trombone [trɔ̃bɔn] nm trombone; (agrafe) paper-clip.

trompe [trɔ̃p] nf (éléphant) trunk; (musique) horn.

tromper [trɔ̃pe] v deceive; (par accident) mislead; (poursuivant) elude; (duper) fool, trick. **se tromper** be wrong, make a mistake. **tromperie** nf deception, deceit. **trompeur, -euse** adj (apparence) deceptive, misleading; (personne) deceitful.

trompette [trɔ̃pɛt] nf trumpet. **trompettiste** n(m+f) trumpeter.

tronc [trɔ̃] nm trunk.

tronçon [trɔ̃sɔ̃] nm section.

trône [tron] nm throne.

tronquer [trɔ̃ke] v truncate; (texte) cut down; (détails) cut out.

trop [tro] adv too, too much. **de trop** (quantité) too much; (nombre) too many;

(importun) in the way. **trop de** too much; too many. **trop-plein** nm overflow. nm excess.

trophée [trɔfe] nm trophy.

tropique [trɔpik] nm tropic. **tropical** adj tropical.

troquer [trɔke] v exchange, swap; (transaction commerciale) barter.

trot [tro] nm trot; (souris) scamper. **trotter** v trot. **trottinette** nf scooter.

trottoir [trɔtwar] nm pavement.

trou [tru] nm hole; (vide) gap. **trou de serrure** keyhole. **trou d'homme** manhole.

trouble¹ [trublə] adj (eau) cloudy; (vue) blurred, misty; (affaire) shady.

trouble² [trublə] nm (agitation) turmoil; discord; embarrassment; (inquiétude) distress; (méd) disorder.

troubler [truble] v disturb, trouble; (eau) make cloudy. **se troubler** (personne) get flustered; (eau) become cloudy. **trouble-fête** n(m+f) invar spoilsport.

trouer [true] v make a hole in; pierce; (parsemer) dot. **trouée** nf gap; (mil) breach.

troupe [trup] nf (mil) troop; (chanteurs, etc.) troupe; band, group. **troupeau** nm herd; (moutons) flock.

trousse [trus] nf case, kit; (sac) bag. **trousseau** nm (clefs) bunch; (mariée) trousseau. **trousser** v truss.

trouver [truve] v find. **se trouver** be; (se sentir) feel; (arriver) happen. **trouvaille** nf find.

truc [tryk] nm trick; (fam: combine) knack; (fam: chose) thing; (fam: machin) whatsit, thingummy.

truelle [tryɛl] nf trowel.

truffe [tryf] nf truffle.

truie [trɥi] nf sow.

truite [trɥit] nf trout.

truquer [tryke] v rig, fix. **truquage** nm rigging, fixing; (cinéma) trick photography, special effects pl.

tsar [dzar] nm tsar.

tu [ty] pron you.

tuba [tyba] nm tuba.

tube [tyb] nm tube; pipe; (fam: chanson, disque) hit.

tuberculose [tyberkyloz] nf tuberculosis.

tuer [tɥe] v kill. **à tue-tête** at the top of one's voice. **tuerie** nf slaughter. **tueur, -euse** nm killer.

tuile [tɥil] nf tile; (fam) blow.

tulipe [tylip] *nf* tulip.

tumeur [tymœr] *nf* tumour.

tumulte [tymylt] *nm* tumult, commotion. **tumultueux** *adj* turbulent, stormy.

tunique [tynik] *nf* tunic.

tunnel [tynεl] *nm* tunnel.

turban [tyrbã] *nm* turban.

turbine [tyrbin] *nf* turbine.

turbot [tyrbo] *nm* turbot.

turbulent [tyrbylã] *adj* turbulent; (*agité*) boisterous, unruly. **turbulence** *nf* turbulence.

turf [tyrf] *nm* (*hippisme*) racing; (*terrain*) racecourse.

turquoise [tyrkwaz] *nf, adj invar* turquoise.

tutelle [tytεl] *nf* (*surveillance*) supervision; protection; (*jur*) guardianship.

tuteur, -trice [tytœr, -tris] *nm, nf* guardian. *nm* stake.

tutoyer [tytwaje] *v* address as 'tu'. **tutoiement** *nm* use of the 'tu' form.

tuyau [t^чijo] *nm* pipe; (*d'arrosage*) hose; (*fam*) tip. **tuyau d'échappement** exhaust pipe.

tympan [tɛ̃pɑ̃] *nm* eardrum.

type [tip] *nm* type; (*représentant*) classic example; (*fam*) bloke, chap.

typhoïde [tifɔid] *nf, adj* typhoid.

typhon [tifɔ̃] *nm* typhoon.

typique [tipik] *adj* typical.

tyran [tirã] *nm* tyrant. **tyrannie** *nf* tyranny. **tyrannique** *adj* tyrannical.

U

ulcérer [ylsere] *v* (*méd*) ulcerate; (*blesser*) wound, embitter. **ulcère** *nm* ulcer.

ultérieur, -e [ylterjœr] *adj* later, subsequent.

ultimatum [yltimatɔm] *nm* ultimatum.

ultime [yltim] *adj* ultimate, final.

ultrasonique [yltrasɔnik] *adj* ultrasonic.

ultraviolet, -ette [yltravjɔlε, -εt] *adj* ultraviolet.

un [œ̃], **une** *art a, an. n, adj, pron* one. **les uns** some. **l'un et l'autre** both. **l'un ou l'autre** either. **unième** *adj* first.

unanime [ynanim] *adj* unanimous. **unanimité** *nf* unanimity.

uni [yni] *adj* (*tissu, couleur*) plain; (*famille*) close; (*lisse*) smooth, even.

unifier [ynifje] *v* unify. **unification** *nf* unification.

uniforme [ynifɔrm] *adj* uniform; (*surface*) even. *nm* uniform. **uniformité** *nf* uniformity.

union [ynjɔ̃] *nf* union; association; combination.

unique [ynik] *adj* (*seul*) only; (*exceptionnel*) unique. **uniquement** *adv* only.

unir [ynir] *v* unite; combine; join. **unité** *nf* (*élément*) unit; (*cohésion*) unity.

unisexe [yniseks] *adj invar* unisex.

unisson [ynisɔ̃] *nm* unison. **à l'unisson** in unison.

univers [ynivεr] *nm* universe. **universel** *adj* universal; (*outil*) all-purpose.

université [yniversite] *nf* university. **universitaire** *adj* university.

urbain [yrbɛ̃] *adj* urban, town. **urbanisme** *nm* town planning. **urbaniste** *n(m + f)* town planner.

urgent [yrʒã] *adj* urgent. **urgence** *nf* urgency; (*cas urgent*) emergency.

uriner [yrine] *v* urinate. **urine** *nf* urine. **urinoir** *nm* urinal.

urne [yrn] *nf* (*vase*) urn; (*pol*) ballot-box.

usage [yzaʒ] *nm* use; custom; (*gramm*) usage; (*politesse*) breeding. **usagé** *adj* (*usé*) worn, old; (*d'occasion*) second-hand, used.

user [yze] *v* wear out; (*consommer*) use. **user de** use, make use of. **usé** *adj* worn; (*banal*) hackneyed; (*râpé*) threadbare. **usure** *nf* wear.

usine [yzin] *nf* factory, works.

ustensile [ystãsil] *nm* implement; (*de cuisine*) utensil.

usuel [yz^чεl] *adj* common, everyday; (*d'usage*) usual.

usurper [yzyrpe] *v* usurp. **usurpateur, -trice** *nm, nf* usurper. **usurpation** *nf* usurpation.

utérus [yterys] *nm* womb, uterus.

utile [ytil] *adj* useful. **utilité** *nf* use, usefulness.

utiliser [ytilize] *v* use, utilize. **utilisable** *adj* usable.

V

vacance [vakãs] *nf* vacancy. **vacances** *nf pl* holiday *sing*, vacation *sing*. **en vacances** on holiday. **vacant** *adj* vacant.

vacarme [vakarm] *nm* din, row.

vaccin [vaksɛ̃] *nm* vaccine. **vaccination** *nf* vaccination. **vacciner** *v* vaccinate.

vache [vaʃ] *nf* cow; (*argot*) bitch, swine. *adj* (*argot*) rotten. **vachement** *adv* (*argot*) bloody.

vaciller [vasije] *v* wobble, sway; (*flamme*) flicker; (*courage*) falter, fail. **vacillant** *adj* unsteady; flickering; (*santé*) shaky; indecisive.

va-et-vient [vaevjɛ̃] *nm invar* comings and goings *pl*; (*mécanisme*) movement to and fro.

vagabond [vagabɔ̃], **-e** *adj* (*errant*) roaming, restless; (*nomade*) wandering. *nm, nf* tramp, vagrant. **vagabondage** *nm* wandering; vagrancy. **vagabonder** *v* roam, wander.

vagin [vaʒɛ̃] *nm* vagina. **vaginal** *adj* vaginal.

vague[1] [vag] *adj* vague. *nm* vagueness. **regarder dans le vague** stare into space.

vague[2] [vag] *nf* wave; (*montée*) surge. **vague de chaleur** heat wave.

vaillant [vajã] *adj* brave, valiant; vigorous, robust.

vain [vɛ̃] *adj* vain; empty, futile. **en vain** in vain.

*****vaincre** [vɛ̃krə] *v* conquer, defeat, overcome.

vainqueur [vɛ̃kœr] *nm* conqueror; (*sport*) winner. *adj* victorious.

vaisseau [veso] *nm* vessel; (*naut*) ship.

vaisselle [vesɛl] *nf* crockery, dishes *pl*; (*lavage*) washing-up. **faire la vaisselle** wash up.

val [val] *nm* valley.

valable [valablə] *adj* valid; (*notable*) worthwhile.

valet [valɛ] *nm* servant, valet; (*cartes*) jack. **valet d'écurie** groom. **valet de ferme** farm-hand.

valeur [valœr] *nf* value; (*qualité*) worth. **de valeur** valuable. **mettre en valeur** exploit; (*détail*) bring out, highlight. **objets de valeur** *nm pl* valuables *pl*. **valeurs** *nf pl* (*bourse*) securities *pl*.

valide [valid] *adj* (*billet*) valid; (*personne*) fit; able-bodied. **validité** *nf* validity.

valise [valiz] *nf* suitcase.

vallée [vale] *nf* valley.

*****valoir** [valwar] *v* be worth; be valid, apply; (*équivaloir à*) be as good as; (*causer*) bring, earn. **faire valoir** exploit; (*caractéristique*) bring out, highlight. **il vaut mieux** it is better. **valoir la peine** be worth it.

valse [vals] *nf* waltz. **valser** *v* waltz.

valve [valv] *nf* valve.

vampire [vãpir] *nm* vampire.

vandale [vãdal] *n(m+f)* vandal. **vandalisme** *nm* vandalism.

vanille [vanij] *nf* vanilla.

vanité [vanite] *nf* vanity, conceit; futility. **vaniteux** *adj* vain, conceited.

vanter [vãte] *v* praise. **se vanter** boast. **se vanter de** pride oneself on. **vantard** *adj* boastful. **vantardise** *nf* boasting, boastfulness; (*propos*) boast.

vapeur [vapœr] *nf* vapour, steam. **bateau à vapeur** steamer. **cuire à la vapeur** steam. **vaporiser** *v* (*parfum*) spray; (*phys*) vaporize.

varice [varis] *nf* varicose vein.

varicelle [varisɛl] *nf* chicken-pox.

varier [varje] *v* vary. **variable** *nf, adj* variable. **variante** *nf* variant. **variation** *nf* variation. **variété** *nf* variety.

variole [varjɔl] *nf* smallpox.

Varsovie [varsɔvi] *n* Warsaw.

vase[1] [vaz] *nm* vase.

vase[2] [vaz] *nf* mud, sludge.

vaste [vast] *adj* vast, immense.

Vatican [vatikã] *nm* Vatican.

vau [vo] *nm* **à vau-l'eau** with the current; (*projets, etc.*) down the drain. **aller à vau-l'eau** be on the road to ruin.

vaudou [vodu] *nm, adj invar* voodoo.

vaurien [vorjɛ̃], **-enne** *nm, nf* good-for-nothing.

vautour [votur] *nm* vulture.

se vautrer [votre] *v* sprawl. **se vautrer dans** wallow in.

veau [vo] *nm* calf; (*cuisine*) veal.

vedette [vədɛt] *nf* (*cinéma, etc.*) star; (*bateau*) launch.

végétal [veʒetal] *adj* plant, vegetable.

végétation [veʒetasjɔ̃] *nf* vegetation. **végétations adénoïdes** adenoids *pl*.

véhément [veemã] *adj* vehement. **véhémence** *nf* vehemence.

véhicule [veikyl] *nm* vehicle.
veille [vɛj] *nf* (*garde*) watch, vigil; (*jour précédent*) eve, day before; (*état*) wakefulness. **veillée** *nf* evening; (*mort*) watch. **veiller** *v* (*mort, malade*) sit up with, watch over; (*rester éveillé*) stay awake; be vigilant. **veiller à** attend to, see to. **veiller sur** watch over. **veilleuse** *nf* (*flamme*) pilot-light; (*lampe*) night-light.
veine [vɛn] *nf* vein; (*fam*) luck.
vélo [velo] *nm* (*fam*) bike.
vélocité [velɔsite] *nf* swiftness, nimbleness; (*vitesse*) velocity.
velours [valur] *nm* velvet. **velours côtelé** corduroy. **velouté** *adj* velvety, smooth.
velu [valy] *adj* hairy.
venaison [vɛnɛzɔ̃] *nf* venison.
vendange [vɑ̃dɑ̃ʒ] *nf* grape harvest.
vendre [vɑ̃dr] *v* sell. **vendre la mèche** (*fam*) give the game away. **vendeur, -euse** *nm, nf* seller; (*magasin*) shop assistant.
vendredi [vɑ̃dradi] *nm* Friday. **vendredi saint** Good Friday.
vénéneux [venenø] *adj* poisonous.
vénérer [venere] *v* venerate, revere. **vénérable** *adj* venerable. **vénération** *nf* veneration.
vénérien [venerjɛ̃] *adj* venereal. **maladie vénérienne** venereal disease.
venger [vɑ̃ʒe] *v* avenge. **se venger** take one's revenge. **vengeance** *nf* vengeance, revenge.
venin [vənɛ̃] *nm* venom. **venimeux** *adj* venomous.
*****venir** [vanir] *v* come. **en venir à** come to, resort to. **faire venir** send for. **venir de** come from; (*suivi d'un infinitif*) have just.
vent [vɑ̃] *nm* wind. **dans le vent** (*fam*) trendy, fashionable. **il fait du vent** it is windy. **venteux** *adj* windswept.
vente [vɑ̃t] *nf* sale. **vente aux enchères** auction. **vente de charité** bazaar, jumble sale.
ventiler [vɑ̃tile] *v* ventilate. **ventilateur** *nm* fan, ventilator. **ventilation** *nf* ventilation.
ventouse [vɑ̃tuz] *nf* sucker, suction pad.
ventre [vɑ̃tr] *nm* stomach, belly.
ventriloque [vɑ̃trilɔk] *n(m+f)* ventriloquist.
venue [vəny] *nf* coming.
ver [vɛr] *nm* worm; (*larve*) grub; (*asticot*) maggot. **ver à soie** silkworm. **ver du bois** woodworm.
véranda [verɑ̃da] *nf* veranda.
verbe [verb] *nm* verb. **verbal** *adj* verbal.

verdict [verdikt] *nm* verdict.
verdir [verdir] *v* turn green. **verdure** *nf* greenery.
verge [verʒ] *nf* rod; penis.
verger [verʒe] *nm* orchard.
verglas [vergla] *nm* black ice.
vergogne [vergɔɲ] *nf* shame.
véridique [veridik] *adj* truthful.
vérifier [verifje] *v* check, verify; (*comptes*) audit; confirm, prove. **vérification** *nf* check, verification; auditing; confirmation.
vérité [verite] *nf* truth; (*sincérité*) truthfulness. **véritable** *adj* real, true, genuine.
vermeil, -eille [vermɛj] *adj* bright red.
vermine [vermin] *nf* vermin.
vermouth [vermut] *nm* vermouth.
vernaculaire [vernakyler] *adj* vernacular.
vernir [vernir] *v* varnish. **verni** *adj* varnished; (*luisant*) glossy. **cuir verni** patent leather. **vernis** *nm* varnish; (*poterie*) glaze; (*éclat*) gloss; (*apparence*) veneer. **vernis à ongles** nail varnish *or* polish. **vernisser** *v* glaze.
vérole [verɔl] *nf* **petite vérole** smallpox.
verre [ver] *nm* glass; (*optique*) lens; (*boisson*) drink. **verres de contact** contact lenses *pl*.
verrou [veru] *nm* bolt.
verrouiller [veruje] *v* bolt.
verrue [very] *nf* wart.
vers[1] [ver] *prep* towards, to; (*approximation*) about, around.
vers[2] [ver] *nm* line. *nm pl* verse *sing*.
versant [versɑ̃] *nm* side, slope.
verse [vers] *nf* **à verse** in torrents. **il pleut à verse** it is pouring down.
Verseau [verso] *nm* Aquarius.
verser [verse] *v* pour; (*sang, larmes*) shed; pay; (*basculer*) overturn. **versement** *nm* payment; (*échelonné*) instalment.
version [versjɔ̃] *nf* version; (*traduction*) translation.
verso [verso] *nm* back.
vert [ver] *adj* green; (*fruit*) unripe; (*propos*) spicy. *nm* green.
vertèbre [vertɛbr] *nf* vertebra (*pl* -brae). **vertébral** *adj* vertebral. **vertébré** *nm, adj* vertebrate.
vertical [vertikal] *adj* vertical. **verticale** *nf* vertical.
vertige [vertiʒ] *nm* vertigo, dizziness. **avoir le vertige** feel dizzy. **pris de vertige** dizzy, giddy. **vertigineux** *adj* breathtaking; (*hauteur*) giddy.

vertu [vɛrty] nf virtue. **vertueux** adj virtuous.

verve [vɛrv] nf vigour, zest; eloquence.

vessie [vesi] nf bladder.

veste [vɛst] nf jacket.

vestiaire [vɛstjɛr] nm cloakroom; (piscine, etc.) changing-room.

vestibule [vɛstibyl] nm hall, vestibule.

vestige [vɛstiʒ] nm vestige, remnant, trace.

veston [vɛstɔ̃] nm jacket.

vêtement [vɛtmɑ̃] nm garment. **vêtements** nm pl clothes pl, clothing sing.

vétéran [veterɑ̃] nm veteran.

vétérinaire [veterinɛr] nm vet. adj veterinary.

vétille [vetij] nf trifle.

*vêtir [vetir] v clothe, dress. **vêtu de** wearing.

veto [veto] nm veto. **mettre son veto à** veto.

vétuste [vetyst] adj ancient, decrepit. **vétusté** nf age, decay.

veuf [vœf] adj widowed. nm widower. **veuve** nf widow. **veuvage** nm widowhood.

veule [vøl] adj spineless, weak.

vexer [vɛkse] v upset, hurt. **vexant** adj hurtful; (contrariant) annoying.

via [vja] prep via.

viable [vjablə] adj viable. **viabilité** nf viability; (chemin) practicability.

viaduc [vjadyk] nm viaduct.

viager [vjaʒe] adj for life.

viande [vjɑ̃d] nf meat.

vibrer [vibre] v vibrate; (voix) quiver. **vibration** nf vibration.

vicaire [vikɛr] nm curate.

vice [vis] nm vice; fault.

vice-chancelier nm vice-chancellor.

vice-consul nm vice-consul.

vice-président, -e nm, nf (état) vice-president; (réunion) vice-chairman.

vice versa [viseversa] adv vice versa.

vicier [visje] v pollute, taint; (jur) invalidate.

vicieux [visjø] adj licentious, depraved; (animal) unruly; (fautif) incorrect.

vicomte [vikɔ̃t] nm viscount. **vicomtesse** nf viscountess.

victime [viktim] nf victim.

victoire [viktwar] nf victory. **victorieux** adj victorious.

vidange [vidɑ̃ʒ] nf emptying; (auto) oil change. **vidanges** nf pl sewage sing. **vidanger** v empty, drain.

vide [vid] adj empty; (disponible) vacant. nm emptiness; (espace) void; (sans air) vacuum; (creux) gap. **vider** v empty; (bassin, etc.) drain; (quitter) vacate; (cuisine) gut; (fam: épuiser) wear out; (fam: expulser) throw out.

vie [vi] nf life; (moyens) living.

vieil [vjɛj] form of **vieux** used before a vowel or mute h.

vieillir [vjejir] v age, grow old. **vieillard** nm old man. **vieillesse** nf old age.

Vienne [vjɛn] n Vienna.

vierge [vjɛrʒ] nf virgin. **Vierge** nf Virgo. adj (terre, etc.) virgin; (papier) blank.

vieux, vieille [vjø, vjɛj] adj old. **vieille fille** spinster. **vieux jeu** adj invar old-fashioned. nm old man. nf old woman.

vif, vive [vif, viv] adj lively; brusque; (aigu) sharp, keen; intense, vivid; (fort) strong, great; (froid) biting; (éclat) bright; (allure) brisk. nm quick.

vigile [viʒil] nf vigil. **vigilance** nf vigilance. **vigilant** adj vigilant.

vigne [viɲ] nf vi...e. **vignoble** nm vineyard.

vignette [viɲɛt] nf label; (auto) tax disc.

vigoureux [vigurø] adj vigorous; robust, sturdy.

vigueur [vigœr] nf vigour; (robustesse) sturdiness; (force) strength. **entrer en vigueur** come into effect. **en vigueur** in force, current.

vil [vil] adj vile, base.

vilain [vilɛ̃] adj nasty; (laid) ugly; (méchant) mean, wicked.

vilebrequin [vilbrəkɛ̃] nm (auto) crankshaft; (tech) brace.

villa [vila] nf villa, detached house.

village [vilaʒ] nm village. **villageois, -e** nm, nf villager.

ville [vil] nf town; (plus grande) city. **ville d'eau** spa.

villégiature [vileʒatyr] nf holiday; (lieu) holiday resort.

vin [vɛ̃] nm wine. **grand vin** vintage wine.

vinaigre [vinɛgrə] nm vinegar. **vinaigrette** nf French dressing, vinaigrette.

vindicatif [vɛ̃dikatif] adj vindictive.

vingt [vɛ̃] nm, adj twenty. **vingtième** n(m+f), adj twentieth.

vinyle [vinil] nm vinyl.

viol [vjɔl] nm rape.

violent [vjɔlɑ̃] adj violent; (effort) strenuous; (fort) strong, intense. **violence** nf violence.

violer [vjɔle] v violate; (*femme*) rape; (*loi, promesse*) break. **violation** nf violation.

violet, -ette [vjɔlɛ, -ɛt] adj purple, violet. nm purple. nf violet.

violon [vjɔlɔ̃] nm violin. **violoncelle** nm cello. **violoniste** n(m+f) violinist.

vipère [vipɛr] nf adder, viper.

virage [viraʒ] nm bend, turn.

virer [vire] v turn; change; (*argent*) transfer. **virement** nm transfer.

virginité [virʒinite] nf virginity.

virgule [virgyl] nf comma; (*math*) decimal point.

viril [viril] adj virile, manly; masculine. **virilité** nf virility.

virtuel [virtɥɛl] adj potential. **virtuellement** adv potentially; (*pratiquement*) virtually.

virus [virys] nm virus.

vis [vis] nf screw.

visa [viza] nm (*passeport*) visa; (*timbre*) stamp; (*de censure*) certificate.

visage [vizaʒ] nm face.

vis-à-vis [vizavi] adv opposite, face to face. nm en vis-à-vis opposite each other. prep vis-à-vis de opposite; (*comparaison*) beside, next to; (*envers*) towards.

viser [vize] v aim (at); (*remarque*) be directed at. **visée** nf aim; design.

visible [vizibl] adj visible; (*évident*) obvious. **visibilité** nf visibility.

visière [vizjɛr] nf (*casquette*) peak; (*armure*) visor.

vision [vizjɔ̃] nf vision; (*faculté*) eyesight. **visionnaire** n(m+f), adj visionary.

visiter [vizite] v visit; (*ville, château*) go round; examine; (*fouiller*) search. **visite** nf visit; tour; inspection, examination. **rendre visite à** visit, call on. **visiteur, -euse** nm, nf visitor.

vison [vizɔ̃] nm mink.

visser [vise] v screw down or on.

visuel [vizɥɛl] adj visual.

vital [vital] adj vital. **vitalité** nf vitality, energy.

vitamine [vitamin] nf vitamin.

vite [vit] adv fast, quickly; (*tôt*) soon. interj quick! **vitesse** nf speed; (*auto*) gear; velocity.

vitrer [vitre] v put glass in, glaze. **vitrail** nm, pl -aux stained-glass window. **vitre** nf pane of glass; (*fenêtre*) window. **vitrine** nf (*magasin*) shop-window; (*armoire*) display cabinet, glass case.

vivace [vivas] adj (*plante*) hardy; (*foi,*

haine) undying. **vivacité** nf vivacity, liveliness; (*éclat*) brightness; (*mordant*) sharpness; intensity.

vivant [vivɑ̃] adj alive, living; (*vivace*) lively. nm living person; (*vie*) lifetime.

vivier [vivje] nm fish-pond.

vivifier [vivifje] v invigorate.

vivisection [vivisɛksjɔ̃] nf vivisection.

****vivre** [vivr] v live, be alive. **vive ... !** interj long live ... ! three cheers for ... ! **vivre de** live on. nm board. **vivres** nm pl provisions pl.

vocabulaire [vɔkabylɛr] nm vocabulary.

vocal [vɔkal] adj vocal.

vocation [vɔkasjɔ̃] nf vocation, calling.

vodka [vɔdka] nf vodka.

vœu [vø] nm (*souhait*) wish; (*promesse*) vow.

vogue [vɔg] nf fashion, vogue. **en vogue** fashionable.

voguer [vɔge] v sail; (*pensées, etc.*) drift.

voici [vwasi] prep (*sing*) here is, this is; (*pl*) here are, these are. **voici ...** que it is ... since. **voici une heure** an hour ago.

voie [vwa] nf way, road; (*rail*) track, line; (*autoroute, etc.*) lane. **voie d'eau** leak. **voie ferrée** railway line. **voie publique** public highway. **voie sans issue** no through road.

voilà [vwala] prep (*sing*) there is, that is; (*pl*) there are, those are. **voilà ...** que it is ... since. **voilà une heure** an hour ago.

voile[1] [vwal] nf sail; (*sport*) sailing. **voilier** nm sailing ship or boat.

voile[2] [vwal] nm veil; (*tissu*) net.

voiler [vwale] v veil, shroud. **se voiler** mist over, grow hazy.

****voir** [vwar] v see. **aller voir** call on, visit. **faire voir** show. **n'avoir rien à voir avec** have nothing to do with. **se voir** show, be obvious.

voire [vwar] adv indeed.

voirie [vwari] nf (*voies*) highways pl; (*entretien*) highway maintenance; (*enlèvement des ordures*) refuse collection; (*dépotoir*) refuse dump.

voisin, -e [vwazɛ̃] adj neighbouring; (*adjacent*) adjoining; (*ressemblant*) akin. nm, nf neighbour. **voisinage** nm neighbourhood; proximity.

voiture [vwatyr] nf car; (*wagon*) coach, carriage. **voiture d'enfant** pram.

voix [vwa] nf voice; (*pol*) vote. **à voix basse/haute** in a low/loud voice. **être sans voix** be speechless.

vol¹ [vɔl] nm flight. **à vol d'oiseau** as the crow flies. **vol à voile** gliding. **vol libre** hang-gliding.

vol² [vɔl] nm theft. **vol à l'étalage** shoplifting. **vol à main armée** armed robbery.

volaille [vɔlɑj] nf poultry, fowl.

volant [vɔlɑ̃] nm (auto) steering wheel; (tech) flywheel; (sport) shuttlecock; (robe) flounce. adj flying.

volatil [vɔlatil] adj volatile.

volcan [vɔlkɑ̃] nm volcano. **volcanique** adj volcanic.

voler¹ [vɔle] v fly. **volée** nf flight; (groupe) flock, swarm; (coups, sport) volley.

voler² [vɔle] v (chose) steal; (personne) rob. **voleur, -euse** nm, nf thief. **au voleur!** stop thief!

volet [vɔlɛ] nm shutter; (tech) flap.

volière [vɔljɛr] nf aviary.

volontaire [vɔlɔ̃tɛr] adj voluntary; intentional; (décidé) headstrong, determined. n(m+f) volunteer.

volonté [vɔlɔ̃te] nf will; (détermination) willpower. **bonne volonté** goodwill, willingness. **volontiers** adv gladly, willingly.

volt [vɔlt] nm volt. **voltage** nm voltage.

volte-face [vɔltəfas] nf invar about-turn.

voltiger [vɔltiʒe] v flutter about.

volume [vɔlym] nm volume.

volupté [vɔlypte] nf sensual delight, voluptuousness. **voluptueux** adj voluptuous.

vomir [vɔmir] v vomit. **vomissement** nm vomiting; (matière) vomit.

vorace [vɔras] adj voracious. **voracité** nf voracity.

vos [vo] V votre.

voter [vɔte] v vote; (loi) pass. **vote** nm vote.

votre [vɔtrə] adj, pl vos your.

vôtre [votrə] pron le or la vôtre yours.

vouer [vwe] v (promettre) vow; (consacrer) devote; (condamner) doom.

***vouloir** [vulwar] v want; (essayer) try; require, need. **en vouloir à** have a grudge against. **vouloir bien** be willing. **vouloir dire** mean. nm will.

vous [vu] pron you, to you; (réfléchi) yourselves, each other. **vous-mêmes** pron yourselves.

voûter [vute] v arch. **voûte** nf vault, arch. **voûté** adj arched; (personne) stooped.

vouvoyer [vuvwaje] v address as 'vous'. **vouvoiement** nm use of the 'vous' form.

voyage [vwajaʒ] nm (course) journey, trip; (action) travel, travelling; (par mer, d'exploration) voyage. **voyage de noces** honeymoon. **voyage organisé** package tour. **voyager** v travel. **voyageur, -euse** nm, nf traveller; passenger.

voyant [vwajɑ̃] adj gaudy, garish.

voyelle [vwajɛl] nf vowel.

voyou [vwaju] nm hooligan, lout.

vrai [vrɛ] adj true; real. nm truth. **à vrai dire** to tell the truth, in actual fact. **pour de vrai** (fam) for real. **vraiment** adv really.

vraisemblable [vrɛsɑ̃blablə] adj likely, probable; (histoire) convincing, plausible. **vraisemblance** nf likelihood, probability; plausibility.

vrille [vrij] nf (bot) tendril; (tech) gimlet; spiral.

vrombir [vrɔ̃bir] v hum. **vrombissement** nm humming.

vu [vy] adj **bien vu** highly regarded. **mal vu** poorly thought of. prep in view of. conj **vu que** seeing that. **vue** nf view; (sens, spectacle) sight; (projet) plan, design.

vulgaire [vylgɛr] adj (grossier) vulgar; (banal) common. **vulgarité** nf vulgarity.

vulnérable [vylnerablə] adj vulnerable.

W

wagon [vagɔ̃] nm (marchandises) truck, wagon; (voyageurs) carriage. **wagon-lit** nm sleeping-car. **wagon-restaurant** nm restaurant-car.

watt [wat] nm watt.

week-end [wikɛnd] nm weekend.

western [wɛstɛrn] nm western.

whisky [wiski] nm whisky.

whist [wist] nm whist.

X

xénophobe [ksenɔfɔb] *adj* xenophobic. *n(m+f)* xenophobe. **xénophobie** *nf* xenophobia.

xérès [gzeres] *nm* sherry.

xylophone [ksilɔfɔn] *nm* xylophone.

Y

y [i] *adv* there. *pron* it, about it, to it, in it. **n'y être pour rien** have nothing to do with it.

yacht [jɔt] *nm* yacht.

yaourt [jaurt] *nm* yoghurt.

yeux [jø] *V* œil.

yoga [jɔga] *nm* yoga.

Yougoslavie [jugɔslavi] *nf* Yugoslavia. **yougoslave** *adj* Yugoslav, Yugoslavian. **Yougoslave** *n(m+f)* Yugoslav.

youyou [juju] *nm* dinghy.

yo-yo [jojo] *nm invar* yo-yo.

Z

zèbre [zɛbrə] *nm* zebra. **zébrer** *v* stripe. **zébrure** *nf* stripe; (*d'un coup*) weal.

zèle [zɛl] *nm* zeal. **zélé** *adj* zealous.

zéro [zero] *nm* zero, nought.

zeste [zɛst] *nm* peel, zest.

zézayer [zezeje] *v* lisp. **zézaiement** *nm* lisp.

zibeline [ziblin] *nf* sable.

zigzag [zigzag] *nm* zigzag. **zigzaguer** *v* zigzag.

zinc [zɛg] *nm* zinc; (*fam*) bar, counter.

zodiaque [zɔdjak] *nm* zodiac.

zone [zon] *nf* zone, area.

zoo [zoo] *nm* zoo.

zoologie [zɔlɔʒi] *nf* zoology. **zoologique** *adj* zoological